Making Europe

SINCE 1300

Making Europe

PEOPLE, POLITICS, AND CULTURE

Frank L. Kidner
San Francisco State University

Maria Bucur
Indiana University

Ralph Mathisen
University of Illinois at Urbana-Champaign

Sally McKee
University of California, Davis

Theodore R. Weeks
Southern Illinois University, Carbondale

Houghton Mifflin Company

Boston   New York

Publisher: *Suzanne Jeans*
Senior Sponsoring Editor: *Nancy Blaine*
Senior Marketing Manager: *Katherine Bates*
Senior Developmental Editor: *Jeffrey Greene*
Senior Project Editor: *Jane Lee*
Art and Design Manager: *Jill Haber*
Cover Design Director: *Tony Saizon*
Senior Photo Editor: *Jennifer Meyer Dare*
Composition Buyer: *Chuck Dutton*
New Title Project Manager: *James Lonergan*
Editorial Associate: *Adrienne Zicht*
Marketing Associate: *Lauren Bussard*
Editorial Assistant: *Anne Finley*

Cover image: *Portrait of Lady Mary Wortley Montagu* (1689–1782) by Gervase Spencer (1740–1783). Lincolnshire County Council, Usher Gallery, Lincoln UK/Bridgeman Art Library.

Printed in the U.S.A.

Library of Congress Catalog Number: 2007938069

ISBN 13: 978-0-618-00482-9
ISBN 10: 0-618-00482-3

1 2 3 4 5 6 7 8 9-CRK-11 10 09 08 07

Brief Contents

Contents

Maps

Features

Choice

Voice

Echo

For years we five professors from across the country have taught Western Civilization courses without the textbook we really wanted to have—a textbook with a coherent strategy for helping students to study and learn. In 1999 we commenced to develop such a text. This book is the result.

The five of us bring to this book a variety of backgrounds, interests, and historical approaches, as well as a combined total of nearly one hundred years of teaching history. Two of us completed graduate degrees in literature before turning to history. We have all studied, worked, or lived on three continents; we are all American citizens, but not all of us were born in the United States. Although we come from different parts of the country and have different historical specializations, all of us teach in large state university systems. We have a strong commitment to the kinds of students who enroll in our schools and in community colleges—young people and nontraditional students from richly diverse cultural and ethnic backgrounds who are enthusiastic and prepared to work but have little knowledge of history and few formal skills in historical analysis. We were gratified to be developing a new kind of textbook that met their needs.

We conceived of a textbook that would be lively and absolutely up-to-date but did not presume a great deal of prior knowledge of western civilization. We also wanted to include new types of learning aids that were fully integrated into the text itself. Our greatest hope is that students who use this book will come to understand how the West has developed and, at the same time, to see the importance of the past for the present. In other words, we want to help them value the past as well as understand it and thus to think historically.

Approaches and Themes

This textbook introduces the cultural unit we call "the West" from its beginnings in the ancient Near East to the present. It is focused around five themes: politics, religion, social history, biography and personality, and individual and collective identity.

Politics: Our book's first theme centers on western politics, states, and the state system from the emergence of civilization in Mesopotamia and Egypt down to our own century. Politics provides the underlying chronological backbone of the text. Our experience has taught us that a politically centered chronology is the most effective way to help inexperienced students get a sense of what came before and what came after and why. Political chronology helps them perceive trends and recognize the forces for historical continuity and change.

If there are sensible reasons for organizing the text around a political chronology, there are pitfalls as well. The chief one is the disaffection many students may have felt in the past with a history that seems little more than a list of persons, reigns, and wars ("Kings and Things") needing to be memorized. To avoid this pitfall we have adopted an approach that centers on dynamic exchanges between states and political elites on the one hand and citizens or subjects on the other. In this textbook students will read and think about the ways taxation, the need for armies, and judicial protection affect ordinary people and vice versa—how the marginal and unrepresented affect the politically powerful. Our approach focuses both on what states and their political elites want from the people who live in them and on what benefits they provide to those people. In turn, we also consider what ordinary people do or do not want from the state, and what kinds of people benefit and do not benefit from the state's policies. When relevant, we also treat the state's lack of impact.

Religion: Our second theme takes up the history of western religion. We have aimed for an expansive treatment of religious activity that includes its institutions and beliefs but is not confined to them. Our textbook ranges widely over issues of polytheism, monotheism, civic religion, philosophically inspired religion, normative religion, orthodoxy and heresy, popular practices, ultimate spiritual values, and systematically articulated agnosticism or atheism. Since from beginning to end we emphasize religious issues, this book is set apart from most Western Civilization texts that treat religious matters fairly consistently up through the sixteenth century but then drop them.

Our distinctive post–1600 emphasis on religion arises from our sense that religious beliefs, values, and affiliations have continued to play a central role in European life up to and including the twenty-first century. Although in part compartmentalized or privatized in the last several centuries as states pursued various secularizing agendas, religious sensibilities still have had considerable impact on economic behavior, social values, and political action, while simultaneously adjusting to or resisting changes in other aspects of life. In addition, of course, they regularly influenced European activity in colonies and empires.

In our treatment of religion we do not focus simply on the dominant religion of any time or place. Judaism, for example, is discussed throughout the text, while Islam, introduced in Chapter 8, is discussed again in connection with such issues as the Moriscos of Spain, the Habsburg re-conquest of Hungary, tension in Russian Central Asia and the Balkans before World War I, Soviet campaigns against religion, the arrival of Muslim immigrants in post–World War II Europe, and the dissolution of Yugoslavia. In addition, an emphasis on religious pluralism in European life leads to discussions of the variety of subcultures found in the West, many of which believe that their religious and ethnic identity is integral to their other values and practices. Indeed, our belief that religion continues to play an important role in modern European history rests in large part on the abundant evidence showing it to be a core component of life for subcultures within the larger western context. Catholic and Protestant Irish, Protestant northern Germans and Catholic southern Germans, Orthodox Russians, and Bosnian Muslims stand as examples of communities whose values and actions have been significantly shaped by ongoing religious allegiances and whose interactions with those practicing other religions have had lasting repercussions. Our intention is to present the religious past of the West in all its complex, multifold voices to students who are more and more self-consciously aware of racial, cultural, and ethnic diversity in their own world.

We also believe that attention to religion reflects the current public debate over values, using students' experience of this contested territory to stimulate their interest. Their awareness of current values-based programs can serve as a springboard for a study of the past. Does one choose aggression, persuasion, or passive resistance and nonaggression?

Social History: The theme of social history is integrated into the text as consideration is given to the way politics and religion affect people and societies. Discussions of daily lives and family structures are illuminated through occasional spotlights on the experience of a single, typical individual. We also pay close attention to issues of gender norms and roles in the past, drawing on the work of a generation of historians concerned with the history of ordinary men, women, and children. We see many possibilities for engaging the interest of students in this approach. We hope our book will stimulate productive class discussions of what it meant to live as a woman or a (male) citizen in the Athenian city-state, as a peasant or a landlord in the relatively stateless world of the early Western Middle Ages, as a man or woman during the French Revolution, and as a soldier or nurse in the trenches of World War I.

Biography and Personality: To give focus and immediacy to the themes we emphasize, we have chosen to highlight the biographies of important or representative figures in the past and, when possible, to give students a sense of their personalities. We want key figures to live for students through their choices and actions and pronouncements. Biography and personality are the focus of chapter openings and are integrated into the chapter narratives. Portraits of cities occasionally stand in for biographies by providing a picture of the places and spaces that have been important in a particular era or have continuing significance across centuries.

Identity: An emphasis on individual and collective identity is another distinctive feature of our book. By addressing matters of identity for each era, we believe that we can help students see themselves in—or as against—the experiences of those who preceded them. To this end, the relationship between the individual and the group is examined as well as changing categories of identity, such as religion, class, gender, ethnicity, nationality, citizenship, occupation or profession, generation, and race. In a real sense, this emphasis flows from the preceding four themes. It means that the political narrative is personalized, that history is not only an account of states, institutions, and policies, but also of people.

The West and the World

In addition to emphasizing the themes outlined above, we have adopted a view about the West that shapes this volume. It derives from our rejection of the tendency to treat the West as a monolithic entity or to imply that the West is "really" western Europe after 500 and, after 1500, specifically northwestern Europe. We define the West more broadly. Throughout the book, students remain informed about developments in eastern Europe, western Asia, and Africa. We show that, far from being homogeneous, the West represents a diversity of cultures. By taking this approach we hope to be able to engage students in a way that will lead them to understanding the causes, effects, and significance of the cultural diversity that exists in the modern world.

We also address the issue of cultural diversity by looking at the impact of the non-western world on the West from antiquity to the present. We discuss both western knowledge and western fantasies about non-western peoples, the actual contact or lack of contact with non-western societies, and the growing global impact of Europe and Europeans during the last five hundred years. The emphasis is always on the West—on how the West did or did not make contact with other societies and, in the case of contacts, on their consequences for everyone involved—but the effect is to place the West in its larger global context as one of humanity's many cultural units.

Pedagogy and Features

One of the most common questions our students ask is: "What's important?" This textbook aims to help them answer that question for themselves. We have found that students can profit from a text that takes less for granted, provides a consistent and clear structure for each chapter, and incorporates primary documents. For both teachers and students, "Western Civ" is often the most difficult history course in the curriculum. With this textbook, we hope to change its reputation. We have developed a strong pedagogy realized through a series of innovative features that will assist students in understanding the book's content and help them master it. We also kept instructors in mind, because we believe that carefully constructed chapters that convey basic information are the best support for teaching. Instructors may then build on the text or modify it to meet specific needs.

Chapter Opening Feature: "Choice": Each chapter opens with an account of an individual making a crucial choice that mattered, that had important consequences, and that can be used to introduce the chapter's central concerns. Our intention in this feature is to foreground human agency, to spark the interest of students, and to guide them on into the chapter. Thus, Chapter 5, which introduces students to the rise of Rome, opens with Spartacus' revolt in 73 B.C.E. to help them understand the role of slavery in Roman political and social history. Chapter 22, which discusses the "triumph" of the nation-state in the late nineteenth century, opens with an account of Theodor Herzl's endorsement of Zionism as a way to discuss the impact of nationalist ideology and to carry out the book's emphasis on religious diversity in the West.

Primary Source Feature: "Voice": Each chapter has a document from an individual who lived during the era of the chapter, sometimes from the same individual featured at the beginning of the chapter in "Choice." An explanatory headnote sets the context for the document. Students are then helped to analyze it historically through a series of marginal notes called "Exploration Points." The points are also designed to aid instructors seeking to integrate primary sources into their classrooms.

End-of-Chapter Feature: "Echo": This feature is a brief exploration of an interesting and often fun connection between the chapter's era and the student's life today. Topics often relate to material culture, identity and memory, and technology. For example, Chapter 14, which deals with sixteenth-century reform movements in the western church, picks up on the important role of the new technology of the printing press in reformers' programs to discuss "Media Revolutions" down to the present. Chapter 28 takes us on a journey in the post–World War II Volkswagen Transporter minibus as it caught on with Europeans on both sides of the "Iron Curtain," then with American hippies of the 1960s, and finally morphed into the suburban minivan of today.

In addition, we have built into each chapter a strong framework of pedagogical aids to help students navigate the text. Each chapter opens with a **map** that provides a geographical orientation to political content. A **timeline** highlights seven to nine landmark events that define the time frame. Each chapter opening also has an **outline** of chapter topics and subtopics, listed together with chapter features. A chapter **introduction** provides an overview of chapter topics and themes. Chapter openings also include a **chronology** that lists events and serves as a guide to the text and as a study aid. Each major chapter division begins with two **focus questions** that direct students' attention to the central concerns and issues about to be examined. Where events follow thick and fast, **brief boxed chronologies** outline their sequence. At the end of the chapter is a **summary,** preceded by three synthetic **review questions** that prompt students to draw connections among the chapter's focus questions. One review question in every chapter highlights the identity theme. Basic answers to these questions can be found in the summary, which reinforces what the students have read, but instructors will find that the review and focus questions prompt students to do more than regurgitate pat answers. Their aim has been to prompt critical thinking. At the end of the summary is a **thinking back, thinking ahead question** that asks students to extend their thinking to previous eras or into the eras to come. At the end of each chapter is a short list of **suggested readings,** classic or important publications that students can easily locate as well as three especially good **websites** that they might find helpful. Additional sources for each chapter will be listed on the book's website. The most distinctive feature of our text is the **glossary**—a system whereby boldfaced names, terms, organizations, concepts, and events are explained or defined on the same page where they are introduced. These definitions support students whose vocabulary and knowledge of history are weak, enhance the background a better-prepared student may have, and serve as a convenient review and study aid. In the printed book each chapter will have a rich array of maps and illustrations that will expand the chapter contents through informative captions.

Flexible Format

Western Civilization courses differ widely in chronological structure from one campus to another. To accommodate the differing divisions of historical time into intervals for various academic year divisions, *Making Europe: People, Politics, and Culture* is published in three print versions, two of which embrace the complete work, and two electronic versions:

- One-volume hardcover edition: *Making Europe: People, Politics, and Culture*
- Two-volume paperback: *Making Europe: People, Politics, and Culture, Volume I: To 1790* (Chapters 1–17); *Volume II: Since 1550* (Chapters 15–30)
- *Making Europe: People, Politics, and Culture, Since 1300* (Chapters 12–30), for courses on Europe since the Renaissance
- An ebook of the complete one-volume edition
- A two-volume ebook of volumes one and two

Ancillaries

A wide array of supplements accompany this text to help students better master the material and to help instructors in teaching from the book:

- Student Website
- Instructor Website
- *HM Testing* CD-ROM (powered by *Diploma*)
- Online *Instructor's Resource Manual*
- Online *Study Guide* (powered by eCommerce)
- *PowerPoint* maps, images, and lecture outlines
- *PowerPoint* questions for personal response systems
- *Blackboard*™ and *WebCT*™ course cartridges
- *Eduspace*™ (powered by *Blackboard*™)

- Interactive ebook
- *HistoryFinder*

The student website, HM HistorySPACE™, which is accessible by visiting **college.hmco.com/pic/kidner1e,** is a companion website for students that features a wide array of resources to help students master the subject matter. The website, prepared by Craig Pilant of the County College of Morris, and Mark Seidl, is divided into three major sections:

- "Prepare for Class" includes material such as learning objectives, chapter outlines, and pre-class quizzes for a student to consult before going to class.
- "Improve Your Grade" includes practice review materials such as interactive flashcards, chronological ordering exercises, primary sources, and interactive map exercises.
- "ACE the Test" features our successful ACE brand of practice tests as well as other self-testing materials.

Students can also find additional text resources such as an online glossary, audio mp3 files of chapter summaries, and material on how to study more effectively in the "General Resources" section.

The instructor website, HM HistorySPACE™, also accessible by visiting **college.hmco.com/pic/kidner1e,** is a companion website for instructors. It features all of the material on the student website plus additional password-protected resources that help instructors teach the course, such as an electronic version of the *Instructor's Resource Manual* and *PowerPoint* slides.

The *Instructor's Resource Manual,* prepared by Doug McGetchin of Florida Atlantic University, contains instructional objectives, chapter outlines, lecture suggestions, suggestions on using primary sources, activities for the Choice feature, activities for the Voice feature, activities for the Echo feature, map activities, audio-visual bibliographies, and internet resources.

HM Testing (powered by *Diploma*) offers instructors a flexible and powerful tool for test generation and test management. Now supported by the Brownstone Research Group's market-leading *Diploma* software, this new version of *HM Testing* significantly improves on functionality and ease of use by offering all the tools needed to create, author, deliver, and customize multiple types of tests. Diploma is currently in use at thousands of college and university campuses throughout the United States and Canada. The *HM Testing* content for this text was developed by Kathleen Addison of California State University at Northridge and offers key term identification, essay questions (with guidelines for how to effectively write the essay), and multiple-choice questions (with page references to the correct response).

The *Online Study Guide* (powered by eCommerce) offers students additional materials to aid their study and mastery of the text. The *Study Guide* content was developed by Robert Shannon Sumner of the University of West Georgia and offers learning objectives, chapter key points, topics for essay and discussion, fill-in-the-blank activities, matching activities, multiple-choice questions, chronology exercises, literary analysis, geography questions, and map activities.

We are pleased to offer a collection of Western Civilization *PowerPoint* lecture outlines, maps, and images for use in classroom presentations. Detailed lecture outlines correspond to the book's chapters and make it easier for instructors to cover the major topics in class. The art collection includes all of the photos and maps in the text, as well as numerous other images from our Western Civilization titles. *PowerPoint* questions and answers for use with personal response system software are also offered to adopters free of charge.

A variety of assignable homework and testing material has been developed to work with the *Blackboard*™ and *WebCT*™ course management systems, as well as with *Eduspace*™: Houghton Mifflin's Online Learning Tool (Powered by **Blackboard**™). *Eduspace*™ is a web-based online learning environment that provides instructors with a gradebook and communication capabilities, such as synchronous and asynchronous chats and announcement postings. It offers access to assignments such as over six hundred and fifty gradable homework exercises, writing assignments, interactive maps with questions, primary sources, discussion questions for online discussion boards, and tests, which all come ready-to-use. Instructors can choose to use the content as is, modify it, or even add their own. *Eduspace*™ also contains an interactive ebook, which contains in-text links to interactive maps, primary sources, and audio pronunciation files, as well as review and self-testing material for students.

HistoryFinder, a new Houghton Mifflin technology initiative, helps instructors create rich and exciting classroom presentations. This online tool offers thousands of online resources, including art, photographs, maps, primary sources, multimedia content, Associated Press interactive modules, and ready-made PowerPoint slides. HistoryFinder's assets can easily be searched by keyword, or browsed from pull-down menus of topic, media type, or by textbook. Instructors can then browse, preview, and download resources straight from the website.

Acknowledgments

It is a pleasure to thank the many instructors who read and critiqued the manuscript through its development:

Patricia E. Behre, Fairfield University
Robert J. Brennan, Cape Fear Community College
Dorothy L. Brown, Columbia College
Peter Buhler, Boise State University
Christine Caldwell, St. Louis University
Susan Carrafiello, Wright State University
Maryanne Cline Horowitz, Occidental College
Luanne Dagley, Pellissippi State Technical Community College
A. Dudley Gardner, Western Wyoming College
Kathryn A. Edwards, University of South Carolina
Carla C. Falkner, Northeast Mississippi Community College
Joanne M. Ferraro, San Diego State
Carlos R. Galvao-Sobrinho, University of Wisconsin, Milwaukee
Paul S. George, Ph.D., Miami-Dade Community College
Eva Giloi, Rutgers University, Newark
Jay Harmon, Catholic High School
Robert Henry, Skyline College
John Howe, Texas Technical University
Paul J. L. Hughes, Ph.D., Sussex County Community College
Theodore M. Kluz, Troy State University
Craig Koslofsky, University of Illinois, Urbana
Michael Kulikowski, University of Tennessee
Tom Lansburg, Front Range Community College
F. Thomas Luongo, Tulane University
Molly McClain, University of San Diego
Andrew McMichael, Western Kentucky University
T. Mills Kelly, George Mason University
Prudence Moylan, Loyola University
Charlotte Newman Goldy, Miami University
Patricia O. O'Neill, Central Oregon Community College
William A. Paquette, Tidewater Community College
Ricky E. Parrish, Brevard Community College
Brian A. Pavlac, King's College
Ty M. Reese, University of North Dakota
Paula M. Rieder, University of Nebraska, Kearney

James B. Robinson, University of Northern Iowa

Jim Roderick, Truckee Meadows Community College

Ian Rush, Washtenaw Community College

Philip Schaeffer, Olympic College

Stuart Smyth, State University of New York, Albany

David R. Stone, Kansas State University

Dale R. Streeter, Southwest Missouri State University

Laura Trauth, Community College of Baltimore County, Essex

Alice N. Walters, University of Massachusetts, Lowell

Andrea Wilford, Muscatine High School

In addition, we would like to thank the History 205A and 205B classes at Southern Illinois University at Carbondale who used this text, in preliminary form, during Fall 2006 and Spring 2007. Thanks to all the students, and in particular, thanks to:

Matt Adelman
Stephanie Borrelli
James Bradley
Jeffrey M. Cap
Kyrus Daugherty
Jill L. Genovese
Jacob Heath
Ashley Jones
Sheri Keller
Viridiana Ortega
Daniel Polivka
Craig Rose

Joseph Schmelter
Savannah Short
Jaron Smith
Anran Wang

Frank Kidner wishes to thank his colleagues Bob Cherney, Trevor Getz, Pi-Ching Hsu, Julyana Peard, and Jarbel Rodriguez for their help at various points in *Making Europe*'s development.

Maria Bucur wishes to thank her husband, Daniel Deckard, for continued support and inspiration in matters intellectual and musical, and her children Dylan and Elvin, for putting up with the many hours mommy had to be away from them and reinvigorating her in the hours she was lucky to be with them.

Ralph Mathisen wishes to thank Frank Kidner for getting this project going and keeping it on track. He would also like to thank his two children, Katherine and David Mathisen, for putting up with piles of civ texts, notes, and drafts spread all over for these past eight years.

Sally McKee wishes to thank her fellow authors for their mutual support, epicurean disposition, and good cheer over the years.

All of us wish to express our deepest thanks to our development editor, Ann Hofstra Grogg, who worked with us throughout the writing of this book. A thousand thanks, Ann!

F. L. K.
M. B.
R. M.
S. M.
T. R. W.

About the Authors

Frank L. Kidner is Professor of History Emeritus at San Francisco State University, where he taught from 1968 until his retirement in 2006. He has also taught in the Western Civilization program at Stanford University and at Amherst College. His courses include Western Civilization, undergraduate and graduate courses in Early Modern Europe, and the history of the Christian Church as well as a graduate course in historical methodology. He has authored articles on topics in Late Antiquity and co-edited *Travel, Communication and Geography in Late Antiquity.*

Maria Bucur is Associate Professor and John V. Hill Chair in East European History at Indiana University, where she teaches an undergraduate course on "The Idea of Europe" and other topics in nineteenth- and twentieth-century eastern Europe. Her research focus is on social and cultural developments in eastern Europe, with a special interest in Romania (geographically) and gender (thematically). Her publications include *Eugenics and Modernization in Interwar Romania* and the co-edited volumes *Staging the Past: The Politics of Commemoration in Habsburg Central Europe, 1848 to the Present* and *Gender and War in Twentieth-Century Eastern Europe.*

Ralph Mathisen is Professor of History, Classics, and Medieval Studies at the University of Illinois at Urbana-Champaign. He is a specialist in the ancient world with a particular interest in the society, culture, and religion of Late Antiquity. His teaching experience includes Western Civilization and topics in the Ancient Near East, Greece, Rome, Byzantium, coinage, and Roman law. He has written more than seventy scholarly articles and written or edited ten books, the most recent of which is *People, Personal Expression, and Social Relations in Late Antiquity.* He is also the editor of the *Journal of Late Antiquity.*

Sally McKee is Associate Professor of History at the University of California at Davis, where she teaches courses on Western Civilization and medieval history. Her research focus has been Venice and its colonies and Mediterranean slavery, but her new project centers on nineteenth-century France. She is the author of articles that have won prizes and been anthologized, and she has also published a three-volume edition of Venetian-Cretan wills and a monograph, *Uncommon Dominion: Venetian Crete and the Myth of Ethnic Purity.*

Theodore R. Weeks is Professor of History at Southern Illinois University at Carbondale, where he teaches Western Civilization and world and European history. His research centers on nationality, inter-ethnic relations, and antisemitism in eastern Europe. He is the author of *Nation and State in Late Imperial Russia* and *From Assimilation to Antisemitism: The "Jewish Question" in Poland, 1850–1914,* and his articles have appeared in several languages, including Lithuanian and Belarusian.

Making Europe

The Renaissance in Italy and Northern Europe, 1350–1550

CHAPTER 12

CHAPTER OUTLINE

1500 B.C.E.	1000 B.C.E.	500 B.C.E.	1 B.C.E./1 C.E.

	1347 Black Death first appears in Italy				1417 Great Schism ends	1440s Gutenberg invents printing process

1340	1360	1380	1400	1420	1440

The Spread of New Cultural Expression, 1300–1500

In the fifteenth century, artists and thinkers across northern Italy produced extraordinary artistic and intellectual work that attracted attention throughout Europe. Byzantine refugee scholars brought previously unknown classical works with them to Italy. Which Italian cities played important roles in the promotion of the new forms of cultural expression?

Largest cities, ca. 1500

- ■ Over 125,000
- ◆ 100,000 to 125,000
- ● 50,000 to 100,000
- ○ 25,000 to 50,000
- • Other cities
- — Boundary of Holy Roman Empire

ATLANTIC OCEAN

IRELAND
Dublin
Edinburgh
ENGLAND
London
North Sea
NORWAY
Oslo
Stockholm
SWEDEN
Baltic Sea
DENMARK
Lübeck
Danzig
Riga
TEUTONIC KNIGHTS
MUSCOVY
Warsaw
POLAND-LITHUANIA
Kiev
KHANATE OF THE GOLDEN HORDE
Rotterdam
Antwerp
Ghent
FLANDERS
Rouen
Paris
Fontainebleau
FRANCE
Mainz
HOLY ROMAN EMPIRE
BOHEMIA
Prague
Cracow
Vienna
AUSTRIA
Buda Pest
HUNGARY
MOLDAVIA
Lyons
SWISS CONF.
SAVOY
Brescia
Verona
MILAN
Milan
Cremona
Genoa
Venice
VENICE
Bologna
Florence
Pisa
Urbino
Siena
Black Sea
NAVARRE
Marseilles
GENOA
PORTUGAL
KINGDOM OF CASTILE AND ARAGON
Valencia
Córdoba
Seville
Granada
Cádiz
Ceuta
Corsica (Genoa)
Sardinia
PAPAL STATES
Rome
Naples
Ragusa
OTTOMAN EMPIRE
Constantinople
Salonica
Smyrna
Algiers
Palermo
Sicily
Tunis
MOORISH EMIRATES
Mediterranean Sea
Crete (Venice)
Cyprus (Venice)

0 200 400 Km.
0 200 400 Mi.

500 C.E.	1000 C.E.	1500 C.E.	2000 C.E.

1492 Columbus sets sail

1508 Michelangelo begins painting ceiling of the Sistine Chapel

1485 Henry Tudor defeats Richard III of England

1494 Savonarola institutes reforms in Florence

1516 Erasmus translates the Greek New Testament

1517 Luther condemns indulgences

1532 Machiavelli publishes *The Prince*

1460	1480	1500	1520	1540	1560

Choic Choice Choice

Although a few Renaissance painters matched his skill and talent, Leonardo da Vinci surpassed them all in vision, curiosity, learning, and expertise in an impressive range of subjects. In 1513, when he was sixty-one years old and living in Rome, Leonardo drew this self-portrait that shows the flowing hair and beard of an old man. (Alinari/Art Resource, NY)

Leonardo da Vinci Seeks Employment

In the spring of 1519, at the great age of sixty-seven, Leonardo da Vinci made his will. He died several days later, leaving his long-time trusted assistant, Francesco Melzi, a treasure trove of paintings and drawings. Their power to move and evoke awe has not diminished with the passing of centuries. Today, they are among the most valuable works of art in the world.

It may have been that this master draftsman and painter would have preferred to be remembered for his engineering feats, especially those applicable to the so-called art of waging war. Leonardo had long applied his talents to the service of the state, and since 1516 he had been living in a house granted him by the French king in Fontainebleau, France. He was far from Milan, where he had spent nearly two decades in the service first of Duke Ludovico Sforza and then of the military governor after the French invaded that city in 1499 and forced Sforza out. His deathbed was equally far from Tuscany, where he had been born in 1452 and spent his childhood and youth. After spending his teenage years and his twenties working as an apprentice to the master painter Andrea del Verrochio, the thirty-year-old Leonardo composed a letter to Ludovico Sforza, in which he detailed the skills he hoped to put to use in the duke's service. He offered to design bridges that could bear the weight of cannon and weaponry; to instruct Milanese captains in the techniques of siege warfare; to make a transportable cannon that fired rocks; and to build ships more suitable to naval warfare, as well as siege engines, catapults, and even an armored vehicle to transport troops. In the end, none of these plans were ever executed, but they demonstrate Leonardo's extraordinary imagination. Only in an incidental way did he mention the very talents for which he was already acquiring a reputation, painting and sculpture.

By portraying himself in this fashion, Leonardo ensured that he would not have to choose among his many and varied interests. Noble men and women all over Italy wanted him to paint their portraits. Monasteries commissioned him to paint altarpieces and frescoes. The city of Florence hired him to paint a large and complicated fresco painting of a battle for the city's freedom. The pope ordered paintings from him. But Leonardo simultaneously pursued his military interests. He drew topographical maps of contested territory for his employers. The government of Genoa paid him to survey the landscape in the city's hinterland and make recommendations on its defenses. In 1500, he inspected and suggested improvements to the eastern defenses of the Republic of Venice. Two years later, he prepared military maps and charts of the Papal States for the pope.

Leonardo's decision to emphasize his talent for military engineering in his letter to the duke of Milan was in his mind not much different from his decision to put his talent for painting in the service of the French king. Both rulers were willing to give him employment to create what the world

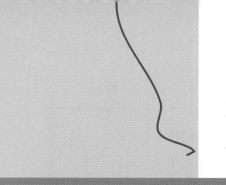

perceived to be the work of an artisan. In Leonardo's lifetime, the work of engineers and artists overlapped to a great degree. Wealthy patrons saw in the talents of artisans like Leonardo an opportunity to enhance their own prestige and social status. The cities of Italy were utterly transformed in the process.

Introduction

Even before Leonardo died, his fame was secured for his work as an artist, and it would soon be seen as part of the cultural flowering of art and literature that began in Italy and is known as the Renaissance. By the early sixteenth century, the new forms of expression affirming faith in God and the worth of human creativity had been developing for more than a century. Even before famine and plague afflicted Italy in the fourteenth century, its intellectuals and artisans had begun to explore new techniques, new ideas, and new ways to analyze old texts, and the hardships ahead did not hinder them. Over time, commerce and industry revitalize the Italian urban economies hurt by crop failures and population loss. A mutually beneficial relationship developed between wealthy families looking to display their high social status and talented scholars and artisans. The products of those relationships—extraordinary, lifelike paintings and bronze statuary, philosophical treatises displaying great learning, and breathtaking monuments to God or man—caught the attention of the rest of the continent.

No longer confined to the world of the clergy, scholars rejected the old methods of analysis in favor of a rigorous, questioning approach to the study of classical and Christian texts. In Italy, intellectuals discovered new joy in reading ancient Latin texts, taking pleasure foremost in the literary qualities of Cicero and Virgil instead of testing their compatibility with Christian doctrine. When Greek texts that no one in the west had previously read arrived in the baggage of refugees from the east, the scholars dedicated themselves with enthusiasm to the study of Greek. In northern Europe, the same love of inquiry drove scholars to reexamine with newly critical eyes authoritative Christian texts. The invention of the printing press made all these texts widely available to a far greater number of readers than ever before, prompting new levels of scholarly debate.

Both in Italy and in the north, painters, sculptors, and architects approached their work with the same open mind with which scholars viewed their texts. An enhanced appreciation of human potential and a desire to highlight in the human form the image of God inspired them to represent in their work men and women with a realism not seen in paintings and sculpture since ancient Rome. Italian painters relied on the precision of perspective, while the Flemish painters achieved similar effect with the warmth of color. The results stunned the whole of western Europe. Guided by scholarly insight into God's relationship to humanity and inspired by the astonishing creativity of the artisans now become artists, the rulers of Europe might now act like the wise princes so many of their subjects hoped they would become. They hoped in vain.

A New Climate of Cultural Expression

⬇ How did the humanists differ from monks and scholastic thinkers?

⬇ What factors caused artisans to emerge as artists?

Even before the Black Death completely subsided, an entirely new spirit began to be felt in Italy. Between the middle of the fourteenth and the middle of the fifteenth centuries, an explosion of cultural expression of astonishing and extravagant proportions permeated every aspect of life. No one, no matter how poor, could fail to notice. Whether passing the construction site of an enormous cathedral dome rising to an awe-inspiring height, praying before an altar painting of an unusually lifelike and colorful scene, or watching a bejeweled husband and wife clothed in rich fabric trimmed with gold embroidery, surrounded by a large entourage, pass by on a city street, even the most ordinary person was aware of living in an extraordinary time. People believed they, or at least their societies, had reached unprecedented wealth and ease. This impression was only partly an illusion.

The Spirit of Humanism

The new spirit began with a broadening of learning. Universities no longer held a monopoly on intellectual pursuits. Now laymen studied texts with private

Chronology

1356	Emperor Charles IV issues Golden Bull
1362	Lithuanians capture Kiev
1380	Venice and Genoa fight War of Chioggia
1417	Great Schism ends
1436	Brunelleschi's dome atop the cathedral of Florence is consecrated
1440	Lorenzo Valla refutes authenticity of Donation of Constantine
1440s	Gutenberg invents printing press
1450	Francesco Sforza becomes duke of Milan
1455–1485	House of Lancaster and House of York fight Wars of the Roses
ca. 1455	Gutenberg Bible is published
1470	Thomas Malory writes *Le Morte d'Arthur (The Death of Arthur)*
1478	Lorenzo de' Medici survives assassination attempt
1485	William Caxton publishes Malory's *Le Morte D'Arthur;* Henry Tudor defeats Richard III of England
1494	Ludovico Sforza becomes duke of Milan; The Medici of Florence enter exile
1496	Savonarola assumes power in Florence
1498	Savonarola is burned at the stake
1508	Pope Julius II reconquers Papal States
1508–1512	Michelangelo paints ceiling of Sistine Chapel
1512	Medici return to power
1516	Erasmus translates Greek New Testament into Latin; Leonardo settles in France
1520	Francis I becomes king of France
1532	Publication of Machiavelli's *The Prince*

tutors in the hopes of employment in the governments of Italian cities. Women from well-to-do families, too, studied philosophy and theology, but solely out of a love of learning, since careers outside of home and marriage were closed to them. Lay scholars became interested in exploring the question of what it meant to be human. They were called humanists because their intellectual interests centered on the study of humanity (*studium humanitatis*), or **humanism.** They esteemed the works of ancient Romans for their literary qualities rather than their usefulness for Christian theology. Their interest in language and the technical aspects of literature led them to criticize Scholastic thinkers for not paying closer attention to grammar and vocabulary in their interpretation of biblical texts. In general, however, they celebrated human potential and downplayed the theological emphasis on the sinful nature of humanity.

One of the earliest humanists, Francesco Petrarca, born in 1304 in Tuscany and known as **Petrarch,** belonged to the generation of scholars that joined the clergy to acquire a higher education. His father wanted him to study canon law, but a love of literature directed the young scholar toward poetry both in Latin and in the everyday **vernacular** language. Petrarch's poems made him famous throughout Italy, southern France, and eventually all of Europe, but his love of manuscripts made a greater impact on literature. As ambassador to the Avignon popes, Petrarch traveled all over Europe, stopping in monasteries along his way. A **bibliophile** of the first order, Petrarch searched

humanism Philosophical and literary study of what it means to be human.

Petrarch (1304–1374) Francesco Petrarca, one of the first humanist scholars, who was responsible for the recovery of numerous works of classical Latin Roman writers.

vernacular In medieval and Renaissance Europe, the dialects spoken in everyday life, in contrast to the literary language of Latin.

bibliophile Lover and collector of books.

through their libraries for old manuscripts and discovered lost works by Cicero. Writing to the ancient Roman as if he were alive, Petrarch chastised Cicero for contributing to the downfall of the Roman Republic. He emulated the style and content of the ancients with such success that readers took a new interest in the language and texts associated with Rome.

Ancient Greek texts benefited from the arrival of refugees from the Byzantine Empire in the 1390s. Fleeing the Ottomans, they emigrated to Italy and stimulated a great interest in the literature of the past. After a tour of Europe in 1394, the great Greek scholar **Emmanuel Chrysoloras** made Florence a new center of Greek learning, thanks to his skills as a teacher and to the manuscripts he brought with him. Other Byzantine scholars found employment elsewhere in Italy, where they not only taught Greek but also introduced intellectuals to the previously unknown body of scientific works by Plato, Aristotle, and others.

Not all intellectuals worked as papal secretaries or scribes in city government. Some worked directly for **autocratic** rulers and wealthy merchants who enjoyed the prestige that came with being **patrons** of humanists. These men employed scholars in their households, to instruct their children or to converse when visitors came to call. Humanist **clients** encouraged their patrons to collect manuscripts and, later, books that would form the basis of some of Europe's most important libraries. **Lorenzo de' Medici,** the ruler of Florence in the late fifteenth century, amassed an important collection of manuscripts and books under the guidance of the humanist scholars whose patron he was. Although humanists tended to embrace the values of the patrons for whom they worked, they admired Cicero's involvement in Roman public affairs and valued political engagement in city life. The Florentine humanists took from Cicero an appreciation for republicanism, which rejected autocractic rule in favor of government by the people. **Civic humanism,** the study of ancient texts to develop ideological support for Florence's republican government, gave the humanists an opportunity to express their patriotism. Through the study of these texts, the humanists sought to bring what they perceived to be the best of the ancient world to life again in their own time—hence their conviction that they lived in a period of rebirth, or **renaissance.**

From Artisan to Artist

By the end of the fifteenth century, when the Renaissance in Italy was at its height, patrons like Lorenzo de' Medici would have viewed the painter, sculptor, and architect **Michelangelo** much as we do today, as an artist of outstanding genius. Two centuries earlier, the early-fourteenth-century Italian painter **Giotto** would have been viewed as an **artisan** of exceptional talent. The emergence of artists from the world of artisans had everything to do with the same cultural climate in which humanist scholars worked.

Giotto painted in a time when the function of a painting mattered as much as the beauty or creativity it displayed. The male and female patrons who hired Giotto would have specified what they wanted to see in the painting. Giotto's role in the process was simply to execute the patron's desire. Although Giotto received much praise for the beauty and spiritual qualities of his painting, he was only a craftsman in the eyes of the people who employed him. Religious and secular patrons hired artisan painters, sculptors, and architects to create devotional objects whose beauty was meant to enhance, reinforce, and remind viewers of what they should believe or do. Painted frescoes like the ones Giotto painted celebrating the life of Saint Francis in the basilica at Assisi (see image on page 271) depicted stories that taught the laity the elements of Christian belief. Sculptors created statues out of stone or bronze that portrayed holy or historical figures, celebrated warriors, or secular rulers. Craftsmen builders designed churches, government buildings, and private residences whose size or grandeur suggested the glory of God or its occupants. Even the finely crafted gold and silver objects on display in churches had practical uses in the Mass. All artistic creations had a purpose and a function.

Emmanuel Chrysoloras (1355–1415) Important Greek scholar who introduced the scientific works of ancient Greek philosophers to the west.

autocrat Ruler who possesses absolute power.

patron Person, usually wealthy or powerful, who financially supports the intellectual or artistic work of a client.

client Artist or intellectual supported by a wealthy patron.

Lorenzo de' Medici (r. 1469–1492, "the Magnificent") Ruler of Florence and patron of artists, poets, and humanist scholars during the Italian Renaissance.

civic humanism Study and appreciation of classical republican forms of government.

renaissance Literally, "rebirth," signifying a revival.

Michelangelo Buonarotti (1475–1564) Painter, sculptor, poet, and architect, considered in his time to be the greatest artist Italy had ever produced.

Giotto di Bondone (1267–1334) Best-known and most influential painter of the Middle Ages.

artisan Skilled craftsmen, such as a cabinetmaker, painter, or shoemaker.

For these reasons, those who painted portraits or religious works, made statues, and designed buildings would have described themselves as artisans, not as painters, sculptors, or architects. They were also businessmen. If a painter was successful, he very likely owned and operated his own workshop and employed other painters who assisted him, even to the extent of painting the background of a scene that would eventually be associated with his name alone. **Gentile Bellini,** a renowned Venetian painter and the son and brother of two other famous painters, was the master of his own workshop, where he and his assistants together painted scenes of Venice's ceremonial life. The contract he signed with his patrons specified precisely what images the painting would contain, the pigment colors that would be used, and the date when the project would be completed. Once all the conditions had been agreed upon, Bellini's assistants worked on drafting and painting the buildings in the background while the master focused his creative attention on the figures that required technical precision and artistic vision. Sculptors and architects made similar contractual arrangements with their patrons, who tended to view themselves as the real creative force behind artistic productions.

The workmanlike relationship between a painter and his patron changed slowly over the fifteenth century as the creative expression of the artisan became more highly valued. By the end of the century, not only did people think of painters, sculptors, and architects as artists, as we understand the term, but the artisans also began to regard their skills and talent more highly than previously. Michelangelo, a devoutly religious man, who painted the ceiling of the Sistine Chapel and designed Saint Peter's Church, both at the **Vatican,** evoked the highest praise of any artist in his time from his contemporaries, yet he revealed his ambivalence about the life of an artist in a poem:

My cherished art, my season in the sun,
name, fame, acclaim—that cant I made a run for,
left me in servitude, poor, old, alone.
O death, relieve me soon. Or soon I'm done for.

By the sixteenth century, the artisan had become an artist, and his work was now art. This change is reflected clearly in a collection of biographical sketches by a painter whose reputation rests more firmly on his writings than on his paintings. **Giorgio Vasari's** *The Lives of the Most Eminent Painters, Sculptors, and Architects,* published in 1550, preserves details about the life, work, and character of Renaissance Italy's most famous artists, from Giotto in the thirteenth century to Michelangelo in the sixteenth. In this work, the stereotype of artist as temperamental genius emerges clearly for the first time.

Perspectives and Techniques

One man's career best personifies the changes in cultural expression and production during the Italian Renaissance. **Filippo Brunelleschi,** like most of his colleagues, did not confine himself exclusively to one creative medium. He was an exceptionally talented painter, metalworker, engineer, and architect, all in one. Born and raised in Florence, Brunelleschi became even in his own day one of the most famous artists Italy ever produced. His two most significant contributions to the cultural movements of his time related to his experiments with **linear perspective** in painting and to his engineering innovations in architecture.

Like the humanists, Brunelleschi believed the ancient Romans had much to teach him. His studies in the art and architecture of Rome led him to develop the mathematical principles of linear perspective that the Romans had used in their wall paintings to convey a sense of depth. Linear perspective creates the illusion of three dimensions on a two-dimensional surface. To convey a sense of depth or distance, the painter drew lines on the flat surface of his canvas or wall that all converged on one point, called the **vanishing point.** Brunelleschi's own paintings in which he demonstrated this technique have not survived, but his peers credit him with bringing the principles of linear perspective to the attention of working painters and sculptors. Among the very first to make use of perspective were **Masaccio** in Florence and Ja-

Gentile Bellini   (ca. 1429–1507) Important Venetian painter whose subject matter mainly concerned Venetian political and religious history.

Vatican   Area on the north side of the Tiber in Rome where the pope was living by the end of the fifteenth century.

Giorgio Vasari   (1511–1574) Italian architect and artist who wrote biographies of Renaissance artists.

Filippo Brunelleschi   (1377–1446) Outstanding architect, painter, and engineer who introduced linear perspective in painting and designed the dome of Florence's cathedral.

linear perspective   Illusion of depth and three-dimensional space in an image achieved by drawing the lines of the composition toward a vanishing point.

vanishing point   In a painting, the point at which all the lines converge to give the illusion of depth and three dimensions.

Masaccio   (1401–1428) Italian artist notable for his early experimentation with linear perspective.

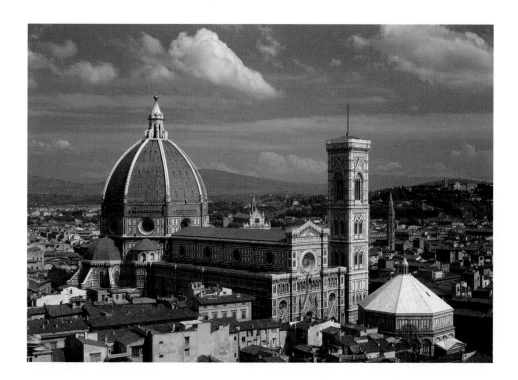

Brunelleschi's reputation rests on his engineering of the dome of Florence's cathedral, finished in 1436 and pictured here. Italians refer to cathedrals by their word for "dome," *duomo*. The Duomo stands out so clearly in Florence's skyline that it epitomizes the city today as much as it did in the fifteenth century. *(Scala/Art Resource, NY)*

copo Bellini, the father of Gentile Bellini, the prominent Venetian painter.

Brunelleschi's fame, in his own time and today, however, stems mainly from his architectural and engineering accomplishments. Although the foundation of Florence's cathedral was laid at the very end of the thirteenth century, it still lacked a roof and a dome in the first decades of the fifteenth century. In 1420, Brunelleschi, chief architect of the ongoing construction, implemented his plan to build an enormous and immensely heavy octagonal dome on top of the completed cathedral walls. It was a daring project, involving updated Roman engineering equipment and ancient brick and stone methods of construction. In the end, Brunelleschi's plan worked, and the dome was consecrated in 1436. A friend of all the great artists at the time, Brunelleschi represents the extraordinary combination of talent, skill, and great learning found in many of the artists who emerged in the fifteenth century.

Leonardo da Vinci rivaled Brunelleschi and Michelangelo in breadth of knowledge, skill, and talent. He worked as a painter of portraits and of the large frescoes in monasteries and civic buildings that only ecclesiastical institutions and governments could afford to commission. His skills as a military engineer made him just as well known (see Choice). He was a scholar, too, who read widely in many fields. The humanist quest to celebrate all that was human inspired Leonardo to investigate the inner workings of the human body through dissections of cadavers, an illegal practice condemned by the church. Understanding how tendons connected muscle to bone enabled him to depict human forms with detailed accuracy. Everything that was human fascinated Leonardo. His wide range of expertise and his genius made him the prototype of the Renaissance man.

The Pleasure of Things

The explosion of cultural creativity in Renaissance Italy was not confined to the works of art in churches and government buildings. All wanted to adorn themselves and their surroundings with more possessions than had ever been available before, but, as always, only a minority could afford to. When the economy began to revive after the reversals and disasters of the fourteenth century, a new acquisitive spirit took hold in Italian cities as trade, manufacturing, and a rise in imported goods provided people with opportunities to spend money on objects that pleased them, enhanced their status, or both.

Leonardo da Vinci (1452–1519) One of the world's greatest artists and engineers, most famous for his painting the *Mona Lisa*.

Before beginning his painting in 1482, the Adoration of the Magi, Leonardo sketched on paper its composition, using linear perspective in the architectural elements. The painting was never finished, but Leonardo's sketches have taught art historians much about how painters in the fifteenth century worked. *(Scala/Art Resource, NY)*

Domestic interiors in the late fourteenth century would have seemed as uncomfortable to someone at the start of the sixteenth century as they would to someone today. Medieval homes lacked good seating. Most families of modest means in the fourteenth century owned very few pieces of furniture. One or two beds sufficed for all members of the family; the servants slept on rushes piled on the floor. One table provided a surface to eat on, socialize around, or write on. Perhaps there was a stool or a wooden bench to sit on. Against a wall might be a rough-hewn wooden chest for storage. With so little furniture, families spent most of their days outside in the courtyard of a house, working in the fields, or sitting under a tree with their neighbors, whether they lived in the countryside or in a city. When they had to come indoors, family members piled on the bed for seating.

The home of a well-to-do family would not have contained a greater variety of furniture, although there were likely to be a few more seats, wooden chests, and tables. Nor was there much in the way of decoration. Only wealthy families could afford to have their walls hung with tapestries, whose main function was, in any case, to retain heat. Everyday utensils, like serving dishes and cookware, tended to be uniform and utilitarian in shape, color, and material.

As the fifteenth century progressed, people bought more and more things, because, in large part, there were now more things to buy. Italian cities were becoming societies of consumers, intent on spending money in ways that would show off their status and taste. The wealthiest families directed their money toward building palaces that would reflect their social status. Domestic architecture emerged as a style distinct from ecclesiastic and governmental architecture. Builders designed palaces for their patrons that looked magnificent and imposing from the outside and luxurious and ceremonial on the inside. Spacious reception rooms, where the members of the family met with visitors, now contained more kinds of furniture than before. Larger and more ornately decorated wooden storage chests lined the wall. More chairs were available. A sideboard held the family's silverplate in a room now specifically designated for eating. Framed devotional paintings or frescoes depicting all the members of the family and their patron saints filled in the spots on the wall not covered by tapestries. People spent their money on luxury goods that would impress a visitor with the family's wealth, prestige, and cultivated taste.

In addition to decorating their homes, consumers also spent a good deal of money on what they wore. Until the fifteenth century, people's social status could be judged by the quality of their clothes. Renaissance Italians now had a greater variety of apparel to choose from, and the clothes themselves became more ornate, more complex in design, and made of expensive material. This greater availability of luxurious clothing, however, caused social tension. When a greater variety of fabrics came on the market at prices humble people could afford, even the wife of a shoemaker could look like a member of the upper classes. People could no longer be sure of a stranger's social rank from his or her clothing. Many city governments in Italy passed **sumptuary laws** that prohibited people of middle and low social status from wearing the kinds of fabrics and accessories associated with the rich. Ordinary women, for instance, could not use mink to trim the necklines of their dresses. In Venice, only patrician men could wear a red *giubba,* the gown worn by men of the city's highest rank. Of course, these laws proved very difficult to enforce. The consumer societies coming into being in the fifteenth century had the unintended effect of blurring some social distinctions that the ruling elites depended on to maintain order in society and themselves in power.

The Northern European Renaissance

⬇ What distinguished Flemish from Italian painters?
⬇ How did the invention of movable type and the printing press bring about a revolution?

The Renaissance in northern Europe contrasted sharply with the busy, chaotic workshops of Italian artists and the offices in government palaces occupied by busy scribes. In Flanders, France, and England, quiet chambers in universities and libraries lined with tall bookcases—with the soft light of northern Europe streaming through glass windows—characterized the more tranquil environment of intellectuals and artists at work. What was produced in the northern Renaissance struck contemporary observers as no less stunning, however, for its less dramatic and less noisy emergence onto the cultural scene. If northern Europe benefited much from exposure to Italian scholars and artists, then the people of the north more than balanced the exchange of innovation by providing everyone with the printing press.

In this study in Anderlecht, in modern-day Belgium, the humanist theologian, Desiderius Erasmus wrote his best-known works at this desk. The shelves above his desk hold books of a size typical in his time. On the writing stand, an inkwell holds a feather quill, like Erasmus would have used to write. *(Erich Lessing/Art Resource, NY)*

Northern European Art

The other center of artistic innovation in the fifteenth century lay in northern Europe, particularly in the cities of Flanders, where a style of painting and decoration very much different from Italian painting evolved. Although Flemish and Italian painters were interested in one another's work, they took from the other basic ideas and molded them to fit their own cultural environment. So subtle was the cultural exchange that it has been a matter of considerable debate as to whether the fifteenth-century fashion for portrait painting began in Italy or in Flanders. By the end of that century, however, two distinct styles of painting and sculpture had emerged.

sumptuary laws   Municipal legislation restricting modes and expense of attire according to social status, profession, and, in the case of Jews, religion.

Manuscripts from the late fourteenth century reveal the earliest signs of northern European artists' unique approach to representing the world around them. Wealthy women and men paid copyists to compile prayer books for use in daily worship and artists to illuminate the pages with designs and figures in brilliant colors and gold leaf. A so-called **Book of Hours** contained a calendar with feast days and saints' days marked, the Psalms, and readings from the Gospels. Typically, illuminating the calendar offered the artist an opportunity to use bright and costly blue, red, and gold pigments to illustrate a month. In the manuscript collections of the Psalms (**Psalters**) and the schedule of church services throughout the year, which were small enough to fit conveniently in the hand, artists rendered painstakingly detailed scenes of the banquets, hunts, and other recreations of the nobility and urban elites. *The Very Rich Hours of the Duke of Berry*, executed around 1416, offers an exquisite example of the artistry to be seen in northern Europe.

From the detailed miniature manuscript illuminations to oil paintings was a short step. Unlike Italian artists, who used paints made of pigments mixed with egg yolks—known as **tempera**—either on fresh wall plaster or on wooden boards joined to form a smooth surface, Flemish painters set their scenes in pigments mixed with linseed oil and on linen canvas. The practice of painting in oil migrated from Flanders to Italy by the start of the sixteenth century, once Italian artists saw the superb work of **Jan van Eyck**, court painter to Philip, duke of Burgundy, and other Flemish artists. Apart from this difference in painting medium, two other differences in technique between the Italians and the Flemish are immediately noticeable. Whereas Italian painters relied on linear perspective to convey depth and dimension, the Flemish used gradations in color and the optical effect of painted light to achieve the same effect. And Italian painters presented their paintings in an architectural frame within the painting that separated the viewers from the painting's subject, while Flemish painters placed their subjects in a setting that seemed to include the viewer of the painting in the same space.

In contrast to the monumental, spare quality of Italian painting, the oil painting of Flanders looked cluttered and busy, with too many objects claiming the viewer's attention. Nothing in the world around them—from sacred figures to the buttons on the jacket worn by a portrait's subject—seemed insignificant to van Eyck and his fellow painters. They sought to realistically depict things and people as they looked to the human eye. It was the ordinariness of life that interested them. Not everyone appreciated the effort.

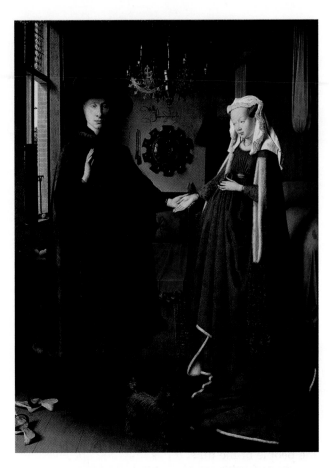

Above, in his 1434 portrait of a newly-married couple, the Flemish painter Jan Van Eyck used light and color to achieve depth of field. In contrast, the Italian Fra Angelico, a painter and Dominican friar, employed linear perspective—the use of lines converging on a vanishing point—for a similar effect in his fresco of the Annunciation from the 1440s on the right (page 333). *(Above: Reproduced by courtesy of the Trustees, the National Gallery, London; Right: Erich Lessing/Art Resource, NY)*

Michelangelo, for one, thought Flemish painters were far too obsessed with the minutiae of life and not attentive enough to its spiritual essence. Yet the things that cluttered Flemish paintings possessed meanings not

Book of Hours   Book or manuscript containing a calendar, prayers, and biblical passages for private devotion.

Psalter   Book or manuscript containing the Psalms.

tempera   Egg-based medium that binds paint pigments, used in Renaissance Italy.

Jan van Eyck   (ca. 1390–1441) Influential Flemish painter whose pioneering use of rich colors and light conveyed unprecedented depth of field.

easily apparent. In his portrait commemorating the marriage of an Italian merchant residing in Bruges, the objects van Eyck placed around the wedding couple standing beside a bed include a little dog and one lighted candle in the chandelier, both objects seemingly irrelevant to the event the painting honored. To the people of the time, it has long been believed, the bed was a familiar symbol of the sexual union in marriage, the little dog recalled fidelity, and the candle signaled the presence of Christ at the marriage. Thus, the painting works on both literal and symbolic levels at the same time. Flemish artists invited viewers to look not just at the objects in their paintings but through the objects to find their symbolic meaning.

Northern Humanists

Scholars from all over Europe undertook the arduous journey through the mountain passes into Italy to learn from the humanist scholars, especially those in Florence, whose works displayed a refreshing approach to classical literature. Frenchmen, Englishmen, and scholars from the Low Countries, in particular, came to Florence, Pisa, Venice, and other cities, where they found tutors in Greek and specialists in Latin literature to study with. When they returned home, they took with them new methods for the analysis of texts, a deeper appreciation for Greek and Roman literature, and plans to apply their newly acquired learning in the service of the church. In contrast to the Italian humanists, who believed public

service was as important as private study, the scholars from the north mostly came from and returned to either the cloister or the university. Because they were not in the public eye, the impact they had on their societies was less obvious and provoked less fanfare, but it was equally profound.

Like many of the Italian humanists, the humanists of northern Europe focused on the languages and literature of the past, but their interests reflected their close ties to the church and universities. By examining the language and history of texts written by early Christian writers more closely than had been done before, these fifteenth-century Christian humanists placed Christianity in history. They traced the evolution of doctrine from the church's earliest days to their present. In France, Italian-trained humanists such as Jacques Lefèvre d'Étaples produced new editions of texts written by the early church fathers. Others, like John Colet at Oxford University in England, studied early Christian texts written in Greek and Latin. They were the first generation of scholars to question the accuracy of the translations from Greek into Latin of scripture and the writings of early church thinkers. These editing projects and textual analyses formed the basis of a new field, **patristics.** Likewise, German scholars studied early Hebrew texts to gauge their influence on the development of early Christian thought.

The new fields and methods of study were controversial. From the perspective of the Christian humanists, the texts they studied and edited suggested that the church had wandered far from its original mission. More controversially, a few questioned the translation of certain words and verses in the New Testament, a text whose accuracy the church prohibited anyone from questioning. **Desiderius Erasmus,** a theologian born in Rotterdam in the Low Countries,

---

patristics Study of the writings of the early church fathers, such as Jerome, Ambrose, Augustine, and Pope Gregory I.

Desiderius Erasmus (1469–1536) Dutch humanist, theologian, and textual scholar whose writings influenced the movement for church reform.

In 1523, Hans Holbein the Younger, one of the best known painters in northern Europe, painted this portrait of Erasmus. Even though he is shown indoors, he wears heavy robes and a hat. The interiors of houses in northern Europe were so difficult to heat that people dressed very warmly while indoors. *(Erich Lessing/Art Resource, NY)*

believed not only that literate lay Christians ought to read scripture in the languages they spoke, but also, that scholars ought to reexamine the Vulgate Bible, which he found to contain errors in translation from the Greek New Testament. After a number of years of comparing manuscripts of the Greek New Testament he found in western Europe, Erasmus produced in 1516 a corrected Greek version with an updated Latin translation and extensive notes. Even this corrected version did not satisfy the standards set by humanist scholars, including Erasmus himself, and in 1522 he issued an improved edition of his Greek Testament that corrected his own errors. Erasmus faced stiff criticism from church leaders, most of whom objected to his undertaking the translation without the authorization of the church. They also felt ambivalent about making scripture available in vernacular languages to people liable to read whatever they wished into the translations. Even many of Erasmus's friends warned him that allowing laypeople to read and interpret the Bible for themselves would lead to disorder and rebellion. Although he and his fellow humanists believed that reading scripture for themselves in their own language would strengthen laypeople's faith, Erasmus came to see that it would not necessarily lead to continued obedience to church authority.

Jewish scholars, too, participated in the humanist study of texts. Their works incorporating humanist principles into the study of Judaism and the Hebrew Bible drew the interest of some Christian scholars. The study of Hebrew texts posed a challenge to those who objected in principle to the idea that Judaism had any influence on Christianity. Anti-Jewish senti-

Voice

Erasmus Defends His Translation of the Greek New Testament

Erasmus, a theologian and editor and translator of the Greek New Testament, faced strong criticism for undertaking his translation from church leaders and other theologians, who feared what would happen if laypeople studied the text on their own. Erasmus had an enormous circle of friends throughout Europe. All his life, he wrote letters to them in which he discussed whichever work he was composing at the time, debated with them about political trends, and defended his belief in church reform. In the following letter, written in 1515, he responds to Martin Dorp, a Dutch theologian who in a previous letter had questioned the need for and legitimacy of the New Testament translation that Erasmus was about to begin. In his reply, Erasmus aggressively defends his translation at the same time as he insinuates that someone like Dorp, who could not read scripture in its original language of Greek, was in no position to lecture a theologian who could.

What you write about the New Testament really makes me wonder what's happened to you. . . . You don't want me to change a single thing unless an idea is expressed more significantly in the Greek, and you deny that in the edition we know as the Vulgate there is any error at all. You think it would be sacrilege to alter in any way a text authenticated by agreement over so many centuries and endorsed by so many councils. 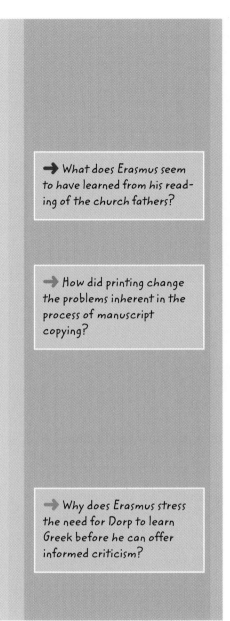 But if what you say is true, let me ask you, most learned Dorp, why Jerome often cites scripture in a form that varies from ours, and Augustine in another form, and Ambrose in still another? Why does Jerome censure and correct many specific passages which still remain uncorrected in the Vulgate?. . . . Are you going to dismiss all these authorities to follow a manuscript that may be full of scribal errors? Nobody says that the scriptures contain lies, though you seem to assume this is my attitude; nor does the matter relate in any way to the various controversies between Jerome and Augustine. 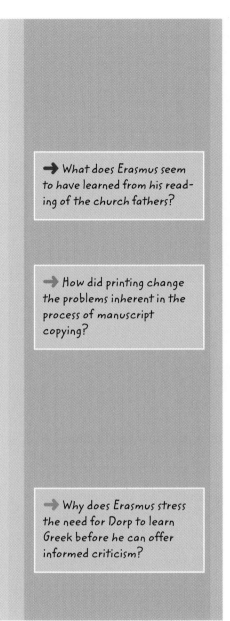 But the situation cries aloud; it would be plain, as they say, to a blind man: often, because of the ignorance or carelessness of a translator, the Greek has been imperfectly rendered, and often the original true reading has been corrupted by an ignorant copyist. We see this happen every day: texts are changed by thoughtless or sleepy scribes. Who does more to promote a lie, the man who corrects and removes a mistake, or the man who, out of reluctance to make a change, lets it stand? Besides, it's the nature of corrupt texts that one error leads to another. For a fact, more of these changes that I've made relate to the emphasis than to the basic sense, though frequently the emphasis is itself part of the sense, and not infrequently the whole passage has been drawn out of shape. When such a thing happens, I ask you, where does Augustine turn, where do Ambrose, Hilary, and Jerome look, if not to the Greek original? . . .

. . . I have translated the entire New Testament afresh from the Greek originals with a Greek text across the page for easy comparison. My annotations are separate; they show, partly on the evidence and partly on the authority of ancient theologians, that my emendations were not rashly undertaken, that they can be accepted with confidence, and that they cannot be lightly dismissed. I only hope I have succeeded in a venture which has cost me so much labor. . . . 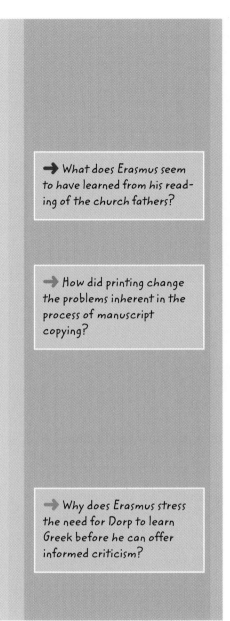 Finally, I don't doubt that you too will congratulate me on the book you now deplore, provided only that you acquire a little taste of that language without which you can't possibly form a reasonable judgment of the matter.

The sidebar questions in the image:

➡ What does Erasmus seem to have learned from his reading of the church fathers?

➡ How did printing change the problems inherent in the process of manuscript copying?

➡ Why does Erasmus stress the need for Dorp to learn Greek before he can offer informed criticism?

ment within the church and among traditional scholars made ecclesiastical authorities look with suspicion on scholars like Johannes Reuchlin, a German theologian at the university in Württemberg, who studied the **kabbala,** a Jewish mystical text.

Neither northern humanists nor their Italian counterparts sought to challenge the authority of the church and the papacy. But to varying degrees, the humanist project in northern Europe and in Italy helped to create the conditions out of which powerful critiques of the church emerged in the sixteenth century.

Printing, a New Medium

Scholarship in both northern Europe and in Italy underwent a profound change when a new invention, the printing press, made it possible to reproduce

kabbalah   (From Hebrew, "tradition") Field of Jewish mysticism dating to the twelfth century but of greater interest in the sixteenth.

Printer's shops, like this recreation of Johannes Gutenberg's in Mainz, Germany, pictured here, were crowded places. The printing press took up most of the room. Printers hung freshly-printed pages on lines across the shop so that the ink would dry. In the background appear frames with many compartments in which letter types were stored *(Erich Lessing/Art Resource, NY)*

many identical copies of a work quickly for distribution. A goldsmith from the German city of Mainz, **Johannes Gutenberg,** is believed to have invented in the 1440s the process in which a printer pressed ink-coated movable type onto paper. Although the Chinese had centuries before devised a printing process by carving the characters that made up their written language onto blocks of wood, Gutenberg's innovation was, first, to cast small pieces of metal type, each with a raised face in the shape of a letter. A typesetter arranged the metal type, letter by letter, in horizontal rows to spell out the text to be published. Setting the type was the most time-consuming part of the printing process. After the rows were locked within a frame, the printer brushed the set type with ink, laid paper on it, and then slid it under a heavy press. When all the pages of the text had been printed, the metal type was disassembled so that it could be set again for another text.

The development of the printing process depended on the availability and low cost of paper in western Europe. Originally a product from China that Muslim merchants brought back along the caravan routes to the Mediterranean, paper attracted the attention of Christian merchants—and possibly the crusaders—who had dealings in the Muslim world. They recognized that paper, made from pulverized cotton cloth,

cost far less to produce than parchment and vellum, the treated sheep or calf skins that served as writing surfaces in western Europe. Depending on its size, a complete Bible consisting entirely of parchment or vellum pages could require the skins of nearly two hundred sheep or calves, which explains why manuscripts were so expensive to produce. By the late thirteenth century, paper production in Italy had begun. Scribes continued to use parchment and vellum for their luxury manuscripts, but in everyday life people increasingly used paper for their account books, records, and private documents.

The affordability of paper and the speed of printing on it brought about a revolution in ideas and beliefs in the sixteenth century, as unprecedented amounts of information were put into circulation. The first products of the printing press certainly included books, but short and inexpensive political pamphlets, religious tracts, and bureaucratic forms appeared for sale in Mainz's first printshops right away. The artistry and craftsmanship that went into large luxury books, like the beautiful three-volume Bibles Gutenberg printed around 1455, kept their price prohibitively high.

Johannes Gutenberg   (d. 1468) Inventor of the printing press, and printing from movable type, in the west.

MAP 12.1 **The Growth of Printing** Bills of sale, sermons, bibles, and scholarly works were among the first printed texts that printers produced. The new invention quickly spread across western Europe. Within fifty years, Venice had more printing presses than any other city in Europe.

Printing shops spread quickly, first across Germany and then throughout Europe. Within a few years of Gutenberg's Bibles, the printing press reached other German cities—Strasbourg in 1460, Cologne in 1464. Sixty towns in Germany had printing shops by 1500. But in that same year Venice could boast of 150 printing presses. One Venetian printer, **Aldus Manutius**, joined with humanist scholars to print texts in the Greek alphabet that refugee scholars from the Byzantine Empire had brought to Italy.

Less than a century following the invention of movable type and the printing press, an estimated 9 million books were in circulation. Moreover, a great

many more people knew how to read, especially in Italy, where literacy had accompanied the expansion of commerce and lay education. As the print culture expanded, reliance on memory and recitation diminished. The very way people thought and learned and remembered was changing.

Aldus Manutius (1449–1515) Important Venetian printer noted for publishing Byzantine texts in the Greek alphabet.

The Cities of Renaissance Italy

↓ How were the cities of Italy governed?
↓ What was the relation of the Papal States to the politics of Renaissance Italy?

The cities of the northern Italian peninsula took pride in their nearly complete autonomy, although in theory the German Holy Roman emperor still ruled them. For some, like the city of Milan, that autonomy had come at a bloody price. The end of the fourteenth century brought an end to that autonomy. Now military strongmen, wealthy merchants, and royal foreigners each saw a chance to grab as much Italian territory as they could manage. While an army brought some to power, fabulous wealth put others in charge of their cities. The republican liberty and human potential that humanist scholars and artists celebrated remained an ideal that the reality of politics in the cities of Italy nearly always defeated.

The Medici of Florence

Florentine merchants considered themselves the inheritors of the ideals of the Roman Republic, which they read about in history books now being written for their pleasure by a new generation of humanist intellectuals espousing the ideals of civic humanism. In reality, these city governments only inadvertently resembled the Roman Republic, because, like the small elite that had ruled Rome more than fifteen hundred years before, they, too, constituted a small minority of wealthy men who monopolized the political life of their cities. Within those small groups of mercantile families, competition to exert the most influence on the government was fierce. Wealthy patrons granted business and political favors to less wealthy clients, who then were expected to vote according to the interests of their patrons. A family's political power stemmed from such supporters, friends, and relatives who felt beholden to their benefactors and their families.

In Florence, the Medici family came to power through the steady and generous distribution of fiscal, political, and commercial favors to those less fortunate than they. Those favors bought the political loyalty of those who accepted the Medici's help. The first member to achieve nearly complete but unofficial dominance of the Florentine government was **Cosimo de' Medici,** who inherited his father's lucrative role as banker to the pope in addition to the responsibility of representing the family in Florence's public life. Cosimo was elected to the Signoria and other city councils, like many of his peers, but his real

power far exceeded the authority of any public office he held. Through his network of clients, Cosimo directed—out of sight from public view—Florentine fiscal and diplomatic affairs. He dressed modestly, ate sparingly, and often retreated to Florence's most exclusive monastery, San Marco, spending days in quiet reflection and prayer. Behind that humble exterior lay a hunger for power as sharp as his splendid palace was opulent. The city governing councils did nothing relating to taxation, foreign policy, or the economy without taking their direction from Cosimo de' Medici. His supreme authority was so taken for granted—even if an open secret and resented by many—that foreign powers knew to negotiate directly with him, not the elected councils.

Despite opposition, Cosimo's grandson, Lorenzo, strengthened his family's hold on power. Called "the Magnificent" for the grandeur of his palaces and building projects, Lorenzo shared with his grandfather a similar passion for power. Displaying a subtle diplomatic skill, he prevented the pope and other Italian rulers from banding together against him, but within his own city he faced continual challenges to his power, including an attempted assassination in 1478. Although severely wounded, he lived to exact revenge on his would-be killers. Opponents of Medici rule had to wait until two years after Lorenzo's death in 1492 before they ousted the family from power and exiled them from the city.

After the ouster of the Medici in 1494, **Girolamo Savonarola,** a friar from the monastery of San Marco, used his great popularity as a church reform–minded preacher to become the next ruler of Florence. Savonarola's establishment of a new government dedicated to eradicating the corruption associated with the Medici and the papal court alarmed both the Medici allies and the pope. He ruled Florence with the support of the majority of Florentines, while a small faction of families conspired with the papacy to bring about his downfall. On the grounds that his calls for church reform constituted heresy, Savonarola was tried and burned at the stake in 1498. After four more years of turmoil in the city, the Medici returned to power in 1512.

Cosimo de' Medici (1389–1464) First important member of this wealthy family to make himself ruler of the city of Florence.

Girolamo Savonarola (1452–1498) Italian Dominican friar who tried to carry out church reform in Florence.

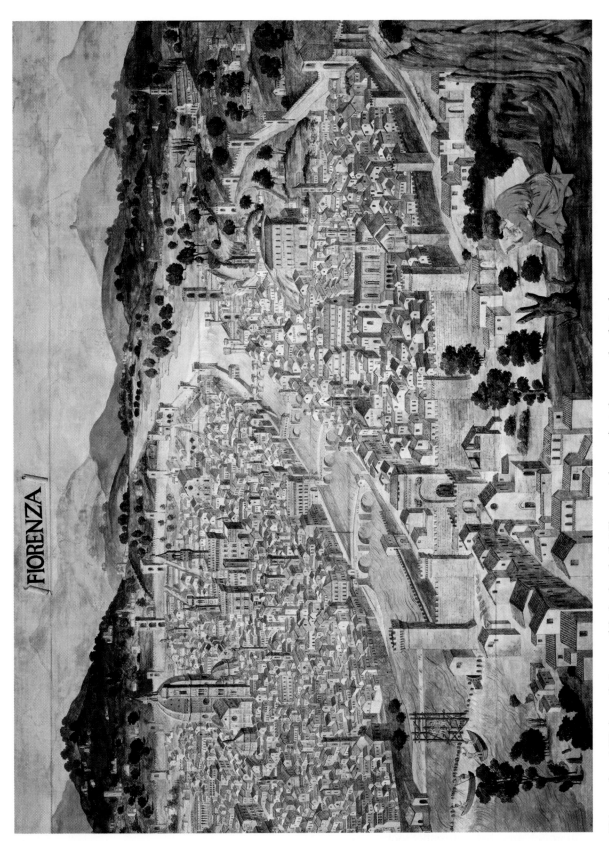

FIORENZA

This map from 1480 shows that many of the landmarks that Florence is known for today were already in place. The Duomo and the public buildings appear in the center of the map. The expansion of the city across the river Arno, to the right, required extending the city walls. *(Erich Lessing/Art Resource, NY)*

Maritime Republics

The Florentines were not the only people of Italy who claimed their city embodied the classical virtues of civic humanism. Similar to the elites of Florence, small, hereditary groups of merchant families ruled the republics of Venice and Genoa by the end of the fourteenth century. The governments of both city-states consisted of councils, over each of which a **doge** presided as the official head of state. In Venice, the members of the ruling councils considered themselves to be nobles, but the term they used to describe themselves was reminiscent of ancient Rome—patricians. They represented only about 1 percent of the population of Venice, which fluctuated just above and below 100,000. A similarly tiny percentage of Genoa's population exercised complete political authority there. The families that rose to the top of Venetian and Genoese societies became wealthy through long-distance trade. Trading companies had extensive networks of branch offices around the Mediterranean and in the ports of northern Europe.

Economic competition between Genoa and Venice at times led to open hostilities and even warfare between the two republics. Four times—in 1258, 1298, 1350, and 1380—the fleets of the two cities met in sea battles in the vicinity of their trading operations in the east and in the Venetian lagoon. They fought over access to and commercial dominance of the Aegean Islands and the Black Sea. During the last and decisive conflict known as the **War of Chioggia** in 1380, the Venetians relied on cutting-edge military technology by mounting cannon on their war galleys, which they aimed both at attacking ships and at on-shore military defenses. Venice's victory over Genoa had as much to do with its advanced weaponry as it did with Genoa's internal weaknesses. Factional fighting among Genoa's ruling elite led to frequent changes in Genoa's government and the shifting of the responsibility for the city's overseas trade to the **Maona,** a private mercantile company in Genoa that assumed the role of the state in the Aegean Islands under Genoese rule. Genoa's instability gave the edge to Venetian merchants, who benefited from the stable and mature institutions of their government, which maintained a war fleet in the region that protected them. By the turn of the fifteenth century, Venice had emerged as the stronger power.

Of the two cities, Venice had the more illustrious—certainly the more notorious—reputation. By the fifteenth century, Venetians lived as much by means of the sea as literally in the sea. A city made up of more than a hundred tiny islands connected by bridges, Venice had thoroughfares that were either footpaths or navigable canals, punctuated now and then by a campo, or field, with a public well in its center. In the seventeenth century, when the campi were paved, the Venetian government banned horses and compelled Venetians to move around the city either on foot or by gondola, a long, black vessel propelled by an upright oarsman. Even in the fifteenth century, Venice exerted a fascination on people from elsewhere. Its jewel-like appearance, lying off the mainland and surrounded by a shimmering sea, impressed visitors. So did its growing reputation for vice. Contemporaries expressed astonishment as the number of prostitutes and **courtesans** in public view in certain quarters of the city.

Beginning with Petrarch in the 1360s, humanists received a warm welcome in Venice, provided they did nothing to disturb the oligarchic serenity of Venice's patricians. In the city itself, the lack of visible social unrest among the humble sections of its population and its ruling elite impressed visitors and Venetians themselves to such an extent that its government proudly called itself The Most Serene Republic in its official documents. The Aegean islands occupied by Venetian troops in the fourteenth century and the mainland Italian cities subordinated to Venetian authority in the fifteenth had a different experience of Venice's serenity. By the middle of the fifteenth century, as Ottoman Turks undermined Venetian authority in the eastern Mediterranean and Venice attempted to extend its territory on the mainland, the other Italian powers felt increasingly threatened.

Autocrats and Humanists

In the late fourteenth century, northern Italian city dwellers lived in fear of rioting workers, bloody **vendettas** between warring families, and the violent overthrow of civic institutions by ambitious men. Personal and collective liberty required from the city residents constant vigilance and active defense. Urban violence reached such alarming levels that city

doge   (from Latin *dux*, "leader") Head of state in Venice and Genoa.

War of Chioggia   Conflict between Venice and Genoa in 1380, in which Venice won a decisive victory.

Maona   Private mercantile company in Genoa that assumed the role of the state in the Aegean Islands under Genoese rule.

courtesan   A woman, very often highly educated and refined, who served as a mistress to wealthy men in exchange for support.

vendetta   Campaign of revenge fought between two factions or families.

authorities resorted to the services of professional military men—**condottieri**—to keep the peace. These captains and their salaried armies acted at first like a police force and a militia, but they soon made themselves lords of the cities whose safety they had been hired to defend.

These military rulers of Italian cities owed their power to brute force, but disguised it behind the elegant and refined behavior typical of a Renaissance court. Among humanists, two types of the ideal ruler took shape. *The Courtier,* a widely-read work published in 1528 by **Baldassare Castiglione,** a diplomat and intellectual from Milan, described the ideal ruler as a battle-tested as well as a highly educated commander with elegant manners. Castiglione's "Renaissance man" combined a chivalrous knight with a humanist scholar.

A Florentine presented another type of ideal ruler that reflected a grittier understanding of how the world worked. The son of a poor Florentine lawyer who belonged to a distinguished family, **Niccolò Machiavelli** gained considerable experience as a diplomat in Florence's government between the death of Savonarola in 1498 and the Medici's return to power in 1512. On the grounds that employment in Florence's government prior to their return made Machiavelli their enemy, the Medici family had him arrested and tortured. After a brief, painful period in prison, he went into exile. To win his way back to Florence, Machiavelli dedicated to the new Medici ruler his work *The Prince.* Published in 1532 only after Machiavelli died, *The Prince* offers political advice on how heads of states, particularly those who seize power, should govern. Machiavelli advanced a strategy for domination requiring rulers to show no mercy to their enemies, to act decisively and ruthlessly, and to rule by expediency rather than morality. The ends, Machiavelli famously argued, justified the means. Like the humanists, he looked to ancient Roman writers for solutions to the problems he saw plaguing the cities of Italy. But he studied those texts with the autocratic behavior he had witnessed when on diplomatic business for Florence in Milan and the Papal States in mind and came to conclusions that sat uneasily with humanist ideals.

Milan in the province of Lombardy enjoyed the rights and privileges of an autonomous city. A council made up of the leading Milanese families governed the city until 1311, when the **Visconti** family imposed its rule on the population. Under their rule, Milan grew into a powerful state founded on its rulers' military requirements. Its armaments and textile industries made the city wealthy. Milanese armor was in demand throughout Europe, and its silk cloth rivaled what Florentine weavers produced.

The Visconti family's ambition to govern did not stop, however, at the city walls. Throughout the 1380s and 1390s, Visconti forces conquered Siena and Pisa (both near Florence) as well as Verona and Vicenza (close to Venice), subdued the city of Bologna (a papal possession), and took control of the commercially important passes over the Alps. The alliance formed by Florence, Venice, and the pope to stop the Visconti was only partly successful. In 1447, when Filippo Maria Visconti died without a legitimate male heir, the people of Milan saw an opportunity to form a republic. Filippo Maria's son-in-law, **Francesco Sforza,** the condottiere hired to keep public order, had other plans. By 1450, attempts to form a republic had failed and Sforza had declared himself duke of Milan.

The new autocratic rulers of Milan enjoyed the prestige that came from patronizing the humanists and artists inspired by Renaissance ideals of republican liberty. In return, the republican-minded humanists, painters, and architects did not object to working in the military state that Milan had become. They easily found employment in the city's monasteries and ducal government. The most prominent artist of all, Leonardo da Vinci, spent nearly two decades in Milan in the employ of Ludovico Sforza, duke of Milan, who asked him to cast a bronze equestrian statue commemorating his father, Francesco, the first Sforza duke of Milan. His fresco of the Last Supper in the Convent of Santa Maria delle Grazie in Milan remains to this day one of the most recognizable paintings in the world.

The Papal States and the Church

Unlike Florence and Milan, where many people clung to republican ideals even when ruled by autocrats, the Papal States made no accommodation to those who would have preferred to live in a republic. In all of western Europe, only the pope could claim

condottieri Mercenary captains employed by Italian city-states to maintain internal order.

Baldassare Castiglione (1478–1529) Diplomat and humanist who wrote The Courtier (1528), in which he describes the "Renaissance man."

Niccolò Machiavelli (1469–1527) Diplomat and political writer most famous for *The Prince,* a work instructing rulers on how to govern.

Visconti The family of ruling Milanese dukes from 1395 until 1447, when replaced by the Sforza family.

Francesco Sforza (r. 1447–1466) Mercenary captain hired to protect Milan; the first of a dynasty to rule Milan.

legitimacy dating back to Emperor Constantine in the third century, even if that claim had been discredited in certain circles. Over half a century before, in 1440, the humanist **Lorenzo Valla** performed a feat of scholarship that drew the admiration of scholars all across Europe, including Erasmus. Using humanist methods of textual analysis, he convincingly proved that the Donation of Constantine, on the basis of which the papacy laid claim to central Italy, was forged. Valla's work had little practical impact, as the papacy's power had been reinforced simply by the passage of centuries and the weight of tradition. The Papal States remained a theocratic and autocratic dominion until the nineteenth century.

When the papacy left Rome and settled in Avignon, the nobles who governed the Papal States on behalf of the papacy took the opportunity to extricate themselves from its lordship. During the fourteenth century, several of the cities and towns under papal rule, such as Bologna, refused to recognize the lordship of the Avignon popes. The Visconti family of Milan, whose territory abutted the northwestern borders of the pope's lands, also saw an opportunity to add to their territory. Resistance to papal overlordship grew so strong that the papacy's income dropped significantly. Hiring an army in the 1350s to reimpose papal rule over the rebel lands sapped the pope's treasury even more.

Initially, restoring order in the Papal States was the first order of business when the popes returned to Rome permanently at the end of the Great Schism in 1417. The popes of the fifteenth century appointed their own family members to secular and ecclesiastic offices in the cities of central Italy as a way of securing the loyalty of public authorities there. At the end of the century, Pope **Alexander VI** of the Borgia family put family loyalty ahead of the papacy's interests by creating a new, independent state carved out of the Papal States for his illegitimate son, Cesare Borgia, whom he had made a cardinal in 1493 when Cesare was not yet twenty. Five years later, Cesare exchanged his position as cardinal for that of military commander. The army he led conquered the three principal regions in the Papal States: Emilia, Romagna, and Umbria. When his father died in 1503, Cesare lost access to the funding he needed to pay his army. Without an army, and with a new pope intent on restoring dignity to the papacy and its lands, Cesare fell from power.

The death of Alexander VI's successor within a year of his election put Pope **Julius II** in charge of imposing papal rule over central Italy. Not content with hiring a mercenary army to enter battle for him, Julius led his own troops in 1508 to restore papal authority in the cities of Bologna and Perugia, contrary to church law, which forbade clergy to fight in wars.

Alexander VI's death and Cesare Borgia's inability to defend his possession of the Papal States had given Venice an opportunity to expand its mainland holdings. Now, in an alliance with other powers in Italy, Julius forced the Venetians out of his lands in 1509. Julius, the patron of the arts responsible for Michelangelo's ceiling in the Sistine Chapel, conquered the land that had been lost to the papacy since the Avignon popes of the fourteenth century.

Renaissance Ideals in Transition, 1400–1550

↓ How did many of the cultural benefits of the Italian Renaissance reach France?

↓ What factors contributed to their slow passage to England?

Pope Julius, the Sforza dukes, and the Medici demonstrated that the appreciation of humanist ideals could coexist with autocratic domination over their subjects. Similarly, the people of other countries and their rulers absorbed the cultural and intellectual innovations of Italy and Flanders at different rates and in their own ways. The French king admired the Italian Renaissance so much that, when he invaded the peninsula to conquer it, he made sure to acquire as many works of art—and artists—as he could along the way. For most of the fifteenth century, civil war distracted the nobility of England from the pleasures of patronage. In Germany, painters took some notice of the Italian and Flemish artists, but farther east, the Russians clung to the stylized forms icon painters had absorbed from the Byzantines long ago.

The Court of Francis I

Chivalry—the medieval code of heroism, piety, and the idealization of noblewomen—was the consuming passion of one man, whose interests and predilections shaped the character of the Renaissance in France:

Lorenzo Valla (1407–1457) Humanist scholar whose influential treatise, written in 1440, showed the Donation of Constantine to be a forgery.

Alexander VI (r. 1492–1503) Pope who was a member of the Spanish Borgia family and notorious for the promotion of his illegitimate children and the corruption of his papal court.

Julius II (r. 1503–1513) Pope who was a great patron of artists, especially Michelangelo, and who restored the Papal States to papal control.

King **Francis I.** As a fatherless teenager, heir to his cousin Louis XII, Francis took no interest in academic learning. Warfare and the ceremony associated with aristocratic knighthood absorbed all of the spoiled boy's attention. With no one able to guide him or restrain him apart from his mother, Francis trained himself to wage war rather than to rule.

When he succeeded to the throne in 1520, Francis I made his mother, Louise, regent so that she could rule in his absence and then left to conquer Italy. His first target was the duchy of Milan, under the rule of the Sforza family, whose forces he defeated. The French king was outmaneuvered by the adroit Pope Leo X, who took back possession of his territories in central Italy while recognizing Francis's overlordship. The Sforza duke of Milan achieved the same arrangement.

Francis failed to conquer Italy, but Italy, in a sense, conquered him. During his time at the papal court, the French king was deeply impressed with the culture of the Italian Renaissance and, over time, patronized some of its leading artists. He drew to his court in France the finest painters, poets, musicians, and scholars, who, perceiving their patron's chivalric passions, produced paintings, poetry, and songs that glorified the arts of war. Leonardo da Vinci and the sculptor Benvenuto Cellini were his guests. The royal place at **Fontainebleau** melded traditional French architecture with the new Italian style, and the king's lavish court life there was modeled on the magnificence of the great Italian courts in Florence and Milan. Moreover, Francis took an interest in the Christian humanists and their reform-minded critiques of the church. As an adult, he acquired the intellectual interests that his martial training in youth had precluded. The combination of chivalric ceremonial displays and his promotion of the arts and learning created a lasting legacy for Francis as his kingdom's Renaissance king.

England Before Its Renaissance

After the last battles of the Hundred Years' War in the mid-fifteenth century, English men and women associated king with country more than they had ever done, partly as a result of patriotic pageants, popular **ballads**, and other propaganda meant to rally financial and moral support for the war against France. Throughout the war, the **Arthurian legends** idealized knighthood and offered a powerful model of chivalric kingship in the character of King Arthur. After the war, in the 1470s, **Thomas Malory** reworked many of the old tales about the legendary king and his knights for the first time in English in an epic account of the Knights of the Round Table, *Le Morte d'Arthur* (*The Death of Arthur*). The printer **William Caxton** pub-

lished it in 1485, making it one of the earliest printed works of English literature. The stories about the adventures of King Arthur, Lancelot, Guinevere, and the knights offered a model of heroic kingship that the English looked for in their own king.

Henry V's son and heir, Henry VI (r. 1421–1461, 1470–1471), did not, however, inspire much confidence. Mentally unstable and unfit to rule for periods of time, he survived repeated attempts to remove him from power until kinsmen and rival claimants to the throne deposed him in 1461. The leader of his opponents and his cousin from the House of York ascended the throne as Edward IV (r. 1461–1470, 1471–1483). Henry fled to allies in Scotland but was captured and confined in the **Tower of London** in 1465. The new king Edward spent his entire reign fighting off supporters of the deposed Henry in the ongoing series of civil wars known collectively as the **Wars of the Roses** (1455–1485), after the red and white roses symbolizing Edward IV's York and Henry VI's Lancaster families. After his coronation, Edward ruled for ten years before his early death put his young son, Edward V (r. 1483), on the throne.

The young king's reign, too, soon ended. His uncle, Richard of York, imprisoned the young king and his younger brother in the Tower of London, where they both died under mysterious circumstances. Rumors that their uncle, now **Richard III**, had had his

Francis I (r. 1515–1547) King of France who centralized royal rule, created at his court a vibrant Renaissance culture, and unsuccessfully fought Charles V for control of Italy.

Fontainebleau Castle, or château, and chief residence of Francis I, king of France.

ballad Popular song that usually told a story.

Arthurian legends Stories associated with the deeds and lives of the mythical King Arthur and the Knights of the Round Table.

Thomas Malory (d. 1471) Author of *Le Morte d'Arthur,* an English-language collection of the Arthurian legends, published in 1485.

William Caxton (ca.1415–1492) England's first printer, who published Malory's *Le Morte d'Arthur.*

Tower of London Norman fortification situated on the banks of the Thames River where political prisoners were confined.

Wars of the Roses Civil wars between the descendants of Edward III for the throne of England, 1455–1485.

Richard III (r. 1483–1485) King of England after his young nephew, Edward V, died in captivity; defeated and killed by Henry Tudor at the Battle of Bosworth Field.

nephews murdered turned the nobles and the population against the king, thus presenting an opportunity for the supporters of Henry VI's House of Lancaster to reassert their claim to the throne. In 1485, Richard's chief Lancastrian opponent, Henry Tudor of Wales, defeated Richard at **Bosworth Field.** When Henry married Elizabeth of York in 1486, he united the Lancastrian and Yorkist factions. Crowned **Henry VII,** the founder of the **Tudor** dynasty set out to restore stability to England and replenish the nearly empty royal treasury. Only under later Tudors would England achieve its Renaissance.

The Holy Roman Empire and Eastern Europe

In the lands to the east of the French kingdom in the late fourteenth and fifteenth centuries, the flourishing trade among the Baltic Sea countries inspired the rulers in the region to consolidate their authority and claim their share of the profits. The Holy Roman emperors concentrated their efforts on their German lands. The princes of Moscow wrested control over their lands from their Mongol conquerors. The kings of Bohemia and Hungary insinuated themselves into the center of the Holy Roman Empire's political life, while new states were emerging along the northern shorelines of the Baltic Sea.

Unlike his predecessors, the Holy Roman emperor Charles IV (r. 1347–1378) faced the difficult truth that he could not sustain an empire that stretched from Germany in the north to Italy in the south. In a proclamation issued in 1356 and known as the **Golden Bull,** he laid out a system by which his successors would be chosen by seven permanent electors: the archbishops of three German cities and the rulers of four principalities. Three of the **prince electors** were German; the fourth was the king of Bohemia. Although Charles's plan provided political stability to the civil war–prone empire, the permanent exclusion of certain princely families deepened resentments and competition among the German nobles that had already led to sporadic warfare. Charles's choice of electors, however, had an unforeseen but timely impact on the empire's security. After deposing Charles' son and successor, the electors chose as emperor his grandson, Sigimund, king of Bohemia and Hungary in 1410 largely because his kingdom was viewed as the front line in the effort to hold back the Ottoman Turks, whose armies pushed the empire's eastern borders in the first half of the fifteenth century.

While the system of prince electors offered some stability to the empire, merchants in German and

Slavic territories competed fiercely over trade in Scandinavian and Baltic lands. In the final decades of the thirteenth century, guilds of German merchants with branch offices in England and Flanders joined with German merchants based in the Baltic and Scandinavian regions to form the Hanseatic League, a commercial association whose purpose was to provide its members with protection against piracy at sea and to regulate trade in German cities and in the Baltic states farther north. They specialized in the major commodities of the Baltic region, especially in fish, timber, and furs. Because public order was conducive to trade, league members served as city managers and police forces in the hundred-odd cities in which they were based during the fourteenth century. But the lack of centralization among the branches of the Hanseatic League led to their decline in the face of the growing power of the states around them, particularly to the east.

On the eastern borders of the empire and the Hanseatic cities of Prussia lay Poland and, beyond it, Lithuania, whose duke, Jagiello, became king of Poland in 1386 when he married Poland's heiress to the throne, Jadwiga. Jagiello's conversion to the Roman church at his marriage ensured that the majority of Lithuanians adhered to the Roman Catholic Church rather than the Eastern Orthodox tradition. Although the two countries were ruled by the same man, they did not merge into one kingdom. Within a generation, Poland had one grandson of Jagiello's as king and Lithuania had another as grand prince. The power of conjoined Poland-Lithuania succeeded in defeating the military order of Teutonic Knights, the major competitor for conquering and ruling the unchristianized Baltic territory to the north. Based in Prussia, to the west of Poland and Lithuania, the order protected the Hanseatic cities and made incursions into Polish territory in

---

Bosworth Field   Battle in 1485 in which the Yorkist forces, led by the English king Richard III, was defeated by the Lancastrian faction commanded by Henry Tudor.

Henry VII   (r. 1485–1509) First Tudor king of England, who ended the Wars of the Roses and consolidated royal power.

Tudor   Dynastic family ruling England from 1485 to 1603.

Golden Bull   Decree issued by Emperor Charles IV in 1356 that established the method for electing the Holy Roman emperor.

prince electors   Noblemen and bishops with the hereditary right to elect the Holy Roman emperor.

an effort to claim land there. In 1410, Jagiello defeated the order in a battle that set back its efforts to occupy the northern parts of Lithuania. But it was only at the conclusion of a thirteen-year war in 1466 that the Teutonic Knights were finally and decisively defeated.

Even farther to the east, the grand prince of Moscow, **Basil I**, brought together Russian principalities under his rule by conquering his neighbors between 1392 and 1398. To discourage an invasion of his lands by the Mongol Empire of the Golden Horde—to whom he paid tribute to prevent just that possibility—he made an alliance with Lithuania in 1392. Within three years, a larger threat appeared on his eastern borders: Timur, the Tartar ruler, who attacked Basil's lands and inflicted even more damage on the Mongols. Basil's death in 1425 left his ten-year-old son, Basil II

(r. 1425–1462), to defend his inheritance of his father's lands from his uncles. Political stability came to Basil's Russian lands only after decades of warfare against his uncles and cousins, the slow collapse of the Golden Horde, and, once Basil had died in 1462, the coming to power of his capable son, Ivan III. By the end of the fifteenth century, Basil's heirs had transformed Moscow into the strongest power in the east, beholden to no other.

> **Basil I** (r. 1389–1425) Grand prince of Moscow who expelled the Mongols from Russia and maintained his independence from Lithuania.

Summary

Review Questions
- ↑ How did Renaissance ideals affect the expectations of the people and behavior of rulers?
- ↑ How did ideas about painters, sculptors, and architects change over the course of the Renaissance?
- ↑ What was the impact of printing?

Out of the long, bleak period of high mortality rates emerged a cultural movement that emphasized humanity's essential worth. Individually and collectively, the human species found its champions in the humanists, painters, sculptors, and architects who celebrated mind and body in their work. In the birthplace of the long-gone Roman Republic, scholars found a new inspiration that to many felt like a rebirth, a renaissance. The rediscovery of classical texts refreshed knowledge of a past world and stimulated a new type of critical textual analysis. Greek refugees from the east brought the opportunity to incorporate new knowledge from the even older Greek civilization.

Artisans, too, underwent an evolution in how they approached their work. As humanists, painters strove to depict the human form in lifelike dimensions, which included situating figures realistically within a painted scene. The human image was no longer an ideal type with indistinguishable, anonymous features but was now, in the hands of a master

painter, a recognizable figure with a name. The skills required were more than those of a technician. It took an artist to render the soul in human form.

In northern Europe scholars also found a new appreciation of ancient Roman authors, but their intellectual audacity led them to focus on the Bible and the writings of the church fathers. Humanists such as Erasmus came to believe that it was time to review the translations from Greek of the New Testament. They also believed that the main consequence of more people reading the Bible in the vernacular would be the strengthening of Christian faith. The spread of printing presses across western Europe assisted the humanists in their goals. Communities of scholars now had identical texts to study. The scientific works of ancient Greek philosophers reached a far wider audience of scholars than they would have in manuscript form. The greater availability of inexpensive printed texts created an incentive to learn how to read.

The work of humanists and artists appealed to the autocratic rulers of western Europe in spite of its ideals rather than because of them. The Medici family of Florence had no intention of sharing power with any others in a state that was republican in the Roman sense of the word. The republics of Venice and Genoa also discouraged dissent within their populations and conducted campaigns of conquest. When military strongmen assumed control of Milan, they ruthlessly squashed republican sentiment. Pope Julius II crushed all resistance to papal rule in the

Papal States. In ruling circles, the appeal of civic humanism was limited.

Elsewhere in Europe, the news of these cultural movements led slowly to similar changes. Francis I of France could not conquer Italy, but he returned with a great appreciation of the Renaissance and lured many of its artisans, like Leonardo, to follow him. The absorption of Renaissance ideals by the peoples of England, the Holy Roman Empire, and Russia occurred at a slower pace. Political stability and peace had to return to those war-torn regions before the influence of the Renaissance could be felt.

← **Thinking Back, Thinking Ahead** →

What were the possible consequences of the greater availability of printed Bibles in vernacular languages?

ECHO

Renaissance Art, Modern Art

What is art? If you walk into a museum today, you might find one gallery filled with huge canvases covered with stripes of color or splattered paint. In the next room might be portraits and religious scenes painted centuries ago. One kind of art seems like child's play, while the other seems to have required much skill in its creation. Can they both really be art? Must art involve craftsmanship and fine technique as well as beauty, as in a Renaissance painting? Or does anything that an artist does or makes that stimulates a response in a viewer qualify as art?

Such questions have long preoccupied artists, art critics, and the public. Renaissance artists meant to glorify God, in the first place, and humanity, in the second. Their aim was to faithfully represent the world they saw around them, and by "faithfully" they would have intended faithfulness to God and nature. In later centuries, artists abandoned the goal of accurately depicting the human form and expression and sought instead to depict an interior reality—what an emotion felt like, for example, or the fragmentation of modern life, or the chilling efficiency of machines and technology.

Since the Renaissance, the purpose or role of art in society has never ceased to change. Pablo Picasso, one of the most influential artists of the twentieth century, insisted that when he incorporated African and Asian-Pacific elements into his paintings and sculptures, he was seeking only to broaden the range of what was considered beautiful. His goal was to render new models of beauty accessible to people in the west. Still other modern artists renounced the ideal of beauty in art altogether. Barnett Newman, a twentieth-century artist, wrote in 1948, "The impulse of modern art is the desire to destroy beauty," a sentiment that stands in strong contrast to the objectives of Renaissance artists, whose aim was to exalt the human form.

Today the desire to create—even if to do so is to suggest destruction—continues to motivate artists to put their works before the public. The concept of art has become so broad that it can encompass the altarpiece painting that appeals to religious and nonreligious people alike and an abstract painting that consists of a solid block of color.

Suggested Readings

Abulafia, David. *The Western Mediterranean Kingdoms, 1200–1500.* London and New York: Longman, 1997. A useful study of mainly Italy and Spain.

Baxandall, Michael. *Painting and Experience in Fifteenth-Century Italy.* 2nd ed. Oxford: Oxford University Press, 1988. A work that helped establish the social history of Renaissance art.

Brucker, Gene. *Florence, the Golden Age, 1138–1737.* Berkeley and Los Angeles: University of California Press, 1998. A classic overview of Florentine history.

Epstein, Steven. *Genoa and the Genoese, 958–1528.* Chapel Hill, N.C.: University of North Carolina Press, 2001. A good introduction to the history of this merchant republic.

Goldthwaite, Richard A. *Wealth and the Demand for Art in Italy, 1300–1600.* Baltimore: Johns Hopkins University Press, 1995. An account of the rise of consumer culture that emphasizes Florence.

Lane, Frederic C. *Venice, a Maritime Republic.* Baltimore: Johns Hopkins University Press, 1973. Still the place to begin, despite having been written more than thirty years ago.

Nuttall, Paula. *From Flanders to Florence: The Impact of Netherlandish Painting, 1400–1500.* New Haven, Conn.: Yale University Press, 2004. A good introduction to northern influence on Italian art.

Websites

On Leonardo, a museum in his birthplace, **The Leonardo Museum,** at www.leonet.it/comuni/vinci

An excellent site to look at images of artwork, organized by the artist's name, **Web Gallery of Art,** at www.wga.hu/frames-e.html?/html

A group seeking to vindicate Richard III of the charge of murder offers many interesting features relating to the Wars of the Roses, **The Richard III Society, American Branch,** at www.r3.org/intro.html

Europe's Age of Expansion, 1450–1550

1500 B.C.E.	1000 B.C.E.	500 B.C.E.	1 B.C.E./1 C.E.

| 1440s Gutenberg invents printing process | 1462 Ivan III becomes tsar | 1469 Marriage of Ferdinand of Aragon and Isabella of Castile | 1485 Henry VII becomes king of England | 1492 Columbus sets sail Jews expelled from Spain |

| 1440 | 1450 | 1460 | 1470 | 1480 | 1490 |

Europe in 1556
The political boundaries of Europe in the year of Emperor Charles V's abdication indicate the power of the Habsburgs. In what ways do the size and location of his lands suggest potential threats to the independence and stability of other European states?

Lands of Charles V, by 1556
France
England
Ottoman Empire
—— Boundary of Holy Roman Empire

NORWAY
SWEDEN
ESTONIA
TEUTONIC KNIGHTS
RUSSIA
SCOTLAND
Baltic Sea
PRUSSIA
North Sea
DENMARK
POLAND-LITHUANIA
IRELAND
Vistula
Dnieper
WALES ENGLAND
Cambridge
Oxford
Amsterdam
Hamburg
Elbe
BRANDENBURG
London
NETHERLANDS
ANHALT
LUSATIA
Antwerp
HESSE-KASSEL
SAXONY
SILESIA
ATLANTIC
LUXEMBOURG
Rhine
BOHEMIA
OCEAN
RHINE PALATINATE
Paris
UPPER PALATINATE
MORAVIA
LORRAINE
WÜRTTEMBERG
FRANCE
BURGUNDY
BAVARIA
HUNGARY
FRANCHE-COMTÉ
Vienna
AUSTRIA
CHAROLAIS
SWISS CONFED.
TYROL
SALZBURG
SAVOY
MILAN
Po
REP. OF VENICE
GENOA
Danube
Black Sea
MODENA
TUSCANY
PAPAL STATES
OTTOMAN EMPIRE
PORTUGAL
ANDORRA
Corsica (Genoa)
MONTENEGRO
Ebro
Madrid
Rome
Constantinople
Lisbon
Tagus
SPAIN
NAPLES
Palos
Seville
SARDINIA
Naples
Otranto
BALEARIC IS.
Tangiers
SICILY
Melilla
Algiers
Bougie
Bona
Tunis
Oran
Mediterranean Sea
Crete (Rep. of Venice)
NORTH AFRICA
OTTOMAN EMPIRE

0   200   400 Km.
0   200   400 Mi.

500 C.E.   1000 C.E.   1500 C.E.   2000 C.E.

1515
Francis I crowned king of France

1552
Las Casas publishes *Brief Account of the Destruction of the Indies*

1510
Albuquerque conquers Goa

1517
Charles V begins to rule in Spain

Luther condemns indulgences

1500   1510   1520   1530   1540   1550

Choice Choice Choice

Isabella of Castile

In this painting by an unknown artist, Queen Isabella is presented in modest dress, head covered. There is no hint of royal splendor in her appearance or expression. She appears, rather, as the woman head of household, a role she emphasized for her subjects. (Institut Amatller d'Art Hispanic)

Isabella of Castile Finances Columbus's Voyage Across the Atlantic

In January 1492, a forty-year-old Genoese sailor, Cristoforo Colombo, known in the English-speaking world as Christopher Columbus, appeared before Queen Isabella of Castile and her husband, King Ferdinand of Aragon. Columbus was seeking Spanish support for an ocean voyage to the eastern shores of Asia, which he believed were on the far side of the Atlantic Ocean. Twice before, Isabella had turned the Italian down. His third audience with the queen in 1492 was a desperate last attempt. Once again he presented his plans and described the benefits of the voyage. Once again, the queen refused. In despair, Columbus fled the court and galloped north, intending to ask the French king for help. But six miles out of town, royal guards stopped him and brought him back to the city. Isabella had changed her mind.

Later, Ferdinand would claim that he had convinced his wife to finance the voyage. Perhaps. As the only woman in the fifteenth century who ruled as a monarch, Isabella had to assert her royal will while not breaking the conventions of womanliness, which required submission to her husband. Throughout her reign, she acted as a dutiful wife involved in the traditional tasks of running a household, weaving cloth for the family's clothing, and repairing worn garments. Isabella also emphasized her faithfulness to Ferdinand despite his frequent infidelities. Ferdinand's claim that he had the final say in authorizing Columbus's voyage would fit with Isabella's role as the subordinate partner in their marriage.

But Ferdinand's account was challenged by one of Isabella's earliest biographers, the Dominican friar and bishop Bartolomé de Las Casas. Las Casas was an influential person at the court of Isabella's grandson, King Charles I, and had access to official documents and family papers. After Isabella's death, he wrote that the queen took the advice of her financial advisers when she recalled Columbus to court. This, too, is possible. Although Isabella embraced the gender expectations of her age, she was also highly effective in charting her own course of action. She herself had chosen Ferdinand as her husband, defying the wishes of her half brother, the king. The bride and groom were technically ineligible for marriage because, as cousins, they were too closely related in the eyes of the church. But Isabella went ahead with the union after documents were forged in the pope's name permitting an exception to Catholic marriage laws. Although independent when she needed to be, she preferred to work as a partner with Ferdinand, adopting as her motto, "The worth of one is the worth of the other—Isabella as Ferdinand." Isabella's motto cleverly proclaimed both her independence and her wifely relation to Ferdinand. It also emphasized the union of the two Spanish kingdoms that her marriage had achieved.

However she made her decision, Isabella announced that she would pawn her jewels to finance the voyage. (Pawning valuables was one way fifteenth-century monarchs could raise quick cash.) Finances settled, the queen could relish the gains from Columbus's voyage. Spain, like the rest of Europe, was hungry for the gold and spices of the east. But the country was cut off from a land route across Asia by the Venetians and their Muslim trading partners, and from a sea route around Africa by treaties with the Portuguese. A direct westward route was therefore the only one available to the Spanish. Moreover, both the Spanish and Portuguese had discovered and colonized islands in the Atlantic during the past seventy years. Perhaps Columbus would find more on the way to Asia, increasing the likelihood of riches.

Columbus's proposal also appealed to Isabella's fervent Catholic faith; a Spanish presence in eastern Asia would open the way for a Christian encirclement of the Muslim world and even the recapture of the holy city of Jerusalem. This vision exerted a powerful influence on a Spanish queen whose ancestors had extended their rule over a Muslim-dominated Iberian Peninsula. In fact, at the very moment Columbus appeared at court in 1492, Isabella and Ferdinand were celebrating their conquest of Granada, the last independent Muslim state on the peninsula. The Muslim defeat also provoked an attack on the other non-Christian people of the peninsula, the Jews. Shortly after Isabella offered Columbus the money he needed, she ordered the forced conversion or expulsion of all Jews in her lands. In the spring of 1492, just as the unconverted Jews were being shipped out of Spain, Columbus began preparing for his westward voyage.

Introduction

The Europe Columbus left in 1492 was bustling with renewed energy. The economic stagnation and population decline that had followed the trauma of the Black Death, the turmoil of the Hundred Years' War in France, and the Wars of the Roses in England was easing. By 1450, Europe's population was once again growing, and commerce revived. Both rural and urban dwellers profited from these upswings as increased demand for labor resulted in good wages, laying the foundation for an economically prosperous and expanding Europe.

The years after 1450 also saw a vigorous new generation of rulers in Spain, France, and England who consolidated state power and increased their control over their subjects, often with the help of new, professionally trained legal and financial experts. At the same time, these rulers continued to fight wars that drained their treasuries and forced them to tax and borrow at unprecedented levels. These European states were stronger and more centralized in 1550 than they had been in 1450 and exercised increasingly effective control over their inhabitants. In other parts of Europe, however, especially in Germany and Italy, the trend was toward smaller regional states instead of large, centralized ones. In the east, the rulers of

Moscow broke free from their Mongol overlords, conquered vast territories, and established a Russian empire that stretched from Poland to Siberia.

Europeans also extended their political and economic power over Africa, Asia, and the Americas. When the decline of the Mongol Empire disrupted Europe's land routes to Asia, the Portuguese sought new sea routes to the east and created a trading empire that stretched down the west coast of Africa, where they purchased gold and slaves. They also crossed the Indian Ocean to India and China, where they traded for spices, silks, and porcelain to sell in Europe, and ventured to the Western Hemisphere, where they established a colonial empire in Brazil based on African slave labor. The Spanish established an empire in the Caribbean, Mexico, and Peru that exploited the labor of Indians and then African slaves. Europe's territorial and economic expansion created the first global economy and turned many European states into colonial powers. It also raised the troubling issue of the relation of Europeans to the non-European peoples encountered in imperial expansion. While the peoples of Africa and the Americas experienced cataclysmic changes, the century between 1450 and 1550 was, for Europeans, marked by economic, political and territorial expansion. It was Europe's first modern age.

Chronology

1420	Portuguese begin the colonization of Atlantic islands
1462	Ivan III becomes tsar
1469	Ferdinand of Aragon and Isabella of Castile marry
1480	Ivan III declares Moscow's independence from Mongol rule
1485	Henry VII (Tudor) becomes King of England
1488	Bartholomew Diaz rounds southern tip of Africa and enters Indian Ocean
1492	Jews are expelled from Spain; Columbus sets sail
1500–1502	Muslims are expelled from Spain
1509	Henry VIII becomes king of England
1510	Alfonso de Albuquerque conquers Goa
1515	Francis I becomes king of France
1517	Charles V (Habsburg) begins rule in Spain
1519	Cortés lands in Mexico
1531	Pizarro invades Inca Empire
1533	Ivan IV becomes tsar
1542	Charles V issues New Laws for the Indies
1552	Las Casas publishes *Brief Account of the Destruction of the Indies*
1556	Charles V abdicates
1557	Portuguese establish trading colony at Macau
1559	French and Spanish sign Peace of Cateau-Cambrésis
1565–1572	Ivan the Terrible purges enemies in *oprichnina*

Economic and Social Change

⬇ What effects did the rise in population after 1450 have on rural and urban communities?

⬇ How did the revival of the European economy affect the lives of men and women?

From 1347 to 1351, between a third and a half of Europe's people died from the Black Death. For the next hundred years, population declined; outbreaks of plague, devastation caused by war, and failures of the grain harvest raised death rates to crisis levels and prevented a recovery. Then, about 1450, as plague, war, and famine subsided, the population once again started to grow. Population growth was also accompanied by an economic revival in both the countryside and towns.

Population Increase

Historians using the techniques of modern **demography** have determined that even in the good times after 1450, European death rates were shockingly high. Half the children born died before they reached their twenties. If a person made it to adulthood, however, the chances were good that he or she would live on for another thirty-five years. People over sixty, however, were rare, and the older they were, the stranger they were thought to be. Old people aroused fears: Why had they lived so long? Were they especially blessed by God, or (more likely!) had they made deals with the Devil? No social or economic group escaped these high **mortality rates.** Death cut down the families of kings and queens along with those of their humblest subjects, with no consideration of social distinctions or levels of wealth.

Once the crisis conditions in the century following the Black Death eased, the low population level created favorable economic conditions for those who had survived. Fewer people meant more available agricultural land, greater food supplies, and a higher demand for labor, which in turn produced higher wages. These favorable economic conditions affected marriage rates. In the lands of the Roman Catholic Church, a distinctive marriage pattern had emerged by the mid-fifteenth century. Women married in their

demography   Statistical study of populations.

mortality rate   The number of deaths per thousand in a given population.

Peter Bruegel the Elder's *The Harvesters* (1556) captures the beauty of a good harvest. Grain stalks shimmer in the sun as men scythe them, while men and women bind them. Other workers take a meal under a tree. This painting presents a powerful image of agricultural abundance and human wellbeing. *(Copyright © The Metropolitan Museum of Art/Art Resource, NY, The Metropolitan Museum of Art, New York, NY, USA)*

mid-twenties and men somewhat later, and about 10 percent of both men and women never married. This pattern contrasted with that of European Jews and Eastern Orthodox Christians, for whom marriage for women coincided with the onset of sexual maturity in the teenage years and was nearly universal. The reason for late marriage and significant rates of celibacy among the Christians of western Europe lay in the expectation that people should marry only when they could afford to set up their own household; it took time to establish economic independence, and some people never achieved it. After 1450, when land, food, and wages were abundant, more young people married and established their own households. When these better-fed, healthier people started their families, the **birthrate** rose in much of western Europe. The rise in

marriage and birth rates caused the increase in Europe's population. In 1450, Europe's population was about 60 million. In 1550, it was nearly 69 million.

Recovery in the Countryside

In 1450, Europe was still an overwhelmingly agricultural society. Ninety percent of Europeans lived in rural areas, where they engaged in some kind of farming. As in the past, agriculture depended on unpredictable weather conditions that could lead to

birthrate   The number of live births per thousand in a given population.

either abundant harvests or devastating crop failures. Yet despite the precarious nature of agricultural activity, times were good for rural people between 1450 and 1550.

After the Black Death, when population fell and labor was scarce, landlords' power over their peasants often decreased. Serfdom virtually disappeared in western Europe, where it was replaced with communities of free peasants who either owned their land, rented it from their lords, or worked as wage laborers. Below the lord was the peasants' **commune**, which set dates for planting crops and managed the meadows and woodlands belonging to the community as a whole. If the local lord tried to seize these common lands for his own use, the commune would organize villagers' resistance and even encourage riots in defense of them. In eastern Europe, however, landlords successfully reimposed serfdom on their peasants, seizing peasant lands, setting heavy work requirements, and forbidding peasants to leave their estates. Landlords were able to do this because the kings and other rulers in the region supported their actions.

In western Europe, the village of Langlade in southeast France shows how rural people responded to improved economic conditions. Like most communities, Langlade increased agricultural production to provide for a rising population. In addition to cultivating their grain fields, the villagers grew grapes for wine and moved into nearby hills, where they chopped down scrubby oaks and uprooted wild rosemary bushes. After pack animals had carried off the wood to nearby towns to meet a growing demand for fuel, the community planted the new land with wheat and olive trees.

In 1450, many rural communities were largely self-sufficient economically, since they produced most of the food, clothing, and other basic necessities they needed. Over the next hundred years, however, many rural people sold their agricultural surplus and bought many goods they had previously produced for themselves. Thus, they became integrated into regional or international markets. When the villagers of Langlade, for example, sold the wood they had cleared from their new fields to townspeople, they were losing their economic independence and becoming integrated in a market economy.

The growth of a market economy affected the value of people's economic activity. Previously, everything men and women did to maintain the material well-being of their families was considered work. With the growth of markets, however, the definition of work began to change. It was now defined simply as activity that produced goods for the market. This narrower definition of work affected men and women differently. Because women's economic activity focused primarily on their households, they no longer "worked." They simply did "housekeeping." Men were the "workers" because they raised crops for the market.

The devaluation of women's traditional household work was accompanied by the belief that women were incapable of skilled work. They were thought to be too awkward or ignorant to do complicated jobs. Therefore, anything they did was, by definition, unskilled. In fact, however, much of their activity involved considerable skill. For example, many rural women made butter or cheese. But the skill involved was not recognized. The same attitudes shaped men's and women's wages. At harvest time, when there was a high demand for labor in the fields, men were regularly paid twice what women were although they performed similar tasks.

Growth in the Cities

The developing market economy was also closely linked to the growth of cities. Beginning in 1450, Europe's cities grew until by 1550 about 10 percent of the total population lived in them. Since most cities were surrounded by their old walls, the rise in population made them ever more crowded. Houses were crammed next to each other, and streets were full of garbage. Sometimes garbage was dumped into wells, canals, or the local river, polluting the city's water supply, while at others it was piled just outside the city walls. These garbage piles could become so high that they threatened the city's defenses, since they could be used for scaling the walls. Human excrement also presented problems. Feces were placed next to front doors for sale to manure peddlers, who used them to fertilize nearby fields. Urine was sometimes collected in barrels outside leather shops, where it was used in the tanning process. All this waste created a huge stench; often travelers could smell a city long before they could see it. Overcrowding and filth also led to high urban disease and death rates. Throughout the sixteenth century, cities could never sustain their population levels but relied on a continuous stream of migrants from the countryside. Because of Europe's expanding population, the stream never dried up. Although cities were crowded and dirty, their inhabitants thought of them as organic wholes

commune An association of peasants supervising and coordinating the collective life of their village.

whose well-being depended on the harmonious interaction of all the people living in them. It was therefore the responsibility of the well-off to care for the needy by founding hospitals, orphanages, and homes for the elderly.

Men's work in sixteenth-century cities can be classified into four categories. Some men turned agricultural products like grain into food such as bread, the basic element in the urban diet. Bread was such a basic necessity that urban governments strictly regulated its price and tried to assure its availability in times of grain shortages, since they feared riots if the supply gave out. Others manufactured cloth and leather goods for clothing. Still others were engaged in construction; with urban populations growing and more buildings under construction, these men were in constant demand. Finally, some men made household furnishings or fashioned the tools that builders used. The most prestigious workers in a city, such as weavers of fine woolen or silk cloth or workers in gold, were organized into guilds. Guilds had originated in the Middle Ages but were in their heyday from 1450 to 1550. Like society at large, the guilds were organized on hierarchical lines; the men admitted to them were divided into masters, journeymen, and apprentices. Journeymen hoped someday to be admitted to the ranks of the masters, but often they were not, since masters worked to keep their membership limited. Guilds had originated as social clubs for artisans, providing opportunities for drinking and offering protection from a saint adopted as the guild's patron. In the sixteenth century, these older functions were still important, but the guild's main purpose was to regulate the manufacture of specific goods for the marketplace.

Membership in a guild was a prized source of male identity, and members proclaimed their skills and the perfection of their products. They thought of themselves as the backbone of the urban world and were concerned with maintaining an honorable position in society. To this end they carefully policed themselves, punishing the wayward for indecent or immoral behavior. Also, in line with the idea that the community should function as a harmonious whole, the guilds were required by law to maintain the quality of their products in the interests of consumer protection.

Guild work was considered skilled and, therefore, usually open only to men. In the Middle Ages, a few women had participated in guilds, but after 1500, most lost their place in them. As in the countryside, most women were confined to housekeeping or low-paid work. Women did, however, have a significant role in retail trade, operating stalls in marketplaces and serving as city-appointed officers to certify weights, measures, and grain quality. They also worked as seamstresses and lace makers, skilled activities that, like butter and cheese making, were usually undervalued and poorly paid. Many women spun thread for weaving. Spinning was the slowest process in cloth production, and the need for spinners rose dramatically as weavers tried to meet the growing demand for cloth from a rising population. In the countryside, both men and women worked as spinners. In cities, however, men avoided this occupation as too low paying.

One group did break through the restrictions on women's economic activity—widows. A widowed woman could step in as the head of her dead husband's business and run it on her own. But if she remarried, or had male children who wanted to take it over, she usually returned to a subordinate economic position. Finally, prostitution was the one occupation always open to women. Because it dishonored her, a woman usually chose it only when nothing else was available.

The Port of Antwerp

Although cities all over Europe were growing, none could rival **Antwerp** in wealth and importance. Located at the western end of the North Sea, Antwerp was an ideal transfer point for the east-west trade that moved through the English Channel and the North Sea to the Baltic Sea. It was also a transfer point between northern Europe, the Iberian Peninsula, and the Mediterranean. By 1500, it was the most important commercial center in Europe. With its rise, European trade networks shifted northward, from the Mediterranean. Although Italian cities and merchants continued to play a central role in European trade, Mediterranean cities would never again dominate it.

The wharves of Antwerp were piled high with goods from Europe and Asia. One hundred thousand pieces of English woolen cloth were imported each year, and the city was ringed with huge bleaching vats preparing the cloth for finishing in the city's cloth guilds. Spain also sent its prized wool north for spinning and weaving. Next to the bales of cloth and wool were sacks of wheat, along with wood for

Antwerp City in the Netherlands that functioned in the first half of the sixteenth century as Europe's main trading center.

This painting by an unknown artist from the Netherlands shows the bustling commercial activity of Antwerp. The crowds examining goods for sale, the groups of men talking, and the carts carrying barrels of beer or wine give a lively sense of the city as Europe's leading commercial center in the sixteenth century. (*Musées Royaux des Beaux-Arts de Belgique*)

urban construction and shipyards, all from eastern Germany and Poland. The sixteenth-century population surge turned eastern Europe into a major supplier of grain and timber for the west. Bars of copper and silver from mines in south Germany were securely locked away in Antwerp's warehouses, waiting the arrival of Portuguese ships laden with spices brought around the southern tip of Africa from India and Southeast Asia. The metals would be exchanged for cinnamon, nutmeg, and pepper, and then exported to the Far East, where they would pay for another cargo of spices. Vaults also held chests of diamonds waiting to be cut and sold. Over a thousand representatives of foreign trading companies jostled each other on the city's streets as they inspected cargoes and bargained over prices.

In 1500, Antwerp boasted a population of over 100,000, making it one of Europe's largest cities. The city center was dominated by the Cathedral of Our Lady, the largest in the Netherlands, which covered more than two acres. Begun in the mid-fourteenth century, it was finished in the sixteenth and stood as a symbol of the city's wealth and pride. Nearby was the great square with its monumental city hall and imposing guild offices. On the city's outskirts were breweries supplying beer for thousands of thirsty workers.

The complex trade networks converging on Antwerp, involving thousands of merchant businesses spread over long distances, stimulated the development of the banking and credit networks, developed in the twelfth century, through which traders avoided the inconvenience of hauling about large sums of coins to cover their transactions. Instead, they signed notes promising payment from money kept at home. If a merchant's reputation was good, the notes would be accepted as a kind of paper money. The use of these notes laid the foundations for modern banking practices. Because Antwerp was the center for both inter-European and Far Eastern trade, it functioned as a center of exchange for an emerging world economy.

Resurgent Monarchies

⬇ What steps did rulers take to strengthen their realms?
⬇ What role did religion play in the advancement of royal authority?

While Europe's population and economy were expanding after 1450, new, energetic rulers extended their control over their subjects and centralized their governments. Civil wars were brought to an end, state control of justice increased, new officials enforced government decrees, and new sources of revenue were created. Above all, a period of warfare erupted in Italy, where the rulers of Spain and the Holy Roman Empire fought the kings of France for control of the peninsula.

Ferdinand and Isabella and the Rise of Spain

In 1469, **Isabella of Castile,** aged eighteen, married the seventeen-year-old **Ferdinand of Aragon.** Their kingdoms shared the Iberian Peninsula with Muslim **Granada** and Christian Portugal and Navarre, and neither was a first-rate state. Moreover, on Ferdinand and Isabella's wedding day, their kingdoms were torn apart by civil war as great nobles challenged the young monarchs' rule. Yet the marriage of these two teenagers laid the foundations for a spectacular rise in the power of Spain.

Within ten years, Ferdinand and Isabella had secured their rule, embarking on a tireless campaign of travel and direct appearances and relying on the persuasive power of face-to-face meetings with their unruly subjects. In early modern Europe, kings and queens, God's appointed rulers, were bathed in a sacred aura. As a result, even the most rebellious subjects could be coaxed into obedience when brought personally before the monarch. As a boy, the future historian of Isabella's reign, **Bartolomé de Las Casas,** was part of the crowd cheering the royal couple as they passed through his hometown of Seville on one of these journeys. In addition, the two rulers shrewdly calculated that their success depended as much on negotiation with their people and respect for each kingdom's traditional political institutions as it did on a show of royal grandeur. Thus they did not try to fuse Aragon and Castile into a single monarchy but respected the political independence of each kingdom.

In Aragon, Ferdinand accepted traditions that made him a limited, constitutional monarch. In Castile, the larger and more populous kingdom, he and Isabella took specific measures to strengthen royal power. The nobility was confirmed in its privileges and landed estates, and new titles of nobility were awarded to men who cooperated with the monarchs. At the same time, powerful but rebellious nobles were excluded from a direct role in government and were replaced by lesser nobles or commoners. These men were more dependent on royal favor for their success than the great nobles. Many had been trained as lawyers. Their legal training gave them orderly habits of mind and a commitment to carefully defined routines for state administration that made the monarchy more efficient. One of the first benefits of this rule of orderly lawyers was a more effective collection of royal taxes. Isabella and Ferdinand also worked out a policy of cooperation with the towns of Castile. They knew that they were tightly knit communities, jealous of their traditions and suspicious of outsiders who might upset them. Painstaking negotiation in the interests of peace after civil war was the way to bring them into working relations with the royal government. The monarchs also revived urban police forces to clear the country of bandits and established a workable local judicial system.

In 1482, Ferdinand and Isabella went to war with Granada, the last Muslim kingdom on the Iberian Peninsula, using the revitalized urban police forces as their army. The pope declared the war a crusade and sent a huge silver cross for troops to carry in battle. In 1492, the Spanish monarchs stood with their glittering court before the gates of the city of Granada to receive the defeated Muslim king, who came forward, kissed the hands of the monarchs, and surrendered the keys to the city. By the end of the day, Christian flags flew from the highest tower of Alhambra, the royal palace. With Granada's fall, the centuries-long Christian Reconquista of the Iberian Peninsula was complete.

The fall of Granada coincided with a new Spanish policy of religious intolerance. In the spring of 1492, Isabella and Ferdinand decreed that Jews were to convert to Christianity or leave their kingdoms. A century earlier, anti-Jewish riots had provoked mass

Isabella of Castile (r. 1474–1504) and **Ferdinand of Aragon** (r. 1479–1516) Rulers who launched Spain's rise as a major European power in control of a vast overseas empire.

Granada Last Muslim state on the Iberian Peninsula, conquered by Ferdinand and Isabella in 1492.

Bartolomé de Las Casas (1474–1566) Soldier turned priest and bishop who criticized the brutality of the Spanish conquest of America.

conversions to Christianity. But these **New Christians,** or **Conversos,** were often accused of secretly holding to their old Jewish ways. In response, the monarchs created the **Spanish Inquisition,** a church court authorized to examine Conversos about the genuineness of their Christian faith. Over the next dozen years, hundreds of them failed to prove their sincerity and were burned alive as heretics. Then, in 1491, news of a supposed atrocity swept across Castile. Some New Christians and unconverted Jews in the town of La Guardia were accused of murdering a Christian boy and ripping out his heart for use in magic. A story like this was a standard element in late medieval Christian attacks on Jews, and in 1491 it led to the execution of the accused men, despite the fact that no one in La Guardia reported a missing child. Faced with rising anti-Jewish passions, some Jews responded in kind, repeating old arguments that Christians' souls were created by the Devil. It was against this background that Ferdinand and Isabella ordered the forced conversion or expulsion of all remaining Jews. About fifty thousand converted, while some forty thousand fled to Portugal, Italy, and North Africa. Many of these refugees eventually returned and submitted to baptism. Thus the edict eliminated Jewish communities but greatly increased the number of New Christians, who continued to be accused of half-hearted conversion. The Jews who had fled to Portugal were expelled from that kingdom in 1497. Some then moved to Antwerp, where they established a thriving merchant community that prospered from the revival of European commerce. In 1494, Pope Alexander VI proclaimed Ferdinand and Isabella "Catholic Rulers" in recognition of their efforts to suppress non-Christian religions.

Finally, between 1500 and 1502, all remaining Muslims in Granada and Castile were also ordered to convert to Christianity or leave. Some, like the Jews, became Christians. But these **Moriscos** were no more well received than the Conversos, since the sincerity of their conversions was also questioned. Most who left went to North Africa. The forced conversion or expulsion of Jews and Muslims ended the religious pluralism and cultural diversity of Castile and Aragon. The war against Granada had united Castilians and Aragonese in a common Spanish crusade. The expulsion of the Jews and Muslims created a new, exclusively Christian Spanish identity.

As they consolidated their power and promoted a new identity among their subjects, Ferdinand and Isabella searched for a husband for their eldest surviving child, Joan. They themselves had made a good political marriage, and they wanted one for their daughter. Fortunately, they found an ideal match in the son of the Holy Roman emperor, Philip the Handsome. Joan brought Castile, Aragon, Granada, Naples, Sicily, and Sardinia to the marriage, while Philip brought the **Habsburg** family's land of Austria, inherited from his father, along with the Netherlands, inherited from his mother. Theirs was the royal wedding of the century. All that was needed was a child who would inherit this vast collection of territories.

Charles I of Spain, Charles V of the Holy Roman Empire

That child was born in 1500 and named Charles. Charles spent his early years in the Netherlands, where Joan moved after her wedding. A sickly boy, he inherited from his father a large lower jaw that stuck out beyond the upper one and made it difficult to chew food. This "Habsburg jaw" continued to be passed on in the family and can be seen in many paintings of Habsburg rulers, despite artists' attempt to downplay it. In 1517, after the death of his father, Philip, and grandfather, Ferdinand, Charles journeyed for the first time to Spain, where he was to rule as Charles I in place of Joan, who had developed mental problems that prevented her from governing. Charles quickly made Spain his primary place of residence, spending more time there than in his other lands. When not in Spain, he was usually back in the Netherlands, the country he loved the most.

The lands Charles inherited rivaled Charlemagne's empire in size, but they were never a united state. Like Ferdinand and Isabella, Charles recognized the political independence of each, respecting its local laws and traditions. Also, like his grandparents, he realized the importance of appearing personally before his subjects. Unlike them, however, he ruled over so many lands that he could never be in one of them long enough to satisfy people's desire to see him. This was a constant source of friction. "My life," he complained, "has been one long journey."

New Christians/Conversos   Jews whom the state forced to convert to Christianity or face persecution and expulsion from Spanish territory.

Spanish Inquisition   Church court originally established to try New Christians suspected of observing their old Jewish practices in secret.

Moriscos   Muslims in Spain who were forced to convert to Christianity or leave.

Habsburgs   Dynastic family originating in Austria that provided many rulers there, and also in the Netherlands, Spain, and the Holy Roman Empire.

This portrait of Emperor Charles V by the Venetian painter Titian (1548) presents him as a warrior, a convention for depicting rulers that stretches back to the pharaohs of ancient Egypt. Charles' forceful gaze, the horse's prancing and fine plumes, and the thrusting lance all point to the Emperor's might. *(Museo del Prado)*

feudal armies no longer worked in the face of highly trained soldiers who made warfare their permanent profession. Moreover, weapons technology had changed with the introduction of gunpowder from China, brought west by Arab traders, which made bows and arrows obsolete. But mercenaries and firearms were expensive, and state budgets strained to finance them. For his Italian wars, Charles managed to field an army of 150,000 men, the largest Europe had ever seen, but he had to scramble to find ways to pay for it. One way was to push heavily on traditional sources of income like sales taxes and grants from representative assemblies of subjects like the Castilian **Cortes.** Gold also started to pour in from the Caribbean after Spanish conquests there. But taxes and **New World** wealth never provided enough, so Charles sold **Crown lands.** This was still not enough. He then turned to borrowing and contracted ever-larger debts

The journeys became even more frequent in 1519, when he was elected Holy Roman emperor on the death of his paternal grandfather, the emperor Maximilian. In the empire he was called **Charles V.**

Although Charles never united his territories into a single state, he did develop a common policy for them by consolidating his rule in each and making sure that none worked at cross-purposes with the others. Coordinating a common policy became particularly important during the long wars with France over Italy, where his role as Holy Roman emperor, along with his inherited lands in southern Italy, made him a central player. For sixty-five years, France and Spain fought for control of the Italian peninsula.

These wars were costly, and they were only one series of Charles's wars. By 1500, Europe's rulers faced a new military world. To win a war, it was necessary to fight with the best military forces, and that meant hiring **mercenary armies,** since the medieval

Charles V (r. 1516–1556) Heir of Ferdinand and Isabella in Spain and of the emperor Maximilian in the Holy Roman Empire; the most powerful European ruler during the first half of the sixteenth century.

mercenary armies Skilled professional armies under the command of generals who sold their services to European rulers.

Cortes In Castile, a representative assembly of Isabella's subjects that advised the queen and negotiated over taxes.

New World Term that Europeans used to refer to the Americas.

Crown lands Lands owned by a ruler as his or her family estate.

in the forms of **annuities**—long-term loans that guaranteed an annual payment to the lender.

Annuities turned out to be the way that cash-hungry sixteenth-century states managed to meet their financial obligations. The success of annuities depended on two things: the availability of lenders and the recruitment of managers to supervise states' growing indebtedness. The demographic and economic expansion of Europe from 1450 to 1550 ensured the former; prosperous times put money in the pockets of many people who then looked for relatively safe ways to invest it. Lending to a state seemed one way. Charles borrowed from bankers in Germany and the Netherlands who were financing the growing trade networks centered on Antwerp, the prize jewel in his inheritance. He also turned to individual subjects who had money to invest.

The rise of a professionally trained class of bureaucrats began with Ferdinand and Isabella's lawyers. Under Charles, men with expert skills were recruited to collect taxes more efficiently. Increasingly, trained managers supervised governments' growing debts and oversaw the new complexity of state borrowing in a time of escalating military costs. Borrowing from banks and subjects turned Charles, and other rulers who did the same, into royal credit risks whose credit ratings were closely watched by would-be lenders.

By 1550, Charles V was growing weary of rule. He had been personally involved in the Italian and French wars for thirty years. Moreover, the political and religious situation in the Holy Roman Empire was becoming destabilized with the rise of **Protestantism**. He suffered from gout and insomnia. During the sleepless nights, he tinkered with his collection of clocks, taking them apart and reassembling them over and over again. He sank into depression and wept like a child. Finally, in 1556, he decided to abdicate. He granted the position of emperor and his Austrian lands to his younger brother, Ferdinand. His son Philip received the Netherlands, the Italian possessions, the Spanish states, and Spain's vast new American empire. Charles then retired to a monastery in southwestern Spain, where he died in 1558.

Francis I and the Kingdom of France

In 1500, the French state, like Spain, was undergoing profound transformations. The Hundred Years' War had strengthened the French monarchy, which now possessed a regular source of revenue from the *taille* tax, a permanent royal army, and the beginnings of a state bureaucracy staffed by experts. But France was fragmented. Although the English had been driven

out, except for a toehold around Calais, large swaths of territory, each ruled by a branch of the extended royal family, functioned as virtually independent units within the theoretically unified kingdom. Over the second half of the fifteenth century, however, these branches died out, their lands reverted to the Crown, and the amount of territory directly ruled over by the king almost doubled between 1450 and 1500. Habsburg lands had grown as a result of spectacularly successful marriages; the French state grew as a result of lucky deaths.

Francis I, who ruled from 1515 to 1547, was the most vigorous of the newly powerful French kings. His court was famous for its Renaissance culture. Like Charles V, he traveled throughout his realm, showing himself to his subjects and thereby cementing his rule. Unlike Charles, however, he ruled over a more unified state, since political centralization had increased when each previously independent territory reverted to direct royal rule. To further this new centralization, Francis ordered all courts, except church ones, to use the French dialect of Paris in their proceedings. Since this French was only one of several dialects spoken at the time, the edict promoted a single common language for use in public affairs throughout the kingdom. At the same time, French nobles stopped using their local dialects and started to speak the refined French of Francis's royal court. The growing use of standardized French, along with political centralization, created a new national identity for the people of the kingdom that slowly replaced older identities rooted in local customs and dialects.

Francis also increased royal power when he signed a **concordat** with Pope Leo X in 1516 that gave the king the right to nominate candidates for hundreds of high offices in the French church, thereby increasing the Crown's control of church personnel. In return, Francis repudiated the earlier French position that

---

annuities Long-term loans to European states guaranteeing an annual interest payment to the lender.

Protestantism Beliefs and practices of Christians who broke with the Roman Church in the sixteenth century.

taille French royal tax first levied during the Hundred Years' War.

Francis I (r. 1515–1547) King of France who centralized royal rule, created at his court a vibrant Renaissance culture, and unsuccessfully fought Charles V for control of Italy.

concordat Formal agreement between a pope and a ruler of a Catholic state.

the pope was subject to the authority of general church councils and recognized him as the supreme head of the Roman Church. Having reestablished good relations with the papacy, the king was now free to pursue his military ambitions in Italy.

By 1519, when Charles V had inherited the lands ruled over by his two grandfathers, Francis had one great fear: the Habsburgs. From the northeast to the southwest, wherever he looked beyond French borders, he saw Habsburg lands. Francis had tried to break Habsburg power by bribing the imperial electors in the Holy Roman Empire to choose him as emperor, but Charles was the grandson of the emperor Maximilian, and he had bribed the electors as well. Francis then turned to Italy and tried to make good the French claims to Milan and Naples. But he fared poorly, being captured on a battlefield and taken as a prisoner to Madrid. As the price for his freedom, he was forced to sign a humiliating peace in which he repudiated all his Italian claims and promised Charles the duchy of Burgundy, one of the territories that had reverted to the French Crown.

Back in Paris, Francis repudiated the peace and laid plans to continue the fight. Charles's victories in Italy had created a backlash that allowed Francis to form an anti-Spanish alliance with a number of Italian rulers, including the pope. Then in 1527, Charles won another victory when Spanish and German mercenary armies descended on Rome and sacked the city. Charles's reputation suffered badly from his troops' brutality, and he took his anger out on Francis, proposing, unrealistically, that the two should meet in a duel to settle their dispute.

After 1527, Francis continued the fight against the Habsburgs, but his strategy changed. Now Charles faced the threat of an expanding Protestant movement in the empire and the Netherlands. Although he was no friend of the Protestants in France, Francis allied with the German Protestants and then with the Ottoman Turks in his attempts to weaken Habsburg power. Francis's foreign policy undermined the medieval notion that Europe was held together by a common Catholic Christian faith. Now, it seemed, it was composed of a number of independent states, each of which advanced its own interests without regard to religious allegiance.

In 1547, Francis died, aged fifty-three and wracked by syphilis, a new disease from America. He was succeeded by his son, **Henry II**, who ruled until 1559. Although the king was new, French policy remained the same, since Henry continued the war against the Habsburgs. Finally, in 1559, the French and the Spanish signed the **Peace of Cateau-Cambrésis,** which brought

the long conflict to an end. The French renounced claims in Italy and ceded some territory to Spain. This settlement caused a good deal of grumbling among powerful French nobles who had shed their blood over three generations on behalf of the "king's just cause" in Italy. Henry, however, ordered festivities to celebrate the peace and participated in one of them, a joust in which men on horseback holding lances charged each other in hopes of dismounting their opponent. As the king's opponent made contact with him, his lance shot into a slit in the king's helmet and pierced his eye. Ten days later Henry was dead.

Consolidation in England Under the First Tudors

Defeat in the Hundred Years' War forced England's kings, for the first time in four hundred years, to confine their rule to their island possessions, except for the French port city of Calais. In 1485, when the Wars of the Roses ended with the death in battle of Richard III, **Henry VII** ascended the throne as the first king of a new royal dynasty, the Tudors. Like his counterparts in Spain and France, Henry embarked on a policy of consolidating royal power. Henry, a Lancastrian, also united Lancastrian and Yorkist factions by marrying Elizabeth of York in 1486.

The Tudors' roots lay in Wales, a semi-independent territory under English rule. Henry emphasized his Welsh heritage and presented himself as a truly homegrown ruler, the first since the Norman Conquest in 1066. In the year he became king, Sir Thomas Malory's *Le Morte d'Arthur* was published, recounting the legends about the Welsh king Arthur and his Knights of the Round Table. Drawing on them, Henry named his first son Arthur to emphasize his ancient British background. When Arthur was of age, Henry arranged his marriage to Catherine of Aragon, the younger daughter of Ferdinand and Isabella, to forge a Spanish alliance against England's old enemy, France. Henry ruled in conjunction with the Parliament, which

Henry II (r. 1547–1559) French king who pursued Francis I's wars in Italy.

Peace of Cateau-Cambrésis (1559) Treaty that ended the Spanish and French war for the control of Italy and established Spanish dominance there.

Henry VII (r. 1485–1509) First Tudor king of England, who ended the Wars of the Roses and consolidated royal power.

had gained power during the Hundred Years' War by granting the king taxes to pay for his military expenses. Like Ferdinand and Isabella with the towns of Castile, Henry coaxed the Parliament to cooperate in consolidating the new dynasty.

Henry became king at a particularly favorable time. England, like the rest of Europe, was experiencing demographic expansion and economic growth. Its heartland, the southeast, centered on London, was bustling with agricultural and commercial activity as population rose and ships loaded with wool crossed the North Sea to Antwerp. Henry took advantage of prosperous times to increase his royal income. He confiscated the property of his opponents in the Wars of the Roses and then made sure his new estates produced maximum revenue. Yet more money came from import and export fees, which rose with expanding overseas trade. The administration of justice also produced revenue, since courts charged fees and levied fines. Henry established a series of judicial councils that operated with streamlined rules and speedy efficiency. Understandably, they were popular with his subjects since they offered justice more quickly than older courts bogged down in top-heavy procedures.

Perhaps Henry VII's most important achievement was his imposition of English power on the other parts of the British Isles—Scotland and Ireland. Although Scotland was an independent kingdom, English kings had tried for centuries to bind it closely to their realm. Henry continued this policy by arranging for the marriage of his daughter, Margaret, to the Scots king, a marriage that laid the foundation for a union of the two kingdoms under a single ruler. Ireland had been under English rule since the twelfth century, when the pope had confirmed Henry II as its lord. In fact, effective English control was confined only to the area around Dublin. But even this area had slipped from the English during the Hundred Years' War and the Wars of the Roses. During his reign, Henry reestablished royal control there.

In 1509, Henry VII died and was succeeded by his younger son, **Henry VIII**, since Arthur had also died. Henry VIII had married Arthur's widow, Catherine of Aragon, to keep his father's Spanish alliance intact. He had to obtain a special papal dispensation to do so, since the church forbade marriage between a widow and her brother-in-law. Henry VIII wanted the marriage with Catherine for dynastic reasons: Catherine's chief job was to produce a male heir to the throne. At this she failed, since she gave birth to only one child who survived infancy, and it was a daughter, Mary. By the late 1520s, Henry was convinced that Catherine could no longer conceive and sought an annulment of his marriage. Eventually, in the 1530s, Henry

broke with the pope over the issue. He forbade papal control of the church in England, got Parliament to approve his divorce from Catherine of Aragon, and married a new wife, Anne Boleyn, the second of six, as it turned out. Like his father, Henry VIII expanded English control over the rest of the British Isles. He abolished Wales's semi-independent status and gave it seats in the English Parliament and got the Irish parliament in Dublin to decree that Ireland was an independent kingdom ruled by the king of England.

England's political control of ever-larger parts of the British Isles was accompanied by a growing cultural dominance as the English dialect of the court and the southeast spread throughout the Tudor realm. The rise of English was partly the result of a new literature, like Malory's Arthurian legends, which was printed in London and distributed throughout the kingdom. English was also spread by men graduating from the country's two universities, Cambridge and Oxford, which started to use it instead of Latin. The introduction of an English prayer book in churches after Henry VIII's break with Rome spread the use of the language even more. Political centralization and cultural unification laid the foundations for a new English identity that would develop fully during the long reign of Henry VIII's daughter Elizabeth I.

From 1450 to 1550, the monarchs of Spain, France, and England embarked on a policy of consolidating their political power at home by ending civil wars and strengthening royal government. If they fought foreign wars, they faced financial strains that forced them to search for new sources of revenue. The most important source came from borrowing. As a result, a new group of state creditors emerged in Europe. The management of strengthened royal governments and complex state finances fell increasingly on a new class of legally trained experts, often of non-noble birth. Finally, these states created new forms of collective identity for their subjects based on a common religion or a common language. As these developments took place, the older ideal of Europe united into one community, Christendom, gave way to a new reality, a Europe made up of independent states whose ambitions often brought them into armed conflict with one another.

Henry VIII (r. 1509–1547) King who consolidated Tudor rule over the British Isles and, breaking with the pope over his divorce, launched the English Reformation.

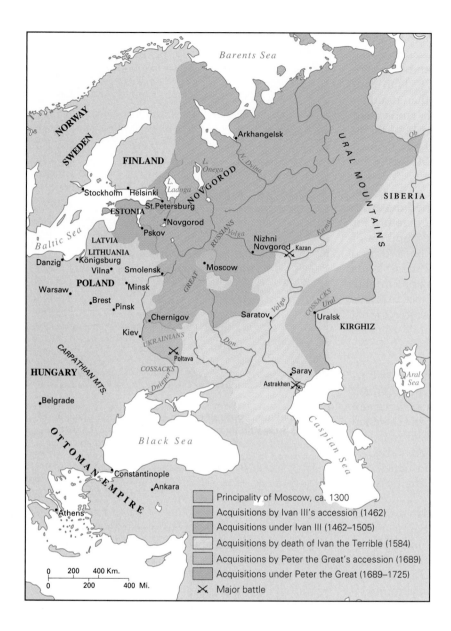

MAP 13.1 **The Expansion of Russia, to 1725** From its beginnings as the small Principality of Moscow, Russia expanded to become one of the world's largest states. Ivan III's and Ivan the Terrible's acquisitions made Russia both a European and a central Asian power.

characterized the political life of the peninsula for the next three hundred years.

Germany was even more politically fragmented. In theory, the Holy Roman Empire bound all of north-central Europe into a single state. But Emperor Charles IV's Golden Bull of 1356 had given the imperial electors a good deal of political independence, which was gradually claimed by the other rulers of the empire's more than three thousand separate territories, some large and powerful like Saxony or Bavaria, others comprising only a few acres. The Protestant Reformation of the sixteenth century added religious fragmentation to the previously existing political decentralization as the empire's states split into hostile Protestant and Catholic camps. As in Italy, regionalism was to characterize German political life until the nineteenth century.

In far eastern Europe, the decline of the Mongol Empire allowed peoples under Mongol rule to assert their independence. In 1462, the grand prince of Moscow, **Ivan III the Great**, began to consolidate power in a centralized Russian state. Ivan, who married the niece of the last Byzantine emperor, took the title of **tsar**, the Russian form of caesar, to proclaim that he

Italy, Germany, and Russia

By 1550, large centralized states covered parts of Europe, but other parts continued to be characterized by political fragmentation. Chief among them were Italy and Germany. In 1450, the Italian peninsula was dominated by five states: Milan, Venice, Tuscany, the Papal States, and the kingdom of Naples. In 1559, when the French and Spanish wars in Italy ended, Spain controlled Milan in the north and the kingdom of Naples in the south and thereby exercised the greatest influence over the peninsula as a whole, but the other states maintained their political independence. Thus regionalism, rather than centralization,

Ivan III the Great (r. 1462–1505) Grand prince of Moscow who conquered lands, took the title of tsar, and established a centralized state.

tsar (in Russian, "Caesar") Title taken by the early consolidators of a unified Russian state.

was the successor of the Byzantine emperors, whose court ceremonial he adopted. Moscow was to be the "Third Rome," succeeding Old Rome and Constantinople, now in Muslim hands. In 1478, Ivan conquered the city of Novgorod and more than doubled his territory, since Novgorod ruled lands that stretched east to the **Ural Mountains.** In 1480, he refused to pay tribute to the khanate of the Golden Horde and thereby formally declared Moscow's independence from Mongol rule.

Ivan III's conquests required a large army to defend his territories. He therefore expanded the army by awarding new soldiers grants of land in return for military service. He also resettled large numbers of landlords: men from Novgorod were moved into older Russian lands, while men from those lands were awarded land in Novgorod. This shift in elite populations lowered the chance of resistance to Ivan's rule by cutting landlords' ties with their old regional power bases while creating clusters of landlord elites in new territories, where they administered justice and collected taxes.

Throughout his reign, Ivan increased the tax burden of his subjects, starting a trend that continued into the sixteenth century. In fact, the government was so aggressive in raising taxes that it exhausted the ability of its subjects to pay. By the late sixteenth century, landlords and their peasants had started to flee east and south into frontier lands in hopes of a better life. The state responded by ordering peasants to remain where they were to guarantee landlords a workforce for their estates. The result was to turn more and more Russian peasants into serfs bound to the land. Raising armies, administering justice, and collecting taxes were tasks like those of the centralized monarchies of western Europe. But Ivan's wholesale resettlement of landlords involved a governmental interference in the lives of elite subjects that was unlike anything done in the west.

In 1533, Ivan III's grandson, **Ivan IV the Terrible,** became tsar. He continued his grandfather's policy of territorial conquest when he marched southeast to the Volga River to seize Mongol **Kazan** and **Astrakhan.** During his reign, Russians also started crossing the Urals to establish settlements in western Siberia.

In theory, Ivan IV's state was organized like a great family with the tsar as its stern but just patriarch. Thus the whole family suffered when the tsar went mad. In the 1560s, Ivan was engaged in the **Livonian War** against Livonia and Lithuania to gain access to the Baltic Sea. When the war went badly, Ivan blamed his nobles, some of whom he accused of treason. He then started to terrorize his subjects in a bloody episode

This anonymous portrait of Ivan the Terrible employs traditions of Russian religious art to depict the tsar. The text around his head and the stylized hair and beard echo the icons found in Russian churches. The artist's use of icon techniques is a way of depicting Ivan's majesty and divinely sanctioned rule. (*National Museum, Copenhagen, Denmark*)

known as the *oprichnina,* an ever-widening purge of the tsar's supposed enemies, carried out by some six thousand state agents. As the purge expanded, thousands were tortured and killed. Ivan exhibited violent mood swings, doing public penance for his sins by beating his head on church floors until the blood ran

Ural Mountains   Mountain range marking the border between the European and Asian parts of Eurasia.

Ivan IV the Terrible   (r. 1533–1584) Ruler of Russia and conqueror of Mongol Kazan and Astrakhan along the Volga River, southeast of Moscow.

Kazan and **Astrakhan**   Mongol khanates along the Volga River conquered by Ivan the Terrible.

Livonian War   (1558–1583) Russian war against Livonia and Lithuania, two states blocking Russia's access to the Baltic Sea.

oprichnina   (in Russian, "domain") (1565–1572) A period of mass terror and executions perpetrated by Ivan the Terrible that resulted in the deaths of thousands.

and then rushing to his palace, where he would preside over bands of executioners engaging in drunken, blasphemous orgies. The *oprichnina* convulsed Russia for seven years and then subsided. Ivan continued to suffer from fits of violent rage, during one of which he brutally killed his son and heir. He died in 1584, a year after his defeat in the Livonian War.

Despite its violence, the *oprichnina*'s lasting effects on Russia were minimal. Many old noble and landlord families survived the purge, while some of Ivan's agents, temporarily raised to power during this terrible episode, sank back into the class of modest provincial landowners. Ivan's attempt to rule despotically had failed. Like their counterparts in the west, Russia's rulers were most successful when they cooperated with their social and economic elites instead of trying to crush them.

When Ivan IV died, the tsar ruled over vast, culturally diverse lands. The northern peoples and those in western Siberia were non-Russians who spoke their own distinct languages and worshiped local, non-Christian gods. The people of the center were Slavs who had converted to Orthodox Christianity, while the peoples of the south, in the former Mongol lands, were either Muslims or pagans. The tsars' policy was to respect these religious differences. Although they were Orthodox Christian in religion, and claimed descent from the Christian rulers of Kiev and Constantinople, Ivan III and his successors officially forbade the Orthodox Church from systematic missionary activity among the non-Christian peoples of the emerging Russian Empire. This policy contrasted sharply with that adopted farther west by Ferdinand and Isabella of Spain.

Europe's Global Expansion

⬇ What were the motivations of Europeans who sought long-distance trade and far-off territories?
⬇ What were the unexpected outcomes of expansion?

Population and economic growth in Europe, along with the rise of strong states headed by energetic rulers, contributed to Europe's global expansion in the sixteenth century. Rising population and a strong economy led to increased demand for the products of Asia and Africa, while vigorous governments helped to organize and finance new commercial ventures. When technological developments turned the wish for new long-distance trade routes on the open seas into a practical possibility, a global economy based on trade began to emerge. At the same time, Portugal

and Spain created Europe's first overseas empires in Asia and the Western Hemisphere.

The Motives and the Means

Economic, political, and religious factors, along with technological developments, combined to bring about Europe's overseas expansion. After 1450, when population rose and the economy strengthened, Europeans once again demanded goods from Asia and Africa. By 1450, however, the realities of trade with those places had changed. Gone were the days when Marco Polo and other Europeans could travel under Mongol protection across Eurasia to trade directly with the Chinese. Now the Ottoman Turks barred the way, while Muslims in Africa kept Europeans out of trade there. Some Europeans benefited from the new realities; the Venetians established profitable trading posts in Syria and Egypt, where they worked with local Arabs to bring Asian goods to Europe. Others, jealous of the Venetians' success, sought new routes to the east. The Genoese, especially, looked for ways to recover the trade they had lost to the Ottomans on the Black Sea.

The rise of strong governments after 1450 also prepared the way for expansion. State sponsorship and financing were crucial in the search for new trade routes. The first states to offer this support were Portugal and Castile. Their location on the Iberian Peninsula positioned them for explorations down the coast of Africa and across the Atlantic. Moreover, Portuguese and Spanish sailors, who had fished in Atlantic waters for centuries and carried cargoes to and from northern trading centers like Antwerp, were accustomed to sailing ocean waters outside the protected Mediterranean. Often, it was the Genoese who organized this rising seaborne commerce. Columbus himself was Genoese.

Economic considerations drove states to support the ventures of their merchants, but religious motives were equally important. As Christians, most Europeans believed they were required to spread their faith to all parts of the world, following Jesus's command in the Gospel of Matthew: "Go therefore and make disciples of all nations, baptizing them in the name of the Father and of the Son and of the Holy Spirit." Kings, queens, merchants, and priests all wished to promote Christianity along with trade. Many believed that worldwide conversion to Christianity would prepare for the Second Coming—Jesus's return to earth, when he would judge the world and reign with his saints. Hopes for profits, the spread of Christianity, and Jesus's return, however,

MAP 13.2 **Map of Martin Beheim, 1492** Martin Beheim, a fifteenth-century German map maker, showed the world as round in 1492. Africa and part of Europe are on the far right. The Madeira and Cape Verde Islands are identified, and then Cipongu (Japan). This is the information Columbus had when he set sail. *(From* Admiral of the Ocean Sea *by Samuel Eliot Morison. Copyright © 1942 by Samuel Eliot Morison; Copyright © renewed 1970 by Samuel Eliot Morison. By permission of Little, Brown and Company, Inc.)*

would have gotten nowhere had it not been for technological developments that made long-distance sailing on the open seas a practical possibility.

In the Middle Ages, Europe's ships were ill suited to long voyages on rough Atlantic waters. Propelled by oars or a simple sail, they were small, with only crude steering devices. By the end of the fifteenth century, however, ships had improved. They were larger, better constructed, fitted with improved rudders for steering, and supplied with a triangular **lateen sail**, popularized by Arab sailors, that allowed them to pick up the wind regardless of the direction from which it was blowing. They could also carry cannons and thus take advantage of the new gunpowder technology.

Navigational aids had also improved. Mapmaking became more accurate with the spread of navigational manuals and the development of **cartography**, which

allowed mapmakers to accurately draw large portions of the known world. Sailors were also able to determine their north/south position (latitude) with greater accuracy, using **astrolabes** or **quadrants** for measuring the distance of heavenly bodies (the sun or known stars) from the horizon. Finding one's east/west position (longitude) was more difficult, but a skilled sailor could calculate it using a magnetic com-

lateen sail Triangular sail, first used by Arab sailors, that could swing to pick up wind coming from different directions.

cartography Science of mapmaking.

astrolabes and **quadrants** Devices allowing sailors to use the stars to find their north/south position (latitude) on the ocean.

pass, first developed by both Chinese and Arab sailors, along with an hourglass to mark off time and observations about the speed of the ship through the waters.

With improved ships, navigational manuals, maps, quadrants, compasses, and hourglasses, sailors ventured farther into the Atlantic and gained knowledge of ocean sailing. By the time of Columbus, they had a good sense of the wind patterns on the Atlantic and were learning how to use them to travel north and south as well as east and west. They had also discarded some earlier theories about global climate. In the Middle Ages, geographers knew that when one traveled south from Europe, it got hotter and hotter. They therefore reasoned that continuing south would eventually lead to parts of the earth so hot that no human being could survive there. Voyages down the coast of Africa gradually proved this theory wrong.

The Portuguese Empire

Sailors from the kingdom of Portugal, the westernmost state on the Iberian Peninsula, were the first Europeans to systematically explore Africa's west coast. For years, the Portuguese had resented Muslim control of the overland trade routes that carried gold from Africa to the Mediterranean. They were also eager to participate in the spice trade from Asia. In 1415, they captured the Muslim port of Ceuta in Morocco. Portuguese seamen then began inching down the African coast, looking for trading partners who would supply them directly with gold. At the same time, they bought black African slaves from local merchants. Both gold and slaves brought high prices back home, spurring other adventurers to join in the voyages. By the 1480s, the Portuguese had set up trading posts in **Guinea,** the center of the gold and slave trade. From the start, the kings of Portugal took an active part in the explorations, working closely with merchants and finally declaring a royal monopoly over the African trade. A member of the royal family, **Prince Henry the Navigator,** promoted the new technologies that made Atlantic sailing possible.

Portuguese traders did not seize large territories in Africa. Instead, they established fortified trading posts along the coast where they could exchange wine, guns, and wheat for gold and slaves. Life in these posts was difficult; the climate was harsh, and many traders died of tropical diseases, against which they had no immunity. Nevertheless, the trade prospered, and by 1500 Portugal was the chief supplier of gold and slaves to Europeans. In 1488, **Bartholomew Diaz** made it to the southern tip of Africa, rounding the Cape of Good Hope, as he called it, and sailing into the Indian Ocean. Faced with a mutiny by his crew,

he turned back to Portugal before reaching India itself. Then in 1497, **Vasco da Gama** landed on the west coast of India, returning to Portugal in 1499 with a shipload of spices and cotton cloth. Da Gama's success launched the Portuguese drive into the Indian Ocean. Sailors soon discovered that the best winds for getting around southern Africa were picked up far out in the Atlantic. They therefore sailed due west of the Cape Verde Islands, found these winds, and then turned around and sailed to the southeast past the Cape of Good Hope. In 1500, on one of these trips, the ships sailed farther west than usual and sighted the coast of South America. Soon the Portuguese settled there, calling it Brazil after a local wood used for dying cloth.

The founder of the Portuguese Empire in Asia was **Alfonso de Albuquerque.** Appointed governor-general of Portuguese possessions along the Indian Ocean, Albuquerque sought to take over the spice trade with Europe. He attacked local Muslim merchants' ships at sea, pounding them with his superior shipboard cannons, and led armed expeditions on land against key trading posts. In 1510, he captured **Goa** on India's west coast, killing the Muslim men there and forcing their widows to marry his sailors to establish a Portuguese community. With Goa secured, he attacked the spice-trading center of **Malacca** on the Malay Peninsula. In 1557, the Portuguese established the first European settlement in China at **Macau.** Albuquerque mixed a passion for trade with hatred of Muslims. To him, they were liars and cheats; force, not friendship, was the only thing they understood.

Guinea Area near the western bulge of Africa; in the sixteenth century, the center of gold and slave trade.

Prince Henry the Navigator (1394–1460) Member of the Portuguese royal family who encouraged explorations along the coast of Africa.

Bartholomew Diaz (ca. 1450–1500) Portuguese sailor who in 1488 rounded the southern tip of Africa and sailed into the Indian Ocean.

Vasco da Gama (1460–1524) First Portuguese trader to land in India and establish direct European trade.

Alfonso de Albuquerque (1453–1515) Governor-general of Portuguese possessions along the Indian Ocean; founder of Portuguese Empire in Asia.

Goa Portuguese colony on the west coast of India.

Malacca Muslim port on the Malay Peninsula where goods from spice-growing islands farther east were collected and shipped westward.

Macau Trading post on the south coast of China near Hong Kong.

His dispatches to Portugal reveal the kind of stereotyping that would feed western imaginations for centuries to come. For Albuquerque, smashing infidel control of Far Eastern commerce would allow for the triumphant planting of the cross of Christ in heathen lands. He was the perfect crusader trader.

The Spanish Empire

In the spring of 1492, **Christopher Columbus** began preparations for his westward voyage across the Atlantic. Columbus was no stranger to Atlantic waters. He had lived in Portugal for many years, marrying a Portuguese woman and sailing to the **Canary Islands**, the African coast, and the Madeira Islands, where his wife's family had estates. After failing to get Portuguese backing for a voyage across the Atlantic, he turned to Spain for help (see Choice). When that finally came, he began collecting crews and supplies for the three small ships Queen Isabella had given him. Local sailors were reluctant to sign on, not because they thought the world was flat and they would soon fall off its western edge (most Europeans knew the world was round) but because they were local tuna fishermen already making a good living in waters close to home. So Columbus had a hard time recruiting the ninety men he needed, some of which, in the end, were convicts. His task was made especially difficult because he had to work out of the small Spanish port of Palos; the larger ports were clogged with ships carrying away the recently expelled Spanish Jews. Finally, on August 3, 1492, just as a ship carrying the last of the Jews sailed from Palos, Columbus headed out of the port.

After reprovisioning his ships in the Canary Islands, in early September Columbus sailed west for thirty-three days, landing in the Bahamas on October 12. Since the Spaniards believed they had found islands in the East Indies, they called the local people Indians. Columbus then explored the islands of Hispaniola and Cuba, hoping to set up Portuguese-style trading posts. Finding no cities, he returned to Spain in January 1493, leaving some men behind on Hispaniola. Following a triumphant procession across Spain, witnessed by Bartolomé de Las Casas and his family, Columbus presented Isabella and Ferdinand with gold, parrots, spices, and captives, along with a pineapple, which Ferdinand happily ate. This was modest booty, but Columbus played up the potential for future profits and managed to get royal backing for three more voyages between 1493 and 1504. Las Casas's father, excited by the sight of Columbus's captives and booty, embarked on the first of them. In 1494, Spain and Portugal, with the blessing of the pope, signed the **Treaty of Tordesillas**, granting Spain control of Central and South America except for Brazil, which went to Portugal, along with Africa and Asia. Thus the entire world was divided into two zones for these first European empires.

Christopher Columbus   (1451–1506) Genoese sailor and explorer who captained the first European voyages to the Caribbean and South America and claimed lands there for Spain.

Canary Islands   Islands in the Atlantic Ocean colonized by Spain.

Treaty of Tordesillas   Arrangement in 1494 between Spain and Portugal drawing a north-south line west of the Azores; lands west of it went to Spain and lands east (plus Brazil) to Portugal.

VoidVoiceVoiceVoice

Isabella of Castile Writes Her Last Will and Testament

On October 12, 1504, twelve years to the day after Columbus landed in the Bahamas, the dying Isabella began to dictate her last will and testament. In it she made arrangements for her burial and the disposition of her worldly goods. She also summed up the major achievements of her reign and asked her successors to honor them.

→ I ask and order that my body be buried in the monastery of Saint Francis which is in the Alhambra in the city of Granada . . . dressed in the habit of the very blessed poor man of Jesus Christ, Saint Francis, in a lowly grave without any bust and only a plain slab on the ground containing an inscription.

→ Why would Isabella ask to be buried in a plain grave in Granada?

→ In addition, because I have wanted to order a simplification of the laws . . . , identifying the doubtful ones and eliminating the superfluous ones, in order to avoid doubts and any contradictions that have arisen concerning them and the expenses that they might impose on my kingdoms . . . I beg the king my lord, and I order and enjoin the said princess, my daughter, and the said prince, her husband, to bring together a learned and conscientious prelate with persons who are educated, wise, and expert in law, to examine the said laws and to reduce them into a briefer and less cumbersome code.

→ Why does Isabella "beg" her husband and "lord" to carry out her wishes while "ordering" her daughter and son-in-law to do so?

→ I command that the jewels which the said princess and prince, my children, have given me be returned to them. And that the relic I have of Our Lord's loincloth be given to the monastery of Saint Anthony in the city of Segovia. And that all my other relics be given to the Cathedral in the city of Granada.

→ How does Isabella's gift of relics to Granada relate to her instructions for her burial?

And I entreat and command the said princess, my daughter, and the said prince, her husband, as Catholic princes, to take great care concerning the things that honor God and His holy faith, watching over and securing the faith's safety, defense, and glorification, since for it we are obliged to pledge our persons, lives, and possessions as is necessary. And that they be very obedient to the commandments of holy mother church, as they are obliged to be its protectors and defenders. And that they will not cease the conquest of Africa to fight for the faith against the infidels. And that they will always favor the work of the Holy Inquisition against heretical depravity.

→ From the time when the Holy Apostolic See granted us the Islands and Mainland of the Ocean Sea . . . our first intention was, from the time we entreated pope Alexander VI, of blessed memory, who gave us the said grant, to attempt to persuade and cause the inhabitants there to convert to our holy Catholic faith, and to send to the said islands and mainland prelates and members of religious orders and clergy, and other learned and God-fearing persons, to instruct the inhabitants and residents there in the Catholic faith, and to teach and instruct them in good behavior, and to put in them the necessary diligence, taking the care stated more fully in the letters of the grant. To this end, I most affectionately beseech the king my lord and I charge and command the said princess, my daughter, and the said prince, her husband, to carry this out as their principal goal with much diligence. → They must not in any way allow the Indians, the inhabitants, and the residents in the said islands and mainland to suffer any injury to their persons or property, but must be well and justly treated. And if they have received any injury, they must set it right.

→ Notice Isabella's description of her motive for conquering new territories. To what degree was it shared by the Spaniards who went to these new territories?

→ Why would Isabella express her concerns for the Indians in her will?

This drawing from about 1550 by an unknown Aztec artist shows the devastation that smallpox brought to the indigenous populations of the Western Hemisphere. At the upper left a local healer speaks to a sick person while others lie dying on mats. *(Biblioteca Medicea Laurenziana; Photo: MicroFoto, Florence)*

The **Taíno** people Columbus encountered on the islands of the Caribbean were friendly and provided him with food and information, but relations deteriorated when the Spaniards started to claim their land for Spain and rape women. Over the next twenty-five years, as more land was seized for farms, the Taíno, now virtually enslaved, were forced to work it. Even worse were the diseases, such as smallpox and influenza, that swept through the local population. Since the Western Hemisphere was isolated from Europe, local peoples had no immunity from the diseases the Spaniards brought, and millions died as epidemics swept through Central and South America, often in advance of any European's arrival. The Taíno, who may have numbered 300,000 in 1492, were virtually extinct by 1550, and, overall, the native population of the Americas fell by 90 percent in the century after Columbus's voyages—the greatest demographic catastrophe in recorded history.

For a quarter century after 1492, few Spaniards migrated to the Caribbean. Although some gold was found, it was difficult to grow sufficient food, and Spanish mortality rates were high as men succumbed to local diseases. Columbus himself died in Spain in 1506, disappointed by the meager results of his discoveries. Everything changed, however, in 1519, when a Spanish nobleman, **Hernán Cortés,** landed on the east coast of Mexico with six hundred men, sixteen horses, and six cannons.

Like those before him, Cortés was looking for gold. Unlike them, he embarked on territorial conquest; in two and a half years his small force conquered the **Aztec Empire** of central Mexico. The Aztecs ruled over many states, which had to supply men and tribute to the emperor in the capital of Tenochtitlán. Cortés formed alliances with the most discontented states and augmented his own force with their soldiers. If local states refused to join the anti-Aztec coalition, they were intimidated by the invaders, who were mounted on horses, which the local people had never seen before, wore strange body armor, and wielded steel swords. In addition, the noise, smoke, and fire of Cortés's artillery, which was also unknown to the Aztecs, panicked the enemy, as did the attack dogs used in battle. (The Aztecs' only dogs were tiny, resembling modern-day chihuahuas.)

In November 1519, Cortés and his allies entered Tenochtitlán at the invitation of the emperor, Moctezuma II, who may have been influenced by Aztec traditions that prophesied the arrival by sea of a pale-

Taíno Native people inhabiting the Caribbean islands visited by the Spaniards in the first period of encounter between Europeans and American Indians.

Hernán Cortés (1485–1547) Spanish nobleman and conquistador (conqueror) who in 1519 conquered the Aztec Empire.

Aztec Empire Federation of states in central Mexico ruled by an emperor from his capital, Tenochtitlán, the present-day Mexico City.

In this engraving, the Inca prince Atahualpa rises from his throne on his litter just before his capture by the Spanish at Cajamarca. He attempts to fend off a soldier while a Spanish friar raises a cross either in blessing or as protection against a pagan. The cannon in the foreground reminds the viewer of the withering Spanish fire power. *(Biblioteca Nazionale Marciana Venice/Dagli Orti/The Art Archive)*

skinned god, Quetzalcoatl. In June 1520, Moctezuma died under mysterious circumstances. Although probably murdered by his own people, the Aztecs blamed the Spaniards for his death and attacked Cortés. Withdrawing from the city, the Spaniards regrouped and made a successful assault in August 1521. Cortés now controlled the Aztec Empire, and one of his first acts was to demolish the sacred pyramid in the center of Tenochtitlán and replace it with a cathedral.

Cortés's conquest of the Aztecs launched the first New World gold rush. When news of Tenochtitlán's capture reached Europe, along with gold from Moctezuma's treasury, thousands of Spaniards flocked to Mexico in search of bounty. Among them was **Francisco Pizarro**, an illiterate laborer who had migrated to Hispaniola in 1502 and served in expeditions to Central America, including **Vaso Núñez de Balboa**'s trek across Panama to the Pacific Ocean. In

1531, Pizarro launched an expedition of 280 men and 55 horses against the **Inca Empire**, taking advantage of a political crisis among the Inca to conquer them.

In the late 1520s, the Inca emperor died, a victim of the European-induced epidemics that were raging though Central and South America. Two of his sons, Atahualpa and Huáscar, then fought each other for

Francisco Pizarro   (ca. 1475–1541) Soldier who in 1531 conquered the Inca Empire with a small Spanish force.

Vaso Núñez de Balboa   (1475–1519) Spanish explorer who crossed the isthmus of Panama in 1513 and sighted the Pacific Ocean.

Inca Empire   Empire stretching from Ecuador to northern Chile and from the Pacific Ocean to the upper Amazon River.

MAP 13.3   **World Expansion, 1492–1535**   By 1535, Europe's worldwide sea-lanes were well established, following the voyages of Vasco da Gama, Christopher Columbus, and Ferdinand Magellan. Compare the size of Spain and Portugal with the size of their overseas empires.

control of the empire. Arriving during the civil war sparked by the sons' rivalry, Pizarro played the brothers against each other. He used his horses, cannon, and steel swords to slaughter over three thousand Inca soldiers at Cajamarca in present-day Peru after Atahualpa had unwittingly led them into an ambush. Atahualpa was taken prisoner. Huáscar was murdered in 1532, and a year later Atahualpa was also. Pizarro then set up a third brother as a puppet emperor.

Cortés's conquest of the Aztecs and Pizarro's of the Incas finally produced the precious metals that had driven the search for direct trade routes to Asia. It was silver, however, rather than gold, that flowed in ever-increasing quantities toward Spain from mines at Zacatecas in Mexico and Potosí in present-day Bolivia, both started in the 1540s. Following **Ferdinand Magellan**'s circumnavigation of the globe in 1519–1521, the magnitude of Columbus's voyages and subsequent Spanish conquests began to sink into the European consciousness.

Exploration, Expansion, and European Identity

> ↓ How did Europeans come to terms with the peoples of Africa and the Americas, whom they perceived as not like them?
>
> ↓ How did African slavery develop, and how was it justified?

Once it became clear that the peoples of the Western Hemisphere were not Asians but previously unknown inhabitants of a "New World," travelers' and missionaries' accounts appeared offering conflicting descriptions of these "Indians." In addition, the creation of Portuguese and Spanish Empires in the New World led to the importation of millions of black African slaves to replace the declining native populations as a labor force. Confronted with strange New World people and the emergence of African slavery in overseas empires, people in Europe were forced to rethink who they were in relation to others and outsiders.

Native Americans in the European Imagination

European attempts to understand Native Americans started with the assumption that there were universal standards for proper human behavior. Early travelers' and missionaries' accounts of New World people based on this assumption were positive. Native Americans were pictured as simple people who lived virtu-

ous lives. They had no private property and no money, and hence no reason to be greedy. They lived in harmony with nature and each other, solving disputes without need of laws and courts. They waged war, but only for just cause. In a word, the Indians were what Europeans ought to be. And so, in the end, these accounts were really about Europe, with the Indians providing a way for moralists to condemn abuses in their own society.

Alongside the picture of the "good Indian," an image of the "bad Indian" soon emerged. Indians were accused of eating disgusting things like spiders and worms. Because they wore no European clothes, they were accused of engaging in what Europeans thought were the vilest kinds of sexual behavior, including homosexuality and intercourse with animals. They had no true religion but worshiped satanically inspired idols. Worst of all, they practiced human sacrifice and cannibalism. Both the good and bad pictures of the Indians wove together bits of accurate information with misinformation and a host of European fantasies and fears, and both were believed. Gradually, however, the negative picture gained ground, and by the mid-sixteenth century, arguments were made that the Indians were not really human beings but **"natural slaves."**

The theory of the natural slave went back to the Greek philosopher Aristotle, who stated that there were creatures resembling human beings who nevertheless lacked fully rational minds. Although they could understand and communicate with real humans, they needed human masters to control them. If Indian behavior was as bad as some people said, then it was clear that the Indians were natural slaves, since fully rational human beings would reject the things the Indians supposedly did. Moreover, when the theory of natural slavery was applied to the Indians, the Spanish conquest and exploitation of them was fully justified.

The attack on the Indians reached a climax in the late 1540s, when Charles V's chaplain, **Juan Ginés de Sepúlveda**, defended the theory that they were natural slaves. Sepúlveda's endorsement of the "bad In-

Ferdinand Magellan   (1480–1521) Portuguese commander of a Spanish fleet who circumnavigated the globe in 1519–1521.

"natural slaves"   As theorized by the Greek philosopher Aristotle, semirational creatures resembling human beings who needed human masters to control them.

Juan Ginés de Sepúlveda   (1494–1573) Charles V's chaplain, who denounced the American Indians as less than human.

This idealized portrait of Bartolomé de Las Casas is shows Las Casas as a Dominican friar. The artist gives him a noble but kindly face. He sits quietly writing in defense of the Indian populations he encountered first as a conquistador and then as a priest and bishop. *(Archivo de Indias, Seville/Mithra-Index/The Bridgeman Art Library)*

dian" theory provoked a response from Bartolomé de Las Casas. Las Casas was also an influential member of Charles V's court who had known both Ferdinand and Isabella. After 1492, he followed his father to the Caribbean, where he became a landowner, with many Indians working for him. But his true calling was to the church, and he became the first man to be ordained a priest in the Americas. Las Casas's experiences as a landowner had shown him just how brutally the Indians were exploited, and as a priest he campaigned for their better treatment. In 1542, he persuaded Charles V to stop the worst abuses by issuing the **New Laws for the Indies.** In 1545, Las Casas was consecrated a bishop and sent to Guatemala to introduce the New Laws, but local landlords' opposition to the reforms forced him to return to Spain. When Las Casas read Sepúlveda's attack, he demanded to face him in a debate.

Las Casas argued that men like himself, who had observed Indian culture directly, were the only per-

sons qualified to determine whether Indians were fully human. And he argued eloquently that they were. Las Casas admitted that the Indians often behaved "badly," but he explained that this did not prove a lack of humanity. Their behavior resulted from evil customs that had taken root in their societies. In the past, Christianity had corrected Greek and Roman errors, and it would also correct Indian ones. In 1552, following his debate with Sepúlveda, Las Casas published his *Brief Account of the Destruction of the Indies*, a fiery description of Spanish brutality in the New World that was widely read and influenced many Europeans.

New Laws for the Indies   (1542) Laws issued by Charles V that attempted to stop Spanish exploitation of New World populations.

Las Casas's arguments were thoroughly **Eurocentric.** He believed in the superiority of European civilization and thought that the Indians' conversion to Christianity was the only way to save them from eternal damnation. His recognition of their full humanity and his demands for a just treatment of them, along with his sense of the superiority of European culture and religion, gave voice to many of the principles that guided European colonial expansion in subsequent centuries. Finally, Las Casas, aware of the labor shortage in the Americas created by the decline in local populations, urged his fellow Europeans to import African slaves to fill the gap, a position he later regretted.

The Labor of Africans

New World slavery had its origins in Portuguese exploration of Africa. Beginning in 1420, the Portuguese settled on **Atlantic islands** off Africa's west coast, while the Spanish occupied the Canary Islands. The islands' volcanic soil was ideal for growing sugar cane, and large **plantations** were established to produce it. During the Middle Ages, honey was Europe's chief sweetener. Medieval Europeans had known of sugar, which was imported in small quantities from Muslim lands and used as medicine or a sexual stimulant. With the colonization of the Atlantic islands, sugar became a European-controlled commodity and the demand for it rose rapidly. At first, the plantations' workforce consisted of Portuguese settlers as well as **indentured servants** fulfilling the terms of their contracts and slaves from the eastern Mediterranean and sub-Saharan Africa. By 1500, however, black African slaves predominated. For years, tribal warfare in West Africa had involved the capture and enslavement of enemies. Portuguese traders bought these slaves from Africans because they were relatively cheap and could be forced to do the harsh work on the island plantations that free Europeans eventually rejected.

Some African rulers opposed the Portuguese slave trade, but coastal merchants found it economically profitable and even invested in the sugar plantations. Over the sixteenth century, tens of thousands of slaves were brought to the Atlantic islands. Because they came from parts of Africa where agriculture was widespread, they were familiar with field work and could be trained to handle sugar cane. Soon the islands were the main sugar producers for Europe, sending sugar to Antwerp and other markets.

The Portuguese and Spanish not only pioneered the use of African slaves in a plantation system, they also adopted stereotypes about Africans developed first in the Muslim world, where a trade in sub-Saharan African slaves had persisted throughout the Middle Ages. These stereotypes condemned Africans as ugly, lazy, sexually promiscuous, stupid, and evil smelling. Christians had also long identified the color black with sin and the Devil and the color white with purity. The combination of these Muslim and Christian stereotypes laid the foundations for arguments about the racial inferiority of blacks to whites that were to have a long and vicious history.

Columbus, who had lived on the Madeira Islands before coming to Spain, took sugar-cane plants with him on his return to the Western Hemisphere in 1493. When settlers realized that cane grew well in Brazil and the Caribbean islands, plantations were established there, and the transatlantic importation of African slaves began. For the next three hundred years, more than 11 million Africans were carried across the Atlantic in one of the largest forced migrations in history.

Europeans justified African slavery in various ways. Some appealed to Aristotle's theory of natural slaves, while others cited Christian scripture, which showed that both the Israelites and the first Christians owned slaves. Others turned to Genesis and argued that Africans were the descendants of Noah's son Ham, cursed as a slave because he had seen his father drunk and naked. In a world that believed all human beings were slaves to sin, the idea that some were slaves to other men was easily accepted. In addition, Europe's hierarchical and patriarchal social order, in which wives, children, and servants were subject to the male head of household, made slavery seem like an extension of the general structure of society. As a result, few Europeans questioned it.

Slavery in the Western Hemisphere differed in important respects from the kind practiced in European and Muslim lands. First, slaves were increasingly thought of as black and African. Earlier forms of slavery had been colorblind, since people of many different racial and ethnic communities had been enslaved.

Eurocentric   Idea that Europe and European culture are either superior to or more important than the lands and cultures of other peoples.

Atlantic islands   The Azores, the Cape Verde Islands, the Madeira Islands, and São Tomé, where the Portuguese used African slaves to cultivate sugar for the European market.

plantation   A large-scale agricultural enterprise producing goods for the European market, often using slave labor.

indentured servants   Servants who agreed to compulsory service for a fixed period of time, often in exchange for passage to a colony.

376 CHAPTER 13 Europe's Age of Expansion, 1450–1550

In the Americas, most slaves worked on plantations or, after silver was discovered in the Spanish Empire, in mines. This work was in contrast to European and Muslim slavery, in which many different types of work were performed by slaves. Most important, slavery was increasingly considered a lifelong status and one that children inherited from their parents, thus creating a perpetually enslaved class of persons. The idea that one was "born" a slave, not "made" one by capture or some other force, fitted in with European ideas of Africans' racial inferiority.

The Problem of "the Other"

At the end of the sixteenth century, the new peoples Europeans had encountered in their expeditions for trade and wealth were so broadly recognized that the great playwright of the English Renaissance, **William Shakespeare**, put them on stage in his dramas. In Shylock the Jew, Caliban the slave, and Othello the African, Shakespeare provides insights into Europeans' thoughts about **"the other."** These unforgettable stage characters reveal traditional stereotypes but also portray the playwright's sense of their humanity and the injustices done to them.

In *The Merchant of Venice*, Shakespeare used traditional Christian stereotypes of the Jew to create Shylock, a miserly moneylender who proclaimed his hatred of Christians and wanted to destroy the Christian merchant Antonio. When Antonio's finances falter, Shylock agrees to loan him money, but at a price—a pound of his flesh if he fails to repay. This gruesome demand echoed traditional Christian fantasies and fears, like those that had surfaced at La Guardia in Spain, where Jews were accused of killing a child for magical purposes. The Christians of Venice repay Shylock's hatred in kind, spitting on him and calling him "dog" and "the devil in the likeness of a Jew."

When Antonio goes broke, Shylock demands his pound of flesh—to use as fish bait. But just at this point, Shakespeare gives Shylock one of the most famous speeches in the play:

> *Hath not a Jew eyes? hath not a Jew affections, passions? if you tickle us, do we not laugh? if you poison us, do we not die?*

Here, Shakespeare shows Shylock not as a monster but as a man crushed by Christian slander and contempt, and his words cut through the mutual hatred like a cry. Nevertheless, Shylock continues to demand his payment. In the end, he loses in court; Antonio keeps his flesh, and Shylock must surrender half his fortune to his daughter, who has run away with a Christian. Then he is forced to convert to Christianity.

Shakespeare used common anti-Jewish stereotypes to construct Shylock. But two details were his own: Shylock's plea to be treated as a human being and the renunciation of his religion by force. These both complicate the stereotype of the wicked and hated Jew.

Like Shylock, Caliban in *The Tempest* is a complex character. He was "king" of the island where he lived alone until Prospero, the deposed duke of Milan, was exiled there with his daughter. At first, Prospero befriended Caliban, teaching him to speak like a human. But when Caliban attempted to rape his daughter, he turned against him, enslaving him and calling him "a born devil, on whose nature nurture can never stick." Prospero also calls himself "lord" of Caliban's island.

Shakespeare had read European accounts of Native Americans. References in *The Tempest* show that he drew on them when he created Caliban, who has all the qualities of a natural slave—he is physically deformed, without speech until taught by a European, and a would-be rapist who must be ruled by force. Throughout the play Caliban uses his newfound speech to curse Prospero while plotting to murder him. He is dangerous and despicable. And yet, when Caliban describes the beauties of his island, which Prospero has seized from him, Shakespeare gave him some of the most beautiful lines in the play, and they are in poetry. Shakespeare normally reserved poetic lines for high-born or noble characters, while the low and bad ones speak prose. Caliban, like Shylock, embodied stereotypes of the hated "other." But, like *The Merchant of Venice*, there are occasions in *The Tempest* when Shakespeare cast the stereotypes aside to show the humanity of the injured character, if only for a moment.

In *Othello*, Shakespeare returned to Venice for the setting of his play. The title character is an African ex-slave serving as the mercenary commander of Venetian forces on Cyprus to defend the island against the "malignant and turbaned Turk." Shakespeare again used current stereotypes to create Othello, who is described by other characters in the play as having thick lips and being "sooty," "lascivious," "an old black ram," and "ignorant as dirt." He also drew on a contemporary account of Africans in English that called them savage, jealous, and easily deceived. The play

William Shakespeare (1564–1616) England's greatest playwright, author of *The Merchant of Venice, The Tempest, Othello,* and many other plays and poems.

"the other" Religious, ethnic, racial, or other outsiders who are feared and hated because they are said to embody all that a community rejects as bad or inhuman.

revolves around Othello's growing belief that his beloved Venetian wife, Desdemona, who is white, has been unfaithful to him. Once convinced of Desdemona's infidelity, Othello flies into a wild, jealous rage. In the end he strangles his wife. When he learns that she was, in fact, innocent, he kills himself. Othello is a great sinner, guilty of rage, murder, and suicide. But he is not the villain of the play. That label goes to Iago, who is white, Christian, and Venetian. Out of jealousy and hatred for Othello, Iago seduces the "Moor" into believing that Desdemona is an adulteress. He is one of Shakespeare's greatest villains—intelligent, crafty, and supremely evil. In the end, Othello the black outsider is a tragic hero, while Iago, the white insider, is led offstage in chains.

In Shakespeare's plays, debates about "others," carried on in learned circles by Las Casas and Sepúlveda, were presented to a wider audience in vividly dramatic form. Like Las Casas, Shakespeare wrestled with the problem by starting with assumptions of his own culture's superiority. But also like him, Shakespeare could argue that the hated and savage "other" was part of humanity. Medieval people had identified themselves as Christians and thought of the "other"—that is, Jews and Muslims—mainly in religious terms as people who had heard of but rejected the Christian gospel. Now "others" came to include Indians and African slaves, who had no prior knowledge of Christianity, and the problem of understanding who they were became acute.

Summary

Review Questions

↑ How did Europe's economic expansion create a global economy?

↑ What strategies did European rulers use to increase control over their territories?

↑ What factors shaped the formation of Europeans' individual and collective identities and those of the peoples they encountered in global expansion?

The growth of Europe's population, which began after 1450, stimulated an economic expansion based on increasing agricultural activity and the growth of new trading networks. From 1450 to 1550, most urban and rural workers benefited from a rise in wages, although rates of pay were sharply different for men and women because of prevailing notions about the relative value of men's and women's work. The gendered distribution of wages echoed the general patriarchal organization of society. Both urban and rural communities were headed by men. In addition, these communities were arranged hierarchically from the better sort to the lesser sort.

Although many communities became less economically self-sufficient as they were linked to large-scale trading networks, a strong sense of community identity and mutual responsibility characterized Europe's villages, towns, and cities. The community was conceived of as an organic whole in which anyone's fate was everyone's business. This view explains Europeans' commitment to public hospitals and welfare institutions. Communities also carefully guarded their local ways of life against outside intrusions.

Rulers in this early modern world benefited from Europe's rising economy, which allowed them to tax and borrow to meet their needs, but they also had to be careful to respect their subjects' rights and traditions, even as they sought to increase their control over them. Successful government involved cooperating and negotiating with local elites, whether nobles, landowners, or town fathers, in order to develop working relations with them. Rulers like Ivan IV, who tried to govern despotically, could throw their societies into turmoil, but their extreme policies usually met with failure.

One trend in government was the attempt to forge more centralized states. The means to this end varied. In Spain, a policy to respect the political independence of Castile and Aragon was balanced against the creation of a new, more homogeneous national identity. In France and England, it involved the introduction of standardized languages. In many states, it involved tying rulers as borrowers to subjects as lenders. It also involved administrative centralization in the hands of experts.

The creation of empires after 1450 was the most dramatic example of Europe's age of expansion. For Portugal and Spain, empire building was directly linked to trade. The creation of empires had enormous consequences for both Europeans and non-Europeans. For Africans, it had the disastrous effect of expanding and extending the trade in slaves from the small Atlantic islands to the huge plantation economies of the New World. In the New World, it involved not only conquest but also the destruction of whole societies, through the unforeseen and largely uncontrollable spread of new diseases. For Europeans like Cortés and Pizarro, empire brought new riches. For those like Las Casas and Shakespeare, it brought a new urgency to think through the problems of colonial domination and Europeans' relations with other peoples.

← Thinking Back, Thinking Ahead →

What were the long-term consequences of European overseas expansion during the sixteenth century?

ECHO

Christopher Columbus

Cristoforo Colombo, a Genoese sailor, died before the full impact of his voyages was understood in Europe. He certainly could not have known how famous he would become—or that he would be a symbol for all that later generations admired or condemned in the complex encounter between the "New World" and Europe that his voyages set in motion.

Curiously, this Italian who sailed for a Spanish Catholic monarch became a hero for nineteenth-century Americans, most of whom were staunchly Protestant. In their eyes, Columbus embodied all the virtues they most admired in themselves. He seemed to represent the rugged individualist whose contempt for hidebound traditionalists arguing that the world was flat led him on a heroic adventure across the unknown frontier of the Atlantic. This way of thinking reached a climax in 1892, when President Benjamin Harrison issued a proclamation for a national observance of the four-hundredth anniversary of Columbus's "discovery" of America.

In the first half of the twentieth century, Columbus was returned to his ethnic roots and became the darling of Americans of Italian descent, who campaigned for an annual national holiday in his honor. In 1937, President Franklin D. Roosevelt, who had recently won a landslide reelection victory with many Italian American votes, created the present holiday. (In 1971, the observance was changed to the second Monday in October to give workers the chance for a three-day weekend.)

In the second half of the twentieth century, Columbus became a contested symbol. Italian Americans continued to venerate him, but so did Hispanics, claiming that his voyages were "a thoroughly Spanish event." In 1996, both groups organized rival Columbus Day parades in New York City. On the other hand, Scandinavians complained that Columbus was a latecomer and called for a holiday honoring the first Norse "discoverers," who landed in North America around the year 1000. All three groups have also had to compete with Native Americans' counterimage of Columbus as the man who brought devastating disease, followed by slavery, to the peoples of the Western Hemisphere. In 1992, on the five-hundredth anniversary of his voyages, a protest holiday, Indigenous Peoples Day, was observed in some places by Native Americans and their supporters. Although seventy towns or districts in the United States are today named in honor of Columbus, the Genoese sailor continues to be a contested figure for people with different ethnic loyalties and conflicting historical memories.

Suggested Readings

Cameron, Euan, ed. *Early Modern Europe: An Oxford History.* Oxford: Oxford University Press, 2000. A recent general account.

Kamen, Henry. *Empire: How Spain Became a World Power, 1492–1763.* New York: HarperCollins Publishers, 2003. Detailed account of Spanish empire building in the Western Hemisphere.

Musgrave, Peter. *The Early Modern European Economy.* New York: St. Martin's Press, 1999. A recent survey.

Phillips, William D., Jr., and Carla Rahn Phillips. *The Worlds of Christopher Columbus.* New York: Cambridge University Press, 1992. Excellent on Columbus's life and times.

Postma, Johannes. *The Atlantic Slave Trade.* Westport, Conn.: Greenwood Press, 2003. An excellent introduction.

Riasanovsky, Nicholas V. *A History of Russia.* 6th ed. New York: Oxford University Press, 2000. The standard account in English.

Zinsser, Judith P., and Bonnie S. Anderson. *Women in Early Modern and Modern Europe.* Washington, D.C.: American Historical Association, 2001. A brief introduction.

Websites

For sections and links to readings on many of the topics discussed in this chapter, **Internet Modern History Sourcebook,** at www.fordham.edu/halsall/mod/modsbook03.html

A detailed listing of products traded in the emerging world economy, **Trade Products in Early Modern History,** at www.bell.lib.umn.edu/Products.html

More than a thousand images relating to the slave trade and slave life, **The Atlantic Slave Trade and Slave Life in the Americas: A Visual Record,** at www.hitchcock.itc.virginia.edu/Slavery/index.php

CHAPTER 14

Reform in the Western Church, 1490–1570

1500 B.C.E.	1000 B.C.E.	500 B.C.E.	1 B.C.E./1 C.E.

| | 1494 Savonarola institutes reforms in Florence | | | 1516 Erasmus translates the Greek New Testament | 1517 Luther condemns indulgences | | 1527 Henry VIII breaks with the pope |

1490	1495	1500	1505	1510	1515	1520	1525	1530

Catholics, Protestants, and the Eastern Orthodox in 1555

The Religious Peace of Augsburg in 1555 confirmed the division of western Christendom. Which religious community or communities were able to win over the majority of the population in the most parts of Europe, north and south, east and west?

Predominant religion in 1555

- Lutheran
- Calvinist (Reformed)
- Church of England
- Roman Catholic
- Orthodox
- Muslim
- → Spread of Calvinism
- ▲ Huguenot centers
- — Boundary of Ottoman Empire, 1566
- — Boundary of Holy Roman Empire

NORWAY

SWEDEN

Bergen

Helsinki

Stockholm

ESTONIA

Baltic Sea

RUSSIA

LIVONIA

Riga

SCOTLAND

Edinburgh
John Knox

Penetration of Calvinism
to England after 1558

DENMARK

Copenhagen

PRUSSIA

POLAND-LITHUANIA

IRELAND

Dublin

North Sea

Hamburg

Warsaw

WALES

ENGLAND

Oxford

London
Thomas More

Plymouth

Amsterdam

NETHERLANDS
Menno Simons

Antwerp

Brussels

Münster
Slaughter of
Anabaptists,
1535

BRANDENBURG

Wittenberg
Martin Luther

Leipzig

SAXONY

SILESIA

Marburg

Erfurt

Prague

BOHEMIA

MORAVIA
Jacob Hutter

ATLANTIC
OCEAN

Rennes

Paris

Worms
Edict of Worms,
1521

HOLY ROMAN
EMPIRE

Speyer

Nuremberg

Stuttgart

Orléans

Strasbourg

Augsburg

Munich

HUNGARY

Nantes
Edict of Nantes,
1598

Basel

Zurich
Ulrich Zwingli

Vienna

AUSTRIA

Buda

Pest

TRANSYLVANIA

La Rochelle

FRANCE

Geneva
John Calvin

Council of Trent,
1545–1563

Trent

Bordeaux

Milan

Pavia

Venice
Jewish
Ghetto,
1516

Belgrade

Black Sea

Loyola
Ignatius Loyola

Toulouse

Avignon

Genoa

PAPAL
STATES

OTTOMAN

Marseilles

Pisa

Florence
Girolama Savanorola

EMPIRE

PORTUGAL

Ávila
Teresa
of Avila

Madrid

ANDORRA

Corsica

Rome
Roman Inquisition
established, 1542

Constantinople

Lisbon

Toledo

SPAIN

Barcelona

Naples

NAPLES

Seville

Valencia

Sardinia

Granada

Balearic Is.

Sicily

ALGIERS

Mediterranean Sea

TUNIS

OTTOMAN
EMPIRE

0   200   400 Km.

0   200   400 Mi.

| 500 C.E. | 1000 C.E. | 1500 C.E. | 2000 C.E. |

1535
Anabaptists slaughtered at Münster

1536
Calvin's
Institutes
published

1540
Pope approves
Jesuits

1545
Council of
Trent opens

1555
Peace of Augsburg
accepts split in
western Christianity

1563
Council of
Trent ends

| 1535 | 1540 | 1545 | 1550 | 1555 | 1560 | 1565 | 1570 | 1575 |

Choice Choice Choice

Teresa of Ávila

Teresa of Ávila, one of the Catholic Church's great reformers, reinvigorated her religious order, the Carmelites, and wrote spiritual works that were quickly recognized as masterpieces of devotion. As a woman, she faced huge obstacles because women were thought to be unsuited for such serious work. But she won over even her fiercest opponents and at her death was recognized as one of the pillars of the Roman Catholic Church. (Institut Amatller d'Art Hispanic)

Teresa of Ávila Chooses to Reform the Carmelites

In 1535, a twenty-year-old woman, defying her father, secretly left her family's house and entered a convent of the Carmelites, a religious order founded in the Middle Ages. There, as "Teresa of Jesus," she did not cease to follow her heart—challenging the male church authorities who oversaw orders of nuns, urging the Carmelites to adhere to poverty, and inaugurating a renewal of church life based in prayer and a personal union with God. Her accomplishments are testimony to the power of one woman's persistence and the strength of personal conviction even in an era dominated by an authoritarian church hierarchy.

Teresa de Cepeda y Ahumada was an unlikely candidate for a nunnery. She was born in 1515 to a wealthy Spanish family, aristocratic in status but also suspect for its recent conversion to Catholicism from Judaism. Many Spaniards thought that Jewish ancestry was a blot that not even Christian baptism could wash away. But Teresa's commitment to Christianity was genuine; even as a child she showed signs of the choice she would make later in life. She liked to "play church" with her brothers and sisters, pretending to be a holy hermit living in a cave. She even dreamed of a trip to North Africa, where she hoped Muslims would chop off her head and make her a Christian martyr.

As a nun, Teresa contended not only with her Jewish background but also with stereotypes that cast women as weak, the playthings of the Devil, and therefore especially prone to error and sin. Clerical enemies dismissed her as a "silly little woman" who had no business writing about monastic reform and the life of prayer. In a clever response, Teresa accepted these charges but turned them upside down, arguing that her ideas and plans must have come directly from God, since she herself was so weak, ignorant, and sinful.

At the same time, Teresa undertook a drastic reform of the Carmelite Order, which had not strictly obeyed its own rules concerning separation from the world. With support from the bishop of Ávila, her hometown, Teresa saw that it did. The nuns were to become the Discalced, or "Barefoot," Carmelites, giving up shoes for sandals and living a life of poverty. These reforms also provoked strong opposition, but she pursued them with firmness and common sense. Although she suffered from ill health, she traveled all over Spain seeking support from the rich and powerful. She regularly rose at five in the morning but often stayed up past midnight to write letters to those who could help or harm her cause. The turning point came when she won the support of the Spanish king, Philip II. Fourteen Carmelite convents accepted her reform program.

Like Catherine of Siena, Teresa was a mystic. Beginning in 1554, she started to experience visions of Christ during her prayers. "His Majesty," as she called Jesus, appeared to her frequently and spoke to her in her heart, as one friend to another. When Teresa told her father confessor and other male clergymen of these visions, they were alarmed and ordered her to write them down in detail so they could examine them for errors. She obeyed. These writings, which described her visions and offered advice on how to pray, soon brought her to the attention of the Spanish Inquisition. But she was able to convince the inquisitors and others that there was nothing heretical or devilish in her experiences or writings.

Soon after Teresa died in 1582, her friends collected her writings and published them. The recently invented printing press, which could rapidly spread an author's works throughout Europe, made Teresa famous. She was immediately recognized as a masterful guide for Catholics who sought a more perfect life of prayer and a closer union with God. In 1612, she was declared a saint of the Catholic Church. But the gender expectations of her age, which classified women lower than men, even shaped the decrees proclaiming her sainthood. She was labeled a "virile woman" with a "manly soul," as male clerics believed that, before Teresa could become an object of public devotion, she had to be made manlike. But her life and writings carried a different message. Here was an intelligent, capable woman who counteracted deep prejudices to renew the life of her religious order, write treatises on prayer that became instant classics of Christian spirituality, and lead church reform. In 1969, Teresa was the first woman to be proclaimed a doctor, or authoritative teacher, of the Roman Catholic Church.

Introduction

Teresa of Ávila's reform of the Carmelite religious order was part of a larger church renewal movement sweeping over Europe in the sixteenth century. Church reform had been a feature of Christian life throughout the Middle Ages, but the movement that gained strength around the year 1500 was unparalleled in intensity and scope. It also split the Catholic Church apart. One branch of reform, known as Protestantism, rejected the authority of the pope, who until then had been the head of western Christianity. The other branch remained loyal to the pope while insisting, like Teresa, on the need for basic change within the Catholic Church. Only the Orthodox churches of eastern Europe and the Middle East were largely untouched by these reforms.

In Germany, Martin Luther launched Protestant reform. He was followed by other Protestants who began reforms of their own that sometimes disagreed with Luther's. Thus Protestants had to choose which reformer to follow. The leaders in Catholic reform were the religious orders of the church and the Roman popes. Together they refashioned Catholicism in ways that lasted until the mid-twentieth century. Because Catholics could rally around the person of the pope, they remained more united than the Protestants, although they, too, experienced division and controversy, as Teresa of Ávila's struggles show.

As reform touched more and more people's lives, both Protestants and Catholics had to rethink what it meant to be a Christian. Both forged new identities while imposing undesirable stereotypes on their opponents. Catholics also launched the first worldwide Christian missionary movement, as priests followed conquerors and merchants into the Americas and East Asia. Both Protestants and Catholics expected Jews to be swept up into church renewal and looked for their conversion to Christianity. When this did not happen, a backlash developed that worsened the living conditions of Jews in western Europe.

In both Protestant and Catholic Europe, reformers expected the mass of Christians to accept the changes they proposed. Often Christians did, since there was wide popular support for many of the reforms. Sometimes, however, ordinary people had expectations of their own. When these clashed with those of the reformers, a period of unofficial negotiation took place in which reforms were modified or rejected by the community as a whole.

Chronology

1494	Savonarola institutes moral reforms in Florence
1516	Jewish Ghetto is established in Venice
1517	Luther condemns church indulgences
1521	Luther is excommunicated and declared an outlaw in the empire
1522	Ignatius of Loyola becomes a church reformer
1524	Peasants' War breaks out in Germany
1525	Luther marries Katherine von Bora
1527	Henry VIII breaks with pope
1535	Catholic and Lutheran rulers slaughter Anabaptists at Münster Teresa of Ávila becomes a nun
1536	Calvin publishes *Institutes of the Christian Religion*
1540	Pope approves Jesuits
1541	Calvin initiates reform in Geneva
1545	Council of Trent opens
1549	Francis Xavier introduces Christianity into Japan
1555	Peace of Augsburg allows Lutheranism
1558	John Knox introduces Calvinism into Scotland; Elizabeth I becomes queen of England
1563	Council of Trent ends

The Context of Church Reform, 1490–1517

⬇ What developments prepared the way for the church reform of the sixteenth century?

⬇ What were the similarities and differences between Savonarola's and Erasmus's church reform programs?

The famine and plague that beset Europe in the fourteenth century intensified religious concerns and raised anxieties about God's wrath and judgment. Above all, people looked to the traditional head of the western church, the pope, for spiritual leadership, but when he did not provide it, they turned elsewhere for religious guidance. Some found it in the sermons of fiery preachers predicting God's punishment on sinful humankind, while others turned to new forms of piety and to the humanist movement for inspiration. By 1500, spiritual hunger and a growing sense that the western church was ineffective and worldly had set the stage for the waves of religious reform that swept over Europe in the sixteenth century.

Growing Discontent in the Western Church

Around 1500, a number of developments converged to provide the context for the reforming movements that spread throughout the western church during the sixteenth century. After 1450, the Roman papacy, the focal point of the church, tried to recover from the decline in prestige it had suffered during papal residence in Avignon and the Great Schism. Although the papacy successfully countered conciliarism's challenge that church councils held more authority than the pope, the popes of the late fifteenth century did not inspire confidence. People were looking for a pastor, but none of the men elected to the papacy lived up to their expectations. Some, like Alexander VI, shocked contemporaries with their sexual immorality by keeping mistresses who gave birth to their children. Others, like Leo X, behaved more like Renaissance princes than devout bishops. On hearing of his election to the papacy, Leo reportedly said, "God has given us the papacy and we intend to enjoy it!" Lack of spiritual leadership convinced many that the papacy had become corrupt and worldly.

Hope for a spiritual leader in Rome was fueled by the spread of **Christian humanism**, which emphasized the need to recover pure Christianity by turning to the Bible and the ancient church fathers. At the same

Christian humanism Humanist movement in northern Europe emphasizing study of the Bible and the early church fathers.

These two prints attack Pope Alexander VI. The left image, the first a viewer would see, shows the "official" Alexander in his papal robes, carrying a ceremonial cross and wearing the papal triple tiara. The caption reads "Alexander VI Supreme Pontiff." After lifting up the first image the viewer would see the right image of the "real" Alexander, a hideous, hellish monster. The caption reads "I am the pope." (*University Library Bern, Switzerland. Biblia. (lat.) Interprete Sebastiano Castalione, Basel; Johannes Oprinus, 1550, sign. Hosp. 44*)

time, laymen and -women in the Netherlands joined clergy to form the **Brothers and Sisters of the Common Life.** The brothers and sisters tried to live the life of Jesus's first disciples—a life of poverty while caring for the sick and feeding the hungry. Their activities and their intense personal devotion to Jesus offered religious comfort to a generation hungry for spiritual renewal. Their devotion also prompted a growing popular interest in the life of Jesus and in the Bible and a greater demand for preachers who could talk about scripture and describe Jesus's life and death.

Although the popes did not respond vigorously to rising demands for spiritual leadership, the lower clergy did. By 1500, many clergymen were better educated and more effective in performing their duties than they had been in the Middle Ages. Some installed **pulpits** in their churches to respond to the de-

mand for preaching. Traditionally, preaching had been the task of religious orders like the Franciscans and Dominicans. When **parish priests** began to preach, these orders resented their intrusion, and tensions led to charges of incompetence and immorality from both sides. Friars complained that parish priests were badly educated, while parish priests accused the friars of preaching to lure women into confession and then

Brothers and Sisters of the Common Life   Religious community founded in the Netherlands that cared for the needy, following the example of Jesus.

pulpit   Raised and enclosed platform for preaching.

parish priests   Clergymen in charge of church life in the basic local unit of the church, the parish.

use them sexually. Although many of these accusations were exaggerated, they fed a growing belief that the clergy as a whole, not just the pope, was corrupt.

In the absence of strong papal leadership, rulers in many parts of Europe tried to meet their subjects' religious expectations while strengthening their own control over the church in their lands. Ferdinand and Isabella in Spain, along with Francis I of France, showed what determined rulers could do in reforming perceived abuses and regulating relations with the pope. Their efforts inspired others to look to the state as an agent of religious reform.

Finally, the printing revolution that swept over Europe during the fifteenth century allowed for fast reproduction of inexpensive texts and illustrations in large numbers. It was in the Rhineland and the Netherlands that printing first became widespread. In the fifty years between 1450 and 1500, more books were produced using the new technology than during the previous thousand years. After 1500, church reformers quickly exploited the possibilities of rapid, widespread dissemination of their views that the printing press made possible.

God's Wrath and Church Reform

Fear of God's wrath, which lay behind movements like the medieval flagellants, continued to inspire movements of reform. In the 1490s, a Dominican friar in Florence, **Girolamo Savonarola**, denounced corruption in the city and church. He proclaimed that a divine day of reckoning was just around the corner on which the church would be judged and then renewed. Condemning the Florentines' worldliness, he organized "burnings of vanities." In a frenzy of communal purification, people tossed their fancy clothes and jewels onto public bonfires along with playing cards, gambling tables, and pornographic pictures. For Savonarola, this was the first act in a divinely scripted drama in which Florence would become a truly holy Christian city. He proclaimed that reform would increase Florence's wealth and prestige and would inaugurate a purification of the church throughout the world. Savonarola also prophesied that a French army would invade Italy and win an easy victory over the Italians. When, in fact, the French king Charles VIII invaded in 1494, many Florentines believed that Savonarola's prophesy had come true, and his prestige in the city soared. For the next four years he was Florence's spiritual dictator.

Savonarola denounced not only the "vanities" of the Florentines but also Pope Alexander VI's sexual immorality. Angered by the attack, Alexander looked for ways to silence him. Faced with mounting papal hostility, Savonarola called for a general council of the church to judge Alexander, thus resurrecting the theology of the conciliar movement that Rome had tried to quash. This was too much for the pope; in 1498, at Alexander's instigation, a church court condemned Savonarola. He was then tortured and burned at the stake.

Savonarola's dictatorship, which had widespread popular support, mixed Christian reform with a strong dose of local patriotism and a belief that a truly Christian Florence could prosper in this world. It expressed a yearning for Christ's return to earth as judge of the living and the dead that was as old as Christianity itself. It also reflected the traditional Christian view that earthly and heavenly things were inseparable; right relations with God led to an orderly, prosperous community life. Savonarola's commitment to a purified Christian community, his belief in a coming day of reckoning with God, and his sense that religion and all other aspects of life were tied together reappeared regularly in the later church reform movements of the sixteenth century.

Humanism and Church Reform

Humanism also contributed to the movement for church reform, thanks to **Desiderius Erasmus** of Rotterdam, the greatest Christian humanist of his generation. The illegitimate son of a priest, Erasmus lost both his parents to the plague when he was a child. His new guardians sent him to various schools, including one run by the Brothers of the Common Life. Later, he complained about the brothers' harsh routine, but their piety deeply influenced him. When his guardians insisted that Erasmus become a monk, he joined a religious order and was ordained a priest. The monastic life, however, was not to his taste, and in 1516 he obtained papal permission to live outside his monastery. Although he attended the University of Paris and lectured at Cambridge University in England, he was never drawn to the academic life. Rejecting both the monastery and the university, he set himself up as an independent scholar and traveled widely throughout western Europe. Erasmus shared the humanists' interest in studying the pagan and Christian literature of antiquity. His writings com-

Girolamo Savonarola (1452–1498) Italian Dominican friar who tried to carry out church reform in Florence.
Desiderius Erasmus (1469–1536) Dutch humanist, theologian, and textual scholar whose writings influenced the movement for church reform.

bined an elegant Latin style with biting humor. Like Savonarola, he was fiercely opposed to immorality, but unlike him, he expressed his opposition in wit and satire instead of fiery preaching. Also, like Savonarola, he wanted a reform but not a rejection of the Catholic Church, since he accepted the basic teachings of Catholicism, including the pope's preeminence.

Erasmus's version of reformed Christianity centered on what he called the philosophy of Christ, which was found in the ancient sources of Christianity—the scriptures and the commentaries of the early church fathers. Erasmus believed that the fathers, who were closer in time to Christ than his own generation, were also closer to the original meaning of scripture. Therefore, people should follow the example of Christ in the Gospels as the fathers presented it. Erasmus argued that if certain practices were not found in these early sources, like confession to a priest or clerical celibacy, they were not essential to Christianity.

Erasmus believed that education was the way to get people to accept the philosophy of Christ. He had huge faith in the power of education to change people's lives; study did not simply make people informed or skilled—it made them good. He therefore told teachers that they should teach the young by persuasion, not fear, and should avoid whipping bad students unless absolutely necessary. Since education was to teach the philosophy of Christ based on the scriptures, Erasmus prepared an accurate printed edition of the New Testament in its original Greek and made a correct translation into the more familiar Latin.

During his visit to England, Erasmus met the English lawyer and humanist **Sir Thomas More.** More was famous for his *Utopia,* a witty account of a fictional country where there was no private property, men and women saw each other naked before marriage to show that they were physically sound, and the incurably ill were encouraged to take their own lives. More, a devout Catholic, was not advocating these practices (*utopia* in Greek means "no place"). His intentions were to amuse his readers and to unmask the stupidity and greed of his own society. More also served in the English king's government as chancellor, the highest judicial official in the realm. His service appealed to Erasmus, who believed that Europe's rulers should be agents for church reform.

By the time Erasmus died in 1536, the Protestant Reformation was well under way. Although he remained a Catholic, his emphasis on scripture as the foundation of Christianity, his call for Christians to return to their ancient roots for standards of belief and action, and his faith in the power of education to make a better world were all embraced by reformers after him.

Martin Luther and the Protestant Reformation, 1517–1550

↓ How was Martin Luther's reform agenda similar to and different from that of his predecessors?
↓ What was the impact of Luther's reforms?

By the time Erasmus was a well-established critic of the church, another reformer, Martin Luther, had emerged and was carrying the reforming agenda in new directions. Eventually, Luther argued that reform of the church required a complete rejection of the Roman pope, and rupture with Rome, therefore, became the central feature of his movement. Historians call reformers who broke with the pope Protestants. With the establishment of Lutheran Protestant churches in north Germany and Scandinavia, the religious unity of western Europe was shattered.

Luther's Challenge to the Church

Martin Luther was a broad-faced German monk from peasant stock with a sharp tongue and a brilliant mind whose father had wanted him to become a lawyer. Like Savonarola, Luther was troubled by fears of sin, God's wrath, and judgment. In the summer of 1505, the fears came to a head when he was caught in a violent thunderstorm, during which a bolt of lightning threw him to the ground. He cried out in terror, "Help me Saint Anne! I shall become a monk!" After Luther gave up the law and took monastic vows, the head of his monastery ordered him to study theology, and in 1508 he was appointed professor of New Testament studies at the new University of Wittenberg.

For the next seven years, Luther studied the Bible. He had become a monk to lessen his fears about his sinfulness before God, but the old doubts continued to haunt him. He carefully observed the monastic life and regularly confessed his sins, but the promise of God's forgiveness, which came with the priest's **absolution,** seemed hollow, since he continued to feel

Thomas More   (1477–1535) English lawyer and humanist, author of *Utopia* and friend of Erasmus.
Martin Luther   (1483–1546) German monk who led a church reform movement in Germany that became the Lutheran form of Protestantism.
absolution   At the end of confession, words spoken by a Catholic priest, acting as God's agent, that grant forgiveness of a person's sins.

Luther was fifty when Lucas Cranach the Elder painted this portrait in 1533. By then Lutheranism was spreading through much of Germany and Scandinavia. Luther gazes out of the picture toward something that would be on the viewer's right. His sturdy face and serene expression convey confidence and calm. *(Scala/Art Resource, NY)*

that they had performed a superabundance of good works, which overflowed into a treasury that Christians could draw on to supplement their own less abundant righteousness. An indulgence, issued by the pope, allowed the person obtaining it to use the righteousness of Christ and the saints to cancel out his or her own sins. At its best, the system of indulgences was something like a mutual-aid society based on compassion for sinners, but it often degenerated into an accountant's game of credit (works) and debit (sins) in which specific sums were shifted from the treasury to the sinful man or woman. Moreover, indulgences could be obtained for someone else, like a spouse or parent, who had died. These dead people were thought to be in **Purgatory**, where they were being punished for their earthly sins. An indulgence for them would cancel some of that punishment and thus hasten their passage into Heaven.

Luther's study of the Bible led him to reject the premises on which the practice of indulgences was based. For him, righteousness before God, called **justification**, did not begin when humans chose to do good works, which then earned God's grace. In fact, Luther believed that

unrighteous before God. In 1517, these private doubts burst into public protest when a Dominican friar, **Johannes Tetzel**, began to sell **indulgences** in the territories of the empire.

Indulgences were at the heart of late medieval Catholic religion, and they raised a particularly troubling question for Luther: "How can I become righteous in God's eyes?" The Catholic Church taught that righteousness resulted from two things: human effort and God's help, called **grace**. People could become righteous before God by choosing to do good deeds, called **works**—giving to the poor, going on a religious pilgrimage, and fasting. Above all, righteousness began when one received the **sacraments** of the church, like baptism, Communion, and confession, most of which had to be administered by a priest. When God saw this human effort, he rewarded it with grace, thus helping one to do even better.

In addition to one's own good works, one could become righteous by drawing on the good works of Christ and the saints. They had been so righteous

Johannes Tetzel (ca. 1465–1519) Dominican friar whose sale of indulgences angered Martin Luther.

indulgences Documents applying the good works of Christ and his saints to cancel the divine punishment of one's own sins or those of a dead friend or relative.

grace God's help in making a person righteous.

works Good deeds performed to become righteous in the sight of God.

sacrament Religious practice or ceremony that symbolizes a deeper religious reality; the seven sacraments are baptism, Communion (Eucharist), confirmation, confession (penance), ordination, marriage, and unction in sickness.

Purgatory The place where the souls of the departed were punished for their earthly sins before entering heaven.

justification Luther's teaching that righteousness before God comes from God alone, not from a combination of God's grace and human works.

while humans had **free will** in the sense that they could choose what they ate for breakfast, when it came to doing things that were good in God's eyes, they had no free will—their sinfulness always made them choose unrighteousness and made them incapable of doing good works. Justification therefore had no connection to good works. It was simply God's gift to human beings that made them righteous even though they were still sinners. Christians were simply to trust in this gift and the additional gift of faith that God alone made them righteous. Luther based his position on the apostle Paul, who had written, "He who through faith is righteous shall live" (Romans 1:17).

Tetzel came to the vicinity of Wittenberg selling indulgences to fund the building of the new Saint Peter's Church in Rome. He even had a slogan to motivate potential buyers: "When the coin in the change box rings, the soul from Purgatory springs!" When Luther heard of this, he was outraged. Tetzel stirred up the issues of works, grace, faith, and righteousness before God that had preoccupied Luther for years. Luther's response was to pen the **Ninety-five Theses,** propositions attacking indulgences, which were quickly printed up and distributed throughout Germany. They caused a sensation. At first the pope dismissed Luther as just another "drunken monk," but, as the seriousness of his challenge to indulgences sank in, a gulf opened up between Luther and the papacy.

The Impact of Luther's Challenge

The implications of Luther's teaching were profound: if works were irrelevant, and people were justified by faith alone, the whole structure of medieval Catholic piety—based on pilgrimages, fasting, alms to the poor, and indulgences—came tumbling down. Moreover, the sacraments administered by priests were no longer so central. Over the next five years, the rift between Luther and the Catholic Church deepened. In 1518, the pope condemned him as a heretic. In 1519, during the **Imperial Diet,** the Holy Roman Empire's legislative body, which elected **Charles V** emperor, Luther debated publicly with a papal representative, John Eck, and declared that neither the pope nor church councils had final authority to settle theological disputes. The pope then excommunicated Luther, who in turn publicly appealed to the princes of the empire to initiate reforms against indulgences. He argued that all believers, not just the clergy, were priests who were responsible for the well-being of the church. This doctrine of the **priesthood of all believers** posed another threat to Catholic Christianity, which made a sharp distinction between the ordained priesthood

and ordinary Christians. To gain support, Luther printed four thousand copies of his appeal. They sold out in a few days.

In 1521, Charles V, who had remained in Spain during these confrontations, made his first trip to Germany as emperor and summoned Luther to another Imperial Diet in the city of Worms. Asked directly to renounce his teachings, Luther refused, arguing that **scripture alone** was the only authority he would obey. He concluded dramatically, "Here I stand. May God help me! Amen." The emperor then declared him an outlaw, and Luther went into hiding.

The local ruler of Wittenberg, who had embraced Luther's theology, shielded him from the imperial authorities. Luther continued to develop his theology, arguing that in the Gospels, Christ had instituted only two sacraments, baptism and Communion, not the other rites that Catholics considered sacraments. Soon afterward, Luther began to translate the Bible into German, using Erasmus's edition of the Greek New Testament to make the ancient scriptural sources of Christianity available to ordinary men and women. He also composed hymns like "A Mighty Fortress Is Our God" for people to sing, thus bringing them directly into community worship and strengthening their sense of God's presence among them. And he continued to publish his protests; some three hundred thousand copies of his works were printed and distributed throughout the empire.

The Spread of Reform

Luther's ideas, spread by the printing press, inspired local reformers in both town and countryside. Like Savonarola, they believed that religion was linked to all other aspects of life, and their reform programs had political and social dimensions along with religious

free will   Teaching that people can freely will to do good works and thereby merit God's grace.

Ninety-five Theses   Luther's public attack on indulgences.

Imperial Diet   Holy Roman Empire's legislative body.

Charles V   (r. 1516–1556) Heir of Ferdinand and Isabella in Spain and of the emperor Maximilian in the Holy Roman Empire; the most powerful European ruler during the first half of the sixteenth century.

priesthood of all believers   Luther's teaching that all Christians exercised priestly functions in the Christian church.

scripture alone   Luther's teaching that the Bible was the only authoritative guide for Christian belief and conduct.

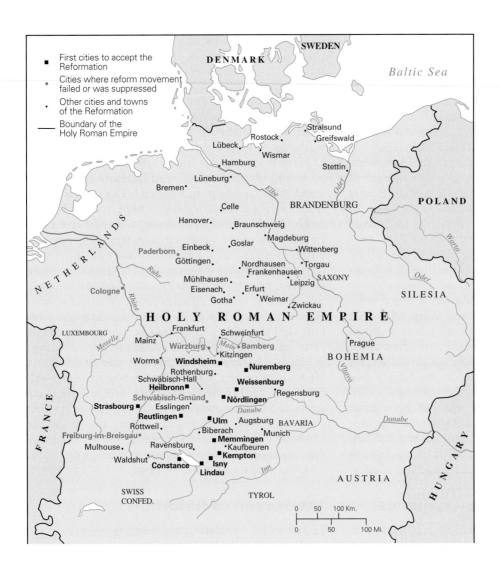

MAP 14.1 Cities and Towns of the Reformation in Germany This map shows the early spread of Protestantism in the cities and towns of the Holy Roman Empire. It also shows where the supporters of Roman Catholicism stopped the spread. At first, Protestantism was concentrated mainly in the center and southwest of the Empire. Eventually, it spread to the north and east, where it set down its most lasting roots.

ones. In the cities of southern Germany and Switzerland, local religious or political leaders encouraged men and women from the middle ranks of urban society to support reform. These were hardworking people who resented their exclusion from the ruling elite and thought of themselves as the backbone of the town on whom its collective well-being depended. After 1520, they produced a flood of printed pamphlets that, like Luther's, were circulated throughout Germany and constitute a kind of sixteenth-century public opinion poll. It shows that Luther's criticism of the pope and his priests was widely accepted. In the decentralized political world of Germany, papal taxes and clerical exemptions from them were often easily imposed and deeply resented. As a result, urban reformers attacked the privileges of the Catholic clergy, demanding that they be taxed like all other citizens.

The urban reformers also believed that community

life should be regulated by what they called the **pure gospel**, which stressed the equality of all Christians and rejected the idea that clergy or members of religious orders were somehow more genuinely Christian than laypeople. A number of specific reforms flowed from the idea of the pure gospel. The community, not the local bishop, would appoint clergy. Preachers were to preach on the Bible and nothing else. If disputes arose about the correct interpretation of scripture, the community would decide who was right. Acceptance of the pure gospel, which called for love of neighbor and commitment to the common

> **pure gospel** Reform program of German Protestant reformers in the cities of the empire endorsing some of Luther's reforms but rejecting others.

good, would reinvigorate the collective identity and social solidarity of city dwellers. The reformers were, therefore, particularly receptive to Luther's theology of the authority of scripture alone and the priesthood of all believers. Faced with the demands of these urban reformers, which were often introduced with a wave of rioting, local municipal authorities had to decide what to do. Since they were concerned with maintaining public order, they more or less willingly went along with the reforms.

Events in the Swiss city of Zurich show how urban reform progressed. There, a local priest, **Huldrych Zwingli,** after reading Erasmus's attacks on corrupt clergy, urged the town council to inaugurate reform. Zwingli was supported by many townsfolk who believed that both the material and spiritual welfare of the city depended on a purifying reform of the church. Luther's actions influenced Zwingli, but he went beyond Luther when he banished images of Christ and the saints from the churches and argued that the bread and wine of Communion were not the body and blood of Christ but simple memorials of Jesus's Last Supper with his disciples. Protestant reform thus started to take different and sometimes conflicting paths.

By 1523, there were signs that urban reform was attracting rural followers. Calls for religious renewal to create a more just Christian community also appealed to German peasants, many of whom were experiencing economic hard times following crop failures and landlords' demands for more rent. Invoking the pure gospel, peasants demanded that their payments to landlords be lowered, that serfdom be abolished, and that they have greater access to common lands. During the summer of 1524, violence broke out in the **Peasants' War,** which engulfed much of southern Germany. In May 1525, an imperial army defeated a peasant force and massacred five to six thousand rebels. After that, the uprising collapsed.

The war shocked Luther, who had a firm respect for social order and obedience to civil authorities. In a pamphlet, *Against the Robbing and Murdering Hordes of Peasants,* he urged the troops to "smite, slay, and stab" the rebels. Because of the radical nature of its demands, historians have often regarded the Peasants' War as a revolution, though a failed one. It testified to a widespread hunger for fundamental religious and social reform that touched hundreds of thousands of ordinary men and women by the mid-1520s.

The years after 1525 saw the continuing spread of Luther's reforms, but the dynamic behind them had changed. No longer were church-based reformers the leaders in the movement, and no longer were German cities in its vanguard. Now the princes of the empire, like the dukes of Saxony and Bavaria, deter-mined whether Protestantism would be adopted in their territories. Rulers also introduced Lutheran reforms in Denmark and Sweden. The state's increasing leadership in reform was partly a backlash following the Peasants' War, as princes and city councils decided that a popular reformation by peasants or the urban middle classes was too dangerous to tolerate. But Luther, under Erasmus's influence, had also prepared the way by calling on rulers to carry out reform.

As the empire split into hostile Catholic and Lutheran states, the emperor Charles V looked on in dismay. Although he wanted to stamp out the Lutheran movement, he was only one of many imperial princes, and he was never able to implement his policy, largely because of distractions from warfare with the Turks in the east and the French in the west. Between 1531 and his abdication in 1556, Charles tried many solutions to the problem of growing religious disunity in the empire: gaining time with a truce between the competing factions; calling for a general church council to resolve the matter; trying to establish a dialogue with the Lutherans; and, finally, in 1546, going to war against the Lutheran princes. None of these strategies worked, and in 1555 he turned the problem over to his younger brother, the archduke Ferdinand, who accepted the **Peace of Augsburg** in that year. It acknowledged Lutheranism as a religious option in the empire and allowed the rulers of each imperial state to determine whether the state would be Lutheran or Catholic. If the ruler chose Lutheranism, Catholics were free to emigrate to a Catholic state, and vice versa. In fact, emigration was often impossible because of family or economic reasons, and secret Catholic or Lutheran communities developed in a number of states. Thus, dissenting German Christians were forced into a situation rather like that of the Jews and Moors after their expulsions from Spain and Portugal—convert, leave, or practice one's religion in secret. State rulers now took the lead in reorganizing the church, policing the behavior of clergy, and maintaining Christian morality in the general population. In Catholic states, they still had to share

Huldrych Zwingli (1484–1531) Swiss reformer who accepted some of Luther's theological points but rejected others.

Peasants' War Uprising, 1524–1525, in southern Germany inspired by Protestant calls for a reform of church and society.

Peace of Augsburg First major treaty, 1555, to accept the split in western Christianity between Protestants and Catholics.

government of the church with the pope. In Lutheran ones, they ruled largely unchecked. Thus, the Peace of Augsburg permanently shattered the religious unity of Germany and established a pattern of Christian religious pluralism that would be one of the hallmarks of European life in subsequent centuries.

The Protestant Reformation Across Europe, 1520–1570

⬇ What were the similarities and differences among the reform programs of Luther, the Anabaptists, and Calvin?
⬇ What were the distinctive features of Protestant reform in England?

Along with Lutheranism, other forms of Protestantism developed. One movement, led by radicals, went even further than Luther and Zwingli in rejecting traditional Catholicism. Another, founded by the Frenchman John Calvin, proved to be the most rapidly expanding form of Protestantism. In England, an ambiguous type of reform was eventually introduced from above by the state.

The Anabaptists and Radical Reform

In the early 1520s, when Luther was condemned by the church for pushing church reform too far, he was also attacked by people who thought he had not gone far enough. These were the Protestant radicals. Though never a unified movement, the radicals shared a deep dislike of the ordained clergy and a strong sense that the church should exist for the benefit of ordinary men and women. They were at odds with Luther—a clergyman and university scholar—in rejecting scriptural interpretation by trained professionals. While Luther proclaimed the priesthood of all believers and wanted the Bible in people's hands, he believed the people needed expert guidance in understanding scripture. The radicals replied that every Christian man and woman was capable of correctly interpreting it under the direct guidance of the Holy Spirit.

The radicals were also deeply suspicious of Luther's policy of turning to city or state rulers to help introduce Protestantism. Arguing for a sharp separation of church and state, some also believed that true Christians should be completely separated from the sinful world surrounding them. Only adults who had received a divine call should become church members; consequently, the ancient practice of infant baptism should be abolished because babies were incapable of

receiving or responding to such a call. Soon these radicals were being denounced as **Anabaptists,** since they insisted on being rebaptized as adults in a true, voluntary baptism.

Anabaptism first emerged among the craftsmen of the Swiss city of Zurich. They preached adult baptism, called for a separated church, and refused to honor customary civic obligations like paying church taxes, holding public office, or serving in the militia. They even began to hold all their material goods in common, inspired by the first-century church in Jerusalem, which had implemented this form of Christian communalism, as described in the New Testament book of Acts. Anabaptist separatism was thus deeply subversive because it rejected the generally accepted idea that everyone in a given place should be a church member and that society would fall apart without the unifying force of a common religion. To suppress Anabaptism, Charles V issued an imperial edict in 1529 decreeing the death penalty for anyone who held a separatist view of church-state relations. In some states, executions were carried out by drowning, a punishment thought to fit the crime.

In the northwestern German city of **Münster,** the Anabaptists would not be suppressed. Elected to the city government in 1534, they declared all real estate common property, banned money, and decreed that house doors were to be unlocked and open day and night. Then polygamy was introduced. The reformers justified the practice of men's taking multiple spouses by citing the Old Testament, but the practice may have had more to do with remedying a gender imbalance in the Anabaptist community and the need to put women under male rule in individual households. When Münster's expelled bishop tried to retake the city by force but was defeated, the Anabaptists proclaimed the impending end of the world, with Münster designated as the New Jerusalem. As executions of the wayward began, Catholic and Lutheran rulers were so alarmed that they set aside their differences and joined forces to recapture Münster. Following their victory in 1535, they slaughtered almost all Münster's inhabitants in one of the greatest bloodbaths of the century.

The catastrophe in Münster permanently discredited all forms of violent Anabaptism. Following it, the

Anabaptists   (from Greek, "repeated dippers") Radical Protestants who practiced a second, adult baptism.

Münster   City in northwestern Germany where a violent Anabaptist movement was defeated by a combined Protestant and Catholic army.

radical remnant turned to leaders who denounced violence and embraced **pacifism**. **Jacob Hutter** provided the inspiration for those who fled to Moravia, where they continued to practice Christian communalism and prospered economically in the later years of the sixteenth century. By 1600, about 20,000 Hutterites lived in peaceful coexistence with their Catholic and Protestant neighbors.

In the northern Netherlands, **Menno Simons**, a Dutch ex-priest, organized churches as a refuge for those Anabaptists who had survived the slaughter of 1535. Simons's churches were based on voluntary membership and adult baptism, but he gave up the New Testament ideal of Christian communalism and called simply for mutual aid among church members. These Mennonites numbered about one hundred thousand at the end of the century. Like the Hutterites, they gained a degree of respectability in the eyes of their non-Anabaptist neighbors. Beginning in the eighteenth century, many began to emigrate to North America, where their descendants today make up the Amish and Mennonite communities of Pennsylvania and parts of the Midwest. They still live a life separated from the larger world.

John Calvin and Calvinism

John Calvin founded the third major Protestant community of the sixteenth century, **Calvinism**. Luther was already thirty-six when Calvin was born in northeastern France; Calvinism was thus a second-generation Protestant movement. Calvin was sent to the University of Paris to study theology, since his father wanted him to become a priest. Then, his father changed his mind and sent him to law school. During his school years, Calvin met men who had embraced Protestant reform. His father's death in 1531 freed him to make his own future plans, and he became a reformer. Calvin was more reserved and private than Luther, who talked openly about his spiritual trials. But he, too, believed that he had undergone a "sudden conversion" in which God subdued his "stubborn heart" and called him to Protestantism. In 1535, the pro-Catholic French government attacked Protestants in Paris, and Calvin was forced to flee under a false name.

In 1536, Calvin was in Switzerland, beyond the reach of French authorities. There he published the first edition of the *Institutes of the Christian Religion,* a work he revised and expanded for the next twenty-three years. It gained him an immediate European reputation. The *Institutes,* which presented Calvin's version of theology, came to serve as the blueprint for Calvinist reform. Calvin followed Luther on a number of points, condemning the pope and ar-

PROMPTE   ET SINCERE ·

IOHANNES · CALVINVS · ANNO · ÆTATIS · 53 · · B ·

René Boivin's engraving (1562) shows Calvin at age fifty-three, as the Latin inscription at the bottom of the portrait indicates. The caption at the top, in French, asserts that Calvin is "active and honest," affirming his success as a religious leader. *(Genève, Département Iconographique, Bibliothèque de Genève)*

guing that scripture was the only source of authority for Christians. He did not, however, accept Luther's teaching on the priesthood of all believers. For Calvin,

pacifism   Opposition to armed force and warfare.

Jacob Hutter   (1500–1536) Anabaptist leader in Moravia who embraced pacifism and the practice of Christian communalism.

Menno Simons   (1495–1561) Leader of the Mennonite Anabaptist communities in the Netherlands who embraced pacifism but rejected Christian communalism.

John Calvin   (1509–1564) Frenchman who founded the Protestant movement known as Calvinism.

Calvinism   Teachings and church organization of Protestant churches that considered John Calvin their founder.

Institutes of the Christian Religion   Calvin's systematic presentation of his Protestant teachings, which served as a blueprint for Calvinist reform.

the clergy were placed above ordinary church members to teach and administer discipline in the community. His insistence that the church alone should appoint the clergy was closer to traditional Catholic practice than the procedures adopted in Lutheran lands, where the state controlled clergy recruitment. But Calvin joined Luther in increasing worshipers' personal participation in church services by translating the book of Psalms into French and setting the Psalms to simple tunes that the congregation could sing.

Calvin also agreed with Luther that everyone in a given territory should belong to the same church. But, because of his belief in the doctrine of **double predestination,** he did not think that all church members were necessarily saved. Predestination taught that before the world was created, God foresaw that human beings would sin and thereby merit damnation as the just punishment for their sin. God then decreed that some of these sinners were predestined for Hell while others were predestined for Heaven. Those predestined for Hell suffered just punishment for their sins, testifying to God's justice. Those predestined for Heaven were forgiven their sins and would be reunited with God, testifying to God's mercy. Calvin often argued that probably only one in a hundred would be saved. Like Luther, he believed that sin had corrupted people's wills so that they could do nothing that contributed to their salvation. Therefore, they were saved not through any merit or works of their own but solely as a result of God's loving kindness. Although a person's good works did not earn salvation, Calvin taught that they were a sign that God had chosen the person as one of **the elect** destined for salvation. Since impulses to act as good Christians were an assurance of salvation, Calvinists were quick to nurture their desire for church and state reform. Calvin also argued that hard work and thrift were signs of election. He believed that the doctrine of double predestination explained why some people refused to join the reformed churches. It also assured believers that, in the end, God would triumph over sinners' opposition to him.

Calvin's opportunity to put his theology into practice came in 1541, when the town council of the little city-state of Geneva called him to reform the local church. For the next fourteen years, he argued, threatened, and maneuvered to get a reform to his liking. Calvin's cause was helped by an influx of religious refugees from his native country who fled to Geneva to avoid persecution by the French government. These Frenchmen, solidly behind their fellow countryman's agenda, were able to take over Geneva's government in 1555. It was then that Calvin finally gained full control over the church.

Because Calvin thought of the church in territorial terms, everyone in Geneva had to conform to church standards. To enforce reform, he created the **Consistory,** a body made up of Calvinist ministers and members of the city government. The Consistory scrutinized every aspect of Genevans' behavior, imposing fines or imprisonment for infractions. Everything people said or did was to be supervised and controlled. Like the advocates of the pure gospel, Calvinists in Geneva were trying to forge a new Christian identity based strictly on Protestant religious principles.

Throughout the period of Calvin's rule in Geneva, religious refugees from all over Europe continued to stream into the city. It is estimated that between 1550 and 1562 about seven thousand of the city's ten thousand inhabitants were foreigners. These refugees,

double predestination   Belief that God has predestined some human beings for damnation and others for salvation.

the elect   Those whom God has chosen (elected) for salvation.

Consistory   Assembly made up of Calvinist ministers and members of city government that enforced Calvinist standards of behavior in Geneva.

Voice

The Pastors of Geneva Establish Rules for Proper Christian Conduct

Beginning in 1541, the reformed clergy of Geneva, under the guidance of John Calvin, published rules governing the behavior of clergy and laity in Geneva. Calvinism's great strength lay in its ability to forge strong bonds and loyalties between members of a Calvinist community. This could be done by rewarding behav-

ior that conformed to Calvinist community norms while punishing behavior that did not. It could also be done by trying to reconcile quarreling members of the community. The rules of 1541 provided guidelines for carrying out all aspects of Calvinism's community building agenda.

➡ Vices which are intolerable in a pastor: Heresy . . . Rebellion against ecclesiastical order . . . Drunkenness . . . Dancing and similar dissoluteness. Vices which can be endured provided they are rebuked: Strange methods of treating Scripture which result in scandal . . . Buffoonery, Deceitfulness . . . Rashness, Evil scheming . . . Uncontrolled anger, Brawling and quarreling.

➡ What picture of the pastor emerges from the prohibition of these vices?

➡ FAULTS WHICH CONTRAVENE THE REFORMATION . . .

Those who are found in possession of . . . images for the purpose of worshipping them shall be sent before the Consistory, and besides the discipline which shall be imposed on them, they shall be sent to [the government].

Those who have been on pilgrimages or similar journeys.

➡ Any person who curses or denies God or his baptism shall on the first occasion be placed on bread and water for nine days; and for the second or third occasions he shall be punished with a more rigorous physical punishment, . . .

If anyone is found drunk he shall pay three sous on the first occasion and shall be summoned before the Consistory; on the second occasion he shall pay the sum of five sous; and on the third he shall be fined ten sous and be put in prison.

Anyone who sings indecent, dissolute, or outrageous songs or dances the fling or some similar dance shall be imprisoned for three days and shall be sent before the Consistory.

No one shall stir up rowdy scenes or altercations, under penalty of being punished according to the seriousness of the case.

If there is ill-will or altercation between any, the minister shall call the guards and shall endeavor, as is his duty, to bring the parties concerned to agreement, and if he is unable to achieve this, the matter shall be brought before the Consistory.

No one shall play dissolute games or any game for gold or silver or excessive stakes, under penalty of five sous and the forfeiture of the money staked.

Any who are found practicing fornication, if they are an unmarried man or an unmarried woman, shall be imprisoned for six days on bread and water and shall pay sixty sous into the public funds.

Although in ancient times the right of the wife was not equal with that of the husband where divorce was concerned, yet since, as the Apostle says, the obligation is mutual and reciprocal regarding the intercourse of the bed, and since in this the wife is no more subject to the husband than the husband to the wife, if a man is convicted of adultery and his wife demands to be separated from him, this shall be granted to her also, provided it proves impossible by good counsel to reconcile them to each other.

➡ On Sunday July 28 [1549] an ordinance . . . was announced in St. Pierre ordering that girls who had not kept their honor should not henceforward present themselves in church for marriage with the hat which virgins are accustomed to wear, but that they should have their heads veiled; otherwise they could be sent away.

➡ Against whom are these prohibitions directed?

➡ What is the picture of the model Calvinist that emerges from these rules?

➡ Why would this shaming technique be necessary?

Source: The Register of the Company of Pastors of Geneva in the Time of Calvin, ed. and trans. Philip Edgcumbe Hughes (Grand Rapids, Mich.: William B. Eerdmans Publishing Company, 1966), pp. 38–39, 56–59.

many of whom were nobility, wanted to introduce Calvin's reforms into their homelands, and their status was particularly important for Calvinism's future success. To meet the refugees' needs, Calvin founded a training institute for future Calvinist pastors, the Genevan Academy, where men were taught the theology of the *Institutes* and the best ways to form church communities, especially under persecution.

The Spread of Calvinism

Calvinism was the most dynamic form of Protestantism after 1550, becoming an international movement with headquarters in Geneva as missionaries left the city to establish Calvinist communities in their native lands. The first to return home were the French. In France, most Calvinists were recruited from the urban middle class, but members of powerful noble families also converted. It was often the women in these families who convinced their relations to embrace Calvinism. For example, **Jeanne d'Albret** introduced Calvinism into the tiny kingdom of Navarre, on the border between France and Spain. By 1560, about 10 percent of the overall French population was **Huguenot**, as the French Calvinists were called, while about 50 percent of the nobility had embraced the new faith. As the Huguenots' numbers grew, confrontations with Catholics also increased, and soon France was on the verge of civil war.

In the Netherlands, Protestantism was fiercely resisted by Charles V. Unlike in Germany, where he was often checked by other powerful imperial princes, Charles governed the Netherlands directly as the local prince, and no powerful noble factions emerged to promote the Protestant cause. When the Lutherans and Anabaptists tried to establish communities in the Netherlands, Charles's government effectively repressed them. By the time he abdicated in 1556, some five hundred dissidents had been executed for heresy. Nevertheless, Calvinist missionaries began to infiltrate the region, establishing secret communities, and, like France, the Netherlands was moving toward armed clashes between Protestants and Catholics.

In 1558, **John Knox**, returning from Geneva, successfully introduced Calvinist theology into his native Scotland and created a **Presbyterian** form of church administration that eliminated bishops. Knox had the help of powerful nobles who opposed the rule of Mary, Queen of Scots, widow of the French king Francis II and a committed Catholic. In 1559, Knox published *The First Blast Against the Monstrous Regiment of Women*, in which he attacked Mary and argued that female rule was unnatural. Knox's attack appealed to Scottish Calvinists, whose leaders, hard-

ened by organized persecution from Catholic authorities, were prepared to resist rulers if they opposed Calvinist reform. This position directly conflicted with Luther's views about obedience to rulers.

Reform in England

Calvinists in Scotland introduced religious reform from the bottom up. To the south, in England, it was introduced from the top down. In 1521, King **Henry VIII** published a treatise condemning Lutheranism. Shortly thereafter, the pope granted him the title Defender of the Faith in recognition of his service to Catholicism. Twelve years later, however, Rome excommunicated Henry, a surprising turn of events that occurred because succession problems were plaguing the king.

When the pope refused to grant Henry an annulment from Catherine of Aragon, the daughter of Ferdinand and Isabella, the king turned to the English clergy. With their support, he divorced Catherine and married her lady-in-waiting, Anne Boleyn, who was already pregnant with his child. Anne gave birth to Henry's second daughter, Elizabeth. When the pope learned of Henry's action, he excommunicated him. In retaliation, Henry, in the **Act of Supremacy**, proclaimed himself "the only supreme head on earth of the church of England," a title still held today by British monarchs. In 1536, Henry, still in search of a male heir, had Anne convicted of adultery and beheaded. Following her execution, Henry married four more times, finally having a son, Edward, by his fourth wife. All three of Henry's children were to rule England, as Edward VI, Mary, and Elizabeth I.

Although Henry VIII broke with Rome, he had no intention of breaking with traditional Catholicism.

Jeanne d'Albret (1528–1572) French noblewoman who introduced Calvinism into the kingdom of Navarre.

Huguenots (from German, "confederation") French Calvinists, so called because they formed a network of Protestant churches.

John Knox (1505–1572) Leader of Calvinist reform of the church in Scotland.

Presbyterian Form of church organization used in the Calvinist Church of Scotland in which ministers known as presbyters or elders were church leaders, eliminating bishops.

Henry VIII (r. 1509–1547) King who broke with the pope over his divorce from Catherine of Aragon and marriage to Anne Boleyn, launching the English Reformation.

Act of Supremacy Henry VIII's declaration that the king of England was the earthly head of the English church.

Throughout his reign, he resisted any attempt to turn the English church into a Protestant one. Nevertheless, the rift with the pope opened the door to more radical reform, which actually began under Henry. The greatest change came when the king ordered the abolition of English monasteries and the confiscation of their lands on the grounds that the monks and nuns in them were too closely tied to the pope. Most of these lands were then sold to aristocrats to pay for England's foreign wars, and these new owners—who constituted the kingdom's political, social, and economic elite—thus had a vested interest in keeping Roman Catholicism out of England. So Henry's divorce had huge consequences he had not intended.

When Henry died in 1547, he was succeeded by his son, Edward VI. Because the boy was a minor, a Regency Council, controlled by Protestant noblemen, was created to govern in his name. In 1552, the council instituted a compromise form of Protestantism in the English church when it imposed the **Book of Common Prayer**, a blend of Lutheran and Calvinist theology. Now congregations could participate directly in worship, using their own language instead of Latin. Had Edward VI lived, the reforms might have succeeded, but in 1553 he died, at the age of sixteen, and was succeeded by his older half sister, Mary, Catherine's daughter.

Mary had never accepted Henry's divorce of her mother and his break with the pope, and as queen she promptly restored the Catholic Church. To seal the restoration, she married Philip II of Spain, the Catholic Church's most energetic defender. Mary then proceeded to execute some three hundred Protestants, many of them Anabaptists, earning her the nickname "Bloody Mary," which has stuck to this day. In the end, England's return to Catholicism was short lived. In 1558, Mary died childless and was succeeded by the last of Henry VIII's children, **Elizabeth I**, the daughter of Anne Boleyn.

When she became queen, Elizabeth endorsed Protestantism and ended the decade-long alternations between the two forms of Christianity, depending on the ruler. Elizabeth's forty-three-year reign proved decisive in establishing an ambiguous form of Protestantism in England. In 1571, an official theology for the **Church of England** was proclaimed in the **Thirty-nine Articles**, which were silent on a number of hotly contested theological issues, such as Calvin's doctrine of predestination.

Elizabeth and her religious advisers were trying to find a middle ground between Catholicism, Lutheranism, and Calvinism. Political calculations played a central role in this policy. The queen feared a powerful Catholic faction in the English Parliament. She also feared popular agitation if reform went too far. It was Elizabeth's accomplishment to make England Protestant while keeping Catholic opposition fairly well contained. As her reign progressed, more and more Anglicans identified with the queen's theological middle way, seeing it as a distinctively English solution to the huge rift between Protestantism and Catholicism that had engulfed the western church.

By 1570, religious warfare between Catholics and Protestants had broken out in France and the Netherlands. These developments ruled out the possibility of any reconciliation between the rival forms of Christianity on the continent, where, for the next eighty years, there would be armed conflict between Protestants and Catholics.

Catholic Reform, 1500–1570

↓ What did Catholic reformers want to change in the church?

↓ What were the most important outcomes of Catholic Church reform?

As Protestantism spread in Europe, the Catholic Church underwent its own reform. In addition to the reform programs of Savonarola and Erasmus, an early sign of Catholic reform was the founding of new religious orders and the reform of old ones. By the 1530s, the papacy had also become involved in reform. Its most important act was to convene a church council in the northern Italian city of Trent. The Council of Trent defined traditional Catholic theology and condemned the Protestants. It also laid down guidelines for the internal reform of the church. Finally, the Catholics inaugurated Christianity's first major missionary campaigns overseas in the Spanish and Portuguese Empires.

Reform by Religious Orders

The reform of old religious orders and the foundation of new ones signaled renewal within the Catholic

Book of Common Prayer   Official service book of the reformed English church.

Elizabeth I   (r. 1558–1603) Daughter of Henry VIII and Anne Bolyn who ruled after the deaths of her half brother Edward VI and half sister Mary.

Church of England   Name given to the reformed church in England; also called the Anglican Church.

Thirty-nine Articles   Statement of the official theology of the Church of England during Elizabeth I's reign.

Church. Although their specific goals were often different, all the reforms aimed to increase Catholics' commitment to the moral and spiritual teachings of the church. Most began in Italy or Spain, where Protestantism was less widespread than in northern Europe. None was founded to counteract Protestantism, although some later took up the fight against it.

Teresa of Ávila's reformed **Carmelites** set the tone for women's orders (see Choice). Her convents were strictly separated from the larger world because of traditional disapproval of women working actively as teachers or preachers. These nuns maintained their dwellings and prepared their community's food, depending on donations to help with their upkeep. Social distinctions between rich and poor nuns, or noble and common ones, observed in many convents, were abolished. Although not all reformed women's orders adopted the strict poverty of Teresa's Carmelites, most followed separation from the world and a rigorous life of prayer, which, they believed, would strengthen the church as a whole. Recruitment to women's orders rose during the sixteenth century. For example, in 1427 two out of a hundred people living in Florence were nuns; in 1622, six out of a hundred were.

The largest reformed male order was the **Capuchins**, a branch of the Franciscans. The Capuchins took strict vows of poverty. They lived in mud huts, went barefoot, and begged in public for their food to show their detachment from worldly possessions and pleasures. They also preached lively sermons on street corners and in churches, urging Catholics to live more in accordance with Jesus's teachings and setting an example by caring for plague victims. In 1542, scandal rocked the order when its head moved to Geneva and became a Calvinist. Nevertheless, the Capuchins continued to attract new members. By 1600, there were almost nine thousand; by 1700, twenty-seven thousand.

The most dynamic new religious order was the **Society of Jesus**, or the **Jesuits**. Its founder was **Ignatius of Loyola**, a nobleman from northern Spain. As a young man he embarked on the classic noble career, service in the army. In 1521, aged thirty, he was badly wounded and forced into a long convalescence. During this period, Ignatius had a profound religious conversion and decided to become a spiritual soldier instead of a military one. In 1522, he offered his old sword to the Virgin Mary and symbolized his new life of dedication to God by exchanging his fine clothes for those of a beggar.

Ignatius wanted to convert Muslims to Christianity in the Holy Land, but an outbreak of plague delayed his departure. As he waited for better travel conditions, he formulated his *Spiritual Exercises*, a training program designed to strengthen one's will to

Jacopino del Conte painted this portrait of Ignatius of Loyola shortly after Ignatius' death in 1556. The artist bathes Ignatius's face in light to convey his holiness. Like the artists who depicted Luther and Calvin, Conte wished to show Ignatius's gentleness as well as his authority. *(Courtesy, Archivio A.R.S.I., Rome)*

fight for Christ. For thirty days, persons taking the *Exercises* examined their conscience to see where their will to obey God was weak and then concentrated on a word or deed of Christ to strengthen their resolve to

Teresa of Ávila   (1515–1582) Spanish monastic reformer and spiritual teacher.

Carmelites   Order of nuns reformed by Teresa of Ávila to be strictly separated from the larger world.

Capuchins   (from Italian, *cappuccio*, "hood") Largest reformed male religious order, named after the hood the friars wore as part of their religious garb.

Society of Jesus/Jesuits   Most important reforming religious order in the sixteenth-century Catholic Church.

Ignatius of Loyola   (1491–1556) Spanish nobleman and ex-soldier, founder of the Society of Jesus.

Spiritual Exercises   Ignatius of Loyola's training program, designed to strengthen one's resolve to serve Christ and his church.

follow him. Ignatius's emphasis on training the will to follow Christ was based on the traditional Catholic view that both human effort and God's grace brought about a person's salvation. This view contrasted with Luther's and Calvin's belief in the deep sinfulness of human wills.

For Ignatius, strengthening the will involved a form of prayer called **meditation,** in which one concentrated on a scene from Jesus's life as recounted in the Gospels, breathing the air, feeling the heat, and becoming part of the crowd in order mentally to meet Jesus face to face. Thus Ignatius, like Luther and Calvin, turned to the Bible for inspiration. But he never embraced their doctrine of scripture alone. In fact, part of the *Exercises* laid down "rules for thinking with the church." As a Catholic, Ignatius looked to church tradition and papal authority, as well as scripture, for religious guidance.

As Ignatius formulated the *Exercises,* he also modified his future plans, deciding that more education was necessary to be a successful missionary in the Holy Land. He, therefore, enrolled in a Spanish elementary school (as a nobleman, he had learned how to fight, but not how to read and write). Later he transferred to the University of Paris, where he began his studies in 1528, the year John Calvin entered law school. In Paris, he joined seven fellow students to found the Society of Jesus. In 1537, they were ordained priests and set off for Venice, intending to sail for the Holy Land. Once again, the trip was canceled, this time because of a war between Venice and the Turks. In 1540, the pope officially recognized the Jesuits, and Ignatius moved to Rome. From there he ran the order in a highly centralized way, rather like a general running his army. He also placed the order at the pope's disposal. From then on, it expanded rapidly and became the single most important reforming order in the church. Like the Capuchins, it concentrated on active service in the world.

The Jesuits' most successful service was in education. They founded secondary schools throughout the Catholic world, for boys from the middle and upper classes. They believed that, by instilling a deep sense of Catholic identity in these future social and political leaders, they could reinvigorate Catholicism and push back Protestantism. The Jesuits did not charge students tuition; instead, they expected local authorities to finance their schools and thereby build community involvement in their educational program. They also gave Ignatius's *Exercises* to students and their families, as well as to interested local clergy. The Jesuit schools were spectacularly successful. The quality of instruction was so good that even some Protestants went to them. The Jesuits attacked Protestants in print and from the pulpit, but they welcomed them into their schools in hopes of converting them.

Like the Protestants, the Jesuits and other Catholic reformers also promoted new forms of devotion for the laity. One of the most popular was the recitation of the rosary. Combining traditional veneration for Mary with meditation on Christ's life, death, and Resurrection, the rosary was a widely used means for instructing ordinary Catholics in the church's teachings, heightening their sense of spiritual union with God and forging a strong sense of Catholic identity. In 1556, when Ignatius of Loyola died, the Jesuits had almost a thousand members. Seventy years later, they had fifteen thousand members across the globe and ran 450 schools.

Reform in the Papacy

The pope who recognized the Jesuits was **Paul III.** Paul cautiously embraced church reform, and his reign proved a turning point for the Catholic Church. One of his first reforms was to appoint a special commission to evaluate papal administration. The commission's secret report, issued in 1537, argued that corruption in the church was caused mainly by abuses of papal power. Paul tried to ignore the report, but it was smuggled out to a local printer who made it public, once again demonstrating the power of the printing press. Shortly thereafter, Luther published it with his own scathing comments. Publicly, Paul appeared unruffled by the uproar, but privately he began appointing reformers to the **College of Cardinals,** the body charged with the election of future popes.

In 1542, Paul established the Roman Inquisition. Modeled on Ferdinand and Isabella's Spanish Inquisition, it investigated and punished heretics in Catholic lands. In 1549, another instrument of repression was set up, **The Index of Prohibited Books,** which listed works Catholics were forbidden to read. Eventually, many of Erasmus's works appeared on it. The creation of the Roman Inquisition and the *Index* signaled a change in outlook for the Catholic Church. Faced

meditation   Form of mental prayer developed by Ignatius that concentrated on a scene from the life of Jesus as recounted in the Gospels.

Paul III   (r. 1534–1549) Most important reforming pope of the Catholic Church.

College of Cardinals   Body charged with the election of new popes.

The Index of Prohibited Books   A list of books that Catholics were forbidden to read.

Titian painted *Pope Paul III and His Grandsons* (1546). The old pope, with an arresting face and piercing eyes, looks toward one grandson, an elegant courtier who bows to him, while the other grandson, a cleric, raises his hand in blessing while looking out at the viewer. Paul made both grandsons cardinals. *(Erich Lessing/Art Resource, NY)*

justification by faith alone, the council decreed that while God's grace saved people, Christians could choose whether they would cooperate with grace or resist it. This position was based on a verse in the Old Testament: "Thus says the Lord of hosts, 'Return to me . . . and I will return to you'" (Zechariah 1:3). The council, therefore, quoted scripture against Protestants to justify Catholic teaching about the roles of free will, works, and grace in determining a person's salvation and to counteract Protestant teaching about corrupted human wills and double predestination. The council's defense of traditional Catholic belief and practice dismayed Charles V, who saw his hope of reconciliation with the Protestants slipping away.

When the council next met, in 1561–1563, it reaffirmed the practice of indulgences while discouraging their sale, and it endorsed the traditional organization of the church with the pope as its head. Under him were the clergy and then—standing sharply apart—the laity. This last point was reinforced symbolically when the council decreed that at the Mass, the clergy alone would receive the cup of wine, the laity only the bread—a rejection of Luther's priesthood of all believers. The council also reaffirmed the church's seven traditional sacraments. In addition to restating doctrine, the council's last session also established guidelines for a thoroughgoing reform of the church. Trent ordered the establishment of **seminaries** in all

with Protestantism, it developed a fortresslike mentality, identifying itself as a militant church guarding against heresy. This new emphasis had a chilling effect on what many Catholics did or said in public.

Paul III's most significant act was to convene a church council in the city of Trent to address Protestantism and Catholic Church reform. He was not eager to convene the council, fearing it would get out of control or be ineffective, but he conceded to pressure from Charles V, who still hoped to restore religious unity in the empire. The **Council of Trent** met in three separate sessions from 1545 to 1563. The first two sessions (1545–1547 and 1551–1552) reaffirmed traditional Catholic theology. To counter Luther's doctrine of scripture alone, the council declared that *both* scripture *and* the traditions of the church were authoritative for Catholics. Moreover, it decreed that only the Roman Catholic Church, headed by the pope, had the right to interpret scripture. To counter the doctrine of

Council of Trent Catholic Church council, meeting 1545–1563, that reasserted traditional Catholic teaching and created guidelines for Catholic Church reform.

In this engraving of the Council of Trent, cardinals, bishops, and papal representatives are shown on either side of the Council's Chancellor, who sits at a desk while the king of Spain's representative speaks. Representatives of other Catholic rulers are seated in the center. Behind them is a crowd of observers. (*Courtesy of the Trustees of the British Museum*)

Catholic **dioceses** for the training of new clergy. It also ordered bishops to visit every church in their diocese to make sure that the buildings were in good repair, that services were properly conducted, and that the clergy were living moral lives. Another decree reaffirmed the traditional position that all women in religious orders were to stay within their convents, separated from society. In 1564, the pope accepted all Trent's decrees while announcing that he alone had the authority to interpret them.

The reforms of Trent were implemented, slowly and unevenly, throughout the Catholic world. The greatest gains were made in dioceses where the bishop was a committed reformer. One of the first successes came in the northern Italian city of Milan, where the archbishop, **Carlo Borromeo**, founded a diocesan seminary, set up Sunday schools to teach the young the basics of Christian belief and practice, and established religious associations for laymen and -women. He also gained control over local religious orders, conducted thorough visitations throughout the diocese, and cared personally for the sick and needy. Despite strong opposition from people who profited

from the old system, including an assassination attempt, Borromeo was remarkably successful in making Milan a showcase of reform. He died in 1584, at age forty-six. In 1610, the pope proclaimed him a Catholic saint.

Borromeo showed the way for reforming bishops elsewhere in the Catholic world. A hundred years after the Council of Trent, that world had been largely transformed. The Catholic Church was more centralized than ever before. Vigorous leadership after 1534 strengthened the position of the Roman popes, while centralized and dynamic orders like the Capuchins and Jesuits spread new ideals and practices to Catholic communities all over the globe. Religious devotion

seminaries   Schools for the training of the Christian clergy.

diocese   Territory presided over by a bishop of the church.

Carlo Borromeo   (1538–1584) Catholic archbishop of Milan who implemented the reforms of the Council of Trent in his diocese.

intensified as Teresa of Ávila's treatises on prayer were more and more widely read. Finally, a reformed Catholic identity was further advanced when the church issued new books for worship services that put Catholics literally on the same page throughout the year; all over the Catholic world, on any given day, people in church read and heard the same words during worship. Like the Muslims, whose worship was always in Arabic, the Catholics also shared a common religious language, Latin.

Catholic Missions Overseas

The Catholics were the first Europeans to embark on overseas missionary activity in the Americas and East Asia, believing that converts there could make up for the souls lost in Europe to the Protestant "heresy." Some also thought that spreading Christianity overseas meant the end of the world was near, since Christ's command "to make disciples of all nations" (Matthew 28:19) would finally be realized.

In the Americas, Spanish missionaries debated the best strategy for Christianizing the local people. Some followed Bartholomé de Las Casas in trying to protect them from harsh treatment by fellow Europeans and to preserve those features of their pre-Christian cultures that were compatible with Christianity. Others believed that local peoples were so lacking in human reason that they should be viewed as stubborn unbelievers, like Jews and Muslims. They should be forced to learn Spanish and live in settlements that reproduced European life, thereby replacing their old values and customs with European ones.

If missionaries in the Americas disagreed over strategies for converting local peoples, they all agreed that the process of conversion should be in European hands. Only in the eighteenth century did the church start to train large numbers of Indian men for the clergy. Before then, even the most well-disposed priests doubted that the Indians were ready to lead the church on their own. This attitude resulted from three factors: bewilderment at the complexity and strangeness of the Indians' cultures, a paternalistic sense of the church's obligation to protect or correct local peoples, and a racist sense of the innate superiority of Europeans.

Local peoples reacted to the missionaries' activities in various ways. Some tried to resist any changes in traditional culture. Others, particularly those who came from the old Indian elite, converted fairly easily to both Christianity and European customs. Many, however, found a middle way. They adopted those aspects of Catholicism and European culture that seemed useful and melded them with their older beliefs and practices, creating a new religious identity.

Thus, in Peru, local people went to church—after protecting the building by smearing animal blood on its foundations, an old Inca ritual. This modified Latin American Catholicism still exists, illustrating the complexity of the encounter that took place as the Catholic Church established itself in the Americas.

In Asia, Portuguese missionaries led in spreading Catholicism. One of the first was **Francis Xavier**, who with Ignatius of Loyola had founded the Jesuits. Xavier was active in India and Japan, using as his base the Portuguese trading post at Goa. In 1549, he also traveled to Japan and stayed two years, leaving behind a small Christian community made up of Jesuits and Japanese converts. This mission's success depended on the Japanese political elite. Some local rulers supported the missionaries in hopes of strengthening their commercial ties with the Portuguese. For their part, the Jesuits were careful to respect Japanese customs by dressing appropriately, bathing frequently, and eating only locally acceptable foods. The result was the establishment of a Christian community that numbered some 250,000 by 1600, or about 0.5 percent of the total population. But after 1593, when Spanish missionaries arrived from the Philippines, quarrels with the Portuguese caused the missionary effort to collapse in the face of imperial rivalries. In 1616, the Japanese government began suppressing Christianity and ultimately executed almost forty thousand men, women, and children, some by crucifixion. Japan then closed its doors to the west. Christianity was driven underground, where it survived for centuries as a secret religion passed on in families and local communities from generation to generation.

The Jesuits also initiated missionary activity in China. In 1552, Francis Xavier arrived there but died shortly after landing on an island near Hong Kong. The real founder of the Chinese mission was an Italian Jesuit, **Matteo Ricci**, who was born in the year Xavier died. Ricci learned Mandarin, dressed in Chinese clothes, and emphasized the similarities between Catholicism and the traditional Chinese philosophy of Confucianism. Like the Jesuits in Europe, Ricci concentrated on Chinese political and social elites, hoping for conversions in powerful places. He eventually resided at the imperial court in Beijing, where he gained a few converts, though most refused baptism. Thus, Ricci's influence in China was small, but his influence in Eu-

Francis Xavier (1506–1552) Jesuit who led Catholic missions in India and Japan.

Matteo Ricci (1552–1610) Italian Jesuit missionary in China who sent new information on Chinese civilization back to Europe.

Reformation and Society 1517–1570

↓ How was religious reform put into practice?
↓ How did the actions of ordinary men and women shape the outcomes of reform?

From Savonarola on, both Catholic and Protestant reformers hoped that church renewal would bring about a renewal of society as a whole. Reformers, therefore, tried to impose new codes of conduct on their communities, and people had to decide whether to accept or reject them. The result was a negotiation between reformers and the population at large, during which some changes were accepted and others were modified or rejected. This process was at work in three areas: children's education, poor relief, and family life. Finally, both Protestants and Catholics reassessed their relations with the largest religious and social minority in Europe, the Jews.

Educating the Young

In the Middle Ages, primary schooling was mainly reserved for boys destined for careers in the church, the state, law, and medicine. As a result, many men, like Ignatius of Loyola before he decided to become a missionary, saw no reason why they should study or learn to read and write. Protestant reformers, however, began to question these traditional ways and to argue for popular educational reform. Luther's belief in the priesthood of all believers led him to promote elementary education for both boys and girls, along with the establishment of public libraries. His goal was to turn children into good Christians by teaching them how to read the Bible. In 1529, he also published a *Small Catechism* for them, which contained the **Lord's Prayer** along with simple statements of Lutheran theology. Calvin adopted a similar program in his *Geneva Catechism* of 1545.

Leaders in a number of communities adopted Luther's and Calvin's educational agendas, but only after modifying them. While primary schools for boys were established, those for girls lagged behind, reflecting current social values. Few people, including many girls, thought that women's social or work roles were the same as men's; their education could be limited to training as wives and mothers, since these were the only respectable roles left for them after the Protestants abolished religious orders.

Adam Schall, a German Jesuit dressed as a mandarin, was court astronomer for the Chinese emperor in Beijing. Schall calculated the astrologically best dates for the performance of Confucian rites at court. In assimilating aspects of Chinese culture, Schall represents the style of missionary activity in China that his fellow Jesuit, Matteo Ricci, established. *(Bettmann/Corbis)*

rope was considerable. The reports he and other Jesuits sent to Rome were soon published, providing a flood of new information about Chinese culture, philosophy, and history. Here was a people who were unquestionably "civilized" like the Europeans but who had developed without the benefit of Christianity. Debates over the meaning of this puzzle were to swirl about in European intellectual circles for decades to come.

After Ricci's death, the Catholic community in China continued to expand. By the early eighteenth century, Christians numbered somewhere between two hundred thousand and five hundred thousand, or about 0.2 percent of the total population. Chinese Christians never faced government repression like Japanese Christians, but they achieved only a marginal place in the larger Chinese world.

Lord's Prayer   The prayer Jesus taught his followers to use, found in the Gospel of Luke and the Gospel of Matthew.

Catholic reformers sometimes endorsed education for both boys and girls, often for the same reasons as Protestants. A new *Roman Catechism*, published in 1566, taught young people throughout the Catholic world how to recite the Lord's Prayer, the creeds, and the **Hail Mary**. Nevertheless, Catholics established even fewer schools for girls than the Protestants; a late-sixteenth-century educational survey in Venice listed 4,600 boy students but only 30 girls. Catholics, too, thought that cooking, sewing, and other household activities, all requiring little formal education, were women's usual work, although they continued to see life in a religious order as another option.

Catholic boys fared better than girls, since efforts were sometimes made to educate more of them than before. For example, the **Piarists**, a religious order founded in 1597 by a blacksmith's son, established primary schools for poor boys so they could meet the entry qualifications for the more advanced Jesuit schools. Since Piarist schools were free, the poor would be given an equal chance with the rich for a quality education. The Piarists met with opposition from people who thought that the lowborn should stay where they were. Overall, both Catholic and Protestant reforms of elementary education, along with the availability of printed reading material, hastened the spread of **literacy** throughout Europe.

Poor Relief

In Europe, the number of poor people grew during the sixteenth century, rising to nearly half the population in the hardest-hit urban and rural areas. It is, therefore, not surprising that Protestant and Catholic reformers called for a rethinking of the problem of poverty. The outcome was a change in attitudes about the poor and the ways communities should deal with them.

In the Middle Ages, the poor were given sacred significance. In the Gospel of Matthew, Jesus identified the hungry, the naked, and the sick with himself. Anyone, therefore, who cared for them was also caring for him. As a result, charity toward the needy made up a major portion of the good works medieval people performed; they looked after the sick and dying and provided food and shelter for the destitute. Above all, they gave to beggars. These practices came under attack from both Protestants and Catholics during the sixteenth century.

As early as 1522, Martin Luther issued an ordinance governing poor relief in Wittenberg. It outlawed all public begging and mandated that care of the poor was to be transferred from private individuals or groups to the city. Funds for poor relief were to be collected in all the city's churches and then distributed by the municipal government. Only those identified by the authorities as "deserving" would receive help, thus restricting aid to those who were truly unable to work because of age, disability, or sickness. People who simply chose not to work would be left to fend for themselves.

The guiding principle behind Luther's ordinance was his rejection of good works as a means toward salvation. No longer were people to think that giving to the poor helped to save them. Charity was simply a free act of love performed by Christian people for the benefit of other Christians. Luther's reform was rooted in his theology, but his decision to turn poor relief over to the city government had profound consequences: from then on, the state, not the church, was responsible for care of the destitute.

Catholic reformers also argued that the state should assume the task of poor relief. In 1526, **Juan Luis Vives**, a Spanish humanist living in the Netherlands, argued that municipal governments should administer all funds for the poor. Vives's work won the support of other Catholics, but his proposals were never fully implemented in Catholic lands. The old practice of individual giving to the poor was too strong to be swept away completely, as the success of the begging Capuchins shows. Moreover, the idea that charity was a praiseworthy good work was reinforced by the Council of Trent. As a result, Catholics tended to create a variety of different systems for poor relief. State authorities administered some funds, religious confraternities collected and distributed others, and private individuals continued to give. Like the Lutherans, Catholics usually tried to distinguish between the deserving and undeserving poor.

Calvin's program for the poor resembled both Luther's and Vives's, since the government of Geneva took responsibility for the needy. Calvin believed that all wealth came from God and was to be used for the benefit of the community as a whole. Thus the state should tax the rich for the benefit of the poor. He also thought that poverty was a sign of God's anger over sin, but he did not place the sin simply on the shoulders of the poor themselves. If there was poverty, it

---

Hail Mary Roman Catholic prayer praising Mary and asking her to pray to Jesus on behalf of the one reciting it.

Piarists Catholic religious order dedicated to the education of poor boys.

literacy Ability to read and write.

Juan Luis Vives (1492–1540) Spanish Catholic humanist living in the Netherlands who supported a state takeover of relief for the poor.

was because the community as a whole had sinned. Like Luther and Vives, Calvin was shifting poor relief from the church to the state. In the long run, state administration of poverty programs was to be a central feature of the modern European world.

Family Life

A third area in which Protestant and Catholic reformers tried to introduce new social attitudes and practices was family life. As with primary education and poor relief, communities accepted some reforms while modifying or rejecting others. The result was a melding of old and new that resulted from a prolonged contest between reforming elites and ordinary people.

In the western Catholic Church during the Middle Ages, family life was based on the institution of marriage. The church taught that the purpose of marriage was twofold: to provide an outlet for sexual impulses and to bring children into the world. Both purposes were considered acceptable but not ideal. The highest state for Christians was that of permanent sexual abstinence expressed in a life of celibacy, following the example of Jesus and the apostle Paul. Thus clergymen, monks, and nuns were thought to live a better kind of Christian life than married people. For the married, sexual intercourse was permissible only between husband and wife, only on certain days, and only in certain positions. Of course, there were many who failed to live up to these ideals, and some clergymen even expected that people would find it impossible to observe them. Thus many city governments established brothels, arguing that men, especially, were incapable of controlling their sexual passions and that use of brothels was better than rape and adultery.

Marriage itself was considered a sacrament that the bride and groom administered to each other through the exchange of vows. The free consent of the partners to marriage was thus required. The Council of Trent also required that the marriage take place in public before witnesses, including the priest in the parish where the agreement to marry had taken place. Marriages contracted secretly were not recognized as binding on the couple. Once a proper marriage had taken place, it would last until the death of one of the spouses, since divorce was prohibited. It was also widely agreed that after marriage, the husband was head of the family, with his wife and all others subject to him.

As in other areas of life, Martin Luther swept away many of these traditional attitudes and practices. He declared that marriage was not a sacrament but simply a God-given social institution. He saw it as the foundation of all social order, since it created the basic social unit, the family. All men and women, including the clergy, were now to be married, and religious orders, which promoted celibacy, were to be abolished. In 1525, he set the example by marrying an ex-nun, Katherine von Bora. Marriages were to be public events, and they had to be sanctioned by the couple's parents, not just the future spouses themselves. In these ways Luther narrowed the freedom of choice for couples. In another way, however, he expanded it by allowing for divorce under special circumstances. Although divorces were frowned on and expensive to obtain, they could be granted for such reasons as adultery, male impotence, a spouse's refusal of sexual relations, desertion, and conviction of a capital crime. Finally, Luther ordered the closure of brothels, arguing that men could control their sexual impulses and confine their sexual activities to marriage. Luther's reform of marriage served as a model for most other Protestant churches, although some modified various points. For example, the Church of England forbade divorce, while the Anabaptists often insisted on community, not just parental, approval of marriages.

Protestant reform brought changes to the lives of husbands and wives. On the one hand, those Protestants who married were no longer viewed as second-class Christians, since the old ideal of a celibate life was no longer accepted. In addition, marriage was viewed more positively than before. Its purpose was to increase affection and cooperation between spouses, not just to provide an outlet for sexual impulses or to bring babies into the world. Women were viewed as real partners with their husbands in running a household, increasing their honor in society. On the other hand, women lost some of their older religious options, since they could no longer enter a women's religious order. From then on, their adult roles were limited to those of spouse or spinster. Even legal prostitution as a choice was taken away when brothels closed.

Catholics also reformed marriage practices, although they kept more of the old ways than Protestants. Marriage was still viewed as a sacrament. In addition, the free consent of bride and groom remained the only essential act leading to marriage; parental consent was encouraged but not required. Marriages could not be secret; they had to take place in public before a priest. Divorce was still not allowed. The best one could hope for in a failed marriage was either a permanent separation or an annulment declaring that the marriage had never really existed. While Catholics differed from Protestants on the matter of divorce, they both agreed that marriage existed for something more than the release of sexual passion and the production of offspring. It was also the place where individuals could find companionship and

The woman in this sixteenth-century engraving represents, according to the caption, "A Virtuous Woman of Geneva." Her dress is sober and her head is covered. Her bowed head and clasped hands convey a prayerful attitude and the submissiveness that embodied Calvinist gender norms. *(Genève, Departement Iconographique, Bibliothèque de Genève)*

mutual support. Moreover, women's religious options were greater for Catholics than for Protestants. Special female saints could be invoked during conception, pregnancy, and childbirth, and women could still enter their own religious orders, where they largely governed themselves. In contrast, Protestant authorities had abolished religious orders and prohibited asking saints for their prayers.

Faced with the reforming agendas of both Catholic and Protestant clergy, the mass of people had to decide how to react. Many reforms were well received. There was popular support among Catholics and Protestants for closing brothels and for punishment of sexually promiscuous people. Public anger was highest against sexual acts that threatened to disrupt the family or bring dishonor on it, like adultery. Others, like same-sex acts, while technically capital offenses that were deeply offensive to most people, were less of a challenge to social order since they did not result in the birth of children and usually did not tear families apart.

Other reforms were less well received, especially if they seemed too novel or threatening. For example, Luther wanted early marriages as a safeguard against lust. In Germany, where marriages were usually late and took place only when the couple had saved enough money to establish their own households, this reform was rejected. Popular opinion also often won out over the issue of premarital sex. Reformers wanted sexual relations to begin only after marriage, but many couples began them right after their engagement to prevent ill-wishers from using magic that would prevent desired pregnancies, since most people believed that their enemies could draw on the Devil's power to inflict harm.

Jews in the Age of the Reformation

The late-fifteenth-century expulsions from Spain and Portugal left western Europe almost empty of Jews, since the Iberian Jewish communities were the largest in the Christian world. As Protestant and Catholic reform developed, anti-Jewish sentiment increased and led to further expulsions. In some states, however, authorities permitted Jews to live under severe restrictions.

Like Savonarola, Martin Luther believed that church reform would usher in Christ's return to earth. This belief led to attacks on the Jews. With the end of the world at hand, why did they still refuse to convert to Christianity and acknowledge Jesus as their Messiah? In 1543, Luther gave his answer in a pamphlet, *Concerning the Jews and Their Lies*, where he repeated all the anti-Jewish arguments Christians had made in the Middle Ages. As a result, the Lutheran reformation turned sharply against the Jews; rulers of Lutheran states in the empire ordered their expulsion along with Catholics. Calvin also endorsed the medieval view of Jews as Christ killers and therefore enemies of God. Protestant Europe, therefore, became increasingly hostile toward Jews. It was only in Catholic Italy that Jews found new places to resettle in the west.

In 1516, the government of the Republic of Venice allowed a permanent Jewish community on its territory. Jews were confined to one area of Venice, the **Ghetto**. As a result, some Spanish and Portuguese Jews migrated there from the Muslim lands where they had gone after the expulsions. Those who had been forced to convert to Christianity now returned to Judaism. "Ghettos," modeled on the one in Venice, were also established in Rome and other Italian cities.

Like Luther, reform-minded popes believed that the Jews' refusal to convert to Christianity made them God's enemies. The low point came in 1593, when the pope placed severe restrictions on Jews living in his territories. They were forbidden to sell meat or unleavened bread to Christians. They could not bathe or shave with Christians and could not employ them as servants. Cases they had previously settled in Jewish law courts were now transferred to the state's law courts, run by Christians. Jews could no longer serve as physicians to non-Jews, a role traditionally played by Jewish men in the Middle Ages. Now, their economic activity was confined to the secondhand clothes trade. Finally, they continued to be publicly identified and shamed by the yellow badges they were forced to wear on their clothing. The pope intended to humiliate the Jews, isolate them socially, and attack them economically. But Jews were not expelled from the Papal States. They were also allowed to live in other states in Italy, often on terms more favorable than those offered by the popes. While Rome shaped its policy for religious reasons, the other states took economic considerations into account. They wanted Jewish settlements for commercial reasons, since Jews had good business connections in the Muslim world.

Ghetto Originally, a district in Venice where Jews were allowed to settle in the sixteenth century.

Summary

Review Questions

↑ What motivated the leaders of church reform, whether Protestant or Catholic?

↑ How did Protestant and Catholic reform reshape the religious identities of both Christians and non-Christians in western Europe and overseas?

↑ How did religious reformers, rulers, and ordinary people interact in the business of reform?

Savonarola's and Erasmus's hopes for church reform were symptomatic of a growing demand for religious renewal in the western church, brought about by the spread of humanism, a decline in the prestige of the papacy and the clergy, a rise in lay-inspired devotion to Christ, and the ability of reformers to use the new technology of the printing press. Savonarola and Erasmus raised issues and proposed changes that shaped the programs of many later reformers. One of the first was Martin Luther, the founder of Protestant reform. Although other Protestants, like the radicals and Calvinists, disagreed with Luther on some points, their programs were similar enough to create a general Protestant movement. Lutheranism was the dominant form of Protestantism in northern Germany and Scandinavia. But in the second half of the sixteenth century, Calvinism became the most dynamic Protestant movement, spreading throughout Europe. After the fall of Münster, the radicals renounced violence and followed leaders who embraced pacifism. The outcome of Protestant reform was a permanent split in the western church, characterized by deep hostility on both sides.

Initially, Catholics who shared the general expectation of church reform did not shape their programs with an eye to the Protestant challenge. In the end, however, orders such as the Capuchins and the Jesuits combated Protestantism while reforming the Catholic Church from within. Along with the religious orders, the papacy led Catholic Church reform when Paul III convened the Council of Trent. The council reaffirmed Catholic teaching, thereby cementing the division between Catholics and Protestants, and created a blueprint for reform that was implemented over the next hundred years throughout the Catholic world. Finally, Catholics inaugurated the first overseas missions by western Christians. Missionaries often tried to impose European values on converts as they sought to make up for the souls lost in Europe to Protestantism. Some local people accepted Christian teachings wholeheartedly, while others rejected them or blended them into their old religions.

In Europe, the decisive factors determining the success of reform, whether Protestant or Catholic, were the choices made by rulers, nobles, and ordinary people. The choices of the elite were the most important in determining whether communities would become Protestant or remain Catholic, but the long-term success of reform within a community depended on popular reception. Many reformers thought their programs would restore a united church to a state of purity they believed had existed formerly. In this sense, they were looking backward. Some reformers thought that church reform and overseas missions would usher in Christ's Second Coming and thus the end of the world. One outcome of reform was the introduction into European life of some basic features of the emerging modern world—the spread of literacy, new state administration of poverty programs, and changing standards for family life.

← Thinking Back, Thinking Ahead →

What were the consequences of religious reform in Catholic and Protestant Europe for future generations of Europeans?

ECHO ECHO ECHO ECHO ECHO

Media Revolutions

The first modern media revolution took place in the second half of the fifteenth century with the invention of printing using movable type. Studies of printed material in the sixteenth century show that most publications dealt with religious matters. Catechisms, prayer books, Bibles, and saints' lives were turned out in ever-increasing numbers. Not only were more religious texts produced in shorter time, *mistakes* in texts were produced in a different way. When a scribe made one copy of a manuscript, his mistakes were in that copy alone. When the printing press churned out many identical copies of a single work, mistakes were repeated over and over again. In England, for example, a printer was summoned before a church court on the charge of blasphemy because of a mistake in his edition of the Bible. His text read, "Thou shalt commit adultery."

The use of print media to promote Catholic or Protestant reform meant that, for the first time, reading skills were necessary for the mass of Europeans. The ability to read and write therefore became a central aspect of European identity. Historians measure the growth of literacy by noting the percentage of personally signed documents in the surviving sources. By this indicator, literacy spread gradually throughout Europe in the seventeenth and eighteenth centuries, first in the northwest and then in the south and east.

Beginning in the late nineteenth century, when literacy was widespread in all parts of Europe, media revolutions followed each other in rapid succession. The silent motion picture and the phonograph, which were invented at about the same time, emphasized different channels of communication—sight and sound. In the early twentieth century, radio expanded sound communication even further. Then the two were united in the talking motion pictures. After World War II, the development of television brought sight and sound into the home. Now it was possible to get the daily news or enjoy a story without having to use reading skills, and some critics complained that people's reading ability would decline.

Today, communication via e-mail, online newspapers, and audiovisual streaming in real time links millions of people around the globe in radically new ways. But the Internet revolution is only the latest in a series of media revolutions that have changed people's lives. Compared to the Internet revolution, the printing revolution looks pretty primitive. But, in its time, its impact was equally profound.

Suggested Readings

Donnelly, John Patrick. *Ignatius of Loyola: Founder of the Jesuits.* New York: Pearson/Longman, 2004. A good biography.

Hsia, Ronnie Po-chia. *The World of Catholic Renewal, 1540–1770.* 2nd ed. New York: Cambridge University Press, 1998. A comprehensive guide to Catholic reform in Europe and overseas.

Kittelson, James M. *Luther the Reformer.* Minneapolis: Augsburg Publishing House, 1986. A readable biography.

McGrath, Alister E. *A Life of John Calvin.* Malden, Mass.: Blackwell Publishers, 1990. A biography that places Calvin's life and thought within the larger context of church reform.

Tracy, James D. *Europe's Reformations, 1450–1650.* 2nd ed. New York: Rowman & Littlefield, 2006. Good general coverage.

Wiesner-Hanks, Merry. *Christianity and Sexuality in the Early Modern World.* New York: Routledge, 2000. A wide-ranging study that examines the impact of church reform on ordinary people.

Williams, Rowan. *Teresa of Avila.* New York: Continuum, 1991. A brief account of Teresa's life and thought.

Websites

Basic information and many links to more specialized topics, **Internet Modern History Sourcebook / Reformation Europe,** at www.fordham.edu/halsall/mod/modsbook02.html#Protestant

More basic information and links, **The Reformation Guide,** at www.educ.msu.edu/homepages/laurence/reformation/index.htm

Illustrations of important Reformation people, **Reformation Picture Gallery—People,** at www.mun.ca/rels/reform/pics/people/people.html

CHAPTER

15

A Century of War and Wonder, 1550–1650

1500 B.C.E.	1000 B.C.E.	500 B.C.E.	1 B.C.E./1 C.E.

| | 1555 Peace of Augsburg accepts split in western Christianity | 1562 French Wars of Religion begin | | | | | 1598 Edict of Nantes grants tolerance for French Protestants | |
| | | 1566 Calvinist revolt in the Netherlands | | | | | | |

1550	1560	1570	1580	1590	1600	1610

Europe in the Age of the Religious Wars

From 1550 to 1650, Europe was engulfed in a series of religious wars. One of the last was the Thirty Years' War, fought from 1618 to 1648 in the Holy Roman Empire. It pitted the Catholic Habsburgs and their German allies against the Protestants of the Empire. During the war Sweden, Denmark, the Dutch Republic, Spain and France were drawn into the fighting. Does the position of the Empire in relation to the other states of Europe suggest why this happened?

Austrian Hapsburg lands
Spanish Hapsburg lands
Other German states
Swedish lands by 1648
Ottoman and Tributary States
Boundary of Holy Roman Empire
Major battle
Siege

500 C.E.   1000 C.E.   1500 C.E.   2000 C.E.

1648
Thirty Years' War ends

1660
Monarchy is restored
in the British Isles

1618
Thirty Years'
War begins

1629
French Wars of
Religion end

1649
Charles I is executed,
England becomes
a republic

1665
Sabbatai Sevi is
proclaimed the Messiah

1620   1630   1640   1650   1660   1670

Choic Choice Choice

IACOBVS CALLOT
CALCOGRAPHVS AQVA FORTI NANCEII IN LOTHARINGIA.
NOBILIS.

Jacques Callot

Jacques Callot was one of the greatest artists and printmakers of his generation. Born into a noble family, he spent his early years documenting the pageants and festivities of European rulers in works that pioneered remarkable new techniques of fine line etching and were printed on the new printing press. In his last years, Callot produced scenes portraying the horrors of war that have inspired generations of antiwar protesters. (Lucas Vorsterman, Flemish, 1595–1675, *Portrait of a Man* [Jacob Callot]. Princeton University Art Museum. Gift of Junius S. Morgan. x1934-367a. © 2007 Trustees of Princeton University)

Jacques Callot Publishes "The Miseries and Misfortunes of War"

In 1633, Jacques Callot, nearing the end of his life and suffering from a painful stomach disorder, published eighteen large etchings depicting "The Miseries and Misfortunes of War." Military scenes had always been part of his artistic repertory, but the "Miseries" were something different. With them, the respected portrayer of elite life in early-seventeenth-century Europe revealed himself as one of the most powerful protesters against the dark side of war.

Callot was born in 1592 into a noble and devout Roman Catholic family in the duchy of Lorraine. His artistic talent was apparent at an early age, and in his teens he joined a band of gypsies heading south to Rome, where he worked as an assistant in a printshop specializing in religious images at a time when the campaign against Protestantism gripped the city. The papacy urged the Catholic faithful to come to Rome to reinforce their faith through visits to the tombs of saints and the city's magnificent churches. When they left, these pilgrims were eager to take home souvenirs, and prints like Callot's of the famous paintings they had seen in churches were especially prized.

In 1611, Callot moved to Florence to serve the grand duke Cosimo II and his mother, the grand duchess Christine, who, like Callot, was from Lorraine. Cosimo's court was one of the most brilliant and intellectually distinguished in Europe, and Florence was filled with artists and scientists in the grand duke's employ. Here Callot perfected his etching technique using the extra-hard varnish Italian violin makers put on their instruments. This varnish allowed Callot to prepare his copper printing plates by cutting fine, clear lines with his etching needle. The result was a remarkably detailed and precise etching ready to pick up ink for printing. In Florence, Callot continued to produce religious prints, but he also documented the lives of the grand dukes and their lavish court—scenes of operas, precision marching, and tournaments. Soldiers also figured prominently in these works because the rulers of the time were expected to project an image of warrior power. Callot's soldiers were dashing and heroic, mounted on prancing horses and glittering with finely polished armor.

In 1621, Cosimo II died, and the grand duchess Christine, reducing state expenditures, dismissed Callot and other court artists. Callot returned to his father's house in Lorraine, which, in 1630, the French invaded. They invaded again in 1632 and in 1633, when they finally annexed the duchy to France and demanded an oath of loyalty from all locally prominent people, including Callot.

The invasion of Lorraine brought the harsh facts of warfare directly into Callot's family. Plague swept through the duchy, brought in by French soldiers, and Callot's father fell victim to it. It was in this context that Callot decided to create his "Miseries and Misfortunes of War." The series of prints were published in 1633. The first shows an army recruiter luring men to sign up with promises of good pay. A fierce battle scene follows, and then come five prints showing the cruelty of soldiers against civilians as troops pillage a farm, attack a monastery, burn a village, and seize a stagecoach. In these scenes people are stabbed, shot, and burned alive. The next prints show the tables turned on the soldiers, who are tortured and killed by their commanders for military crimes such as desertion. Here men are tied to a rope and hurled earthward from a great height, shot by a firing squad, torn apart on a rack, or burned at the stake, while others hang by their necks like human fruit on the branches of a great tree. We then see wounded and mangled soldiers crowding a hospital, people dying by a roadside, and peasants attacking soldiers in revenge for their atrocities. The series ends with a conqueror rewarding his troops, implying that the horrors, now celebrated as a "victory," will start all over again. Callot presented his prints without any commentary, intending that his artistic skill alone should carry his bitter message; the moralizing lines now seen on many of them were added later.

In 1635, at the age of forty-three, Jacques Callot died in a Lorraine that was ravaged by wartime disease and famine. But his prints endured. They struck home to many of his generation who, like him, were deeply committed Christians, whether Catholic or Protestant, and who were also appalled by the horror and futility of the warfare that had torn Europe apart for nearly a century.

Introduction

Callot's Europe was indeed troubled and turbulent. Rulers fought increasingly expensive and destructive wars and, not content with battling their enemies at home, carried the struggles overseas. The Spanish and Portuguese fought to maintain their empires, while the French, English, and Dutch attempted to seize their rivals' wealth or establish competing empires of their own in the Western Hemisphere and Asia.

After 1550, the prosperity Europeans had experienced since the mid-fourteenth century ended. In both town and country, the numbers of the poor grew, while a small, well-to-do elite struggled to maintain control over the increasingly restless and riot-prone masses. Hard times produced widespread anxiety. People became obsessed with witches, who were feared as agents of the Devil bent on ruining society. Many believed that the troubles they were experiencing were a prelude to Christ's Second Coming to judge the world.

The church reforms of the sixteenth century had created two mutually hostile religious communities in western Europe. Neither the Protestants nor the Catholics accepted that religious unity had been shattered, and both fought ferociously to impose their own ways on their opponents. Capitalizing on his New World wealth and extensive European territories, Philip II of Spain, the son of Charles V, took the lead in the fight for Catholicism. The Netherlands, France, Germany, and the British Isles all saw religious warfare. In some wars, all Protestants joined to fight Catholics; in others, different types of Protestants fought each other. Both Protestants and Catholics committed terrible atrocities. The fierceness of the fighting shows how central the principle of religious unity was for the culture of early modern Europe.

Warfare accelerated economic decline, producing widespread famine and disease. In parts of Europe, population dropped by 50 percent. In the end, neither Protestants nor Catholics succeeded in eliminating their opponents, and religious disunity prevailed. By 1650, most Europeans had accepted it, often unwillingly, as a fact of life. Also by 1650, Spain, having exhausted its resources in the fight against Protestantism, had lost its preeminent position in Europe. France, weathering the crisis of its religious wars, now emerged as the dominant European power.

Although the Jews were not directly involved in disputes between Christians, they, too, experienced hard times when wars broke out in the lands where they lived. Nevertheless, the Jews' condition improved in western Europe, where they settled once again and often prospered. Yet, as a despised minority, Jews were sometimes subjected to terrible attacks. Some Jews saw the troubled times after 1550 as a sign that the long-awaited Jewish Messiah was about to appear and lead them to victory.

Chronology

1540s	Spain's silver mines in the Americas open
1555	Peace of Augsburg allows Lutheranism
1556	Philip II becomes king of Spain; Ferdinand I becomes Holy Roman emperor
1558	Elizabeth I becomes queen of England
1559	Francis II becomes king of France
1562	French Wars of Religion begin
1564	Maximilian II becomes Holy Roman emperor
1566	Calvinists rebel in the Netherlands
1571	Spain defeats Turkish navy at Battle of Lepanto
1572	French Catholics attack Protestants in Saint Bartholomew's Day Massacre
1588	Spanish Armada attacks England
1589	Henry IV becomes king of France
1598	Edict of Nantes grants religious toleration to Huguenots

1603	James VI of Scotland becomes James I of England and Ireland
1610	Louis XIII becomes king of France
1618	Thirty Years' War begins
1625	Charles I becomes king of Scotland, England, and Ireland
1629	Peace of Alès ends French Wars of Religion
1642	English civil war begins
1643	Louis XIV becomes king of France
1648	Peace of Westphalia ends Thirty Years' War
1649	England becomes a republic
1659	France and Spain sign Treaty of the Pyrenees
1660	Monarchy is restored in the British Isles
1665	Sabbatai Sevi proclaimed the Jewish Messiah
1667	War ends in Poland

Europe's Economy and Society

↓ What were the effects of overseas empire building and global trading on Europe's economy?

↓ What caused the decline in the standard of living for most Europeans, and what effect did this decline have on society?

Between 1550 and 1650, Europe's economy, which had boomed in the previous hundred years, began to stagnate. Silver from Spanish mines in the Americas caused inflation, which, combined with overpopulation, reduced the standard of living for most Europeans. Hardship was widespread, evident in protests and riots. As communities' traditional sense of solidarity crumbled, the well-to-do became obsessed with maintaining social order. Panic over witches was another symptom of the hard times that struck after 1550.

Europe's Continuing Overseas Expansion

During the sixteenth century, Portuguese and Spanish success in creating empires stirred similar ambi-tions in France and England. At first, the French and English were content to conduct raids against Spanish shipping. In 1523, a French ship sized three ships loaded with Moctezuma's personal treasure and the booty collected by Hernán Cortés's army. Since France and Spain were at war for most of the sixteenth century, this attack was considered part of the larger struggle. In the late sixteenth century, when relations between England and Spain deteriorated, Queen Elizabeth I commissioned the **privateer** Sir Francis Drake to seize Spanish treasure. These raids constituted the first phase of France's and England's entry into empire building in the New World, and by the early seventeenth century, permanent English and French colonies were being established.

In 1607, businessmen financed the first permanent English settlement in North America at Jamestown in

privateer Private vessel commissioned by a state to attack the commercial and naval ships of another country.

present-day Virginia. In 1625, the English colonized the Caribbean island of Barbados and imported African slaves to work sugar plantations there. The French state also sponsored colonial ventures in America. In 1608, Samuel de Champlain founded the city of Quebec on the Saint Lawrence River as the center of the new colony of Canada. In 1683, a French nobleman, Robert Cavalier, Sieur de La Salle, led an expedition from the Great Lakes down the Mississippi River to the Gulf of Mexico and claimed the lands along the river for France, naming them **Louisiana** in honor of the French king, Louis XIV. At the very end of the century, France claimed the western half of the island of Hispaniola and established sugar plantations there. The Dutch also established sugar plantations in the Caribbean as, like the English and French, they seized islands originally claimed by Spain. In Asia, the Dutch attacked the Portuguese and gradually replaced them as the major power in the spice trade.

Establishing colonies and attacking empires were costly adventures involving large investments and high risks. To raise the necessary money, Europeans developed a new form of business organization, the **joint-stock company,** in which individuals pooled their capital and received stock shares in proportion to the size of their investment. The joint-stock technique raised huge sums of money but limited the risk factor for each investor. Jamestown was founded by a joint-stock venture, the Virginia Company. The English **East India Company,** founded in 1600, established trading posts on the subcontinent of India, while the Dutch United East India Company, founded in 1602, was profitable for more than a century.

Nowhere were the effects of trade and colonization more far reaching than in the exchange between Europe and the Western Hemisphere. In the century after Columbus's voyages, many new food items were introduced into Europe: chili peppers, beans, pumpkins, squashes, tomatoes, peanuts, chocolate, maize, and potatoes. Maize and potatoes were to become staples in the diets of southern and northern Europeans, respectively. These strange foods provoked doubt and debate. Some argued that people should eat only foods mentioned in the Bible. Others wondered if potatoes and peanuts, which grew underground, should be fed to animals but not to humans, who were higher up in the ladder of creation. Tobacco, cultivated early in Virginia, provided a satisfying New World smoke, sniff, or chew after a New World turkey dinner, washed down with rum, an alcoholic drink made from American-grown sugar.

The exchange brought even more dramatic changes to the Americas. On his second voyage, Columbus brought wheat, melons, onions, radishes, grapevines, sugar cane, cauliflower, cabbages, lemons (originally from Asia), and figs to the Western Hemisphere, along with the European rat. Horses, cattle, pigs, goats, dogs, sheep, and chickens came as well, changing forever the animal population of the Americas. Later European arrivals unknowingly brought weed seed with them in the form of Kentucky bluegrass, daisies, and dandelions, as well as the European honeybee. The European ox pulled plows through soils that had been too heavy to turn over with the Indians' hand-held tools.

Trade with Asia also brought more new products to Europe. The first shipment of tea from China arrived at the beginning of the seventeenth century, and rice, a staple in some Asian diets, was soon widely grown in Italy. By the end of the century, coffee, native to the Arabian Peninsula, was grown in the East Indies and then shipped to Europe. Soon it would also be grown in the Americas. The rich prized Asian ebony wood for furniture and delicate Chinese porcelains for their collections of rare items. At a less exotic level, Chinese zinc and Indian tin were imported in ever-increasing quantities. Thus, the entry of new states and private companies into Europe's overseas trade expanded the global trading networks linking America, Europe, and Asia that had begun in the sixteenth century. The result was the beginning of a new era in Europe's economic life based on commerce.

A River of Silver

Spain's silver mines in the Americas, opened in the 1540s, produced huge quantities of precious metal that flowed to Europe and Asia. Contemporary official estimates of silver exports from the Spanish Empire place the figure at some 17,800 tons, but smuggling and unofficial exports may have pushed it as high as 29,000 tons. This amount would have tripled silver supplies in Europe, where the metal was used mainly as money; when news of silver's discovery reached Europe, Charles V's credit rating soared. The most productive mine was in present-day Bolivia at San Luis de Potosí. The other main source was at Zacatecas in northern Mexico. Gold and emeralds were also mined.

The silver of Potosí was either minted into coins or

Louisiana   French colony in the Mississippi valley named after King Louis XIV.

joint-stock company   Company in which individuals pool their capital and receive stock shares in proportion to the size of their investment.

East India Company   English joint-stock company founded in 1600 to establish trading posts on the Indian subcontinent.

melted into bars and then transported to the Peruvian port of Lima. From there it went by ship to Panama, where it was hauled overland to the Caribbean for transfer to Spain. Some silver from northern Mexico was also carried to the Caribbean while the rest went to Acapulco on the Pacific, where it was loaded onto the **Manila galleon,** a large, square-rigged sailing ship sent to the Philippine Islands to purchase Chinese silks and porcelains. The galleon's annual round trip was the single most profitable voyage in the Spanish Empire, and the millions of silver coins used to pay for trade goods flooded Southeast Asia, where they became the standard international currency.

The silver for Europe, along with goods from China, was collected once a year by armed Spanish ships that arrived in the Caribbean in late summer. After wintering there, they joined up in Havana for the voyage home. This was the most perilous part of the trip, since the fleet's valuable cargo made it subject to seizure by independently operating pirates or privateers commissioned by the governments of Spain's enemies.

If the Spanish fleet managed to dodge attacks and survive storms at sea, it headed for **Seville,** Spain's largest and richest city. In theory, all precious metals from the Americas had to be registered with the port authorities and then taxed, but smuggling, bribery, false declarations of value, and other techniques were routinely used to evade this requirement. Nevertheless, the government *quinto,* or fifth tax on gold and silver, made up a quarter of the royal income. Other goods were stored on the wharves, but few merchants gathered there to buy them. Instead, goods were shipped north to the trading centers of Antwerp and Amsterdam. Thus, Seville never became a major hub in the global commercial network but served simply as a transit point for Spanish overseas riches.

Despite the sizable sum provided by the royal *quinto,* Charles V and then his son, **Philip II,** found that the ruling of their lands created costs even the river of silver from the New World could not completely pay. So Philip, like his father, borrowed. During his reign he overextended himself, borrowing more than he could repay and declaring bankruptcy four times. Each bankruptcy created a financial crisis throughout Europe. Lenders disappeared, and expenses piled up until a renegotiation of Spain's debt was worked out. The crisis solved, lenders returned—until the next bankruptcy.

A Revolution in Prices

Around the middle of the sixteenth century, Europe experienced **inflation,** a sharp rise in prices for land, food, and other basic necessities that had major ef-

fects on Europeans' day-to-day lives. Several factors explain this **price revolution.** The New World silver flowing into Spain soon spread through Europe, since the Spanish government sent it out of the country in the form of coins to pay for the costs of warfare in Italy, the Netherlands, and elsewhere, which never seemed to stop. As silver coins became more and more common, the value of the metal in them declined, and their purchasing power diminished. To counteract the declining value of silver, people with things to sell raised their prices.

The continuing rise in Europe's population after 1450 also caused the price revolution. At first, population growth stimulated the economy and led to increased agricultural and commercial activity, which benefited many urban and rural workers. By the mid-sixteenth century, however, as population continued to grow, Europe was experiencing a crisis of overpopulation that put pressure on the ability of people to sustain themselves. For example, in agriculture, the growing population required that more and more land had to be cultivated. By about 1550, good land was running out, and cultivation moved to marginal, less productive land. This process is evident in the little French village of Langlade. Vineyards were converted into wheatfields, and hilly land, once thought too poor for cultivation, was cleared and planted with wheat. But these efforts were still not enough to meet the surge in population. The result was an inadequate food supply and a rise in food prices.

The rise in the price of food led, in turn, to two other developments: first, fierce competition for food-producing acreage caused land prices to rise sharply, and second, a glut of workers in need of jobs caused wages to decline. The impact of declining wages might have been offset if rural workers could have raised enough food for themselves on their own plots, but most could not because their landholdings were too

Manila galleon   Spanish sailing ship that carried Spanish silver from Mexico to exchange for Chinese silks and porcelains in the Philippine Islands.

Seville   Spain's largest city and government-mandated port for all goods going to or coming from the Spanish Empire.

Philip II   (r. 1556–1598) King of Spain, the most powerful ruler in late sixteenth-century Europe and leader of the Catholic crusade against Protestantism.

inflation   Process by which the cost of goods and services increases and the value of money declines.

price revolution   Rise in prices for land, food, and other basic necessities in mid-sixteenth-century Europe.

In this etching by Jacques Callot, a blind beggar stands with his begging cup and canine companion. His attitude is humble; with head bowed, he quietly waits for help from passersby. The man's blindness would qualify him as one of the "deserving poor." (*Callot, Jacques,* Beggar with Dog. *Rosenwald Collection, Image © 2007 Board of Trustees, National Gallery of Art, Washington, D.C., 1949.5.302*)

declining wages brought on by overpopulation. Guild members in the textile industry, which employed thousands in cities across Europe, were particularly hard hit because they faced fierce competition from merchants who hired needy peasants to weave in their homes for low wages and to produce cloth that was not subject to guild regulations. The result was a growing gap between the urban rich and poor that strained relief agencies.

To make matters worse, Europe was experiencing a period of climate change known as the **Little Ice Age.** Winters were colder and longer than previously; glaciers in the Alps advanced to cover inhabited land; in England, the Thames froze over. Colder, wetter years damaged crops, causing food shortages. Epidemics increased. Declining standards of living, vulnerability to disease, and the growing polarization between rich and poor weakened both rural and urban communities' sense of solidarity and mutual responsibility. The needy protested and rioted more frequently, while the well-off became obsessed with maintaining order among the masses.

The Hunt for Witches

Local political leaders shared the concern for maintaining popular order. In addition to economic hard times and social unrest, they also faced religious turmoil and spiritual anxiety as Europe split permanently into hostile Protestant and Catholic camps. Religious uncertainty lay behind rising beliefs that the world was coming to an end and that the Devil's attempt to destroy good Christians was intensifying. These fears led in turn to a search for **scapegoats** who could be blamed for the troubled times.

For centuries, Europeans thought that some people possessed magical skills that allowed them to cast harmful or helpful spells. These so-called cunning men and women were consulted by people at all levels of society. Both Catholic and Protestant reformers considered them nuisances and tried to draw their followers away from their "superstitious" practices, usually with little effect. By the sixteenth century, however, a belief spread that these cunning folk were not just magicians, but Devil worshippers. As it did, authorities in many parts of Europe inaugurated a crusade against **witches.**

Little Ice Age   Period of cooler weather in Europe beginning around the start of the fourteenth century.

scapegoats   People blamed for other people's bad behavior or embodying their fears.

witches   People, usually women, who were believed to have made a pact with the Devil, whom they worshiped.

small. To make ends meet, peasants borrowed from local moneylenders. As collateral, they would put up their land or anything else they owned. If they defaulted on the loan, the lender would seize the collateral. So another problem was rising peasant debt. Over the hundred years from 1550 to 1650, rural communities were gradually polarized between a few rich peasants who managed to keep or increase their landholdings and a mass of poor small-scale landowners, landless wage laborers, and sharecroppers who paid rent for the land they farmed by sharing its produce with their landlord.

Urban workers also suffered from rising prices and

Belief in witches was long standing, but it was only in this period that a sustained campaign against them was launched. After 1550, a stereotype of the witch emerged. Witches were said to be cunning folk who sold their souls to the Devil. In their obscene night rituals, called witches' Sabbaths, they sacrificed infants to Satan, engaged in cannibalism, and performed disgusting sexual acts. In a world where most people's lives were increasingly insecure, fear of bad magic skyrocketed, encouraging people to accuse their neighbors of satanic witchcraft. As many as 200,000 witchcraft trials were held all over Europe, most leading to convictions. The number of trials varied from place to place. Where lawyers and church officials had strict standards for accepting accusations or were skeptical of them, there were fewer trials. In England, for example, legal procedures prohibiting torture to procure confessions lowered the rates of self-incrimination. Rates were also low in Spain, where the Inquisition held that the Devil had no power to seduce people into witchcraft. The greatest number of trials—three-quarters of all known cases—occurred in the Holy Roman Empire, in areas where local officials, rather than state or church authorities, were in charge of the process. There, community leaders, clergymen, and other members of the local social elite, fearing social disorder and panicked by their belief in Satan's subversion of society, carried out wholesale prosecutions of people accused of witchcraft.

The vast majority of those accused were older women, most of whom were widowed or single and therefore lacked male protection. Some had served as midwives. Most were poor, but some controlled their own property. Those who were quarrelsome or sexually independent were seen as transgressors against prevailing patriarchal values. Women accused of witchcraft were, therefore, associated with dangerous activities, or seen as an economic burden to their communities, or envied for their material wealth, or despised as violators of the community's norms of behavior. Their trials often involved torture to get them to confess their activity and then more torture to force them to name accomplices. In cities, torture often produced a chain reaction of accusations. As the numbers of accused grew, the victims bore less and less resemblance to the stereotypical poor-woman witch: men, the rich, and children were named. On average, half of those convicted were executed, while the rest were imprisoned or subject to other forms of punishment.

Beginning in 1650, witch trials declined dramatically, as more and more centralized states took jurisdiction away from local authorities. Lawyers also worked to end persecutions. Although most lawyers still believed in witches, they also believed that legal standards for accusing and trying them had been too lax. Some people also believed in newly proposed scientific views of the world that questioned the Devil's active intervention in human affairs. Thus, a sense of fairness, along with doubts about Satan's power, won out over the fear of the Devil's subversion of society by means of witchcraft.

The Fate of Spain and the Flourishing of the Netherlands

↓ What were Philip II's successes and failures?
↓ What explains the success of the Dutch economy?

In 1550, Spain, with its silver and empire, was the most powerful state in Europe. Philip II dominated international affairs, making war on Muslims and attempting to eliminate Protestantism throughout his lands. Philip also sought to defend the western Mediterranean from the Ottomans while making war on his own Moriscos and laying the grounds for their expulsion from the Iberian Peninsula. His greatest failure came in the Netherlands, where his attempt to crush Protestantism provoked a rebellion during which the northern provinces declared their independence. These provinces, now organized as the Dutch Republic, soon dominated the European economy.

Philip II

In 1556, Philip II succeeded his father, Charles V, as head of the **Habsburg** dynasty. Despite Charles's grant of the Holy Roman emperorship to his younger brother, Ferdinand I, Philip ruled over a vast assembly of territories: Castile, Aragon, and Granada in Spain; the Netherlands; Franche-Comté on the Rhine; Naples, Sicily, and Milan on the Italian peninsula; Spanish America; and the Philippine Islands (named after him) in East Asia. His global empire was the wonder of the world, and he was the most powerful ruler of his age.

Philip used marriage to increase his political power. His short-lived first wife, Mary of Portugal, allied him with the other great imperial power of his time, while his second wife, Mary Tudor of England,

---

Habsburgs   Dynastic family originating in Austria that provided many rulers there and in the Netherlands, Spain, and the Holy Roman Empire.

This portrait of Philip II by Sanchez Coello (1583) shows the king in the somber dress favored at the Spanish court. His commitment to Roman Catholicism is symbolized by the rosary he holds. Contrast this style of royal portrait with the one of his father, Charles V, in Chapter 13. *(Museo del Prado, Madrid)*

prayed and meditated with the monks. His most important advisers were the priests who heard his confessions and the theologians he kept at his side.

In appearance, Philip hardly looked like the self-appointed leader of the Catholic world. Short and soft-spoken, he presided over a somber court and rarely left the area around Madrid, since he thought that "traveling about one's kingdom is neither useful nor decent." In this he unwisely rejected the policy of his predecessors, whose frequent travels throughout their lands kept them in touch with their subjects. Cautious by nature, he kept tight personal control over government, making every important policy decision and spending hours alone in his office pouring over the mountains of memoranda that had to be prepared for his approval. Before his death, Charles V had urged Philip to fight heresy and to hold onto the lands God had given him. Philip followed this advice. The money he amassed through taxes and borrowing was spent in pursuit of these aims.

The Spanish War Against Islam

In the early sixteenth century, the Ottoman Turks continued to push into Christian territory. Hungary fell in 1521, and in 1529 a Turkish army laid siege, unsuccessfully, to Vienna. When the Ottomans conquered Christian peoples in the Balkans, they organized them as a **millet**, or non-Muslim subject people. Millet Christians had to pay special taxes and accept that some of their boys would be recruited into the army as **janissaries.** But they were allowed to practice their religion, and conversion to Islam was discouraged because the taxes Christians paid were an important source of state revenue. Nevertheless, many Christians did convert to improve their position in society. The Christian millet was dominated by Greeks in Constantinople, headed by the Orthodox patriarch there. Jews under the Ottomans were not organized into a millet but were encouraged to immigrate to Turkish lands when western Christian states expelled them.

offered an English and Catholic alliance. When this Mary died childless in 1558 and was succeeded by her Protestant half sister, Elizabeth I, Philip wed Elizabeth Valois of France to cement relations with that kingdom. On her death, he married a cousin, Ann of Austria, who bore him his son and heir, Philip III.

By the time Philip became king, Protestantism was challenging the Catholic Church throughout central and northern Europe, and Philip undertook its defense, using both military and diplomatic means. He also continued Christian Spain's attack on the Muslim world, now dominated in the west by the **Ottoman Turks.** In Spain, he adopted the title of His Most Catholic Majesty and supported Teresa of Ávila's reform of the Carmelites while collecting manuscripts of her religious writings for his library. He also built a residence, just outside Madrid, the new Spanish capital. Called the **Escorial**, it housed both the royal palace and a monastery where Philip frequently

Ottoman Turks   Muslims who captured Constantinople in 1453, ending the Byzantine Empire and founding the Ottoman Empire.

Escorial   Philip II's palace and monastery complex outside of Madrid.

millet   Legally defined community for non-Muslims living within the Ottoman Empire.

janissaries   Ottoman infantry composed mainly of Christian boys either captured or given in tribute to the sultan to be raised as Muslim soldiers.

The Turks also established contact with the **Moriscos.** Following Ferdinand and Isabella's conquest of Granada in 1492, its Muslim population, now called Moriscos, had been forced to convert to Christianity. Then Christians seized their lands and sought to stamp out their culture along with their religion. Speaking Arabic and bathing on Fridays, along with traditional dancing and eating couscous, were forbidden as signs of heresy. Faced with this repression, the Moriscos rose up in 1569. The revolt lasted two years and involved thirty thousand rebels joined by four thousand Turks and North Africans. Each side outdid the other in cruelty, since each believed that its enemy was God's enemy. The revolt was put down in 1571, but hatred remained on both sides. Finally, in 1609, Philip's son, Philip III, ordered all three hundred thousand Moriscos expelled from Spain. Many went to North Africa, while some went to northern Greece and Constantinople. The expulsion of the Moriscos was the last step in the dismantling of the cultural and religious diversity that had characterized medieval Spain. Some Spaniards hailed the expulsion as a purification of the land, but others, like the great novelist **Miguel de Cervantes** condemned it. In *Don Quixote*, Ricote, an expelled Morisco, laments, "Wherever we are, we weep for Spain, because we were born there and it is our native land."

In 1571, the last year of the Morisco revolt, Philip destroyed the Turkish navy at **Lepanto** off the coast of Greece; 195 ships in the Turkish fleet of 230 were captured or sunk, thirty thousand Turks were killed or wounded, and three thousand were taken prisoner. Although the Turks assembled another fleet in 1572 and continued to harass the coasts of Italy and Sicily, their dominance of the Mediterranean had been weakened. Then, in 1580, Philip became ruler of Portugal and its empire when the Portuguese king disappeared on a crusade in Morocco against the Muslims. Philip was now at the height of his power.

The Revolt in the Netherlands

Even as Spanish might awed Europe, Protestant forces in England and the Netherlands were rising to challenge it. Protestantism had not spread to Spain, but it had to the Netherlands, the Habsburgs' richest territory. Charles V had tried without success to eliminate it there, and Philip tried as well, with even worse results. Philip viewed his Protestant subjects as damnable heretics, but at first he recognized that their growing numbers required a political solution. Therefore, in 1566, on the advice of his court theologians, he granted religious **toleration** to the Protestants. Shortly thereafter, militant Calvinists went on a rampage across the country, destroying Catholic churches and religious images. Philip now decided on a military solution.

In 1567, a Spanish army marched north to subdue the Protestants. Its commander, the duke of Alba, then tried and executed more than a thousand people. To pay for his army, Alba also imposed a tax on the Netherlanders. Both Protestants and Catholics condemned it and rebelled when it was not withdrawn. Then, in 1572, Calvinist exiles in England returned home and joined the rebellion, seizing the country's northern provinces and electing **William of Orange** as their leader. The general rebellion in the Netherlands forced Philip to recall Alba in 1573.

In 1575, Philip declared a bankruptcy that delayed pay for his troops in the Netherlands. In response, his army mutinied and sacked Antwerp, destroying property and leaving eight thousand dead. This "Spanish Fury" signaled the end of Antwerp as Europe's leading commercial hub. Finally, in 1579, Philip's new military governor was able to consolidate Spain's rule in the southern provinces, thereafter known as the Spanish Netherlands. But the northern provinces were lost when rebels there forced the Spanish army to retreat by opening the dikes that kept the sea out, flooding large parts of the country. Having declared their independence from Spain, the northern provinces reconstituted themselves as the **United Provinces,** or **Dutch Republic.**

Queen Elizabeth I of England had aided the Dutch Protestants, and Philip decided to attack her. In 1588, he sent the **Spanish Armada**—130 ships and thirty thousand men—to join with his loyal forces in the Spanish Netherlands and then conquer the island kingdom. The Spanish met a slightly larger and much faster English fleet in the English Channel, where

Moriscos   Muslims in Spain who were forced to convert to Christianity or leave.

Miguel de Cervantes   (1547–1616) Spanish writer and critic of Philip II who wrote *Don Quixote*.

Lepanto   Naval battle won by Spain over the Ottomans in October 1571.

toleration   Recognition of the right to hold dissenting beliefs.

William of Orange   (1533–1584) Calvinist nobleman, also known as William the Silent, who led the Protestant rebellion against the Spanish in the Netherlands.

United Provinces/Dutch Republic   Northern Netherlands provinces that successfully threw off Spanish rule.

Spanish Armada   Unsuccessful armed fleet sent by Philip II in 1588 to conquer England.

MAP 15.1 **The Netherlands** When the Twelve Years' Truce was signed in 1609, the seven northern provinces of the Netherlands , along with parts of the Duchy of Brabant and the County of Flanders, were put under Dutch control. Spain continued to control the remaining southern provinces.

stormy weather and superior English cannon fire broke up the Armada. Only half the Spanish ships returned to their ports. The defeat was the beginning of Spain's decline. The failure to stamp out Protestantism in the Netherlands, followed by the loss of the northern provinces, was a bitter blow to Philip, who grieved that he had betrayed his father's trust.

The Dutch Miracle

It would take decades for Spain to acknowledge Dutch independence, but from the 1590s on, the breakaway provinces were free from serious invasion. Distracted by other wars, Spain was never able to conquer the north. Finally, in 1609, the Spanish signed the Twelve Years' Truce with the rebels. The Dutch Republic was founded by Calvinists who sought to reform church and state. But William of Orange and his successors feared that the rebellion's success would be

jeopardized if the Catholics of the north, who made up a third of the population, were alienated. So a policy of partial toleration was instituted. Calvinism was recognized as the state religion, but the church was not allowed to control state policy. Although Catholics were forbidden to worship publicly, they were allowed unofficially to open private chapels. Anabaptists, Lutherans, and Jews also had their places of worship. None of these communities really welcomed the others; each tended to mix socially and marry only with its own kind. But a grudging live-and-let-live attitude prevailed in the country that was far different from the atmosphere in Philip II's Spain.

Although Calvinist church members were a minority of the Dutch population, Calvinist values were widely shared. Chief among them was the idea of the **calling.** Calvin had rejected Catholic practices such as renouncing the sinful world by joining religious orders or giving one's wealth to the church or the poor. Like Luther, he believed these acts were useless for salvation. Instead, he urged people to treat their ordinary work as a divine calling through which they could serve God with diligence and to avoid sinful idleness, luxury, and waste. When giving this advice, Calvin did not have a particular economic agenda in mind, but his ideal of a sober and serious attitude toward one's calling in the world encouraged attentive, thrifty behavior among the merchants, manufacturers, and artisans who heeded it. This attitude was one of the factors behind the Dutch economic miracle of the late sixteenth century.

The revolt against Spain hurt the economy of the southern Netherlands and hastened the decline of Antwerp. But while the economy faltered in the south, it boomed in the north. Unlike most of Europe, which experienced hard times after 1550, the Dutch Republic flourished. As both population and workers' wages rose, the Dutch economy became the wonder of the age. Its success rested on an adequate grain supply from Poland that prevented the food shortages plaguing other parts of Europe. With this staple assured, Dutch farmers were free to specialize in other foodstuffs: butter, cheese, hops for beer, and livestock for meat. In addition, the North Sea provided catches of nutritious herring. Half the labor force was engaged in agriculture, the rest in a variety of industries. There was a need for labor, and workers' wages rose as a consequence. Men worked on large reclamation projects as coastal land was pumped dry with windmills

calling Calvinist belief that ordinary work was a means for serving God.

This engraving from 1647 shows fluteships in a Dutch harbor. The fluteship's deck is narrower than the bulging hull below it, which will be filled with the goods shipped in what the Dutch called the "mother trade" between Dutch ports and Baltic ports in the east. *(Courtesy, Stichting Atlas van Stolk [Historisch Museum Het Schielandhuis, The Netherlands])*

for agricultural use. Dutch cities grew and with them a demand for servants, carpenters, masons, and other urban workers. High literacy rates and lax censorship created a demand for books, news sheets, and pamphlets offering a wide range of opinions on often-controversial subjects like religion. These, in turn, called for printers and engravers. Shipyards employed others, while the ships they built needed crews. In fact, ships and shipping did the most to stimulate the economy.

After 1550, the Dutch became the best shipbuilders in Europe. They also created an international trading network and used their ships to move their goods. The success of Dutch shipbuilding and trade rested on the **fluteship,** a large-hulled boat with a shallow draft. Fluteships carried salt, herring, and cloth east to Poland and other Baltic ports and brought back grain and timber. Some of the imports were used locally, while the rest were sold abroad. Interestingly, Spain was one of the Dutch Republic's best customers. Although at war with the rebels for much of the time, Spain could not do without Dutch-shipped

timber for its navy and grain for its food-hungry territories in Italy. So the Spanish swallowed their principles and traded.

The Dutch also entered the East Asian trade. In 1602, the government licensed the United East India Company to set up trading posts from Persia to Japan. Because Portugal was ruled by Spain after 1580, the Dutch aimed to reduce Spanish power by supplanting Portuguese traders in Asia. After the Portuguese were driven out, the company dominated the spice trade with Europe. It also dominated the inter-Asian trade, picking up cotton cloth in India and trading it elsewhere for goods like porcelain and silk that were then sold in Europe. After the Japanese government began persecuting Japanese Christian converts and shut off contact with the outside world, the Dutch

> **fluteship** Merchant ship with an enlarged cargo hold and shallow draft used in Dutch trade with eastern Europe.

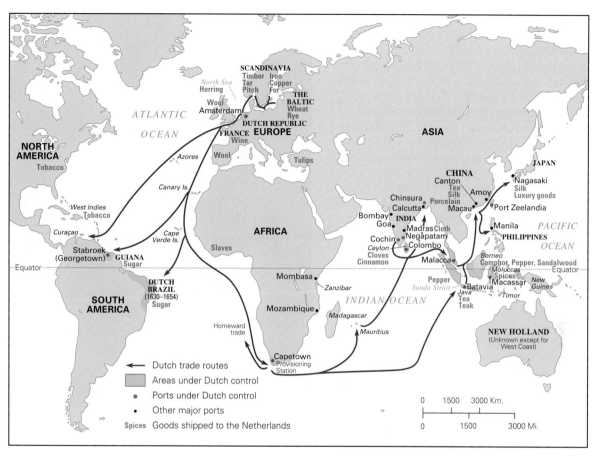

MAP 15.2   **Dutch Commerce in the Seventeenth Century** By the seventeenth century the Dutch had developed a complex global trading network. They took over Europe's East Asia trade from the Portuguese, dominated the European seaborne trade routes, traded with their New World colonies, and became the major trading partner with the Portuguese in Brazil.

alone were allowed a trading post there. In 1621, the Dutch government also chartered the Dutch West India Company, which set up posts in Curaçao on the Caribbean and Surinam on the South American coast. Soon the Dutch were trading with Brazil, exporting European goods to the colony and importing African slaves in return for sugar. Dutch settlers also founded the colony of New Amsterdam on Manhattan Island at the mouth of the Hudson River.

Dutch Civilization

Science flourished in the Dutch Republic, where scientific experimenters tried to develop practical devices that would aid people in their worldly callings. The Dutch scientist **Anton van Leeuwenhoek,** who perfected the magnifying lenses of the microscope, was the first to describe the world of microorganisms, drawing the protozoa he found in rainwater, the bac-

teria in the human mouth, and spermatozoa. As one scientist put it, the microscope opened a world "in which you will find wonder heaped upon wonder, and will be amazed at the Wisdom of God manifest in a most minute matter."

The hub of Dutch life was **Amsterdam** in the province of Holland. By the early seventeenth century, Amsterdam had replaced Antwerp as Europe's chief commercial and banking center. Because the republic's commercial activity spread across Europe and the world, involving people in complex, long-distance economic activity, the Dutch can be seen as

Anton van Leeuwenhoek (1632–1723) Dutch scientist who perfected the microscope to see and describe the world of microorganisms.

Amsterdam Capital of the Dutch province of Holland and commercial center of the Dutch Republic.

the creators of the first truly modern economy. Like modern economies that followed it, the Dutch experienced speculative frenzies like the "tulip mania" of the early seventeenth century. In the sixteenth century, tulip bulbs had been imported from Turkey, where they quickly became the flower of choice for wealthy Dutch gardeners. The most prized blooms were multicolored ones, which occurred in the offspring of single-colored bulbs if invaded by a particular virus. Since no one knew in advance if any new bulb would produce multicolored flowers, trade in them was a gamble. In the mid-1630s, a speculative frenzy in tulip bulbs swept across the United Provinces as thousands of people bought lots of bulbs that had not yet flowered in hopes of selling them at a profit to eager buyers. Thousands were risked in hopes of hitting on the most prized blooms. Then, suddenly, the craze collapsed, and those unlucky enough to hold unsold lots of bulbs suffered huge losses. But the complicated trade in these commodity "futures" was to be a feature of all modern economies.

More lasting was the rise in Dutch purchasing power. The republic's prosperity allowed people to spend more of their income on things other than food and shelter. In particular, middle-class Dutch families spent disposable income on furnishing their homes; Chinese porcelains and Turkish carpets became standard decorative items. But no item was more popular than paintings, and demand for them led to a remarkable flowering of Dutch art in the seventeenth century. Since Calvinists refused to decorate their churches with images of Christ and the saints, considering them idolatrous, the home became the setting for works of art. The paintings of **Jan Vermeer,** small in size, were made for household walls; they often depict household scenes that radiate with light and domestic peacefulness. More versatile was **Rembrandt van Rijn,** an artistic whirlwind who painted, drew, and etched throughout his long career. Rembrandt painted the great merchants of his generation along with ordinary people while also undertaking commissions for paintings of town councils and other public bodies that hung them in guild offices and town halls. He also painted religious scenes for purchasers who were less reluctant than the Calvinists to accept sacred art. In all his work, he was a master in depicting the contrasts of shade and light.

The art that hung in people's homes often drew its themes from domestic life, but it was never simply a reproduction of that life. It was also filled with symbols and associations that pointed to the complexity of Dutch civilization in its "Golden Age." Take, for instance, the Flemish artist Clara Peeters' 24 by 19.5

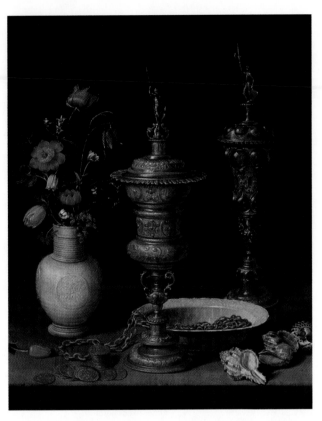

Women artists like the Flemish Clara Peeters were unusual. Peeters painted her tiny reflection on the goblet to the right. Dutch trade and wealth, the shortness of life and the certainty of death, the wonders of creation, and the wonders of little things—all are conjured up in her painting. *(Staatliche Kunsthalle Karlsruhe)*

inch *Still Life with Golden Goblets and Collectibles* (1612), This small picture is remarkable for the precision with which even the smallest details are painted, calling to mind the wondrous world that van Leeuwenhoek revealed. The bouquet contains a tulip and resonates with the tulip mania that would sweep over the Dutch Republic in 1637, as well as the beauty of God's creation and the fragility of life, for the flowers' petals will soon drop and dry up. The coins and the Chinese bowl point to Dutch commercial activity and reach, as do the shells, for they come from the

Jan Vermeer (ca.1632—1675) Dutch painter of peaceful household scenes that radiate with light.

Rembrandt van Rijn (1606–1669) Greatest Dutch painter of the seventeenth century; also a skilled printmaker.

François Dubois' painting of the Saint Bartholomew's Day Massacre, August 24, 1572, graphically depicts the chaos of this event. Note the killings, the corpses, the raised swords and clubs, the blood on the ground, and the men on horseback. The barking dog, at center left, seems to give voice to the violence. *(Musée Cantonal des Beaux-Arts de Lausanne, Switzerland/The Art Archive)*

non-European waters into which the Dutch sailed. And, like the flower, the shells call to mind the beauty of creation.

Political Contests and More Religious Wars

⬇ What explains the violence of Europe's political contests and religious wars?

⬇ What were the outcomes of the wars?

In 1562, France was plunged into religious warfare between Catholics and Protestants that lasted for nearly seventy years. In the end, the Protestants were granted limited religious toleration, but their attempts to create their own semi-independent political communities within France failed. The Holy Roman Empire also experienced a religious war. The German war lasted fewer years than the war in France, but it brought non-German states into the fighting, and its destruction was far greater. The peace settlement ending the war granted religious toleration to Calvinists, Lutherans, and Catholics and reduced the emperor's power. Like the French, the Germans had to learn to live with a new religious pluralism. The conflict also accelerated Spain's decline and France's rise as the most powerful state in Europe.

France's Wars of Religion

When Henry II died in 1559, he left his fourteen-year-old son Francis II to succeed him. In the confusion following Henry's death, the powerful **Guise family**, utterly committed to the extermination of Protestantism, seized control of the government. For the next thirty years, as three of Henry's young sons ruled France in succession, plots and fighting broke out between the Catholic Guises and the Protestant Huguenots. In 1572, a Catholic attack on the Huguenots that began in Paris on Saint Bartholomew's Day—thus known as the **Saint Bartholomew's Day Massacre**—spread to the provinces. Some five thousand people died as violence reached extraordinary levels—heads, hands, and genitals were cut off; pregnant women were stabbed in the stomach; and bodies were burned. The massacres put an end to the growth of Protestantism in France. The brutality of religious conflict demonstrated that both sides believed a fundamental issue was at stake—the belief that all members of a community had to share a common religious commitment for the community to function properly. In early modern Europe, religion was more a matter of community solidarity than of individual belief. Therefore, all religious dissent had to be stamped out to restore communal unity and win God's favor, especially since the Second Coming and Last Judgment were believed to be near at hand. Thus, Huguenots and Catholics saw each other not simply as different, but as dangerous polluters of the community. Killing as a rite of purification was not enough; the very bodies of the enemy had to be degraded.

In 1589, the last of Henry II's sons, Henry III, died, assassinated by a fanatical Catholic monk. Since Henry III had no children, the Crown passed to a cousin, **Henry IV of Navarre**, a Huguenot. Henry was eager to end the fighting, but he faced a dilemma. The law of royal succession made him king, but his coronation oath would require him to attack non-Catholic heretics. In 1593, Henry resolved the issue by converting to Catholicism, supposedly saying that "Paris is well worth a Mass." In 1595, when the pope absolved Henry of his Huguenot errors, Henry was able to win over all but the die-hard Catholics. He reassured the Huguenots by issuing the **Edict of Nantes,** granting official toleration, in 1598. This edict brought an uneasy religious peace to France, but at a high price to community unity. The Huguenots were permitted to worship undisturbed, and they were also granted some two hundred fortified towns, along with troops to defend them. These towns were effectively independent from royal control and became a Huguenot state within the state. To rally support for the edict, Henry showered powerful Catholic and Huguenot nobles with high government positions and large pensions. He also insisted that the king, who was the source of all law and order, should be obeyed regardless of his religion. Henry's emphasis on the importance of law and order vested in the king's authority became one of the basic principles of **absolutism,** which guided French kings' rule for the next two centuries.

The Resurgent French Monarchy

At the grass-roots level, Henry IV built on an expansion of government begun by his predecessors, who had sold administrative offices to middle-class lawyers and then forced them to loan the government money. This strategy raised additional revenue and built loyalty, as the new officeholders had a compelling reason to see that the monarchy remained strong. Henry IV used this expanded administrative force to consolidate royal power and initiated tax reform to erase the royal debt and build up a treasury surplus.

Henry's chief minister, the Huguenot duke of Sully, lowered direct taxes while raising indirect ones. Since the direct tax of the *taille* took one large bite out of incomes while indirect taxes on commodities nibbled slowly away at them, the pain of taxation was obscured. Most important, Sully imposed the annual *paulette* tax on all officials who had bought their offices. Because their numbers were now so large, *paulette* payments raised revenues that eventually rivaled the *taille* as the chief source of royal income.

Although Henry IV won many Huguenots and Catholics over to his policies of religious toleration and administrative consolidation, in 1610 he was stabbed to death by a deranged ex-monk obsessed with the

Guise family   Powerful Catholic nobility committed to eliminating Protestantism in France during the French religious wars of 1559–1588.

Saint Bartholomew's Day Massacre   1572 Catholic massacre of Protestants in Paris and throughout France that ended the growth of Protestantism in the kingdom.

Henry IV of Navarre   (r. 1589–1610) Protestant king of Navarre who became king of France, converted to Catholicism, and started to end the religious wars.

Edict of Nantes   Decree issued by Henry IV in 1598 that allowed the Huguenots to practice their religion and gave them two hundred fortified towns,

absolutism   Doctrine that a king was the sole source of all law in his realm.

continuing presence of heretics in the kingdom. Henry's heir was his nine-year-old son, **Louis XIII**, who, once king in his own right, resumed war against the Huguenots. In 1629, he issued the **Peace of Alès**, which dismantled the Huguenots' fortified towns and ended France's Wars of Religion. But the religious toleration granted the Huguenots in 1598 was reaffirmed.

The Habsburg War Against Islam

Charles V had put his younger brother Ferdinand in charge of the Holy Roman Empire before his abdication in 1556. Thirty years earlier, Ferdinand had also been elected king of Hungary and Bohemia after the previous king died fighting the Ottoman Turks. While Ferdinand had full control of Austria and Bohemia, the Turks conquered most of Hungary, leaving only the northern part in Habsburg hands. Even that was threatened when the Turks, marching up the Danube River, tried in 1529 and again in 1532 to seize all of Hungary and the city of Vienna in Austria. For Ferdinand, a devout Catholic, the Turks posed a greater threat than the Protestants.

Thus, during Ferdinand's reign, and that of his son Maximilian II (r. 1564–1576), various kinds of Protestants increased their followings in all Habsburg lands. Lutherans predominated in Austria, while Lutherans and Calvinists flourished in Bohemia, and Calvinists and **Unitarians** gained converts in Habsburg Hungary. "In affairs of religion everyone does as he pleases," one Catholic complained. After Maximilian died in 1576, effective Habsburg rule declined, as a contest between his two sons encouraged the great nobles who controlled the representative assemblies, or **diets**, to seek increased political independence. Their model for good government was **Poland-Lithuania**, where the nobility elected the king and had the right to rebel against him if he violated his coronation oath. In the Polish Diet, each noble had the right to veto a measure and thus "explode" the diet. They were also free to govern their serfs without royal interference and to choose between Catholicism and some form of Protestantism. When new war with the Turks broke out in 1593, the nobility in the Habsburg lands demanded more religious freedom and greater local control of government in return for funds for the war.

The Thirty Years' War

As Protestantism grew in Habsburg lands, the Catholics launched a counteroffensive. As early as the 1590s, Jesuits from Italy rallied Catholic communities, which soon established a militant anti-Protestant movement. Catholics found their leader in the new emperor, **Ferdinand II**, a fervent Catholic who prayed privately every morning for an hour before dressing and attended two morning Masses, during which he frequently knelt to kiss the ground five times in honor of Christ's five wounds on the cross. His determination to put an end to Protestantism launched the **Thirty Years' War**, the most devastating conflict of the seventeenth century. At first confined to Bohemia, it soon engulfed the Holy Roman Empire and drew in many European states as it went through Bohemian, Danish, Swedish, and French phases.

In 1617, after he was elected king of Bohemia, Ferdinand II ordered Protestant churches closed in two Bohemian towns. Enraged Protestants confronted two of Ferdinand's officials in Prague, the capital of the kingdom, and threw them out of an upper-story window. Surprisingly, they survived. Catholics claimed they had been wafted gently to earth on angels' wings, while Protestants protested that a pile of dung had broken their fall. This "defenestration of Prague" prompted a Bohemian rebellion, which Ferdinand subdued with help from the Spanish Habsburgs. Ferdinand seized rebel lands and gave them to Habsburg supporters. Believing that religious dissent polluted society and offended God, he banned Protestant worship, ordering Protestants to convert or leave. In 1627, a subdued Bohemian Diet declared that the Crown was no longer elective, but rather hereditary in the Habsburg family. The abolition of elective monarchy marked the high point in Ferdinand's reconquest of Bohemia.

Louis XIII (r. 1610–1643) King of France who made war on the Huguenots and took France into the Thirty Years' War to weaken France's political rival, Spain.

Peace of Alès Treaty in 1629 that ended France's religious wars, allowed Huguenots freedom of worship, but took away their fortified towns.

Unitarians Christians who denied the traditional doctrine of the Trinity.

diets In the Holy Roman Empire under Habsburg rule, representative assemblies dominated by the great nobility that sought increased control of government.

Poland-Lithuania Kingdom formed in 1569 from two previously independent states; included modern Poland, the Baltic states, Belarus, and most of Ukraine.

Ferdinand II (r. 1619–1637) Habsburg emperor who reestablished Catholicism in Bohemia and Austria but failed to do so in the empire as a whole.

Thirty Years' War General war, 1618–1648, between German Protestant princes and their foreign allies against the Habsburgs, who were allied with Catholic princes.

A la fin ces Voleurs infames et perdus ,   *Monstrent bien que le crime (horrible et noire engeance)*   *Et que cest le Destin des hommes vicieux*
Comme fruits malheureux a cet arbre pendus   *Est luy mesme instrument de honte et de vengeance ,*   *Desprouuer tost ou tard la iustice des Cieux .*

Thieving soldiers are executed in this etching from Jacques Callot's *Miseries of War*. A priest blesses the men as they are led up a ladder to be hung. A caption describes the executed as "infamous lost souls . . . hung like unhappy fruit." *(Erich Lessing/Art Resource, NY)*

The Habsburg victory in Bohemia had repercussions throughout Europe. The Spanish branch of the family used it to seize the Palatinate, a state on the Rhine River, and thereby expand its control of the "Spanish Road" that led north from Habsburg, Italy, to the Spanish Netherlands. Soon the king of Denmark entered the war as leader of the Protestants. But he was defeated and driven out of the empire in 1629. Victorious, Ferdinand II supposedly reaffirmed the 1555 Peace of Augsburg but in reality sought to strengthen Catholicism, not only in Habsburg lands but throughout the Empire. At this point, the Swedish phase of the war began, when the Lutheran king of Sweden, **Gustavus II Adolphus**, assumed leadership of the Protestant cause.

Gustavus Adolphus was a seasoned warrior, having already fought the Danes, the Russians, and the Poles. His chief concern was to expand Swedish power in the Baltic, as he feared that a Catholic Habsburg victory in Germany would threaten his interests. But his death in battle in 1632 spread confusion. When Ferdinand, realizing he would never be able to eradicate Protestantism, offered toleration for Lutherans, the war entered its French phase.

Although Louis XIII and his chief minister, **Cardinal Richelieu**, were devout Catholics, they feared that Ferdinand's reconciliation with the Protestants would increase the power of France's long-standing Habsburg enemy. They, therefore, entered the war, and for the next eleven years, French and Swedish troops continued to fight the Habsburgs. Almost all the fighting was done on German soil, and the devastation was terrible. The Thirty Years' War made the region's economic decline immeasurably worse. Overall, the population of the empire fell between 15 and 20 percent as the warring armies disrupted agriculture, sacked villages and cities, and spread disease among the civilian population. In areas of the worst fighting, such as Bohemia and the southern Baltic coast, population declined by 50 percent as people died or fled. Cities fell into debt because of the huge bribes they paid the warring armies, whether friend or foe, in hopes of averting pillaging by the troops.

The Peace of Westphalia

The war finally came to an end in 1648 with the **Peace of Westphalia.** It amended the 1555 Peace of Augsburg to allow rulers to choose Catholicism, Calvinism, or

Gustavus II Adolphus (r. 1594–1632) King of Sweden who led Protestant forces against the Habsburgs until his death in battle in 1632.

Cardinal Richelieu (1585–1642) Louis XIII's chief minister, who persuaded Louis to enter the Thirty Years' War against Ferdinand II.

Peace of Westphalia Peace in 1648 ending the Thirty Years' War, allowing states in the Holy Roman Empire to establish their own foreign policies and state religion.

VoiceVoiceVoiceVoice

Simplicius Simplicissimus Encounters Some "Merry Cavalrymen"

Jacques Callot was not alone in commenting on seventeenth-century warfare. In 1669, a German innkeeper, Johann von Grimmelshausen, who had fought as a soldier in the Thirty Years' War, published Simplicius Simplicissimus *(Simplest of Simpletons), a tale that mixes humor and horror in equal measure. It went through three editions in 1669 alone. In the excerpt that follows, young Simplicius/ The Simpleton, while working as a shepherd for his father, meets a band of cavalrymen and accompanies them to his home. Here he tells us what happened next.*

➡️ **Why does the author use these remarks to set up what follows?**

➡️ Though I hadn't intended to take the peace-loving reader into my father's home and farm along with these merry cavalrymen, the orderly progress of my tale requires me to make known to posterity the sort of abysmal and unheard-of cruelties occasionally perpetrated in our German war, and to testify by my own example that all these evils were necessarily required for our own good by the kindness of our Lord. For, my dear reader, who would have told me that there is a God in heaven if the warriors hadn't destroyed my [father's] house. . . .

➡️ **What effect in the reader does the author try to create when he mixes his account of pillaging with humor?**

➡️ The first thing these horsemen did in the nice black rooms of the house was to put in their horses. Then everyone took up a special job, a job having to do with death and destruction. Although some began butchering, heating water, and rendering lard, as if to prepare for a banquet, others raced through the house, ransacking upstairs and down. . . . Still others bundled up big bags of cloth, household goods, and clothes, as if they wanted to hold a rummage sale somewhere. What they did not intend to take along they broke up and spoiled. Some ran their swords into the hay and straw, as if there hadn't been hogs enough to stick. . . . Some shook the feathers out of beds and put bacon slabs, hams, and other stuff in the ticking, as if they might sleep better on these. ➡️ They flattened out copper and pewter dishes and baled the ruined goods. They burned up bedsteads, tables, chairs, and benches, though there were yards and yards of dry firewood outside the kitchen. Jars and crocks, pots and casseroles, all were broken, either because they preferred their meat broiled or because they thought they'd eat only one meal with us. In the barn, the hired girl was handled so roughly that she was unable to walk away, I am ashamed to report. They stretched the hired man out flat on the ground, stuck a wooden wedge in his mouth to keep it open, and emptied a milk bucket full of stinking manure drippings down his throat; they called it a Swedish cocktail. He didn't relish it and made a very wry face. By this means they forced him to take a raiding party to some other place where they carried off men and cattle and brought them to our farm. . . . I can't say much about the captured wives, hired girls, and daughters because the soldiers wouldn't let me watch their doings. But I do remember hearing pitiful screams from various dark corners and I guess that my mother and our Ursula had it no better than the rest. ➡️ Amid all this horror I was busy turning a roasting split and didn't worry about anything, for I didn't know the meaning of it. ➡️ In the afternoon I helped water the horses and that way got to see our hired girl in the barn. She looked wondrously messed up and at first I didn't recognize her. In a sickly voice she said, "Boy, get out of this place, or the soldiers will take you with them."

➡️ **Why does Grimmelshausen order the details of the pillaging in the way he does?**

➡️ **What is the point of this sentence?**

➡️ **Thinking back on this account, why would Grimmelshausen describe the destruction of a clearly prosperous, well-supplied peasant household?**

Source: The Adventures of Simplicius Simplicissimus by Hans Jacob Christoffel van Grimmelshausen. A modern translation with an introduction by George Schultz-Behrend, second revised edition. Rochester, New York: Camden House, 1993. Reprinted with permission.

Lutheranism as their state religion. Thus, Ferdinand II's dream of reestablishing Catholic dominance in the empire died forever. Like the Peace of Alès in France almost twenty years earlier, the Peace of Westphalia ratified a grudging recognition that the state's religious unity had been shattered and that new ways of forming community and community identity would have to be found.

Important political changes also occurred. The empire's boundaries were altered: the Swiss Confederation and the Dutch Republic were now placed outside the empire and recognized as independent states. Within the empire, states were granted the right to develop their own foreign policies without the emperor's approval. Both France and Sweden took imperial territory. Sweden gained control of the southern Baltic shore, while France received three important bishoprics on its eastern frontier.

Although France ended its war in Germany in 1648, war against the Habsburgs continued, with fighting between France and Spain along the borders of the Spanish Netherlands and the Pyrenees Mountains. In 1659, the two countries signed the **Treaty of the Pyrenees.** France extended its rule along the eastern Pyrenees and took important cities in the Spanish Netherlands. To celebrate the peace, the king of Spain agreed to the marriage of his eldest daughter, Anne, to the young king of France, Louis XIV, who had succeeded Louis XIII in 1643. Spain, exhausted by decades of warfare, never regained the position it held under Philip II. France was now the most powerful state in Europe.

Europeans were to fight many more wars after the Treaty of Westphalia, but religious motivations for conflict were never again as strong as they had been in the century before 1648. Now, states formed diplomatic and military alliances to advance their political and economic agendas while curbing those of their rivals, thereby creating an unstable and ever-shifting **balance of power** that prevented any one state from overwhelming the others.

Reformation and Revolution in the British Isles

⬇ How did the expectations of the English people change, or remain the same, from 1558 to 1660?
⬇ What were the relations among the English, Scots, and Irish in this period?

England experienced a golden age during the reign of Elizabeth I, the last Tudor monarch. But during the seventeenth century, the British Isles experienced religious wars when different Protestant groups fought

to control state churches. Like their counterparts on the continent, Protestant Scots and English believed that their communities should be united by a single church. Gradually, however, a party formed that called for toleration of different forms of Protestantism, but not of Catholicism. In Ireland, where Catholics predominated, English and Scots prejudice led to a brutal conquest of the island that established Protestant control. Conflict over religion also involved a struggle between the English monarch and Parliament for control of policy, which led to revolution in England, the execution of the king, and the establishment of a republic. In 1660, the republic came to an end and the monarchy was restored.

Elizabeth I

Elizabeth I was one of England's ablest and most popular rulers. At five feet ten inches, she was exceptionally tall for her time, and her flaming red hair, along with her trim, athletic body, caught everyone's attention. Elizabeth was a shrewd ruler who played on her womanhood, challenging contemporary views about women's weakness with her own force of will and political skill while instilling fear in anyone who challenged her. She was exceptionally well educated, speaking French, German, and Italian as well as reading Latin and Greek with ease. When Philip II, anxious to continue his English alliance, proposed marriage, the "virgin queen" turned him down, as she did everyone else, saying, "I am wedded to England." Her subjects hailed her as Good Queen Bess.

In addition to promoting a moderate form of Protestantism in England, Elizabeth faced two problems—the power of Spain and opposition in Ireland. Philip II's attempt to assert strong Spanish and Catholic control over the Netherlands threatened English economic interests there, since the Netherlands had long been the main market for English wool exports. Thus, in 1585, Elizabeth sent an army to aid the Dutch rebels against Philip. The next year, she sanctioned Sir Francis Drake's raids on Spanish colonial shipping. The English now identified themselves as pro-Protestant, anti-Catholic, and anti-Spanish. Thus religious, economic, and political issues deepened the rift between Spain and England, thereby ending the medieval al-

Treaty of the Pyrenees Treaty in 1659 ending the wars between France and Spain and leaving France the most powerful state in Europe.

balance of power Long-time European diplomatic aim for a distribution of power among several states that would prevent the dominance of any one state.

liance between the two countries that had led to the marriage of Catherine of Aragon to Henry VIII.

Rivalry with Spain also influenced developments in Ireland. Like her father and grandfather, Elizabeth was determined to strengthen English control of the island. But her attempts were met with a local rebellion led by Catholics, who received Spanish help, including the failed Spanish Armada of 1588. In the end, Elizabeth triumphed and transferred vast tracts of Irish land to loyal English Protestants, thus consolidating the conquest of the kingdom.

Elizabeth's England saw a flowering of literature, known as the **English Renaissance. William Shakespeare** wrote many of his plays during her reign, performing them at court and in his own theater, the Globe. Shakespeare's contemporary, **Christopher Marlowe,** wrote equally popular plays, including *The Jew of Malta,* which explored themes Shakespeare developed in *The Merchant of Venice,* and *The Massacre at Paris,* about the Saint Bartholomew's Day slaughter during France's religious wars. Marlowe's greatest play is *Doctor Faustus,* about a man who sells his soul to the Devil in return for power and knowledge.

Poetry also flourished in Elizabeth's reign. **Edmund Spenser** continued the tradition of epic poetry that stretched back to Dante Alighieri, Virgil, and Homer in his *Fairie Queene,* an elaborate allegory celebrating Protestant England's struggle with Catholicism and Spain. Spenser's friend and fellow poet **Sir Walter Raleigh** also extolled Elizabeth and Protestant England in verse. Both Raleigh and Spenser actively pursued politics. As a young man at court, Raleigh became a favorite of the queen, who commissioned him to attack Spanish shipping. In 1587 he founded a short-lived colony on Roanoke Island off present-day North Carolina, and in 1595 he led the first English expedition into South America, sailing up the Orinoco River in search of a fabled kingdom ruled by El Dorado, a man covered in gold. No gold was found, but his account of the expedition established him as a master of the literature of discovery and exploration. When Elizabeth began her conquest of Ireland, both Raleigh and Spenser joined her forces and were rewarded with estates confiscated from the rebels.

Elizabeth's refusal to marry was based more on political calculation than on personal preference; she feared the challenges to her power and independence that submission to a husband might bring. As the years passed, however, the problem of succession became acute since her heir was her cousin, **Mary Stuart, Queen of Scots,** the Catholic widow of King Francis II of France and a relative of the Guises. After Francis's death, Mary had returned to Scotland, where she married a Scots nobleman and had a son,

James. Mary's religion also caused problems in newly Calvinist Scotland, and in 1568 she fled to England after nobles deposed her and seized James. Elizabeth promptly imprisoned Mary because her Catholicism made her a magnet for those who favored the old church. Rumors of Catholic plots swirled around Mary for years. In 1587, when the rumors seemed to stick, Elizabeth had her beheaded.

The Early Stuart Monarchs

In 1603, Mary Stuart's son, **James VI** of Scotland, succeeded the virgin queen as **James I** of England and Ireland, and, for the first time, the separate kingdoms of Scotland and England were ruled by the same person. James had an excellent mind and published ten works, including a *Counterblast to Tobacco* that denounced smoking as "loathsome to the eye, hateful to the nose, harmful to the brain, [and] dangerous to the lungs." His greatest literary achievement was to sponsor a new translation of the Christian Bible for use in the Anglican Church. Published in 1611 and known as the **King James Version,** it has shaped the English language down to the present.

Two issues dominated James's reign and that of his son, **Charles I:** religion and relations between king and Parliament. Henry VIII and Elizabeth had used Parliament to implement the English Reformation, thereby

English Renaissance   Flowering of English literature during Elizabeth I's reign.

William Shakespeare   (1564–1616) England's greatest playwright, author of *The Merchant of Venice, The Tempest, Othello,* and many other plays and poems.

Christopher Marlowe   (ca.1564–1593) Playwright in Elizabeth I's reign, author of the play *Doctor Faustus* and a contemporary of William Shakespeare.

Edmund Spenser   (1553–1599) Poet and author of the epic poem *The Fairie Queene.*

Sir Walter Raleigh   (ca.1554–1618) Privateer, explorer, poet, and favorite of Elizabeth I.

Mary Stuart, Queen of Scots   (r. 1542–1587) Cousin of Elizabeth I and heir to the English throne whose Catholicism led to her execution.

James VI/James I   (r. 1567/1603–1625) Son of Mary, Queen of Scots, king who ruled in Scotland as James VI from 1567 and in England and Ireland as James I from 1603.

King James Version of the Bible   Translation of the Bible sponsored by King James I for use in the Church of England and published in 1611.

Charles I   (r. 1625–1649) King of England, Ireland, and Scotland who was beheaded by order of Parliament in 1649.

giving it a permanent place in the country's political life. But the exact nature of Parliament's authority was disputed. Both James and Charles believed that God appointed kings to rule and that they were accountable to Him alone. But they also knew that Parliament had a traditional right to raise taxes. For its part, Parliament believed the king could formulate state policy, but it claimed the right to criticize policy. James rejected this right. Parliament, he said, was no place "for every rash and hair-brained fellow to propose new laws of his own invention." At stake in these conflicts was a fundamental political issue: Should Parliament simply express opinions, or should it have a voice in policymaking? Traditions of strong kingship, stretching back to the Middle Ages, favored the king, but Parliament's power to grant or withhold taxes enabled it to assess the policies its taxes would finance. James and Charles leaned toward royal absolutism, while Parliament favored a theory of limited royal rule.

Religion regularly divided king and Parliament. Like Elizabeth, James was a moderate Protestant, but he was married to a Catholic. His moderation and his wife raised suspicions among the **Puritans**, Calvinists who thought that the Anglican Church was not completely reformed. Puritans wanted no bishops, no church ceremony, more sermons, policing of people's behavior, and an effective Protestant foreign policy. Their suspicions of James were overcome in 1605 when the government discovered a Catholic plot to blow up the king, along with Parliament. Thereafter, James followed Elizabeth in treating English Catholics as traitors.

Anti-Catholicism also shaped English policy in Ireland. In 1597, another rebellion broke out in **Ulster**, in the northeastern part of the island. It ended just as the plot to blow up the king and Parliament was discovered. In the anti-Catholic backlash, the lands of the rebel Catholic leaders were confiscated and given to English owners, who then colonized them with some one hundred thousand Scottish Protestants. The Catholic Irish, viewed as "savages," were driven onto marginal lands. Later, habits learned in Ireland were transferred to North America, where settlers drove Indian "savages" off the lands they then farmed. Ulster was England's first successful colony.

In North America, the Virginia Colony boomed when tobacco was grown for export. James I may have hated the "pernicious weed," but his subjects loved it and Virginia's economic success was assured. Beginning in the 1620s, other colonies were founded, this time by religious dissidents upset with the monarchy's support of Anglicanism and persecution of Catholics. The Pilgrims, Protestant Separatists who, like the Anabaptists, believed that the church should

be a voluntary association, founded Plymouth Colony in 1620. In 1629, Puritans founded the Massachusetts Bay Colony, while English Catholics emigrated to Maryland in the 1630s. Unlike the colonies of Spain and Portugal, the English settlements were not directly sponsored by the state. Instead, they began as commercial ventures, like the Virginia Colony, or as religious havens.

James died in 1625, and his son became king as Charles I. Like his father, Charles had an unshakeable belief in his right to rule as he pleased. He also shared his father's views about Parliament. Between 1625 and 1629, the king clashed with parliamentary leaders who criticized his policies and refused to grant him money for his wars against Spain and in support of the Huguenots, questioning the success of his campaigns and criticizing the men in charge of them. Finally, in 1630, Charles decided to govern without Parliament and did not convene it for ten years.

Charles ruled well enough on his own for most of the 1630s. One policy, however, provoked growing opposition—reform of the Anglican Church. In 1633, the king appointed **William Laud** archbishop of Canterbury; Laud introduced new church ceremonies and ordered the clergy to adhere strictly to Elizabeth's 1559 Book of Common Prayer. The Puritans were outraged, seeing Laud's program as an attempt to reintroduce Catholic practices. Some of them left for North America, where they joined their fellow Puritans in Massachusetts. Others waited for a chance to turn on Laud. Laud's position was further weakened when he stated that the clergy alone, not the local laity, would control church affairs. He also ordered the restoration of church lands that the laity had taken over. These policies angered a large group of landowners with seats in Parliament, who now had economic and political reasons, as well as religious ones, for opposing the king and his archbishop.

Charles and Laud were not content to revamp the Church of England. In 1637, the king imposed the Book of Common Prayer, along with bishops, on the Presbyterian Church of Scotland. In response, in 1639, the

---

Puritans　Calvinists who wanted to eliminate bishops and favored more sermons, policing of people's behavior, and a strong Protestant foreign policy.

Ulster　Northeastern part of Ireland colonized by Scots and English Protestants after England's defeat of the local Catholics.

William Laud　(1573–1645) Archbishop of Canterbury who enforced Charles I's unpopular religious policies through royal courts.

In this woodcut print of the execution of Charles I, the blindfolded king, his hat set to the side, puts his neck on the chopping block and waits for the executioner's ax. An Anglican clergyman prays while armed guards and a crowd look on. *(Hulton Archive/Getty Images)*

Scots rebelled. Charles, now at war with his Scottish subjects, needed funds for an army. In 1640, he resummoned the English Parliament and demanded money from it.

Civil War, Revolution, and the Commonwealth

The new **Long Parliament** was filled with men angry at Laud and the king. It passed a bill stating that the king could not dissolve Parliament without its own permission (which Charles signed, probably inadvertently). Parliament removed Archbishop Laud and sent him to prison. It also passed an act requiring the king to call Parliament into session on a regular basis. In 1641, Charles was forced to sign a treaty with the Scots that gave the Scottish parliament a role in the appointment of royal ministers and conceded the Scottish parliament's right to oversee policy. The English Parliament promptly demanded the same concessions, and when Charles refused, it proposed a bill abolish-

ing bishops in the Church of England. At this point, another Catholic rebellion broke out in Ireland, and several thousand Protestants were massacred in Ulster. In 1642, Charles demanded money from Parliament for an army to subdue the Irish. When Parliament refused and started to form its own army, Charles declared war on Parliament.

England had now fallen into civil war. For the next seven years, the king and his supporters fought Parliament's army. Troops of both sides damaged crops and disrupted trade, while cold temperatures ruined the harvests of the late 1640s. By war's end, popular rebellions against both sides had broken out in various parts of the country.

In 1643, Parliament reorganized the Church of England along Presbyterian lines and then executed Laud. In 1645, Charles, finally defeated in battle,

Long Parliament English Parliament that sat from 1640 until 1660.

surrendered to the Scots, who turned him over to the English Parliament in 1647. In 1648, the army purged Parliament of those favoring monarchy, and the remaining members brought the king to trial on charges of treason and murder for his role in the civil war. Charles denied the court's legitimacy, proclaiming that "the king cannot be tried by any superior jurisdiction on earth." But Charles was convicted and publicly beheaded in London on January 30, 1649. When the executioner's ax fell on his neck, a huge groan went up from the crowd surrounding the scaffold, for it was a momentous event. Never before had an English court of law removed a monarch or the English people killed their king. Civil war had become revolution. England was now a republic.

Even as the civil war raged, the English engaged in an unprecedented debate over the nature of the state and the role of ordinary people in political life. Charles's growing unpopularity led many to go beyond older arguments about the king's relation to Parliament. The Levellers wanted to establish a democratic republic in England and allow all men to vote. Women activists supporting the Levellers petitioned Parliament on their behalf. Even more radical were the Diggers. Responding to economic hard times, they rejected the institution of private property and supported a form of communal ownership. Levellers and Diggers were always in a minority, but the very fact that they gave public voice to their ideas for reform stimulated popular thought about the nature of England's social order and raised questions about the political and economic identities of English men and women.

Oliver Cromwell

One of Parliament's generals in favor of Charles's execution was **Oliver Cromwell.** In 1649, Cromwell led an army to put down the rebellion in Ireland, where disruptions from fighting and crop failures had produced widespread famine; the Irish population fell by almost 40 percent. Cromwell's invasion delivered the final blows. His army massacred thousands, 80 percent of agricultural land was transferred to the Protestant minority, Catholicism was outlawed, and twelve thousand rebels were deported as penal slaves to Barbados and other English colonies in the West Indies. For the next two hundred years, English Protestant control of Ireland was assured.

With Ireland subdued, Cromwell turned to Scotland. Despite their differences with Charles I, most Scots favored the continuation of monarchy. After the king's execution, **Charles II,** Charles I's elder son, was summoned from exile and crowned Scottish king in 1650. Cromwell then invaded Scotland, forced Charles to flee, and established the rule of the English Parliament there. When Cromwell returned from Scotland, he quickly dominated the new English **Commonwealth,** as the republic was called. Cromwell believed that God had called him to leadership and guided his actions. In this he was exactly like the king he had helped to execute.

In 1651, Parliament attempted to break the Dutch shipping monopoly with the **Navigation Act,** which required overseas goods destined for England to be carried in English ships or ships of English colonies. The next year, Cromwell supported a war against the Dutch, telling them that "the Lord has declared against you." The war was short, and the act did little to limit Dutch trade, but it signaled England's rise as a commercial power and marked the beginning of government control of the emerging English Empire.

In 1653, Cromwell took the title of Lord Protector. Parliament continued to meet, but Cromwell and the army actually ruled. In 1655, after suppressing a royalist rebellion, Cromwell established a military dictatorship. Press censorship was instituted, and traditional local officials were replaced by major generals who ran local government and carried out a moral reform of society along strict Calvinist lines. Although Cromwell ruled as a Calvinist-inspired dictator, he abolished the requirement that everyone attend Calvinist church services, proclaiming, "I meddle not with any man's conscience." He did, however, ban Anglican and Catholic services for political reasons. By the 1650s, growing numbers of Protestants shared Cromwell's embrace of limited toleration.

Cromwell was offered a crown by some followers who wanted him to become King Oliver. He refused it. When he died in 1658, his son Richard became the new lord protector. Richard, however, did not have his father's political skills and soon retired to his country estates. His departure left England leaderless. Once

Oliver Cromwell (1599–1658) General on Parliament's side in English civil war who eventually established a military dictatorship in England.

Charles II (r. 1650/1660–1685) Son of Charles I, crowned king of Scotland in 1650 but ruled there only after 1660, when he was crowned king of England as well.

Commonwealth Name of the English republic from 1649 to 1660.

Navigation Act (1651) Parliamentary act requiring overseas goods destined for England to be carried in English ships or ships of English colonies.

again, a general stepped in; George Monck marched his army on London and negotiated the return of King Charles II, along with the House of Lords, the Church of England, and all its bishops. Oliver Cromwell's corpse was dug up and publicly hanged.

In 1660, it seemed that England's troubles had come full circle. Anglican monarchists viewed the post-1660 regime as a simple "restoration" of older ways. But in the wake of the Anglican Church being outlawed, a king executed, and a republic created, the merits of absolutist monarchy and limited constitutional government had been debated. There had been calls for democracy, communal ownership of property, and religious toleration. The debates and the conflicts unleashed during the civil war and revolution would shape the future of the English-speaking world.

Christian Reform, Religious Wars, and the Jews

> ↓ How did Europe's Jews define themselves as a community in the larger Christian world?
> ↓ What explains the rise and fall of Sabbatai Sevi?

The expulsion of Jews from Spain and Portugal destroyed Europe's largest Jewish community. In the early sixteenth century, Italy alone in western Europe had a significant Jewish population. In eastern Europe, Poland also admitted large numbers of Jews. Then, after 1550, Jews returned to western Europe when the Dutch Republic, Bohemia, France, and England once again admitted them. But the rising religious passions of the Christian reformations led to an upsurge of anti-Jewish attacks, including devastating massacres in eastern Poland. Like some Christians, Jews believed that the troubles they experienced were signs of the world's end. In 1665, thousands of them looked to a young Jew from Smyrna in Ottoman Turkey, Sabbatai Sevi, who proclaimed that he was the long-awaited Jewish Messiah.

Jews in Poland and Western Europe

Following their expulsion from England and France in the late Middle Ages, western European Jews were permitted to settle in Poland-Lithuania, where the Black Death had reduced the number of people on the agricultural estates of the king and the nobility. Soon Jews were working the land as peasants, supplying local needs as craftsmen, and serving as estate managers. Jews prospered with the growth of grain and timber exports to the west, acting as agents in organizing this trade. They also played an important role as moneylenders. By the end of the seventeenth century, Polish Jews numbered some 450,000, or about 4.5 percent of Poland's population and 75 percent of Jews worldwide.

Whether they lived in towns or the countryside, Jews were governed by local councils made up of prominent community members, who often dressed and acted like non-Jews. Like the Christian population, Jewish communities were hierarchically organized. At the top were a few rich and socially prominent people as well as rabbis and Talmudic scholars. Below them were craftsmen, peddlers, and shopkeepers. Lower still were the poor. Most Polish Jews were separated from the larger Christian population not only by religion but also by culture. Like the Arabic-speaking Moriscos of Spain, they spoke their own distinctive language, **Yiddish.** Aware of their minority position, the Jews worked hard to maintain a strong sense of community solidarity that fostered a distinctive Jewish identity. At times, however, internal tensions threatened to fracture the community, as when rich Jews adopted non-Jewish ways or well-to-do moneylenders seized land and other collateral from fellow Jews who defaulted on loans.

Beginning in the mid-sixteenth century, Jews started to return to western Europe. The largest Jewish community in the west, Rome excepted, was in Bohemia, where the Habsburgs encouraged Jewish settlement and used Jews as bankers and moneylenders. Bohemian nobles also courted Jews, who served as estate managers like their counterparts in Poland. Even Emperor Ferdinand II welcomed them, despite his determination to eliminate dissident Protestants. In his eyes, heretics were a greater danger to the Christian community than unbelievers. Throughout the Thirty Years' War, both the Habsburgs and the Swedes turned to the Bohemian Jews for the funds they needed to continue fighting.

The Dutch Republic also welcomed Jews. Both **Ashkenazim,** from Poland and Germany, and **Sephardim,** from Spain and Portugal, congregated in Amsterdam. Overall, some eighteen thousand Jews settled in the

Yiddish German dialect spoken by the Ashkenazim, derived from German and Hebrew and written in Hebrew characters.

Ashkenazim Jews of Europe who settled mainly in the Holy Roman Empire, Poland, Lithuania, and other eastern regions.

Sephardim Jews from the Iberian Peninsula.

Dutch Republic. Although this community was smaller than the ones in Poland and Bohemia, it played a crucial role in the booming Dutch economy. Its original members were Sephardim who had economic ties to merchants in the Iberian Peninsula, the Spanish Empire, and Brazil. The Dutch West India Company exploited these contacts to develop trade with Spain and to push into the profitable trade with the New World. Some four thousand Portuguese Jews eventually settled in the Dutch colonies.

France and England also permitted new Jewish settlements. French kings permitted expelled Portuguese Jews to settle in some cities as part of their struggle with Habsburg Spain. In England, Oliver Cromwell fostered a growing Jewish community in London. Like many Protestants, Cromwell believed that the conversion of the Jews to Christianity, along with the destruction of the Antichrist (that is, the pope), would usher in the Second Coming of Christ. He, therefore, welcomed the visit of an Amsterdam rabbi who came to London seeking formal recognition of a Jewish community there. The rabbi also had a religious agenda; for him, Jews had to settle in all parts of the world as a prelude to the coming of the Jewish Messiah. Although formal recognition of an English Jewish community was not forthcoming, as merchants and clergy resisted, Jews were allowed unofficially to settle in London and engage in trade.

War in Poland

In 1648, the year of the Peace of Westphalia, war broke out in Poland-Lithuania when **Cossacks**, warriors protecting lands bordering on Muslim territory, rebelled in Ukraine. The rebellion was provoked in part by a decision to reduce the number of Cossacks in the Polish army and in part by religious clashes—the Polish Cossacks were Russian Orthodox, while the kings of Poland were Roman Catholics. Catholic-Orthodox tensions were particularly high in the seventeenth century after the **Union of Brest-Litovsk**, which united bishops in Polish Ukraine with the Roman Catholic Church, despite Orthodox Christian opposition.

The Cossack revolt of 1648 inaugurated nineteen years of warfare. Like the Thirty Years' War, it started as a local dispute but was soon internationalized when both Sweden and Russia joined in. In 1655, Sweden, fresh from territorial gains during the Thirty Years' War, hoped to amass more lands on the Baltic's southern shore. The Russian **tsar** also used the war for territorial gain. The Swedes withdrew in 1660 after receiving territory from the king of Denmark, with

whom they were also at war. The Russians signed a peace treaty in 1667 that gave them the eastern half of Ukraine.

The devastation caused by two decades of warfare was immense. The Polish economy was disrupted, and food shortages occurred, followed by periods of famine. Predictably, armies of all sides spread disease, and epidemics ravaged a population already weakened by disruptions in the food supply. At the beginning of the war, the Cossacks slaughtered Catholics, Jews, and signers of the Union of Brest-Litovsk indiscriminately. These atrocities rivaled Ivan the Terrible's mass executions and matched the worst incidents during the French Wars of Religion. Like the French slaughters, those in Poland were intended to ritually degrade the bodies of a socially polluting enemy. Eventually, all warring sides committed atrocities, and all Poles were victims of them, but Polish Jews suffered disproportionately. The lucky ones fled to Jewish communities in western Europe. Others fled south into Muslim lands, where they were enslaved and then sold in Constantinople. In all, some forty to fifty thousand Jews, a quarter of Poland's Jewish population, perished in the war.

Sabbatai Sevi

In some Jewish circles, 1648 was widely held to be the year in which the Jewish Messiah would appear to gather the exiled children of the Covenant, lead them into the land of Israel, and rebuild the Temple in Jerusalem. The greeting "Next year in Jerusalem!" gave voice to this longing for restoration, which grew more intense after the expulsions from Spain and Portugal and the slaughters in Poland. But the Messiah did not appear. Then, in 1665, a twenty-nine-year-old Jew, **Sabbatai Sevi**, proclaimed that he was the Messiah.

Sevi grew up in Izmir, a commercial center on the western coast of Turkey. From an early age, he excelled in Jewish religious studies and was eventually ordained a rabbi. Before Sevi claimed to be the Mes-

Cossacks   Warriors organized locally to protect frontier lands bordering on Muslim territory; also used by Polish kings and Russian tsars as fighting forces.

Union of Brest-Litovsk   Agreement in 1596 uniting Orthodox bishops in Polish Ukraine with the Roman Catholic Church.

tsar   (in Russian, "Caesar") Title of the rulers of Russia.

Sabbatai Sevi   (1626–1676) Jew from Izmir of Sephardic ancestry who proclaimed he was the Messiah.

In the upper part of this engraving, Sabbatai Sevi is enthroned as the Messiah. The Hebrew inscription above his head reads "The Crown of Sabbatai." Below him is an inscription from the prophet Jeremiah, "I will cause to sprout for David the root of righteousness." In the bottom panel the tribes of Israel study Torah under the Messiah's guidance. *(From Freely, John, The Lost Messiah: In Search of Sabbatai Sevi [London: Viking Press, 2001]. Reproduced with permission.)*

siah, he had wandered around the Ottoman Empire from Greece to Egypt. He experienced dramatic shifts in his mental state, ranging from deep depression to frenzied exaltation. He also fell into religious ecstasies that some believed revealed his Messianic status. Although it has been speculated Sevi suffered from bipolar disorder, there were also historical reasons for Sevi's intense spiritual experiences, for they were at the heart of the Jewish mystical tradition centered on the **kabbala** that Spanish Jews had developed during the late Middle Ages.

In 1665, after his return to Izmir, Sevi openly proclaimed that he was the Messiah and started to gather followers. He dressed in royal robes and ordered changes in Jewish worship, turning fast days into feasts and altering synagogue services as signs of the dawning End Time of Jewish restoration. In the past,

other men had claimed to be the Messiah, but none attracted the following that Sevi gained. News of him spread quickly along trade routes. Soon Jews in the Ottoman Empire and Europe were performing the penitential acts prescribed for the time of the Messiah's arrival and saying prayers for Sevi in their worship. People said that Sevi was about to seize the sultan's crown or that he performed miraculous cures. In their own way, these proclamations were like contemporary Christians' belief in the Second Coming.

kabbala (from Hebrew, "tradition") Field of Jewish mysticism dating to the twelfth century but of greater interest in the sixteenth century.

Both Jews and Christians shared a hope for a decisive divine event that would right all wrongs and usher in a golden age of peace and prosperity. The economic hard times after 1550, along with a seemingly endless cycle of war, slaughter, and religious conflict, heightened these expectations in both communities.

In 1666, Sevi set out for Constantinople. Before he arrived, the Turks arrested him for disturbing the peace and jailed him. His followers were allowed to visit, and he continued to act as the Messiah and even signed his letters, "I am your God Sabbatai Sevi." In September, Sevi was brought before the sultan and threatened with execution. He then converted to Islam, and the sultan named him Mehmet Efendi, gave him a pension, and appointed him a doorkeeper in the royal palace. He died ten years later.

As news of Sevi's **apostasy** spread, shocked congregations throughout the Ottoman Empire and Europe erased his name from their records. From the beginning, many Jews had doubted Sevi's claims and had been appalled at his self-deification. A few, however, continued to believe that Sevi was the Messiah. His conversion was part of his Messianic strategy, they thought, by which he burrowed like a worm into Islam with the aim of destroying it from the inside out. Some of his followers also converted to Islam and established communities that lasted into the twentieth century.

The furor over Sabbatai Sevi marked a turning point in Jewish history. Following his apostasy, any claim of Messiahship was severely scrutinized. Forms of Judaism that emphasized present faithfulness to the Law and focused less on the mystery of the Messiah's future appearance gained ground. Nevertheless, the kabbalistic traditions that had inspired Sevi continued to serve as a rich matrix for future mystical movements within Judaism.

apostasy   Act of renouncing one's religious beliefs.

Summary

Review Questions

↑ How did political and religious issues shape the nature of warfare?

↑ How did the meaning of community change during a century of conflict?

↑ How did religious conflict affect the states of Europe?

After 1550, the European economy turned downward. A price revolution aggravated an economic crisis brought on by overpopulation. Hard times produced widespread anxiety, which in turn led to social unrest, fears that the world was coming to an end, and panic about witches. For the next century, religious strife tore Europe apart.

In Spain, Philip II undertook aggressive campaigns against Muslims and Protestants. He defeated his Morisco subjects in Spain and fought the Turks at sea. He also opposed the Protestant movement in England and fought his own Protestant subjects in the Netherlands. When he died in 1598, Protestantism had survived, and Spain's military might was in decline. The Netherlands were split in half, and the economically prosperous Protestant provinces of the north were virtually independent from Spanish rule. England under Elizabeth I was Protestant and prepared to challenge Spain on the seas and in the New World. Henry IV of France had granted religious toleration, along with a good deal of political autonomy, to the Huguenots, but he had also strengthened the French monarchy.

Warfare continued throughout the first half of the seventeenth century. Europeans believed that religious unity was essential for the well-being of the community, but renewed warfare failed to reestablish the unity lost in the sixteenth century. Louis XIII defeated the Huguenots and stripped them of their political autonomy, although they still had the right to worship. In Germany, the Thirty Years' War failed to curb Protestantism in the Holy Roman Empire, where the emperor's power was greatly weakened. When the war ended, German princes now had a third religious option for their states, Calvinism, in addition to the Lutheranism and Catholicism allowed in 1555. In England, Anglicans and Puritans fought each other in a civil war that ended in the execution of Charles I, the dismantling of the Anglican Church, and the establishment of a commonwealth. In 1660, monarchy and Anglicanism were restored when the republican experiment of the 1650s crumbled following Oliver Cromwell's death. All English Protestants agreed that the Catholic Irish must be conquered. The creation of the Ulster colony and Cromwell's campaign in Ireland established England's dominance of the island. By 1660, it was clear that the religious unity of western and central Europe was shattered, despite fierce attempts on all sides to preserve it.

Europe's Jews were allowed once again to settle in the west, where some benefited from the global trading networks established in the sixteenth century. But Jews were still often despised and sometimes suffered catastrophic losses, like the ones occurring in Poland after the Cossack rebellion of 1648. Some Jews, like some Christians, hoped for divine deliverance from the troubled times. But the rapid rise and shocking betrayal of the self-proclaimed Messiah

Sabbatai Sevi turned many Jews away from a belief that their deliverance was at hand. Like the Christians, they now lived in a religiously fractured world.

← Thinking Back, Thinking Ahead →

Once the principle of religious toleration was accepted, what changes would people eventually make in their understanding of religious and political allegiances?

ECHO

War Stories

This chapter opens and ends with a war story. War stories have been told in the western world for thousands of years. Some early ones are found in Homer's *Iliad* and the monuments of Egyptian pharaohs. From the beginning, war stories have been told with words and images. Homer wrote his stories in verse, while the pharaohs had workers carve battle scenes on the walls of their mortuary temples. Homer's warriors lose battles and die in them. In his temple, the pharaoh never loses.

Over the last hundred and fifty years, war stories in ever-greater numbers have circulated more and more quickly during conflicts. In the nineteenth century, American reporters wrote stories about the great battles of the Civil War, and Mathew Brady, following in Jacques Callot's footsteps, took shockingly graphic photographs of battlefield carnage. In World War I and World War II, carefully edited film footage of battle was shown weekly in newsreels to the civilian population in movie theaters. During the Vietnam War, reporters using portable video cameras shot fighting scenes that were shown every night on network television news. Never had scenes of war been seen so often by so many people. Their graphic detail alarmed some, who thought that the news broadcasts weakened the country's resolve to fight the war. During the 1991 Gulf War television cameras and news reporters were not allowed on the battlefield. In 2003, during the war in Iraq, the Department of Defense allowed some reporters and cameramen to be "embedded" with troops entering Iraq. But it also banned television coverage of flag-draped coffins from Iraq arriving at Andrews Air Force Base. Shortly thereafter, the president of the United States flew onto a navy aircraft carrier to be televised in front of a banner announcing "Mission accomplished!" Then pictures of torture at Abu Ghraib Prison in Baghdad appeared on the Internet.

Governments know the power of images in time of war and therefore try to control what people see. But some images seem always to get beyond their control. On the other hand, there is always the suspicion that images have been doctored to make a point. What lies just beyond the camera's frame? Has something been airbrushed out or pasted in? Digital photography, which does away with the fixed film image, makes these questions even more important and faith in the truth of pictures even more risky.

Suggested Readings

Cameron, Euan, ed. *Early Modern Europe: An Oxford History.* New York: Oxford University Press, 2001. A recent general account.

Davies, Norman. *The Isles: A History.* New York: Oxford University Press, 2001. The history of all the British Isles.

Edwards, John. *The Jews in Christian Europe, 1400–1700.* New York: Routledge, 1988. A good general account.

Freely, John. *The Lost Messiah: The Search for the Mystical Rabbi Sabbatai Sevi.* Woodstock, N.Y.: Overlook Press, 2001. The most recent account of Sevi's life and career.

Kamen, Henry. *Spain, 1469–1714: A Society of Conflict.* New York: Longman, 1983. A good study of Philip II.

Schama, Simon. *The Embarrassment of Riches: An Interpretation of Dutch Culture in the Golden Age.* New York: Random House/Vintage Books, 1997. An excellent examination of the formation of Dutch identity in the seventeenth century.

Watts, Sheldon J. *A Social History of Western Europe, 1450–1720.* London: Hutchinson University Library for Africa, 1984. An older account with a great deal of information.

Websites

Sections and links to readings on many of the topics discussed in this chapter, **Internet Modern History Sourcebook,** at www.fordham.edu/halsall/mod/modsbook03.html

On the history of Jews in early modern Europe, **Internet Jewish History Sourcebook,** at http://www.fordham.edu/halsall/jewish/jewishsbook.html

Information on artists and their work in the seventeenth century, **Web Gallery of Art,** at http://www.wga.hu/frames-e.html?/welcome.html

State Building and the European State System, 1648–1789

1500 B.C.E.	1000 B.C.E.	500 B.C.E.	1 B.C.E./1 C.E.

1640
Frederick William becomes elector of Brandenburg

1657
Leopold I becomes Holy Roman emperor

1660
Monarchy is restored in the British Isles

1661
French King Louis XIV becomes his own prime minister

1682
Peter the Great becomes tsar

1688
Glorious Revolution begins

1640	1650	1660	1670	1680	1690	1700	1710

Europe in 1715

In 1715, when Louis XIV died, France was still the dominant power in Europe. But other centers of power—the Austrian Habsburg lands, Great Britain, Russia, and a small newcomer, Prussia—were prepared to challenge France. After 1715, how did the ambitions of all these states affect the goal of maintaining a European wide balance of power?

Austrian Hapsburg lands
Prussian lands
Swedish lands
Boundary of Holy Roman Empire
Major battle

SWEDEN

NORWAY · Oslo

KINGDOM OF DENMARK

North Sea

DENMARK

GREAT BRITAIN

SCOTLAND · Edinburgh

IRELAND · Dublin

ENGLAND

London

UNITED PROVINCES · Utrecht

BRANDENBURG-PRUSSIA · Berlin

SAXONY

HOLY ROMAN EMPIRE

PALATINATE

LORRAINE · Strasbourg

ALSACE

BOHEMIA

AUSTRIA

BAVARIA

Vienna

SILESIA

EAST PRUSSIA

Baltic Sea

Vistula

POLAND · Warsaw

LITHUANIA

ESTONIA

LIVONIA

INGRIA · St. Petersburg

· Moscow

RUSSIAN EMPIRE

Kiev

Dnieper

Poltava 1709

Elbe

Rhine

ATLANTIC OCEAN

FRANCE

Versailles · Paris

Loire

Garonne

· Toulouse

SWITZERLAND

SAVOY

MILAN

GENOA

Po

REPUBLIC OF VENICE · Venice

Danube

Buda · Pest

HUNGARY

Dniester

Black Sea

PORTUGAL

Lisbon ·

SPAIN

Madrid ·

Duero

Tagus

Ebro

CATALONIA

Marseilles ·

Corsica (Genoa)

TUSCANY

Rome ·

PAPAL STATES

KINGDOM OF NAPLES

Naples ·

Adriatic Sea

MONTENEGRO

OTTOMAN EMPIRE

Constantinople ·

GIBRALTAR (Gr. Br.)

Minorca (Gr. Br.)

Balearic Is.

SARDINIA

Corfu (Rep. of Venice)

MOREA (Rep. of Venice)

MOROCCO

ALGERIA

Mediterranean Sea

SICILY (Savoy)

TUNIS

TRIPOLI

OTTOMAN EMPIRE

0   200   400 Km.

0   200   400 Mi.

| 500 C.E. | 1000 C.E. | 1500 C.E. | 2000 C.E. |

1740
Frederick the Great becomes king of Prussia

War of the Austrian Succession begins

1756
Seven Years' War begins

1763
Seven Years' War ends

| 1720 | 1730 | 1740 | 1750 | 1760 | 1770 | 1780 | 1790 |

Choice Choice Choice

Louis XIV

Louis XIV of France embodied the ideal of the vigorous, state-building monarch. Throughout his long reign, he dominated European diplomacy and warfare, and his glittering court established standards of grandeur that other monarchs tried to imitate. As a young man, he seemed more interested in the pleasures of the court than in politics. In fact, however, he emerged as one of Europe's ablest and most disciplined rulers following the death of his prime minister, Cardinal Mazarin. (Château de Versailles/Laurie Platt Winfrey, Inc.)

Louis XIV Decides to Rule France on His Own

On March 9, 1661, France's prime minister, Cardinal Jules Mazarin, wracked by gout, kidney stones, and fluid in his chest cavity, died. When news of Mazarin's death was announced, the royal court was abuzz with rumors about who would be next in line for the position. Within hours of Mazarin's death, King Louis XIV made his choice: himself. Standing before the highest officials in the kingdom he announced: "Up to this moment I have been pleased to entrust the government of my affairs to the late Cardinal. It is now time that I govern them myself. [Monsieur the Chancellor], you will assist me with your counsels when I ask for them. I request and order you to seal no orders except by my command. And you, . . . my secretaries of state, I order you not to sign anything, not even a passport . . . without my command."

Courtiers were astonished by Louis' announcement. The twenty-three-year-old seemed more interested in dancing the role of the god Apollo in court ballets and engaging in sexual escapades with young ladies-in-waiting than sitting at his desk and shuffling through reports on wool weaving in this province or sheep farming in that one. Besides, Louis' announcement that he would rule by himself broke with family tradition. Both his father and grandfather had relied on strong prime ministers to help them with the affairs of state, and since 1643, Cardinal Mazarin had guided France skillfully through the last years of the Thirty Years' War. In the 1640s, France seethed with unrest as taxes rose to pay for the war and great nobles rebelled against Mazarin's policies. There was fearful talk that France—like England—would slip into a civil war. Would monarchy be attacked in France? Would the French king be executed like Charles I? Would the French Calvinists, tolerated but no longer politically independent, rise up like the Puritans and declare a republic? Mazarin had played on these fears of chaos and bloodshed in order to keep the monarchy safe.

By 1653, calm was restored, and the fourteen-year-old Louis XIV's throne was secure. Louis believed that Mazarin had saved the monarchy, and his devotion to his prime minister knew no bounds. For the rest of his life, Mazarin continued to advise the king on policy and even chose his companions, dismissing young men he thought unfit for association with Louis. Mazarin also amassed the largest personal fortune ever known under the monarchy. On his deathbed, he gave it to the king.

Given Mazarin's role in guiding the French monarchy through tumultuous times and the seeming frivolity of the young Louis, it is no wonder that courtiers looked askance at the young king's surprising decision to rule on his own. In the end, however, Louis fooled them all. For the next fifty-four years, until his death in 1715, he refused to appoint a prime minister and directed the affairs of state himself. The discipline, endurance, and stamina this "bureaucrat king" showed in running the government became legendary. Both the successes and the failures of his very long reign rested on his determination to control all the affairs of state.

Introduction

Louis XIV was one of the most successful rulers in the years after the Peace of Westphalia and the very embodiment of absolutism—a style of monarchy that spread across Europe in the seventeenth and eighteenth centuries. Royal absolutism was a way to build the power and effectiveness of the central state. A century of religious warfare had taught Louis and other absolutist rulers that only a strong central government, coupled with a policy of either tolerating or crushing religious dissent, could bring political stability.

Although wars continued to be fought after 1648, religiously motivated warfare declined. Increasingly, the roots of conflict focused on issues of territorial expansion, power, and prestige. By the mid-eighteenth century, European warfare had also taken on global dimensions as states fought each other for control of overseas empires. To meet the challenges of European and global warfare, rulers increased the size of their armies and brought them under tight state control. Absolute monarchs saw war as a means to enlarge their territories and, simultaneously, to deny the territorial ambitions of other states. In their eyes, Europe, and then the world, was like a chessboard on which each state's diplomatic and military moves were met with countermoves from other states. But war and territorial gains were expensive, and throughout the century after the Peace of Westphalia, states increased taxes, tried to collect them more efficiently, and sought to improve their economies to increase their tax base.

All over Europe, the needs of almost continual warfare drove expansion in state administration and improvements in financial and judicial bureaucracies. State authority aimed to direct economies and to reach more aspects of people's lives. Key to these expansions was the creation of officials accountable to the Crown. In western Europe, loyal middle-class people were recruited into these bureaucracies, while in eastern Europe, monarchs drew their officials from the ranks of the lesser nobility. The goodwill of the public in general was also essential, as was the allegiance of the nobles in particular, since they constituted the political and social elite. Some states also tried to increase services to their subjects, such as infrastructure improvement and better policing of town and country.

On the European continent, states tended to develop along the absolutist model pioneered by Louis XIV in France. In Britain, however, the rebellion and revolution of the mid-seventeenth century ended the absolutist ambitions of the early Stuart kings. After 1660, their successors ruled with Parliament in a constitutionally limited monarchy. The joint rule of king and Parliament ensured a high degree of political stability and proved important to Britain's success in empire building, trade, and manufacturing. In some parts of Europe, warfare and state building fostered a strong sense of national identity as people embraced the policy perspectives of their rulers and defined themselves as the opposite of their enemies. In other European states, however, the religious and ethnic roots of collective identity were so strong that a common sense of community centered on the state failed to emerge.

Absolutism in France, 1648–1740

⬇ What were the characteristic features of French royal absolutism?

⬇ What were the outcomes of the French monarchy's attempts to strengthen the state?

Louis XIV of France dominated Europe in the second half of the seventeenth century. After assuming personal rule (see Choice), he launched wars that added to France's territory. He also continued the policy of stamping out Protestantism in his kingdom, tarnishing his image in Protestant Europe. Eventually continual warfare drained his treasury and forced him to reorganize the French state. His successor built on Louis' successes, expanding state activity in several new directions. But France was also rocked by a new religious crisis, which pitted the state against a dissident Catholic movement.

The Sun King at Versailles

Since 1500, Europe's royal courts had grown in size. In the 1520s, the French court had just over five hundred members. **Louis XIV's** court had ten thousand, half of them nobles. For the nobles, closeness to the king brought honor, appointments in the royal army, and pensions. Since nobles had a prickly sense of self-worth, a tradition of military service, and extravagant lifestyles that strained their purses, Louis' attentions were highly prized. Thus nobles flocked to the king's court, and, as he established a working relationship with this powerful elite, Louis was also able to keep his eye on them.

At court, the entire day focused attention on the king. From his rising to his bedtime, great nobles

Louis XIV (r. 1638–1715) King of France and the most powerful ruler in Europe during the second half of the seventeenth century.

Chronology

1640	Frederick William becomes elector of Brandenburg
1657	Leopold I becomes Holy Roman emperor
1660	Charles II is restored as king of England, Ireland, and Scotland
1661	Louis XIV becomes his own prime minister
1672–1679	Dutch War between Louis XIV and the Dutch Republic
1682	Peter I the Great becomes tsar
1685	Louis XIV revokes Edict of Nantes
1688–1689	Glorious Revolution dethrones James II
1700–1721	Great Northern War between Russia and Sweden
1701–1713	War of the Spanish Succession between Louis XIV and most of Europe
1702	Anne becomes queen of England, Ireland, and Scotland
1707	England and Scotland unite to form the kingdom of Great Britain
1711	Charles VI becomes Holy Roman emperor
1713	Pope condemns the Jansenists
1713	Spain grants Britain the *asiento*
1714	George I of Hanover becomes king of Great Britain
1715	Louis XV becomes king of France
1727	George II becomes king of Great Britain
1740–1748	War of the Austrian Succession ends in a draw
1756–1763	Seven Years' War leads to British and Prussian victories
1762	Catherine II the Great becomes empress of Russia
1772	First partition of Poland
1780	Joseph II becomes ruler of the Habsburg lands
1780s	Joseph II abolishes serfdom in the Habsburg lands
1790s	Leopold II reestablishes serfdom in the Habsburg lands

attended him. At midday, Louis ate alone while courtiers stood and watched. The dinner table etiquette was so complicated that it took three men seven minutes to give the king a glass of wine. When Louis went to Mass, he sat in a balcony, looking down at the altar, while the court, turning their backs on the priest, sat looking at Louis. This distinctive arrangement emphasized the king's pivotal position between God and France. Louis believed that he ruled by **divine right** because God had decreed monarchy to be the correct form for France's government and had called Louis to the throne as the eldest legitimately born son of his father. The elaborate court rituals also proclaimed that Louis, as an absolute monarch, was the only real political player in France. He alone made policy and laid down the law. He was also the only person who unified the different regions and peoples of France, since he alone ruled over them all.

Louis was also the perfect gentleman, famous for his politeness and beautiful manners. Courtiers commented that they rarely saw him lose his temper. If someone misbehaved, a simple look or short comment was enough to convey his displeasure. Like court etiquette, the king's gentlemanly behavior had a political purpose, since it reinforced a new trend in noble society that emphasized polite speech and good manners as necessary qualities for the highborn and powerful. Encouraged by noblewomen in Paris, who presided over **salons** in which this conduct was

divine right   Theory that kings were called by God to rule and that opposition to the king was therefore opposition to God.

salons   Meetings in great Parisian homes presided over by well-born women who set the style for discussions of literature, science, and other matters of current interest.

This aerial view of Versailles shows the palace as it appeared toward the end of Louis XIV's reign. Its grandeur is apparent. At the top, the town's boulevards converge on the palace front. The rear façade looks out over the palace's large gardens and park. Louis' personal rooms were located in the center of the central wing to emphasize that everything at Versailles was centered on the king. *(Yann Arthus-Bertrand/Altitude)*

required, the new emphasis on manners disciplined the often violent and crude behavior of nobles.

The setting for Louis' court was **Versailles**, originally a hunting lodge for Louis XIII. Throughout his reign, the king worked to turn his father's modest building into Europe's most magnificent palace. He laid out acres of grounds decorated with lavish fountains. Louis adopted the sun god Apollo as Versailles' symbol and symbolically identified himself with Apollo as the "Sun King," spreading radiance on his lands and subjects. At Versailles, an entire town sprang up to meet the needs of courtiers and their thousands of servants. The palace itself was the centerpiece in a carefully orchestrated propaganda campaign designed to celebrate the king's *gloire*—that is, his glory or renown—in architecture, painting, sculpture, and other artistic media. Above all, Louis' *gloire*

rose when he led his troops into battle and fought other kings for territory, honor, and prestige.

Forty Years of Warfare

The early years of Louis' reign were marked by peace at home and victory abroad. But after 1668, the king, increasingly worried about the weakness of France's eastern border, launched a series of wars. The greatest of these campaigns was the **Dutch War**. Resenting

Versailles   Louis XIV's palace near Paris begun in the 1660s and housing the king after1683.

Dutch War   France's 1672–1678 invasion of the Netherlands aimed at breaking Dutch control of international trade and shipping.

Voice

Louis XIV Advises His Son

In 1666, Louis XIV assembled a team of collaborators to help him write his memoirs, which were intended for his young son, another Louis, when he became king. Such memoirs were common in early modern Europe. Charles V had written one for Philip II, and Cardinal Richelieu had composed one for Louis XIII. Although Louis' son died before the king and, therefore, could never follow his father's advice, the Memoirs *reveal the preoccupations and principles of Louis XIV some five years after he became his own prime minister.*

➡ **What do these remarks say about Louis' understanding of his relationship with his subjects?**

➡ My son, many very important considerations caused me to resolve to leave you, at the cost of much labor in the midst of my most important duties, these memoirs of my reign and principal acts. . . . I even hoped that in this way I might be the most valuable person in the world to you and consequently to my subjects. For no one with more talent and experience has ever reigned in France, and I do not hesitate to say to you that the higher one's position, the more it has qualities that no one may perceive or understand without occupying it . . .

➡ **Why would Louis argue that the happiness and tranquility of France depended on the union of authority in the king?**

➡ For it is generally agreed that nothing preserves the happiness and tranquility of the provinces with greater certainty than the perfect union of all authority in the person of the sovereign. ➡ The slightest division of authority always produces the greatest misfortunes, and whether the alienated portion falls into the hands of individuals or groups, it cannot remain there except in a state of violence . . .

➡ **Why would the king be concerned that a division of political authority would lead to the "greatest misfortunes"?**

➡ As for the work of [governing], my son, . . . I imposed upon myself the rule to labor twice daily. I cannot tell you what benefit I received immediately after making this resolution. I felt elevated in spirit and courage, a changed man, discovering in myself unknown resources and joyfully reproaching myself for having ignored them for so long. . . . I now seemed to be king and born to be so. As for those who were to assist me in my work, I resolved above all else not to appoint a first minister. . . . For in order to unite in myself all sovereign authority, I resolved after I had chosen my ministers to call upon them when they least expected it, even though their duties might involve details to which my role and dignity would not ordinarily allow me to stoop, so as to convince them that I would follow the same procedure regarding other matters at any time. The knowledge that resulted from this small step, which I took but rarely and more for diversion than because of any principle, instructed me gradually without effort regarding a thousand things that were of value in making general decisions. . . .

➡ **What do these remarks tell you about the king's personality?**

➡ Kings are often obliged to do things contrary to their inclinations and good nature. They should enjoy giving pleasure, but they must frequently punish and ruin persons whose good they naturally desire. The interest of the state should take precedence. One should counter one's inclinations and not place oneself

➡ **How did Louis' concern to promote the interest of the state shape his behavior toward others?**

in position to regret mishandling something important because some individual's interest interfered and diverted attention from the aims that one should have for the grandeur, the good, and the power of the state. . . . The mistakes that I have made and have given me infinite pain have been caused by kindness or allowing myself to be too easily guided by others' advice. Nothing is as dangerous as weakness of any kind whatsoever.

Source: From *Louis XIV* by John B. Wolf. Copyright © 1968 by W. W. Norton & Company, Inc. Used by permission of W. W. Norton & Company, Inc.

the "maggots" who dominated European trade and shipping, in 1672 Louis ordered his generals to invade. In response, the Dutch **stadholder, William,** broke the dikes that protected his low-lying country and flooded it, as the government had against the Spanish in 1579. The strategy obviously caused much hardship for the Dutch, but it also bogged down the French. In the end, neither side could defeat the other, and a peace was signed in 1679. The chief consequence of the war was to alienate William, who was now dedicated to the defeat of France.

To further challenge Dutch economic predominance, Louis' financial minister, **Jean-Baptiste Colbert,** developed a strategy for increasing France's national wealth. Known as **mercantilism,** it regulated economic policy for France's benefit. Consumers were encouraged to "buy French," and the state supported porcelain manufacturers capable of competing with imports from Asia. Monopolies were given to trading companies that would challenge the Dutch in overseas markets. Finally, French colonies were encouraged to grow. The population of Canada, known for its exports of furs and fish, rose from three thousand to twenty-five thousand, and the French founded settlements on the Gulf of Mexico at Mobile and New Orleans. These colonies secured the French in the North American heartland watered by the Mississippi and Ohio Rivers. **Saint-Domingue** and other colonies in the Caribbean specialized in cash crops, first tobacco and then sugar. Colbert's mercantilism established a new goal for the monarchy—the development of a national economic policy.

The mid-1680s brought a downturn in Louis' fortunes. In 1683, Louis refused to declare war on the Turks when they besieged Vienna. His decision was in line with France's traditional anti-Habsburg policy, but his refusal to help a Christian state attacked by Muslims scandalized many Europeans. Then, in 1689, Louis again went to war on France's eastern frontier, this time against Austria, a war that was quickly joined by the Dutch. The **War of the League of Augsburg** lasted until 1697. Louis, who had the largest army in Europe, strengthened the eastern frontier by conquering the province of Alsace and the

city of Strasbourg. But his finances were exhausted. In 1693, crop failures, caused by a drop in average yearly temperatures during the Little Ice Age, led to a terrible famine in which over a million people perished from hunger and disease.

Then an even greater political crisis loomed—the succession to the Spanish throne. Spain was ruled by Charles II, who was childless and feeble-minded. On his death, the vast Spanish possessions would have to pass either to the Austrian Habsburgs or to the French Bourbons, since both had claims to the crown. Although on his death in 1701 Charles had willed his lands to the Bourbons (Louis XIV's grandson, Philip), the Austrian Habsburgs disputed the will and went to war. This **War of the Spanish Succession** was the most devastating one Louis ever fought. It further shattered his finances, while a crop failure in 1709 was followed by the coldest winter of the century, leaving thousands frozen to death in their homes or on the roads. At war's end, Philip remained king of Spain and its empire, but the **Treaty of Utrecht** stipulated

stadholder   Chief executive in the Dutch Republic.

William   Stadtholder of the Dutch Republic (1672–1702) who later became king of England as William III (r. 1689–1702).

Jean-Baptiste Colbert   (1619–1683) Louis XIV's financial minister who implemented French mercantilist policies.

mercantilism   State-initiated economic policy encouraging exports, discouraging imports, and stimulating domestic industries.

Saint-Domingue   Sugar-producing French island colony in the Caribbean.

War of the League of Augsburg   (1689–1697) First of Louis XIV's two great wars fought against Austria, England, and the Dutch Republic.

War of the Spanish Succession   (1701–1713) Louis XIV's last great war, with France and Spain allied against the Austrians, Dutch, and English.

Treaty of Utrecht   Treaty signed in 1713 between France and the states fighting France that ended the War of the Spanish Succession.

that France and Spain could not be united as a single state. The Austrians received northern and southern Italy, along with the Spanish (now the Austrian) Netherlands.

Louis' many wars had increased the size of France by 12 percent and strengthened its eastern borders, now protected with state-of-the-art fortifications. But they had left a bitter legacy. In 1713, France was virtually bankrupt and the economy in a shambles. Moreover, other Europeans states, especially the Dutch Republic and Britain, feared that the Sun King was trying to upset the balance of power, which aimed to prevent any one state from establishing permanent military dominance in Europe.

A Unified French State

Within France, however, the wars had a unifying effect. Continuous warfare after 1688 had led Louis to search desperately for new revenue, and he sold waves of new offices. Then, in 1695, he took the unprecedented step of imposing a tax, the **capitation**, on all his subjects without exception. To supervise the collection of these taxes, Louis relied on his **intendants**, chief local royal administrators appointed on the basis of their ability and loyalty to the Crown. The intendants also gathered information about local conditions for the central government, and their reports allowed the king and his ministers to be better informed about the state of the economy. The result was better policymaking.

Thus, in his later years Louis was able to transform the French state. He reduced the power of the royal courts, known as **parlements**, which were now forbidden to criticize royal edicts. But their members were guaranteed their right to hold office and encouraged to enforce the law. As royal administration became more efficient, relations between the king and his subjects improved. Well-run parlements appealed to the king's subjects, who increasingly used them instead of church or landlords' courts, believing that they offered fairer rulings. Although taxation was still resented, the better-organized collection of taxes, along with a continuing shift to indirect taxation on items like paper and tobacco, took some of the sting out of payment. Even the royal armies were appreciated. During the religious wars earlier in the century, royal troops had been hated because of their violence and unruliness, but Louis' army, though huge, was well disciplined. His troops were now seen as protectors, welcomed by civilians and local vendors who supplied their needs. Under Louis, the French government functioned more fairly and efficiently.

The unity of France was important to Louis. As a child, he twice had to flee Paris for his safety, during a noble revolt against royal rule known as the **Fronde.** When he assumed personal rule of France, he was determined to prevent a similar rebellion. His policy of coaxing the most powerful nobles to his court with promises of honors, careers, and money was designed to tie them closely to the fortunes of the Crown.

Louis also sought to secure religious unity in France, believing the kingdom should have "one king, one law, one faith." In Louis' mind, the French Huguenots were potentially rebellious, so in 1685 he revoked the Edict of Nantes, thereby ending the limited religious toleration Louis' grandfather had granted. Huguenots who failed to convert to Catholicism were forced to flee. Around three hundred thousand, many of them middle-class merchants, left for the Dutch Republic, England, and America, spreading tales of the king's brutality. The Huguenot exodus cost France dearly, since it deprived the kingdom of a commercially skilled group just as the Anglo-French struggle for global commerce was beginning. Those still in France were subject to the quartering of troops in their houses, while in the mountainous south, where many Protestant peasants lived, royal troops burned hundreds of villages. In retaliation, peasants carried on a **guerrilla war** against the royal army. In Protestant Europe, news of the army's atrocities, coupled with exiles' grim accounts, produced a new image of Louis. The glorious Sun King was now a vicious tyrant. In France, however, most Catholics supported the king's policy. Louis' campaign against the Huguenots resulted not only from a belief that France should be religiously unified but also from fear that the Huguenots were secretly republicans, a charge that bedeviled them after English Calvinists declared a commonwealth in 1649.

Louis also quarreled with the pope by supporting

capitation Royal tax imposed on all French subjects in 1695 that introduced the idea of taxation of all people in defense of the state.

intendants In the second half of Louis XIV's reign, the most important local royal administrators, appointed by the king.

parlements France's highest royal courts, which enforced the king's edicts.

Fronde (1648–1653) Rebellion of the French nobles against Cardinal Mazarin and the regent, Queen Anne, during Louis' early years as king.

guerrilla war An undeclared, irregularly fought war.

the French clergy's adoption of the **Four Gallican Articles**, which proclaimed that church councils were superior to the pope and that the pope could not alter the way the French church was governed. The attack on the Huguenots was designed in part to heal the rupture with the pope. Relations with the papacy were further improved when Louis supported the pope's condemnation of the **Jansenists**, austere Catholics whose notions about human sinfulness struck some Catholics as too close to the views of John Calvin.

During the famine of 1709, Louis took the unprecedented step of issuing a letter directly asking his subjects for help. This appeal went against the principles of absolutism, in which the king was the only political player, but it was well received. As a result, king and subjects bonded in an effort to meet the crisis, and a new sense of collective identity was forged. Now people started to think of themselves as part of a unified nation facing a common task. Louis XIV's regulation of religious affairs, his control of the French nobility, his efficient royal administration of tax and economic policies, and his establishment of better working relations with his subjects all promoted a growing sense of national unity, exemplifying French royal absolutism in action.

Yet in 1715, seventy-seven years old and dying, Louis reflected on his failings. He told his five-year-old great-grandson and heir, **Louis XV**, "Try to remain at peace with your neighbors. I loved war too much. Do not follow me in that or in overspending."

Louis XV

After 1715, France avoided prolonged warfare. Capitalizing on peaceful times and a smoothly functioning state administration, Louis XV continued his great-grandfather's absolutist policy of expanding the state's activity in new directions. One was policing. Traditionally, cities maintained rudimentary police forces, and the army was the real maintainer of public order. Under Louis XV, the army's policing role declined, and professional police forces were created. Paris saw the first changes. Its police force, which numbered 193 in 1700, grew to 725 by 1760. In the rest of the kingdom, about 3,000 men functioned as police. These forces were spread thinly over a population of 24 million, but they represented the beginning of a modern, professional police network.

Another area of activity concerned poor relief. Increasingly, the state assumed care of poor children and the elderly, who were housed, clothed, and fed in urban "hospitals." Life in the hospitals was strict; attendance at morning and evening prayers was oblig-

atory, and the able-bodied were forced to work. Some historians argue that the new state program aimed to isolate the socially undesirable from society at large, while others see it as the beginning of a modern state-sponsored welfare system.

In religious policy, however, Louis XV struggled, as the problem of the Jansenists remained. While his government continued its predecessor's condemnation of the Jansenists, the Parlement of Paris, following the Four Gallican Articles, declared that the pope was illegally intruding into the French church's affairs. The conflict was intense because in 1715 the Duke of Orléans, the regent for the new child king, had once again permitted the parlements to criticize royal policy. By 1730, the Parlement of Paris was openly defying Louis on the Jansenist issue and challenging the absolutist principle that the king alone made law. Neither side could silence the other, and it now seemed that Louis XV could no longer keep religious peace in the kingdom. Despite this failure, however, absolutism in France had brought the state into new areas of people's lives and made the state more demanding, as well as more responsive, than ever before.

The Austrian Habsburgs, 1648–1740

⬇ How was the Austrian Habsburg form of absolutist kingship similar to and different from French royal absolutism?

⬇ What factors delayed the implementation of state building in the Habsburg lands before 1740?

The Habsburg emperor Leopold, a lifelong rival of Louis XIV, successfully contained France's bid for dominance in European affairs, thus maintaining the balance of power. His reign, too, was marked by warfare. Positioned between the French in the west and the Turks in the east, Leopold often had to fight both at the same time. But unlike France, warfare in the Habsburg lands did not accelerate a drive for unity in

Four Gallican Articles Decrees of 1681 proclaiming church councils superior to the pope and denying Rome's power to alter internal rules governing the French church.

Jansenists Austere Catholic reformers who were accused of holding views about human sin similar to the Protestant John Calvin and were condemned by the pope.

Louis XV (r. 1715–1774) Louis XIV's five-year-old great-grandson who became king on Louis XIV's death.

In this engraving by Caspar Luyken, Emperor Leopold I is shown in the Spanish style dress worn at his court, far more somber than the fashions favored at Versailles. Leopold looks out at the viewer with piercing eyes. The elongated lower jaw, characteristic of the Habsburgs, is also apparent. *(Austrian National Library, Vienna)*

the state, and Austria was not remodeled along absolutist lines. Its reach was simply too great and its population too diverse—particularly after the reconquest of Hungary—to permit the perfect alignment of the king and the law that had been Louis XIV's aim.

Leopold I

In 1657, on the death of his elder brother from smallpox, the seventeen-year-old **Leopold I** unexpectedly became Holy Roman emperor and head of the Austrian Habsburgs. He had been destined for a career in the church, and at first he did not play the role of monarch very well. Throughout his life he remained deeply religious. He married three times and had sixteen sons and daughters, only five of whom outlived him. He was also withdrawn and bookish as well as an accomplished musician who composed many pieces performed at his court in Vienna.

Like most rulers of his day, Leopold was aware of the political implications of Louis XIV's Versailles and set out to rival him by building his own palace, **Schönbrunn,** on the outskirts of Vienna. Plans to convert the building, which like Versailles had been a hunting lodge, were drawn up during his reign. They included an imposing residence of four hundred rooms as well as gardens and fountains in the manner of Versailles. But there were differences. Versailles was situated on high ground, so the gardens sloped down

Leopold I (r. 1657–1705) Head of the Austrian Habsburgs, emperor, ruler in Austria, king of Bohemia, and king of Hungary, which he reconquered from the Turks.

Schönbrunn (in German, "beautiful spring") Leopold I's palace on Vienna's outskirts, built on the model of Versailles.

from the palace, creating long vistas. Schönbrunn sat at the bottom of a hill. This allowed designers to sweep the gardens upward and to incorporate cascading water into their plans. The effect was different from Versailles, but equally impressive.

The Turkish Siege of Vienna and the Reconquest of Hungary

In 1683, a Turkish army, under the leadership of the Ottoman grand vizier, Kara Mustafa, marched up the Danube River and besieged Vienna. Once again, Europe shuddered at the threat of Muslim conquests. Leopold, forced to flee the city, tried to rally support from Christian princes. Many responded, though not Louis XIV, for whom dynastic rivalry was more important than Christian solidarity. In September, after a savage two-month siege of the city, a united force, which had received the pope's blessing, defeated the Turks, and Kara Mustafa fled south. The grand vizier blamed everyone but himself for his failure, executing subordinates as he made his way to winter quarters in Belgrade. There, on Christmas Day, he received a silk scarf signaling the sultan's displeasure. He was strangled on the spot and his head then shipped to Constantinople, to be presented to the sultan on a silver platter.

These dramatic events opened the way for the Habsburgs' reconquest of Hungary. By 1687, Leopold was master of most of the kingdom and the semi-independent principality of Transylvania. Summoning the Hungarian Diet, he convinced the deputies to decree that the Crown was no longer elective but hereditary in the male line of the Habsburg family. The Hungarians also renounced their traditional right of rebellion against a ruler they thought had violated the kingdom's customary laws. Despite these concessions, Leopold did not trust the Hungarians. Earlier in his reign, some of their great nobles had rebelled against him, while others were Protestants. Hungarians were also culturally distinct, dressing in local costumes and speaking their own language—Magyar.

Turkish occupation and the war of reconquest had devastated the Hungarian countryside, and vast stretches of farmland lay unoccupied. To restore agriculture, and also to neutralize possible Hungarian rebellions, Leopold encouraged Serb, Bohemian, and German peasants to resettle the lands, promising them limited freedom from royal taxes and the obligations of serfdom. This resettlement complicated the religious situation in Hungary, where, for a century, Hungarians had been split over religion; along with Catholics, there were Calvinists, Lutherans, Unitari-

ans, Eastern Orthodox, and Muslims. The resettlement also reduced the proportion of Hungarians. In 1526, they had constituted 85 percent of the kingdom's population; by 1700, they made up only 40 percent.

Peace in Europe during the 1680s had freed Leopold to concentrate on Hungary. When the War of the League of Augsburg with France broke out in 1689, he was forced to turn west once again. Then, with Habsburg troop strength reduced in the east, the Turks attempted to retake Hungary, only to be defeated again in 1690. This time a new grand vizier lay among the battlefield dead. Finally, just as war in the west was ending, in 1697 Leopold scored another smashing victory. At Zenta, the vizier and thirty thousand men were slaughtered before the sultan's eyes, for this time the sultan himself had accompanied the Turkish army into Hungary. The Habsburg commander ripped the great seal of the Ottoman Empire from the dead vizier's neck and sent it back to Vienna. In 1699, the Treaty of Carlowitz confirmed the Habsburg conquests. Although the Ottomans had lost Hungary, they continued to hold the Balkans and challenged the Russians in the northern Black Sea region.

During the War of the Spanish Succession, more trouble flared up in the east, this time a rebellion led by a Transylvanian prince, Francis II Rákóczi. Rákóczi typified the touchy Hungarian noble resentful of Leopold's preference for Germans. His father, mother, and stepfather had all led rebellions against the Habsburgs, and he was determined to guarantee Hungary's traditional rights. By 1711, however, he had been defeated, as the Habsburgs were now able to rely on the enlarged non-Hungarian population of the kingdom for support. War and plague devastated the kingdom during the rebellion; almost a half million people perished. Rákóczi eventually sought protection from the sultan and died in exile in Turkey. The Peace of Szatmár (1711) united Hungary to the Habsburg lands through a common ruler.

---

grand vizier   Chief minister of the Ottoman sultan.

Zenta   Battle in 1697 in which the Habsburgs defeated the Turks and reconfirmed Habsburg conquests in Hungary.

Treaty of Carlowitz   Treaty of 1699 between the Austrian Habsburgs and the Ottoman Turks confirming the Habsburg reconquest of Hungary.

Francis II Rákóczi   (1676–1735) Prince of Transylvania who led the last major rebellion against the Habsburgs in Hungary.

Peace of Szatmár   Treaty of 1711 uniting Hungary to the other Habsburg possessions through a common ruler.

The Habsburg Monarchy

The Habsburgs ruled over lands that were far more socially polarized than Louis XIV's France. At the top were the **magnates**, who were often fabulously rich. Visitors to the magnate Esterházys in Hungary could travel for days before they reached the end of their lands, passing through entire towns that were under the family's exclusive control. Magnate families were few in number, but their cooperation with the Habsburgs was essential for the smooth functioning of the government, and they dominated Habsburg administration at the central and local level. Unlike in France, there were few independent cities and towns in the Habsburg lands. The vast majority of people, tied to the land as **serfs**, lived in the countryside.

Serfdom had expanded in the sixteenth and seventeenth centuries as eastern European landlords, all of whom were noble, successfully bound peasants to the soil as a labor force producing grain and timber for the western European market. During the dislocations of the Thirty Years' War, they also bound them to the soil to prevent them from fleeing to more peaceful areas. Landlords used their serfs to work their estates without compensation. Leopold tried to reduce uncompensated work to three days a week, but his success was limited because direct control of serfs lay with the landlord class, not the Habsburgs. Thus, Leopold's policy had to accommodate noble self-interest before it could become effective. Because Leopold's direct rule over the mass of his subjects was very limited, he never established the kind of centralized, intrusive state that Louis XIV and Louis XV created. The Habsburg state was also characterized by a high degree of ethnic and religious diversity, particularly in Hungary. Habsburg rulers manipulated these groups to their own ends, with the result of enhancing the sense of difference between communities. Unlike in France, no sense of common identity emerged that spanned all the people of the Habsburg hereditary lands.

Leopold died in 1705, leaving two sons, Joseph I (r. 1705–1711) and Charles VI (r. 1711–1740), to rule. When Joseph died during the War of the Spanish Succession, Charles, as the sole surviving Austrian *and* Spanish Habsburg male, was poised to inherit the Austrian territories along with Spain and its lands in the Netherlands, Italy, and America, thus reconstituting Charles V's empire. This was too much for the other European states, which feared that an Austrian Habsburg succession in Spain would upset the European balance of power. They, therefore, supported the division of lands between Habsburgs and Bourbons that was written into the Treaty of Utrecht ending the War of the Spanish Succession.

Warfare did not lead Charles to reform the Habsburg state, as it did in France. Instead, during his twenty-nine-year reign, he devoted his mediocre talents to two basic policies: making sure that his brother's daughters did not succeed him and that his own daughter did. The matter was complicated. The emperor had always been male, so Charles's daughter, **Maria Theresa**, could not follow him in that office. But she could succeed him as ruler of the family's hereditary lands. To this end, Charles coaxed the magnates into recognizing her succession and then sought guarantees from the other European rulers that they, too, would recognize it. When Charles died in 1740, his careful plans exploded. In the **War of the Austrian Succession**, another new ruler, **Frederick II** of Prussia, attacked Maria Theresa during the opening phase of the two world wars that convulsed Europe in the mid-eighteenth century. The new war showed just how weak the Habsburgs had become.

The Rise of Prussia, 1640–1740

⬇ What factors accounted for Prussia's rise in power?
⬇ What role did the army play in forging a collective Prussian identity?

North of the Habsburg lands, another state emerged out of the chaos of the Thirty Years' War—Prussia. Prussia was a poor country, lacking the human and material resources of France and the Habsburg lands. But its rulers wanted it to become a major European power. To this end, they consolidated the state's territories, strengthened the state administration, raised revenue, and above all enlarged the army. These am-

magnates Politically powerful nobles in the Habsburg lands who owned vast agricultural estates worked by serfs.

serfs Peasants bound to the land who owed payments and labor service to their landlord.

Maria Theresa (r. 1740–1780) Daughter of Charles VI and ruler of the Habsburgs' hereditary lands whose husband was elected Holy Roman emperor.

War of the Austrian Succession (1740–1748) Mid-eighteenth century world war, fought on land and sea in Europe, the Americas, and India.

Frederick II (r. 1740–1786) King of Prussia during the War of the Austrian Succession and the Seven Years' War.

MAP 16.1 **The Growth of Austria and Prussia to 1748** Both Austria and Brandenburg-Prussia were expanding in the first half of the eighteenth century. The Austrians continued adding territories in their southeast, but in the north lost Silesia to Brandenburg-Prussia. Prussian lands were still scattered; by 1772 however, Brandenburg would be joined to Prussia in the First Partition of Poland under Frederick the Great.

bitious plans meant that the state had to mobilize the country's limited resources to a unique degree.

Territorial Consolidation

In 1640, a twenty-year-old, **Frederick William von Hohenzollern,** known as the Great Elector, became ruler of Brandenburg and a string of other territories that stretched across northern Germany from the Rhineland to the Polish border. In the west, little Cleves and Mark owed him allegiance; in the center were Brandenburg and its capital, Berlin, where he ruled as margrave; to the east was the duchy of Prussia, which he held as a vassal of the king of Poland. These Hohenzollern lands were separated by territories belonging to other rulers, and each had its own jealously guarded political traditions. Because Frederick William was

one of eight German princes entitled to elect the Holy Roman emperor, he had an important place in imperial politics. But his own lands were weak. Those in the center had been devastated during the Thirty Years' War, and some were still under foreign occupation. Overall, the population of his lands had fallen by 50 percent since 1618. But the Peace of Westphalia allowed Frederick William to reestablish princely authority in his territories.

In 1655, when Sweden went to war against Poland in hopes of gaining territory on the southern shore of the Baltic Sea, Frederick William faced his first test

Frederick William von Hohenzollern (r. 1640–1688) Known as the Great Elector, ruler who started to create the modern state of Prussia.

since the Peace of Westphalia in the treacherous game of warfare and diplomacy that was the norm among European states. At first, he proclaimed his neutrality. When the Swedes suffered temporary losses, he allied with them on condition that they recognize the independence of Prussia from Poland. When the Poles started to lose, he joined them, again demanding that they abandon any claim to the duchy. At war's end in 1660, he was master of an independent Prussia. Now the Hohenzollern lands were scattered from the Rhineland to the Russian border.

Taxes to Support an Army

For the rest of his reign, the Great Elector set two policy goals: to build up his army and to reorganize his finances to pay for it. Between 1653 and 1688, the army grew from eighteen hundred to thirty thousand. As the one institution established in all territories from east to west, it became the primary unifying force in the elector's state.

A bigger army called for more taxes, and more taxes led to a confrontation between Frederick William and his diets, local political assemblies dominated by the nobility. Like their Habsburg counterparts, the Hohenzollern diets had traditionally granted taxes to the ruler. The elector had obtained a six-year grant from the Diet of Brandenburg in 1653 that he continued to collect on his own authority during the war of 1655–1660. Also in 1653, he proposed supplementing the grant with a general **excise tax**, taking his cue from the French, who had lowered direct taxes while raising indirect ones. When the local nobility objected that the excise violated their traditional rights of tax exemption, the elector asked only towns to pay it. This solution created two tax systems. The countryside, dominated by nobles, paid a land tax, while towns adopted the excise tax. In creating this twofold system in Brandenburg, the elector split the united opposition of urban and rural taxpayers to new taxes. When Prussia balked at taxes, Frederick William introduced the two-tiered system there with the same results. Shorn of their taxing power, the diets withered away, and, as in France, political power was increasingly consolidated in the hands of the ruler and his government.

Frederick William had another source of revenue from his own domain. All European rulers had these private income streams, but the Hohenzollerns were blessed by very large family landholdings, constituting about one-third of their country's agricultural land and worked by 30 percent of the country's serfs. Under the leadership of an efficient administrator, Dodo zu Knyphausen, these domain lands produced ever-larger amounts for the elector's treasury.

In addition to imposing his right to tax and reorganizing his domain revenues, the elector encouraged economic growth along mercantilist lines by increasing exports and introducing new manufacturing centers. As a youth, he had spent time in the Dutch Republic and seen firsthand the thriving economic life there. After 1685, he welcomed some twenty thousand exiled Huguenots. These French artisans, merchants, and manufacturers played a vital role in the economic recovery after the Thirty Years' War.

During his reign, Frederick William had united his far-flung lands into a single state, imposed his right to tax them on a regular basis, and reinvigorated the economy. His growing army made him the most important military figure in Germany after the Habsburgs. In 1688, the elector was succeeded by his son, Frederick, who ruled until 1713. Frederick spent most of his time in Berlin, presiding over a lavish court in the style of Louis XIV. His one major accomplishment was to adopt the title of King in Prussia in 1701 after obtaining Leopold I's recognition with promises of military aid in the looming War of the Spanish Succession. The title gave Frederick the standing he thought appropriate for his state's new power.

King Frederick William I

In 1713, King Frederick was succeeded by his son, King **Frederick William I**. Although Prussia was Lutheran, Frederick William was a strict Calvinist who believed in the absolutist principle that he was responsible to God alone for his rule. His subjects were to obey him without question. The king hated all elegance and refinement and spent most of his free time with his military men, smoking and getting completely drunk. These "tobacco evenings" sometimes ended with a participant being set on fire, a great joke in the king's eyes. Frederick William also stalked the streets of Berlin, roaring at his subjects, beating them with his cane, and leaving them with broken noses and teeth. The king was obsessed with tall men and scoured the kingdom for fit specimens to fill the ranks of his personal guard. If necessary, he

excise tax   Indirect tax imposed on consumer items and collected at the moment of sale.**Frederick William I** (r. 1713–1740) King of Prussia who further centralized the state administration and continued to build up the army.

Frederick William I   (r. 1713–1740) King of who Prussia who further centralized the state administration and continued to build up the army.

resorted to kidnapping. Frederick William was a strange, violent, and crude man, but he was also a very successful ruler.

Like his grandfather, the Great Elector, Fredrick William I pursued the twin policies of strengthening the royal administration while enlarging the army. The excise tax was expanded to new commodities, and the land tax was imposed directly on the nobility in East Prussia, as the old duchy was now called. Income from the royal domain was further increased through yet more efficient management. Town councils were abolished and new royal officials put in their place. A new administrative body called the **General Directory** was created in 1723 that brought together all officials involved in collecting taxes and revenues from the royal domain and supervising the overall economy of the kingdom. The directory improved administrative centralization and efficiency.

The king stood at the apex of this new administrative system. Unlike his predecessors, Frederick William I did not consult regularly with his top officials because he had a low opinion of the men who worked for him, criticizing them for laziness and greed and paying them poorly. Instead, he worked in private, receiving reports and then secretly making decisions that were transmitted in writing to his officials. His was a system of personal absolutism unknown even in Louis XIV's France, where the king always consulted with a handful of trusted advisers.

The king's government produced what Frederick William I wanted above all else—an enlarged army. At his death in 1740, the Prussian army had eighty thousand men, making it the fourth largest in Europe. Command of the troops was given to the Prussian nobility, who also served in the civil administration. The king thus bound the nobility to his government and created a tradition of loyal state service among his nobles that was to last into the twentieth century. He also guaranteed the nobility's economic preeminence by recognizing their rights as landlords to control the serfs on their estates.

The military had always been the one institution common to all the Hohenzollern lands, and the state's financial administration was geared to its maintenance. The military budget was met with tax and domain revenues, not with borrowing, as in other states. As he enlarged the army, Frederick William drafted more and more of his own subjects. All parts of the kingdom were required to present men, mainly peasants, for service. To lower costs, the soldiers were quartered in civilian homes, where they paid for their food and lodging and thereby stimulated the local economy. Because the rank and file of the growing army was made up of Prussians who lived among the civilian population, historians have described eighteenth-century Prussia as a "barracks state."

When Frederick William died in 1740, he was succeeded by his son, Frederick II. Frederick was everything his father was not—refined, an accomplished flute player and composer, and a lover of philosophical discussion. He and his father had not gotten along. Relations between ruling monarchs and their successors were often stormy because the next in line attracted those who were out of favor in the current reign. But Frederick William I's treatment of his son was particularly violent. At one point, having beaten Frederick bloody with his cane, he put him in solitary confinement and forced him to witness the beheading of his closest friend on largely falsified charges.

Frederick William I had doubled the size of his army, but he was reluctant to use it in war. Frederick II's first act as king was to attack Charles VI's successor, Maria Theresa, seizing Silesia, her richest territory, and thereby starting the War of the Austrian Succession, the first of two world wars that engulfed the major European states in the mid-eighteenth century.

Russia and Europe, 1682–1796

> ↓ How were the state-building efforts of Russia's rulers similar to or different from the reform programs of European rulers farther to the west?
>
> ↓ How were Russian rulers' relations with their nobility similar to and different from relations between monarchs and nobles farther to the west?

Beginning in 1700, Russia began to realize Tsar Ivan the Terrible's dream of turning westward to expand its territory. In addition, rulers restructured Russia's state and church, along with its economy and society, along western lines. By the end of the eighteenth century, Russia was a major player in European politics.

Peter the Great and Westernization

Following Ivan the Terrible's death in 1584, Russia sank into a thirty-year period of political instability during which aristocratic factions fought for control of the state. In 1613, stability was restored when the first **Romanov** tsar, Michael, ascended the throne. At

General Directory Prussian central administrative agency created in 1723.

Romanovs Family that ruled Russia from 1613 to 1917.

the end of the century, another Romanov, **Peter I the Great,** transformed Russia into a major European power. Peter was six feet seven inches tall and powerfully built. His huge size had a personality to match—restless, energetic, and always on the move. Peter was ten when he became tsar in 1682. He shared rule with a half brother, Ivan V, until Ivan's death in 1696 and then ruled alone. The young tsar was fascinated by technology. In 1697, he traveled to western Europe under an assumed name, which fooled no one. Settling in the Dutch Republic, he spent hours visiting sawmills, cloth manufacturers, botanical gardens, and museums. He listened to lectures on anatomy and met with local architects. But, above all, he visited Dutch shipyards to learn about shipbuilding, and then, having bought his own tools, he worked alongside Dutch shipbuilders. On a visit to England, he went to Anglican church services, attended a Quaker meeting, went to the theater, and visited Parliament, which did not impress him. And, again, he studied ships.

Peter worked for the rest of his life to apply what he had learned in the west to Russia. He began with fashion. Immediately on his return to Moscow, he forbade men to grow beards, the traditional sign of manhood in this Orthodox Christian country, and personally cut them off his courtiers. Traditionalists were horrified and protested that their hairless faces made them look like Protestants, Poles, or monkeys. His court was then ordered to dress in western clothes and to meet in "assemblies," where men and women together conversed and engaged in other polite pastimes. This mingling of men and women overturned traditions decreeing the separation of women in special quarters.

In 1700, the tsar began a two-decade struggle with Sweden, the greatest power in northeastern Europe, for control of the Baltic Sea. Since the sixteenth century, tsars had believed that Russian access to the Baltic, the central sea link between eastern and western Europe, was essential if Russia hoped to be a major European power. Peter acted on this belief in the **Great Northern War,** which marked a turning point in Russian history.

After early Russian victories on the Baltic, Peter took the examples of Louis XIV and Leopold I further by building not a palace but a city, **St. Petersburg,** founded in 1703 on swampy coastal land seized from the Swedes at the mouth of the Neva River. The new city proclaimed his success in securing a Baltic port. In 1712, Peter made St. Petersburg the new capital of Russia, and the next year the court and state administration moved there from Moscow. Peter also forced skilled craftsmen to settle there with their families. When they resisted or attempted to flee, the army brought them back in chains and branded them to make flight more difficult. In 1718, well-to-do landowners were required to build a house there and spend some of the year in the city. St. Petersburg was designed using western principles of urban planning, and western architects constructed its beautiful classical buildings.

Peter knew that continuing military success in the war with Sweden depended on an unprecedented refashioning of Russia's fighting forces and tax structure. He therefore reorganized his army along western lines, ordering a draft for soldiers and introducing up-to-date western drill and weapons. By 1715, he had an army of 215,000, supplemented by 100,000 Cossacks, locally organized warrior bands used by tsars as fighting forces. Peter also built a Baltic navy from scratch. To pay for this huge military mobilization, he imposed new taxes on everything from beehives to beards to baths. He abolished the old household tax and imposed a new head tax that all unprivileged people had to pay at higher rates than the old one. Overall, taxes skyrocketed during Peter's reign, as they had in France during the Thirty Years' War. To improve his tax base, Peter inaugurated a mercantilist stimulation of the Russian economy by encouraging exports, discouraging imports, and sponsoring new industries in metallurgy, mining, and textiles.

The decisive battle in the Great Northern War came in 1709 at **Poltava,** where Peter destroyed the Swedish army. Nine thousand Swedes lay dead on the battlefield, and sixteen thousand more surrendered a few days later. The Swedish king, Charles XII, who commanded the army, fled into Turkish territory. Although the war lasted another twelve years, the Swedes never recovered from the disaster at Poltava. At the end of the Great Northern War, in 1721, during a solemn ceremony in St. Petersburg, Peter was proclaimed emperor of Russia, a title taken from Rome that was to supplant the traditional one of tsar.

Peter I the Great   (r. 1682–1725) Greatest Romanov tsar who westernized Russia and made the country a major European power.

Great Northern War   (1700–1721) War between Russia and Sweden that resulted in Russian dominance of the Baltic.

St. Petersburg   City founded by Peter the Great in 1703, which became the Russian capital in 1712.

Poltava   Decisive battle of the Great Northern War in 1709 in which Peter the Great defeated Charles XII of Sweden.

A young Peter is shown in this painting in the workman's clothes he often wore during his tour of western Europe. His dress and demeanor are nothing like the elegance and majesty typical of royal portraits of the eighteenth century. Would his attitude and appearance have made him more, or less, popular with his subjects? *(Collection, Countess Bobrinskoy/ Michael Holford)*

Peter also continued to restructure Russian society. Traditionally, Russians thought of their society as a three-tiered hierarchy. At the base were the millions of serfs who toiled for their landlords. Serfs, who constituted more than half of the Russian population, were under the complete control of their landlord, needing his permission to marry or leave his estate. They also had to work for him without pay, often as many as six days a week. In their lack of freedom of choice, they resembled the African slaves laboring in the fields in the Americas more than the European peasants farther to the west. The landlords in turn worked for the emperor. Peter intensified this traditional pattern, first by demanding more in taxes and military service from the serfs and then by requiring the landlord class to serve for life in either the military or the civilian administration. Candidates for state service had to start at the bottom of their service branch and then work to the top on the basis of personal merit. Peter applied the test of merit to himself when he rose through the ranks of the army and the navy. This sys-

tem was codified in the **Table of Ranks.** Administrators received noble status as they moved up. Peter's reform of his civil and military administration was one of the first attempts in modern European history to overturn the idea that nobles had a right to govern in favor of the notion that government should be in the hands of a civil service staffed by experts whose advancement depended on their performance. To train experts for state service, Peter established engineering, artillery, and medical schools, a school of mathematics and navigation, and a naval academy. In 1725, he established an Academy of Sciences that quickly gained an international reputation for excellence. Peter's insistence on able and expert administrators was central to his program of state building.

Peter loved alcohol, coarse language, and even coarser practical jokes. Throughout most of his reign, he presided over a "Most Drunken Council" that engaged in monumental drinking bouts while mocking Catholic, but not Orthodox, church ceremonies. His practical joking was often violent, as when he forced food down the throat of a courtier, who collapsed in a fit of coughing with blood running from his nose and mouth. Peter's violence matched that of Frederick William I of Prussia and contrasted sharply with the refined manners promoted at the court of Louis XIV and the piety of Leopold I.

Peter's most radical reform was to abolish the office of **patriarch** in the Russian Orthodox Church. In the Orthodox world, patriarchs were bishops with great prestige and influence. The patriarch of Moscow, who had received the title in 1589, had served as a counterweight to tsars and a check on their power. By Peter's time, however, the patriarchate had been weakened by a schism in the church when the **Old Believers** rejected his authority and denounced him as the Antichrist. The patriarch had tried to reform church practice, and although Russian church councils and the other patriarchs approved the reforms, Old Believers rejected them because they had not been used traditionally in "Holy Russia." Moreover, people unhappy about Peter's policy of cultural westerniza-

Table of Ranks   Decree by Peter the Great in 1722 that restructured civil and military administration into a system of advancement based on merit.

patriarch   Title of the most important bishops in the Eastern Orthodox Church.

Old Believers   Orthodox Christians who rejected the Russian patriarch's attempt to alter church ceremony.

tion looked to the patriarch for support of traditional ways. Peter never openly attacked Orthodoxy, but his own theological beliefs were heavily influenced by Lutheranism. In 1721, he abolished the patriarchate and replaced it with a **Holy Synod,** which embodied his Lutheran leanings, since it reduced the church to a simple department of the state.

Peter's plans for the remaking of Russia were far reaching, and many of them looked better on paper than they worked in reality. But his reforms brought a new centralization and rationality to government while demanding more from all Russians and advancing the country as a major European power. Thus, he set Russia on a new course.

Catherine the Great and Russian Expansion

From 1725 to 1762, Russia was allied with Austria against France, the traditional ally of the Poles, the Swedes, and the Turks, all enemies of Russia. The Austrian alliance implemented Peter's policy of bringing Russia directly into the European system of international politics and diplomacy. Domestically, one far-reaching change took place: in 1762, the landlord class was freed from Peter's compulsory state service obligation. From then on, landlords served voluntarily; many did so, since service brought prestige, influence, and wealth.

In 1762, Peter III, Peter I's grandson, became emperor. Peter III was violent, crude, and dimwitted. Raised in Germany, where his Romanov mother had married a duke, Peter feared Russians and loved Germans, thereby alienating many at court. In religion, he also leaned toward Lutheranism and ordered icons removed from Russian churches while demanding that Orthodox clergy dress like Lutheran pastors. No one dared to implement these decrees. Peter was married to Sophie, a princess from a minor German state. Six months after Peter's accession, Sophie plotted with powerful courtiers, one of whom was her lover, to depose Peter in a palace **coup d'état.** He was soon murdered, and the conspirators proclaimed Sophie his successor. For the next thirty-four years, she ruled Russia as **Catherine II the Great.**

Catherine's first major decision was to continue Peter III's seizure of all ecclesiastical lands, thereby further reducing the church's independence from the state. She then granted large tracts of state land and their peasants to her favorites. This action increased the number of serfs because state peasants were reduced to serfdom when their lands passed into private hands. Catherine also continued her predecessors' policies of

For her portrait (c. 1765), Catherine II the Great is dressed in shiny splendor. On her head is the Romanov crown, and in her hands are an orb and scepter, emblems of royal and imperial rule. She gazes straight out at the viewer with a kindly expression, perhaps to convey an image of her womanly concern for her subjects. *(The Granger Collection, New York)*

exempting the landlord class from compulsory state service and freeing them from taxation while forbidding serfs on their lands from directly petitioning the empress for redress of grievances.

Like Peter the Great, Catherine dramatically expanded Russia's borders. In 1772, she joined Prussia

Holy Synod   Council of clergy established by Peter the Great in 1721 that made the church a department of the state.

coup d'état   (in French, "blow of state") Abrupt overthrow of a government by a small group of conspirators.

Catherine II the Great   (r. 1762–1796) German princess who, as Russian empress, was one of Russia's most powerful rulers.

MAP 16.2　The Partition of Poland and the Expansion of Russia Prussia, Russia, and Austria all benefited from the partitions of Poland. By incorporating the part of Poland that had previously separated them, Prussia and Brandenburg were finally united. But Prussian lands further to the west were still separated from those in the east by other states. Russia continued its westward expansion taking present-day Belarus, Lithuania, and Ukraine. Austria took part of southwestern Poland and Galicia, the lands closest to its eastern border.

and Austria, which were also looking to expand their territories, in the first **partition of Poland.** In the 1760s, Prussia and Russia had instigated a civil war in Poland by demanding full toleration for its Protestant and Orthodox inhabitants. Claiming that they were putting an end to that civil war, Austria, Prussia, and Russia proceeded to divide up sections of Poland among

themselves. Two more partitions took place in 1792 and 1795, bringing an end to an independent Poland.

> **partitions of Poland** Divisions of Poland carried out by Austria, Prussia, and Russia in 1772, 1792, and 1795, leading to the end of an independent Polish state.

Catherine also fought two wars with the Turks. In 1792, when the second war ended, Russia seized the north shore of the Black Sea and the Crimean peninsula along with the northern Caucasus. These conquests, along with the partitions of Poland, rivaled Peter the Great's advances in the Baltic region and established the modern western boundaries of Russia. Catherine encouraged colonization in the lands of the south by urging Russian landlords to move there with their serfs and sponsoring German immigrants in the region. At the end of Catherine's reign, the Russian Empire contained dozens of different ethnic and religious communities, 50 percent of whom were Russian. Thus, cultural diversity in the Russian Empire rivaled that of the Habsburg lands and similarly retarded the development of a common identity among the peoples ruled by the empress in St. Petersburg.

The Pugachev Rebellion and Russian Society

In 1773, during the Turkish war, a massive rebellion against the empress broke out in the south. It was led by a Cossack, **Emelian Pugachev,** who claimed to be Peter III. Popular revolts led by men pretending to be long-lost tsars were a feature of early modern Russia's political life. So were Cossack frontier rebellions. What made Pugachev's revolt distinctive was its size and its social composition. Thousands rose with him, including many serfs. In 1774, when the Turkish war ended, Catherine was free to turn her professionally trained army against the insurgents, who were no match for the imperial troops, and the revolt fell apart. Pugachev was taken to Moscow in a cage and then executed. Although the revolt failed, it was a sign of a deep social crisis in Russia. The elimination of compulsory state service for the landlord class had undercut the traditional structure of the Russian community, in which landlords toiled for the state while their serfs toiled for them. When the landlords were freed of their obligations, many peasants believed they should be free as well. When they were not freed, alienation and anger exploded into revolt. Those who followed Pugachev demanded an end to serfdom, taxation, and the military draft. In 1775, Catherine clamped down. She imposed administrative centralization by reorganizing Russia into fifty provinces and putting the landlords in charge of local government, where they had enough force to control peasant protest.

Under Peter I and Catherine II, Russia emerged as a first-rate European military and diplomatic power.

Coercion from above was crucial in this transformation. Modernization and westernization also increased privileges for the landowning class and reduced the condition of the peasant population, which (serfs and free peasants together) constituted more than 90 percent of Russia's inhabitants. The gulf between the landowning elite and the mass of inhabitants was as great as, if not greater than, any in Europe.

The English Constitutional Monarchy, 1660–1740

⬇ How did religion continue to play a role in English politics?
⬇ In what ways did political development in England differ from that in the absolutist regimes on the continent?

In 1660, after eleven years of civil war, religious controversy, republican government, and Oliver Cromwell's dictatorship, monarchy was restored in the British Isles when Charles I's son, already crowned king of Scotland, was crowned king of England and Ireland. Restoration, however, did not bring either political or religious peace. For the next seventy years, the British Isles were torn apart by conflicts pitting king against Parliament. Religious divisions also persisted, as restored Anglicans refused all compromise with the Puritans. When the Catholic king James II seemed to have established a permanent Catholic dynasty, he was overthrown, and his Protestant daughter Mary II, along with her husband, the Dutch stadholder William III, were crowned with Parliament's blessing. But Mary and then her successor, Anne, died without heirs, and Parliament again determined who would rule when it chose a German Protestant prince, George I. In this turbulent period, as Parliament made and unmade monarchs, its power grew. Political stability was achieved in the early eighteenth century, when Crown and Parliament started to cooperate in governing the country.

The Restoration of Charles II

The restoration to the throne of **Charles II** in 1660 sparked a repudiation of Oliver Cromwell's Calvinist moral reform of society. The king led the way. Charles

Emelian Pugachev   (1742?–1775) Cossack who claimed to be Peter III and led an unsuccessful rebellion of thousands of serfs against Catherine the Great.

Charles II   (r. 1660–1685) Elder son of Charles I who became king of England, Scotland, and Ireland.

was a charming, witty man with a taste for good living and an eye for women. A string of mistresses, along with packs of spaniels, shared his bed. "God will not damn a man for taking a little unregular pleasure along the way," he once quipped. In pursuit of pleasure, Charles reopened London theaters and canceled the traditional prohibition against women playing female roles. Now people could revel in worldly comedies like *Love in a Wood* or *The Gentleman Dancing-Master*.

Underneath the glitter of **Restoration** society, the long-standing political conflict between king and Parliament continued to shape events. Like his predecessors, Charles could conduct foreign policy on his own and choose his ministers. He could also call Parliament into session and dismiss it, veto its legislation, and override any parliamentary law by suspending it or dispensing people from its provisions. For its part, Parliament could impeach royal ministers. It also controlled state finances through its right to raise taxes. In sum, both sides had formidable powers, and neither could gain a permanent advantage over the other. This situation contrasted to the absolutist monarchies on the continent, where power was increasingly concentrated in the hands of the king.

The issue that provoked the greatest political fights was religion. Although Charles II was officially Anglican, he favored some form of religious toleration in England. But the Parliament elected in 1661 was determined to promote Anglicanism alone and force conformity to the Book of Common Prayer. Therefore, it enacted the **Clarendon Code,** which required all clergymen to swear an oath supporting Anglican theology and prohibited non-Anglican Protestants from worshiping in public. About 10 percent of the clergy refused to accept it and turned their backs on Anglicanism. These clergymen and their supporters, known as **dissenters,** supported the king's more tolerant attitude. Most Anglicans suspected that the king's policy of religious toleration was shaped by loyalty to his Catholic family—his mother, wife, and younger brother, James, Duke of York, were all Roman Catholics.

These suspicions deepened when Charles allied with his cousin, Louis XIV, in the Dutch War of 1672. In fact, Charles and Louis had signed a secret treaty in 1670 in which Louis granted Charles a subsidy to free him from Parliament's control of the purse. In return, the king promised to convert to Roman Catholicism when the time was ripe. Always politically astute, Charles postponed his conversion until he was on his deathbed.

The problem of Catholic members of the royal family became especially acute in the 1670s. Although

Charles fathered at least seventeen illegitimate children by his many mistresses, he had no legitimate heir to succeed him, so his brother James would be the next king if the rule of strict hereditary succession was applied. The prospect of a Catholic king created a rift among the Anglican elite, which controlled Parliament and ran local government, since Anglicans hated Catholics as well as dissenters. Soon two parties, the **Tories** and the **Whigs,** fought each other over the issue of succession. Tories supported the Duke of York's right to the crown, even if this meant that Protestant England would have a Catholic king, because they believed that hereditary monarchy was divinely instituted and that opposition to it was a sin. Whigs wanted a Protestant monarch at all costs. Following the argument of the English philosopher **John Locke,** they believed in the contractual theory of government. The English monarchy was based on a contract between the ruler and his subjects, represented in Parliament, which could be broken for good reason. As battles between the two parties raged, a new politically active press emerged under the relatively moderate censorship regime of the restored monarchy. Press and parties encouraged the English publicly to discuss politics and take sides on issues in ways that were inconceivable under the absolutist monarchies on the continent.

James II

In 1685, when Charles II died, the principle of hereditary succession won out, and the Duke of York became **James II.** James kept up some Anglican appearances,

Restoration   Name given to the period 1660–1689 in which the restored Stuart kings Charles II and James II ruled.

Clarendon Code   Law of 1661 requiring clergy and officeholders to swear allegiance to the Anglican Church and banning non-Anglican Protestants' public worship.

dissenters   Non-Anglican Protestants.

Tories   Supporters of strict hereditary succession to the crown.

Whigs   People who believed in the necessity of a Protestant monarch, even if this meant that the rule of strict heredity would have to be violated.

John Locke   (1632–1704) Political philosopher who argued that legitimate government rested on a contract between rulers and subjects.

James II   (r. 1685–1689) King of England who was removed from the throne by Parliament.

being crowned in public according to the Anglican rite after being crowned in private according to the Catholic one. When one of Charles II's illegitimate sons, the Protestant Duke of Monmouth, rebelled against his uncle, the duke was taken prisoner and executed. At first, many Tories and Whigs could accept James because his heirs were his two Protestant daughters, Mary and Anne, the children of his first marriage. Although James had remarried, none of the ten children by his second marriage had survived past infancy.

Like his brother, James promoted religious toleration of both dissenters and Catholics, granting them the right to worship in public and using his power of exempting people from the law to override a provision in the Clarendon Code forbidding non-Anglicans from serving in high civil and military office. This action infuriated the Anglicans, who saw the king's actions as a backdoor way of promoting Catholicism. When Anglican bishops objected, James resurrected King Charles I's hated church courts, and purged Anglican opponents from local government office, replacing them with Catholics and dissenters.

In 1688, England was rocked by news that James's wife had given birth to an eleventh child, a baby boy who would rule as James III. Outraged Protestants tried to argue that the queen had faked a pregnancy and that the baby had been smuggled into the palace in a bed-warming pan. Tories and Whigs alike were horrified at the prospect of a perpetual Catholic monarchy and furious with James's high-handed exempting of the law in favor of non-Anglicans. Joining forces, they asked the stadholder William, the husband of James's daughter Mary, to come to England in defense of Protestantism. When William landed, James panicked. Unable to sleep and suffering from endless nosebleeds, he led an army against William but failed to find him because his generals had no maps. After sending wife and baby out of the country, James fled to France.

The Glorious Revolution

When Parliament reconvened in 1689, it determined who would rule, proclaiming that in leaving the country James had abdicated and then offering the crown to Mary, his daughter, who accepted on condition that William rule jointly with her. Parliament then passed the **Bill of Rights,** which upheld the Whig view that monarchs ruled not by hereditary right but by right of a contract with their subjects. It overturned James II's suspension of parliamentary law, stating that "the pretended power of suspending the laws or the execution of laws by regal authority without consent of Parliament is illegal." It also undercut royal power by denying the king the right to raise an army on his own, saying that "raising and keeping a standing army within this kingdom in time of peace without the consent of Parliament [is] contrary to law." This bill also guaranteed subjects' right to petition the government as well as to a jury trial, along with freedom from "cruel and unusual punishments," excessive bail, and excessive court fines. It did not, however, guarantee the right of all subjects to vote for members of Parliament's **House of Commons.** Voting for this lower house, made up of non-nobles, was still limited to a relatively small number of property-owning adult males. Candidates for the Commons also had to meet substantial property qualifications.

In support of Protestantism, Parliament also repealed the most oppressive portions of the Clarendon Code in the **Toleration Act** (1689), which granted religious toleration to all dissenters except Unitarians, people who did not believe in the doctrine of the Trinity. Dissenters, however, were still subject to a law that required all officeholders to take Holy Communion in an Anglican Church. Some dissenters evaded the law by taking Anglican Communion once a year and then going to their chapels for the next twelve months. This "occasional conformity" infuriated Anglicans. Overall, the Bill of Rights and the amendments to the Clarendon Code implemented the contract theory of government by strengthening Parliament while providing subjects of the Crown with a wide range of rights that were spelled out in detail and had the force of law.

Large-scale landowners controlled Parliament. After 1689, these people also enjoyed control of local government in the countryside with little interference from the king. This situation contrasted with the absolutist monarchies on the continent, where royal control of local affairs was implemented. William knew that his predecessor's dismissal of Anglican landlords from local office in favor of Catholics and dissenters had contributed to his overthrow and did not intend to provoke these powerful people again.

Bill of Rights Parliamentary act passed in 1689 stipulating the basic rights of English subjects; based on the contract theory of government.

House of Commons Lower elected house of Parliament made up non-noble men (commoners); nobles sit in the upper house, the House of Lords.

Toleration Act Parliamentary act of 1689 granting religious toleration to all Protestants except Unitarians, and also excepting Catholics.

In this painting of the House of Commons by Karl Anton Hickel, the Speaker of the House sits with his hat on at the center behind secretaries. The MPs (Members of Parliament) flank him on either side. The man standing is the king's first minister, William Pitt the Younger, who is addressing the House. *(National Portrait Gallery, London)*

In 1701, royal judges were given life tenure, subject only to impeachment and removal from office by Parliament. This reform, which created an independent judiciary, was intended to strengthen the **rule of law** called for in the Bill of Rights. William accepted these reforms from below and thereby acknowledged that he ruled by right of contract with his subjects. He had come to England as part of his grand strategy to defeat Louis XIV. As king he could take England into the War of the League of Augsburg on the Dutch side. Mary reluctantly accepted the crown, believing that she was sinning against her father, who led a French landing in Ireland to reclaim the monarchy. When William defeated James, James fled once again to France, where he died in 1701. The changes brought about in 1689 spelled the end of royal absolutism in

the British Isles and laid the foundations for a **constitutional monarchy** in which the monarch and Parliament ruled as partners following the principles of the rule of law.

The reign of William and Mary inaugurated twenty-five years of war against France. Whigs supported William's pursuit of Louis XIV, while Tories grum-

rule of law Principle that law has a higher authority than rulers, governments, and officials; rulers must obey the laws.

constitutional monarchy Form of government in which the monarch and legislature rule as partners following the principles of the rule of law.

bled about rising land taxes. The two parties fiercely contested elections to seats in the House of Commons. In principle, Parliament controlled taxation and the Crown controlled foreign policy. But ongoing warfare forced the two sides to work together, since William had to explain his policies to Parliament if he hoped to get the money he needed.

Mary died childless in 1694, and when William died in 1702, the crown passed to James II's younger Protestant daughter, Anne. Anne had had nineteen children, all of whom were stillborn or died in infancy. She believed this calamity was God's judgment on her father's removal from the throne. As Anne had no heirs, Parliament determined who would rule when Anne died. In 1701, fifty-seven Catholic Stuarts were passed over in favor of a Protestant granddaughter of James I, Sophia, of the German state of Hanover. In 1707, Scotland, still an independent kingdom ruled by the English monarch, but suffering from an economic depression and a financial collapse, agreed to accept the **Act of Union** with England to create a united Great Britain ruled over by a Protestant monarch. In 1714, when Anne died, Sophia's son George became king. Later generations in England referred to the events of 1688 and 1689 as the **Glorious Revolution,** which kept the state Protestant while advancing the power of Parliament and repudiating absolutist and divine right theories of kingship.

The Georges from Germany

George I was already middle aged when he became king of Great Britain in 1714. He spoke no English and had to communicate with his ministers in French. He also spent half his time in Hanover. The Great Britain he presided over had emerged victorious from the wars against Louis XIV, and his right to be British throne had been recognized by the Treaty of Utrecht ending the War of the Spanish Succession in 1713. The treaty had also awarded Britain Gibraltar, Hudson's Bay, Nova Scotia, Newfoundland, and the *asiento,* which gave the British the exclusive right to import African slaves into Spanish America. In addition to the *asiento,* Britain was allowed limited rights of trade with the Spanish colonies. These concessions spurred development of the British navy and the establishment of trading posts that were vital to the kingdom's growing colonial empire. The territorial grants in North America intensified the contest between France and Britain for control of Canada.

Recognition of George as king provoked James II's baby boy, now grown up, to lead an uprising in Scotland to regain the crown. It failed, but when a number of Tories expressed sympathy for the **pretender,** the Whigs accused them of treason. This charge, coupled with George's clear preference for the Whigs, turned the Tories into a minority party for the next forty-five years. The leader of the triumphant Whigs was **Sir Robert Walpole,** a rich landowner and country gentleman. Walpole, unlike his ministerial predecessors, refused the king's offer to ennoble him and give him a seat in the House of Lords, the upper house of Parliament. Walpole preferred to stay in the Commons because he believed he could be more effective there in creating majorities to support royal policies. His skill in winning over both the king and Parliament contributed to the smooth running of the central government, while his decision to remain in the Commons added to the power of that house. Walpole also tried to calm the partisan passions that had agitated the country since 1660. He emphasized good manners in politics and signaled his willingness to accept moderate Tories into his political coalitions. Thus, in his own way, he agreed with Louis XIV that politeness had its political uses. Under Walpole, Britain enjoyed a period of political stability that contrasted sharply with the turmoil preceding George I's reign.

At the same time, a new sense of collective British identity was forming. Britons enjoyed the rights guaranteed in 1689 and were thereby "free-born," in opposition to what they thought were the "slavish" Catholic peoples of France or Spain. This new sense of identity was given voice in the poem "Rule, Britannia," set to music in 1740: "Rule, Britannia! Britannia, rule the waves / Britons never never never shall be slaves." After their union with England, Scots could also identify with this sense of national unity, especially since they profited increasingly from British overseas and colonial trade. The Catholic Irish, however, conquered and impoverished, were excluded from the community of the "free-born."

Act of Union Parliamentary act of 1707 uniting Scotland and England in the one kingdom of Great Britain.

Glorious Revolution (1688–1689) Name given to the events leading to the dethronement of James II and the rule of William and Mary.

George I (r. 1714–1727) Elector of Hanover who became king of Great Britain.

asiento Monopoly on the importation of African slaves into Spanish America granted to English merchants by Spain in 1713.

pretender Claimant to a throne.

Sir Robert Walpole (1676–1745) Leader of the Whigs and the most important minister in England from 1721 to 1742.

When George I died in 1727, Walpole survived the change of reign and continued to serve George II. Throughout his career he promoted a policy of peace with the rest of Europe and used this time to consolidate the religious and political gains of the Glorious Revolution. When he left office in 1742, the principle of mixed monarchy, in which a constitutionally sanctioned Protestant king ruled jointly with Parliament, had become the cornerstone of British political life. Finally, the defeat of James II in Ireland in 1689, along with the union of Scotland and England in 1707, consolidated English dominance.

Two World Wars, 1740–1763

↓ How did the competitive European state system effect the conduct of war?

↓ What were the outcomes of the two world wars for the states that fought in them?

In the middle of the eighteenth century, all the major states of Europe were drawn into two great wars. Warfare, a permanent feature of relations between states in early modern Europe, often ended in stalemate, but the midcentury wars fundamentally altered European power relations. Because they were also fought in the overseas empires of Britain, France, and Spain, they had long-lasting consequences for peoples in the Western Hemisphere and Asia.

The Wars

In 1740, Frederick II of Prussia attacked Maria Theresa of Austria, beginning the War of the Austrian Succession. The rulers of Bavaria and Saxony challenged Maria Theresa's right to rule on the grounds that they were more legitimate heirs to Charles VI than she. Frederick, however, accepted the legitimacy of her succession. What he wanted was Silesia, the richest of Austria's territories. Taking advantage of challenges to Maria Theresa's right of succession, he claimed that Silesia rightfully belonged to Prussia and then seized the province. Britain had been at war with Spain since 1739 over the trading rights conceded to it at the end of the War of the Spanish Succession. In 1740, Britain joined Austria to fight Prussia, renewing the British-Austrian alliance that had been forged in the wars against Louis XIV. The British also attacked the French in North America and India. France, in turn, stood by its traditional ally, Prussia, in order to check Austrian power. In 1748, at war's end, Prussia emerged victorious, keeping Silesia. The war between Britain and France ended indecisively.

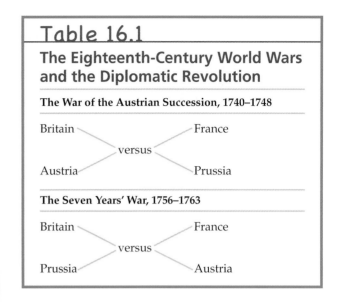

Table 16.1

The Eighteenth-Century World Wars and the Diplomatic Revolution

The War of the Austrian Succession, 1740–1748

Britain ╲╱ France
      ╳ versus
Austria ╱╲ Prussia

The Seven Years' War, 1756–1763

Britain ╲╱ France
      ╳ versus
Prussia ╱╲ Austria

War broke out again in 1756 between Austria and Prussia over Silesia, this time with Russia allied with Austria against Prussia. Since 1754, France and Britain had again been at war in North America along the western frontier of the British colonies there. In 1756, they continued the fight in Europe and India during the **Seven Years' War.** Because Austria had recently concluded an alliance with France, Britain also switched sides and joined with Prussia against the two in the **diplomatic revolution.** The war ended in 1763. The complicated alliances in these two wars are summarized in Table 16.1.

Eighteenth-Century Warfare

The complex, ever-shifting alliances and counteralliances that characterized the world wars of the mid-eighteenth century were typical of the culture of war in early modern Europe. War was accepted as an inevitable and ongoing feature of the relations between European states. Rulers did little to counteract this idea; the old ideal of the king as head of the warrior band was too deeply embedded in European tradition.

The growth of large professional armies in the hundred years between 1650 and 1750 reinforced the idea of the inevitability of ongoing warfare. The profes-

Seven Years' War   (1756–1763) World war fought in Europe, North America, and India.

diplomatic revolution   Shift in alliances between European states that preceded the Seven Years' War.

In this engraving from a Prussian army manual of 1726 a drill master supervises the marching and field maneuvers for which the Prussian army was famous. Soldiers who fail to follow his commands will have to mount the donkey punishment device shown on the left. By emphasizing the stark simplicity of the surrounding buildings, the engraver reinforces the precision and orderliness of the troops at drill. *(Bildarchiv Preussischer Kulturbesitz/Art Resource, NY)*

sional standing army, pioneered by Louis XIV, became a standard feature in eighteenth-century states. The one exception was Britain, which preferred to keep its army small while offering financial aid to its continental allies' forces. Armies were now better provisioned and disciplined than they had been during the period of religious warfare and were, therefore, less of a danger to the civilian population. Although troops were sometimes quartered in civilians' homes and taxes were imposed for the armies' upkeep, the fear of military pillaging lessened.

A science of warfare also emerged, taking several forms. One was an interest in military engineering. In France, Sébastien le Prestre de Vauban improved the architecture of fortresses and supervised their construction along France's northern and eastern frontiers. The idea that impregnable fortresses could protect France from its enemies was to shape French military planning into the twentieth century. Military scientists also produced new drill manuals for soldiers, specifying a series of increasingly complicated battlefield maneuvers, including the Prussian "goose step," which kept soldiers in a straight line. Not surprisingly, Frederick William I was a pioneer in this field, earning him the nickname "the royal drill sergeant." Soon, other armies were training their troops in similar ways. Army officers, almost always drawn from the nobility, received instruction in drill and battlefield tactics in new military academies and then applied them to the common soldiers under their command.

Eighteenth-century statesmen used warfare to enforce the doctrine of the balance of power, based on the assumption that Europe's international system functioned best when power was evenly distributed among states, thereby preventing any one of them from achieving dominance over the others. Thus, the coalitions against Louis XIV were explained as restoring the balance that the Sun King's aggressive military activity had threatened. Of course, agreement on the balance rested on the agreement of all the interested players. And that was where the problems began.

Since one player's "balance" was often another's "domination," European states were thrown into a never-ending defensive and offensive scramble. Religious division played a smaller role in the wars of midcentury than it had a century earlier. Now issues of territory, power, and prestige were central.

Winners and Losers

When war ended in 1763, there were clear winners and losers. In central Europe, Frederick II was a winner; Silesia was never returned to Austria. But the wars put huge strains on Prussia's finances and military, and at times it looked as if the kingdom would be defeated. In 1762, Frederick was saved when the pro-German emperor Peter III broke Russia's alliance with Austria and signed a peace with Prussia. This was the most consequential act of his short reign. After 1763, Prussia rested. "Old Fritz," as his subjects called the king, lost his taste for wars of conquest. Now he preferred more

In this painting by R. Warthmülle, Frederick II of Prussia inspects a potato field. Potatoes grew well in the sandy soils of Frederick's lands, and he promoted the cultivation of this New World vegetable for its high nutritional value and abundant yield. Well-fed Prussians, he knew, would live to pay taxes and serve in the army. *(Private Collection, Hamburg/akg-images)*

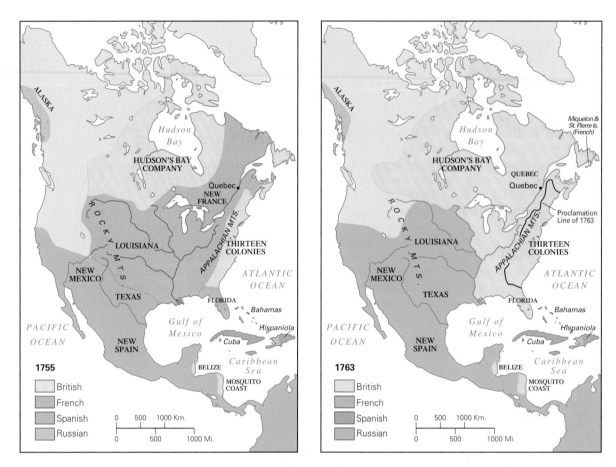

MAP 16.3 **European Claims in North America Before and After the Seven Years' War** In losing the Seven Years' War, France lost its continental North American empire. New France went to Britain, and Louisiana went to Spain. France retained only Newfoundland and its island colonies in the Caribbean.

peaceful means for gaining territory, such as joining with Austria and Russia in 1772 to partition Poland and finally link Prussia with Brandenburg.

Austria was a loser. Before 1740, the Habsburgs had not followed Prussia and Russia in reforming state finances, strengthening the central administration, and updating the army. The shock of Silesia's loss galvanized Maria Theresa into a frenzy of state building. She began with the army, founding a military academy, introducing advanced drill and maneuvering techniques, and expanding the government's ability to house and supply its troops. To pay for reform, she overhauled the state's tax structure. Beginning in 1748, she coaxed the diets of Bohemia and Austria to grant taxes for ten years. In effect, this action made state taxation permanent, and the power of the magnates in the diets to control state finances waned, just

as it had in Prussia under the Great Elector. To increase government efficiency, she founded a school to train state administrators. In 1761, she decreed that her state council, staffed by experts, could make policy decisions that were binding on her and the state administration. She, therefore, repudiated the king-centered decision making that Louis XIV and Frederick William I of Prussia had developed.

In 1756, when the Seven Years' War began, Maria Theresa's reforms were put to the test and failed. With Silesia still in Frederick's hands at war's end, Austria initiated more reforms, primarily to increase revenue to pay for a better army. This time, however, Maria Theresa tackled the problem by focusing on the economic improvement of the mass of her subjects, the serfs. Like Leopold I, she tried to reduce serfs' uncompensated work for their landlords, de-

Some official portraits of Maria Theresa show her with her husband and children, emphasizing her role as wife and mother. This one, by Martin Meyhens (c. 1743). shows her in military dress as commander of the Austrian army. *(Erich Lessing/Art Resource, NY)*

creeing that the traditional minimum of three days a week would now be the maximum. Reform of serfs' lives pitted Maria Theresa against the interests of the landlord class, but she made headway, especially in Austria and Bohemia, when serfs took matters into their own hands by going on rent strikes and fomenting local rebellions against landlord demands.

Maria Theresa also imposed new taxes on the Catholic Church. Although she was a pious Roman Catholic who hated heresy, she believed that the church should assume a greater part of the expenses needed to defend the state against competitors. The clergy were taxed without the pope's permission, and the church was forbidden to acquire new land that would be tax-free.

Defense of the Habsburg lands against enemies went hand in hand with attacks on weaker states, as the Polish partition of 1772 shows. Maria Theresa had moral scruples about the partition, but fear of continuing vulnerability in the competitive international system overcame her qualms. Frederick II of Prussia remarked unkindly, "The more she weeps, the more she takes."

Maria Theresa died in 1780 and was succeeded by her son, **Joseph II**, who was also determined to strengthen Austria against Prussia. But as his foreign policy never resulted in clear victories, he pushed domestic reforms in a more radical direction. In the 1780s he abolished serfdom. Then, in 1789, using new property tax rolls, he abolished the rents and uncompensated work obligations peasants owed their landlords, replacing them with a single cash payment. He also imposed state taxes on the ex-serfs. Traditional procedures had denied the state direct jurisdiction over peasants; the state had to work through the noble landlord class. But Joseph's reforms asserted direct state control. Peasants were to keep 70 percent of their income, the rest going in payments to the landlord and the state. Predictably, landlords resisted his radical restructuring of political and social relations, but peasants rose up in support of the reforms. The result was widespread rebellion when Joseph died in 1790. His brother, who succeeded him as Leopold II, restored order by making concessions to the landlords. He reinstituted serfdom and landlords' control of peasants. Serfdom was not permanently abolished until 1848.

Austria's defeat in war led to radical social reforms intended to increase peasant prosperity, which in turn would allow for higher taxes and more money for the army. Thus, the dynamics of Europe's fiercely competitive international system fundamentally shaped the course of Austrian state building over the second half of the eighteenth century.

Although Britain and France fought each other in Europe alongside their respective allies, their real contest was overseas in North America and India. In 1763, at the end of the Seven Years' War, Britain was the undisputed winner. British victories drove the French off the North American mainland. Britain also secured its predominant place in India. But the victory in North America created problems of its own that led directly to the American Revolution and indirectly to revolution in France.

Joseph II   (r. 1780–1790) Holy Roman emperor and head of the Austrian Habsburg lands who tried to strengthen his realm through radical reform of its social structure.

Summary

Review Questions

↑ How did governments try to establish good working relations with the people?

↑ What effect did state building have on the various religious communities of Europe?

↑ What factors worked to develop or retard a collective sense of national identity?

After 1648, Europe's rulers engaged in vigorous state building. In France, Louis XIV pressed change from above based on the principle of royal absolutism, as did rulers in Prussia, Russia, and, eventually, Austria. In the British Isles, absolutism gave way to limited constitutional monarchy after the Glorious Revolution, but William III's wars against Louis XIV increased the effectiveness of the central government in Britain while strengthening Parliament's role in policymaking and administration. In all cases, the frequent warfare fostered by the competitive European state system was the prime incentive for strengthening the state.

Successful state building involved establishing good working relations between rulers and elite groups. In France and Prussia, nobles' political independence was curbed while their social preeminence was confirmed with honors and opportunities for state service. In England, after the failure of royal absolutism in 1689, the monarch had to cooperate with the landowning classes who controlled Parliament as well as local government. In Russia, rulers after Peter the Great wooed the landlord class by canceling compulsory state service but confirming landlords' rights over the serfs on their estates. Failure to establish working relations with the elite could lead to rebellion, as it did in Austria when Joseph II antagonized the nobility with his attacks on serfdom.

Joseph's abolition of serfdom was motivated in part by a desire to use state power to improve the lives of ordinary people, and the serfs responded by cooperating in the updating of property rolls and rising in support of reform when nobles resisted change. In France, Louis XIV's reforms also had the same effect; control of the army eased fears of violence and looting, and efficient and fair royal courts encouraged confidence. Louis XV's reforms of police forces and poor relief offered new services to his subjects. But when ordinary people's needs were overlooked by rulers, revolt could follow, as Pugachev's rebellion in Russia shows.

After 1648, religious commitments continued to shape identity and sometimes led to conflicts. Although Protestants throughout Europe denounced Louis XIV's revocation of the Edict of Nantes, the French Catholic population supported it. In England and Scotland, attacks on Catholics had widespread popular support. The Old Believers in Russia refused any cooperation with the state-supported Russian Orthodox Church. In France, Huguenots who refused conversion to Catholicism were also brutally dealt with. In general, however, the trend after 1648 was toward limited toleration of religious dissenters. In addition, forms of collective identity shifted from religion toward the national community. Wars between Britain and France produced a surge of patriotism in each country. While religious difference contributed to the stereotyping of the enemy, more state-centered issues, such as control of colonies or prosperity in trade, also whipped up patriotic fervor.

← **Thinking Back, Thinking Ahead** →

How were the European states of the eighteenth century similar to and different from the states of previous centuries?

ECHO ECHO ECHO ECHO ECHO

Palaces

The word *palace* derives from the name for the hill in Rome, the Palatium, where the Emperor Augustus resided. In the Middle Ages, *palatium* ("palace") referred to the temporary lodgings of kings on the move. It was also used for a monastery's guesthouse for royalty. Charlemagne's residence at Aachen was a palace of sorts. At Fontainebleau, Francis I of France built a palace blending Italian Renaissance architectural principles with traditional French design. In the late sixteenth century, Philip II of Spain built the Escorial, a grand palace-monastery complex outside Madrid. In the late seventeenth century, Louis XIV's Versailles outdid them all and set the standard for later palaces throughout Europe.

In the eighteenth century, Frederick II, following Leopold I's Schönbrunn, built a palace at Potsdam to show that Prussia also knew how to keep up with the Bourbons. The British monarchs lagged behind these palace makers. In 1762, George III bought the run-down townhouse of the Duke of Buckingham for his wife. It was only in the nineteenth and twentieth centuries that remodeling made it into the Buckingham Palace of today. British monarchs from Queen Victoria on have lived there.

Although Versailles was Europe's grandest palace, it was not very clean. Men used areas under stairways as urinals, and contemporaries remarked on the stench when they climbed the stairs. Interestingly, Versailles was open to the public. All a man needed to stroll the gardens and walk through the public rooms was a hat, gloves, and sword. If you forgot yours or did not own them, they could be rented at the gate. Visitors could also watch the king eat at midday; they got in line and filed through the far end of the room. Easy public access to the ruler's residence contrasts with the strict security that now surrounds almost all political leaders.

Today, most government heads do not live in palaces. The president of the United States lives in the White House, not the White Palace. The prime minister of Britain lives at 10 Downing Street. One exception is the president of France, who lives in Paris in the Élysée Palace, decorated in the style of Louis XIV and Louis XV. By the twenty-first century, many old palaces had undergone democratization. The Louvre Palace in Paris, the Winter Palace in St. Petersburg, and even Versailles have been turned into public monuments or museums. You can stroll through them for the price of a ticket.

Suggested Readings

Collins, James B. *The State in Early Modern France.* New York: Cambridge University Press, 2001. A good introduction to state building.

Gagliardo, John. *Germany Under the Old Regime, 1600–1790.* New York: Longman, 1991. A good general account.

Ingrao, Charles. *The Habsburg Monarchy, 1618–1715.* 2nd ed. New York: Cambridge University Press, 2000. A history of state building in the Habsburg lands.

Riasanovsky, Nicholas V., and Mark Steinberg. *A History of Russia.* 7th ed. New York: Oxford University Press, 2005. The standard account in English.

Smith, Lacey Baldwin. *This Realm of England, 1399–1688.* 8th ed. Boston: Houghton Mifflin Company, 2001. A standard account.

Spielman, John P. *Leopold I of Austria.* London: Thames and Hudson, 1977. A good biography.

Willcox, William B., and Walter L. Arnstein. *The Age of Aristocracy, 1688–1830.* 8th ed. Boston: Houghton Mifflin Company, 2001. A standard account of British history after the Glorious Revolution.

Websites

On early modern absolutism, **Structures of Politics–Absolutism,** at www.fordham.edu/halsall/mod/modsbook1.html#Structures%20of%20Politics%20-%20Absolutism

On politics in the Dutch Republic and the British Isles, **England, Holland, and America—Alternative Polities and Economies,** at www.fordham.edu/halsall/mod/modsbook1.html#England,%20Holland,%20and%20America

On early modern Russia, **Romanov Dynasty,** at www.mnsu.edu/museum/historyrussia/romanov.html

The Scientific Revolution and the Enlightenment, 1550–1790

1500 B.C.E.	1000 B.C.E.	500 B.C.E.	1 B.C.E./1 C.E.

	1543 Copernicus, *On the Revolution of the Heavenly Bodies*				1637 Descartes, *The Discourse on Method*	
1540	1560	1580	1600	1620	1640	1660

Europe During the Scientific Revolution and the Enlightenment

This map shows that most scientific and Enlightenment centers were in the cities of western and central Europe. What factors explain this geographical spread? Why do you think intellectual life was focused in cities?

Legend:
- Major university
- Scientific society
- **S** Salon
- Tea/coffee house
- Boundary of Holy Roman Empire

KINGDOM OF SWEDEN
Stockholm
Oslo

KINGDOM OF DENMARK AND NORWAY
Copenhagen
Brahe

RUSSIAN EMPIRE
St. Petersburg — Catherine II
Moscow

GREAT BRITAIN
Edinburgh
Dublin

Bacon
Harvey
Hobbes
Boyle
Locke
Behn
Newton
Pope
Lady Montagu
Wollstonecraft
Cook

North Sea

Vesalius
van Leeuwenhoek

UNITED STATES OF AMERICA
Franklin
Jefferson

ATLANTIC OCEAN

Oxford
London
Cambridge

DUTCH REPUBLIC
Amsterdam
Leiden

AUSTRIAN NETHERLANDS

PRUSSIA
Königsberg
Copernicus
Kant

POLAND
Warsaw

Kepler
Mendelssohn
Frederick II

S Berlin

Göttingen

Descartes
Pascal
Baron de Montesquieu
Voltaire
Châtelet
La Mettrie
Abbé Raynal
Diderot
Vigeé-Lebrun

FRANCE
Paris **S**

Heidelberg
Tübingen

Prague

AUSTRIA
Vienna
Rudolph II
Mozart

SWITZERLAND
Rousseau
Geneva
Lyons
Freiburg Bern

Venice
Padua

Budapest
HUNGARY

Baltic Sea

Black Sea

OTTOMAN EMPIRE

Toulouse
Montpellier

Genoa
Bologna

REPUBLIC OF VENICE

Gallileo
Cosimo II
Florence

PORTUGAL
Lisbon

Salamanca
Madrid

SPAIN

PAPAL STATES
Rome

Constantinople

Naples

KINGDOM OF THE TWO SICILIES

Mediterranean Sea

OTTOMAN EMPIRE

0   200   400 Km.
0   200   400 Mi.

---

500 C.E.	1000 C.E.	1500 C.E.	2000 C.E.

1687
Newton, *Mathematical Principles of Natural Philosophy*

1690
Locke, *An Essay Concerning Human Understanding*

1733
Voltaire, *Philosophical Letters on the English*

1748
Montesquieu, *The Spirit of the Laws*

1751
Diderot, *Encyclopédie, volume 1*

1776
American Declaration of Independence

1784
Kant, *What Is Enlightenment?*

1680	1700	1720	1740	1760	1780	1800

477

Choice Choice Choice Choice

Lady Mary Wortley Montague

Lady Mary Wortley Montagu, an aristocrat, moved in England's literary circles as well, publishing poems and pamphlets anonymously. Her letters to friends and family were eventually collected and published, since letter writing was considered an art form in her day. She was also the wife of the British ambassador to the Ottoman Turkish sultan's court in Constantinople. In 1718, she witnessed the Turkish practice of inoculating people against the deadly disease of smallpox. (Boston Athenaeum)

Lady Mary Wortley Montagu Introduces Smallpox Inoculation in England

In March 1718, an aged Greek woman, her hands shaking, reached for the arms of the six-year-old son of the British ambassador to the sultan's court in Constantinople. After opening veins in the boy's arms with a blunt, rusty needle, she smeared pus into the cuts. The pus, carried in a nutshell, had come from a victim of smallpox. The old woman then bound up the wounds with more nutshells. A day later, the boy's arms began to swell, and on the third day bright spots appeared on his face and quickly turned into a hundred pustules. For a week he lay in bed with a fever. Then the pustules subsided, the fever fell, and the boy was well. He had survived a mild case of smallpox and would not get the disease again.

The boy's mother had supervised this "engrafting," as the procedure was then called. Lady Mary Wortley Montagu had seen it performed and had written home that Turks and Greeks in the sultan's lands often held engrafting parties, at which ten or fifteen people were infected with "the best sort of smallpox." Some Greeks liked to have the cuts made on their foreheads, arms, and chest to make the sign of the cross. For the Protestant Lady Mary, this was pure superstition; she preferred cuts in hidden places so that the scars they caused would not be seen. After contracting a mild form of the disease, almost everyone survived in complete health. Impressed with the procedure's success, Lady Mary decided on engrafting for her son to protect him from the death or disfigurement that smallpox so often brought.

Lady Mary knew, personally, the ravages of smallpox. In 1713, a beloved brother had died from the disease. Three years later, she contracted it. Luckily, she lived, but she lost her eyelashes and had deep pits on her face from scars the pustules had left. When her son survived his inoculation unblemished, Lady Mary became a strong advocate for the procedure. After her return to England in 1718, she encouraged friends and family to undergo inoculation and set the example again by having her infant daughter engrafted. As an aristocrat, she moved in Britain's highest social and political circles, and in 1721 the Princess of Wales joined her cause. At the princess's command, six volunteers were recruited at London's notorious Newgate Prison, and promised freedom if they survived. Physicians, surgeons, and members of the Royal Society, England's leading scientific institute, witnessed the engrafting, which was successful. The princess then ordered more experiments on London orphans. When they, too, were successful, she had two of her own daughters inoculated. Members of the royal court then began to inoculate themselves and their children. However, when two of them died, a huge controversy erupted over the wisdom of the procedure.

Some Anglican clergymen attacked inoculation on the grounds that it was contrary to God's will. But six Puritan clergy from Boston wrote that they found nothing theologically offensive in the treatment. Physicians attacked it on all fronts: inoculation's protective power was not satisfactorily demonstrated; the disease might be spread through it; the procedure was the work of amateurs who should leave such matters to the medical professionals. Worst of all, not only was it foreign, it was Turkish! As one doctor fumed, inoculation was the work of "*Ignorant Women* amongst an illiterate and unthinking People."

Faced with these attacks, Lady Mary wrote a scathing article in which she accused physicians of opposing the procedure out of greed and snobbery. Here she made public the speculation she had stated privately in a letter to her sister— whether doctors would be willing "to destroy such a considerable branch of their revenue for the good of mankind." The article, printed in a leading London newspaper, was published anonymously, for Lady Mary did not believe that a person of high breeding, like herself, should write for the public. Nevertheless, her campaign "for the good of mankind" continued to flourish. The practice of inoculation spread, and improvements, such as using cowpox, a milder variant of smallpox, made it safer.

In the nineteenth and twentieth centuries, wide use of vaccine essentially eradicated smallpox, a lethal disease that had long ravaged human populations. Therefore, routine vaccination is no longer necessary today for prevention.

Introduction

Lady Mary was caught up in many of the intellectual currents of the seventeenth and eighteenth centuries. Her interest in medicine and her attention to observation and experimentation were part of a general shift in scientific theory and method that had begun in the sixteenth century. This Scientific Revolution, which first occurred in astronomy, physics, and anatomy, had fundamentally altered people's view of the universe and led to the development of a scientific method that relied more on human reason to arrive at truth and less on the authority of ancient authors and sacred scripture. Now a new intellectual figure, the scientific expert, began to challenge the views of traditional theologians and those who believed that the best human knowledge was found in the works of ancient Greeks and Romans.

The New Science also inspired attempts to apply scientific methods to other fields of inquiry in an intellectual movement known as the Enlightenment. Relying on the scientific method's use of human reason to arrive at truth, the Enlightenment created the modern social sciences. Traditional Christianity also came under scrutiny; Lady Mary's scorn for religious "superstition" was shared by many supporters of the Enlightenment, who thought that religion should be based on observation of the natural world and the exercise of human reason. Some abandoned traditional Christianity altogether. As a result, the Christian worldview that had dominated European thought for more than a thousand years now competed with non-Christian and even nonreligious alternatives.

The principles of both the New Science and the Enlightenment were spread through new communication networks. Scientific societies, polite salon gatherings, coffeehouses, Masonic lodges, and debating clubs, for all their differences, created environments for discussion of the ideas and methods of both movements. Discussion also filled the pages of a growing number of books, newspapers, and pamphlets, as writers and publishers produced a wide variety of reading material for increasing numbers of literate Europeans. As more and more people engaged in public discussion of current affairs, a new intellectual and political force arose—public opinion—that could determine an author's success or failure and even sway the policies of kings.

When Lady Mary entered the debate over inoculation, she acted as a woman defending a Turkish medical practice carried out by other women. Debate was a central feature of both the Scientific Revolution and the Enlightenment. Women participated in these debates, and soon their increasing presence in European intellectual life led to a debate over issues of gender equality and the relations between men and women. Growth in commerce and the establishment of overseas colonies around the world also provoked debate about Europe's place in the larger world. By the end of the century, debate also centered on a central feature of commerce and colonization—the institution of slavery. In these debates, as in religion, Christian ideas had to compete with approaches that paid more attention to nature, climate, and biology than to traditional theology.

Chronology

Year	Event
1543	Copernicus publishes *On the Revolution of the Heavenly Bodies*
1637	Descartes publishes *The Discourse on Method*
1651	Hobbes publishes *Leviathan*
1687	Newton publishes *Mathematical Principles of Natural Philosophy*
1688	Behn publishes *Oroonoko*
1690	Locke publishes *An Essay Concerning Human Understanding* and *Two Treatises on Government*
1717	First Masonic lodge opens in London
1718	Lady Mary Wortley Montagu introduces smallpox inoculation in England
1733	Voltaire publishes *Philosophical Letters on the English*
1746	La Mettrie publishes *Man the Machine*
1748	Montesquieu publishes *The Spirit of the Laws*
1751	First volume of Diderot's *Encyclopédie* is published
1761	Voltaire takes up the case of Jean Calas; Rousseau publishes *The New Heloise*
1762	Rousseau publishes *The Social Contract* and *Emile*
1770	Raynal publishes *The Philosophical History of the Two Indies*
1772	Diderot publishes *The Supplement to the Voyage of Bougainville*
1775	Pierre Roussel publishes *The Physical and Moral Makeup of Women*
1776	Declaration of Independence states independence of American colonies from England
1778	Voltaire returns in triumph to Paris
1781	Thomas Jefferson publishes *Notes on the State of Virginia*
1784	Emmanuel Kant publishes *What Is Enlightenment?*
1789	Olaudah Equiano publishes his *Life*
1791	Mozart's opera *The Magic Flute* is performed in Vienna

A Revolution in Astronomy

↓ What were the central features of the new scientific method?

↓ What factors explain the rise of the New Science?

The religious crises that shook Europe in the sixteenth and seventeenth centuries were accompanied by an intellectual crisis. Beginning as a new theory of the universe that placed the sun, not the earth, at its center, it grew into a questioning of the traditional sources of authority guiding European thought about the natural world—ancient authors, and Christian scripture. Gradually, as the new view of the universe gained acceptance, new sources of authority based on close observation of natural phenomena and the use of independent human reasoning were embraced. These changes are usually described as the Scientific Revolution.

Ancient and Medieval Astronomy

Following the translation of classical works in the twelfth century, Europeans' views of the universe had been shaped by two ancient Greek authorities: the philosopher Aristotle and the astronomer Ptolemy. For centuries, medieval universities had synthesized their teaching with Christian theology to describe how the universe worked. In this system, the earth was at the center, created by God to be fixed and unmoving. But in terms of worth, earth was the lowest element in the cosmic scheme. It was the place of decay; as one philosopher put it, our world was "the worst, the lowest, most lifeless part of the universe, the bottom story of the house." It was only in this region, which stretched upward to the moon, that change took place. Here night turned to day; plants sprouted, bloomed, and died; and human beings moved from cradle to grave. The innate nature of objects determined some of the movement in this region. Thus acorns grew into oaks and kittens into cats because both strove to realize their potential and reach their goal as mature organisms. The same striving toward their goals also characterized nonliving things; fire leapt upward because its proper place was in the heights, while a rock thrown in the air fell because its place was on the earth. Essentially, objects were urged along by their inner natures to come to rest in their rightful place. Rest was the natural state of being for objects; it was only motion that had to be explained. In the case of human beings, God's decrees determined the movement of their lives; they hurtled toward death and decay because of their sinful rebellion against God until Christ redeemed them and they found their place of rest in Heaven.

Above the moon, a radically different part of the universe reigned. In these regions there was no change or decay. The sun and the planets, made of a uniquely pure and perfect substance, moved endlessly in circles (the noblest form of motion, as Plato had taught). Above them were the fixed stars, which also moved in a circle, propelled by the angels. As all these bodies moved, they created a wondrous music, the harmony of the spheres. Beyond the stars the universe ended, and the mysterious realm of God's Heaven began.

This picture of the natural world seemed to work because it was confirmed in multiple ways. First, it corresponded with common sense (sun, moon, and planets *did* move across the sky.) Common sense was in turn reinforced by prediction. Ptolemy had shown that it was possible to calculate the trajectories of the planets in advance, and astronomers in the centuries after him had confirmed and refined his calculations. Finally, this view corresponded with what were taken as the revealed truths of Christian scripture.

A New View of the Universe

In the sixteenth century, a new view of the universe challenged the traditional one. As it spread, an intellectual crisis developed, rivaling the crises in faith and certainty created by the Protestant Reformation, the Wars of Religion, and the discovery of the New World—an entire hemisphere with previously unknown plants, animals, and human beings.

The challenge began with a Polish clergyman in East Prussia, **Nicholas Copernicus.** Seeking to improve Ptolemy's predictions of planetary movement by making them simpler, Copernicus started with the assumption that earth and the planets moved about the sun. His *On the Revolutions of the Heavenly Bodies,* published in 1543, was quickly denounced by both

In an engraving from Johannes Hevelius' *Selenographia* (1647), an astronomer, perhaps Hevelius himself, looks at the heavens through a telescope. After Galileo's pioneering efforts, observatories sprang up all over Europe. Hevelius' observatory, on the roof of his house in Danzig, was one of the best. *(The Syndics of the Cambridge University Library)*

Protestants and Catholics. Nevertheless, Copernicus caught the attention of some astronomers, who began building on his work.

One of the first was a Dane, **Tycho Brahe,** who spent years producing the best logs of planetary movement yet compiled. He also described in detail a new star that appeared in 1572 and, thereby, disturbed the traditional view that the universe above the moon was changeless. But Brahe held the traditional view that the earth was the unmoving center of the universe; for him, the planets moved around the sun, but

Nicholas Copernicus (1473–1543) Polish astronomer who posited a sun-centered universe in which earth and the other planets move around the sun.

Tycho Brahe (1546–1601) Danish astronomer who partly confirmed Copernicus's theory of a sun-centered universe.

Sir Isaac Newton was sixty-years-old when this portrait was painted by Sir Godfrey Kneller in 1702. He had published his *Mathematical Principles* some fifteen years earlier and was at the height of his fame. *(By courtesy of the National Portrait Gallery, London)*

the sun moved around the earth. Brahe's work was continued by his pupil, **Johannes Kepler,** who used Brahe's calculations to argue that the planets moved in elliptical, not circular, orbits around the sun and that the speed of their movement varied. Both points also challenged older ideas about the unchanging nature of the upper universe.

Galileo Galilei, a professor of mathematics from Florence, continued the work of Copernicus, Brahe, and Kepler. While these men had viewed the heavens with the naked eye, Galileo used the newly invented telescope to see craters and other "imperfections" on the moon and describe sunspots for the first time. He also confirmed Copernicus's theory that the planets and the sun rotated on their own axes and posited that earth did the same. These phenomena further undermined traditional ideas. Galileo also conducted carefully controlled experiments on earthly bodies, rolling metal balls down slopes of varying degrees. He argued that material bodies were naturally in motion, thereby questioning the older idea that they moved only when

they were displaced from their homes and rested once they arrived there. A brilliant writer, Galileo knew how to present his findings to a broad public. Despite his cordial relations with Pope Urban VIII, Galileo eventually caught the eye of the Roman Inquisition, which ordered him to stop arguing in favor of the sun-centered universe and placed him under house arrest.

The Inquisition's condemnation of Galileo virtually guaranteed that sympathetic Protestants would take up his cause. The greatest of them was the Englishman **Sir Isaac Newton.** In his *Mathematical Principles of Natural Philosophy* (1687), Newton brought together the work of Copernicus, Brahe, Kepler, and Galileo to present a complete picture of the universe. Planets, rotating on their axes, traveled around the sun in elliptical orbit. Their orbits and the variations in their speed were controlled by gravity, a force of mutual attraction that kept the planets from flying off into space. Gravity also explained the behavior of bodies on earth, as described by Galileo. Beyond the solar system, the universe stretched out infinitely. Newton presented his picture mathematically. Although only a handful of his contemporaries understood his advanced equations, his ability to knit the work of his predecessors into an all-encompassing description of the universe proved compelling and established the modern science of physics.

Models of Scientific Knowledge

Just as important as the new view of the universe were the methods developed for proposing it. Taken together, they radically altered traditional European views of how human beings know anything. **Sir Francis Bacon,** lord chancellor of England under James I, was an early advocate of an approach to knowledge grounded in careful observation and experimentation. For him, the source of authority for knowledge about the natural world was found in that world itself, not in the writings of Greeks or Romans. He was, there-

Johannes Kepler (1571–1630) German student of Brahe who argued that the planets moved in elliptical orbits around the sun.

Galileo Galilei (1564–1642) Italian astronomer who first used the telescope to view the heavens and argued in favor of the Copernican system.

Sir Isaac Newton (1642–1727) English mathematician and philosopher who established the modern science of physics.

Sir Francis Bacon (1561–1626) English defender of the New Science who endorsed the inductive method of inquiry.

fore, an early defender of a purely **inductive method** of reasoning, which based general statements on observation of phenomena as the only proper way to gain knowledge.

Just as influential was a French mathematician and the inventor of analytic geometry, **René Descartes.** Descartes was deeply affected by the intellectual crisis the Protestant-Catholic split had created in western Christendom. The constant attacks of each side against the other had led to massive intellectual confusion. Some maintained that since no human opinion could ever be shown to be definitively true, one had to take a leap of faith and submit to the authority of the church and its teachings. Others embraced a thoroughgoing skepticism about the truth of any human argument. Descartes began by examining himself.

Self-examination was something Christians had practiced for centuries, but Descartes struck off in a new direction. He decided that he would submit every statement he had heard about humans and their world to radical doubt. If there was any reason, no matter how small, to doubt it, he would treat it as worthless. Statement after statement was tossed aside until, finally, Descartes came upon something that, try as he would, he simply could not doubt: "I think." This undoubted truth became his principle of knowledge. From it he drew another equally firm conclusion: "Therefore I am." I exist as a thinker—that was the starting place for knowledge. Descartes then went on to reconstruct the world, moving from previously established points to new ones that followed logically from them. This **deductive method,** modeled on geometry, lay behind his *Discourse on Method* (1637).

In arriving at reliable knowledge, Descartes departed from Bacon. Instead of looking out at the natural world, he looked inside himself and found an authoritative source for all knowledge—the principle of autonomous, or independent, human reason. Human reason had always played an important role in traditional Christian views about the sources for human knowledge; the medieval Scholastic movement had placed a premium on logically presented argument. But in the older view, reason was also supplemented by divine revelation, which corrected or completed what human beings could think on their own. For Descartes, human reason stood alone as a reliable source for human knowledge.

Newton combined Bacon's and Descartes' methods to argue that any statement about the natural world had to pass two tests. First, it had to correspond to what was found by observation and experimentation. Second, it had to fit logically with all else that was known about the phenomenon being investigated. He thus combined inductive and deductive

methods to arrive at knowledge about the world and thereby laid the foundations for the modern **scientific method.** Newton's method impressed people as much as his description of the universe. His mighty mind had swept heaven and earth, revealing for the first time how the universe worked. As the English poet **Alexander Pope** exclaimed:

> *Nature and Nature's laws lay hid in Night:*
> *God said, Let Newton be! and all was light.*

Why Change Occurred

Many factors contributed to the new view of the universe. One stemmed from Renaissance humanists' rediscovery of ancient authors, including Plato. In the medieval west, Aristotle had reigned supreme. With the recovery of other ancient works, it became clear that Aristotle's theories had been contested in their own times and could be challenged again by new approaches to nature.

Another factor concerned the people engaged in the study of nature. Traditionally, philosophers pursued natural studies in a university setting. Much of the new work, however, was done by mathematicians working outside the universities. Copernicus, Kepler, and Descartes worked on their own or sought support from princely patrons.

Mathematicians' prestige rose when they were called on to help with land reclamation and canal building in places like the Dutch Republic or land surveys for taxation purposes in states trying to raise more revenue. Applying mathematics to solve specific problems was also in tune with humanist emphasis on useful knowledge.

Usefulness also lay at the heart of another tradition contributing to the New Science, that of craftsmen. As

inductive method   Method starting with observation of phenomena and then making general statements about them based on the observations.

René Descartes   (1596–1650) French philosopher who argued for the principle of autonomous human reason as the basis for human knowledge.

deductive method   The process of drawing logically coherent conclusions from self-evident first principles.

scientific method   Newton's combination of the inductive and deductive methods to establish a twofold method for scientific inquiry.

Alexander Pope   (1688–1744) English poet and literary critic who championed Newtonian physics and the Enlightenment's emphasis on the study of human beings.

sailors ventured out into the Atlantic, the need for precise astrolabes and quadrants to measure their positions had enhanced the work of those who produced these instruments and improved them through experimentation. Thinkers such as Galileo employed craft traditions of experimentation using metal balls, telescopes, and other devices to examine natural phenomena more precisely. They then wedded observation and experimentation to mathematics.

Another intellectual pursuit fostering experimentation was **alchemy**. Alchemists believed that nature contained hidden powers that influenced how the world worked and that these powers might be revealed through careful observation of and experimentation with chemical and other natural processes. Isaac Newton, for example, was an accomplished alchemist, and his experiments in a little shed outside his rooms at the University of Cambridge contributed to his endorsement of the inductive method in physics. In addition, his theory of gravity was influenced by the belief that hidden forces determined how the universe functioned.

Developments in anatomy also fostered increased attention to observation and experimentation. **Andreas Vesalius**, a Flemish professor at the University of Padua in Italy, broke with medieval tradition by conducting his own dissections of corpses during his lectures. Previously, anatomists had lectured from ancient authorities on what dissections would reveal but left the actual cutting to surgeons, who were considered inferior to professors. Vesalius's dissections, which students loved, revealed that Galen, the greatest ancient medical authority, was incorrect when he stated that the interior wall of the heart separating the ventricles was perforated, allowing for the circulation of the blood. That the heart wall was solid now required a whole new theory of blood circulation. An English student at Padua, **William Harvey**, worked one out in 1628 after examining animals slaughtered for their meat. Harvey combined Vesalius's insistence on direct observation with the craft traditions of butchers to develop his theory and thereby laid the foundation for modern physiology.

Defenders of the New Science argued that it stood in sharp opposition to the rigid, unalterable medieval version. In fact, however, the relationship was more complex. For example, both the old and new science insisted on the importance of a logical presentation of an argument. Medieval science had also raised issues like the nature of the terrestrial and celestial realms that preoccupied the New Scientists, and medieval terminology continued in use. But as the **Scientific Revolution** progressed, the criteria for making arguments shifted. Scientists who relied more on mathe-matics, craft traditions, and careful experimentation were developing a new view of the universe as a place full of motion, with much still to be discovered, a view in stark contrast to the unchanging and unchangeable world of Aristotle, Ptolemy, or the Bible.

The Impact of the New Science

↓ Who participated in the Scientific Revolution and how did the participants characterize themselves?
↓ What was the impact of the New Science on theology and political theory?

Those practicing the New Science were from many regions of Europe. Their findings were spread by means of a new institution, the scientific society, made up of well-to-do men who thought of themselves as a new type of educated person, the modern man of science. The societies developed procedures for presenting and verifying scientific experiments. They also provided guidelines for reproducing them and published new information for the interested public. As new views of the universe spread, along with the new scientific method and the principle of autonomous human reason, traditional European religious and political thought expanded in new ways.

Scientific Networks

The first scientific societies developed in princely courts. In Prague, the emperor Rudolf II (r. 1576–1612) established one of the first. Rudolph was a moody, reclusive man who fought with his brother for control of the Habsburg Empire, but he was also interested in artistic and scientific developments and joined with the king of Denmark to support Tycho Brahe's work. In Florence, Cosimo II not only patronized artists such as the French printmaker Jacques Callot but also supported Galileo and encouraged scientific discus-

---

alchemy Discipline practiced in the Middle Ages that searched for the hidden relations between natural phenomena.

Andreas Vesalius (1514–1564) Flemish physician who dissected human corpses and corrected some ancient statements about human anatomy.

William Harvey (1578–1657) English physician who described the circulation of blood in the human body.

Scientific Revolution Name given to the new views of the natural world and the new methods for obtaining them that began in the sixteenth century.

sion. In England, Bacon called for a research institute whose members would be royal employees collecting information to enhance state power. In fact, no such institute was created. Scientists' connections with the state were therefore looser than Bacon had hoped. Although Charles II of England and Louis XIV of France granted charters to the **Royal Society** of London and the French Royal Academy of Sciences, respectively, scientists generally worked free of direct royal control.

Membership in scientific organizations was overwhelmingly male. That men interested in science had to have a formal education further limited membership to the economically well-off. Members met to discuss issues of method and to learn what experiments others in the organization had performed. Some societies followed the lead of the English Royal Society and published reports of scientific findings.

Demonstrations of observable physical phenomena played an important role in scientific meetings. The correctness and accuracy of observations could be confirmed when many members agreed on them. During meetings, orderly procedures and polite behavior were insisted on. In addition, gentlemanly codes of honor and honesty helped to guarantee that the experimenters could be taken at their word. In printed presentations of experiments, detailed descriptions of equipment, procedures, and results were given so that readers could feel that they, too, had been present when the experiment took place. Detailed description also made possible the reproduction of the experiment.

Members of scientific societies believed they were a new class of people called to interpret the book of nature. **Robert Boyle,** a founder of the Royal Society of London who made important contributions to the study of air pressure and chemistry, called its members "priests of nature," because they revealed God's work through experimentation and observation. Boyle was a deeply religious man. He believed that men performing experiments must be modest and unassuming, in contrast to university debates, which had traditionally been conducted in public with lots of verbal fireworks. Personal ambition, prejudice, and passion had no place in proper scientific work. From these ideas emerged the modern concept of scientific objectivity.

Science and Religion

Newton's theory bound earth to the heavens, describing both as operating under laws that made motion as natural as rest. In his view, the universe seemed to function like a machine or a huge self-regulating clock. After being wound up, clocks ticked away in orderly fashion, following the laws governing their construction. The universe, he proposed, operated in the same way. In addition, Descartes and others argued that everything in the universe was made up of tiny particles that moved mechanically by universal laws of attraction and repulsion. Rocks, plants, animals, and human beings were like the planets—matter in motion. So it now seemed that there was a man-machine as well as a universe-machine. If all this was true, where did God fit in? For a few, the answer was clear: he didn't. For the great majority, however, there was definitely a place for God in the new order.

Clocks required a clockmaker, and, by analogy, the universe required a universe maker. This widely held belief was reinforced by the **argument from design.** Newton's wonderfully regulated universe could not have come into being without a designer. The microscope, perfected by the Dutch lensmaker Anton van Leeuwenhoek, was also important in this regard, since it revealed previously unknown worlds, small in size but intricate in detail, that also pointed to a divine designer.

Descartes' view that all bodies, including human ones, were simply matter in motion struck many as **atheistic.** But Descartes, a Catholic, believed in the Christian God. He argued that humans were unique. Not only did they have bodies made of matter, which were governed by the laws of attraction and repulsion; they also had minds, which were nonmaterial. God endowed human minds with the ability to reason, and Descartes reasoned his way to God's existence. For example, he argued that humans were finite beings who yet had a clear and distinct idea of God as an infinite being. Since the idea of an infinite being cannot be conceived by a finite one, it must be an **innate idea** given to humans by God himself. Arguments like these were meant to preserve the basic features of traditional Christian theology while relying solely on the principle of autonomous human reason for arriving at them.

Royal Society   One of the earliest scientific academies, founded in London in 1660.

Robert Boyle   (1627–1691) Founder of the Royal Society who advanced understanding of air pressure and chemistry.

argument from design   Widely held belief in the seventeenth century that the complex and beautiful design of nature was proof of a divine designer's existence.

atheism   Belief that there is no God.

innate ideas   Ideas about God, the human mind, or anything else that seem to be a primary part of human mental equipment.

If the universe was like a huge clock, did God wind it up at the beginning and then allow it to run on its own? Some of Descartes' arguments seemed to imply this belief, while others made room for ongoing divine intervention. Newton also insisted on God's regular activity in keeping the universe running and denounced the idea of a "dwarf-god" who did nothing more than set the world machine in motion.

For the New Scientists of the seventeenth century, the universe was not only a great machine; it was also the book of nature. Like the book of scripture, it could be consulted for knowledge of the Christian God. Protestants argued that the book of nature could be enlisted in the battle against Catholic error. A universe operating in a regular way under natural laws had no place for Catholics' superstitious beliefs in miracles performed by saints. Lady Mary Wortley Montagu's dismissal of smallpox inoculation in the form of the cross fitted into this rejection of "superstition" (see Choice). The Catholic Galileo argued that knowledge of nature led to a proper interpretation of scripture. Biblical references to the sun's motion around the earth should not be taken literally; they were simply God's concession to "the shallow minds of the common people."

One mathematician and scientist, **Blaise Pascal**, took issue with the heavy reliance on observation and reason as the best guides for religious thought. Pascal was a devout Jansenist who worried that Descartes' emphasis on autonomous human reason and innate ideas improperly downplayed the traditional Christian emphasis on revelation as a source of religious knowledge. Pascal gave reason and observation their proper place in the construction of human knowledge: although humans were mere specks in an infinite universe, and frail as reeds tossed about in the wind, they were thinking reeds. But Pascal introduced another source of knowledge: "heart." Heart drew on intuition, allowing a deeper view into the human condition than either reason or observation. "Heart has its reasons that Reason does not know," Pascal explained. For him, the human condition was characterized by both wretchedness and grandeur. Human wretchedness manifested itself in people's selfish, passion-driven, sin-filled lives as they hurtled toward the abyss of death. Grandeur manifested itself in the deep self-awareness of that wretchedness that "heart" opened up. Life as it is is not life as God originally meant it to be. Pascal died before he could present his ideas in a defense of traditional Christianity, but his notes have survived in his *Pensées* (*Thoughts*), one of the great philosophical and religious statements of the seventeenth century and published in various editions since 1670.

Pascal was one of many seventeenth-century scientists whose beliefs were shot through with traditional Christian values and concerns. Bacon believed that the accumulation of natural knowledge would prepare for Christ's return to earth, while Newton believed that human mastery of nature was a step in restoring the human race to Paradise, where Adam was master of the world before he fell into sin.

Science and the State

On April 2, 1662, Jacques-Bénigne Bossuet, a bishop in the Catholic Church, preached a sermon "On the Duties of Kings" before Louis XIV in which he celebrated the theory of absolute monarchy. "You are gods," he said to Louis. "You are all sons of the Most High." These flattering words came from Psalm 82. Bossuet then went on to describe how the king ruled without any human check on his power. Each point was justified by an appropriate quotation from Christian scripture. Basing politics on the Bible had been practiced since the days of the first Christian emperors of fourth-century Rome. Bossuet was, therefore, the heir to centuries of European political thought. At the same time, however, justifications for absolutism based on the New Science were also being proposed. Descartes' endorsement of the sun-centered universe, for example, was adopted as a model for Louis XIV's monarchy. Just as the planets orbited around the sun, so French subjects should be obedient to the Sun King.

The Englishman **Thomas Hobbes** also drew on scientific thought to argue for absolutism. Hobbes had lived through the turmoil of the English civil war and Commonwealth and had accepted Descartes' idea that human beings were matter in motion. Combining his experience of political instability and violence with his mechanical view of human beings, he argued in *Leviathan* (1651) that people, if left to themselves, would simply attack each other. The prepolitical, or natural, state was "every man against every man," because each human piece of matter in motion would try to fulfill its desires at the expense of the others. "Man is a wolf to his fellow man," he concluded, and all life "nasty, brutish, and short." The solution was to submit to an ironclad authority, a "mortal God," who would rule over everyone and force obedience to

Blaise Pascal (1623–1662) Scientist and defender of traditional Christianity who stated that "heart" could lead one to the deepest religious truths.

Thomas Hobbes (1588–1679) English political theorist who tried to defend absolutism on scientific grounds.

laws that restrained the aggressive impulses in people. Hobbes's defense of absolutism differed from traditional ones by not being based on the ruler's divine right to rule. He believed that the people created the absolute ruler (who might be a king or a parliament) to end the self-defeating violence of prepolitical society. Absolutism was, therefore, based on a contract between ruler and ruled, not on God's will.

Another Englishman, **John Locke,** also argued that government rested on a contract between ruler and ruled. But he drew quite different conclusions from this premise. Locke was an opponent of absolutism and had fled to Holland when James II became king in 1685. Returning to England with William and Mary, he published *Two Treatises on Government* (1690), in which he justified the Glorious Revolution. Locke had a more optimistic view of human nature than Hobbes. He believed that people could curb their aggressive impulses without coercion from an absolutist government. People entered into a political contract voluntarily and could withdraw from it when it no longer suited their purposes. The chief purpose of government was to protect private property rights. Locke's notions of contractual government and rights of private property supported the overthrow of James II, the repudiation of absolutism, and landowners' control of Parliament under a constitutional monarchy. His thought also had an impact on the American revolutionaries of the eighteenth century.

Although Hobbes and Locke had different views of human nature and endorsed different kinds of states, both tried to construct their politics on the basis of experience and reason rather than tradition and scripture. Their work represents some of the first attempts to construct a "political science."

The Nature of History

Growing enthusiasm for the New Science also provoked a sharp argument over the nature of human history. Traditional seventeenth-century understandings of history were pessimistic. Some stated that history was the sad story of decline and decay from an original high point, sometimes identified as the Garden of Eden and sometimes as Greek and Roman culture. In either case, humanity's passage through time was simply a slide downhill from an earlier golden age. A less dismal view presented history in cyclical terms. Humanity passed through high stages and then slid into decay until, once again, it started to ascend to a high point that, in turn, would provoke another period of decline. Thus, in a Protestant version of the cyclical theory, the high point of Christianity's first days was followed by a decline as Catholicism spread,

until Martin Luther's or John Calvin's day, when Protestantism returned Christianity to its original purity and a high point was once again reached. Traditionalists sometimes argued that the natural world was subject to decay as well; plants and animals, along with people, had degenerated over time. People who held these traditional views of natural and human history were called Ancients.

Beginning in the late seventeenth century, a new view of history gained ground, held by people dubbed Moderns. Inspired by the New Science, the Moderns argued against a decay over time of the natural world, citing the timeless, universal laws that Newton had discovered. Moderns also optimistically argued that human history was the story of intellectual progress. Although ancient Greek and Roman poets and playwrights were as good as contemporary ones, ancient scientists had been surpassed. Progress pointed to the overall superiority of Moderns. The battle between Ancients and Moderns continued on into the eighteenth century.

The Enlightenment

↓ How did the Enlightenment employ the methods of the New Science?
↓ What were the major items on the Enlightenment's agenda for reform?

Isaac Newton was the inspiration for a new European intellectual movement that emerged in the last years of the seventeenth century. People who joined it described themselves as enlightened, because they had embraced Newton's view of the universe along with his scientific method. Historians have adopted the term for the movement itself. The Enlightenment was the most energetic current in European thought during the eighteenth century.

The Early Enlightenment

England, the home of Isaac Newton, was one center for the early **Enlightenment.** The power of Newton's scientific method inspired his fellow countryman,

John Locke (1632–1704) English political theorist who argued, like Hobbes, that government rested on a contract between ruler and ruled.

Enlightenment European intellectual movement of the eighteenth century using the scientific method of the New Science.

John Locke, to apply it to a new field of study, the human mind. In 1690, Locke published *An Essay Concerning Human Understanding,* in which he took issue with Descartes' belief that God had planted some innate ideas in the mind. Instead, Locke argued, our minds at birth are like "white paper, void of all characters, without any ideas." Ideas arise only through experience of the world around us. And that experience comes through our senses of sight, hearing, taste, touch, and smell.

Locke's *Essay* was one of the foundational documents of the Enlightenment. It showed how Newton's scientific method could be used to establish a new science, that of the human mind, and thereby laid the foundations for the modern discipline of psychology. At the same time, it ratified a central tenet of the scientific method—reasoning on the basis of experience and observation. The *Essay* also had one profound implication. Sense knowledge can come only from the physical, material world, since it alone is capable of registering on the senses. That meant that human beings could not directly know the immaterial or supernatural world, even if it exists. Thus, the *Essay,* repudiating the notion of innate ideas and limiting human knowledge to sense impressions, cast serious doubt on the reality of divine revelation as an authority for guiding people's lives. Messages from the supernatural beyond seemed less and less likely in Locke's world.

Locke's interest in the mind testifies to a central concern of the Enlightenment: the study of human beings. In the sixteenth century, when the western Christian world split into two warring camps—Catholic and Protestant—the problem of God was a central intellectual issue. The Scientific Revolution brought the study of nature to the fore. In the Enlightenment, attention shifted once again. As Alexander Pope put it:

> *Know then thyself, presume not God to scan;*
> *The Proper study of Mankind is Man.*

Another center of the Enlightenment was France, where the **Baron de Montesquieu** took the study of humans in a different direction. A nobleman and a lawyer, Montesquieu sat in the French Parlement of Bordeaux. He made his literary debut in 1721 with *The Persian Letters,* a witty critique of French society supposedly written by Persian tourists. In 1748, he published one of the great works of the Enlightenment, *The Spirit of the Laws.* Unlike Locke, who had studied the individual human mind, Montesquieu focused on human beings as a group. Assuming that there was a universal human nature, he then sought the causes for the great variety of human political arrangements—monarchies, republics, despotic states—and found them in environmental factors. A comparative analysis led him to argue that climate and geography played an important role in shaping the features of any given society. He concluded that a society's traditions concerning religion, government, and economic activity also contributed to its distinctive shape, or "spirit."

Montesquieu argued that good government in France depended on the nobility, seated in institutions like the parlements, which put restraints on both the monarchy and the common people. He also greatly admired the constitutional monarchy of Britain. Montesquieu's interest in the role of natural and historical factors in shaping a society laid the foundations for the modern discipline of sociology.

Voltaire

If any person embodied the Enlightenment, it was the French philosopher and author **Voltaire.** The son of a middle-class Parisian lawyer, Voltaire attended the prestigious Jesuit school of Louis-le-Grand. He then defied his father, who wanted him to enter the law, by deciding to make his living as a writer. In 1718, his first play, *Oedipus,* which recounted the Greek legend of the king who killed his father and slept with his mother, ran on the Paris stage for an unprecedented forty-five nights. This success established the young man as France's foremost author of tragedies. A few years later, he published an epic poem on the reign of Henry IV of France, the *Henriade,* his most popular work.

In late 1725, a quarrel with a descendant of one of France's greatest noble families landed Voltaire in the **Bastille,** a notorious royal prison. He was released in 1726, on the condition that he go into exile in England. He did, and his exile set him on the path that made him France's greatest **philosophe,** the name French supporters of Enlightenment gave themselves.

Voltaire stayed in England until 1729, becoming familiar with Newton's and Locke's writings and learning about the English form of monarchical and parliamentary government. In 1733, he published *Philosophical Letters on the English,* a seemingly inno-

Baron de Montesquieu (1689–1755) One of the founders of the modern discipline of sociology and author of *The Spirit of the Laws.*

Voltaire (1694–1778) Social critic, attacker of Christianity, defender of the principle of autonomous human reason, and author of *Candide.*

Bastille Medieval fortress in Paris serving as a royal prison.

philosophes (in French, "philosophers") Name French supporters of Enlightenment ideas gave themselves.

In this contemporary portrait, Voltaire is fashionably dressed and wears a wig. His eyes have moved slightly to his right so he can look directly at the viewer as if in conversation, a pose that would have pleased this master of salon culture. *(Mary Evans Picture Library/The Image Works)*

cent account of English politics, religion, and society that was, in fact, a scathing denunciation of contemporary France. The issues Voltaire raised in the *Letters* formed the basis for his subsequent career as a reformer. The subversive tone of the book was not lost on the French authorities, who ordered it burned in public by the royal executioner and issued a warrant for Voltaire's arrest. Fleeing Paris with his new mistress, **Emilie du Chatelet,** he took up residence near the French border in case a quick getaway was needed. Mme. du Chatelet, an accomplished physicist and mathematician, helped Voltaire deepen his understanding of Newton. In 1738, he published *Elements of Newton's Philosophy,* which helped to establish Newton's reputation in France.

Voltaire was also interested in the improvement of French society. He sought reform of the criminal justice system, especially an end to the use of torture. In 1761, he heard of the perfect case to make his points. In the southern French town of Toulouse, a young Huguenot, Marc-Antoine Calas, was found hanged in his father's

shop. It was rumored that Calas was about to convert to Catholicism. Although his family claimed that Calas had committed suicide, the Parlement of Toulouse, dominated by Catholics, charged his father, Jean, with murdering him to prevent his conversion. The elder Calas was found guilty and then subjected to excruciating torture to get him to confess to his crime before his execution. The elder Calas refused, even when his bones were broken, and he was finally strangled to death. Was the father guilty or not? If he was, for Voltaire he demonstrated Protestant fanaticism; if not, the court demonstrated Catholic fanaticism. Either way, the case demonstrated the barbarity of judicially sanctioned torture. Voltaire turned the **Calas affair** into a European scandal that widely discredited the use of torture in criminal proceedings.

The affair also gave Voltaire the opportunity to attack traditional Christianity, whether Protestant or Catholic. For years he had rejected Christian teaching. Now he openly subjected Christianity to withering ridicule and began closing his letters with the phrase "Stamp out the infamous thing," by which he meant the churches, their ministers and priests, and their teachings. The Jesuits, in particular, came under heavy attack, perhaps because, as Voltaire told Alexander Pope, they had sexually molested him while he was a student at Louis-le-Grand. Although most supporters of the Enlightenment remained Christians, Voltaire's public, passionate attack on Christianity marked a turning point in the religious history of Europe.

Voltaire's campaign to improve human society was waged despite his sense of the limits of reform. When a huge earthquake destroyed the city of Lisbon in Portugal, he published his most famous work, *Candide, or Optimism,* which ridiculed the German philosopher Gottfried Wilhelm Leibnitz and the English poet Alexander Pope, who argued that we live in the best of all possible worlds. Nevertheless, Voltaire endorsed a limited optimism. As Candide says at the end of the novel, "We must cultivate our gardens," by which Voltaire meant that despite calamities like the Lisbon earthquake, which are beyond any human control, some things can and should be changed. Voltaire also carried on a huge correspondence, exchanging letters with his fellow philosophes, and also with Catherine

Emilie du Chatelet (1706–1749) Voltaire's mistress and intellectual companion who was an expert in Newtonian physics and mathematics.

Calas affair Trial, torture, and execution of Jean Calas, who was accused of killing his Huguenot son to prevent his conversion to Catholicism.

Void Voice eVoice Voice

Voltaire Attacks Christianity

Voltaire wanted to present the ideas of the Enlightenment to a large reading public. He therefore polished a literary style that sparkled with wit and was laced with biting satire and moral outrage. The two pieces presented below illustrate Voltaire's attack on traditional Christianity, "the infamous thing." They were published anonymously, without the approval of the French royal censors, and represent the Enlightenment attack on Christianity in its most radical form. They offended many traditionalists, who dismissed Voltaire as a "filthy little atheist," but they expressed views that many people repeated in the years after Voltaire published his attack.

On the Trinity

Here is an incomprehensible question which for over sixteen hundred years has exercised curiosity, sophistical subtlety, bitterness, the spirit of cabal, the rage to dominate, the rage to persecute, blind and bloodthirsty fanaticism, barbaric credulity, and which has produced more horrors than the ambition of princes, which indeed has produced enough.

➡ Is Jesus Word? If he is Word, did he emanate from God, is he co-eternal and consubstantial with him, or is he of a similar substance? Is he distinct from him or not? Is he created or engendered? Can he engender in turn? Has he paternity, or productive virtue without paternity? Is the holy ghost created or engendered or produced? Does he proceed from the father, or from the son, or from both? Can he engender, can he produce? Is his hypostasis consubstantial with the hypostasis of the father and the son? And why, having precisely the same nature, the same essence as the father and the son, can he not do the same things as these two persons who are himself?

I certainly do not understand any of this; nobody has ever understood any of this, and this is the reason for which people have slaughtered one another.

The Story of the Banishing of the Jesuits from China

Brother Rigolet: ➡ Our God was born in a stable, seventeen hundred and twenty-three years ago, between an ox and an ass. . . . [His mother] was not a woman, but a girl. It is true that she was married, and that she had two other children, named James as the old gospels say, but she was a virgin none the less.

The Emperor: What! She was a virgin and she had children!

Brother Rigolet: To be sure. This is the nub of the story: it was God who gave this girl a child.

The Emperor: I don't understand you. You have just told me that she was the mother of God. So God slept with his mother in order to be born of her?

Brother Rigolet: You've got it Your Sacred Majesty; grace was already in operation. You've got it I say; God changed himself into a pigeon to give a child to a carpenter's wife, and that child was God himself.

The Emperor: But then we have two Gods to take into account: a carpenter and a pigeon.

➡ How does Voltaire turn the technical theological terms he uses here against the doctrine of the Trinity?

➡ Why would Voltaire choose to mock the Jesuits in this little dialogue?

Brother Rigolet: ➡️ Without a doubt, Sire; but there is also a third, who is the father of these two, and whom we always paint with a majestic beard: it was this God who ordered the pigeon to give a child to the carpenter's wife, from whom the God-carpenter was born; but at the bottom these three make only one. The father had engendered the son before he was in the world, the son was then engendered by the pigeon, and the pigeon proceeds from the father and the son. Now you see that the pigeon who proceeds, the carpenter who is born of the pigeon, and the father who has engendered the son of the pigeon, can only be a single God; and that a man who doesn't believe this story should be burned in this world and the other.

The Emperor: That is as clear as day.

> ➡️ How does Voltaire develop this story for comic effect?

Source: Extract from Peter Gay, *Voltaire's Politics: The Poet as Realist* (New Haven, CT: Yale University Press, 1959), pp. 246–247. Reprinted by Yale University Press.

II of Russia and Frederick II of Prussia, who invited him to his court outside Berlin. No European writer since Erasmus in the sixteenth century was as well connected as Voltaire.

In early 1778, Voltaire, now eighty-three, returned in triumph to Paris. The city's most prestigious theatrical company, the Comédie-Française, performed his tragedy *Irene* and placed his statue in their theater, the only living author to be so honored. At his death, in May of that year, he was arguably the most famous man in Europe. The modern edition of his works fills more than 135 volumes.

Enlightenment Religion

Although Voltaire declared war on Christianity, he was no atheist. He embraced **deism,** a rational religion based solely on the observation of nature. Deism drew on Locke's sense-based psychology, the argument from design, and Newton's clocklike universe. As a religious movement, it denied Christian doctrines of the Trinity, the divinity of Jesus, and the divine authority of the Bible. Most deists also rejected Newton's notion that God intervenes in the universe to keep it going. Deists emphasized the need for humane treatment of human beings, supporting the campaign against judicial torture.

For Voltaire and other deists, like Benjamin Franklin and Thomas Jefferson, deism and religious toleration went hand in hand. Since traditional religion, whether Jewish or Christian, was based on fraud and foolishness, it could never be legitimately defended by attacking those who rejected it. Even acceptable religious belief, like deism, was a matter of individual conscience over which no state or church authority ought to have jurisdiction. Voltaire's pursuit of these points in the Calas affair met with growing sympathy, and,

in 1787, on the eve of revolution in France, Louis XVI signed an edict granting limited religious toleration to the Huguenots. Deist-inspired calls for religious toleration also spread in Britain's North American colonies. After gaining independence, the new United States proclaimed religious toleration in its own Bill of Rights (1791).

In addition to battling traditional Christians, Voltaire also denounced atheists. On this score, however, he was fighting a losing battle. By the mid-eighteenth century, more and more philosophes believed that the existence of God could never be proved by an argument from design or demonstrated as necessary for explaining the world and human beings. The **materialism** of Descartes, stripped of its Christian beliefs, could account for everything. The universe simply was, and humans were wholly material beings without souls or immaterial minds. At death, they ceased to exist. In 1746, a French physician, **Julien Offroy de La Mettrie,** argued these points in *Man the Machine.* His work caused a scandal in conservative circles, but, undaunted, he followed it up in 1749 with *Man the Plant.* La Mettrie also preached a gospel of pure physical pleasure, which made him doubly scandalous. In 1751, when he died after gorging himself on pheasant pâté, his enemies said the punishment fitted the crime.

deism Religious belief that rejected traditional Christian teachings and tried to base its theology on scientific method.

materialism Argument that material things alone exist, therefore denying the existence of a soul or of an immaterial world.

Julien Offroy de La Mettrie (1709–1751) French author of the materialist and atheistic works *Man the Machine* and *Man the Plant.*

This engraving of a craft process from Diderot's *Encyclopédie* shows a printer's shop. From left to right men set type for a page, arrange lines, and lock the type in place. The type will print four pages at once. Previously printed pages are drying on lines above workmen's heads; when dry, they will be folded to arrange the pages in proper sequence. Diderot's emphasis on craft and manufacturing processes reminded readers of their importance and gave them a new dignity. *(Division of Rare & Manuscript Collections, Cornell University Library)*

Some Jewish thinkers were also caught up in the debates over revealed versus natural religion and atheism. One of the most important was the German Jew **Moses Mendelssohn.** Mendelssohn argued for a Judaism stripped of miracles and other supernatural phenomena. Its basic truths could be proved by reason. He also rejected the idea of Jewish uniqueness, denying that the Jews were a chosen people. But he asserted that, in the larger Christian world, they were an oppressed people, and he worked tirelessly to end discriminatory legislation against them. He also urged Jews to be more open to the larger European culture. They should stop using Yiddish as a literary language and follow his example of writing in German. They should also stop persecuting Jewish sects, like the followers of the seventeenth-century self-proclaimed Messiah Sabbatai Sevi. If Jews demanded toleration from Christians, they should grant it themselves. Mendelssohn shocked many Jewish traditionalists, but his views appealed to others and were to be influential in the nineteenth century.

Diderot and the *Encyclopédie*

While Voltaire was crusading against Christians and atheists, some of his fellow philosophes were embarking on a highly successful publishing venture. In 1751, the first volume of the *Encyclopédie* appeared. Under the editorial leadership of **Denis Diderot,** sixteen more volumes followed over the next twenty-

Moses Mendelssohn   (1729–1786) German Jew who said that Judaism's basic beliefs were rationally provable and who worked to end discrimination against Jews.

Encyclopédie   Multivolume work with contributions from philosophes throughout Europe that summed up the philosophy of the Enlightenment.

Denis Diderot   (1713–1784) French writer and editor of the *Encyclopédie.*

one years. The *Encyclopédie* was a huge commercial success, making millions for its publishers. Diderot wished to present current knowledge on all subjects in a single multivolume reference work. He also wanted to show how all knowledge was interconnected and that the key to it rested on observation, experiment, and autonomous reason. Throughout the *Encyclopédie,* Diderot drew on the works of Bacon, Descartes, Locke, and Newton. He also got major Enlightenment writers, such as Montesquieu and Voltaire, to contribute articles. In addition to standard articles on religious, philosophical, scientific, and artistic subjects, the *Encyclopédie* also had groundbreaking contributions on craft and manufacturing processes such as brassmaking, printing, tapestry weaving, and fishing with nets. Inclusion of these articles testified to the importance that craft traditions had played in the emergence of the Scientific Revolution. They also met Diderot's insistence that the *Encyclopédie* should be useful. Usefulness also lay behind articles like "Asparagus," which not only described the plant and its cultivation but gave five recipes as well.

Diderot had to work under conditions of government press censorship, which was always on the lookout for unorthodox political or religious ideas and often forced him to make controversial points in subtle ways. One device he and his associates perfected for sneaking in inflammatory material was a system of clever cross-referencing. For example, in the article on "France," when Louis XIV's revocation of the Edict of Nantes was described, a cross reference to "Toleration" was given. If Voltaire was the one man who best embodied the ideals of Enlightenment, the *Encyclopédie* was the one work that summed them up.

The Late Enlightenment

As editor of the *Encyclopédie,* Diderot had to be discreet in voicing his own opinions, but his works make clear that he, too, had embraced materialism and atheism. The leading philosophe of the late Enlightenment, however, did not. He was **Jean-Jacques Rousseau,** the son of a Genevan watchmaker. Rousseau was a Calvinist who converted to Catholicism and then embraced deism. His *Profession of Faith of a Savoyard Vicar,* an emotional defense of deism, won Voltaire's praise.

Rousseau was touchy, paranoid, and blunt. In the 1750s, he attacked the refined world of the philosophes and their aristocratic patrons. Rejecting the Christian idea of original sin, Rousseau believed that human beings were good by nature but that civilization had

In this etching Jean-Jacques Rousseau is depicted as a "man of nature" who rejected the refined world of the salons. Leaning against a tree and holding a bunch of wildflowers, he contemplates the beauty of the natural world, which his deist God had created. *(The Granger Collection, New York)*

corrupted them because it encouraged injustice and inequality. His attacks alienated Voltaire, Diderot, and others who believed that civilization was a sign of human progress, not degeneration. Voltaire said he thought Rousseau wanted him to walk around on all fours. In fact, however, Rousseau did not want to abolish civilization; he wanted to reform it.

In 1762 Rousseau published *The Social Contract,* which advocated a democratic society and pioneered modern democratic theory. This work set him apart from other philosophes. For all their radicalism, Vol-

Jean-Jacques Rousseau (1712–1778) Genevan Swiss social critic, philosophe, and novelist who pioneered modern democratic theory in his *Social Contract.*

taire and Diderot were part of the eighteenth-century literary establishment. Like the gentlemen who gathered in the scientific societies of the seventeenth century, they criticized society but did not want to overturn it. In contrast, Rousseau wanted fundamental change. He argued that the good society is one in which all members voluntarily give up their individual rights and submit to what he called the general will. Usually, the general will amounted to the will of the community's majority, although Rousseau was careful to say that sometimes it did not. This point has confused some of his readers. What Rousseau really wanted was a community in which people participated in politics and acted openly for the true good of all the community's members. This ideal has served as a benchmark for democratic societies ever since.

Rousseau's hunger for openness in human relations prompted him to write his *Confessions*. Published in 1781, three years after his death, the *Confessions* recounted in detail many of the most private facts of his life, among them acts of theft, sex with a sailor, and the abandonment of a child he had fathered. While some were shocked by these revelations, Rousseau's real intent was to demonstrate that he was a man who hid nothing but presented himself fully to other human beings. If all people were as open, society could be fundamentally transformed.

Rousseau's radicalism and rejection of refined aristocratic society was also endorsed by a host of pamphleteers and writers for hire who never made it into Voltaire's or Diderot's elite publishing circles. These people produced political criticism that mixed opposition to government policies with pornographic accounts of the degenerate lives of kings, queens, and nobility. Although these works had roots in earlier traditions of satire and slander, their volume and intensity increased in the late eighteenth century, especially in France after its defeat in the Seven Years' War. Overall, they undermined the legitimacy of traditional government as much as Rousseau's democratic criticisms did.

Other parts of Europe were less receptive to the radicalism that swept over France after 1750. In Prussia, **Immanuel Kant** summed up the philosophes' program in *What Is Enlightenment?* (1784): "Dare to know. . . . Have the courage to use your own understanding is . . . the motto of enlightenment." Kant, however, never advocated democracy or any real social or political reform. People were free to use their minds to seek the truth but, according to Kant, should submit to the current political, social, and economic orders in which they found themselves.

Society and the Enlightenment

↓ What impact did developments in publishing and reading habits have on European intellectual life?
↓ What additional trends promoted the Enlightenment?

Just as scientific societies helped to spread Newtonian physics, so new institutions served to popularize the Enlightenment. Publishers expanded the types of books they produced from religious works to new literary forms like the novel. Newspapers also became increasingly available to readers. This wider array of reading materials, which encouraged readers to digest the news of the day or enter into the world of the novel, offered new ways of thinking about human experience. The Enlightenment's insistence on rational discussion of topics spread through society as new opportunities opened for comment on current affairs in coffeehouses, salons, and Masonic lodges. Critical discussion of issues also spilled over into the political realm as ordinary people commented on rulers' policies and required rulers to justify their actions before a new political force, public opinion.

The New World of Reading

The invention of the printing press in the mid-fifteenth century, along with the Protestant Reformation and Catholic reforms of the sixteenth, ushered in a new era in the history of European book reading. Both Protestants and Catholics used print to attack their opponents and to present their co-religionists with catechisms and prayer books. Most of this popular literature was written in the languages spoken by the people rather than Latin, which was still the official language of learning. In Protestant countries, translations of the Bible also multiplied. Prayer books, catechisms, and Bibles were read reverently and reread many times; Bible study required returning to passages over and over again, while prayers for the morning and evening were repeated daily. Habits of devout, repetitive reading, a reading style intimately linked to Christian belief, were predominant among literate people in the sixteenth and seventeenth centuries as religious publications multiplied.

In the eighteenth century, both the types of litera-

Immanuel Kant   (1724–1804) Leading German philosophe of the late Enlightenment.

In Pierre-Antoine Baudoin's *Reading,* the woman reads in private. Note how the screen behind her would prevent anyone coming through the door to see directly into the room. Her book, a novel, has fallen from her left hand as she swoons over it, thinking of the scene she has just read. *(P.A. Baudoin, La Lecture. Les Arts Decoratifs, Musée des Arts decoratifs, Paris. Photo Laurent Sully Jaulmes. All rights reserved.)*

ture available to people and styles of reading changed. Throughout the century, religious publications declined dramatically, and **novels,** a new literary type, rose to first place. Novels were particularly popular with women, who were now more likely to read than they had been earlier. Women like the Englishwoman **Aphra Behn** also figured prominently as authors of novels. Although some people seemed to have read and reread novels many times, and thereby used the same technique for reading them as for Bibles or prayer books, most readers read the latest bestseller only once, then turned to something else.

In addition to novels, newspapers and political pamphlets became increasingly available in the eighteenth century, especially in Britain and the Dutch Republic, where censorship laws were relaxed or abolished. Reading newspapers had often been a collective activity in which one person read aloud to a group, but increasingly newspapers were read privately and silently, like novels, and passed along un-

til the next day's newspaper was available. As the variety of reading material expanded, it is likely that Europeans received more information about the world and, often lost in the contents of the page in front of them, had a wider range of imaginative reading experiences than people had ever had before. One of the clearest signs of Europeans' expanding reading habits was the spread of **lending libraries,** which al-

novel   Literary form of prose fiction that was popular in the eighteenth century and sometimes used to promote social criticism and programs for reform.

Aphra Behn   (1640–1689) English novelist who pioneered the form and made a financial success of writing.

lending libraries   Institutions allowing readers to borrow books from their shelves and then return them, thus avoiding the need to buy them.

In this London coffee-house, as the elegantly dressed owner looks on, a waiter pours coffee for the well-to-do men sitting at tables. They are reading and conversing and may be transacting business. Note the coffee pots being kept warm in front of the fire. (© *Michael Holford*)

lowed anyone who joined to check books out to read where they wished and thus eliminated the cost of purchasing them.

The nature of writing and publishing changed with new reading habits. Formerly, writers had either worked as economically self-sufficient gentlemen or had sought commissions from wealthy patrons. In the eighteenth century, some, like Lady Mary Wortley Montagu, thought that the profession of author was beneath the well-born, but others, like Voltaire and Diderot, were eager to make a living from writing. Few became as rich or famous as they, but many managed to survive on wages paid for their work.

Those wages came from publishers. Publishing became big business in the eighteenth century. Publishing houses often specialized in certain types of literature. Some produced cheap editions of fairy tales or almanacs, which peddlers carried in their packs throughout town and countryside. Others, especially in the Dutch Republic, concentrated on controversial works that might be censored in other countries; Diderot, for example, used a publisher in the Netherlands for the *Encyclopédie.* Many of these works were then smuggled into places like France, where censors were sometimes bribed to look the other way when the books went on sale. Authors also tried to evade censors when they wrote something particularly scan-

dalous; Voltaire was fond of blaming his literary rivals for his anti-Christian works.

Publishers stayed in business by both meeting and shaping readers' demands and tastes. When a particular type of novel sold, they urged other writers to produce similar works. This worked well for Rousseau, whose *The New Heloise,* a runaway bestseller in 1761, fed a growing late-eighteenth-century taste for novels describing domestic settings that were full of romance, heartbreak, and feeling. His *Emile* (1762), a novel that advocated a "natural" course for children's education based on direct observation and experience at the various stages of a child's development, also sold well. In fact, during his life, Rousseau was better known for these novels than for *The Social Contract.*

Increasing numbers of Europeans could afford books and newspapers, or lending library fees, in part because their disposable incomes rose as Europe entered a new period of prosperity in the early eighteenth century. Moreover, printed material was viewed less as an avenue to God or a source for spiritual improvement than as a means to worldly information and pleasure. The new world of reading, writing, and publishing constituted a major shift in the intellectual activities of Europeans that the philosophes put to good use for popularizing their ideas and advocating programs of reform. Reading still remained, however, a practice that only a minority of Europeans engaged in, and the ideas of the philosophes were embraced by only a part of this reading public.

Enlightenment Sociability

Along with new types of literature and changing styles of reading, new institutions sprang up in which people could discuss what they read and put into practice the central method of the Enlightenment—thought based on autonomous human reason. Chief among them were coffee and tea houses. Europeans' consumption of coffee and tea rose significantly during the eighteenth century as a result of expanded colonial trade and an improving European economy. While both beverages were drunk at home, many people, especially men, liked to take them in cafés where there were newspapers and pamphlets to read, opportunities to buy and sell stocks in joint-stock companies, and people to talk to. The coffeehouse phenomenon had begun in Restoration London when Whigs took tea or coffee and discussed politics at Old Slaughter's, while the Tories gathered at the Cocoa Tree. Coffeehouses then sprouted up in Paris, Vienna, and other major European cities. The atmosphere in them was informal; one dropped in and left at will. Originally patronized by the rich and fashionable, coffeehouses became more socially inclusive over the century. Men of different backgrounds who would normally be separated on more formal occasions mixed easily with one another in the coffeehouse atmosphere. And always, politics and other current events were discussed. Because coffee is a stimulant, animated discussion was the rule. Unlike taverns, however, where drinking often led to brawling, coffeehouse conversation was supposed to be orderly and polite, even if heated.

Conversation was also the rule in salons. Invented in Paris during the seventeenth century, the **salon** became a central Enlightenment institution for the educated and well-born. Women like Madame du Deffand, the wife of a rich Parisian financier, presided over salons that met in their homes on specified days and discussed topics that the hostess announced. The hostess also set rules for conversation that prohibited shouting, swearing, and name calling. Guests were to converse politely, intelligently, and amusingly about the scientific, artistic, or political matters assigned for discussion. Anyone able to do this would be admitted. Thus, men and women, nobles and commoners, joined in. Although the hostess was usually rich and often noble, salons, like coffeehouses, were relatively informal institutions in which an ability to converse well counted more than wealth or social background.

Even religious differences were overlooked in salons, especially in Berlin, where Jewish hostesses brought together Jews and Christians.

Masonic lodges also offered a new form of social interaction in which religious or class differences played a minor role. Guilds of masons who laid brick or stone had existed since the Middle Ages, but modern **Freemasonry** began in London in 1717, when a group of middle-class men formed a club in which Newton's science and other issues of current interest were discussed. By the 1720s, 75 percent of the London lodge members also belonged to the Royal Society. Although Masonic lodges modified old rituals from the medieval guilds when they initiated new members, their main purpose was to create an environment like that of the salons, in which polite conversation on issues could occur. Masonic lodges spread throughout Europe in both Catholic and Protestant countries, despite the pope's condemnation of the movement in 1738 on the grounds that it advocated anti-Catholic ideas. Like the salons, the lodges downplayed the social and economic differences of their membership. Brotherhood in the lodge made all members equal. These Masonic ideals were articulated in one of the century's great operas, *The Magic Flute,* written by **Wolfgang Amadeus Mozart** and performed in the last year of the composer's life. Mozart made a point of stressing Masonic ideals of human equality. At one point, when a priest exclaims that the hero is a prince, the high priest corrects him: "More than that! He is a man!"

The Enlightenment and Politics

The rational discussion taking place in new social settings also extended to politics, taking different forms in eastern and western Europe. In Scandinavia, Germany, and Russia, Enlightenment rationalism melded with an older political tradition, **cameralism.** Devel-

salon   Meeting place where current ideas are discussed, in the eighteenth century presided over by a woman.

Freemasonry   Social and intellectual movement that originated in England during the eighteenth century and spread across Europe.

Wolfgang Amadeus Mozart   (1756–1791) Composer of symphonies, operas, and many other works who perfected the classical style in music.

cameralism   Eastern European tradition of political thought emphasizing rational government policymaking that melded with Enlightenment principles.

oping in the seventeenth century, cameralism aimed at increasing a state's wealth through direct management of people and resources. Government should intervene in people's lives to make them better fed, better housed, and better behaved so that they could become more productive. Cameralism also emphasized the need for a rational assessment of a state's strengths, weaknesses, and needs as the basis for good government policy. The state itself was compared to a machine. When properly managed it could regulate society in the interests of increasing its wealth.

Cameralism was taught in eastern European universities to candidates for posts in the state bureaucracy. At the head of the bureaucracy was the ruler, whose job was to see that the machine of government ran smoothly and produced good results. Thus, kings were viewed more as supreme political managers than God-appointed rulers endowed with the sacred authority to govern. Many of the policies of Frederick William I and Frederick II of Prussia, as well as Peter the Great of Russia, were inspired by cameralist principles. Cameralism's emphasis on rational assessment of political needs, along with its conception of government as a well-run machine improving people's lives, fitted into many Enlightenment principles.

In western Europe, greater discussion of politics by ordinary people gave rise to increased popular participation in politics. In Britain, the political turmoil of the seventeenth century, which led to constitutional monarchy and a permanent role for Parliament in shaping government policy, fostered ordinary people's discussion of political affairs. Elections to the House of Commons also stimulated political debate, and, occasionally, commoners with widespread popular support could force the king to accept them as government ministers. In 1757, George II thus accepted **William Pitt the Elder**, though he despised Pitt's insistence that Britain's imperial interests were more important than Hanover's, the German principality from which the king and his father had come. It was Pitt who later masterminded the British victories in the Seven Years' War.

For its part, Parliament tried to shield its debates from the public by forbidding publication of its proceedings. But intense interest in the kingdom's politics, along with the growth of the press, forced Parliament to back down in the early 1770s. With parliamentary proceedings now publicly distributed, popular discussion of politics intensified.

Similar developments also occurred in France. There the monarchy still clung to its absolutist principles, which proclaimed that there was only one political player in the realm, the king. Everyone else was supposed to be a mere spectator watching royal politics from the sidelines. While court etiquette at Versailles and official press accounts of the king's daily activities reinforced this view, it proved increasingly difficult to maintain. Prolonged conflicts between the French king and the parlements over Jansenism, during which the parlements published their grievances, made it clear that others beside the king claimed a political role. The growth of the newspaper press and the rise of rational discussion in new social settings also encouraged the king's subjects to become actively engaged in discussion of policies and events.

In both England and France, therefore, public opinion played a growing role in politics. Its advent constituted a major shift in European political life. Monarchs who had previously argued that they ruled by divine grace and operated in a political world, whose rules could not be understood by the mass of their subjects, now had to contend with a growing chorus of voices commenting on and even criticizing what they did. Although criticism of rulers could lead to charges of treason, it also forced governments to become more open in explaining and justifying their policies. As states made increasing demands on their subjects, rulers were increasingly expected to account for their actions.

Enlightenment Debates

↓ How did ideas about Europe's place in the world change during the Enlightenment?
↓ How did Enlightenment thinkers confront ideas about difference among human beings?

Discussion and debate were at the heart of Enlightenment intellectual life. Debating clubs, where men and women could hear opposing views on subjects of current concern, often addressed the degree of likeness and difference in the human community. The philosophes believed in universal natural laws and a universal human nature. At the same time, they lived in a world where difference separated some people from others and thereby challenged universalism. Debates on human likeness and difference, which raged throughout the eighteenth century, focused especially on three issues: the relation between Europeans and non-Europeans; the institution of slavery; and the relation between men and women.

William Pitt the Elder (1708–1778) British minister during the Seven Years' War.

This painting of a New Zealand warrior was made by Sydney Parkinson who accompanied James Cook on his first voyage to the South Pacific. It would seem both familiar and odd to Europeans. Their warriors often wore plumes on their hats, but a cape of fluffy flax and dog skins would never be seen on Europe's battlefields. *(Plate XV, "A New Zealand Warrior in His Proper Dress, & Completely Armed, According to Their Manner," from Sydney Parkinson,* Journal of a Voyage to the South Seas. *Department of Special Collections, Charles E. Young Research Library, UCLA)*

Europeans and Non-Europeans

As early as the 1540s, the debate over the humanity of non-European people had pitted Bartolomé de Las Casas against Juan Guinés de Sepúlveda. Las Casas argued that New World Indians were fully human, while Sepúlveda said they were not. In the sixteenth century, Europeans thought of their culture primarily in religious terms; they lived in Christendom, while others were either infidels (Jews and Muslims) or pagans (everyone else). During the Enlightenment, as the debate continued, the terms in which it was conducted started to change. Under the influence of the New Science, natural factors like geology and climate, rather than the traditional religious categories of Christian and non-Christian, were used increasingly to explain diversity in the human community and to shape separate collective identities.

Debate centered on two sets of people: those in the New World and those in the South Pacific. In 1770, a French priest and philosophe, the **Abbé Raynal**, published *The Philosophical History of the Two Indies*, which quickly became a runaway bestseller. Raynal argued, like Sepúlveda, that the Indian natives of the Western Hemisphere were inferior human beings. But Raynal went further, arguing that the natural world in America was as degenerate as the human one. America, he wrote, had been formed later than Europe, rising from the sea in the recent past. This explained why the climate was damp and cold, making New England, which was on the same latitude as Spain, so snowy in winter. This chilly, watery New World produced plants and animals that were puny compared to their counterparts in Europe. Going even further, Raynal stated that Europeans who migrated to North America soon degenerated. Thus, America's geological history produced a climate that was inhospitable to all forms of life.

Raynal's attack provoked a sharp response from the North Americans. In 1781, **Thomas Jefferson** published his *Notes on the State of Virginia,* a spirited refutation of Raynal's work. Was Raynal correct when he wrote that Virginia's Indian men were less manly than Europeans because they had no facial hair? No. The Indians simply chose to pluck out their beards, and such warlike men could not be considered unmanly. Did the New World produce puny animals? No. Look at the newly discovered bones of a huge American elephant, the **mammoth**. Were Americans of European origin degenerate descendants of their ancestors across the ocean? No. Look at **Benjamin Franklin**.

Franklin was Raynal's cleverest opponent. When the Continental Congress sent him to France in 1776 to seek French aid for the American Revolution, he made a point of refuting Raynal at every turn. Franklin's earlier experiments with electricity made him the ideal man of science, someone who, like Newton, revealed the workings of nature. His invention of the lightning rod made him the philosophe who worked for the betterment of humanity. At Versailles, Franklin shunned the silks and lace fashionable men favored and dressed in plain brown, presenting himself as a simple American who was, nevertheless, the intellectual equal of any European. The French court was charmed. Franklin was a natural but noble man who showed no trace of deformity. One evening, he and other Americans found themselves at a dinner party with Raynal. When the theory of American degeneracy came up, Franklin asked all the Americans at the table to stand, and then all the Frenchmen. The Americans towered over the French, and especially over Raynal, whom Franklin dismissed as a "mere shrimp." Soon afterward, Raynal retracted his unflattering picture of America. Franklin triumphed again in 1777, when France signed an alliance with the Americans in their war for independence from Britain.

Debate about non-Europeans also focused on the peoples of the South Pacific. In the 1770s, an Englishman, **James Cook**, and a Frenchman, **Louis-Antoine de Bougainville**, led scientific voyages through the region and published accounts of their expeditions, feeding French and British thirst for travel literature. The South Pacific was a new frontier for Europeans, and these accounts sparked interest in the local peoples. Diderot wrote a fictional *Supplement to the Voyage of Bougainville* (1772) in which he used Bougainville's account of Tahitians' free and open sexual activity to attack traditional Christian sexual morality as cruel and unnatural.

Raynal's denunciation of a degenerate America and Diderot's titillating account of the Tahitians' erotic freedom were part of a sustained discussion of European civilization and Europe's proper place in the larger world. One central issue was the nature of civilization itself. Many Europeans continued to think in **Eurocentric** terms and to assert the superiority of their way of life, and most philosophes encouraged this view. Kant declared that the spread of Enlightenment and of reliance on autonomous human reason was a sign that Europeans, after centuries of immaturity, had finally reached adulthood. Voltaire celebrated the refined world of salon conversation, seeing it as a sign of a truly civilized world. But Rousseau attacked civilization as a corrupter of humanity's original goodness and purity. Pointing to the tea and coffee drunk in Enlightenment salons, he claimed that overseas trade and colonies promoted an improper love of luxury and harmed other peoples. Raynal also had his doubts. His depiction of America as an alien and

hostile place that Europeans should have avoided arose in part from his belief that colonization had harmed **indigenous people,** as indeed it had. Following their first encounters with Europeans, the native populations of the Americas declined by 90 percent, largely as the result of epidemic diseases that swept through their communities, a demographic catastrophe unparalleled in human history. Diderot's Tahitians also suffered from European intrusion into their world. In the *Supplement,* a Tahitian complains to Bougainville that "the idea of crime and the fear of disease entered among us only with you." Diderot rejected Rousseau's attack on all civilization but agreed that European colonization had introduced corruption and inequality to other peoples.

As philosophes like Rousseau, Raynal, and Diderot debated the nature of non-European peoples and the worth of commerce and colonies, they increasingly sought nonreligious explanations for differences among human beings and tried to articulate a sense of European identity in non-Eurocentric terms. Europe was simply one human community among many others in the world and could make no valid claims for superiority on religious, cultural, or commercial grounds.

Slavery

"We hold these truths to be self-evident: That all men are created equal; that they are endowed by their Creator with certain inalienable rights; that among these are life, liberty, and the pursuit of happiness." These words in one of the Enlightenment's most famous documents, the **Declaration of Independence** (1776), were written by Thomas Jefferson and proclaimed the philosophes' belief in universal **human rights.**

James Cook (1728–1779) Head of three British Royal Society–financed expeditions into the South Pacific.

Louis-Antoine de Bougainville (1729–1811) French explorer in the South Pacific who gave his name to the bougainvillea, a flowering vine he discovered there.

Eurocentric Idea that Europe and European culture are either superior to or more important than the lands and cultures of other peoples.

indigenous people Original inhabitants of a region, or "natives."

Declaration of Independence Document justifying separation of American colonies from Britain in 1776 and defending the theory of self-government.

human rights Rights given to all human beings by God or the natural order and that neither the state nor society may take away.

But Jefferson was a Virginia plantation owner who never freed his slaves. This contradiction lay at the heart of Enlightenment debates over slavery.

By the eighteenth century, trade in slaves from sub-Saharan Africa had gone on for more than a thousand years. During the Middle Ages, Arab traders had brought millions of them into the Islamic world. Beginning in the fourteenth century, the Portuguese brought African slaves to the Atlantic islands. Later Spanish, English, French, and Dutch traders transported Africans to Europe's colonies in the Western Hemisphere, where they worked the plantations that produced the coffee that Europeans drank in their coffeehouses and the sugar that sweetened their tea. By the end of the eighteenth century, 11 million slaves had been forcibly taken to the Americas to labor for the 2 million Europeans who had migrated there. As demand for slave-produced commodities rose, the slave trade rose also, justified again and again with traditional arguments about biblical passages accepting the practice and the subhuman nature of Africans.

The philosophes' attitude toward slavery was mixed. Both Hobbes and Locke endorsed the practice. Although Voltaire had attacked slavery in *Candide,* he came, reluctantly, to accept it as a fact of human life. Montesquieu argued against it, claiming that it undermined a society's moral well-being by oppressing the slaves while giving slave owners too much power. On the other hand, supporters of slavery could point to Montesquieu's argument that the hot, humid climate of the tropics had conditioned the people who lived there to resist work unless forced to do it.

Moral objections had been raised against slavery since the late seventeenth century. In England, several Protestant groups called for its abolition. For example, **Quakers,** who believed that God's "inner light" shone in every human being's heart, argued that the taking of slaves was simply kidnapping and should be stopped, while Quakers in America who owned slaves were urged to free them. Some Anglicans also condemned the trade, arguing that slavery was incompatible with Jesus's gospel of love, despite scriptural passages that sanctioned it. Thus, both Christian and Enlightenment arguments could be made for or against slavery. Over the course of the eighteenth century, however, the balance tipped toward the antislavery position.

Novelists, poets, and playwrights played a crucial role in this development. Writers of fiction took the lead in arousing sympathy for slaves and an imaginative understanding of the conditions in which they lived. One of the first was Aphra Behn. Her novel *Oroonoko,* published in 1688, described the enslavement of an African prince and his beautiful love, Imoinda. Prince Oroonoko is a physically handsome

and morally upright man with an unquenchable love for freedom, while Imoinda displays all the womanly virtues. Showing her readers that Oroonoko and Imoinda possessed the physical traits and moral qualities that Europeans admired, Behn wanted to evoke admiration for them and outrage over their enslavement. Her novel was eventually turned into a play, and its themes were repeated in a growing body of antislavery literature.

Works like *Oroonoko* and later narratives by slaves who escaped to tell their story drew readers into a world in which slaves were upright and blameless human beings who had suffered terrible cruelty and injustice. The effect was to cut through centuries of dehumanizing stereotypes and indifferent or hostile theological traditions. By the late 1780s, both the London Committee for the Abolition of the Slave Trade and the French Society of the Friends of the Blacks were campaigning tirelessly for an end to the slave trade and the abolition of slavery. Although both the trade and slavery itself ended only gradually, the antislavery momentum would not, from this point, be reversed.

Men and Women

The problem of difference and likeness in human beings, which shaped the debate on slavery, was also addressed in debates over the nature and roles of men and women. Women participated actively in the Enlightenment. Those who, like Madame du Deffand, presided over Europe's salons were arbiters of intellectual discussion. Those who, like Aphra Behn, joined men as professional writers became respectable public figures. Women also wrote some of the pamphlets that increasingly shaped public opinion, while others, like Mme. du Chatelet, contributed to the spread of Newtonian science. In the arts, France's most sought-after society painter was a woman, **Elisabeth Vigée-Lebrun.** Women's new social, intellectual, and professional activities raised the issue of similarity and difference between men and women and the proper relations between them.

To Descartes and Locke, it seemed self-evident that men and women not only possessed a common human nature but were intellectual equals. Descartes had

---

Quakers An English Protestant sect that rejected ceremony and an ordained ministry, relying instead on a mystical "inner light" to guide conscience.

Elisabeth Vigée-Lebrun (1755–1842) French society painter.

coupled his arguments about the power of autonomous human reason with a discussion of the mind's relation to the body. He argued that the two were radically different; humans' bodies were wholly material and were subject to the laws of matter in motion. The mind, however, was nonmaterial. This **Cartesian dualism** made one thing perfectly clear: mind was not shaped by the body it went with, whether male or female. It floated free in a nonmaterial and, therefore, sexless world. Locke's picture of the human mind pointed to similar conclusions. If the mind was like a blank sheet of paper, there seemed no good reason to argue for different male and female minds, since both were subject to the same stimulus from sense experience.

Many philosophes accepted the implications of Locke's and Descartes' arguments. Diderot did not think that men and women were all that different and agreed with Montesquieu that a woman's sexually based role as a mother was only one part of her life, not its defining characteristic. Voltaire rejected the idea of distinct male and female minds; men and women were intellectual equals, as his collaborator, Mme. du Chatelet, demonstrated.

Acceptance of intellectual equality between men and women, however, did not prevent many philosophes from assigning them separate social roles. Rejecting the traditional idea that men had to rule women because women were prone to irrational and unruly behavior, the philosophes now argued that women should enforce the rules of civilization in society and thereby tame *men's* unruly behavior. The salon hostess performed this task and did so in women's traditional sphere, the household, while other women performed it as mothers who educated their children in proper behavior.

Some philosophes rejected outright the idea of gender equality. Chief among them was Rousseau. Resurrecting old ideas about women's inferiority, Rousseau argued that women were irrational. Above all, they should play no public role in society as salon hostesses or commentators in the realm of public opinion. Their actual roles in this regard were simply another symptom of civilization's corrupting effect. Women belonged at home, breast-feeding their children and obeying their husbands. As creatures of feeling, they played a central role in training children. Men alone, however, should carry on rational discussion and engage in politics.

A growing body of medical literature seemed to support Rousseau's denial of women's equality to men and their banishment from public life. Works by physicians, such as Pierre Roussel's *The Physical and Moral Makeup of Women* (1775), offered a new view of male and female difference that in good Enlightenment fashion claimed to be based on scientific observation. Rejecting the traditional view that women were simply incomplete men, Roussel and others argued that women were completely different from them. For example, their nervous system, which included smaller brains, made it impossible for them to develop men's rational capacities. Their job was to nurture their babies and their husbands.

Rousseau and the medical men found their opponent in **Mary Wollstonecraft**, the author of *A Vindication of the Rights of Woman* (1792) and the ablest defender of women's equality. Wollstonecraft pointed out the basic paradox of their views on women. These men attacked the despotism of kings and rejected the institution of slavery but endorsed the subordination of some human beings to others on the basis of gender. Wollstonecraft believed with Rousseau that women as mothers should take charge of the moral and emotional education of their children, but she denied that they were inferior to men. If defects existed, she pointed out, they came from the inadequate education women received in a world where the best teaching was available only to men. Wollstonecraft argued that if women were educated with men on an equal basis, their seeming deficiencies would disappear.

In the Enlightenment, ideas about a universal human nature and gender-neutral minds mixed ambiguously with older ideas about women's inferiority and their proper place in the private, domestic sphere. But the debate among people like Rousseau, Roussel, and Wollstonecraft was conducted in increasingly nonreligious terms. Despite their differences, all sides looked less to Christian scripture and traditional church teaching on gender issues and turned instead to biology, psychology, and an examination of social conventions to demonstrate their respective positions.

Cartesian dualism Descartes' idea of the radical difference between material human bodies and nonmaterial human minds.

Mary Wollstonecraft (1759–1797) English writer and feminist who rejected the idea that women were physically and mentally inferior to men.

Summary

Review Questions

↑ What were the basic differences between traditional Christianity and the New Science on views of God, the natural world, and the human world?

↑ How did the Enlightenment draw on and expand the method and findings of the Scientific Revolution?

↑ How did Enlightenment debates reshape Europeans' sense of identity?

The Scientific Revolution changed European views of earth in fundamental ways. No longer were humans at the center of things; now they spun around the sun in an infinite universe. "These vast spaces terrify me," Pascal lamented in his *Pensées (Thoughts)*. Many others, however, were excited by the new understanding of the universe. It rested on a scientific method that relied on autonomous human reason and careful observation to demonstrate that it was true, thereby advancing knowledge far beyond anything achieved in the ancient world. So great was the prestige of the New Science that its method was quickly applied to other fields of learning in hopes of turning them into sciences as well.

The application of scientific method to an ever-expanding set of problems was at the heart of the intellectual movement known as the Enlightenment. The philosophes employed autonomous human reason and careful observation to establish the modern disciplines of political science, psychology, and sociology. At the same time, they subjected traditional Christian views on politics, human beings, and human society to systematic criticism. Above all, traditional Christian theology was scrutinized and often rejected, wholly or in part.

The Enlightenment promoted the principle of ra-tional discussion in a variety of ways. Discussion and debate were put into practice firsthand in salons, coffeehouses, Masonic lodges, and debating clubs, where people met as equal intellectual partners regardless of their social backgrounds. As more and more people gathered in these new institutions, the habit of collective discussion of and participation in matters of current interest spread. The growing numbers of books, newspapers, and pamphlets also aided this sense of participation in current affairs as readers learned of debate and discussion going on in other parts of Europe. Although gossip and misinformation jostled uncomfortably with accurate information in this new world of talk and print, participation gradually turned people into a public whose opinions mattered. The growing activity of an engaged public would soon manifest itself in demands for more popular participation in political life, a fact that states recognized when they began appealing to public opinion for support of their policies.

Although rational discussion was central to both the New Science and the Enlightenment, it did not always resolve problems to everyone's satisfaction, as ongoing debates over Europe's place in the world, the nature of non-European peoples, the acceptability of slavery, and issues of gender equality demonstrated. That these debates were conducted in increasingly nonreligious terms indicates a profound shift in western culture and an erosion of Christianity's dominance in Europe's intellectual life.

← **Thinking Back, Thinking Ahead** →

To what degree do the scientific method of the New Science and the values and agendas of the Enlightenment still shape western people in the twenty-first century?

ECHO ECHO ECHO ECHO ECHO ECHO

Coffeehouses

Coffeehouses were a central Enlightenment institution. They soon came to specialize in certain areas of discussion and information, some offering commercial or political news and others concentrating on reviews of recent plays, poems, and books. Still others were simply places where you could be seen. The famous British insurance company Lloyd's of London began in a coffeehouse. Also in London, by the end of the eighteenth century, some coffeehouses had begun to charge dues for membership, gradually becoming private clubs.

On the continent, public coffeehouses also underwent change. By the late nineteenth century, they were no longer meeting places for men only; whole families would now go to them for coffee and sweets. One of the grandest nineteenth-century coffeehouses was the Café Sacher in Vienna, which offered patrons slices of its famous sacher torte, a chocolate cake with chocolate icing and an apricot filling, topped with whipped cream. In the twentieth century, two Paris coffeehouses, Les Deux Magots and its rival next door, the Café de Flore, became meeting places for famous writers such as the American Ernest Hemingway, the French philosopher Jean-Paul Sartre, and the French feminist Simone de Beauvoir. People still throng their sidewalk tables, trying to recapture something of the earlier intellectual atmosphere.

Today coffeehouses have been rediscovered and are booming throughout the world. Starbucks, which started in Seattle, can now be found across the United States as well as in London and Hong Kong. Independent owners challenge the large franchise chains, and some advertise particular specialties—organic coffee, or fair-trade coffee, or coffee in a Christian atmosphere. Recently, the English magazine *The Economist* suggested that the Internet was a new version of the coffeehouse, serving as a virtual meeting place for the exchange of information, opinion, and gossip. Since the Internet is available in Internet cafés, the old coffeehouse and the virtual one sometimes occupy the same space.

Suggested Readings

Black, Jeremy, and Roy Porter, eds. *The Penguin Dictionary of Eighteenth-Century History.* New York: Penguin, 2001. A useful one-volume handbook.

Gay, Peter. *The Enlightenment: An Interpretation.* 2 vols. New York: Knopf, 1966–1969. A classic interpretation written in a very engaging style.

Henry, John. *The Scientific Revolution and the Origins of Modern Science.* 2nd ed. New York: Palgrave, 2002. A recent introductory account.

Jacob, Margaret C. *The Cultural Meaning of the Scientific Revolution.* New York: Knopf, 1988. An account placing the Scientific Revolution in its larger European cultural context.

_____. *The Enlightenment: A Brief History with Documents.* Boston: Bedford/St. Martin's, 2001. A recent introduction.

Shapin, Steven. *The Scientific Revolution.* Chicago: University of Chicago Press, 1996. An excellent recent analysis.

Voltaire, *Candide.* Edited by Daniel Gordon. Boston: Bedford/St. Martin's, 1999. A recent edition of Voltaire's best-known novel.

Websites

A useful site for the New Science , **Scientific Revolution,** at http://web.clas.ufl.edu/users/rhatch/pages/03-Sci-Rev/SCI-REV-Home

Another site for the New Science, **Scientific Revolution,** at www.fordham.edu/halsall/mod/modsbook09.html

A site for the philosophes, **Enlightenment,** at www.fordham.edu/halsall/mod/modsbook10.html

CHAPTER 18

Trade and Empire, 1700–1800

CHAPTER OUTLINE

1500 B.C.E.	1000 B.C.E.	500 B.C.E.	1 B.C.E./1 C.E.

		1713 Spain cedes *asiento* to Britain	1720 Last plague epidemic breaks out in France			

1700	1710	1720	1730	1740	1750

The Atlantic World, 1700–1789

By the eighteenth century Europe's trade had expanded beyond the routes from an earlier time between northern and southern Europe and eastern and western Europe. It now refocused on a cross-Atlantic trade that united Europe, Africa, and the Americas in new trading patterns. What role did agricultural products, raw materials, metals, manufactured goods, and human beings play in this Atlantic economy?

Great Britain
France
Portugal
Spain
Netherlands

ARCTIC OCEAN

ASIA

EUROPE

NORTH AMERICA

MEXICO

LOUISIANA

Hudson Bay

Silver (to the Philippines)

Silks, spices, porcelain

Acapulco

Veracruz

NEW FRANCE

QUEBEC

NEWFOUNDLAND
(To Gr. Br., 1713)

GREAT BRITAIN

NETHERLANDS

FLORIDA

Tobacco

NOVA SCOTIA
(ACADIA)
(To Gr. Br., 1713)

Furs

Colonial products

FRANCE

Havana

CUBA

Silver

Manufactured goods

SPAIN

JAMAICA

Sugar

PORTUGAL

Porto Bello

Silver

HISPANIOLA

SAINT DOMINGUE
(Fr.)

SANTO DOMINGO
(Sp.)

CANARY IS.
(Spain)

GUADELOUPE
(Fr.)

MARTINIQUE
(Fr.)

BARBADOS
(Gr. Br.)

Manufactured goods

Gold

AFRICA

NEW GRANADA

Lima

PERU

Amazon

DUTCH GUIANA

FRENCH GUIANA

Sugar

NORTH ATLANTIC OCEAN

CAPE VERDE IS.
(Port.)

Cape Verde

SLAVE COAST

GOLD COAST

Silver

SOUTH AMERICA

BRAZIL

Slaves

ANGOLA

Buenos Aires

SOUTH ATLANTIC OCEAN

| 500 C.E. | 1000 C.E. | 1500 C.E. | 2000 C.E. |

1776
Smith publishes *The Wealth of Nations*
American Revolution begins

1780
Gordon Riots attack Catholics in London

1760s
Industrial Revolution
begins in Britain

1763
France loses its empire
in North America

1783
American
independence
is won

1791
Prussian General
Code becomes law

| 1760 | 1770 | 1780 | 1790 | 1800 |

507

Choice Choice Choice

Samuel Gamble

Samuel Gamble was a ship's captain who contracted with British merchants to carry slaves from Africa to the Caribbean and return home with New World goods for the European market. Profit was foremost in his mind and the minds of those who backed him. In 1793, he set sail from London to buy slaves in Africa for the West Indian market. On this trip, things did not go as well as he had hoped. (Visual Connection Archive)

Samuel Gamble Sets Out from London on a Slaving Voyage

On April 7, 1793, Samuel Gamble weighed anchor and eased his ship, the *Sandown,* along the Thames River to the North Sea. Gamble had contracted with a group of British investors in January to gather a cargo of slaves in Africa for sale in the British colony of Jamaica. He had been in the slave trade for years, but this time business conditions were dangerous. France and Britain were once again at war, and the French were attacking British ships on the high seas. The Royal Navy was seizing ships' crews for its men-of-war, and Gamble had replaced twelve seized sailors only days before he set sail. Despite the dangers, Gamble and his backers were willing to put down money for the voyage. High risk meant high yield if the venture was successful.

The *Sandown* was provisioned for long sailing, since a roundtrip could last for a year or more. For weeks, supplies had been taken on board: beef, pork, pigs, tripe, potatoes, butter, and beer to feed the captain and crew; lead bars, gunpowder, earthenware dishes, and brandy to trade for slaves; and "big Iron Handcuffs, Neck chains & collars" to bind the slave cargo on the voyage to the West Indies. After leaving the Thames estuary, Gamble sailed along the southern coast of England in a convoy of merchant ships protected by the Royal Navy. Then they headed southwest into the Atlantic. On May 16, some of the ships veered off for the West Indies, while Gamble sailed south for the west coast of Africa. After stopping in Portugal's Cape Verde Islands, where he picked up cotton cloth to trade in Africa, Gamble arrived in what is today Sierra Leone on June 12, prepared to trade his cargo for slaves.

From then on, things went badly. June was the beginning of the rainy season in West Africa, and wet ground brought swarms of disease-carrying mosquitoes. Already, yellow fever was ravaging the coastal areas. This disease often killed within a week, as victims, vomiting blackish blood, fell into a coma while their liver deteriorated, causing them to turn yellow from jaundice. Gamble's stop in Africa had to be short if profits were to be made. He had contracted to carry 250 slaves to Jamaica in time for the beginning of sugar-cane cutting in December, when market demand for new slaves would be high. But yellow fever had disrupted the African trading networks, and Gamble had to wait nine and a half months before he could collect 234 slaves, 16 short of his contract. They were listed in his journal simply by age, sex, and an assigned number.

As Gamble tried to fill his ship with slaves, and he himself began to shake with fever, some of his sailors fell ill or died. The crew as a whole became, he wrote in his journal, "quite Peevish, fraxious, ill natur'd and Childish." In mid-January 1794, a slave uprising broke out on board, and eight Africans drowned, most likely as they tried to swim to freedom. Troubles continued after the *Sandown* set sail across the Atlantic in March—yellow fever, fights between sailors and slaves, more deaths. The ship's water kegs were leaking, and the *Sandown* had to make an unplanned stop in Barbados to take on more. There sixteen crew members abandoned ship and hired lawyers to get their back wages from Gamble. With the lawyers demanding the removal of *Sandown*'s sails and rudder to prevent it from leaving, Gamble sneaked out of port before daybreak and limped into Kingston, Jamaica, with a crew of five.

Yellow fever awaited him there. It had swirled across the Atlantic on other ships, disrupting the Jamaican slave markets and leaving Kingston's harbor crowded with earlier arrivals from Africa. In any case, Gamble had arrived too late to take advantage of high prices at the beginning of the cane-cutting season. "Slaves complaining of pains in their Bowells," he wrote glumly in his journal on May 25. The next day's entry read, "Slaves as before, they go off very slow (Market glutted)." After taking on provisions and a new cargo, probably of sugar and rum, the *Sandown* joined an armed convoy for the return trip to London, arriving there on October 11, 1794, a year and a half after the outbound voyage.

Gamble and his backers were disappointed in their profits. In a trade economy that pitted high gain against high risk, they had lost.

Introduction

Gamble saw slaves as one trade good—a very lucrative one—in the bustling transatlantic economy that was fueling Europe's economic growth. During the eighteenth century, Europe once again experienced population growth, which in turn stimulated economic production and a rise in consumption of goods and services at all levels of society as people bought more clothing, household items, and food. Increased economic activity led European thinkers to explore the reasons for economic growth and to lay the foundations for the modern discipline of economics. These new economists viewed people primarily as rational beings who exercised individual choice as consumers of the goods available in the marketplace.

The Atlantic economy also reshaped the European empires that had been formed in the Western Hemisphere beginning in the sixteenth century. Portugal, founder of the first overseas empire, relied more and more on the riches of Brazil for its continuing prosperity. The Spanish and French Empires declined as the British Empire rose, outstripping all others in vitality and prosperity and making London the commercial center of Europe. Britain's leading role in the Atlantic economy stimulated manufacturing and early forms of industrialization, thus laying the foundations for the modern economic world. But for the British as for every other New World empire, commerce and wealth depended on the labor of enslaved Africans.

Prosperity in Europe was accompanied by changes in upper- and middle-class behavior, as the well-to-do, influenced by Enlightenment ideas, began to expect greater privacy and comfort in the home and indulged in more spontaneous displays of affection among family members. The poor continued to live more tradition-bound lives, and the social and cultural gap between them and the rich widened. Government officials developed new theories about the causes of poverty and new institutions to eliminate them, while the poor took action by rioting. Food shortages and unacceptable working conditions could provoke popular rioting. So could long-simmering religious hatred. Europeans also began to rethink the basic nature of society, rejecting traditional ideas that emphasized group membership more than individual autonomy. Some people argued that wealth, not birth, was the proper basis for social ranking, while others maintained that society was made up of individual citizens bound together in a unified nation.

Economic Recovery

↓ What new ideas about economic development and the value of work accompanied Europe's economic recovery?

↓ What effects did the consumer revolution have on the daily lives of Europeans?

After 1700, Europe's population began to grow once again. Unlike the sixteenth-century demographic expansion, the eighteenth-century growth did not produce a crisis of overpopulation and economic hard times. Instead, it produced prosperity. But economic growth also caused people to question older ideas about how wealth was generated and to search for

Chronology

1665 Last plague breaks out in Britain	**1768** James Hargreaves invents the spinning jenny
1666 Great Fire in London	**1769** Richard Arkwright invents the water frame
1711 Last plague breaks out in Germany	**1771** Arkwright opens the first water-powered factory
1713 Spain grants Britain the *asiento*	**1776** Adam Smith publishes *The Wealth of Nations*
1720 Last plague outbreak in France	**1778** British Parliament grants limited rights to Catholics
1721 Calico Act restricts the import of cotton cloth from India	**1780** Gordon Riots destroy Catholic property in London
1733 Flying shuttle doubles weavers' speed	**1780s** James Watt's improved steam engines are introduced in Britain; Prussian General Code becomes law
1750 Treaty of Madrid between Spain and Portugal	**1793** Eli Whitney invents the cotton gin
1760s Industrial Revolution begins in Britain	

the laws that made the economic world function. Europeans also began to consume a greater variety of products than ever before, thus further stimulating the economy.

The Expanding Population of Europe

Europe's sixteenth-century overpopulation crisis was followed in the seventeenth century by a stagnating or declining population in many places. Then, in the early eighteenth century, population again began to grow, increasing from 95 million in 1700 to 146 million in 1800—by more than 50 percent. Growth was greatest in England and France; in general, western Europe experienced more growth than eastern Europe.

Historians have identified several factors contributing to population increase. The first was the disappearance of bubonic plague. London's last plague outbreak was in 1665, and the last outbreaks in Germany and France were in 1711 and 1720, respectively. Over the eighteenth century, the disease also disappeared from eastern and southern Europe. The likely cause for the plague's decline is found in Europe's shifting rodent population as large brown rats, carrying fleas that stayed on them, overtook the earlier black rat population, which hosted fleas that jumped onto human beings. The fleas carried the plague bacillus. This change in the rat population coincided with better government quarantines of infected areas that reduced the spread of disease.

Other killers, like smallpox, dysentery, and typhoid fever, periodically exploded into epidemics, but their effects were moderated by a growing interest in community and personal hygiene. Recognizing that filth bred disease, urban governments launched campaigns to clear out the garbage and human waste from the cities. In the eighteenth century, Europeans also began to bathe regularly. Bathing had been common in the Middle Ages, at least in towns with communal baths. After the Black Death, however, many cities closed their baths, thinking that they spread the disease. Later, Protestant and Catholic reformers campaigned to shut them down, arguing that baths promoted lewdness and sexual license. As a result, Europeans became dirtier and smellier than their medieval ancestors. By the eighteenth century, doctors had started to prescribe cold baths to build up the body, and the resumption of bathing improved hygiene and reduced disease.

Changing patterns of European warfare also encouraged population growth. The religious wars of the sixteenth and seventeenth centuries devastated the civilian population where they were fought. Armies were huge breeding grounds for disease, which spread beyond their own quarters. Battle also disrupted agriculture and brought on food shortages in a population already straining Europe's agricultural resources. Shortages, in turn, weakened people's resistance to disease. In the eighteenth century, Europe fought some of its wars elsewhere—in the Western Hemisphere and in Asia—and those fought in Europe were shorter

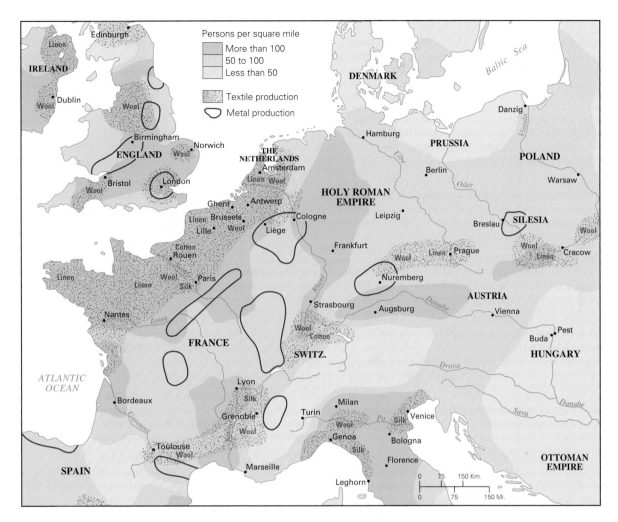

MAP 18.1 **Industry and Population in Eighteenth-Century Europe** In the eighteenth century most people lived in the countryside and many manufacturing processes, like textile weaving, were concentrated there in the putting out system. Metal production, especially iron and copper, were also located in the countryside.

and therefore less disruptive that earlier wars. Moreover, troops were better fed, better supplied, and better disciplined than they had been, making their presence less dangerous to the surrounding civilian population.

Finally, improvements in Europeans' diets encouraged population growth. Better climatological conditions gradually set in after 1700 as the Little Ice Age ended and harvests improved. In addition, some farmers kept up with rising demand by changing the agricultural practices in what has been described as an **agricultural revolution**. The changes developed first in the Rhineland and the Netherlands and then spread to England in the seventeenth and eighteenth centuries.

Traditionally, farmers had let fields lie fallow, or uncultivated, to restore their fertility. Beginning in

the sixteenth century, farmers discovered that instead of taking fields out of production, they could plant clover or turnips, which not only replenished the soil but could also be used as fodder for livestock. Now larger herds could be developed for milk, hides, and meat, so people began breeding livestock to improve quality. In England, local cows were bred with Dutch cattle to increase milk yield, and sheep were bred with specimens that were bigger than normal or that

agricultural revolution Improvements in agricultural method and livestock breeding in the sixteenth to the eighteenth centuries that greatly increased crop yields.

had fine wool coats. Growing herds meant nitrogen-rich manure that could be spread on fields to further increase their productivity. With fallowing eliminated and more manure available as fertilizer, land could be kept in continual production, thus greatly increasing the yield.

Increased yields created surpluses; so did a reorganization of farmland for agricultural production that ended the open-field system. In the past, cropland was usually divided into individually owned plots that were small but had no barriers between them. Sometimes people owned plots separated from each other by other owners' land. This exposed and fragmented pattern of landholding worked as long as the farming community operated as a single unit, planting and harvesting crops in the same sequence and at the same time. Village councils or the local landlord usually regulated planting and harvesting. After harvest, the community's livestock was allowed to range freely over the fields, grazing on what was left in them. This system discouraged experimentation with new crops and agricultural techniques.

Beginning in the middle of the eighteenth century, Britain's Parliament encouraged more efficient and productive use of farmland by passing laws permitting **enclosure** in a given area. Single strips were bought or traded to create large, consolidated blocs of land that were fenced off. Enclosure allowed for economies of scale in agricultural production and made experimentation with different crops and crop rotations possible. New land was also brought under cultivation and improved with new techniques. Underground drainage systems were installed in waterlogged fields, and heavy clays were lightened by working in crushed limestone. Improvements in crops, land organization, and soil quality also greatly increased yields. During the eighteenth century, improvements in agriculture spared Europeans from the devastating famines of earlier centuries, like the ones that struck France during the reign of Louis XIV.

Enclosure increased agricultural productivity, but it came at a social cost. Small-scale owners and poor squatters were forced off their plots, and traditional rights to common grazing after harvest were eclipsed. As the rural poor lost even the chance to maintain livestock, many became landless wageworkers on enclosed farms.

Nevertheless, the decline in epidemic diseases, coupled with improvements in military behavior, people's diet, and agricultural production, reduced mortality rates. During the eighteenth century, more people could count on their children surviving infancy and then living longer, healthier lives. In addition, people had more children because they were marrying earlier than before. In previous centuries, death had been the great social equalizer because rich and poor were equally defenseless in the face of disease. Now, the rich began to live longer than the poor because they were better fed and lived in the cleanest, healthiest environments.

The World of Work

For many Europeans, patterns of work remained as they had been in previous centuries. Despite innovations in agriculture, most peasants toiled in the countryside using age-old techniques for planting and harvesting crops. In cities, guild members continued to think of themselves as the elite of the working world and jealously guarded their privileges. Alongside this traditional world, however, other types of work began to engage growing numbers of people.

During the economic slump of the seventeenth century, Europe's peasants and urban working poor, especially in the west, supplemented their incomes by making things at home. Many women spun wool into yarn and sold the surplus—the yarns they did not use themselves. Most likely, they would put their children to work cleaning and carding (combing) the wool, while husbands would weave on hand looms. Eventually, merchants delivered raw wool to the household and paid cash for finished cloth. This arrangement, known as the **putting-out system,** was Europe's first means of manufacturing. Merchants got involved because they could pay low and sell high. They might buy raw wool in large volume from sheep farmers, put it out to many different households, and pick up spun yarn or even woven cloth for a pittance—so much for a certain amount, or by the piece. Linen cloth—both coarse and fine—and nails were also produced in the putting-out system. Workers accepted the arrangement because the entire family could be put to work. But the spread of the system, in which household workers only occasionally saw the merchant who bought their **piecework,** created a personal and physical distance between workers and merchants that did not exist in the older owner-operated workshop of the guild system.

When Europe's population once again began to

enclosure   Process of consolidating agricultural land and enclosing it with hedges or fences.

putting-out system   System whereby workers manufactured consumer goods for a merchant who supplied them with raw material.

piecework   Work paid for by the number of pieces produced.

grow in the early eighteenth century, demand for manufactured products rose, offering people further employment. Because prices for food and other basic products tended to rise faster than workers' incomes, there were always people willing to do piecework. But the putting-out system also carried risks. Merchants would pay for products as long as demand was high, but an unpredictable decline in demand, often in a distant market, would lead to drastically fewer pieces bought and a sharp decline in income for workers. Overall, however, the putting-out system dynamically increased Europe's manufacturing capacity. For example, English linen exports jumped from 180,000 yards in 1730 to 9.6 million yards in 1760.

Other new types of work were urban based. Europe's cities were growing in the eighteenth century, offering work for architects, engineers, bricklayers, stonemasons, street repairers, plumbers, and those who catered to them. In Paris, a kind of "take-out" developed, as people bought prepared food for their meals. Women found work as dressmakers, seamstresses, linen workers, and clothes washers. Paris had two thousand washerwomen scrubbing along the banks of the Seine River. Women also operated stalls in outdoor markets. As in the past, women's wages lagged noticeably behind men's.

All over Europe, migrants from the countryside to the city often ended up as servants, since servants regularly made up a city's largest single group of workers: Paris may have had more than ninety thousand of them. Usually, they constituted about 10 percent of the total urban population. Servants benefited from some job security since their employment was continuous and they were given room and board and sometimes clothing. But work in an employer's house could also be dangerous. Angry masters might accuse their servants of theft, and women could be seduced or raped by their employer or fellow servants and then abandoned.

The servant world was divided into the skilled few and the mass of the unskilled. The skilled worked as butlers, cooks, and personal attendants. They often served the same employer for many years and then retired into the middle class. Most servants, however, worked as footmen, stable boys, or chamber and kitchen maids. These lower servants usually calculated employment opportunities carefully, regularly leaving one employer for another if the new job promised a better wage, a new set of clothes, or better food and lodging. Male servants viewed their work as a temporary measure until something better came along. Many women worked to save a dowry and then marry a prosperous peasant or artisan in their home village or in the city where they worked.

At the bottom of the urban world were the underemployed. These were men and women who passed in and out of work. Men looked for odd jobs, hauling water or carrying messages across town. Women washed clothes, or took up prostitution when nothing else was available. All of them eked out a life through begging, petty thievery, and occasional work, depending on what seemed the best opportunity from day to day. With Europe's population rising, their numbers probably grew over the century.

Changing Notions of Wealth

As work diversified and patterns of work changed during the eighteenth century, Europeans debated the nature of the economic world. Gradually, new ways of thinking about work and the economy emerged. During the seventeenth century, states had adopted mercantilism as an economic policy. Mercantilists believed that the world's wealth was limited and that a state needed to increase its overall share at the expense of others. This belief led to programs for stimulating domestic prosperity and establishing favorable trade balances. Mercantilism emphasized the needs of states and their rulers above all else; economic policy was a means of strengthening states locked in the competitive struggle for dominance in Europe. Europe's colonies were absorbed into this mercantilist agenda; their purpose was to provide the things that the mother country needed to secure a greater share of the world's wealth and to increase its competitive advantage at home and abroad.

In the eighteenth century, economists started to argue that economic activity did not simply shift wealth from one state to another. Economies were capable of growing, and new wealth could be generated if states stopped interfering in economic life. In France, the **Physiocrats** argued that the government's traditional regulation of the grain trade harmed agricultural productivity and that the economy would work best if the government left it alone. *"Laissez faire, laissez aller!"* ("Leave it alone, let it go!"), they cried; the term **laissez-faire** coming to stand in for a government policy of noninterference in the economy. The Physiocrats also thought of the economy as a complex mechanism, each part of which depended on the others. In this way it was like the natural

Physiocrats   French economists who argued against mercantilist regulation of the economy.

laissez-faire   (in French, "leave it alone") Economic principle that economies develop best when free of government interference.

34

In this print, Adam Smith, a professor at the University of Glasgow in Scotland, points to a book, perhaps one of his own. Near the book are feather pens and letter paper. Like most writers in the eighteenth century, Smith would have carried on an extensive correspondence with people who shared his intellectual interests. *(Special Collections/Glasgow University Library)*

world. And, like the natural world, the economy was governed by laws. Just as Isaac Newton had discovered the laws of physics, the Physiocrats proposed to discover the laws of economic activity and to construct a science of economics.

When **Adam Smith,** professor of moral philosophy at the University of Glasgow, visited with the Physiocrats on a trip to France, he became interested in this new science. His *Inquiry into the Nature and Causes of the Wealth of Nations,* published in 1776, quickly became a foundational text for modern economic thought based on the Physiocrats' idea that economies could grow. Smith adopted the laissez-faire principles of the Physiocrats. Governments, he argued, should regulate economic activity as little as possible, restricting themselves to defending the community against foreign attackers, establishing a judicial system to police people's behavior, and supporting improvements in transportation, such as roads and canals, that would facilitate commerce.

Smith believed that human beings wanted to acquire material goods to make their lives more comfortable. They were consumers by nature. Their economic activity was driven by their own needs and those of their immediate families, not by any concern for the public good. Nevertheless, as individuals pursued their private and often-selfish economic interests, the larger economy benefited. An "invisible hand" linked all these private pursuits into an overall economic dynamic that brought prosperity to the whole community. So, when tea drinkers satisfied their desire for tea by buying tea leaves, a teapot, and teacups, they enriched the merchant who had brought the tea from Asia and the workers in porcelain who had made the pot and cups. These people then used their profits to satisfy their own desires, thereby enriching yet another group of merchants and manufacturers.

Smith knew that satisfying consumers' desires meant that production of goods had to keep up with them, and he argued that production could grow with the **division of labor.** Each stage in the production of a commodity—Smith used the example of pins—should be done by specialists. Division and specialization would result in a greater volume of production than when one person made one pin, start to finish. This division of labor was already happening in the putting-out system, as merchants brought raw wool to spinners, picked up yarn and took it to weavers, and then picked up woven cloth to sell on the market. In their writings, Smith and the Physiocrats analyzed economic behavior on its own terms, and, like the philosophes, they formulated the laws underlying it.

Adam Smith (ca.1723–1790) Scottish philosopher and economist whose *Wealth of Nations* (1776) became a foundational text for modern economic theory and economic liberalism.

division of labor Manufacturing arrangement whereby each stage in production is done by specialists, thus increasing volume of production.

Attitudes toward manual work were also changing during the eighteenth century. Traditionally, manual labor was held in contempt because it involved working with material things like dirt, wood, or animal skins. The material world was thought to be lower than the spiritual world, and, following the story of Adam in Genesis, manual labor was believed to be punishment for sin. But when the philosophes rejected traditional Christian ideas about human beings' inherent wickedness, they also cast aside the idea of work as punishment. No one did this more forcefully than Denis Diderot. His *Encyclopédie* extolled the social usefulness of crafts that depended on working with one's hands and presented readers with detailed articles, accompanied by engravings, of manufacturing processes.

Thus Smith's idea that people could increase their productivity through division of labor was coupled with Diderot's celebration of the workers who produced goods for consumption. Throughout the eighteenth century, a surge in consumer demand across all economic groups created new employment opportunities in a wide range of firms manufacturing consumer products. New attitudes help to explain why the manufacturing sector of the European economy grew so dynamically during the eighteenth century.

The Consumer Revolution

Smith's and Diderot's interest in the production of goods was connected to an important shift in many Europeans' economic behavior that has been described as the **consumer revolution.** As more goods became available, people bought more than ever before, stimulating the production of even more, and more varied, kinds of things to buy. Consumer demand rose over most of Europe, but especially in the states of the northwest—Britain, the Netherlands, western Germany, and France. Imported goods made the array of items to purchase even more enticing. The rich purchased wallpaper, paintings, mirrors, and elaborate clocks, as well as expensive furniture. Fine porcelain began to replace pottery on dining tables and was used for such things as candlesticks that earlier had been made from wood or metal. Cotton clothing, made from fiber imported from India and Europe's American colonies, became increasingly popular, replacing wool and rivaling linen and silk as the fabric of fashion. Snuffboxes for men, elegant scarves for women, and bejeweled walking sticks for both came increasingly into fashion.

The rich had always spent heavily on decorative and luxury commodities, and their spending habits in the eighteenth century represented a quantitative

Olof Fridsberg's painting of *Ulla Tessin in Her Study* shows a rich Swedish women caught up in the consumer revolution. Her study is crammed with luxury goods—an oriental rug, two desks, a clock, figurines, a Chinese vase, a Chinese lacquered cabinet on a shelf, and much more. (*The National Museum of Fine Arts, Stockholm*)

but not a qualitative increase in conspicuous consumption. The real change over the century occurred among the middle and lower economic groups in European society; now, for the first time, they bought many of the same items, copying the tastes of the rich. The change is reflected in wills and lists from estate sales. Now a merchant would have a set of razors for shaving, along with porcelain shaving mugs and washbowls, all of which sat on a wooden stand made of fine wood in the latest fashion. His wife would have several changes of clothes, hung in a new wooden clothes closet set against a wall. Chamber pots placed in toilet chairs became a common feature of their well-appointed bedroom. By the end of the

> **consumer revolution** Term used for the eighteenth-century rise in consumer demand that stimulated the economy, especially in northwestern Europe.

century, some people were installing indoor plumbing and flush toilets that connected to improved sewer systems. Even the working poor furnished and decorated their rented rooms. Inexpensive prints hung on their walls, and pieces of pretty porcelain were brought out for special occasions. They bought more bed frames and mattresses than ever before and started to put their children in their own beds instead of adding them to the parental bed, as they had in the past. They also accumulated several changes of clothes, buying from secondhand dealers who sold the used clothes of the rich.

Several factors lay behind working people's accumulation of possessions. Increasingly, workers were paid in cash rather than kind. The growth of a cash economy offered new forms of investment. Extra clothing and nonessential household items served as a hedge against catastrophic poverty during hard economic times. If demand for textiles in the putting-out system declined, workers could take their new possessions, purchased when work and incomes were good, and pawn them for cash in the growing number of **pawnshops** that emerged during the eighteenth century. When good economic times returned, the pawned items were redeemed, enjoyed once again, and held in reserve for the inevitable bad times. Moreover, as people became consumers of a variety of products, they developed a sense of empowerment. They saw their choices in the marketplace as reflecting their taste, and they sought to cultivate their taste through knowledge of goods and markets. As they made personal choices about what they wanted to buy, they increased their role as individual actors in the marketplace. Adam Smith's picture of an economy based on private individuals' pursuit of their own interests was embodied in the consumer revolution.

In addition to buying more clothes, accessories, and household items, Europeans also added new foodstuffs to their daily diets. Four items, in particular, stand out: coffee, tea, and chocolate, all of which were drunk, and cane sugar, which started to replace honey as a sweetener. All four depended on the growth in overseas trade and the establishment of colonies. Tea was imported from East Asia, while coffee came from either the Middle East or the Western Hemisphere. Chocolate was raised in tropical colonies. Above all, sugar was produced in ever-larger quantities in the plantations of the Caribbean and Brazil. By century's end, sugar had become a standard item on the tables of both the rich and the poor. The introduction of these new foodstuffs often stimulated European manufacturing. Take tea. As its consumption rose, so did demand for teapots and teacups. A well-to-do hostess, preparing for a tea party, would also

have purchased many other new goods—canisters to store the tea, special clippers to cut sugar from the cones in which it came, a tea table, a porcelain pitcher for cream, a sugar basket and tongs for the cut sugar, and teaspoons for stirring.

London

On September 2, 1666, a fire in London destroyed more than thirteen thousand homes and eighty-seven churches, including the medieval Cathedral of Saint Paul. As the city recovered from the disaster of what was called the Great Fire, new building codes required the use of brick instead of wood for dwellings. The architect **Christopher Wren** designed a new Saint Paul's Cathedral as the city's centerpiece. By 1801, London had a population of about 1 million, making it the largest city in Europe. This "overgrown monster," as one Londoner called it, was covered with soot and engulfed in smog that came from the smoke of coal fires that heated everything from St. Paul's Cathedral to the dingy rooms of the city's slums. When the smoke mixed with river fog, it created the city's notorious "pea soup" atmosphere that persisted well into the twentieth century. In this densely packed, polluted environment, only one in four babies could expect to survive to adulthood. The city's population could not replace itself, so it depended on migration; over three-quarters of its population was not London-born.

From everywhere in Britain, people came. Despite London's unhealthy environment, outsiders plunged into the city to make money and seek excitement. Tens of thousands toiled away in the city's shipyards, textile manufacturers, and breweries. Thousands more worked on the docks that bordered the Thames, where over a thousand ships at any given time were unloading cargo from Asia, Africa, and the Americas or loading goods destined for the Atlantic world. Stalls in the city's huge markets were tended by thousands more. The city also teemed with government employees, lawyers, bankers, and stockbrokers, all engaged in the business of running the commercial, financial, and legal business of Britain and its empire. Physicians, surgeons, and clergymen attended to the physical and spiritual well-being of the populace. The building trades boomed throughout the city as its growing population clamored for more accommodations.

pawnshops Institutions that lend money to persons who deposit goods there as security against the loan.
Christopher Wren (1632–1723) English architect who designed the new Saint Paul's Cathedral after the London fire of 1666.

Leicester Square in London, shown here in an engraving by William Henry Prior, was in the fashionable western part of the eighteenth-century city. The houses, built from a common plan, open onto a large, clean square, where people ride or stroll. *(Mary Evans Picture Library/The Image Works)*

Over the century, the city became divided between poor working districts to the east of Saint Paul's, which also housed many Jews, and fashionable new districts west of the cathedral. The eastern districts continued to be built with narrow streets and shoddy, windowless buildings. In the western districts, however, radically new design standards were employed. Wide streets lined with stately houses opened onto great squares where the wealthy strolled or rolled by in their carriages. These houses had large rooms and windows that let in light and fresh air.

No city in Europe experienced the consumer revolution more than London. Every type of good and entertainment was available for a price. New shops were built with large glass display windows that allowed people to scrutinize the enticing goods for sale inside: clothes, shoes, umbrellas, watches, furniture, paintings, clocks, hats, gloves, walking sticks, pistols, fans, tea, Chinese porcelain, East Indian cotton cloth—everything.

One of London's most popular consumer items was gin. In the early eighteenth century, improvements in **distilling** and lower grain prices made the production of gin at cheap prices possible, and the poor of London took to it with gusto. A wave of binge drinking and public drunkenness swept over the city in the 1730s and 1740s that ended only in the 1750s, when Parliament passed strict licensing laws for gin shops and the price of grain rose, making the drink more expensive.

> **distilling** Process in which fermented grain is heated to turn its alcohol content into vapor that is then siphoned off and allowed to cool into liquid form.

If one wished entertainment, there were dozens of theaters performing the latest plays or one of **George Fredrick Handel**'s operas or oratorios. Or one could spend an evening at the cockfights or the ring where scantily clad women wrestled. Or one could go to sideshows where one could look at dwarves, bearded ladies, and Siamese twins. There were the pleasure gardens of **Vauxhall** and **Ranelagh,** where the price of admission allowed visitors to stroll the lamp-lit gardens at night to hear singers and musicians or enjoy food and drink in a pavilion while waiting for the fireworks. Or there was the **Tower of London,** where the crown jewels were on display. There was everything to see and do.

London was not the only city that grew over the eighteenth century and was transformed by the consumer revolution. Paris, with a population of 600,000, also underwent a building boom and urban renovation. Like London, the working poor lived in crowded quarters in the eastern parts of the city, while the rich and well-born occupied newly constructed western quarters where public squares and large townhouses were built. One contemporary observer of the Parisian scene stated that more than 30 percent of the city's buildings had been constructed between 1760 and 1780. The Duke of Orléans, a cousin of the king, made a fortune selling wood from his estates to feed the building boom. Improvements were made in street lighting and sewage disposal. The city also ordered property owners to provide street numbers for their buildings and tried to place street names on corner buildings. But London was in a class by itself. And underpinning all its bustle, buying, pleasure, and wealth was the complex web of the Atlantic trade that depended on the seizure, shipping, sale, and labor of thousands of African slaves.

The Atlantic World

↓ How did the Atlantic trade link Europe, Africa, and the Americas in an integrated economy?
↓ What explains Britain's leading role in this trade?

During the eighteenth century, trading networks across the Atlantic, which had formed during the sixteenth century, reached their fullest development. Northern Europe's trade with the Mediterranean and East Asia flourished, but the dynamic center shifted decisively to the Atlantic Ocean. The older empires of Spain and Portugal continued to send products to Europe, but they were being overtaken by the French and the British. In the end, it was the British who occupied the central place in an Atlantic trade system.

This system was based on the seizure and transport of, ultimately, millions of Africans to the Western Hemisphere, where they labored as slaves to produce agricultural commodities, especially sugar, to satisfy rising consumer demand in Europe. In return, Europeans manufactured shoes and cheap clothing for slaves and a variety of household items, tools, and luxuries for colonists.

The Atlantic Economy

Samuel Gamble's triangular voyage (see Choice) was commonplace in the eighteenth century. British, French, Dutch, and Portuguese slavers sailing from Europe headed to the West African coast. There, like Gamble, they turned to resident Europeans with links to local African rulers, who supplied the slaves. Guns and gunpowder, alcohol, cloth, tobacco, and iron bars were traded for the human cargo. Once slaves were collected, the voyage across the Atlantic, the dreaded **Middle Passage,** began. For weeks, the ship sailed west, following the trade wind patterns of the North Atlantic. As with Gamble's voyage, death stalked the slave ships. On average 10 to 20 percent of the Africans died before reaching the Caribbean, along with 20 to 25 percent of the ship's crew, from diseases contracted in Africa or on board. The Portuguese called these slave ships hearses. Death rates were even higher for Europeans who manned the outposts on the African coast because of malaria and other diseases.

The European colonies' import of slaves reshaped the communities of West Africa. Slaves were sometimes captives taken in warfare, while others were simply kidnapped. Some rulers, anxious to take advantage of European demand, extended their power and created centralized kingdoms, like Dahomey and Ashanti, where the capture and sale of slaves was a central feature of the local economy. The rich soils of West Africa assured a good food supply, especially after manioc, a nutritious root vegetable, was imported

---

George Fredrick Handel (1685–1759) German composer who resided in England and wrote operas and oratorios, including *The Messiah*.

Vauxhall and **Ranelagh** Pleasure gardens open to the paying public where people could stroll, eat, listen to music, and watch fireworks.

Tower of London Medieval fortress on the banks of the Thames that became a popular tourist attraction in the eighteenth century.

Middle Passage Slave ships' weeks-long voyage across the Atlantic from West Africa to the Caribbean.

MAP 18.2 **The Worldwide Slave Trade** In the eighteenth century, slave trading out of Africa went in many directions. Africans from central Africa were taken north to Muslim ports on the Mediterranean, while the Arab-controlled slave trade east from Mozambique to Asia also flourished. Most slaves bound for the New World were taken from Mozambique and from the central and southern west African coast.

from America. In turn, the food supply encouraged growth of the local population, which slavers could seize for the transatlantic trade. Overall, some 11 million slaves were taken across the Atlantic to toil in American plantations, mainly in the Caribbean and Brazil. The colonies' importation of slaves resulted from an insatiable demand for labor and slaves' high mortality rate; perhaps one-third died within a few years of arriving in the Western Hemisphere. An imbalanced sex ratio also worked against a stabilization of the slave population. Male slaves, considered more desirable for plantation labor because of their strength, outnumbered female ones, and adults were enslaved more frequently than children.

Voice Voice Voice Voice

Olaudah Equiano Describes Passage on a Slave Ship

In 1789, Olaudah Equiano, a freed slave, published The Interesting Narrative of the Life of Olaudah Equiano, or Gustavus Vassa, the African. *He claimed that his account was based on his own memories as an African boy of ten taken aboard a slave ship. The claim is currently disputed, but there is no doubt that Equiano's narrative, whether fact or fiction, helped to gain support in England for the abolition of the slave trade.*

➡ The first object which saluted my eyes when I arrived on the coast was the sea, and a slave ship . . . waiting for its cargo. These filled me with astonishment, which was soon converted into terror. . . . When I was carried on board I was immediately handled, and tossed up, to see if I were sound by some of the crew, and I was now persuaded that I had gotten into a world of bad spirits and that they were going to kill me. Their complexions too differing so much from ours, their long hair, and the language they spoke, which was very different from any I ever heard, united to confirm me in this belief. . . . When I looked round the ship too, and saw a large furnace or copper boiling and a multitude of black people of every description chained together, every one of their countenances expressing dejection and sorrow, I no longer doubted of my fate; and, quite overpowered with horror and anguish, I fell motionless on the deck and fainted. . . . I became so sick and low that I was not able to eat, nor had I the least desire to taste anything. ➡ I now wished for the last friend, Death, to relieve me; but soon, to my grief, two of the white men offered me eatables, and, on my refusing to eat, one of them held me fast by the hands and laid me across, I think, the windlass, and tied my feet, while the other flogged me severely. . . . ➡ I had never seen among my people such instances of brutal cruelty; and this not only shewn towards us blacks, but also to some of the whites themselves. One white man in particular I saw, when we were permitted [*sic*] to be on deck, flogged so unmerci-

➡ How does Equiano manage to convey these experiences from the point of view of a ten-year-old child?

➡ Why would Equiano be flogged for not eating?

➡ Why does Equiano make these remarks?

fully that he died in consequence of it; and they tossed him over the side as they would have done to a brute. . . .

The stench of the hold while we were on the coast was . . . intolerably loathsome. . . . The closeness of the place, and the heat of the climate, added to the number in the ship, which was so crowded that each had scarcely room to turn himself, almost suffocated us. This produced copious perspirations, so that the air soon became unfit for respiration, from a variety of loathsome smells, and brought on a sickness among the slaves, of which many died, thus falling victims to the improvident avarice, as I may call it, of their purchasers. This wretched situation was again aggravated by the galling of the chains, now become insupportable; and the filth of the necessary tubs, into which the children often fell, and were almost suffocated. The shrieks of the women and the groans of the dying, rendered the whole a scene of horror almost inconceivable. ➜ Happily perhaps for myself I was soon reduced so low here that it was thought necessary to keep me on deck; and from my extreme youth I was not put in fetters.

➜ *Does this act of kindness lessen or sharpen the horrors of Equiano's account?*

Source: "Olaudah Equiano Describes Passage on a Slave Ship" from Northrup, David, ed., *The Atlantic Slave Trade,* 2nd edition. Copyright © 2002 by Houghton Mifflin Company. Reprinted with permission.

This engraving of Olaudah Equiano appeared in his autobiography, which was published in 1789. In European dress, he looks out thoughtfully toward the reader. (*National Portrait Gallery, Smithsonian Institution/Art Resource, NY*)

Slavers like Gamble returned to their home ports loaded with New World products: coffee, chocolate, cocoa, and sugar from the tropics as well as fish, tobacco, and furs from farther north. Above all, it was Europe's demand for sugar that fueled plantation owners' demand for slaves. Sugar raising and refining was a highly complex process that required hundreds of workers laboring in lockstep. When the cane was ripe, it had to be quickly cut and crushed between giant rollers before it dried out and the sap deteriorated. Huge vats heated by roaring fires reduced the sap to a syrup that could be further refined into cones and loaves. Slaves' frenzied cutting and crushing of cane, along with the unbearable heat of the fires beneath the vats, led one Portuguese priest in Brazil to write that "a sugar mill is hell, and all the masters of them are damned."

The need to clothe the huge slave populations of the Americas stimulated the shoe and textile manufacturers of Europe. Food for slave populations was produced in the tropics where they worked, but dried fish was also shipped in from New England. Thus all the lands that bordered the Atlantic—Africa, the Americas, and Europe—were linked in a complex trading system that depended on the forced labor of African slaves.

Sugar was processed on Caribbean plantations where it was grown. In this painting, sugar cane stalks are on the left. In the right rear some slaves crush the stalks for their juice, while in the foreground others tend the vats in which the juice is boiled down until the sugar crystallizes. *(Mary Evans Picture Library/The Image Works)*

The Spanish and Portuguese Empires

After a decline in production during the mid-seventeenth century, Spain's colonial silver mines boomed and produced half of the world's silver in the 1700s. The silver and other trades were organized as they had been in the sixteenth century; the Manila galleon sailed once a year to the west coast of Mexico, from which its goods were transferred to the Caribbean and then shipped with New World silver to Spain in a convoy of merchant ships guarded by men-of-war. This highly centralized system no longer worked well. By 1700, some 2 million Spaniards had migrated to the Spanish colonies, and their demand for European goods could not be met by the annual trips to and from Spain. Although Spanish law forbade trade with foreigners, smuggling flourished in the empire's ports, where French and British traders brought needed goods from Europe or other parts of the Western Hemisphere and returned to their ports with emeralds, pearls, and cocoa.

The British benefited most from Spain's inadequate trading network. In 1709, during the War of the Spanish Succession, when Britain was fighting both France and Spain, merchants in the western port of Bristol financed a privateer to capture the Manila galleon. The venture was successful, and the galleon's cargo brought a profit of £786,000 to the overjoyed in-vestors. The ship itself was sailed to London, where it became a tourist attraction. In 1713, at the end of the war, the Spanish granted the British the *asiento*, permission to sell slaves in Spanish colonies. In addition, the right to sail into Spanish ports enhanced the possibility for trade in other goods.

In the fifteenth and sixteenth centuries, Portugal had created an empire that stretched westward from India to outposts in Africa and then across the Atlantic to Brazil. In the seventeenth century, Brazil had produced most of the sugar for Europe. By the 1680s, however, competition from French and British colonies in the Caribbean had led to a decline in prices for Brazilian sugar, and the industry slumped. Soon afterward, gold was discovered. During the first half of the eighteenth century, gold became the main export, and Brazil was Portugal's most profitable colony. Each new find sparked a fevered gold rush as people from Portugal and the Atlantic islands joined local people in the hunt for treasure. The influx of these fortune seekers greatly increased the European population in the colony. The slave population also increased because Africans were brought in to work the mines. The largest gold strikes were in Brazil's interior, so, for the first time, Europeans started to move away from the coast, where the sugar plantations were located. The push inland also brought increasing contact between whites and the local Indian population, which declined, like Indians in the Spanish Empire, as the result of disease and exploitation. Historians estimate that the Indian population of Brazil fell by 75 percent during the Brazilian colonial period. Unlike the Spanish, who studied Indian culture even as they exploited the local peoples, the Portuguese showed hardly any interest in the Brazilian Indians except as a labor force.

Portuguese occupation of the Brazilian interior was capped off by the **Treaty of Madrid,** signed in 1750, which adjusted the boundary between Spanish and Portuguese America, set by the Treaty of Tordesillas, in Portugal's favor. The territory assigned to Portugal west of the old line of demarcation created a colony that covered roughly the same territory as modern Brazil. By the time the treaty was signed, gold mining was in decline, but the sugar industry was on the upswing as demand and prices rose. Diamonds were also found and sent to Europe in such numbers that their price fell by 75 percent. Sugar, gold, and diamonds ended up making Brazil far richer in resources and income from trade than its mother country.

The French and British Empires

In theory, the French New World Empire was vast, stretching from Quebec in eastern Canada to the Great Lakes and down the Mississippi River to Louisiana and the Gulf of Mexico. It also included the Caribbean islands of Saint-Domingue, Guadeloupe, and Martinique. In fact, however, these lands were sparsely inhabited by European colonists. In the mid-eighteenth century, Canada contained 60,000 Frenchmen as compared to the 1.8 million European inhabitants of the British mainland colonies. Canada's main export to Europe was furs, especially beaver pelts, which were used for making hats because their tight nap allowed them to shed water easily. French traders paid local trappers and Indians with guns and woolen clothes manufactured in the mother country. The Canadians also supplied the sugar islands with grain, timber, and leather goods. The sugar produced there was shipped back to France for refining, along with locally grown coffee. Seventy-five percent of the sugar and 80 percent of the coffee were then reexported to markets in northern and eastern Europe. The slave population in the French Caribbean, which far outnumbered the white colonists, stimulated French manufacturing, since textiles were shipped overseas to clothe the African workforce. The sugar island of Saint-Domingue was the single most productive colony of any European empire in the eighteenth century. Despite its profitability, the French, like the Spanish and Portuguese, lost ground to the British. Smaller European populations in the French colonies meant a less dynamic transatlantic economy.

The French also established trading posts in India, supplanting the Portuguese and Dutch and rivaling the English, who were also expanding their trade on the subcontinent. The main French post was at **Pondicherry,** on the southeast coast, from which silk and pepper were exported to France. In addition to these traditional commodities, printed cotton cloth was also exported to supply the growing demand for cotton clothing in Europe.

Britain benefited most from the Atlantic trade. Its success rested on two things: a slave-worked plantation economy in the Caribbean and the southern half of the mainland colonies combined with a thriving colonial demand for the products of the mother country. In addition, the needs of the mainland colonies' many coastal cities provided other trading opportunities across the Atlantic world. Beginning in 1651, a series of Navigation Acts passed by Parliament excluded foreigners from the trade between British colonies and the mother country, decreed that all shipping must be in British or colonial vessels, and prohibited American manufacturers from sending their products to Britain if the products would compete there with locally made products.

London and the ports on Britain's west coast prospered from the trade goods they shipped to all parts of the Atlantic world. In addition to those sent to West Africa for slaves, merchant vessels carried textiles, tools, metal utensils, and a variety of household items to West Indian and North American consumers. Cheap cloth was in demand to provide clothing for the thousands of slaves, while household items like desks, chairs, wallpaper, curtains, china, carriages, and silverware were bought by the white population, who were caught up in Europe's consumer revolution. Colonial demand also increased because of a rising population. Not only did Britons continue to migrate to the American colonies; birthrates there were exceptionally high and large families the rule. The relatively easy availability of land for agriculture resulted in a high standard of living, perhaps the highest in the world at the time, that allowed colonials to buy nonessential items that pleased them or made their lives more comfortable. British manufacturers responded to this overseas demand by producing more and more for the overseas market.

Treaty of Madrid Treaty between Spain and Portugal in 1750 that revised the boundaries of Brazil by adding more land in the west to the colony.

Pondicherry Most important French trading post in India.

Colonials also produced products that were shipped either to the mother country for consumption or re-export, or to other parts of the empire. In addition to the sugar, coffee, and chocolate that went from the Caribbean colonies to Britain, rice grown in South Carolina and Georgia on slave-labor plantations was shipped to markets in Portugal, Spain, and Mediter-ranean ports, where it was a staple in local diets. Indigo from the two colonies was also a highly prized blue dye for textiles. Beaver pelts were also shipped—eighty thousand of them by midcentury. Tobacco grown on slave-labor plantations in Maryland and Virginia was sent to Europe as demand rose. Euro-peans had imported 9 million pounds of New World tobacco in the 1660s; in 1775, they imported 220 mil-lion pounds.

No region in British North America prospered more from Britain's Atlantic trade than New England. Despite their cool climate and rocky soil, the New England colonies played a vital role in imperial com-merce as the American center for the **carrying trade.** The abundant timber in the region gave rise to a local shipbuilding industry as well as supplying tall fir trees as masts for ships built in Britain. Corn and salt fish were shipped to the sugar plantations of the West Indies in return for tropical fruits, spices, and slaves taken to the mainland colonies. Barrels made from lo-cal wood were also sent to the West Indies and filled there with molasses, which New Englanders turned into rum. The rum was then shipped to Africa as payment for slaves who were brought to the Carib-bean. Newport, Rhode Island, was the capital of this molasses-rum-slaves trading triangle. Molasses were also sent to the **wine islands** off the northern coast of Africa as payment for **Madeira,** which became the drink of choice for well-heeled Americans. Thus the New England ports of Boston and Newport rivaled British ones in the scope and complexity of their trad-ing networks.

The merchants who managed the Atlantic trading network had to master the dynamics of moving many different cargoes over long distances to multiple de-livery points. None of them could personally know all the people they had to deal with, and all of them knew, like Gamble's investors, that risk was high. To lessen the dangers of a failed voyage, merchants tried to establish reliable correspondence networks based on kinship, religion, or ethnic identity. Thus, merchant families often had members stationed across the world at crucial trading junctures, while Jews and Quakers relied on co-religionists and Scots tended to stick to fellow Scots. Traders also tried to establish a reputation for creditworthiness—a reputation for keeping one's word and being a sound financial risk.

World War and Britain Victorious

The British Navigation Acts had been aimed against the preeminence of Dutch shipping in the emerging global trading networks of the seventeenth century. By 1700, Dutch power was on the wane and England was the major maritime power, thanks to the growth of the Royal Navy. In 1664, the Royal Navy seized the Dutch colony of **New Amsterdam** on Manhattan Is-land and renamed it New York. The War of the Span-ish Succession, known in British America as Queen Anne's War, gave Britain control of Hudson's Bay, Newfoundland, and Nova Scotia (Acadia) in present-day Canada. Territorial gains in Canada, along with trade rivalries in India, set the stage for renewed war-fare between Britain and France. By the mid-eighteenth century, fur traders in Britain's mainland North Amer-ican colonies started to cross the Allegheny Mountains into the Ohio River Valley and thereby threatened French control of the Mississippi valley. In response, the French built forts and allied with local Indians. War between the two sides broke out in 1754 when a young George Washington led Virginia troops into the Ohio River valley to block French expansion there. He was defeated, but the event was soon embroiled in a larger conflict, the Seven Years' War, known as the French and Indian War in British America. The war's decisive turning point came in 1759, when the British captured Quebec. At war's end, France was forced to cede Canada and all lands east of the Mississippi River to Britain. Louisiana—lands west of the river—was ceded to Spain in compensation for its ceding Florida to Britain. France also lost in India, where it surrendered almost all its trading posts to the British, who consolidated their rule there.

The American Revolution and Britain Subdued

The world wars of the mid-eighteenth century had put huge strains on the finances of all belligerent states. After 1763, the new king, **George III,** and Par-

carrying trade   Shipping enterprise that moved com-modities from one part of the empire to another.

wine islands   Portuguese islands of Madeira and Porto Santo.

Madeira   Wine fortified with brandy.

New Amsterdam   Dutch colony on Manhattan Island seized by the English in 1664 and renamed New York.

George III   (r. 1760–1820) British king during whose reign the American Revolution occurred.

liament decided that the American colonies should contribute to the expenses of running an enlarged British Empire. In 1765 the **Stamp Act** levied the first direct tax on the colonies, and the Americans howled in protest. It seemed to them that Parliament was acting in a high-handed, unconstitutional way, just like James II before 1688. The Americans had embraced the Whig notion that government involved the consent of the governed. But Parliament had no members from the colonies. "No taxation without representation!" summed up the colonists' objections to British policy. Protests over taxes and a lack of parliamentary representation led, within a decade, to the **American Revolution** and, in 1783, to Britain's loss of thirteen very profitable North American colonies.

Crucial to the American victory was help from the French, who had been looking for an opportunity to redress the power balance that tipped in Britain's favor after 1763. The losses at the end of the Seven Years' War had reshaped French notions of what was at stake. In French eyes, the English had violently seized what rightfully belonged to France. In 1777, the French entered the war on the revolutionaries' side, but they paid dearly for their involvement. War costs imposed a crushing debt on the monarchy that led to an unraveling of French state finances and the collapse of the royal government in the late 1780s.

The British fared better in India than they did in America. After driving the French out of most of their trading posts, Britain's East India Company, which had carried on trade there since the seventeenth century, extended its control indirectly by forming alliances with Indian princes who allowed the company trading rights. Gradually, this indirect rule gave way to direct British control of the country.

European Society in the Age of Enlightenment

↓ How did European ideas of home life change in the eighteenth century?
↓ What caused Europeans to rethink the nature of society?

The consumer revolution coincided with a new emphasis on privacy, comfort, and displays of affection. As population rose, governments began to rethink the problem of poverty, but the poor were not simply an object of study. They also took matters into their own hands through rioting. New ways of thinking about society challenged traditional views emphasizing group membership more than individual autonomy. At the same time, many Europeans also started to think of themselves as members of distinct nations.

Comfort and Privacy

The consumer revolution coincided with new standards of privacy and comfort that changed the lives of Europe's upper and middle classes. Traditionally, nobles and other people of high social standing believed they had to make a public display of their grandeur. They surrounded themselves with many servants dressed in **livery.** They also acted as patrons to networks of clients who joined the servants in waiting publicly on their patron. In this world of display, privacy meant little, and the houses of the great reflected their public nature. Rooms served multiple purposes; people ate, slept, and received guests in the same space. Servants slept in the rooms of their masters, and both shared their beds with other people of similar standing. The lack of concern for privacy extended to the dining table, where people dipped their fingers into a common bowl, shared drinking cups, and used the edge of the tablecloth as a common napkin.

Beginning in the eighteenth century, the traditional emphasis on public display began to change. In Europe's cities, the houses of the rich were built for greater privacy. Multipurpose rooms gave way to specialized ones—bedrooms for sleeping; dining rooms for eating; and drawing rooms for conversation, card games, and music. Houses also incorporated a new architectural feature, the hallway. Hallways allowed people to pass from one part of the house to another without entering every room in between, thus increasing each room's privacy. To ensure even greater privacy, servants were no longer housed in the same space as their masters but placed in restricted servants' quarters, and their numbers were reduced to keep domestic space as free from them as possible.

Bedrooms also became more private. Now people slept one to a bed and often one to a room. Dining also became a more private affair. People no longer shared food and utensils. Each person at the table had separate silverware, glasses, and dishes. Food was served onto plates with specialized spoons and forks so that no person's silverware went into prepared food that everyone was eating.

Stamp Act British revenue-raising measure imposed in 1765 on the American colonies at the end of the Seven Years' War, provoking American resistance.
American Revolution Rebellion of thirteen British colonies on mainland North America leading to their independence in 1783 as the United States of America.
livery Clothing with distinctive colors worn by servants of an important person.

Michel Barthélemy Olliver's, *Supper at the Prince of Conti's Residence in the Temple* (1766) shows the prince and his guests enjoying supper in an informal atmosphere. Some people talk while others read or listen to the harpist. Conti belonged to a junior branch of the French royal family. *(Réunion des Musées Nationaux/Art Resource, NY)*

The growing demand for privacy among Europe's upper and middle classes was accompanied by a demand for comfortable domestic spaces. The older display society had emphasized grandeur, even if that meant that people had to live in uncomfortable surroundings. Although the rich and well-born still put elegance above comfort in dress on formal occasions, they now preferred a more relaxed pattern at home. Men wore dressing gowns in their private rooms, while women favored looser clothes when they read or visited with friends. Little tea or supper tables covered with simple cloths were placed in front of soft upholstered chairs. Rooms were smaller than before, and thus fires could keep them warmer. Dinner parties also tended to become more informal.

The emphasis on domestic privacy and comfort also affected family life. Families, now enclosed in the cocoon of the home, often welcomed more openly spontaneous displays of affection and intimacy. Mothers increasingly breast-fed their babies instead of sending them away to **wet nurses** in the country. Parents had always loved their children and shown concern for their futures, but traditional child-rearing practices had stressed discipline: parents punished children's failures and mistakes to prepare them for the rough-

and-tumble of the adult world. During the eighteenth century, however, aristocratic and middle-class parents began to express love more openly, and they praised their children more frequently than before. One reason for Jean-Jacques Rousseau's popularity was his endorsement of these displays of feeling.

Historians have debated the causes for the rise in domestic privacy, comfort, and displays of familial affection. In part, they resulted from examples given at the highest levels of society, at royal courts. Louis XV of France toned down the public court ritual of his great-grandfather Louis XIV and spent much time in his private apartments with a few close friends. Stiff and silent at formal court events, Louis XV was relaxed and chatty in his private rooms, where he sat with cats on his lap. No one promoted a comfortable lifestyle more than the French queen Marie Antoinette, wife of Louis XVI. Turning her back on the marble and gilt of Versailles, she built a play village, Le Hameau, on the palace grounds. There she and her

wet nurses Women who nursed other women's babies for a fee.

ladies-in-waiting dressed in country clothes and pretended to be milkmaids. Rousseau's rejection of corrupt civilization and his call for people to live closer to nature inspired Le Hameau. So did the enthusiasm for the "natural" natives of the South Pacific pictured in the travel reports of James Cook and Louis-Antoine de Bougainville. But the new standards for simpler living also shaped it.

Some historians attribute the new privacy to a growing sense of individualism fostered by the Enlightenment's emphasis on each person as an autonomous rational being. Others look to Protestant and Catholic reformers, who called for more modesty in people's daily lives. These reformers also preached that Christians should be bound together by love, thus encouraging an open affection within the family and the idea that affection should take precedence over financial considerations or social advancement when it came to marriage and children. The new emphasis on privacy, comfort, and family affection represented a profound shift in people's sense of how they should relate to others.

The Problem of the Poor

The changes in domestic life in Europe's upper and middle classes had little impact on the mass of working people, whose lives, as in the past, continued to be lived more in public view and were, therefore, shaped by community opinion and standards. Farthest removed from the world of the well-to-do were the poor. About 10 percent of Europe's population lived in permanent conditions of poverty.

As in the past, people made a distinction between the "deserving" and "undeserving" poor. Old or sick people, along with the disabled, deserved support, but able-bodied beggars and vagabonds should be forced into work. Throughout the century, these undeserving poor were treated both as a social problem and as a criminal threat. British authorities regularly rounded up beggars along with convicted felons and transported them to its overseas colonies, first to America and then to Australia. In the early eighteenth century, France adopted the same policy and shipped poor men and women to Louisiana.

Another way of handling the able-bodied poor was to place them in publicly sponsored **workhouses**, where they were forced to be productive and reeducated in the value of labor. After the German state of Bavaria cleared its territory of beggars and vagabonds by building a huge workhouse that confined them, other European governments ordered similar institutions. In England, the law allowed two or more parishes to build a common workhouse for the poor.

In France, Louis XV's government ordered a workhouse for each province. Their inmates either engaged in unskilled work, spinning wool and unwinding silk cocoons, or were drafted to do roadwork.

During the eighteenth century, the problem of poverty began to be looked at in new ways. When church reformers of the sixteenth century had called on the state to administer poverty programs, they had argued that it was the government's duty to care for the poor just as a father cared for his needy children. By the eighteenth century, the view that the state had a fatherly obligation toward the poor was giving way to the argument that poverty relief was a *right* that human beings could demand. The idea of the rights of the poor was stimulated by the Enlightenment notion that human beings were endowed with natural rights that society had to acknowledge. People who accepted this view sometimes argued that poor relief should be supplemented by old-age and medical insurance for the needy. Although insurance programs were never implemented and policymakers concentrated solely on relief or forced work, the idea of a comprehensive state-sponsored welfare system had entered European thought about society.

The Enlightenment also lay behind another new aspect of thought about the poor. Previously, Europeans believed that poverty was the result of human sin, which made the rich greedy and the poor lazy. Programs to eliminate poverty aimed, therefore, to reform the sinner. In the eighteenth century, a more secular approach developed. The Englishman Gregory King and the Frenchman Sébastien de Vauban signaled the change when they called for a careful count of the number of poor people. Once the magnitude of the problem had been established, the state could determine its causes and develop rational policies to deal with it. The Enlightenment idea that people were naturally good undermined the notion that human sinfulness lay at the root of poverty. Now people looked for social and economic causes and argued that poverty resulted from such things as the rise in the cost of living, shifts in the demand for workers, and problems of overpopulation. On the European continent, the central state took direct control of poverty programs, while in England the state turned the problem over to local government and ordered parishes in the kingdom to undertake the care of the poor. Overall, government-sponsored poor relief was confined to western and central Europe. Farther east,

workhouses State-run prisonlike institutions housing vagabonds and beggars.

In 1780, anti-Catholic sentiment in London exploded in a week of violence known as the Gordon Riots. Rioters destroyed Catholic establishments and homes. In this engraving, they set fire to London's notorious Newgate Prison after freeing the inmates. Attacks on public buildings, including prisons, were common in eighteenth-century riots. *(Guildhall Library, City of London/The Bridgeman Art Library)*

the family or the village commune was called on to deal with its destitute members.

Popular Social Protest

In times of economic crisis—when harvests failed and the food supply dropped or demand for goods produced in the putting-out system declined—the ranks of the poor could swell to almost 50 percent of the population in an affected area. During these bad times, Europeans rioted. A sudden rise in grain and bread prices often triggered food riots. Because many peasants did not produce enough grain to feed themselves, they had to buy it. When prices shot up, they would lie in wait for wagon convoys carrying grain and attack them—often at stream fords or during the loading of cargo onto riverboats. In cities, the working poor attacked bakeries. Although the attacks sometimes involved looting, many people, after seizing bread, paid what they thought was a fair price. Records testify to people returning to bakeries following a riot to put their money down on the counter, saying that they had forgotten to pay in the heat of the moment. Rioters did not think of themselves as thieves and maintained their honor by paying what they could. In times of

need, honor was often the only thing poor people possessed, and it was, therefore, carefully protected. Women always played a prominent role in food riots. As the family's food providers, it was their duty to take the lead in putting bread on the table.

Laborers also rioted to obtain higher wages or better working conditions. Secretly forming organizations with ominous names like "The Conquering and Bold Defiance," weavers destroyed their employers' looms or cut the threads in them. Coal miners also destroyed machinery, throwing it down mineshafts while trying to set fire to the coal. Employers regularly denounced these riots as the work of wild mobs, and governments looked unfavorably on any form of labor organization. In 1791, the French revolutionary legislature passed the **Le Chapelier Law** outlawing labor unions, while the British **Combination Act** of 1799 made unions unlawful conspiracies. Workers themselves, however, viewed riots and unions as nec-

Le Chapelier Law (1791) and **Combination Act** (1799) French and British legislation, respectively, that outlawed labor unions.

essary negotiating tactics in a world where they had no legal rights to **collective bargaining.**

In 1780, London experienced violent anti-Catholic rioting following a 1778 act of Parliament that allowed Roman Catholics who took an oath of loyalty to the king to serve in the army and own land. Many Protestants, horrified at this leniency, joined a Scot, Lord George Gordon, in organizing the Protestant Association, which gathered sixty thousand signatures on a petition demanding the act's repeal. When Parliament refused to receive the petition, rioting began. For a week, rioters ran through the city destroying Catholic chapels, schools, and **pubs.** In the city's fashionable western districts, homes of rich Catholics were invaded and their furnishings thrown into the street and burned. The houses were then vandalized or destroyed. For these people, withdrawal into an upper-class world of privacy counted for little when their front doors were smashed in, their rooms invaded, and their comfortable furnishings thrown out the window. The Royal Army's intervention finally ended the riots. Two hundred eighty-five rioters were shot by the troops, and twenty-five more were hanged. The **Gordon Riots** were the most violent eighteenth-century upheaval in London, destroying more property than any event since the Great Fire of 1666.

Government authorities held complicated views about riots. Generally, they took a dim view of popular disturbance in any form and severely punished those they caught. At times, however, they had some sympathy for rioters who seemed to be truly hard pressed by food shortages or deteriorating working conditions and would soften the punishments. Authorities also held women less accountable than men because of widespread beliefs that women by nature were emotional and disorderly. Male protesters took advantage of this view by occasionally disguising their faces with charcoal dust and then putting on women's clothes to protect themselves by symbolically assuming female disorderliness.

The Social Order

In the eighteenth century, most Europeans lived in a society made up of **orders**, also sometimes called **estates.** These were social groupings based largely on hereditary principles. Thus, one was born into the estate of nobles or the estate of commoners. Some orders were entered through recruitment; clergy, for example entered their order through the rite of ordination. Orders could include the family, the official residents of a certain city, and professional or occupational groups like lawyers or members of guilds. People in a society of estates and orders could belong to many of them si-

multaneously. For example, a French duke living in Paris would be a member of his ducal family, the order of the nobility, and an official resident of Paris. To a large degree, peoples' sense of self, along with other peoples' recognition of their place in the community, was defined by their participation in these groups. As a consequence, individuality was less noticed or regarded than group membership. To enforce this point, European governments defined the orders legally and issued laws stating who were proper members of them. Thus, illegitimate children were not legally family members, and vagabonds or the floating population of underemployed poor people were not legally recognized as residents of cities.

Each order and estate had certain rights that belonged exclusively to it. For example, in France the male head of family had the legal right to request the imprisonment of a disobedient son or daughter, and in eastern Europe the nobility alone had the right to own land. The distinctive legal rights belonging to an order were known as **privileges.** Privilege was something one had a right to that others did not have, because it belonged only to one's order. Thus, the clergy of France had the right to be exempt from state taxation, while nobles and commoners were taxed in varying degrees. In a society of orders, one's right to enjoy one's privileges was as strong as other peoples' right to enjoy theirs, but the privileges varied from order to order. As the conservative English political philosopher **Edmund Burke** put it, "Everyone has equal rights, but not to equal things."

A society of orders and estates was also hierarchical. Orders were not only unequal in privileges; they were also unequal in social status. Thus, the **Prussian General Code** of 1791 assigned the top position to the

collective bargaining Negotiations over working conditions between an employer and an organized group of workers.

pubs "Public houses" where food and alcoholic beverages were sold.

Gordon Riots Named after Lord George Gordon, anti-Catholic rioting in London in 1780.

orders/estates Form of social organization in which people's identity was largely defined by the groups to which the law assigns them.

privileges Exclusive rights that belonged to members of an order or estate.

Edmund Burke (1729–1797) Political writer and member of Parliament, Britain's leading opponent of the French Revolution, and the founder of modern conservatism.

Prussian General Code (1791) State law code that defined Prussia as a society of estates.

nobility, while the middle classes were placed below nobles, and the mass of peasant serfs made up the lowest social order. The law codes of France, the largest society of orders in western Europe, did the same. Societies organized this way recognized that the orders occupied the same general space, such as the kingdom of Prussia or the kingdom of France, but within that space they were walled off from each other by their legally defined privileges and ranked hierarchically. The only thing they had in common was obedience to the king, who presided over all the orders and held them together as a unit—a principle of royal absolutism. The view of society as comprising orders encouraged people to signal their position in the social hierarchy by surrounding themselves with liveried servants or insisting on their right to wear distinctive kinds of clothing—swords, lace, and bright clothing for nobles; dark-colored, simply cut clothes for commoners. Supporters of the society of orders argued that it was the divinely established form of social organization. People had a duty to live within their order and to respect the hierarchical arrangement of society.

During the eighteenth century, the idea of society as a hierarchy of orders and estates based on privilege increasingly had to compete with other ways of thinking about the human community. In Britain, the older structure of society had been largely dismantled during the religious and political turmoil of the seventeenth century. Although a privileged nobility, the **peerage,** continued to exist, its numbers were small and its boundaries weak since the younger sons and daughters of peers were classified as commoners. In its place, a new social structure emerged in which money largely determined people's social position. In this **plutocracy,** an aristocracy made up of peers and commoners, or **gentry,** occupied the highest social position. Membership in it depended on land ownership. Although old landed families often looked down on recent purchasers of land, the newly arrived could count on a general acceptance of their place in the aristocracy.

Britain's dominant position in the Atlantic economy led to the growth of a middle-class engaging in trade, manufacturing, and banking. Aristocrats invested in their businesses, sent their younger sons to work in their firms, and welcomed their daughters into their families as well-heeled brides. At the end of the century, the British emphasis on money as a social marker shaped the novels of **Jane Austen,** which are full of discussions about the annual incomes of their heroes and heroines.

French society was legally organized as a society of orders and estates, but money also played an increasingly important role in determining people's social standing. Wealth bought noble titles for commoners and opened the doors to the best schools for the sons and daughters of the rich, whether noble or not. The consumer revolution, with its emphasis on people as buyers of products, fostered plutocratic conceptions of society, and the increasing importance of money in determining social standing broke down traditional ideas that birth determined one's place in society. In addition, the choices the consumer revolution gave to individuals also undermined the idea that people's identity was largely determined by membership in group-based orders.

The Nation

By the middle years of the eighteenth century, yet another way of thinking about society emerged in which people now argued that a primary component of a person's identity derived from being a citizen of a distinct **nation.** The idea of the nation emerged in both the plutocratic society of Britain and the more traditional society of France. The world wars of the mid-eighteenth century between these two peoples fed a growing sense of national unity on each side. For the British, their common identity was rooted in the belief that they were a unique "island race" united behind a Protestant monarchy and church. The king fostered the sense of national unity by traveling throughout his realm and appearing at carefully staged events that brought rich and poor and men and women together. For many Britons, war with France was a war between antagonistic religious communities. Britons, as defenders of Protestantism, were a free, peaceful, righteous nation, while the French were slaves who groveled before a tyrannical monarchy and an oppressive Catholic Church.

The French took an equally dim view of the British. They saw themselves as the defenders of enlightened civilization, while the British were addicted to a vulgar materialism that concentrated simply on trade

---

peerage Legally recognized British titled nobility.

plutocracy Society in which wealth is the main determinant of social standing.

gentry British landowning aristocracy composed of commoners and peers.

Jane Austen (1775–1817) British novelist who depicted provincial life in classics such as *Sense and Sensibility* (1811) and *Pride and Prejudice* (1813).

nation Way of thinking about society that emphasizes common citizenship in a community as a primary component of a person's identity.

and making money. Hadn't Adam Smith himself referred to them as a "nation of shopkeepers"? French losses in the Seven Years' War fueled the notion that Britain was bent on world domination. The conflict had not been one of king against king, or Protestant against Catholic, but of nation against nation. Thus, by midcentury, the French had forged a new sense of collective identity as they embraced the ideal of a united nation fighting a wicked foreign enemy whose culture and values were incompatible with their own. The French monarchy, like that of the British, fostered this sense of national identity in the face of a dangerous enemy. But religious concerns were less prominent in the French concept of the nation. While the British thought that Protestantism had united the English, Welsh, and Scots into a single nation, the French thought that the nation was a purely human construction that the French people themselves had willed into existence. Its task was to resist British power and arrogance. In both France and Britain, people thought that each individual had an active role to play in protecting the nation from enemy outsiders. This sense of individual engagement, along with the rising political importance of public opinion, contributed to a growing popular interest in politics and a desire to participate more directly in the political process.

The Beginning of Industrial Production

⬇ What factors favored industrialization in Great Britain?
⬇ How did new manufacturing processes revolutionize the production of goods?

As antagonism between the French and British increased over trade and empire, the beginning of industrialization in Great Britain gave the British the upper hand. At the same time, industrialization had a radical impact on Britons' everyday life, altering the living habits and psychology of people touched by it—sometimes positively, often negatively, but in all cases unavoidably and without any possibility of returning to an earlier, less complicated era.

Mechanization and Mass Production

Increased international trade and rising consumer demand had fueled growth in British manufacturing under the putting-out system. During the second half of the eighteenth century, continuing increases in population and trade created a need for innovations that would increase productivity, standardize quality,

and lower the cost of products. These innovations altered British manufacturing.

Cotton cloth weaving was one of the first areas to see radical changes in production. In 1733, the **flying shuttle** doubled the speed at which a weaver could work. The quicker looms demanded more thread, leading James Hargreaves to invent the **spinning jenny** in the 1760s. Previously, spinners produced only one thread at a time; with one person operating Hargreaves's jenny, eight to eleven threads could be spun simultaneously, although the thread produced was unevenly strong. The spinning jenny was further improved by Richard Arkwright, the son of a tailor and a one-time barber, wigmaker, and tavern owner who invented the **water frame,** which produced a uniformly strong thread, thereby standardizing quality. Unlike the hand-powered spinning jenny, the water frame relied on a water mill for power. Its size and complexity required construction of a special building, the **factory.** Now spinners had to leave their cottages and report to a workplace where their work was supervised, regulated, and timed. Arkwright set up his first factory in 1771, employing nearly six hundred spinners. In 1785, Samuel Crompton patented the **spinning mule,** which combined the best qualities of the jenny and water frame and produced a thread that was both strong and fine. Weavers now could make high-priced, thin cotton cloth as well as cheaper, coarser cloth. Improvements in thread production, however, outstripped the ability of weavers using hand looms to convert thread into cloth, creating a bottleneck in production. In 1785, Edmund Cartwright, an Anglican clergyman, invented the steam-driven **power loom,** eliminating this bottleneck. The power loom also required weavers to leave their homes for

flying shuttle Weaving device invented in 1733 that doubled a weaver's speed.

spinning jenny Hand-operated spinning device invented by James Hargreaves in 1768 that allowed multiple strands of yarn (or thread) to be spun at the same time.

water frame Water-operated spinning device invented by Richard Arkwright in 1769 that improved the spinning jenny by producing a uniformly strong thread.

factory Building or series of buildings where workers in a particular industry are gathered together to increase the speed and volume of production.

spinning mule Spinning device invented by Samuel Crompton in 1785 that combined features of the jenny and water frame.

power loom Steam-driven loom invented by Edmund Cartwright in 1785 that doubled the speed of weaving.

At Josiah Wedgwood's pottery manufactory in Staffordshire, kilns belching coal smoke fired thousands of pieces of china at the same time. The china was then stacked and packed in special containers for distribution around England. In early industrial enterprises, housing for workers was built in the midst of factory buildings. *(Mary Evans Picture Library)*

power-driven factories. With the power loom, the **mechanization** of the cotton cloth industry was complete; machines now did work that had previously been done by hand. In 1793, the American Eli Whitney invented the **cotton gin,** which quickly separated seed from fiber in the cotton boll. As American cotton cultivation expanded, British cotton cloth production soared. Between 1750 and 1800, alone, it increased tenfold. The British navy, improved to deal with colonial rivalries, and the merchant marine, which boomed in the Atlantic economy, played an important role by transporting raw cotton from the American South and India to the spinning machines and looms in Britain.

In addition to cotton cloth, pottery making was at the heart of what would be described as the **Industrial Revolution.** In 1759, **Josiah Wedgwood** transformed British porcelain production. Using the good clay of the English Midlands, Wedgwood opened a porcelain factory, based on Adam Smith's theory of the division of labor. Each stage in production—unloading the clay, mixing it, shaping it into pieces, dipping it in a glaze, placing it in kilns, and firing it—was carried out by specialized worker groups. In addition, Wedgwood

bypassed the individual potter's wheel, which had been used in pottery production for millennia, and shaped his pieces using molds of standardized size. The finished pieces were therefore identical, allowing for easy stacking and storage. Wedgwood hired salesmen to crisscross the country, demonstrating his wares. True to Smith's prediction, division of labor ensured quality control and lowered production costs; for the first time, English porcelain could compete with Asian imports because of lower price. Eventually, Wedgwood replaced workers with steam engines to mix his clay. Division of labor, uniform products, and competitive prices were central to **mass production,** another feature of the early Industrial Revolution.

The development of steam power was also vital to industrialization. The **steam engine** had been invented by Thomas Newcomen in 1702 and had found practical application in pumping water out of coal mines. But its inefficiency limited use away from coal fields. Broader use of steam power in industry had to wait for the improvements of **James Watt.** Like Arkwright, Watt had a relatively modest education. Unlike most inventors, he actually worked as an "instrument maker" (at Glasgow University); he improved on Newcomen's invention, developing a steam engine that was efficient and safe enough to be used in industry. By the 1780s, Watt's engines were pumping water out of mines, driving cotton looms, and powering Wedgwood's clay mixers. The engine's steam was produced by a fire fueled with coke—coal, abundant in England, that had been heated to eliminate impurities preventing it from burning hotly and evenly. Steam

mechanization Manufacturing process in which machines replace hand work.

cotton gin Device invented by Eli Whitney in 1793 that allowed easy removal of seeds from raw cotton, thereby making cotton more easily processed for cloth.

Industrial Revolution Changes in manufacturing involving mechanization of production and the use of power sources other than human or animal muscle.

Josiah Wedgwood (1730–1795) English pottery manufacturer whose success came from an efficient division of labor in his manufactory.

mass production Production technique based on the division of labor, uniform products, and competitive prices that increased both quantity and quality of production.

steam engine Engine that uses steam power to supply energy, invented in 1702 by Thomas Newcomen and perfected by James Watt.

James Watt (1736–1819) Scottish inventor who improved Newcomen's steam engine, making it safe enough to be used in industry.

engines were made of iron, and their spreading use stimulated iron production in Britain. Steam, coal, and iron, along with mechanization and mass production, were at the heart of the early Industrial Revolution.

Why Britain?

Britain was the first country in the world to experience the Industrial Revolution. Six important factors made industrialization possible: high levels of agricultural productivity, available skilled workers, ease of transportation, natural resources, political stability, and **capital** for industry. Before industrialization can take place anywhere, that area's agriculture must be efficient enough to be able to spare workers to leave agriculture for industry. Britain's agricultural revolution had fulfilled that condition, freeing up surplus labor in the countryside that would be absorbed into the industrial working class.

Another precondition for industrialization was the availability of skilled workers. In Britain this precondition was also present. The growth of the putting-out system, stimulated by Britain's leading role in the Atlantic economy, increased the number of merchant **entrepreneurs** as well as the pool of workers who had mastered many basic processes in the production of goods. Industrialization would build on this basis by using the existing skills of both entrepreneurs and workers. Water and steam power also supplemented human and animal muscles.

Geography also helped Britain to industrialize. Because Britain was an island country with many navigable rivers and a well-developed canal system, British industry could transport both raw materials and finished products more economically than its continental competitors. Before the development of the railroad, transporting bulk materials such as coal, wool, or cotton by land was very expensive. Mass industrial production demanded that these materials either be located near the factory (as in the case of coal) or that they be transported cheaply—that is, by water.

Britain was also blessed by nature with a large supply of the raw material that fueled the early Industrial Revolution: coal. The coal belt that extends across Europe from northern England to southern Poland was first exploited in Britain, particularly in such early industrial cities as Manchester, Birmingham, Glasgow, and Sheffield. Because of their endless appetite for coal, the first factories were usually built on top of or next to existing coal fields. Britain was also lucky in that the coal deposits lay relatively close to the surface, allowing easy exploitation of this fuel source.

Political factors were no less important. Since the Glorious Revolution of 1688, England had enjoyed peace and political stability. Unlike the continent, Britain was one unified market: no tolls or internal **duties** had to be paid to ship goods from Scotland to England or Wales. The British government also actively encouraged industrial development by such laws as the **Calico Act** of 1721, which restricted the import of cotton cloth, called calico, from India.

Britain was also ahead of other European states in the accumulation of capital, thanks to the economic growth produced by the Atlantic trade. Some of this capital came directly from profits in the slave trade, but most of it came from other sources. While per capita income in Britain in the mid-eighteenth century was probably not significantly greater than that in France, this income was better distributed among larger groups in the population. More important still, access to capital was easier in Britain than in any other European country, in large part because of the existence of a central national bank. The **Bank of England**, founded in 1694, remained for over a century the only central bank in any major European country. The Bank of England loaned money to smaller banks, thereby helping increase the circulation of capital by making it easier for savings to be funneled into investment. This well-developed system of banks and credit made it relatively easy for British entrepreneurs to obtain financing—venture capital—to build factories, purchase steam engines or power looms, advance credit to purchasers, and the like. The combination of accumulated capital (that is, savings) and a well-developed system of credit helped Britain to industrialize. For all these reasons—agriculture, labor supply, transportation system, natural resources, politics, and capital—Britain managed to take the industrial leap before the rest of the world. Some scholars have pointed out that *revolution* might be an inappropriate term for this process, which began around 1760 but only really took off during the period of French Revolution and the Napoleonic Wars. The impact of industrialization was revolutionary, however, as in time it would alter work patterns, family

capital   Wealth available for investment in the production of goods for the market.

entrepreneur   Person who manages economic activity by assuming the risks and enjoying the profits.

duties   Taxes, usually charged on products crossing a regional or national boundary.

Calico Act   (1721) British act that limited the importation of cotton cloth (calico) from India.

Bank of England   National bank established in 1694 that facilitated the circulation of capital during the Industrial Revolution.

life, income distribution, society and culture, the availability of material goods, wealth and poverty, and the thinking of intellectuals and politicians about all these developments.

Summary

Review Questions

↑ How did changes in overseas empires and trading networks contribute to Europe's economic development in the eighteenth century?

↑ How did Enlightenment thinking influence Europe's economic and social development?

↑ What new forms of individual and collective identity emerged?

Europe's eighteenth-century population growth stimulated economic growth and led to new forms of work, especially in manufacturing. As a result, some theorists began to argue that economies were capable of ongoing expansion, and they searched for the laws that made growth possible, founding the modern discipline of economics. As the consumer revolution took root, some economists began to praise all forms of work equally, repudiating the older view that the mental work of philosophers or theologians was superior to manual labor.

Trading networks across the Atlantic, which had formed during the sixteenth century, reached their fullest development in the eighteenth century and also fueled European economic growth, as the French and then the British Empire overtook the older Spanish and Portuguese Empires. Because of their populous colonies in North America and their sugar islands in the Caribbean, the British developed the most far-reaching and profitable Atlantic trading networks, making London the commercial center of Europe. African slaves made possible the commercial exchanges of the Atlantic trading system. They were forcibly imported by the millions to labor in the plantations of the New World, where they cultivated the crops and mined the silver and gold that Europe's people and economies demanded. As part of the trading system, Europeans sent manufactured goods to colonies in the New World.

Well-to-do European consumers developed new standards of domestic life during the eighteenth century. Older behaviors emphasizing public display as a sign of high social standing gave way to a concern for privacy and comfort. Enlightenment ideals, which stressed life in this world, were partly responsible for these new ways of life. Farther down the social scale, the poor continued to live as in the past, since their lives were more in public view and were shaped by community-enforced norms. The Enlightenment also inspired European governments to reconceive poverty less as a consequence of sin than as the product of social, economic, and demographic conditions. The poor also shaped their place in society by means of the riot, the classic form of social protest in the eighteenth-century world. Rethinking the problem of poverty was symptomatic of a larger change in social thought, as corporate and hierarchical understandings of society now competed with ideas of status based on land and wealth. Some argued that each individual's primary identity was as a citizen of a nation, whose rights and values had to be defended from threatening outsiders.

Nationalist antagonism between the French and British increased with the beginning of industrialization, which in Britain started as a mechanization of textile production and spread to other forms of manufacture.

← **Thinking Back, Thinking Ahead** →

How did European society and economic life change between 1500 and 1800?

ECHO

Trafficking in Human Beings

At the beginning of the nineteenth century, Europeans ended the African slave trade and then abolished slavery. Britain banned the international trade in 1807, the United States in 1808. The abolition of slavery took more time. France abolished it in the 1790s but reintroduced it under Napoleon Bonaparte; permanent abolition had to wait until 1848. Britain's abolition came in 1833. In the United States it came after a civil war, in 1865. Spain did not abolish slavery in all its Caribbean territories until 1886. In 1888, Brazil was the last New World country to end slavery. In the eastern Mediterranean, where it had been practiced since ancient times, slavery ended in the 1890s.

In the nineteenth century, the term *slave* was sometimes used for people who were neither African nor legally classified as slaves. Early in the century, U.S. Marines landed in the North African state of Tripoli to stop its ruler's practice of seizing American seamen and selling them into slavery. By mid-century Southern defenders of the U.S. slave system described factory workers as "wage slaves." Working girls in a London match factory were described as "white slaves" because of their low wages and hazardous working conditions. Women forced into prostitution were also called "white slaves." The charge of white slavery was particularly horrifying to Americans and Europeans because it inverted the "usual" racial equation of white master/black slave.

Today various forms of slavery are still practiced, despite global condemnation. Exploitation of some kind is always involved. After the fall of the Soviet Union, traffickers used false papers and promises of work to lure young women to western Europe. Their papers were then seized, and they were forced to work in sweatshops or brothels. In Southeast Asia, impoverished parents sometimes sell their children into slavery or are tricked into turning them over to traffickers, who use them for a child sex industry that attracts pedophiles from around the world. In Haiti, poor parents sometimes give their children to well-to-do families, who use them for household work. As many as 12 million children globally may serve as child laborers under abusive conditions, 2 million of them in Europe. And traditional forms of slavery are still with us—CNN and the BBC have recently reported on a flourishing slave trade in the war-torn regions of Sudan. Sadly, wherever people are desperate and profits are to be made in the traffic of humans, slavery persists.

Suggested Readings

Bell, David A. *The Cult of the Nation in France: Inventing Nationalism, 1680–1800.* Cambridge, Mass.: Harvard University Press, 2001. An important recent study.

Black, Jeremy, and Roy Porter, eds. *The Penguin Dictionary of Eighteenth-Century History.* New York: Penguin Books, 1994. Brief entries with bibliographies on important persons, events, and economic and social developments.

Cameron, Euan, ed. *Early Modern Europe: An Oxford History.* New York: Oxford University Press, 1999. Chapters on various topics, including an excellent one by James C. Riley titled "A Widening Market in Consumer Goods."

Colley, Linda. *Britons: Forging the Nation, 1707–1837.* 2nd ed. New Haven, Conn.: Yale University Press, 2005. The standard account.

Rudé, George. *The Crowd in History: A Study of Popular Disturbances in France and England, 1730–1848.* New York: Wiley, 1964. A classic account of popular social protest.

Sarti, Raffaella. *Europe at Home: Family and Material Culture, 1500–1800.* Translated by Allan Cameron. New Haven, Conn.: Yale University Press, 2002. A good introduction to domestic life in early modern Europe.

Willcox, William B., and Walter L. Arnstein. *The Age of Aristocracy, 1688–1830.* 8th ed. Boston: Houghton Mifflin, 2001. A lively and readable history of eighteenth-century Britain.

Websites

Information on eighteenth-century economy and society plus much more, **Modern History Source Book: The Early Modern West,** at www.fordham.edu/halsall/mod/modsbook1.html

Many images related to the slave trade, **The Atlantic Slave Trade and Slave Life in the Americas: A Visual Record,** at http://hitchcock.itc.virginia.edu/Slavery

A good site for more information, **Industrial Revolution,** at www.fordham.edu/halsall/mod/modsbook14.html

Revolutionary France and Napoleonic Europe, 1775–1815

1500 B.C.E.	1000 B.C.E.	500 B.C.E.	1 B.C.E./1 C.E.

1792
French Republic proclaimed

1776
American
Revolution begins

1789
French
Revolution
begins

1793
Louis XVI is executed

1794
Reign of Terror ends

1775	1780	1785	1790	1795

Europe in 1789

In 1789, France was only one of Europe's great powers. Compare its size here to what it became by 1810 (see map on page 561). What other changes had France brought to the continent of Europe by this time?

ATLANTIC OCEAN

SWEDEN

• St. Petersburg

KINGDOM OF DENMARK AND NORWAY

Christiania

• Stockholm

ESTONIA

• Moscow

LIVONIA

Riga

RUSSIAN EMPIRE

North Sea

Baltic Sea

LITHUANIA

GREAT BRITAIN

SCOTLAND

IRELAND

ENGLAND

London

DUTCH REPUBLIC

Amsterdam

Utrecht

HANOVER

BRANDENBURG

Berlin

PRUSSIA

POLAND

Warsaw

France
Austrian Hapsburg lands
Prussia
Spanish Bourbon lands
Great Britain
Russian Empire
Ottoman Empire

Antwerp

AUSTRIAN NETHERLANDS

Cologne

SAXONY

SILESIA

Varennes

Versailles • Paris

LORRAINE

BOHEMIA

AUSTRIA

BAVARIA

Vienna

BESSARABIA

CRIMEA

VENDÉE

FRANCE

Lyons

SWITZERLAND

SAVOY

Avignon

GENOA

MILAN

REPUBLIC OF VENICE

TYROL

Venice

Buda

Pest

HUNGARY

MOLDAVIA

WALLACHIA

Black Sea

PORTUGAL

Lisbon

Madrid

SPAIN

Duero

Tagus

TUSCANY

PAPAL STATES

Corsica

Rome

BOSNIA

SERBIA

BULGARIA

Constantinople

Minorca (Gr. Br.)

Balearic Is.

SARDINIA

KINGDOM OF NAPLES AND SICILY

ALBANIA

OTTOMAN EMPIRE

GREECE

GILBRALTAR (Gr. Br.)

Mediterranean Sea

CRETE

CYPRUS

TUNIS

0   200   400 Km.

0   200   400 Mi.

TRIPOLI

OTTOMAN EMPIRE

| 500 C.E. | 1000 C.E. | 1500 C.E. | 2000 C.E. |

1799
Napoleon seizes power

1804
Napoleon becomes emperor

1812
Napoleon invades Russia

1814
Congress of Vienna opens

1815
Napoleon is finally defeated at Waterloo

| 1800 | 1805 | 1810 | 1815 | 1820 |

Choic Choice Choice

Olympe de Gouges

Olympe de Gouges was a playwright and political pamphleteer who pursued a career as an independent woman of letters. Caught up in the French Revolution, she became an outspoken advocate of women's rights. She was executed by the revolutionary government in 1793. (Musée de la Ville de Paris, Musée Carnavalet, Paris, France/The Bridgeman Art Library)

Olympe de Gouges Becomes a Revolutionary

In 1768, a twenty-year-old widow left her hometown in southern France and headed for Paris to make her fortune. For the next twenty years, Olympe de Gouges struggled to live independently and to establish herself as a playwright in a world dominated by male privilege and aristocratic intrigue. When the French Revolution broke out, she sided with the revolutionaries, calling for a new political and social order based on equality—including equality between men and women.

As a single woman alone in Paris, Madame de Gouges found few respectable options open to her; she could either remarry or work. Vowing not to marry again, she relied on her beauty and wit to get ahead and offered love to men of means, who gave her financial help in return.

For ten years, she lived a life of pleasure while quietly amassing enough money to obtain what she truly desired—economic independence. Then, at the age of thirty, she announced she would devote the rest of her life to philosophy by writing plays that praised the ideals of the Enlightenment.

The theatrical world Gouges threw herself into was lively, but not open to new talent. The Crown had granted a monopoly on theatrical performances in Paris to a handful of privileged theaters, which used their power ruthlessly to promote the work of favorites while denying access to others. As a woman without powerful connections, time and again Gouges had the theater doors slammed in her face. She therefore took to publishing her work, often at her own expense, in hopes of building support for the performance of her plays.

In 1789, she wrote *The Slavery of the Blacks,* a controversial play in which the hero, a black, murdered a white man to prevent him from raping the hero's mistress. Finally, this play made it to the stage when the Comédie-Française, the most prestigious theater in Paris, performed it. But after just three performances, it closed. Perhaps the plot was too controversial, or perhaps, as Gouges claimed, the theater management had sabotaged the play to avoid paying her.

By this time, France was in the midst of revolution, and Gouges turned to applying Enlightenment ideals to the crisis at hand. To solve the monarchy's bankruptcy, she called for a voluntary tax to be paid equally by all. She called for a state system of social security and government employment to care for the poor. She denounced the filthy conditions in the maternity wards of hospitals and called for local community ownership of agricultural land to help poor peasants. Above all, she demanded complete political and social equality for men and women. In 1791, she published *The Rights of Woman,* the most important feminist statement of the French Revolution. "Woman," she wrote, "is born free and remains equal to man in rights." This single sentence summed up her years of struggle against the injustices she had experienced and seen around her.

Olympe de Gouges promoted the ideals of France's Revolution, but she never joined revolutionary clubs and refused to take part in the street violence that erupted periodically in Paris. She also never gave up her belief in the French monarchy. She did her best to save the king, even offering to defend him in the trial that led to his execution. For this, she herself was executed. Olympe de Gouges's life was caught up in many of the forces that shaped revolutionary France—resentment at aristocratic privilege, anger at social injustice, excitement over the possibility of fundamental change, and anxiety over the violence that so often accompanied revolutionary action. Most of all, her defense of women's rights raised issues that remained at the center of political debate long after her death.

Introduction

On June 11, 1775, in the Gothic cathedral of Rheims, a young man of twenty was crowned king of France. The coronation was an ancient ceremony in the kingdom's collective life that bound the French people to the king as his loyal subjects. At the climax of the ceremony, when the archbishop of Rheims lowered the jeweled crown of Charlemagne onto the head of the new king, Louis XVI prayed, "O Christ, may You Yourself crown this king!" Eighteen years later, in Paris, that very same head was severed from its body and lifted from a bloodstained basket to be displayed triumphantly to thousands of the king's former subjects.

In 1775, no one could foresee the king's execution. In retrospect, however, it is clear that the new king faced a growing political crisis. Finally, in 1789, revolution broke out, and thousands of French men and women, Olympe de Gouges among them, joined in the movement to reshape the French community from the bottom up. First France's absolute monarchy was modified into a limited constitutional monarchy. Then, the monarchy was abolished and a republic proclaimed. When the conservative states of Europe sought to restrain the republic, a revolutionary dictatorship was established to crush France's foreign and domestic enemies. Then, France was a republic again. Then, Napoleon Bonaparte took control and shortly proclaimed himself emperor. During all these years, almost all of Europe was at war against France. France gained control of most of the continent, then lost it all. Napoleon was defeated and exiled. In 1814, the monarchy was back, as Louis XVI's youngest brother was proclaimed king. Then, for a hundred days, Napoleon was back, then gone, and the king returned and remained.

Beneath this dizzying change of regimes in France, fundamental change was taking place that would alter Europe forever. The French revolutionaries created Europe's first modern representative democracy, sweeping away the old world of orders and estates and creating a new world of citizens bound together in a single nation. The revolutionary regime also broke with the Catholic Church, rejecting the centuries-old ties between church and state and creating a secular political and social order. War led to Europe's first mass mobilization of citizens to defend the country from external enemies as well as to a harsh dictatorship that crushed opposition at home.

France's wars spread the revolution outside France, and as victorious French armies occupied foreign territory, Napoleon enforced revolutionary reform across the continent. Written constitutions were introduced, state-sponsored religious discrimination was ended, the principle of equality before the law for all citizens was advanced, and a military draft was imposed. When Louis XVI's brother was restored as king of France, it looked as though the clock had been turned backward. But it had not, and Europe was never again as it had been in 1775 when Louis XVI was crowned.

From Crisis to Constitution, 1775–1789

↓ What were the causes of the French Revolution?
↓ At the end of 1789, how had the political and social order in France changed?

In 1775, the year Louis XVI was crowned king of France, American colonists began a revolution that challenged British royal authority. Many in France, which aided America's revolutionary war, embraced America's revolutionary rhetoric about fairness in taxation, the rights of citizens, and representative government. At the same time, the French monarchy, nearly bankrupt and facing challenges to its own royal authority, was poised to unravel. Its financial problems peaked in the late 1780s, just as bad harvests forced up the price of bread. An unprecedented crisis quickly escalated into revolution.

Chronology

1775	Louis XVI is crowned king of France
1776	American Revolution begins
1788	Parlement summons Estates-General; France declares bankruptcy
1789	Estates-General meets; National Assembly is formed
1790	National Assembly decrees the Civil Constitution of the Clergy
1791	Slaves revolt in Saint-Domingue
1792	France becomes a republic; France declares war on Austria and Prussia
1793	Louis XVI is executed; Reign of Terror begins
1794	France abolishes slavery; Reign of Terror ends
1795	Directory is created
1799	Napoleon seizes power
1800	Napoleon reorganizes French administration
1801	Napoleon and Pius VII sign Concordat
1802	Napoleon makes himself consul for life; Slavery is reestablished in French colonies
1804	Napoleonic Code reforms French law; Napoleon becomes emperor
1806	Continental System closes French ports to British shipping
1812	Napoleon invades Russia
1814	Napoleon is defeated by European allies, abdicates; Louis XVIII becomes king of France

The French Monarchy in Crisis

Louis XVI intended to use his absolute political power to rule for the good of his subjects. But absolutism worked only as long as people did not question the king's exercise of that power. By the 1780s, however, many people were questioning it, accusing the king and his ministers of everything from indecisiveness to despotism. The chief problem was the king's inability to manage state finances. The cost of the world wars of midcentury had put huge strains on the French treasury, and for naught, as France lost its overseas possessions. French involvement in the American Revolution was also expensive. The French government was forced to raise taxes, distributing the burden unequally among its subjects, because nobles and clergy were traditionally exempt from some taxes. But state income still regularly fell short of state expenses, so new loans were required. As loans increased, so did interest on them, which only increased shortfalls in revenue. The result was a policy muddle indicating to many that the monarchy had lost its grip on the country's affairs.

By the mid-1780s, the king had realized that a complete overhaul of royal finances was needed to solve the problem of declining revenues and rising debt. Hoping to gain the support of the greatest nobles and churchmen, Louis appealed to them to join in a reform of the system. But these powerful people demanded to see the royal accounts before they agreed. Louis took their demand as a direct challenge to his absolute authority and turned it down. The king then turned for support to the **Parlement of Paris,** but this royal court, too, was reluctant to help and engaged in a fierce struggle over control of policy, claiming that it alone could protect the people of France from government mismanagement. By July 1788, the conflict between Louis and the Parlement had become so severe that public order started to break down as pro-Parlement rioters and royal troops clashed in several provinces of the kingdom.

Failure to resolve the financial crisis drove the king

Louis XVI   (r. 1775–1792) King of France whose monarchy was abolished by the creation of the French Republic.

Parlement of Paris   France's most important royal court, which resisted the king's absolute rule.

into a deep depression. He frequently burst into tears and ate and drank excessively. He also turned increasingly to his wife, Queen **Marie Antoinette,** for political advice. The queen, an Austrian princess, had never been popular; her marriage to Louis in 1770 had been intended to forge an alliance with France's longstanding Austrian Habsburg enemy. Now her extravagant personal spending on clothes and hairdos was also blamed for the financial crisis. Her enemies started calling her Madame Deficit. The queen's new political role, therefore, further enflamed people who had lost confidence in the king's ability to govern.

On July 13, 1788, an unexpected turn in the weather deepened the crisis. A massive hailstorm swept across much of France, with hailstones so big that they killed humans and animals alike. Much of the grain ripening in the fields was destroyed, ruining chances for a good harvest and substantial tax revenues. The losses, the worst incurred in a series of mediocre harvests from the 1760s on, also meant that bread prices would rise sharply, threatening many with starvation. Grain and bread were diet staples; ordinary people spent between a third and a half of their income on them. Now the government's creditors, individuals and banks at home and abroad, lost confidence in France's ability to pay interest on its debts and refused to lend any more money to the king. In a desperate move to restore confidence, Louis announced that a traditional assembly of his subjects, the **Estates-General,** would convene in May 1789, to deal with the crisis. But lenders were not reassured, and on August 16, 1788, France went bankrupt, suspending payments on its loans.

The Estates-General

The Estates-General had not met in 175 years, and no one in 1788 had a clear idea how it should be organized. In September, the Parlement of Paris resolved the question by ordering the Estates-General to convene as it had in 1614, in three orders, corresponding to the three estates of the realm. The First Estate was the clergy and religious orders, and the Second Estate was the nobility; together they stood at the top of France's society of orders and accounted for about 3 percent of France's population. The Third Estate was everyone else—the 97 percent of the French population that included merchants, lawyers, shopkeepers, urban workers, landowning peasants, and rural laborers. The estates would meet separately, and each would have one vote, though the Crown allowed the Third Estate to elect as many delegates as the First and Second Estates combined.

At this very moment, the Crown also decided to suspend the old system of royal press censorship. Hun-

A FAUT ESPERER Q'EU JEU LA FINIRA BEN TOT.

V'tuleur en Campagne Ap. 1789.

A man of the Third Estate staggers under the burden of a priest and an aristocrat, representatives of the parasitic First and Second Estates. Cartoons like this were common in 1789. *(Réunion des Musée Nationaux/Art Resource, NY)*

dreds of pamphlets debated the implications of the arrangements for the Estates-General: voting by delegates instead of by orders would give the Third Estate a voice. The most widely read pamphlet was *What Is the Third Estate?,* written by a Catholic clergyman, **Joseph Emmanuel Sieyès.** Though a member of the

Marie Antoinette   (r. 1775–1792) Austrian Habsburg princess married to Louis XVI who as queen of France was his controversial political adviser.

Estates-General   Kingdomwide deliberative body convened in 1789 to deal with the Crown's financial collapse and to reform the government.

Joseph Emmanuel Sieyès   (1748–1836) Catholic priest who championed the political rights of the Third Estate.

First Estate, Sieyès argued that the clergy and nobility were parasites in French society. They contributed nothing to the wealth and skills of the kingdom but simply lived off the labor and talents of the Third Estate even as they monopolized political power. "What is the Third Estate? Everything," he exclaimed. "What has it been up to this point in the political order? Nothing." Sieyès wanted the Third Estate's political power to match its economic productivity and social usefulness.

In this supercharged atmosphere, France went to the polls to elect deputies to the Estates-General. The elections, which took place from January to April 1789, represented the greatest experiment in democratic politics that Europe had ever seen. They were also the largest public opinion poll to be carried out in Europe until the twentieth century, as voters—taxpaying men who were at least age twenty-five—were asked to state their suggestions for reform in books called **cahiers**. Generally, the cahiers of all three estates called for an end to absolutism and the creation of a representative assembly of citizens that would join with the king in governing. There was also agreement that taxes needed to be restructured and that the exemptions the clergy and nobility traditionally enjoyed should end. (Table 19.1 summarizes the unfolding of the French Revolution in 1789.)

On May 4, 1789, nearly one thousand newly elected deputies to the Estates-General gathered at Versailles. Most looked to the king for leadership in the question of whether the estates would vote by order or by delegate, but it was not forthcoming. Well-intentioned but timid, Louis XVI feared to take the initiative. The deputies, left to figure things out on their own, could do no more than disagree. Weeks passed in stalemate, and tensions mounted dangerously. Finally, in June, the deputies of the Third Estate followed the lead of a minority of self-styled "**patriots**," including Sieyès, who had been elected a deputy of the Third Estate, and declared that they were the **National Assembly**, the true representatives of the whole of the French people. Inviting the clergy and nobility to join them in a common meeting, they aimed to proceed with the business of reform. This step was the beginning of the constitutional revolution, since the deputies' action had no justification in either law or precedent. Over the next several days, a significant number of clergy from commoner families, along with a few members of the nobility, joined the new National Assembly. Some of these privileged defectors were influenced by Enlightenment ideas that government should be based on a contract with the governed. Others joined the patriots out of political calculation, recognizing that there was no other realistic course of action.

Table 19.1

The Revolution Unfolds in 1789

January–April	Elections to Estates-General
May	Estates-General meets
June	National Assembly formed
	Tennis Court Oath
July	Storming of the Bastille
July–August	Great Fear
August	Night of August 4
	Declaration of the Rights of Man and the Citizen (Late August)
	October Days

These events finally shook Louis XVI into action. He announced that he would address the estates in a special "royal session," but, in the meantime, he prohibited any further meetings of deputies. The problem was that no one informed the deputies of the prohibition! So, on June 21, when the National Assembly tried to reconvene in its usual meeting place, it found the doors locked and barred by royal troops. In a frenzy of excitement and anger, the deputies seized a nearby indoor tennis court and took a solemn oath—the **Tennis Court Oath**—not to disband until they had written a constitution for France. Two days later, Louis held his royal session, which accomplished nothing, and the Assembly went on meeting. On June 27, the king faced the inevitable and ordered all members of the clergy and nobility to join the deputies of the National Assembly. Reluctantly, they did. But the king was humiliated, and at the end of the month he changed his mind again, ordering his soldiers to disband the National Assembly by force. When these troop movements were reported in Paris, fear combined with tension to explode in ways that were to have huge, if unforeseen, consequences for the emerging revolution.

cahiers Lists of grievances drawn up by voters electing deputies to the Estates-General in 1789.

patriots People who rejected absolutism and supported revolutionary reform of France.

National Assembly First French revolutionary legislature, in session from 1789 to 1791.

Tennis Court Oath Oath of the National Assembly not to disband before a written constitution had been drafted.

This painting of the Tennis Court Oath, based on an unfinished painting of Jacques-Louis David, enshrines the moment in French collective memory. Here representatives of the revolutionary nation stretch out their hands to swear that they will not disband until they have written a constitution. Notice the curtains billowing in the fresh air and the shaft of light shining directly upon the figure in the center who is reading the oath. *(Réunion des Musées Nationaux/Art Resource, NY)*

Trouble in Paris, Trouble in the Countryside, Trouble in Versailles

By late June 1789, Paris had become a hotbed of politics as patriot orators, fearful for the fate of the National Assembly, whipped up a feverish state of excitement. Anxiety intensified as food prices skyrocketed following the hailstorm and bad harvest of 1788. Then, on July 11, the king dismissed his latest finance minister, **Jacques Necker**, thought to be the most pro-patriot person in the government.

Paris panicked. Rioters, convinced that the king was about to attack the people, broke into arsenals, seizing weapons and ammunition. Soon up to a quarter million people were carrying weapons. On July 14, a huge crowd, armed with cannons, headed toward the Bastille, a medieval fortress that served as a royal prison and had long been a symbol of the king's ab-

solute power. At first the insurgents tried to negotiate with the prison governor for a surrender of the ammunition they sought. When this failed, they took the Bastille by force, releasing prisoners (there were only seven) and killing the governor, whose head, hacked off with a pocketknife, they paraded triumphantly about the city on the end of a pike. Frightened by the disorder, on July 15, the king recalled Necker to office and ordered the troops around Versailles and Paris to disband. Thus, the uprising in Paris saved the National Assembly at Versailles.

But immediately there was a new crisis, as peasant

Jacques Necker (1732–1804) Louis XVI's financial minister whose dismissal provoked the uprising in Paris on July 14, 1789.

Claude Cholat, one of the "conquerors of the Bastille," painted this picture, thereby enshrining another moment in the collective memory of the French people. The awkward perspective indicates that Cholat was not trained in an art academy, but the work captures the drama of the moment as Cholat remembered it. *(Réunion des Musées Nationaux/Art Resource, NY)*

revolts erupted throughout most of the kingdom. Called the **Great Fear**, these uprisings in the countryside were sparked by the same high food prices and political excitement that had ignited Paris. The peasants believed that they were about to be attacked by people they called brigands and aristocrats. Rising up in self-defense, they vented their fury against their landlords, looting manor houses and ransacking the offices that housed records of payments to the landlord. These payments, often cited in the peasants' cahiers, included fees for the use of the landlord's mill or bake ovens, which all peasants paid in addition to their regular land rents. Even peasants who owned their own land had to pay them. In the Great Fear, rural communities all over France spontaneously attacked these symbols of remaining feudal dues.

Faced with the peasant uprising, the National Assembly feared that all public order was about to collapse. In May, most deputies had wanted a reform of

government. Now they realized that fundamental changes were needed. Therefore, on the **Night of August 4**, 1789, in an evening session of the Assembly, some deputies proposed to abolish the feudal dues that peasants were attacking. As it turned out, this limited proposal quickly turned into something extraordinary. In a flash of enthusiasm, the deputies rushed to renounce all sorts of traditional taxes, payments, and privileges: the clergy gave up the **tithe**,

Great Fear Widespread peasant uprisings in July and August 1789 that abolished feudal dues to landlords.

Night of August 4 French legislative session in 1789 that abolished many traditional taxes, payments, and privileges.

tithe (From Middle English: "tenth") Payment required by the Catholic Church from all owners of nonchurch lands.

military appointments previously reserved for nobles were opened to commoners, and the tax privileges of many towns and provinces were abolished. By dawn, when the session ended, the deputies had swept away virtually all of France's old society of orders and privilege.

The all-night meeting on August 4 dismantled the old social order of France, just as events in Versailles and Paris, culminating in the storming of the Bastille, had dismantled the old political order. But what was to replace them? Three weeks later, the National Assembly, led by Sieyès and other patriots, gave its answer when it issued the **Declaration of the Rights of Man and the Citizen,** the single most important document produced during the Revolution. In it, France's new regime was laid down in principle. The declaration drew on both Enlightenment thought and the language of the American Revolution, especially as expressed in the Declaration of Independence. It proclaimed the "natural, inalienable, and sacred rights of man," which included the rights to "freedom, property, safety, and the right to resist oppression." It also guaranteed security from arbitrary arrest and freedom of speech and religion. France was still to have a king, but he was no longer to be absolute, since he was to govern according to a new written constitution. One word summed up the content of the declaration: liberty. Human rights guaranteed by a government representing the people, limited by a constitution, and promoting the rule of law would make liberty possible. The declaration's affirmation that "all people shall have equal rights upon birth and ever after" would have a huge impact across Europe and eventually the world.

The National Assembly's program for a constitutional monarchy was worked out during August 1789. Now it was up to Louis XVI to state his position on it, and, once again, the king hesitated. Then, in early October, the initiative passed to a new element of the population—the workingwomen of Paris, who were furious about the high cost of bread and believed the king should do something about it. On October 5, six thousand women seized cannons and in pouring rain marched to Versailles to demand food. As the patriots joined them in the streets, the king capitulated. He promised flour for bread and agreed to accompany the marchers back to Paris, where he and his family were resettled in an old palace. A few days later, the National Assembly also moved to the city. These **October Days** shifted the center of power from aristocratic Versailles to turbulent Paris, where the king and the new National Assembly were under the watchful eye of the most militant revolutionaries.

By this time, the events of the previous months were well on their way to becoming legends. The Tennis Court Oath came to symbolize the defiance of the French people in the face of royal despotism, while the storming of the Bastille became the symbol for the overthrow of royal oppression. The Night of August 4 stood for the destruction of the **Old Regime** and the inauguration of the new. These events were memorialized in monumental paintings, like *The Tennis Court Oath* by **Jacques-Louis David,** and celebrated as national festivals. To this day, July 14, Bastille Day, is France's chief national holiday. The message these events conveyed was clear: In the Old Regime, politics was something done by the king and the court. In the new, politics would be done by the people. This momentous shift in the understanding of politics was at the heart of the French Revolution.

The Constitutional Monarchy, 1789–1792

↓ What was new in the revolutionary concepts of the citizen and the nation?

↓ What were the causes and effects of the Revolution's break with the Catholic Church?

From the fall of 1789 to the summer of 1792, France was a constitutional monarchy, with rule by the king and the National Assembly, the new national legislature. Writing a constitution, the Assembly scrapped the old haphazard administrative system, replacing it with uniform institutions and procedures. It also redefined French collective identity, reshaping France as a new nation made up of a community of citizens while defining the nature of citizenship. Many of these changes remain in place today. At the same time, however, new conflicts arose that were equally long lasting. One centered on the rights of women in the new regime. Another raised the problem of slavery in a reformed France. A crucial conflict was the rupture between the Revolution and the Roman Catholic

Declaration of the Rights of Man and the Citizen Statement of revolutionary principles, proclaiming universal and inalienable human rights.

October Days Uprising of Parisian workingwomen in 1789 that brought the royal family to Paris.

Old Regime Revolutionary name for prerevolutionary France.

Jacques-Louis David (1748–1825) Important artist who celebrated the Revolution's great turning points in monumental paintings.

Church. These issues increased the hostility between the revolutionaries and Louis XVI, who never really accepted his new constitutional role. Other European rulers, frightened by revolutionary radicalism, turned against France's new regime. After war broke out between revolutionary France and conservative Europe, France's monarchy fell.

The New Constitution

By November 1789, fear of hunger began to subside following a good harvest that reduced grain prices. Political excitement nevertheless remained high. Dozens of newspapers appeared, with names like *The Daily Thermometer* and *The National Whip*. New political clubs sprang up in Paris, where deputies and their supporters passionately debated legislative proposals. The most famous club was the Society of the Friends of the Constitution, nicknamed the **Jacobin Club** for the building in which it met, once owned by Jacobin Dominican friars. The Jacobins were mainly middle class and often well-to-do. While they supported the democratization of politics, they also defended the rights of private property and favored an economy free from government regulation. The Jacobin leader **Maximilien Robespierre**, a prim provincial lawyer called "the Incorruptible" because of his dedication to the revolutionary agenda, praised the street violence that had led to the storming of the Bastille and the October march on Versailles.

By late 1789, the old political and social structures of France had been swept away. Now the National Assembly, following Article 3 of the Declaration of the Rights of Man and the Citizen, which stated that "the principle of all sovereignty resides in the Nation," began to write a constitution for the new regime. The **Constitution of 1791** reinvented French society and politics and redefined what it meant to be French. It discarded the old estates and orders, declaring France to be a single nation, uniting all people who resided permanently on French soil. **Sovereignty** now resided in the nation, no longer in the king. The goal of the constitution was to create a community in which each person was equal, with equal natural rights. Ability, not birth, proclaimed the deputies, should determine success and status. Thus, the National Assembly abolished all titles of nobility.

As French society was pushed to be uniform and unified, the administration of government was made uniform and unified, too. The Assembly swept away the overlapping muddle of administrative districts and replaced it with **departments.** Departments were to be alike in size and organized into standardized subdivisions. The departments reflected the revolu-

Maximilien Robespierre, the "incorruptible," is shown here at a writing desk. Although a supporter of the radical democratic left in the revolutionary movement, Robespierre never adopted revolutionary clothing. As shown here, he continued to wear knee breeches and to powder his hair. He also continued to address men as "monsieur" rather than "citizen." *(Réunion des Musées Nationaux/Art Resource, NY)*

tionaries' goal of creating efficient administrative districts and implemented the Enlightenment ideal that good government should be based on rational principles. Rationality also lay behind the introduction of

Jacobin Club   Most important French revolutionary political club, whose members were called Jacobins.

Maximilien Robespierre   (1758–1794) Important and powerful leader in the French Revolution and one of the instigators of the Reign of Terror.

Constitution of 1791   Written document establishing a constitutional monarchy in France that went into effect in October 1791.

sovereignty   Supreme political power and authority; also a nation's independence or freedom from control of another state.

departments   Local French administrative districts, uniform in size.

MAP 19.1   The Ratonalization of French Administration, 1789 and 1790 These maps show the reorganization of French territory. The map on the left shows the traditional provinces of the monarchy as they were in 1789. Note that they are very unequal in size. The map on the right shows the new departments, uniform in size and named after geographical features of the French landscape. They were created in 1790.

the **metric system,** based on the meter, calculated as one ten-millionth of the quarter meridian. From now on, length was to be measured naturally, with a uniform unit based on the size of earth itself.

The National Assembly also addressed the issue of citizenship. The idea of citizenship had been discussed during the Enlightenment and was associated with self-government in the tradition of ancient Rome. It had been put into practice during the American Revolution. When it came to implementing citizenship in France, the Assembly, on the advice of Sieyès, backtracked on its principles of unity and uniformity by decreeing that people in the one nation were to be divided into two categories, **active and passive citizens.** Only men who owned or otherwise controlled a certain amount of property could be active citizens, and only active citizens could vote and hold public office. The deputies believed that property ownership gave men a stake in society that would make them a band of citizen brothers who would act responsibly when making political decisions. Women and non-property-holding men were to be passive citizens. Despite these restrictions, these formulations secured France a level of participatory democracy that would not be reached elsewhere in Europe for many decades. About two-

thirds of adult French males met the qualifications for active citizens, and Protestants and Jews, who had been discriminated against during the Old Regime, were now admitted to full rights of citizenship.

The restructuring of France as a nation composed of equal (male) citizens was summed up in a new revolutionary slogan: "Liberty, Equality, Fraternity." Although women like Olympe de Gouges (see Choice), with the support of a few deputies in the Assembly, protested their exclusion from active citizenship, they were not able to change the categories. Most male revolutionaries, influenced by philosophes such as Jean-Jacques Rousseau, considered women too emotional and illogical to participate in political life. Their place was in the home, where they could serve as wives to their patriot husbands and raise children to serve the

metric system   Standardized system of weights and measurements based on the unit of ten, introduced following the French Revolution.

active and passive citizens   Two categories of citizenship in which only property-owning men (active citizens) were allowed to vote and hold public office.

nation. For working-class women, Gouges' agenda had little appeal. Food for their families and wages in their traditional occupations were much more important.

When these were threatened, workingwomen could be roused to public action that often had profound political consequences, as the October Days had proved.

Voice

Olympe de Gouges Asserts the Rights of Women

In September 1791, just before the Constitution of 1791 went into effect, Olympe de Gouges published her most famous pamphlet, The Rights of Woman. *In it she demanded equality for both men and women in the new revolutionary regime and asked the outgoing legislature, or the new one created by the constitution, to enact this program. Her decision to model her demands on the Declaration of the Rights of Man and the Citizen of 1789, often following that text word for word while adding the word* women, *revealed the omissions in that earlier document. She was thus attempting to use the ideals of the Revolution for the benefit of women.*

➡ Why would Gouges address her "Rights of Woman" to the French Queen?

➡ Why does Gouges use the label "Citizeness"?

➡ How is Gouges turning the ideals of the Revolution as stated in her list of demands to the benefit of women?

➡ The Rights of Woman: To the Queen
Mothers, daughters, sisters, female representatives of the nation, ask to be constituted as a national assembly. Considering that ignorance, neglect, or contempt for the rights of women are the sole causes for public misfortune and governmental corruption of Governments, they have resolved to set forth in a solemn declaration the natural, inalienable, and sacred rights of woman. . . .

➡ In consequence, the sex that is superior in beauty as in courage, needed in maternal sufferings, recognizes and declares in the presence and under the auspices of the Supreme Being, the following rights of woman and the citizeness:

1. Woman is born free and remains equal to man in rights. Social distinctions may be based only on common utility.

2. The purpose of all political association is the preservation of the natural and imprescriptable rights of woman and man. These rights are liberty, property, security, and, especially, resistance to oppression.

3. The principle of all sovereignty rests essentially in the nation, which is but the reuniting of woman and man. No body and no individual may exercise authority which does not emanate expressly from the nation.

4. Liberty and justice consist in restoring all that belongs to another; hence the exercise of the natural rights of woman has no other limits than those that the perpetual tyranny of man opposes to them; these limits must be reformed according to the laws of nature and reason. . . .

6. ➡ The law should be the expression of the general will. All citizenesses and citizens should take part, in person or by their representatives, in its formation. It must be the same for everyone. All citizenesses and citizens, being equal in its eyes, should be equally admissible to all public dignities, offices, and employments, according to their ability, and with no other distinction than that of their virtues and talents.

→ What is the importance of this article?

7. → No woman is exempted; she is indicted, arrested, and detained in the cases determined by the law. Women, like men obey this rigorous law. . . .

→ Why did Gouges include this article in her declaration?

10. No one should be disturbed for his fundamental opinions; woman has the right to mount the scaffold, so she should have the right equally to mount the tribune, provided that these manifestations do not trouble public order as established by law.

11. → The free communication of thoughts and opinions is one of the most precious rights of the woman since this liberty assures the recognition of children by their fathers. Every citeness may therefore say freely, "I am the mother of your child"; a barbarous prejudice [against unmarried women having children] should not force her to hide the truth, so long as responsibility is accepted for any abuse of this liberty in cases determined by the law. . . .

13. For maintenance of public authority and for expenses of administration, taxation of women and men is equal; she takes part in all forced labor services; in all painful tasks; she must therefore have the same proportion in the distribution of places, employments, offices, dignities, and in industry. . . .

Olympe de Gouges is the original French pamphlet of 1791 (Olympe de Gouges, "Les droits de la femme. À la reine." As found in Lynn Hunt, ed. and trans., *The French Revolution and Human Rights: A Brief Documentary History* (Boston: Bedford Books of St. Martin's Press, 1996). pp. 124–126.

Although the deputies denied women the vote and the right to hold public office, the legislature eventually endorsed other elements of Gouges's program by expanding women's rights in the important areas of domestic relations and inheritance law. In 1792, divorce, advocated by Gouges but forbidden by the Catholic Church, was legalized. Both women and men were allowed to file for divorce by mutual consent or on account of "incompatibility of temperament." Many women used the new law to separate from their husbands. Another law benefiting women ordered the equal division of estates among all heirs, male and female. These new divorce and property laws reflected the emphasis on individual rights and the freedom to act even in opposition to Catholic Church teaching or traditional family values.

Debates over the nation and its citizens sparked a reconsideration of slavery. France had long been considered "free land," but slavery was practiced in French colonies in the Caribbean. There the Declaration of the Rights of Man and the Citizen was a bombshell; white colonials denied that it applied to slaves, while the slaves considered it a signal for revolt. Trouble continued into the spring of 1791, when the Assembly cautiously granted citizenship to a small number of free blacks on Saint-Domingue, France's most important remaining colony, where 57,000 whites and free blacks ruled more than 465,000 African slaves. In August, there followed a massive uprising led by **François Dominique Toussaint L'Ouverture**, a former slave inspired by Enlightenment thought. Many plantation owners were slain, while others fled to the new United States. The uprising, which ended French control of the island and France's Atlantic trade, was the first successful slave revolt in history. In early 1794, France became the first European country to abolish slavery and to grant full rights of citizenship to ex-slaves. Because citizenship touched on so many aspects of reform, both at home and overseas, it became the central issue in defining the new regime.

The Break with the Catholic Church

The French church had been involved in the new regime from the beginning. Clergy like Sieyès continued to sit in the new National Assembly. Many welcomed the reordering of society into a nation of equal citizens as a fulfillment of the "gentle fraternity" of Jesus, which incorporated everyone equally. The clergymen who were deputies, therefore, accepted the Assembly's increasingly radical restructuring of the church.

After abolishing the tithe on the Night of August 4, the Assembly decided to confiscate church property, which constituted about 10 percent of French land, and to use it to back new government bonds and restore confidence in the state's finances. It also withdrew

François Dominique Toussaint L'Ouverture (1743–1803) Former slave who led the first successful slave revolt in history in the French colony of Saint-Domingue.

state enforcement of monks' and nuns' religious vows and forbade all future vows. Then, in 1790, the Assembly took even more drastic action, decreeing the **Civil Constitution of the Clergy.** Dioceses were adjusted to conform to new departments, clergy were put on state salary, and parish priests were to be elected by active citizens, including Protestants and Jews.

The Assembly issued the Civil Constitution of the Clergy without formal consultation with the church, and while the clergy generally were grudgingly prepared to accept it, they were not prepared to have it imposed on them. In the Old Regime, the king had always consulted with the First Estate over religious affairs. The Assembly argued that since the estates were abolished, consultation was no longer possible. The issue of consultation was solved, temporarily, by turning to the pope. He was a power outside the nation, but a positive word from him could be taken as final. When the Assembly ordered all French clergy to take a solemn oath in favor of the Civil Constitution, only 7 out of 160 bishops complied, though half of the lower clergy stepped forward to take it. Then in May 1791, Pope Pius VI publicly condemned the Civil Constitution.

Instantly, the French church was split between those who had taken the oath and those who had rejected it. Because the oath had been phrased to demand loyalty to the Revolution as a whole, clergy who refused it, called **nonjurors,** were quickly branded counterrevolutionaries. Thus, the failure to consult the church led to a rupture between the church and the new regime. This was a fateful development. There had been opposition to the Revolution from the beginning, but it was never widespread. Now it increased and solidified. Traditionally minded Catholics who opposed the Civil Constitution harassed the "constitutional clergy" who supported it, jeering at them in the streets, shooting at their houses, or throwing dead animals onto their doorsteps. The police force representing the new regime attacked these protesters, identifying them as enemies of the nation, and arresting and imprisoning them. As these conflicts widened, opposition to the course of events in the capital mounted, especially in western France, where support for the nonjurors was strongest.

Foreign Intervention

On June 20, 1791, Louis XVI and his family, shocked by the rupture between the new regime and the Catholic Church and fearing for their personal safety, attempted to flee France. The next day they were caught east of Paris, in the town of Varennes. People had recognized the king along the way, but it was the postmaster at Varennes who claimed public credit for

the identification after he compared the face of the man before him to the one on a banknote in his pocket. Louis and his family were immediately returned to Paris under armed guard. With the king back in the capital, the deputies made the best of the situation by claiming that Louis had been "kidnapped." Nobody really believed this accusation, since the king had written a letter condemning the new regime in harsh terms. The fiction of kidnapping, however, allowed the deputies to proceed with their constitution making.

Those who shared the king's doubts, however, now thought it best to get out of France. These **émigrés** had first started to leave the country in the summer of 1789. In all, about 150,000 people, out of a total population of 28 million, fled France during the 1790s. Thus, another kind of opponent of the Revolution, unhappy with the revolutionaries' treatment of the king, emerged alongside those unhappy with their treatment of the Catholic Church. These two opposition movements soon joined forces to oppose the Revolution both at home and abroad.

Public opinion outside France was sharply divided over the merits of France's revolution. The newly independent Americans fiercely debated the meaning of events in France and formed pro- and anti-French political parties. In Britain, Edmund Burke, a political theorist and member of Parliament, denounced the Revolution's headlong rush to change. "Liberty without wisdom," he argued in his *Reflections on the Revolution in France* (1790), "is folly, vice, and madness." Burke in turn was quickly attacked by **Thomas Paine,** an Englishman who had defended the American Revolution in his *Common Sense* and now defended the French in *The Rights of Man.* "From what we now see," Paine wrote, "nothing of reform in the political world ought to be held improbable. It is an age of Revolutions, in which everything may be looked for." The English poet **William Wordsworth,** twenty-one years old and visiting France, also championed the Revolution's assertion of reason and rights: "Bliss was

Civil Constitution of the Clergy Legislative decree of 1790 radically reforming the Catholic Church in France.

nonjurors Clergy refusing to take an oath supporting the Civil Constitution of the Clergy.

émigrés Counterrevolutionaries who fled France during the Revolution.

Thomas Paine (1737–1809) Englishman who defended both the American and French Revolutions.

William Wordsworth (1770–1850) English poet famous for his nature poetry and his defense of the French Revolution.

it at that dawn to be alive," he later wrote, "but to be young was very Heaven!" Mary Wollstonecraft not only attacked Burke's views in *A Vindication of the Rights of Man* (1790) but went further in her *Vindication of the Rights of Woman* (1792) to argue, like Olympe de Gouges, for women's full participation in public life.

While politicians and intellectuals debated France's Revolution, Europe's governments, based on traditions of royal rule over societies of estates and orders, became increasingly alarmed by the implications of universal human rights and the example of France's democratic government. Monarchs began to suppress local pro-French ferment. For example, the Austrian emperor Joseph II, Marie-Antoinette's brother, ordered the state police to arrest revolutionary sympathizers in Vienna. The king of Prussia, Frederick William II, also considered crushing the Revolution and restoring Louis XVI's authority. Indeed Louis hoped for just such an invasion, and war between the conservative European states and the Revolution began to seem inevitable. In France, most revolutionaries thought that a war against Austria would end agitation by the émigrés, consolidate the Revolution, and unmask any plotting by the king. In April 1792, in a preemptive strike, France declared war on Austria and its ally Prussia.

As it turned out, the war set the stage for the fall of the French monarchy. Austrian troops quickly crossed into France and moved on Paris, with the announced intention of rescuing Louis XVI. Just then, a poor harvest once again sent food prices skyrocketing. Faced with these crises, radical deputies in the legislature, convinced that the king was at the heart of all their problems, started to plan the overthrow of the monarchy. For their muscle, they turned to the old militants of July 1789, now nicknamed the **sans-culottes** (literally, "without knee-breeches") because they advertised their democratic principles by wearing long laborers' trousers rather than the shorter breeches with hose favored by the well-to-do.

The sans-culottes were a cross-section of Parisian society. Many were artisans and day laborers, but the movement's leaders were often well educated and economically well-off. They championed "equality" over the "liberty" celebrated in the Declaration of the Rights of Man and the Citizen. Before 1792, many sans-culottes had fallen into the category of passive citizens. Now they demanded full political participation in the Revolution and the right to advance themselves economically and socially. They denounced the "idle" rich, demanding government regulation of private property rights and state-sponsored welfare programs that would provide them with basic necessities like food and jobs. They also called for government controls on the price of bread. The sans-culottes' advo-

cacy of government regulation of the economy put them at odds with the Jacobins and most deputies in the revolutionary legislatures, who favored the laissez-faire principles of the Physiocrats and Adam Smith. To achieve their ends, the sans-culottes advocated the direct use of violence. For the next two years, they played a major role in Paris politics, mobilizing mass street demonstrations and marching on the legislature to demand more and more equality.

On August 10, the sans-culottes invaded the palace where the king and his family were held. Palace guards put up a bloody fight, but in the end Louis XVI was imprisoned and the Constitution of 1791, in effect for less than a year, was scrapped. New elections took place for yet another legislature, the **National Convention.** In these elections, property and occupational qualifications for voters were abolished. All adult males could go to the polls. This arrangement responded to sans-culotte demands for a more thoroughly democratic regime.

The Republic and the Reign of Terror, 1792–1795

⬇ What measures did France's new republican government take to secure the Revolution??
⬇ By 1795, how far had the Revolution traveled since the Estates-General was called to initiate tax reform?

The National Convention, which met in Paris in September 1792, served as France's government until October 1795. These years saw the proclamation of a republic and the execution of Louis XVI. At the same time, revolutionary France faced both the ongoing foreign war and a new civil war that broke out in 1793. In the end, the republic triumphed, but at a terrible cost, when the Convention created a revolutionary dictatorship that ruthlessly pursued its enemies by means of state-controlled terror. The dictatorship's repression set in motion the forces of its own destruction.

The End of Monarchy and Monarchs

Following the imprisonment of the king and queen, as enemy troops moved closer to Paris, panic swept through the city. A fiery orator from the Jacobin Club,

sans-culottes   (in French, "without knee breeches") Parisian militants who overthrew the French monarchy in 1792.

National Convention   First republican legislature in France, governing from 1792 to 1795.

Georges Danton, proclaiming that the Revolution needed "boldness, boldness, boldness forever," persuaded the out-going Assembly to create a special tribunal to try people who continued to support the monarchy. Those found guilty of opposition to the new regime were beheaded high on a platform in a public square by a new execution device—the **guillotine**, invented by a French doctor who argued that the fast fall of its heavy blade resulted in a painless and efficient means of execution. By early September 1792, the Paris prisons were full of people accused of counterrevolutionary activity. Fearful that they were still plotting in their jail cells, the sans-culottes invaded the prisons and slaughtered 1,300 inmates, sometimes mutilating the corpses. These **September Massacres** were publicly defended by Danton and Robespierre as the will of the people, but some who had thus far supported the Revolution were secretly alarmed, seeing in them a chilling example of brutal popular violence. When news of the massacres spread, people throughout Europe and America turned against the Revolution in horror.

On September 22, the National Convention proclaimed France a republic. Now the problem was what to do with the king. In December, Louis was put on trial before the Convention, where he mounted a dignified defense. But the deputies overwhelmingly found him guilty of "conspiracy against the general security of the state." Now debate turned to the king's punishment. Deputies who argued for execution were known as the **Mountain** because they occupied a steeply rising set of seats in the Convention's meeting hall. The Mountain was also the dominant faction in the Jacobin Club. Robespierre took the lead in pressing the Mountain's case for execution, declaring that the king's conviction required it. Some deputies, however, wanted a punishment that fell short of execution— perhaps banishment to the United States, as Paine, now a deputy in the Convention, argued. The opponents of execution were known as **Girondins**, because their leaders were from the department of the Gironde. They argued that Louis' execution would energize the Revolution's enemies at home and abroad, thereby increasing the dangers France faced. Both the Mountain and the Girondins were committed to the new republic, but their power bases were different. The Mountain relied increasingly on the radical Parisian sans-culottes, who had overthrown the king on August 10, while the Girondins looked to revolutionary moderates in the provinces. By a narrow vote, including that of Sieyès, the Convention sided with the Mountain and ordered the king's execution. On January 21, 1793, Louis XVI went to the guillotine. His last words to his subjects were deliberately drowned out by a drumroll from the execution squad.

Foreign War and Civil War

The execution of the king caught the attention of Europe's royalty, who now condemned the revolutionaries as "king killers." Shortly after Louis' death, Great Britain and Spain joined the war against France. Austria and Prussia regrouped with a coalition that now included the Dutch Republic and the Italian kingdom of Sardinia.

Facing enemies on every border, the National Convention formed the **Committee of Public Safety**, made up of twelve deputies, led first by Danton and then by Robespierre, who were given dictatorial powers to deal with the wartime emergency. The committee ordered a mass mobilization of French citizens to defend the Revolution: unmarried men were drafted to fight in the army, married men were to make weapons, women were to sew clothes and nurse the wounded, while children and the elderly were to make bandages. Never before had a European government tried to harness the energy of a whole people in the service of the state. In ordering this mass mobilization, the National Convention appealed to the revolutionary principle of fraternity. Now the revolutionaries identified themselves as a "Nation, one and indivisible" and put this slogan on their flags, their stationery, and even their dinner plates.

The most important effect of the mass mobilization of 1793 was the reorganization of the French army. **Conscription** greatly increased the number of men under arms. They were badly needed, since the old royal army, which numbered about 165,000 in 1789, had fallen to approximately 130,000 in 1793, owing to deaths, desertions, and the resignations of noble officers who opposed the Revolution. The new recruits brought the numbers up to 750,000—the largest army

Georges Danton (1759–1794) Radical Jacobin revolutionary who rose to prominence after the overthrow of the monarchy.

guillotine Execution device used by the French revolutionaries for beheading, invented by a doctor as a humane way of executing people.

September Massacres Slaughter of 1,300 prisoners by the sans-culottes in Paris in 1792 that alienated many early supporters of the Revolution.

the Mountain and the Girondins Two revolutionary factions vying for control of the National Convention in late 1792 and early 1793.

Committee of Public Safety Committee of the National Convention created in 1793 and granted dictatorial powers to implement the Terror.

conscription Military draft, or forced enrollment of soldiers from among the people.

In this engraving of Louis XVI's execution, the executioner displays the king's head to the soldiers and citizens witnessing the event. The king's body still lies on the plank of the guillotine. A basket beside it will receive the head and the body after a priest prays for Louis's soul. *(Dagli Orti/Bibliothèque des Arts Décoratifs, Paris/The Art Archive)*

In the Vendée, the execution of the king and the break with the Catholic Church were especially unpopular. The Vendée was one example of a gulf opening up between parts of provincial France and Paris, where militant revolutionaries continued to push for ever more radical change. Another hotbed of discontent was the southeastern city of Lyon, second largest in France, where opposition to the Convention's emergency measures sparked a rebellion against the central government. With the Vendée and Lyon in rebellion, the National Convention found itself fighting both a civil war and a foreign war.

In early 1793, the Mountain blamed the Girondins for both the foreign war and the civil war. Robespierre, Danton, and other members of the Mountain accused the Girondins of being secret counterrevolutionaries. This accusation outraged the Girondins' supporters, who denounced Robespierre as an "insect wallowing in the filth of corruption." Finally, in May 1793, the Mountain purged the Girondins from the Convention with sans-culotte support. In return, the sans-culottes expected the Mountain to enact yet more economic controls and measures against those accused of counterrevolutionary activity.

The Republic of Virtue

Maximilien Robespierre had been active in the Revolution from the beginning, first as a deputy to the Estates-General and then as a fiery orator in the Jacobin Club and a deputy in the National Convention. Now "the Incorruptible" became the Revolution's leader. Elected

Europe had ever seen. It was also Europe's first citizen army, in which volunteers or draftees replaced the professional soldiers of the Old Regime. The new army also offered career advancement on the basis of talent, not birth or wealth, fulfilling one of the principles of 1789. After 1793, many of France's best generals rose up from the rank and file on the basis of ability, and many soldiers were fired up with revolutionary patriotism. As one put it, "The war which we are fighting is not a war between king and king or nation and nation. It is the war of liberty against despotism. There can be no doubt that we shall be victorious. A nation that is just and free is invincible." Over the next two years, this new revolutionary army launched mass assaults that crushed opponents and drove enemy troops from French soil, thus ending the foreign threat, and then carried the war outside of France by invading the Dutch Republic and northern Italy.

If the reorganization of the army saved the Revolution in the long run, it also created dangerous short-term problems. In March 1793, when the draft was imposed on peasant communities in western France, the **Vendée** burst into open insurrection against the National Convention. In 1789, peasants throughout France had supported the Revolution, but after the Great Fear ended feudal payments to their landlords, many turned conservative and resisted further change.

> **Vendée**   Part of western France in open rebellion against the National Convention in early 1793 following the break with the Catholic Church and the execution of the king.

to the Committee of Public Safety in July 1793, Robespierre and the other committee members moved to crush opposition to the Revolution at home, just as the republic's reorganized armies were crushing France's foreign enemies. In early September, the Convention declared that "terror is the order of the day": enemies of the Revolution would be ruthlessly suppressed by force. Robespierre saw terror as necessary for the establishment of a truly virtuous republican regime: "If the mainspring of popular government in time of peace is virtue, the mainspring of popular government in time of revolution is both *virtue and terror*. Terror is nothing but justice, prompt, severe, and inflexible; it is therefore an emanation of virtue." In practice, the **Reign of Terror** meant government control of the economy and the execution of those deemed counterrevolutionaries. New laws greatly expanded offenses against the Revolution. Now people the committee identified as high-profile counterrevolutionaries were tried and guillotined, including the imprisoned Girondins, Marie-Antoinette, and Olympe de Gouges. Their public beheadings attracted huge crowds. In the provinces, the committee moved against the rebels in the Vendée, where the army crushed opposition, as self-styled revolutionary "columns from hell" burned, looted, and killed indiscriminately. Tens of thousands of people, mostly peasants, died. The army also besieged Lyon, and when the city surrendered, more executions followed. "Lyon no longer exists," wrote the triumphant agent of the Committee. What remained of the city after the siege was renamed Freed City.

A crisis mentality seized the revolutionaries as they moved to defeat their enemies at home and abroad, and everything took on political meaning. Now revolutionaries scrutinized how people dressed, looking to see if they wore the sans-culottes' long trousers and no longer powdered their hair as men of means had done before 1789. They listened to how people spoke, making sure they treated each other as equals, using "Citizen," instead of "Monsieur" and "Madame," and addressing each other with *tu*, the familiar French form for "you," instead of the polite form *vous*. They looked to see if people ate and drank from plates and cups with revolutionary slogans on them. They formed processions and marched to the singing of revolutionary songs like the *Marseillaise*—to this day the national anthem of France. This politicization of all facets of everyday life was one of the most striking features of the Reign of Terror, and one of the most threatening, since it narrowed choices down to two—those who were united with the revolutionaries 100 percent and those who weren't. The revolutionary ideal of fraternity had now taken on a grimly exclusive meaning.

Jacques-Louis David drew this sketch of Marie Antoinette as she passed by his window on her way to execution in 1793. She sits tall, but her face is drawn. Her hands are tied behind her back so she can easily be positioned on the guillotine's plank, and her hair has been cut to give the blade access to her neck. *(Réunion des Musées Nationaux/Art Resource, NY)*

The most ambitious attempt to ensure that the new republic broke with the monarchical and aristocratic past was the creation of a new calendar. No longer were years to be counted from the birth of Christ. Now they began with the birth of the republic. Thus September 22, 1792, the day the republic was proclaimed, became the First Day of the Year One. Months were renamed after the seasons of the year, and weeks were lengthened from the biblical seven days to ten

Reign of Terror   Government's systematic coercion to defeat the Revolution's enemies, implemented in 1793 and 1794.

Marseillaise   Revolutionary battle song favored by the san-culottes, now the national anthem of France.

to accord with the metric system. Thus, time and the seasons were reconfigured in a new republican way.

In the prerevolutionary past, Catholicism had been the official religion of France. It, too, was radically repudiated in a movement known as **de-Christianization.** Unlike earlier attacks on the nonjurors, the de-Christianizers made no distinction between supporters and opponents of the Civil Constitution of the Clergy. All priests and their congregations were roughed up and their churches pillaged. As a result, Catholics were driven underground in much of France. Protestants fared no better; their pastors were assaulted and their meeting places vandalized.

As an alternative to Christianity, the Committee of Public Safety sponsored new republican religious observances that celebrated the deist divinity of the philosophes. In Paris, a singer from the Paris Opera, dressed as Liberty, presided over a celebration in the former Cathedral of Notre Dame, renamed the Temple of Reason. Robespierre himself presided over a Festival of the Supreme Being. This new religion aimed to cement the unity of all true revolutionaries and provide the republic with its base of virtue.

By early 1794, the crises France had faced during the previous year had subsided. Yet state terror increased as the Committee of Public Safety began to root out fellow revolutionaries accused of deviating from correct republican principles. Thus, the Revolution was now devouring its own. Then in June 1794, at Robespierre's urging, the Convention passed a law that denied accused persons any right of self-defense in court, inaugurating the **Great Terror** in Paris. During the next month, more than thirteen hundred people were convicted and executed. The guillotine had to be moved to the edge of the city following complaints about the amount of blood in the streets and the stench from rotting corpses.

Faced with the end of rebellion at home and improved conditions abroad, many deputies believed that the Terror, instituted to meet the crises of civil and foreign war, was no longer needed. They supported yet another uprising in Paris in the revolutionary month of Thermidor (July), during which some members of the Committee of Public Safety, including Robespierre, were arrested and executed. The fall of Robespierre inaugurated a wave of reaction against the Terror, known as the **Thermidorian reaction.** The Convention released political prisoners and closed the Jacobin Club, which was identified with Robespierre. It also dismantled the price and wage controls of the previous year, restoring free-market conditions.

The Reign of Terror of 1793–1794 was the product of two factors. The first was the pressure of foreign and civil war, to which the Committee of Public Safety

responded with realistic, if bloody, repression. But this is not the whole story. The second factor contributing to the Terror had more to do with revolutionary politics than with outside pressures. Since 1789, the identity of the revolutionary nation had rested on its oneness and indivisibility. The nation could not be divided against itself. If opposition arose, it therefore had to come from somewhere outside the nation and from people who were opposed to the republic. These people, condemned as counterrevolutionaries, were to be stamped out. It was this kind of thinking that led the Committee of Public Safety to execute fellow revolutionaries who questioned its policies and made Robespierre inaugurate the Great Terror in June. By the end of the Revolution, some 17,000 people had been officially executed. Another 10,000 to 12,000 were lynched or assassinated for political reasons, and between 6,000 and 11,000 died in prison awaiting trial for political crimes. In all, some 35,000 to 40,000 people perished out of a population of 28 million.

The Rise of Napoleon, 1794–1804

↓ How did the Revolution make possible the rise of Napoleon?
↓ Which parts of the revolutionary heritage did Napoleon Bonaparte accept and which ones did he repudiate?

The revolutionary republic survived for five years following the overthrow of the Committee of Public Safety. France's citizen armies continued to win on the battlefield until, in 1797, all the continental states warring against France made peace with the republic. Only England remained to fight at sea. In 1799, continental war broke out again when Austria and Russia attacked France. That same year, France's leading general, Napoleon Bonaparte, seized power. The early years of Napoleon's rule were marked by significant achievements. He reorganized the French state, brought an end to the war, healed the break with the Catholic Church, and instituted a new law code. In these years there was widespread support for Bonaparte's regime. Some émigrés even returned to France.

de-Christianization Attack on all forms of Christianity initiated by the sans-culottes in 1793.

Great Terror Culminating phase of the Reign of Terror in 1794, when more than 1,300 people were convicted and executed in Paris.

Thermidorian reaction Period in 1794–1795 during which the Terror was dismantled.

French Expansion

The restoration of free-market conditions following the collapse of the Committee of Public Safety had dire consequences for many sans-culottes. The fall harvest of 1794 proved one of the worst of the decade, creating economic hard times in the capital as the price of bread once again soared. By spring 1795, hardship had provoked two sans-culotte uprisings, which were put down by the army. From then on, a new Ministry of Police kept a sharp eye on sans-culotte leaders and periodically rounded them up for "preventive detention" in the city's prisons. Both the Terror and the Thermidorian reaction used coercion to control political enemies, and both whittled away at the human rights proclaimed in the Declaration of the Rights of Man and the Citizen.

In October 1795, the National Convention installed a new regime, which consisted of a two-house legislature and a five-man executive committee, the **Directory.** In another retreat from the Revolution, only men owning property could vote and hold public office. The Directory skillfully alternated in supporting republicans and royalists, who reemerged after the dismantling of the Terror. The Directory tried to keep either from dominating, but the result was permanent political instability and increasing cynicism about a government that stifled dissent.

Yet during this time, the French achieved significant gains in the foreign war. In 1795, Prussia, preoccupied once again with Poland, dropped out of the coalition, as did an exhausted Spain. For France, the next four years saw spectacular military victories and territorial expansion, as the Directory pursued a high-minded desire to create a ring of republics around France and a hard-headed aim to make France the leading power in western Europe. French generals, eager for increased military and political power, also drove the conquests. The most ambitious was **Napoleon Bonaparte.**

Bonaparte was born to a minor noble family on the island of Corsica, which France had annexed in 1768. Sent to a French military school at age ten, he was a good student but a loner, hazed by his classmates because of his odd name and modest origins. In 1789, the year the Revolution began, Napoleon was twenty and a lieutenant in the royal army. The Revolution gave him his great chance when it opened careers to talent. Bonaparte sided with the revolutionaries, and by 1793, he had risen to the rank of general. In 1795, his role in putting down a royalist uprising in Paris led to his appointment as commander of the Army of Italy. In that same year he married Josephine de Beauharnais, the widow of a French nobleman who had been executed during the Terror. Napoleon was

deeply in love with Josephine and devastated when he learned of her love affairs with other men after their marriage. From then on, he shut himself off from close relations with people and concentrated on advancing his career. In 1797, he drove Austria out of northern Italy and negotiated a treaty, thus bringing peace to the European continent for the first time since 1792. Britain alone remained to fight. Bonaparte's Italian victories displayed his qualities as a military commander. He planned carefully, struck fast, and was not afraid to take risks. He also knew how to gain maximum military and political advantage from a win.

Following the invasion of northern Italy, Bonaparte reorganized his conquered territory into a new state, the Cisalpine Republic, staffed by pro-French locals under his control, following the pattern established in 1795, when the French had invaded the Dutch Republic and set up the Batavian Republic. In 1797, Napoleon would also establish another republic in Switzerland. The old society of estates and orders was abolished in these **sister republics,** replaced by the French model of a nation composed of citizens. The sister republics were required to pay France for its war costs, to provide supplies to French troops in their territory, and to maintain their own armies at local expense. In Italy, Bonaparte also organized wholesale looting of churches and palaces, seizing statues and paintings that were shipped to Paris for display in the new **Louvre Museum,** where many can still be seen today.

When land fighting ended in late 1797, Bonaparte feared his career would falter, so he began angling for a new command. In early 1798, he and the Directory decided on a campaign in Egypt. If the French had access to the Red Sea, they could threaten the British in India. The French force set off by sea in May, landed near Alexandria, and soon occupied Cairo. Then disaster struck. On August 1, the British navy under Horatio Nelson destroyed the French fleet off Alexandria. With his line of supplies now cut, Bonaparte was bottled up in Egypt. To make matters worse, the Austrians and Russians, alarmed at France's creation of sister republics and a French presence in the Middle East, declared war on France in early 1799.

Directory Executive committee that ruled France from 1795 to 1799.

Napoleon Bonaparte (1769–1821) French general who seized power in 1799 and ruled France until 1814.

sister republics French satellite states formed from territories conquered between 1795 and 1799.

Louvre Museum Paris museum of art founded in 1793 and housed in a former royal palace, one of the great museums of the world.

Now the French were put on the defensive, just as they had been in 1792. The military crisis galvanized a group of politicians disgusted by the failure of the Directory to establish domestic stability. One was a new member of the Directory, Joseph Emmanuel Sieyès, whose pamphlet had touched off the furious debate over the Estates-General exactly ten years before. Sieyès did not have the power or popularity to lead a plot against the government, so he turned to someone who did: Napoleon Bonaparte. Leaving his army in Egypt, Napoleon had slipped through the British naval blockade off the coast and arrived back in France. In November 1799, after the conspirators overthrew the Directory in a coup d'état, Napoleon quickly assumed unchallenged leadership of the government. Now all Napoleon's talents came to the fore—his charm and intelligence, his ability to awe people and inspire their loyalty, and his sense of his own exceptional abilities and destiny.

Order and Administration

The new constitution of December 1799 made Napoleon **First Consul** in a three-man consulate. In fact, however, he was the only one with real power. Members of the new legislature had little say in government, since Napoleon, assisted by a council of experts, made all the important decisions. The new constitution did not include the Declaration of the Rights of Man and the Citizen. Opposition to the new government was silenced when a rigid press censorship was instituted. All these changes signaled a repudiation of the Revolution's participatory politics. Yet the repudiation was ambiguous, since Napoleon kept up appearances by submitting the new constitution to a carefully controlled popular vote of adult males.

In early 1800, Bonaparte reorganized administration throughout France. **Prefects**, put in charge of the departments, were under the strict control of the minister of the interior in Paris, who was second only to Napoleon himself. The prefects were chosen on the basis of administrative experience and political leanings. The First Consul was deliberately upholding the revolutionary ideal of careers open to talent, from which he himself had benefited, while trying to win over all factions except die-hard royalists and radical republicans. Influenced by Enlightenment thought, Napoleon also believed that governing was a science based on reason and careful observation, which allowed administrators to act logically by objectively analyzing problems and finding rational solutions to them. With this system in place, far less stood between the state and the citizen in 1801 than had stood between the Crown and its subjects in 1789.

One of Napoleon's biggest problems was the continuing crisis in state finances, which had been the immediate cause of the Revolution in the first place. Each revolutionary regime since 1789 had assumed the debts of the old monarchy, but by the late 1790s, these debts had become intolerable. To stabilize the state's finances, Napoleon instituted a standardized system of taxation that fell on all citizens in accordance with the revolutionary principle of equality. Remembering what had happened to the monarchy in 1788, he refused to put his government at the mercy of financiers who could indirectly dictate policy by their lending strategies.

In 1801 and 1802, peace returned to Europe as Napoleon signed treaties with the Austrians and the British, confirming France's territorial gains and acknowledging the sister republics. Another peace, which proved more lasting than the others, was signed with the Catholic Church in the form of a new **concordat** between Napoleon and Pius VII, elected pope in 1800. The Concordat of 1801 established French Catholics' right to worship publicly, but it did not renew the ancient connection between church and state. Catholicism was simply recognized as the "religion of the majority of the French," and the state remained separate from the church. Napoleon himself was a nominal Catholic who thought of religion as a tool for maintaining social and political order. He believed that religious toleration for Catholics was a way to end the political headache caused by the Civil Constitution of the Clergy and de-Christianization. But the Concordat also gave the state tight control over church activities, including the regulation of seminaries. A new national catechism for religious instruction secured church endorsement of the regime. Many French people returned to Catholic worship with fervor, especially in the countryside, where women led the revival, demanding the return of priests and urging neighbors to join once again in communal worship.

Protestants also benefited from Napoleon's religious policies, since they, too, were allowed to worship openly without harassment. The fate of the Jews,

First Consul   Title taken by Napoleon Bonaparte when he seized power in 1799.

prefects   Napoleon's local government administrators in France.

concordat   Formal agreement between the pope and the ruler of a Catholic state; Concordat of 1801 reestablished Catholics' rights of worship in France but separated church and state.

however, was somewhat different. Like the revolutionaries, Napoleon wanted to integrate Jews into society. But he also wanted to place them under state supervision. Although Jews were granted freedom of worship, laws put limits on their economic activities and increased their military obligations. The government assumed control of Jewish moneylending, forbade foreign Jews from settling in France, and ordered Jewish men serving in the army to obey all military rules and regulations, even if these conflicted with Jewish religious observance.

While French Jews received limited benefits from Napoleon's regime, another group saw its condition worsen catastrophically. These were the ex-slaves in the Caribbean. In 1801, Toussaint L'Ouverture, who had led black resistance to French rule a decade earlier, conquered the Spanish half of Santo Domingo and proclaimed himself president of the united island. Initially, L'Ouverture had French support, but in 1802, Napoleon turned against him and sent an army to Santo Domingo. It captured and executed L'Ouverture yet was unable to reassert French control over the former colony, now called Haiti. In the course of the campaign, however, Napoleon restored slavery in Martinique and Guadeloupe, France's other Caribbean possessions. Thus France, which had been the first European state to abolish slavery in 1794, reinstituted it in 1802. It was not finally abolished until 1848. This act was Napoleon's clearest repudiation of the revolutionary heritage. In 1803, he sold Louisiana, which France had received back from a defeated Spain, to the United States. His failure to retake Haiti convinced him that there was no hope for reestablishing a French empire on the North American continent.

The Napoleonic Code

Napoleon's most lasting achievement was a reform of French law codes. Faced with a confusing and contradictory tangle of laws developed over centuries under the old monarchy, the revolutionary governments of the 1790s had declared in principle that French law needed to be rationalized and standardized as part of the great reorganization of the country into a single, undivided nation. Napoleon carried the principle into practice.

The most important new code was the Civil Code of 1804, later renamed the **Napoleonic Code.** In it the revolutionary principles of equality before the law and security of persons from arbitrary arrest were reaffirmed. Private property rights were guaranteed, as well as the principle of a free-market economy in which individual economic initiative was encouraged. Workers' rights to form unions or other associations were again prohibited as a form of interference with market forces.

The code reversed many of the gains women had made during the 1790s. Laws relating to families upheld patriarchal authority; the male head of household stood over all other family members and controlled their property. The revolutionary equality between spouses in filing for divorce was revoked, giving men more grounds for divorce than women. Many of these provisions remained a part of French law until 1965. They reflected Napoleon's view that women belonged in the private sphere, where, he said, men would protect them and make them happy.

Overall, Napoleon's reworking of the revolutionary legacy, culminating in the Civil Code, promoted what he called "order." In 1789, the rallying cry of revolutionaries had been "liberty." In 1793, the sansculottes had called for "equality," and the Committee of Public Safety had promoted "fraternity" to unite citizens against internal and external enemies. Now liberty, equality, and fraternity were condemned as excuses for **anarchy.** Under Napoleon, democratic politics ceased. Freedom of speech was silenced by censorship and police surveillance. Society was dominated by the **notables,** a class of landowners created by Napoleon from the middle classes and the old nobility. Along with civilian administrators and army generals, they were the real powers in France. Once again, French national identity was based on the Old Regime model of a pyramid with a small and powerful elite at the top.

In 1802, at the height of his popularity, Napoleon modified the constitution to make himself consul for life. In 1803, after a peace that had lasted a mere fourteen months, France and England went to war again. Britain wanted more access to continental markets for its manufactured goods, while France feared English preeminence at sea. Soon afterward, Napoleon moved closer toward hereditary rule. In December 1804, he summoned Pius VII from Rome to preside over a coronation ceremony in Paris in which he became Emperor Napoleon I. When it was time to place the new imperial crown on his head, Napoleon crowned himself, asserting the separation of the state from the church. He then whispered to his brother, "If only our

Napoleonic Code Code of civil law implemented in 1804, applied first to France and then to French-occupied territories in Europe.

anarchy Absence of government, marked by disorder and lawlessness.

notables Elite group of large-scale landowners created by Napoleon.

Jacques-Louis David painted this official representation of Napoleon's coronation as emperor. Having crowned himself, Napoleon now crowns his wife Josephine. Pope Pius VII, seated, is simply one of the spectators. The painting emphasizes two of Napoleon's governing principles: the separation of church and state and the subordination of women to men. *(Réunion des Musées Nationaux/Art Resource, NY)*

father could see us now!" The new emperor modeled his court on the old one at Versailles and started referring to Louis XVI as "my uncle." In 1808, he created a new imperial nobility. Thus, the republican state was eroded, but never completely destroyed: the Napoleonic Code was still in place; legislatures met, even though they had little to do; a written constitution still existed; and changes in the regime were carefully submitted to popular ratification in special elections.

The Napoleonic Empire, 1804–1815

⬇ What did Napoleon demand from the men who administered his empire and its satellite states?

⬇ What impact did Napoleon's rule have on Europeans outside of France?

From 1803 until 1815, France was again at war with the rest of Europe. Beginning in 1805, France won spectac-ular victories on the continent, crushing Austria, Prussia, and Russia and occupying most of Germany. Conquered territories were added to the ever-expanding French Empire. In 1807, when he controlled Europe from the Atlantic to Russia, Napoleon attempted the economic ruin of his sole remaining enemy, Great Britain. But his policy of closing this vast territory to British manufactured goods stirred up resistance. In 1812, Napoleon invaded Russia, a disaster from which he never recovered. In 1814, a renewed coalition defeated Napoleon and drove him from his throne. Napoleon's empire was short lived, but it had a lasting impact.

Renewed War on the Continent

In 1805, continental war broke out again when Austria and Russia joined Great Britain, at war with France since 1803. Austria was soon defeated for the third time, and the Holy Roman Empire formally came to an end when Napoleon decreed its demise.

But the British navy defeated the French navy in the Battle of **Trafalgar** off the Spanish coast. Admiral Nelson, who had destroyed Napoleon's fleet in Egypt, destroyed it once again in this battle, losing his life in the process. From now on, Britain enjoyed unchallenged control of the high seas and imposed a blockade on Napoleon's ports to stop France's international trade. On the continent, Napoleon fared better; Prussia, which joined the Allies in 1806, was quickly defeated, and in 1807 Russia, too, succumbed.

Emperor Napoleon, now at the height of his power, redrew the map of much of Europe. All the states in the old Holy Roman Empire, except Prussia and Austria, were made French allies and consolidated in the **Confederation of the Rhine**, a prelude to German unification in the nineteenth century. An independent Poland reemerged as the **Grand Duchy of Warsaw**. To organize his vast territory, Napoleon used the techniques of the Directory: the creation of satellite states, now called kingdoms instead of republics, and annexation to France. Napoleon made his numerous brothers and sisters the heads of the satellite kingdoms or relied on close confidants to rule them—Joseph Bonaparte went to Spain, Louis to the kingdom of Holland, and Jerome to the new kingdom of Westphalia. Napoleon expected unquestioning obedience from them.

Rulers were to remake their kingdoms using France as a model. Written constitutions formed the basis of government. The Napoleonic Code was imposed, sweeping away the society of estates and orders and establishing the principle of equality before the law, careers open to talent, and trial by jury. Local legislatures usually controlled taxation rates, which were lower than those in France. Religious discrimination ended, and Jews were admitted to full citizenship. This last reform was particularly important in Holland and Germany, where there were large Jewish populations. Except in Russia, serfdom was abolished. Government administration was to be based on the scientific principles employed in France. Military conscription was imposed everywhere, and local people were required to pay the costs of French troops stationed in their territory. Napoleon discouraged concessions to local customs, since he thought that the French model of government was universally applicable. Many of these reforms outlasted the Napoleonic period, particularly in Holland, Germany, and northern Italy. Even Prussia and Austria adopted some of them, in hopes of combating the French challenge by strengthening their states.

Napoleon's stunning victories between 1805 and 1807 were the result of his skill as a general and his ability to raise huge armies by means of conscription.

In 1793, France had relied on the mass mobilization of the nation to build up the army to 750,000 men. By 1797, however, the army had fallen to about half this number because of death and desertion. The Directory, therefore, resorted to annual conscription. Napoleon continued the new practice. Some 2 million French men were conscripted between 1799 and 1814. At first, the draft was fiercely resisted. Since married men were exempt, potential draftees rushed to marry, sometimes taking wives as old as eighty. If marriage was not an option, men cut off their trigger fingers or hacked away at their shins and testicles to induce debilitating infections. Slowly, however, through persistence and power, the state made its policy stick. By 1806, when the war against Prussia began, the battle against the draft was over; from then on the French submitted to this permanent new intrusion into their lives. Overall, in both the revolutionary and Napoleonic wars, about 916,000 men were lost to the French army, half from death and half from desertion.

In late 1806, Napoleon undertook economic warfare against Great Britain. This program, the **Continental System,** closed European ports in French-dominated areas to British merchant shipping. Napoleon reasoned that Britain's economy would slump and its government revenues decline when its traditional continental markets were taken away. As a bonus, French manufacturers would benefit from a market now closed to British competition. But the system's success depended on the closure of *all* ports, and here the problems began. While France itself could be brought into compliance, in the satellite states merchants who had profited from trade with Britain protested. Even Napoleon's siblings, under pressure from their subjects, complained. The emperor's response was to annex more territory to France: the kingdom of Holland was absorbed in 1810, as was the north German coast. When Pope Pius VII refused to join the system and excommunicated Napoleon, the pope was put under house arrest and then deported to France, where he lived as Napoleon's prisoner. Italy as far south as Rome was annexed. Pius's imprisonment

Trafalgar Naval battle fought 1805 in which the British destroyed the French navy and gained unchallenged control of the high seas.

Confederation of the Rhine Napoleon's union of all German states except Prussia and Austria.

Grand Duchy of Warsaw Napoleon's restored independent Poland.

Continental System Closure of all French-controlled ports to British merchant shipping initiated by Napoleon in 1807 as a form of economic warfare.

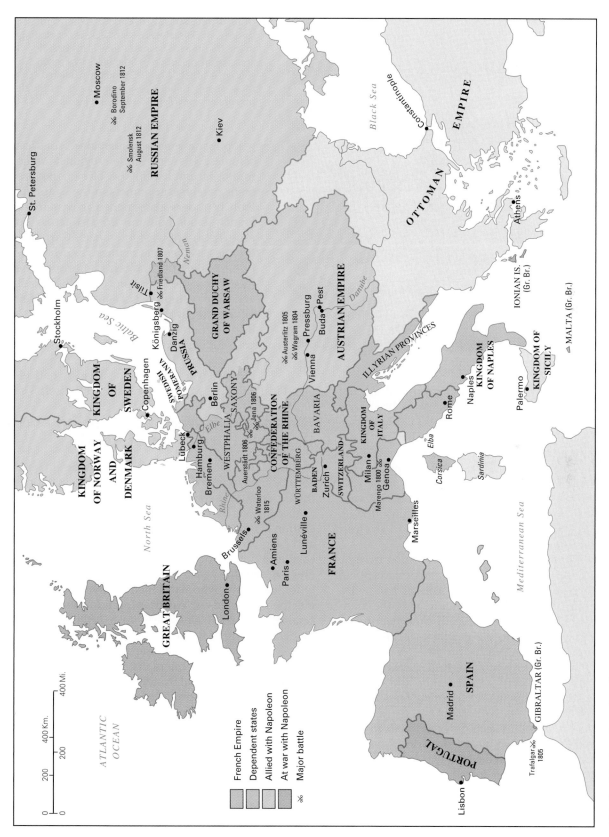

MAP 19.2 Napoleonic Europe, 1810 By 1810, France was an empire whose boundaries had absorbed many small states to its east. Other states were French allies or dependencies. In all of Europe only Britain, Portugal, Sardinia, Sicily, and the Ottoman Empire remained independent. Napoleon's domination of Europe rivaled Charlemagne's empire and the empire of ancient Rome.

RUSSIAN EMPIRE

Moscow

Borodino September 1812

Smolensk August 1812

Kiev

Black Sea

Constantinople

OTTOMAN EMPIRE

St. Petersburg

Neman

Friedland 1807

Tilsit

Königsberg

Danzig

GRAND DUCHY OF WARSAW

AUSTRIAN EMPIRE

Danube

Stockholm

Baltic Sea

PRUSSIA

SWEDISH POMERANIA

Copenhagen

KINGDOM OF SWEDEN

Berlin

SAXONY

Jena 1806

Austerlitz 1805

Wagram 1804

Pressburg

Vienna

Buda Pest

ILLYRIAN PROVINCES

IONIAN IS. (Gr. Br.)

Athens

MALTA (Gr. Br.)

KINGDOM OF NORWAY AND DENMARK

Lübeck

Hamburg

Bremen

WESTPHALIA

Auerstädt 1806

Elbe

CONFEDERATION OF THE RHINE

BAVARIA

WÜRTTEMBERG

BADEN

Zurich

SWITZERLAND

KINGDOM OF ITALY

Milan

Genoa

Marengo 1800

KINGDOM OF NAPLES

Rome

Naples

Palermo

KINGDOM OF SICILY

Elba

Corsica

Sardinia

North Sea

Rhine

Waterloo 1815

Brussels

Amiens

Paris

Lunéville

FRANCE

Marseilles

Mediterranean Sea

GREAT BRITAIN

London

ATLANTIC OCEAN

400 Mi.

400 Km.

200

200

0

0

SPAIN

Madrid

GIBRALTAR (Gr. Br.)

PORTUGAL

Lisbon

Trafalgar 1805

French Empire

Dependent states

Allied with Napoleon

At war with Napoleon

Major battle

In 1810, the Spanish artist Francisco Goya produced "The Disasters of War," a series of etchings in the tradition of Jacques Callot. This brutal scene of an execution of Spaniards by French solders is titled "And It Cannot Be Changed," thus echoing Callot's pessimism about ending the horrors of war. *(Foto Marburg/Art Resource, NY)*

veloping new markets in Spain's American colonies, where regulations against foreign traders crumbled in the face of government paralysis at home. On the continent, French traders also opened new markets. French goods now moved east across Europe instead of west to France's Caribbean colonies, as they had before 1789. Manufacturers in Belgium and central Europe benefited from the exclusion of British goods and the development of a unified continental market. In Poland, however, the loss of British grain markets caused an economic crisis for landlords and their peasants. Overall, French trade advanced under Napoleon, but it never reached the level it had enjoyed in 1789. That would not return until the 1830s.

shocked European Catholics and produced a great wave of sympathy for the suffering pope. Britain responded to the Continental System by tightening its blockade on French-controlled ports. The French responded by authorizing privateers to slip through the blockade and harass British merchant shipping. The new United States, a self-declared neutral in the war, was hurt by the blockades and saw its trade with both France and Britain decline. Eventually, in 1812, the United States declared war on Britain in an effort to assert its economic independence.

As military intervention and annexation became the means of enforcing the Continental System, Spain entered a period of crisis. Ever since it had withdrawn from the war against France in 1795, the country had been unstable. In 1808, a French army of occupation was sent to close Spain's ports to the British, and Napoleon put his brother Joseph on the Spanish throne. But a riot in Madrid quickly spread into open rebellion across the country, and cries for Spanish national unity in the face of the French occupier grew ever more insistent. More and more French troops were required to keep order. While Napoleon denounced the "Spanish ulcer," the British saw it as an opportunity to reopen the land war against France and sent an expeditionary force to aid the rebels.

Despite the problems in Spain, the Continental System was a considerable success. Although British overseas trade never collapsed, it was badly damaged. At the worst of the crisis, Britain survived only by de-

The Austrian War of Liberation and the French Invasion of Russia

In late 1808, Napoleon marched into Spain with 150,000 men to take direct command of French forces there. Austria seized the opportunity to attack France, urging all Germans to rise up in a "war of liberation." Few German states responded, however, and Napoleon had time to return to France, march east, and defeat Austria for the fourth time. Shortly after signing the peace treaty, Napoleon divorced his wife, Josephine, who had failed to give him an heir. He then married an Austrian archduchess, Marie-Louise, who soon gave birth to a little Napoleon, named the king of Rome.

In Russia, far to the east, Tsar **Alexander I** watched these events and laid his plans. Though required to enforce the Continental System on his coasts, he now believed Russia was strong enough to shake off French domination. He therefore withdrew from the French alliance and resumed trade with the British. Napoleon was furious and began preparing to invade Russia. In June 1812, he moved east with a force of 650,000 troops

Alexander I (r. 1801–1825) Russian emperor defeated by Napoleon who then broke with the French, provoking the Russian campaign of 1812.

drawn from twenty countries. It was the largest single army in the field that Europe had ever seen.

Throughout the summer, French troops marched farther and farther into Russia, as the Russians withdrew, since their army numbered only about 200,000. In August, they fought Napoleon at Smolensk, and in early September, they fought again at Borodino, seventy-five miles west of Moscow. These were the bloodiest battles of the revolutionary and Napoleonic wars. After Smolensk, wagons were piled high with amputated arms and legs. Wounded and survivors alike crumpled as food supplies ran out, while hundreds of men died by the roadside from exposure as they slipped into vodka-induced comas. Battle dead and wounded from both sides at Borodino stood at 75,000, including 47 French generals.

Technically, the French won at Borodino, and the road to Moscow lay open. When Napoleon arrived there in mid-September, however, he found the city practically deserted; once again the Russians had retreated. The French stayed in Moscow for six weeks, waiting for Alexander to sue for peace. But the tsar, in his palace in St. Petersburg, refused. In the meantime, a fire, perhaps started by the Russians, destroyed most of Moscow. With his army exhausted and badly depleted, and with no hope of adequate winter quarters in a burned-out city, Napoleon ordered a retreat to Germany. What happened next is the stuff of legends: the troops stumbled westward, harassed continuously by Russian units and frozen by the bitter winter that arrived in November. Only 15 percent of Napoleon's army made it back to Germany. For Napoleon, defeat in Russia was the beginning of the end.

Europe's Defeat of Napoleon

In 1813, Austria and Prussia, subsidized by Great Britain, reentered the war after reforming their armies and introducing a French-style draft. Napoleon realized that the next campaign was the one he had to win. The conscription machine in France and the other imperial territories pressed down harder than ever; by the summer of 1813, the emperor had raised an army of 400,000, including 100,000 rounded-up French draft evaders and deserters. In October, it engaged the Allies in eastern Germany. Napoleon lost and began to retreat westward. As he drew back, the Germans finally rose up in an anti-French revolt, rallying behind their traditional rulers. Years of taxes, conscription, and the hardships of the Continental System were taking their toll. In addition, the French ideal of a united nation of citizens had spread to the occupied peoples. Now they countered the French with their own nationalist fervor.

After he returned to Paris, Napoleon tried once again to rally his generals and ministers, but they refused to fight on. Finally, in April 1814, he abdicated. The Allies marched into Paris, with Alexander I of Russia at their head. Not far behind was Louis XVI's brother, who had fled France twenty-five years earlier. He was installed as King **Louis XVIII**. Louis XVI's son, who had died in a Paris prison in 1795, was thus honored as Louis XVII.

The Allies exiled Napoleon to the island of Elba, off the coast of Italy not far from his native Corsica. But Napoleon outwitted them one last time. In 1799, he had slipped away from his enemies in Egypt, and now he did it again, secretly setting sail for the south of France. Louis XVIII sent troops to intercept the ex-emperor, but they joined him instead; once again, his fame as a commander carried the day. The new king then fled to Belgium, and Napoleon triumphantly reentered Paris, where he was to rule again for a **Hundred Days**. He quickly reorganized the government and prepared yet again for battle. Miraculously, the conscription machine pulled up 100,000 men. On June 18, 1815, Napoleon engaged his old enemies at **Waterloo** in present-day Belgium, where he was defeated for the last time by an English general, the Duke of Wellington, leading a coalition of Prussians, Austrians, and Russians. Once again Napoleon abdicated, Louis XVIII entered Paris, and Napoleon was sent into exile. This time, however, the Allies shipped him into the far South Atlantic, to the island of St. Helena, where he died in 1821 at the age of fifty-two.

Throughout his years in exile in Allied lands, Louis XVIII had promised a full restoration of the prerevolutionary monarchy if he returned to France as king. But that proved to be impossible; too much had changed since 1789. He therefore issued a Constitutional Charter, which bore a marked resemblance to the Constitution of 1791, as the basis for his rule. The one thing from the past that Louis wanted was a coronation like the one held in 1775 for his brother. But it never took place. The king was old, Rheims was far away, and the revolutionaries had destroyed most of the sacred implements used in the ceremony.

Louis XVIII   (r. 1814–1824) Younger brother of Louis XVI of France who became king after Napoleon's defeat.

Hundred Days   Period in 1815 of Napoleon's briefly restored rule in France between his return from exile on Elba and his permanent exile on St. Helena.

Waterloo   Napoleon's last battle, fought in Belgium in 1815 against an international coalition headed by the British Duke of Wellington.

Summary

Review Questions

↑ From 1789 to 1815, what changed and what remained the same in French political, social, and religious life?

↑ How did revolutionaries and opponents of the Revolution in France define their collective identities and those of their enemies?

↑ What was the impact of revolutionary France and Napoleonic rule on Europe?

At one level, the era of the French Revolution and Napoleon was characterized by political instability as regimes came and went in a matter of years. From 1775 to 1815, France moved from an absolute monarchy to a constitutional one, and then to a republic, an empire, and back to a restored monarchy. Beginning in 1792, the wars between France and conservative Europe deeply influenced the policies of these shifting regimes. A similar instability affected the territories France occupied, as lands became sister republics and then kingdoms, or were annexed outright. On another level, however, it was clear by 1815 that despite political instability, the revolutionary and Napoleonic years had brought about fundamental changes in three areas of European life.

First, the democratic experiments of the 1790s, despite their limitations and failures, introduced a new model for political life that was lasting. Frenchmen, endowed with inalienable human rights, became citizens of the state and participants in government. Even Napoleon, who detested this democratic world, could not quite stamp it out. Both at home and in the occupied lands, he relied on written constitutions to give legitimacy to his regime, recognizing the necessity of legislatures and popular voting. Although women did not achieve the same level of political participation that men did, demands for their inclusion, first made by revolutionaries like Olympe de Gouges, were to remain central to political debate in the years after 1815.

Second, the old society of orders and estates based on privilege, abolished first in France and then in Napoleonic Europe, never really returned. The inhabitants of a country were constituted as citizens of a nation. Even Napoleon's reintroduction of nobility did little to alter this new form of society. The notables ignored the old distinctions between commoners and nobles, and the revolutionary ideal of careers open to talent, which had so benefited Napoleon himself in the 1790s, persisted. In the end, the occupied peoples adopted the nationalist ideals of France and then turned them against the French.

Finally, the state's power had grown enormously. The abolition of orders and estates had swept away institutions like the Parlement of Paris that had stood between the state and its subjects. The state had also freed itself from its attachment to the Catholic Church. The process of centralized state control, begun by the Committee of Public Safety, was continued after 1799. Both at home and abroad, Napoleon used the reorganization of France into standardized units to extend the state's reach into ordinary people's lives. The chief sign of the state's expanded power was conscription. The ideals of the Revolution—broad political participation, the end of privilege and the beginning of merit-based advancement, and the increased power of the state—have had repercussions throughout the world.

← **Thinking Back, Thinking Ahead** →

How were the English revolution of the 1640s and the French Revolution of the 1790s similar to and different from each other? Keep these revolutions, and this question, in mind when you get to the Russian Revolution of 1917.

ECHO

"Left" and "Right"

Today when we speak about the political "left" and "right," we use terms that originated accidentally in the early years of the French Revolution. When the deputies to the Estates-General assembled at Versailles, the king and his court sat on a platform at one end of the meeting room. The orders of the clergy and the nobility sat directly in front of the royal party, while the Third Estate was crammed into a space at the back end of the hall, separated by a low railing from everyone else. This organization of the meeting space symbolized the king's belief in a hierarchically arranged society of estates and orders.

After the Third Estate became the National Assembly, the meeting hall was rearranged to eliminate the separation of the three estates. Now the room had benches placed in an oval so there could be no more "front" for privileged people and "back" for commoners. Nevertheless, a new politically charged use of this space quickly developed. In the middle of the oval was the desk of the Assembly's president. The patriots, who had created the National Assembly, wanted to be in contact with each other, so they sat as a group on benches to the left of the president. The patriots' opponents symbolized their political differences by sitting to the president's right. Political preference, in combination with the configuration of the meeting space, led to the accidental identification of "left" (of the president) as the place for liberals who favored thoroughgoing revolutionary change and "right" (of the president) as the place for conservatives who wanted less change.

When the National Assembly moved to Paris, the deputies met in a converted indoor riding stable. This space was long and narrow. The desks of the president and his assistants were placed in the middle of the hall, where they took up almost all available room. This meant that the only places where deputies could sit were either on the president's left or his right. Once again, the patriots sat on the left, while their opponents gravitated to the right.

When the National Convention convened, the radical Jacobins occupied the upper rows of benches, again to the left of the president, and became the Mountain. Noncommitted deputies occupied lower rows and became the Swamp. Here was a new configuration with potential political meaning—"high" seats for thoroughgoing revolutionaries and "low" ones for moderates. But "high" and "low" never replaced "left" and "right" as political markers. These have lasted to this day.

Suggested Readings

Censer, Jack R., and Lynn Hunt. *Liberty, Equality, Fraternity: Exploring the French Revolution.* University Park: Pennsylvania State University Press, 2001. A recent introduction.

Holtman, Robert B. *The Napoleonic Revolution.* Philadelphia: J. B.Lippincott Company, 1967. A clear account of Napoleon's reorganization of France.

Hufton, Olwyn. *Women and the Limits of Citizenship in the French Revolution.* Toronto: University of Toronto Press, 1992. A recent study of women's gains and losses during the revolutionary decade.

McManners, John. *The French Revolution and the Church.* New York: Harper and Row, 1969. A short but masterful history of the relations between French Catholics and the Revolution.

Palmer, R. R. *Twelve Who Ruled.* Princeton, N.J.: Princeton University Press, 1941. A classic account of the Committee of Public Safety.

Tackett, Timothy. *When the King Took Flight.* Cambridge, Mass.: Harvard University Press, 2003. A vivid account of the king's attempt to flee France and its consequences.

Woolf, Stuart. *Napoleon's Integration of Europe.* New York: Routledge, 1991. A useful work on the Napoleonic empire.

Websites

A useful site with much information, **Internet Modern History Sourcebook: IV, American and French Revolutions,** at www.fordham.edu/halsall/mod/modsbook2.html#revol18c

Another useful site, **Liberty, Equality, Fraternity: Exploring the French Revolution,** at www.chnm.gmu.edu/revolution/

A fun site with information on reenactments as well as historical material, **Napoleon.Org,** at www.napoleon.org/en/home.asp

CHAPTER 20

Restoration and Reform: Conservative and Liberal Europe, 1814–1847

1500 B.C.E.	1000 B.C.E.	500 B.C.E.	1 B.C.E./1 C.E.

1815
Napoleon is finally
defeated at Waterloo

1814
Congress of
Vienna opens

1817
Wartburg Festival celebrates
German history, life, and culture

1810	1815	1820	1825

Europe After the Congress of Vienna, 1815
The Congress of Vienna redrew the map of Europe in an effort to strengthen conservative governments. What changes can you see comparing this map with Europe before the Napoleonic Wars (page 561) and in 1918 (page 743)?

ATLANTIC
OCEAN

KINGDOM OF
SWEDEN AND
NORWAY

Oslo

Helsinki

St. Petersburg

Stockholm

Moscow

SCOTLAND

North
Sea

Baltic
Sea

Riga

RUSSIAN
EMPIRE

UNITED KINGDOM
OF GREAT BRITAIN
AND IRELAND

Dublin

Manchester

IRELAND

DENMARK

Copenhagen

SCHLESWIG

HOLSTEIN

Danzig

ENGLAND

WALES

KINGDOM OF THE
NETHERLANDS

HANOVER

London

Amsterdam

KINGDOM OF PRUSSIA

Berlin

Warsaw

KINGDOM OF
POLAND
(Russia)

Kiev

— Boundary of German Confederation

Antwerp

Waterloo

Göttingen

Cologne

SAXONY

Frankfurt

Prague

BOHEMIA

GALICIA

Cracow

UKRAINE

Luxembourg

Paris

LORRAINE

ALSACE

BADEN

BAVARIA

WÜRTTEMBURG

Munich

Vienna

AUSTRIAN EMPIRE

BESSARABIA

FRANCE

SWITZERLAND

LOMBARDY

PIEDMONT

Milan

VENETZIA

Venice

Buda

Pest

MOLDAVIA

HUNGARY

WALLACHIA

CROATIA

Black
Sea

PARMA

MODENA

PORTUGAL

Madrid

Marseilles

LUCCA

TUSCANY

PAPAL
STATES

SERBIA

Belgrade

Danube

BOSNIA

BULGARIA

Elba

KINGDOM OF
PIEDMONT-
SARDINIA

SPAIN

Corsica
(Fr.)

Rome

Istanbul

NAPLES

ALBANIA

OTTOMAN

EMPIRE

Adriatic
Sea

GILBRALTAR
(Gr. Br.)

Sardinia

KINGDOM
OF THE
TWO SICILIES

GREECE

Athens

MOROCCO

ALGIERS

TUNIS

Mediterranean

Sicily

Malta
(Gr. Br.)

Sea

0   200   400 Km.

0   200   400 Mi.

500 C.E.   1000 C.E.   1500 C.E.   2000 C.E.

1830 Revolutions break out in Paris, Brussels, and Warsaw

1831 Independent Belgium is established

1832 Reform Bill in Britain expands suffrage

1845
Irish potato famine begins

1833
Factory Act in Britain
restricts child labor

1837 Victoria becomes Queen of England

1838
Anti–Corn Law League is established

1846
Corn Laws are abolished

1830   1835   1840   1845   1850

Choice Choice Choice

The Grimm Brothers

For Americans, the Grimm brothers are most famous for their collection of fairy tales. But their role in helping create a standardized German language went far beyond editing volumes of children's stories. Together they helped define the grammar and vocabulary of the standard German spoken today—a pioneering feat of linguistic standardization that would be copied in other countries and equal in significance to Martin Luther's translating the New Testament into German three centuries earlier. (akg-images)

The Grimm Brothers Begin Work on Their German Dictionary

In 1838, Jacob and Wilhelm Grimm were middle-aged professors—expelled from their university. They were well known in academic circles for their many path-breaking studies in the field of linguistics and German philology, the study of words and texts. Individually and together, they had published dozens of studies, including a book on German mythology, a grammar of the German language, and collections of German stories, fairy tales, and myths. And linguists speak of "Grimm's Law" to describe a regular shift in consonant sounds (*p* : *v* : *f*) in the development of European languages; for example, *pater* in Latin became *Vater* in German and *father* in English. The Grimms' analysis revealed connections among languages derived from Indo-European roots.

The Grimms' collection of German fairy tales was first published in 1812—just as Napoleon was on his way to Moscow. They oversaw the collection of hundreds of stories, often venturing into villages to hear the tales that had been passed down orally from generation to generation. By writing down these narratives for the first time, the Grimm brothers saw themselves as carrying out a patriotic duty to preserve German folk traditions. By the end of the century, these stories would be published in hundreds of editions and dozens of languages.

The Grimms' work aimed to elevate the prestige of German culture and language. They wanted to prove that German culture was every bit as rich as the cultures of unified nations such as England and France. Throughout the century, similar research with the same patriotic purpose would be carried out by Russian, Hungarian, Irish, and Slavic folklorists. In a similar way, the American Noah Webster published his *American Dictionary of the English Language* in 1828 to emphasize the legitimacy of American English. All these early nationalists believed that the development of individual national cultures contributed directly to the enrichment of world culture.

The Grimm brothers' political views combined liberalism and nationalism. When, in 1837, the new king of Hannover (the German kingdom where their university, Georg-August-Universität, was located) cast aside the constitution in effect since 1833, the Grimm brothers, along with five other Göttingen professors, protested. The "Göttingen Seven," as they came to be known, refused to swear an oath to the despotic new king. For daring to stand up for their political principles, they were expelled from the university. Their fame as scholars was now enhanced by admiration for them as political martyrs, and a public collection helped fund their continuing research.

In the same year as their expulsion, the Grimm brothers embarked on their most ambitious project of all: a German dictionary that would "contain the endless richness of our fatherland's language from Luther to Goethe." The Grimms aimed not just to compile definitions of German words but to document the history of the German language and the changing usage of words from late medieval times to the present day. Their *Deutsches Wörterbuch* (*German Dictionary*) was a monumental undertaking. The work went forward slowly, and the first volume (*A* to *Biermolke*) was published after sixteen years of work. Wilhelm died in 1859, a year before the second volume appeared. The third volume (*E* to *Forsche*) appeared in 1862, one year before Jacob's death. The massive project started by the Grimm brothers was continued by their students and was not completed until the early 1970s. In the twenty-first century, this enormous historical dictionary remains one of the marvels of nineteenth-century philology and a valuable research tool for specialists in German language and literature.

Introduction

In the decades after Napoleon's final defeat, Europeans like the Grimms lived in the shadow of the French Revolution and its ideologies. In 1815, it appeared that the French Revolution had failed. Monarchs held fast to power throughout Europe, from London to St. Petersburg and even in Paris, where a successor to the Bourbons occupied the throne. The peace conference ending the Napoleonic Wars, held in Vienna, established a conservative political system aimed specifically at preventing the spread of liberal and revolutionary ideas. However, appearances were deceiving, as the French Revolution had changed European politics forever. The revolutionary ideals of "Liberty, Equality, Fraternity" continued to inspire active political participation. These ideas dominated the development of political ideologies during these decades.

These ideologies were conservatism, liberalism, and nationalism. Conservatives aimed to retain the power of monarchs, despite the fact that few still believed in the divine right of kings. Liberals called for parliaments, constitutionalism, civil rights, the rule of law, and a withdrawal of the state from economic matters. Nationalists denounced kings and princes, naming the nation—that is, the entire people—as the ultimate authority in politics. Until 1848, liberals and nationalists often joined forces; most liberals were nationalists. Nationalist movements in the Balkan Peninsula attempted to gain independence from Ottoman rule, and the Greeks succeeded. In central Europe, German and Italian nationalists sought to bring together existing small states into large, unified nation-states. Later in the century they would succeed.

Paralleling and crisscrossing these national movements was a literary and artistic movement known as Romanticism, which championed the individual human spirit. The Romantics rejected the cold rationality of the Enlightenment and looked back in longing to the preindustrial, deeply religious world of the Middle Ages. They celebrated the strong and dynamic individual who—like Napoleon—could change the world. Romantic thinkers and artists also challenged social conventions of the day, openly calling for more freedom in love and sexuality, even as they experimented with new forms of artistic and poetic expression. The Romantics' mystical brand of Christianity clashed with conventional religious institutions and dogmas.

While most governments in the post-Napoleonic period were conservative, the ideas of the French Revolution continued to influence politics and culture. A series of uprisings in 1830 realized some national and constitutional ambitions, while in Great Britain political reform was achieved through a series of parliamentary acts. Even in conservative-dominated central Europe, liberal and nationalist ideas were spreading and gaining in strength. In 1848, these new ideologies would burst forth in a wave of revolutionary uprisings across the European continent.

The Old Order and New Challenges

↓ What were the main aims and outcomes of the Congress of Vienna?
↓ How did Romantic poets and artists challenge the existing social order?

A quarter century of revolution and war was brought to a close by the defeat of Napoleon at Waterloo in June 1815. But even before Napoleon's defeat, monarchs and diplomats from all over Europe were meeting in the Austrian capital to hammer out a peace

Chronology

1814–1815	Congress of Vienna restores prerevolutionary rulers
1815	Napoleon is defeated at Waterloo; British Parliament passes Corn Laws
1817	Wartburg Festival
1818	Mary Wollstonecraft Shelley publishes *Frankenstein*
1819	Peterloo Massacre in Manchester kills eleven, wounds hundreds
1821	Greek War of Independence begins
1823	United States issues Monroe Doctrine
1825	Nicholas I becomes tsar
1828	Noah Webster publishes his *American Dictionary of the English Language*
1829	Catholic Emancipation Act furthers religious tolerance in Britain
1830	Greece achieves independence; Revolutions break out in Paris and Brussels
1832	Reform Bill in Britain expands suffrage; Giuseppe Mazzini forms Young Italy
1833	Slavery Abolition Act initiates emancipation of slaves in British Empire; Serbia wins independence
1837	Victoria becomes queen of England
1838	Grimm brothers begin work on their *German Dictionary*
1838	Richard Cobden forms Anti–Corn Law League in Manchester
1845–1849	Potato famine sweeps Ireland
1846	Corn Laws are abolished
1847	Factory Act in Britain reduces working hours for women and children
1848	Revolutions topple governments from Paris to Budapest

settlement. Presided over by the Austrian prime minister Prince Clemens von Metternich, this would be a conservative peace, guided by the principle of legitimacy. The Congress of Vienna restored prerevolutionary rulers and drew borders that lasted into the twentieth century. Metternich wanted to restore, as much as possible, the preindustrial, absolutist social and political order of the eighteenth century, but he was realistic enough to recognize that he could not set the political clock back to 1788. Instead, he aimed to prevent revolutionary outbreaks and to suppress the new ideologies of liberalism and nationalism by strengthening traditional rulers and the landowning nobility. Even as he did this, however, the new cultural and artistic movement called Romanticism was challenging the conventions of this conservative world.

The Congress of Vienna

After Napoleon's catastrophic Russian campaign of 1812, it was clear that his control of France was weakening. In 1814, as allied troops from Russia and the various German states marched into Paris, Napoleon was exiled—courteously sent to govern the pleasant island of Elba off the Italian coast. But the question of the postrevolutionary order in Europe was open. The **Congress of Vienna**, called by the Austrian prime minister **Clemens von Metternich** in mid-1814, aimed to set that order. Metternich was a brilliant and complex man who combined wit and charm with cold calculation. As representatives from all over Europe arrived in the Austrian capital, its grand palaces glittered with the gold braid of officers' uniforms and the jewels of diplomats' wives. There were so many festivities that one French prince quipped, "The Congress

Congress of Vienna (1814–1815) International meeting that redrew the European map and restored order after the Napoleonic Wars.

Clemens von Metternich (1773–1859) Austrian statesman, architect of the Congress of Vienna and the Congress System, foreign minister and then prime minister of Austria, 1809–1848.

In this painting from the early 1820s, Metternich gazes haughtily past the viewer, his rich clothing and self-assured posture reflecting the power he exerted in Austria and throughout Europe. The papers he holds in his left hand suggest that even while sitting for a painting he was engaged in important state business. *(The Royal Collection, © 2004 Her Majesty Queen Elizabeth II)*

danced," implying that little work was getting done. In fact, however, Metternich was working hard behind the scenes to make sure that the outcome of this first modern diplomatic gathering would reflect his conservative political principles. When the congress disbanded in 1815 a new, conservative, post-Napoleonic Europe had been established.

Besides Metternich, two other statesmen played important roles in the congress's work: the foreign minister of Great Britain, Robert Castlereagh, and Tsar Alexander I of Russia. Prussia's king Frederick William III seemed reluctant to press his concerns, perhaps remembering his military humiliation at the hands of Napoleon and salvation with Russian help. Surprisingly, even defeated France was allowed to send a representative, the cunning but utterly cynical survivor Charles Maurice de Talleyrand, once memorably described as "a piece of dung in a silk stocking."

Talleyrand cleverly exploited divisions among the Allies, particularly the widespread fear of growing Russian power, to gain better conditions for France. Castlereagh expressed no interest in territorial gain but aimed to restore a European balance of power in which no European state would ever again be able to dominate the continent. Tsar Alexander I hoped to extend Russian influence in Europe, while Metternich aimed to neutralize it. Talleyrand made the case that only a strong France could ensure each ally's goals.

Competing interests came to a head over the issue of Poland. Alexander felt that the partitions of Poland of the late eighteenth century had been immoral and wished to resurrect Poland in some way. More practically, he knew that a reconstituted Poland connected to Russia would considerably enhance Russian influence in central Europe. Understandably, Prussia and Austria opposed this extension of Russian power, though they agreed that Russia should be compensated for its important role in defeating Napoleon. This dispute almost split the congress apart, but in the end a compromise was reached. The kingdom of Poland (or **Congress Poland**) was established as an **autonomous** kingdom, with Alexander as king and Warsaw as its capital. While Russia gained the largest amount of Polish territory, millions of Poles continued to live in Prussia and Austria.

Talleyrand succeeded in keeping France from being punished. The Bourbons, in the person of Louis XVIII, were restored to France's throne, though not to absolute rule. The king was subject to a constitution and had to share power with a legislature. France had to give up lands occupied after 1795 and to pay a war **indemnity** but remained intact, an important player in European politics.

The German states and principalities that had fought against Napoleon were restored to their rulers, but their total number was reduced from around three hundred to thirty-nine. These ranged in size and importance from Prussia and Austria (the Habsburg Empire contained, of course, much non-German territory as well) to tiny Liechtenstein with only five

Congress Poland   Polish kingdom under the Russian tsar created at the Congress of Vienna (1815), enjoying until 1831 its own constitution, legislature, army, and bureaucracy.

autonomous   Self-governing but not entirely independent, usually in a certain region or for a certain ethnic/national group.

indemnity   Money or goods paid by the losing side after a war to compensate for the cost and damage of military action.

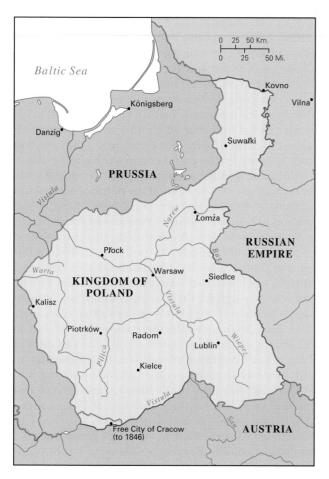

MAP 20.1   **Kingdom of Poland, 1815** The Kingdom of Poland was created at the Congress of Vienna and attached to the Russian Empire; the Russian tsar was also the king of Poland. The kingdom was ruled by a viceroy and a parliament in the capital, Warsaw. While most Poles lived in this so-called Congress Kingdom, millions continued to live under Austrian and Prussian rule.

thousand residents. These German states were loosely connected in a confederation but remained independent entities. Prussia gained the territory west of the Rhine River that Napoleon had incorporated into France. The Netherlands regained independence and acquired the southern provinces that had belonged to Spain and then to Austria. The Spanish Bourbons were restored to power in the person of King Ferdinand VII, who at first promised to work together with liberals, then turned on them and ruled as an absolute monarch. The congress restored the Papal States, including the city of Rome and covering much of central Italy, to the papacy. Thus, the diplomats gathered in Vienna redrew the map of Europe in a settlement that would set the political course for nearly a century.

Besides the territorial changes set down at the

Congress of Vienna, the powers also agreed to work together in concert—the so-called Concert of Europe—to prevent future military and civil disturbances. In this they were astonishingly successful: Europe would see no general war for nearly a century.

The Congress System

The four Great Powers of Prussia, Austria, Russia, and Great Britain (later joined by France) planned regular congresses, like the one at Vienna. Their **Congress System** aimed to root out revolution, even if it meant interference in the internal affairs of sovereign states. Such interference was considered less dangerous than allowing liberal and radical ideas to grow.

The guiding principle of the Congress System, urged by Tsar Alexander I, was to be the **Holy Alliance.** Alexander, very much under the influence of Christian mysticism, proposed to his fellow monarchs (not just those present in Vienna) that henceforth they model their policies on principles of the Christian faith. That this suggestion was greeted—at least in private—with a good deal of skepticism and even ridicule reveals that even Christian statesmen and monarchs considered international relations a realm distant from Christian morality. Castlereagh denounced the Holy Alliance as "nonsense," and Metternich called it "a loud-sounding nothing." Nonetheless, the diplomats were reluctant to offend the tsar and at least pretended to be sympathetic to Alexander's proposal.

In fact, the system's real guiding power was Metternich, who sought to limit Russian power in Europe, to expand Austrian influence, and to suppress all the ideas that had come out of the French Revolution. For Metternich, constitutionalism, civil rights, and the rule of law all amounted to the same thing—revolution. For a **multinational state** like Austria, nationalism was every bit as much of a threat as liberal ideas. The Congress System was a deeply conservative, even **reactionary,** set of policies that aimed mainly at preventing change.

> **Congress System**   Conservative political system put in place at the Congress of Vienna aiming to preserve peace and prevent the spread of nationalism and liberalism.
>
> **Holy Alliance**   Political agreement advocated by Tsar Alexander I at the Congress of Vienna calling for international relations to be based on Christian morals.
>
> **multinational state**   Country in which more than one ethnic group ("nation") resides—for example, the Habsburg, Ottoman, and Russian Empires.
>
> **reactionary**   Exceedingly conservative, wishing not only to prevent change but to retreat into the past.

From the start, however, there were serious practical problems with the Congress System. When the Greeks rebelled against their Ottoman rulers in 1821, setting off the Greek War of Independence, their cause was championed by Tsar Alexander of Russia, but Metternich and Castlereagh opposed any measures that could increase Russian power. The strain between British insular interests and the obligations of the Congress System proved too much for the already unstable Castlereagh; he took his own life in the midst of the Greek crisis. In the end, Metternich's savvy diplomacy prevented Russia from declaring war on the Ottoman Empire, and the Greeks had to wait another decade for independence.

Castlereagh's suicide pointed to a fundamental contradiction between British interests and European unity in the form of the Congress System. Following more than twenty years of warfare on the continent, the British were extremely reluctant to get involved in European affairs, especially in military action. When, in 1823, France intervened against a more liberal order in Spain, Britain openly broke with the alliance. Across the Atlantic, the United States also sought to guard against European intervention. President James Monroe issued what became known as the Monroe Doctrine, declaring that European meddling in the Western Hemisphere would not be tolerated. Alexander I died two years later, and his successor, Tsar **Nicholas I**, was much less interested in European affairs than his elder brother had been. From this point on, the Congress System became little more than a weapon in the hands of Metternich to suppress nationalist and revolutionary movements in central Europe and Italy.

The Age of Romanticism

In his attempts to root out nationalism, Metternich set himself against a new cultural movement that was sweeping Europe and would eventually, in a political form, tear apart Austria and the multinational states he sought to preserve. Metternich embraced tradition, privilege, and the existing political order. In contrast, the artistic and literary movement **Romanticism** embraced emotion, individuality, and new forms of expression. Romanticism was everything Metternich was not: mystical, antirational, and passionate. While often deeply religious, the Romantics opposed most existing institutions—even the church—and demanded freedom for human beings to realize their emotional, cultural, and even sexual potential. Reacting against what it saw as the cold rationality and dull universalism of the Enlightenment, Romanticism celebrated the human soul and mystical nature that connected directly

with God. The Romantics also rejected Enlightenment ideals such as parliamentarianism and codified legal systems. Their rejection of fundamental liberal politics, combined with religious mysticism, was probably one reason that many of them who did not die young ended up as extreme conservatives, as did William Wordsworth.

The Romantics saw God in nature, as Wordsworth conveyed in his poetry and **Caspar David Friedrich** expressed in his starkly beautiful landscapes. Wordsworth would wander lonely through England's Lake District and return to his cottage to write poems about the glories of nature—and the deeply felt sense of God's majesty in such things as daffodils, clouds, or landscapes. The German poet Friedrich von Hardenberg, better known as Novalis, portrayed man, woman, nature, and God as merged in an infinite unity. Romantic art also sought out exotic localities, tempestuous nature, and common people as its subjects. In France, Eugène Delacroix's paintings showed exotic scenes (especially in northern Africa and the Muslim world), stormy seas, and his most famous painting of all—a bare-breasted Liberty leading the people to victory over their oppressors. One common aspect of nearly all Romantic art is a burning desire to overcome feelings of personal loneliness and alienation, to submerge individual identity in a cosmic whole combining human, natural, and divine elements.

The Romantics—and it is not by chance that most of these were poets or painters, not stockbrokers or college professors—rejected the Enlightenment's mechanical universe and its method of seeking the truth through studied observation, experimentation, and reason. They were profoundly disturbed by the idea of a clockwork universe in which human beings were just a cog. The most important aspects of life, they contended, cannot be understood by rational scientific experimentation. Rather, the irrational—powerful emotions, the sense of beauty, the ecstasy of love—makes us human. In "The Tables Turned," Wordsworth called on a friend to "quit your books," "Our

Nicholas I   (r. 1825–1855) Russian tsar noted for conservatism and his hatred for the political ideals of the French Revolution.

Romanticism   Literary and artistic movement of the late eighteenth and early nineteenth centuries that extolled artistic genius and opposed many traditional social conventions.

Caspar David Friedrich   (1774–1840) German artist whose landscapes often featured craggy mountains, mighty forests, and Romantic ruins that overwhelmed small human figures.

Caspar David Friedrich's paintings exemplify the romantic sensibility. Often, as in his "Wanderer Above a Sea of Fog" (1818) to the left, the lone human figures are overwhelmed by the rough and beautiful natural world. In "Abbey Surrounded by Oak Trees" (1809) to the right, the eerie image of craggy oak trees surrounding the ruins of a monastery in winter reflects the Romantic obsession with death and religion. *(left: Preussischer Kunstbesitz/Art Resource, NY; right: Galerie der Romantik, Berlin/akg-images)*

meddling intellect / Mis-shapes the beauteous forms of things—We murder to dissect." In the Romantic view, the scientific method can never fathom the mystery of life or answer fundamental moral questions such as why human beings are here, why we love, and why we suffer. The English poet John Keats, in his famous "Ode on a Grecian Urn," proclaimed: "'Beauty is truth, truth beauty,'—that is all / Ye know on earth, and all ye need to know."

Romantics also rejected the restraints of middle-class respectability. They mocked hardworking, narrow-minded pillars of society. Instead, they extolled the Romantic hero, a dashing figure who often ended tragically, like **Alexander Pushkin**'s Eugene Onegin and Lord Byron's Don Juan. The German poet Fried-

rich Schlegel praised sexual love even outside marriage in his poem *Lucinde*. Novalis's *Hymns to the Night* were inspired by a teenaged girl, though it is clear that his feelings for her were more spiritually exalted than physical. Intellectual women figured prominently in the Romantic movement as organizers of salons where Romantic writers gathered as well as writing themselves. Women like Dorothea (Veit) Schlegel and Mary Wollstonecraft Shelley (daughter of the early feminist Mary Wollstonecraft) worked as

Alexander Pushkin (1799–1837) Russian nobleman and poet considered Russia's national writer.

equal partners with their writer-husbands and published works of their own. In their art—and sometimes in their personal lives—the Romantics created a world where man and woman interacted in full equality, the female and the male principles supplementing and inspiring each other. The German writer Johann Wolfgang von Goethe, who had been a great influence on the Romantics, had concluded his epic poem, *Faust*: "The eternally feminine leads us forward." At the same time, the Romantics' conception of "artistic genius" took for granted that most people would not be able to understand or appreciate him—or her! The image of the starving and alienated artist so familiar to us today took on modern form with the Romantics.

Romanticism was an all-embracing philosophy of life that emphasized unity, organic growth, inspiration, and creative genius. While Romantics often combined their mystical longings for the unity of all nature and humanity with religious sentiments, they were rarely Christians in any conventional sense. Furthermore, their emphasis on creative genius bordered on blasphemy: geniuses became in their own way gods, creating new worlds. The established churches could hardly embrace such ideas, even from individuals who opposed the anticlerical Enlightenment. The Romantics were fundamentally **utopian**—visionaries who believed perfectibility was possible in human relationships and societies. But they lacked the detachment and willingness to compromise that are essential to achieving reform in the political arena. Even those Romantic figures like Friedrich Schlegel who wrote on political subjects were not successful in influencing contemporary politics.

Despite its fundamentally utopian nature, Romanticism had an important impact on future politics through its influence of nationalism. Nationalists, embracing the Romantic spirit, rejected universalism and glorified the individual—in this case, the individual language, culture, and nation. Like the Romantics, nationalists in the early nineteenth century rejected existing institutions and looked forward to a golden age in which not just French and German but also languages like Czech, Lithuanian, and Serbian would

utopian   (from Greek, "no place") Consisting of unrealistic attempts at reforming human life.

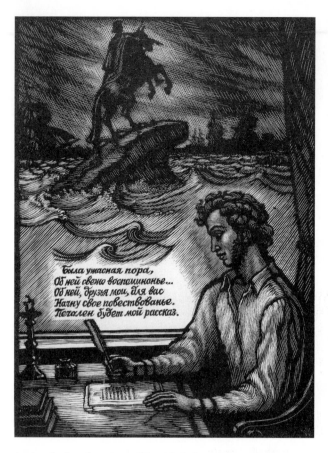

Active during the reign of Tsar Nicholas I, Russian poet Alexander Pushkin's works reflect the romantic temperament of the age. In this engraving he sits at his desk creating his historical poem "The Bronze Horseman" (1833) in which the famous statue of Peter the Great comes to life and pursues the poem's hero through the gloomy streets of St. Petersburg. (*The Visual Connection Archive*)

be cultivated and respected. The Romantics themselves welcomed the French Revolution in its early stages—a nation coming to power—though the bloodshed soon disillusioned them. For many, Napoleon Bonaparte resembled the ideal Romantic hero who swept away old institutions and ideas and brought the ideals of liberty, equality, and brotherhood to the lands he "liberated" (not "conquered").

In different forms, Romanticism spread across the European continent. The homeland of Romanticism is arguably either Germany or England, but Poles put forth their national poet, **Adam Mickiewicz**, or the patriotic composer and pianist **Frederic Chopin** as archetypical Romantics. Mickiewicz's poetic masterpiece, *Pan Tadeusz*, evokes a lost homeland and a world that no longer exists. Even today it is a rare

Pole who cannot recite the poem's first lines: "Lithuania [for Mickiewicz, a province of Poland], my homeland! You are like health; only he who has lost you can appreciate your true worth." Chopin was born in Warsaw but, like Mickiewicz, spent most of his life in France. His most famous works used traditional Polish folk melodies and musical forms. Both Chopin and Mickiewicz exemplify a fusing of Romanticism and nationalism. Among Russian writers, Pushkin exhibits Romantic strains, and even more typically Romantic are Mikhail Lermontov's rousing stories and poems of dashing young soldiers, beautiful maidens, unrequited love, and exotic locales along the Black Sea and in the Caucasus Mountains.

The Beginnings of Modern Ideology

↓ On what points did liberals and conservatives of this period differ?
↓ Why did conservatives in the early nineteenth century oppose nationalism?

The nineteenth century has been called the century of "isms." Besides the literary and artistic movement of Romanticism, the most important among these are conservatism, liberalism, nationalism, and socialism. All these modern political ideologies trace their origins back to the French Revolution. Conservatives opposed the Revolution and favored traditional authority and a slow rate of change, carefully directed from above. Liberals generally supported the Revolution's ideals of "Liberty, Equality, Fraternity," though they rejected the violent excesses of the Reign of Terror and Napoleonic period. Nationalists latched onto the Revolution's idea of the "great French nation" in which all citizens were equal in rights and responsibilities. In central and eastern Europe, nationalists—almost always political liberals or radicals—called for democratic nation-states on the French revolutionary model to replace the old multinational states. Conservatives like Metternich, on the other hand, rejected nationalist arguments as destructive for existing state structures.

Adam Mickiewicz   (1798–1855) Polish writer, mainly of lyric and patriotic poetry, born in Polish Lithuania but spending most of his life in exile.

Frederic Chopin   (1810–1849) Polish composer and pianist, best known for his expressive Romantic piano works and his dances, especially polonaises, that celebrated Polish nationalism.

Conservatism

Conservatism is often understood as the political ideology that opposes change. In fact, conservatives recognize that some degree of change in human society is inevitable. In these years, they did, however, oppose the rapid and thoroughgoing change advocated by the French Revolution. Most conservatives were not so much ideological as practical: they saw that change threatened their own position. Metternich is a good example. He believed that "the people" were not capable of choosing their government or governing themselves. Only royalty or the nobility were **legitimate** rulers, and they would direct change from above, based on existing traditions and institutions. For conservatives, religion and the Catholic Church played a fundamental role in maintaining respect for established rules of conduct and obedience to authority. The people themselves are not to be trusted. Conservatives have a pessimistic view of human nature and believe the people must be held in check and told how to behave.

Perhaps the greatest ideological conservative was the Irish philosopher, political theorist, and member of Parliament Edmund Burke. When the French Revolution broke out, he was almost sixty, and his most famous book, *Reflections on the Revolution in France*, was published in 1790. Burke argued that the French Revolution was doomed to descend into violence and anarchy because it was based on abstract principles instead of firmly rooted institutions. Having swept away the king's legitimacy, Burke warned, the revolutionaries had nothing to put in its place except the abstraction of popular rule that would mean a despotism far worse than Louis XVI's bumbling. Burke did not reject change out of hand but insisted that it must be "organic"—that is, growing naturally out of existing ideas, institutions, and individuals. This metaphor of organic change was to become very common among conservatives.

Burke was certainly no admirer of absolutism. After all, he had defended the American colonists in their revolt against the British monarch. He valued highly the rights enjoyed by British men of his class, talents, and education. He did reject, however, the idea that all men should be treated as equal and should participate on an equal footing in politics. This, he argued, was a recipe for disaster and the worst kind of tyranny. Describing the National Assembly in Paris, Burke wrote, "Their liberty is not liberal. Their science is presumptuous ignorance. Their humanity is savage and brutal." Burke did not reject the ideal of political liberty but insisted that most men—ignorant, lazy, and undisciplined—were not yet ready to appreciate this lofty sentiment. By eliminating the political and moral institutions that helped keep the masses of humanity in line, the French Revolution threatened to unleash a flood of destructive brutality and anarchy.

Burke, like Thomas Hobbes before him, thought pessimistically that unfettered liberty would inevitably lead to lawlessness. The terrible events of the Reign of Terror and Napoleonic Wars only served to confirm this pessimism. Perhaps the most extreme political conservative of the post-Napoleonic period was **Joseph de Maistre.** This nobleman from Savoy, on the border between France and Italy, fled his homeland when it was invaded by French armies under General Napoleon in 1792. For the rest of his life, much of which was spent in St. Petersburg, Maistre wrote against the ideals of the French Revolution and liberalism. Like Burke, Maistre based his political ideology on authority, religion, and tradition. Unlike Burke, Maistre emphasized the pope and the Catholic Church as central to legitimate authority. Maistre argued directly against certain central tenets of the Enlightenment, and in particular despised Jean Jacques Rousseau's famous line "Man was born free, and everywhere he is in chains." Maistre rejected the idea of natural freedom put forth by Rousseau; for him, men were brutish and violent in a state of nature and, without Christianity, were no better than slaves. Only accepting and obeying existing authorities, first among them the pope, prevented the "natural bondage" of humanity from reasserting itself. In other words, mankind's base and sinful nature required the strict control of church and legitimate rulers. Like Burke, Maistre stressed the importance of history and tradition, rejecting written constitutions as harmful abstractions: "Man cannot make a constitution, and no legitimate constitution can be written." In other words, political legitimacy comes only through the slow evolution of traditional authority, never from abstract principles.

A unique kind of European conservatism in this period arose in Russia, the most conservative of Europe's Great Powers, under Tsar Nicholas I. In the Russian context, **Slavophilism** called for a return to

conservatism Political ideology emphasizing tradition, slow change from above, and respect for existing institutions.

legitimacy Conservative view of the political and social order that assumes the right of kings and the nobility to rule.

Joseph de Maistre (1753–1821) Conservative theorist whose pessimistic outlook on human nature led him to advocate severe limits on human freedom.

Slavophilism ("love of Slavs") Russian social philosophy of the 1830s and 1840s, calling for a return to religious values and a rejection of Tsar Peter the Great's reforms.

pure Russian Orthodox religious values and a rejection of foreign—specifically western—influences. The Slavophiles demanded the abolition of Tsar Peter the Great's Europeanizing reforms in order to restore Russia's inner harmony and religious purity. The Slavophiles rejected representative government, institutionalized democracy, and industrial development, arguing in a Romantic vein that such rational western institutions were alien to the Russian soul. At the same time, they argued for the abolition of serfdom, but from a uniquely conservative point of view. By ending serfdom, the tsar could reestablish the mystical unity that had existed between the Russian people (that is, the peasantry) and himself. The Slavophiles' central principle was *sobornost,* a word that has no equivalent in English and that connects religiosity (*sobor* = "cathedral"), collectivity (*sobrat* = "to collect"), and a unifying mysticism. Like the Romantics in other parts of Europe, the Slavophiles yearned for mystical unity while championing the uniqueness of their own Russian historical and religious experience. While Slavophilism had little effect on Russian governmental policy, the Slavophiles demonstrated that one could oppose the Russian status quo not only from a left-wing, radical perspective but also out of conservative conviction and religious belief.

The era 1815–1847 was in most respects a conservative, even reactionary one. It is remarkable that this conservatism owed very little to the thinkers discussed here and much more to Metternich's practical politics. These thinkers did, however, share with Metternich many fundamental attitudes. All rejected the legitimacy of written constitutions, representative government, and political change based on abstract rights and reasoning. In this way conservatism both in theory and in practice lined itself up directly against the most important traditions of the Enlightenment.

Liberalism

Where conservatism rejected the Enlightenment, **liberalism** embraced it wholeheartedly. Liberalism enthusiastically took up the Enlightenment's call to "dare to know," to transform knowledge into practical measures that improve the world. Classical liberalism, like the Enlightenment, put the individual at the center of its political ideology. Unlike conservatism (and socialism), liberalism emphasized above all constitutionalism and civil rights, including the right to own property, express one's opinions freely, and profess any religion—or no religion at all. The abstractions of law and constitutions so despised by the conservatives lay at the very center of liberal politics. Only through the impersonal rule of law could true liberty

be guaranteed for all citizens. Standing above all individuals—rich or poor, noble or peasant—law would regulate the relations of the individual citizen and society as a whole. In this way, the liberals argued, the rule of law assured true equality of rights. Laws also restrict the individual's actions, of course, but liberal theorists recognized that some individual freedoms must be sacrificed for the good of society as a whole. Liberals also stressed the importance of private property for a free society. Owning property gave an individual a stake in the existing order and transformed the abstractions of law into concrete rights and duties.

Unlike conservatives, liberals were fundamentally optimistic about human nature and the possibility for transforming the world for the better. The liberals were middle-class men (and, increasingly after mid-century, women) whose political ideology may be termed the politics of the industrial **bourgeoisie** and educated middle class. Liberals opposed traditional forms of authority like royal absolutism or the pope. On the economy, they differed fundamentally from what present-day Americans understand as liberal, as they firmly opposed government interference. In principle, liberals were in favor of the equality and fraternity of all humanity, though in practice they remained wary of granting full political rights to poorer and less educated elements in the population. Similarly, very few liberals indeed thought that women were truly equal to men. Rather like the Enlightenment thinkers themselves, they argued that "in time" even these strata would be ready for full political rights—when they were educated. With its insistent call for constitutionalism, civil rights, protection of private property, and the rule of law, liberalism was for this period a markedly progressive political ideology.

Great Britain was the homeland of classical liberalism. Classical economic liberalism rests mainly on Adam Smith's renowned work *The Wealth of Nations* (1776). Smith argued that nations enrich themselves not by amassing precious metals and restricting their exports, a central tenet of mercantilism, but by allowing the greatest possible freedom for market forces, in other words, **free trade.** Government should stay out

---

liberalism   Political ideology emphasizing constitutionalism, civil rights, private property, and the rule of law.

bourgeoisie   The middle class, especially capitalists, well-to-do investors, factory owners, and educated professionals.

free trade   Unrestricted trade between different countries, not hindered by high tariffs or taxes.

of economic matters, avoid high taxes and tariffs, and let markets set prices. Smith spoke of the "invisible hand" of the market mechanism that through the **law of supply and demand** would maximize economic efficiency. Smith did concede that government could not stay out of the economy entirely because of the need for infrastructure, such as roads and harbors, which the profit motive would not create. On the whole, however, Smith thought that by limiting government expenditures, keeping taxes low, and encouraging free markets, a country would prosper. Economic liberals demanded a laissez-faire economic policy from the state, calling on government to keep out of the economy and let it develop naturally according to market forces.

Political liberalism grew out of Jeremy Bentham's *Introduction to the Principles of Morals and Legislation* (1789), which contained the now famous statement that the aim of legislation should be the greatest happiness for the greatest number of citizens. Bentham, like Adam Smith, believed that enlightened self-interest was the best guide for reforming institutions and politics. Not abstract principles but practical applications should be the reformer's primary goal. Because of his emphasis on practical reforms, Bentham's thought has been called **utilitarianism.** His influence may be seen clearly in the political demands of liberals like James Mill and also more radical thinkers. Like Smith, Bentham held a basically optimistic outlook: if human beings followed their own interests in an enlightened way, a better society would result.

James Mill developed this argument further, emphasizing the role that proper education would play in enabling individuals to recognize their own proper self-interest. Mill argued that the greatest happiness for the greatest numbers may not necessarily require **universal suffrage,** in which everyone had the right to vote, but it certainly did demand a political system in which the participation of educated and propertied individuals was guaranteed. Mill took his own ideas on education seriously enough to apply them to his son, **John Stuart Mill,** perhaps the most famous liberal of all. The younger Mill began to study Greek at the age of three, Latin at eight, and by twelve had read through most of the ancient classics, as well as studying mathematics, history, and philosophy. While morality was a central aspect of this education, religion and poetry were specifically excluded from it. Not surprisingly, given his father's intense educational regime, as a young man John Stuart Mill underwent a shattering spiritual crisis from which he only gradually recovered. Mill's most famous work, *On Liberty* (1859), forcefully made the case for individual liberty, justice, and toleration. Unlike his father, John Stuart

Mill was greatly troubled by the possibility that the spread of democracy could strengthen a tyrannical majority that would limit and crush individual freedoms. Mill defended the right to minority views, which he feared majority rule could threaten. Mill also believed that women must be recognized as intellectual and political equals—if not superiors—of men, a radical view that he expounded in his *Subjection of Women* (1869). As a philosopher, moralist, and political thinker, Mill was the epitome of liberalism. At the same time, his works reflected the progress of industrialization, mass society, and even socialism that challenged the basic tenets of liberalism: individualism, the rule of law, and private property.

Mill's life was intimately related to that of the woman he described in his autobiography as "the most admirable person I had ever known," Harriet Taylor (later Harriet Taylor Mill). Taylor herself published relatively little, but her impact on John Stuart Mill's works was enormous. Mill himself wrote in a highly Romantic vein that when two persons are so close in spirit and mind and spend so much time together conversing on topics of interest to both, then "it is of little consequence in respect to the question of originality, which of them holds of the pen." Mill dedicated *On Liberty* to her, calling it "our joint production."

Nationalism

Like liberalism, **nationalism** underwent profound changes as a political philosophy in the course of the nineteenth century. Before 1848, nationalism was generally associated with liberalism and democracy. In the second half of the century, nationalism became more and more closely aligned with conservative forces. The realignment of nationalism after 1848 reflects its triumph, and our present-day acceptance of

---

law of supply and demand   Economic law according to which prices increase when supply is low and demand high.

utilitarianism   Practical philosophy, usually associated with Jeremy Bentham (1748–1832), whose goal was the greatest happiness for the greatest number of people.

universal suffrage   Right to vote for everyone.

John Stuart Mill   (1806–1873) Liberal philosopher who supported universal suffrage, including for women; son of James Mill and author of *On Liberty* and *Utilitarianism.*

nationalism   Political ideology arising in the late eighteenth century that demanded that the nation (a group of people) have control of its own state.

the **nation-state** (in principle, at least) as the political norm is part of this triumph.

To understand the political ideology that nationalists propagated, two often-confusing terms need to be distinguished: *nation* and *state*. In English, as in French, these words are often used as synonyms, but in most of Europe in the nineteenth century, they were completely distinct concepts. Indeed, in most European languages it is impossible to confuse the two: German, for example, distinguishes *Staat* ("state") and *Volk* ("nation"). The state is easiest to define: it is a political entity that levies taxes; finances an army and a state bureaucracy; issues passports; and demands certain obligations of its citizens such as military service, payment of taxes, and obedience to laws. In the classic phrase of the German sociologist Max Weber, the state "holds the monopoly on legitimate violence." Examples of present-day states include Japan, Germany, the Russian Federation, Zambia, Israel, and the United States. It is an example of the linguistic confusion in English mentioned above that the so-called United Nations is in fact an organization of independent *states*.

While states are political units, the term *nations* refers to groups of people bound together by common language, culture, religion, history, ancestry—or some combination of these factors. The Romantics glorified the distinctive qualities of each nation, rejecting the idea that any one nation (like the French) had the right to consider its language or culture better than any other. In the nineteenth century, one of the most important markers for claiming nationhood was ethnic and linguistic. Thus, Germans—like the Grimm brothers—championed their own language as the element that made them a single national group, despite the fact that they lived in dozens of separate states. German nationalists in Vienna, Munich, Hamburg, or Berlin all demanded a united Germany. Similarly, Italian nationalists in Rome, Palermo, Venice, and Turin wanted to bring all Italians together in one political unit: Italy.

But in central and eastern Europe there were nations that lacked states altogether. Congress Poland was not truly independent of Russia, and Poles lived elsewhere in Russia, Austria, and Prussia. For Polish nationalists, all Poles should live together in a single Polish state. At least Poles had the historical memory of a strong Polish state; many nations, such as Latvians, Ukrainians, and Romanians, lacked even that.

On a practical level, it was often difficult to decide just where a given nation's boundaries lay, and nations did not usually live in compact, easily defined regions. The people now known as Belarusians and Ukrainians were considered by the Russian government to be branches of the Russian nation, and there was considerable debate on whether they could, or should, be considered separate nations, as they are today. It was also debated whether Croats were a nation or should join an "Illyrian" or **Yugoslav** nation with Serbs, who spoke the same language but followed a different religion. Hence nationalism pulled in opposite directions. Even as it called for members of a nation to live together in one state, it threatened the territorial integrity of such multinational states as the Russian, Habsburg, and Ottoman Empires.

Nationalists also faced difficulties created by class. Some nationalities consisted almost exclusively of peasants, while the upper classes belonged to a different national group. Such was the case for Latvians, whose landlords were German. And there remained the problem of where to put the Jews, who in the context of east-central Europe, at least, certainly fit the criteria of a separate nation with their distinct language (Yiddish), religion, culture, and forms of everyday life. Where—and even whether—Jews would fit in the emerging nation-states of Europe would be known in the late nineteenth century as the Jewish question. Before 1848, however, these practical difficulties were rarely considered. Nationalists overwhelmingly felt that national liberation would engender cooperation among different ethnic groups. Like the liberals (and most nationalists were liberals), nationalists were optimistic about human nature, predicting that education and economic development would help put an end to strife and wars.

Before 1848, nationalism often did not yet take a specifically political form. At this point, nationalists emphasized the need to develop the nation's culture and language and worked to expand national consciousness—that is, the feeling of belonging to a nation. In the early nineteenth century, most Europeans, aside from a thin (though growing) stratum of educated people, lacked strong national consciousness: their identity was based rather on belonging to a religion and social group (peasant, noble, artisan, and so on) and having origins in a certain village or town. They often did not think much about the language they spoke, as they had no experience with foreigners. The concept that a peasant speaking some form of German in, say, Bavaria, belonged to the same na-

nation-state Independent political unit, usually dominated by one culture or ethnicity, in which the ultimate political legitimacy rests with the people (the nation).

Yugoslav (literally, "south Slav") Group of related languages and ethnicities, including Slovenes, Croats, Serbs, and sometimes Macedonians and Bulgarians.

Voice Voice Voice Voice

Jacob Grimm Writes a Foreword to the German Dictionary

Before the mid-nineteenth century, the German language suffered from an inferiority complex. Even the celebrated Prussian king Frederick the Great had preferred speaking French over his native German. Most educated Europeans knew little about German literature and culture. And even Germans themselves were not always certain about the correct usage and pronunciation of their language— indeed, often there was no single standard language to guide them, only dozens of dialects. The Grimm brothers set out to change this situation. They worked to establish a standardized form of German that everyone could accept as "correct." Part of this enterprise was the publishing of a mammoth dictionary. The dictionary would have two main purposes: to document the richness of the German tongue and to standardize usage and spelling of German words. This text is taken from the foreword to the Grimm brothers' German Dictionary.

What is the purpose of a dictionary?

➡ It should establish a shrine to the language, preserve its treasure intact, open up the language to everyone. The written word, like the honeycomb, grows and becomes a sublime monument for the folk whose past and present are tied up with it.

➡ Language is known by everyone and is at the same time a mystery. Just as language powerfully attracts the scholar, so too do common folk feel an affinity and interest toward it. "What is that word I can't think of right now?" "There must be better ways of expressing this—let's look it up."

Beloved German compatriots, no matter what your religion or country, come together in the open halls of your ancient ancestral tongue! ➡ Sanctify it and hold fast to language; the strength and endurance of your nation depends on it. ➡ The German language still reaches beyond the Rhine to Alsace and Lorraine, north to Schleswig-Holstein, on the Baltic to Riga and Reval (Tallinn), beyond the Carpathians to Transylvania. And for you, too, German émigrés beyond the salty sea, this book will bring wistful yet pleasant thoughts of your homeland's language.

➡ *Grimm uses words like treasure, shrine, sublime monument. Why do you suppose language is so precious for him as a German? Why might language be more important to a German in this era than, say, someone from England or France?*

➡ *Why does Grimm claim that the "endurance of your nation" depends on holding fast to the German language? What does he mean by "nation"? What other European ethnic groups might place similar emphasis on the development of their language?*

➡ *Grimm describes language as a "mystery" and speaks of the "common folk." How do these two concepts fit into the ideas of Romanticism and nationalism?*

➡ *Look at the map at the beginning of the chapter. How do the geographical limits of the German nation mentioned by Grimm differ from the area where German is spoken today? What happened to bring about this change?*

tion as the king of Prussia would have been completely incomprehensible to these people. Nationalists set out to change this mindset.

Jacob and Wilhelm Grimm, the German brothers who studied the German language and folk culture, were nationalists with these aims (see Choice). So was **Johann Gottfried von Herder**, a German who spent much of his life in Riga on the Baltic. Herder wrote widely on the philosophy of history, language, and literature and insisted that all cultures and languages have something to add to world culture and world history. All ethnic groups, Herder argued, should develop their own culture, enrich their own language, and create their own literature. Just as Herder demanded that the German language be treated on an equal footing with French or English, later in the nineteenth century, young Lithuanians would refuse to use Polish, Czechs would reject German, and Jews would insist on using Yiddish or, even more radically, Hebrew in daily life. In his own way, Herder was an individualist Romantic challenging the universalist assumptions of the Enlightenment. He was both a nationalist and a democrat, arguing for equal rights and respect not just for individuals, but for entire cultures.

Nationalism contained in its very essence a strong democratic element. For nationalists, the legitimacy of the state arose out of its unity with the nation. The term *nation-state* describes this unity. Hence politics must be influenced by the sentiments of the nation as a whole. Obviously, very few of those in power in the early nineteenth century could accept such an ideology. Kings might claim to rule for the good of their people, but they rarely welcomed the people's interference in their policies. Nationalists and liberals thus shared an interest in breaking down the royal status quo. Conversely, kings and conservatives like Metternich saw in nationalism one of their greatest enemies.

Political Pressures on the Continent

↓ How did nationalist ideology affect politics during this era?

↓ Where, and why, did liberal ideas succeed in this era? Where, and why, were they suppressed?

These new political ideologies of conservatism, liberalism, and nationalism had a direct impact on politics in continental Europe. Conservatism was the driving principle at the Congress of Vienna, but even where monarchs were restored, concessions were made to liberalism in the form of constitutions and elected legislatures. In France, the restored Bourbon king was overthrown by a middle-class revolt in 1830. In Russia, Tsar Nicholas I's conservative regime refused to allow any kind of political reform. But even there and in the Ottoman Empire, nationalist movements challenged the authority of the tsar and sultan by demanding political and cultural rights for specific nations. Across the continent, the growing attraction of liberal and nationalist ideas caused kings and emperors to sit uncomfortably on their thrones.

Restoration and Liberal Revolt in France

The French Revolution and the guillotining of Louis XVI in 1793 changed French politics forever. Even conservatives like Metternich and Talleyrand at the Congress of Vienna recognized this fact. Hence they worked not to restore the absolutist monarchy of 1788 but to put in place a system that would keep most power in royal hands while allowing a measure of political participation to the wealthiest (and most conservative) elements of French society. Even before the congress began, the Bourbon dynasty had been restored to the French throne in the person of Louis XVIII, the younger brother of the ill-fated Louis XVI. Louis XVIII did not rule as an absolute monarch: he had to share power with a legislature. Louis was a narrow-minded and selfish person whose obesity and atrocious table manners made a horrible impression on Parisian society. He was also a terrible politician. In a few months, he had so alienated the political elite that when Napoleon reappeared on the scene, having escaped from Elba in March 1815, the entire Bourbon court fled. No one was willing to take up arms in defense of Louis XVIII.

Luckily for Louis, Napoleon was soon defeated by the Allies at Waterloo, and Louis returned to Paris. For the next decade and a half, French politics was dominated by Louis and his conservative royalist supporters. Under pressure from Britain and Russia, whose troops were occupying Paris at the time, Louis allowed more moderates into the legislature. In 1818, France paid off its war indemnity, foreign troops left Paris, and, for all practical purposes, France was once

Jacob and Wilhelm Grimm (1785–1863, 1786–1859) German linguists famous for their collections of fairy tales and monumental dictionary of the German language.

Johann Gottfried von Herder (1744–1803) German critic and historian who urged small nations to develop their language and culture.

again accepted as a fully legitimate Great Power in the Concert of Europe.

The following decade was a period of calm and growing prosperity. The royalists aimed to restore the Catholic Church to dominance in French society, roll back the revolutionary changes of the previous decades, and combat the specter of "democracy" (at this point the word was nearly always used in a negative sense, suggesting mob rule). The French liberals were hindered by a lack of effective leadership and by the vivid memories of chaos and bloodshed during the revolutionary period.

In 1820, Louis XVIII died. The new king was his elderly brother, **Charles X,** who was intent on restoring royal absolutism. His coronation at Rheims was a medieval extravaganza; more seriously threatening to the interests of the middle class were his plans to give financial compensation to émigrés who had lost property during the revolutionary years. Other laws considerably tightened censorship and threatened those guilty of sacrilege with severe punishments, even death. Tensions between Charles X and the Parliament came to a head in 1830, when elections failed to secure a majority for Charles's supporters. Instead of compromise, Charles chose the path of direct confrontation—in effect, a royal coup d'état. He dissolved the legislature and prepared a new electoral law that would deprive even the wealthy bourgeoisie of the vote. This was too much. Led by the brilliant journalist Adolphe Thiers, the liberals demanded a truly constitutional monarchy and the replacement of Charles X by his cousin, the Duke of Orléans. Faced with barricades, street fighting, and a clear lack of broad support, Charles X abdicated in favor of his grandson and left France to spend the rest of his days in Prague. Thus, began the reign of the "bourgeois king" **Louis Philippe**—so-called for modest habits and reliance on middle-class political support—which would last for almost twenty years.

Nationalist Movements in Belgium, Italy, and Germany

In France, nationalism played very little role in politics. After all, the French nation and the French state were closely identified with each other, with non-French ethnic groups such as Basques, Bretons, and Catalans far from the capital and not politically organized. In other parts of Europe, however, nationalism was often the single greatest rallying cry for change of the political status quo. Just to the north of France, nationalism provided the driving force for a revolution in Belgium in 1830. At the Congress of Vienna,

the Belgian provinces had been united with the Netherlands. Both economically and religiously, however, these southern provinces differed significantly from Holland. The Belgian provinces were rich in coal, and the textile industry in this region had always been closely linked with England. By 1830, this region was, after England, the most industrialized area in Europe. The Belgian provinces were also predominantly Catholic—unlike the much more Calvinist north—and in great part did not use the Dutch (or Flemish) language, but French.

Discontent with rule from Amsterdam broke into open insurrection in Brussels in late August 1830. When the Dutch king William I was unable to restore order, the Congress System went into action, and the Great Powers called an international conference to decide the fate of the Belgian provinces. Essentially the British and French decided to support Belgian independence. France was happy to see the Netherlands weakened but was also wary of allowing Great Britain to gain influence in the region. When Louis Philippe sent an army against the Dutch, they were obliged to give way and abandon Antwerp to the newly independent state. The international agreement of 1831 made Belgium a constitutional monarchy, with Leopold of Saxe-Coburg (related not only to German royalty but also to the British ruling house) as its first king. The Great Powers also decreed that Belgium would always remain neutral in international disputes. The creation of Belgium was a triumph for liberal nationalist forces.

Elsewhere liberal nationalists fared more poorly. In Italy, underground nationalist organizations like the radical *carbonari* opposed clericalism and the conservative order. In 1832, **Giuseppe Mazzini** called for all Italians to unite and create a liberal nation-state. In a famous appeal, he urged liberal Italians to

Charles X (r. 1824–1830) French king renowned for his refusal to compromise with modern political ideas; swept from power by the July Revolution of 1830.

Louis Philippe (r. 1830–1848) French constitutional monarch, known as the "bourgeois king" for his unpretentious lifestyle and political connections with the bourgeoisie.

carbonari Members of secret societies existing throughout Europe, but especially in Italy, aiming to fight political reaction and work for liberal political reform.

Giuseppe Mazzini (1805–1872) Italian political thinker and revolutionary who advocated bringing together all Italians under a single republican government.

The liberal Italian nationalist Giuseppe Mazzini (left) dedicated his life to the cause of Italian nationalism. Compare his middle-class attire and scholarly expression to the excitingly unconventional dress of his contemporary Giuseppe Garibaldi (right). Mazzini was the thinker most responsible for the resurgence of Italian national feeling while Garibaldi was the fighter who helped put Mazzini's ideals into practice. *(left: The Granger Collection, New York; right: Alinari Archives/The Image Works)*

form Young Italy—"a brotherhood of Italians who believe in a law of *progress* and *duty*, and are convinced that Italy is destined to become one nation." His writings inspired the **Risorgimento**, a movement calling for a renewal of Italian culture and nationalism. Mazzini organized Young Italy throughout the Italian peninsula, often in dangerous circumstances, and gathered funds for the cause from wealthy supporters. Though Mazzini's supporters often had to operate in secret to avoid arrest, even in the 1830s the membership of Young Italy was estimated at more than fifty thousand people.

One of those inspired by Mazzini's Young Italy was **Giuseppe Garibaldi.** Garibaldi and Mazzini shared more than a first name. They were both born in northern Italy, barely two years apart. Both dedicated their lives to the Italian nation and were key figures in the unification of Italy. But there were also significant differences between the two men. While Mazzini was of

middle-class origins (his father had been a physician and professor at the University of Genoa), Garibaldi came from a poor fisherman's family. Mazzini was a writer, thinker, and organizer. Garibaldi was an enthusiast, a revolutionary, and a military man. Indeed, few men so resembled the Romantic hero—passionate, handsome, dedicated to a cause—as Garibaldi did. During the 1830s and 1840s, Garibaldi worked as a sailor, fighting for republican liberties in Italy and South America. Only in 1848 would he return from

Risorgimento (from Italian, "to rise again") Era of political and cultural nationalism in early nineteenth-century Italy calling for Italian unification and political liberalization.

Giuseppe Garibaldi (1807–1882) Italian political leader who worked to translate Mazzini's nationalist ideas of Italian unification into reality.

Uruguay to Europe in hopes of destroying the conservative order set down at the Congress of Vienna. Garibaldi and Mazzini helped pave the way for future upheavals, but during the 1830s and up to 1848, politics in the Italian principalities remained firmly in the hands of conservatives and clericals.

Like supporters of Mazzini and Garibaldi in Italy, young educated Germans opposed the existing political order, calling for a liberal united Germany. German universities were hotbeds of nationalist thought and agitation. There young men (no women would enter German universities until the twentieth century) gathered together in fraternities to discuss politics over beer. After the patriotic fervor of the Napoleonic Wars—in German known as the Wars of Liberation (reflecting French influence)—they found it difficult to accept the conservative and antinationalist Congress System. Liberal nationalists called the first all-German gathering in October 1817 at the Wartburg, the castle where Luther had translated the New Testament into German. At this **Wartburg Festival** they celebrated German history, life, and culture—Luther's challenge to the pope in 1517, the German victory over Napoleon at Leipzig in 1814, and the beauty of the German language. Speeches called on Germans to transcend the political boundaries that divided them. But transforming speeches into political reality proved difficult. When the somewhat addled young patriot Karl Sand assassinated the reactionary poet August von Kotzebue in 1819, the German authorities moved to restrict the activities of the nationalists. The Carlsbad Decrees of 1819 put severe restrictions on freedom of expression in the press and especially in the universities, which were known for their strong support of nationalist and liberal ideals.

Yet they would not be suppressed. In 1832, at the ruins of a medieval castle in southwest Germany, some twenty to thirty thousand young people gathered and marched, carrying the national black-red-gold national banner. At the Hambach Festival, named after the castle where they gathered, German patriotic youth called for national liberation: both from foreign influences—from French culture—but even more importantly from the conservative policies of Metternich. As in Italy, these young radicals organized themselves into a group loosely called Young Germany. And as in the Italian case, Metternich worried over the ideas and appeal of these liberal nationalist groups and set his police to gather information about their subversive actions. It was in this repressive atmosphere that the Grimm brothers, who shared many of the ideals of Young Germany, were harassed and ultimately dismissed from their jobs.

National Liberation Movements in the Balkans

While the Ottoman sultan officially still ruled over most of the **Balkan Peninsula,** from the Adriatic Sea to the borders of Austria-Hungary, local elites held most of the power. These elites were more often Greek than Turkish in culture, though, in some areas, Slavic-speaking Muslims held local control. By the 1790s, many were unhappy with Ottoman rule, with its high taxes, general lawlessness, and the arbitrary behavior of troops and local officials who could not assure public order and would not be controlled by Istanbul. Complicating the disorder was competition among the extremely diverse ethnic and religious groups who made their home in the Balkans. Greeks, Romanians, "Turks" (as all Muslims tended to be called), Germans, Hungarians, and many groups of Slavic peoples lived in close proximity. They were Roman Catholic, Orthodox Christian, Muslim, and Jewish, with religion playing a central role in national identity. For example, Croats and Serbs spoke the same language: it was their religion (Catholic or Orthodox, respectively) that divided them. The Muslims of the Balkan Peninsula—who numbered in the hundreds of thousands—were often mistrusted by the nationalists and in many cases fled as nationalists gained power. The small numbers of Jews in the Balkans were significant in the region's commerce and trade. Most Balkan Jews traced their roots to the expulsion of Jews from Spain in 1492 and continued to speak Ladino, a version of Spanish written in Hebrew letters.

Nationalism not only presented a huge challenge for the Ottoman overlords; it also threatened to destabilize traditional life entirely. As throughout eastern Europe, nationalists formed a quite small group of educated, relatively privileged individuals who thought it their duty to agitate for rights on behalf of the entire Serbian, Romanian, or Greek nations. These first nationalists were fervently concerned with developing their own culture, and especially their language. In the nineteenth century, the languages spoken in the Balkan Peninsula were mainly peasant tongues, lacking many words and expressions necessary to express

Wartburg Festival   Patriotic meeting at Wartburg castle in central Germany in 1817, promoting German national and liberal ideals.

Balkan Peninsula   Region between the Black and Adriatic Seas where present-day Bulgaria, Serbia, and Greece are located.

abstract concepts and to carry out modern scientific research. More crucially still, these languages were seldom written and were not standardized. Each tongue had many local dialects, and speakers of different dialects often had great difficulty understanding one another. Hence the early Balkan nationalists were obliged to push their program on at least two fronts: the cultural (to develop a modern written language and literature) and the political (to gain their own state or autonomy).

Nationalists' programs also had a social component. Elites often differed in ethnicity and religion from the peasant majority, a situation typical in eastern Europe and much of the world. In many regions, such as the future Yugoslavia and Bulgaria, Christian peasants were ruled by Muslim landlords and officials. Thus, nationalists combined demands for political independence, cultural rights, and social development of the impoverished masses.

Nationalist aspirations first came to a head in the Pashalik ("district") of Belgrade, where discontent with Ottoman rule among Serbs ran high. When the Austrians attacked Bosnia and Serbia (then part of the Ottoman Empire) and captured Belgrade in 1789, some Serbs fought on the Austrian side. At the conclusion of these wars in 1791, Serbs gained nothing. The formation of Serbian military units, aimed against the violence of Ottoman troops, culminated in a full-scale revolt beginning in 1804, a revolt not against the sultan but against his rebellious military units. Seeking support from abroad, the Serbs turned to Russia, whose similar language and Orthodox religion made it a natural ally, and the Russians were sympathetic—interested, as always, in weakening the Ottomans. While Serb forces led by the remarkable peasant leader Karadjordje Petrović scored initial successes, after several years of fighting their resistance was worn down. In 1813 Karadjordje and his lieutenants retreated across the Danube to Austria, but the struggle was not lost. In 1815, another Serbian leader, Miloš Obrenović, gained from the sultan the title of supreme prince of Serbia. While Serbia officially remained under Ottoman rule, for most practical purposes, local affairs in the Pashalik of Belgrade were now in the hands of Serbs. Official independence came in 1833, along with an expansion of the borders of Serbia and the establishment of the Obrenović dynasty on the Serbian throne. For the next century, descendants of the two original Serbian rebels, Karadjordje and Miloš Obrenović, would occupy the Serbian (and later Yugoslav) thrones.

To the east of Belgrade, in the Danubian provinces of Walachia and Moldavia (now in Romania), an impoverished peasantry was ruled by a Greek upper class so corrupt and violent that the Greek middle class cobbled together an opposition that included Romanian landlords and the peasants. The subsequent revolt of 1821 was based on neither Greek nor Romanian ethnicity but on a general call for justice and an end to oppression. The rebels hoped for Russian assistance, but Tsar Nicholas I remained cool to their cause, thus enabling the Ottoman army to crush the rebellion. While the revolt did not bring independence to the provinces, it did strengthen the position of local nobles, who replaced Greeks in high church and administrative offices. Full autonomy was attained in 1829, and in February 1862 the modern state of Romania was created, officially still under Ottoman control but in practical terms an independent constitutional monarchy. The choice of the name Romania aimed to underscore the new state's connection to classical civilization and the European mainstream.

Nationalist feelings also strengthened in Greek provinces of the Ottoman Empire. Greek nationalists took pride in the heritage of classical Greece, though the language of Plato and Aristotle had splintered into a bewildering array of mutually incomprehensible dialects, their speakers divided by mountainous terrain. The question of what form of Greek to adopt as the official, standard tongue continued to plague Greeks long after political independence had been won. Further complicating matters was the fact that Greek merchants lived all around the Black Sea, including in territory ruled by the Russian tsar.

The Greek War of Independence broke out in April 1821. Greek independence fighters attacked both Ottoman authorities and local Muslims. Christian atrocities were matched by Ottoman reprisals, including the slaughter of thousands of Greeks on the island of Chios and the hanging of the Greek Orthodox patriarch. Reports in the European press of Ottoman atrocities (Christian atrocities against Muslims were generally ignored) pushed the Concert of Europe to intervene in support of the Greeks. England's Romantic poet Lord Byron and other idealists set off for Greece to fight for the Greek independence, often—like Byron—sacrificing their lives. The rebellion ended with a treaty signed in London that created an autonomous (but not independent) Greek state. The new state proved unworkable, and in 1830—in another Concert of Europe action—France and Russia established Greek independence. Greece, like Belgium, was to be a constitutional monarchy, and Prince Otto of Bavaria became its first king. The new Greek state was small; impoverished; and lacked a common language, administration, or educational system. The Greek nationalists had their state; they had now to create the Greek nation.

Eugene Delacroix's 1824 painting *The Massacre of Chios* romantically depicts a terrible episode of the Greek War of Independence during which Ottoman soldiers massacred thousands of Greeks. Paintings like this one influenced western Europeans to support the Greek struggle against the Ottoman Turks. *(Réunion des Musées Nationaux/Art Resource, NY)*

Autocracy in Russia

While liberal and nationalist ideologies blossomed in much of Europe, Russia's rulers did what they could to insulate their empire from such ideas. After Napoleon's invasion of Russia, Tsar Alexander I became mystical and suspicious of change. Meanwhile, Russian society—at least at the educated upper levels—did not stagnate. Young Russian officers who had participated in the campaign against Napoleon returned home from Paris with new liberal ideas. They desired a greater voice in the affairs of their native land. Some even spoke of constitutions and legislatures, though censorship prevented open discussion of such revolutionary ideas. When Alexander I died in 1825, the conspirators decided it was time to act, especially as the question of who should replace Alexander on the throne was confusing. He had left no male heirs, and by law his eldest brother, Constantine, should have succeeded him. But Constantine had given up his right to be tsar when he married a nonroyal woman, though his renunciation of the throne had never been made public. Most Russians

were unaware that the younger brother Nicholas was in line to be tsar.

In this confused situation, conspirators aimed to seize power in the name of Constantine and demand a constitution for Russia. But Nicholas was well informed of their plans. These liberal revolutionaries, who have gone down in history as the **Decembrists**, called on the army not to swear allegiance to Nicholas. The Decembrist-led rebels were surrounded by troops loyal to Nicholas on the banks of the Neva River in St. Petersburg. After several hours of fruitless negotiations, Nicholas gave the order to open fire, and the revolt disintegrated on the spot. The conspirators were soon arrested, tried, and exiled to Siberia or executed. The Decembrists quickly entered into Russian liberal and radical mythology as the "first Russian revolutionaries," but the practical effect of their revolt was negative. Nicholas had always been suspicious of

Decembrists Supporters of liberal reforms in Russia whose plot was crushed by Nicholas I in 1825.

liberal movements, and indeed of any abstract political ideologies, and now his worst fears were confirmed. His rule would be marked by an unwillingness to compromise with these new ideologies. Nicholas insisted that the Russian Empire would remain an **autocracy** and that he alone would decide the country's political future.

Nowhere was the contrast between liberal nationalism and the forces of conservatism so stark as in Russian Poland. It was perhaps inevitable that the Russian autocracy would clash with the leaders of the autonomous Congress Poland also ruled by Nicholas I, where many Poles believed that the new tsar was violating their constitutional rights. A rebellion against Russian rule broke out in Warsaw in November 1830, but the rebels, counting on French help for their independence struggle, miscalculated badly. The French were unwilling to provide more than verbal support, and, after initial Polish successes, the Russian army crushed the rebellion. Most Polish peasants refused to support the rebels, seeing in them not national kin but hated landlords. Nicholas abolished the Polish legislature and army and incorporated the Polish provinces more closely into the Russian Empire. But the Polish national spirit remained unvanquished, celebrated in the poetry of Mickiewicz and the music of Chopin. Polish patriots continued to sing the now forbidden Polish national anthem, dating from the Napoleonic period, in secret: "Poland is not yet lost / As long as we are alive."

The Polish uprising confirmed Nicholas's hatred for political abstractions and strengthened his determination to base his rule on tradition and the army. He was never so happy as when inspecting his troops, and woe to any soldier found with a button unshined or a medal out of place. At one such review, it was said, the tsar was considerably vexed because while the soldiers were lined up in exact rows, their continued breathing upset perfect symmetry. Nicholas wanted the entire country to be just as orderly as his army on the parade grounds. To prevent the spread of liberal or revolutionary ideas (Nicholas made little distinction between the two), the tsar created a secret police force—the Third Section of the Tsar's Chancellery. Censorship was tightened, reaching truly paranoid levels in the late 1840s, when the phrase "free air" in a cookbook was struck as possibly subversive and censors examined musical scores for signs of secret revolutionary codes.

Yet Russian society under Nicholas could not be shielded from change and foreign influence. It was during Nicholas's reign that there occurred what one historian has called a "parting of ways" between Russian educated society and the Russian government.

The Russian **intelligentsia** emerged, a social group whose identity derived not from birth (unlike the nobility or peasantry) but from education and a desire to work for the good of Russia and the Russian people. Such aspirations brought these reformers into direct conflict with the inefficient but all-powerful Russian state—and Nicholas's secret police. After midcentury, the Russian intelligentsia would split into liberals who wished to reform Russia and revolutionaries who saw the present system as completely rotten and looked forward to its complete destruction. Nicholas was successful in driving dissent underground during his reign. In the long run, however, his refusal to accommodate new ideas or to share power even on a limited level alienated most educated Russians from their rulers and helped pave the way for a far more destructive revolution.

Reform in Great Britain

↓ Why did the British establishment agree to political reform?
↓ What specific liberal reforms allowed Britain to avoid revolutionary outbreaks?

While Russia staunchly opposed any change in the first half of the nineteenth century, the course of political reform in Great Britain presents a strong contrast. The British middle classes—stronger here in numbers and wealth than anywhere else in Europe—gained significant political rights. These wealthy merchants and industrialists demanded and received a voice in British politics. In triumphs for political and economic liberalism, the parliamentary system was reformed, suffrage considerably broadened, and restrictions on religious minorities reduced.

But even in Britain, many groups remained outside the political system. Reform barely touched the lives of Britain's peasants and factory workers, an impoverished class that expanded rapidly as Britain industrialized. Living and laboring in dangerous conditions, workers sought to organize to improve their lives, but their efforts were opposed by a government committed to a free-market economy. Still, in Great Britain, the existing order was able to bend and mod-

---

autocracy Form of government headed by a ruler whose power is not limited by constitutional or other political restraints, as in Russia before 1917.

intelligentsia Social class of educated, progressive individuals wanting liberal reforms in Russia; later also applied to Russian revolutionaries.

ify itself to accommodate new ideologies and social classes, and in the second half of the century most worker demands would be realized. By agreeing to timely reforms, Great Britain avoided the social and political turmoil that occurred in other parts of Europe.

Conservative Domination and Reform

At the beginning of the nineteenth century, political participation in Great Britain was limited to an extremely small group of men (women would continue to be shut out for another century). Both political parties—the conservative **Tories** and the more liberal **Whigs**—were dominated by the aristocracy, but the Whigs were more sympathetic to opening the political system to wealthy middle-class men. King George III was still on the throne, though his off-and-on insanity meant that his son, crowned **George IV** in 1820, often carried out his father's duties. Ruling in his own right, George IV discredited the Crown (and thereby played into the hands of political reformers) by his immoral behavior, including his notorious attempt to divorce his estranged wife, Caroline, and his unwillingness to allow her to be crowned queen.

The first decade after 1815 was dominated by the Tories, who set a very conservative course by passing the **Corn Laws.** These laws, which for all practical purposes prevented the import of cheap grain ("corn") into Great Britain, were designed to reduce British dependence on foreign foodstuffs, but they had a disastrous effect on the poor. By keeping the price of grain—and thus bread—high, they impoverished working people, who had to spend most of their tiny wages on food. In Manchester, which tripled in size between 1801 and 1831 (to a population of 238,000) as peasants from the countryside took jobs in new textile factories, a series of public meetings culminated in 1819 with the notorious **Peterloo Massacre.** A cavalry charge dispersing the more than sixty thousand people gathered to petition Parliament for political representation and repeal of the Corn Laws ended with eleven dead and hundreds injured. The government's answer to the public uproar after Peterloo was to restrict civil liberties and free speech. In 1824, however, Parliament repealed the Combination Acts, which had forbidden workers from forming unions. Strikes were still illegal, but the important right of labor to organize had been won.

The Tory administration also took an important step toward fulfilling the liberal principle that religion should not bar an individual from full participation in political and social life. In 1829, with the

Catholic Emancipation Act, Catholics and dissenters (non-Anglican Christians) gained the right to participate in Parliament and to occupy all public offices in the realm, with the exception of lord chancellor of England and lord lieutenant of Ireland. The practical effect of this measure was not immediately great—very few Catholics in England and Ireland were wealthy enough to qualify for the vote—but the measure was significant as a further step toward religious toleration in Britain. English Jews also gained rights in this period. The first bill for Jewish emancipation (that is, completely equal rights with Christians) passed the House of Commons in 1833 but was defeated in the House of Lords. However, individual Jews were knighted (Moses Montefiore, in 1837), admitted to the bar, and elevated into the hereditary nobility (Isaac Goldsmid, in 1841). The process of Jewish emancipation was completed in 1858 when Lionel de Rothschild was—after more than a decade of debate—allowed to take the oath on a Hebrew Bible and take his seat in the House of Commons.

The Reform Bill of 1832 and the Abolition Act of 1833

King George IV died in 1830 and was succeeded by his son William IV. In the parliamentary elections that, by tradition, accompanied the ascension of a new king, the position of the more liberal Whigs and their middle-class supporters was strengthened by the example of France, where the conservative Bourbon dynasty had been toppled, replaced by a new political order under the "bourgeois king" Louis Philippe.

Tories   Conservatives, one of the two ruling parties in nineteenth-century Britain.

Whigs   Liberals, the Tories' rivals in the British Parliament.

George IV   (r. 1820–1830) King of Great Britain and Ireland, hated for his sexual immorality; most notorious for his failed attempt to divorce his wife, Caroline, in 1820.

Corn Laws   Series of laws passed in 1815 that prevented the import of grain ("corn") until prices reached a certain (high) level; kept grain and bread prices high; repealed in 1846.

Peterloo massacre   Repression of workers' gathering at St. Peter's Fields outside Manchester in 1819, leaving eleven killed and hundreds injured.

Catholic Emancipation Act   Act of 1829 allowing Catholics to be elected to Parliament and to serve in most public offices in Great Britain.

Britain's captains of industry likewise wanted to make their importance felt, arguing for a government that would support the interests of manufacturing and trade rather than representing only landowners and landowning interests. To accommodate the wealthy manufacturers, parliamentary districts, unchanged since the seventeenth century, had to be modernized. Since that time, the huge shifts in population that accompanied industrialization had created entire districts controlled by a few large landowners (**pocket boroughs**) and depopulated districts where only a few dozen people lived (**rotten boroughs**), while large industrial cities like Manchester and Birmingham had no representatives in Parliament at all.

Once in power, the Whigs pushed the **Reform Bill of 1832** through Parliament. Though suffrage was still tied to a property qualification, the new law increased the number of voters by 50 percent and significantly redistributed parliamentary representation to benefit the heavily populated new industrial cities. In short, the Reform Bill of 1832 was a triumph for English liberalism, the first step in a gradual expansion of the political system set in motion by an enlightened class of relatively privileged individuals. Men espousing the liberal ideals of constitutional rule, free trade, and a gradually expanding electorate now increasingly took seats in Parliament. Still, only one in five Englishmen could vote. Reform bills in 1867 and 1884 further extended the franchise, but not until the twentieth century was universal suffrage—for all men and women—achieved.

Liberals had long championed the cause of abolishing slavery. British law did not recognize slavery within England, Scotland, Ireland, and Wales, and in 1807 Parliament had forbidden British vessels and captains from engaging in the slave trade. But in demanding the complete abolition of slavery, liberals found themselves in a perplexing ideological position. The demand for human liberty was, of course, central to liberalism. But so was the protection of private property, and slaves were, after all, a form of property. In 1833, this contradiction was overcome when Parliament passed the Slavery Abolition Act, which abolished slavery throughout the British Empire. At the same time, the enormous amount of 20 million was appropriated by Parliament to pay slave owners for their freed "property." In this way, British liberals succeeded in extending basic human liberty to slaves while compensating their former owners.

The Repeal of the Corn Laws

The expanded Parliament now included middle-class manufacturers who opposed the Corn Laws both out of general commitment to free trade and because the higher cost of bread put pressure on the wages they had to pay workers. Two outspoken opponents to the Corn Laws elected to Parliament in the 1840s were John Bright, son of a cotton manufacturer in Lancashire, and **Richard Cobden,** a calico printer from Manchester. Both proponents of laissez-faire economics, they had founded the Anti–Corn Law League in 1838, an effective and well-financed pressure group that rapidly came to exert influence even on the Tory prime minister, Sir Robert Peel. The league was also extremely successful in appealing to the working class with slogans such as "Give Us This Day Our Daily Bread," taken from scripture. The actual repeal of the Corn Laws came, however, as a direct result of one of the most tragic events of the nineteenth century—the **Irish potato famine.**

Ireland was, at the time, an impoverished and backward colony of England. The landed gentry was almost entirely Protestant, and often absentee, while the Catholic peasantry eked out a miserable existence on shrinking plots of land, living entirely on potatoes, a New World vegetable adopted by Irish peasants because it produced more calories per planted acre than any other crop. By 1840, it was clear that the land and people were stretched to their utmost limits. Then fungus struck the Irish potato crop, wiping out sustenance for millions. The Protestant landowners and English Parliament seemed indifferent to the famine, and from 1845 to the end of the decade millions in Ireland either starved or left their homes for England or the United States. Around one-third of the Irish population perished or emigrated. To this day, the population of Ireland remains lower than it was two hundred years ago—a fact unparalleled in European demographic history.

In the public mind, the Corn Laws had been a decisive factor in causing the famine by preventing grain

pocket boroughs and **rotten boroughs**   Electoral districts in Britain that were controlled by a single landowner or where few people lived, respectively, abolished by the 1832 Reform Bill.

Reform Bill of 1832   British reform increasing suffrage and redistributing electoral districts to reflect actual population, thereby giving more representation to industrial cities.

Richard Cobden   (1804–1865) English liberal who in 1838 formed the Anti–Corn Law League to fight for free trade in grain.

Irish potato famine   Demographic catastrophe in the mid- to late 1840s caused by a fungus infection, or blight, of the Irish peasantry's staple food, the potato.

The Irish Potato Famine not only devastated the population of Ireland but also called into question British rule there. In cartoons like this one published in many European countries, the unfeeling and well-fed English ("John Bull") were contrasted with the starving Irish. *(The Granger Collection, New York)*

imports from abroad. The tragedy thus dealt the Corn Laws a decisive blow, and they were abolished in 1846. This triumph for free trade could not, unfortunately, help the victims of the famine. While grain prices did drop after the abolition of the Corn Laws, not Irish peasants but factory workers in Britain were able to take advantage of cheaper bread. From 1846 until the First World War, free trade and liberalism dominated British economic policy. Presided over by **Queen Victoria**, the Victorian Age represented the pinnacle of British prosperity and prestige. As the first fully industrialized country, Great Britain had a significant economic advantage, while other countries—such as the United States, Germany, and Russia—erected trade barriers to protect their own industries from a flood of cheap British imports. Not until the end of the nineteenth century did the United States and Germany catch up with Britain's industrial head start. The Victorian Age was also the pinnacle of British imperialism. With colonies and dominions in Asia, Africa, and North America, the British were proud to claim that "the sun never sets on the British Empire."

The Chartist Movement and the Factory Acts

Yet not all of Victoria's subjects were content. The middle classes could point to solid gains in political and economic aspects of their lives, but most workers continued in dangerous jobs for little pay. Their discontents were translated into political action by **Chartism**, a workingmen's reform movement that agitated for increased political rights. The movement took its name from the People's Charter, a document published in 1838 that announced six demands: annual Parliaments, universal male suffrage, voting by secret ballot, the elimination of property requirements for members of Parliament, salaries for members of Parliament, and equal electoral districts. Using modern techniques of political agitation such as mass meetings, pamphlets, and a popular newspaper, the *Northern Star,* the Chartists took their case to Parliament in the form of a petition with several hundred thousand signatures. Parliament rejected the petition overwhelmingly, and when some of the more radical Chartists made statements about armed resistance, the movement's leadership was arrested and jailed. Thus ended the first Chartist movement. Two more petitions were brought to Parliament—and rejected—in the 1840s; afterward, the movement fell apart.

Though Chartists appeared to have failed in their efforts to improve the political situation of workers, by the early twentieth century five of their six demands had been met. Perhaps even more important for workers' everyday lives, the government continued to intervene—despite laissez-faire liberalism—to improve conditions in mines and factories, which were revealed in a series of government investigations and reports to be appalling. A series of **Factory Acts** passed in the first decades of the nineteenth century had intended to restrict child labor but lacked enforcement. In 1833, a new Factory Act ruled that children under nine years of age were not to be employed in textile works and set maximum work hours for workers under eighteen. Most important, these laws were to be enforced by a newly created factory inspectorate.

Queen Victoria   (r. 1837–1901) English queen whose reign was a period of British prominence in world politics, the world economy, science, trade, and culture.

Chartism   Workers' political movement in Britain, 1838–1848, that demanded a People's Charter guaranteeing universal male suffrage and other reforms.

Factory Acts   British laws of 1833, 1842, and 1847 that limited the number of hours manufacturers could require children and women to work.

An 1842 law prohibited women from underground work in the mines. Most path-breaking of all, an 1847 act forbade women and children from working more than ten hours a day. Government's responsibility for regulating the conditions of labor was now firmly established, as the interests of public order and safety triumphed over the interests of the manufacturers. Thus, in England parliamentary rule proved capable of reform and of responding to the needs of the people in time to prevent either the middle-class revolt that reformed France or the working-class revolution that in the next century would convulse Russia.

Summary

Review Questions

↑ In what ways did the Congress of Vienna help shape Europe and European politics?

↑ What were the major demands of nationalists? Which governments felt particularly threatened by such demands?

↑ In what ways did national identity expand and deepen in this period? What effect did Romanticism have on this process?

The period 1814–1847, unlike the years preceding and following, was not one marked by great upheaval or striking events. It makes sense to think of these decades as a "breathing space," a rest between the exhilarating and terrifying years of revolution and war before 1814 and the revolutions and growing political ferment after 1847. Yet there were local wars and a series of revolts in 1830–1831 that registered growing discontent, as did the writings of intellectuals and the responses of politicians. Meanwhile, the most important political ideologies of the modern era began to take shape.

While conservatives like Metternich aimed to restore the political institutions of the Old Regime as much as possible, middle-class liberals had markedly different political goals. They opposed the privileges and exclusivity of the aristocratic order upheld by Metternich and argued that the limitations placed on their political rights harmed not just themselves but the entire nation. Only through constitutions enshrining the rule of law under which all were equal, the liberals insisted, could the entire nation live in freedom, justice, and prosperity. Progressive reforms, argued liberals, would unite and uplift the entire nation. For liberals throughout Europe, the constitutional monarchy in Great Britain represented the ideal. While conservative forces continued to rule over most of Europe, a rapid expansion of the middle class and the circulation of liberal ideas by educated professional people laid the ground for political reforms in the second half of the nineteenth century.

Closely linked with liberalism were the new and increasingly important nationalist movements. Nationalists promoted new identities based on common language, culture, religion, history, and ancestry and demanded new, ethnically homogeneous states that would have to be carved from the existing multinational imperial states. In this era, Belgians, Greeks, Serbs, and Romanians had varying degrees of success in establishing autonomous nation-states. Nationalists in German, Italian, and Polish lands demanded unitary liberal nation-states that would unite their peoples, setting in motion trends that would be realized for an increasing number of nations after 1848.

An exception to the conservative domination in this period was Great Britain. Here middle-class liberals were successful in passing many significant reforms—broadening the suffrage, reforming parliamentary representation, eliminating legal discrimination against non-Anglican Christians, and ending slavery in the British Empire. Even so, in midcentury Great Britain was hardly a democracy, and full voting rights for the working class and for women would not come until the next century. Yet Britain's series of reforms, gradually expanding political participation and government protections for workers, modeled a political process that contrasted sharply with politics elsewhere in Europe. In Britain, political leaders responded to the needs and demands of those who did not have the vote in order to control reform from the top down. Elsewhere in Europe, rulers suppressed calls for increased political participation, forcing liberals and nationalists to take to the streets in armed revolts. Reform—if it happened—was directed from the bottom up. In 1848 and through the rest of the nineteenth century, the patterns of revolution and progressive reform would bring sweeping changes to European politics and society.

← Thinking Back, Thinking Ahead →

How did the political ideals of nineteenth-century liberals reflect ideals of the Enlightenment?

How did these ideals differ from the political ideology of absolutism?

ECHO ~~ECHO ECHO ECHO ECHO~~

Frankenstein

The story of a man-made monster who turns on his creator is both a nightmare and a metaphor for the destructive potential of human creativity. An early version is a sixteenth-century story in which Rabbi Loew of Prague creates a servant for himself out of clay. He breathes life into it—with the help of a few strategically placed Hebrew letters. As with the later and more famous Frankenstein, Rabbi Loew's creation gets out of hand and has to be destroyed.

The famous Frankenstein comes from a novel by the English writer Mary Wollstonecraft Shelley, daughter of the writer and feminist Mary Wollstonecraft and wife of the Romantic poet Percy Bysshe Shelley. Mary Shelley was only eighteen years old when, one night, the poet Lord Byron challenged his guests to come up with a ghost story. In response, Mary Shelley wrote her masterpiece, *Frankenstein; or, The Modern Prometheus* (1818). It tells of a Swiss chemist, Dr. Victor Frankenstein, who in his anatomical research discovers the secret of life. Working secretly at night, the scientist stitches together a human form to which he gives life. Dr. Frankenstein's pride in his creation turns to horror when "the monster" escapes and carries out a series of murders. But who is to blame? Confronting his creation on a mountain glacier, Dr. Frankenstein reproaches the monster, who retorts that it is not his fault that he is not "Adam"—a good man—but "the fallen angel," seeking joy but forever shut out and persecuted. Unfortunately, the good Dr. Frankenstein's efforts to redeem his creation and "friend" (as he calls the monster) come to nothing. After more (implied) sex and (explicit) violence, the guilt-wracked creature destroys himself.

Mary Shelley's story reflects both its own time and ours. The Romantics of the early nineteenth century were deeply troubled by a world in which religion and spirituality seemed to be losing ground to crass materialism and cold scientific rationality. In their own poetic works, they extravagantly compared themselves to God: they, too, were creating new worlds. Dr. Frankenstein's creation is motivated by the same kind of search for knowledge, but the outcome of his experiment is tragic for all concerned. In our time, too, we both enjoy and mistrust the consequences of scientific research. Looking at the mushroom cloud of the first successful atomic bomb test in 1945, the physicist Robert Oppenheimer recalled a phrase from the Bhagavad Gita: "I am become death, the destroyer of worlds."

Suggested Readings

Blum, Jerome. *In the Beginning—The Advent of the Modern Age: Europe in the 1840s.* New York: Scribner's, 1994. An account arguing that "modernity" begins in the 1840s; excellent on political and intellectual history, with many fascinating anecdotes.

Chapman, Tim. *The Congress of Vienna: Origins, Processes and Results.* London and New York: Routledge, 1998. Very clear and concise discussion of the congress itself and diplomacy to 1848.

Gellner, Ernest. *Nations and Nationalism.* Ithaca, N.Y.: Cornell University Press, 1983. A challenging and extremely influential theoretical work.

Hobsbawm, Eric. *The Age of Revolution: Europe 1789–1848.* New York: Barnes & Noble, 1996. A path-breaking synthesis.

Ó Gráda, Cormac. *The Great Irish Famine.* Basingstoke, England: Macmillan Education, 1989. Concise treatment of the famine itself and its effect on Irish history.

Riasanovsky, Nicholas. *Nicholas I and Official Nationality in Russia, 1825–1855.* Berkeley and Los Angeles: University of California Press, 1959. Still the best account of politics and intellectual life under Nicholas I.

Thompson, Dorothy. *The Chartists.* London: Temple Smith, 1984. A detailed history of the movement.

Websites

Web resources on Romanticism, **Prometheus Unplugged,** at http://prometheus.cc.emory.edu/library.html

The Austrian statesman and his place in history, **Graf Clemens Wenzel Lothar Metternich,** at www.aeiou.at/aeiou.encyclop .m/m583439.htm

Clearinghouse of information on the Brothers Grim, **The Grimm Brothers' Home Page,** at www.pitt.edu/~dash/grimm.html

CHAPTER 21

Industrialization and Society, 1800–1850

1500 B.C.E.	1000 B.C.E.	500 B.C.E.	1 B.C.E./1 C.E.

		1810s Luddite revolts protest industrialization in England	1815 Napoleon is finally defeated at Waterloo	1820s Industrialization begins in Belgium and northern France	1824 British Combination Acts are repealed

1800	1805	1810	1815	1820	1825

Railroads and Industrial Development in Europe in 1850

By 1850 industrialization had spread from western to central Europe and railroad construction expanded outward from major cities from Moscow to Manchester. Where was industry most developed? Which country had densest railroad system?

Legend:
- ⎯ Railroads
- ▨ Coalfields
- ◯ Industrial areas
- ⚒ Scattered iron works
- ⬓ Textile production
- ■ City with population over 500,000

**Labels on map:**

ATLANTIC OCEAN

KINGDOM OF SWEDEN AND NORWAY

Oslo
Stockholm
St. Petersburg
Moscow
Riga

North Sea

DENMARK
Copenhagen

Baltic Sea

Danzig

RUSSIAN EMPIRE

UNITED KINGDOM OF GREAT BRITAIN AND IRELAND
Newcastle
Dublin
IRELAND
Liverpool
Leeds
Manchester
Birmingham
London

KINGDOM OF THE NETHERLANDS
Amsterdam
Antwerp
Essen
Cologne
Liège
Luxembourg
Paris
LORRAINE
ALSACE
Mulhouse
Le Creusot
FRANCE
Lyons

KINGDOM OF PRUSSIA
Berlin
Göttingen
SAXONY
Frankfurt
Prague
Warsaw
Kiev
Cracow

AUSTRIAN EMPIRE
Munich
Zürich
SWITZERLAND
Vienna
Buda
Pest
Turin
Milan
Venice

PORTUGAL
Madrid
SPAIN

KINGDOM OF SARDINIA AND PIEDMONT
Marseilles
TUSCANY
PAPAL STATES
Elba
Corsica (Fr.)
Rome

Sardinia

KINGDOM OF THE TWO SICILIES

Belgrade
Istanbul
OTTOMAN EMPIRE
Athens

Adriatic Sea
Black Sea

Danube
Dnieper
Dniester
Vistula
Elbe
Seine
Loire
Garonne
Ebro
Rhône
Po

Sicily
Malta (Gr. Br.)

Mediterranean Sea

MOROCCO
ALGIERS

0   200   400 Km.
0   200   400 Mi.

Timeline (upper):

500 C.E.   1000 C.E.   1500 C.E.   2000 C.E.

Timeline (lower):

1833
Factory Act in Britain restricts child labor

1840s
Industrialization begins in central Europe

1848
Political uprisings sweep Europe
Marx publishes the *Communist Manifesto*

1851
Half of English population lives in cities

1830   1835   1840   1845   1850   1855

Choice Choice Choice

Friedrich Engels

The impact of industrialization was dramatic and in many ways appalling. Friedrich Engels (1820–1895) came from Germany to England as a young man to work at his father's textile plant in Manchester. What he saw there made him condemn industrial capitalism as cruel and inhumane. His first major work, *The Condition of the Working-Class in England in 1844,* revealed the miserable conditions of industrial workers and became a classic of socialist literature. (Bettmann/Corbis)

Friedrich Engels Denounces Capitalist Exploitation

Friedrich Engels was just twenty-two when his father sent him away from home to keep him out of trouble. Home was Barmen (now Wuppertal), Germany, where the family owned textile mills. The "trouble" was Friedrich's interest in philosophy, which caused him to reject his father's stern brand of Christianity. Hoping to distract his son from such irreligious studies, the elder Engels sent young Friedrich to manage a textile mill outside Manchester, England, in which the family had an interest.

Once in Manchester, young Engels was appalled by what he saw: over-crowded housing; entire districts lacking sewers and clean drinking water; families competing for foul, half-rotten food. The horrifying conditions in which the working people of Manchester lived changed Engels's life, causing him to dedicate his life to exposing the misery caused by industrial capitalism and to helping workers organize to improve their lives. Engels decided to write a book. Though he represented his father's interests at the mill during the day, at night he roamed the slums of Manchester, gathering material for what would be published as *The Condition of the Working Class in England in 1844.*

Engels documented entire families living in a single room, sleeping together in a single bed that was alive with lice and vermin. He recorded the physical effects of grueling work, poor nutrition, and lack of hygiene. These terrible living conditions meant that the majority of industrial workers died before they reached the age of twenty. Even as he gathered his data, Engels was asking himself more fundamental questions: What factors cause such poverty? How could factories that were so efficient at increasing production make the lives of their workers so miserable? In short, Engels wanted to understand the workings of industrial capitalism.

In 1844, Engels returned home to Germany, stopping on the way in Paris to meet Karl Marx. Within two years, the two young men (Marx was only two years older than Engels) would be calling themselves communists and calling for an overthrow of the present economic and political order. But for now Engels went home to write his book. It was published the next year in German, but its dedication was in English: "To the Working Classes of Great-Britain." Engels praised English workers, dedicated his book to them, and urged them to fight for their rights against "the middle classes [who] intend to enrich themselves by your labour."

This was more than a documented report; it was a political manifesto, and Engels called on England's workers to take control of their own destiny. Scholars at the time and later complained that Engels exaggerated the misery wrought by industrialization, provided a one-sided picture of life in Manchester, and based his sweeping accusations against the middle class on his own narrow experience in Barmen and Manchester. These criticisms are reasonable, but on another level they miss the point. Engels was not writing a scholarly analysis; he was trying to change the world. His conclusion was a warning: "The war of the poor against the rich will be the most bloodthirsty the world has ever seen." This war would be a revolution, he claimed, that would usher in a world of justice and dignity for all.

In 1848, only three years after the book's publication, revolutions did sweep the European continent, including Germany. In the same year, Marx and Engels published the famous *Communist Manifesto,* in which they argued that a workers' revolution would soon put an end to capitalism. The workers' revolution did not come in 1848. For political reasons, both Marx and Engels had to flee their native Germany and live in permanent exile in England. There they maintained a fruitful partnership and friendship that lasted until Marx's death in 1883.

While Engels's *Conditions of the Working Class in England* made him famous among German radicals, it was not published in England until 1891. Still, the book's impact was enormous. For some young Russian socialists, Engels's descriptions of the degradations of industrial capitalism made them hope to avoid industrialism altogether—an aim that Marx and Engels firmly rejected as impossible and undesirable. Instead, Engels argued, radicals needed to harness industrialization's wealth-generating power for the good of all workers and all society. In a sense Engels did this himself as an individual: he worked all his life as a businessman and manufacturer, devoting much of his income to radical causes and supporting the ever-impoverished Marx family. Ironically, industrial capitalism made Engels a radical and also financed his quest to destroy it.

Introduction

Like many other radicals, Engels was reacting to the rapid and far-reaching changes in European society and everyday life that occurred during the first half of the nineteenth century—all of them the consequences of industrialization. Populations grew rapidly, economies boomed, and millions of people migrated from the countryside to the city in search of factory employment. Industrialization, starting first in Great Britain, soon took the continent by storm, affecting all segments of society, transforming every aspect of life. Skilled artisans and craftsmen found their jobs threatened by mass production in factories, where dozens and even hundreds of workers labored side by side, doing repetitive and monotonous tasks in dangerous conditions. At the same time, the economic power of the middle classes, from factory owners to professional people, grew rapidly, increasing their political power.

The Industrial Revolution transformed Europe on various levels. On a physical level, the coal mines, coal-burning factories, and railroad tracks and trestles altered the European landscape. Soot and pollution literally blanketed industrial cities and their outskirts. Other effects were more subtle. Middle-class people came to think of themselves as "self-made"—that is, they perceived their identity as derived from their work, accomplishments, or training. The thousands of men and women congregated in factories also began to perceive themselves differently: as members of a new and potentially powerful working class. In both cases, this class consciousness meant that identity was derived not from birth but primarily from one's position within the economy.

Industrialization revolutionized production, efficiently mass-producing huge numbers of items far more cheaply than could be done by hand. But the wealth produced by industrialization was uneven, and the gap between wealthy industrialists and their workers grew. Reformers like Friedrich Engels fought against terrible working conditions, poverty, and exploitation of the workers by the capitalist system. Other reformers thought that justice for workers could be attained by government intervention, cooperation, and reforms. The Factory Acts in Britain in the 1830s seemed to remedy the worst conditions, and eventually workers' pay also rose. But Karl Marx argued forcefully that only revolution would end exploitation of the working class and create a truly just and humane society.

In many ways the world we know—running by the clock, fast paced, full of mass-produced consumer goods, accepting constant change as normal—is a direct outcome of the Industrial Revolution, which began in the late eighteenth century and continued throughout the nineteenth. Industrialization rearranged economies, altered the rhythm of daily life, and changed attitudes, first in Europe and North America, then around the world.

Chronology

1799–1800	English Combination Acts prohibit strikes and unions
1801	Joseph Marie Jacquard invents the automated loom
1810s	Luddites revolt in England
1815	British Parliament passes Corn Laws
1815	End of Napoleonic Wars
1824	Repeal of Combination Acts permits labor unions
1820s	Industrialization begins in Belgium, northern France
1829	First steam locomotive, the *Rocket,* travels from Liverpool to Manchester in test race
1830s–early 1840s	Chartists protest British Corn Laws
1831	Belgium's independence encourages industry
1831	Workers in Lyon Destroy Jacquard loom to protest industrialization
1834	Zollverein (German Customs Union) established to promote trade
1835	First German railroad opens
1838	Iron steamships compete in race across the Atlantic to New York
1839	Prussia forbids the employment of children under nine in factories
1840s	Beginnings of industrialization in central Europe
1847	British Factory Act limits the number of hours women and children can work in textile factories
1848	Revolutions sweep Europe; Marx and Engels publish *The Communist Manifesto*
1859	Samuel Smiles publishes *Self-Help*
1851	First major Russian railway opens, linking Moscow and St. Petersburg; Half of English population lives in cities

The Spread of Industrialization

⬇ How did the process of industrialization differ in Britain and in continental Europe?

⬇ How did industrialization create class identities?

In Britain, the Industrial Revolution took place over several decades in the late eighteenth century, fueled mainly by technological innovation and private capital. In other parts of Europe, industrialization came later but often developed even more quickly, pushed along by government investment and subsidies. Technology continued to develop rapidly, and new means of transportation—especially the railroad and steamships—seemed to shrink distance and time, encouraging intercontinental trade and migration. The initial effects of industrialization were usually horrible—pollution, crowded and unsanitary cities, and the disruption of family life. While peasants had lived by the natural rhythms of the seasons, sunrise, and sunset, the industrial world was regulated by the clock. By the mid-nineteenth century, some benefits of industrialization were evident—an increase in affordable consumer goods, the growth of middle-class prosperity, and, in some cases, even higher wages for industrial workers. Thus, in just half a century, industrialization altered both lifestyles and attitudes, sometimes positively, often negatively, but always permanently. After industrialization, there was no returning to an earlier, less complicated time.

Industrialization on the Continent

In the late eighteenth century, as Britain's manufactured goods began to enter continental European markets in increasing numbers, European states became alarmed. Believing that a strong economy was the basis of political power, France restricted British imports until the **Eden Treaty** of 1786, after which

Eden Treaty   Treaty between France and Great Britain in 1786 permitting the import of British manufactured goods into France.

British cloth swamped the French market. Some French manufacturers responded to the competition by introducing spinning jennies and water frames in local production. Others blamed the failure of French manufactures to compete on Britain's passion for world economic domination, which French nationalists had always denounced.

But continental European states soon found that developing their own industries would be more complicated than just copying Britain's model. First of all, Britain jealously guarded its artisans and inventors, making it illegal for them to leave the country. Moreover, on the European continent, water transport was less widely available and more expensive than in Britain. Coal was also in short supply. European guilds were stronger, and their members often actively opposed industrialization as a threat to their livelihood. Finally, much of Europe was simply too poor to provide a market for mass-produced industrial goods. In France, where wealth and educational standards rivaled those in Britain, different taxation systems in various provinces and the innumerable tolls that had to be paid when shipping goods across the kingdom severely handicapped commerce. And just as Britain was making its **industrial take-off** in the 1780s and 1790s, France exploded in revolution.

On the European continent, industrialization had to wait for the end of the Napoleonic wars in 1815. Even then, few regions had the capital, skilled laborers, or resources required for industrializing. From the 1820s, Belgium, northern France, and western Germany began to experience the economic and social transformations of industrialization. By 1850 industry had spread to central Europe, and in 1851 a railroad connected the two largest Russian cities, St. Petersburg and Moscow. Railroads were built, coal mined, and factories and corporations founded. Despite these developments, most of Europe—in particular, the continent's southern and eastern regions—remained mainly agricultural and without significant industry in 1850. British industry remained the most advanced in Europe, as shown by the fact that in 1851 more than half of the English population lived in cities. But by 1850, Britain no longer monopolized European industrial textile production, coal mining, or railroad building.

Belgium was the first region on the continent to industrialize. Just across the English Channel, it had long had close commercial ties with Britain, and since the late eighteenth century, British manufactures destined for the continent often passed through Belgium. The country also possessed the building blocks of industrialization: good communications by water; raw materials like coal, lumber, and iron ore; a well-trained population with many artisans; and, from

MAP 21.1   Industrialization in England, ca. 1859 By the middle of the nineteenth century, England was heavily industrialized. Most industrial regions were close to the sea or other waterways and near coal fields. Locate Manchester on the map. What about its location made it a prime industrial site?

1831, a government favorable to the development of industry. By 1850, Belgium could boast a degree of industrialization unrivaled by any other continental country. At first, Belgian industry concentrated on textiles, but by midcentury a boom in railway building spurred growth in mining and iron production.

Industrialization in France followed a different road. As a large and diverse country, quite unlike Belgium, and with its historical suspicion of Britain, France could hardly be expected to follow the British example closely. France did possess the prerequisites for industrialization, such as agricultural efficiency, natural

industrial take-off The point at which industrialization continues to grow on its own—that is, becomes self-perpetuating.

Founded in the late eighteenth century by an English entrepreneur, the Le Creusot ironworks in the Burgundy region to the southeast of Paris became one of the most advanced in France. The company would later develop into France's largest arms manufacturer. The enormous amount of pollution generated by the ironworks is evident in this image. *(Roger-Viollet/The Image Works)*

resources including coal and iron, and sophisticated scientists and artisans. For example, French gunsmith Honoré Le Blanc had pioneered the use of **interchangeable parts** in the mid-eighteenth century, and in 1801 inventor **Joseph Marie Jacquard** invented a power loom that could be programmed to produce different patterns of cloth. On the other hand, most French peasants continued to live on their own small farms and were not interested in becoming industrial workers, whereas in England large numbers of landless peasants had little alternative. The French government, again unlike the British, did little to encourage a "pro-industrialization climate"; Le Blanc's innovation of interchangeable parts was not taken up in France and had to wait for another inventor, the American Eli Whitney, to be introduced into manufacturing. The size of France and the lack of economical transport delayed industrialization in many regions until the coming of the railroads.

Traditionally, French manufacturing had concentrated on high-quality luxury items like silk, fine carpets, and exquisite furniture. Entrepreneurs and skilled workers in these traditional manufactures were hostile to the idea of mass production, which, they claimed, was capable of producing only cheap and shoddy articles. Jacquard's looms were attacked and destroyed by angry weavers. Despite the resistance of skilled artisans, industrialization did advance in France. In the Paris region, modern textile factories were established, and the long-standing silk industry in France's second-largest city, Lyon, began

to use modern industrial techniques, such as the Jacquard loom. On the whole, however, most French manufacturers continued to produce small amounts of high-quality luxury items rather than the cheap mass-produced articles of the industrial age.

French industrialization before 1850 was concentrated in **Alsace-Lorraine,** in the northeast, and in the northern part of the country, where coal and iron reserves were located. In the 1830s the first French railroads were built, and in 1842 the government set down a master plan for railroad construction. Private firms built the lines, but with considerable government aid and, later, profit guarantees. This cooperation between government and private business would become typical for the construction of railroads from France to Russia. By 1850, one could go by rail from Paris to Brussels, Frankfurt, Bordeaux, and Marseilles via Lyon. Even greater railroad expansion would come in the second half of the nineteenth century.

interchangeable parts Precision manufacture of identical parts so that if the original part breaks or wears out, it can be replaced.

Joseph Marie Jacquard (1752–1834) French inventor and businessman who used punch cards to "program" complicated weaving styles on the power looms called by his name.

Alsace-Lorraine Region of northeastern France in which French industrialization was concentrated before 1850.

In the German lands, industry grew up on top of coal fields in the **Ruhr** and **Saxony**, and entrepreneurs built small factories in the Prussian capital, Berlin. In 1837, August Borsig set up a machine shop there that would become one of the largest locomotive factories in Europe. Ten years later, **Werner Siemens** established a company in Berlin to manufacture telegraph equipment; Siemens remains a major manufacturer of electronic goods in the twenty-first century. Despite the fact that industrialization had come to many German regions in the 1840s, most Germans continued to live on the countryside and earn their livelihood from the soil. In Prussia, less than 10 percent of the population lived in cities larger than 20,000, even in 1849, and only two Prussian cities boasted populations above 100,000.

At the same time, the German Customs Union (**Zollverein**), established in 1834, helped push German industrialization forward by enabling industrialists to sell their products freely across a large area. While the Zollverein did not include all German states, it laid the groundwork for an economically and politically united Germany. Economically, it created a market of 26 million potential customers. Railroads followed rapidly. The first German line ran from Nuremberg to Fürth in Bavaria—a distance of only a few kilometers—in 1835, but by 1850, Germany could boast of nearly six thousand kilometers of railroad lines, nearly double that of France. As in France, in central Europe governments promoted railroad building. Often the Prussian, Saxon, or Austrian governments would guarantee profits for a certain stretch of track to the company willing to undertake its construction. Private investors would then provide the capital for railroad building, confident that their investment would make a reasonable return. In this way, the construction of German railroads involved much more state support than had been the case in Britain.

Industrialization on the continent always looked to the example of Britain. For many, like **Friedrich Engels**, this example was negative (see Choice). Industrialization in Britain had caused misery for thousands of workers, who crowded into the new industrial towns and lived in dark and squalid slums. From the start, continental governments feared the revolutionary potential of impoverished industrial workers, or the **proletariat,** a word that rapidly appeared in many European languages. And they took action in a way that Britain, devoted to laissez-faire economics, did not. Not only did continental governments promote railroads; they restricted the use of child labor and more closely regulated the conditions of industrial work than in Britain, hoping to reduce working-class discontent. In short, governments on the continent always took a much more active role in regulating relations between **capitalists** and industrial workers. They also protected their new industries through high **tariffs** that discouraged the consumption of imported goods by increasing their price. Many argued that Britain's great head start in industrialization made it necessary to shield developing industry from a flood of cheap British manufactures. Britain, in contrast, had long been a promoter of free trade—that is, British trade.

The Revolution in Transportation

New industries required the transport of both raw materials and manufactured goods. At first, rivers and canals were sufficient, but they were rapidly supplanted by railroads. Railroads originated in the coal mines of Britain, where the difficulty of bringing the heavy, bulky coal to the surface called forth a simple but ingenious solution: coal wagons on metal rails. Soon the principle was transferred outside the mines. At first, horses pulled these wagons on metal tracks, but it was only logical that animal power would be replaced by steam. The culmination of this process occurred in 1829, when **George Stephenson**'s locomotive, the *Rocket,* won a competition for the new

Ruhr   Region in western Germany that became a center of industrial production and metal industry.

Saxony   Region in southeastern Germany, formerly an independent kingdom, important in German industrialization.

Werner Siemens   (1816–1892) German inventor and businessman who established his first factory in Berlin in 1847 and was a major figure in the manufacture of electrical goods.

Zollverein   German Customs Union, or free-trade area, dominated by Prussia and important in Prussian unification of Germany in 1871.

Friedrich Engels   (1820–1895) Karl Marx's closest collaborator, son of a German industrialist who spent most of his life in England.

proletariat   Industrial workers or, more generally, people who own absolutely nothing except their own labor.

capitalists   Individuals whose income comes from capital—wealth in money rather than land—invested in factories and commerce for profit.

tariffs   Taxes charged on imported goods that raise consumer costs and add to government revenues.

George Stephenson   (1781–1848) English railroad pioneer, inventor, and engineer responsible for some of Britain's earliest locomotives and rail lines in the 1820s and 1830s.

The railroad sliced through the countryside, serving as a constant reminder to rural people of the great industrial changes taking place. The rural landscape was transformed by the "iron road" itself, with its bridges and viaducts. The loud, sooty, and dangerous trains that rushed through what had been quiet agricultural regions must have seemed like monsters from another world. *(NRM/Pictorial Collection/SSPL/The Image Works)*

Manchester-Liverpool line by traveling at a top speed of twenty-nine miles per hour over thirty-five miles. The railroad age had begun.

In next two decades, more than six thousand miles of track were laid in Britain. On the European continent, railroad construction was also impressive: by 1850, Berlin, Paris, Vienna, Frankfurt, and other major cities were linked by rail. The first railroad entrepreneurs envisioned these new "iron roads" mainly as means of bringing bulky raw materials like coal or iron ore to factories and manufactured products to market (such as textiles from Manchester to the port of Liverpool). Very soon, however, railroads were carrying not just freight but also large numbers of people. Railroads made it easier for country people to migrate to the city in search of work, thereby increasing the labor pool for further industrialization.

Steam engines proved easier to use in locomotives than in ships. Harnessing steam to propel watercraft was plagued by two separate difficulties. First, a high degree of efficiency was required because of a boat's limited ability to carry coal. Second, for an onboard steam engine, safety was extremely important, as an explosion could well mean the destruction of the entire ship, possibly far out at sea. These problems were effectively solved by the late 1830s, however, and by midcentury steamships were replacing even the swift-sailing clippers on the open seas. Steamships were innovative not only in their use of steam propulsion but also in their construction, being made of iron instead of wood. The use of iron in shipbuilding allowed ships to be larger, more durable, and economically more ef-

ficient. In 1838, two iron steamships, the *Great Western* and the *Sirius,* raced across the Atlantic to New York, making the journey in a record-breaking fifteen days. Rapidly, wooden sailing vessels were retired, no longer able to compete.

Industrialization spurred improvements in roads and overland transport as well. At the beginning of the century, roads in most parts of Europe were worse than they had been during the Roman Empire eighteen centuries earlier. But by 1850, significant improvements had been made, partly in connection with the creation of a European-wide postal system. Post roads with stations where horses could be changed were established along major trade routes from England to Russia. In Britain, by 1830 more than a thousand private "turnpike trusts" had built roads and were then charging tolls to recover their investment. **John McAdam**, surveyor for the Bristol Turnpike Trust, developed a method of road construction that improved foundations and drainage. His method, using gravel and broken rock, formed a hard surface that was more durable and less muddy than dirt roads. Soon similar roads were being built throughout Europe, called in many different languages "macadam."

Water transport was also important for transporting raw materials and manufactured goods. Though the Bridgewater Canal, built in 1761 to carry coal by

John McAdam (1756—1836) Scottish engineer who developed a technique for a harder, less muddy road surface known as "macadam" in various languages.

barge to Manchester, was hard pressed by competition from the Liverpool and Manchester Railroad, the canal's success in generating an entire network of canals around Manchester inspired the Erie Canal in New York State. This canal's completion in 1825, connecting the Hudson River and Lake Erie, opened the American interior to overseas commerce. Even backward Russia improved its canal system, in 1808 rebuilding the Moscow-Petersburg canal first constructed by Peter the Great, and linking the Vistula, Bug, and Dnieper Rivers by canal in 1841 to allow the passage of goods by water from the Baltic to the Black Sea. Many smaller canals throughout Europe connected industry with raw materials and markets, increasingly working together with railroads.

The Social Impacts of Industrialization

The most noticeable—even shocking—impact of industrialization was **urbanization,** the rapid growth of cities. In the first half of the nineteenth century, hundreds of thousands of individuals both in Britain and on the continent left the countryside for work in cities. Factory owners needed large numbers of workers, and these were most readily available in large population centers. New factories built in the countryside to take advantage of waterpower, such as the mills established at the falls of the Clyde in Scotland, soon drew so many workers that mills became towns—in this case **New Lanark, Robert Owen**'s model factory town. Because workers required food, clothing, medical care, and housing, yet more people migrated to the industrialized towns to provide these services. Factory owners and managers in their large houses

required servants, who added to the population. For all these reasons, industrial cities grew at breathtaking rates, so fast that available housing was overwhelmed. As thousands of strangers were forced to live and work together in small, cramped spaces, disease and crime were the inevitable result.

The English city of **Manchester** offers a spectacular example of population growth. Located some thirty miles from the English port of Liverpool, Manchester had long been a center of wool cloth production, powered mainly by human muscle. But directly under and surrounding the city were huge coal deposits that would fuel the transition to steam power, and the opening of the Bridgewater Canal made coal transport cheap. These three factors—closeness to a port, large reserves of coal, and available skilled laborers—made Manchester the birthplace of industrialization. In 1750, the city's population was 20,000. In the next twenty-five years, the population doubled, but that was before industrial take-off. By 1831, the population had soared to more than 250,000, and by 1850, it was 400,000.

---

urbanization   Process by which cities grow as population shifts from rural to urban areas; a major effect of industrialization.

New Lanark   Cotton mill town on Clyde River in Scotland where Robert Owen combined profit making with efforts to improve workers' lives.

Robert Owen   (1771–1858) Scottish industrialist and utopian socialist who attempted to incorporate cooperative principles in his factories.

Manchester   Textile manufacturing city in northern England.

VoiceVoiceVoiceVoice

Friedrich Engels Describes the Condition of the Working Class in England

Friedrich Engels, the son of a German textile manufacturer, saw the impact of industrialization in England firsthand when his father sent him to work in a family-owned textile mill there. The conditions in which working-class people labored in England appalled Engels, compelling him to write his first book, The Condition of the Working Class in England in 1844. *Engels was only twenty-five when the book was published. It gained widespread attention and favorably impressed young Karl Marx, who soon became Engels's friend and collaborator.*

> ➜ *Name some of the ways that industrialization transformed England's society. According to Engels, how typical was England in this respect in 1844?*

> ➜ *Why would artisans be attracted to a growing town around a factory?*

> ➜ *What did Engels have in mind when he wrote of London's "marvels of civilisation"?*

Sixty, eighty years ago, England was a country like every other, with small towns, few and simple industries, and a thin but *proportionally* large agricultural population. ➜ Today it is a country like *no* other; with a capital of two and a half million inhabitants; with vast manufacturing cities; with an industry that supplies the world and produces almost everything by means of the most complex machinery; with an industrious, intelligent, dense population, of which two-thirds are employed in trade and commerce, ➜ and composed of classes wholly different; forming, in fact, with other customs and other needs, a different nation from the England of those days. The Industrial Revolution is of the same importance for England as the political revolution for France.

A manufacturing establishment requires many workers employed together in a single building, living near each other and forming a village of themselves in the case of a good-sized factory. ➜ They have needs for satisfying which other people are necessary; handicraftsmen, shoemakers, tailors, bakers, carpenters, stonemasons, settle at hand. ➜ The inhabitants of the village, especially the younger generation, accustom themselves to factory work, grow skilful in it, and when the first mill can no longer employ them all, wages fall, and the immigration of fresh manufacturers is the consequence. So the village grows into a small town, and the small town into a large one.

➜ Londoners have been forced to sacrifice the best qualities of their human nature, to bring to pass all the marvels of civilisation which crowd their city. . . . What is true of London, is true of Manchester, Birmingham, Leeds, is true of all great towns. ➜ The dwellings of the workers are everywhere badly planned, badly built, and kept in the worst condition, badly ventilated, damp, and unwholesome. The inhabitants are confined to the smallest possible space, and at least one family usually sleeps in each room. . . . The clothing of the workers, too, is generally scanty, and that of great multitudes is in rags. The food is in general, bad.

> ➜ *What does Engels mean when he claims that England is "composed of classes wholly different" and "a different nation" in 1844 than it had been sixty years earlier?*

> ➜ *Describe the steps by which a factory town becomes an industrial city, according to Engels.*

> ➜ *Why do you think that workers' housing, clothing, and food was of such bad quality?*

This rapid growth came at an enormous price: overcrowding, industrial pollution, and filth in the streets that made the stench of Manchester fabled. The air was full of soot and exhaust gases from the coal-powered engines in the factories. A French visitor in midcentury, the journalist Hippolite Taine, described the "dreary streets," full of "masses of livid children, dirty and flabby of flesh. Even to walk in the rich quarter of town is depressing." A medical doctor described this poverty in 1833: "Too often the dwelling of the factory family is no home; it sometimes is a cellar, which includes no cooking, no washing, no making, no mending, no decencies of life." But as the liberal French writer Alexis de Tocqueville observed, "From this filthy sewer pure gold flows."

Unscrupulous landlords threw up cheap, unventilated, and crowded **tenements** in which several families lived in a single room. Water had to be fetched from outdoor wells, often contaminated by outdoor privies. Food was expensive, in part because Britain's

tenements   Cheaply built, crowded, and often squalid multistory dwellings, often constructed by factory owners to house workers.

This painting of the industrial city of Manchester in 1851 graphically depicts the enormous impact of industrialization with the dozens of smokestacks pouring pollution into the air, rendering the city's air hazy and difficult to breath. The stunted trees in the foreground suggest the impact of industrialization on nature.
(The Royal Collection, © 2004 Her Majesty Queen Elizabeth II)

1815 Corn Laws forbade the import of grain. The lack of clean water and the overcrowding made epidemics of diseases like cholera and typhoid common; the polluted air caused respiratory problems that often developed into diseases such as asthma and **tuberculosis.** By the 1830s, British reformers had realized that only government intervention could help solve the problems associated with industrialization.

The pollution and environmental degradation was, literally, breathtaking. Industrial cities were black with soot; light-colored clothing would be filthy by the end of the day. One early solution to the problems of air pollution in Manchester and other industrial towns was to build factory chimneys ever higher so that winds would carry the fumes far away from the city. But this method simply spread pollution farther from the factories themselves. Mining ripped up the face of the earth and brought to the surface toxic substances that were simply dumped aside unless they had commercial value. Rainwater ran through these slag heaps, spreading the poison into rivers. In the absence of municipal water treatment plants—no industrial city

of the time had any—people were obliged to drink this foul, polluted water. Little wonder that in industrial towns, infant mortality was high and life expectancy low.

Industrialization changed the human sense of space and time. With railroads, cities were hours apart instead of days. But railroads and factories also demanded a more precise keeping of time and spurred on another industry—the manufacture of clocks and watches—as well as standardized time. Railways not only linked major cities but cut through less developed agricultural regions, ending their isolation. The physical presence of rails traversing the countryside reminded rural people that the excitement and economic promise of the big city lay mere hours away.

The Duke of Wellington worried that railways "would encourage the lower classes to move about,"

tuberculosis Infectious disease that affects the lungs and if untreated often leads to death; a common killer in the nineteenth century, now treatable with antibiotics.

and they did. Inexpensive fares in third-class carriages made possible travel on a scale hitherto unheard of: in 1844, 27.7 million railroad journeys were taken in Britain. Cheap fares encouraged the migration of impoverished rural people into the growing industrial cities, further accelerating their growth. By midcentury, more-distant journeys to America and Australia usually began with a train ride to the port, where emigrants boarded a steamship. Thus, the transportation revolution wrought by industrialization had a major impact not just on Europe but on the world.

One of the most far-reaching effects of the Industrial Revolution was the creation of social categories based on economic, not legal, status. Until industrialization, most people identified themselves by the social category of their birth—peasant, noble, artisan, merchant. These were legal, not merely economic, categories. It was quite possible for nobles to be poor and even (though more rarely) for peasants to be wealthy. Industrial societies, however, are ordered along class lines. One's class derives primarily from one's economic position in society, or as **Karl Marx** would later describe it, one's relation to the **means of production.** The factory owner controlled the means of production (the factory) and derived profit from it; the workers were an element in the means of production, much like the machine they tended.

The idea of class also implies a feeling of belonging together, or **class consciousness.** This consciousness was new in the early Industrial Revolution. Nobles had long distinguished themselves from commoners by dress, manners, and luxurious lifestyle. Now the growing middle classes, or bourgeoisie, differentiated themselves from nobles by their emphasis on the dignity of work and self-improvement, and from the working class by their accent, clean clothes, and soft hands. Workers, crammed together on factory floors and tenement houses, began to recognize their shared interests, too. With the coming of industrialization, society was no longer divided into three estates—the nobles, clergy, and peasants of France—or the lords and commoners of England. Now it was divided into capitalists, who had wealth available to invest in the means of production, and workers, the proletariat, who had no source of income other than their labor.

Industrialization also enhanced the possibility for social mobility. An intelligent, hardworking peasant boy could go to work in the city and hope to rise into the lower middle class or, if not he, then at least his children. To be sure, most of those born poor died that way—and died much earlier than their middle- and upper-class contemporaries. But the possibility of becoming a "self-made man" and rising above the

class of one's birth was an aspiration—and a reality—for many in this era.

The Middle Classes

↓ Who belonged to the middle classes?
↓ What moral and political values characterized the middle classes?

In the classic formulation, the middle class was, of course, in the middle—between the aristocracy on the one hand and the peasants on the other. In the nineteenth century, the middle classes distinguished themselves from the working classes, too. This group grew rapidly as industrialization progressed, and as they prospered, their political importance and influence grew as well. Speaking of "middle classes" in the plural suggests the great variety of occupations and mentalities that this category embraced. But all middle-class people defined themselves not by their birth but also by what they did—their occupation and, increasingly, their education. Their shared interests included pride in their respectability, sobriety, and hard work, often contrasting these "middle-class virtues" with the drunken and wasteful behavior of both workers and those born into great wealth. The middle-class home reflected this proud, sober, and somewhat smug attitude, with a wife who devoted herself entirely to her family, not needing to earn money outside the home. To be sure, this was an ideal not always realized in reality.

A Variety of Middle Classes

Europe had had a strong and growing class of merchants since the Middle Ages, and as commerce grew, so did banking, investing, and shipping. In the eighteenth century, lawyers, doctors, professors, and other educated professionals might have felt that their income and lifestyle gave them something in common with those who had grown rich from trade. And in the nineteenth century, these middle classes expanded

Karl Marx (1818–1883) German-born radical scholar and writer, long-time collaborator with Friedrich Engels, and author of *Capital* and *The Communist Manifesto.*

means of production Factories, workshops, and other tools that produce wealth.

class consciousness Identification with other members of one's economic class—for example, industrial workers or middle-class professionals.

rapidly. The spread of industrialism demanded and created capitalists with the liquid wealth, or capital, to invest in new factories. Complex machinery, production methods, and business arrangements created an increased need for engineers, skilled technicians, foremen, and managers as well as distributors and salesmen. All those who filled these positions were members of the middle classes.

Some of those who established new enterprises were aristocrats, such as the Duke of Bridgewater, who sank his fortune into the Bridgewater Canal. The canal returned an even greater fortune and also brought great earnings to the duke's engineer, James Brindley, a craftsman's son with little education. Brindley was a self-made man who achieved success through this own effort; in fact, biographers attributed his early death to diabetes and overwork. He is representative of a new class of men whose fame and fortune derived directly from industrialization. Richard Arkwright, a barber whose water frame made him rich, and James Watt, whose improvements on the steam engine made him wealthy, are others. So are Richard Cobden, son of a farmer who gained wealth as a calico printer and prominence as a member of Parliament from Stockport, near Manchester. His close associate in the Anti–Corn Law League, John Bright, was the grandson of a farmer. For these men, social status and identity derived not from birth but from accomplishment. The middle classes were varied and fluid enough to be open to newcomers. Industrialization increased social mobility.

Differences within the middle classes were huge. The richest industrialists, for example, married their daughters into aristocratic families; thus their grandchildren would be "upper class" and frequently embarrassed by grandfather's coarse, unrefined manners. On the other hand, impoverished clerks, owners of small shops, teachers, governesses—the so-called petty bourgeoisie—were in constant peril of sinking down into the "lower depths" of society. The greater possibility for social mobility brought about by industrialization thus cut both ways, enabling the strong, intelligent, and lucky to rise but also making it easy to fall from respected middle-class status into poverty and social disgrace.

Middle-Class Culture

While some of the self-made men in the new middle classes had limited school-

Accommodations in railroad coaches reflected social class divisions. Aristocrats and the rich traveled in first-class coaches, "respectable" middle-class people in second, and everyone else in third. While passengers in third (above) and first (below) classes traveled in very different style, the railroad aided social leveling by the simple fact that everyone left and arrived at the same time. *(above: Mary Evans Picture Library/The Image Works; below: Roger-Viollet/Getty Images)*

ing themselves, they all believed firmly in the value of learning, and they made certain that their sons—and, increasingly, their daughters—had good educations. A secondary or university education almost guaranteed middle-class status, and university enrollments grew steadily throughout the nineteenth century. New universities were founded, often specifically to fulfill the requirements of the new, industrializing society, such as University College London, which provided practical educational opportunities to middle-class men and women. In Berlin, a *Bauakademie*—academy of architecture and engineering—was founded by the Prussian state in 1799 and was joined in 1821 by a *Gewerbeakademie*, or business or trade school. These institutions were merged in 1879 to form the Royal Technical Higher School of Berlin, the forerunner of today's Technical University of Berlin. Significantly, these university-level institutions to train engineers and businessmen in Berlin were founded by the government whereas University College London arose from private initiative.

In central Europe, the emerging class of the *Bildungsbürgertum*, the educated bourgeoisie, testifies to the importance of education for middle-class status. Despite **Wilhelm von Humboldt**'s revitalization of German universities in the first years of the nineteenth century, training entrepreneurs or technicians was not seen as the university's role. Rather, individuals wishing to pursue such practical studies enrolled in institutions like the business or engineering academies in Berlin. In the decades between 1830 and 1860, the most popular subjects at German universities were theology and law (around 30 percent of students each), medicine and liberal arts (15 percent each), with only 5 percent of German students majoring in science.

While a university education secured one's middle-class status, most likely as a member of a profession such as law, medicine, or the church, middle-class people valued hard work equally. The enterprising writer, physician, and editor **Samuel Smiles** provided a formula for success in his 1859 book *Self-Help*. Thrift, hard work, and sobriety were important, as were self-denial, good habits, and the ability to learn from mistakes. "Life will always be to a large extent what we ourselves make it," wrote Smiles. As inspiration, he also wrote biographies of self-made men, such as potter Josiah Wedgwood and engineer George Stephenson. Smiles also believed that self-improvement would contribute to the improvement of society as a whole.

In their emphasis on practical knowledge, middle-class people may be seen as the heirs of the Enlightenment, but their strict views on sobriety and sexual

morality derive rather from Protestant Christian traditions. Young people were admonished to avoid the temptations not only of sexual intercourse before marriage but even of sexual thoughts or masturbation. Many manuals and self-help books for parents and young people warned that "self-abuse" would lead to bad eyesight, insanity, and other misfortunes, including death. Ideally, men and women were to find sexual pleasure only within the bounds of marriage. Sexual love between members of the same sex was literally unspeakable: the word *homosexuality* was not coined until 1869. It is not by chance that later generations would use the word **Victorian**—referring to the reign of British queen Victoria—to mean preachy, sexually repressed, hypocritical, and narrow minded. Still, this characterization is at best one sided. Middle-class ideology in the nineteenth century did have its humorless, self-righteous aspects, but its grinding emphasis on work reflected a desire to validate middle-class identity and to assert that individual dignity should be gauged not by birth but by service to society.

As members of a largely new and growing social grouping, middle-class people felt keenly the need to establish and augment their prestige and respectability, often by promoting their values of self-improvement, education, and sobriety among the less fortunate. Smiles argued that only by adopting middle-class values and habits could workers lift themselves out of poverty. Many middle-class women, especially, engaged actively in charity work, sometimes alienating those they intended to help with their strident self-righteousness. The **temperance movement**, for example, was a middle-class reform directed mainly at the working class. Alcoholism was a problem, but workers were often put off by the well-dressed preachy women who scolded them for their drinking habits.

The middle-class belief in hard work as the key to success implied that poverty was something that those who would not work hard enough brought on

Wilhelm von Humboldt (1767–1835) German philosopher, linguist, and statesman, after whom Berlin's main university is named.

Samuel Smiles (1812–1904) Scottish writer who achieved fame through books promising success through hard work, such as *Self-Help, Thrift, Character,* and *Duty.*

Victorian Term referring to the reign of Queen Victoria (r. 1837–1901) and carrying a connotation of sexual restraint, humorlessness, and social conservatism.

temperance movement Movement to ban the use of alcoholic beverages, often affiliated with Christian churches and led by middle-class women.

themselves. Thus, the structural causes of poverty, unleashed by industrialization, were obscured. The historian **François Guizot**, who dominated French politics in the 1840s, believed that the opportunity for riches was open to all and that failure to achieve wealth reflected an individual's own limitations and weaknesses. Rather than blaming society for their misery, Guizot argued, the poor had only themselves to blame. If they would stay sober, work hard, and live frugally, they would better their social condition. Many middle-class liberals would have agreed, pointing to their own success as proof that hard work alone brought prosperity and social status.

Middle-class respectability involved both self-control and self-righteousness—overall, an avoidance of extremes. In their churches, the middle classes avoided ostentatious ceremonies, mysticism, and overly emotional displays of devotion. The Church of England and the official Protestant churches in central Europe and Scandinavia reprimanded clergy who showed excessive "enthusiasm" or religious fervor, and pastors who pressed their middle-class parishioners too strongly about their sins might find themselves snubbed by the parish. But some Protestants found worship without ceremony and emotion arid and devoid of profound religious meaning. A few left the Church of England for dissenting chapels, and at Oxford, a group of prominent Anglican clergymen who sought to revive certain Roman Catholic rituals drew much attention, particularly when some of them converted to Catholicism.

As Jews began to assimilate into the middle class, dressing and speaking like other members of that class, they also sought to reform their religious practices. The traditional long caftan of the rabbi was exchanged for a sober outfit resembling that of a Protestant pastor. Within the synagogue, a more orderly religious service was inaugurated, sometimes even with choirs and organs, which were quite foreign to Jewish religious traditions. While generally remaining true to their religious laws, avoiding certain foods and keeping the Sabbath (Saturday) holy, these middle-class Jews attempted in all other ways to resemble their Gentile neighbors. Their **Reform Judaism** was strongest in German areas, but even among the overwhelmingly traditional and Orthodox Polish Jews in Warsaw and Lwów, Reform synagogues were opened in the 1840s. More traditional Jews saw these innovations as the first step to conversion to Christianity, and in their own way, they were right. Later Reform Judaism was to significantly relax the strict requirements to eat only kosher food, to abstain from work on Saturdays, and to orient one's life around prayer, worship, and study. Moreover, many

of the middle-class Jews who shed their traditional Jewish garb and habits later abandoned Judaism altogether, as did the children of the preeminent Jewish Enlightenment figure, Moses Mendelssohn. For them, as for the fathers of Karl Marx, English conservative statesman **Benjamin Disraeli**, and many others, social **assimilation** was the first step toward conversion.

The Middle-Class Home

As industrialization spread, concepts of home and work became increasingly separated. In a preindustrial society, artisans lived in or near their workshops, and peasants lived near the fields they tilled, sometimes even sharing their lodgings with their domestic animals. But in industrial societies, just as "work" became associated with a "workplace"—a factory—so, for the middle classes, did the home become distinctly apart from the dirt and noise of manufacturing and the fast-paced and high-pressure world of business. The newly wealthy industrialists built large houses away from their factories, and their wives were expected to create a restful and pleasant haven for their hardworking husbands to return to after a hard day's work. To be sure, these **separate spheres** of home and work were more an ideal than a reality for all middle-class homes, but this ideal had a strong influence on middle-class identity and on ideas of a woman's "proper place." Women's legal status remained unchanged; legally, women were an extension of their fathers or husbands.

Marriage was a vital and central institution of middle-class life; this society rejected as peculiar, and even suspicious, the idea of remaining unmarried, with a few exceptions, such as Roman Catholic priests.

François Guizot (1787–1874) French historian and politician who believed that the poor must improve their own economic condition through hard work without government aid.

Reform Judaism Movement to modernize Jewish life, retaining the religious core of Judaism but eliminating many differences from Gentiles in everyday life.

Benjamin Disraeli (1804—1881) English writer and conservative statesman who was a favorite of Queen Victoria; the son of a converted Jew but very proud of his Jewish origins.

assimilation Process by which one ethnic or cultural group takes on the attributes of another.

separate spheres Middle-class ideal whereby home life was strictly separated from the workplace, with women running the household and men earning money outside it.

The first line of Jane Austen's *Pride and Prejudice* reflects this fact: "It is a truth universally acknowledged, that a single man in possession of a good fortune must be in want of a wife." Founding a family was of vital importance, but first of all, a middle-class man had to establish himself in business—in effect, earn his fortune. Men were typically older than the women they married and were expected to guide and train their wives as well as to love them. The husband had to earn a sufficient amount to pay for a middle-class home and servants and—of course—to allow his wife to devote herself exclusively to her family with needing to earn money.

Middle-class girls were raised to see marriage as their main purpose in life. Not making a suitable marriage was also feared, as it might mean an unpleasant dependency on wealthier relations or a meager livelihood as a "genteel" lady's maid or governess. Once she was married, a middle-class woman's role included running the household, supervising servants, educating her children, and in some cases helping her husband in his professional or scientific endeavors. Outside the home, it was considered proper for a middle-class woman to be active in charitable and religious organizations. Women did not have careers, though they might make their own way as teachers, seamstresses, or milliners—the latter two professions perilously near "working class." Nineteenth-century novels often examine the dilemmas of bright and sensitive young women of marriageable age. Their authors were themselves women who were trying to make their way as writers—**Charlotte Brontë**, author of *Jane Eyre*, is one example. She and her sister **Emily** published under male names, as did **George Sand** (Amandine Aurore Lucile Dupin) in France and **George Eliot** (Mary Ann Evans) in England. By publishing under male names, these pioneering women writers aimed to force readers to take their writing more seriously, and they also sought to avoid criticism by their own middle-class families about earning money with their pen. While some women published—at times with great success—under their own (female) names, they often found that their work was considered by male critics a mere pastime, not real literature.

Middle-class women were not supposed to earn money—just to spend it. While servants usually did the shopping, it was the "lady of the house" who ordered goods, checked prices, kept accounts, and made sure that neither servants nor merchants were cheating her. Even when she had a housekeeper to perform most of these duties, she was expected by her husband to make sure that all of these activities were carried out properly. The middle-class woman also had to purchase clothes for herself and her fam-

The *Englishwoman's Domestic Magazine*'s illustrations reflected middle class women's desire for respectability and even extravagance in fashion. Increasingly able to afford new outfits frequently, women of the middle class consulted such magazines to learn the latest style. *(Corporation of London/HIP/The Image Works)*

ily and to furnish her home tastefully. To help homemakers make choices in their selection of furnishings and clothing, entrepreneurs began to publish books and periodicals devoted to proper, respectable fashions, such as *The Englishwoman's Domestic Magazine*, which began appearing in 1852.

Charlotte and **Emily Brontë** (1816–1855, 1818–1848) English novelists and poets, authors of novels including *Jane Eyre* (Charlotte) and *Wuthering Heights* (Emily).

George Sand (1804–1876) French female author of more than eighty novels who took a man's name and dressed in male attire to protest the treatment of women.

George Eliot (1819–1880) Major English novelist, born Mary Ann Evans, whose novels portrayed social and moral problems of the lower middle class.

Children in middle-class families were trained to be obedient, clean, respectful, and orderly. Physical punishment of children was considered normal, indeed inevitable, though usually the task of the man: respectable French fathers had a small whip for that purpose. At the same time, the ideas of Jean Jacques Rousseau on education and allowing children free time for play and physical development were spreading. Middle-class children were usually educated at home by governesses and tutors, as there was not yet a well-developed educational system. Looking back at their childhood later in the century, many middle-class people recalled the great freedom they had enjoyed compared with later youths, who would be obliged to spend more regimented days in schoolrooms. Because of improved nutrition and sanitation, middle-class families were likely to have many children; it was not unusual for a woman to have ten or more pregnancies in her lifetime. As the century progressed, infant mortality decreased, and the size of middle-class families grew.

Working Classes

⬇ How did industrialization and urbanization change everyday and family life?

⬇ How did industrial workers attempt to improve their work situations?

Industrialization created the working class—or classes. This large group included miners, industrial workers, servants, and artisans, who worked and lived in conditions that were often appalling. Industrialization and urbanization disrupted working-class family life. Increasingly, mothers, fathers, and children went to different workplaces, carrying out separate tasks. The crowded conditions, combined with the city's many temptations, made the proper upbringing and discipline of children all the more difficult. But workers did not simply accept their lot passively. Working-class people banded together to protect themselves from the worst aspects of early industrialization, organizing unions, demanding better working and living conditions, and insisting on their own dignity in the face of what they saw as middle-class indifference.

Diversity Within the Working Class

Manchester exemplifies the triumphs and contradictions of early industrialization better than any other city. Here huge amounts of money were made by a few, but for the workers, life was harsh, brutal, and short. The workday was long—sometimes stretching to fourteen and sixteen hours, six and even seven days

a week. Workers who arrived late were beaten and fined or their pay was docked. Slippery factory floors, complex systems of gears and transmission belts, and the constant presence of fumes endangered life and limb. If injured, workers could expect to be fired instantly. Workers' health also suffered from damp and dank workplaces, sometimes overheated, sometimes chilled by open windows. The air was always filled with smells, fibers, and particles of cloth. Tuberculosis and cholera were always common. The reformer and Manchester native **Edwin Chadwick** pointed out in 1842 that smoke in Manchester was killing vegetation. In the same report he described workers' housing in another industrial city, Leeds: "walls unwhitewashed for years, black with the smoke of foul chimneys, without water, . . . and sacking for bed-clothes, with floors unwashed from year to year."

As industrialization proceeded, artisans often found themselves out of work, replaced by machines. In the early years, artisans' skills had been essential to factory design and operations. But soon mass production deprived tailors, clockmakers, and shoemakers of their livelihood and way or life. Even more directly threatened were weavers and others engaged in textile production. Those who found new employment in mechanized, power-driven textile factories often perceived the change from artisan to worker as painful and humiliating. They resented the constant surveillance of foremen and felt dehumanized by the need to adapt their skills and their personal rhythms to the tempo of the machine. The life of a hand-loom weaver had not been easy, but at least he (weavers were usually men) worked his own hours and was paid a living wage. As artisans were driven out of work and forced to accept factory jobs, they no longer had these satisfactions.

The working classes also included servants. The majority of servants were women, often young girls who came from the countryside to seek employment in the growing number of middle-class households. Hannah Cullwick of Shropshire, for example, lost her parents as a teenager, moved to London, and took a job in the house of a middle-class beer merchant. Remembering her experiences, Hannah described the great gulf between her drudgery as a servant and the life of a "real lady," who "couldn't wash a plate or a saucepan or peal a tato." But the servant class was itself divided into classes. At the very bottom was the harried "girl of all work" who scrubbed, fetched water,

Edwin Chadwick (1800–1890) English social reformer who worked to improve conditions for the poor through better hygiene and government programs.

Realist artist Vasily Perov portrays the misery of the Russian serfs and the indifference of a respectable Russian Orthodox clergyman in this bitter painting, *Tea Drinking at Mytishchi near Moscow* (1862). Juxtaposing impoverished peasants or workers and unfeeling middle- and upper-class people was a common means by which realist artists conveyed a message. *(Tretjakov Gallery, Moscow/akg-images)*

Peasant girls often spent several years "in service" before returning home to marry. Servants might take factory jobs, which paid better and gave them more personal freedom. Generally, however, the flow of country people to the city was one way: after living in the city, few young people wished to return to the strict supervision of elders in the boring village. Despite the crowded and unhygienic conditions of early industrial cities, for many workers, life there brought a degree of personal freedom unknown in the countryside.

washed dishes, and generally carried out any tasks the housekeeper or cook ordered her to do. The cook and chambermaid were her superiors, and they enjoyed a bit more respect. At the very top of the servant class were the housekeeper and butler, who not only dressed and spoke (or attempted to) like the master and mistress but also supervised their fellow servants.

In the new economy-based social divisions, peasants can be considered working class as well. In Britain, while thousands of peasants left the countryside for work in the cities, some farmers who remained on the land enjoyed increasing prosperity. But peasants in Ireland lived in extreme poverty and suffered from malnutrition and catastrophic famine in the 1840s. French peasants, on the whole, lived more comfortably than peasants elsewhere, a condition that explains in part their reluctance to leave their farms and migrate to cities to work in industry. Conditions for peasants were worst of all in eastern Europe, where serfdom remained. Serfs were not only impoverished but could not even leave their village without their landlord's permission. In Russia, the Habsburg Empire, and the Balkan Peninsula, serfdom was not abolished until 1848 or later. Legal serfdom, combined with the extreme poverty of these countries, constituted a severe hindrance to industrial development.

Employment for the working classes was fluid. Some young men sought temporary work in the cities before returning to the village to establish a family.

Working Families

On farms and in farming villages, families worked together; in artisan shops, families were often productive units. Early factories transferred this pattern to a new location. Men, women, and children continued to work side by side. The heavier physical work, such as operating looms, was usually carried out by men. Women predominated among spinners and in other tasks that required less heavy work, as they were assumed to have more manual dexterity than men. And children worked at a variety of light jobs, handling small spools of thread and reaching into places where adult hands could not fit. Even as industry developed, parents often chose to bring their children along with them to work rather than leave them alone at home.

Long before the factory system, women had worked alongside their menfolk in the putting-out system. Spinning wool (later, cotton) into yarn was an almost exclusively female occupation. Factory owners also liked to hire entire families as a means of reducing individual wages. Sometimes men and women would work in the same factory but in different workshops. Men always predominated in metalworking and mining. Children also worked in coal mines, where boys and girls as young as age eight pushed carts laden with coal up from narrow shafts.

Children's labor brought in much-needed income for their families, but increasingly the working family was separated by work. It no longer functioned as an economic unit. From 1802 onward, the British Parliament passed laws limiting child labor, but it was only after 1833 that these laws were really enforced. Eventually child labor was banned altogether, as reformers argued that childhood should be spent in school or at play—not in mines or textile mills. But few children actually went to school. Instead, they were excluded from factory work largely because of the increasing complexity of machines and industrial processes. In Prussia the employment of children under nine in factories was forbidden in 1839. In France, the Child Labor Law of 1841 forbade the employment of children under eight years of age and set down that children under age twelve could not work more than eight hours daily. King Leopold of Belgium proclaimed a similar law limiting child labor in 1842. But such laws were very hard to enforce, in particular because governments seldom wanted to pay for inspectors who would actually check factories for violations.

The employment of women was a different matter. Factory owners often preferred to hire women over men because they could pay women lower wages. Women were also less likely to cause trouble, being much less inclined to alcoholism, insubordination, and union activity. But as industrialization developed, women's work in industry was limited to certain occupational categories, especially in textiles, and was the subject of considerable debate. Middle-class women were almost entirely shut out of paid labor. But some commentators—usually middle-class men—denounced work outside the home as endangering healthy family life for the working class as well. Others argued that women needed to be protected from the bad effects of factory work on the delicate female body and possible harm to their ability to produce healthy children. Midwives did, in fact, note that the babies of factory women were often delicate and prone to illness, and in 1847 Parliament limited the working day of women and children in textiles to ten hours. Nevertheless, women continued to work, as their wages were often necessary for the family's survival and, if single, they enjoyed the independence wage work gave them.

Working families' domestic life was vastly different from life in middle-class homes. Workingwomen kept their own house and did their own washing and cooking in dwellings that were sparse and at times even squalid. Young babies had to be "farmed out" to wet nurses so that the mother could continue work-ing. Frequently these babies died in their first months of life, and estimates of child mortality up to the age of five reach as high as 50 percent in the early to mid-nineteenth century. One common practice for keeping infants still was to give them drugs such as **laudanum** or a highly alcoholic "cordial." Malnutrition and the conditions of early factory work had very negative consequences for these children's health. One doctor wrote that children working in the Manchester cotton mills were "almost universally ill-looking, small, sickly, barefoot and ill-clad . . . a degenerate race." Military leaders also complained that young men who had grown up in working-class families were smaller in stature, thinner, and less hearty than peasant lads. More generally, parents came to recognize that children—despite the pennies they might earn working in a factory—were a drain on the family's resources. As industrialization and urbanization progressed, birthrates almost always declined.

Workingmen sought refuge from the conditions of factory and tenement in the taverns, which were generally off-limits for respectable women. Drinking was more than an attempt to forget one's misery in an alcoholic haze; visiting the pub was an integral part of male working-class comraderie. A workingman who never visited the tavern would be considered abnormal—asocial and probably thinking too highly of himself. But the money spent on drink meant that much less remained for the family's support. Not by chance women spearheaded the temperance movement, calling on men to abandon the bottle and spend more time with and money on their families.

Many working families barely earned a living, and the lures of the criminal world described in nineteenth-century novels were real. Like Fagin's band of boy thieves in **Charles Dickens**'s *Oliver Twist,* orphans in London's slums engaged in pickpocketing and other petty crime. Like Sonya Marmeladov in **Fyodor Dostoevsky**'s *Crime and Punishment,* young women turned to prostitution to support their families. Gin, opium, games of chance, cockfights, bearbaiting: a variety of unsavory and illegal pastimes were available in industrial cities, enriching some but impoverishing

laudanum   Opium dissolved in alcohol, a popular though habit-forming sleep aid in the nineteenth century.

Charles Dickens   (1812–1870) Famous English novelist, author of *Oliver Twist, A Tale of Two Cities,* and *A Christmas Carol,* among many others.

Fyodor Dostoevsky   (1821–1881) Russian writer, author of *Crime and Punishment, The Brothers Karamazov,* and other novels.

many. Yet the industrial cities held opportunities that peasant life could not offer: taverns, theaters, coffee-houses, and the dream of advancement—the chance, however slim, of making one's fortune.

Moreover, family life was not entirely dismal. Parents and children celebrated holidays and played games together. Religion provided comfort and companionship. Working-class people in Britain were often attracted to **Methodism,** a religious movement founded by John Wesley in the eighteenth century that preached self-control, frugality, hard work, and self-respect. Methodism gave working-class people a sense of mission, dignity, and community. Methodist preachers (often themselves of working-class origin) emphasized that working people were separate from, but in no way inferior to, members of the middle and upper classes. Methodism stressed the fundamental Christian beliefs that honored the meek and humble over the rich and powerful, specifically identifying working people with Christ's teaching that the "poor in spirit" would inherit the "kingdom of heaven" and the "meek" would "inherit the earth." On a practical level, Methodist preachers often set up Sunday schools to teach workers and their children how to read and write. Methodist worship services were emotional occasions during which preachers and congregation would shout, groan, leap up, faint, and sing praises. Methodist revival meetings, often held in the open air, attracted thousands of enthusiastic worshipers in the early decades of the nineteenth century.

Working-Class Consciousness and Trade Unionism

Industrialization brought workers together in densely packed spaces. Most did not enjoy the work. Their lives were constricted by factory rules and hours, and whatever independence they might have formerly enjoyed as farmers or artisans was gone. So was pride in their craft and in the products they made: many early mass-produced goods were less durable and attractive than items produced by skilled artisans. Moreover, in the factory no one worker made something from start to finish. In a textile factory, for example, spinners spun the thread and weavers wove it into cloth. In a garment factory, one person cut the cloth, another stitched only sleeves, another finished buttonholes. This division of labor was efficient, but it made work repetitive and monotonous. Workers often felt like they were cogs in a machine. Without any control over their work, they sensed they had lost a part of their humanity. Karl Marx would later attribute this sense to what he described as factory workers' **alienation** from the product of their labor.

Increasingly, working people recognized their common interests and joined together to press for political changes that would aid them. The workers of Manchester who gathered at St. Peter's Field in 1819 were protesting the Corn Laws that kept the price of grain artificially high. Chartist protests of the 1830s and 1840s were democratic, aiming to gain political rights for workingmen, though women also participated. **William Cobbett,** the most famous working-class radical, argued tirelessly against child labor and the unfairness of a society in which some enjoyed great wealth while many could not provide for their most basic needs. "No society," he proclaimed, "ought to exist where the labourers live in a hog-like sort of way." Cobbett's protests help bring about Britain's 1832 Reform Act, but for many political change was too slow and not enough.

Some workers resorted to violence. In the second decade of the nineteenth century, textile workers in Britain's industrial cities occasionally destroyed their machines. As they claimed to be followers of "General Ludd," a mythical figure, they came to be known as **Luddites.** In France, artisans attacked the hated symbol of industrialization, the Jacquard loom. In the city of Lyon, the weavers' guild staged a public execution for the Jacquard loom in 1806, smashing it to bits, then setting the fragments ablaze. A generation later, worker dissatisfaction boiled over in a series of bloody riots and insurrections. The largest uprising occurred in 1831, again in Lyon, where thousands of workers, most from the silk industry, took to the streets. Government repression of these outbreaks took hundreds of lives. On a more personal level, workers avenged themselves on hated foremen by waylaying them after work, sometimes stuffing them headfirst into a sack, then soundly beating it.

Other forms of worker resistance took milder forms. Common was the practice of "blue Monday," in which

Methodism   Religious movement in nineteenth-century Britain that preached self-control, frugality, and hard work, appealing primarily to working-class people.

alienation   Marx's concept of the breakdown, under capitalism, of workers' pride in and identification with the product of their labor.

William Cobbett   (1763–1835) English political reformer who advocated radical working-class politics, elected to Parliament after the Reform Act of 1832.

Luddites   Workers and artisans who destroyed the machines depriving them of a livelihood during early stages of industrialization; now anyone who opposes technological change.

workers—often hung over from overindulgence on their one day of rest—failed to show up for work. Workers also engaged in petty theft or purposely worked at a slow pace. But all these methods had one great disadvantage: the employer could at any moment, without justification, fire workers. Thus, any kind of protest, absence, or work slowdown could bring unemployment—a word that is itself a product of industrialization.

Machine breaking and other forms of resistance were random and unorganized, and so were many strikes, when workers just illegally walked off the job. But coordinated efforts increasingly testified to a strengthening working-class consciousness. In Britain the Combination Acts of 1799 and 1800 severely limited workers' ability to "combine"—that is, to organize for better wages and working conditions. This law made it necessary to disguise workers' organizations as self-help societies that collected money from members to provide support in case of injury, illness, or family emergencies. In Russia, even these organizations were illegal, and in most of Europe, **trade unions**, worker organizations that demanded higher wages and better working conditions, were suppressed until after 1850. Britain, however, repealed the Combination Acts in 1824, allowing workers to organize openly. The repeal also permitted strikes in certain cases, but while the number of strikes did increase after 1824, most often factory owners found it easy to intimidate or simply fire union organizers and other troublemakers. Nevertheless, Parliament also took action, passing Conspiracy Laws in 1825 that again restricted the right to strike.

British unions concentrated on trying to limit work hours. The 1847 act that limited the workday for women and children to ten hours was an early success, though somewhat ironic, as women were excluded from union membership. Trade unionists claimed that workingwomen depressed workingmen's wages, preferring instead to press for a "family wage," sufficient for a husband to allow his wife to stay home and raise a family. Most trade unions combined practical activities like schools and clubs with larger appeals for international working-class solidarity. So did the working-class newspapers that began to appear in France in the 1830s and 1840s, though their readership was limited.

Before 1850, working-class organizations were weak and largely ineffective. In most European countries, such as Russia and Germany, workers had no right to organize whatsoever. In Britain and France, laws restricted the ability of workers to organize and strike. Governments tended to side with factory owners against the workers, seeing investors and capitalists as necessary for economic development of the state.

Improvements for workers would not come until their organizations were stronger and their perspective put forward in a coherent ideology.

Critics of Industrialization

↓ How did society's view of poverty change with industrialization?
↓ What were the main differences between utopian socialism and Marx's scientific socialism?

Industrialization created enormous wealth and great poverty at the same time, and the inequality between capitalist entrepreneurs and wageworkers struck many thinking people as outrageous. These critics of industrialization called for a more equal sharing of profits and even created complex schemes for perfect societies. These first socialists later were themselves criticized by Karl Marx, who insisted that their cooperative, nonviolent methods were doomed to failure. Only by organization and violent revolution, he argued, could the injustices of industrialization be righted.

Poverty in Industrial Societies

Poverty has existed as long as human society, but the poverty created by industrialization was not only more noticeable but also more frightening than rural poverty because it was concentrated in cities, close to the institutions of government and to the ruler's residence. Early concepts of the deserving (hardworking, but unlucky) and undeserving (lazy, drunken, unruly) poor were hard to apply to the situation in industrial cities. Workers had much more money than peasants; but they also had to pay for everything, at prices that were very high, whereas peasants usually paid little or nothing for their hut or humble housing and often grew at least some of their own food. Peasant poverty fluctuated with crop yield, but there was always a social safety net, as relatives, neighbors, and even the landlord would usually help out in cases of extreme need. In the anonymous industrial city, no such safety net existed. Unlike the noble landlord, the factory owner rarely knew his workers and did not consider himself responsible for them.

Worker poverty also fluctuated with the success or failure of industrial enterprises and economies increasingly subject to boom-and-bust cycles. Because

trade unions   Organizations having the aim of protecting workers' rights, improving working conditions, and enhancing workers' prosperity.

of the difficulty of obtaining reliable credit, businesses often went bankrupt, throwing all their employees out of work. Sometimes, as in the U.S. Panic of 1819, overproduction caused a general depression throughout the economy as one factory after another was forced to close down. But one very great difference between poverty before and after the Industrial Revolution must be noted. Previously, poverty meant being on the edge of starvation, and the periodic famines that swept Europe killed thousands. After industrialization, such famines no longer occurred. England and Ireland offer an example; both experienced bad harvests in the early 1840s, but industrialized England did not experience famine, while agricultural Ireland, also beset by the potato blight, did.

The criticisms of industrialization focused less on absolute poverty than on the sharp difference in conditions of life between factory owners and their workers. These critics pointed out the inequitable distribution of wealth in a capitalist system, though they did not generally use that word. **Capitalism** is an economic system in which the means of production are privately owned and operated by individuals for a profit and in which the market plays a dominant role. Modern capitalism developed alongside industrialization, increasing the efficiency of production, extending markets around the world, but also bringing with it new social problems.

Early Socialists

The liberal response to the poverty caused by industrialization was to promote a free market that would, liberals believed, eventually increase prosperity for all. Middle-class liberals extolled individual rights, property, and rule by the most competent. They were inherently **elitist** in their insistence that wealthier and better-educated segments of society dominate in politics but at the same time potentially **egalitarian** in their emphasis on self-help, education, and hard work as the means for improving one's own economic and social condition. Other political thinkers held that the economic and political system itself made it impossible for workers to improve their lives. The discrepancy between the egalitarian ideals of middle-class liberalism and its elitism in practice fueled political **radicalism**, in particular in the form of **socialism**. Many early socialist writers and leaders were themselves from middle-class backgrounds, most famous among them Karl Marx and Friedrich Engels.

While liberalism championed the individual's right to property, socialism put the primary emphasis on the welfare of society as a whole. Socialists disagreed on the status and morality of private property, but all agreed that the rich should share their wealth, for both moral and practical reasons. Such a social sharing was moral because every human being had a right to minimal standards of decent food and housing. It was practical because by lessening the misery of the working masses, the more fortunate classes would defuse anger and hostility that could otherwise explode into violence.

Like liberalism and nationalism, modern concepts of socialism derive from the French Revolution, which proclaimed "fraternity," or solidarity among all citizens, whether rich or poor. During the French Revolution, socialist ideas were championed by the radical **François Babeuf.** Shocked by the continued existence of poor and rich, Babeuf demanded not just legal equality for all citizens but "real equality"—that is, an elimination of differences in wealth and social status. Real equality could be achieved, Babeuf argued, only by a total elimination of private property and by state control of goods and even state-sponsored employment programs. While Babeuf made little impact at the time—he was executed in 1797—his ideas of a state in which all material goods would be shared formed a cornerstone of socialist thought.

Babeuf's ideas influenced the so-called **utopian socialists** of the early nineteenth century. The term itself comes from Karl Marx, who described these thinkers as "utopian"—that is, naive, unrealistic, and impractical—to distinguish them from his own thought, which Marx termed "scientific." Like Babeuf, the utopians looked forward to a harmonious society

capitalism Economic system characterized by private property and a market economy developed by industrialization in the nineteenth and twentieth centuries.

elitist Belief that a small and superior group of individuals (the elite) has the moral right and responsibility to make important social and political decisions.

egalitarianism (from French, "equal") Belief that all people should have the same social, political, and—in its most radical version—economic rights.

radicalism Political ideologies that strive for thoroughgoing political and social changes.

socialism Political movement of nineteenth and twentieth centuries that aimed to end industrial poverty by spreading profits throughout society.

François Babeuf (1760–1797) French revolutionary who demanded not only legal but also economic equality among all citizens.

utopian socialists Early socialists such as Saint-Simon, Fourier, and Owen who believed that the profits of industrialization should be used to improve living conditions throughout society.

in which material differences would be minimized. They did not, however, advocate the total abolition of private property, nor did they foresee a violent revolution that would overturn capitalism. In the details of the social transformation they proposed, the three main utopian socialists—**Claude Henri de Saint-Simon, Charles Fourier,** and Robert Owen—differed significantly. What united them was a desire to harness industrialization to improve life for all classes, to avoid social conflicts, and in the end to create a just, attractive, and humane society.

Claude Henri de Saint-Simon, born in 1760 to a noble family, was a grown man during the French Revolution and as an aristocrat came close to meeting his end at the guillotine. He fought on the American side during the Revolutionary War, made a fortune as a speculator during the 1790s, went bankrupt, and spent time in an insane asylum. Despite his aristocratic background, Saint-Simon detested kings, the nobility, and bishops. He admired British society, seeing it as a system that rewarded merit and hard work. Like the British liberals, Saint-Simon admired intelligence and the entrepreneurial spirit. But in contrast to the liberal belief that competition in a free market would benefit all, Saint-Simon emphasized social cooperation and planning, led by a dedicated, well-educated elite.

Saint-Simon's last major work, *The New Christianity* (incomplete at the time of his death in 1825), attempted to place his ideas on economic justice and a new society in a Christian framework. Surveying the history of Catholicism and Protestantism, he criticized both for failing to respond to the problem of poverty. His New Christianity, he claimed, would rejuvenate Christianity's fundamental rejection of violence and call for compassion. He charged rulers to: "Hearken to the voice of God that speaks through me. Return to the path of Christianity. . . . Remember that Christianity commands you to use all your powers to increase as rapidly as possible the welfare of the poor." These ideas gained considerable prominence among businessmen, intellectuals, and politicians in France, but Saint-Simon's most significant contribution was his linking of industrial growth to general social improvement rather than simply to individual enrichment.

Charles Fourier, the most visionary of the utopians, demanded a far more thorough transformation of society than Saint-Simon. Fourier was an eccentric and difficult man. He came from a family of cloth merchants and earned his living in trade. At the same time, he spent his free moments concocting a utopian scheme of grandiose proportions aimed to solve the economic, social, and even spiritual problems of society. Human beings are motivated, Fourier proposed,

by twelve main passions, ranging from friendship and ambition to love of intrigue and the five senses (taste, smell, touch, sight, and hearing). While all of these passions are present in every human being, the proportion of each differs greatly. Using complex and quite incomprehensible mathematical principles (Fourier left behind several notebooks containing nothing but equations and mathematical notations), he arrived at the idea of the *phalange.*

Each *phalange* would include 1,620 individuals, carefully selected to include a variety of "passionate types." These small communities would live and work together, each carrying out the tasks best suited to his or her (Fourier firmly believed in women's equality) passions and abilities. For example, children, who love muck and filth, would carry out trash and clean sewers. While the division of labor would be retained, it would be based on the most fundamental drives and desires of human beings and would thus enhance, not suppress, their humanity. While inequalities in income and wealth would continue to exist in the *phalange,* these differences would not cause social discontent because all individuals would freely choose their own jobs and income. Children would be brought up and educated communally within the *phalange,* total equality would exist between women and men, and restrictions on sexual relations would disappear. Best of all, because the *phalange* would put human passions to their best use in a just and cooperative community, the need for coercive government, police, armies, and prisons would disappear. Fourier believed fervently that if only one *phalange* could be set up, its success would rapidly transform the world into a community of *phalanges.*

Fourier's scheme seems eccentric, but it addressed real social problems and proposed serious methods of combating them. Industrialization had condemned millions to boring, repetitive, and meaningless work in which they themselves became like machines. It had destroyed social networks that protected the poor. It had also had a devastating effect on the natural environment. Fourier's scheme attempted to give people back their humanity, to end exploitation, and to create a social order consistent with fundamental human psychology (Fourier's "passions"). While no *phalange* was ever set up, Fourier's ideas in various forms certainly

Claude Henri de Saint-Simon (1760–1825) Early socialist of noble birth whose ideal society was led by an elite of technocrats.

Charles Fourier (1768–1830) French thinker who envisioned socialist communities (*phalanges*) having a division of labor based on passions and abilities.

Robert Owen's community of New Lanark, in the Scottish lowlands, was an example of utopian socialism that worked. A practical businessman with a social conscience, Owen built huge brick textile factories at the falls of the River Clyde. He also provided brick dwellings for workers, paid them fair wages, and ran schools for their children. *(British Library)*

influenced actual egalitarian communal settlements, such as Brook Farm and the Oneida community in the United States as well as the Israeli **kibbutzim.**

Robert Owen, like Fourier, believed in the inherent goodness of human nature, but Owen attempted to build practical cooperative communities. He was himself a successful industrialist who used his cotton mill at New Lanark to try out his principles. Owen believed that cooperation rather than competition would enable him to make a profit while spreading industry-generated wealth among the workers. Under his management, New Lanark became a model community in which workers enjoyed high living standards in the apartments he built for them, pleasant and hygienic surroundings, and free education for their children. Owen tried to interest his fellow industrialists in his cooperative principles, but with little success. The community he set up in New Harmony, Indiana, failed after only a few years. In his later years, Owen was active in the trade union movement and encouraged the establishment of **consumer cooperatives** for workers, but he died a disillusioned man. Despite his failure to persuade contemporary businessmen to adopt the system of factory-paid housing and schools, his ideas influenced later industrial-residential complexes from the Soviet Union to Fiat's factory city of Turin, Italy.

The importance of the utopian socialists lies not so much in the communities that applied their ideas but in their ideas themselves, which later socialists would build on and develop. For example, Fourier's idea that a unified economic system would create a more

efficient and humane society was taken up by Karl Marx and later in the Soviet Union. Fourier was also one of the first to advocate total equality between the sexes and to denounce bourgeois marriage as a form of prostitution, ideas that would be further developed by Friedrich Engels and later socialist and feminist thinkers. Saint-Simon's ideas were extremely influential in mid-nineteenth-century France (many cabinet ministers and businessmen considered themselves "Saint-Simonists"), and he can be seen as an early advocate of "technocracy," or rule by technologically trained elites. Owen's ideas have found practical application in various cooperative communities.

Karl Marx

Like most socialist thinkers, Karl Marx was middle class, not working class. His father was a lawyer of Jewish origin who converted to Christianity when Karl was a young boy, growing up in western Germany. Marx attended university in Bonn and Berlin, where he studied philosophy under **G. W. F. Hegel**, whose systematic thought would prove an important source for Marx's own ideas. Marx's passionate personality, which gained him many friends and many bitter enemies. developed early. As a university stu-

kibbutzim Collective agricultural settlements set up by Jewish settlers in what is now Israel in the late nineteenth century and continuing to the present.

consumer cooperatives Organizations of consumers who band together to obtain better prices from producers and share any profits derived from sales.

G. W. F. Hegel (1770–1831) Important philosopher of the nineteenth century whose philosophy of historical progress was crucial for Marx.

dent, he believed that philosophy was the best method for understanding the world. Soon, however, Marx was ready to go beyond philosophy: "Philosophers have only interpreted the world in various ways," he stated. "The point, however, is to change it." Marx's quest to change the world would make him one of the most loved and hated figures in the late nineteenth and twentieth centuries.

Threatened with arrest by the Prussian authorities in the 1840s because of his radical views, Marx left his homeland. After the publication of *The Communist Manifesto* in 1848, he always lived abroad. During this decade he also married, started a family, and began his famous collaboration with Friedrich Engels. Meeting first in Paris in 1844, the two men quickly formed one of the closest and most productive friendships in history. Engels's *Condition of the Working Class in England* (1845) showed that he was far more familiar with the actual conditions of industrial workers than Marx was, but Marx possessed the greater theoretical mind. Engels was less of an original thinker than Marx but far more practical and easygoing—and much more successful in business. Few days in the next four decades went by without letters between the "Moor" (Marx) and the "General" (Engels), as they jokingly referred to each other.

Marx's most famous early work, coauthored with Engels, *The Communist Manifesto,* appeared during the revolutions of 1848. In a few dozen pages, the *Manifesto* denounced bourgeois society as hypocritical, exploitative, and doomed to destruction: "A specter is haunting Europe—the specter of Communism." Marx used the term **communism** to distinguish his more radical thinking—based on class struggle and an inevitable violent revolution—from the less confrontational schemes of earlier socialists. *The Communist Manifesto* set down in stirring language both an ideological justification and a practical program for a thoroughgoing revolution: "Workers of the world unite!" Marx's program was based on the philosophy of Hegel, who had argued that history progresses in a **dialectical** way. That is, in history, an idea that becomes prominent is inevitably challenged by its opposite, and the resolution of these two opposing principles produces a higher idea. Marx's philosophical innovation was to apply this principle to the material world and to argue that this struggle over ideas would produce revolutionary change in the economic, political, and social structure of society. For Marx, history could be understood as class struggle: slaves versus slave owners, serfs versus lords, and now the proletariat versus the capitalists. Marx allowed that the capitalists had previously played a progressive and even revolutionary role in history by challenging the old economic order based on landed wealth and replacing it with industrial capitalism. Now, however, the leading position had to shift away from the capitalists—the bourgeois middle class to the industrial workers, the proletariat. In the end, Marx insisted, the working masses would rise in revolt, strip the bourgeoisie of their wealth and power, and create a just, egalitarian society.

Marx's practical program was violent revolution, which he saw as the natural outcome of inevitable class struggle. It would be naive, he wrote scornfully, to imagine that the bourgeoisie would relinquish their wealth and power without a fight. Here Marx differed significantly from the utopian socialists, who stressed cooperation over violence, and he termed his program "scientific" to distinguish it from theirs. The utopian socialists, Marx claimed, had a faulty understanding of history, economics, and society. Thinking that persuasion and cooperative efforts could do away with the proletariat's misery, Marx thundered, was both absurd and reactionary. Rather, workers had to organize and seize power themselves to achieve a just society. The contours of this future society may be seen by the specific goals mentioned in *The Communist Manifesto:* free education for all children, the abolition of inheritance and landed property, state control of credit and transportation, a **progressive income tax,** and an end to the distinction between urban and rural areas by spreading cultural and educational institutions outside of cities.

The impact of Marx's writing on the revolutions of 1848 was minimal. But Marx put forth his ideas about class struggle and the need for revolution at this time and then spent the rest of his life gathering and analyzing data to support his thesis. In the second half of the nineteenth century, the influence of his and Engels's ideas would grow. By the end of the century, self-proclaimed Marxist parties existed in most European countries. Even more important, liberals and even conservatives came to recognize that to avoid "communist revolution," they needed to respond to worker demands for improved working conditions and increased pay.

communism Radical political philosophy proposed by Karl Marx, advocating the abolition of private property and an inevitable violent workers' revolution.

dialectical Process of thought that achieves a higher synthesis by reconciling two contradictory ideas ("thesis" and "anti-thesis").

progressive income tax Tax on money earned, with high earners paying a greater percentage of income than individuals earning less.

Summary

Review Questions

↑ What were the most important economic and social effects of industrialization?

↑ Describe the rise of class consciousness in diverging middle-class and working-class identities.

↑ Compare and contrast the remedies proposed by reformers and socialists.

Industrialization revolutionized economic and social relations in the first half of the nineteenth century. Beginning in Great Britain in the late eighteenth century, industrialization had by 1850 spread to many parts of western and central Europe. The development of large factories, often linked to their raw materials and markets by railroads, produced both great wealth and great poverty. One direct impact of industrialization was urbanization, as hundreds of thousands of workers streamed from the countryside into cities, creating problems of sanitation, crime, pollution, and sheer human misery that had not been previously experienced on such a scale. While industrialization produced greater wealth in the larger economy, in industrial cities it appeared that the opposite was true. The great differences in wealth and poverty caused by industrialization brought forth new conceptions of poverty and new ideas about social reform.

Industrialization created new economic and social divisions based on economic position and source of wealth. Now wealth came from manufacturing instead of from land and trades, as in earlier centuries. In principle, at least, one could rise out of one class into another by hard work—self-help. In this way, industrialization encouraged social mobility. The middle classes identified themselves not by their birth but by their accomplishments—by what they had made of their lives. They emphasized education, sobriety, intelligence, and hard work to justify their increasing wealth and political power.

Industrialization also created a working class of mainly impoverished factory laborers who worked and lived in dangerous conditions. Crowded together in the unhygienic, polluted new industrial cities, workers began to develop their own consciousness— that is, an identity of belonging together and sharing common goals, often in direct opposition to the goals of the middle class. Some radical workers organized to improve working and living conditions. But they faced severe legal and practical limits on their efforts to unionize or to gain political rights.

Industrial capitalism created both enormous wealth and great poverty. Liberal reformers sought improvements in legislated incremental steps. Socialists argued that the current economic and social order should be restructured so that wealth created by industrialization could improve life for all. The utopian socialists believed that the benefits of industrialization could be better distributed throughout society if only the will existed to make that choice. Karl Marx, on the other hand, insisted that only violent revolution could bring about an end to class-based inequality. The vision of the future held by middle-class liberal reformers, utopian socialists, and Marxists had much in common—a prosperous, just, and humane society— but the methods they proposed for achieving this vision differed enormously and are still argued in contemporary political debates.

← Thinking Back, Thinking Ahead →

Compare the society that industrialization created with working and living conditions in societies that preceded it.

ECHO ECHO ECHO ECHO

Standardized Time

What time is it? The question is for us simple and natural, but our sense of time is historically new. The idea of time as precise—registering minutes and seconds around the globe—derives from the needs of industrialization. In traditional agricultural societies, there was no need for precise time. People followed the natural rhythms of sunrise and sunset, working longer during the longer daylight hours of summer than during the shorter daylight hours of winter. And if the church tower clock in one village said 12:30 while the clock in the village two miles down the road said 12:40, it did not matter.

New industrial factories, however, demanded more precise timekeeping. Expensive machines could not be left idle for even a few minutes, so it was crucial that workers arrive on time to start their shifts. Anyone arriving late was subject to stiff penalties—loss of an hour's pay, or even a half day's wages, for a minute's tardiness. Working families now had to have a clock in their dwelling, and often the father carried a small one—called a "watch"—in his pocket (not on his wrist, as this was seen as effeminate).

Even more than factories, however, railroads required timekeeping to be precise and standardized. Differences in village church clocks could not be tolerated, because a difference of even a minute could mean catching, or missing, a train. Rail lines announced their timetables, and the village clocks had to comply. Following some confusion when different rail lines themselves used different times, a nationwide uniform time was established in Britain. By 1850, all clocks showed the same time—at least in theory.

For large countries such as India, Russia, and the United States, however, a single time zone was impractical. This problem was solved by the creation of time zones in 1883 and the establishment of Greenwich (after the Naval Observatory outside London located on the prime meridian, or 0 degrees longitude) Mean Time (GMT) a year later. From then on, time anywhere on the globe could be calculated by GMT plus or minus any number of hours: New York is GMT minus five hours; New Zealand, GMT plus twelve hours. At first, the French set their standard based on Paris rather than Greenwich, but by the early twentieth century, they, too, had accepted GMT. Today we take standardized times for granted, and atomic clocks are accurate to one second in 20 million years—precise enough to catch any train.

Suggested Readings

Chamberlin, E. R. *The Awakening Giant: Britain in the Industrial Revolution.* London: Batsford, 1976. An engaging illustrated study.

Henderson, W. O. *Britain and Industrial Europe, 1750–1870.* Leicester, England: Leicester University Press, 1972. And account of how British techniques and entrepreneurs helped industrialize the continent.

Kolokowski, Leszek. *Main Currents of Marxism.* 3 vols. New York: W.W. Norton and Co., 2005. Everything you ever wanted to know, from Marx's philosophical sources to post-Stalinism.

Pollard, Sidney. *Peaceful Conquest: The Industrialization of Europe, 1760–1970.* Oxford: Oxford University Press, 1981. Sophisticated explanation of how Europe industrialized.

Thompson, E. P. *The Making of the English Working Class.* New York: Pantheon Books, 1963. A classic work, written with passion and empathy.

Thompson, F. M. L. *The Rise of Respectable Society: A Social History of Victorian Britain, 1830–1900.* Cambridge, Mass.: Harvard University Press, 1988. A study that is important for understanding middle-class morality.

Trebilcock, Clive. *The Industrialization of the Continental Powers 1780–1914.* London and New York: Longman, 1981. An account that is especially detailed on Germany, France, and Russia.

Websites

Huge amount of information on Marx, Engels, and company, with a definite political agenda, **Marxists Internet Archive,** at www.marxists.org

All about the Industrial Revolution in Britain, from inventors to places to workers, **Cotton Times,** at www.cottontimes.co.uk

A listing of dozens of different sites on topics from literature to art to Jack the Ripper, **Victorian Literary Studies Archive: Victorian Websites,** at http://www.lang.nagoya-u.ac.jp/~matsuoka/Victorian.html

The Triumph of the Nation-State, 1848–1900

CHAPTER OUTLINE

1500 B.C.E.	1000 B.C.E.	500 B.C.E.	1 B.C.E./1 C.E.

		1810s Luddite revolts protest industrialization in England	1815 Napoleon is finally defeated at Waterloo	1820s Industrialization begins in Belgium and northern France	1824 British Combination Acts are repealed

1800	1805	1810	1815	1820	1825

Political Europe in 1900

The force of nationalism can be seen in the changing boundaries of European states between 1815 and 1900. Observe the political boundaries on this map from 1900, then compare it with the map of Europe after the Congress of Vienna (p. 567). What are the most significant changes between these maps? What new countries appeared over that time?

— Pale of Settlement

FINLAND

KINGDOM OF SWEDEN AND NORWAY

Oslo

Stockholm

St. Petersburg

ESTONIANS

LATVIANS

Moscow

Riga

SCOTLAND

North Sea

DENMARK

Copenhagen

Baltic Sea

LITHUANIANS

RUSSIAN EMPIRE

UNITED KINGDOM OF GREAT BRITAIN AND IRELAND

Dublin

IRELAND

Manchester

WALES

ENGLAND

London

NETHERLANDS

Amsterdam

SCHLESWIG
HOLSTEIN

Elbe

Danzig

BELARUSIANS

GERMAN EMPIRE

Berlin

Warsaw

KINGDOM OF POLAND (Russia)

Kiev

Dnieper

ATLANTIC OCEAN

BELGIUM

Cologne

Rhine

Luxembourg

LUX.

Frankfurt

Prague

CZECHS

Cracow

GALICIA

UKRAINIANS

Dniester

Paris

Seine

ALSACE-LORRAINE

Munich

Vienna

AUSTRO-HUNGARIAN EMPIRE

SLOVAKS

BESSARABIA

FRANCE

Loire

Zurich

SWITZERLAND

Buda Pest

HUNGARY

MOLDAVIA

Lyons

Garonne

Rhône

Milan

Po

Venice

DALMATIA

CROATIA

TRANSYLVANIA

Belgrade

ROMANIA

Black Sea

Marseilles

ITALY

Adriatic Sea

BOSNIA

HERZE-GOVINA

SERBIA

Danube

WALLACHIA

BULGARIA

PORTUGAL

Ebro

Madrid

SPAIN

Corsica (Fr.)

Elba

Rome

MONTENEGRO

Istanbul

OTTOMAN EMPIRE

Sardinia

Naples

ALBANIA

Baleric Is. (Sp.)

GREECE

Tangier

GILBRALTAR (Gr. Br.)

Algiers

Mediterranean Sea

Sicily

Malta (Gr. Br.)

Athens

CRETE

MOROCCO

ALGERIA (France)

Tunis

TUNIS (France)

0   200   400 Km.
0   200   400 Mi.

500 C.E.   1000 C.E.   1500 C.E.   2000 C.E.

1870
Franco-Prussian War begins

1871
Germany is unified

1878
Bulgaria gains autonomy

1896
Herzl publishes *The Jewish State*

1870   1875   1880   1885   1890   1895   1900

Choic Choice Choice

Theodor Herzl

Theodor Herzl, here depicted in a poster announcing the fifty-year anniversary of the Histadrut Zionist trade union, proclaimed a proud new Jewish identity. Herzl's Zionism insisted that Jews were not just a religious group but a nation and that they could never live in freedom until they obtained their own state. His dignified bearing symbolized the demand that Jews be treated with respect. (Library of Congress)

Theodor Herzl Creates Modern Zionism

In 1895 journalist Theodor Herzl was in Paris covering the trial of Captain Alfred Dreyfus, who had been accused of spying for the Germans. Like Herzl himself, Dreyfus was an assimilated, Europeanized Jew. The trial was held more than a century after the French Revolution had promised equal rights to Jewish citizens. But the trial was unfair: Dreyfus's Jewish background was held against him. In the streets crowds shouted "Death to the Jews!" Herzl was shocked, and he wrote in his diary, "I recognized the emptiness and futility of trying to 'combat' antisemitism." He concluded that Jews would always be outsiders in the European countries in which they dwelled. They would be exiles—as Hebrew teachings phrased it—until they had their own Jewish state. Jews were not just a religious group; they were a nation.

Herzl had experienced antisemitism. As a student at the University of Vienna in the early 1880s, he had been denied admission into a prestigious fraternity because of his Jewish origins. He had been furious, for he felt himself Austrian by culture, upbringing, and language, and more patriotic than most. Being Jewish was just a personal religious matter. But the young Herzl learned a hard lesson: for a Jew, no matter how assimilated, wealthy, and intelligent, some avenues were closed. Herzl graduated and became a well-known playwright and journalist in Vienna, indistinguishable from other middle-class Viennese, with an unhappy marriage, a lifestyle that outstripped his income, and a love for wit and culture.

Vienna was a thriving center for German Jewish culture, with such distinguished writers as Stefan Zweig and Arthur Schnitzler, composers like Alban Berg and Arnold Schoenberg, and of course the renowned psychiatrist Sigmund Freud. In this environment, surrounded by other Jews like him—German speaking, cultured, successful—Herzl tried to believe that Jews could retain their religion and still live in harmony with their Christian neighbors. But that was before he covered what became known as the Dreyfus affair.

Despite the absurdity of the accusation and the flimsy evidence against him, Dreyfus was court-martialed and exiled to Devil's Island off the coast of South America. It was later discovered that the army had manipulated and forged evidence against him. By that time, Herzl was already a Jewish nationalist, a Zionist. In 1896 he published a small book entitled *The Jewish State,* which proposed a political solution to what Europeans called the Jewish question—the proper relation between Jews and the states where they lived. Once Jews had their own state, Herzl argued, the other nations of the world would respect them. Other central and eastern European Jewish thinkers had reached similar conclusions before Herzl—in part, in reaction to the shock of the 1881 wave of anti-Jewish violence in the Russian Empire—but he apparently did not know any of them. Even the term *Zionism* had been used before Herzl, but he gave the movement new political force and vigor.

In 1897, Herzl summoned a "symbolic parliament" of European Jews to the Swiss city of Basel. At this First Zionist Congress he issued a call for all Jews to unite to create a Jewish state. Though he did not specify where that state would be founded, the obvious place was Palestine—for Jews, Eretz Israel ("land of Israel"), an Ottoman province between Egypt and Syria. After all, Jews prayed every year at Passover to meet again "next year in Jerusalem." Most Jews in western Europe did not respond to Herzl's call. Feeling secure and patriotic in France, Britain, and Germany, they firmly rejected the idea of a Jewish nation and feared that Zionism could worsen anti-Jewish feelings. But in eastern Europe, particularly in the Russian Empire, Herzl's call was received with joy. Visiting Russia in 1903, Herzl was lauded as "king of the Jews" in towns throughout the Pale of Settlement, where Russian Jews were forced to reside.

Herzl did not live to see his ideal realized. When he died in 1904, very few people believed that Zionism could succeed—the political, economic, and religious obstacles seemed too great. But, as Herzl once remarked, "If you believe it, it is not a dream." Forty-four years after Herzl's death, two thousand years after the Jewish people were sent into exile, the state of Israel declared its independence. The Jewish people had their own state.

Introduction

The world as we know it—politically, economically, socially—took shape in the second half of the nineteenth century. While political "isms" like nationalism, liberalism, and socialism can be traced back to the French Revolution and earlier, from the 1850s onward these ideologies fundamentally altered political and social life. It was precisely during this period that many Europeans, like Herzl, identified with and demanded rights for their nations. Similarly, while the Industrial Revolution had started in Britain in the late eighteenth century, only during this period did large-scale industrialization begin to affect the lives of people all over Europe and elsewhere in the world. The growth of technology and industrialization came together with new forms of politics to create a new and more democratic Europe after 1848. In that year, liberal democratic institutions existed in few European countries, and constitutionalism as a practical political program was almost unknown. By 1906, even conservative states like the German and Russian Empires had adopted some aspects of constitutional government.

Perhaps the single most potent political force of this period was nationalism. Increasingly, people identified themselves with a national group instead of with their village, social class, or religion. Europeans came to accept the nationalist principle that all members of one nation should live together politically as citizens of a single state. At the same time, the definition of who belonged in a certain nation was contested, and many conservative multinational states opposed nationalism as a dangerous, even revolutionary, idea.

During this period, political leaders, recognizing the force of nationalism, began to define their actions in terms of the "national will." The spread of nationalist rhetoric had the paradoxical outcome that even kings and emperors found it necessary to wrap themselves in the national banner. Before 1848, nationalism and liberalism tended to be aligned, both opposing the prevailing conservative and monarchist order symbolized by Clemens von Metternich in Vienna. After 1848, it was the conservatives who used nationalist ideology for their own political aims.

By the end of the nineteenth century, nationalism had gained broad acceptance, especially in western and central Europe. Even so, nationalism was not without its opponents. The growing socialist movement argued against the aggressive demands and divisions of nationalism, calling for workingmen of all nations to unite against the capitalists. Socialists emphasized class identity over nationality. The Catholic Church also opposed nationalism, particularly after the formation of the secular and implicitly anticlerical Italian state in the 1860s. The rulers of conservative multinational empires in central and eastern Europe understood that nationalism threatened their empires' very existence. In different and often contradictory ways, Habsburg, Ottoman, and Romanov rulers attempted to neutralize the growing power of nationalist ideology. In the end, however, not nationalism but these empires were swept away.

The Revolutions of 1848

↓ What changes did the revolutionaries of 1848 demand?
↓ What were the short- and long-term outcomes of 1848?

In 1848, revolutions across Europe ended the conservative, antiliberal, and antinational period initiated at the Congress of Vienna and symbolized by the Austrian

Chronology

1848 Marx and Engels publish *Communist Manifesto*	**1870–1871** Franco-Prussian War ends with French defeat
1848–1849 Political uprisings sweep Europe	**1871** Prussian king William I becomes emperor of Germany; Paris Commune is crushed by French government
1852 Louis Napoleon declares himself Emperor Napoleon III	
1854–1856 France and Britain defeat Russia in Crimean War	**1875** Ottomans crush Bulgarian uprising
	1877–1878 Russians defeat Turks in Russo-Turkish War
1859 Napoleon III and Piedmont defeat Austria in northern Italy; Italian unification begins	**1878** Bulgaria wins autonomy from Ottoman Empire
	1894 Dreyfus is convicted of espionage
1861 Victor Emmanuel II is crowned king of Italy; Tsar Alexander II emancipates Russian serfs	**1896** Herzl publishes *The Jewish State*
1861–1865 America fights Civil War	**1897** First Zionist Congress is held in Basel, Switzerland
1863 Polish rebellion against Russian rule fails	**1901** First Nobel prizes (for peace, chemistry, medicine, and literature) are awarded
1866 Prussia defeats Austria, opening the way for German unification	**1901** Queen Victoria dies; end of Victorian age
1867 Austria grants Hungary semi-autonomy	

prime minister Clemens von Metternich. While different circumstances in each capital city and region sparked the uprisings, all demanded a broadening of political rights and recognition of nationalist concerns. In the short run, all were unsuccessful. The Prussian king and Austrian emperor were threatened but remained on their thrones. In France, the newly elected president, Louis Napoleon, declared himself Emperor Napoleon III and crushed political opposition. Still, the failure of 1848 helped pave the way for the triumph of national ideas—though not of liberalism—some twenty years later, when the nation-states of Italy and Germany were created. Similarly, while the constitutions granted in 1848 were not always respected, the precedent of constitutional rule had been established and would gain political authority in subsequent decades.

The Tide of Revolution

The **revolutions of 1848** swept through nearly every European country. Only those on the periphery—Great Britain, Scandinavia, Russia, the Ottoman Empire—were spared. But even in these undisturbed regions, rulers and privileged classes were shocked and terri-

fied. In Russia, for example, the government increased censorship and repressed radical thinkers. In Britain, increased police surveillance following the Chartist agitation prevented revolution, but Queen Victoria regarded the events on the continent with worry.

The first uprising began in January 1848 in Sicily. Street demonstrations in Palermo and Naples forced the reactionary ruler of the Kingdom of the Two Sicilies, as the southern Italian state was known, to form a liberal government and issue a constitution. These liberal concessions in one of the most conservative regions of Europe electrified rulers and liberals alike.

Then, in February 1848, Louis Philippe, France's "bourgeois king," was forced to **abdicate**. Since his coronation in 1830 as "King of the French," Louis Philippe had attempted to steer a compromise course

revolutions of 1848 Series of upheavals that shook Europe from Sicily to Paris to Berlin to Vienna, bringing first liberal change, then generally conservative reaction.

abdicate To give up one's position as ruler, usually said of kings.

between the demands of royalist aristocrats and the new, wealthy bourgeoisie. Most Frenchmen, even of the middle class, continued to be shut out of the political process. In the mid-1840s, middle-class protesters began to join with broader peasant and working-class movements demanding relief in the face of bad harvests and unemployment. Because political meetings were illegal, in 1847 a banquet campaign was launched. The king could hardly forbid Frenchmen from eating! As everyone understood, the main purpose of these banquets was not cuisine but politics; banquet speakers called for an extension of the vote, even universal male suffrage. When the government tried to prevent a "monster banquet" in February 1848, clashes with police and would-be banqueters and students escalated into major street battles. Seeing no way out of the situation, Louis Philippe abdicated and fled to London. France was declared a republic, and the revolutionaries began the task of creating a new government.

With the monarchy swept away, the liberals and radicals began to quarrel. When the **national workshops**, set up in March 1848 to provide relief and work for the jobless, could not keep pace with growing unemployment, moderate liberals began to grumble about supporting the lazy at the taxpayers' expense. Business leaders, too, denounced the national workshops as unfair competition and an unbearable tax burden. Yet thousands of impoverished men continued to stream into Paris, and many feared the collapse of public order. Elections in April revealed another growing divide—between Paris and the provinces. Voters in the provinces overwhelmingly supported moderate or even conservative candidates, while in Paris radicals managed—barely—to send radical and socialist delegates such as **Louis Blanc** to the National Assembly. Meanwhile the turmoil on the streets of Paris intensified. On May 15, large crowds declared the parliament dissolved and attempted to set up their own radical government. This attempt ended in failure and arrests. But tensions continued.

As Metternich once quipped, "When Paris sneezes, Europe catches cold." News of the Paris upheavals quickly reached Berlin, Vienna, and other central European cities, where liberals soon demanded similar political concessions from their rulers. In the Habsburg lands, street fighting in May forced the imperial family to abandon Vienna for a more easily guarded country estate. Metternich resigned and fled the city alone. In Berlin clashes between the army and local citizens left many dead. The outrage over the killings was so great that Prussian king **Frederick William IV** felt himself compelled to issue a constitution and salute as heroes the bodies of those shot by his own troops.

Liberal Germans, casting themselves as representatives of the German nation, demanded a unified Germany and organized elections for a **constituent assembly**, which met in late spring at Saint Paul's Church in Frankfurt. Among the more than four hundred elected representatives who gathered to write a constitution, with political rights for all, were lawyers, government officials, and professors, including the Grimm brothers, now at work on their German dictionary. Although there were also four artisans, thirty-four landowners, and one peasant, this **Frankfurt Assembly**, in which 90 percent of the representatives were educated, was indeed a "parliament of scholars."

The nationalism apparent in the Frankfurt Assembly's anticipation of a unified Germany was also at work in Hungary. The Hungarian elite, especially, resented the power of the central government in Vienna. In March, led by the fiery speaker **Louis (Lájos) Kossuth**, they demanded an end to imperial rule and the establishment of a Hungarian parliament. The Austrian Habsburgs were at first conciliatory, but when the newly elected Hungarian parliament voted to create its own army and currency, the emperor sent in troops, and a regular war ensued between Austrian (imperial) and Hungarian forces.

In the Italian states, revolution also seemed to triumph in the spring of 1848. The insurrections spread from Naples to Milan (then belonging to the Habsburg Empire), Venice (where a republic was declared), and Rome. In Rome, the rebels took over the city as traditional authorities fled—while the pope sought refuge outside of town in the fortress of Gaeta. Giuseppe Mazzini and Giuseppe Garibaldi worked together to build a "Rome of the People," establishing

national workshops   Paris institutions set up in 1848 to give work to the unemployed at government expense.

Louis Blanc   (1811–1882) French socialist who advocated the right to work and the abolition of competition.

Frederick William IV   King of Prussia (r. 1840–1861) who issued a constitution during the Berlin revolution of 1848.

constituent assembly   Meeting to draw up a constitution or to agree on basic fundamentals of a governing system.

Frankfurt Assembly   Representatives elected throughout German states who met in Frankfurt (1848–1849) to draft a liberal constitution for a united German Empire.

Louis (Lájos) Kossuth   (1802–1894) Hungarian statesman who led his people in revolt against the Habsburg (Austrian) Empire during 1848–1849.

During 1848, revolutionaries built barricades in the streets of many cities, as in this image of a barricade built during the March 1848 uprising in Berlin. The rebels fly the black-red-gold tricolor of German liberalism and fight for a united, liberal Germany against the Prussian king's troops. *(Landesarchiv, Berlin/akg-images)*

freedom of the press, setting up secular schools, and handing over some church property to the poor.

The Restoration of Authority

If in spring the revolutionaries seemed to be winning, by early summer the forces of traditional authority had gained strength, and by fall the revolutions had been stamped out nearly everywhere. In Paris, tensions between moderates and radicals led to a bloody clash set off by the moderates' abolition of the national workshops in late June. These might have been dismantled without bloodshed had the government moved slowly. Instead, the overnight action sparked an armed workers' uprising, in which more than 1,500 people, including the archbishop of Paris, were killed. After suppressing the uprising, government forces massacred more than three thousand workers.

The violence, known as the June Days, demonstrated that liberal governments, like monarchies and conservative regimes, were willing to use violence against political opponents. After June 1848, the forces of moderation and order were firmly in control in Paris.

In December 1848, French voters overwhelmingly chose Louis Napoleon, a nephew of the great Napoleon, as president of the French Republic. Their longing for order after a year of revolution would help pave the way to his dictatorship as Emperor **Napoleon III**, beginning in 1852. Thus, the immediate outcome in France of the 1848 revolution was not a

Napoleon III   (r. 1852–1870) Louis Napoleon, nephew of Napoleon Bonaparte, who was elected president of France in 1848 and declared himself emperor in 1852.

liberal republic but the Second Empire, which lasted until 1870.

The situation in the Habsburg Empire was complicated by its numerous nationalities and the strife between them. When the Hungarians declared their independence from Vienna, the Hungarian dependency of Croatia aligned itself with the Habsburg emperor. Similarly, German liberals in Prague were offended when the eminent Czech historian František Palacký refused to participate in elections to the Frankfurt Assembly. Palacký pointed out that he was not a German but a Czech who was loyal to the Habsburg Empire. Believing that cultural and political rights of small nations like his were better assured in a large multinational empire than in a nation-state like the one the representatives at Frankfurt envisioned, Palacký declared, "If Austria did not exist," he wrote, "it would be necessary to invent her." Unlike the Germans and Hungarians, smaller national groups in the Habsburg Empire did not aspire to political independence but hoped only to be allowed to use their own language in schools, publishing, and perhaps in government offices. The **Slavic Congress,** held in Prague in June 1848, asserted its loyalty to the Habsburg Empire while advocating recognition for Slavic languages (Czech, Slovak, Croatian) as equals of German. It also called for closer relations between the Slavic peoples of the Habsburg Empire and Slavs in the Russian and Ottoman Empires. The congress was dissolved at gunpoint by forces loyal to the new Habsburg emperor, **Francis Joseph.**

By late 1848, the emperor was back in a now subdued Vienna. The imperial army had established order in northern Italy and in the Czech lands and was gearing up for battle with the Hungarians. But the Hungarians proved hard to defeat, surrendering only after Russian units had come to the aid of the Austrians. Francis Joseph repudiated the constitution he had agreed to in 1848 and vowed to rule as an absolute ruler. As in France, in the Habsburg lands it appeared that the upheavals had all been for nothing.

In the German Confederation, the revolution ended less violently. Except in Berlin, German states had generally avoided clashes with their citizens. Most German princes retained power after 1848, though mainly after promising liberal political reforms. Since May, the Frankfurt Assembly had been debating plans to unify Germany: Should Germans unite under Habsburg rule, the so-called *grossdeutsch,* or "big German," solution, or should a new German Empire be formed with the Prussian king at its head, the *kleindeutsch,* or "small German," solution? At first, most delegates favored the *grossdeutsch* solution. But Francis Joseph could not agree to being the head of a German national state when over half of his subjects in the Austrian and Hungarian lands were non-Germans. After this refusal, the Frankfurt Assembly offered the crown of the future German Empire to King Frederick William IV of Prussia. Frederick William indignantly refused, calling the offer "from the gutter" and the crown a "diadem moulded out of the dirt and dregs of revolution, disloyalty and treason."

Rebutted by Austrian emperor and Prussian king, the Frankfurt Assembly found itself in an impossible position. Lacking the will or ability to revolt against existing German princes, it was attacked as too conservative by radicals and workers. Ironically, the assembly was rescued by Prussian troops, and the "scholars" were unceremoniously sent home. Sporadic attempts at revolution were countered everywhere in the German lands by military action.

By the end of 1849, the revolutions were over. In Paris, a moderate liberal government had demonstrated brutality toward its opponents. In the Italian lands, most of the same rulers were in place, despite a flurry of granted constitutions and promised political rights. In Berlin, the Prussian king was in control, and thousands of liberals and radicals were under arrest, in hiding, or already in exile. Friedrich Engels and Karl Marx would live the rest of their lives in England, but many "Forty-Eighters" fled to the United States. In Vienna, the Habsburg emperor was once again firmly in power. Despite the apparent calm, however, few of the political, national, or social demands of the revolutionaries had been dealt with, and the issues would be raised again. In retrospect, 1848 was a watershed.

1848 As a Watershed Year

The role of ideology in the revolutions of 1848 is complex. There is no doubt about the importance of liberal ideals such as constitutionalism, civil rights, and the rule of law to those who tried to overthrow regimes in Sicily, Paris, Vienna, and Berlin. But when moderate liberals were confronted with radical and socialist demands and the destruction of private property, they joined with conservatives in calling for order. In central Europe, nationalist revolutionaries

Slavic Congress Assembly of Slavic nations—Poles, Balkan peoples, Czechs, Ukrainians, and one Russian—in Prague in 1848 that called for cultural recognition for Slavs.

Francis Joseph (r. 1848–1916) Habsburg emperor of Austria from 1848 and king of Hungary from 1867.

promoted liberal ideas, only to find themselves opposed by other liberal nationalists who remained loyal to traditional authority. In central Europe, nationalist slogans combined with liberal ideas and proposals. Socialist ideas were also discussed, though the actual influence of socialism in 1848 was small.

Liberalism was certainly the most important political ideology in 1848. The revolutionaries called for constitutions, popular representation, and an end to censorship. In Paris, liberalism momentarily triumphed, then was challenged from the left. In central Europe, middle-class liberals learned that the masses of workers and peasants were not always willing to follow their lead, especially if liberal policies did not also promote low bread prices, decent wages, and employment opportunities.

Marx and Engels's *Communist Manifesto,* published in 1848, had been written before the revolutionary outbreaks, and its influence was small, in part because it was available only in German. Socialist ideas such as the abolition of inheritance and landed property, state control of credit and transportation, and free education had not yet gained broad support. Only in Paris did avowed socialists like Louis Blanc, father of the national workshops, play a significant part in the revolutions. On the whole, however, rebelling workers and peasants in 1848 knew nothing about socialism. Their demands were more tangible: lower taxes, cheaper food, jobs. Only later in the nineteenth century would Marx's pamphlet become basic reading for a mass audience.

Nationalism played a very visible role in 1848, though it scored few victories. Neither Germany nor Italy was united, the Hungarian attempt to secure autonomy and national rights was put down by Vienna, and the Slavic Congress in Prague was dissolved. In most parts of Europe, most people did not yet think in national terms. People spoke local dialects that were often far from standard written forms of, say, the German language that the Grimm brothers were working so hard to define. People identified themselves more often as inhabitants of a village, as Catholics, or as Jews than as Hungarians or Czechs or Germans. But nationalist movements in 1848 helped popularize the idea that languages like Czech, Ukrainian, Romanian, Slovak, and Croatian deserved respect—and rights. Crucially, the central idea of nationalism—that a state must defend the values of a nation—was expressed by revolutionaries from Paris to Berlin, from Palermo to Budapest. While the revolutions of 1848 did not establish nation-states in central Europe, they helped spread the ideals of nationalism.

After 1848, the political center shifted significantly to the left. Few thinking Europeans continued to defend divine-right monarchy, and increasing numbers of educated middle-class people embraced political liberalism or even socialism as solutions to society's problems. The liberals are particularly interesting in this context. Before 1848, they constituted a small minority in the politics of every European country save Britain. After midcentury, liberal ideas and liberal figures took on new importance not only in Britain, France, and other western European countries, but even in Russia, the Habsburg lands (after 1867, Austria-Hungary), and southern Europe. Thus, the liberals who were defeated in 1848 had by 1900 become an important—in some cases, a predominant—part of the political landscape. And by this time they recognized that the greatest challenge to liberalism came not from conservatives but from the growing socialist movement.

Yet conservatism was not dead. The peasant unrest of 1848 convinced rulers to abolish the last vestiges of serfdom in Europe, except in Russia. After 1848, the peasantry in western and central Europe became a bulwark of conservative and religious forces. The Catholic Church, badly shaken by the year's events, which had temporarily forced Pope **Pius IX** to flee from Rome, turned away from any kind of liberal reform. Until nearly the end of the century, the Catholic Church would be a solid bulwark of traditional authority, condemning constitutions, nationalism, and popular representation in government.

Many of the rejected national demands of 1848 were resurrected a generation or so later. Italian unification took place in the 1860s, partly through Garibaldi's continued efforts. The Hungarian demands to Vienna in 1848 were granted two decades later in the **Compromise of 1867,** which gave the Hungarians domestic autonomy in the empire. The Slavic Congress of 1848 can be seen as a precursor of the Pan-Slav movement of the 1870s that aimed to unite all Slavic peoples from the Adriatic to the Pacific under the Romanovs. Thus, immediate failures of 1848 masked future triumphs.

Pius IX (r. 1846–1878) Pope who became a staunch conservative, refusing to acknowledge Italian unification and condemning all forms of modernity.

Compromise of 1867 Agreement between Austria and Hungary dividing the country into two autonomous parts, linked by a common budget, military, and foreign policy.

New Nation-States and Nationalist Tensions

↓ How, in politics and personalities, were the processes of German and Italian unification similar?

↓ How did national identity differ in the United States from nationality identity in Poland, Bulgaria, and Norway? How do you explain these differences?

In the second half of the nineteenth century, nationalists translated their ideas into political realities. The greatest triumph of the national principle was the creation of two large, unified states in the middle of Europe: Italy and Germany. Both had conservative constitutions under powerful monarchs (the Prussian king took on the title of Kaiser (emperor), to the disappointment of liberal nationalists. Norway and Bulgaria also became independent states in this era. Nations lacking states stressed ethnic unity and linguistic solidarity. Throughout Europe, nationalism became exclusionary. Across the Atlantic, the United States experienced a mass immigration of European peoples.

The Unification of Italy

Since the 1830s, the idea of the Italian nation had been promoted by Giuseppe Mazzini, who exemplified the enthusiasm and almost mystical quality of early, liberal nationalism. His impassioned writings reminded Italians of their glorious Roman past and called for national unity, democracy, and equal rights for all. Mazzini inspired thousands of his countrymen to think beyond the boundaries of their local town or community and aspire to be "Italians." He demanded "a sacred devotion to the fatherland" and urged Italian men to "cancel from your minds every idea of superiority over Women." Mazzini's importance lies in his writings and the enthusiasm for the Italian idea he spread.

The idea of a united Italy had a lot to overcome, as following the revolutions of 1848 it was still divided into numerous sovereign political units. In the northwest, centered on the city of Turin, was the small but stable kingdom of Piedmont-Sardinia, ruled by the House of Savoy. Southern Italy was dominated by the Kingdom of the Two Sicilies, which stretched from the island of Sicily to Naples. In between were the Papal States, including Rome and Bologna, an area in which the pope not only was the spiritual head but also ruled as a secular lord, much like the dukes of Milan or Modena. In the northeast, the provinces of Veneto and Lombardy remained under Austrian rule. As Metternich had famously put it, Italy was no more than a "geographical expression."

In 1859, Napoleon III, who supported the idea of an Italian state in the hopes of strengthening French influence in the region, agreed to help Piedmont drive Austria out of northern Italy. The prime minister of Piedmont, **Camille Cavour**, saw the alliance with France as a means to position his state as the nucleus of a future united Italy. In his own personal beliefs, Cavour reflected the changes in nationalism before and after 1848. In that year, he had urged the king to issue a constitution, had sponsored some liberal policies, and had worked to end Austrian rule in northern Italy. Ten years later, Cavour continued to pursue the goal of expelling the Austrians from Milan and Veneto, but now specifically with the aim of enhancing the power of his king, Victor Emmanuel II.

First Lombardy (with its capital of Milan), in 1859, and then Veneto, in 1866, were ceded by Austria to the kingdom of Piedmont-Sardinia. In the south the unification movement was spearheaded by Garibaldi, backed up by his famous Red Shirts. This informal—though effective—army fought its way across Sicily, defeating the kingdom of the Two Sicilies. In 1860, this vast region joined Piedmont, as did the central Italian states of Tuscany and Parma. Thus by 1860, the entire Italian peninsula except for Veneto in the north and the Papal States around Rome were under the rule of Victor Emmanuel II, who would be crowned king of Italy in 1861. These last two areas would become part of the new kingdom of Italy by 1870, though the pope would not reconcile himself to the new political situation. Surrounded by Italian territory that he refused to recognize, Pope Pius IX remained in self-imposed imprisonment in the **Vatican** for the rest of his life.

Italian unity had been achieved, but the resulting constitutional monarchy was very far from the democratic ideal envisioned by Mazzini and Garibaldi. Mazzini died in 1872, bitterly disappointed by the form in which his dream had been realized by the less idealistic—but more realistic—Cavour. The new Italy was a constitutional monarchy with universal male suffrage, but the king and his ministers held much more power than the parliament. The problems of illiteracy and poverty, especially in the southern half of the country, were an enormous challenge to the new rulers and would continue to be so well into the

Camille Cavour (1810–1861) Prime minister and adviser to the King of Sardinia, Victor Emmanuel II, who in 1861 became the first king of united Italy.

Vatican Seat of the Catholic Church and the pope's residence, in central Rome on the Tiber River.

MAP 22.1 **Revolutions of 1848** During 1848 uprisings occurred throughout the continent, with the major exceptions of England and Russia.

twentieth century. In 1870, most subjects of King Victor Emmanuel spoke not standard Italian, but dialects, and retained strong regional identities. As one statesman put it, "We have made Italy; now we must make Italians."

The Unification of Germany

"Germany" immediately after 1848 was like Italy: no more than a geographical or cultural expression. Dozens of German states existed, from powerful Prussia to the tiny city-state of Hamburg. When the 1848 revolutionaries offered the crown of a new German Empire to the king of Prussia, he rejected it. His brother would accept it in 1871 as William I, but under vastly changed circumstances. As in Italy, conservatives gained most from German unification. In particular, one man was responsible for Prussia's rapid rise to

dominate a unified Germany. This was the Prussian chancellor **Otto von Bismarck.**

Bismarck combined great energy, determination, and loyalty to the Prussian ruling house with cold calculation. He resembled Metternich in intelligence and ruthlessness, though Bismarck lacked Metternich's elegance and refined manners. Born into a moderately wealthy landowning family, Bismarck had been shocked by the revolutions of 1848 and disappointed by the king's concessions to the liberals. A staunch conservative who had served in the Prussian Landtag (parliament) and as ambassador to Russia

Otto von Bismarck (1815–1898) Prominent conservative Prussian statesman, chancellor (prime minister) and architect of German unification in 1871.

MAP 22.2 **Unification of Italy** In the decade between 1860 and 1870, Italy was united. This process brought together regions of great economic and social diversity under the rule of Rome, which officially became the capital of the newly united Italy in 1871.

and France, Bismarck rose to power by chance. In 1862, King William I became entangled in a dispute with the Landtag over the state budget, in particular the funding for the Prussian army. In despair, the king appointed Bismarck chancellor, hoping that he would be able to find a compromise. Instead, Bis-

marck directly defied the Landtag, acting as if it did not exist. Bismarck's brash behavior revealed the weakness of Prussia's parliament in the face of a strong and ruthless statesman.

Bismarck declared that the biggest mistake of the 1848 liberals was their attempt to unite Germany

With his bald head and bushy mustache, German chancellor Otto von Bismarck was a favorite of caricaturists, as in this cartoon from the early 1890's. Bismarck is shown getting ready to leave (he was forced to resign by the new Kaiser) and looking in disgust at the new Kaiser William II, who gazes lovingly at a newborn labeled "socialism" while reclining on a throne bristling with weaponry. The goddsss of Germania looks on in consternation. *(Bettmann/ Corbis)*

through "speeches and majority resolutions" rather than "blood and iron." By this he meant military might and warfare. In the next decade, Bismarck waged three wars that would realize the primary goal of the liberals in the Frankfurt Assembly—a united Germany. The first war came as Denmark attempted to take over the province of Schleswig, previously an independent duchy. Prussian and Austrian troops invaded Schleswig early in 1864, forcing the king of Denmark to withdraw his claims. Austria and Prussia were to administer the territory jointly, an arrangement Bismarck knew would soon lead to conflict. After various frictions and provocations, Austria and Prussia went to war in mid-1866.

The Prussians humiliated the Austrians at a single decisive battle. The peace terms Bismarck offered were mild: Austria lost no territory and paid no war indemnity, but henceforth Austria would be excluded from the North German Confederation carved by Prussia from the old Austrian-dominated German Confederation set up at the Congress of Vienna. Now the North German Confederation, dominated by Prussia, stretched from the Dutch border in the west

to the Russian Empire in the east; to the south Austria remained isolated.

Bismarck had eliminated his chief rival in the German lands. Now he looked to eliminate his chief rival on the continent—France—which felt threatened by the rise of a unified, aggressive German state. Again Bismarck skillfully manipulated events—the candidacy of a Hohenzollern prince for the throne of Spain—to push strained Franco-Prussian relations over the brink. In a brilliant, though dishonest, media maneuver, Bismarck took a telegram—the Ems Dispatch—he had received from King William I on this matter, doctored it in a way that was insulting to the French, and leaked the provocative document to the press. Napoleon III foolishly took Bismarck's bait and declared war on Prussia.

The **Franco-Prussian War** (1870—1871) was a dis-

Franco-Prussian War (1870–1871) Conflict provoked by Bismarck, resulting in the defeat of France and end of Napoleon III's reign; also led to German unification.

The French government's repression of the Paris Commune in June 1871 left thousands dead. Photographs such as this one showing the massacred supporters of the commune lined up in their coffins served to preserve the memory of government brutality among working class people. *(Adolphe-Eugene Disderi/ akg-images)*

aster for France and for Napoleon III personally. The French badly underestimated the training and equipment of the Prussian forces and were further hampered by poor military leadership. At the Battle of Sedan in early September 1870, the Germans encircled a large French force, capturing more than a hundred thousand men, including Emperor Napoleon III himself. The French declared their emperor deposed and formed a provisional government, which sued for peace.

Radical Paris, though surrounded by German troops, was outraged and disgusted by the actions of the provisional government. Rather than surrender, the adult male citizens of Paris voted in March 1871 to declare the **Paris Commune.** The Commune passed legislation granting free education, moderating rents, reducing church power, and generally supporting the working class. Two months later the provisional government, which had temporarily withdrawn to Versailles, sent troops to storm Paris and crush the Commune. More than twenty thousand people were killed, more than during the entire Reign of Terror of the French Revolution. This slaughter of mainly working-class people by the middle-class government would long be remembered by socialists, as would the myth of the Commune as the first workers' state. Writing immediately after the crushing of the Commune, Marx exclaimed, "Within sight of the Prussian army that had annexed to Germany two French pro-

vinces, the Commune annexed to France the working people all over the world."

In January 1871, before the Commune and even before a peace treaty could be negotiated, King William I had himself crowned "Emperor of the Germans"—symbolically—in Louis XIV's magnificent Hall of Mirrors in the Palace of Versailles. Bismarck had achieved his goal—a united German Empire. In the peace settlement, Germany took from France two German-speaking provinces along the Rhine River—Alsace and Lorraine—and received from France an indemnity of $2 billion. Germany was united, but the French swore revenge.

The American president, Ulysses S. Grant, congratulated the new German government on forming a federal union like the United States and expressed the hope that Germans would soon enjoy the benefits of democracy. In fact, the German constitution did grant universal male suffrage (to those aged twenty-five and older) in elections to the **Reichstag,** or federal parliament, but German states retained considerable

Paris Commune Radical regime in Paris after Franco-Prussian War, brutally suppressed by the French government in May 1871.

Reichstag German federal parliament for united Germany that met in Berlin starting in 1871 and was elected by universal male suffrage.

autonomy. The Reichstag's power was balanced by that of the Bundesrat, or federal council, in which Prussia exercised great influence. Most of all, the emperor—or Kaiser—held enormous power, dictating foreign policy, acting as commander in chief of all armies, and having the right to declare **martial law**, close down parliament, and interpret the constitution. In short, while German states such as Bavaria, Baden, and Saxony could maintain their own armies and issue their own postage stamps, Prussia and its Kaiser dominated German politics. The authoritarianism and militarism traditional to Prussia would often—if unfairly—be perceived by outsiders as "typically German."

Having engineered unification, Bismarck was secure in his position as—now—*federal* chancellor, though Kaiser William sometimes grumbled that Bismarck wielded more power than he. But Bismarck had to contend with a Reichstag considerably more diverse and demanding than the Prussian Landtag. Representatives from the Catholic south of Germany and the organization of the Catholic **Center Party** inspired fears of undue influence from the Vatican, so Bismarck embarked on an anti-Catholic campaign, the **Kulturkampf.** New laws removed priests from the state bureaucracy (most were teachers), closed down Catholic schools, outlawed Jesuit institutions, and instituted **civil marriage.** German Catholics in the south and the millions of Polish subjects of the Kaiser in the east saw these measures as a direct attack on their religion. The Vatican supported their resistance with an 1875 declaration threatening to excommunicate anyone who complied with these laws. At this point, Bismarck sought a compromise with Catholic leaders, but Catholic Germans continued to view rule from Berlin with suspicion.

After the failure of the Kulturkampf, Bismarck sought to suppress what he perceived an even greater threat to the German Empire—the socialists. He had long mistrusted working-class organizations, and after two unsuccessful attempts on the life of Kaiser William I in 1878, Bismarck pushed the Reichstag to forbid German socialists to organize, meet, and publish their programs. Despite this law, which remained in force until 1890, German socialists steadily gained votes in Reichstag elections, from just over 300,000 in 1881 to almost 1.5 million in 1890. Cleverly, Bismarck then implemented some of their demands, including state-sponsored unemployment insurance, healthcare, and retirement benefits, to undercut their appeal and ensure workers' loyalty to the state. Germany's social welfare programs were the first, but in the twentieth century nearly every European state would adopt similar policies, advancing government responsibility for aiding sick and poor citizens.

Nations Seeking States

By 1871, Italy and Germany were unified nation-states in which conservative nationalism had triumphed. Hungary, too, had achieved a degree of independence. After its defeat by Prussia, Austria conceded to the Hungarians essentially what they had demanded in 1848. In the Compromise of 1867, Hungarians gained almost complete autonomy, a fact reflected in the country's new name: Austria-Hungary. Hungarians handled domestic affairs independently. They had their own parliament, used their own language without restriction throughout their part of the empire, and obliged non-Hungarians to use that language in schools and government offices. Only in matters of foreign policy, state defense, and the overall budget did Hungary have to compromise with Austria. Austria and Hungary also shared the same ruler.

But many, perhaps most, nationalities in eastern and southeastern Europe lacked political autonomy. They lived as **national minorities** in the multinational empires of Russia, Austria-Hungary, and the Ottomans. As groups such as Ukrainians, Estonians, Romanians (in Hungary), Croatians, and Slovaks pressed their demands for autonomy, the multinational states were forced to give increasing attention to their **minorities question**—how does a state deal with a minority that refuses assimilation, insisting on using its own language and maintaining its own separate national culture instead of blending in with the majority? Newly independent states like Romania also wrestled with this problem—in Romania, particularly with regard to its Jewish and **Roma** ("gypsy")

martial law Temporary strengthening of government powers, including the suspension of certain civil rights, during public disturbances or other emergencies.

Center Party Catholic political party in Germany, organized in 1870.

Kulturkampf (in German, "struggle for culture") Bismarck's attack on Catholic schools, institutions, and political influence in the 1870s.

civil marriage Legal bond between two persons, usually man and wife, recognized by the state but not necessarily by religious authorities.

national minority Ethnic/national group not making up the majority of a state's population—e.g., in the Russian Empire, Jews, Poles, Ukrainians, and Latvians.

minorities question Problem of what cultural and political rights to give to national minorities.

Roma Nomadic people living especially in eastern Europe who trace their origins back to India, sometimes incorrectly referred to as "Gypsies."

citizens. Despite pressure from the western powers, Romania refused to grant full citizenship to members of these ethnic groups, treating them like foreigners.

Poles were a unique national minority in nineteenth-century Europe. They looked back to a large and powerful Polish state in the medieval and early modern period, before it was partitioned by Russia, Austria, and Prussia in the late eighteenth century. Polish written culture was well developed, and a Polish nobility continued to exist, despite the disappearance of the Polish state. While the Polish peasantry did not always identify with the "Polish nation" in midcentury, the existence of a Polish nation—without a state— could not be questioned, even by hostile Russians and Prussians like Bismarck. The Polish case stood in marked contrast to that of neighboring Slovaks, Belarusians, and Ukrainians, who lacked a long tradition of statehood or written culture.

The majority of Poles lived under Russian rule in the so-called kingdom of Poland, but after the Polish insurrection of 1830, little remained of its autonomy. A second insurrection in 1863 failed disastrously. In its aftermath, thousands of Poles were arrested, had their property confiscated, and were exiled to Siberia or fled abroad. Government schools used Russian as the language of instruction, Poles were excluded from many government jobs, and strict censorship was applied to the Polish press. The next generation of Polish intellectuals, known as the Warsaw positivists after the French intellectual movement of that name, emphasized economic and cultural development over national unity. They recognized that developing a strong, literate, and prosperous Polish nation was under present circumstances more important than fighting for independence.

From the 1890s onward, however, the cautious approach of the positivists did not satisfy the more impatient socialist and nationalist Polish youth. They argued for direct action against the repressive Russian Empire, even for revolution. The **Polish Socialist Party** was both nationalist in its political ideas (demanding an independent Polish state) and socialist in its economic ideas (demanding state ownership of factories and means of communication). At the end of the 1890s, it was challenged by the **National Democratic Party**, which stressed nationalism and rejected socialism. Led by **Roman Dmowski,** the National Democrats were aggressive and exclusivist in their approach, refusing to accept non-Poles, and especially Jews, as a part of the Polish nation. Dmowski, a biologist, was influenced by the social sciences. He argued that the large Jewish minority living among the Poles had taken over middle-class occupations, pushing out Poles. Thus, for a healthy Polish nation to

develop, Dmowski's argument continued, the Jews must either assimilate totally—shedding Jewish culture and identity—or leave Poland. Dmowski's appeals exemplified the beginnings of mass politics in Poland. On the one hand, he and his National Democrats helped organize Poles against Russian and Prussian cultural and political oppression; on the other, he rallied Poles to reject their Jewish neighbors and to embrace an aggressive, almost biological, form of nationalism.

While the Poles would have to wait until the twentieth century for independence, Bulgarian religious and national leaders wrested their own state from the Ottoman Empire by manipulating international tensions. The Ottomans tolerated Bulgarian Orthodox Christianity, but the ruling class in the region was made up primarily of Muslims. By the late nineteenth century, growing numbers of middle-class Bulgarians, most educated in missionary or church schools, came to resent their subordination to Muslim Ottoman authorities. They turned to Russia, which shared its religious traditions, spoke a similar language, and also used the Cyrillic alphabet. Russia had long seen itself as the protector of Orthodox Christians in the Ottoman Empire.

Launching an uprising in the spring of 1875, Bulgarian nationalist leaders drew all Europe's attention to their oppression, especially after violent reprisals by Ottoman forces took the lives of many thousands of Christian Bulgarians. Britain's former prime minister **William Gladstone** produced an overwrought account of the massacre, *The Bulgarian Horrors and the Question of the East*. When, in 1876, another Slavic people in the mountainous province of Bosnia-Herzegovina rose up against Ottoman rule, Russia intervened, in defense of Orthodox Christian Serbs and Montenegrans. In the **Russo-Turkish War**, Russian

Polish Socialist Party   Political party founded in 1892 that combined socialist ideology with the demand for an independent Polish state.

National Democratic Party   Nationalist and antisemitic Polish party formed in 1897 that advocated limiting the number of non-Poles—especially Jews—in a future Polish state.

Roman Dmowski   (1864–1939) Polish politician and leader of the nationalist and antisemitic National Democratic Party.

William Gladstone   (1809–1898) British politician and prime minister; important figure in the Liberal Party.

Russo-Turkish War   (1877–1878) Major war in the Balkans with Serbia and Russia fighting against the Ottoman Empire.

Patriotic images like this one inspired Bulgarians to fight for their independence from the Ottoman Empire in the late 1870s. In this poster, as in many others, the nation was depicted as a woman surrounded by symbols of state. Here we see the Bulgarian flag and the two-headed eagle that represented Bulgaria's link to the Russian Empire. *(1900 poster, courtesy of the Russion State Library print collection)*

troops crossed neutral Romania, invaded Bulgaria in the spring of 1877, and the following year defeated the Turks.

The terms Russia imposed on the Ottomans included a huge independent Bulgaria stretching from the Black Sea to the Aegean. This prospect alarmed Europe's Great Powers, which feared Russia would now gain undue influence in the Balkans and upset the balance of power. At the Congress of Berlin in 1878, Germany, Austria-Hungary, Great Britain, and France forced Russia to accept a much smaller Bulgaria with a German prince, Alexander of Battenberg, as its king. The Bulgarians had received their state not because of popular agitation or nationalist revolution, but through the intervention of Russia. The Ottoman province of Bosnia-Herzegovina was placed under Austrian administration.

Norway gained its independence in an entirely different way. Assigned to the Swedish Crown in 1815 at the Congress of Vienna, Norwegians cherished a separate identity derived from their rugged terrain, folk culture, and historical traditions linked to Denmark. The language used by educated Norwegians differed little from Danish, while the folk dialect was closer to Swedish. As subjects of the Swedish king, Norwegians enjoyed political and civil rights found in few other European countries. Still, Norwegian nationalists insisted on an independent Norway. After some negotiation, the Swedes agreed to a "divorce," and Norway became independent in 1905. This achievement of statehood by peaceful means stands out as a historical rarity.

National Identity in the United States

From 1861 to 1865, the United States fought a bitter civil war over the issues of states' rights and slavery. But the Civil War was also a war over American identity. The separation of the country into slave and free states underscored regional identities as Southerner or Yankee, rural and agrarian or urban and industrial. By seceding from the United States in 1861, eleven southern and slave-holding states had declared themselves a separate and distinct nation—the Confederate States of America. The Confederates' defeat meant the triumph of a more unified political and cultural nation under northern leadership.

After the war, the nation, which already stretched from the Atlantic to the Pacific, subdued its remaining indigenous peoples. Most Americans viewed Indians with hostility or at best as an obstacle for westward expansion, though some tried to assimilate—or Americanize—them in mission schools that forced them to accept American speech, dress, and standards of behavior. The position of African Americans released from slavery by the Civil War created the "Negro problem." Most Americans did not believe African Americans could be assimilated. Local laws enforced segregation of the races and sought to restrict black people to menial jobs and marginal housing. Educator, editor, and writer Booker T. Washington advised his fellow African Americans to gain a practical education and improve their economic standing. The first black American to earn a Ph.D. at Harvard University, W. E. B. Du Bois, disagreed sharply, refusing to limit his people's ambitions to economic betterment and specifically rejecting the segregation of the races common in the southern American states at that time. To push for full social and political equality for

MAP 22.3 **Unification of Germany, 1871** Germany was unified in great part through the efforts of Prussian Chancellor Otto von Bismarck. The creation of this large German state in central Europe put severe strains on the diplomatic balance of power existing in Europe since the Congress of Vienna.

African Americans, Du Bois helped found the National Association for the Advancement of Colored People (NAACP) in 1909. Asians who had migrated to the United States' West Coast in large numbers beginning in the mid-nineteenth century were also subject to discrimination. Congress ended Chinese immigration in 1882, and a diplomatic arrangement ended Japanese immigration in 1907. Asians were denied American citizenship well into the twentieth century.

As a nation of immigrants, American national identity was complex and problematic. For those with white skin, it was a chosen identity. By the end of the nineteenth century, more and more Europeans chose the United States as a new homeland. Millions left Ireland, Germany, Italy, Russia, and other European countries to take up a new life in the New World. America was particularly attractive to those who suffered political repression in their native land or who longed for greater economic opportunity. As great numbers of Poles, Italians, eastern Europeans, and Jews began to arrive, some of the earlier immigrants and their descendants opposed further immigration, claiming that people from southern and eastern Europe could not be assimilated into the American nation. They were wrong. While immigrants often worked long hours in unhealthy conditions and fought off feelings of alienation and homesickness, many prospered and proudly watched their children grew up "100 percent American." Most European immigrants to the United States quickly became great patriots, proud of their American citizenship and their American identity. For Americans of African or Asian descent, however, both political rights and social acceptance were denied.

The Expanding Role of the State

↓ In what ways did states expand their role in the life of their citizens? What role did nationalism play in this expansion of state power?

↓ How did education aim to incorporate citizens into the national cultural of the state?

After 1848, political participation increased throughout Europe. By the end of the century, almost all males in Britain and France could vote, as they also could in newly united Italy and Germany. In the stateless nations in the Ottoman and Habsburg Empires, agitation for political rights strengthened. Everywhere leaders used education as a means of influencing citizens to identify with the state, its culture, and its interests. States also intruded into the economy to encourage local industry and keep out foreign competition. Across Europe, the role of the state in citizen's lives expanded.

Mass Politics and Nation Building

The term **nation building** cannot be separated from the concept of nation-state. It describes the process by which the political unit (state) attempts to transform its population into a "nation." Nation building was also connected with new legislative assemblies and the expansion of political participation after 1848. As individuals voted in elections, held office, debated

political issues, read newspapers, and traveled (often seeking employment) throughout their countries, they gained a sense of national identity that transcended local and religious ties.

In Britain the nation-state was firmly established by the nineteenth century, and parliamentary traditions were strong. In 1832, in a triumph of British liberalism, the Reform Acts had granted the vote to middle-class men. The Reform Acts of 1867 and 1884 extended suffrage to male heads of households; further extensions brought almost universal male suffrage by the early twentieth century. Regional identities remained strong, but they did not challenge the dominance of a British identity fostered by London.

Throughout this period, Great Britain was plagued by the Irish question—what to do with the Irish, poverty-stricken, Catholic peasants in a mainly Protestant and industrialized British nation. The horrific famine of the mid-1840s had reduced the population of Ireland by over one-third and poisoned relations between Irish Catholic peasants and their Protestant landlords. One proposed solution to the Irish question was home rule—autonomy for the Irish provinces with their own parliament in Dublin. Irish demands for home rule increased at the end of the nineteenth century.

France also enjoyed a strong national tradition, prestigious culture, and prosperity. The centrality of Paris and the strength of the central state apparatus and of French culture overshadowed the linguistic and cultural diversity (Basque, Breton, Provençal) existing within France's borders. The extensive rebuilding of Paris in the decades before 1870 added to its glamour and attraction as the center of French nation. To be French meant to be part of the "great nation" that included all citizens of the French Republic. Local identities hardly had a chance to take shape as separatist or national movements. After the French Revolution, being French had nothing to do with religion. French identity was political: one could "become" French by accepting the responsibilities of being a loyal citizen.

The expansion of the electorate in France followed a more abrupt path than in Britain. Following the 1848 revolution, universal male suffrage was established, but under Emperor Napoleon III, starting in 1851, democracy ended in France for two decades. The disastrous Franco-Prussian war ushered in the

nation building Creation of a strong nation-state, with institutions to educate the population in obedience and patriotism.

The "Grand Boulevards" of Paris, planned and built during the reign of Emperor Napoleon III, today give the impression of a well-ordered city. But at the time they entailed an enormous amount of destruction, demolishing much of medieval Paris and pushing many working-class people out of the central city to the suburbs. This photograph, from 1852, shows the clearing of the area near the Louvre. (*Bibliothèque Historique de la Ville de Paris; Photo: UCSC Slide Collection*)

Third Republic, and from 1871 onward, Frenchmen would always enjoy voting rights.

Elsewhere in Europe political rights also increased. In newly unified Italy and Germany, all men could vote. Even in backward Russia, most men could vote in **Duma** elections after 1906, though the votes of the wealthy counted far more than those of peasants and workers. Universal male suffrage came to Austria (though not to Hungary) in 1907. In Finland, still an autonomous principality within the Russian Empire, women were granted the vote in 1906. Women could also vote in local elections in some western states in the United States. Democracy was far from universal even in the early twentieth century, but great strides had been made in that direction since 1848.

Technology played a role in nation building. Steam presses and advances in papermaking technology made newspapers cheap and abundant after the 1860s, and increased literacy meant that more people read them. Newspaper reading helped establish and spread a standard form of the language and thus weakened local dialects. Industrial development also strengthened national feelings. Railroads encouraged mobility between town and countryside and reduced differences between peasants and town dwellers, reinforcing the idea that "we are all Frenchmen" (or Germans, or Russians, or Italians). The telegraph, which dates from 1844, twenty years later spanned the European and American continents, helping bring citizens in closer contact and aiding governments in administering their territories.

The impact of this expanding political participation was enormous. With mass political participation came the need for governments to respond to public opinion. Some governments used secret subsidies to influence the opinions newspapers expressed. For example, it was an open secret that the Russian government paid large sums to the Belgian daily *Le Nord*, which then gave favorable coverage of Russian affairs. Governments also paid editors to print favorable news and suppress embarrassing information. Most governments attempted to limit the information reaching their citizens through censorship, but as the amount of information freely available to citizens grew, politics could no longer remain confined to a few wealthy families.

The new political power of peasant and working-class men changed the agendas of political parties. Conservative parties attempted to gain peasant support by appealing to Christian (often Catholic) values and denouncing "godless" urban socialists and, in some cases, the Jews. Liberal parties increasingly modified their laissez-faire attitudes to support limits

Third Republic (1870–1940) Longest continuous republic in French history, beginning with the defeat in the Franco-Prussian war and ending with military defeat by Hitler.

Duma Russian legislature, granted by Tsar Nicholas II in 1906 and lasting until the Revolution of 1917.

on employment of children and the length of the working day and provision of assistance to ill or injured workers. Nationalist politicians often took up antisemitic slogans, blaming Jews as responsible for higher prices.

Working-class political organizations grew steadily. In England, the **Labour Party**, founded in 1900, rapidly challenged both the Tories and the Liberals, whose party had developed from the Whigs. In other countries, socialist parties sought to represent labor, though they were often harassed or disbanded by governments. The **Social Democratic Party of Germany** was powerful enough to attract more votes than any other party in the 1913 elections, but it was still kept out of the government. In France, when a socialist, Alexandre Millerand, accepted a cabinet post in 1899, he was soundly criticized by other socialists for participating in a bourgeois government. Russian socialists, on the other hand, were forced to operate underground. These illegal groupings were split between the peasant-based **Socialist Revolutionaries**, who embraced terrorist methods, and the Marxist Social Democrats, who themselves split into **Bolshevik** and **Menshevik** factions in 1903 over questions of party strategy. Everywhere, socialists believed that as the numbers of working-class people grew, their triumph over capitalism was increasingly certain.

Mass politics took varied and even contradictory forms. When the British prime minister William Gladstone, a Liberal, toured the country by rail in the 1870s to influence voters, he was participating in mass politics. When, in the 1890s, the Polish political leader Roman Dmowski and the National Democrats published the newspaper *Kurier Wszechpolski* in Austrian Galicia, in part so it could be smuggled into the Russian Empire, they were also participating in mass politics. Mass-circulation newspapers attempted to influence public opinion with their coverage of events and exposés of political corruption. French writer **Émile Zola**'s article denouncing the French army's attempt to frame Captain Alfred Dreyfus, "J'Accuse!" ("I Accuse"), is a famous example of such an exposé.

Education and the Nation-State

Before 1848, few European states compelled their citizens to attend school. By 1914, universal schooling was accepted as a goal—though it was not yet a reality—throughout Europe and increasingly around the world. By the early twentieth century, literacy and access to education were coming to be seen as a primary responsibility of governments. In most countries of western, northern, and central Europe, parents were obliged to send their children to school. States recog-

nized the importance of schools for forming the population into well-trained workers and patriotic citizens.

Everywhere, literacy improved, though at unequal rates. At midcentury, more than 70 percent of the population in Scandinavia, Germany, Scotland, and the United States was literate; by 1913, the figure was over 90 percent, not only in those countries but also in Great Britain (including Ireland), Australia, New Zealand, Austria, and France. Even in backward Russia, nearly half of the population was literate by this time. Generally, literacy rates were higher in urban than rural areas, among men than women, and in Protestant countries than in Catholic countries, probably because of Protestantism's emphasis on Bible reading.

The spread of mandatory elementary education, though not rapid, was steady. From the late eighteenth century onward, Prussia obliged parents to send their children to school. In France, a law promising free, compulsory, and universal elementary education was passed in the wake of the 1848 revolution, though it took several decades to be implemented. Great Britain instituted universal primary education in 1871, and this system grew rapidly in the next few decades. Even in Russia, where the spread of literacy was hampered by poverty and the government's distrust of teachers, who were suspected of revolutionary sympathies, the numbers of primary schools increased significantly in the decades up to 1914, and plans were under way to introduce free and universal primary education.

The nature and philosophy of education changed radically, with its practical—rather than moral or religious—aspects getting more attention. In Prussia, traditional classical high schools, or *Gymnasien*, that emphasized Latin and Greek were supplemented by more practical secondary schools teaching mathematics and science to prepare workers for a new industrial economy. New institutions of higher learning—in

Labour Party   British political party founded in 1900 with the help of trade unions to represent the interests of the urban working class.

Social Democratic Party of Germany   Europe's most powerful and popular socialist party in the late nineteenth and early twentieth centuries.

Socialist Revolutionaries   Russian underground political party, founded in 1901, that carried out terrorist acts against tsarist government.

Bolsheviks and Mensheviks   Two branches of the underground Russian Social-Democratic Party, the more radical of which was the Bolsheviks.

Émile Zola   (1840–1902) French writer, author of "J'Accuse," an article accusing the French army of trying to frame Dreyfus.

particular the technological universities—concentrated on producing well-trained chemists, engineers, and other specialists vital to Germany's growing industries. In other countries, too, science and technology found a place in the curriculum, and technological institutes were set up in St. Petersburg, Warsaw, and Boston, where the Massachusetts Institute of Technology was founded in 1861.

In many parts of Europe, the state sought to reduce the influence of the church on education. The secular French state instituted state-run primary schools with state-employed teachers, the *instituteurs,* who saw themselves as countering the forces of backwardness and reaction they perceived as embodied in the Catholic Church and the local priest. In Germany, one purpose of Bismarck's Kulturkampf was to eject the Catholic priest from the classroom. In other European countries, the tension between state education and religious authority was less open, but everywhere conservatives and traditional religious leaders felt uneasy about mass education, worrying that it could promote radical thinking and atheism.

Mass education also aimed to strengthen patriotism. Italian schools insisted that the pupils use standard Italian, a language that children in many regions could barely understand. Ukrainian and Belarusian children were taught—if at all—in Russian, since the government claimed that their languages were only dialects of Russian. But the patriotic lessens taught in schools went beyond language. In Italian schools, children learned that they had inherited the glories of ancient Rome. Russian pupils were taught that the tsar was a kindly father looking out for all his subjects in their broad motherland, which covered one-fifth of the earth's surface. British children learned pride in their democratic traditions and love for the queen and the British Empire, on which "the sun never sets." In Prussia, the values of order and discipline were stressed.

Even while opening up opportunity for a few gifted individuals, mass education also reinforced existing class lines. While more peasants and workers now sent their children to school, few could afford secondary or higher education. The British public school system prepared the sons of the gentry and upper middle class to enter Oxford and Cambridge and from there to occupy positions of power in government and industry. There, and elsewhere, university students came overwhelmingly from the middle class and upper levels of society, and higher education was far from common. In 1900 there were fewer than thirty thousand university students in France and fewer than fifty thousand in Germany—less than 1 percent of the population in both cases. At the same time, less privileged people were getting more and more education that allowed hundreds of thousands to take up jobs as bank clerks, government bureaucrats, teachers, and telegraph operators. Mass education thus helped expand the middle class, which in turn increased demands for broader political rights.

The Growing Power of the State

Nation building aims to convince citizens that they have a stake and a voice in the nation-state. The nation-state's political legitimacy derives in the end from the nation—that is, all citizens taken as a whole. But the state also demands that citizens fulfill various obligations: paying taxes, serving in the military, obeying the law. Now citizens were asked to fulfill these obligations as part of a social contract between themselves and the nation-state. At the same time, citizens increasingly expected the state to protect them not only from domestic or foreign enemies but from the devastation of sickness, poverty, and old age. In the second half of the nineteenth century, state power expanded in the form of increased government intervention in everyday life, but in return the state promised order, more protection for weaker segments of society, and international prestige.

Classical liberalism argued that the state should interfere as little as possible in economic matters, holding that legal equality would give all citizens equal access to fame and fortune. By the last decades of the nineteenth century, even liberals allowed that the state had a role to play in the economy. The failed example of France's national workshops of 1848 began to seem like a reasonable idea during periods of high unemployment. Most state intervention in the economy, however, aimed to assure investors' profits. In the building of railroads in Russia and Austria, for example, where investors put forth capital, the state guaranteed a certain percentage return, at least for a specific period. The state also sought to assure decent working conditions. From Britain to Russia, government factory inspectors examined working conditions with the power to fine or even shut down workplaces that were dangerous. For some factory owners, such measures seemed an outrageous example of government interference in their businesses.

The technology of war also contributed to nation building and the growth of state power. By the 1870s, nearly every European country, with the exception of Britain, demanded military service from its male citizens. Serving in the Russian or French or Italian army helped young peasant lads to see themselves as part of a larger group—the nation. Before 1917, more Russian boys were taught to read in the army than in schools. Similarly, bringing together young men from different parts of France and Italy helped encourage use of the standard language rather than local dialects and impressed on the soldiers that they served not only their family, village, or region but the entire nation. And the existence of a strong national army was a matter of pride and international prestige: few Europeans could imagine a self-respecting nation-state without a well-trained army in flashy and distinctive uniforms. Throughout Europe the cost of these armies was nearly universally the largest item on the state budget.

To intervene in industrial development, educate citizens, and build strong armies, states needed taxes. With the exception of Great Britain, which introduced an income tax—levied only on those with higher incomes—in 1842, European states collected revenue from tariffs and **indirect taxes,** such as taxes on salt, kerosene, and matches. In Austria-Hungary the state had a monopoly on the sales of tobacco products, and in Russia the state budget was covered in large part by taxation on vodka. Tariffs and indirect taxes pushed up prices and fell disproportionately on the poor. Throughout Europe taxes rose in the course of the nineteenth century.

Nationalism and its Opponents

> ↓ What links developed in the later nineteenth century between nationalism and racism?
>
> ↓ Why did anarchists, socialists, and the Catholic Church oppose nationalism? In each case, what aspects of nationalism did they dislike?

Despite its growing influence, nationalism was not without opponents in this period. Some objected to its increasingly aggressive, even racist, aspects, which pitted nation against nation in contests that defined some as inferior, others as superior. Both conservatives and radicals, for different reasons, saw nationalism as a destructive, even evil, movement. The conservative multinational empires in central and eastern Europe opposed nationalism as a threat to their continued survival. The Catholic Church condemned both the democratic politics of some nationalists and the racism of others. Socialists denounced nationalism as a tool of the ruling classes to distract ordinary people from real social and economic issues, to disguise exploitation with nationalist slogans, and to increase profits through the sale of armaments.

Integral Nationalism, Racism, Antisemitism, Zionism

After 1848, conservatives took up the nationalist ideas and slogans that had been the hallmarks of liberalism before the uprisings. After 1860, nationalists began to preach a more exclusionary and aggressive creed, stressing struggle and dominance rather than cooperation and mutual assistance. At the same time, conservatives recognized the utility of nationalism as a tool for rallying the masses. By painting radicals and socialists as internationalists, the conservatives suggested that leftists would support foreign interests over patriotism. Most important of all, now everyone was expected to identify with one nation, not with a local village or religious faith. This growth in national self-consciousness was encouraged by government schools, mass publications such as newspapers and calendars, and various political parties.

Toward the end of the nineteenth century, nationalism took on increasingly narrow and aggressive forms. This phenomenon has been termed **integral nationalism,** to stress its all-encompassing character and distinguish it from earlier liberal nationalism. These nonliberal nationalists stressed struggle between nations and domination of other nations. Dmowski in Poland, for example, argued that only a struggle between Poles and Ukrainians would determine whether the Ukrainians would survive as a nation. Another key ingredient of integral nationalism was a narrow definition of the nation, focusing in particular on who *did not* belong and usually seeing a nation as a community of birth, not an identity that one could choose. German nationalists came to insist that birth determined German identity. Although France and the United States theoretically defined their nations as open to anyone accepting their political ideals, discrimination belied this open, liberal attitude.

Narrow and exclusionary definitions of the nation came together with the rise of racialist thought. As Europeans engaged in a new wave of colonizing in Africa and Asia, the idea of race emerged as a biological reality and object of study. Though race is now understood as lacking a scientific basis and the

---

indirect taxes Taxes levied on products of common use, like salt, alcoholic beverages, or kerosene, as opposed to direct taxes, such as income tax.

integral nationalism Form of nationalism common in the later nineteenth century, characterized by an aggressive stance toward other ethnic groups.

Voice Voice Voice Voice

Theodor Herzl Speculates on the Impact of Jewish Immigration to Palestine

When Theodor Herzl proposed the creation of a Jewish state in 1896, he focused not on a location or an exact form of government but on the simple fact that Jews should have their own state to shelter them from persecution and to foster their national pride. In his writings, however, he envisioned an economically modern state that would be liberal and democratic in its politics. He also envisioned good relations between Jews and Arabs. In this passage from Old-New Land, *a fictional English visitor speaks with an Arab landowner about the impact of Jewish immigration to Palestine.*

➡ Why does Herzl have an English visitor address this question to an Arab?

➡ "One question, Reschid Bey," interrupted Kingscourt. . . . "Were not the older inhabitants of Palestine ruined by the Jewish immigration? And didn't they have to leave the country?" . . .

➡ Why, according to Reschid, do the Palestinian Arabs appreciate their new Jewish neighbors?

➡ "What a question! It was a great blessing for all of us," returned Reschid. "Naturally, the land-owners gained most because they were able to sell to the Jewish society at high prices. . . ."

"But I wanted to ask you, my dear Bey, how the former inhabitants fared—those who had nothing, the numerous Moslem Arabs."

"'Your question answers itself, Mr. Kingscourt," replied Reschid. "Those who had nothing stood to lose nothing, and could only gain. And they did gain: Opportunities to work, means of livelihood, prosperity. Nothing could have been more wretched than an Arab village at the end of the nineteenth century. . . . Now everything is different. They benefited from the progressive measures of the New Society whether they wanted to or not. . . ."

"You're queer fellows, you Moslems. Don't you regard these Jews as intruders?"

"You speak strangely, Christian," responded the friendly Reschid. "Would you call a man a robber who takes nothing from you, but brings you something instead? The Jews have enriched us. Why should we be angry with them? They dwell among us like brothers. Why should we not love them? . . ."

Reschid's gentle words had moved everyone, Kingscourt included. That gentleman cleared his throat. "Hm-hm! Quite right. Very fine. Sounds reasonable. ➡ But you're an educated man, you've studied in Europe. I hardly think the simple country or town folk will be likely to think as you do."

➡ Why does Herzl have Kingscourt comment on Reschid's European education? Which culture does Kingscourt see as superior?

➡ "They more than anyone else, Mr. Kingscourt. You must excuse my saying so, but I did not learn tolerance in the Occident [the West]. We Moslems have always had better relations with the Jews than you Christians."

➡ Who is the target of Herzl's indirect criticism here?

UN DINER EN FAMILLE

— Surtout ! ne parlons pas de l'affaire Dreyfus !

Ils en ont parlé

A pair of French cartoons illustrates the bitter controversy caused by the Dreyfus Affair within French society—and even within individual families. The first cartoon reads "Above all let's not talk about the Dreyfus Affair"; the second—"They talked about it." *(Archives Charmet/The Bridgeman Art Library)* diversity of humankind as being unclassifiable in such terms, scientists and philosophers in late-nineteenth-century Europe developed a racial system of human classification based on a strict hierarchy, with white Europeans on top. This **scientific racism** claimed that humanity was divided into three races with different physical, mental, and sexual capacities.

Racism and integral nationalism fused most notoriously in **antisemitism.** The word itself was first used by the obscure German writer **Wilhelm Marr** in 1879 in his pamphlet *Victory of the Jews over the Germans* to describe a new phenomenon. While religious hatred and discrimination against Jews had long existed in Christian Europe, antisemitism attacked not the Jewish religion but all those of Jewish birth ("race"), no matter what their religious beliefs, as enemies of all Europeans and their society (the term **Aryan** was often used in this context to mean non-Jews). Antisemites insisted that Jews by their very nature could not be part of European nations, much to the anger of middle-class Jews, who, believing in assimilation, considered their religion no obstacle to their strongly felt identity as patriotic Frenchmen, Germans, or Poles

Antisemites held that Jews unfairly monopolized commerce and banking; were dishonest in their dealings with non-Jews; and exercised a corrupting moral influence through their activities as journalists, lawyers, and doctors. Jews were identified with modern capitalist society—disrespectful of social traditions while energetically and unscrupulously accumulating wealth and power. Antisemitic political parties, such as Dmowski's National Democrats, appealed to workers and lower-middle-class voters, whose economic and social position were threatened by industrialization and large-scale capitalist commerce. Antisemitism gained significant popular support in the 1870s and 1880s in places where Jewish populations were substantial, as in Austria-Hungary and Russian Poland, and where Jews were noticeable in society, despite their small numbers, because of their achievements in business or the free professions, as in Germany. But antisemitism within European society was so general that when the Austrian journalist **Theodor Herzl**, covering the **Dreyfus affair** in Paris, witnessed public demonstrations of hatred toward all Jews, he concluded that no Jew was safe, not even in enlightened, republican France (see Choice). Declaring that Jews constituted a nation, not just a religious community, Herzl initiated a movement, known as **Zionism**, calling for the establishment of a Jewish state in the historical home of the Hebrews in Palestine.

The final decades of the nineteenth century were traumatic for Europe's Jews. In 1881, in the wake of the assassination of Tsar Alexander II in St. Petersburg, a wave of **pogroms**, or organized attacks on Jewish life and property, swept the southwestern provinces of the Russian Empire (today's Ukraine). Despite the small number of deaths in the pogroms, their moral impact was devastating. Most Jews—and Russian liberals—concluded that the Russian government itself was behind the attacks (a view now rejected by historians), and by the end of the 1880s, tens of thousands of Jews were leaving Russia every year, mainly for the United States.

Strains in the Multinational Empires

While Jews felt directly threatened by the new aggressive nationalism, the conservative multinational empires of eastern and central Europe were indirectly threatened. The Ottoman Empire, Austria-Hungary, and Russia were all defined by dynastic loyalties and contained within their borders a wide diversity of groups increasingly conscious of their national and ethnic identities. Their demands for cultural and political rights undermined the stability of these empires.

The Ottoman Empire was a kaleidoscope of ethnic diversity, including, at midcentury, Slavs, Albanians, Arabs, and others—it was not a "Turkish" state. Sultan

scientific racism   Nineteenth-century biological theory that claimed humanity is divided into three races with different physical, mental, and sexual capacities.

antisemitism   Anti-Jewish political movement arising in Germany in the 1870s and spreading to many countries, in particular in eastern Europe.

Wilhelm Marr   (1819–1904) German writer who coined the word *antisemitism,* arguing that Jews posed a major threat to European peoples and culture.

Aryan   Designation for non-Jews, implying that Jews belonged in a specific "semitic" race, while other white Europeans belonged to the "Aryan" race.

Theodor Herzl   (1860–1904) Viennese journalist who founded modern Zionism.

Dreyfus affair   Series of trials between 1894 and 1906 involving the false accusation of Captain Alfred Dreyfus, a Jewish officer on the French general staff, of spying for the Germans.

Zionism   View that Jews were not merely a religious community, but a nation; also a movement advocating the formation of a modern Jewish state in Palestine.

pogrom   In Russia in 1881 and later, organized attacks on Jews and Jewish property.

The ethnic diversity of the Russian Empire is reflected in this 1900 poster showing representatives of a half-dozen peoples (including a Georgian, Chechen, Armenian, and Lezgin) all in native dress. These peoples lived in the Caucasus Mountains that separated Russia from the Ottoman Empire, a region conquered by the Russian Empire in the nineteenth century. *(Courtesy, Russian State Library)*

Abdul Hamid II himself was born to an **Armenian** mother, and among his wives were women of various ethnic groups. In the Ottoman Empire, religion was much more important than nationality. Religious toleration was practiced, though Islam was considered the most perfect religion. In practice, business and commerce were dominated by Christians and Jews, and the population of Istanbul—the former Constantinople—was more Christian than Muslim in 1900. National and ethnic strife was not entirely absent, however, in the Ottoman state. When Armenians, for example, were suspected of disloyalty to the sultan, they were subjected to violent attacks.

In the course of the nineteenth century, Greeks, Romanians, Serbs, and Bulgarians gained their independence from the Ottoman Empire, while Bosnia-Herzegovina was transferred to Austria. These territorial losses were just one sign of Ottoman weakness. Though the sultan exercised absolute power in principle; in reality the empire's unwieldy size and inefficient bureaucracy meant that he could never be sure his orders would be carried out in distant provinces. Local elites from the Balkans to northern Africa often took control into their own hands. Eventually, the economic problems of the Ottoman state became so acute that in effect the empire went bank-

rupt, and state budgets had to be approved by the empire's European creditors.

The Russian Empire was even larger and more diverse than the Ottoman Empire. Stretching from Finland to the Pacific Ocean, it covered one-fifth of the earth's dry land. Like the Ottoman Empire, Russia was not a nation-state. The census of 1897 indicates that not quite half of Nicholas's subjects were ethnically Russian. The empire encompassed Ukrainians, Poles, Jews, Lithuanians, Germans, pagan Udmurts, and Muslim Tartars. Germans predominated among Russia's diplomats, and German names—Benckendorff, Totleben, Kaufmann—were common among the highest officials and generals of the empire. The Finns enjoyed broad autonomy, having their own coinage, postal system, and legislature. The legal status of most non-Russians in the empire was, however, far less favorable.

Russia had been considered a major European power only since the Napoleonic Wars, and this sta-

Armenians Christian ethnic group living in the Russian and Ottoman Empires, subject to violent attacks under Sultan Abdul Hamid II.

tus was severely shaken by its defeat in the **Crimean War** (1854–1856). Tsar Nicholas I died a broken man in the midst of the war, admonishing his son Alexander II to learn from his mistakes. While no liberal, Tsar Alexander II recognized that only sweeping reforms could save Russia's status as a great power. In 1861, he emancipated the serfs in the first of a series of **Great Reforms** that ended in 1876 with universal military service. Censorship was also lightened, but Alexander refused to consider the creation of any kind of elected legislature, even of an advisory sort.

Even before the Great Reforms, religious toleration had been practiced in the Russian Empire, but the Russian Orthodox Church was officially the "reigning religion," its primacy taken for granted. Catholics were regarded as untrustworthy, and Russian officials closely monitored the movements and actions of Catholic priests and bishops. The Jews were worst off: their residence, with few exceptions, was restricted to the southwestern part of the empire, the so-called **Pale of Settlement**; they were discriminated against in government jobs and secondary and higher education.

Russia differed from the Ottoman or Habsburg Empires, however, in the predominance of one religion and one language. While the tsar's subjects were generally free to speak their native tongues at home, Russian was the usual language in government offices and schools, courts, and universities. The Russian tsar had to be Russian Orthodox in religion, but in the nineteenth century, every tsar married a foreign princess, though they all converted to Orthodoxy as a condition of marriage. The last tsar, Nicholas II, married a German princess, Alix—or Aleksandra Fyodorovna, as she was known after her conversion—who had been brought up in England at the court of Queen Victoria. At home, the imperial family usually spoke English, though sometimes German and French, as well as Russian.

In the second half of the nineteenth century, the tsar attempted to introduce a more centralized administration using Russian. This process, usually described as **russification**, did not aim to make Finns, Poles, Jews, and others into Russians, but rather to create a more unified empire where Russian could serve as the means of communication among all of the empire's inhabitants. Nevertheless, russification caused great resentment among non-Russian elites who, like Dmowski, would form the nucleus of nationalist movements throughout the empire. By 1900, nationalism was a powerful antigovernment force, in particular in the empire's western borderlands. At the same time, Russian nationalism was also growing, often exhibiting an aggressive anti-Polish and anti-Jewish attitude. Among the many problems facing the Russian Empire in the early twentieth century, nationalism was one of the most threatening.

Whereas the Russian Empire adopted a policy of russification and repression, Austria-Hungary attempted reconciliation. After the Compromise of 1867 divided the empire into two separate halves, Austria and Hungary ran their own domestic affairs separately, sharing military and diplomatic affairs. They also shared, of course, a ruler: Francis Joseph was emperor (Kaiser) in Vienna, but king (*király*) in Budapest. The rights of minority nationalities were assured by law throughout Austria-Hungary, but in practice the Hungarians tried to impose their language on the Slovaks and Romanians who lived in Hungary. Anyone wishing to gain an education and rise socially would have to master the difficult Hungarian language. Rather like in Russia, this harsh policy had the opposite effect of what Budapest hoped for. Slovak and Romanian peasants were easily propagandized by nationalists, who pointed out that they would have better economic, cultural, and educational opportunities in their own national states.

In Austria, the national issue was a source of constant political complications. Among the larger non-German groups were Czechs, Poles, and Ukrainians (Ruthenians). Poles were given broad autonomy in the eastern region of Galicia, where they lived in large numbers. Somewhat later, the Ukrainians of eastern Galicia were granted special language rights. Little by little, Czechs also made significant gains, such as being able to use their language in schools and state offices. The 1882 split of Prague University into German and Czech institutions was also a major achievement for the Czechs. These concessions served to embolden rather than pacify the nationalists. At the same time, German nationalism was on the rise, and in Vienna it was difficult to piece together a lasting government coalition from the various battling

Crimean War (1854–1856) War fought on the Crimean peninsula in which Russia's defeat by France and Britain led to Tsar Alexander II's Great Reforms.

Great Reforms (1861–1876) Series of Russian reforms that included emancipation of the serfs, lessening of censorship, and reform of the military and judicial systems.

Pale of Settlement Area in the southwestern Russian Empire—roughly equivalent to present-day Belarus, Lithuania, and western Ukraine—where Jews were allowed to reside.

russification Effort to culturally assimilate minority national groups in the Russian Empire, in particular in the second half of the nineteenth century.

parties. Some were already predicting that the Habsburg Empire would not survive the death of its elderly ruler, Francis Joseph, who had been on the throne since 1848.

Universalism in the Roman Catholic Church

The Roman Catholic Church had no reason to favor nationalism. When Rome was incorporated into Italy in 1870, Pope Pius IX refused to acknowledge the Italian state. At the time, he was pushing the Vatican Council to adopt the doctrine of papal infallibility, which holds that papal pronouncements on matters of faith and dogma must be accepted by all Catholics. With this new doctrine, Pius hoped to strengthen the church's position against all forms of modernism, from nationalism and socialism to progress, liberalism, and lay education. Pius's negative opinion of nearly all aspects of modernity may be seen in his *Syllabus of Errors* of late 1864. Here he condemned, among other things, rationalism, socialism, liberalism, and attempts to reconcile church doctrine with scientific discoveries. Pius's total rejection of constitutionalism and modern politics cut the ground out from under moderate Catholics who had been attempting to reconcile their faith with modern life.

In 1878, Pius IX died and was succeeded by a far more conciliatory pope, **Leo XIII**. He was no less an enemy of nationalism, socialism, and rationalism than his predecessor, but he recognized that the church needed to find a compromise that would allow Catholics both to participate in modern life, including politics, and to remain faithful to their religion. Pope Leo's social views were set down in his encyclical *De rerum novarum* of 1891. Here he took a moderate position, though he condemned socialism and the liberal principle of absolute property ownership rights. True Catholics, he set down, must neither support socialist movements nor exploit others economically. Capitalist exploitation was, Leo stressed, every bit as sinful as socialism. The pope called on the Catholic faithful to support those parties that best exemplified Christian values—for example the Center Party in Germany. Nonetheless, the church continued to emphasize its international, indeed universal, role in human affairs.

Internationalism in Politics

Socialists were even more opposed to nationalism than the Catholic Church. In 1864 socialists set up the "International," bringing together socialists from different countries. In particular the **Second Socialist**

Pope Pius IX started his papacy as a liberal, but the Revolutions of 1848 transformed him into a staunch conservative. He opposed liberalism, socialism, and nationalism—including the unification of Italy. His rejection of Italian unification led to tensions between the Catholic Church and the Italian nation-state that were not resolved until the twentieth century. *(Hulton Deutsch Collection/Corbis)*

International, organized in 1889 after Marx's death, worked to strengthen ties between socialists of various nationalities in different countries. Socialists pledged

Syllabus of Errors Document issued by Pope Pius IX in 1864 condemning many modern beliefs, including rationalism, socialism, communism, and liberalism.

Leo XIII (r. 1878–1903) Successor of Pius IX, pope who attempted to find ways of reconciling Catholic faith and the modern world.

De rerum novarum (*About Modern Things*) Document issued by Pope Leo XIII in 1891 condemning socialism and the exploitation of workers and calling for cooperation between classes.

Second Socialist International (1889–1914) Loose organization of working-class political parties dominated by Marxists.

themselves to international solidarity and solemnly declared that they would never go to war. Practically speaking, however, they admitted that socialist organizations would need to be created on a national level. Sometimes national and socialist agendas were pursued simultaneously. The Polish Socialist Party, for example, aimed to overthrow the existing political order and establish an independent—and socialist—Polish republic.

Some who sought to overthrow the political order described themselves as **anarchists.** Like the socialists, anarchists looked forward to a world of shared prosperity, diffusion of political power, and the destruction of the powerful centralized state. But while socialists increasingly accepted the Marxist program of industrial development and a worldwide revolution, anarchists used more flexible tactics, from education and propaganda to **terrorism** and assassination. Some anarchists thought that killing a powerful political leader would strike a blow against state repression. The most famous anarchist, **Mikhail Bakunin,** once famously declared, "The urge to destroy is also a creative urge!" Among the victims of anarchist attacks were Tsar Alexander II (1881), President Sadi Carnot of France (1894), Spanish premier Antonio Canovas de Castillo (1897), Empress Elisabeth of Austria (1898), and U.S. president William McKinley (1901).

Where the anarchists often used violent means to achieve peaceful ends, **pacifists** aimed to prevent war at all costs. As technology and militarism advanced, the prospect of war became ever more horrific. Why not, the pacifists argued, take the millions spent on armies and weapons and use it for better housing, sanitation, cultural facilities, and education? Perhaps the most famous pacifist of this period was the **Baroness Bertha von Suttner.** Daughter of an Austrian field marshal, Suttner became a worldwide celebrity

in 1889 with the publication of her best-selling novel *Lay Down Your Arms!* Suttner dedicated the remainder of her life to encouraging pacifism and working to prevent war. One of her greatest achievements was to persuade the Swedish industrialist and inventor of dynamite, **Alfred Nobel,** to fund an annual prize for those promoting the cause of peace. The Nobel Peace Prize, along with prizes for chemistry, medicine, and literature, was first awarded in 1901. Appropriately, Suttner herself was awarded the Nobel Peace Prize in 1905. The pacifist movement could point to several successes during this period, including the establishment of international treaties on the conduct of war known collectively as the Geneva Conventions that resulted from meetings called by Tsar Nicholas II in 1899, and the Hague conferences and tribunals (1899–1907), which used arbitration as one method of settling diplomatic disputes.

anarchists   Political radicals of late nineteenth century who distrusted central government authority and advocated violent means to overthrow the existing political order.

terrorism   Use of violence to intimidate individuals, ruling groups, or entire nations to achieve an individual's or group's political-ideological goals.

Mikhail Bakunin   (1814–1876) Russian anarchist and revolutionary who espoused a political ideology opposed to all forms of state authority.

pacifists   Individuals who oppose war and violence on principle and seek peaceful solutions to state conflicts.

Baroness Bertha von Suttner   (1843–1914) Austrian writer and pacifist organizer whose novel *Lay Down Your Arms!* (1889) gained her an international reputation.

Alfred Nobel   (1833–1896) Swedish industrialist who funded the Nobel prizes, which he hoped would encourage world peace and the development of culture.

Summary

Review Questions

↑ Why were the revolutions of 1848 so important for political and national histories in Europe?

↑ How was nationalism transformed as an ideology from the early to late nineteenth century?

↑ How did European national and religious identities change during this period?

European history in the nineteenth century is traditionally divided at 1848. In that year, people across

the continent revolted against the existing political order. While the 1848 revolutions failed, the ideas behind the revolutions—nationalism, constitutionalism, liberalism, and the nation-state—would soon be translated into reality. Rulers granted their subjects constitutions in most of central Europe in 1848, and by the end of the century, absolute rule had given way to parliamentary politics almost everywhere. Liberalism in its political and economic form achieved great influence and political power in the second half of the nineteenth century, even while challenged by a newly invigorated nationalist conservatism on the right and socialism on the left.

The idea of the nation-state triumphed in central

Europe with the unification of Italy in the 1860s and of Germany in 1871. Nationalism became an almost universal political program throughout the continent, as stateless peoples from Ireland to Estonia demanded cultural and political rights for their nations. The success of nationalism also caused it to be adopted by conservative forces. Increasingly, nationalists expected struggle and domination, not harmonious cooperation, among different nations.

Both the newly unified Italian and German states, and older ones like Russia, Britain, and France, used various means to strengthen their influence on their people. This process of nation building included the establishment of free public education, the extension of suffrage, and the imposition of military service. The state also intervened increasingly in the economy, whether to encourage industrial development through tariffs or through programs of health and old-age insurance. Increased government responsibilities meant larger government budgets and higher taxes. States promoted nationalist loyalties to convince their citizens that such increased burdens were necessary.

In eastern Europe's great multinational empires, however, nationalism posed a direct threat to stability. Despite their efforts to reduce cultural differences among their subjects through policies such as russification, these multinational empires could not subdue the nationalist movements that aimed to split up the empires. The political and national identities of these empires' ruling classes increasingly diverged from those of the empires' subject masses.

Socialists, pacifists, and even the Catholic Church also criticized nationalism as an aggressive and divisive movement. Still, the idea that every culture deserves respect and perhaps even political rights was gaining ground. At the same time, more and more Europeans came to see their own nation as superior to others and proclaimed the right of "superior nations" to dominate the "inferior." Such conceptions, transferred from the national to the racial sphere, also influenced the course of European imperialism.

← Thinking Back, Thinking Ahead →

How do you imagine that early liberal nationalists such as the Grimm brothers viewed the actual shape nationalism took during and after the unification of Germany?

ECHO

National Anthems and National Identity

We take national anthems for granted, but they are largely nineteenth-century inventions. France led the way during the Revolution, when "La Marseillaise" was sung during the march on Paris in 1792 and decreed the national anthem in 1795. Its stirring phrases about defending the homeland against the forces of tyranny, whose "impure blood" should "water our fields," led Emperor Napoleon to ban it during his time. Authorized after the July Revolution of 1830, it was again banned by Napoleon III and not reinstated until 1879. The German national anthem, a poem written in 1841 and sung to the music of Joseph Haydn, originally began with the words "Deutschland, Deutschland, über alles / Über alles in der Welt" ("Germany, Germany above all / Above everything in the world"). By this the poet expressed a longing for German unity and a German identity above all local identities. But during the Nazi era, the words were taken to express an aim of German world domination, and at the end of World War II, the Allies banned this verse, which also cited German boundaries along rivers that were now solidly in France, Germany, Italy, and the Soviet Union. Today only the poem's third verse is sung on occasions when a national anthem is called for.

Thus, national anthems reflect not only national identity but national history. The Polish national anthem, written after Poland was partitioned, portrays a spirit undaunted: "Poland is not lost, as long as we are alive." Sweden's anthem praises the old, free, and mountainous north—even though many of the mountains were lost to Norway in 1905. Israel's "Ha-Tikva" ("The Hope"), written in 1878, expresses the two-thousand-year-old hope for a return to Zion and Jerusalem. Czechoslovakia had two quite distinct national anthems, both sung to the same melody. The Czech anthem stated, "Czech land is my fatherland!" while the Slovak version declared, "Slovaks are awakening." After the Russian revolution, the new Soviet Union took "The Internationale" of the world socialist movement as its anthem. Only later was a Soviet anthem written, praising the Union of Soviet Socialist Republics as a bulwark of peace and harmony led by the party of V. I. Lenin and Joseph Stalin. After Stalin's death, the text underwent some revision.

Americans are generally more emotional about their national anthem than are Europeans. Typically Europeans stand silently when their anthems are played, while Americans stand with their hands over their hearts, sometime even joining along in song.

Suggested Readings

Brubaker, Rogers. *Citizenship and Nationhood in France and Germany.* Cambridge, Mass.: Harvard University Press, 1992. A well-documented presentation of two opposing concepts of nationhood.

Hobsbawm, Eric J. *Nations and Nationalism Since 1780: Programme, Myth, Reality.* Cambridge, England: Cambridge University Press, 1992. A well-argued synthesis that combines theory and history.

Lindemann, Albert S. *Esau's Tears: Modern Anti-Semitism and the Rise of the Jews.* Cambridge, England: Cambridge University Press, 2000. An argument for the close connection between social change and the rise of antisemitism.

Mack Smith, Denis. *Cavour and Garibaldi, 1860: A Study in Political Conflict.* New York: Cambridge University Press, 1985. An account that captures the two main personalities of Italian unification.

Sperber, Jonathan. *The European Revolutions, 1848–1851.* 2nd ed. New York: Cambridge University Press, 2005. A well-written synthesis.

Taylor, A. J. P. *Bismarck, the Man and the Statesman.* London: New English Library, 1974. A readable and balanced account.

Weeks, Theodore R. *Nation and State in Late Imperial Russia.* DeKalb: Northern Illinois University Press, 1996. A look at russification in the western part of the empire.

Websites

On the history of anarchism, with a definite political agenda, **Anarchist History,** at http://struggle.ws/history.html

An encyclopedia of people, places, and events of the 1848 revolutions, **Encyclopedia of Revolutions of 1848,** at www.ohiou.edu/~Chastain/contents.htm

Excellent material on the unification of Italy, part of a rich site on the Victorian Age, **The Risorgimento or Unification of Italy (1815–1871),** at http://www.victorianweb.org/history/risorgimento/1.html

CHAPTER 23

The Culture of Industrial Europe, 1850–1914

1500 B.C.E.	1000 B.C.E.	500 B.C.E.	1 B.C.E./1 C.E.

| | 1851 Crystal Palace Exhibition opens in London | | 1867 Nobel patents dynamite | 1869 Suez Canal opens in Egypt | 1872 Nietzsche publishes *The Birth of Tragedy* | | 1879 Edison invents the electric lightbulb |
| | Half of English population lives in cities | | | | | | |

1850	1855	1860	1865	1870	1875	1880

Industrialization and Railroads, 1870–1914

Industrialization and railroads went hand in hand. By 1870, nearly all major European cities were connected by rail and even provincial towns usually had a rail connection. Where was industrialization concentrated at the end of the century, and how did that differ from the situation at mid-century (p. 595)?

— Railroads, 1870
— Railroads, 1914
▨ Industrialized area, 1914
━━ Boundaries, 1914

NORWAY SWEDEN
Oslo
Helsinki St. Petersburg
Stockholm
Riga
Moscow
North Sea
Glasgow Edinburgh
Belfast Newcastle DENMARK
Dublin Copenhagen *Baltic Sea*
GREAT BRITAIN
Manchester Hamburg Danzig
Birmingham
London NETHERLANDS GERMANY
Amsterdam Berlin Warsaw Lodz
Antwerp RUSSIA
BELGIUM Brussels Kiev
ATLANTIC OCEAN Liège Cologne
Luxembourg LUX. Frankfurt Prague Cracow
Paris Stuttgart
Munich AUSTRIA-HUNGARY
Zurich Vienna
SWITZERLAND Budapest
FRANCE
Lyons
Oviedo Turin Milan
Bilbao Genoa Venice ROMANIA
PORTUGAL SPAIN Marseilles Florence Belgrade Bucharest *Black Sea*
Madrid *Corsica* Elba SERBIA BULGARIA
Lisbon Rome ITALY MONTENEGRO
Adriatic Sea Istanbul
Baleric Is. *Sardinia* Naples ALBANIA OTTOMAN EMPIRE
GREECE
Tangier GIBRALTAR (Gr. Br.)
Algiers *Sicily* Athens
ALGERIA (France) Tunis *Malta* *Crete* Cyprus
MOROCCO (France) *Mediterranean Sea*
TUNISIA (France)
Suez Canal 1869
LIBYA (Italy) EGYPT (Gr. Br.) *Red Sea*

0 200 400 Km.
0 200 400 Mi.

| 500 C.E. | 1000 C.E. | 1500 C.E. | 2000 C.E. |

1885
First skyscraper is completed

1900
Planck formulates quantum theory

1907
Bakelite, first plastic, is invented

1908
Ford Motor Company produces first Model T

| 1885 | 1890 | 1895 | 1900 | 1905 | 1910 | 1915 |

Marie Curie

Maria Curie-Skłodowska, known as Madame Curie, was the first woman to receive the Nobel Prize in Physics and the first person to receive the Nobel Prize twice (the second time in chemistry). Her important discoveries in the field of radioactivity are remembered in the name of two elements, polonium (after Poland, her native land) and curium (for Curie) One of the largest universities in Poland, in the eastern city of Lublin, also bears her name. (Bettmann/Corbis)

Marie Curie-Skłodowska Chooses to Study Physics

Maria Skłodowska, better known to the world as Madame Curie, chose to dedicate her life to science. Born at a time when women scientists were rare and almost unthinkable, she left her native land, obtained a university education, and made her mark in scientific research. Her life reflects a period when dynamic women could defy social norms and succeed. Her career parallels the enormous growth in the importance of scientific discovery for the economy and everyday life.

Maria was born into an educated middle-class family in Warsaw in late 1867. Her father taught physics and mathematics at a Warsaw gymnasium. Her mother was also educated and served as the director of a local school for girls. But, as Poles, her parents could not teach in government schools, and the salaries they received in private schools were meager. Education in Poland was, at the time, under severe restraints. Following the Polish insurrection of 1863, Russian authorities curtailed the use of the Polish language in schools. Almost all teachers had to be native Russians, and they treated Poles with contempt and hostility. It was in this atmosphere that Maria Skłodowska received her primary and secondary education. Then, when Maria was only nine, her mother died, leaving behind four children.

Finishing high school at age fifteen, at the top of her class, Maria was forced by family circumstances to seek employment as a governess. Many years later, she remembered these years with pleasure, recalling that she had set up secret circles to teach children literacy in Polish, an activity strictly forbidden by the Russian authorities. She also studied at the underground "flying university" that Polish intellectuals had set up for young Poles. But even so, educational opportunities in Russian Poland were limited, so Maria vowed to continue her education abroad as soon as possible. Gathering her meager savings, she left for Paris in 1891 and two years later met Pierre Curie. The two married in July 1895.

Pierre Curie had just completed his doctorate in physics and was teaching at a Paris secondary school. The Curies' economic situation was far from enviable, but their work carried them through. Soon they had two daughters, but Marie (as she was now known) refused to give up her scientific work. With the help of a servant, she balanced her roles as mother and scientist. Pierre's teaching position and Marie's occasional tutoring brought in modest sums, and they were forced to carry out their research in their spare time and in a small laboratory that was little more than a shack outfitted with homemade equipment. Marie was interested in the study of x-rays—peculiar rays emitted by uranium salts—and, as she put it, "decided to undertake an investigation."

For several years the Curies studied the nature of what we now call radioactivity. In 1903 they were awarded the Nobel Prize in Physics along with the French physicist Antoine Becquerel. When Pierre was killed in an automobile accident in 1906, Marie continued their work on her own. She discovered two new elements, polonium and radium, for which she was awarded the Nobel Prize in Chemistry in

1911. At this time she was named to the faculty of the prestigious Sorbonne in Paris, the first woman to be so honored. Under her leadership, research in chemistry and physics blossomed there. Her daughter Irène Joliot-Curie also became a distinguished scientist. Marie Curie died in 1934, one year before Irène and her husband Frédéric were awarded the Nobel Prize in Chemistry.

Marie Curie's discoveries advanced scientific knowledge of radioactivity that would be later expanded on to produce both nuclear power and atomic arms. But her choice to dedicate her life to science had other important consequences. Her dedication to science challenged conventional views of national minorities and the capabilities of women. After Marie Curie, young women could more easily envision their own place as scientists, professors, and even Nobel Prize winners.

Introduction

Marie Curie's life and work reflect the vast and rapid changes throughout Europe in the three generations after 1850. Scientific advances challenged old modes of understanding and even social norms. Science quickened the pace of industrialization, which by the end of the century had spread across the continent, from northern Spain to Sweden to Russia. Industrialization generated profound shifts in social, political, and cultural ideas. New technological advances from the telegraph to the bicycle radically changed the rhythm of everyday life. No less radical were new intellectual movements that rejected religion and attempted to apply the scientific method to all realms of human experience, from social relations to the body and sex. Artists and musicians challenged accepted modes of expression, creating works of art that shocked and enraged conservative critics. Women—like Marie Curie—sought a more visible place in society, even demanding political rights. The clash between traditional social and cultural expectations and new ways of experiencing the world led some to fear that the old and the new could never be reconciled.

New technology and the spread of industrial production had a broad impact on the population, helping to create what we know as mass society. Significant numbers of workers and peasants came to enjoy a certain level of political freedom, comfort, and leisure time. Despite economic differences and class prejudices, increasing numbers of people came to expect that their children would be better educated, healthier, and better off materially than they had been. The idea of progress gained broad support. Yet not everyone enjoyed social advancement, political participation, and cultural development, especially those in central and eastern Europe. And not everyone welcomed the leveling effect on culture that the growth of mass society brought with it. Some denounced it as soulless, shallow, and mediocre.

Art and science also changed radically. Realism in art, which aimed to reproduce images found in nature, gave way to abstraction, which aimed to express the artist's individual perceptions of the world. Scientific research in new fields, such as the Curies' work on radioactivity, compelled scientists to completely reexamine previous understandings of the physical world. The theories of Charles Darwin and Sigmund Freud sparked great controversies.

This was a period of contrasts and contradictions. Economic and industrial developments utterly transformed some regions while others—in particular, the Balkan and Iberian Peninsulas, southern Italy, and much of the Russian Empire—changed relatively little. The growth of mass culture clashed with individualistic ideologies. Atheistic materialism gained many adherents, but the majority of Europeans retained their religious faith. Changes in economies, in technology, and in science, society, and everyday life were rapid and overwhelming, and yet, looking back after 1918, many who lived through these decades wistfully recalled the stability of the era. For most Europeans, this was a time of prosperity, peace, and cultural richness.

The Second Industrial Revolution

⬇ What technological advances were made during the Second Industrial Revolution?
⬇ How did technological advances alter work and leisure?

In the second half of the nineteenth century, in particular after 1870, industrial and technological changes so profoundly altered European life that the era is called

Chronology

1851	Crystal Palace Exhibition takes place in London
1859	Charles Darwin publishes *On the Origin of Species*
1862	Ivan Turgenev publishes *Fathers and Sons*
1863	Edouard Manet paints *The Luncheon on the Grass* and *Olympia*
1867	Alfred Nobel patents dynamite
1867	Karl Marx publishes volume 1 of *Capital*
1869	Suez Canal opens in Egypt
1872	Friedrich Nietzsche publishes *The Birth of Tragedy*
1876	Alexander Graham Bell invents the telephone
1879	Thomas Edison invents the electric light bulb
1885	First skyscraper, the Home Insurance Building in Chicago, is completed
1888	Kodak box camera is perfected by George Eastman
1891	Work begins on Trans-Siberian Railroad
1892	Rudolf Diesel patents internal-combustion engine
1899	Sigmund Freud publishes *The Interpretation of Dreams*
1900	Max Planck formulates quantum theory
1903	Wright brothers successfully fly the first airplane
1904	Max Weber begins publication of *The Protestant Ethic and the Birth of Capitalism*
1905	Albert Einstein publishes paper on special theory of relativity
1907	Bakelite, the first plastic, is invented
1908	Ford Motor Company produces first Model T

the Second Industrial Revolution. These innovations included the widespread use of steel and electricity in industry, major breakthroughs in chemistry, the increasing use of petroleum to supplement coal and other power sources, and a variety of new inventions that revolutionized transportation and communications. All these new industries created new categories of jobs and required corporate organization on a scale previously unknown. Industrial advances increased pay and decreased working hours, allowing Europeans to consume more material goods and enjoy more leisure than ever before. The prosperity of the period gave new possibilities to artists and writers, whose works were viewed and purchased by large numbers of people. Science played a dual role in these changes, both enabling new, more efficient industrial techniques and calling into question long-held views about humanity's place in the world. For some, the discoveries and claims of science threatened traditional religious beliefs. This was an optimistic era, believing in progress and eagerly anticipating new advances. At the same time, some worried darkly that cold scientific rationality and mediocre mass society could destroy the very foundations of moral life and society.

New Materials, New Industries, New Technologies

The stages of early industrialization in Britain and on the continent had been driven by the mass production of textiles in factories using first water power and then coal-driven steam engines. The railroad was a second driving factor in the economic upsurge that spread to the continent following the Napoleonic Wars. In the second half of the nineteenth century, however, while textiles and iron continued to be vital to the industrial economy, new products and processes—steel, chemicals, petroleum—revolutionized industrial production.

The most important of these was mass-produced steel. Steel combines the advantages of pig iron (being hard and durable) and wrought iron (being flexible and resistant to cracking). The advantages of steel had long been known, but before the mid-nineteenth century, there had been no economical method of mass-producing steel. Then, in the 1850s and 1860s, the **Siemens-Martin (open-hearth) process** revolu-

Siemens-Martin (open-hearth) process Technological advance that allowed mass production of steel.

When the Flatiron Building in New York City was completed in 1902, it was the tallest building in the world. The use of steel girders allowed the construction of such "skyscrapers" that became emblematic for Europeans' vision of America. (*Alan Schein/zefa/Corbis*)

tionized steel production. In 1861, before these innovations had begun to spread throughout Europe, the total steel output in Britain, France, Germany, and Belgium was around 125,000 tons. By 1871, production had more than tripled and in 1913 topped 30 million tons—over eighty times the figure of 1871. This massive output went into rails, railroad engines and cars, steamships, and increasingly sophisticated weaponry. Steel also allowed new forms in architecture: its strength and flexibility meant that buildings could expand upward to an unprecedented degree. The skyscraper—an American invention—was the result. The ten-story Home Insurance Building in Chicago was erected in 1885, but expansion skyward was limited by the need to climb stairs. In 1887, this problem was solved with the invention of the high-speed ele-

vator, and by the early twentieth century New York City had a number of skyscrapers, including the beautiful Flatiron Building with twenty-one stories, completed 1902.

Rapid advances in textile production during the first half of the nineteenth century created a need for dyes, which scientists in Britain, France, and Germany figured out how to synthesize from coal tar. The first artificial dye of purple hue was given the French name *mauve*. Soon red ("magenta"), brown, and other colors were synthesized. These cheap new dyes meant that now inexpensive brightly colored clothing could be mass-produced. By the late nineteenth century the German chemical industry had far outstripped all competitors, producing some 90 percent of the world output of synthetic dyes as well as new medicines (most famous of all was aspirin), artificial materials such as Bakelite (an early plastic, 1907), and cellophane (1912). Artificial fertilizers began to be produced in the 1840s, and chemists found new uses for poisons—such as the insecticide DDT, discovered in 1874, though not used until much later. The poisonous gas ammonia that formed an important part of many fertilizers was also used in the development of explosives. In 1867, Swedish businessman Alfred Nobel took out a patent for dynamite, which allowed highly explosive liquid nitroglycerine to be used more safely by combining it with a fine powder and packaging the mixture in tubes. The German firms founded in this era—such as BASF, Bayer, and Hoechst—continue today to be among the largest multinational chemical firms in the world.

Another innovation in chemistry was the process that produced cheap paper from wood pulp, which fostered the growth of mass-circulation newspapers and journals. The use of this cheap paper and mechanized printing, using steam-powered presses, made possible cheap newspapers such as *La Presse* in Paris (founded 1836) and the *Daily Telegraph* in London (founded 1855). The telegraph allowed fast-breaking stories from around the world to be reported almost instantly, and newspapers often printed special editions to cover major events. The invention of the linotype machine in 1886, which mechanized typesetting, allowed newspapers to get stories into print faster. Advances in printing allowed more illustrations in newspapers and magazines. And the use of **lithography** from the 1830s onward allowed artists to create

lithography Printing method used widely from the 1830s that produced text and color images used in posters and illustrated magazines.

Early automobiles, like this 1899 Renault, were expensive and unreliable. Ford's Model-T would use mass-production techniques to produce a cheaper vehicle. Until well into the twentieth century, automobiles were a luxury item that few Europeans could hope to afford. *(National Motor Museum/ HIP/The Image Works)*

drawings, etchings, and other artworks in multiple copies, making artwork more affordable for a mass audience.

The original Industrial Revolution was fueled mainly by coal, but coal was difficult to mine and expensive to transport, especially to countries that lacked natural deposits, so industrialists sought new forms of energy. Coal gas came to be used for streetlights in all major cities early in the nineteenth century. Later it was replaced by natural gas, often discovered when drilling for oil, and petroleum products, from kerosene to gasoline, became increasingly sought after. Kerosene was widely used in lamps, where it produced greater light with less danger of fire than candles. Petroleum was also adopted for use aboard steamships, where the liquid fuel eliminated the need for stokers, and the reduction in labor costs helped offset the higher cost of the fuel itself. Two other distillations of petroleum, gasoline and diesel fuel, were used to propel the first automobiles; the diesel engine was patented in 1892, and the Ford Motor Company's Model T—the first mass-produced automobile—rolled off the assembly line in 1908. By 1900, the petroleum industry was growing enormously, especially in Russia and the United States, making **John D. Rockefeller** one of the world's richest men.

Electricity is not so much a source of energy as a novel means of transmitting power over distance. Knowledge of electricity was not new, but the innovation of the later nineteenth century was to harness electricity for practical use and to perfect methods of generating and supplying it over large distances. The harnessing of electricity meant that industrial plants could be located away from coal fields or other sources of energy, such as water power. Unlike bulky steam engines, small electric motors could be transported from one location to another.

Within the factory, the use of electricity eliminated many of the dangerous belts and pulleys that had connected the steam engine to machinery. As cables and insulation to carry electricity became more efficient, hydroelectric power could be generated and used over a broad area. The spread of electric light, using **Thomas Edison**'s invention of the light bulb (1879), proceeded in tandem with the establishment

John D. Rockefeller   (1839–1937) Founder of the Standard Oil Company, which dominated the American petroleum market.

Thomas Edison   (1847–1931) American inventor of the microphone, record player, and the first commercially practical light bulb.

of public power stations. The first of these was set up in England by the **Siemens brothers** in 1881, and by 1914, electricity for offices, industry, and households was available in all major cities of Europe, though only the richest and most up-to-date families had electricity in the home.

Werner von Siemens created a family dynasty through his inventions and business know-how in the growing field of electrical devices. Trained as an engineer, Siemens quickly saw the commercial possibilities in the electrical telegraph, and in 1847, with his partner Johann Halske, he founded Siemens and Halske Telegraph Construction Company in Berlin. At first the firm mainly built telegraphs for the Prussian army and railroads (Werner was also a Prussian military officer), but by the 1860s, the Siemens family expanded into long-distance telegraphs and other businesses based on Werner's patents, such as the Siemens-Martin open-hearth steel manufacturing process (1869), electric trams in Berlin (1881), and electrical power stations. Founders of a company that is still one of the largest in Berlin, the Siemens family showed how scientific research could lead to technological advances that could, in turn, be translated into business success.

Communications and Transportation Networks

Perhaps no invention symbolized the compression of time and space during this period better than the telegraph, invented in the United States in the late 1830s. By the late 1860s, telegraph lines ran from one end of Europe to the other and were even connected by transatlantic cable to the United States. By the end of the century, all continents were connected by underwater cable, meaning that a message could go from London to Johannesburg to Calcutta to Sydney to Vancouver in a matter of minutes. Telegrams were sent using **Morse code,** a system of dots and dashes representing letters invented for this purpose, and flew through wires as electrical impulses. The telegraph required skilled operators who could translate the dots and dashes into words, offices where individuals could send messages, and messenger boys (in this period, nearly always male) to bring telegrams—often with bad news—to offices and residences. The impact on government, industry, and private life was enormous. At the beginning of the nineteenth century, news could travel no faster than horses or pigeons. By 1900, news traveled at the speed of light from one corner of the globe to the other. On a practical level, the telegraph enabled, for example, the tsar

in St. Petersburg to check up on governors in distant Kamchatka or Tashkent, businessmen to keep in touch with offices abroad, and ordinary people to contact loved ones, though usually only in emergencies because of the high cost.

In 1876, the American Alexander Graham Bell perfected a device that carried not just electrical impulses but actual sounds over a wire: the telephone. Unlike the telegraph, the telephone provided a direct link from person to person, though few working-class people could afford the new invention at first and some aristocrats, such as Emperor Francis Joseph of Austria-Hungary, refused to speak on the telephone at all. Still, many in business and government quickly recognized the advantages of the telephone, and by 1900 telephone exchanges had been set up throughout Europe and North America, from London to Moscow, Berlin to Los Angeles. In Germany, the Siemens and Halske Company enjoyed a near monopoly in building telephone networks. In 1912, among the ten cities with the most telephones per capita, five were in the United States, three in Scandinavia, and two in Germany. The invention was also used to transmit other forms of sound, such as musical performances and news. By the 1890s, the *théâtrophone* in Paris allowed subscribers to hear the latest operas and concerts, while in Budapest thousands subscribed to a service providing news, musical performances, plays, stock market reports, and lectures by telephone.

Soon another invention of the 1890s, the wireless or radio, made telephonic concert and news services obsolete. Perfected for practical purposes by the Italian **Guglielmo Marconi,** wireless telegraphy, as it was then called, seemed useful primarily for communication between ships at sea. In 1899, the first distress signal from a ship at sea was sent. When the state-of-the-art ocean liner the *Titanic* went down on its first voyage on the night of April 14, 1912, it sent out distress signals; unfortunately the telegraph operator on the nearest ship was not on duty. A ship

Siemens brothers German brothers (Werner, Wilhelm, and Carl Heinrich) who, starting in 1847, established branches of their electrical firm in England, Germany, and Russia.

Morse code System combining dots and dashes representing letters, invented by the American Samuel Morse for sending messages over the electrical telegraph.

Guglielmo Marconi (1874–1937) Italian physicist best known for perfection of radio ("wireless telegraphy"); awarded the Nobel Prize in Physics in 1909.

three times as far away did receive the signals, but when it arrived some two hours later, most of the *Titanic* passengers were already dead in the frigid waters of the North Atlantic. Wireless and telegraph communications meant that by the following morning, people all over the world could read in their local newspapers that the ship had struck an iceberg and had sunk rapidly with the loss of more than 1,500 lives. But few heard of the tragedy by radio, which did not become a common household appliance until the 1920s or later.

The world was connected not only by telegraph wires and cables but also increasingly by steamship service and railroads during these decades. For the British, the steamship was vital in linking the homeland with India, though in the 1850s the one-way trip took around a month. The opening of the **Suez Canal** in 1869 cut travel between the Mediterranean Sea and the Indian Ocean in half and speeded up mail service between Britain and its colony India. Steamship travel between Europe and the Americas became increasingly rapid, cheap, and—in the first- and second-class cabins—comfortable. By the 1890s, a steamship ticket from Italy to Argentina had become so inexpensive that many Italians traveled to Argentina to work as agricultural workers there during spring and summer, then returned to do the same in Italy, taking advantage of the reversed seasons in the Northern and Southern Hemispheres. Travel from northern Europe to New York took less than two weeks, and millions of immigrants made that journey in search of economic and political freedom. The **Panama Canal,** opened in 1914, connected the Atlantic and Pacific Oceans. Cutting through mountainous terrain, it was a marvel of engineering.

By the 1870s, railroads linked all the European capitals (Istanbul, or Constantinople, the name used by nineteenth-century Europeans for the city, followed in 1883). European capital and engineers also extended railroads through South America, India, Africa, and Russia. The **Trans-Siberian Railroad,** begun in 1891, helped Russia transport hundreds of thousands of soldiers to Manchuria to fight the Japanese in the Russo-Japanese War a little more than a decade later. Military planners recognized the key role that efficient railroad transportation could play in warfare. The fact that Germany had the most developed railroad network in Europe was perceived as a direct threat by the French and Russian general staffs.

The increased traffic on rail and road required new bridges. In 1849, Buda and Pest were finally linked by a permanent bridge over the Danube, a first step to the unification of the two cities. The Royal Albert Bridge, designed by engineer and railroad innovator

Isambard Kingdom Brunel, opened in 1859, stretching 455 feet over the river Tamar in southern England. Most famous of all was the Brooklyn Bridge, completed in 1883 after a decade of construction. Spanning almost 1,600 feet, it connected Manhattan with what was then a still mainly rural Brooklyn. Building bridges involved new materials like dynamite and steel; similar techniques and materials were used by Gustave Eiffel in the tower named for him in Paris, completed in 1889.

New forms of transportation also took to the air. Germany became a leader in the production of dirigibles or blimps, flying an airship called a zeppelin (named for the German Count Zeppelin) for the first time in 1900. An even more startling development was the Wright brothers' successful flight in 1903, opening the skies to heavier-than-air flying machines. While few people actually traveled by air, thousands watched in awe at dirigibles and primitive airplanes whose impact on warfare, the economy, and culture in the new century would be profound.

New Places and Patterns of Work

As Europe industrialized, it also urbanized as hundreds of thousands of people left farms and villages for better wages and a more exciting life in the cities. In 1800 there was only one city—London—with a population of over 1 million; only twenty-three cities had more than 100,000 inhabitants. By 1900, London's population had grown to over 4 million and five more European cities had over 1 million inhabitants (Paris, Berlin, Moscow, St. Petersburg, and Vienna); 135 cities had populations over 100,000. Manchester had by then topped 600,000.

The population of Berlin increased from around 500,000 at midcentury to over 2 million sixty years later. The Polish textile town of Łód (not by chance known as the Polish Manchester) exploded in size, from a mere 519 inhabitants in 1809 to more than 300,000 at the end of the century. Throughout Europe,

Suez Canal An artificial waterway connecting the Red Sea and the Mediterranean, built by the British and French and opened in 1869.

Panama Canal An artificial waterway connecting the Atlantic and Pacific Oceans, built from 1904 to 1914 by American military engineers.

Trans-Siberian Railroad Russia's ambitious railway project connecting Moscow with the Pacific Ocean, begun in 1891 and completed in 1916, which caused friction with Japan.

MAP 23.1 **European Cities with Populations over 100,000, 1800 and 1900** The rapid growth of population combined with migration from rural to urban areas in Europe is reflected in the significant increase in large cities during the course of the nineteenth century, as shown in this map.

cities such as Budapest, Rome, Madrid, and Hamburg grew impressively.

Most of the newcomers to cities lived in wretched and expensive lodgings and tenements. In some cases, overcrowding was so severe that beds were rented out in two or more "sleeping shifts" on a twenty-four-hour basis. Hygiene and health suffered greatly in such places, and tuberculosis was rampant, claiming thousands of lives yearly, including that of Marie Curie's mother. But running water and central heat were increasingly available, even for the less well-off, and electric tramways and—in Paris and London—subways made it possible for workers to live in less crowded, leafy suburbs and commute to work. London's "underground" was the first to open, in the 1860s, and the Paris "metro" dates from the first decade of the twentieth century. By that time, even smaller cities such as Warsaw and Stockholm had streetcars and trams connecting the suburbs and downtown. Public transportation allowed workers to live farther from the factories, and cities became increasingly differentiated by social class. In Berlin's West End, the bourgeoisie built villas, while workers lived across town in tenements.

Many of the people riding the streetcars to work were employed in new **white-collar** positions. As prosperity increased, so did the places to spend or save that money. Department stores, such as the **Bon Marché** in Paris and KdW (Kaufhaus des Westens) in

Berlin, also opened in Budapest, Milan, and elsewhere. But saving money was also a middle-class concern; the number of banks increased and, with them, the number of clerks. Similarly, the number of lawyers, physicians, and dentists went up markedly, and these professionals employed even larger numbers as receptionists and assistants. Government bureaucracies also burgeoned as the state's role in the economy and everyday life grew. While most of these new positions were filled by young men, women were also able to find employment in banks, department stores, and professional offices. They were, however, expected to quit work upon marrying.

In western and central Europe, by the late nineteenth century the average workday had shrunk, partly because of technological innovations and partly under pressure from organized labor. As fewer workers, both in offices and in factories, lived adjacent to their places of work and workdays shrank to ten and even eight hours, the routine of transport/work/transport became common. Through all layers of society in the

white-collar Employment that does not involve physical labor, such as that of professionals (lawyers, doctors, teachers) and office workers.

Bon Marché First department store, opened in Paris in 1852 and catered primarily to middle-class people.

industrialized countries, one fact was constant: the entire day was no longer taken up by work, freeing up precious hours for **leisure.**

The New Concept of Leisure

As the predominant form of work became employment with a fixed number of hours per day, contracted to an employer, employees also found they had "free time," time after work that was open to other pursuits. The concept of leisure was new, and it was much enjoyed in the second half of the nineteenth century, especially as the workday shrank to about ten hours and the idea of a work-free weekend took hold. Most Europeans had both more time and more money for leisure activities than had their grandparents' generation. Electric lighting meant that dance halls and nightclubs could stay open well into and even through the night. Alcohol consumption increased considerably, worrying religious authorities and middle-class moralists who had chosen for themselves more "high-brow" entertainment such as concerts, operas, and plays.

Nearly everyone in large cities frequented cafés and dance halls. There one could eat and drink, listen to music, experience light comic and dramatic performances, and, of course, dance. Some cafés catered to a select middle-class audience, but for commercial reasons, most desired the largest possible number of patrons and served anyone who enjoyed drinking, dancing, listening to music, and watching clown shows and comedy acts. By the 1890s, the Spanish flamenco and Argentine tango competed with more traditional popular music and dance for public attention. **Magic lantern** slide shows were increasingly popular, allowing mass audiences to experience—at least visually—travels to exotic destinations around the world. Around 1900, the moving picture became technically and commercially viable, and cinema houses sprang up in all major European cities. In the United States, by far the leader in this new technology, millions went to the "picture show" every week. The early picture shows were often long on sensation and short on memorable artistic value, but the new medium of film opened up vast possibilities for artists in the new century.

The new technology of photography, perfected in the late nineteenth century, allowed amateurs to make pictures with their own cameras. The word *Kodak,* specially created by American businessman George Eastman in 1888 to market his small cameras, passed into several languages. Photographic technology, which produced an image as exact as the best sketch or painting, had an important impact on artists, who no longer needed to copy the world but could instead portray their own impressions of light, color, and shadow. Photography also facilitated the spread of another popular diversion: pornography.

Railroads made travel for pleasure possible for the masses. When the Great Exhibition of the Works of Industry of All Nations, better known as the **Crystal Palace Exhibition,** was opened in London in 1851, about one-fifth of the people of England visited, in part on package tours from the travel entrepreneur Thomas Cook. Many of the visitors had never been far from their hometown or village. After the St. Petersburg–Warsaw railroad opened in 1862, travelers could embark from Moscow in a sleeping car and emerge in Paris a few days later. From 1883 onward, they could take the Orient Express from Paris through six countries, ending up in the exotic Ottoman capital, Istanbul. Russian aristocrats could now spend their summers on the French Riviera. Wealthy Europeans traveled by railroad to spas such as Baden-Baden and Karlsbad (Karlovy Vary in the Czech Republic), where they "took the waters," relaxed, played cards, flirted, and engaged in other diversions. Christian pilgrims numbering in the hundreds of thousands annually took the train to Lourdes, where the peasant girl Bernadette Soubirous claimed to have seen a vision of Virgin Mary in 1858. And even workers of modest means could take suburban railroads for day trips to the countryside. The rich could travel in comfort, riding in first class or even hitching their own private railcars onto trains. They stayed in new and magnificent luxury hotels such as the Hotel Adlon in Berlin, where the Kaiser put up his own guests.

Workers also enjoyed sports, both as active participants and as spectators. First in Britain, then throughout Europe, football in the forms of soccer and rugby brought together enthusiasts in increasing numbers. By the early twentieth century, it is estimated, some half million British men regularly played. Golf, spreading outside Scotland, became the sport of choice for the well-to-do. After the chain-driven bicycle was perfected in the early 1890s, cycling swept western Europe. Social conservatives were outraged by the mobility and personal freedom that bicycles gave

leisure   Time for relaxation or recreation, new in the later nineteenth century owing to industrial and social advances.

magic lantern   Early form of the modern slide projector that projected images painted on glass plates onto a screen.

Crystal Palace Exhibition   Great Exhibition of the Works of Industry of All Nations, opened in London's Crystal Palace in 1851.

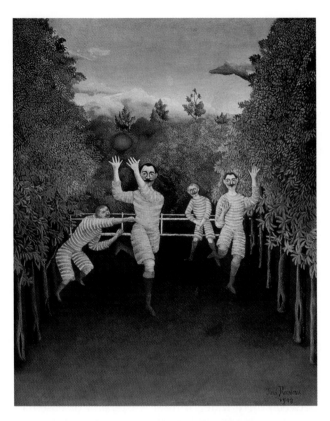

Henri Rousseau's 1908 painting, *The Football Players,* reflects a growing interest in sports and other leisure-time activities among middle- and even working-class Europeans. Not only the football itself was mass-produced but also the outfits worn by the players. One or two generations earlier, before the second industrial revolution, games would have been much less standardized. *(Solomon R. Guggenheim Museum, New York/The Bridgeman Art Library)*

women, as well as by the new fashions that allowed them to ride astride these new iron horses. Tennis in its modern form was invented in the 1870s and rapidly gained popularity, not least of all because it was the rare sport—golf was another—that middle-class men and women could play together.

Like industrialization itself, most modern forms of leisure, tourism, and sport began in England and spread to the rest of Europe in the second half of the nineteenth century. English words themselves invaded other languages, so that Russians and Germans speak of "sport," Swedes enjoy "fotboll," Italians engage in "turismo," and Poles refer to a bicycle as a "rower" after one British company (Rover) that manufactured them. In fact, leisure created new industries. Originally blown-up pig's bladders were used as soccer balls, but their irregular shape made the game unpredictable. In 1855, the American inventor Charles

Goodyear applied the process of vulcanizing rubber that he had invented a decade earlier to the manufacture of soccer balls. This first "modern" soccer ball did not yet have the familiar white-and-black pattern of today's balls but was regular in shape. Soon others adopted Goodyear's technique, and a new industry was born. The same desire for a more regular, predictable game led to the mass production of baseballs, bicycles, tennis rackets, and sports outfits.

Mass Society

↓ How did economic changes alter society and family life?
↓ What impact did science have on society?

In the second half of the nineteenth century mass production in industry and mass consumption in department stores influenced the social order. High levels of literacy, political participation, and (relatively speaking) material affluence in western Europe reduced differences between social classes and expanded opportunities for social advancement. Measured by these criteria, mass society appeared first in Britain (excluding Ireland), Scandinavia, France, Belgium, and the Netherlands. Central and southern Europe, Russia, and the Balkans lagged behind. By the early twentieth century, access to education and to some level of political participation had come to be expected, increasingly by women as well as men. Greater numbers of people were now able to enjoy better food, brighter clothes, and a longer life. Advances in the biological sciences led to new medicines and vaccines. The new opportunities for employment and consumption also influenced women's place in the home and in society, opening the way for a new movement, feminism.

Mass Consumption

The benefits of technological innovation came first to the wealthy, but in the second half of the nineteenth century, they expanded rapidly to the urban poor and peasants out in the countryside. Mass production created a **mass society** in which prosperity spread among different classes. This heightened affluence and widespread education meant that obvious external differences between "high" and "low," such as clothes and

> **mass society**   Modern society characterized by universal legal rights, education, a large middle class, and a high level of equality among classes.

speech, were reduced. Factory-produced textiles and manufacture of garments made clothing so cheap and colorful—reflecting the availability of cheap synthetic dyes—that few peasants even in less developed countries like Russia continued to make their own clothes. In fact, peasants could now afford several changes of clothes, including undergarments—a novelty at the beginning of the century, but a basic by 1900.

Cheap newspapers and magazines, distributed widely by the thickening rail networks, meant that even people in remote regions could see and seek to imitate the latest fashions from Paris or St. Petersburg. And mass production brought prices down so that more and more middle- and sometimes working-class people could afford to dress fashionably. The famous department store Bon Marché was hailed as "a cathedral of commerce for a congregation of consumers" by the ironic French writer Émile Zola. The name Bon Marché means both "good market" and "inexpensive" in French—and the idea of a store for the masses was the creation of a self-made man, Aristide Boucicaut, and his wife, Marguerite. Their first store, opened just after the 1848 revolutions, introduced the novelty of clearly marked prices and welcomed people—mainly women—to come and look over the merchandise without obligation to purchase. The revolutionary concept of allowing potential customers to look without necessarily buying amounted to the invention of shopping as a pastime—and was wildly successful. In 1869, Boucicaut resolved to build a large new store using the most modern architecture. When the palatial structure opened in 1887, it delighted customers with its sumptuous decorations, sweeping marble staircases, and electric elevators. Shoppers are still delighted by Bon Marché, a palace in which to shop and be seen shopping. Boucicaut was a masterful businessman, offering such novel services as a catalogue of merchandise, free delivery, a money-back guarantee, and various sales like the "white month" in January. Zola wrote a novel about the department store—*The Ladies' Paradise* (1883)—and a metro station was given Boucicaut's name.

Thousands of attractive young women were hired as department store clerks, though previously selling had been regarded as unseemly for women. Women also joined the growing lower middle class as teachers, nurses, postal clerks, typists, and telephone operators. Although large numbers of young women continued to work as servants into the twentieth century, the higher pay, greater personal autonomy, and social prestige of these new occupations attracted many. While the salaries were low, the job allowed—indeed required—women to dress and behave like members of a more privileged class. Conservatives found this blurring of social distinctions outrageous and complained that it was becoming impossible to distinguish "people of good family" from servants by dress, and increasingly even by speech and manners.

Public Health

The population of Europe more than doubled between 1800 and 1900 (from around 200 million to 430 million), despite the departure of millions of emigrants for the Americas. This population explosion can be explained partly by better nutrition and the lack of massive epidemics or major wars after 1815, but improvements in medical knowledge and treatment were also a factor. Medical research paralleled work in physics: both were searching for invisible causes for certain phenomena. In physics, these were gamma rays, x-rays, and radiation; in medical science, the invisible cause was the germ, which was discovered in the 1880s. But long before that, scientists knew that *something* spread diseases, and they devised practical programs to prevent disease transmission. In the eighteenth century it had been discovered that using matter from cowpox pustules created an effective vaccine against smallpox. Similarly, the connection between dirty water, rotting waste, and disease had long been made—but most continued to think that disease was spread by foul smells.

Around 1820 cholera, a disease spread by unclean water, spread from India and Central Asia to Russia and western Europe. Crowded towns with minimal hygiene and limited access to clean water were an ideal breeding ground for the disease, which caused epidemics in a number of cities. In London a major outbreak in 1854 allowed the physician **John Snow** to promote his theory that the disease spread not through the air but by bad water. Snow's data showing that all the cholera victims had drunk water from a single source, the Broad Street pump, convinced even his critics. Snow was also one of the first physicians to use chloroform and ether to deaden pain. His most famous patient was Queen Victoria, who was grateful for his treatments during childbirth.

Around the same time in France, **Louis Pasteur** was demonstrating that heating wine to 55 degrees

John Snow (1813–1858) English physician who proved that cholera is spread by drinking water and who pioneered the use of chloroform to deaden pain.

Louis Pasteur (1822–1895) French scientist who developed a process for heating liquids to kill disease-causing organisms, now known as pasteurization.

Celsius killed the disease-causing microorganisms in it. His technique, called pasteurization, was later applied to beer and milk. Pasteur also pioneered methods for vaccinating against a number of diseases, including rabies and anthrax. Perhaps most important for medical practice, Pasteur demonstrated methods of sterilization that reduced the risk of infection in surgery and hospitals. Pasteur's suggestion that tiny particles of organic matter floating through the air could contaminate matter and cause fermentation was seized on by the English surgeon Joseph Lister, who showed that treating wounds with carbolic acid significantly reduced infections. Lister's antiseptic technique cut in half the number of deaths from infection following surgery and was later immortalized in the mouthwash Listerine.

Pasteur's path-breaking work in microbiology was continued by **Robert Koch** in Germany. While previously scientists had suspected the existence of microorganisms too small to be seen under the microscope; Koch proved their existence by isolating the cholera bacillus in 1883. He showed that every disease had its own microbiological cause and devised treatments and vaccines for these diseases. During the last part of his life, Koch devoted himself to the cause and treatment of the infectious lung disease tuberculosis, that plague of factory workers and city dwellers. In 1905 Koch was awarded the Nobel Prize in Medicine in recognition of his achievements.

Until the mid-nineteenth century, a sick person was *more* likely to die if admitted to a hospital, where unhygienic conditions often led to infections and death, than if treated at home. **Florence Nightingale**, who helped organize military hospitals in Istanbul during the Crimean War, returned to Britain to improve hospital care there. She virtually invented the profession of nursing, which from the start was an almost exclusively female occupation—and in Catholic countries often carried out by nuns. Building on the discoveries of Snow, Pasteur, and Lister, Nightingale worked throughout her long life to create modern, antiseptic, but welcoming hospitals. By the early twentieth century, the chances of dying after surgery, during childbirth, or in a hospital had been much reduced.

Families and Feminism

The technological and economic changes wrought by industrialization penetrated all aspects of public and private life. In the industrial cities, families no longer functioned as production units, and children came to be recognized as more of an economic burden than a benefit. Medical advances reduced infant mortality rates, so a woman who gave birth to, say, a dozen children could reasonably assume (at least in western and central Europe) that ten would survive to adulthood. But these children would be expensive to raise and educate, especially as the number of years required for a good education increased. In these decades, family planning in the form of contraception and medical abortions became widespread. Nearly everywhere, both were illegal, but laws did not prevent women from attempting to limit the number of their offspring.

Throughout Europe, birthrates went down, but unevenly. French politicians, not coincidentally all male, expressed grave concern at France's falling birthrate, the lowest among the Great Powers. The German birthrate, though relatively high, went down steadily in this period. Birthrates remained high in the least developed areas, such as Russia, Italy, Spain, and the Balkan Peninsula.

Among the middle classes, having fewer children meant that women had more time for other activities. Before 1848, women could not study at most universities, but during the second half of the nineteenth century these barriers gradually broke down. Women seeking higher education often went to Switzerland to receive training as doctors, lawyers, or economists, such as the famous Polish-Jewish socialist **Rosa Luxemburg**. Other exceptional women, like **Marie Curie**, studied in Paris, though not all professors—or male students—were comfortable with women students. While few women actually succeeded in surmounting the great economic and social obstacles and completing the university course, these first successful pioneers demonstrated that women were in no way intellectually inferior to men.

Yet women's educational opportunities, especially in secondary and higher education, remained limited, and it was often difficult for an educated woman to earn her own living. The laws of most European countries did not recognize women as adults. Very

Robert Koch (1843–1910) German bacteriologist who established that many diseases like anthrax, tuberculosis, and cholera were caused by bacterial infections.

Florence Nightingale (1820–1910) English reformer and creator of nursing as a profession who was instrumental in creating hygienic, well-organized hospitals.

Rosa Luxemburg (1871–1919) Polish-Jewish socialist who worked with V. I. Lenin and was murdered in 1919 by right-wing nationalists after a communist uprising in Berlin.

Marie Curie (1867–1934) Polish-born chemist and physicist who studied radioactivity and radium, the winner of two Nobel prizes.

often a woman could not even open a bank account, sign a contract, or purchase property without her husband's (or, if single, her father's) permission. Women also had little protection against abusive husbands. Despite the passage of the Matrimonial Causes Act in Britain in 1857, which allowed divorces without separate acts of Parliament (previously any divorce needed to be approved by Parliament as a specific, separate act), few women could afford the expense—and social scandal—of a divorce trial. Similarly, in France, divorce was made legal from 1884 onward, but the procedure was so complicated and

Marie Curie Recalls Her Youth in Russian Poland

In an autobiographical memoir that appeared in 1930, Marie Curie described the major events and milestones of her life. This memoir was published together with autobiographical sketches by American activist Jane Addams, Japanese feminist Sugimoto Etsu Inagaki, and other women. The editor of this volume, Helen Ferris, wanted to provide young women with positive role models and evidence that women could make their mark on society. In this passage, Marie Curie recalls teaching Polish children under repressive Russian rule in the 1880s.

➡ Why did the Russian government oppose education for these Polish children? Why might the Russian government see education as dangerous?

➡ Since my duties with my pupils did not take up all my time, I organized a small class for the children of the village who could not be educated under the Russian government. . . . We taught the little children and the girls who wished to come how to read and write, and we put in circulation Polish books which were appreciated, too, by the parents. Even this innocent work presented danger, as all initiative of this kind was forbidden by the government and might bring imprisonment or deportation to Siberia.

My evenings I generally devoted to study. ➡ I had heard that a few women had succeeded in following certain courses in Petrograd or in foreign countries, and I was determined to prepare myself by preliminary work to follow their example. . . .

➡ What were the advantages and drawbacks of solitary study for Curie?

➡ My solitary study was beset with difficulties. The scientific education I had received at the lyceum [high school] was very incomplete; it was well under the bachelorship program [high school curriculum] of a French lyceum; I tried to add to it in my own way, with the help of books picked up at random. This method could not be greatly productive, yet it was not without results. I acquired the habit of independent work, and learned a few things which were to be used later on.

➡ I had to modify my plans for the future when my eldest sister decided to go to Paris to study medicine. We had promised each other mutual aid, but our means did not permit our leaving together. So I kept my position for three and a half years, and, having finished my work with my pupils, I returned to Warsaw,

➡ How important do you think the example of other successful women was for inspiring Maria to try to find a way to study abroad? What do you think motivated Madame Curie to write this short memoir?

➡ What does this passage reveal about family responsibilities in this period? How do they differ from family obligations today?

> **→ Why could Polish young people in the 1880s think of study as a patriotic activity? Can you imagine any students in the twenty-first century having the same attitude, and, if so, where and why?**

where a position, similar to the one I had left, was awaiting me. . . .

→ Another means of instruction came to me through my being one of an enthusiastic group of young men and women of Warsaw, who united in a common desire to study, and whose activities were at the same time social and patriotic. It was one of those groups of Polish youths who believed that the hope of their country lay in a great effort to develop the intellectual and moral strength of the nation, and that such an effort would lead to a better national situation. . . . → We agreed among ourselves to give evening courses, each one teaching what he knew best. There is no need to say that this was a secret organization, which made everything extremely difficult.

> **→ How does this belief in study as a moral force compare with the teachings of Comte and the positivists?**

Source: Helen Ferris, ed., *When I was a Girl: The Stories of Five Famous Women as Told by Themselves* (New York: MacMillan, 1930).

expensive that few actually used it. In many countries, like Russia, divorce was not a possibility and men who grew tired of their wives often simply abandoned them, along with their children. Socialists like Friedrich Engels mocked the morality of middle-class sexuality and family life, calling it little more than a legalized form of enslavement and prostitution.

Despite their legal disabilities, women were increasingly literate and active in society. Whether raising children or working in factories, hospitals, or offices, women were increasingly well informed on contemporary cultural and scientific subjects. Some, like Florence Nightingale, chose to forgo marriage to devote themselves to other causes. Others, like the middle-class feminist **Emmeline Pankhurst**, dedicated themselves to achieving equal rights and opportunities for women, including the vote. Pankhurst, whose daughters Christabel and Sylvia also became notable feminists, embraced radical tactics such as arson, vandalism (like dumping jam into mailboxes), and public protests. For these activities Pankhurst was arrested several times, going on hunger strikes in jail and being force-fed. While such activities were controversial, they attracted attention to women's unequal status before the law and in the economy. Feminists in other European countries and the United States did not always agree with these tactics, but they recognized that such radical actions forced the male establishment to take women seriously. **Feminism**—use of the word to refer to the struggle for women's rights dates from this period—was mainly a middle-class phenomenon, for women workers and peasants were usually more concerned with better wages and work conditions than specific gender-based demands. Socialists denounced feminism as a bourgeois diversion, arguing that true equal rights for women would

come only with socialist revolution. But the idea that women should have the same professional and political rights as men was gaining ground.

Art and Industrial Society

> ↓ What impact did the economic and social changes of the late nineteenth century have on the visions and techniques of artists and writers?
> ↓ How did mass production and mass society influence art and literature?

Industrialization so deeply permeated all aspects of life in the late nineteenth century that art was profoundly altered as well. Art reflected the new industrial mass society both in its subjects and, even more strongly, in its techniques and artistic vision. Photography and the mass production of images through lithography and other techniques called into question the need for realistic art. Artists also worried that the mass production of cheap objects would degrade people's ability to appreciate the beautiful. Yet though artists experimented with new techniques, most people continued to prefer traditional realism and bought mass-produced images in the thousands and millions. Increasingly, artists found themselves out of tune with mass society.

> **Emmeline Pankhurst** (1858–1928) English crusader for women's suffrage who was often arrested for her radical activities.
> **feminism** Movement for equal rights for women, including legal equality and the right to vote.

Jean-François Millet's 1857 painting *The Gleaners* depicts women's back-breaking work of gleaning fields after harvest. Like many other realist works by Millet, this painting shows a scene from the everyday life of poor peasants. *(Musée d'Orsay, Paris/Giraudon/The Bridgeman Art Library)*

From Realism to Abstraction in Art

The scientific and technological advances of the mid-nineteenth century made artists look at the world in a new way, leading to a new artistic movement calling itself **Realism.** Realists rejected conventions dictating that the proper subjects for painting should be lofty—scenes from classical Greece, for example, or the Bible. Instead, they took their subjects from among working people, the peasantry, and events of everyday life. Among the most famous Realists was **Jean-François Millet,** whose paintings often depicted peasants at work, their faces grim and resigned. Realist painters were often political radicals who wanted to convey social and political opinions in their works. The caricatures of **Honoré Daumier,** for example, acidly criticized the existing social order. In Russia, the paintings of **Ilya Repin** revealed the stark misery of the Russian lower classes.

The paintings of **Edouard Manet** also laid open society's more sordid side. He shocked his contemporaries by making a well-known prostitute the subject of his painting *Olympia.* In the same year, 1863, Manet again outraged critics by painting together a pair of fully dressed gentlemen and an unabashedly naked woman in *The Luncheon on the Grass,* alluding to the hypocrisy existing in relations between men and women. Manet's technique remained Realist in his careful and objective attention to detail, but his subjects were deemed scandalous.

Mid-century French art had two main centers, both in Paris: the Academy of Painting and Sculpture, where young artists learned realistic techniques and painted exalted scenes; and the **Salon de Paris,** which exhibited new paintings sponsored by the academy every other year. Having one's work accepted for display at the Salon was the ambition of all young artists, as it meant success and often wealth. But the works of Manet and others who did not accept the Academy's narrow view of art had no chance of being accepted to the Salon. Angry at this conservatism, the rejected artists organized their own Salon des Refusés—an exhibition of refused paintings beginning in 1863.

In the 1870s, artists began to experiment with new ways of depicting reality. Instead of striving for pho-

Realism Movement in literature and painting that aimed at the objective reproduction of reality without idealization.

Jean-François Millet (1814–1875) French painter concerned with depicting social problems in a realistic style.

Honoré Daumier (1808–1879) French artist best known for his bitingly sarcastic caricatures of contemporary political figures and bourgeois society.

Ilya Repin (1844–1930) Russian Realist artist who specialized in painting enormous scenes from Russian past and contemporary life.

Edouard Manet (1832–1883) French painter who chose scandalous subjects and influenced the later Impressionists.

Salon de Paris Exhibition of paintings sponsored every other year by the Academy of Painting and Sculpture.

Ilya Repin's works exemplify the realist style in Russian art and often portray the poorest Russians, as in this painting, *Volga Barge-Haulers,* 1870–73. Like other realists, Repin did not intend merely to show a scene from Russian life: he wanted to shock viewers and remind them of the grinding poverty and social injustice present in their country. *(State Russian Museum, St. Petersburg/The Bridgeman Art Library)*

tographic realism, artists like **Claude Monet** sought to capture the artist's perception of light and shadows—a technique labeled **Impressionism** by a hostile critic. The label stuck but soon lost its negative connotation. The Impressionists sought to convey not an image of an object but rather the artist's perception and technique for depicting color, light, and shadow. Monet's paintings of haystacks at different times of day showed how the play of light created entirely different colors and images. Impressionists such as Edgar Degas, Auguste Renoir, and Georges Seurat painted the new amusements of the day—dance halls, boating trips, and cafés. The great graphic artist **Henri de Toulouse-Lautrec,** who was close to the Impressionists, raised the poster to an artistic form, thereby blurring the distinction between art and advertising. Toulouse-Lautrec's posters advertising the Chat Noir (Black Cat) nightclub, the singer Jean Avril, and the Le Moulin Rouge (Red Mill) dance hall became classics.

During the last decades of the nineteenth century, Paris became the center of the entire art world. American painters like James McNeill Whistler and Mary Cassat came to live and paint there; Cassat remained in France all her life. The Spaniard **Pablo Picasso** arrived in Paris in 1899 and also spent most of his life there. With its academic traditions, the masses of young artists rebelling against those traditions, government support for the arts, and a large wealthy and sophisticated society of art lovers, Paris attracted thousands of artists from everywhere in Europe and throughout the world.

Claude Monet (1840–1926) French Impressionist painter best known for his studies of light on landscapes, such as haystacks and the Rouen Cathedral.

Impressionism Artistic movement in France beginning in the 1870s that aimed to reproduce the painter's impression of light on a scene.

Henri de Toulouse-Lautrec (1864–1901) French artist who created bright and compelling posters advertising nightclub singers and dance halls.

Pablo Picasso (1881–1973) Spanish painter, founder of the Cubist school, and lifelong experimenter with abstract techniques.

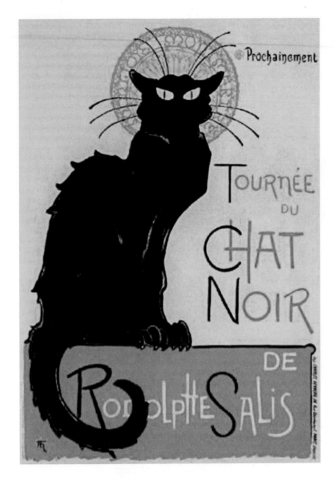

Henri Toulouse-Lautrec's poster art, often advertising cafes and dancehalls as here for the "Black Cat" cabaret, mingled art and commercialism. The striking colors and simple shapes used in these images were designed both to catch the viewer's eye and to facilitate the mass production of these posters. *(Suzanne Visser/Visual Connection Archive)*

While the Impressionists emphasized the artist's perception over any single objective vision of reality, at the beginning of the twentieth century new movements progressed even further from visual realism. The Viennese painter **Gustav Klimt** combined realistic and abstract elements in such works as *The Kiss* (1907–1908), in which the kissing faces of a couple are surrounded by colorful geometric patterns. Increasingly, artists aimed to go beyond surface reality. Picasso's influential and shocking *Demoiselles d'Avignon* of 1907 portrays the "Young Ladies of Avignon" as flat expanses of pink paint with exaggerated eyes and noses. Picasso and other so-called **Cubists** depicted the same object as seen simultaneously from various angles, resulting in a multifaceted, fractured image that represented the mind more than the eye. The

movement away from realism in art culminated in **abstract art.** In abstract works, such as those of the Russian Vasily Kandinsky and the Swiss Paul Klee, swirling shapes and colors do not represent any specific "real" objects but aim instead to depict the artist's emotions and perceptions of the world. The **Futurists,** who published their "Manifesto" in 1909, took these new artistic techniques and added a political twist, provocatively calling for the destruction of past artistic and literary works to open the way for the new. In *Nude Descending a Staircase* (1912), the Futurist Marcel Duchamp used Cubist techniques to portray his subject—movement. These new trends in nonrepresentational art would have a great influence on the art of the twentieth century but failed to find broad acceptance or understanding in their own time.

Realism and Naturalism in Literature

Realism was not limited to the visual arts. Writers such as Charles Dickens in England, Ivan Turgenev in Russia, and Gustave Flaubert in France all wrote realist fiction, aiming to describe life objectively and with an eye toward social criticism. Dickens's heroes like the orphans Oliver in *Oliver Twist* (1838) and Pip in *Great Expectations* (1861) struggle to improve their social position, eventually succeeding in being accepted in middle-class society. Turgenev's most famous novel, *Fathers and Sons* (1862), highlights the generational conflict between the liberal gentry "fathers" and the radical younger generation during the Great Reform period in Russia. In Flaubert's *Madame Bovary* (1856), a woman locked in a loveless marriage to a dreary though not evil man seeks joy by taking a lover and is ultimately destroyed by her choice. Flaubert's sympathetic description of an adulteress led in 1857 to a court case against the novel for obscenity, but the writer was acquitted.

Gustav Klimt (1862–1918) Viennese painter whose portraits integrated rich abstract patterns with realistic and expressive human faces.

Cubists Painters who challenged traditional realism by breaking up three-dimensional figures into different "cubes."

abstract art Art depicting the artist's view of the world through free use of color and shapes.

Futurists Artistic movement beginning in 1909 with a "Manifesto" that stressed energy, movement, even violence in visual and literary art.

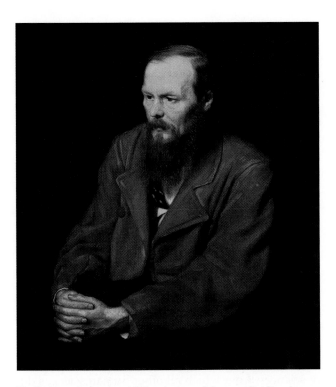

Vasily Perov's famous 1872 painting of the novelist Fyodor Dostoevsky shows the writer's intense gaze and haggard expression. Subject to epileptic seizures and plagued by an addiction to gambling that never allowed him to achieve material prosperity, in certain ways Dostoevsky resembled one of his own tortured characters. *(Tretyakov Gallery, Moscow/ The Bridgeman Art Library)*

Turgenev's contemporary **Fyodor Dostoevsky** also wrote novels in the realist style. But Dostoevsky, who despised Turgenev as a weak liberal overly fond of western European culture, combined psychological depth with political and religious passion. As a young man in the 1840s, Dostoevsky had been condemned to death for his involvement in a liberal reading circle. The death sentence was called off at the very last moment, after the first of the condemned had already been bound to a post to be shot. Dostoevsky was exiled to Siberia, where he rejected liberalism and rediscovered his Christian faith. In his best-known novel, *Crime and Punishment* (1866), an impoverished university dropout, a would-be great man like Napoleon, plans the perfect crime—the killing of a vile moneylender. After carrying out the murder, his guilt proves that no man is above God's law. In another work, *The Possessed* (or, translated more accurately, *The Devils*, 1871–1872), Dostoevsky delves into the psychology of Russian radical terrorists of the late 1860s.

Going beyond realism, Émile Zola described his own approach as "naturalist," and he exposed—in extensive scientific detail—the unhealthy aspects of modern society. In a series of very popular novels, he depicted several generations of two families beset by poverty, alcohol, prostitution, and other social ills, implying that their ills are inherited and inevitable. His characters are miners, café owners, prostitutes, and their clients, whose lives are described without moralizing. Zola dismissed criticism that his novels were rough, inelegantly written, and full of the sordid. "I am little concerned with beauty of perfection," he wrote. "All I care about is life, struggle, intensity. I am at ease in my generation."

Literature was also mass-produced. All the works mentioned here were bestsellers both in their original language and in translation. Inexpensively produced books were readily available, and bookshops in railroad stations provided reading material for travelers. Nearly all novels were first published in newspapers in serial form, helping boost circulation. Unfortunately for authors, it was very difficult to make a living from writing, as effective international **copyright** protection dates only from 1887.

Art for the Masses

Advances in technology—especially lithography and photography—were both welcomed and denounced by artists. On the one hand, lithography allowed a work of art like Toulouse-Lautrec's posters to be printed by the thousands. On the other, artists were disturbed when their images were poorly copied and distributed in distorted, cheapened form. Some purists also attacked Toulouse-Lautrec and the Czech poster artist Alphonse Mucha for "prostituting" their art in posters that advertised cigarettes, bicycles, singers, and dance halls. For others, the brightly colored posters were a form of art available for the enjoyment of those who could never afford a painting. Posters bridged the gap between "high" and "low"—a single, dynamic, brightly colored figure presented in a style unconventional enough to catch the attention. The success of these poster artists is apparent in the continued popularity of their images a century later.

Lithography and photography also made possible a great proliferation of illustrations in books, periodicals, and as prints. In Russia, hardly a peasant home was

Fyodor Dostoevsky (1821–1881) Russian Realist novelist whose expansive narratives examine conscience, character, and redemption.

copyright Legal protection for authors and artists, giving them specific rights to profit from the works they create.

without the *lubok:* a cheap lithographed print sold by peddlers. These prints were mass-produced on zinc plates and then often brightly colored by hand. Favorite subjects for the *lubok* were popular heroes, images from Russian history or mythology, and religious scenes. Similar mass-produced prints brightened the homes of the poor in other parts of Europe, though middle-class critics complained of their low artistic value, crude workmanship, and garish colors.

But it would be wrong to distinguish too sharply between "popular art" for the masses and works by "great artists" such as the Impressionists and Cubists. In Paris, tens of thousands flocked to the Salon, especially on days when admission was free. Poster art was broadly exhibited and accepted, and even the paintings of great artists were quickly available in prints and popular magazine illustrations. Some artists seized on mass production to argue that it should aim to produce beautiful things. William Morris, founder of the **Arts and Crafts movement** in Britain, designed books, tapestries, and even wallpaper, applying medieval designs to modern uses. His burning desire to see artistic beauty incorporated into everyday life came together with his commitment to equality as a socialist who worked with Karl Marx's daughter. Morris aimed to merge the useful and the beautiful. "Have nothing in your house that you do not know to be useful or believe to be beautiful," he advised. But Morris and his followers failed to find a broad following. His decorations and graceful designs were simply too expensive for most peasants and working-class people.

Science and Social Science

↓ How did science expand and change in the late nineteenth century?

↓ How did new scientific theories challenge religious ideas, and how did religion accommodate science?

During the nineteenth century it appeared that the Enlightenment promise of understanding the world entirely through scientific observation was being fulfilled. The application of the scientific method to the study of human behavior and society created new academic disciplines—the fields of anthropology, psychology, and especially sociology. Some argued that the natural world and human society could be understood without recourse to any metaphysical basis—that is, without any belief in God. Geological discoveries that the earth was far older than had been thought called into question the literal interpretation of the Bible. Even more shocking to traditional religious sensibilities was the theory of evolution ad-

vanced by Charles Darwin. By suggesting that human beings evolved from less complex animals, evolution struck at the very heart of traditional religion: the idea that humanity was created in God's image. Even time and space were no longer constants, as Albert Einstein's theories in the field of physics showed. While some religious leaders of nearly every faith furiously attacked the new science, others pointed out that scientific observation cannot provide a basis for morality and argued for a reconciliation between science and religious faith. The arguments that started in these decades continue to fuel controversy more than a century later.

The Science of Society

Sociology was the newest and perhaps the most ambitious of the new fields of inquiry into human existence. As its name suggests, sociology saw itself as the "science of society," claiming that human society can be studied, quantified, and understood like any other part of the natural world. Indeed, nineteenth-century sociologists called their discipline the queen of sciences, from which all other human sciences derived. Others were less sure that scientific methods could explain the inner workings of human society, and some feared that trying to do so would strip away the mysteries of human relations and impoverish life.

The beginnings of sociology may be found in the philosophy of **Auguste Comte,** a student of Claude Henri de Saint-Simon. To understand world history, Comte proposed the law of three stages, which explained history as the steady progress of humanity's understanding of the world through rational observation. The first stage of history he called the "theological," the era when people's primary means of explaining the world was through reference to God. The second stage was the "metaphysical," during which religious explanations were supplanted by a belief in ideas as reality—for example, G. W. F. Hegel's theory of history. The third and final stage, and one that Comte wanted to usher in with his own work, he named the "positive"—thus, his philosophy came to

lubok Brightly colored print, often of a religious or historical scene, mass-produced and sold by peddlers to Russian peasants.

Arts and Crafts movement Effort led by English artist and designer William Morris to merge beautiful design and workmanship with industrial techniques.

Auguste Comte (1798–1857) French thinker, inventor of the word *sociology* and proponent of positivism.

be known as **positivism.** In the positive era, the world would be explained exclusively by verifiable scientific data and method, and all branches of human knowledge would come together in a unified scientific system. The natural and social sciences would supplement each other, but both would share a common methodology based on mathematics and the scientific method.

Comte's call for a scientific study of society and the idea and method of positivism were widely influential. In the second half of the nineteenth century, the discipline we now know as sociology was created in great part along Comtian lines. Among its most famous practitioners was **Émile Durkheim,** who used **empirical** methods and statistics to examine the common values that held societies together. In his *Division of Labor in Society* (1893), he argued that the division of labor—so hated by Marx—actually had positive effects on society by allowing "organic solidarity" to arise, in which the various parts of society worked together like organs in a healthy body. His classic work on suicide, first published in 1897, attributed rising suicide rates (a widespread fascination of the period) to a breakdown in commonly held values.

Comte's insights also found resonance in Germany. There, two sociologists, Friedrich Tönnies and Georg Simmel, made the now classic distinction between *Gemeinschaft,* a traditional community of shared values, and *Gesellschaft,* modern industrial society in which individuals seldom knew their neighbors and felt no strong emotional attachment to the people around them. **Max Weber** looked into the inner workings of authority and obedience. He coined the term *charisma* to explain why some political leaders are successful in commanding respect and power. His short work *The Protestant Ethic and the Spirit of Capitalism* (1904–1905) aimed to explain the role that religious and moral values played in the development of modern capitalism. In their own ways, all of these early sociologists were attempting to come to terms with the social change and dislocation of this era. Their work reflected concerns also present in the works of Karl Marx, whose *Das Kapital* (*Capital*) appeared in three volumes between 1867 and the 1880s.

The Influence of Charles Darwin

Perhaps the greatest challenge to traditional values and outlooks on the world was presented by the thought of **Charles Darwin.** Darwin was the son of a self-made man, a physician who grew wealthy from his tireless work and financed his son's studies and, crucially, a trip around the world on the HMS *Beagle* (1831–1836), during which Darwin sketched and gath-

ered samples of thousands of exotic species. He wrote many books on topics ranging from fossils to barnacles, orchids to carnivorous plants, worms to coral reefs, and, most famously, *On the Origin of Species* (1859) and *The Descent of Man* (1871).

Darwin's primary contribution to science was not the idea of **evolution**—many previous thinkers, including his own grandfather, Erasmus Darwin, had noted the possibility of evolutionary change in nature. What Darwin offered, however, was an explanation of how evolution took place: **natural selection.** In his revolutionary *On the Origin of Species,* Darwin suggested, on the basis of a wealth of examples taken from his extensive career as a naturalist, that in any population of animals, certain features give individuals a greater chance for survival. For example, a bird that feeds mainly on nuts and seeds needs a strong bill to crack these open. Over time, natural selection favors these strong-billed birds, and the species evolves in that direction. For birds feeding on fruit or insects, however, other characteristics are more important.

Random mutations that enhanced survival played a key role in evolution. At the time, Darwin could not explain just how mutations arose and how these changes were transmitted to future generations. The discovery of the gene and the rediscovery in 1900 of the experiments in genetics carried out earlier by **Gregor Mendel** helped buttress Darwin's theories. *The Descent of Man* put forth the even more controversial

positivism   Comte's philosophy of knowledge emphasizing empirical observation and the idea that all natural and human phenomena can be explained in scientific terms.

Émile Durkheim   (1858–1917) French sociologist influenced by positivism who used empirical methods and statistics to study society.

empiricism   Belief that all knowledge can be derived from scientific observation.

Max Weber   (1864–1920) German sociologist who considered religious belief, charisma, and bureaucracy central influences on political and social life.

Charles Darwin   (1809–1882) English scientist who formulated the theory of natural selection and authored *On the Origin of Species* (1859).

evolution   Biological theory that diverse animal and plant species developed over time through a combination of genetic mutation and environmental influence.

natural selection   Darwin's theory that better-adapted species survive (and reproduce) while others are eliminated.

Gregor Mendel   (1822–1884) Austrian monk credited with the discovery of theory of genetic heredity.

Darwin's controversial theory of evolution made him a world-wide celebrity—though he had to endure many caricatures of himself as a "monkey man," as in this August 1878 issue of the French satirical journal, *La Petite Lune*. *(Archivo Iconografico, S.A./Corbis)*

ology, however, came from those who applied the concept of natural selection to human society. So-called **social Darwinists** such as **Herbert Spencer** argued that human societies also evolved through struggle, what Spencer called "the survival of the fittest," and that a society's health depended on the strongest elements' being allowed to develop themselves freely. While Spencer was careful not to equate the "fittest" with the most aggressive or physically able, others used these ideas to oppose social programs that aided the poor and weaker elements in society. Social Darwinists now used the language of science to validate the long-held opinion that the poor were to blame for their own poverty. Many social Darwinists also advanced arguments about European "racial superiority" over the peoples of Asia and Africa. Allied with such ideas was the new discipline of **eugenics**, which sought to improve society by discouraging the reproduction of "undesirable elements." Increasingly in the early twentieth century, advocates of eugenics and scientific racism argued that certain races were inferior not only because of environment but in their very genes. Some even called for the sterilization of those judged to be physically or mentally inferior.

The new field of anthropology also sought to describe and explain human diversity, especially as Europeans encountered different societies, religions, political structures, and kinship patterns in their colonies. Russian anthropologists and ethnographers, for example, described the everyday life and beliefs of Siberian and Central Asian native peoples. In St. Petersburg, exhibitions of the dress, art, and lifestyle of these exotic peoples were organized—showing not only artifacts like clothing, carpets, and dwellings but sometimes individuals of these ethnic groups as well. Peasants also interested anthropologists, such as **Olga Semyonova Tian-Shanskaia**, who studied Russian peasant life. Anthropologists generally saw themselves

thesis that humanity had descended from less advanced primates. Darwin's theory described a state of constant struggle for survival. Thus, even the smallest genetic advantages, he posited, could favor the survival of one species over another. Darwin's notion of the gradual improvement of species over time—the less favored individuals dying outwent along with the era's belief in the progress of human society.

Darwin's theories had a huge impact, and not only on the scientific community. His ideas were broadly debated by fellow scientists, who compared him with Galileo and Isaac Newton, and in the popular press, where he was ridiculed as "the monkey-man." The greatest long-term effect of Darwinism outside of bi-

social Darwinists Theorists who applied Darwin's theory of natural selection to human society, arguing that poorer and weaker segments of society deserved their fate.

Herbert Spencer (1820–1903) English philosopher and political theorist who coined the phrase "survival of the fittest."

eugenics Pseudoscience aiming to improve humanity by encouraging those with "desirable traits" to reproduce; now discredited as racist.

Olga Semyonova Tian-Shanskaia (1863–1906) Russian ethnographer who collected folk songs and important data on the Russian peasantry.

as representatives of a superior civilization, which they contrasted with the object of their research, so-called primitive or savage peoples, doomed to extinction by human progress, whose culture was put on display in museums and exhibitions.

Chemistry and the New Physics

In chemistry and physics, too, new research was fundamentally changing the understanding of the physical world. Dmitri Mendeleev's periodic table, first published in 1869, advanced chemistry by classifying elements according to atomic weight and periodical—that is, recurring—properties. Mendeleev's arrangement of the elements allowed chemists to predict characteristics of unknown elements according to their atomic weight and place in the table, thus paving the way for later discoveries, such as Marie Curie's radium.

Up to this time, following Isaac Newton, physics had understood all phenomena and motion as the result of the action of one particle on another. But this mechanical view made it difficult to understand the action of light and other invisible rays that traveled rapidly across space and appeared to have no mass. For Newtonian physics to work, scientists had theorized that a substance called ether permeated the universe, though it had never been discovered or measured. The search for ether would lead to the discovery of many other invisible rays and forces that in the end would establish the existence of fields of force that operated over great distances. Through experimentation and rational analysis, scientists postulated a physical world more complex than previous generations had imagined.

One practical challenge was to understand the nature of electricity. The work of James Clerk Maxwell, though mainly on a theoretical level, paved the way for practical applications of electricity for use in lighting and motors. Maxwell also predicted the existence of radio waves and theorized that light itself was a form of electromagnetism. The German scientist Heinrich Hertz proved Maxwell correct by broadcasting and receiving radio waves in the late 1880s. In late 1895, Wilhelm Röntgen discovered x-rays, a form of electromagnetic radiation. This discovery spurred others—the Curies among them—to search for other forms of radiation (see Choice). All of these discoveries were rapidly developed into practical inventions by other scientists and by industry: electricity was put to work in the electric light bulb, phonograph, and innumerable other inventions by Edison; Hertz's findings were translated into the radio by Marconi; Röntgen's x-rays found practical application in healthcare and his name became the German word for "to x-ray."

The revolutionary work of **Albert Einstein** built on these scientists' research but, in another sense, completely reformulated physicists' understanding of the universe. In 1905, the young scientist published a paper proposing the **special theory of relativity**, suggesting that as particles approach the speed of light, their speed cannot be predicted by Newton's laws of motion. Two years later Einstein developed these ideas further, leading to the now famous equation $E = mc^2$—energy is equivalent to mass multiplied by the square of the speed of light. Einstein postulated that light travels through empty space at a constant speed, thereby eliminating the need for any medium like ether. Einstein's theory of relativity also challenged concepts of absolute space and time because these were shown to depend on the relative velocity of the particle and the observer.

Within a few years, Einstein's theory was being hotly debated by scientists, many of whom attempted to verify or discredit relativity experimentally. As Einstein's special theory of relativity gained acceptance on both sides of the Atlantic, he followed it with the general theory of relativity in 1915, which dealt with gravity. In this theory, Einstein predicted that starlight passing near the sun would be curved by the pull of gravity. This prediction was verified in 1919 during a solar eclipse, and Einstein suddenly became an international celebrity. He was awarded the Nobel Prize in Physics in 1921.

Few scientists at the time could appreciate Einstein's relativity theories or the radical new understanding of the atom, the quantum theory, advanced by the German physicist **Max Planck** in 1900 to explain the behavior of energy within the atom. While physicists struggled with the implications of relativity and quantum theory, for many in the general public these disturbing new ideas symbolized a destruction of certainty. Just as Darwin had called into question accepted notions about the natural world and its origins, Einstein and Planck stripped away certainty from even the most fundamental elements of perception: time and space.

Albert Einstein   (1879–1955) German physicist most famous for his theory of relativity.

special theory of relativity   Einstein's theory stating, among other things, that the speed of light is always constant while distance and time are relative to the observer.

Max Planck   (1858–1947) German physicist and author of quantum theory who won the Nobel Prize in Physics in 1918.

The Battle Between Science and Religion

Darwin's theories, especially regarding human evolution, stirred great controversy, and some of his main opponents were religious leaders who understood evolution as directly challenging not only the biblical story of creation but the majesty of God. Anglican bishop Samuel Wilberforce of Oxford decried Darwin's work as "a tendency to limit God's glory in creation," while the Catholic cardinal Henry Edward Manning denounced Darwin's ideas as "a brutal philosophy—to wit, there is no God, and the ape is our Adam." But the controversy between science and religion went far deeper, representing a profound crisis of consciousness in the nineteenth century. Geological discoveries, in particular those associated with the British geologist **Sir Charles Lyell**, had already proved that the earth was vastly older than the number of generations in the Bible between Adam and Jesus Christ. In addition, the fossil remains of dinosaurs and other animals not mentioned in the Bible further eroded conventional Christian faith in literal biblical truth. While most Europeans still professed Christianity, the content of their beliefs changed under the weight of scientific evidence. The biblical account of creation came, for example, to be understood more and more in a symbolic rather than a literal way.

In second half of the nineteenth century, many young Europeans rejected religious belief as unscientific, irrelevant, or even immoral. As early as the 1840s, Marx had exclaimed that religion was the "opiate of the people." In other words, religion diverted people's attention from the real causes of their poverty and, most important, hindered their action to bring about social justice. While Marx and other socialists were atheists, rejecting religion, they believed fervently in progress, science, and humanity's ability to better itself. This radical rejection of a religious worldview was also shared by the fictional hero in Turgenev's *Fathers and Sons*, Evgeny Bazarov, whose views were summed up by a friend: "He doesn't believe in principles, but he believes in frogs [to dissect]." Like Bazarov, many young radicals rejected religious authority and demanded that any principles, whether moral, political, or scientific, be proven by empirical methods. In a sense, they were simply reformulating Comte's positivism. Not religion but empirical scientific methods—in both the social and physical sciences—would bring about true progress.

For most people, however, a world without God was unthinkable. Even scientists were not generally atheists, though they often did not accept all aspects of church dogma. Most continued at least to cherish a belief in a Supreme Being, however defined. While Pope Pius IX condemned materialism in the *Syllabus of Errors* of 1864, and "modernism" was denounced by the later Pope Pius X in 1907, many educated Catholics sought to reconcile their religious beliefs and elements of modern thought.

In the **shtetls** of eastern Europe, Jewish boys were punished for daring to read "modern" authors—even in Hebrew translation. Traditional Jews claimed that the Torah, Talmud, and other religious works contained enough of human wisdom to satisfy anyone, but their attempt to shut out the modern world was in the long run doomed to failure. Some Jews discarded religious beliefs entirely in their desire to become modern, rational Europeans, while others pointed out that great Jewish scholars from earlier ages had studied natural science, claiming that the study of science was but another way of understanding the greatness of God's creation. While religion could not ignore new scientific discoveries, neither could scientific materialism be entirely satisfying for most people. While the scientific method could explain much, it was mute when faced with life's most basic question: why are we here? Even Comte conceded the existence of a Supreme Being in his positivism, and Darwin fudged: "There is a grandeur in this view of life, with its several powers, having been originally breathed by the Creator into a few forms or into one." Rationality and empirical experimentation could only explain so much of human existence.

Critiques of Reason

Toward the end of the nineteenth century, the optimism that came with prosperity, scientific advances, and the philosophy of positivism began to falter. Some thinkers saw mass production less as a triumph than a threat, burying differences and local peculiarities in sterile uniformity. Max Weber warned darkly about the "iron cage" of bureaucracy. The German philosopher **Friedrich Nietzsche** called on gifted individuals to resist mass society, which he termed "the

Sir Charles Lyell (1797–1875) English geologist whose *Principles of Geology* (1830–1833) suggested that the world must be far older than hitherto imagined.

shtetls (in Yiddish, "small cities") Towns inhabited mainly or exclusively by Jews, in particular in eastern Europe.

Friedrich Nietzsche (1844–1900) German philosopher renowned for his demand for a complete revision of human ethics and who notoriously despised mass society.

common herd." Austrian psychiatrist **Sigmund Freud** used scientific methodology to probe into the irrational motivations of human behavior. Just as artists were rejecting representations of the external world for explorations of individual perceptions, writers such as Gustave Le Bon and Henri Bergson described the limits of rationality in human experience, arguing that passion and intuition played a key role in social and individual behavior. Despite advances in science, politics, and technology, both seemed to say, human behavior remains profoundly determined by basic, even primitive, drives and passions.

Nietzsche himself bore both physical and psychological scars from his service as a medical orderly in the Franco-Prussian War. Returning home, he rapidly published his first book, *The Birth of Tragedy* (1872), which gained him a professorship at the University of Basel, an almost unheard-of distinction for a man under thirty. *The Birth of Tragedy* emphasized the role of passion and ecstasy (which Nietzsche associated with the Greek god Dionysus) in the genesis of Greek tragedy, an argument that was so novel and suggestive that Nietzsche became a celebrity outside of academic circles as well.

In the next decade and a half, Nietzsche produced thousands of pages of books, essays, polemics, and poetry, returning time and again to the themes of personal freedom and intellectual and moral self-reliance. He despised many aspects of modern life, including mass society, and lashed out against liberal democracy, German nationalism, antisemitism, and traditional moral standards—in particular, the "slave morality" of Christianity. He denounced mass society, which he perceived as his era's "herd mentality" and preference for the safe and comfortable. Instead, he demanded that human beings recognize their own freedom, admit that "God is dead," and then celebrate the enormous liberation that this fact implies. Nietzsche's philosophy emphasized the role of the will and passion over cool, calculated reason, and his insistence that humans discard all traditional values and create their own moral world is perhaps the most radical modern restatement of Immanuel Kant's famous dictum, "Dare to know!"

Nietzsche was never a systematic philosopher, and the sheer sparkle and wit of his writing may get in the way of his ideas. These qualities, combined with his meandering writing style, open his works to many different interpretations. In the twentieth century, the German National Socialists (Nazis) tried to appropriate his ideas for their cause, claiming that Nietzsche's superman—a man whose passion and will would create a new moral world—was identical to the Nazi Aryan ideal. But this interpretation is directly contradicted by Nietzsche's denunciation of Germany's antisemites as typical of the herd mentality. Nietzsche scorned biological explanations of human differences. On the other hand, his no less vehement attacks on such Christian values as forgiveness, charity, kindness, and mercy seem at times to parallel Nazi ruthlessness. In the light of rationality, elements of Nietzsche's thought seem contradictory, but he claimed that his philosophy operated at a higher—or deeper—level, concerning the innermost reaches of the human soul.

Nietzsche died in 1900, one year after Sigmund Freud's most famous work, *The Interpretation of Dreams*, appeared. While the two men were utterly different in background, professional training, and temperament, both had an enormous impact on modern consciousness. Freud was born into a lower-middle-class Jewish family and lived nearly his entire life in Vienna. Like many young Jews of his generation, he studied medicine, aiming to dedicate his life to medical practice and research and discarding traditional religious belief along the way. As early as the 1880s, Freud noticed in some of his patients—who were primarily middle-class women—symptoms that could not be explained by physical illness alone. Gradually he developed his theory of **repression**, claiming that patients repressed—that is, denied and refused to acknowledge on a conscious level—traumatic memories, usually of a sexual nature. Having diagnosed the problem, Freud began to develop a treatment. Like others before him, Freud differentiated between conscious and subconscious levels in the human psyche. On the conscious level, we may be rational, considering pros and cons and thinking through the consequences of our actions. But Freud insisted that our rational decisions were always liable to be influenced and sometimes overpowered by the subconscious. His "talking cure" (today we know it as psychoanalysis) aimed to reveal the subconscious by a steady probing of a patient's memories, reactions, behavior, and dreams. Dreams were a key component because for Freud they often revealed repressed desires that existed at a subconscious level.

To describe the human personality, Freud divided the psyche into three components: the id, ego, and superego. The id consists entirely of drives, hungers,

Sigmund Freud (1856–1939) Austrian psychiatrist who emphasized the role of fundamental and prerational drives, including sexual desire, in human behavior.

repression Freud's theory that memories and desires not acknowledged by a person's conscious thought can lead to physical and mental disorders.

and desires; a baby, for example, may be seen as an example of pure id. The ego develops as the child encounters reality and realizes that not all wants can be filled. The superego, the last part of the personality to develop, incorporates the moral values, taboos, and behavioral models that children internalize as they mature. According to Freud, all three components exist in every human being; none are inherently bad or good. Hysteria and other neuroses appear, however, when the three are out of balance. For example, in any society, individuals must control and regulate their instinctual drives. But for some neurotics the demands of the superego become so demanding as to make normal life impossible.

Freud's thought combines the rationalist method of the later nineteenth century with a recognition of the limitations of rationality. In his own life, Freud was very much the model of the positivist scientist, rejecting the idea of a Supreme Being and insisting on an empirical approach in psychology. But he also recognized that in human behavior, irrational—or at least subconscious and prerational—elements often prevailed.

Summary

Review Questions

↑ What was the Second Industrial Revolution? What impact did it have on society and culture?

↑ How did the cultural and scientific changes of the late nineteenth century affect religious identity?

↑ Describe some of the positive and negative aspects of mass society.

As industrialization spread, Europe changed irrevocably. Between 1850 and 1914, major technological advances in communications, chemistry, steel, electricity, and energy transformed the nature of industrialization itself. The so-called Second Industrial Revolution, based on electricity, steel, and modern chemistry, changed Europe, and the world, profoundly. Scientific discoveries were rapidly translated into technological advances that in turn had a great impact on people's daily lives. Discoveries in the field of electricity led to the construction of undersea telegraph cables that by the early twentieth century kept citizens informed of the latest news from around the world. New technologies producing cheap wood-fiber paper translated into cheap newspapers read by all segments of society. Gains in mass production considerably increased the material prosperity of the broad masses, who could now purchase a wide range of goods from garments to cooking utensils to prints to hang on their walls. Shorter working hours meant increased possibilities for various forms of leisure—travel, sports, music, and cinema.

Political and social attitudes changed no less radically. By 1914, nearly every country in Europe allowed some degree of political participation by all classes, including peasants and workers, and in many places women demanded political rights equal to those of males. In education, expectations increased: literacy became the norm, not the exception. Technological advances—in particular, steamships and the extension of the railroad network—opened the way for mass travel and tourism. Millions of Europeans left Europe forever, to seek a new and better life in overseas colonies and the Americas.

The arts and sciences likewise exhibited great and thoroughgoing changes. Artists challenged traditional modes of depicting reality. This shift in perception and artistic method created the new movements of Impressionism and abstraction. The new science of sociology aimed to bring together all branches of human knowledge. Rejecting religion, the positivists argued that applying empirical methods to studying human society would bring a more rational, happier, and better world. Charles Darwin's theory of natural selection radically challenged traditional religious beliefs. Other thinkers, such as Sigmund Freud and Friedrich Nietzsche, pointed out that rationality was always in conflict with deeper instinctual drives. Even scientific certainty was called into question by the theories of Albert Einstein. After Einstein, even time and space had to be thought of as relative.

Europe's great advances in the period from 1850 to 1914 shaped its politics, art and music, industrial production, social sciences, and objects of everyday life. In 1914 Europeans were, for the most part, immensely proud of their achievements and optimistic about the future.

← **Thinking Back, Thinking Ahead** →

Compare the Second Industrial Revolution with the original Industrial Revolution of the late eighteenth and early nineteenth centuries. Which had the greater social and cultural impact?

ECHO HO ECHO ECHO ECHO

Tourism

In the twenty-first century, tourism is one of the largest and most rapidly growing industries in the world. But although there have been travelers throughout history, mass tourism is a product of the late nineteenth century. Starting in the late eighteenth century, wealthy and adventurous individuals traveled to cultural and historic cities. These "Grand Tours," often lasting months, were an integral part of any gentleman's—and even young lady's—education. Wealthy travelers in Florence and Rome, sketching artwork and rereading Latin classics, or in Istanbul and Jerusalem, usually with Bible in hand, can be seen as the precursors of modern tourists. In that age, before the lithograph or photography had been invented, the only way to see famous paintings or works of architecture was to visit them.

But for tourism to become a mass phenomenon required something more. It was the railroad that allowed middle-class people—and even artisans and laborers—to become tourists. One man can be fairly called the father of modern tourism. The devout Baptist Thomas Cook began organizing tours in the hopes of diverting workers from more sinful entertainment, especially of the alcoholic variety. In 1851, Cook organized his first package tour, a day trip from the central English town of Leicester featuring an eleven-mile journey by train, musical entertainment, lunch, and temperance speeches. Cook's Tours took thousands to visit the Crystal Palace Exhibition in London. By the time of his death in 1892, thousands more had traveled on Cook's Tours to Europe, Africa, Asia, and even around the world. Cook made travel not only more affordable but fun and carefree. By paying one fee, tourists rid themselves of worries about tickets, customs, rude innkeepers, and inedible restaurant food. Perhaps even more important, Cook's Tours allowed middle-class people to meet others like themselves and insulated them from encounters with local people. In an age when strangers did not normally address one another, the organized tour created a kind of tourist community in which travelers felt safe and at home.

The term *Cook's tour* also entered the English language, defined as "a rapid or cursory survey or review." Even today Cook's Tours offers tens of thousands of package holidays, and competitors like American Express, Wagons-Lits, Neckermann, and Club Med send hundreds of thousands to all corners of the globe.

Suggested Readings

Gay, Peter. *The Bourgeois Experience: Victoria to Freud.* 5 vols. New York: Norton, 1984–1998. An ambitious study looking into various aspects of middle-class life in the nineteenth century.

Himmelfarb, Gertrude. *Darwin and the Darwinian Revolution.* Chicago: Ivan R. Dee, 1996. A well-written, clear narrative.

Kern, Stephen. *The Culture of Time and Space, 1880–1918.* Cambridge, Mass.: Harvard University Press, 2003. A fascinating synthesis of culture, technology, ideas, and everyday life.

Landes, David S. *The Unbound Prometheus: Technological Change and Industrial Development in Western Europe from* *1750 to the Present.* 2nd ed. New York: Cambridge University Press, 2003. A path-breaking work with clear explanations.

Romein, Jan. *The Watershed of Two Eras: Europe in 1900.* Middletown, Conn.: Wesleyan University Press, 1978. A huge volume full of interesting facts and arguments.

Schorske, Carl. *Fin-de-Siècle Vienna: Politics and Culture.* New York: Vintage Books, 1981. A modern classic of cultural history.

Trebilcock, Clive. *The Industrialization of the Continental Powers, 1780–1914.* London: Longman, 1981. A work that combines theoretical models with lots and lots of facts.

Websites

Information in French and English about August Comte, the founder of sociology, **Auguste Comte and Positivism,** at http://membres.lycos.fr/clotilde

Detailed chronicle of Friedrich Nietzsche's life, **Nietzsche Chronicle,** at www.dartmouth.edu/~fnchron

Charles Darwin's life, travels, and works, **About Darwin.com,** at www.aboutdarwin.com

CHAPTER
24

The Age of Imperialism, 1870–1914

1500 B.C.E.	1000 B.C.E.	500 B.C.E.	1 B.C.E./1 C.E.

1865
Tashkent falls to the Russians

1857
Sepoy Rebellion begins

1867
French annex Cochinchina

1869
Suez Canal opens in Egypt

1877
Queen Victoria becomes empress of India

1850	1855	1860	1865	1870	1875	1880

European Colonies Around the World, 1900

By 1900, European countries had established colonies on every inhabited continent. On which continents were the majority of European colonies? Which European countries had the greatest number of colonies?

| 0 | 2000 | 4000 Km. |
| 0 | 1000 | 2000 | 3000 | 4000 Mi. |

GREENLAND
(Denmark)

ALASKA

CANADA

UNITED STATES

ATLANTIC OCEAN

GREAT BRITAIN

NETH. GERMANY
BELG.
FRANCE
AUSTRIA-HUNGARY
SPAIN
ITALY
OTTOMAN EMPIRE
PORTUGAL
CYPRUS

RUSSIA

Sakhalin
KARAFUTO
MANCHURIA
KOREA   JAPAN

PACIFIC OCEAN

MOROCCO
TUNISIA
AFGHANISTAN
PERSIA
CHINA

BAHAMA IS.

RIO DE ORO
ALGERIA
LIBYA
EGYPT
INDIA
BURMA
Taiwan

BR. HONDURAS

HAWAII

ERITREA
ANGLO-EGYPTIAN SUDAN
HADHRAMAUT

FRENCH INDOCHINA

PHILIPPINE IS.

Mariana Is.

FRENCH WEST AFRICA
GAMBIA
TOGO
NIGERIA
GOLD COAST
KAMERUN
BR. SOMALILAND
FR. SOMALILAND
IT. SOMALILAND
CEYLON
MALAY STATES
SARAWAK
BR. NORTH BORNEO
Marshall Is.
Caroline Is.

PORT. GUINEA
SIERRA LEONE
SP. GUINEA

BRITISH GUIANA
DUTCH GUIANA
FRENCH GUIANA

UGANDA
BRITISH EAST AFRICA
GERMAN EAST AFRICA
BELGIAN CONGO

DUTCH EAST INDIES

PAPUA

SOUTH AMERICA

Solomon Is.
New Hebrides
(Gr. Br. and France)

PACIFIC OCEAN

ANGOLA
NORTHERN RHODESIA
NYASALAND
MOZAMBIQUE
SOUTHERN RHODESIA
MADAGASCAR

INDIAN OCEAN

New Caledonia
(France)

GERMAN SOUTHWEST AFRICA
BECHUANALAND
SWAZILAND
UNION OF SOUTH AFRICA
LESOTHO

AUSTRALIA

NEW ZEALAND

ANTARCTICA

The colonial powers and their possessions

Germany	Russia	Belgium	Italy
France	United States	Netherlands	Spain
Great Britain	Japan	Portugal	— Major shipping routes

| 500 C.E. | 1000 C.E. | 1500 C.E. | 2000 C.E. |

1884
Congress of Berlin regulates trade and empire in Africa

1885
Congo Free State is established

1899
Boer War begins

1900
Foreign powers crush Boxer Rebellion in China

| 1885 | 1890 | 1895 | 1900 | 1905 | 1910 | 1915 |

683

Choic Choice Choice

Cecil Rhodes

Cecil Rhodes was one of the best-known advocates of the new imperialism of the late nineteenth century, and he reflected the mindset of the age. A cartoon in the English humor magazine *Punch* showed Rhodes as a colossus whose mighty stride took in the entire African continent. It related specifically to Rhodes's pet project of a railroad running the length of Africa, from Cairo to the Cape of Good Hope, a project that was never realized. (Punch Limited)

Cecil Rhodes Creates the Rhodes Scholarship

For Cecil Rhodes, as for many other young, energetic Europeans of the late nineteenth century, establishing colonies around the world was not just an adventure or means of gaining wealth but a moral duty. They wanted to spread European values and culture around the world.

Born in 1853 into a middle-class family in a country town in England, Rhodes had been singled out early as an intelligent boy. His adoring and powerful mother sheltered him in his early years, and he grew up self-confident, sure of his own destiny. At age of sixteen, he set off for Africa with his parents' blessing. In the 1870s, he divided his time between Africa and Oxford, earning his degree in 1881. Already by this time—before his thirtieth birthday—he had made a fortune in South African diamonds. His ambitions helped extend British power far to the north, into a region named Rhodesia (today Zambia and Zimbabwe) in his honor.

As a businessman and government official, Rhodes was known for ruthlessness and an authoritarian style that created enemies among his white contacts and fear among Africans. As prime minister of Cape Colony, he authorized a military excursion that he hoped would unite South Africa as a British colony. Its failure led the House of Commons to pronounce him guilty of grave breaches of duty, and he was forced to resign. Rhodes died a rich but embittered man in 1902, not even fifty years old.

But Rhodes had already made provision for funding the Rhodes Scholarships, for which he is best known today. Though a businessman and colonial official, Rhodes was also a visionary who believed that English culture should conquer the world. Convinced of English superiority, Rhodes maintained that the more the world came to resemble England, the better. So to preserve and spread English culture, Rhodes funded scholarships that would allow the most talented men (women could not enter most British universities at the time) to study in England—at the oldest of English universities, Oxford.

At first, Rhodes proposed thirty-six scholarships for "young colonials" from New Zealand, Australia, Canada, and South Africa. Later, scholarships were added for young men from the United States and Germany. In all cases, Rhodes's aim was the same: to produce cultured, educated English gentlemen. Rhodes had little interest in producing scholars or independent thinkers: among the qualifications he listed for selecting scholarship winners were "manly sports," "qualities of manhood," and "moral force of character," as well as "literary and scholastic" excellence. Rhodes Scholars, he hoped, would not be mere bookworms but would carry on his own values and those of upper-class, wealthy Britons dedicated to the good of the empire.

Rhodes set down that the scholarships would be open to all male candidates, regardless of "race or religious opinions." Rhodes did not mean race as it is understood today; he meant nationality, and by this he intended that the Dutch in South Africa—Britain's rivals for control—should be eligible. He certainly never expected

Africans or Asians to apply. In practice, however, the scholarships have been awarded to individuals of diverse races and backgrounds and from many countries.

Rhodes's legacy has enabled hundreds of young men and women (the latter only since 1977) to complete their education at Oxford. Among Rhodes Scholars are some of the most distinguished scholars, political leaders, and social activists of the twentieth century: Count Bernstorff, a German diplomat executed for conspiring against Hitler; Edwin Hubble, the astronomer after whom the Hubble Space Telescope is named; Daniel Boorstin, former librarian of Congress; David Souter, Supreme Court justice; and former U.S. president William J. Clinton. Add to this list hundreds of distinguished scholars, diplomats, and politicians from Pakistan, India, Canada, Australia, and other countries.

Introduction

European expansion and colonialism did not start in the late nineteenth century. Spain and Portugal had established American colonies in the late fifteenth century, and Russian domination of Siberia in northern Asia dates from the seventeenth century. But the imperialism of the late nineteenth century was new. Europe's industrialization and new technologies made it possible, and more of Europe's nations than ever before got involved in the race for expansion. In little more than a generation, Europeans extended colonial rule over much of the globe. Colonies provided Europeans with raw materials and markets. They were good for European economies. Imperial rule also fascinated Europeans, whose very identity became linked with their countries' role as overlords in Africa, Asia, and the Muslim world. Europeans were proud of their culture and believed it superior to any other civilization in the world. The scientific and technological advances of the nineteenth century, rising literacy rates, and the general advance in standards of living convinced them that their rule of other lands was a benefit.

In 1870, there were a few European colonies and settlements on the edges of Africa. By 1900, the entire continent had been divided up among the European powers. The largest colonial territories were held by Britain and France, but Portugal, Belgium, and Germany also ruled over thousands of square miles and hundreds of thousands of Africans. Only two independent states remained in Africa by 1914—Ethiopia in East Africa and Liberia on the west coast.

Asia was also colonized by Europeans. The largest and richest colony of all was there: British India. France extended colonial rule in Indochina (now Vietnam, Laos, and Cambodia), and the Dutch exerted control over the islands now known as Indonesia. While China was never colonized directly, western powers interfered in Chinese domestic affairs. And Japan, industrializing from the 1870s onward, became a colonial power in its own right, conquering Taiwan at the end of the century. In all, around half a billion Asians and Africans fell under colonial rule.

The new imperialism extended to the Muslim world, as the Ottoman Empire, the most important Muslim state of the time, was challenged by incursions from Russia and other European powers. An even larger number of Muslims lived under imperial rule in British India and, by the end of the nineteenth century, in Russian Central Asia. Muslim intellectuals, who wondered why their culture had been unable to withstand these threats, formulated programs of reform to meet the challenge of imperialism.

Some Europeans, too, opposed and criticized imperialism, denouncing it as a highly exploitative and racist form of capitalism. These opinions would be influential into the twenty-first century.

Motives and Methods of the New Imperialism

⬇ What political and technological advances paved the way for the new imperialism?
⬇ How did Europeans attempt to justify imperialist expansion?

Many explanations have been offered for European expansion during between 1870 and 1914. These include economic motivations, political and demographic factors, national rivalries, a desire to spread Christianity, and the idea that Europeans (and North Americans) had a moral responsibility to spread their culture and technology around the world. European governments did not follow any well-thought-out plan in expanding their colonial empires. Rather, they

Chronology

1836–1846	Boers take Great Trek north away from English colonists in southern Africa
1839–1842	British defeat the Chinese in the Opium Wars
1853–1854	United States forces Japan to open to foreign trade
1857–1858	British put down Sepoy Rebellion in India
1865	Tashkent falls to the Russians
1867	French annex Cochinchina (southern Indochina)
1869	Suez Canal opens
1877	Queen Victoria becomes empress of India
1882	British occupy Egypt
1884–1886	Germany establishes African colonies
1885	Indian National Congress is founded; Congo Free State is established
1887	Russia completes conquest of Turkestan (Central Asia)
1894–1895	Japanese annex Formosa (Taiwan);
1898	Spanish-American War begins
1899–1902	British defeat Boers in the Boer War
1900	Foreign powers crush Boxer Rebellion in China
1902	Hobson publishes *Imperialism*
1904	Japanese attack on Russian naval base at Port Arthur
1905–1907	Herero Revolt takes place in German Southwest Africa
1908	Leopold II turns over the Congo Free State to Belgium
1910	Union of South Africa is established
1912	South African Native National Congress is established; Italy invades Libya
1916	Lenin publishes *Imperialism, the Highest Stage of Capitalism*

reacted to specific circumstances, always seeking to prevent other European powers from gaining on them. The conviction of European superiority also pushed imperialism forward. So did the new technologies of the Second Industrial Revolution. All these factors help explain how, and why, millions of non-Europeans were brought under European rule.

Economic Motivations

The desire for new markets and the need for the raw materials of industry certainly fueled the **new imperialism**. Britain looked to India as a market for its textiles and other industrial products. King **Leopold II** of Belgium derived huge profits from rubber plantations in the Congo, and **Cecil Rhodes** (see Choice) became vastly wealthy from exploiting African labor in the gold and diamond mines of southern Africa. Industrial society demanded rubber for industrial uses, but also for tires on bicycles and a new invention, the automobile. Similarly, palm oil was in great demand as a machine lubricant. Fruits such as bananas and pineapples were also imported from colonized areas.

These products could be obtained only in tropical regions, many of which fell under European rule at this time.

Still, the direct connection between economic motivations and the establishment of political control is not often clear. Britain already enjoyed economic and political dominance of India and southern Africa *before* imperialist domination was established. For Germany, the establishment of colonies in Africa and the Pacific made no economic sense; these colonies cost German taxpayers millions. Furthermore, throughout this period, more western European capital flowed to

new imperialism   Extension and strengthening of European colonial rule, mainly in Africa and Asia, from approximately 1870 to 1914.

Leopold II   (r. 1865–1909) Belgian king who established personal rule over a large part of central Africa (later the Belgian Congo).

Cecil Rhodes   (1853–1902) British businessman and colonial official who made a fortune in diamonds and was prime minister of Cape Colony in Africa.

Russia, the United States, and South America than to territories under formal colonial rule. Thus, economic motivations alone cannot explain the late-nineteenth-century drive for colonial rule.

Domestic Politics and National Rivalries

A more convincing explanation of imperialism is found in the domestic politics of the major European powers. Large numbers of Britons, Frenchmen, Germans, and others came to identify their own national pride with colonial possessions. After their humiliating defeat in the Franco-Prussian War, the French, for example, were able to take pride in an expanding colonial empire. But Germans, who had won the war, felt the need for a colonial empire, too. Having failed to suppress the Social Democrats even through the strategy of adopting some of their programs, Chancellor Otto von Bismarck turned to empire to enhance his political popularity. In the late nineteenth century Europe was swept by "imperialist fever." Even sober politicians not usually concerned with popular opinion—such as Bismarck in Berlin—found it necessary, or at least useful, to adopt imperialism as a political program.

National rivalries contributed to imperial expansion. The establishment of one colony almost inevitably led to the perceived need to grab more territory to "protect" it. In this way, European rivalries contributed to European expansion. For example, in the early 1880s, the French government declared formal control over Tunisia in northern Africa mainly because it feared Italian expansion westward from Libya. Similarly, the British occupied Egypt in 1882 partly to deny the French any influence. At first, they did not intend to maintain permanent political control, but facing a power vacuum and fearing that hostile Egyptian groups would take over, the British stayed. Control of Egypt also allowed the British to secure the sea route to India once the Suez Canal was constructed. Protection of the canal then became an end in itself. Thus, securing access to existing colonies also served as a justification for taking new ones. All along the route to India, the British secured stopping and fueling points for ships. Aden, at the tip of the Arabian Peninsula, was deliberately taken for this purpose.

As Britain and France carved up Africa, other European powers demanded their place in the sun. Italy grabbed Libya from the Ottoman Empire in 1912 and established control over Eritrea and Somaliland in East Africa. Germany occupied Cameroon, German Southwest Africa (now Namibia), and German East Africa (roughly today's Tanzania). Germany also took control of a large group on Pacific islands, thereby coming into conflict with another young imperial power, the United States. None of these colonies brought wealth or significant new markets to the home country. Rather, their main purpose was to satisfy the patriotic fever of Germans and Italians who felt that without colonies their countries would be second-rate powers. In this way, domestic politics pushed imperialism, often against the wishes and advice of the imperialist powers' foreign ministers and foreign policy experts.

Christian Missions

Churches and missionaries also played a vital role in imperialist expansion. Most often, Christian missionaries had established footholds before official colonial control was declared. To be sure, missionaries sincerely desired to bring education, healthcare, and other benefits of European culture to Africans and Asians. They often built schools and hospitals. Missionaries seldom forced Christianity on the native peoples, hoping instead to win converts by good example. At the same time, they taught European concepts of sexual morality and gender relations and often insisted that natives dress in a "modest" European manner, all of which undermined native cultural values. When local rulers attempted to restrict or expel missionaries, even without using violence, the European powers often intervened. Thousands and eventually millions of Asians and Africans embraced Christianity, but these numbers represented a grave loss to native cultures and religions.

One well-known missionary was **David Livingstone.** As a small boy in Scotland, born to a working-class family in 1813, young David was influenced by accounts he heard and read of Christian missionaries in China and the Muslim world. In 1840, he left England for Africa, where he was to spend the rest of his life spreading the gospel, healing the sick, and fighting European exploitation—including enslavement—of Africans. Livingstone became famous for his expedition seeking the source of the Nile River and his discovery of Victoria Falls, now shared by Zimbabwe and Zambia. His life in the African bush and his dedication to helping Africans, even against other Europeans, made him a controversial figure, however. In 1871, the American reporter Henry Stanley went to Africa in search of Livingstone, famously greeting

David Livingstone   (1813–1873) Scottish missionary, explorer of Africa, and discoverer of Victoria Falls.

him with the words, "Dr. Livingstone, I presume?" Stanley described the elderly missionary as "a living skeleton"; Livingstone died in his tent in 1873 and was buried in London, in Westminster Abbey. At his funeral, he was praised for his efforts to spread Christian morality through good example. Livingstone's motivations for the extension of European culture contrast sharply with those of Rhodes, indicating the complexities of imperialist motivations.

Missionaries translated the Gospels into African languages, wrote grammars and dictionaries, and thereby helped transform tongues previously only spoken into written languages. Many stood up for native rights against European administrators. They did not always get along with European traders, but their example—the clothes they wore and houses they kept—provided Africans with incentive to purchase European manufactured goods. Thus, in spite of their own kindly intentions, missionaries encouraged economic links between industrial Europe and underdeveloped colonies.

"The White Man's Burden"

Many Europeans, not only missionaries, saw the spread of European civilization as a precious gift to "dark peoples" of African and Asia: the figure of speech referred to alleged intellectual and cultural backwardness as much as to skin color. The English poet **Rudyard Kipling** called this impulse "**the white man's burden.**" Kipling was born in India, which is the setting for his well-known children's books, such as *The Jungle Book* (1894) and *Kim* (1901). In 1899, in the context of the Spanish-American War that had begun a year earlier, he addressed these lines to the United States, urging Americans to join in the imperialist enterprise:

Take up the White Man's burden—
Send forth the best ye breed—
Go bind your sons to exile
To serve your captives' need;
To wait in heavy harness
On fluttered folk and wild—
Your new-caught, sullen peoples,
Half-devil and half-child.

The condescending attitude of the imperialists is evident here. At the same time, Kipling emphasizes that imperialism is not a program for exploitation and self-aggrandizement but a duty: "to serve your captives' need." He sees imperialism as a "civilizing mission" that is self-sacrificing. The next stanza describes it as: "To seek another's profit, / And work another's gain." Kipling may be termed a romantic imperialist who perceived imperialism as an uplifting moral crusade that, while not always so understood by the natives ("new-caught, sullen peoples"), would in the end bring about better conditions for their lives.

Rudyard Kipling (1865–1936) English writer and poet, born in India, best known for his adventure stories, which often took place in exotic colonial locations.

white man's burden Phrase taken from a poem by Rudyard Kipling urging Americans—but implicitly all "white men"—to spread western civilization.

Cecil Rhodes Writes His Own "Confession of Faith"

From an early age, Cecil Rhodes had a mission—to spread British culture, values, and education. Rhodes never wavered in his belief that the world would be better off under British rule. In 1877, at age twenty-four, Rhodes set down his ideas in a "Confession of Faith" for himself. The document was never published in his lifetime.

➜ What do you think Rhodes meant by "the most despicable specimens of human beings"?

➜ I contend that we [English] are the finest race in the world and that the more of the world we inhabit the better it is for the human race. Just fancy those parts that are at present inhabited by the most despicable specimens of human beings what an alteration there would be if they were brought under Anglo-Saxon influ-

➡️ What would happen to these people if Rhodes's plan was realized?

➡️ What does Rhodes mean when he speaks of "race"? How does his usage differ from our present-day understanding of that word?

➡️ Why do you suppose that Rhodes proposed a secret society to pursue his aims?

➡️ What kind of "extra employment" do you think Rhodes had in mind here? How did imperialism increase jobs at home?

➡️ Do you think that Rhodes's emphasis on duty was typical of the nineteenth century? Typical of someone twenty-four years old? Why or why not?

ence, look again at the extra employment a new country added to our dominions gives. I contend that every acre added to our territory means in the future birth to some more of the English race who otherwise would not be brought into existence. Added to this the absorption of the greater portion of the world under our rule simply means the end of all wars. . . .

➡️ Why should we not form a secret society with but one object the furtherance of the British Empire and the bringing of the whole uncivilised world under British rule for the recovery of the United States for the making the Anglo-Saxon race but one Empire. . . .

➡️ Africa is still lying ready for us it is our duty to take it. It is our duty to seize every opportunity of acquiring more territory and we should keep this one idea steadily before our eyes that more territory simply means more of the Anglo-Saxon race more of the best, the most human, most honourable race the world possesses. ➡️ To forward such a scheme what a splendid help a secret society would be a society not openly acknowledged but who would work in secret for such an object. . . .

What has been the main cause of the success of the Romish [Roman Catholic] Church? The fact that every enthusiast, call it if you like every madman finds employment in it. Let us form the same kind of society a Church for the extension of the British Empire. A society which should have its members in every part of the British Empire working with one object and one idea. . . .

Imperialists firmly believed in western superiority in civilization, culture, and even genetic makeup. Earlier in the nineteenth century, Americans had justified their expansion from the Atlantic to the Pacific Ocean as **manifest destiny,** claiming that God and the natural order had ordained American control over the entire continent. In a similar way, Europeans extolled the virtues of their social order, technology, and religious beliefs and assumed that non-Europeans would be grateful to be "uplifted" and assimilated into the European political and economic systems and moral values.

Scholars such as the French sociologist and journalist Paul Leroy-Beaulieu argued that France had a "civilizing mission" to the world. In other words, French culture was a valuable commodity that could improve the lives of Asians and Africans. The British politician Joseph Chamberlain argued much the same for British culture. In a speech to Parliament in 1897 he exclaimed, "I maintain that our rule does, and has, brought security and peace and comparative prosperity to countries that never knew these blessings before." Chamberlain praised the "work of civilization" that British imperialists carried out in India, Africa, and other lands.

But these attitudes contained within them a contradiction. Even as imperialists claimed that they brought civilization to colonized peoples, they frequently exploited the labor of those peoples, denying them the rights and privileges taken for granted by Europeans. The large gap between the rhetoric of imperialism and its more brutal reality meant that sooner or later imperialism would collapse.

Racism certainly played a part in the ideology and practice of imperialism. By the second half of the nineteenth century, scientific theories of race had divided humanity into Caucasian, Negroid, and Mongoloid races, which some argued were different species

manifest destiny   North American ideology that saw the extension of the United States to the Pacific Ocean as fulfillment of a divine plan.

and others arranged in a strict hierarchy, with Europeans (Caucasians) on top. European racial theorists believed it was self-evident that the white, or Caucasian, race had progressed further than the others. Both the categories and the argumentation revealed not scientific facts but prejudices and convenient self-justifications for European dominance. Nonetheless, these ideas about the races were widely held.

Beaulieu and Chamberlain were not overtly racist, but their assumption that European culture was superior to that of Asia or Africa was paternalistic. **Paternalism**'s greatest blind spot was its inability to recognize and respect the humanity of non-Europeans. Kipling's description of native people as "half-devil and half-child" reflects this view. Imperialists did not understand that their values were not necessarily universal and that from the colonized people's point of view, imperialist efforts to "enlighten" might well be experienced as oppression and even as the destruction of time-hallowed traditions. Hypocrisy was inherent in this system that claimed to protect and nurture native peoples while in reality privileging European economic and political interests.

The Importance of Technology

European domination over most of the world's surface would have been impossible without the technological advances of the Second Industrial Revolution. Among these, advances in communications, transportation, and medicine are most important.

The telegraph vastly simplified the administration of world empires by making nearly instantaneous communication possible. By the 1860s, England was connected to India by telegraph over land lines, but messages had to be sent and retransmitted many times, often by operators not entirely fluent in English. When underwater cables were laid in the late 1860s and 1870, communications between Britain and India became far faster and reliable. By 1895, nearly two hundred thousand miles of underwater cables connected Europe with America, Asia, Africa, and Australia, and more than six hundred thousand miles of land telegraph cables sped messages to their destinations. When, at the end of the nineteenth century, the increasingly dense telegraph network was supplemented by a growing telephone network, colonial administrators were able to be in continuous and almost instant communication. At any sign of unrest, an administrator out in the countryside could telegraph the nearest military outpost with a request for troops. In this way the telegraph helped imperial administrators stifle resistance and revolt.

Developments in transportation similarly facilitated

imperial administration. The imperial powers constructed railroads in the colonies, most impressively in India, which by 1900 had more than twenty-five thousand miles of railway lines—more than France or Britain itself. Just as Rhodes dreamed of connecting British colonies throughout East Africa by a Cairo-to-Capetown rail line, German imperialists dreamed of a Berlin-to-Baghdad railroad that would strengthen German influence in the Ottoman Empire. Neither line was completed, but railroads were built in many African colonies, making the extraction of raw materials and the penetration of European military control possible. Steamship lines, too, shortened distances. The trip from England to Australia, which had taken more than four months in the early nineteenth century, was down to a month by the century's end.

As Europeans ventured into new climates in Africa and Asia, they encountered new microbes. In Africa, particularly, death rates among European explorers up to the mid-nineteenth century were extremely high. Among the diseases, **malaria** was probably the most devastating. Before the late nineteenth century, little was understood about germs. The disease was attributed to "bad air"—in Italian, *mal'aria*—because it was not yet understood that the disease was spread by germ-carrying mosquitoes. Still, by trial and error, Europeans came to recognize that constant doses of the bark of the cinchona tree were effective in staving off the worst symptoms of malaria. The bark contained quinine, which began to be commercially produced in the 1830s. Quinine became the constant companion of the imperialist in tropical areas, and the typical imperialist cocktail, a gin and tonic (containing quinine), became a pleasant means of administering a daily dose. By the end of the century, the role of germs in sickness was established, and British scientists made significant advances in studying tropical diseases. For all that, mortality continued to be high among Europeans serving in tropical regions, in particular in equatorial Africa.

Political, ideological, economic, and technological factors all contributed to the new imperialism's massive extension of European power around the globe. Imperialists saw themselves as the bearers of a superior cultural and political order. At the same time, many

paternalism   Attitude toward or control of one group (here, colonialized people) by another (here, Europeans) that resembles a father's rule over his children.

malaria   Infectious parasitic disease transmitted by mosquitoes, particularly widespread in tropical areas but preventable by constant doses of quinine.

of them gained huge profits and prestige derived from the labor and natural resources of the colonized lands. Imperialists took for granted the superiority of European thought and culture, seeing in the native populations as ignorant and backward savages to be "brought up" to European standards. Despite the imperialists' often sincere belief in their own "civilizing mission," their failure to appreciate the validity of other cultures led quickly to conflicts, resentment, and resistance.

The Scramble for Africa

↓ How did settler colonies in Africa differ from other kinds of colonies?

↓ What economic factors propelled Europeans to colonize Africa?

Africa provides the most startling example of the new imperialism. In 1870, while there were European outposts along the coasts, the African interior was almost totally unknown to Europeans. By 1914, the continent was almost completely colonized. Africans resisted imperialism, but the superiority of European weaponry doomed resistance to failure. But competition for control led two groups of European settlers to fight against each other, in the Boer War.

Settler Colonies in South and North Africa

Historians differentiate between **settler colonies**, in which colonists came in large numbers, often including entire families, and settled permanently, and colonies where only a few, usually male, administrators lived temporarily and then returned to Europe. Settler colonies were usually located in temperate regions such as Argentina, the United States, and Australia, where the majority of the current population is descended from settlers, not native to that place. In Africa in the nineteenth century, there were only two large-scale European settler colonies. One was located at the temperate southern tip of Africa, where Dutch farmers (or Boers) had originally settled in the seventeenth century, later joined by English colonists. During the Great Trek of 1836–1846, the Boers moved north into land previously inhabited by Africans. Around 1900, perhaps 10 percent of the total population in South Africa was of European descent, but they dominated the economy and political system there. It was these white settlers who gained most from the establishment of the Union of South Africa in 1900.

Thousands of Indian laborers and professionals also made these colonies their home. Most numerous, of course, were the native African peoples of the region, who often saw their land and livelihoods taken over by Europeans in this period. To fight against these injustices of colonial rule, the South African Native National Congress was established in 1912. This organization, later called simply the **African National Congress,** helped abolish white privilege and establish a more democratic order in South Africa in 1994.

In northern Africa, French Algeria can be considered a settler colony. By 1848, around one hundred thousand Europeans had settled there, and by the early twentieth century, around 1 million French men and women made their home along Africa's Mediterranean coast. Some 40 percent of the population was of European descent. Unlike South Africa, Algeria was from the 1840s onward considered by the French government to be an integral part of that country. However, the native Arabic-speaking Muslim population had no political rights under the French, and Europeans also dominated the economy.

The Belgian Congo

One of the largest and most remarkable colonies in Africa was established by the private initiative (and funds) of the king of Belgium, Leopold II. Neither the Belgian government nor the Belgian public showed much interest in an African possession when Leopold, acting on his own, established the Association Internationale du Congo in 1876 for what he called humanitarian purposes. In fact, he financed private expeditions—sending Henry Stanley, among others—throughout the Congo River basin for his own economic gain. By the late 1880s, the Congo was in essence Leopold's own private estate, an estate of some nine hundred thousand square miles with millions of inhabitants.

Though he set up the Congo Free State in 1885, Leopold ruled the area directly, with the help of his Force Publique, a brutal and corrupt mercenary army. Treating the Congo as a financial investment, Leopold extracted as much rubber, ivory, and palm oil as possible with a minimum of expense, gaining vast riches

settler colonies   Colonies inhabited by settlers of European origin, always located in temperate regions such as North America, Australia, and South Africa.

African National Congress   Organization established by Africans in 1912 to defend their rights that eventually brought a more democratic order to South Africa.

These two youths were among the many in King Leopold's Congo colony whose hands were cut off by soldiers and policemen who forced local people to produce rubber for export—or else. The printing of photographs like this one in European newspapers and magazines helped publicize the brutality of imperial rule in central Africa. *(Courtesy, Anti-Slavery International)*

in the process. African workers were forced to produce quotas of rubber. Failure to do so brought brutal punishments, including the hacking off of hands and feet. Though the king and investors grew rich, the brutality appalled Europeans, and in 1908 European pressure obliged Leopold to turn over the colony to the Belgian state, which would rule over the area as the Belgian Congo until 1960. The cruelty and inhumanity of exploitation in the Congo inspired **Joseph Conrad**'s novella *Heart of Darkness*.

The Berlin Conference and German Colonies

In Germany, Chancellor Bismarck seized on tensions among Africa's colonial powers to enter Germany in what has been described as the scramble for Africa. In 1884, he called the **Berlin Conference**, specifically to press Leopold to agree to free trade in the Congo. At this congress, the United States joined Great Britain,

France, Russian, Austria-Hungary, and the Ottoman Empire in recognizing Leopold's authority over the Congo in exchange for the right to trade there. Bismarck used the occasion to declare German control over Southwest Africa, Togo, and Cameroon, to be followed by East Africa (today's Tanzania) a year later. Also during these years, 1884–1886, Germany established colonies in the South Pacific, straining relations with the United States.

By establishing colonies, Bismarck was pursuing both international and domestic goals. In foreign policy, he aimed to enhance German power and prestige in the world. At home, Bismarck was responding to pressure from the **German Colonial Union**. By 1884 it appeared that if the German state did not act quickly, all chances for African colonies would be gone, the continent taken over by the British and French. So Bismarck acted swiftly and, in the short run, very successfully, as his popularity soared.

But the new German colonies lacked any obvious economic or political rationale. It was not clear how they would be administered or whether the tiny German navy could defend them. Furthermore, Bismarck's action infuriated the British, from Queen Victoria to the common laborer, all of whom identified closely with the idea of empire. The new German colonies in Africa were both a challenge and a threat to British colonies there.

The German colonial empire was off to an inauspicious start. For the next few years, Bismarck attempted to administer the territories through private chartered companies. After this policy failed, in the 1890s the German government took over the colonies directly. In their effort to crush native resistance and establish control of German Southwest Africa, German colonial officials, small in number and inexperienced, carried out horrifying massacres, especially after the **Herero Revolt** of 1905–1907. This policy of **genocide**

Joseph Conrad   (1857–1924) English writer of Polish origin whose novels such as *Heart of Darkness* and *Lord Jim* often examined the morality of colonialism.

Berlin Conference   Meeting in Berlin of the United States and European powers in 1884 that regulated European trade and imperial control in Africa.

German Colonial Union   Political pressure group formed in 1882 to press the German government to seek overseas colonies.

Herero Revolt   Rebellion against colonial rule in German Southwest Africa followed by a German massacre of the Herero people in 1905–1907.

genocide   Attempt to kill an entire people or nation.

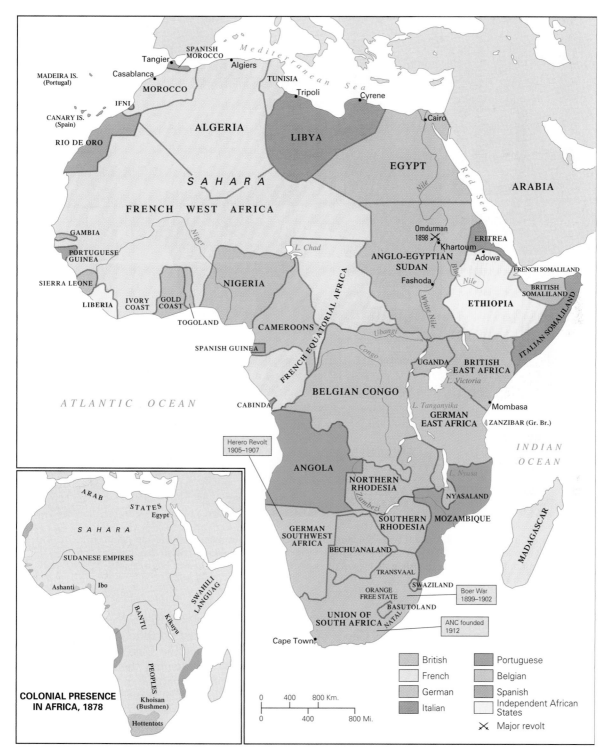

MAP 24.1   **Partition of Africa, 1870–1914** Between 1870 and 1914 nearly all of Africa came under European colonial rule. As these maps show, British and French colonies predominated, but several other European powers also participated in "the scramble for Africa."

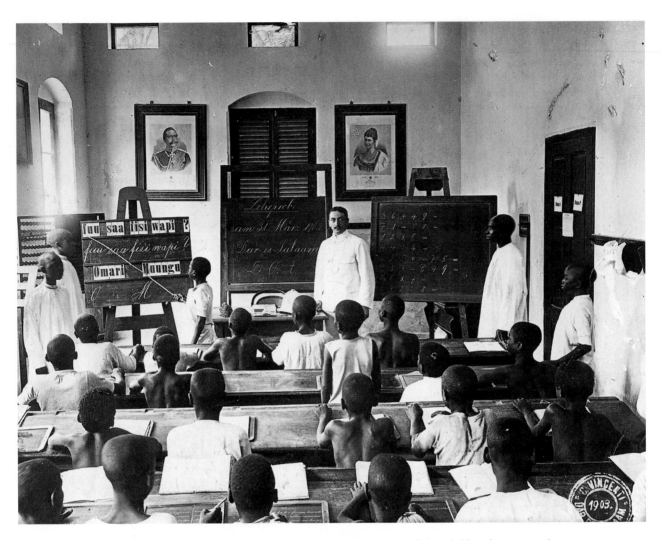

In this missionary school in German East Africa (Dar Es Salaam, now Tanzania), African children learn to read under the gaze of the German Kaiser and his wife. As the writing on the chalkboard indicates, these children were learning to read not only in German but also in their own native African language. *(Ullstein Bilderdienst/ The Granger Collection, New York)*

was widely criticized in Europe. On the whole, German colonies in Africa failed to bring Germany either economic or political gains.

The Boer War

In South Africa, the discovery of gold and diamonds in the 1880s attracted thousands of Englishmen and other Europeans to the region. Among these new arrivals was Cecil Rhodes, whose investments in the gold and diamond mines of Kimberley made him a millionaire. The huge influx of prospectors caused the Dutch farmers, or Boers, great worries. They had earlier left their original colony near the Cape of Good Hope and trekked north to avoid English rule. Now it appeared that the English were pursuing them once again, threatening their farms and way of life. To preserve their independence, in 1899 the Boers, led by their gruff leader Paul Kruger, took a stand against the British.

The resulting Boer War of 1899–1902 caused great suffering and death among Africans, but the central

Boer War Conflict between British Empire and Dutch settlers (Boers) in South Africa in 1899–1902, ending in a costly British victory.

dispute was between Europeans, in particular, the Boer's desire to retain their own autonomy and the British insistence on extending their rule to include areas of Boer settlement. The British expected to win quickly and easily, but they were wrong. Nearly five hundred thousand British men fought in the Boer War; around one-tenth of these lost their lives. In the end the British prevailed, however, and they granted the Boers broad autonomy and home rule. But after this expensive and bloody war between Europeans in a colonized country, many Europeans began to question whether imperialism was economically or morally defensible.

The British Raj in India

⬇ What was the nature of British rule in India?
⬇ Why was British rule in India so important for the empire?

British dominion over India was always a special case, with its specific mystique and tradition. Even the language used to refer to this colony was unique—"the jewel in the crown" of empire. The British presence in India dated from the seventeenth century, and domination continued in various forms until 1947. Besides the unprecedented length of British control, the huge size and complex culture of the territory made India a colony unlike any other. The enormous diversity of religions, languages, and customs in India complicated British rule, especially as the extension of British colonial power in India did not follow a well-considered plan. Rather, economic interests were gradually transformed into political dominion in reaction to threats of foreign encroachment, the perceived and real weaknesses of native Indian administrations, and resistance to British rule. More than any other colony, India influenced British home politics, national identity, and culture. The impact of British rule on Indian culture was no less significant.

Commerce and Trade

European traders had visited the Indian **subcontinent** from the sixteenth century onward. By the eighteenth century, both French and English traders were competing over Indian goods like calico cloth, spices, and luxury items. At first, British interests in India were strictly commercial. The British East India Company had one aim: profit. It operated through warehouses and posts along the Indian coast, where agents traded with Indian merchants, but by the early eighteenth century the trading posts in Bombay, Madras,

and Calcutta were fortified. Following Britian's victory in the Seven Years' War (1756–1763), French competition ended. Still, as the **Mughal Empire** weakened, company officials continued to worry about their own safety and the future of trade there. In this insecure political situation, British state institutions gradually moved in.

A governor-general of India was first named in the late eighteenth century. Though supposedly just the agent of the British Parliament and the Crown, he ruled in the absolutist style. Some regions he ruled directly; in others he ruled through subordinate Indian princes. But from the first, the ideological basis of British rule in India was contradictory. British liberals saw it as aiming to produce Indians capable of self-rule, "a class of persons Indian in colour and blood, but English in tastes, in opinions, in morals, and in intellect," explained Thomas Babington Macauley, a Whig member of Parliament and East India Company leader. Until this class could be trained, however, India was controlled by a British administration that, while generally honest and efficient, was conservative and on the whole quite alien, even hostile, to Indian traditions.

The Sepoy Rebellion

The **Sepoy Rebellion** of 1857 demonstrated that Indian soldiers in British service, called sepoys, had long been dissatisfied over issues of pay and rumors that the British would force them to convert to Christianity. When they were issued new cartridges greased with fat made from cows (sacred to Hindus) and pigs (forbidden to Muslims), they refused to load their weapons. The mutiny spread rapidly through northern India. British response was brutal: thousands of Indian soldiers were massacred and entire villages were destroyed. This response was justified by pointing to lurid stories of sepoys committing murder and rape, specifically of "dark men" sexually abusing English women. The British believed they had to protect both "the white race" and "English womanhood."

Following the rebellion, British rule of Indian was fundamentally transformed. The British East India

---

subcontinent   British India, including present-day Pakistan and Bangladesh ("sub" refers to its location on Asia's bottom edge).

Mughal Empire   Muslim empire in India lasting from 1526 to 1857.

Sepoy Rebellion   Revolt of Indian soldiers (sepoys) in northern India in 1857–1858, put down with brutality by the British.

MAP 24.2 **Growth of British India** India was by far the largest and most important British colony from the late eighteenth to the mid-twentieth century. As this map shows, British India—which included the present-day countries of India, Pakistan, Bangladesh, and Burma—was partly under direct British rule and partly ruled by Indian princes subordinate to the British.

Company was disbanded and control of the colony transferred to the Crown. Large numbers British soldiers were sent to the colony. Whereas in 1857 European soldiers were outnumbered ten to one by native troops, by 1885 there were 73,000 British and 154,000 Indian soldiers. The costs of administration and the army were a heavy burden for Indian taxpayers.

Official British policy aimed to avoid interference in religious matters, but, as the mutiny demonstrated, few British administrators understood the complexi-

The Delhi Dunbar of 1903 was an enormous celebration of British rule in India that brought together dozens of Indian princes, hundreds of British soldiers and officials, and huge crowds who watched the splendid processions and ceremonies. *(British Library)*

ties of religious relations in India, where traditional religions involved the worship of many gods, while the large Muslim population, making up a significant proportion of native rulers, was strictly **monotheistic**. The Church of England, while not a militant missionary force, was influential through its influence on British administrators. As Christians, they found it difficult to understand and appreciate a religion based not on belief in a single God, Wishing to rationalize administration, the British encouraged the creation of a more coherent Hindu religion out of thousands of separate, often local, rites, beliefs, and rituals. At the same time, Hindus perceived British rule as favoring monotheistic Muslim Indians, thereby exacerbating relations between the diverse religious groups of the subcontinent.

The Jewel in the Crown

In the late nineteenth century, the British **Raj** in India continued to expand. Steamships brought officials and their families back and forth between England and Calcutta, the capital of British India. It became common for ambitious young men to make a career in India, amassing a fortune or pension, then returning

to England in retirement. Some Englishmen, however, remained in India their whole lives. Their children were known as "Anglo-Indians," the most famous of whom was probably the writer Rudyard Kipling.

Even for Anglo-Indians, however, relations with Indians were seldom on an equal basis. With only a few exceptions at the highest levels of society, the English in India knew native people as servants. An Englishwoman could not be alone with an Indian man without endangering her reputation. Racial categories and hierarchies—with the Englishman on top—dominated English colonial identity in India as well as at home. The injustice of this racially defined colonial rule helped bring about the formation of the **Indian National Congress** in 1885, an organization that would work to free India from British rule.

The allure of India also affected Englishmen who would never leave home. Visual art, songs, and

monotheism   Belief in the existence of only one God.
Raj   (from Hindi, "rule") British Empire in India.
Indian National Congress   Organization formed in 1885 demanding the end of colonial rule in India.

literature—like Kipling's *Jungle Book* and *Kim*—created an image of India as a place both familiar and alien, full of exotic scenes, wild animals, and exquisite dangers. British identity derived great pride in the domination and influence over this vast region, so many times larger than England itself. In 1877, Queen Victoria took the title of Empress of India in well-orchestrated ceremonies both at home and in India itself. The stately processions of Indian princes, elephants, and native soldiers in uniforms thrilled Englishmen in Manchester and Leeds. Their own lives might be dull and routine, but as Englishmen they, too, were part of these imperial pageants.

British Order and Indian Culture

British liberals claimed that in India their goal was an honest administration, a market economy, and individual self-development. They aimed to reduce corruption, to increase efficiency, and in the long run to bring prosperity and enlightenment to the peoples of India. The British regime sought to uplift and educate, rooting out customs such as the isolation of upper-class women from men (purdah) and the suicidal burning of widows on their deceased husbands' funeral pyres (suttee). In time, the British hoped, all aspects of life, from administrative practices to religion to social roles, would be transformed by their benevolent rule.

Rapidly, however, the British liberals recognized that to introduce their own ideas of culture and standards of hygiene in India, they would have to oppose the popular will. They justified these measures as "for the Indians," though not "through them." In the words of the English liberal John Stuart Mill, "Despotism is a legitimate mode of government in dealing with barbarians, provided the end be their improvement." But when Indians wished to retain traditional ways and their own cultural values, the British denigrated them as backward and ignorant. Some British administrators were disillusioned by the perceived lack of interest in the Indian community for "self-betterment."

Even those Indians who embraced British education, values, and the English language discovered that they were not accepted as equals by most Europeans. The group most receptive to British culture, the middle-class Bengali babus, were mocked as being effeminate and incapable of independent action. The word *babu*, which in Bengali denoted a respected educated figure, when used by the British meant a half-educated, slavish, and rather contemptible figure who was neither British nor Indian and neither man nor woman. The **gendering** of British colonialism differentiated sharply between the manly "martial races" such as the Sikhs and the "effeminate" Bengalis. Predictably, imperialists equated manliness with strength, goodness, and progress, while so-called effeminate tendencies bore a negative connotation of corruption, weakness, and backwardness. The British ascribed to themselves manly virtues such as bravery, decisiveness, and energy. The Indian masses, in contrast, were denigrated as passive, backward, and unambitious.

British rule did have some positive aspects for Indians. It united the subcontinent as never before. The educational system, while still leaving most Indians illiterate, made significant strides in creating an educated Indian elite—the very class that would be instrumental in challenging and ending British rule in the twentieth century. By 1857 there were five universities in India, and increasing numbers of young Indians entered the civil service. In 1900, Calcutta University, with eight thousand students, was the largest university in the world. Even earlier, privileged Indians had begun to attend elite British universities. In 1888, **Mohandas Gandhi,** who would lead India's independence movement and preach nonviolent resistance to colonialism, left India to study law in London.

The English language provided a common means of communication for educated Indians, who spoke hundreds of different native languages. As this new middle class of Indians developed, they could not help contrasting the liberal British ideals of democracy and equal rights with their own situation. The most talented Indians, even if trained at Oxford, could not reach the highest levels in the colonial bureaucracy or in private British firms. Nor could native Indians join exclusive British associations like the Bengal Club. The resentment and frustration of the educated Indian middle class fueled demands for an end to British colonial rule that would come in the twentieth century. Economically, British rule in India brought mixed results. One was a **deindustrializing** of the subcontinent, even as railroads and telegraph lines were built. British manufacturers, particularly of cheap British cloth, put native industries out of

gendering   Considering certain peoples or activities intrinsically linked with the male or female gender, in the latter case often with a negative connotation.

Mohandas Gandhi   (1869–1948) Indian political and spiritual leader who fought for Indian independence and emphasized nonviolent struggle.

deindustrialization   Process of reducing the level of industry in a country, generally in colonized regions, especially India.

business. On the other hand, British rule connected India to the world economy.

Imperialism and the Muslim World

↓ Where did Muslims come under colonial rule in the late nineteenth century?

↓ In what ways did the Russian and Ottoman Empires confront imperialism differently?

The Muslim world also felt the impact of the new imperialism, and not only in India. As Russia expanded its influence in southeastern Europe (the Balkans) and beyond the Caucasus Mountains on its southern border, hundreds of thousands of Muslims were affected. Nor could the Ottoman Empire, the only major Muslim state in the world at this time, defend itself from European imperialists. In northern Africa, southeast Europe, and elsewhere, Ottoman influence was replaced by European influence. At the very end of the nineteenth century, a new challenge to the Muslim world arose—the Zionist movement, which called on Jews to return to their ancestral homeland, Palestine, at the time an Ottoman province. European successes called forth new movements among Muslims that aimed for new forms of modern, nationalist, and democratic politics.

Russian Expansion

After the British in India, Russians had more contact with Muslims than any other Europeans. From the sixteenth century onward, the tsar had counted among his subjects Tartars and other Muslim peoples. As Russia expanded, a variety of religious and national groups came under Russian rule, including many Muslims. By 1700, Russia had extended its dominion over thinly populated Siberia all the way to the Pacific. A century and a half later, Russian control stretched across the Bering Strait, over Alaska, and down the American west coast as far south as present-day California. Amid the Great Reforms of the mid-1860s, however, Russia abandoned its American territories, selling Alaska to the United States in 1867. Russian expansion would now take place not in the New World but in the heart of the old: **Central Asia.**

The boundary between "southern Siberia" and "Central Asia" is fluid, and Russian settlers had been moving gradually into what is now Kazakhstan at least from around 1800. In the second half of the nineteenth century, however, the Russian Empire—already the largest on earth—took over vast territories in

Central Asia. Like the European colonial powers in Africa, the Russians did not set out to control this region. They did not intend to settle Russians in Central Asia, only to prevent any other power from gaining a foothold there. In this respect, Russian expansion into Central Asia followed a common colonial pattern.

In 1865, Tashkent fell to the Russians, followed later in the decade by the khanates of Bukhara and Khiva. The ruling **khans** remained in place but now formally recognized the tsar's authority. In the 1870s, Russian troops engaged in military action against the warlike Turkmen who dominated the territory to the east of the Caspian Sea, establishing Russian control there by the end of the decade. Thus, by 1887 the conquest of **Turkestan** (the contemporary Russian term for Central Asia) was completed and Russian rule extended to the borders of Persia and Afghanistan. The Russian advance did not go unnoticed by other western powers. In particular, the British were deeply concerned about the possibility of Russian influence in Central Asia and how it might affect British rule over India. These fears were rather exaggerated: the Russians had neither the intention nor the means of threatening the British colony. In the end, Afghanistan remained as a buffer between Russian and British **spheres of influences,** and in the early twentieth century Persia was partitioned between a northern Russian zone and a southern British zone.

Russia's new possessions in Central Asia did little to enhance the Russian economy, despite some cotton exports. The Russians did build railroads and extend telegraph lines to the new territory in the interests of more efficient administration. On the whole, however, few Russian merchants appeared in these new lands, and local economies experienced little change. The costs of administering these regions far exceeded any new tax revenues.

These territories were dominated by Muslim culture and populated by peoples speaking **Turkic** languages (as well as Tadjik, which is related to Persian). Persian

Central Asia Geographical area including present-day states of Kazakhstan, Tajikistan, Uzbekistan, Kyrgyzstan, and Turkmenistan.

khan (in Turkic, "lord" or "ruler") Term used to describe Islamic rulers in Central Asia.

Turkestan (in Turkic, "Turk-land") Central Asian region inhabited by Turkic peoples.

sphere of influence Region over which a state exerts indirect political power, usually to prevent another state from extending its influence there.

Turkic Designation for a number of related languages such as Tartar, Uzbek, Kyrgyz, Turkmen, and Kazakh.

Vasily Vereshchagin's artistic works often showed scenes from regions in Central Asia that had recently been incorporated into the Russian Empire. This 1869 painting of the exquisite tomb in Samarkand of Timur or Tamerlaine, the Mongol conquerer who died in 1405, combined exoticism with a deep interest and respect for Central Asian culture. *(Tretyakov Gallery, Russia/The Bridgeman Art Library)*

and Arabic remained the most powerful languages in written culture; local languages were spoken but rarely written. The Russian rulers and settlers did not make serious attempts to russify or convert local populations. Like the British in India, they tended to live apart from native peoples and to return to Russia once their service was completed.

Central Asia exerted a powerful influence on Russian artists and ethnographers, many of whom visited the newly conquered lands to study the peoples and the architectural monuments there. The popular artist **Vasily Vereshchagin,** for example, resided for a time in Tashkent and produced many drawings and paintings on Central Asian themes. The region was

also hailed by Russian nationalists. "Asia will prove the outlet for our future destiny," proclaimed the popular novelist Fyodor Dostoevsky. But well into the twentieth century, Central Asia remained impoverished, remote, and, aside from a few large cities, largely untouched by Russian or other western influences.

Nevertheless, Orthodox missionaries increased their activity in Central Asia following the sale of

Vasily Vereshchagin　(1842–1904) Russian realist painter, best known for his paintings of exotic Central Asia scenes.

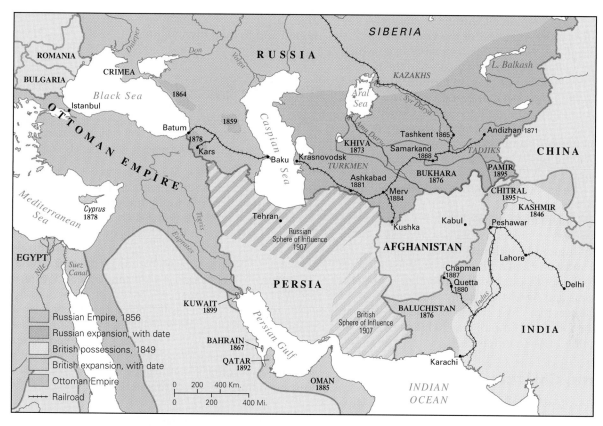

MAP 24.3   Central Asia The Russian Empire extended its borders southward from the 1860s to include most of Central Asia. By the late nineteenth century, the Russian Empire extended to border Afghanistan on the south, causing great concern among British officials in India.

Alaska to the United States. They had had some success in Alaska, as the prevalence of Orthodoxy among today's Alaska Natives indicates. But efforts by the government to convert Muslims, mainly Tartars living along the Volga River, had not worked. Few missionaries ventured out into the harsh and sparsely populated regions of Siberia. Those who did, however, did not attempt to convert the native populations directly. Instead, they established schools, where they taught in non-Russian languages as a first step toward "civilizing" native peoples. Only a few such schools were set up, however, and in the late 1860s the governor-general of Turkestan, Konstantin Kaufman, banned missionary activity in this huge, newly conquered Russian colony. Instead of gaining converts, Russian rule in Central Asia indirectly encouraged a movement for modern Islamic education known as **Jadidism.** As in colonized areas elsewhere in the world, the Russian presence in Central Asia ended up provoking the development of local nationalisms aimed against the imperial power.

The Ottoman Empire

In the nineteenth century, Muslims around the world looked to the Ottoman Empire as the religious and political center for their religion. The sultan held the title of Caliph, the spiritual head of all Muslims. Even more important, the holy cities of Mecca, Medina, and Jerusalem were all located in Ottoman territory. Thus, the decline of Ottoman political power and loss of Ottoman territory were of concern to all Muslims.

In 1800, the richest and most populous lands of the Ottoman Empire were located in Europe, on the Balkan Peninsula. By midcentury, Ottoman influence over these lands had been considerably reduced, though the officially Romanian, Greek, Serbian, and

Jadidism (from Arabic, "new method") Movement attempting to reconcile Islam with modernity, especially in the Russian Empire from the 1870s.

Bulgarian regions remained within the empire. A key event showing the weakness of the Ottoman Empire was the Crimean War, fought ostensibly over which European power—Russia or France—had the right to protect Christians in the Ottoman Empire. Russia lost the war, but the very fact that European powers could demand—and get—the right to protect Christian Ottoman subjects showed the empire's weakness. The sultan could not, of course, offer similar protection to Muslims living under colonial rule in Egypt, French Algeria, or Russian Central Asia.

During the era of new imperialism, Ottoman influence was further reduced. The creation or expansion of Greek, Romanian, Serbian, and Bulgarian states in the Balkans was accompanied by the migration—often forced—of hundreds of thousands of Muslims to the Ottoman interior. Similarly, as Russia expanded its borders to the south, establishing control over present-day Armenia and Azerbaijan, many Muslims preferred to flee rather than live under the new Christian rulers. The Ottoman Empire was helpless to oppose the widening Russian influence.

Muslims, Christians, and Zionists

Another challenge to the Ottoman Empire and Muslim world was the new Jewish nationalist movement, Zionism. This movement, led by Theodor Herzl, aimed at the establishment of a Jewish state in ancient Palestine, or what Jews called Eretz Israel, centered on Jerusalem. In the 1890s, this region was under Ottoman rule, and although numerous Jews and Christians lived there, the majority of the population (except in Jerusalem) was Muslim. The first Zionist settlers arrived in Palestine in the 1880s, and after that, large groups of Zionist pioneers came from Europe to establish Jewish settlements in this Ottoman province.

Initially, neither local Muslims nor the Ottoman authorities were concerned about the Zionists. After all, their numbers were small—around twenty thousand by 1903—and Jews had long lived in the region, even constituting the majority in Jerusalem. Still, the Ottoman sultan refused to grant the Zionist leader Herzl a charter officially sanctioning Zionist settlement, preferring to allow or forbid such activity on a case-by-case basis.

In the early twentieth century, **Arab nationalism** was beginning to take form. At first, however, this movement was primarily anti-Ottoman, wishing to foster an Arab identity based primarily on language and culture and only secondarily on the Muslim religion shared with the Turks. Not until the second decade of the twentieth century would Arab nationalists begin to see Zionism as a serious threat to the region and to their own identity.

The Far East

> ↓ How did economic and administrative practices differ in Asia and Africa, and between different colonial powers?
> ↓ How did Japan and China react to the threat of European imperialism?

In East Asia or, to use an imperialist term, the Far East (far, of course, from Europe), imperialism also had a major impact. Some regions, such as Indochina and Indonesia, were controlled directly by European powers. But even in the two large East Asian countries that were not directly colonized, Japan and China, European influence had a profound effect. Western ideas as diverse as constitutionalism and Christianity entered these societies, influencing some Asians in a positive way while calling forth resentment and resistance from others. Both the violent and failed Boxer Rebellion in China and the peaceful reform of Japan's military and political institutions reflect the power of European imperialism of this period.

The French in Indochina

While the French had long held colonial outposts in Asia, including India, French expansion into Southeast Asia dated from the 1850s. French missionaries in the region caused friction with local rulers, whose anti-Christian measures induced the French emperor Napoleon III to intervene. A treaty of 1862 forced local rulers in **Indochina** (today Vietnam, Cambodia, and Laos) to concede religious toleration for Christians. The treaty gave France a foothold in the southern part of what is now Vietnam, including the city of Saigon, and in 1867 France annexed this territory, known as Cochinchina. From there the French extended direct rule into most of present-day Cambodia and Laos to protect Catholic missions, establish naval bases, and defend French commercial interests in China. Emperor Napoleon III's foreign policy was explicitly imperialist, as he sought to enhance French prestige in the world.

Arab nationalism   Movement beginning in late nineteenth century declaring that all Arabs constitute one nation and should be liberated from foreign rule.

Indochina   Region in Southeast Asia under French colonial rule in the later nineteenth century, today Vietnam, Laos, and Cambodia.

This French board game, based on Jules Verne's novel *Around the World in Eighty Days,* emphasized the exotic territories now colonized by European powers like France. (*Archives Charmet/The Bridgeman Art Library*)

Economically, the most important product of Indochina was raw silk, but reports of rich mineral wealth in the hills of Vietnam also lured French investors and adventurers. A small group of French settlers derived profit from plantations that produced rubber and teak wood. On the whole, however, French taxpayers paid a heavy price for France's colonial ventures. Few Frenchmen were interested in settling in the new colony, though many hundreds served there in administrative and military roles. The French also set up schools where, by the end of the century, young Vietnamese, Laotians, and Cambodians were learning to read and write French from the same textbooks used in Paris. Among the students were future leaders of Indochinese liberation movements, including **Ho Chi Minh.**

In India, higher British administrators brought their wives and raised their families, but French administrators in Indochina generally did not, often taking wives and mistresses from the local population. So-called native wives and their offspring did not receive equal political protection. Very often, at the end of their tour of duty, the men simply returned to Europe, abandoning their local wives and children.

In contrast to the British colonies, which were often ruled using already-existing political structures and local rulers, the French had a more ambitious agenda. At least initially, they hoped to assimilate their colonial subjects and to make them into genuine Frenchmen.

Soon, however, the realities of colonial administration, the difficulties in financing an adequate school system, and resistance from native peoples considerably interfered with this aim. Moreover, racial and nationalist prejudices made the French unwilling to allow native peoples in Indochina the same legal rights and financial advantages enjoyed by French colonists and officials.

The Dutch in Indonesia

The Dutch had been active in Southeast Asia since the sixteenth century, when Dutch explorers had opened the way for the spice trade that had been a great source of Dutch wealth. Like the British in India, the Dutch managed trading posts and spice warehouses through a trading company—the Dutch West India Company—but did not exercise direct rule over the region that is today Indonesia. In contrast to the French, the Dutch were not interested in "civilizing" the native population, whose Islamic faith had been brought to the region centuries earlier by Arab

Ho Chi Minh (1890–1969) Vietnamese national leader who in Paris helped found the French Communist Party and later led the Vietnamese independence movement.

traders. The Dutch carried out little missionary activity and, on the whole, left existing native political and judicial structures and Muslim institutions in place. At no time did the Dutch attempt to influence the mainly Muslim Indonesian population to abandon their faith. Dutch schools for natives aimed primarily to train minor officials to serve in the local colonial bureaucracy.

Between 1830 and 1870, the Dutch West Indies produced huge profits for the Netherlands, but only by exploiting native labor and generating serious local discontent. After about 1870, Dutch trade with the Dutch West Indies declined. In contrast to Vietnam, where French influence may still be discerned a half century after the end of French colonial rule there, Dutch colonial control left few traces in Indonesia.

Concessions in China

China, the largest and most populous country in Asia, had long been a major cultural influence. By the mid-nineteenth century, however, under the corrupt and weak **Qing dynasty**, China could not compete against the military and economic might of the European imperialists. China's defeat in the 1840s by the British during the **Opium Wars** revealed its weakness. Subsequently, the Chinese accepted massive imports of opium from British India, enriching British merchants but weakening Chinese society.

Thus, began the era of **unequal treaties**. Western imperialist powers negotiated concessions at treaty ports that assured them favorable trade arrangements and a minimum of Chinese interference. As part of the concessions, the Chinese agreed that the imperialist power could administer its own tax system and legal system. The British took over Hong Kong and had a concession in the major city of Shanghai. The Germans received a concession in the port city of Qingdao (Tsingtao), establishing a beer factory that continues in operation today. The French also gained favored treatment in China. In many areas in China, foreign businessmen could trade without interference or taxation from the Chinese government. Concessions deprived the Chinese state of much-needed taxes, while westerners—and some well-placed Chinese businessmen—reaped huge profits.

China's political weakness was also apparent in foreign policy. Defeat in the Sino-Japanese War of 1894–1895 forced China to relinquish the island of Formosa (Taiwan) to Japan. In the early twentieth century, with Russian and Japanese power growing in northeast Asia, China lost its influence over Korea. A few years later, China bowed to Russian pressure, allowing the Russians to build a railroad across its

Manchurian province to the north and to establish nearby naval bases. By the early twentieth century, foreign influence in the form of concessions, naval bases, and trade privileges had compromised Chinese sovereignty.

Christian missionaries set up schools and health clinics throughout China, winning a significant number of converts. For ambitious Chinese parents, missionary schools provided some education for daughters and, for sons, a means to a higher education, usually abroad. Following this path, the future nationalist leader **Sun Yatsen** received a Christian education and then left China to attend medical school in Hawaii.

Despite the missionaries' sincere desire to educate and help the Chinese people, their teachings inevitably came into conflict with Chinese customs. For example, the ancestor worship so important for Chinese culture was seen by Christians as a form of idolatry. Christian missionaries also encouraged not only education for females but an end to female infanticide and the traditional practice of binding young girls' feet so they would be the desirable tiny size in adulthood. Foreign missionaries worked with their Chinese pupils and converts to translate western ideas into Chinese, but often without any understanding of the implications of western practices within Chinese society. Many Chinese thus feared and resented the spread of Christianity. In 1870, in Tianjin, these feelings exploded into attacks on foreigners. The so-called Tianjin Massacre did not, however, reduce missionary activity in China.

By the late nineteenth century, this enormous cultural and economic influence of foreigners had called forth a strong and violent reaction from Chinese patriots, the **Boxer Rebellion**. The Boxers were a group of young Chinese men who combined training in martial arts with a burning desire to free China from foreign domination, which they found humiliating. In

Qing dynasty   Ruling house of China from 1644 to 1912, also known as Manchus.

Opium Wars   Conflict between Britain and China from 1839 to 1842 that ended in Chinese defeat.

unequal treaties   Treaties favorable to western powers (and Japan) extorted by force or threat from China during the nineteenth and early twentieth centuries.

Sun Yatsen   (1866–1925) Chinese physician and political leader who aimed to transform China with patriotic, democratic, and economically progressive reforms.

Boxer Rebellion   Antiforeign revolt in China in 1898–1900.

In this Japanese print of the Meiji period (ca. 1860), traditionally dressed samurai set out in boats to confront Commodore Matthew Perry's looming "black ships." By signing a treaty in 1854 opening Japan to foreign trade, the Japanese reversed centuries of isolation and began a rapid process of industrialization and westernization in their country. *(Courtesy of the Trustees of the British Museum/The Art Archive)*

1900 the Boxers attacked foreign missionaries, businessmen, diplomats, Chinese converts to Christianity, and generally all forms of foreign influence. Their violence alarmed westerners, and the imperialist powers reacted swiftly to put down the rebellion. Thousands of German, French, American, British, Japanese, and Russian troops rushed to Beijing, where they ended a siege of foreign embassies. Order was restored, but the prestige of the Qing dynasty was fatally weakened. Young Chinese intellectuals increasingly called for limitations on foreign influences and the restoration of Chinese sovereignty throughout the entire territory of China.

The Westernization of Japan

Japan forms an exception to many generalizations about late-nineteenth-century imperialism. While Japanese history shows strong western influences in this period, the Japanese were successful in using western models to their own advantage and, in the end,

against the western powers themselves. For the previous two centuries, foreign entry into Japan had been limited to two small trading posts. Then, in 1853, the American commodore **Matthew Perry** arrived in Tokyo harbor and, after months of negotiation, forced the Japanese to open up to foreign trade in 1854.

The Japanese were shocked at the foreigners' command of new and unfamiliar technology, in particular modern firearms. Rather than falling under foreign rule, however, the Japanese under a new emperor known as Meiji ("the enlightened one") carried out their own administrative, military, and economic reforms. By the end of the century, Japan was rapidly industrializing. Railroads connected the most important Japanese cities, and the Japanese army had been

Matthew Perry (1794–1858) American naval officer who in 1854 persuaded the Japanese government to allow American trade with previously closed-off Japan.

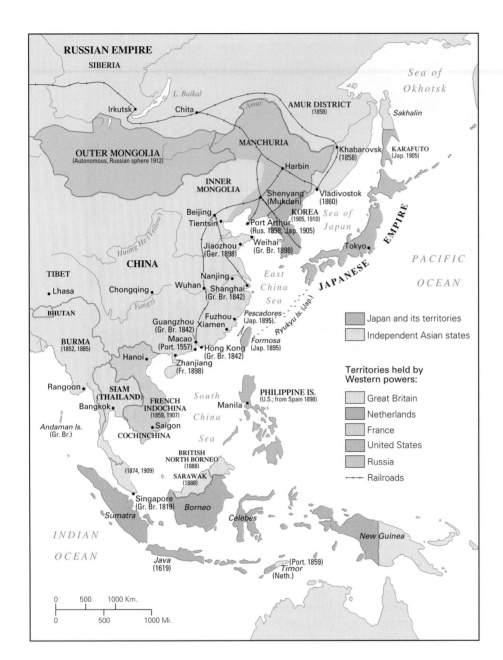

MAP 24.4   Asia in 1914 In 1914 one found both independent countries (Japan, China, Siam [Thailand]) and a number of European colonies (British, French, Dutch) in East Asia. Japan had also extended its rule over Korea to the north and Taiwan to the south.

reconstituted along Prussian lines. The success of the **Meiji Restoration** may be seen in the Japanese defeat of China in the Sino-Japanese War.

Japanese influence in Korea led inevitably to frictions with Russia, which was also seeking to expand its power in East Asia. Beginning in the 1890s, construction of the Trans-Siberian Railroad, linking Moscow and the Pacific Ocean, was one means by which Russia hoped to promote its influence in Siberia and even settlement of the region. The railroad's terminus at Vladivostok was just a few hundred miles from Japan

and even closer to Korea. Russia obtained the right to build the railroad directly across the northeastern Chinese province of Manchuria, to Japan's considerable annoyance. The Chinese also allowed the Russians to build a naval base on Chinese territory at Port Arthur (now Lüshun), to the south of Korea,

Meiji Restoration Reform of Japanese politics and economy under Emperor Meiji (r. 1867–1912).

which Japan could only see as a direct threat. Fearing further Russian inroads into China and Korea, in 1904 Japan carried out a surprise attack on the Russian base at Port Arthur.

The **Russo-Japanese War** that ensued turned out to be an international and domestic disaster for Russia. To the shock of not only Russians, but all Europeans, the Japanese prevailed on the seas—destroying two Russia fleet and on land. For the first time in centuries, a European power was defeated by an Asian country. The success of Japan's modernization was evident in its army trained on the Prussian model and its navy of western-style warships. The American president Theodore Roosevelt helped negotiate a peace between Japan and Russia, which ended the war in 1905. The Japanese used their victory to extend their power in the region, and in 1910 they formally annexed Korea.

In Russia, the war caused a crisis, the **Russian Revolution of 1905.** When marchers who had peacefully gathered outside the Winter Palace in St. Petersburg were brutally dispersed, causing dozens of deaths, the country exploded into violent protest and strikes. **Tsar Nicholas II** seemed completely out of touch—unable to influence events and unwilling to compromise with widespread demands for political reform. General strikes that paralyzed the country in October forced him to reduce censorship, increase religious freedom, and grant a parliament, the Duma. While limited in its powers, the Duma provided a place for political debate until 1917.

Consequences and Critics

> ↓ What impact did imperialism have on the global economy and European culture?
> ↓ Who opposed imperialism in Europe and elsewhere, and why?

Even as the new imperialism extended European influence throughout the world, it also called forth resistance and condemnation. Its benefits were greatly unequal, as western powers profited while colonized regions did not. Ironically, the western ideals of liberty and democracy that the imperial powers boasted they were bringing to the unenlightened peoples of the world inspired anticolonial movements among African and Asian intellectuals. But critics in Europe, too, argued that imperialism was a capitalist sham, an attempt to divert attention from injustice and inequality at home. In both negative and positive ways, imperialism had a profound effect on European politics and culture.

A Global Economy

In the late nineteenth century, European colonial empires did much to link up the world and to create a single global economy. But the linkage was uneven. Raw materials like cotton flowed from the colonies to Europe, and European goods like cloth were purchased by the colonies. British textiles were exported to Africa and India. The Indian railways used rails and locomotives that for the most part were imported from England. Textiles from Russia found a market in Central and East Asia. Because the European colonizers had little interest in developing colonial industry, the colonies became economically dependent on European industry. In some cases, colonies deindustrialized. So as profits flowed to Europe, wages and living standards remained very low in nearly all colonial areas.

In addition, colonial economies were reshaped to meet the needs and desires of western imperialist powers. Tea, sugar, and chocolate had become staples in the European diet; in this era even Russian peasants began to drink tea daily. The plantations that produced these commodities expanded, and the economies of entire colonies and tropical nations were built around a single export. Bananas, which began to appear on tables in North America and Europe, are only the most prominent example. The companies that managed these commodities were western; the laborers were native peoples. Again, the profits flowed to Europe.

Now guano from Peru and nitrites from Chile enriched the fields of European farmers. Rubber for tires, belts, and gaskets, indispensable for modern machinery, had to be extracted from trees that grew only in tropical regions such as Malaya (a British colony, now Malaysia), Indochina, and the Belgian Congo. Palm oil, another tropical commodity, was used in the manufacture of soap—a product then exported back to the colonies. Cinchona trees were also cultivated to provide the quinine on which the health of Europeans in tropical regions depended. Copper was imported from mines in the Belgian Congo; tin

Russo-Japanese War Conflict in 1904–1905 that began with a Japanese surprise attack on a Russian naval base and ended in Russian defeat.

Russian Revolution of 1905 Insurrection in Russia set off by military defeats in the Russo-Japanese War that forced political concessions from Tsar Nicholas II.

Tsar Nicholas II (r. 1894–1918) Russian emperor and cousin by marriage of Kaiser William II, killed by the Bolsheviks in 1918, after the Russian Revolution.

came from Malaya. Huge amounts of Indian cotton were imported to be transformed into cloth in British mills. Diamonds and gold from South African mines adorned wealthy Europeans.

New inventions and technological innovations facilitated global exchange. Starting in the late 1870s, for example, refrigerated steamships carried frozen meat from the United States, Argentina, and even New Zealand to the ports of Europe, pushing out less efficient meat producers. But on the whole, European economies were not challenged by colonial economies. Colonial markets were relatively small compared to European markets, and Europeans sold far more manufactured goods to each other and in the Americas than they did to their colonies. Europeans did invest in colonies, however. Global links were economic; they were only partly the result of direct colonial rule.

Indigenous Resistance

As the Sepoy Rebellion and the Boxer Rebellion indicate, colonized peoples in Asia did not simply accept European colonial domination. In the Battle of **Omdurman,** too, Africans fought against European colonizers. But native troops, armed with traditional weapons, were massacred there by British troops using machine guns and other modern weapons. European technological superiority meant that native peoples needed to seek other means of resistance.

After European colonies had been established, the colonized had to struggle for their rights within the existing colonial system. Some resistance assumed a heroic public form, such as Gandhi's organizing of Indian residents in South Africa to demand their rights in the 1890s. Other resistance was more subtle. Indigenous peoples might refuse to carry out the orders of colonial administrators, avoid paying colonial taxes, or shun European cultural and educational institutions. Some resisters insisted on wearing native clothing, despite imports from Europe, or on speaking native languages, despite schools that taught English or French.

The education that colonized peoples received at colonial schools proved to provide them with the most effective weapon of resistance. Learning of European constitutional government and political rights, native peoples came to challenge the racial hierarchies evident in the colonies. Pointing out the contradictions of a system that promised civilization and justice but refused equal rights to native peoples, resistance leaders exposed the hypocrisy of imperialism and demanded rights for themselves and their peoples. To the European imperialists they quoted European thinkers and ideals such as liberty, democracy, and individual

rights. They pointed to the vast contrast between the luxury in which colonial officials lived and the impoverishment of natives.

Before 1914, however, resistance to imperialism was only beginning to be organized. In most African and Asian colonies, European administrators continued to dominate, at least officially. Away from cities and European settlements, however, life generally continued along traditional lines. At the same time, increasing numbers of educated Asians and Africans were formulating ways of resisting European dominance. Full-fledged independence movements would emerge in the middle decades of the twentieth century.

Imperialism and European Culture

Though the dominators, not the dominated, Europeans were affected by the lands they ruled. Literature, music, visual arts, architecture, and even advertising took up themes and images of imperialism. Popular novels praised the bravery of the colonists while hinting at forbidden romantic attachments. Painters produced scenes of entrancing foreign places, often featuring ruins, exotic vegetation, and—of course—beautiful native women. In music, the most "imperial opera," *Aïda*, by Giuseppe Verdi, was commissioned specifically for the opening of the Suez Canal in 1869. The story hinges on a beautiful Ethiopian slave, Aïda, and her love for an Egyptian general in the era of the pharaohs. The opera was a hit: apparently few minded the absurdity of a made-up story about ancient Africans sung in Italian for the benefit of European audiences.

Literature of the late nineteenth and early twentieth centuries reflects imperialist themes. Kipling's many stories and novels about life in British India were bestsellers of the day. The poet Alfred, Lord Tennyson celebrated the empire in verses such as "The Fleet" (1885) and "On the Jubilee of Queen Victoria" (1887). In France, **Pierre Loti** published dozens of novels that reflect the European fascination with the peoples and customs of the colonies. Set in exotic regions, they nearly always involve a romance between a strong European man and a beautiful non-European woman. The plots are unrealistic, but Loti's novels were very

Omdurman Battle in 1898 in present-day Sudan, in which thousands of African warriors were massacred by a British army using machine guns.

Pierre Loti (1850–1923) French writer who authored novels set in exotic climes and featuring romances between a European man and a non-European woman.

Jean-Léon Gérôme's *The Snake Charmer* (1883) reveals an imperialist gaze, combining exoticism, titillation, and the suggestion of sexual decadence. In this scene from Central Asia, a naked boy with a tame snake dances for bearded elders. *(© Sterling and Francine Clark, Art Institute, Williamstown, Massachusetts)*

popular, and in 1891 he was elected to the **French Academy,** the prestigious scholarly and literary society, at the unprecedented young age of forty-one.

International exhibitions in Paris in 1867 and 1900 also reflect European fascination with the colonies. Here Parisians and visitors could "experience" an African village, listen to Tunisian musicians, or wander through a reproduction of a Cairo street. These exhibitions aimed both to educate the populace about the colonies and to promote European superiority. Ethnographic museums served similar purposes. In Paris at the Museum of the Colonies, and in museums in Moscow and St. Petersburg, colonial peoples themselves were put on display. The purpose was always to demonstrate the "savage" ways of "the uncivilized" and to reassure Europeans of their superiority.

The interests of imperialism were evident in the visual arts as well. In Russia the painter Vereshchagin depicted the land and peoples of Russia's newly conquered territory in Central Asia. After French stockbroker **Paul Gauguin** abandoned his family and went to live in Tahiti, he painted Tahitians in their own environment. Popular postcards and prints familiarized Europeans with far-off colonies and spurred interest in the colonial endeavor. Images in advertising, too, drew on imperialist themes. In Britain advertisements extolled Pear's Soap as one of the benefits that Britons could bring to Africa and Asia.

French Academy   French cultural institution established in 1635 whose members make judgments on the proper use of the French language.

Paul Gauguin   (1848–1903) French painter who painted Tahitian life and culture.

Many of Paul Gauguin's paintings from Tahiti, like *Arearea* (1892), depict beautiful Tahitian women in an exotic tropical landscape. Gauguin's own biography—abandoning a respectable middle-class profession and leaving his family to pursue pleasure and painting in the South Seas—reflects the lure colonial regions had for nineteenth-century Europeans. Gauguin rejected photographic realism; his bold colors and broad brushstrokes were influenced by Tahitian models. *(Musée d'Orsay, Paris/Giraudon/The Bridgeman Art Library)*

Capitalism and Imperialism

The heyday of imperialism lasted barely two decades, ending with the Boer War. While no crisis of European imperialism was obvious in the first decade of the twentieth century, the arguments of the anti-imperialists were already being developed. The first critiques concentrated on its cruelty toward subject populations. Later these were overshadowed by Marxist critics who portrayed imperialism as part of a decaying capitalist world order.

In 1902, **John A. Hobson** argued in *Imperialism: A Study* that Britain's imperial expansion was a short-

term attempt to avoid social conflict. British workers at first benefited from the cheap produce and labor of the colonies, but Hobson predicted that soon their position would be undermined by this vast pool of cheap labor. Hobson saw a major cause for imperialism in the search for markets and investment opportunities abroad. For him, imperialism was both hypocritical and dangerous. Imperialists falsely claimed to be

John A. Hobson (1858–1940) English economist and influential critic of imperialism.

bringing higher culture to subject peoples, and Britain's nondemocratic rule over the colonies posed a threat to democracy at home. By placing colonial peoples at the very bottom of the social hierarchy, Hobson claimed, imperialism falsely elevated the status of England's working class.

Some of Hobson's arguments were taken up a bit more than a decade later by the Russian Marxist **Vladimir Ilyich Lenin.** Lenin's *Imperialism: The Highest Stage of Capitalism* (1916) portrayed imperialism as a symptom of a larger ill: capitalism. Thus, when capitalism would be overthrown by socialism, imperialism would also be destroyed. Following Karl Marx, Lenin pointed out that since the early years of industrializa-tion, profit levels had declined steadily. Capitalists were thus forced to seek new and more lucrative investment opportunities outside Europe. Although in retrospect it is evident that colonial markets and investment were of secondary importance even in the heyday of imperialism, Lenin's exposure of imperialism as an economic, political, and moral dead end seemed convincing to many contemporary Europeans.

Vladimir Ilyich Lenin   (1870–1924) Russian Marxist revolutionary and leader of the Bolsheviks.

Summary

Review Questions

↑ What were the major causes of the new imperialism?

↑ How did colonial rule work, and how did colonized peoples resist?

↑ How did imperialism influence European identity in politics, culture, and everyday life?

In the decades before World War I, European countries established direct colonial rule over huge parts of the globe. Nearly the entire continent of Africa was divided up among the European powers. In Asia, merchants and administrators from Britain, France, Germany, the Netherlands, and Russia established new colonies or strengthened existing colonial control. The imperialism of this period differs from earlier European colonialism. First, few Europeans moved permanently to these new colonies of the late nineteenth century. While millions left Europe during these years, most chose a new life in the Americas or Australia, not in the Congo or India. Second, the scale of imperial rule was quite different from that in earlier periods. The colonial powers came to rule over millions of non-Europeans, accepting their status as both a duty and an opportunity. Third, technological advances reduced practical constraints. Steamships radically reduced transit time between Europe and all corners of the globe. Telegraph lines and undersea cables allowed officials in London and Paris to communicate almost instantly with their colonies in Africa and Asia. The use of quinine to prevent malaria and advances in bacteriology and tropical medicine permitted Europeans to venture into tropical regions where earlier they would have been struck down by disease.

Imperialism was propelled by feelings of European superiority, including the false idea that the Caucasian race (a term invented in this period) was superior to other races. Whether they consciously believed these ideas or not, most Europeans accepted their role as "big brother" or "parent" over the "childlike" colonized peoples. This paternalist attitude, combined with the ignorance of Europeans about African and Asian cultures, created resentment and animosity. Imperialism also spread European culture, languages, democratic values, and the Christian religion.

The new imperialism transformed the world in ways that remain controversial. The brutality of European imperialists produced horrors that devastated native populations and shocked the European public. While many European businessmen and missionaries sincerely desired to improve the lives of Africans and Asians, others were more interested in profits or adventure. At the same time, the medical advances and schools that Europeans brought with them had some positive effects. Ideas of political liberalism, democracy, and industrial development also arrived with the imperialists. African, Australian, and Asian peoples were incorporated more fully into world culture, though their own cultures, religions, and languages suffered as a consequence.

Imperialists claimed to improve conditions in the colonies, making them and their populations more like the European homeland. But their undemocratic rule and failure to create balanced economies made it impossible to re-create the European experience in a faraway land. Rather, imperialist regimes created divided and racially stratified societies that lacked experience in self-governance and suffered from economic underdevelopment. In the early twenty-first century, the legacies of these problems remain.

← **Thinking Back, Thinking Ahead** →

What present-day conflicts find their roots in the new imperialism of the late nineteenth century?

ECHO ECHO ECHO ECHO ECHO

Imperialism and the English Language

In the early twentieth-first century, more than 500 million people around the world speak English. Some two-thirds of them are native speakers; the rest learned English as a foreign language. While more people speak Mandarin (Chinese), Hindi, and even Spanish as a native language, no other language in the world can compete with English as a language of international communication. Not only do Americans, Canadians, Englishmen, and Australians speak English—of differing varieties—among themselves, but English serves as the principal language of communication between different ethnic and linguistic groups in places as diverse as Jamaica, Nigeria, and India. And, as any traveler to Helsinki, Tokyo, Tel Aviv, Singapore, or any large city anywhere in the world can attest, an English-speaker is seldom far away. This dominance of English is a product of imperialism.

Early British settlers in North America, South Africa, and Australia took their native tongue with them and taught it—sometimes forcibly—to other immigrants and to native peoples. In the late nineteenth century, English businessmen and administrators spread English in Africa and Asia. From Burma to Botswana, as people living under British imperial rule went to English-language schools, English became their means of communication.

In many of these areas, hybrid languages developed, called Pidgin English in Nigeria, India, and the Caribbean. And English absorbed new words. As the largest British colony, India contributed perhaps the largest number, including, for example, *loot, punch, bungalow, thug,* and *pajama*. From Chinese came *tycoon* and *kow-tow*. From Arabic, old entries into English such as *alcohol* and *algebra* were joined by new words like *assassin* (a hashish-smoking bandit). The parting words *So long* are a mangling of the greeting *Salaam* ("peace"), brought home by British soldiers serving in Muslim Malaya.

Today, almost everywhere, a good knowledge of English is considered vital for a successful career. In the former Soviet Union, where Russian used to be the main second language, young Lithuanians, Estonians, and Kazakhs are now more likely to speak English. The Internet and global marketing have contributed to the dominance of English, as terms like *XXL* (meaning "very big"), *McDrive* (attached to European McDonald's restaurants) indicate. Russians recognize such brand names as Uncle Ben's and Snickers, and everywhere pilots and air traffic controllers communicate in English. For all its illogic, absurd spellings, and complex verb system, it seems likely that English dominance in international diplomacy, trade, and culture is here to stay.

Suggested Readings

Fieldhouse, D. K. *The Colonial Empires: A Comparative Study from the Eighteenth Century.* New York: Delacorte Press, 1967. An excellent overall introduction.

Headrick, Daniel R. *The Tools of Empire.* New York: Oxford University Press, 1981. An examination of links between technology and imperialism.

Hochschild, Adam. *King Leopold's Ghost.* Boston: Houghton Mifflin, 1999. A page-turning account of Leopold of Belgium's Congo colony and the journalists who exposed its horrific brutalities.

Metcalf, Thomas R. *Ideologies of the Raj.* New York: Cambridge University Press, 1997. A concise and well-written introduction to British India.

Mommsen, Wolfgang. *Theories of Imperialism.* Chicago: University of Chicago Press, 1982. An investigation of the "why" of imperialism.

Poliakov, Leon. *The Aryan Myth: A History of Racist and Nationalist Ideas in Europe.* New York: Basic Books, 1974. An examination of the racism that often accompanied imperialism.

Sinha, Mrinalini. *Colonial Masculinity.* Manchester, England: Manchester University Press, 1995. A study of gendering in British imperialism in India.

Websites

Maps, pictures, biographies, discussion room focusing on the British Empire, **The British Empire,** at www.britishempire.co.uk

Information about Cecil J. Rhodes, Rhodes Scholarships, and Indian Rhodes Scholars, **Rhodes Scholarships India,** at www.rhodesindia.com

Sources and information about Islamic history, including imperialism, **Internet Islamic Sourcebook,** at http://www.fordham.edu/halsall/islam/islamsbook.html

CHAPTER 25

War and Revolution, 1900–1918

CHAPTER OUTLINE

1500 B.C.E.	1000 B.C.E.	500 B.C.E.	1 B.C.E./1 C.E.

1905
Tsar Nicholas II
crushes revolt
in Russia

1908
Austria-Hungary
annexes
Bosnia-Herzegovina

1902	1904	1906	1908	1910

Europe in World War I, 1914–1918

The First World War divided Europe into two warring camps. Only the edges of the continent—Ireland, Scandinavia, and the Iberian Peninsula—were not affected. What differences can you see on this map between the war's progress on the Eastern and Western fronts? Where was Germany most successful?

Legend:
- Triple Entente and its Allies
- Central Powers
- Neutral nations
- Farthest German-Austrian advance
- ✕ Major battle
- Battle lines

FINLAND

NORWAY

SWEDEN

Helsinki

Petrograd (St. Petersburg)

ESTONIA

LATVIA

Moscow

COURLAND

Riga

British blockade line

Jutland 1916

DENMARK

North Sea

Baltic Sea

LITHUANIA

Wilno (Vilnius)

Treaty of Brest-Litovsk, March 1918

IRELAND

GREAT BRITAIN

London

Kiel

NETHERLANDS

GERMANY

Berlin

Farthest Russian Advance, 1914

Masurian Lakes 1914

E. P RUSSIA

Tannenberg 1914

Warsaw

KINGDOM OF POLAND (Russia)

Brest-Litovsk

BELARUS

RUSSIA

Kiev

Armistice line, December 1917

Don

ATLANTIC OCEAN

Louvain

BELGIUM

LUXEMBOURG

Paris

Seine

ALSACE-LORRAINE

Western Front

FRANCE

Loire

Munich

Bern

SWITZERLAND

Rhine

AUG. 1917

MAR. 1918

Caporetto 1917

Italian Front

Po

Vienna

AUSTRIA-HUNGARY

Budapest

MAY 1915

Dniester

GALICIA

Dnieper

UKRAINE

Garonne

Ebro

SPAIN

Corsica

Elba

ITALY

Rome

Adriatic Sea

MONTENEGRO

SERBIA

TRANSYLVANIA

ROMANIA

Bucharest

Danube

BULGARIA

Black Sea

Armenian massacre, 1915–1916

GILBRALTAR (Gr. Br.)

Baleric Is.

Sardinia

Sicily

ALBANIA

1917–1918

1916

1915

Balkan Front

GREECE

Dardanelles

Gallipoli 1915

Istanbul

OTTOMAN EMPIRE

MOROCCO (France)

ALGERIA (France)

Tunis

TUNISIA (France)

Malta

Mediterranean Sea

Crete

Cyprus

0 200 400 Km.
0 200 400 Mi.

| 500 C.E. | 1000 C.E. | 1500 C.E. | 2000 C.E. |

1912 First Balkan War begins

1914 Serbian nationalist assassinates archduke of Austria
World War I begins

1915 Italy joins the Allies

1916 Allies suffer 1 million casualties at the Battle of the Somme
Lenin publishes *Imperialism*

1917 Tsar Nicholas II abdicates
Bolsheviks seize power in Petrograd

1918 Germany imposes harsh peace on Russia
Germany signs armistice with Allies

1919 Allies impose harsh peace on Germany

| 1912 | 1914 | 1916 | 1918 | 1920 |

Choice Choice Choice

Vladimir Ilyich Lenin

Vladimir Ilyich Lenin changed the course of history in the early twentieth century. Without him, it is difficult to imagine the Bolshevik Revolution in Russia, the rise of the Soviet Union, and the spread of world communism. Love him or hate him, Lenin had an indisputable impact on his native land and the entire world when he chose to dedicate his life entirely to the fulfillment of the Marxist revolution. (Bettmann/Corbis)

Vladimir Ilyich Lenin Leads the Russian Revolution

When Vladimir Ilyich Ulyanov, better known by his pen name Lenin, was just seventeen, his older brother Alexander was executed for involvement in a plot to assassinate the Russian tsar. As a grown man and revolutionary, Lenin would oppose such terrorist tactics as ineffective for achieving revolutionary goals, but on a more profound level, his life was dedicated to showing that his brother had not died in vain.

As the brother of a convicted revolutionary, Lenin came to the attention of the educational authorities while he was in high school in Simbirsk, a provincial city on the Volga River. He was nearly expelled for reading banned literature. Later he studied law at Kazan and St. Petersburg Universities, though he never practiced as a lawyer. In his early twenties, Lenin was already known as *starik*—"the old man"—more for his serious dedication to the revolutionary cause than for his receding hairline.

All political parties were forbidden in Russia before 1905, and the tsarist secret police were especially vigilant in sniffing out socialist circles. In these circumstances, it was inevitable that Lenin would be arrested. In 1897, he was sentenced to three years in Siberia, where he continued his studies and writing despite his official status as a political exile. In 1890, he returned to European Russia and soon left for western Europe. He would live abroad continually, aside from a short visit to Russia in 1905, until the fateful year of 1917. Like Karl Marx, he spent his days in libraries, especially London's British Museum, where he read and wrote newspaper articles, commentaries, books, and letters. In his brochure *What Is to Be Done?* (1902) he sketched out his belief that only a small, dedicated revolutionary party could engineer the world revolution that would overthrow capitalism. Whereas other socialists of the period, including Rosa Luxemburg and Leon Trotsky (before 1917) sought broad-based support, Lenin argued for a narrow but intense cadre who would educate workers, explaining why they should reject material advances such as better pay and shorter working hours in favor of complete political revolution. Critics said Lenin's cadre would be a socialist party acting in the name of the working class rather than led by the working class.

By 1917, the world was engulfed in what Lenin hoped was the final, desperate convulsion of the outdated and doomed capitalist system. He had opposed the war from the outset, reading and writing and lecturing in Zurich, in neutral Switzerland, and working to spread revolutionary ideas. Though, in 1916, he told a meeting of socialists that his own generation might not see the triumph of revolution, he was shortly to bring it about. In April 1917 he accepted Germany's offer to transport him, in a sealed train, back to Russia, where the Germans hoped the presence of this radical would weaken the resolve of the new liberal government, which had just overthrown the tsar, to continue in the war. In November, Lenin gambled that support for this new government was so low that it would fall if attacked by a small but well-organized revolutionary party. He was right. Four months later, he reasoned that Germany would lose the war in the end, so the humiliating peace treaty he signed would soon cease to matter. Again he was right, and taking Russia out of the war gave him the chance to stabilize his revolution. The cadre of dedicated revolutionaries he had foreseen two decades before soon forced a new economic, social, and political order on the world's largest, and formerly most conservative, empire. Lenin's commitment to a revolution of his own making changed the course of history.

Introduction

The revolution that Lenin brought to Russia would not have happened had Europe not tumbled, in 1914, into a general and worldwide war that proved to be far more destructive than any of the conflicts of the nineteenth century. Growing nationalism, advances in military technology, and strains on the balance of power established at the Congress of Vienna made many in Europe fear that war was coming. But no one anticipated the length and breadth of this war when it came.

Using the technologies developed during the Second Industrial Revolution, World War I devoured the financial and human resources of Europe. To manage the Great War, as it was called at the time, governments harnessed civilian populations as never before. State intervention in the economy and society grew considerably during the war and changed everyday life. State propaganda ceaselessly reminded citizens why they needed to continue the fight. Throughout Europe—and the world—women took up jobs vacated by men sent to the trenches.

In August 1914, many Europeans welcomed war. For some, the chance for heroism and glory appeared attractive. Nationalists saw the war as a chance to enhance the prestige and strength of their nation-state or even to achieve a long-desired independence. Some radicals—like V. I. Lenin—saw the war as an opportunity to overthrow the old order with socialist revolution.

Europe at war's end looked very different from anyone's expectation in 1914. The horrific and senseless massacres of trench warfare convinced many Europeans that nothing could ever justify war again. Millions and millions of soldiers and civilians had died, and an influenza epidemic killed millions more. Poverty and political unrest, as well as the Bolshevik Revolution in Russia, threatened to further destabilize the entire continent. Nothing was as it had been. The safe, secure world of aristocratic and middle-class Europeans was gone forever. But if the world was more dangerous, it also had the potential, at least, to be more democratic.

A New Century, 1900–1914

↓ In the early years of the twentieth century, what made a general European war seem likely?

↓ How did nationalism help cause the outbreak of World War I?

By 1900, three generations had passed since a major war had swept Europe. The balance of power set down at the Congress of Vienna, though rattled by the unification of Germany and Italy, seemed to be effective in keeping the peace. But relations between the Great Powers were strained, in particular by the huge growth of German industry and the aggressive style of the German Kaiser William II. Wars in the Balkan Peninsula threatened to draw Russia into local conflicts. Advances in technology meant that any new war would be far more deadly—and more expensive—than any previous war. Optimists hoped that the threat of the enormous killing power of modern weaponry would make states find peaceful solutions. Others pointed to the system of alliances as a factor that would prevent war: every major power knew it would be very difficult to localize a conflict, and even a small outbreak threatened a continent-wide conflagration. Ironically, the very alliances that were intended to protect Europe from war ended up playing a major role in the continent's descent into war in 1914.

An Unbalanced Balance of Power

As the twentieth century began, the balance of power established at the Congress of Vienna almost a century earlier remained shakily in place. France, Austria (since 1867 Austria-Hungary), Britain, and Russia continued to play important roles on the European continent. After 1871, however, following Germany's

Chronology

1904–1905	Japan defeats Russia in Russo-Japanese War
1905	Dissatisfaction with tsarist rule sparks empirewide revolution in Russia
1908	Austria-Hungary annexes Bosnia-Herzegovina
1912	First Balkan War weakens Ottoman Empire
1913	Second Balkan War strengthens Serbia
1914	Archduke Ferdinand is assassinated (June 28); Austria presents Serbia with an ultimatum (July 23); Austria-Hungary declares war on Serbia (July 28); Germany declares war on Russia (August 1); Germany declares war on France and invades Belgium (August 3); Great Britain declares war on Germany (August 4); World War I begins (August); Germany defeats Russia at the Battle of Tannenberg (mid-August); French defeat Germans in the First Battle of the Marne (September)
1915	Turks defeat Allies at the Battle of Gallipoli; Italy declares war on Austria-Hungary (May 23)
1916	Battle of the Somme ends without significant advances (July–November)
1917	Russian Revolution begins; Tsar Nicholas II abdicates (March); United States enters World War I on Allied side (April); Bolsheviks attempt coup in Petrograd (July); Bolsheviks seize power in Petrograd (November)
1918	Treaty of Brest-Litovsk ends war for Russia (March); Germans launch offensives on the western front (spring); Armistice ends World War I (November 11)
1918–1919	Worldwide influenza epidemic kills millions

victory in the Franco-Prussian War, the balance was increasingly threatened by the growing might of the Prussian-dominated German Empire. Germany, with a population of nearly 70 million and an industrial output rivaling Great Britain's and exceeding that of France, sought to expand its economic, political, and cultural power. A latecomer to imperial ambitions, it seized colonies in Africa after the Berlin Conference in 1884. Ruled since 1890 by the insecure and belligerent **Kaiser William II**, Germany directly threatened the European status quo. Newly independent states like Italy, Romania, Serbia, and Bulgaria also complicated the international scene. Major powers scrambled to form new alliances that would retain the balance of power under greatly changed circumstances.

The French felt most threatened by a powerful Germany. Since the end of the Thirty Years' War in 1648, France's foreign policy had aimed to keep the Habsburgs to the east divided and weak. But Otto von Bismarck had successfully isolated Austria and then united German-speaking lands under Prussian leadership. Germany's victory over France in 1871 had gained it Alsace-Lorraine and its king the title of Emperor. Avenging this national humiliation remained a burning issue in French politics. With their low birth-

rate, moderate industrial growth, and underdeveloped railroad network, the French could not hope to take on the German army alone: they needed an ally.

The obvious candidate was Russia, whose large population, enormous territory, and long border with Germany offset its technological and economic backwardness. Although relations between Russia and Germany had traditionally been friendly, Russia was disturbed by Germany's growing industrial and military power. France courted Russia, and in 1894 the two signed a military alliance in which each promised to come to the other's aid if attacked by Germany. Thus, the most conservative major power in Europe, Russia, joined forces with its ideological opposite, republican France. Ideology mattered less than the menace of a common foe.

This agreement, however, heightened the prospect of Germany's worst strategic nightmare: a two-front war. To counter this threat, Germany sought alliances

Kaiser William II (r. 1890–1918) Prussian king and German Kaiser, noted for his impetuous and unsteady character.

with Austria-Hungary and Italy, both second-rate military powers. Austria-Hungary was continuously embroiled in domestic crises between the Austrian and Hungarian halves of the empire, and in Austria proper there were clashes over the use of local languages in schools and administration. Austria-Hungary was also concerned about the pro-Russian regimes in Serbia and Bulgaria, new states in the Balkans, and thus welcomed German military support against these Slavic nations. The junior member in this alliance, Italy, had its own troubles trying to hold together the mainly rural and impoverished south with the wealthier and industrialized north. In 1896, eager to seize an African colony for itself, Italy had been defeated by Ethiopia. The military pact Germany signed with Austria-Hungary and then, in 1882, with Italy was known as the **Triple Alliance.**

The wild card in international politics was Britain. Traditionally wary of continental entanglements, the British refused to join any military alliance. But the rapid growth of German industrial and military strength deeply disturbed British leaders. From the time of the Napoleonic Wars, British policy had aimed to prevent the domination of the European continent by any one power. Now Germany seemed ready to do just that, especially after it began an aggressive program of naval construction in 1907. Germany's belligerent behavior in international affairs had already alienated British public opinion as well as its Foreign Office, especially Germany's seizure of colonies in Africa. While Britain held back from a formal alliance, it reached a friendly understanding, known as the **Entente Cordiale,** with France in 1904. It reached a similar agreement with Russia in 1907. Now the **Triple Entente** balanced the Triple Alliance, but instead of ensuring general peace, the new alliance system seemed headed for war.

To prepare for the two-front war it feared, in the early twentieth century the German General Staff adopted the **Schlieffen Plan,** named for the general who developed it. In case of war, German armies were to strike quickly and decisively against the French before wheeling to the east and taking on the Russians. Thus, Germany could fight each enemy separately rather than dividing its forces between the two fronts. To knock out the French army, the Germans would march through Belgium toward the North Sea, bypassing the French border fortresses, then swing around toward Paris. For the plan to work—for hundreds of thousands of troops to move into position to threaten Paris—speed was of crucial importance. The Germans would also have to count on Belgium's cooperation or at least hope that Britain would not object to this violation of Belgian neutrality, guaranteed by Britain and the other major powers at the time Belgium won independence in 1831. In 1914, this proved to be a fatal miscalculation.

Rivalries

The alliance system seemed to stabilize the strains in international relations caused by national pride and imperial rivalries. For the French, regaining Alsace-Lorraine was a matter of pride. For Russia, there was a worry that the Ottomans were so weak that another power might seize the Bosporus and Dardanelles Straits, thereby cutting off Russian access to the Mediterranean Sea. In Africa, German and British interests came into direct conflict. In the 1890s, Kaiser William II made matters worse by publicly expressing his support for the anti-British Boers of South Africa.

National identity in Britain was connected closely with imperial prestige. In central and eastern Europe, however, nationalism was directed *against* existing empires—both Russia and Austria-Hungary. In Russian lands, Poles and Finns sought concessions or even independence; Poles, especially, aspired to the resurrection of Poland, which had been partitioned into oblivion in the eighteenth century. In Austria-Hungary, Romanians, Serbs, Czechs, and Italians hoped to gain broader political and cultural rights. Young nation-states in the region, such as Romania, Serbia, and Bulgaria, further encouraged such nationalist agendas. Russia considered itself the protector of the ethnically Slavic and religiously Orthodox peoples in the Balkans, including Bulgarians, Montenegrans, and Serbs. Russian public opinion strongly supported such **Pan-Slav** sentiments.

European rivalries were not only political, however. They were also economic. Since 1870, both Germany and Russia had experienced very significant industrial growth, including the building of railroads that often served strategic aims. The rapid growth of

---

Triple Alliance   Military alliance concluded in 1882 by Germany, Austria-Hungary, and Italy.

Entente Cordiale   Set of agreements signed between France and Great Britain in 1904 pledging cooperation, but not a formal military alliance.

Triple Entente   Agreement signed in 1907 by Russia, France, and Great Britain pledging closer relations.

Schlieffen Plan   German war plan of early twentieth century that aimed to avoid a two-front war by a quick and massive attack first on France, then on Russia.

Pan-Slavism   Movement from later nineteenth century emphasizing Russia's kinship with other Slavic nations, especially those under Ottoman and Habsburg rule.

German manufacturing presented French and British firms with a frighteningly efficient competitor, while modern industry in Moscow, St. Petersburg, Warsaw, and other cities of the Russian Empire had the potential to threaten Germany directly. Thus, Germans felt great relief at the poor showing of the Russian army and navy in the Russo-Japanese War of 1904–1905. When the Revolution of 1905 shook the political order in Russia to its foundations, Germans mistakenly concluded that it would take Russia at least a decade to recover. Then, when the Russian economy shortly boomed again, German leaders became alarmed.

Of Europe's many industries, arms manufacturing was among the biggest, employing thousands of workers and producing large profits. National and imperial rivalries generated an arms race that was good business for these manufacturers, which successfully lobbied their governments against any reductions in military budgets. New technologies meant that a country's weaponry had to be replaced quickly. Among the military innovations of the years before 1914 were airplanes, the machine gun, poison gas (though an agreement had been signed promising not to use it), and enormous artillery pieces that could destroy the most massive fortifications.

Nationalism in the Balkans

By the end of the nineteenth century, formerly Ottoman territories on the Balkan Peninsula were now independent states: Romania, Serbia, Bulgaria, Greece, Montenegro, and Albania. Bosnia-Herzegovina, occupied by Austria-Hungary since 1878, was formally annexed to that country in 1908. The Russians were furious, but their army, much weakened following defeat by Japan, was unable to help their Slavic allies. Both Russians and Balkan Slavs—especially Serbs—were now convinced that Austria-Hungary harbored aggressive intentions.

Each of the states in the Balkans had contested borders with its neighbors and significant numbers of national minorities inside its borders. All were united, however, in hatred for the Ottoman Empire. Religious loyalties added to the tensions, as, except for Albania, which had large numbers of Roman Catholics and Muslims, the people of the Balkans were Eastern Orthodox, whereas the Ottomans were Muslims. During the First Balkan War of 1912, the Balkan League of Serbia, Montenegro, Greece, and Bulgaria attacked the Ottoman territories of Kosovo and Macedonia and nearly swept the Ottoman forces out of Europe. Austria-Hungary, which had significant interests in the Balkans, prepared for war until the threat of Russian intervention caused it to back down.

MAP 25.1 **Balkans, 1912–1913** The two Balkan Wars of 1912–1913 both weakened the Ottoman Empire and revealed hostilities among the young Balkan states. Bulgaria's territorial loss to Serbia was one reason Bulgaria sided with Germany and Austria during World War I.

But the Balkan League could not hold together for long. The large territorial gains by Bulgaria excited the anger and resentment of its neighbors. In 1913, the Second Balkan War broke out when Serbia, Greece, Romania, and Montenegro banded together and attacked Bulgaria. When the Bulgarian armies had already been severely weakened, Ottoman forces crossed the border to take back some of the territory lost in 1912. The end result of the two **Balkan Wars** was a weaker Bulgaria, a stronger Serbia, and anger in

Balkan Wars Two wars, in 1912 and 1913, among countries of the Balkan Peninsula, the first ending with defeat for the Ottoman Empire, the second with defeat for Bulgaria.

Austria-Hungary over growing Serbian power, which was promoted by Russia. The 1913 peace established in the Balkans seemed temporary.

The Unexpected War, 1914

↓ How did the reality of war differ from expectations?
↓ Why, and how, did Europe's conflict engage the entire world?

On June 28, 1914, a young Serbian nationalist named Gavrilo Princip shot and killed the heir to the Austro-Hungarian throne, Archduke Francis Ferdinand. The archduke had not been popular, and at first little notice was taken of the assassination. Foreign ministers and other dignitaries continued their vacations, not suspecting a major crisis. Only some weeks later, when Austria-Hungary presented harsh demands to the Serbian government, did European leaders begin to realize the danger of the situation. By then it was already too late: within days, Europe was at war.

Imperial rivalries and military competition among European states had heightened international tensions to the point that any compromise seemed like fatal weakness. The complex alliance system, designed to prevent war, instead increased the likelihood that a small, regional conflict would become general. Economic interests such as those of major armament manufacturers backed up the alliance system. Individual states hoped that war would bring territorial gains, while stateless nationalities like the Poles saw war as a chance to gain their own nation-state. The causes of the general war were multiple, but no one expected it to turn out like it did. Rather than the quick, patriotic war Europeans expected, the war became a drawn-out, murderous international conflict, the first genuine world war in which battles took place around the globe. Both on the front and at home every element of society was called upon to serve the war effort.

The Slide into War

The assassination of the Austrian archduke Francis Ferdinand set off a fatal chain of events, tied to alliances and war plans. The shooting took place in Sarajevo, capital of Bosnia-Herzegovina, the province annexed by Austria-Hungary just six years earlier. The assassin, Gavrilo Princip, was connected with the Black Hand, a nationalist group with ties to Serbia that dreamed of a unified Slavic state. On July 23, encouraged by its German ally, Austria presented Serbia with an **ultimatum**, a set of non-negotiable demands

so harsh that they could not be accepted by a sovereign state. For example, the Austrians demanded not only that all forms of anti-Austrian **propaganda** be stamped out but that this campaign be carried out by Austro-Hungarian officials. As expected, the Serbians could not accept all the ultimatum's demands, and on July 28, exactly a month after the assassination, Austria-Hungary declared war on Serbia.

Russia felt obliged to support its Serbian ally, though Tsar Nicholas II recognized that military action against Austria-Hungary would compel its ally, Germany, to declare war. Yet to abandon Serbia at this moment would have meant a humiliation for Serbia's Great Power protector, Russia, and so, on July 30, reluctantly, the tsar ordered general **mobilization.** Now he hoped to avert a war through a personal appeal to Kaiser William, his cousin by marriage. Unfortunately, two days of frantic telegrams between "Nicky" in St. Petersburg and "Willy" in Berlin (the two communicated in English) came to nothing, and on August 1, Germany declared war on Russia. On August 3, convinced that France was about to attack from the west, Germany declared war on France and, following the Schlieffen Plan, marched into neutral Belgium. Technically in defense of Belgium, on August 4, Great Britain (whose king was also a cousin of "Nicky" and "Willy") declared war on Germany. "The lamps are going out all over Europe," observed British foreign minister Sir Edward Grey, "We shall not see them lit again in our lifetime."

Europe quickly divided into two warring camps: the **Allied Powers,** led by France, Great Britain, and Russia; and the **Central Powers,** Germany and Austria-Hungary, joined by Bulgaria and the Ottoman Empire. Serbia, Romania, and Belgium sided with the Allies, while Spain, Greece, Switzerland, Holland, and the Scandinavian countries remained neutral. Italy infuriated the Central Powers by refusing to honor its alliance and then, on May 23, 1915, declaring war on

ultimatum   Harsh demand requiring an immediate positive answer to avoid dire consequences.

propaganda   Efforts to influence public opinion, often using dishonest or misleading means.

mobilization   Calling up of military reserves and putting armies in place for battle that generally precedes a war.

Allied Powers   Wartime coalition of France, Great Britain, Russia, Serbia, and others, in the end a total of twenty-four countries including the United States.

Central Powers   Opponents of the Allies in World War I, most importantly Germany and Austria-Hungary, later joined by the Ottoman Empire and Bulgaria.

Among the crowd on Odeonsplatz in Munich cheering the outbreak of war on August 2, 1914 was a delighted Adolf Hitler. Like many men throughout Europe, the young Austrian welcomed war as an exciting adventure and an opportunity to put his nationalist sentiments into action. *(Heinrich Hoffmann/ Hulton Archive/Getty Images)*

Austria-Hungary and thereby joining the Allies, lured by promises of territorial gain in a postwar settlement. Both the Allies and the Central Powers promised territorial gains and other enticements to bring neutral powers onto their side, a fact that would complicate postwar settlements.

War Enthusiasm

Europeans from London to Moscow greeted the outbreak of war in August 1914 with patriotic demonstrations. Huge crowds gathered in the public squares of cities. In St. Petersburg, Russians attacked and gutted the German Embassy, and it became dangerous to be heard speaking German. In Munich, a twenty-five-year-old Austrian named Adolf Hitler cheered with the crowds on Odeonsplatz, then returned home and thanked God that he had lived to see the outbreak of war. In Paris, men rode to war in train cars marked "To Berlin!" In Berlin, Kaiser William II told the Reichstag that he "no longer recognized parties, only Germans."

European men rushed to polling stations to enlist, while women showered them with flowers. Mothers, wives, and sweethearts dutifully sent their men off to war. Patriotism, a longing for adventure, and a desire for revenge came together in a feverish enthusiasm for war. The young soldiers expected to be home, triumphant, by Christmas. Military planners, too, expected a quick, mobile war with one or two decisive

battles, like all the smaller wars that had been fought since Napoleon was finally defeated in 1815.

The war was initially so popular that even pacifists hesitated to oppose it, and those who did often brought trouble on themselves. In Russia, the Social-Democrats who refused to vote to fund the war were promptly arrested. The Russian socialist **Alexandra Kollontai** openly called for resistance to the war—from the safety of neutral Scandinavia. Others, following the idea of the long-time pacifist Bertha von Suttner, who had recently died, agitated for a "peace without victory." In the summer of 1915, an International Congress of Women in the neutral Netherlands called on all warring countries to lay down their arms. By that point, however, none of the warring countries were ready to compromise and make peace.

As the Schlieffen Plan dictated, the German army advanced rapidly and by September 1, 1914, threatened Paris. At this point, the French army and the British Expeditionary Force launched a counteroffensive. This **First Battle of the Marne** forced the ex-

Alexandra Kollontai (1872–1952) Russian revolutionary and diplomat, commissar for social welfare in 1918 and head of the women's section of the Communist Party.

First Battle of the Marne Crucial battle near the Marne River, just north of Paris, in early September 1914, in which the French stopped the German advance.

MAP 25.2 Western Front, 1914–1918 The Western Front remained mainly stable from autumn 1914 to spring 1918 with trenches stretching from the English Channel to Switzerland. The horrors of trench warfare experienced here inspired literary and artistic works by soldiers of all nationalities.

hausted and overextended German troops to retreat. By mid-September the opposing sides began to dig themselves in along a line stretching from the English Channel to the border of Switzerland. The stalemate of trench warfare on the western front had begun.

On the eastern front, Russia mobilized more rapidly than expected. Pressed by their French allies to attack, on August 15 two Russian armies invaded East Prussia, forcing the German high command to transfer troops from France to the eastern front, a transfer that may have been decisive in the Schlieffen Plan's failure. Russian troops still outnumbered the Germans in East Prussia, but they were poorly led and supplied. At **Tannenberg,** the Germans won a decisive victory, with some 100,000 Russian soldiers taken prisoner. Never again in this conflict would Russian troops threaten German soil. Austria was a different matter. Russian armies invaded the Austrian province of Galicia, remaining there until 1916. Even more embarrassing for Austria, the small Serbian army successfully defended the Serbian capital, Belgrade, until finally defeated by a much larger combined Austrian and German force in October 1914.

It was already clear that expectations for a short, glorious war were an illusion. **Casualties** had mounted to the hundreds of thousands, and ammunition had begun to run short. Governments were forced to take drastic measures to boost arms production. On all sides, military planners and civilian authorities had known huge amounts of resources would be needed at the start, but no one had anticipated the need for long-term military and economic organization. The war they had expected developed in a way they did not expect.

Trench Warfare

No one had anticipated that movement on the western front would stop altogether, but by fall 1914 soldiers on both sides had dug in. Across northern France were hundreds of miles of trenches in which thousands of men lived, fought, and died in a sea of mud, blood, rats, and vermin. The great technological advances in weaponry produced by the armaments industry were countered by primitive defenses built

Tannenberg Battle in East Prussia in August 1914 in which the Germans decisively defeated the Russian army.

casualties Deaths and injuries in battle.

In this photograph taken by French photographer Jacques Moreau in 1916, soldiers in a forward trench in the Champaign region of northern France have a quick bite to eat. Note the different levels in the trench, enabling men to walk safely in the middle but allowing the use of periscopes to peer out over the top of the trench facing no man's land. *(Archives Larousse, Paris/Giraudon/The Bridgeman Art Library)*

of earth and barbed wire. Generals continued to use old tactics of massive frontal assaults, however. Periodically, an attempt to break through to the enemies' front trench would end in slaughter and failure or, at best, the gain of a few yards of territory.

On the Allied side, a typical front trench was about six to eight feet deep, about four feet wide, and separated from the German front trench by a narrow strip of land—**no man's land**—fifty yards to a mile wide, with masses of coiled barbed wire in front of each set of trenches. A few hundred yards behind front, or firing, trenches were parallel support and reserve trenches. All these trenches were connected by perpendicular communication trenches that allowed men to move between the rear and the front. German trenches were similar but, in general, deeper and more elaborate. British and French soldiers who saw them were impressed by their neatness. Behind the trenches were rail lines that brought in fresh troops and supplies and evacuated the wounded and men on leave. Between the two lines of enemy trenches were the killing fields. During the day, stepping into no man's land would mean instant death, but at night this area was busy with scouting expeditions and soldiers repairing defenses.

Those who experienced trench warfare and survived recalled filth, stench, and constant noise. Imagine thousands of men living in close quarters in a muddy hole in the ground with few opportunities for personal hygiene. Add a climate in which rainfall and dark gloomy weather are the norm. Then there's the odor of decomposing corpses fed upon by large rats. The racket of constant artillery and small-arms fire, together with flares illuminating the night sky, made sleep difficult. The nervous strain of trench warfare produced a psychological disorder newly described as **shell shock**, which left thousands of men incapable of fighting any longer or carrying out everyday activities at home. Constant shelling pulverized farmhouses, barns and yards, roads and forests. Chemicals from thousands of explosive shells poisoned the earth itself, leaving it useless for agriculture. Once-familiar landscapes became eerie, lifeless moonscapes later depicted by painters like **Paul Nash.** Tense monotony

no man's land Territory between the two opposing enemy lines of trenches that had to be crossed in an attack.

shell shock Psychological disorder, sometimes lasting decades, caused by the extreme stress faced by men under the constant barrage of explosions during war.

Paul Nash (1889–1946) English painter whose disorienting, surreal paintings depicted the bizarre world of the trenches.

Paul Nash's ironically entitled painting *We Are Making a New World* (1918) shows a landscape devastated by shelling with the sun rising ominously over the horizon. Nash was a volunteer in the British Army who was later promoted to officer and experienced trench warfare firsthand. *(Imperial War Museum, London/The Bridgeman Art Library)*

alternated with solitary deaths (if, for example, one forgot to crouch down in the more shallow parts of the trench) and, periodically, the mass slaughter of an offensive.

Attempts to break through the line followed a common pattern. First, artillery shelling, often lasting days, aimed to destroy forward machine-gun placements and barbed-wire defenses and force the enemy back from the front trenches. Relentless shelling also aimed to wear down and "soften" the enemy psychologically. Then, always at dawn, came the order to advance. The nervous men were awakened and given a stiff drink to buck up their nerves. The artillery would cease its shelling, a clear signal of impending attack. At the sound of a whistle, hundreds of men would "go over the top" of the front trench and run headlong into no man's land—and into machine-gun fire. Only a few made it as far as the barbed-wire barriers in front of the enemy trenches. Fewer still actually made it into the empty enemy trench, where they could do little more than sit tight, hoping for the arrival of reinforcements before enemy soldiers were able to rush back to their front trenches. Usually death arrived before reinforcements, and the stalemate was reestablished. Desperate to break this stalemate, in the spring of 1915 the Germans lobbed canisters of poison gas into enemy trenches, inflicting blindness

and miserable deaths on unprepared French and British soldiers. Gas attacks and gas masks soon became standard on both sides.

Two battles in 1916, each lasting months, epitomize the desperation and gruesome absurdity of warfare on the western front. In February, the Germans launched a massive assault, aiming to capture the French fortress at **Verdun.** Calculating that the French would go to extreme lengths to defend this town, which had been fortified after defeat in the Franco-Prussian War, the German command aimed simply to kill as many French soldiers as possible. The propaganda value of the fortress far overshadowed its military importance. "They shall not pass!" declared the French general **Henri Pétain.** But the French lost more than 350,000 men, and before the battle was over, ten months later, the Germans had lost 330,000. Today Verdun is a mausoleum and a cemetery, its defenses still harboring live mines and closed to visitors.

Verdun French fortress attacked by Germans in 1916, resulting in almost 700,000 casualties.

Henri Pétain (1856–1951) French general in World War I who later, during World War II, served as president of Vichy France, the Nazi puppet state.

On July 1, to take the pressure off the French at Verdun, the British launched a massive attack at the **Somme** River, along a twenty-mile front, and were later joined in the battle by the French. Despite the use of a new weapon, the tank, the Allies were unable to dislodge the Germans. When the fighting finally ended in mid-November, the Allies had suffered 1 million casualties—and had advanced six miles.

War on the Seas and in the Air

With the British army bogged down in the trenches, the British Admiralty, headed by young **Winston Churchill**, urged an assault on the Central Powers' southern ally, the Ottoman Empire. Churchill calculated that an attack on the **Gallipoli** peninsula would break through Turkish defenses and open the way to Istanbul, knocking Turkey out of the war. In this largest **amphibious** operation of the war, troops from Australia and New Zealand under British command seized the beaches of Gallipoli in late April 1915. Contrary to expectations, however, Turkish troops on bluffs overlooking the beach rained down bullets and shells on the Allied positions. In the end, Churchill could not muster sufficient troops and **materiel** to break Turkish defenses, and the British gave up the attempt. Churchill and Britain were humiliated by the defeat, and Turkey remained in the war. Together the belligerents suffered more than 500,000 casualties.

Despite this setback, the British navy continued to dominate the seas, blockading Germany's North Sea harbors. Given British naval superiority, the German navy preferred caution to bold moves until mid-1916, when the two fleets clashed at Battle of **Jutland**, off the west coast of Denmark. While the German fleet was smaller, it inflicted heavy losses on the British. In the end, the battle was indecisive. The British blockade continued, but the German navy still dominated the Baltic, standing between the British navy and its Russian allies.

Vastly more important than this conventional naval battle was what the Germans called the war on commerce, carried out almost entirely by a new type of warship, the submarine, or **U-boat**. The British could be starved into submission, thought the Germans, if their submarines could prevent the delivery of food and raw materials, and Britain's naval blockade of Germany justified this measure. In early 1915, the Germans announced **unrestricted submarine warfare**, warning that any ship entering British waters, including those of neutral countries, could be attacked and sunk. Because of the vulnerability of submarines when on the surface, there would be no warning before an attack. This policy, which violated traditional rules of war for engagements on the high seas, antagonized the United States, which had declared neutrality but traded actively with Britain. Although millions of tons of Britain-bound shipping fell prey to submarines, it was the sinking of the British passenger liner *Lusitania* on May 7, 1915, with the loss of over a hundred American lives, that intensified anti-German feeling in the United States, despite the Germans' contention that the ship had been carrying an illegal cargo of arms. Rapidly the British developed antisubmarine measures, including mines, aerial surveillance, depth charges, and, most effective of all, the use of armed escorts of naval shipping—the **convoy system**—which was introduced in May 1917.

While not as effective as U-boats, "flying machines" also played a part in World War I. Airplanes scouted out enemy positions, attacked enemy troops, and dropped bombs and propaganda leaflets. Their pilots were known as aces; perhaps the most famous was Manfred von Richthofen, the "Red Baron." Aces engaged in aerial "dogfights," but in the final year of the war airplanes were also used in mass formation to support ground troops—an actual military advance.

Somme Battle in 1916 near the Somme River in which the British and French failed to break through German lines, resulting in 1 million Allied casualties.

Winston Churchill (1874–1965) English politician of aristocratic background who backed the disastrous Gallipoli campaign, nearly destroying his political career; as prime minister during World War II, he inspired British victory.

Gallipoli Peninsula in western Turkey where an Allied attack using Australian and New Zealander troops in April to December 1915 ended in failure.

amphibious Military action using both land and sea troops.

materiel Military hardware such as guns, tanks, and ammunition.

Jutland Naval battle in 1916 between Britain and Germany off the coast of Denmark that ended in a draw.

U-boat (from German *Unterseeboot*, "undersea boat") Submarine.

unrestricted submarine warfare German policy of attacking without warning any ship entering British waters during World War I.

Lusitania British passenger ship torpedoed by a German submarine off the coast of Ireland in May 1915, drowning over 1,000 passengers, including 120 Americans.

convoy system Grouping merchant ships together with an escort of armed naval vessels, successfully used to protect shipping from U-boats.

World War I was the first war fought in the air as well as on the ground and on the seas. Mortality among pilots like these flyers of the British SE-5A biplane fighter was very high. *(Courtesy of the Trustees of the Imperial War Museum)*

Both sides also developed anti-aircraft guns. The planes themselves changed rapidly in these four years, as tens of thousands were built and destroyed. By 1918 the first all-metal fighters were appearing. German airships, called zeppelins after their inventor, were used to bomb London and military targets in England. Bulky, slow, and inflated with flammable gas, they were extremely vulnerable to attack by aircraft. This bombing of civilian areas blurred the traditional line between the fighting front and the "home front." World War I was the first **total war.**

A World at War

Many eighteenth- and nineteenth-century European conflicts had taken place far from Europe, but this war in Europe's heartland affected the entire world. At the same time, technological advances, such as the submarine, brought warfare to the high seas. More than anything else, Europe's unprecedented economic and colonial domination of the world brought nearly every continent into the conflict and made it difficult for independent states to remain neutral. Eventually twenty-four states were drawn in on the Allied side— from the African Republic of Liberia to China, Japan, and Siam (Thailand) in Asia; Brazil, Cuba, Guatemala, and Honduras in South and Central America; and, eventually, the United States. Of the total world pop-

ulation of 1.6 billion, some 1.4 billion lived in states officially engaged in the conflict.

Thousands of Asians and Africans from Europe's colonies fought on the western front, where their bravery was noted, challenging Europeans' sense of racial superiority. Young men from Australia and New Zealand fought at Gallipoli; Canadians and South Africans also helped the British war effort. Battles also took place in the colonies. In Africa, the Allies attacked the German colonies of East Africa, Togoland, and Southwest Africa. Fighting was particularly bitter in East Africa, involving British Kenya in the north down to present-day Zambia. Both European and African troops fought in these regions, and many African homes, crops, and herds were destroyed.

National and ethnic groups took advantage of warfare to press their own ambitions. In Russian Central Asia, Kazakhs revolted in 1916 against forced labor and war taxation, venting their anger on recently arrived Russian colonists. The revolt was put down with massive bloodshed. Half a world away in Dublin, on Easter Day 1916, Irish nationalists led a revolt

> **total war** War in which all elements of population, economy, and politics are obliged to serve the military effort.

against British rule, demanding an independent Ireland. The **Easter Uprising** was quickly repressed, but the anxiety of the British government over the Irish question increased.

Both Allied and Central Powers attempted to incite the minority national groups under enemy rule. The Russian tsar and German Kaiser, for example, each sought to gain Polish loyalty by promising the Poles increased national rights after the war. In the Ottoman Empire, the British encouraged nationalist Arabs to revolt against their Turkish overlords as the young English officer **T. E. Lawrence**—"Lawrence of Arabia"—dressed in Arab garb to lead Arab troops against Turkish positions. Today the military cemetery at Mount Scopus, Jerusalem, bears witness to the thousands of British and Arab troops that died in that conflict. But even before the fighting had ended, the future of the region had been decided. In 1916 the British and French negotiated the **Sykes-Picot Agreement**, dividing up former Ottoman territories in the Middle East between themselves. When it became clear that the British government did not intend to grant the Arabs real independence, Lawrence resigned in disgust. An even more complicated appeal to a national minority in the region was the **Balfour Declaration** of November 1917, in which the British government indicated its willingness to set up a Jewish "national home" in Palestine. Support for Zionism, the British thought, would strengthen Jewish sympathy throughout the world for the Allied cause.

In another part of the Ottoman Empire, the border region between Russia and Turkey, an unprecedented attack on a civilian population occurred: the **Armenian Massacre.** Relations between Christian Armenians and Muslim Turks (and Kurds), never cordial, had become severely strained by accusations that the Armenians had been spying for the Russians. During the winter of 1915–1916, Ottoman authorities gave orders to deport Armenians from their native villages near the front with Russia. In the course of these deportations, Turkish military units killed many unarmed Armenians or allowed them to perish in the harsh winter. Up to 1.5 million Armenians died in these operations, which nearly wiped out the Armenian community in Turkey. As an instance of genocide, the Armenian Massacre stands as a precursor to even more horrific ethnically based attacks on civilian populations later in the twentieth century.

The participation by colonized people in the European war effort radicalized movements opposing European rule and weakened the legitimacy of imperialism. If Indians, for example, could shed blood for the Allied cause, Indian nationalists argued, why could they not also rule themselves? In Africa, too, the eco-nomic effects of the war fueled nationalist and anti-colonial sentiments after 1918.

Total War, 1914–1918

↓ How did war influence everyday life and family relationships?
↓ In what ways did governments aim to control their citizens?

The Great War broke down the distinction between the military and noncombatants. Entire societies were harnessed for the war effort. Governments intruded into the economy and everyday life of their citizens as never before, making this the first total war. The right to free speech was limited. Shortages affected households and diets. Women took up new jobs as millions of men left for the front, unions and employers agreed to avoid conflicts to increase war production, and political parties vowed to work together. Like the mass mobilization during the French Revolution, but far more encompassing, the state demanded that citizens devote full energies to crushing the enemy.

State Control and Intervention

Within months of the outbreak of war, all governments realized that supplies of foodstuffs and raw materials were threatened. The German government rapidly set up a Raw Materials Department in the War Ministry to secure raw materials vital to war industries. In Russia, Tsar Nicholas II proclaimed that, for the duration of the war, no vodka would be distilled. This measure, designed to reserve millions of tons of grain to feed Russian soldiers, had the unintended

Easter Uprising   Nationalist rebellion in Dublin 1916 that demanded Irish independence and was bloodily suppressed by British authorities.

T. E. Lawrence   (1888–1935) English soldier and scholar known as "Lawrence of Arabia" who led the Arabs against Turkish domination during World War I.

Sykes-Picot Agreement   Treaty of 1916 dividing up Ottoman territory in the Middle East between Great Britain and France.

Balfour Declaration   Official statement by British government in November 1917 in favor of a Jewish "national home" in Palestine, a major victory for Zionism.

Armenian Massacre   Killing of as many as 1.5 million Christian Armenians by the Muslim Turkish military and Muslim Kurds in 1915–1916.

side effect of eliminating the government's largest source of income, the tax on vodka. In Britain, the government negotiated a settlement between unions and big business to assure that war production would not be interrupted by strikes. As the war dragged on, government intervention in the economy became more radical. In 1915, Britain **nationalized** the railroads. In May 1916, the British government moved the clock forward one hour to take advantage of summer daylight—the first daylight savings time.

To prevent hunger, governments stepped in to manage the production and sale of foodstuffs. With overseas food supplies cut off by the British naval blockade, Germany began to ration bread in early 1915. By mid-1916, labor shortages in agriculture and the effect of German submarine attacks forced the French and British governments, also, to introduce food rationing. In France, the beloved baguette was outlawed as wasteful, as were ice cream and most forms of candy. By late 1916, Germans had ration cards not only for bread but for meat, potatoes, milk, sugar, butter, soap, and eggs. Even so, supply could not keep up with demand. Governments introduced various food substitutes, such as vegetable beefsteaks, artificial eggs, and "war bread," which contained a limited amount of white flour.

Government intervention was most direct in military conscription. Compulsory military service, long in force in most countries, was expanded. Britain's 1916 Military Service Act drafted men between eighteen and forty. All across Europe, almost all young men were either serving in the army or working in war industries. Those not serving in the armed forces found themselves scorned or even physically attacked as cowards.

To pay for the costs of the war, governments raised taxes and took out loans. For the Allies, most loans came from the United States. Even these measures could not cover war costs, however, and everywhere governments printed money, thereby starting an inflationary cycle that would continue into the 1920s.

War Propaganda

Throughout Europe, governments attempted to control what citizens could know about the war's progress. The German people did not know that German troops had destroyed the priceless library at Louvain, in Belgium, while the people of England and France did not know that the Allies had bombed civilians in Karlsruhe, Germany. Propaganda campaigns sought to keep up morale and convince citizens that right was on their side. The enemy was always characterized as vicious, cunning, and hardly human. The Allies por-

Propaganda merged with commercial purposes during World War I. This advertisement for a Hungarian brewery suggests that its beer was so delicious that the enemy soldiers would come running—and surrender—just to get a glass. *(Hoover Institution Archives)*

trayed German troops as "the Hun," murderous creatures bent on looting and destruction. German atrocities in Belgium were said to include bayoneted children and raped nuns. German propaganda countered with stories of German prisoners being tortured by Allied captors, all the while depicting German soldiers as defenders of culture pitted against effeminate French decadence and Russian barbarism.

Politicians' speeches, press editorials, posters, and even songs warned citizens to be ever vigilant, to avoid defeatism, and to work for the war effort. In

nationalization The taking over of private enterprise by a government, sometimes with compensation, sometimes not, often in emergencies.

Germany, the poetic "hit" of the war was Ernst Lissauer's "Song of Hatred Against England," for which the author was awarded the **Iron Cross,** a military decoration. Postcards bore such gruesome rhymed inscriptions as "Jeder Schuss ein Russ'" ("Every shot, a Russian") and "Jeder Stoss ein Franzos'" ("Every bayonet thrust, a Frenchman"). Similarly, patriotically minded Russians could send New Year's greetings on cards depicting a Cossack lopping off a German soldier's head and bearing the message, "Happy New Year! A successful blow!" French posters called on citizens to save wine for the troops and to support the war by buying war bonds.

Films also bolstered spirits, and since one-third or more of the people of Europe—at least those in cities—attended the movies at least once a week, their effect was significant. In Germany, melodramatic war films, such as *How Max Won the Iron Cross,* inspired patriotism. Among the Allies, **Charlie Chaplin**'s comedies enjoyed immense popularity, including his rare, unheroic portrayal of a frontline soldier in *Shoulder Arms,* produced in 1918. Moviegoers were also treated to newsreels, which showed a very sanitized and upbeat version of the week's military developments.

Propaganda everywhere dealt in half-truths and some outright lies. In London one could visit a model trench that, as returning soldiers complained, hardly resembled the real thing. In fact, soldiers found the patriotic falsehoods spread at home to be sickening. Even civilians on the home front grew weary of the emphasis on the positive and upbeat as news of casualties mounted and food in the cities grew scarce. In the end, it is doubtful that the large expenditures on propaganda had any significant effect on the final outcome of the war.

Besides controlling the flow of information, governments restricted civil rights. Fearing civil unrest immediately after the declaration of war, in August 1914 the British Parliament passed the Defence of the Realm Act, known as **DORA.** This act essentially placed Britain under martial law for the duration of the war, allowing police to question and arrest individuals without a warrant and severely restricting freedom of speech. Individuals like the philosopher **Bertrand Russell** who dared to question the war or to advocate pacifism were harassed and even imprisoned. In Germany, when the radical socialists **Karl Liebknecht** and Rosa Luxemburg denounced the war at a **May Day** rally in 1916, calling for it to be transformed into a class war, they were arrested, tried for treason, and imprisoned. Even in the United States, the declaration of war in 1917 was quickly followed by the **Espionage and Sedition Acts,** which outlawed agitation against the war effort or criticism of the government.

Domestic and Family Life

In this war, every segment of society fought in one way or another. All were admonished to "do your part." Wealthy and middle-class women volunteered as nurses. Retired people put their savings into war bonds to help finance the purchase of weaponry. Schoolteachers instilled patriotic and military virtues in their pupils and encouraged their students to prepare "care packages" to be sent to the men on the front. From the top to the bottom of society, people tried to economize and waste less, with more modest meals for the British royal family setting an example. The deterioration in quality and quantity of basic consumer goods and foodstuffs meant that most German women were fully occupied simply finding food for their families and mending clothing that could not be replaced. German women also supplemented their income by taking in work, such as the home production of gas masks, uniform items, and sandbags. Numerous posters called on women to subscribe to war bonds as one way of doing their part to help their men in the trenches.

Women also began to take jobs previously reserved for men. In Britain, female "postmen" and bus conductors startled onlookers at first. In Russia, a famous propaganda poster showed a women working at a lathe. German women also worked in armament factories, and everywhere women worked as nurses. With doctors overwhelmingly occupied at the front, nurses took their place at home in treating civilian ailments.

While no army put women into combat, the British organized auxiliary units, such as the WAACs (Women's Army Auxiliary Corps) and Wrens (British

Iron Cross   High military honor awarded for bravery to Prussian and German soldiers from 1813 to 1945.

Charlie Chaplin   (1889–1977) British film actor and producer who created the Little Tramp character and whose silent comedies were extremely popular.

DORA   Defence of the Realm Act, a law that curtailed civil liberties in Britain during World War I.

Bertrand Russell   (1872–1970) British mathematician, philosopher, and pacifist.

Karl Liebknecht   (1871–1919) German left-wing socialist who spent most of the war in jail for his socialist and antiwar agitation.

May Day   International labor holiday, celebrated since the late nineteenth century throughout the world except in the United States.

Espionage and Sedition Acts   Laws in United States passed in 1917 restricting free speech to prevent antiwar statements ("sedition") and spying ("espionage").

Women's Royal Naval Service), in which women carried out office duties and also served as nurses. In Germany, the military command established the "Women's Home Army" to keep up morale and detect spies. Strikingly, Russia formed and trained a "Women's Battalion of Death," a volunteer unit that also functioned to shame male soldiers whose morale was low.

Even the most intimate spheres of life were militarized. A French poster showed a newborn baby lamenting "Alas! I arrived too late." Another showed a soldier surrounded by beaming women proclaiming, "Let's do our part for repopulation." In this way, even the newborn and the unborn were mobilized for the war effort.

Old family patterns were disrupted by the absence of fathers at the front. Women assumed new responsibilities that helped break down old stereotypes and encouraged demands for economic and political equality. In Britain, greater numbers of women in wage work outside the home strengthened the arguments of women's suffrage activists. By war's end, they had achieved the vote for women. Children, too, became more independent and self-reliant. Men returning from the front were sometimes shocked by the new attitudes of their wives, sisters, and children. Entire societies felt the impact of the new social and economic roles for women that developed during wartime.

Russia in Revolution, 1917

⬇ What caused the Russian monarchy to collapse?
⬇ What caused the Provisional Government to collapse in November 1917?

Stalemate, scarcities, mounting casualties, and millions of deaths: war stalked all of Europe, but the Russians were most miserable of all. Russia was the largest, poorest, least industrialized, and most politically repressive of the large European states. Russia also had the largest army in Europe, a heavy burden on its limited resources. By late 1916, overwhelmed by rising prices and widespread shortages of food and fuel, and facing another cold, dark winter, Russians were desperate. Strikes broke out as workers protested the excessive profits earned by arms manufacturers while their own low wages failed to keep up with inflation. Anger with the tsarist regime mounted with military disasters and the seeming indifference of the tsar and his German-born wife. In March 1917, popular discontent exploded to sweep the tsar from power. Suddenly Russia found itself without a real government. As rival groups competed, a small band of radical socialists took advantage of the political instability to seize control and impose a new economic, social, and political order. Denouncing the "imperialist war," the new leaders of Russia urged soldiers on all sides to join in a class struggle that would topple corrupt empires and destroy capitalism itself. Exhilarating for some and horrifying for others, the Russian Revolution posed a direct challenge to existing economic, social, and political powers around the world.

The March Revolution

Repeated military setbacks made the tsar's many subjects heartily sick of war and bitter about the failures of his leadership. They believed that his German wife, Alexandra, sympathized with the enemy. Suspicions of treason at the highest level of government were reinforced by the presence in the imperial palace of a notorious peasant healer, **Grigory Rasputin.** The tsar and his wife appreciated Rasputin's ability to ease the bleeding of young Alexis, the heir to the Romanov throne, who suffered from hemophilia. Most Russians, however, falsely believed Rasputin to be a German spy and Alexandra's secret lover. Foolishly, Nicholas refused to send Rasputin away.

Nicholas's refusal to acknowledge ugly facts made him unable to deal effectively with Russia's deteriorating military situation and rising social unrest. A man who hated conflict, the tsar politely banished strong personalities from his presence and simply ignored criticism or advice from public figures or the press. In September 1915, he made a fatal decision when, in direct opposition to his advisers and despite his complete lack of military expertise, he left Petrograd—the new, more Russian-sounding name given to St. Petersburg in 1914—to join the general-staff headquarters near the front lines. As his advisers had feared, the tsar's presence at headquarters both distracted the officers there and meant that the Russian public connected every military defeat with the tsar's person. Back in Petrograd, Alexandra and Rasputin, together in the imperial palace, fueled more rumors that the "German woman" and her degenerate peasant lover were the real rulers of Russia. The truth was simpler: Russia lacked any effective leadership.

Every morning in the Russian capital, women lined up before dawn in front of shops that might have

Grigory Rasputin   (1869–1916) Siberian peasant healer whose ability to ease the suffering of Tsar Nicholas's son Alexis gained him entry to the Russian imperial family.

This wartime cartoon mocked Tsar Nicholas II and his wife Alexandra as mere pawns in the hands of the sinister bearded Rasputin. In fact the Siberian peasant healer's influence on policy was negligible, despite what many Russians thought. *(Stock Montage)*

some bread and milk to sell. On March 8, 1917, however, many shops had received no food at all, and women were turned away empty handed. As they trudged home, worrying how they would feed their families, they came upon radical women demonstrating in support of **International Women's Day.** The two groups came together, and soon the entire capital city was in an uproar, with ten thousand women demanding equal rights for women, a Russian republic, and an end to the war—demands summed up in the slogan "Bread and Peace." As workers went out on strike and even middle-class professionals took to the streets, the local chief of police telegraphed news of the riots to Nicholas. The president of the Duma sent

a similar telegram, begging Nicholas to take notice of the people's demands. Instead, the tsar chose repression, commanding the local authorities to crack down on demonstrators.

Nicholas failed to appreciate how much the power of local authorities had eroded. Very quickly, control of the city passed over to the rebels. It soon became dangerous for those associated with the tsarist regime to show themselves in public. Policemen were beaten to death. When Nicholas finally decided to return, railway workers sabotaged the route, stranding the emperor outside the capital. Conservative Duma members persuaded the tsar to abdicate to preserve Russia. His patriotism touched, Nicholas signed away his power and thus ended more than three centuries of Romanov rule in Russia.

The Provisional Government

News of the tsar's abdication was greeted in the streets with shouts of "Long live the Russian republic!" Support for the monarchy seemed to evaporate overnight. Former Duma members of the center and moderate left formed a new government that was rapidly recognized by the Allied Powers. This **Provisional Government** was to rule Russia for most of 1917. Its leaders proclaimed a free, liberal, and democratic Russia. They issued a blanket **amnesty** for political prisoners, ended all restrictions on non-Russians (thereby giving Russia's Jews and Muslims equal rights), and promised to convene a constituent assembly to draw up a constitution for the new republic. The Provisional Government also pledged to continue the war effort against Germany, hoping that the Allies would offer significant material support to the new, democratic Russia. Outside of Petrograd, however, the end of tsarist rule brought little change; even local administrators were seldom replaced.

The Provisional Government, representing mainly middle-class Duma members, espoused such liberal ideals as the rule of law, civil liberties, and private property. Almost immediately, it was challenged by

International Women's Day International holiday celebrating the achievements of women, whose demonstrations for "bread and peace" in Petrograd on March 8, 1917, grew into workers' riots that deposed Tsar Alexander II.

Provisional Government Temporary Russian government in March–November 1917 that was led by former Duma members and deposed by the Bolshevik Revolution.

amnesty General pardon by government.

the more radical, socialist **Petrograd Soviet,** a council that represented factory workers and soldiers. Issuing Order No. 1 in early March, the soviet called on each military unit to form committees of elected representatives, demanded that officers show proper respect to the common soldiers, and proclaimed that no military orders were to be honored unless approved by the Petrograd Soviet. The Provisional Government felt unable to oppose this order directly. As unpopular officers were killed or, more frequently, simply warned to disappear, the conservative officer corps found it exceedingly difficult to maintain discipline.

As Order No. 1 vividly demonstrates, after March 1917 there were two centers of power in Russia. While the Provisional Government was the internationally recognized government, it lacked power and legitimacy at home. It saw itself as a caretaker, in place only until a permanent constitution could be drafted and put into effect. The Petrograd Soviet, on the other hand, had little time for such liberal and parliamentary niceties. Inspired by the Petrograd Soviet, workers' councils sprang up in other cities and in the countryside to push for a radical solution to Russia's wartime problems.

Soon after the blanket amnesty, political prisoners in Siberia and political exiles around the world began to make their way home. In April, Vladimir Ilyich Lenin, the leader of the radical **Bolsheviks,** arrived in Petrograd after a complicated journey, supported by the German authorities, from his exile in Switzerland (see Choice). Quickly he published a fiery article demanding an end to the war in the Bolshevik newspaper *Pravda*. His clear and radical program appealed to many, and support for the Bolsheviks grew. The Bolsheviks had two things other political parties in Russia lacked: the dynamic leadership of Lenin and an easily understood program summed up in the slogan "Peace, Land, and Bread." But the Bolsheviks were a small and extreme group, and no one thought they would eventually triumph.

Petrograd Soviet   (in Russian, "council") Radical council that represented socialist workers and soldiers and shared power with the more moderate Provisional Government.

Bolsheviks   Radical wing of the Russian Social-Democratic Party in 1917 led by Vladimir Lenin, whose program called for "Peace, Land, and Bread."

Voic**Voice**eVoiceVoice

Lenin Proposes His "April Theses"

When V. I. Lenin returned to Petrograd in April 1917, the enthusiasm for the democratic revolution of March had not yet worn off. Even socialist parties—including Lenin's own Bolsheviks—had agreed to support the Provisional Government until the war was won. Within days of his return, Lenin shocked his Bolshevik colleagues with his "April Theses," which demanded a far more radical and confrontational course of action. In any other country at war—including the United States—Lenin would have been arrested for his demands to end the war and for revolution. The fact that he was able to publish these radical comments openly shows that, indeed, as he himself commented, Russia after the March revolution was "the freest country in the world."

➡ Why did Lenin term the war "predatory"? What did capitalism have to do with that?

➡ Why would overthrowing capitalism bring about a "truly democratic peace"?

[Thesis 1: Against the war]
➡ The war . . . unquestionably remains on Russia's part a predatory imperialist war owing to the capitalist nature of that [provisional] government. . . .

The class-conscious proletariat can give its consent to a revolutionary war. . . .

➡ It is necessary . . . to explain the inseparable connection existing between capital and the imperialist war, and to prove that without overthrowing capital *it is impossible* to end the war by a truly democratic peace. . . .

[Thesis 3: Against the Provisional Government]

➡ No support for the Provisional Government; the utter falsity of all its promises should be made clear, particularly of those relating to the renunciation of annexations. . . .

[Thesis 5: For revolution]

Not a parliamentary republic—to return to a parliamentary republic from the Soviets of Workers' Deputies would be a retrograde step—but a republic of Soviets of Workers', Agricultural Labourers' and Peasants' Deputies throughout the country, from top to bottom. . . .

Abolition of the police, the army, and the bureaucracy. . . .

[Thesis 6: Re an agrarian program]

➡ Confiscation of all landed estates.

➡ Nationalisation of all lands in the country, the land to be disposed of by the local Soviets of Agricultural Labourers' and Peasants' Deputies. . . .

[Thesis 7: For the nationalization of banks]

➡ The immediate amalgamation of all banks in the country into a single national bank, and the institution of control over it by the Soviet of Workers' Deputies.

➡ What social groups might support Lenin in his call for nationalizing large estates?

➡ Was the Provisional Government conservative or anti-socialist? What does Lenin mean by "annexations" here?

➡ Would peasants welcome the placing of land under the control of local Soviets?

➡ Why did Lenin specifically mention that banks should be nationalized (he does not mention any other kind of business or industry)?

Meanwhile, the Provisional Government was also moving to the left politically. In July, **Alexander Kerensky,** a socialist lawyer and the only man to hold posts in both the Provisional Government and Petrograd Soviet, became prime minister. Kerensky enjoyed great popularity at first. His talents as an orator were considerable, though when he preached to the troops at the front that they had a sacred duty to give their lives for Mother Russia some scorned him as the "persuader-in-chief." Unfortunately for Kerensky, his speeches proved unable to prevent the collapse of the Russian army. A major Russian offensive launched in the summer of 1917 turned into a rout.

As a moderate socialist, Kerensky faced serious enemies on both the right and the left. The military despised him as an illegitimate upstart, and the Bolsheviks saw him as ineffectual. In a sense, both were correct. But Kerensky was in an impossible situation. Having neutralized the Bolshevik threat after a coup attempt in July, in early September Kerensky had to fend off a military coup led by the popular Cossack general Lavr Kornilov. To defeat Kornilov, Kerensky released many Bolsheviks from jail, including **Leon Trotsky,** another dynamic leader. The Bolsheviks regrouped, and within weeks Kerensky faced them again, now more dangerous, well organized, and armed.

The November Revolution

Hiding outside of Petrograd, Lenin pelted his comrades in the capital with enraged letters and instructions. In mid-October he entered Petrograd in disguise to persuade his party comrades that the time had come to seize power. Opposition to Lenin's timetable was considerable, but his powers of persuasion were even stronger. Trotsky's support proved critical. Despite press coverage of the Bolshevik plan to grab power, the Petrograd Soviet refused to believe it could succeed and would not align itself with Kerensky and the Provisional Government.

Alexander Kerensky   (1881–1970) Moderate socialist and prime minister of the Provisional Government who was deposed by the Bolsheviks.

Leon Trotsky   (1879–1940) Russian revolutionary who along with Lenin helped bring the Bolsheviks to power in 1917.

The support of war-weary soldiers like these marching in Petrograd under the banner of communism was crucial for the success of the Bolshevik takeover in November 1917. By continuing to push the war effort, the Provisional Government lost support among many workers, soldiers and peasants. *(RIA/Novosti)*

On the night of November 6, the Bolsheviks executed a carefully planned takeover of Petrograd. Bridges across the river Neva were occupied, and the Bolshevik party's **Red Guards** surrounded the main railway stations, central post office, and other strategic buildings. The Provisional Government found itself trapped inside the Winter Palace, unable to communicate with the outside. Except for a few cadets and the ill-trained Women's Battalion of Death, no one defended Kerensky and the recognized government of Russia. Very much like the tsar's regime some eight months earlier, the Provisional Government collapsed. As Lenin put it later, "Power lay on the street; we merely picked it up." The following day, the Bolsheviks broke into the Winter Palace and arrested the members of the Provisional Government except for Kerensky, who, disguised as a woman, escaped in an American Embassy automobile. Though the Bolsheviks faced stiff opposition and street fighting in Moscow, in the countryside peasants were far more concerned with seizing the land they had been promised by the Bolsheviks. By the end of November,

Lenin and his party comrades found themselves unexpectedly in control of the world's largest country.

The Bolsheviks themselves did not expect their power to last. They hurried to proclaim Russia the first socialist state in history and rapidly issued decrees calling for peace, nationalizing land for peasants, establishing worker control of factories, and affirming equal rights for all religious and national minorities. Alexandra Kollontai became commissar for people's welfare. To the embarrassment of the Allied Powers, the Bolsheviks published secret treaties concerning promises about postwar settlements revealing, among other things, that Russia was to receive territory from Turkey after the war—agreements that the Allies had earlier denied. The long-delayed elections to the constituent assembly were allowed to take place, but when it convened in January 1918, the Bolsheviks shut

Red Guards   Troops organized by the Bolsheviks that were instrumental in their victory in the Russian Revolution of November 1917.

it down after only one day. Already the Bolsheviks were curtailing the liberal freedoms gained by the March revolution.

The Bolsheviks had never pretended to be liberals. They had never advocated equal rights or toleration for all political views. When they came to power, they were well aware of how weak their position was and how many enemies surrounded them. In December 1917, they established the secret police known as the **Cheka**—the Extraordinary Commission to Combat Counterrevolution, Sabotage, and Speculation. The Cheka and its agents, Chekists, ruthlessly sought out and arrested anyone suspected of opposing Bolshevik power. By mid-1918, all conservative and liberal parties had been shut down, their newspapers confiscated, and their leaders driven underground or into exile. By the summer of 1918, the enemies of the Bolsheviks had organized themselves to fight the new order in Russia. The **Russian Civil War**, between the Reds (Bolsheviks) and the Whites (diverse groups opposed to the Bolsheviks), was to last until 1920. Some of the first victims were Nicholas II and his family, killed in July 1918 on the orders of Lenin, who feared that the ex-tsar might fall into the hands of the Whites.

The Turning of the Tide, 1917–1918

↓ What events led to the defeat of Germany and the Central Powers?

↓ Why did so many Germans refuse to believe that they had been defeated?

After two and a half years of war, by early 1917 despair and frustration prevailed on all sides. The ideals and enthusiasm of the summer of 1914 had been long forgotten as governments and military leaders desperately cast about for some way of ending the conflict. Two events of 1917 broke this deadlock: the revolutions in Russia and the decision of the United States to enter the war on the Allied side. With the arrival of American finances, troops, and equipment, chances for a victory of the Central Powers faded. The year 1918 began with German victory on the eastern front but ended with defeat in the west. Few Germans realized at the time how crushing this defeat would be. But even the exhausted Allies had little cause for celebration in 1918.

War Exhaustion

Based on the military situation in early 1917, it would have been difficult to predict World War I's final outcome. Despite the stalemate in the west, the German army had advanced into Russia. Warsaw was taken in mid-1915, and by late 1916 Germans had taken Wilno (now Vilnius, Lithuania) and occupied much of eastern Ukraine, Belarus, and Lithuania. Austrian armies took back Galicia, which had been occupied by the Russians in the first months of the year and, after unexpectedly fierce fighting, succeeded in neutralizing Serbia.

The military and domestic situation in multinational Austria-Hungary, however, was unstable. Czech and other Slavic troops often deserted across the Russian lines, and even German-speakers in the empire questioned openly the utility of continuing "Prussia's" war. Early in 1916, Emperor Francis Joseph died after a reign of nearly seventy years, depriving Austria-Hungary of a unifying symbol. Later that year, a young man entered a Viennese café, approached the Austrian prime minister, cried out, "We want peace," then shot him and waited quietly to be arrested. A Russian offensive in the summer of 1916 had brought the Austro-Hungarian army close to collapse, until German troops intervened. Behind the scenes, the young Austro-Hungarian emperor sent out secret peace feelers to the Allies, only to be found out and severely rebuked by the Kaiser. By 1917, the war enthusiasm of a few years earlier was dead, all sides longed for an end to the bloodletting, but no one could see a way out.

In such a situation, the peace movement gained momentum. In previous years radical socialists, including Lenin, Kollontai, and Luxemburg, had met in Switzerland to issue a manifesto, drafted by Trotsky, calling for "a peace without annexations or war indemnities." These socialists argued that the war should end without any country gaining new territory or demanding payment from their enemies. They believed that the present war was absurd and immoral, serving the interests of the armaments industries, the imperialist powers, and the rich. They demanded, instead, a war against the existing order, in which workingmen and -women of all nations would band together and turn weapons on the hated capitalists and generals. No mainstream socialist party could accept such a radical program, but as the stalemate con-

Cheka   Secret police established in Soviet Russia in December 1917 to eradicate enemies of the Bolshevik regime.

Russian Civil War   War between Bolshevik government ("Reds") and its opponents ("Whites") from 1918 to 1920, ending in victory of Reds.

tinued on the battlefronts, and misery on the home fronts deepened, calls for peace were also issued by mainstream leaders, including U.S. president **Woodrow Wilson** and the pope.

In 1917, in Britain, France, and Germany, hundreds of thousands of workers went out on strike, breaking their no-strike pledges. Even wage increases could not keep up with the steep rise in prices, but strikers were also protesting this senseless war. Influenced by left-wing arguments, they increasingly rejected the idea of shared interests with factory owners. Similarly, soldiers distrusted their generals and loathed the politicians back home. For many, it appeared that incompetent leaders were merely spouting hollow lines about patriotism to mask their inability to end a war that by now nobody wanted. In April 1917, at several places on the western front, French soldiers simply refused to "go over the top." Their disobedience was simply a reasonable unwillingness to carry out unreasonably murderous orders, but these mutinies shook the military leadership, who feared that the soldiers would turn their weapons against their own officers and mutinies would spread.

Russian soldiers, whose morale and material conditions had been shaken by the March revolution in Petrograd, retreated in disorder in the midst of a summer offensive. Shortly after seizing power in November, the Bolsheviks initiated cease-fire talks with the Germans. Germany had already defeated Romania earlier in 1917 and had exacted very harsh peace terms from that country. At the same time, the Central Powers' Bulgarian and Turkish allies were barely hanging on, plagued by low morale and shortages of food and ammunition. The loss of vast Ottoman Middle Eastern territories to the British by late 1917 created a crisis of confidence in the Turkish leadership.

Amid general war weariness, only the Germans appeared to have some reason for hope. In late September 1917, the combined German and Austrian army inflicted a crushing defeat on the Italians at Caporetto. The Italian army nearly disintegrated, thousands deserted, and three hundred thousand men were taken prisoner by the German and Austrian armies. This decisive victory, combined with the Russian collapse, encouraged many Germans to believe that the war would end favorably in 1918. Such wishful thinking failed to appreciate the decisive turn in the war's fortunes caused by the United States' joining the Allies.

The Entry of the United States

Until 1917, the United States had avoided taking sides in the European conflict. Most Americans could not see how their interests were involved in the European war and preferred to remain neutral. Even after the public outrage over the sinking of the *Lusitania* in May 1915, President Wilson remained unwilling to press for American intervention. His election campaign of the following year was conducted under the slogan "He kept us out of war." But just a month after his second inauguration, Wilson signed a declaration of war against Germany.

Two foolish actions by the German government had altered American public opinion. In January 1917, the German foreign minister, Arthur Zimmermann, telegraphed the German ambassador in Mexico, instructing him to offer Mexico the return of lands lost in the 1840s to the United States if Mexico would support Germany against the Americans. The British intercepted the telegram and revealed its contents to the American government. The reaction was predictably furious, and when the telegram was published in the American press in March, anti-German war sentiment ran high.

At the beginning of February, the Germans announced the resumption of unrestricted submarine warfare, disregarding the effect that such a move would have on American public opinion. The sinking of several American merchant ships strengthened calls for intervention. The March revolution in Russia heightened the contrast between the militarist regime in Berlin and democratic governments in Paris, London, and now Petrograd. All these factors came together in Wilson's request on April 2, 1917, for a declaration of war. Wilson stated that world peace was the goal: "The world must be made safe for democracy."

The impact of the American entry into the war was felt first financially. American loans and credits, previously somewhat restrained by considerations of neutrality, opened up fully for the Allied Powers. American factories retooled for war production, and more than 20 million men registered for military service. American soldiers began to arrive in France in June 1917, though it was not until 1918 that American troops actually went into battle. Just as in European countries, the American government intervened in the economy. The War Industries Board in Washington coordinated production and distribution of essential goods. As American troops and manufactured

Woodrow Wilson   (1856–1924) U.S. president, 1913–1921, who brought the United States into war "to make the world safe for democracy" and authored the Fourteen Points.

goods streamed across the Atlantic, the Central Powers were reaching their last reserves.

German Victory over Russia

With the American entry into the war, the Germans knew that their only chance for victory was to crush the Allies before American troops could arrive in significant numbers. That seemed possible when the Bolsheviks pulled Russia out of the war. Lenin recognized that the very survival of his new socialist regime depended on making peace, and the Russian army had essentially ceased to exist. As Lenin himself put it, peasant soldiers had "voted with their feet" by deserting to head home and obtain their share of agricultural land being seized from the landlords.

In the autumn of 1917, the Germans had taken Riga and were threatening the Baltic approaches to Petrograd, with little to stop them. On December 15, 1917, representatives of the Bolsheviks and the Central Powers met in the Belarusian town of Brest-Litovsk and agreed on an **armistice.** Both delegations remained in the city to hammer out details of the peace. The deliberations between Bolsheviks, led by the fiery orator Trotsky, and the German delegation, made up mainly of stiff Prussian generals and sober diplomats, revealed the enormous political differences between the two sides. The Soviet representatives demanded "peace without annexations or war indemnities" and **national self-determination** for Ukrainians, Poles, and other non-Russians under German occupation. The Germans were astounded that the Bolshevik representatives dared make demands, considering their military weakness. When negotiations broke down, the German army simply advanced farther into Russian territory, encountering almost no resistance.

Back in Petrograd, Lenin was furious. He scolded Trotsky for his arrogance and warned that Germany's conditions for peace would now be even harsher. He was right. In March 1918, the Bolsheviks accepted the **Treaty of Brest-Litovsk.** Russia signed away over a quarter of its prewar population and arable land as well as over half its coal fields and iron manufacturing. This vast region, stretching from the Baltic Sea to Ukraine, was carved into new states dependent on Germany. Even though relatively few ethnic Russians lived in these lands, the loss of this huge territory was a severe blow to the young government, one that no democratic government could have survived. The new border with Finland and Estonia ran threateningly close to Petrograd, and for security reasons the Russian capital was moved to Moscow, where it remains to this day.

German Defeat

In January 1918, Woodrow Wilson issued his famous **Fourteen Points**—a plan of the future peace based not on revenge but on the liberal principles of freedom, justice, and free trade. Among the most important of the Fourteen Points were the demands for "open covenants of peace, openly arrived at," national self-determination, an independent Polish state, arms reduction, free navigation of the seas, and the creation of a postwar international body—the **League of Nations**—that would regulate relations between states and prevent future wars. Through private conversations, many Germans and Austrians learned of the speech despite their governments' efforts to suppress the information. For them, the Fourteen Points appeared to open the possibility of peace negotiations. Others, however, denounced Wilson's speech as mere propaganda. As long as there was a chance for military victory, in any case, the German government expressed no interest in Wilson's proposal.

Hoping to win the war quickly, the Germans launched major offensives on the western front in the spring of 1918, but they failed, with several hundred thousand casualties only weakening the Germany military further. By autumn, even the German High Command recognized they had lost the war. Thinking that a civilian government could win milder terms from the Allies, and seeking to evade their own responsibility for the defeat, the military leadership persuaded the Kaiser to abdicate. As strikes and political demonstrations rocked German cities, a new government was formed, dominated by moderate socialists. In this way, the burden of defeat fell not on generals and the Kaiser but on the fledgling democratic government of Germany.

Under the armistice agreement, the Germans promised to withdraw from Belgium, return Alsace-Lorraine

---

armistice   Temporary cease-fire reached before official treaty ending hostilities.

national self-determination   Right of ethnic groups or nations to autonomy, often falsely interpreted to mean the setting up of independent nation-states.

Treaty of Brest-Litovsk   Harsh peace imposed on Soviet Russia by Germany in March 1918 that stripped Russia of large territories on its western borders.

Fourteen Points   President Woodrow Wilson's blueprint for peace and postwar negotiations based on the principles of freedom, justice, and free trade.

League of Nations   Postwar international body proposed by Woodrow Wilson to regulate relations between states with the goal of preventing future wars.

to France, surrender submarines and rail stock, and destroy artillery. All Allied prisoners of war were to be released immediately, and the Treaty of Brest-Litovsk was annulled. The Germans agreed to pay for war damages. The Allied naval blockade of Germany would continue until a final peace settlement was reached. Though the provisions were harsh, the German delegation signed, one member taking comfort by observing, "A nation of seventy million suffers, but does not die." At the eleventh minute of the eleventh hour of the eleventh day of the eleventh month of 1918, the guns went silent on the western front.

The fighting was ended, but the final conditions of peace were still to be negotiated and the German people were already stunned at the harsh armistice terms. Though the German generals knew well that the war had been lost, propaganda at home had predicted victory. Ordinary Germans had no way of knowing that their army was on the brink of collapse. German troops remained in position in northern France, and no Allied troops had crossed onto German soil. Corporal Adolf Hitler, temporarily blinded in action, heard the news in his hospital bed and wept.

Central and eastern Europe were in chaos. The Russian and Austro-Hungarian Empires had ceased to exist. Independence was declared in Poland, Ukraine, Czechoslovakia, Finland, and Lithuania. In Vienna, an Austrian Republic was proclaimed; its parliament asked to be accepted into the German Reich. German sailors mutinied and took over the northern port city of Kiel. In other German cities, from Berlin to Munich, radicalized soldiers and workers set up soviets on the Russian model. Budapest, capital of the new Hungary, also experienced a short-lived soviet government. As workers, soldiers, and sailors took to the streets, the middle classes feared for their property and lives. In Moscow, Lenin hoped this was the dawn of the world revolution. Not just a war had ended, but a world.

End of the European Era

More than 8 million Europeans died in World War I, and about 20 million young men had been wounded, many permanently disabled. The worldwide influenza epidemic of late 1918–1919 killed as many as forty million more. In many areas, public order had broken down, and governments were in disarray. Four empires—German, Russian, Ottoman, and Habsburg—had collapsed, millions of people had been uprooted, and class warfare had broken out in many parts of central and eastern Europe.

The war caused widespread destruction. Roads and railroads were destroyed. Entire villages and towns

Jaroslav Hašek's literary creation, *The Good Soldier Švejk* was an ordinary soldier—a kind of Czech "Sad Sack"—in the Austro-Hungarian army during World War I. Good-natured and portly, Švejk has been seen as a reflection of Czech national character, but the efforts of this "little man" to survive in an absurd war is a universal theme. *(Jaroslav Hašek, Osudy dobrého vojáka Švejka; za svetové valky; [Prague: Československý spisovatel, 1984])*

ceased to exist. Factories were breaking down without proper upkeep and investment. The total cost of the war is difficult to calculate, but the famous English economist John Maynard Keynes estimated that it represented Europe's entire industrial output of several years.

From London to Constantinople, from Moscow to Marseilles, Europeans were poorer in 1918 than in 1914. Except for Britain, industrial production contracted. Commercial trade ceased, and the center of international finance shifted from London to New York. Agriculture also suffered, and food shortages were so widespread, especially as the naval blockade continued, pending the peace settlement, that millions faced starvation in the winter of 1918. On the other side of the world, Japan prospered during the war and increased its influence in the region at the expense of China. The American economy also boomed as its capital and goods streamed into Europe, further reducing the European proportion of world economic output.

The war had a permanent effect on the European psyche. Trench warfare and total war made optimism about the future—and belief in the past—hollow. The notion of human progress was undone. Disorientation, depression, and rage were the surviving emotions, reflected in the paintings of Paul Nash and George Grosz and in the highly unmilitary figure of Jaroslav Hašek's *Good Soldier Švejk.* Literary critic Paul Fussell has suggested that World War I even altered European perceptions of the natural world. Sunrise had long been the symbol of a new day, full of hope and possibilities. But for soldiers in the trenches, dawn was the most terrifying time of all—the time of the call to "go over the top." After World War I, nothing, not even the sunrise, would be the same.

Summary

Review Questions

↑ What role did nationalism play in the outbreak and events of World War I?

↑ How did new technologies make World War I a new type of war, both at the front and at home?

↑ How did World War I alter the way Europeans sense of themselves and their world?

World War I did not come unexpectedly. Europe's Great Powers had been building military budgets, their arms and armies, all through the age of imperialism. While no nation wanted war, each of the major powers was willing to wage war to achieve specific goals. France wanted the return of Alsace-Lorraine, Britain and Russia feared Germany's growing industrial and military might, and Austria-Hungary felt the need to suppress nationalist movements supported by hostile neighbors. The German leadership was threatened by growing Russian and French military power and feared being squeezed between them in a two-front war. Many recognized that ethnic conflict in the Balkans could lead to a European war. And, in the summer of 1914, it did.

Still, the actual war came as a shock. Most Europeans expected an intense but short war. Instead, the fighting soon bogged down in trenches across France that made a mockery of the idea that war could be glorious. On the eastern front, the poor organization and tactics of the Russian army caused many casualties. As the suffering continued, many wondered why the political will could not be found to end this mad destruction. The longing for peace helped bring about the Bolshevik victory in the Russian Revolution of November 1917, thereby ending the war on the eastern front and creating the first socialist state in world history.

To manage this unexpected Great War, states assumed a far greater role in citizens' lives than ever before. Governments coordinated the distribution of raw materials and transformed civilian industry for military purposes. They brokered agreements between labor and big business to prevent strikes. To finance the war, they ran up large deficits, causing prices to rise and purchasing power to decline. To ensure loyalty and bolster morale, they restricted free speech, censored news, and spent large sums on propaganda. In this first total war, governments demanded that citizens work only for total victory.

While the front experience was almost exclusively male, the home front was dominated by women, and it had a major impact on family life. With millions of men gone from the fields and factories, women took jobs outside the home—many for the first time—in munitions manufacturing and nursing. Their increasingly public role strengthened their demands for equal rights and the vote.

On November 11, 1918, the war came to an end. For most Germans, defeat was a shock, as the German armies had won in the east and in the west still held French territory. But there were no real victors. Millions had lost their lives or been crippled. Billions had been spent, bankrupting European governments. The north of France was gutted with shell craters, the earth poisoned. The end of the war was greeted not with rejoicing but with a dull bewilderment.

← **Thinking Back, Thinking Ahead** →

What were some of the consequences of the First World War that caused many Europeans, especially of the middle and upper classes, in 1918 to feel that their entire world had collapsed?

ECHO ECHO ECHO ECHO ECHO ECHO

Propaganda and Advertising

"Fly to Paris for $99!" "Speak Arabic in just two hours!" "Have fuller, sexier hair!" We are constantly bombarded with advertising slogans and appeals. On the radio, on television, and inevitably in our e-mail inbox, we find promises of a better sex life, slimmer hips without hunger, grade-A research papers, and more. We have come to regard such promises with a great deal of skepticism, knowing well that the ticket to Paris will end up costing $900, that after two hours we will barely know ten words in Arabic, and that better sex rarely arrives by e-mail. Similarly, official reports and government statements are no longer accepted as necessarily true—at least not the entire truth. In 1914, however, people were not yet accustomed to this steady stream of lies and half-truths.

Propaganda is a Latin word first used by the Catholic Church to refer to the spreading of the faith, without any negative connotation. When, in 1914, the British set up an agency to keep up public morale and convince citizens of the moral correctness of the war effort, they called it the War Propaganda Bureau. Famous writers such as John Galsworthy, Rudyard Kipling, and Arthur Conan Doyle were recruited to write pamphlets praising British war aims and military leadership, while denouncing German barbarism. Photographers and artists were also recruited for the war effort. Similarly in America, the Committee on Public Information worked to increase public support and enthusiasm for the war, publishing posters and pamphlets showing the Germans to be cruel and inhuman, and even creating films with titles such as *The Kaiser: The Beast of Berlin.*

Advertisers learned a lot from war propaganda. A complete lie is not effective: it is too easily found out. Much better is to present part of the truth as the whole. Just as propagandists made some German atrocities seem universal, advertisers expand an attractive feature into a life-changing virtue. Everyone knows the story of the boy who cried wolf, whose jokes got him in trouble when the real wolf arrived. Similarly, the lies and distortions of war propaganda in World War I convinced many people after 1918 to believe no claims of atrocities or appeals to patriotism issued by the government. Thus, World War I propaganda played a role in the creation of a much more skeptical—or even cynical—attitude, whether toward government pronouncements or advertisers' claims.

Suggested Readings

Ferguson, Niall. *The Pity of War.* New York: Basic Books, 1999. Sophisticated and detailed argument against the inevitability of World War I.

Figes, Orlando. *A People's Tragedy: The Russian Revolution, 1891–1924.* New York: Penguin Books, 1998. A very detailed account of the causes and events of the revolution.

Fischer, Fritz. *Germany's Aims in the First World War.* London: Chatto and Windus, 1967. Controversial and path-breaking work arguing that Germany's aggressive economic and political policies were primarily to blame for World War I.

Fitzpatrick, Sheila. *The Russian Revolution.* New York: Oxford University Press, 2001. A short book covering the period 1917–1932.

Fussell, Paul. *The Great War and Modern Memory.* New York: Oxford University Press, 2000. A brilliant discussion of the experience of the trenches and English poetry.

Keegan, John. *The First World War.* New York: Vintage, 2000. A well-written survey by the dean of British military historians.

Pipes, Richard. *The Russian Revolution.* New York: Vintage, 1991. Massive volume from important conservative historian.

Websites

A huge variety of military, diplomatic, and memoir sources, **The World War I Document Archive,** at http://net.lib.byu.edu/~rdh7/wwi

Images, documents, posters, maps, and a wealth of other information, **An Internet History of the Great War,** at www.worldwar1.com

Paintings, music, writings, information on the Russian Revolution, **Soviet History** at http://www.marxists.org/history/ussr/index.htm

CHAPTER 26

A Decade of Revolutionary Experiments, 1918–1929

1500 B.C.E.	1000 B.C.E.	500 B.C.E.	1 B.C.E./1 C.E.

1916	1917	1918	1919	1920	1921	1922

1918
Russian civil war begins

1919
League of Nations is established
Versailles Treaty imposes a harsh peace on Germany

1922
Mussolini seizes power in Italy

Europe Following World War I

Europe's political map was greatly altered by the peace settlements following World War I. With four empires wiped off the map, and new, smaller states cobbled out of the territories lost by these former great powers, Europe entered a new era of the nation-state. In Europe's new political configuration, what new tensions would be likely to arise?

Legend:
- Boundaries of German, Russian, and Austro-Hungarian empires in 1914
- Areas lost by Austro-Hungarian Empire
- Areas lost by Russian Empire
- Areas lost by German Empire
- Areas lost by Bulgaria
- Areas lost by Ottoman Empire
- Demilitarized Zones
- Boundaries of 1926
- Areas controlled under mandates from the League of Nations, 1920

500 C.E.   1000 C.E.   1500 C.E.   2000 C.E.

1923
French occupy the Ruhr
Hitler's Beer Hall Putsch fails

1926
Germany is admitted to the League of Nations

1928
Kellogg-Briand Pact outlaws war
Stalin assumes leadership of Soviet Union

1929
U.S. stock market crashes
Great Depression begins

1923   1924   1925   1926   1927   1928   1929   1930

Choice Choice Choice

Alexandra Kollontai

Though a role model for many feminists, Bolshevik revolutionary Alexandra Kollontai (1872–1952) never saw herself as such. She considered feminism a product of nineteenth-century capitalism and a misguided ideology for women who wanted liberation. She believed that only by achieving economic power as wage earners would women be able to gain freedom and social equality. (Sovfoto)

Alexandra Kollontai Becomes a Revolutionary

At age twenty-two, Alexandra Kollontai seemed to have achieved everything expected of a young woman from an aristocratic family. As the daughter of a general in Russia's imperial army, she was well educated, privileged, and active in St. Petersburg's high society. She had married an army officer and given him a son. She was obedient and devoted. Then she read August Bebel's *Woman and Socialism.* His ideas that under capitalism women were fundamentally subjugated through the institution of marriage and could achieve full independence only under socialism convinced her that she was enslaved.

Almost instantly she gave it all up. She started attending lectures by radical socialists and visiting factories to see the conditions in which the workers, especially women, of St. Petersburg labored. Her secure and privileged life now seemed nothing more than a gilded cage, and she knew she could never go back to it. At age twenty-five, she abandoned her husband and child, disowned her aristocratic heritage, moved out on her own, and embarked on a remarkable career of revolutionary activism.

Beginning in 1898, she worked with underground Marxist organizations in Russia and abroad. She was an outspoken organizer of women workers, an important opponent of World War I, and leader of the International Women's Day demonstration for bread and peace that triggered the overthrow of the tsar in March 1917. In November 1917, she was at the forefront of the armed Bolshevik uprising.

Although a devoted Bolshevik, Kollontai was never satisfied with simply following the party line; she insisted on speaking her mind and following her convictions, no matter what the consequences. Thus, in 1918, she resigned from her government position as commissar for social welfare when she found herself the sole voice opposing the Treaty of Brest-Litovsk, which she viewed as abandoning the Finnish communist movement. She remained an inconvenience to the Bolshevik leadership throughout the early 1920s, never afraid to stand up to anyone, even V. I. Lenin.

Cleverly, Lenin dealt with Kollontai's inconvenient radicalism by sending her abroad. In November 1922, she was appointed to the Soviet legation in Norway, then sent to Mexico and to Sweden. Far from Moscow, Kollontai was free to criticize the Bolshevik regime without posing a real threat inside the center of power. Yet she continued to play an important role in the Soviet Union. She was among the first female diplomats to serve at such a high level and was regarded in the diplomatic international community as a very able colleague. Even when sidelined, Kollontai was a trendsetter.

Kollontai's radicalism was most remarkable in her choices as the first leader of the Women's Section of the Communist Party (the Zhenotdel). Following Bebel's principles, she advocated an end to marriage and the nuclear family in favor of living in free unions and raising children in communal settings, where domestic chores—cleaning, cooking, and child care—would be shared. She lived by her convictions but was unable to inspire others to do the same. Most women were not ready to abandon the satisfaction and security of marriage and motherhood, and men resisted her radical ideas. Yet Kollontai's choice for freedom and courage to reshape her identity according to her radical beliefs made her a symbol of revolutionary experiments in politics and social relations that marked the decade after the Great War.

Introduction

Like Alexandra Kollontai, many Europeans began, or were forced, to reconsider their social, cultural, and political identities in the decade after 1918. In the same way that Kollontai had shed her aristocratic past like a useless shroud, many others abandoned their allegiance to the nationalist or liberal ideals that had yielded few positive results in the Great War. Women demanded political and economic power, workers fought for social justice, newly created states struggled for recognition, and artists offered entirely new ways of defining beauty and the individual.

This period saw both a rush toward creating a brand-new world from the ashes of war and a withdrawal aimed at imposing stability on a world that had unraveled. As empires collapsed, new states sprang up, forcing a veritable new order. Europe redrew national borders, reformulated the principles of state sovereignty, and redefined the nature of international relations. Democracy became the new foundation for political legitimacy. The postwar peace conference that mapped these changes pleased no one and left many issues unresolved. Mounting economic problems such as postwar payments and debts plagued much of the continent.

To address these new conditions, Europeans tried a broad range of political experiments, from social democracy in Germany and especially in Scandinavia, to fascism in Italy. In Russia, the Bolsheviks won a civil war and embarked on a new and untested communist system. New state institutions forcefully eliminated any real and potential enemies and tried to transform peasants into workers, and women and men into equal participants in the building of communism. Avant-garde artists created a new revolutionary style.

New movements flourished all over Europe, in fact. Women tried on new public identities in popular culture and new political roles in countries where they won the vote. Some challenged economic, social, sexual, and cultural limits. Philosophers, theologians, and artists reacted against the destruction of the war with a renewed commitment to moral values and hope in Christianity. The 1920s also saw the growth of a pacifist movement.

The notion of progress had been strenuously tested by the war and the frailty of the human condition laid bare. Europeans met these challenges in different ways—some by living in the moment and enjoying the freedoms of popular entertainment and consumption, others by searching for absolutes in politics, philosophy, or art. At the heart of many of these responses was the hope that a brand-new world had been born out of the ashes of the war. Some politicians, reformers, and intellectuals tried to find a middle ground, but their voices were not much heard in the chaotic atmosphere of the 1920s. By 1929, Europe was becoming polarized between two extremist political regimes—fascism and communism—and democracy was losing ground.

The Search for Stability, 1918–1924

↓ What various strategies did political leaders use to restore Europe after the war?
↓ What problems stood in the way of political stability?

When European leaders met in 1919 to write the peace treaties, the mood was grim. The war was over, but violence continued. Four empires—the Habsburg, German, Ottoman, and Russian—lay in shambles. Revolution had engulfed Russia and spread in Germany and Hungary. The economies of all the combatants were devastated. Cities, factories, and fields lay in ruin; people starved. Yet few leaders were ready to rebuild Europe and secure a lasting peace through democracy. Instead, they focused on immediate objectives, such as increasing their territory and population, reducing war payments, and solidifying their

Chronology

1918–1922	Reds and Whites engage in Russian Civil War
1919	Comintern is established; Bolshevik revolution in Hungary creates short-lived Soviet Republic; League of Nations is established; Treaty of Versailles officially ends World War I; Fiume Republic is established
1921	Lenin inaugurates the New Economic Policy in Russia
1922	Mussolini seizes power in Italy; Irish Free State is established
1923	Hitler attempts to seize power in Bavarian Beer Hall Putsch

1923–1925	Britain and France occupy Ruhr, precipitate German economic crisis
1924	Ramsay MacDonald becomes first Labour Party prime minister of Great Britain; Dawes Plan resets German reparation payments; First Surrealist manifesto is issued in Paris
1925	Josephine Baker performs American jazz dances in Paris
1926	Germany is admitted into League of Nations
1928	Kellogg-Briand Pact renounces future war in Europe; Stalin assumes leadership of Soviet Union

own political position at home. The peace negotiations were driven as much by internal as by international considerations. They were also driven by secret treaties made during the war. As a consequence, the ideal of national self-determination promoted by U.S. president Woodrow Wilson stood little chance of success. In the end, the victors were dissatisfied, and the defeated were humiliated. Even before the ink dried on the paper of the last peace document (1923), radical movements were undoing the stability of Europe.

The Peace Treaties

As peace negotiations opened in January 1919 at the old royal palace in Versailles, the representatives of the victorious Allied Powers that dominated the agenda—all gray-haired men in tails and top hats—embodied the old European order established a century before at the Congress of Vienna. But revolutionary changes were at hand: the map of Europe would be redrawn, a new international system would redefine state relations, and democracy would replace aristocratic privilege as the fundamental basis for political power.

Wilson arrived in Paris with an idea for a European order based on national self-determination: Poles should govern themselves in an independent Poland, and Italians should live in Italy. This principle seemed a rational and just solution to some of the problems that had caused turmoil in Europe since the end of the nineteenth century and contributed to the beginning of World War I. Ethnic minorities had come to see themselves as fundamentally oppressed because they generally did not receive the same benefits of economic development and state support for their education and culture as members of the majority ethnic group. But the ethnic map of Europe was in reality so complicated as to make self-determination impossible. Polish nationals lived in areas where there were significant Russian and German populations. Italians and South Slavs were mixed in Istria and other areas along the Adriatic Sea. So no matter where the national boundaries were set, some ethnic groups would still be minorities. But, generally, the winners in Europe's Great War liked Wilson's ideas and supported them as a basis for peace and stability in Europe as well as a justification for territorial gains. Those who had sided with the Allies—such as the Poles and Romanians—gained, while those aligned with the Central Powers lost.

One outcome of self-determination was an array of new and significantly reshaped countries. Among the winners, France, Greece, Italy, and Romania gained territories and populations. From the losers, new countries were created: Czechoslovakia was carved out of Austria-Hungary; Finland, Estonia, Latvia, and Lithuania emerged from Russia's western borderlands; Poland was re-created from the unification of territories lost by Germany, Russia, and Austria-Hungary; Turkey was a diminished version of the Ottoman Empire; and Yugoslavia was created by uniting Serbia

In 1919, the old generation of political leaders—Prime Minister *David Lloyd George* of the United Kingdom, *Vittorio Orlando* of Italy, Premier *Georges Clemenceau* of France, and President *Woodrow Wilson* of the United States—met at Versailles to decide the fate of Europe. While Wilson's view of self-determination became an important, if contested, concept after 1918, the political leadership of the other heads of state present in this photograph was subsequently rejected by their voters. *(Bettmann/ Corbis)*

with South Slavic territories lost by Austria-Hungary. The western European states' interest in creating these new countries had a great deal to do with self-determination and also with their fear of Bolshevism. The new countries that bordered the Soviet Union would be a buffer zone against communist contamination from the east.

By contrast, Austria, Bulgaria, Hungary, Germany, and Russia lost territories. Most severely reduced were Germany, held responsible for starting the war, and Russia, whose Bolshevik regime had signed a separate peace with Germany. Neither was represented at the negotiations. For all these countries, save the Soviet Union, revision of the **Versailles Treaty** and the supplemental treaties (see Table 26.1) was an important aim in the internal politics of the next two decades, undermining any quest for stability and democratic government.

Other wartime arrangements undermined the spirit of reconciliation and justice promoted by Wilson. To convince Italy to enter the war, the Allies had secretly offered it Istria, where the majority of the population were South Slavs. Serbia, also an ally of France and Britain, had been promised the same area. In the end, Italy received a good part of this territory, in flagrant disregard for the principle of self-determination. Another victim of the secret treaties was the Ottoman

Table 26.1
World War I Peace Treaties
1918 Brest-Litovsk: Germany with Russia
1919 Versailles: Allies with Germany
1919 St. Germain: Allies with Austria
1919 Neuilly-sur-Seine: Allies with Bulgaria
1920 Trianon: Allies with Hungary
1920 Sèvres: Allies with Turkey
1921 Riga: Poland with Soviet Union
1924 Lausanne: Allies with Turkey and Greece

Empire. The Sykes-Picot Agreement (1916) had promised France and Britain various Ottoman territories in the Middle East. After the war, contradictory promises made by some British leaders, such as T. E. Lawrence, to Arab nationalist groups, and by other British politicians to Jewish Zionist groups (the Balfour Declaration) produced a conflict over Arab and Jewish

Versailles Treaty   First peace treaty of World War I; established Germany's guilt in starting the war and punished it through reparations and demilitarization.

homelands in Palestine that remains unresolved to this day.

Thus, a great deal of debate at Versailles focused on what counted more—the promises made by the Allies during the war or the new and popular principle of self-determination. The solutions varied, and though the states involved in these disputes were pacified, they were not necessarily satisfied. The greatest casualty was, however, the very principle of self-determination. If secret treaties counted more than the rights of ethnic groups who inhabited the disputed territories, the new states learned quickly that they were still at the mercy of Great Powers.

The Great Powers tried to address potential inter-state conflicts in two ways. First, they made sure the peace treaties protected minorities. The borders of Czechoslovakia, Poland, Romania, Yugoslavia, Greece, and Turkey were recognized only if these states agreed to treat ethnic and religious minorities, especially Jews, as equal citizens. Yet these provisions fostered some instability: they gave rise to protests inside states, especially by ethnic majorities, and from outside—from states that had lost populations. On a personal level, consider the dilemma of an educated ethnic Hungarian, a city employee in Kolozsvár, in the heart of Transylvania. After 1919, when Hungarian Kolozsvár became Romanian Cluj, he lost his job because he did not speak the language of the new administration—Romanian. His identity changed overnight: he lost his economic position, his social standing as a respectable government employee, and his cultural position as member of an important European nation, Hungary. Though the same person living in the same place, he was recast as a member of a powerless ethnic minority. It is not difficult to imagine how those who had been part of Europe's privileged old order felt after 1919 and how quickly they looked to revise the peace treaties. **Revisionism** set the stage for future inter-ethnic conflict.

Another way the Great Powers tried to maintain peace was through the new League of Nations, created in the peace settlement. This international organization gave sovereign states the means for communicating and solving problems through open, peaceful negotiations rather than secret treaties. The league also monitored the protection of minorities and various international humanitarian organizations, such as the Red Cross. But it was weak from the beginning, as the United States—fearing European entanglements—refused to join, while Germany, Russia, and Turkey were excluded. Other Great Powers wavered between playing a strong role and disengagement. The league was important for upholding international principles such as human rights and for regulating arms traf-

ficking, labor practices, and the treatment of displaced persons. But it did not have the strength to enforce its decisions. Its most severe punishment was to expel countries that did not comply.

The league did have an important role regarding the status of colonies, however. Former German colonies in Africa and Asia were transferred to Britain, France, Japan, and the United States as **trust territories** or **mandates**, and large parts of the former Ottoman Empire were also placed under British authority. Through its new mandate system, the league monitored the treatment of the native populations by colonial governments and facilitated cooperation among colonial powers, which were now also obligated to report to the league on their colonies. The goal of this system was to prepare native populations for self-government. One prominent example was the role of Britain in facilitating the development of modern political institutions and elites in Iraq, which moved from its **protectorate** position in 1919 to gaining full independence in 1932.

In most cases, the league found it difficult to enforce its supervisory role without a military force. At the same time, the participation of colonial troops in the war and the promises of the league had awakened the hope of self-rule and greater freedom among native peoples, and the league was ineffective in easing the resulting tensions. Especially in Palestine, another British mandate, clashes between the local Arab population and resolute Jewish settlers continued into the 1930s and beyond.

Still, the league represented a major departure from the system of international relations of the nineteenth century, in which small states had been virtual clients of the Great Powers. Some of these uneven power relations continued after the war, but recognition of all member states as equals allowed small and new states to carve out a more independent position in international relations. This more democratic and inclusive setting helped generate a new culture of diplomacy, in which alliances and negotiations were discussed openly. Even though the league was ultimately unsuccessful in preventing another world war, it did

revisionism   Political aim of revising the World War I peace settlements.

trust territories and **mandates**   Former colonies and territories of losing countries given by the League of Nations to the winning countries to oversee.

protectorate   Political entity that formally agrees by treaty to enter into an unequal relationship with another, stronger state.

bring about greater stability in the 1920s. It also served as a learning ground for the creation of the United Nations after World War II.

Revolutionary Upheavals

The Bolshevik threat also shaped the ultimate outcome of the peace negotiations. With revolution in Russia and millions of armed soldiers on their way home to ruined economies and impoverished families throughout Europe, all states were afraid of revolution. In a few cases, this fear was real. In Germany, the Communist and Socialist Parties seemed on the rise, and several bloody uprisings took place between November 1918 and January 1919. They were crushed relatively quickly and violently, with leaders Rosa Luxemburg and Karl Liebknecht brutally murdered on the spot. A young corporal, **Adolf Hitler,** made himself known in the crushing of the communist uprising in Bavaria.

In Hungary, a Bolshevik revolution in March 1919 helped bring about a short-lived (133 days) Soviet Republic under the leadership of **Béla Kun.** The Bolshevik success here owed much to the Hungarians' dissatisfaction with the results of the war. As junior partners of the Austrians, they had endured great material and psychological losses. Kun's regime did not alleviate this suffering, focusing instead on the brutal suppression of its enemies. In a swift reaction, the Great Powers allowed Slovak and Romanian forces to invade the country. The results were disastrous for Hungary. The Kun regime was crushed, but Romania and Czechoslovakia extracted large territorial concessions for their role in "saving" the Hungarian people. The result was the Treaty of Trianon (1920), which reduced Hungary to one-third its prewar size, with large groups of Hungarians living outside its borders. The brief and violent Soviet Republic proved a costly experiment. It rendered Hungary small, landlocked, and vengeful, eager to revise the peace treaties.

Another short-lived revolutionary experiment was the **Republic of Fiume,** the brainchild of Italian poet **Gabriele D'Annunzio.** This small Adriatic port was part of Istria, the area claimed by Italy and Yugoslavia. South Slavs constituted a majority in Istria, but Fiume had an Italian majority. Wilson sided with Yugoslavia. Given the controversy over this city, D'Annunzio decided to take matters into his own hands and seized municipal institutions in September 1919. The poet became a military dictator, revered by his followers and feared by the general public.

Fiume was finally granted to Italy, but its ultimate fate was less important than the style of rule and **charismatic leadership** D'Annunzio modeled for **Benito Mussolini,** the future fascist leader. D'Annunzio's dramatic public speeches swayed huge crowds, more through performance and style than content. His followers marched through the streets in black shirts and leather boots, creating the impression of a highly unified and threatening military force. Adopting a look of youthful vengeance and an aura of absolute obedience, these young men seemed ready to renounce their individuality and devote themselves to their leader. The masterful way in which D'Annunzio reshaped identities impressed Mussolini, who adopted the rhetoric, uniforms, and ideas first experimented in Fiume.

Other victors also confronted revolutionary uprisings. The turmoil in Ireland intensified after 1919. Newly elected members of the Irish parliament declared independence and a bitter civil war ensued (1919–1921), claiming many victims and ending in a peace treaty that laid the foundation of the **Irish Free State** (1922–1937). This state comprised of all of Ireland except the six counties of Northern Ireland and received **dominion** status identical to that of Canada. There was much debate over the requirement to swear allegiance to the British king and especially over the status of Northern Ireland, which remained under direct British rule. The close final vote to ratify the treaty, 64 to 57, virtually ensured that separatist movements, such as the **Irish Republican Army (IRA)**, would con-

Adolf Hitler   (1889–1945) Leader of the Nazi Party and dictatorial ruler of the Third Reich who initiated World War II by attacking Poland.

Béla Kun   (1886–1938) Leader of a short-lived Bolshevik regime in Hungary crushed by Romanian and Slovak forces.

Republic of Fiume   Revolutionary experiment led by Gabriele D'Annunzio, whose dictatorship and militarized police state were precursors of fascism.

Gabriele D'Annunzio   (1863–1938) Italian writer who led the Republic of Fiume.

charismatic leadership   Leadership style that uses emotional appeals to arouse followers and compel loyalty.

Benito Mussolini   (1883–1943) Fascist dictator of Italy, the first to successfully challenge democracy in Europe; after 1936, a close ally of Adolf Hitler.

Irish Free State   Irish state established in 1922 with dominion status, consisting of all of Ireland except Northern Ireland, which remained under direct British rule.

dominion   Status in which former colonies recognize the British monarch as the head of the state but control their internal and foreign affairs.

Irish Republican Army   Military organization recognized in 1919 by the parliament of the *Republic of Ireland* as its army, revived in 1970 as a paramilitary terrorist organization.

tinue against the British. Unlike most other movements for national liberation in Europe at that time, in Ireland religion rather than language identity was at issue. In the Irish Free State, Catholicism was the dominant religion, while Catholics were a religious minority in Northern Ireland, where Protestants dominated. Yet despite tensions, Catholics and Protestants in Northern Ireland lived in relative peace for the next forty years.

Political challenges from the left and right thus threatened peace in Europe. Most governments and parties equated stability and democracy with suppressing Bolshevism. Liberals, social democrats, and nationalists united against this common enemy; yet some nationalist parties were also aggressive and potentially destabilizing, especially when they fought against the peace treaties. German nationalists in both Germany and Czechoslovakia, for example, used the principle of self-determination to argue that Czechoslovakia, with its large German minority, did not respect the peace treaties and would therefore be Bolshevik-friendly. Thus, opponents of the peace treaties also used anti-Bolshevism to argue their cause.

War Reparations and Economic Crisis

While the peace treaties sought political solutions to Europe's turmoil, economic stability proved elusive. The cost of the war had been enormous in financing the military effort and rebuilding destroyed lands and industries. Between the deficits that built up to finance the wars and the overall drop in economic production, all European states emerged from the war with major deficits, looking toward the United States for help. The victorious Allies, wanting the Central Powers to pay these costs, imposed **reparations** as part of the peace treaties. By far the largest reparations were demanded of Germany, both as revenge and as a means for the political leaders at Versailles to gain popular support at home. Coupled with the treaty's war guilt clause, in which Germany had to admit responsibility for starting the war, and its demand for disarmament, including demilitarization of the Rhineland, reparations reinforced Germany's humiliation and aimed to prevent it from becoming a major power again. The notion of making losers pay for the costs of armed conflict was not new, but the size of the payments was unprecedented. An international commission set reparations at 132 billion gold marks (today about $331.79 billion), or two years' worth of Germany's gross national product.

The British and French pressed Germany to start payments immediately, as both needed to repay the United States billions of dollars in war loans. The Americans were in a hurry to see the loans repaid, and with weak economic performance and potential political instability at home, Britain and France were relying on war reparations as an important revenue source. The French were particularly inflexible. But after making its first payment of 2.5 billion gold marks in 1921, the German government defaulted the following year. Great Britain was willing to work out a **moratorium** and potential reduction of the payments, but France and Belgium, which had suffered much greater material and human losses in the war, stood by the Versailles agreement and proceeded to occupy Germany's heavily industrial Ruhr district in order to extract the debt payment in kind.

The **Ruhr occupation** (1923–1925) had a twofold effect on the young German democracy. First, it unified Germans in their opinion of the 1919 Versailles Treaty as unjust and of the victorious powers as abusive. This view fostered the growth of nationalist parties, including the **National Socialist German Worker's Party**—the Nazis. In addition, by extracting from Germany some of its most important economic resources (the Ruhr produced 80 percent of Germany's steel and coal), the occupation helped generate a severe economic crisis. The German government only made things worse by printing more money, which led to **hyperinflation.** For white-collar workers, small-business owners, and the lower middle class generally, buying power vanished overnight. The hard-won savings of a middle-class professional that once might have paid for a car now barely bought a loaf of bread. Suitcases filled with paper money were not enough for a week's groceries. The professionals and small businessmen who had been the backbone Germany's social and economic stability were instantly converted into impassioned and desperate critics of the new German republic.

---

reparations War payments demanded by the victors from the losers.

moratorium Delay in the payment of the war debt.

Ruhr occupation Occupation (1923–1925) by French and Belgian troops of Germany's industrial Ruhr district to enforce the war reparations clause of the Versailles Treaty.

National Socialist German Workers' (Nazi) Party Right-wing party that recruited followers by promoting nationalism-socialism, with a nationalist-racist perspective.

hyperinflation Rapid devaluation of a currency that reduces its buying power overnight.

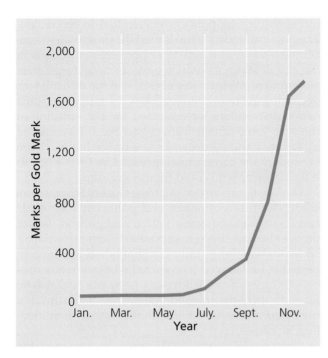

FIGURE 26.1 **German Hyperinflation in 1922**
After 1918 Germany suffered an economic breakdown, due to the punitive war debt payments the state was obligated to assume. It was only after the Dawes Plan came into effect in 1924 that Germany began to recover its economic power. *Source: Wilkinson, James D.; Huges, H. Stuart,* Contemporary Europe: A History, *9th Edition, © 1998, pp. 136. Reprinted by permission of Pearson Education, Inc., Upper Saddle River, NJ.*

The Ruhr crisis brought in other mediators, including a commission headed by American statesman and banker Charles G. Dawes. Its recommendations, known as the **Dawes Plan** (1924), set reparation payments at more realistic levels and helped rebuild the economies of other European countries, including Germany's. The United States loaned money to Germany to finance its war debt. Germany then paid installments to France and Britain as part of its reparations. These payments enabled France and Britain to repay their war loans back to the United States. By the second half of the 1920s, Europe's economies seemed restabilized.

With inflation under control in Germany and reparations payments steady, a new mood of reconciliation dominated Franco-German relations. In 1925, the two countries finally accepted their post-1918 common border. The League of Nations, despite the absence of the United States, was active and had a growing membership that after 1926 included Germany. That same year **Aristide Briand**, the French foreign minister, and **Gustav Stresemann**, his German counterpart, received the Nobel Peace Prize for

their "unprecedented attempt to base politics on the principle of mutual friendship and trust." In 1928, under the leadership of Briand and U.S. Secretary of State Frank B. Kellogg, fifteen countries signed the **Kellogg-Briand Pact**, which "condemned and renounced war as an instrument of national policy." Though the pact suggested greater U.S. involvement in European affairs, it had no means of enforcement, so it represented more a hope for peace than a guarantee. Still, international relations were now conducted in a relatively democratic and open fashion, a major shift from the prewar order.

Postwar Political Experiments, 1924–1929

↓ What new forms and responsibilities of government emerged during this period?
↓ Where and in what ways was democracy successful, and what were its failures?

In the second half of the 1920s, Europe stabilized. Governments rebounded from the disappointments of the peace treaties and hyperinflation. In western Europe, the most successful political parties were conservative and moderate; liberals and social democrats lacked popular trust. New parties tried to take advantage of this vacuum, most prominently the Italian fascists. In eastern Europe, a combination of older liberal and new agrarian parties had the greatest impact on the young states. Only in Scandinavia was there continuity between the prewar and postwar politics. But everywhere, except for Italy, democratic forms of government seemed solidly in place.

Politics in Western Europe

In the five years after 1918, the politicians of the most powerful European countries—Great Britain, France, and Germany—lost the confidence of their constituents.

Dawes Plan Financial agreement concluded by France, Britain, and the United States in 1924 that solved the crisis of war reparations and loans.

Aristide Briand (1862–1932) French foreign minister who orchestrated reconciliation with Germany and the Kellogg-Briand Pact.

Gustav Stresemann (1878–1929) German prime minister and later foreign minister who brought stability to Weimar Germany in the 1920s.

Kellogg-Briand Pact Agreement renouncing war, signed in 1928 by fifteen European countries and the United States and ultimately by sixty-three states.

They had failed to fulfill the promises made before and during the war. Disappointment with the peace treaties and subsequent economic crises further eroded their standing.

In Britain, the most important political casualty of the war was the Liberal Party, which never recovered from the growing division over wartime policies. Though **David Lloyd George** had won at Versailles, his position at the helm of the Liberal Party wavered, as many politicians and followers were displeased with the economic and political costs of his aggressive wartime policies. He tried to rebuild his popularity and the unity of the party, but allying himself with Conservative politicians cost him dearly, sending many followers toward the growing Labour Party. While the Liberals floundered, between 1920 and 1929 the Conservative and Labour Parties fought for political power. The Conservatives provided an economic platform and an ideology of security that spoke to the older basis of this party, the upper classes, and also to many among the middle classes who had lost faith in the Liberals. For most of the decade, the Conservatives controlled Parliament and pushed stringent measures to protect business interests, often at the expense of the working and lower middle classes. Yet the British economy did not fully recover from its wartime losses.

Leading the anti-Conservative opposition was the Labour Party, which developed rapidly from a marginal, class-based party to a more popular and broad-based party with socialist ideological leanings that attracted workers in the public service sector and lower ranks of the middle class. Though the Labour Party held power for only a brief nine-month period under **Ramsay MacDonald** (1924), it forced the Conservatives to confront workers' concerns such as the length of the workweek and unemployment benefits as mainstream issues. Just as important was the growing union movement, loosely coordinated with the Labour Party but institutionally independent, which in 1926 forced the Conservatives to deal with workers' concerns through a general strike. The strike failed, but the work rights demanded by the strikers entered the vocabulary of both dominant parties.

In France, the disappointment that followed the peace treaties produced a quick succession of governments. No party—centrist, conservative, or left wing—was able to keep power for long. Only after 1926, under the Republican centrist **Raymond Poincaré**, did a more secure government emerge. He stabilized the currency and secured prosperity, which gave people hope for the future.

Germany faced the greatest political challenges after 1919. All prewar political leaders were compromised by defeat, and following the collapse of the monarchy, a new political system had to be created. The political leaders who drafted the progressive democratic constitution and other political institutions in the city of Weimar—which gave its name to the new government, **Weimar Republic**—had the difficult task of gaining the trust of an embittered population. Some nationalist leaders were blamed for the outcome of the war, some liberal leaders had been assassinated by radical nationalists, and some on the left had been tainted by the communist uprisings in 1918–1919, so it was unclear who could fill this vacuum.

The key figure turned out to be Gustav Stresemann, a successful businessman and politician who came from a monarchist conservative background. Before the war he had strongly supported German nationalist aspirations and traditions embodied by the emperor but had looked with some favor upon measures benefiting workers. Above all, he was a realist who knew by 1918 that the old system was bankrupt. For him, democracy was a pragmatic, rather than ideological, choice.

Between 1920 and 1923, when he assumed the leadership of the government for one brief year, Stresemann went from opposing the Weimar constitution to supporting it for the sake of stability. After the war, he created the German People's Party to revise the Versailles Treaty, secure economic growth, and offer some support for workers. Stresemann's election as prime minister in 1923 marked a turning point for the Weimar Republic. He stabilized internal politics and, resolving the Ruhr occupation crisis, rebuilt Germany's international stature. Under him, radical right- and left-wing movements were effectively put down, notably the Nazi Party's attempt under Hitler to seize power in Bavaria known as the **Beer Hall Putsch.** Stresemann's successors were able to maintain stability partly because of his achievements. Although the Weimar Republic proved short lived, it was one of the

David Lloyd George   (1863–1945) British politician who led Britain and through World War I and the postwar settlement as the Liberal Party prime minister, 1916–1922.

Ramsay MacDonald   (1866–1937) First leader of Britain's Labour Party to become prime minister.

Raymond Poincaré   (1860–1934) French politician, president between 1913 and 1920, then twice premier.

Weimar Republic   Name of the German state between 1919 and 1933, taken from the city where its democratic constitution was written.

Beer Hall Putsch   (in German, "beer hall riot") Violent failed attempt by Hitler and the Nazi Party to take over the Bavarian local government in 1923.

most democratic and progressive states in Europe, with universal suffrage and protections for workers much more comprehensive than in Great Britain or France, from regulation of the workweek to state unemployment insurance.

Politics in Eastern Europe

After 1918, eastern Europe was responding to dramatic changes in borders and new ethnic compositions and struggling to organize stable governments. Democratic institutions and mass parties were new, so the main concern was order rather than the return to prosperity sought in the west. And while some countries—Czechoslovakia, Poland, the Baltic states, Greece, and Turkey—adopted republican governments to foster democracy, the rest—Hungary, Yugoslavia, Romania, Albania, and Bulgaria—opted for more traditional constitutional monarchies. Neither choice brought stability and democratization, however, as both were compromised by corruption.

The only new state to demonstrate relative political stability and economic growth was Czechoslovakia. Like all the other new states in eastern Europe, Czechoslovakia experienced interethnic tensions (among Czechs, Slovaks, and Germans) and political weakness. There were so many parties that no single one could capture the majority in parliament. In almost every election, it was necessary to form coalitions among two or three parties, rendering any government unlikely to follow a clear political agenda. But, unlike other eastern European states, Czechoslovakia was fortunate to have a visionary president, **Tomáš G. Masaryk,** who followed a policy of tolerance toward ethnic minorities. Masaryk was skillful at negotiating and maintaining the trust of the population. He also kept his country out of regional conflicts. Just as significant was his faith in the democratic institutions created after 1918.

Elsewhere in eastern Europe, leaders manipulated the new democratic institutions to maintain power or sometimes disregarded them altogether in the name of stability. These young democracies had little chance to function properly. In Poland, for instance, **Józef Piłsudski** used his position as leader of the military and war hero to undermine the powers of the parliament. Between 1926, when he executed a military coup to replace the government in power with his own, and until his death in 1935 he sought economic stability, international security, and tolerance for minorities—all worthy goals. But he sacrificed any balanced division of power among the branches of government, showing through his actions that democracy could not work in his country. Piłsudski himself never assumed

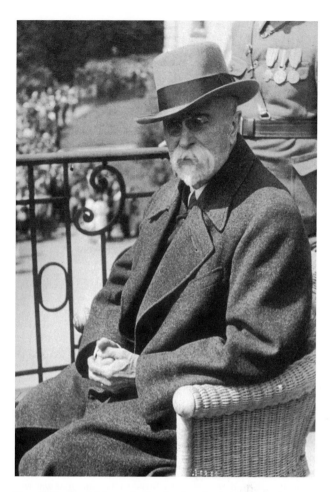

Tomáš Garrigue Masaryk, Czechoslovakia's first president, came to be known as the father of modern Czechoslovak democracy. Many of his ideas about governing through compromise in order to maintain stability came from the years he spent in the United States. He was also a visionary in this part of Europe in his strong feminist convictions. *(Hulton Archive/ Corbis)*

leadership of the country and preferred instead to manipulate policymaking through indirect threats and intrigues. Poland's failure to build democracy was typical of most other eastern European states.

In the former Ottoman lands, Greece and Turkey also aimed for stability and prosperity within their new borders, often disregarding democratic aspirations.

Tomáš G. Masaryk   (1850–1937) First president of Czechoslovakia and a strong supporter of democracy.

Józef Piłsudski   (1867–1935) Military leader of Polish liberation forces in World War I and most important political figure between 1926 and 1935.

Mustafa Kemal took on the surname "Atatürk" to fashion himself as the father of modern Turkey. His main goal was to position Turkey as a modern player in the international arena, rather than a mere survivor of the remnants of the Ottoman Empire. Thus, the secularization of Turkish elites was foremost on his agenda. *(Stock Montage)*

Greece had been the first constitutional government in the Balkans and by 1920 had almost a century of political experience with modern parliamentary rule. But experience did not improve its chances at establishing a stable democracy. Instead, Greece became embroiled in expansionist dreams at the expense of Turkey. After 1918, it pursued a series of disastrous military campaigns, only to be defeated and humiliated by **Mustafa Kemal Atatürk**'s armies. The territorial losses and repatriation of more than 1.2 million Greeks sent Greek politics into turmoil. In the first half of the 1920s, the king was forced to abdicate, and a new republican system was proclaimed, but it proved ineffective and in 1935 the king returned to the throne. The cradle of democracy proved inauspicious ground for building democratic institutions and practices after 1918.

Turkey also failed in its attempt to foster democracy. Atatürk focused his entire career as president of the new republic (1920–1938) on consolidating parliamentary rule, a secular government, and a new type of military. He also pursued modernizing social programs, such as compulsory education for all children and many reforms to empower women. Yet his style of government was not unlike that of Pilsudski, preaching democratization while practicing heavy-handed **authoritarian** tactics. Yet, although substantially diminished in terms of size, during the 1920s Turkey, reshaped by Atatürk, was militarily stronger, more homogeneous, and effectively **secularized.**

Fascism

While eastern Europe struggled to create democratic institutions, Italy abandoned them altogether. Benito Mussolini established a **fascist** dictatorship that was the decade's first successful challenge to democracy. His model was D'Annunzio's police state in Fiume. Born to a blacksmith and a schoolteacher, Mussolini was a talented writer and speaker. In his youth he joined the Socialist Party and edited left-wing publications. His radical pacifism landed him in jail in 1911. Already he was dreaming of organizing a revolutionary mass movement of workers. But in the fall of 1914, he switched to an aggressive pro-war position. In 1917, after he was accidentally wounded by a grenade (not on the battlefield), he turned to writing for a nationalist paper and to promoting his heroic participation in the war.

Having once spoken for the workers, Mussolini was skillful at exploiting postwar fears of unemployment with pro-worker rhetoric. In 1919, when strikes led by communist and socialist unions broke out, Mussolini used the popular anti-Bolshevik rhetoric of the time to depict these actions as a threat to Italy's

Mustafa Kemal Atatürk (1881–1938) President of Turkey from 1920 to 1938 who pursued modernization and secularization in the name of democracy.

authoritarian Concentrating power in the hands of a ruler.

secularization Change in a society from close identification with religious institutions to a more separated relationship, including transfer of institutions from ecclesiastical to civil control.

fascism Radical-right political movement initiated by Benito Mussolini in Italy that replaced parliamentary democracy with authoritarian regimes emphasizing order.

stability. His call attracted young war veterans and other men looking for a good fight. These recruits were organized in closely knit **paramilitary** groups that operated in a strictly hierarchical fashion, copying the army, and took their orders strictly from their leader. They became the *fasci italiani di combattimento,* or "Italian gangs of combat," the predecessors of the Fascist Party.

Mussolini's fascists terrorized members of opposing parties and by 1921 had become a feared group in Italian politics. In October 1922, Mussolini threatened to march on Rome with his fascist troops and seize power from the weakened parliament unless he was named prime minister. King Victor Emmanuel III gave in. Mussolini moved swiftly to eliminate all political parties and establish a one-party authoritarian state in which he personally controlled all branches of the government and a powerful military. On the surface, he continued to maintain a parliamentary system, but only members of his Fascist Party could be elected, and "debate" meant obedience to the party line set by Mussolini himself.

Despite the existence of government institutions that suggested a division of power among the executive, legislative, and judicial branches, all power rested in the hands of Il Duce—"the leader." At times Mussolini held as many as seven positions in government ministries, trying to run everything from public works to propaganda and the army. He was obsessed with managing every aspect of government, even making hiring decisions about minor personnel. The light in his office was kept on for the entire period of his rule, and little boys and girls would be told that Il Duce was always there, laboring to bring happiness to the Italian people.

Italian fascism became an important model for other European politicians critical of democratic parliaments who wished to establish strong authoritarian regimes. Mussolini's regime was particularly attractive because its **corporatist** structure combined political and social stability with the promise of economic growth, thus attempting to solve all the dilemmas of postwar Europe. Eliminating political parties and labor unions, which he claimed were destabilizing, Mussolini instead channeled citizens into corporations run by the state, which would supposedly allow them to express their political views and protect their interests. Corporations would, for example, mediate conflicts between employees and employers without disturbing economic production through strikes. In reality, however, corporations were set up mainly to control workers and to disable protests against business leaders and the state.

The look of Mussolini's "Italian gangs of combat" was modeled after Gabriele D'Annunzio's paramilitary troops in Fiume. They represented a specific aesthetic vision of force, order, and physical beauty, intended to awe supporters and frighten opponents. *(United States Holocaust Memorial Museum)*

Special corporations were created for women. These institutions aimed to control women's public activities and at the same time give the illusion that they were actively contributing to the nation's betterment. Mothers' organizations that promoted child care and household management told women it was their patriotic duty to be good mothers and wives and gave them a sense of pride in their domestic chores. But this propaganda also underscored what was *not* proper for women—to engage in employment outside the home and activities outside the family. Feminist ideas about women's economic and political independence were depicted as antipatriotic and dangerous. Women's corporations were meant as much to shape

paramilitary   Group of civilians trained and organized in a military fashion.

corporatism   System of government that organizes society into industrial, occupational, and professional groups that channel political expression and repress dissent.

the identity of women as solely mothers and wives as to allow women a place to come together in public.

Corporations successfully changed social and political institutions, but the fascists had more trouble with religious institutions. Mussolini was an unabashed atheist, and his paramilitary troops often showed little respect for the Catholic Church. Yet for most people being Italian was the same as being Catholic. The church had such a central role that it was really impossible to either ignore or fight it. It took Mussolini many years to come to an agreement over the status of the church, the clergy, and Catholic organizations in Italy, but in 1929 he signed a concordat with the pope that recognized the autonomy of Vatican and reinforced the dominance of the church in education and marriage law. Relations with the church continued to be rocky in some areas, but most Italians were pleased with this agreement, which greatly increased Mussolini's popularity.

Finally, the fascist government attempted to solve the problem of economic underdevelopment by increasing agricultural productivity, enlarging the male workforce, and creating public works such as roads and irrigation. There was a program to reclaim land, a program to improve wheat production, a program to promote agricultural self-sufficiency (encouraging purchases exclusively from the internal market), a program to increase the birthrate, and a program to improve transportation and build highways and railways. The economy was still primarily in the hands of private entrepreneurs and farmers, but the state played an important role in regulating business practices (for example, by eliminating trade unions and dictating priorities in production), communications, and commerce, especially international trade. To some unstable European states, the fascist government's strong grip over both business and labor seemed to have solved the era's political and economic difficulties.

Yet fascist solutions were neither simply pragmatic nor wholly positive. Workers' rights were reduced for the benefit of industry; farmers' production was closely scrutinized; and women's rights were severely restricted for the benefit of families, their bodies closely monitored for the purpose of reproduction, especially through **pro-natalist** and anti-birth control policies.

Those who were not willing to abide by these restrictions, or who were defined as dangerous on account of their convictions, ethnicity, or religion, were severely persecuted. To be communist, non-Italian, feminist, or, especially after 1936, Jewish was a dangerous identity. These populations were threatened by economic and social discrimination, subsequently by isolation, and, starting in the late 1930s, by extermination. Thus, in addition to positive definitions of

what it meant to be a true Italian, Mussolini imposed categories of unacceptable identities on some.

But in the 1920s Mussolini was able to hide these negative aspects of his regime through masterful propaganda. Newspapers, films, radio broadcasts, parades, museums, and other state institutions and activities portrayed him as a man of the people and a resolute leader ready to listen and respond to the needs of all Italians. Most people could not imagine their country without Mussolini at the helm: "Italians of my generation carried the portrait of Mussolini within themselves, even before they were of an age to recognize it on the walls," remembered a writer who grew up in the 1920s. Mussolini's image was in every government office and classroom, and his personal style directed fashion trends. Both men and women were attracted to Il Duce—the first political leader to turn his baldness into a symbol of virility and strength. In making himself such a vivid model of the new Italian, Mussolini helped transform the ideals of a whole generation. Marching in the streets by the thousands, in their stylish black uniforms, young men experienced power as intoxicating; on the sidewalks, young women swooned. Their emotions rendered them loyal followers in the hands of the charismatic and cunning Duce.

Social Democracy in Scandinavia

A very different approach to the economic and social problems of the postwar period can be seen in the Scandinavian countries, which used the tools of democracy. Here a tradition of charitable work and support for state intervention in matters of employment had existed since the late nineteenth century. Questions regarding the role of government in education, public health, child care, unemployment, and pensions were often the subject of debate in parliament. Social democratic and labor parties had a large presence in Scandinavian parliaments both before and after the war, and they guaranteed that social welfare measures would continue to be on the agenda. In 1923, Norway introduced old-age pensions. Denmark endorsed the principle of full rights for government social services, such as education, healthcare, and pensions for all citizens, irrespective of class or gender. Sweden launched a system of unemployment benefits, state support for health, and life insurance.

pro-natalism   Policy encouraging women to have more children, pursued by most European governments after 1918 to replenish the postwar population.

Scandinavian countries were thus at the forefront in establishing the **welfare state,** and their innovative reforms averted both social unrest and state bankruptcy. Yet the Scandinavian context was unique in Europe. With the exception of Finland, Scandinavia had been sheltered from war. The small size and ethnic homogeneity of these countries also helped preserve their stability. Quite simply, the sense of crisis and despair that dominated most of Europe in early 1919 was not present in Scandinavia. Instead, reforms that built on the prewar social welfare agendas proceeded, as the dominant political parties were never discredited by the war. Continuity, rather than upheaval, best describes the political and social development of Scandinavia in the 1920s.

The New Soviet State

↓ What were the essential components of the Soviet state?

↓ How did the Bolsheviks reshape society and individual identities?

The most radical experiment of the 1920s was the Soviet state. Out of a bloody civil war, the Bolsheviks were able to create a smaller but stronger country in which they reinvented the state and reshaped society according to Marxist-Leninist ideology. The Bolsheviks succeeded because of the unprecedented level of control imposed on every aspect of public life, rendering the Communist Party all-powerful and individuals fearful of the party's every move. The Bolsheviks also tried to attract people to the party by promising a better life for workers and peasants. By 1929, the Soviet Union had consolidated into a stable police state.

The Civil War

Russia left the Great War in 1918 after the Treaty of Brest-Litovsk, but the country was soon embroiled in a civil war between the Bolsheviks and their supporters, known as the Reds, and the Whites—the latter an alliance of supporters of the old order, such as military officers, nobles, and anti-Bolsheviks (supporters of liberalism and democracy) inside Russia and out. In their attempt to stamp out the Bolshevik threat, France, Britain, the United States, and Japan sent troops and financial help to the Whites. In addition, the newly independent Baltic republics and Poland, which wished to secure their territorial gains, also pursued a war against the Bolsheviks.

Though fighting a desperate war on its borderlands—from the Baltic and Siberia to the Crimea—the Bolsheviks won. What they lacked in experience and military power they made up for in organization and unity of purpose. They had charismatic, driven leaders who inspired great loyalty in their followers. Among them was War Commissar Leon Trotsky, described by an American observer as "the most dramatic character" and the "only great organizer" of the Russian Revolution. Trotsky was a skilled military leader who turned some of the most difficult battles of the civil war into victories. With his wild hair and piercing glare behind wire-rimmed glasses, Trotsky inspired many people, especially among the poor, to join the Reds. Like Mussolini, Trotsky represented a new style of leader whose ability to project virility, demand action, and use violence made them attractive to the generation that came of age during the war.

By contrast, the Whites were divided in their aims and strategies, and the foreign aid they received was half-hearted. By 1922, these supporters were pulling out their war-weary armies and the Reds were winning in the Crimea and Siberia. Poland remained a serious threat, but the new states of eastern Europe did not challenge the Bolshevik regime itself. By 1922, the Reds had won the war by simply giving up some territories in the west, then consolidating their control over the rest of the country.

The civil war set in motion some important trends later formalized as components of the Soviet regime. In 1918 the Bolsheviks nationalized almost all industry, legislated the obligation for all adults to work, and placed the government in charge of commercial activities. Another element of the civil war that became permanent was a secret police apparatus, the Cheka, which employed brutal methods to silence enemies. In its first six years, the Cheka killed more than two hundred thousand people. Overall, the human losses in these years, due to military conflict, starvation, and various epidemics, is estimated by some at above 4 million.

In 1919 the Bolsheviks also created the Communist International, or **Comintern,** as a means for promoting world revolution, an extension of Trotsky's belief in the mission of the Soviet Union to transform the world into a "workers' paradise." This organization provided financial support and ideological guidance

welfare state   State in which the government assumes responsibility for social needs such as public health, education, and unemployment insurance; pioneered in Scandinavia.

Comintern   International organization set up by the Russian Bolsheviks in 1919 to promote communist revolutions all over the world.

MAP 26.1   The Russian Civil War, 1918–1922 The Russian Civil War proved to be a second conflict of attrition after World War I, engulfing large parts of Russia and lasting almost three years. The victory of the Reds (Bolsheviks) came at a high human and territorial price, as Russia lost many of its western imperial lands.

Российская Социалистическая Федеративная Советская Республика

ПРОЛЕТАРИИ ВСЕХ СТРАН СОЕДИНЯЙТЕСЬ!

ГОД ПРОЛЕТАРСКОЙ ДИКТАТУРЫ.
ОКТЯБРЬ 1917 - ОКТЯБРЬ 1918

"Workers of the World Unite!" declares this Soviet poster in large red letters. The Soviet propaganda of the 1920s focused on the success of the workers' revolution in crushing the forces of oppression, depicted here through the crown and royal mantle, as well as the shield and broken chains, on which the worker steps with calm confidence. *(Snark/Art Resource, NY)*

to communist movements abroad. In exchange, the Soviets demanded that all Communist Parties of the Comintern abandon cooperation with socialist and other left-wing noncommunist organizations; they were to take orders only from Moscow. These developments prefigured the more aggressive policies of political purging and terror, state-controlled economy, and communist imperialism that came to define the Soviet Union in the 1930s.

But in 1922, the Bolsheviks had the more basic tasks of creating a stable political system and reinvigorating the economy. The communist regime of those years was more open to experiments in economic production, propaganda, and social programs than at any other time.

The Communist Regime

In December 1922, the **Union of Soviet Socialist Republics (USSR)** came into being. The ideological and legal foundations of this state combined the writings of Karl Marx and Friedrich Engels with V. I. Lenin's own ideas. One fundamental principle of the new order was equality, understood very differently from the definition offered in the U.S. Declaration of Independence. Instead of focusing on equal rights for pursuing individual goals, the Soviets focused on economic equality: all people who worked were *equally* entitled to the fruits of their labor. This principle also implied that differences in wealth and class were fundamentally unjust, as they were based on the oppression of one class (the workers) by another (the bourgeoisie). The Soviet state set out to eliminate these injustices, first by taking all property and means of production away from the bourgeoisie and nobility and then by enabling workers to gain control over the economy. The proletariat, or workers, the producers of goods, were to control the fruits of their labor. By 1922, most of the means of production were under state control. The system the Bolsheviks imagined was entirely untested. No other country in the world had attempted such a fundamental transformation of the economic and social system overnight.

The Soviet Union also had to address problems of political stability and control. The revolution took place before workers had achieved full "consciousness" of class conflicts, one of the Marxist prerequisites for a communist revolution. Lenin made it an important goal for the Bolshevik regime to consolidate political power both by inclusive means, educating the workers and peasants, and by exclusionary tactics, eliminating enemies of the Bolsheviks. Propaganda and a secret police with an extensive network of informants were essential for this effort, and both had been solidified during the civil war. By 1922, they were essential in building state institutions and programs.

Finally, the Soviet regime aimed to open opportunities for political participation to people who had lacked a voice before 1917. This goal was also incorporated into Soviet propaganda: the party would listen to the

Union of Soviet Socialist Republics (USSR)   Official name of the Soviet Union, a federation of four, and eventually fifteen, autonomous republics, the largest and most powerful of which was Russia.

needs and problems of the oppressed and defend their rights; these promises would induce people to join the party and its affiliated organizations. The Women's Section of the Communist Party, or **Zhenotdel**, was one such institution. The Bolsheviks had critiqued the inferior status of women in Russian society and attempted to attract them to the Communist Party through this department. Initially led by Alexandra Kollontai (see Choice), it also served as an advocacy group where women could voice social, economic, and political concerns. Though democratic and experimental at the beginning, by 1928 it had become centralized and authoritarian and was eventually dissolved.

For all its positive propaganda, the exclusionary policies of the Soviet regime raised questions even among the faithful. Did the ends justify the means? Supposedly, communism was about democratic equality and justice. Yet the road to it was paved with violence, and the new institutions of the Soviet Union concentrated power in the hands of a small party elite. By the mid-1920s, there were furious debates within the party over centralization, with Trotsky in fierce opposition. In addition, although the party claimed that individuals had choices and that the state was interested in their ideas, most institutions suppressed ideas and actions that were contrary to the official party line. Soviet citizens received protection from the state only insofar as they were willing to serve the state with unquestioning loyalty.

The New Economic Policy and Struggle for Leadership

As the Soviet regime was attempting to deal with enemies at home and in the borderlands, its economy worsened. Nationalizing all industry did not lead to economic growth. In 1921, industrial production was just 13 percent of the prewar volume. Many of the best-trained professionals left the country, peasants refused to work for the state, and workers went on strike. Lenin realized that the regime needed to adopt a pragmatic economic policy to win the civil war and consolidate political control. In the spring of 1921, he inaugurated the **New Economic Policy (NEP),** which allowed for the rebirth of private property and free commerce. The state retained control over large and medium-size industries, such as steel and heavy machinery, but small businesses could be privately owned. Under the NEP, three-quarters of retail trade shifted back into private hands. In the countryside, the state allowed peasants to sell their own harvests rather than have the state requisition them at fixed prices. The recovery of the economy was remarkable.

By the end of the 1920s, the Soviet Union had reached 1914 levels in agricultural production.

But the social and political costs of this recovery seemed too high to many Bolsheviks. The NEP had fostered the rebirth of an entrepreneurial class that was a nuisance to local communist administrators. One the one hand, the regime spoke about the need to eliminate class oppression and give workers control over the means of production. On the other, the state allowed for the kind of exploitation it condemned, based on pragmatic considerations. This double standard weakened the control of the Soviet regime and troubled faithful party members.

A struggle over the political costs of the NEP ensued in the **Politburo,** the highest decision-making body of the Communist Party. Lenin's death in January 1924 rendered this debate more complex, as Politburo members became divided. Trotsky and his leftist supporters wanted to continue revolutionary struggle in the world at all cost. This group also opposed the NEP as a deviation from communism and was concerned about the growing centralization of the state, which clashed with the democratic foundations of communism. Their strongest opponents were the centrists, led by **Joseph Stalin,** who called for building socialism in the Soviet Union, deemphasizing the struggle for worldwide revolution. Stalin stressed the principal role to be played by Russia in the USSR and suggested the need to further centralize the state. This position was favored by Russian communists with nationalist leanings.

In the end, Stalin won the struggle by working behind the scenes in the Politburo and among his loyal lower party appointees. Few anticipated his victory, as he was less respected than Trotsky. Stalin was, however, a cunning man who advanced his career through power politics. Born in the Georgian Caucasus as Joseph Dzhugashvili, he joined a Marxist group while studying to become a priest and later worked with local Bolsheviks. He undertook danger-

Zhenotdel Women's Section of the Soviet Communist Party, which focused on policies and issues such as employment, day care, and domestic work.

New Economic Policy (NEP) Economic plan allowing limited capitalism adopted by Lenin in 1921 to alleviate Russia's deep economic crisis.

Politburo Highest decision-making body of the Soviet Communist Party.

Joseph Stalin (1879–1953) Dictatorial leader of the Soviet Union from 1929 to 1953, who transformed the Soviet Union into a police state run by fear and deceit, and into a military and economic superpower.

ous actions on behalf of the movement, ending up in jail and exile, but he was neither a theoretician like Lenin nor an organizer like Trotsky. He simply happened to have a good instinct for showing up in the right place at the right time and knowing whom to flatter and whose weaknesses to exploit.

By the early 1920s, Stalin had risen to the top of the Bolshevik hierarchy, but neither Lenin nor the other leaders thought he would be Lenin's successor; they assumed that would be Trotsky. Stalin was clever, however, in exploiting Trotsky's criticisms of the NEP and other policies as evidence of disloyalty; eventually Trotsky was eliminated from leadership and sent into exile. Then Stalin removed all remaining opponents. By 1928, he dominated all institutions of the state in dictatorial fashion, much like Mussolini in Italy, but without the fascist leader's personal allure.

The New Soviet Man and Woman

The Bolsheviks wanted nothing short of a complete transformation of society. They depicted capitalism as a system that bred greed, narrow-minded materialism, and pettiness among people and described their own aims in terms of transforming individual and collective identity to foster fairness, selflessness, and dedication to the common good.

To eliminate class differences, supposedly the root of all capitalist problems, the party used brutal policies. In addition to abolishing private property in the early days of the civil war, the Bolsheviks also wished to eliminate all "oppressors," especially the social and economic elites of the tsarist regime—the aristocracy, businessmen, and the professional middle class. In the first phase of this social revolution, the Bolsheviks imprisoned or killed most members of the nobility. The bourgeoisie was also a class enemy, but it was also a larger and less clearly defined category. Initially, the Soviet regime eliminated businessmen, easily targeted as exploiters of workers, by nationalizing their wealth and killing many. But if the bourgeoisie included all those who owned private property, it would include peasants as well.

Class enemies also included white-collar workers, professionals, and some educators. Those employed in state institutions, such as bureaucrats and teachers, became targets because of their allegiance to the tsarist regime. Doctors and engineers were viewed as a threat because they belonged to professions with standards independent of the political regime, and the Soviets could not tolerate independence. Doctors, chemists, and engineers often had to join the party to maintain their professional standing.

As large numbers of qualified individuals were re-moved from professions badly needed in the economy, education, and social services, the party embarked on its own program of education and training to fill gaps. The government considered eliminating illiteracy (above 50 percent in 1918) an important social goal and created many public schools. But quality was poor. Progress and access to higher education were linked to class background, with priority given to sons and daughters of workers, often at the expense of academic qualifications. The first generation of teachers, doctors, and engineers produced by this system were more likely to be faithful party activists than skilled professionals.

The Soviets used education to promote secularization and a rational understanding of Marxist economy. Though presented as scientific, the Marxist worldview was akin to a religious vision of history. Communists described eliminating class struggle as scientifically predictable. Yet there was no way of proving such developments. Instead, it was through a leap of faith that the Bolsheviks spoke of the certain "withering away of the state" and the inevitable victory of communism throughout the world. Like other religious zealots, revolutionaries such as Trotsky and Kollontai were willing to sacrifice both themselves and all who stood in their way for the fulfillment of this destiny.

Organized religion, however, was seen as irrational and a threat to Soviet ideology. The Orthodox Church, the state religion in tsarist Russia, emphasized faith in the afterlife and accepted the hardships of this life as normal, something to be embraced, not overcome. Social inequality was a fact of life. These beliefs clashed with the staunch atheism of the Bolsheviks. In addition, the Orthodox Church was rich and influential. It owned large estates and economic interests and commanded a great deal of respect, even fear, among the Russian population. From the beginning of their struggle in 1918, the Bolsheviks persecuted members of this and all other religious institutions, clergy and lay-people alike. These persecutions continued throughout the 1920s, forcing believers to retreat to private places of worship, including homes and forests. Yet the complete elimination of all religious organizations did not become a goal of the Soviet Union until after 1928.

In their ambition to transform Russian society, the Soviets also sought to reshape private lives, including family and gender relations. The Bolsheviks were quick to replace religious with civil marriage. Young couples now came to city hall to be married before a judge in a ritual that incorporated statements of loyalty to the Soviet regime and the Communist Party. Some party leaders, like Kollontai, believed that marriage itself should be eliminated, as it institutionalized

Voice Voice VoiceVoice

Alexandra Kollontai Advocates a New Type of Woman

Alexandra Kollontai was one of the most active leaders of the communist movement in Russia before 1917 and also an accomplished writer. Her writings depicted radically new female heroines, free from old-fashioned notions of emotional dependency and jealousy, acting as powerful movers and shakers. Yet her ideas regarding women's roles in society and marriage made her unpopular with the communist leadership, so she was sent abroad in 1922. While away from the Soviet Union, Kollontai published other radical writings, including the book from which the following selection is taken, The Autobiography of a Sexually Emancipated Communist Woman, *first published in Norway in 1926.*

But who are they, these single new women? The single woman—she is a child of the large-scale capitalist economic system. ➡ There is no place in the ranks of those earning their own livelihood for the "unfit," that is to say, the women of the old type. Here, too, therefore, a "natural selection" among the women of the different social strata is discernible: only the stronger, more resistant disciplined natures arrive in the ranks of those "earning their own livelihood." ➡ The weak, inwardly passive, cling to the family hearth, and when the insecurity of existence tears them away from the protection of the family, to catapult them into the stream of life, supinely, they let themselves be driven by the waves of legal or illegal prostitution: they enter into a marriage of convenience or they walk the streets.

➡ The influence of women earning their own livelihood spreads far beyond their own circle. With their criticism, they "poison" the minds of their contemporaries, they smash old idols, they raise the banner of revolt against those "truths" with which women have lived for generations. By liberating themselves, the new, single women, earning their own livelihood, also liberate the passive-backward spirit, as this has been molded down the centuries, of their contemporary sisters.

➡ But whereas with the women of the working class, the struggle for the assertion of their rights, the strengthening of their personality, coincides with the interests of the class, the women of other social strata run into unexpected obstacles: the ideology of their class is hostile to the transformation of the feminine type. In the bourgeois milieu, woman's "rebellion" bears a far sharper character, its forms are set in bolder relief, and here the psychological dramas are far sharper, more variegated, and more complicated. ➡ The new type of woman, inwardly self-reliant, independent, and free, corresponds with the morality which

➡ What is Kollontai implying about marriage?

➡ What does Kollontai's criticism here imply about bourgeois women's movements?

➡ Kollontai uses the terms "unfit" and "natural selection" to connect capitalism to a certain scientific theory of the nineteenth century. What is she referring to?

➡ How do working women revolt against past "truths"? Does Kollontai criticize or celebrate this challenge?

➡ Is the women's movement for liberation separate, or does it have to be part of a larger working-class movement?

the working class is elaborating precisely in the interests of its class. For the working class the accomplishment of its mission does not require that she be a handmaid of the husband, an impersonal domestic creature, endowed with passive, feminine traits. Rather, it requires a personality rising and rebelling against every kind of slavery, an active conscious equal member of the community, of the class.

the oppression of one half of humanity, women, by the other half, men. Only free love, without the constrictions of marriage, would end this oppression. There were some early attempts to create communal housing for those who lived together but were not married and also to give children born out of wedlock full legal rights. The more radical leadership of the party envisioned a future in which children would be brought up in communal housing where domestic chores would be shared.

But the Communist Party shied away from such radical change. Bolshevik leaders themselves lived in traditional marriages and considered Kollontai's ideas threatening to social stability. By the end of the 1920s, the party had come around to condemning those who were not married and extolling the virtues of the proletarian family. Nuclear families remained the foundation of social stability, yet with more freedom to enter and exit such unions for both partners. In particular, divorce was liberalized, allowing women protection against domestic violence, which had not been recognized as a basis for dissolving marriages under previous divorce laws.

Women also gained more reproductive control. Early on, the Soviet regime legalized abortion and made it inexpensive. The liberalization of abortion would be short lived, however. By the end of the decade, the Communist Party had revised its policies, partly out of fear of depopulation. Under Stalin, abortion was made illegal again.

A lasting change, however, involved the support for and protection of women's employment and education as well as the creation of state child-care institutions for working mothers. These measures helped women become more economically self-sufficient and can thus be viewed as progressive reforms, similar to social welfare measures in Scandinavia during the 1920s. Yet the Soviet regime was interested only in fashioning loyal citizens through education and in increasing the workforce. The Soviets looked upon women as an important means for fulfilling these aims rather than as oppressed individuals who needed to be liberated. Women would not have a choice of motherhood or employment. Rather, they would have to join the workforce and leave child rearing in part to state institutions such as kindergartens and schools.

Social and Cultural Experiments

↓ How did social reformers and intellectuals respond to the aftermath of war?
↓ How did the war and technology transform culture and entertainment in this era?

Social reformers, intellectuals, and artists throughout Europe tried to cope with the disruptions of war in radical ways as well. The experience of total war forced both men and women to reexamine many assumptions about their roles in the family and society. This process prompted important changes in gender relations, but fewer than reformers, especially feminists, hoped to achieve. Artists grappled with loss and destruction by fashioning entirely new artistic styles, some democratic and socially engaged and others an escape into dream worlds. Widespread violence had become an everyday experience, and many embraced it as a potentially positive force in art. Others recoiled from the memory of this violence and turned to pacifism and religious faith. Some of these trends had started before 1914 but were greatly reshaped by war's destruction and transformation of European society. These experiments produced some of the most remarkable works of literature and art of the twentieth century as well as important developments in popular entertainment.

Change and Frustration in Gender Roles

The war had brought upheaval in gender roles, and with the resumption of peace, many wondered if the changes would continue. More than in any previous conflict, the experiences of soldiers had been so vastly different from those of civilians that a great gap opened between husbands and wives, mothers and sons, fathers and daughters. While the experience of total war had placed both soldiers and civilians in direct contact with violence, the physical and psychological burdens of trench warfare often crippled soldiers in unprecedented ways. Returning soldiers suffered from deep psychological trauma and were unable to communicate their suffering to noncombatants. So many soldiers had gruesome injuries that the sight of a maimed body became commonplace. Deep psychological and physical scars forced veterans to question their masculinity and often strained relationships at home; domestic violence increased. These men yearned to have their old jobs and the prestige they had enjoyed before the war, but nothing could go back to the way it had been.

Many women had entered "male" professions and jobs during the war. After 1918, both government and private businesses preferred to rehire men, however, even for positions in which women had been effective and had accepted lower wages. The idea that men were breadwinners and women were nurturers remained strong, but not all women returned to the home. Many continued to work, but in jobs that were less secure and worse paid, including domestic and secretarial work and factory work in the food industry. Women were also increasingly important as consumers, as evidenced by the greater diversity in goods available at both the low and high ends of the markets. An aggressive fashion industry focused on "working girls" and independent women. The image of the flapper, or "new woman," was plastered all over fashion magazines and movie posters. These changes suggested new identities opening up for women.

Yet little changed for women in the domestic sphere. They were still considered primarily responsible for child care, cooking, and tending to the home. Unlike the Scandinavian welfare experiments and the Bolshevik revolution in women's family responsibilities, governments in the rest of Europe paid little attention to child-care questions. Consequently, women found it difficult to both work and take care of their families, or they did so with enormous effort and little support.

Still, in the realm of politics women made important gains, achieving voting rights except in France, Italy, Spain, and the Balkans, where they could vote only in local elections. The extent of women's suffrage varied and often included educational, marriage, and age criteria at a time when universal male suffrage was the norm. But even as feminists celebrated this victory, they also wondered how much power women had really gained. Though women could vote, their concerns were not necessarily reflected in party platforms, nor were female politicians successful in the first decade after the war. Traditional parties, even liberal and socialist ones with pro-women platforms, were unwilling to put forth female candidates. Questions about women's rights seemed subordinate to the pressing issues of Bolshevik threat, war debt, inflation, unemployment, and revisionism.

Yet politicians appealed to women as mothers and wives, asking them to place family and nation above their individual selves and help rebuild their nation. In France, for instance, a pro-natalist campaign for replenishing the human losses in the war involved a stern government demand that all women of childbearing age, regardless of economic status, produce as many children as possible to regenerate the fighting force. Women were described as patriotic and selfless if they responded to this call and as heartless materialists if they indicated interest in attaining economic independence or limiting their families. There was no comparable campaign to shame men into fatherhood.

Most European governments were concerned with population growth and hoped to revive the birthrate with positive incentives, such as monetary rewards and patriotic propaganda, and negative measures, such as the criminalization of abortion. Some reformers with similar concerns took a different position on reproduction. They saw sexual satisfaction as key to a couple's desire to reproduce and have a happy family. In the decade after the war, a diverse movement advocating sexual reform emerged. It was a response, in part, to the marital problems many couples were having after years of separation during the war. Husbands who came back with psychological traumas and physical disabilities were often unable to perform sexually; and women, who had gained tremendous self-confidence during the war years, found themselves more interested in an active role in sexual relations. Reformers wrote manuals for couples, encouraging the exploration of mutual sexual satisfaction, and doctors provided sex advice to husbands. Sex advice columns began to appear in women's magazines. Even though the ideas about what constituted normal sex and pleasure were conventional, removing the taboo on discussing such matters in public and emphasizing women's sexual needs were important and lasting changes.

Intellectual Responses to the War

The destruction wrought by war prompted the rise of important intellectual movements in the decade after 1918. Among the cries for revenge and revolution, some intellectuals took a stand for peace. The postwar pacifist movement was in part a continuation of prewar pacifism and in part a reflection of Europe's political strategy to keep the peace, but it was no longer linked to particular political ideologies and organizations. It was more of an individual reaction to the horrors of war, a conclusion that no ideology—nationalism, liberalism, communism—could justify the enormous human losses.

Many pacifists came from socialist or religious back-

Hannah Höch's collage *Cut with a Cake Knife* (1919) is an example of the dada movement in art that flourished during and right after World War I. Höch's work explored the contradictions of contemporary society in an aggressively ironic feminist vein. By placing female heads on male bodies and vice versa, and including images of politicians in her collages, Höch forced viewers to confront their own gendered assumptions. The presence of faceless bodies also points toward her struggle with defining identity in postwar Germany. *(Bildarchiv Preussischer Kulturbesitz, © 2007 Artists Rights Society [ARS], NY)*

grounds, but some were completely nonideological. Among the most prominent figures were the German physicist Albert Einstein and British writer **Vera Brittain,** who spent the war as a volunteer nurse and wrote as early as 1914: "The destruction of men seems a crime to the whole march of civilisation." Einstein's strong pacifism was unusual for a prominent scientist. In the following decade, he continued to be an outspoken critic of fascism and antisemitism at a time when other scientists were retreating into their labs or committing their research to the service of states with destructive agendas. The impact of the peace movement was small by comparison to the more forceful and well-organized fascist and communist ones. Yet the personal courage of individuals who stood up

against the aggressive nationalism of the coming decade represents important legacies.

While some intellectuals and artists reacted to the destruction of the war by taking on an overtly atheistic and often Marxist position on religion, others sought spiritual rejuvenation, prompting a revival of Christianity. Among these were several prominent thinkers of the time. In Britain, T. S. Eliot and Aldous Huxley turned away from secularization to find spiritual and intellectual solace in religion. The French philosopher and atheist **Gabriel Marcel** converted to Catholicism. Marcel attempted to find a concrete philosophy of being engaged in the world, but through spirituality, moved away from abstractions such as truth or progress toward a focus on the everyday experience of pain, joy, and other basic human emotions.

Artistic Experiments

In contrast, in the arts, the decade of the 1920s was spectacular. Writers, painters, dancers, musicians—all types of artists and performers—revolutionized both high culture and popular entertainment. These experiments were connected both to a longer tradition of the avant-garde in the arts, dating from the end of the nineteenth century, and to the war, whose trauma had a direct impact on basic questions about beauty and goodness in the face of overwhelming destruction.

Several movements in the art world flourished during this period. The Futurists believed in a future marked by technology, power, and even violence. They saw war as a positive tool for cleansing all that was putrid in society and preparing for an era of strength. Futurists became close allies of radical political movements. In Italy, **Filippo Marinetti,** whose paintings depicted movement and speed on canvas, served as Mussolini's minister of the arts. In Russia, poet **Vladimir Mayakovsky** led a generation of Futurist writers who promoted Bolshevism.

Even though the Futurists were original, they did not produce the lasting masterpieces created by the

Vera Brittain (1893–1970) British author and pacifist who volunteered during World War I as a nurse.

Gabriel Marcel (1889–1973) French philosopher of atheist convictions before 1918 who converted to Catholicism after the war.

Filippo Marinetti (1876–1944) Leader of Italian Futurism who served as minister of arts under Mussolini.

Vladimir Mayakovsky (1893–1930) Russian poet, Bolshevik activist, and leading figure of Russian Futurism.

Surrealists. These visionaries sought alternatives to the "reality" of the visible world in the inner world of dreams and nightmares, the subconscious and suppressed, which they considered more truthful to the human condition and suffering than the decade's obsession with wealth and social stability. Adapting the new interest in psychoanalysis to art, they rebelled against rationality, ignored politics, and explored the mind. The first Surrealist manifesto, authored by the French writer **André Breton,** appeared in Paris in 1924 and declared this movement a revolution, outlining in form and content how Surrealism was to alter human consciousness. Artists, poets, and filmmakers rallied to his call to explore the subconscious and reject immediate reality.

The movement continued to flourish until World War II, with Spanish artist **Salvador Dali** and Belgian painter **René Magritte** as some of its most spectacular practitioners. Dali's haunting work portrayed a dream world, in which distortions of everyday objects were rendered in photographic detail and placed in hallucinatory settings. Dali lived his art, appearing in public in bizarre costumes, sporting a fantastic mustache, immaculate yet always strange. In keeping with Surrealistic principles, he showed no interest in politics. Unlike the colorful Dali, Magritte was far more cerebral and understated, and his paintings reached into dream worlds by a scrupulous, photographic rendition of objects in surprising settings. This paradoxical juxtaposition of the real and unreal, rather than distortion, became Magritte's signature.

Other artists more directly engaged with political and social upheavals became affiliated with **Expressionism.** This movement had been developing since the beginning of the twentieth century but took on more social and political tones after the war. German artist **Käthe Kollwitz,** for example, had been a committed socialist and pacifist before the war, depicting the social problems of the working class, especially women and children. The loss of her son in the early days of the war brought on a deep personal crisis. In contrast to the dream world of the Surrealists, her stark woodcuts projected the pain and suffering of people whose emotions were a direct response to the outside world and real events.

Much more committed to linking artistic experimentation and political engagement were the artists active during the first decade of the Soviet Union. Among early devoted supporters of Bolshevism were writers such as Mayakovsky and artists such as **Marc Chagall.** In the early 1920s, Chagall developed his unique dreamlike combination of color and religious imagery. Cinema directors such as **Sergei Eisenstein** produced remarkable films like *Battleship Potemkin*

that revolutionized cinema. His techniques in framing, lighting, and composition were stark and expressive, unlike anything that had been seen on the silver screen before.

Soviet artists were not, however, free of state control. Chagall fell out of favor with the Soviet leadership and had to leave the country in 1923 because of tensions with the party and increased antisemitism. Mayakovsky committed suicide in 1930 after his work was severely criticized by party officials. Eisenstein was able to pursue his creative work only by making movies that did not challenge the ideology of the Communist Party. His prominent films from the 1920s were, in fact, powerful propaganda for the Soviet regime. Under Stalin's dictatorship, many writers and artists were silenced, imprisoned, or killed for their art.

Experiments in Architecture and Design

After the war, some architects and designers sought to redefine the relationship between the practical and the artistic by simplifying architectural and interior design. Grouped around Walter Gropius in Germany, these designers, artists, and architects became known as the **Bauhaus school,** the most influential design

Surrealism   Artistic movement of the 1920s and 1930s that explored the realm of dreams and altered reality to find the deeper truth of human experience.

André Breton   (1896–1966) French writer and founder of Surrealism.

Salvador Dali   (1904–1989) Spanish-born artist who became the most famous Surrealist.

René Magritte   (1898–1967) Belgian Surrealist painter famous for his superimposition of photographically depicted objects in unrelated three-dimensional spaces.

Expressionism   Artistic movement that aimed to represent the connection between the inner emotional world and outer social reality.

Käthe Kollwitz   (1867–1945) German Expressionist artist who portrayed the plight of working-class women and children.

Marc Chagall   (1887–1985) Russian Jewish painter whose art combined romantic images of lovers, nature, and traditional Jewish symbols with harsh political commentary.

Sergei Eisenstein   (1898–1948) One of the greatest film directors of the twentieth century, who used pioneering film techniques as powerful propaganda for the Bolsheviks.

Bauhaus school   Innovative German movement of architectural and interior design that sought to make living spaces and furniture designs functional and affordable.

movement in the first half of the twentieth century. The motivation of these architects and artists was connected to the horrors of the war. They sought to blend style and functionality, eliminating excesses they identified with the high bourgeois culture before the war and stripping away nationalism in style. Adherents of the Bauhaus school were optimistic: by eliminating the excesses of the past, artists and architects hoped to build a more stable environment accessible to people of different classes.

Another important force in design was **Le Corbusier,** a Swiss-born French engineer and artist—and one of the greatest architects of the twentieth century. Le Corbusier had a vision similar to that of the Bauhaus school—streamlining design, making it affordable and accessible to people of different social classes, and creating a new type of urban environment. Reacting against the cramped and alienating living conditions of the working classes before the war, he envisioned living quarters that were open, transparent, and connected to the community. His aim was to create a new society, and his *Toward a New Architecture* (1923) revolutionized urban planning. The Bauhaus school and Le Corbusier's work helped transform the appearance of old and new cities all over Europe, from Prague to Paris, as well as cities in Brazil, Algeria, and India.

The idea that the best in design should be available to people of all incomes generated the movement known as **Art Deco,** which aimed to make everyday objects simple, sleek, and affordable through mass production. Technological advances and assembly-line methods first introduced by Henry Ford in his Detroit automobile plants helped cut production costs. By the end of the 1920s, Art Deco furniture, china, household appliances, and window treatments graced the grand houses of the rich, the homes of the middle classes, and even the bungalows of the working classes. The gap between highbrow and lowbrow culture in the realm of consumer goods was closing up.

Popular Entertainment

High art joined popular culture in this amazing decade to give new status to entertainment, particularly dance and music. Cabarets had been popular since the 1910s, but after the war they were transformed by new trends, particularly American **jazz,** which swept working-class music halls and high-class art gatherings from Paris to Bucharest. Jazz was electrifying, showcasing improvisation and defying old classifications in its combinations of African rhythms and slave songs with popular ragtime and the blues. Introduced to Europe by African American

The artistic persona of Josephine Baker, the enormously popular African American jazz dancer in Paris, challenged the aesthetic norms of old Europe and reinforced concepts of race in European culture. Baker's freedom and eroticism were depicted as organically tied to her African blood, so that she appeared as modern and primitive, sophisticated and wild. *(Private Collection © DACS/Peter Newark American Pictures/ The Bridgeman Art Library)*

soldiers serving in France, jazz made audiences yearn to know more about American popular culture and entertainment.

Soon Europeans were doing the Charleston, with swings and heel kicks said to have originated with black dance styles on the islands off South Carolina.

Le Corbusier   (1887–1965) Swiss-born French architect whose innovations aiming to eliminate class distinctions influenced city planning throughout the world.

Art Deco   Architectural and design style that emphasized simplicity in style and aimed to make quality designs affordable to all through mass production.

jazz   Innovative American musical form that combined elements of African rhythm and slave songs with popular music and later avant-garde European influences.

Fritz Lang's *Metropolis* (1927) presented an image of modernity and technological progress that was both alluring and foreboding. The icon at the center of the movie was emphatically female, reflecting widespread fears among many men of women's empowerment as de-feminizing and emasculating. *(Schulz-Neudamm,* Metropolis, *1926. Lithograph, 83" x 36½". Gift of Universum-Film-Aktiengesellschaft Digital Image © The Museum of Modern Art/Licensed by Scala/Art Resource, NY)*

And in 1925, dance was further revolutionized when a U.S. traveling show captivated Paris with wild new jazz rhythms and the sensuous dances of its young African American star, **Josephine Baker.** Baker became an idol overnight, appealing to people of all walks of life who sought to discard the stuffiness of the prewar forms of entertainment for a more democratic and participatory type of dance and music. Baker's freedom and sensuality made her a lasting symbol of American culture in Europe.

At the same time, British dancer **Isadora Duncan** was transforming classical ballet into a new form of performance that emphasized expressive movement and grace rather than virtuosity. Duncan appeared on stage barefoot, in willowy silks instead of the stiff classic tutu; her movements aimed to convey emotions rather than showcase technique. Her new style of modern dance connected the Royal Opera House and rowdy cabarets into one seamless continuum of celebrating human creativity and sensuality.

A new invention, the phonograph, also made musical choices more accessible to mass audiences. For a few pennies, anyone could hear the sounds of a favorite band at home, practice trendy new dance steps, and throw a party instead of sitting in the audience at a music hall for an evening's entertainment. Just as revolutionary was the introduction of inexpensive, mass-produced radios, which, starting in the late 1920s, transformed the music industry and news media. Soon the sounds of jazz and other popular music blasted out of windows and courtyards in almost every neighborhood.

Film was by far the most important and inexpensive form of entertainment for the masses during the 1920s. German filmmakers produced some of the most memorable films. The most important directors, such as **Fritz Lang,** were the Expressionists, who used simple plots to exaggerate human emotions, especially suffering, through distorted camera angles, lighting, and creative editing. Lang's best-known movie is *Metropolis* (1927), which examined the relationship be-

Josephine Baker (1906–1975) African American dancer who charmed European audiences in 1925 and popularized the music and dance associated with jazz.

Isadora Duncan (1877–1927) British dancer who transformed traditional ballet technique into a more natural and emotion-filled movement style.

Fritz Lang (1890–1976) German Expressionist film maker, later active in Hollywood.

tween technology and progress by personifying technology as a female with both enticing and ultimately destructive characteristics. The movie also presented the suffering of the lower classes but expressed hope that technology could overcome social problems.

Listening to jazz, dancing the Charleston, and watching movies enabled working people, even the poor, to forget the war and escape the boredom of their hard lives. These forms of popular entertainment also allowed them the freedom to imagine other roles for themselves—as famous dancers, actors, or musicians. The new entertainment styles blurred the distance between the highly educated and privileged elites and the lower masses: fame seemed to be something almost anyone—in the excitement of the 1920s—could achieve.

Summary

↑ How did the destruction of the Great War bring about political and social transformations?

↑ How did the political and cultural experiments of the 1920s challenge the old order and ideas of prewar Europe?

↑ How did political and social identities shift in the aftermath of war and the experiments of the 1920s?

The end of World War I brought relief to Europe but also challenged the old political and social order, relations among states, and the roles of individuals in society. Political leaders, social reformers, intellectuals, artists, workers, and average citizens had to find their place in the new Europe. The experiments of the decade were as much about creating something new as they were about establishing order out of the chaos of the war. Some were more successful than others, but Europe would never be the same.

In the countries where democratic politics already had important roots, there was a struggle to suppress revolutionary attempts against the old system. Democracy was saved, but many of the parties that came out strongest were relatively new; parties with older traditions, especially the liberals, lost ground. In newly created countries, politicians attempted to establish democratic institutions, but political turmoil and economic instability proved difficult to overcome.

In Russia and Italy, political leaders abandoned democracy altogether in favor of communism and fascism, respectively. In both countries, dynamic leaders swept to victory through violent means and then proceeded to eliminate old institutions and create entirely new forms of political organizations and control. The changes in the Soviet Union were more substantial than in Italy, as communist ideology also forcefully sought to reshape all social identities and beliefs. In Italy, fascist propaganda suggested revolutionary changes in the role youth and especially men from the lower classes would play in creating a new Italy, but it also encouraged traditional roles for women. Both fascism and communism provided important models for radical politicians in Europe in the years to come.

The experiments of the 1920s reached into the realm of social identity. In particular, with women having taken on men's roles during the war and men having returned from the trenches with physical and psychological scars, many questioned traditional gender roles in the family, the workplace, and politics. Women experienced empowering changes but also frustration, especially with regard to family relations. And although much was restored with regard to men's economic and social status, they also experienced frustration. There was no going back to the pre-1914 assumptions about gender roles.

Some of the most lasting experiments of this decade were in the realm of the arts, which produced many of the century's masterpieces as well as radically new schools of thought, from dreamy Surrealism to the egalitarian Art Deco. And average people now participated in transforming avant-garde ideas into popular forms of entertainment. Through cabaret, jazz performances and records, new dance styles, and movies, artists now spoke to both elite and mass audiences. These innovations also had an important impact in enabling working-class people to see themselves not as bound to their economic situation but as able to enjoy the fruits of consumption, especially in the realm of entertainment.

← **Thinking Back, Thinking Ahead** →

To what extent did communism in the Soviet Union prove to be a threat to Europe's stability in the twentieth century?

ECHO ECHO ECHO ECHO ECHO ECHO

Sex Advice Columns in Women's Magazines

Today, glossy magazines promising great tips on how to improve and enjoy sex are commonplace at every supermarket checkout. But a century ago, any mention of sex in the media was taboo. Before 1918, women's magazines featured only articles on fashions, home decorations, mothering, and events organized by high-society ladies.

After 1918, however, women's magazines began to reflect the changes women had experienced in wartime. Women appeared in work settings. They were photographed driving cars and operating trams. A radical new feature was the sex advice column. With the rising validity of sexuality as a legitimate area of physiological and psychological research, the sex advice expert was born. Initially, participating in such public discussions about sexuality was seen as demeaning within the medical profession, and physicians were, in fact, discouraged from writing for nonprofessional magazines. More often than not, a layperson, who often sported the title of Dr. without any medical diploma, posed as an expert sexologist. However, as the popularity of the sex advice column surged, more professional physicians, nurses, and psychologists accepted such positions, opening the door for today's Dr. Ruth and Dr. Phil.

In the first years, the questions and advice were rather prudish, though daring for their time, without direct references to specific sexual practices. Most of the questions related to sexual fulfillment as a means for preserving the stability of the marriage and having children. For instance, a woman might ask, "How could I maintain marital bliss after ten years of marriage?" Thus, sexuality was discussed only in its direct link to well-accepted social norms. But the discussion of sex in popular women's magazines signaled to women that it was normal to consider themselves as sexual beings, to seek enjoyment in the intimate aspects of their life, and even to talk about it with their partners and with other women.

Today, the variety of sexual practices discussed in women's magazines in open, direct language has grown tremendously. The endorsement of products like Viagra by respectable politicians is a far cry from the shy and indirect references in the sex advice columns of the 1920s regarding men's ability to perform sexually. Likewise, the notion that women's sexual desire is properly expressed only in marriage and only toward the goal of becoming a mother has also changed dramatically.

Suggested Readings

Berend, Ivan T. *Decades of Crisis: Central and Eastern Europe Before World War II.* Berkeley: University of California Press, 1998. An excellent overview of political, intellectual, and artistic changes in the 1920s and 1930s, as European countries try to cope with challenges of modernization.

Bosworth, R. J. B. *Mussolini.* London: Arnold, 2003. An exhaustive biography of Benito Mussolini's personal and political life.

Marks, Sally. *The Illusion of Peace: Europe's International Relations, 1918–1933.* New York: Palgrave Macmillan, 2003. A succinct and lucid overview of the international changes and challenges in the first decade after the peace treaties.

Meier, Charles S. *Recasting Bourgeois Europe: Stabilization in France, Germany and Italy in the Decade After World War I.* Princeton, N.J.: Princeton University Press, 1998. A comparative analysis of the challenges faced by political elites, liberal democracy, and economies in France, Germany, and Italy in the aftermath of the war.

Siegelbaum, Lewis H. *Soviet State and Society Between Revolutions, 1918–1929.* Cambridge, England: Cambridge University Press, 2004. A close look at the transformations in politics and society in Russia during the first decade of communist rule, highlighting the compromises made by the political elite to secure the state.

Stites, Richard. *Revolutionary Dreams: Utopian Vision and Experimental Life in the Russian Revolution.* Oxford: Oxford University Press, 1991. An excellent analysis of the cultural experimentation of the Bolsheviks during the first decade after the revolution.

Willett, John. *Art and Politics in the Weimar Republic: The New Sobriety, 1917–1930.* New York: Pantheon Books, 1996. A magisterial analysis of the utopian impulses in the artistic life of the German Weimar Republic.

Websites

Links to websites with articles about important events during the 1920s, cultural movements and personalities, maps, and primary documents, **The Inter-War Years,** at www.historyteacher .net/APEuroCourse/WebLinks/WebLinks-Inter-WarYears.htm

Rich, if biased, resource on the most important people, movements, and events linked to the history of communism in the twentieth century, **Marxists Internet Archive,** at www.marxists .org

Links to websites on the political and cultural life of Europe in the 1920s and 1930s, **Internet Modern History Sourcebook: The Age of Anxiety,** at www.fordham.edu/halsall/mod/ modsbook40.html

CHAPTER

Democracy Under Siege, 1929–1945

27

1500 B.C.E.	1000 B.C.E.	500 B.C.E.	1 B.C.E./1 C.E.

1929
Great Depression
begins

1933
Hitler comes to
power in Germany

1936
Civil war begins
in Spain

Great Purges begin
in Soviet Union

1929	1930	1931	1932	1933	1934	1935	1936	1937

Axis Victories in World War II, 1942

World War II tested the limits of European civilization and democratic legacies. The threat was greatest in the spring of 1942, when Adolf Hitler's Axis alliance controlled most of Europe and North Africa. Where would the Allies find Axis weaknesses to exploit? It would take formidable human and material sacrifices to turn around the Nazi war machine.

Hitler's Greater Germany
Allied with Germany
Occupied by Germany and its allies
Grand Alliance
Neutral nations

0   200   400 Km.
0   200   400 Mi.

FINLAND

Helsinki

Leningrad
Siege, Oct. 1941–
Jan. 1944

NORWAY
April 9, 1940

Oslo

SWEDEN

Stockholm

ESTONIA

LATVIA
Riga

Moscow

LITHUANIA

Smolensk

Minsk

SOVIET UNION

Operation Barbarossa
June 1941

North Sea

Baltic Sea

NORTHERN IRELAND

IRELAND

GREAT BRITAIN

Battle of Britain,
July–Oct. 1940

London Blitz,
Sept. 1940–May 1941

London

DENMARK
April 9, 1940

Copenhagen

Elbe

Berlin

Posen

Warsaw

Vistula

Kiev

Stalingrad

Don

Dnieper

ATLANTIC OCEAN

NETHERLANDS
May 10, 1940

BELGIUM
May 10, 1940

GERMANY

Rhine

Seine

FRANCE
May 12, 1940

Paris

LUXEMBOURG
May 10, 1940

Cracow

Dniester

UKRAINE

BESSARABIA

Loire

Vienna

SLOVAKIA

HUNGARY

Budapest

Vichy

VICHY FRANCE
(Occupied Nov. 1942)

SWITZERLAND

Rhône

Garonne

Po

CROATIA

BOSNIA-
HERZEGOVINA

ROMANIA

Belgrade

Bucharest

Danube

Black Sea

PORTUGAL

SPAIN

Madrid

Lisbon

ITALY

*Corsica
(Vichy France)*

Elba

Rome

SERBIA
April 6, 1941

MONTENEGRO

ALBANIA
(Italy)

BULGARIA

Sofia

TURKEY

Ankara

*Sardinia
(Italy)*

Baleric Is.

GREECE
Oct. 28, 1940

Athens

GIBRALTAR
(Gr. Br.)

SPANISH
MOROCCO

Mediterranean Sea

Sicily

Crete

CYPRUS
(Gr. Br.)

SYRIA
(Occupied by Allies)

IRAQ
(Occupied by Allies)

LEBANON
(Occupied by Allies)

FRENCH
MOROCCO
(Vichy France)

ALGERIA
(Vichy France)

TUNISIA
(Vichy France)

MALTA
(Gr. Br.)

PALESTINE
(Br. Mandate)

TRANS-
JORDAN
(Br. Mandate)

SAUDI
ARABIA

Suez Canal

Cairo

LIBYA
(Italy)

EGYPT

Nile

Red Sea

Volga

500 C.E.   1000 C.E.   1500 C.E.   2000 C.E.

1939
Hitler invades
Poland, World
War II begins

1941
Hitler invades
the Soviet Union

1943
Soviets win
the Battle
of Stalingrad

1944
Allies land
at Normandy

1945
World War II
ends

1938   1939   1940   1941   1942   1943   1944   1945

Choic Choice Choice

George Orwell

George Orwell was one of the most powerful voices of Europe to confront the moral collapse and hatred that seemed to engulf the continent in the 1930s and 1940s. From his exposure of the harsh working conditions of miners in England to the atrocities committed during the Spanish Civil War, he criticized those ambitious for unbounded power and the lack of tolerance on both the left and the right. (AP Images)

George Orwell Commits Himself to Socialism

In 1930, Eric Arthur Blair became George Orwell. It wasn't just about choosing a pen name but rather about giving up his privileged identity as the son of a respectable servant of the British Empire in India. Instead of following the path to easy security and middle-class respectability opened by his family, at age nineteen Blair turned his back on elite schools to join the imperial police in India for some adventure. At age twenty-four, disgusted with its racist policies, he quit to live among the poor.

Having decided to follow his dream of writing, Blair, now Orwell, aimed high. He wanted nothing less than to become the moral conscience of his country, writing from conviction and experience, unlike many of the pseudo-bohemian writers of the time who enjoyed material privileges while writing about the poor. He didn't want just to move his audiences but instead aimed to challenge and force them to rethink their identities and act on their beliefs. True to this conviction, Orwell took a job as a dishwasher in Paris and lived in a poorly heated room for many months. It was during these days of self-imposed poverty that he began to understand class inequalities and gain sympathy for socialism as the best direction for democracy.

In his quest to become a good and socially active writer, in 1934 Orwell took on the assignment of writing about the life of coal miners in northern Britain. The result, *The Road to Wigan Pier* (1936), movingly described the appalling conditions of these workers but received mixed reviews from his left-wing editor. Always holding on to his aim of being the moral conscience of his peers, Orwell did not hesitate to criticize British socialists, whom he viewed as armchair critics rather than active reformers.

To demonstrate his own dedication to the cause of democracy through socialism, in 1936 Orwell went to Spain, where a civil war was pitting left-wing forces against a right-wing militarist regime. He arrived as a journalist but couldn't stay away from the action and joined the left-wing armies. His experiences in Spain reinforced his commitment to socialism as profoundly democratic but made him wary of the contribution of the Soviet Union to this cause. Soviet manipulations of the left-wing forces opened his eyes to the controlling and antidemocratic nature of the Soviet regime. These experiences were penned in *Homage to Catalonia* (1938).

Still hungry for action and eager to make a difference, Orwell tried to serve in the British army during World War II but was discharged because of injuries he had received in Spain. Instead, he worked for the British Broadcasting Corporation (BBC) as a reporter, a job that revealed to him the nature of wartime propaganda and the antidemocratic ways in which the British government manipulated information.

Orwell's passionate commitment to "turn political writing into an art" led him to write his last two and most important books, *Animal Farm* (1945) and *1984* (1949). Both reflected his desire to remain the moral conscience of Britain. Exposing the absurdity of sloganeering with expressions such as "war is peace" and "ignorance is strength," he pointed to the deep political corruption, both on the left and on the right, as the root of the tragedies he had witnessed all over Europe in the

1930s and 1940s. These books also represented an impassioned plea on behalf of peace and democracy and against totalitarianism, but they were not exclusively anticommunist, as they came to be depicted later on. Until the end of his life in 1950, Orwell remained committed to his belief in socialism as the most radically democratic ideology of the times, more progressive than liberalism or communism.

Introduction

George Orwell was one of many Europeans who witnessed with alarm the profound political crisis of the 1930s as Europe's democracies plunged into a severe depression. Some, like Orwell, became more committed than ever to socialist ideas. Others rejected democracy itself as the problem and turned toward antidemocratic solutions.

Of the options taken in the 1930s, the dictatorships in Italy, Germany, and the Soviet Union seemed the most successful in managing the economic crisis, eventually restoring full employment and production growth while the democracies struggled. But the success of the Soviets and the Nazis was due largely to their oppressive internal policies, which controlled workers and resources in ways democracies could not. The Nazis' racist ideology and the Stalinist paranoid concept of internal enemies institutionalized terror in both countries. Adolf Hitler and Joseph Stalin also aimed to undo the international system that had been developing through the League of Nations. In particular, Hitler's rearmament and expansionist policies challenged the Versailles Treaty while democratic states stood idle until it was too late.

Still, faced with Hitler's challenge to European international order in 1939, after 1941 the western democracies joined forces with the Soviet Union and by 1945 had defeated Germany and its allies. World War II, with its unmatched carnage, involvement of civilians, use of new military technology, and extermination of innocent people, especially the Jews, radically transformed Europe for a second time in less than a half a century.

Responses to the Great Depression, 1929–1939

⬇ What were the causes of the Great Depression?
⬇ What were the political consequences of the Great Depression?

In the fall of 1929, the bubble of prosperity burst, bringing on severe economic problems and major po-

litical upheaval. After the 1929 stock market crash in the United States, European banks and enterprises lost much of their capital and millions of people lost their jobs. The political impact of the world depression that followed was huge, as most governments lost the trust of the voters, yet starving workers had nowhere else to turn. Everyone looked toward the state for solutions, but no one knew how to deal with this economic and social crisis of unprecedented scale. Only in Britain, France, Belgium, Czechoslovakia, and the Scandinavian countries was democracy able to pass this difficult test. Most other countries slid toward regimes that offered security and strength at the price of democracy. With Italy providing an example of successful management of the economic depression, authoritarian regimes rose all over eastern and southern Europe. Germany also abandoned its fragile republic under the spell of Adolf Hitler.

The Great Depression

By the end of World War I, New York had replaced London as the financial capital of the world, and by 1929, European economies had become highly dependent on the American economy. The Dawes Plan for payment of the war debt tied the finances of Britain, France, and Germany to the economic well-being of the United States. During the 1920s, the growing availability of American goods and lure of American popular culture in Europe also strengthened economic ties across the Atlantic. Thus, when the New York stock market crashed in October 1929, its effects were felt immediately in Europe. American banks and financiers started to call in short-term loans, depleting European banks, especially in Germany and Austria, of sizable resources. By the end of 1930, 1,350 American banks had closed; 2,293 more did so in 1931. Between 1929 and 1934, almost 33 percent of American banks had failed.

In Europe, panic ensued. As people withdrew cash from banks and closed their accounts, the capital available to businesses shrank, leading to the collapse of major European banks, including the Kreditanstalt, Austria's largest bank. Unable to pay their workers,

Chronology

1928–1933	Stalin initiates first five-year plan in Soviet Union
1929	Great Depression begins
1931	United States initiates moratorium on war debts
1933	Hitler comes to power in Germany; Dachau labor camp established in Germany
1934	Soviet Union is admitted to League of Nations
1935	Mussolini invades Ethiopia
1936	Popular Front is formed in France; Spanish Civil War begins; Great Purges begin in Soviet Union
1939	Nazis take over Czechoslovakia; Franco wins Spanish Civil War; Hitler and Stalin sign Molotov-Ribbentrop Pact; World War II begins
1940	Nazis occupy Norway, Denmark, the Netherlands, Belgium, and France; Nazis bomb England in Battle of Britain
1941	U.S. Lend-Lease Act grants war aid to Britain; Nazis invade Soviet Union in Operation Barbarossa United States enters the war after Japanese bomb Pearl Harbor
1942	Wannsee Conference plans Jewish genocide
1943	Soviets win decisive battles at Stalingrad and Kursk
1945	Soviets liberate Auschwitz; Churchill, Roosevelt, and Stalin meet at Yalta Conference; United States drops first atomic bombs in Japan; World War II ends

One of millions of people worldwide left homeless and on the verge of starvation by the Great Depression, this "Migrant Mother" became an iconic image. Florence Thompson was photographed in 1936 in California by the American documentary photographer Dorothea Lange. Thompson's face reflects sadness and worry, but her gestures imply despair. She does not comfort the daughters who hide their faces against her, and the baby on her lap, uncradled, already seems half-dead. *(Library of Congress)*

to almost 6 million by 1932—almost 40 percent of the workforce. In the United States, 25 percent of the workforce was unemployed. By 1933, economic production had fallen by 50 percent in the United States and by 40 percent in Germany. (See Table 27.1.)

Some economists, such as **John Maynard Keynes**, believed that the **Great Depression** was also con-

John Maynard Keynes (1883–1946) British economist whose theories revolutionized the supply-demand equation and inspired government policies to encourage economic growth.

Great Depression Global economic crisis that began in October 1929 and lasted throughout the 1930s.

these businesses started to fire them by the thousands. Even the 1931 American moratorium on war debts could not reverse the downward spiral, though it did ease international tensions. Unemployment in Germany reached 3 million in 1930 and skyrocketed

Table 27.1

The Great Depression

INDICES OF INDUSTRIAL PRODUCTION, 1929–1938, IN MAJOR EUROPEAN COUNTRIES (1937 = 100)

	1929	1930	1931	1932	1933	1934	1935	1936	1937
France	123	123	105	91	94	92	88	95	100
Germany	79	69	56	48	54	67	79	90	100
Italy	90	85	77	77	82	80	86	86	100
Great Britain	77	74	69	69	73	80	82	94	100

UNEMPLOYMENT (IN THOUSANDS)

	1929	1930	1931	1932	1933	1934	1935	1936	1937
France	neglig.	13	64	301	305	368	464	470	380
Germany	1,899	3,070	4,520	5,575	4,804	2,718	2,151	1,593	912
Italy	301	425	734	1,006	1,019	964	—	—	874
Great Britain	1,216	1,917	2,630	2,745	2,521	2,159	2,036	1,755	1,484

Source: Stromberg, Roland N., *Europe in the Twentieth Century,* 4th Edition, © 1997. Reprinted by permission of Pearson Education, Inc., Upper Saddle River, NJ.

nected to the **deflationary** policies of the 1920s, which had followed the hyperinflation scare of the early 1920s. Businesses and individuals had been afraid to borrow, thus slowing economic growth, and banks had also become more conservative, charging higher interest rates. Other scholars have seen the Great Depression as a more acute case of the cyclical process of economic growth and slowdown characteristic of all capitalist economies.

Whatever the causes, the effects of the Great Depression were profound. Many of those who had spent their youth in the trenches of World War I were now middle aged and had families. When they lost their jobs or their businesses, they grew despondent. Some, unable to feed their families or make payments on their homes, slipped into deep depression and abandoned their families. Women's economic status was also badly hurt, though some were able to find part-time work in the service industry—as cooks, servants, and sometimes as sex workers.

Democracies' Responses

If dependency on American investments and banks along with deflationary policies were the initial causes of economic collapse in Europe, the depth and duration of the Great Depression were also a consequence of the choices various states made after 1929. Politicians tried to balance state budgets and avoid expenditures. Following the lead of the United States, European governments quickly imposed higher tariffs to protect their own industries. The result was a decline in international trade that further reduced production and employment. Keynes argued that economic recovery could be achieved only by abandoning the obsession with balanced budgets and the **gold standard** and by instituting government programs to put people back to work. A larger workforce, he pointed out, would increase the tax base, and more taxes would reduce budget deficits. Under President Franklin D. Roosevelt, the United States weathered the Great Depression in part through a broad range of government-supported public works programs that implemented Keynes's ideas.

But in Britain, politicians were not open to these solutions. Labour prime minister Ramsay MacDonald, elected in May 1929 on the promise of securing workers' interests, could not cope with the massive unemployment that hit Britain by 1930 (a 60 percent rise just during that year). His government opted for conservative economic solutions for the economic depression. Hopelessly, it attempted to keep the budget balanced, and it refrained from setting up the kinds of public works programs developed in America. Instead, MacDonald chose to cut compensation for the unemployed. Such a move by a Labour prime minister seemed so much at odds with that party's ideology that half his ministers resigned.

deflationary Referring to a fiscal policy aimed at preventing inflation.

gold standard Fiscal policy that pegs national currency to gold reserves.

In an unprecedented move, MacDonald compromised with the Conservatives to create a **National Unity Government**, with himself as prime minister, which he led until 1935, though he was expelled from the Labour Party for betraying workers' interests. Despite political and economic turmoil, the National Unity Government managed two important accomplishments. First, the Conservatives agreed to support issues important to Labour, such as government-regulated health insurance and Housing Acts that mandated the building of affordable, safe housing. By the late 1930s, politicians of all leanings recognized housing, education, and public health as services for which the state had responsibility, and Britain was on its way to becoming a welfare state. Though private enterprise ran many social services, the government monitored their quality and helped the poor gain access to decent housing and healthcare.

The chief accomplishment of the National Unity Government in Britain, however, was to simply hold on to the principles of democracy. Both communist and fascist movements grew in Britain during the 1930s, gathering strength from the sheer desperation of the economic crisis. But most politicians resisted the temptation to play upon fears in order to increase their following. British politicians followed well-established democratic rules, and average citizens respected this position, although they were often dissatisfied with the results.

France, too, adopted deflationary measures to cope with the downturn in economic production and rise in unemployment. The French were even more conservative than the British, keeping the franc on the gold standard at a time when every other European country and the United States had abandoned it. By 1935, when most European countries had begun to recover, France was registering its highest unemployment rates (464,000, in contrast to 13,000 in 1930) and its lowest index of industrial production since 1929 (30 percent lower).

Yet France, too, resisted the fascist temptation and defended democratic institutions, weathering a major political scandal in 1934 and a demonstration by two hundred thousand protesters that was brutally crushed by the police. Though fascist organizations in France had more than 750,000 members, mainstream politicians and average citizens rejected fascist appeals and in 1936 put a strong antifascist coalition in power.

Authoritarian Solutions

Most of Europe's political elites, however, responded to the Great Depression by undermining or abandoning democratic institutions. Where such institutions were recent, both politicians and ordinary citizens were quick to equate economic problems with a fundamental weakness of democracy and to look for other political solutions.

In Austria, Spain, and Portugal, the response was an alliance between conservative politicians and the Catholic Church. In these countries, the Roman Catholic Church was one of the most stable institutions, shaping not only religious outlook but also political life. In Austria, the Christian Socialists, one of the two largest parties in the country, had a conservative Catholic outlook on moral values and social responsibilities. The party favored government control over education that would be strictly Christian, a traditional social hierarchy with the Catholic aristocracy at the top, and the exclusion of Jews from important positions of public authority. In the early 1930s, both Austria and Portugal replaced democratically elected governments with strong conservative leaders who were devout Catholics. These leaders gave the Catholic Church important educational, propaganda, and social responsibilities. The school curriculum came under the control of the Catholic Church, as did many other social services. Church-controlled censorship of literature and other cultural endeavors was also introduced.

In Spain, the struggle between conservative militarist and Catholic political forces and their secularist left-wing opponents proved more violent and led to a civil war. The **Spanish Civil War** lasted three years (1936–1939) and destroyed trust in democracy in Spain and among many Europeans generally (see Choice). The country went from a republican government in 1931 to, in 1939, a titular monarchy actually headed by the authoritarian general **Francisco Franco**, the leader of the pro-Catholic right-wing forces. The son of a naval postmaster, Franco had, at age thirty-four in 1926, become the youngest general in Europe. Before 1936, he had served under a right-wing nationalist coalition to purge the military of supporters of the left. Through military skill and successful maneuvering among his rivals, he built a reputation as a strong leader and a unifier. Although many regarded Franco

National Unity Government   Coalition government in Britain during the first half of the 1930s, headed by Labour leader Ramsey MacDonald but dominated by the Conservatives.

Spanish Civil War   (1936–1939) War won by the right-wing Nationalists, supported by the Nazis, over republican left-wing forces, supported by the Soviets.

Francisco Franco   (1892–1975) General and leader of the Nationalists in the Spanish Civil War and dictator of Spain from 1939 until his death in 1975.

Pablo Picasso painted *Guernica* (1937) as a political-aesthetic reaction against the mass killings by right-wing forces led by Francisco Franco during the Spanish Civil War. Specifically, Guernica, a small town in northern Spain, was bombed in 1937 by German planes supporting Franco. Though muted in color, the painting became a dramatic symbol of pacifism. Particularly powerful is the image of the mother with the dead child on the left-hand side, screaming upward toward the bull, a symbol of both Spain and of Picasso himself. *(Museo Nacional Centro de Arte Reina Sofía, Madrid/Art Resource, NY, © ARS, NY)*

as a supporter of fascism, he was in fact a pragmatist who used the support of fascist forces, especially from Italy and Germany, to win the civil war. By 1939, when Franco's Nationalists won against the Republicans, over 1 million people had been placed in prison by Franco's victorious dictatorship. The Catholic Church became Franco's right arm in enforcing strict censorship over culture, education, and other public services.

In other young democracies, especially in eastern Europe, political leaders and average citizens blamed democratic institutions and ethnic minorities for the economic crisis. Their solution was to dissolve parliaments, suppress the voice of ethnic minorities, and establish authoritarian ethno-nationalist rule. In Romania, for instance, the young king **Carol II** claimed he was the only leader interested in the unity of the country, thus undermining all political parties. He dealt with the economic crisis by allowing antisemitic propaganda and policies to flourish as he militarized the economy, reviving floundering branches of industry by emphasizing the production of armaments. In 1938, he made himself a virtual dictator. By then, **dictatorships** had replaced parliamentary systems in many eastern European states, including Latvia, Poland, Hungary, Greece, and Yugoslavia. Eastern European leaders used the revisionism of ethnic minorities as an excuse to build up the military. The increasing ob-

session with militarization led to a veritable arms race in the area. Acquiring military equipment from Nazi Germany in return for agricultural goods that could not find a market in western Europe relieved some of the economic crisis for these countries but also rendered them greatly dependent on Germany for their military needs.

The rhetoric and paramilitary organizations of the authoritarian regimes in eastern Europe resembled those in fascist Italy. In fact, fascist movements were particularly strong in Romania, Hungary, and Yugoslavia. But they did not foment fascist coups like Mussolini's. Instead, the dictators of theses countries merely took on a fascist style, with uniformed supporters marching in the streets. Authoritarian regimes in the rest of Europe remained much more conservative in scope and ideology. They were interested in maintaining stability and preventing broad social and political upheaval rather than in generating the kind of changes Mussolini had brought about in 1922.

Carol II   (r. 1930–1940) Romanian king who ruled in authoritarian fashion.

dictatorship   Autocratic form of government headed by a single all-powerful ruler, the dictator.

The Rise of Nazism

By contrast, between 1930 and 1933, Germany experienced a political and social revolution that brought to power the most radical movement since the Bolsheviks—the Nazis. After the 1929 crash, Germany faced obstacles similar to other young democracies. Political parties had a fluid following, and many people had come to question the democratic institutions of the Weimar Republic, which had been set up in the shadow of the much-hated Versailles Treaty and were only a decade old. Just months before the crash, Gustav Stresemann—a central figure for the Weimar's stability—died. Moreover, Germany was hit harder by the depression than any other state in Europe. The Social Democrats, who led the government at the time of the crash, lost power, their representation in parliament shrinking from 30 percent in 1928 to 20 percent in 1932. No other party was strong enough to succeed, so a series of political compromises followed. Various governments tried different approaches, first obtaining a moratorium on war reparations (1931) and then implementing a major land reform. Many politicians were angered by these moves, and average citizens lost faith in the democratic processes that seemed to bring very little stability and even less economic relief to the country. Meanwhile, a political party once marginal and ridiculed by mainstream politicians was growing rapidly. Electoral support for the Nazis increased from 2.5 percent in 1928 to 18 percent in 1930 and to 37 percent in July 1932. The reasons for this meteoric growth were many. First and foremost, the Nazis had a charismatic leader unmatched by any other German politician—Adolf Hitler.

Hitler came from a lower-class Austrian family and had left home at age sixteen to become a bohemian artist in Vienna. Unable to get into the Fine Arts Academy, he became a drifter, living in homeless shelters and eking out a living as a street peddler until 1914, when he volunteered in the German army. Having fought bravely in the war (he was decorated twice), Hitler was dismayed by Germany's loss and looked for a way to continue his service in a paramilitary organization. His ambitions brought him, in 1919, to the organization that became the Nazi Party a year later. Here Hitler discovered his great talent as a speaker and fundraiser, turning the Nazis into a notable party by 1923. His supporters were a motley crew of disillusioned veterans, drifters like himself, and "little men" who were suffering from the effects of the war and postwar inflation. After the failed 1923 Beer Hall Putsch, Hitler was thrown into jail. The Nazis were made illegal but continued their activities, including the publication of Hitler's *Mein Kampf*, written in prison.

Hitler was not a great thinker, as *Mein Kampf* shows. The book is a muddled collection of nationalist and racist, primarily antisemitic, ideas. Using the work of racist theorists of the nineteenth century, Hitler developed a genetically determined hierarchy of ethnicities, with the Aryans (Germans, Scandinavians, Britons) at the top and Slavs and Jews at the bottom, the latter categorized as "subhuman." The book argued for the idea of **Lebensraum**—that because the German nation needed more territory in order to thrive, it ought to expand eastward into Poland, Czechoslovakia, and beyond. Hitler was singularly able to distill the frustrations of many Germans into a few simple messages: Germans had been served poorly by the Weimar Republic, which had been a result of the unfair Versailles Treaty; the enemies of the German people were both outside (especially the Soviets) and inside (communists, Jews, and the capitalists who had profiteered from the postwar economic problems). Eliminating these enemies was the key to bringing Germany back to its former imperial glory.

By the time the Nazis reemerged as an important political party during the Great Depression, Hitler was a seasoned leader and spellbinding speaker, with a loyal paramilitary organization—the storm troopers—and a band of personal bodyguards, the **Schutzstaffel**, or **SS**. His ability to construct a spectacle around the Nazis was another reason for their growing popularity. In a time of growing disaffection and demoralization, Hitler's Brown Shirts marched around as a solid unit—a symbol of Germany's once-great virility and military prowess, now stymied by the Treaty of Versailles and the Social Democrats. Much like Mussolini, whose mastery of ceremony had been a model for the Nazis, Hitler understood well that a powerful show of force sometimes meant more than speeches and ideology. He attracted many students and younger followers simply with the sense of community and strength he seemed to radiate: "Long ago you heard the voice of a man . . . and it struck to your hearts, and it awakened you, and you followed his voice. . . . It is faith in our nation that has made us small people great, that has made us poor people rich, that has

Mein Kampf (*My Struggle*) Book written by Hitler in 1925 in which he formulated his ideas of racial purity and his goal of exterminating the Jews.

Lebensraum (in German, "living space") Idea that Germany needed to expand eastward to secure the healthy growth of the Aryan race.

Schutzstaffel (SS) (in German, "protective squadron") Hitler's personal bodyguards in the early days of the Nazi Party.

made us vacillating, dispirited, anxious people brave and courageous."

The appeal of the Nazis rested on posing simple solutions for complicated problems and playing on the fears of a population caught in a deep economic crisis that other parties could not end. It was not just the die-hard antisemites who voted for the Nazis. The party attracted educated and uneducated, poor and well-to-do, men and women, workers and entrepreneurs, and religious and secularized Germans. But the largest group of Nazi supporters were those either hurt badly by the depression—small artisans and shopkeepers, some workers, farmers—or those who had come to see in the Weimar government only a betrayal of Germany and defeat by outside forces—soldiers who had fought in the war, men laid off while women still worked, students, and antisemites.

By November 1932, the Nazis were the strongest party in the Reichstag. Hitler did not have a mandate to form a single government (the Nazis had received only 33 percent of the vote), but he was not interested in sharing control and no other leaders were willing to give him full powers. Then in January 1933, he became chancellor and embarked on a swift process of undermining all democratic institutions of the Weimar Republic through steps that were technically legal. In February, a mysterious fire in the Reichstag building allowed Hitler to ask for emergency powers to go after the culprits, whom he identified as communists. With the president's approval, Hitler suspended all free speech and asked for new elections, which gave the Nazis 44 percent of the vote. The new parliament moved quickly to outlaw the Communist Party and pass the **Enabling Act**, which gave Hitler extraordinary powers in making executive decisions in all matters of "national security," placing him above accountability to the legal and judicial branches of government. The act enabled Hitler to become a dictator and to begin reshaping Germany according to his vision of a racially pure thousand-year empire—the **Third Reich.**

The Soviet Union Under Stalin, 1929–1939

⬇ What were the Soviet Union's successes and failures in the decade of the Great Depression?
⬇ What were the new elements added by Stalin to turn the Soviet Union into a totalitarian state?

As Europe struggled with the Great Depression and political instability, the Soviet Union seemed on an unstoppable track toward modernization, industrial-

ization, and full employment. With membership in the League of Nation, it gained international respectability. In the 1930s it was a model for many disillusioned people in the west. As a force in the antifascist struggle, the Soviet Union emerged as a first-rank international power. The reality of Stalin's rule, however, was grim: modernization and stability were accomplished only with much brutality. Stalin's newly powerful country was a ruthless police state.

Domestic and Foreign Policies

While the rest of Europe was entering a period of economic crisis, the Soviet Union was relatively free of the vagaries of the free market, as it had not been involved in the Dawes Plan or affected by the rise of American banking in the world of international finance. Fully in control of the country's political apparatus, in the late 1920s Stalin turned his attention toward improving the Soviet Union's international standing and developing the economy.

During the early 1930s, the Soviet Union reversed its policy of fostering world revolution, focusing instead on international security issues. The most important foreign policy concern was to counter the rise of threats in the west (Nazi Germany) and in the east (Japan). The Soviets pursued this goal with a two-pronged strategy: diplomatic and military. In the realm of diplomacy, the foreign commissar **Maxim Litvinov** played the most important role. He was a skillful diplomat who projected an image of cosmopolitan sophistication, unlike most other representatives of the Soviet Union. During the 1920s, when the country was still an international **pariah** and had no diplomatic ties with the Great Powers, Litvinov had become involved in disarmament discussions in the League of Nations. Through his relentless efforts, France (1932) and then the United States (1933) finally reestablished diplomatic relations with the Soviet Union, opening the way for the its admission into the league in 1934 and for increased international economic ties.

Enabling Act   Decree passed by the Reichstag in 1933 that enabled Hitler to legally eliminate all political enemies and assume full dictatorial powers.

Third Reich   Title used for the period of Nazi rule in Germany.

Maxim Litvinov   (1876–1951) Soviet foreign commissar in the 1930s who orchestrated the admission of the Soviet Union to the League of Nations.

pariah   Outcast; a nation that is diplomatically shunned, its leadership and actions not recognized as legitimate.

Another component of the Soviet effort to build up international strength was militarization. While Litvinov was praising disarmament in the League of Nations, Stalin was focusing on the armament industry as an important component of economic planning. The military was building new weapons, such as tanks and new types of bombs. The military leadership was fully committed to this program and conducted intensive campaigns for training and diversifying the fighting forces.

Internally, Stalin's goal was nothing less than turning an agricultural nation into an industrial powerhouse. In 1929 he proclaimed: "We are becoming a land of metals, . . . automobiles, . . . tractors, and when we have put the USSR on an automobile and the peasant on a tractor, let the noble capitalists . . . attempt to catch up." This ambitious goal, however, needed unprecedented planning and government control. Stalin ended the New Economic Policy (NEP) and called on his economic advisers to create a series of **five-year plans** that would set up a **command economy**: all aspects of the economy—from securing natural resources to research and development, employment, and commerce—would be controlled by the state rather than the market. The supply of goods would be determined by ideological goals—industrialization and modernization—rather than by consumer needs and wants. The first five-year plan focused obsessively on high production targets in heavy industries, subordinating production in all other areas to this primary goal: it called for an increase of 300 percent in the production of electricity, coal, pig iron, and steel. "There is no fortress that the Bolsheviks cannot storm," boasted the party leadership.

In the first few years, these industries achieved huge levels of growth because they were so rudimentary at the start. In addition, Stalin empowered factory managers and directors of heavy industry enterprises to use any necessary means, often simply reallocating natural resources and transportation from other economic sectors and using forced labor instead of paid workers for some of the most ambitious projects, such as the Volga–White Sea Canal. But by the third year, the rate of growth had slowed down. Without comprehensive planning for the entire economy, the state risked halting production in some sectors, such as agriculture and light industries, to achieve the official quotas in the heavy industry. For instance, if trains were made available only for mining and steel industries, production and delivery in other sectors of the economy became blocked. In the end, the first five-year plan was a failure by its own goals, but it still produced some outstanding results—a growth of over 100 percent in steel, electricity, and machinery production, although some of these statistics were manipulated. But by the end of the third five-year plan, in 1939, the Soviet Union was outproducing Britain and France, both still mired in depression, and was, after the United States and Germany, the third-largest industrial power in the world.

The greatest failure of the five-year plans pertained to the welfare of the workers. To the Soviet state, the only thing that mattered was the growth of production; the basic material needs of average people were unimportant. Only work and its products—the finished good—had quantifiable value. In practice, this meant that Soviet industries were built without any regard for worker safety. The Soviet workplace looked a lot more like the filthy capitalist enterprises criticized by Friedrich Engels and Karl Marx a century earlier than the workers' paradise envisioned by V. I. Lenin.

The Soviets used both rewards and coercion to mobilize the labor force and increase productivity, especially in heavy industries. Workers who more than met production goals received higher pay and other benefits, such as better housing. In addition, convict labor continued to be used in mining, lumbering, and building roads and waterways. Most workers put up with these measures, some out of conviction and others out of fear or need.

Peasants, however, resisted more stubbornly as the Soviets converted agriculture into a state-owned sector. The five-year plans called for **collectivization**—the confiscation of private land to create state-owned farms where production targets set by the state dictated the crops to be grown and the quantities to be produced. Peasants became wage-laborers who could keep only small plots of land and a few animals around the house for basic household needs. From the perspective of the state, collectivization was a rational way to consolidate small holdings and increase productivity. Large state farms, with machinery unaffordable to most farmers, could produce better crops and larger yields, to everyone's benefit. But for peasants, collectivization robbed them of their identity. To be a

five-year plans Centralized formula for economic planning initiated by Stalin in 1928 to direct and coordinate production in all sectors of economy.

command economy State-controlled economy in which all aspects of the economy are controlled by the state in a centralized manner.

collectivization Soviet policy for turning all agricultural land into state-owned farms and peasants into wage-laborers.

peasant in Russia meant to have land, not just live on it. A man's dignity, in particular, was tied to his ability to feed his family from his land. Communist officials who pushed for collectivization were aware of this problem. But they believed the peasants, especially the newly enriched **kulaks** from the NEP period, needed to be broken. Collectivization was as much an ideological and social goal—eliminating a class enemy and creating a larger proletariat—as it was an economic aim.

Collectivization was accomplished at appalling human costs and failed miserably to reach its economic goals. In the winter of 1932–1933, outrageous production quotas induced a general famine, especially in the Ukraine. Forced by the state to give up even the animals and crops they would have needed to survive through the winter, between 5 and 7 million peasants starved to death. The lucky ones were able to find shelter and food with relatives in the city. Others were reduced to eating tree bark and bugs—and even cannibalism. Young mothers, unable to feed their infants, killed them. But by the end of 1933, ruthless methods had forced most peasants to give up their land. By 1940, all agricultural land was in the hands of the state.

Yet this apparent victory masked important failures. First, peasants had been forced to give up their land through imprisonment, torture, exile in Siberia, and, in many cases, execution. The number of victims of this brutal process is still disputed, but it was certainly in the millions—6 to 10 million, according to various scholars. Some of the best working hands were eliminated in the first years of collectivization, while survivors were broken psychologically and physically. Second, the peasants did not go down without a fight. Many burned their crops and killed their livestock rather than see them in the hands of the government. As a result, the cattle population decreased by over 40 percent and the pig population by almost 50 percent between 1928 and 1931. Such violence continued into the late 1930s because peasants simply could not see collective farms as anything other than theft by the state.

The one goal in which collectivization succeeded was ideological. Peasants were forced to become workers, with no other resources for survival. In the next generation, the very notion of taking pride in one's land was wiped out. The communists had eliminated another social enemy from the old regime and reshaped the identity of the rural population into a subservient, if resentful, category of workers. Using violence, Stalin was on his way to refashioning the New Soviet Man and Woman.

Stalin's Totalitarian State

Having subdued the peasantry, Stalin turned toward intimidating other internal enemies—distrusted members of the party. This campaign began in 1936 and lasted until 1939, starting with the party's upper hierarchy and then widening to include family, friends, and other connections. By 1934, there had been significant disagreement among party leaders over industrialization and collectivization. Most in the Politburo leaned toward slowing down the pace and ending the most brutal policies. Unable to persuade or intimidate his opponents, Stalin turned the **NKVD**, the secret police, on them. The terror employed by the NKVD was not new for the Soviet regime, but the scale of the **Great Purges** that followed was unprecedented.

The first victims were high-ranking old Bolsheviks, some in the Politburo, followed by the most prominent army leaders and eventually the very leaders of the NKVD who had engineered the first purges. Stalin's diabolical system ensured that responsibility for the purges would always fall on the shoulders of his henchmen. Most old Bolshevik elites perished or were exiled, 70 percent of the Central Committee was removed, a significant number of officers were exiled or executed, and most of the leadership of the NKVD was also killed. In 1939, less than 2 percent of the delegates at the party congress remained had attended the 1934 congress. By the end of the decade, the purges had produced a new generation of party, army, and secret police leaders personally subservient to Stalin.

The purges were a conscious policy engineered by Stalin to eliminate all opposition through execution and fear. Most people learned not to speak in public. A comment about how crowded the bus was might land one in jail. Criticism of food in a cafeteria might bring an NKVD agent to the table. Individuals disappeared so often in public places, never to be heard of again, that most people came to believe that the secret police were everywhere and that everyone was a potential informer, including children, spouses, and other close family members.

kulaks Entrepreneurial peasants who enriched themselves during the NEP years.

NKVD (Russian acronym for "People's Commissariat of Internal Affairs") Soviet secret police under Stalin that organized the massive purges of the 1930s.

Great Purges Campaigns of political repression and persecution in the Soviet Union orchestrated by Joseph Stalin during the late 1930s.

By 1939, several million people had been harassed and arrested by the NKVD in connection with alleged opposition. Many were executed; many more were sent to forced-labor camps, the **gulags,** where a majority perished from the brutality of the guards and the dreadful living conditions. An infamous camp was Solovetsky, an island in the Arctic Circle. Those who survived were used as slave labor, building railroads and hydroelectric stations as well as working in coal, gold, and copper mines.

Purges and the NKVD succeeded in transforming high-ranking communist officials and average citizens alike into fearful, powerless pawns in the hands of the state. They completed Stalin's social revolution. Through relentless and arbitrary brutality, the Soviet Union was now a **totalitarian** police state. The fate of all citizens rested in the hands of the party and on the whims of the Great Leader. The party and the state were one. The state controlled the economy and, through the secret police, intruded itself into everyone's daily life. A member of the Politburo could become victim of Stalin's rage as easily as a poor peasant. In fact, the closer one was to the center of power in Moscow, the tighter the control exercised by Stalin's apparatus of fear. His ability to control Soviet society through terror was unmatched by any leader in the twentieth century, save Hitler.

Yet Stalin was not content to project the image of a feared tyrant. He wanted to impress Soviet citizens and the world with his great accomplishments. Through a costly and sophisticated propaganda machine, he built a mythical cult of personality that depicted him as a beloved father of the country. One propaganda ode from this period declared: "O great Stalin, O leader of the peoples, / Thou who broughtest man to birth. / Thou who fructifies the earth, / Thou who restorest to centuries, . . . O thou, / Sun reflected by millions of hearts." Writers were pressed into composing such poems; to write in opposition to Stalin meant certain death.

But many were in awe of Stalin and honest in their praises. A movie producer who later became a critic of the regime confessed: "The strangest thing to me is that I was absolutely sincere. I thought all this was a necessary part of building communism. And then I believed Stalin." Western intellectuals disillusioned with the weak democracies and their inability to fight the fascist threat were also impressed by Soviet accomplishments. The Spanish painter Pablo Picasso, for instance, came to glorify the Soviet Union under Stalin. Engineers and scientists from Europe and the America were likewise enthusiastic. But many of those who went to the Soviet Union during the 1930s also disappeared into the gulag. It was safer to ad-mire the Soviet Union from afar than to experience it up close.

The Third Reich, 1933–1945

↓ What distinguished the Third Reich from other political regimes of the 1930s?
↓ What methods did the Nazis employ to achieve total control over German society?

In Germany, Hitler was also creating a totalitarian state. A pragmatist, he used the economic elites and existing political institutions to gain support and eliminate his enemies. But he was as quick to destroy inconvenient allies, making himself—like Mussolini and Stalin—the supreme leader, the Führer. The Nazis did not come to power with a clear political agenda other than Hitler's concepts of racial purity and the need to revise the Versailles Treaty. But in a few years, violence against internal enemies, in particular Jews, and expansionism became the hallmarks of the Third Reich.

Hitler's Consolidation of Power

Hitler won his mandate in 1933 by vowing to do away with internal enemies. First on the list were the communists, the purported villains behind the Reichstag fire. After the Enabling Act, he eliminated all political parties and trade unions. Labeling his moves as security measures, in 1934 he ordered his SS troops to kill all conservative leaders who had opposed him before 1933 as well as leaders of his own storm troopers. This **Night of Long Knives,** Hitler's first internal purge, paved the way for his dictatorial rule by terror, much like Stalin's purges that began during the same period.

Within six months Hitler had consolidated all political power in his hands. With other political parties gone, the Nazis moved to control civic and public institutions in the name of national and economic reconstruction. The foundation of this policy was the

gulag   (Russian acronym for "Chief Administration of Corrective Labor Camps") Soviet forced-labor camp system in which political enemies of the state were confined and literally worked to death.

totalitarianism   State system in which the state has total control over politics, economic life, and society at large.

Night of Long Knives   First SS purge, in which Hitler's personal political enemies and disloyal followers were killed in one night in 1934.

racist ideology set out in *Mein Kampf*. There Hitler argued that the very racial identity of Jews and Slavs made them a threat to the German nation and its dominant **Aryan race,** which supposedly had superior intellectual, physical, and moral qualities. To ensure the purity and well-being of this race, Jews—whom Hitler considered morally and physically subhuman, materialistic, and physiologically unable to work for the nation's greater good—had to be eliminated. To this end, Hitler used some of the popular ideas at that time, especially eugenics, to suggest swift, "scientific" ways to sort out those who were "desirable" from the rest and to eliminate the biological threat posed by "undesirables." The eugenicist theories adopted by the Nazis considered the health of an individual as a function primarily of genetic makeup, implying that it was impossible to cure or rehabilitate those genetically deficient. Eugenicist solutions ranged from preventing intermarriage with the "healthy" population and denying any social services to the genetically inferior to outright sterilization and **euthanasia.** Under the guise of national reinvigoration—"creating a Germany for Germans"—Hitler's goal was to create a racially pure state.

This irrational ideology worked because it was convenient: it offered an easy scapegoat for Germany's ills and did not force non-Jews to take responsibility or look for difficult solutions. But, in time, Jewishness came to be defined in increasingly complicated ways to include individuals who did not identify themselves as Jews but rather as Germans. Men and women who were Catholics, for example, and had Aryan blond hair and blue eyes, were considered Jewish if the state could uncover one Jewish grandparent. Thus, the Nazis forced all people into trying to conform to racial stereotypes and hide any elements of their identity that might raise the suspicions of the dreaded **Gestapo,** Hitler's secret police.

Hitler's division of people into desirables and undesirables went beyond Aryans and Jews, however. Based on his racist theories, the category of undesirables broadened throughout the 1930s to include all Jews, Roma (Gypsies), and Slavs (for example, Poles) as well as socialists and communists (said to have joined with Jews in a "Judeo-Bolshevik plot" again Germany), homosexuals, members of some religious denominations (for example, Jehovah's Witnesses), feminists, disabled persons, and anyone who supposedly suffered from a genetic disease or from tuberculosis, syphilis, or alcoholism.

The policies for dealing with undesirables aimed to eliminate them. Starting in 1933, the Nazis sterilized Roma and then others deemed "unfit" to reproduce. Doctors and judges, not the Gestapo, were the primary administrators of this policy. In 1933 the first **concentration camp,** meant to advance the elimination of undesirables, was established at Dachau, a town north of Munich. Here initially communist and other left-wing dissidents were taken to perform hard labor in subhuman living conditions intended to starve them to death. Later, these "labor" camps were turned into more effective killing factories, where most of Europe's Jews were exterminated.

The policy of segregating and later eliminating Jews began to take shape in 1935 through the **Nuremberg Laws.** These stripped Jews of citizenship, forbade them to marry non-Jews, and restricted their economic and social activities to the Jewish community. Jewish doctors could treat only Jewish patients; Jews could shop only at Jewish stores. Now Jews who saw themselves as Germans and did not identify with Jewishness in terms of religion, customs, or language were forced to assume a Jewish identity.

But the Nazis were equally intent on controlling the desirables. Aryan women had to abide by the regime's pro-natalist policies, which limited their social role to the home and children. Those who bore no children were considered disloyal to the Führer and punished, while unwed mothers of Aryan children were praised as patriotic Germans. People had to continually show their loyalty to the Nazi state to avoid the terror of the Gestapo, which could at any moment arrest people on the suspicion of treason or for being undesirables. By the late 1930s, the Third Reich had become a totalitarian state under the complete control of the Nazis and their supreme Führer, much like the Soviet Union was under Stalin.

Still, for ethnic Germans there was room for economic and social improvement in Hitler's racist state. During their first five years in power, the Nazis virtually eliminated unemployment, reducing it to less than 1 percent (though that figure did not include more than 1 million noncitizens—Jews and others imprisoned or

Aryan race   Pseudoscientific idea of the racially superior group that made up the German nation.

euthanasia   Forceful termination of one's life in a presumably painless way.

Gestapo   (German contraction for Geheime Staatspolizei, "secret state police") Nazi secret police that implemented Hitler's policies of total control.

concentration camp   Camp for the internment of political prisoners and "undesirables," especially as organized by the Nazi regime.

Nuremberg Laws   Edicts issued by the Nazis in 1935 that deprived Jews of German citizenship and initiated their segregation from German life.

This Jewish synagogue was vandalized by Nazi party members on the night of November 9–10, 1938, which came to be known as Kristallnacht (Night of Broken Glass). Throughout Germany during that night, Nazis destroyed and desecrated Jewish property, often targeting synagogues and other places of Jewish culture and religious significance. *(Mary Evans Picture Library/The Image Works)*

simply stripped of citizenship). For those who were citizens, incomes were going up, business opportunities were growing due to Hitler's remilitarization of the economy, and housing was becoming more affordable. Industrial production rose by nearly 30 percent between 1932 and 1938, a success similar to Stalin's accomplishments. And, like Stalin, Hitler also built these successes on the bodies of those forced to give up their wealth, freedom, and life. But unlike Stalin, Hitler successfully rallied the wealthy business class to engage in his plan of economic recovery. From an economic standpoint, the Nazi regime turned out to be more capitalistic and less socialistic than it had claimed at the beginning.

Intense antisemitic propaganda also worked to justify the actions of the Nazis and gain the cooperation of many average and well-educated Germans. School textbooks were revised to include discussions of racial purity and the threat of marriages with Jews and other "inferior" races. Hitler also skillfully used movies and radio as propaganda tools. The Nazis harnessed the talents of outstanding artists such as film director **Leni Riefenstahl** to produce arousing and flawless documentaries and feature films designed to seduce average citizens into identifying with the ideals of the Third Reich. The most notable was *Triumph of the Will*, a cinematic masterpiece in communicating a racist message with eloquence and in revealing how the Nazis hoped to transform the German people into a homogeneous, energized, militarized, and obedient unit. Hitler also encouraged the production of affordable radios so he could reach most Germans on a regular basis. In addition to mu-

Leni Riefenstahl   (1902–2003) Famous German film director who made propaganda films for the Nazis.

sic, listeners got a daily dose of antisemitic propaganda through newscasts, speeches, and even humor.

Finally, the Nazis turned to sports, already an important pastime in Europe, and determined to demonstrate the superiority of the Aryan race in the Berlin Olympics of 1936. Athletes were carefully selected and trained in a grueling regimen that did produce many medal winners. But the Nazis also suffered some embarrassments, especially in the resounding victories of the African American track-and-field athlete Jesse Owens, whose supposed racial inferiority did not prevent him from breaking eleven Olympic records.

Intense propaganda was successful in transforming German society. By the late 1930s, educated people supported the Nazis. Doctors, for example, were willing to go along with sterilization programs and to pressure those with a good racial "pedigree" to have children. By the late 1930s, German industrial power was second only to that of the United States.

The Nazi Challenge to Europe

Hitler's dream of an Aryan state included an essential expansionist component. He was dedicated to revenging the German losses in World War I and wanted to recover all territories in which German populations lived, to save them from oppression by inferior races such as Slavs and Jews. His concept of Lebensraum aimed to justify the conquest of Poland and Russia so that Germans could resettle these lands and make them productive by using the native populations as slave labor. Not everyone grasped the extent of Hitler's idea of world domination until the beginning of World War II, but most Germans supported revising the Versailles Treaty and strengthening the military.

Initially Hitler focused on projecting a nonconfrontational international position. Germany was isolated in Europe, so he worked to increase trade with countries weakened by the Great Depression, especially in eastern Europe. Although these were also territories slated for occupation, where Slavic people he deemed inferior lived, Hitler was pragmatic. His offers to trade guns for grain and natural resources were received with interest by impoverished authoritarian regimes in Bulgaria, Romania, and Hungary. Such international agreements served to rearm these countries and also to provide Germany with important resources, especially Romania's oil, for its economy and for a future war.

With new markets for their guns, in clear violation of the Versailles Treaty, the Nazis began to rebuild the armament industry, using the very capitalists whom they had criticized before 1933. Starting in 1935 Hitler built a new air force, the Luftwaffe, and encouraged

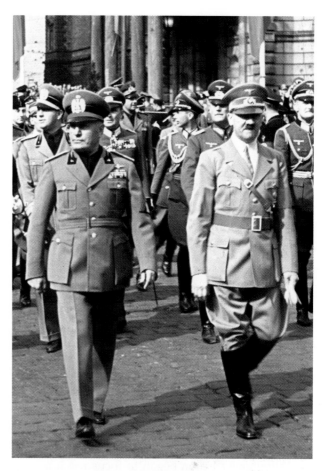

Adolf Hitler and Benito Mussolini appeared together on many occasions to underscore their strong alliance and personal friendship. In reality, Hitler thought of Mussolini as an inferior, if useful partner in his plans for world domination. *(Hugo Jaeger/Time Life Pictures/Getty Images)*

the creation of new offensive weapons through a vast program of research and development. The draft was introduced (1935), increasing the fighting forces to half a million, in flagrant defiance of the Versailles Treaty. But the first significant violation of the treaty came in March 1936, when German troops marched into the Rhineland, the region on the French border that was supposed to remain demilitarized as a buffer zone. The western democracies failed to respond strongly to this challenge, protesting through the League of Nations but taking no action. These violations of the Versailles Treaty are summarized in Table 27.2.

This inaction was a vital mistake because it bolstered Hitler's self-confidence, his popularity at home, and his appeal to similar regimes beyond Germany. Italy also had expansionist ambitions and in 1935 had

Table 27.2

Nazi Challenges to the Versailles Treaty

March 1935	Establishment of German air force and military conscription
March 7, 1936	Occupation of demilitarized Rhineland
March 13, 1938	Annexation of Austria
March 1939	Occupation and dismemberment of Czechoslovakia
August 23, 1939	Molotov-Ribbentrop Pact
September 1, 1939	Invasion of Poland

invaded Ethiopia. By the end of 1936, the **Berlin-Rome Axis** had been formed, an alliance of like-minded states that would later include Japan, a militarist and expansionist power already embarked on conquest in East Asia and the Pacific. The alliance was based on their mutual imperialist interests, their profound disregard for democracy, and their fear of the Soviets.

Resistance and Appeasement

Hitler's rise to power challenged the Soviet Union. In 1935, the Soviet Union began to focus resolutely on the threat Hitler posed to the stability of Europe. The cornerstone of the new Soviet position in international affairs was collective security. The threat of war in both the west and the east forced the Soviets to consider cooperation with capitalist countries, something unthinkable a decade earlier. But Stalin argued that this position did not contradict the goal of world communist revolution. It simply focused on eliminating the most imminent threat, fascism. This position led to his signing of mutual-aid pacts with France and Czechoslovakia in 1935, directed primarily against Germany.

The same pragmatic vision led to a reversal of Comintern policies in 1935 from noncooperation to coalition building with other antifascist parties. This radical change paved the way for the formation of the **Popular Fronts** in Spain and France as well as the coalition in China against the Japanese threat. In France, the Socialist **Léon Blum** was able to talk the Communist, Socialist, and Radical Parties into forming the Popular Front in 1936. Blum was the first Jewish prime minister in France; his victory was an important symbolic challenge to the Nazis and on behalf of democracy, inclusiveness, and social responsibility of the state toward all citizens.

Blum quickly introduced major changes: the forty-hour workweek, the paid two-week vacation, the right of workers to collective bargaining, and other social programs. Under Blum, the Bank of France and the armaments industry were also nationalized. These changes signaled a major shift in defining government responsibilities but were not endorsed by everyone. Blum was attacked by members of his coalition and by opponents on the right. He resigned in June 1937 but remained an important force in the coalition and resumed leadership briefly in 1938, in strong support of the Spanish Republic's struggle against Franco.

While politicians tried ineffectively to defend democracy against radical challenges, writers, popular culture stars, and religious leaders tried to address, if not solve, the crises of the day. The art and literature or the 1930s became more engaged with current events than had been the case in the more escapist 1920s. Writers like the German novelist **Thomas Mann** made it a personal quest to salvage the humanist spirit in Germany and the spirit of tolerance toward Jews. In Britain, **Virginia Woolf** confronted women's continued inequalities and militarization in her book *Three Guineas* (1938).

But a far more powerful and effective critique of the social problems of the times and the rise of fascism came from an unlikely source, the silver screen. Charlie Chaplin effectively depicted social and economic inequalities while offering an amusing and deeply humane picture of the poor. In *Modern Times* (1936), his famous Little Tramp character became a symbol of humanity's vulnerability in a world run by machines and obsessed with mechanized progress. Similarly, *The Great Dictator* (1940) confronted the racist irrationality of Nazi Germany through comedy and farce involving a Jewish barber (the Little Tramp) standing in for Hitler at a Nazi mass rally.

Berlin-Rome Axis Agreement between Mussolini and Hitler in 1936 to support each other in their expansionist goals.

Popular Fronts Moderate left-wing coalition governments during the 1930s that brought political stability, social reforms, and some economic recovery from the Great Depression.

Léon Blum (1872–1950) First Jewish prime minister of France, a Socialist who led the Popular Front government in 1936.

Thomas Mann (1875–1955) Great German writer of the twentieth century who was persecuted by the Nazis for his staunch criticism of their antisemitism.

Virginia Woolf (1882–1941) Pacifist English writer who drew attention to gender inequalities.

MAP 27.1 **The Expansion of Germany** Between 1939 and 1942, Nazi Germany aggressively pursued its goals of acquiring Lebensraum for its Aryan German population. Its success would prove to be short-lived, however, especially as the Axis powers started to overstretch their resources.

Some religious leaders, such as the German Lutheran pastor **Dietrich Bonhoeffer**, attempted both to criticize the inhuman policies of the Nazis and to minister to their religious communities. Bonhoeffer went so far as to establish the underground pacifist Confession Church, which remained active throughout World War II, at great peril to its leader and his following. Throughout the 1930s and the war, Bonhoeffer voiced his strong opposition to the Nazis; he was executed in April 1945 for his role in a plot to assassinate Hitler.

Other prelates, such as Eugenio Cardinal Pacelli,

later Pope **Pius XII**, chose a policy of compromise with the Nazis to protect the Catholic Church. Though Pacelli spoke on several occasions against the Nazis and was critical of their antisemitic policies in some of his writings, he also orchestrated a concordat in

Dietrich Bonhoeffer (1906–1945) German Lutheran pastor who openly criticized the Nazis and organized an underground church during the Third Reich.

Pius XII (r. 1939–1958) Pope who failed to take a strong stance against the Nazis under the pretext of neutrality.

The fate of the world was sealed during this secret meeting in Moscow on August 23, 1939. Soviet Foreign Minister V. M. Molotov and German foreign minister Joachim von Ribbentrop sign a nonaggression pact, while Joseph Stalin, in the back second from the right, smiles as he presides over the proceedings, which were held in an inconspicuous office. *(Bettmann/Corbis)*

1933 that established official relations between the Nazi regime and the Vatican. Critics saw the concordat as condoning the Nazis' assumption of dictatorial powers and the beginning of the Vatican's abandonment of the German Catholics into Hitler's hands. Supporters of Pius XII saw the concordat as a practical means for the Vatican to exercise some pressure on behalf of Catholics in Germany.

Yet many in Europe and America stood idle during this period of increasing tensions and violence. Burdened by their own antisemitism, many democratic countries refused entry to the Jews who were desperately trying to flee the Third Reich. The governments of both Britain and the United States, where many German (and later Austrian and eastern European) Jews sought refuge, were reluctant to lift immigration quotas. One of the most egregious incidents was the refusal by the American government to grant entry to ten thousand Jewish children, a request made insistently by First Lady Eleanor Roosevelt.

As there were no protests from abroad, Hitler continued his quest for aggrandizement. Claiming to respond to the wishes of Austrians—as true Aryans—to be part of the great German nation, in March 1938 he annexed Austria through coercion and manipulation. This action emboldened him to move toward the

next target, Czechoslovakia, where a large German minority was concentrated mainly in the western region of the Sudetenland. But Czechoslovakia could not be easily intimidated. Its democratic government had strong military and mutual assistance pacts with France and the Soviet Union. Hitler gambled and requested that the Sudetenland be ceded to Germany, prompting an international crisis.

At the **Munich Conference** in September 1938, the British and French caved in to the German demands, justifying their desertion of Czechoslovakia as a small price to pay for securing peace. This policy of **appeasement** was meant to reduce the German threat under the misguided notion that Hitler's quest for Lebensraum could be satisfied by the Sudetenland. In fact, appeasement signaled to all countries in the east that the European order and frontiers could be violated and that they could be abandoned by the western democracies at any moment. Within six months, Czechoslovakia was divided into annexed (Sudetenland), occupied (Bohemia and Moravia), and independent (Slovakia) territories controlled by the Nazis. Slovakia became a puppet state ruled by the Catholic priest Josef Tiso, whose full cooperation with the Nazi policies of exterminating Jews was never denounced by the Vatican.

As Hitler was preparing his next step—the invasion of Poland—Britain and France finally determined to stand up to Hitler's challenge by guaranteeing

Munich Conference   Emergency meeting in 1938 in which Britain and France gave in to Hitler's demand for the Czech Sudetenland.

appeasement   Policy of giving in to an opponent's requests to prevent further demands.

Poland's integrity. But it was not clear whether either of these countries was willing or prepared to honor that promise or whether they were merely making a gesture. Either way, Hitler had so much confidence by now that he was completely unimpressed. In addition, he now turned cunningly toward another potential ally, the Soviet Union.

On August 23, 1939, the two mortal enemies, Hitler and Stalin, signed a nonaggression agreement known as the **Molotov-Ribbentrop Pact,** for the foreign ministers who negotiated it. Many were surprised about this about-face in Soviet-Nazi relations. The pact went against the Nazi racist idea that the Slavs and Bolsheviks were enemies of the Third Reich; it also contradicted all the antifascist statements and alliances of the Soviet Union since 1935. Instead, the pact was a pragmatic move. Stalin had been excluded from the Munich Conference, and as the Soviet Union was isolated by France and Britain, he sought another partner in Europe. The Soviets also wanted to recover some of the territories lost in World War I. Thus, the pact included several secret clauses that pertained to the division of Poland and the Baltic countries, as well as to the recovery of Bassarabia from Romania. Hitler wished to pursue his drive toward the east but wanted to ensure that the Soviets would not precipitate a two-front war. The solution was to divide Poland. On September 1, 1939, Germany launched a surprise attach on Poland from the west. On September 3, Britain and France honored their commitment to Poland by declaring war on Germany. World War II had begun.

Table 27.3
Major Events of World War II

September 1939	Poland occupied by Nazis and Soviets
May 1940	Churchill becomes prime minister of Britain
June 1940	Nazis occupy France
Fall 1940	Battle of Britain
March 1941	Lend-Lease Act
April 1941	Nazis occupy Greece and Yugoslavia
June 1941	Operation Barbarossa: Nazis invade Soviet Union
December 1941	Pearl Harbor; United States enters the war
November 1942	Allied invasion of North Africa
February 1943	German surrender at Stalingrad
July 1943	Soviet victory at Kursk
September 1943	Allied invasion of Italy
June 1944	Operation Overlord: Allied invasion of Normandy and liberation of France
August 1944	Warsaw Uprising
February 1945	Yalta Conference
May 8, 1945	Soviets liberate Berlin; Germans surrender
August 6 and 9, 1945	United States drops atomic bombs in Japan
August 14, 1945	Japanese surrender

World War II, 1939–1945

⬇ How did World War II differ from previous wars?
⬇ What military strategies, technological developments, and other factors enabled the Allies to win the war?

World War II was unprecedented in the extent of the destruction it wrought on the entire world, the degree to which it involved civilians, and the depth of the moral questions it raised. New military technologies, fighting strategies, psychological manipulation, and scientific discoveries ensured that this would be a war unlike any other. By the end of the conflict, the entire world had been touched by war; almost 70 million people had perished, most of them in Europe; and democracy had been challenged to the core. Although the Allies defeated the Axis, Europe lay in ruin and democracy was not secure. Communism became Europe's next important challenge, as Stalin emerged victorious in eastern Europe.

Germany's Early Triumphs

Hitler managed to occupy the western half of Poland in four weeks. Tanks and motorized armored troop carriers raced across the border, supported by air power and paratroopers, introducing the world to a new type of warfare, **blitzkrieg.** The Poles fought desperately, but their military strength was inferior to that of the Nazis, and their allies Britain and France

Molotov-Ribbentrop Pact   Nonaggression agreement of 1939 that secretly divided the Baltic countries and Poland between the Soviets and the Germans and allotted part of Romania to the Soviet Union.

blitzkrieg   (in German, "lightning war") German attack strategy involving massed air force cover and rapid, motorized tank and troop movements that overwhelmed opponents.

offered little help. When the Soviets invaded Poland from the east on September 17, the Poles surrendered within ten days. The Soviets also proceeded to occupy Latvia, Estonia, and Lithuania and incorporate them as Soviet Republics. Only Finland resisted Soviet demands, fighting back and scoring some victories, but it, too, was ultimately defeated in the winter of 1939–1940.

In the spring of 1940, Hitler turned west, invading Denmark and Norway and then attacking the Netherlands and Belgium, which fell in two weeks. France was next. In mid-June 1940, German troops marched into Paris, and Henri Pétain, the hero of Verdun, signed over to German occupation the northern three-fifths of the country. The south, **Vichy France,** became a German puppet state under Pétain. This defeat was the greatest humiliation France had ever experienced, and it showed the whole world the aims and methods of the Third Reich.

Britain offered some aid to Belgium in May but had had to evacuate its troops to prevent their capture by the Nazis. In response to the fall of Norway, Winston Churchill assumed leadership of the country and radically shifted the British position from uncertain support for its allies to standing fast against Hitler, who now began an intensive bombardment of Britain's industries and cities in preparation for invasion. During those difficult months, Churchill provided what the British people needed—an unbounded energy and faith in the army, air force, civilians, and democracy that proved inspiring. In June 1941, he declared resolutely: "We shall go on to the end. . . . We shall never surrender."

Churchill had been in British politics for a long time, but he had never made more than a temporary mark. As an officer he had first served in India and Africa, then entered politics in 1901. As head of the British navy, he was responsible for the disastrous loss at Gallipoli early in World War I, which discredited him for the next twenty-five years. By the mid-1930s, he was considered a political maverick, always sure to take unpopular positions and often, critics said, too eager to jump into half-baked plans. But Churchill was also a passionate speaker, and his powerful warnings about the threat to democracy posed by the two great evils of fascism and communism grabbed the attention of the public and politicians alike. By 1940, he seemed the only leader with the vision and courage to change the course of the British policy of appeasement and the magnetism to carry the country with him: "Let us therefore brace ourselves to our duties, and to bear ourselves that, if the British Empire and Its Commonwealth last for a thousand years, they will say, 'That was their finest hour.'"

Between July and October 1940, Britain and Germany engaged in intensive air combat, known as the **Battle of Britain.** Initially the Nazis pursued a policy of strategic bombing of air bases. Their success depended almost exclusively on the strength and versatility of the Luftwaffe, while the British Royal Air Force (RAF) had a sophisticated system of command and coordination among its pilots enhanced by a radar network and good intelligence work in Germany. These advantages gave the RAF great precision in intercepting enemy planes (over 80 percent at times) and coordinating aerial attacks. By contrast, though the Nazis had excellent planes and pilots, they were often less precise and had to resort to riskier blanket bombing. In September, the Nazis shifted to a strategy of bombing civilian targets, bent on terrorizing the population and killing more than 23,000 civilians. But by October 1940, the RAF had outmaneuvered the Germans. The Battle of Britain was significant because it was the first time since 1939 that the Nazis had suffered defeat and it severely weakened the strength of the Luftwaffe. It also convinced Hitler to shift his attention to other areas, though the Nazis continued their attacks on Britain until June 1941.

Churchill also gambled on assistance from the United States and initially received limited help. But the heroic resistance of the British galvanized support from President Roosevelt's government, which in March 1941 passed the **Lend-Lease Act,** granting "all aid short of war" to Britain. Later that year, the two leaders met to formulate a statement of war aims, the **Atlantic Charter,** which announced a commitment to restoring democracy in Europe. Finally, Churchill gambled in sending British troops to the Mediterranean to fight Italian forces bent on conquering Egypt and Greece. This strategy left the British Isles vulnerable but created an important diversion in the south, as Hitler had to send German reinforcements to a new battlefront in North Africa and the Balkans. For the first six months of 1941, German forces concen-

Vichy France Puppet state established by the Nazis in southern France during World War II, named so for its capital in Vichy.

Battle of Britain Nazi air campaign against the British Isles in the fall of 1940 that became Germany's first major defeat.

Lend-Lease Act U.S. commitment in 1941 to grant massive financial and military support to the Allies.

Atlantic Charter Agreement between Churchill and Roosevelt in 1941 stating Allied goals for the war, including the commitment to restoring democracy in Europe.

trated on taking Algeria, Morocco, Tunisia, Greece, and Yugoslavia.

By June 1941, the Axis controlled almost all of Europe, from Norway to the Mediterranean and from France to Poland. Britain stood alone, with support from the United States. The blitzkrieg strategies had worked well for Hitler, and he now prepared to turn east again, toward the Soviet Union, to pursue his Lebensraum policy. The about-face against his former ally was anticipated in Britain, where intelligence concerning **Operation Barbarossa** had leaked in May. Churchill tried to warn Stalin, but to no avail. Other signs made it increasingly clear that Hitler was mounting a large-scale operation against the Soviet Union, especially a series of alliances that drew Hungary, Romania, and Bulgaria into the Axis.

Thus, when the Nazis finally embarked on Operation Barbarossa on June 22, 1941, no one except Stalin was surprised. The campaign was unprecedented in size and scope, including more than 3 million Axis troops, an air force of thousands, and more than three thousand tanks. The Soviets had a formidable army as well, in terms of size and equipment, but they lacked leadership. In addition to the purge of the officer corps, which demoralized the remaining personnel, the military was also paralyzed by Stalin's inability to come to terms with Hitler's betrayal. Quickly, the Germans drove to Kiev, where they took more than six hundred thousand prisoners in just one battle. By the end of October, they were besieging Leningrad and threatening Moscow in the north, while advancing toward oil fields in the south. **Joseph Goebbels**, Hitler's propaganda minister, announced that the war was over: the Soviets had lost more than 2 million soldiers, three hundred thousand square miles of land, and thousands of planes and tanks. Germany seemed invincible, but important developments in 1942 turned the tide of the war.

Allied Victory

The Axis had driven across a large portion of the Russian steppe, but the vast distances, harsh climate, and rudimentary roads proved their greatest obstacles. As winter arrived, the Germans and their allies were unable to get fresh troops and supplies to the front. In addition, the Soviets conducted a scorched-earth policy of burning fields, removing livestock, and disassembling industrial enterprises before retreating east. Blitzkrieg collapsed into a war of attrition. German troops grew demoralized as temperatures plunged to minus 60 degrees Fahrenheit. Many Germans froze to death, while the Russians went into hiding.

Meanwhile, the British and the Soviets soon had a

new and important ally, the United States, which was compelled to declare war on the Axis following Japan's surprise attack on **Pearl Harbor** on December 7, 1941. Roosevelt sent an important infusion of food, supplies, and armament to the Soviets, helping them rebound from the massive losses incurred in 1941. Thus, when the Germans reopened their offensive in August 1942 by attacking **Stalingrad**, an important industrial center at the edge of European Russia, the Soviets were ready to fight back. In addition to Stalingrad's being a gateway to Asian Russia and oil resources in the south, taking the city renamed for the Soviet leader had become an obsession for Hitler.

For Stalin, the city was also symbolic, and he used all available propaganda to promote the idea that saving it was the same as saving the Russian soul. The war was no longer between communism and fascism; it was now the Great Patriotic War, in which soldiers and civilians, men and women, parents and children were called on to help Father Stalin and save Mother Russia from the Germanic invasion. Film director Sergei Eisenstein undertook his masterpiece, *Ivan the Terrible*, at this time, depicting the medieval ruler as both despot and great patriot, the man who saved Russia from foreign threats. Stalin wanted to be seen this way—ruthless against foreigners but an ally of the simple people, who followed him faithfully. The morale of the people proved crucial to the defense of Stalingrad, which withstood months of house-to-house fighting before the Germans surrendered on February 2, 1943, their troop strength diminished from five hundred thousand to eighty thousand. Stalingrad had been reduced to rubble, and Soviet victory came at the great price of over 1.5 million casualties.

The crushing defeat at Stalingrad slowed down the Nazis, but it was fighting at **Kursk**, between February and July 1943, that permanently turned the tide of the war in the east. At Stalingrad, Nazi troops had been at a tactical disadvantage because they were

---

Operation Barbarossa   Code name for the Nazi invasion of the Soviet Union in June 1941.

Joseph Goebbels   (1897–1945) Hitler's propaganda minister who played a central role in the Final Solution.

Pearl Harbor   U.S. naval base in Hawaii bombed by Japan on December 7, 1941, drawing the United States into World War II.

Stalingrad   (today Volgograd) Soviet city held under siege by the Nazis for six months where the Soviets scored one of the most important victories in 1942.

Kursk   Battle in which the Nazis received a crushing defeat through Soviet blitzgrieg tactics.

MAP 27.2 Allied Victory in Europe Soviet, British, and U.S. troops, supported by numerous resistance movements in Axis-occupied territories, turned the tide of war after 1942. The Soviets bore the brunt of the effort, both materially and in terms of lost lives.

engaged in urban warfare, for which they were inadequately prepared; but at Kursk, they could use blitzkrieg techniques. At the same time, however, the Soviets had learned much about Nazi military strategy and been able to upgrade their armaments, especially tank power and antitank guns. Defeated by the Soviets at their best game, the Nazis were profoundly demoralized and began to retreat.

In North Africa, German forces had also been pushed back by the British, now joined by American troops. By May 1943, the Germans had withdrawn entirely from the region. With North Africa secured, the Allies were able to launch an invasion of Sicily, a steppingstone to the invasion of Italy in September 1943. Mussolini was forced from power but remained in the hands of the Germans, at the helm of a puppet republic in northern Italy.

In addition, the Allies pursued a strategy of all-out air attacks on Germany. The policy of strategic bombing—attacking important military, industrial, and transportation centers—failed in its immediate goals of destroying the military capacity of the Nazis, but it did cut production. Night bombing afforded greater protection from anti-aircraft guns but also reduced precision in hitting targets and increased civilian losses. Some 300,000 Germans died and 750,000 were maimed in Allied air raids. But it was clear that Hitler would be defeated only by an invasion.

On June 6, 1944, **Operation Overlord** began. In one of the most intense military operations of the war, the Allies crossed the English Channel to land more than 2 million soldiers (Americans, British, Poles, Belgians, Canadians, Norwegians, Dutch, and French) and millions of tons of military equipment in Nazi-occupied France. Securing the first strip of beach involved heavy casualties, but months of careful planning paid off. Now the Germans had to fight a three-front war—east, west, and south—and could do little more than resist while retreating. Paris was liberated by August, Brussels in September, and that month the first Allied troops crossed into Germany.

In the east, the Soviets were also advancing steadily. In January 1945, they liberated the concentration camp at Auschwitz and took Warsaw; in April, advance units of the American and Soviet armies met south of Berlin on the Elbe River. Mussolini met his end on April 28, killed by Italian partisans while trying to escape. He was then publicly hung so that crowds could freely abuse his body. Two days later, trying to avoid the humiliation of capture, Hitler committed suicide together with his wife, Eva Braun, in his Berlin bunker. On May 8, the Soviets finally liberated Berlin and brought the war to an end on the European front. Three months later, the United States used a newly developed weapon against Japan, the **atomic bomb.** The Japanese surrendered on August 14, and World War II was over.

The total human toll of the war was as high as 70 million people, by some estimates, with Europe suffering roughly half of the casualties. Approximately 20 million of these were soldiers, and the remaining 50 million were civilians. The astronomic number and ratio of civilian to soldier casualties were unprecedented. Those who suffered the most were in eastern Europe: Yugoslavia lost 4.5 million people, a higher ratio of its population than Germany's 7.7 million casualties, while in Poland, Warsaw alone had more casualties in absolute numbers than Britain and the United States combined. The vast majority of the Jewish population exterminated in the war came from eastern Europe. The extent of material destruction was equally unprecedented, with eastern Europe again experiencing the highest losses as two waves of occupation and destruction—the Nazis and then the Soviets—swept through the area between 1939 and 1945.

The Allies won the war by outperforming their enemies in military technology, intelligence gathering, science, diplomacy, and mobilization on the home front. On the eastern front, the Soviets spared no expense and converted more than 50 percent of their industrial production to building tanks that were larger and more powerful than Germany's. The British developed radar technology essential to the RAF success in the Battle of Britain. The Allies also used new technology to break the German and Japanese military codes. And the Americans invested nearly $2 billion and employed more than 130,000 people in the **Manhattan Project,** the vast nuclear engineering complex that worked steadily between 1942 and 1945 to develop the atomic bomb before the Germans did and to use it to force the Japanese surrender.

Another key to Allied victory was diplomacy. The ability of Churchill, Stalin, and Roosevelt to work together, despite their fundamental ideological differences and deep distrust between Stalin and his western allies, was one of the remarkable successes of the war. The three met on two important occasions

---

Operation Overlord   Code name for the Allied invasion of France in June 1944.

atomic bomb   Bomb powered by nuclear energy, with unprecedented destructive capability, developed first by scientists in the United States.

Manhattan Project   Extensive science and development program in the United States in 1942–1945 that produced a nuclear bomb.

MAP 27.3 **War in Asia** In the war against Japan in the Pacific, the United States bore the brunt of the effort. Support from Australia and the Soviet Union were ultimately essential for defeating Japan.

during the war, in Teheran in 1943 and Yalta in 1945. The **Yalta Conference** was particularly important as it laid the foundation for the creation of the United Nations, determined policies for liberating and dividing Germany, allowed postwar Poland and eastern Europe to fall primarily within the Soviet sphere of influence, and arranged for the Soviet Union's entry into the war against Japan. The last two provisions were the result of an informal exchange between the Americans, who desperately wanted support against Japan, and the Soviets, who sought to control the political future of eastern Europe. The Yalta Conference

would play a major role in the political reconfiguration of Europe after the war.

Mobilization, Collaboration, and Resistance

The Allies could not have won the war without the unprecedented mobilization of civilians, who worked

Yalta Conference Meeting of Churchill, Roosevelt, and Stalin in 1945 to discuss postwar peace.

In February 1945, Winston Churchill, Franklin Roosevelt, and Joseph Stalin met in the Russian resort town of Yalta, in the Crimea, to map out plans for ending the war in Asia and for establishing order in postwar Europe. Roosevelt was already ailing; he died in April. In July, Churchill was voted out of office. The Yalta Conference was the last time the leaders of the three great powers were able to work together peacefully for more than forty years. *(Hulton-Deutsch Collection/Corbis)*

in war industries and other essential capacities and, in occupied regimes, participated in resistance movements. Women, especially, served in new capacities. They were allowed to join, and in some cases were even drafted into, the military. But only in the Soviet Union did they serve as combatants, from ambulance drivers to pilots. More important, however, women were mobilized for economic production and auxiliary services, such as medical aid, supplies, and various public service jobs, from secretaries to bus drivers. Their service was significant in Britain and especially in the Soviet Union, where women already constituted almost half of the labor force. During the war, female employment in Soviet industries climbed to an unprecedented 60 percent.

In Germany, the mobilization of civilians was carefully weighed against fears of demoralization. Hitler allowed the production of consumer goods as a means of diverting the anxiety of families whose sons and husbands were away at war. The standard of living of Aryan Germans remained close to the prewar levels long after Soviets, Italians, and Romanians were asked to give up their personal comforts. By contrast, in Britain, people were asked to conserve, give up, and buckle down throughout the war. The constant bombings during the Battle of Britain both frightened civilians and helped build their resolve. The tremendous losses incurred by the Soviets during the first year of combat also worked as powerful propaganda in the hands of the communist government, which used patriotism to recruit the help of civilians and then celebrated their heroism, especially after Stalingrad.

Civilian help was also essential in occupied territo-

ries, such as Slovakia, Vichy France, and Croatia, where the Nazis set up puppet governments. To supply the war machine with much-needed armaments and other industrial products, food supplies, and fuel, the Nazis depended heavily on collaboration with native populations. Even in places like Poland, where the official policy was to exterminate all Jews and where more than 2.5 million non-Jewish Poles perished in the war, the Germans needed to work with the Polish population at the local level. This policy was also implemented in the Czech lands, France, the Netherlands, Serbia, and Greece. The peoples of occupied countries faced difficult choices—either collaborate with the Nazis or become their victims.

Many learned to work within this harsh system and play by its methods. In Prague, for example, a Czech man working for the German authorities stopped saluting his Jewish neighbors on the street, fearful that he might be suspected of being a Jew himself. Soon he asked his son not to play with their Jewish neighbor, until one day the Jewish family was gone. Though he was sad and afraid, he was also relieved. Occupation forced most people to spy, lie, and vilify fellow humans in order to survive, corrupting their human dignity.

Despite fear and violent reprisals, resistance movements developed in all occupied territories and even in Germany, some spectacular in scope and results, others merely symbolic. In Germany, the most remarkable were the efforts of military leaders to assassinate Hitler in 1943 and 1944. These officers were attempting to rescue the German war effort from Hitler's increasingly irrational leadership, but they were not necessarily opposed to either the racist ideology or the expansionist goals of the Third Reich. They all failed, and the officers were executed.

More widespread resistance movements developed in the France, Yugoslavia, the Soviet Union, and Poland. In France, the Free French, under the leadership of **Charles de Gaulle,** provided a focus for courage and hope. The Free French military contributions were modest, but they helped de Gaulle establish himself as the liberator of his people.

The most successful partisan movement in occupied Europe was that of the Yugoslav Communists, led by **Josip Broz Tito.** His well-organized guerilla army liberated Yugoslavia with only indirect assistance from the Allies, and largely independent of the Soviets. This movement was more successful because of broad popular support, Tito's tight leadership, and Germany's weak control in Yugoslavia. But Tito accomplished this remarkable feat by also committing atrocities against other partisan movements and civilians.

In Poland, an underground Polish Home Army acted to thwart German operations with great bravery. They were also able to supply important intelligence to the Allies. In the final months of the war, a large part of this resistance force perished in the **Warsaw Uprising,** which attempted the liberation of the city from Nazi occupation in August 1944. Despite promises to come to the aid of the Poles, Stalin kept the advancing Soviet armies from providing any support to the uprising, which was violently crushed. Though valiant in its efforts to liberate Poland, the Home Army did little to help Polish Jews and was generally reluctant to accept Jews as members.

The Final Solution

The unprecedented level of brutality against civilians is one of the deepest moral challenges posed by World War II. Millions of innocents on both sides of the conflict were imprisoned, placed under siege and starved to death, forced into slave labor, raped, and bombed, initially with conventional artillery and at the very end with nuclear bombs. But by far the most horrifying aspect of World War II was the Nazi policy of destroying the Jews of Europe. Eliminating the Jews from German society had been a fundamental concept of the Nazis since before 1933. And yet the technologies to bring about the **Final Solution**—the physical extermination of all Jews—did not come together until the war. This diabolical policy came into being in a combination of Hitler's irrational theories of racial purity with the expertise of architects, engineers, doctors, biologists, and other people well grounded in the foundations of science and reason, many of whom sub-

scribed to the long-held assumption that there was a "Jewish problem" in Europe. The progression of the Final Solution is summarized in Table 27.4.

The decision to pursue a policy of genocide against all Jews was made official at the **Wannsee Conference** in January 1942, though the specific means by which the estimated 11 million Jews of Europe were to be killed was not discussed. Experiments with mass killings through conventional and chemical weapons had already been tried both before the war in Germany and during the eastern campaigns in Poland, Byelorussia, Ukraine, and Russia. The rounding up of the Jews was assigned to special troops, the **Einsatzgruppen,** small mobile killing units made up of the cruelest SS and Gestapo recruits. The Einsatzgruppen were to eliminate other undesirables also, including communists, Roma, Jehovah's Witnesses, and Slavs.

Another important policy was to place all Jews in occupied territories in **ghettos,** where they were sealed off from the non-Jewish population. In Warsaw, for instance, the European city with the largest Jewish population, several thousand Poles were moved out to make room for around half a million Jews, crowded into a few city blocks. Before being sent to concentration camps, these people were first stripped of all possessions and forced into crowded, unheated, and lice-infested rooms. Jews unable to leave the ghettos were gradually starved to death through inadequate food supplies. Some also perished because of unsanitary and overcrowded conditions, which fostered tuberculosis and other epidemics.

The Nazis used deceit and fear to manage the ghettos. They set up Jewish councils and police, dividing communities by forcing Jews to monitor one another

---

Charles de Gaulle (1890–1970) Leader of the Free French, the partisan movement that worked to liberate France, and first president of postwar France.

Josip Broz Tito (1892–1980) Leader of the Yugoslav Communist Party and of the most successful partisan movement in World War II.

Warsaw Uprising Revolt by the partisan Polish Home Army in the fall of 1944 against the Nazis.

Final Solution Nazi concept of exterminating all European Jews as a response to the so-called Jewish problem in Europe.

Wannsee Conference Meeting of high-ranking Nazis in early 1942 that officially decided to exterminate all Jews.

Einsatzgruppen (in German, "mission groups") Nazi death squads created at the beginning of the war to round up and execute Jews and other "undesirables."

ghetto Small, sealed-off areas in Nazi-controlled cities where the Jewish population was forced to live.

MAP 27.4   The Holocaust
Nazi genocidal policies toward
European Jewry resulted in the
murder of more than six million
Jews. Most were from eastern
Europe, where all of the death
camps were located.

Table 27.4

The Final Solution

March 1933	Dachau concentration camp opens
September 1935	Nuremberg Laws
October 1939	First Polish ghetto
October 1941	Auschwitz concentration camp is opened for the extermination of Jews
January 1942	Wannsee Conference
January 27, 1945	Soviets liberate Auschwitz and its remaining 7,000 inmates
April 1945	Allies liberate last concentration camps

and compete for inadequate food supplies and menial
jobs, while Nazi death squads periodically entered
the ghettos to kill people at random. Jewish leaders
were required to select and round up those who would
be sent to concentration camps. Some of these leaders
committed suicide; others were killed by their own
communities. Upon his arrival at Auschwitz, the
leader of the Lódz ghetto was beaten to death by Jewish inmates, who viewed him as the filthy tool of the
Germans. The Nazis were clever in setting Jews
against Jews, forcing them to victimize each other
and question the very core of their identity.

In the camps, Nazi engineers and architects designed gas chambers made to look like shower rooms,

and scientists identified **Zyklon B,** an insecticide, as a cheap and effective lethal gas. Labor camps in Poland were transformed into extermination camps; at Auschwitz alone, 1.5 million Jews perished. By April 1945, when the last camps were liberated, over 6 million Jews had been killed as well as more than 4.6 million other people classified by the Nazis as undesirables.

The tragedy of European Jewry is incomprehensible in rational terms and raises questions about what could have been done to save Jews and others and why such efforts failed. Those who committed these crimes against humanity abound. In Germany, they were not just Nazi fanatics but ordinary citizens who either willingly helped or looked the other way. In oc-

> **Zyklon B** Type of insecticide used by the Nazis for efficient extermination of the Jews in the death camps.

Voice

George Orwell Reflects on Nationalism

In May 1945, Europe lay in ruins, beyond recognition. George Orwell had reported on the war for the BBC and had seen both Nazi racism and British nationalist propaganda take their turn at vilifying the enemy. To Orwell, it seemed hardly suitable to stand proud because the Allies had just won the war in Europe. Instead, he wrote a sobering reevaluation of the nationalism that had fueled the war effort on both sides.

➔ *Do you agree with Orwell's distinction between patriotism and nationalism? Are there instances when defending oneself can actually mean military aggression and securing more power for one's nation?*

➔ By "nationalism" I mean first of all the habit of assuming that human beings can be classified like insects and that whole blocks of millions or tens of millions of people can be confidently labeled "good" or "bad". But secondly—and this is much more important—I mean the habit of identifying oneself with a single national or other unit, its interests. Nationalism is not to be confused with patriotism. By "patriotism" I mean devotion to a particular place and a particular way of life, which one believes to be the best in the world but has no wish to force on other people. Patriotism is of its nature defensive, both militarily and culturally. Nationalism, on the other hand, is inseparable from the desire for power. The abiding purpose of every nationalist is to secure more power and more prestige, not for himself but for the nation or other unit in which he has chosen to sink his own individuality.

➔ *Do you agree with this statement? How, then, is one to explain the popularity of the Nazis?*

➔ Confronted with a phenomenon like Nazism, which we can observe from the outside, nearly all of us would say much the same things about it. But here I must repeat what I said above, that I am only using the word "nationalism" for lack of a better. Nationalism includes such movements and tendencies as communism, political Catholicism, Zionism, antisemitism, Trotskyism and Pacifism. It does not necessarily mean loyalty to a government or a country, still less to one's own country, and it is not even strictly necessary that the units in which it deals should actually exist. ➔ To name a few obvious examples, Jewry, Islam, Christendom, the Proletariat and the White Race are all of them objects of passionate nationalistic feeling: but their existence can be seriously questioned, and there is not definition of any one of them that would be universally accepted.

➔ *How can the proletariat be the object of passionate nationalist feeling? Is it equivalent to hold a religious, versus racist, versus class identity at the heart of one's nationalism? Are there important differences among these categories of identity?*

It is also worth emphasizing once again that nationalist feeling can be purely negative. There are, for example, Trotskyists who have become simply enemies of the USSR without developing a corresponding loyalty to any other unit. . . . A nationalist is one who thinks solely, or mainly, in terms of competitive prestige. . . . He sees history, especially contemporary history, as the endless rise and decline of great

➡ Looking back at the case studies before Orwell's eyes in 1945, do you see this combination of self-delusion and intense passion as a strength or a weakness of nationalist movements?

power units, and every event that happens seems to him a demonstration that his own side is on the upgrade and some hated rival is on the downgrade. . . . ➡ Nationalism is power-hunger tempered by self-deception. Every nationalist is capable of the most flagrant dishonesty, but he is also—since he is conscious of serving something bigger than himself—unshakably certain of being in the right.

British troops liberated the Nazi concentration camp at Bergen-Belsen in April 1945, too late to save young Anne Frank, who had died there, of typhus, in March, but British food and medical care did help some, such as these starving prisoners, to survive. Bergen-Belsen, in Germany proper, was initially a detention and transit camp, but an estimated 50,000 people died there, largely of disease. Those who survived the camps were physically, emotionally, and psychologically traumatized, and had great difficulty adjusting to life in postwar Europe. Some committed suicide, ridden by guilt for having survived the camps, while loved ones had perished. *(Bettmann/Corbis)*

cupied territories, non-Jews were hard pressed to collaborate with the Germans, and some did so more easily than others. The Allies had detailed knowledge of concentration camps and atrocities as early as 1942, but they failed to impede the program by bombing the camps or the railroads that led to them. Pope Pius XII, who was aware of antisemitic laws and violence committed by Catholics in Italy, Poland, Germany, and Slovakia, did not condemn these actions, failing in his role as moral and spiritual leader of the Roman Catholic Church. The general public in Europe and the United States was more concerned to defeat Hitler than to save the Jews. Antisemitism was a mainstream attitude in the western world. Though it did not necessarily translate into support for Hitler's ideas, it meant that sympathy for the Jews was limited and Jews themselves, like the American secretary of the treasury Henry Morgenthau, hesitated to use the example of the Jewish plight to mobilize support for the war.

Yet individuals and communities also acted courageously to assist Jews and others persecuted by the Nazis. Towns in France helped Jews escape to Switzerland, and several were wiped out by the Nazis as a consequence. The Danes and Bulgarians were notable for their efforts to hide Jews and their refusal to hand them over to the Germans. But brave acts were rare, and no effort, it seems, could stop the Nazi intention to exterminate the Jews of Europe.

Finally, the Jews of Europe were themselves in disbelief about the Final Solution. Many German, Hungarian, Polish, and French citizens of Jewish ancestry had become culturally integrated into their national cultures and thought of themselves as part of the nation rather than as a racially defined group. Only under the Nazis were they forced to identify themselves as Jews. Jewish resistance against the Holocaust developed rather slowly and with limited effect, partly because of the dangers involved and partly because Jews were themselves a diverse group.

The failure to stop the Holocaust had significant consequences in Europe after the end of the war. Although democracy was saved, Europeans and Americans were forced to look within themselves for the source of this profound failure of western civilization. Genocide had succeeded in advanced European countries because the technology was available to implement it, and the people generally were willing to use or allow it.

In Belorussia, as the Nazis and their local collaborators began implementing Nazi genocidal policies, Jewish men and women organized military units that struck back, with the support of the Soviet Union. *(Courtesy, Leonid Smilovitsky)*

Summary

Review Questions

↑ How did the challenges to democracy from 1929 to 1945 help transform European identity and civilization?

↑ Were the experiments of the Hitler and Stalin an aberration of western civilization or the product of its ideas, science, and technology?

↑ At what price did the Allies win the war?

From 1929 to 1945, democracy was severely tried in Europe. The Great Depression was the initial test, baffling politicians and economists with its unprecedented scale and repercussions in all areas of life. Politicians everywhere who were unwilling to try risky inflationary policies may have prolonged the crisis. But the political impact varied widely across Europe. In countries such as Britain and France, where democratic institutions were well established, there was a willingness to uphold democratic ideals at the risk of losing political power. In younger democracies, like Germany, too many lost faith in the value of elected institutions in times of crisis. People wanted stability and economic security more than democracy and freedom.

During and following the Great Depression, the two totalitarian dictatorships, Germany and the Soviet Union, were able to address economic needs more successfully than democratic countries. But remilitarization was key to their economic recovery. Preparing for war seemed to offer more economic stability and prosperity than upholding democracy. Unfortunately, the resulting arms race was not between rational leaders with limited goals but between irrational leaders with expansionist goals and outrageous dreams of world domination. Between Hitler's drive for Lebensraum in the east and Stalin's attempt to turn his country into a communist world power, war became unavoidable. The failure of the western democracies to stand up to Hitler's early defiance of the Versailles Treaty also played a role in emboldening him.

The ensuing total war brought unprecedented destruction and transformed the relationship between civilian and military involvement in war, now encompassing the entire populations of the combatant countries. New military technology also widened the scope and intensity of destruction and made military operations more complex than ever before. Finally, the Nazi extermination of entire populations and the atrocities committed by both occupiers and liberators (especially the Soviets) laid bare horrors that belied all concepts of civilization and progress in Europe. Those who survived the terrible conflict now had to confront its deep moral dilemmas.

← **Thinking Back, Thinking Ahead** →

What did Europeans learn from the totalitarian and genocidal experiences of this period?

ECHO ECHO ECHO ECHO ECHO

The U.S. Holocaust Memorial Museum in Washington, D.C.

"We must draw a veil over all the horrors of the past," concluded Winston Churchill after World War II. Indeed, for more than two decades few people wanted to talk about the Holocaust. For some, it was an uncomfortable feeling of guilt for not having done enough; for others, the victims, it was the unbearable memories of the camps. The word *Holocaust* did not begin to enter mainstream vocabulary with reference to the genocide against the Jews until the 1960s. In the next decades, trials of Nazi officials for crimes against humanity, interest in the stories of survivors, the establishment of Holocaust archives, and the declassification of many World War II archives increased interest in the events of the war years and permitted details, long hidden or suppressed, to be uncovered.

It was in the spirit of preserving the memory of the victims, educating future generations about this tragedy, and encouraging individuals to "reflect upon the moral and spiritual questions raised by the events of the Holocaust as well as their own responsibilities as citizens of a democracy" that in 1978 U.S. President Jimmy Carter established the Holocaust Memorial Commission in Washington, D.C., which led to the building of the U.S. Holocaust Memorial Museum. Open since 1993, this museum is a unique presence on the National Mall, home to the Smithsonian Institution, as it focuses on one historical event that did not take place in the United States or primarily involve Americans.

The museum houses a permanent exhibit, a number of temporary exhibits such as "Nazi Olympics Berlin 1936" (1996–1997), and a research institute on the history of the Holocaust and genocide. It has had more than 19 million visitors, of which almost 6 million have been children. The most impressive feature of the museum is the identity each visitor is asked to assume at the beginning. By following the fate of one real victim step by step, each visitor is able to feel something of the powerlessness and dehumanization suffered by innocent women, men, and children. The museum carries the clear message that "this could happen to you," a sobering reflection on the value of democracy.

Suggested Readings

Bartov, Omer, ed. *The Holocaust: Origins, Implementation and Aftermath.* New York: Routledge, 2000. A critical study of the Holocaust that summarizes the state of the field and offers major reinterpretations by leading Holocaust authors.

Dülffer, Jost. *Nazi Germany, 1933–1945: Faith and Annihilation.* New York: E. Arnold, 1996. A general introduction to the Third Reich reflecting the latest research, including the author's, and emphasizing the preparation for and conduct of the war.

Kindleberger, Charles P. *The World in Depression, 1929–1939.* Berkeley and Los Angeles: University of California Press, 1986. A broad comparative look at the impact of the Great Depression.

Payne, Stanley. *A History of Fascism, 1914–1943.* Madison: University of Wisconsin Press, 1996. A classic comparative history of fascism in Europe, from Italy to Romania.

Tucker, Robert. *Stalin in Power: The Revolution from Above, 1928–1941.* New York: Norton, 1992. A close look at the totalitarian policies of Stalin and the cult of personality before World War II.

Weinberg, Gerhard. *A World at Arms: A Global History of World War II.* Cambridge, England: Cambridge University Press, 2005. A comprehensive examination of World War II that looks at grand strategy and diplomacy.

Weintraub, Stanley. *The Last Great Cause: The Intellectuals and the Spanish Civil War.* New York: Weybright and Talley, 1975. An illuminating collection of stories about the war.

Websites

A Library of Congress virtual exhibit on politics and daily life under Soviet control with many interesting documents and useful links, **Soviet Archives Exhibit,** at www.ibiblio.org/expo/soviet.exhibit/entrance.html#tour

Detailed timeline of World War II with related articles, web links, and good photographs, **World War II Timeline,** at http://history.sandiego.edu/gen/WW2Timeline/start.html

Multimedia teaching site of the Simon Wiesenthal Center's online Museum of Tolerance containing brief articles and indepth analyses of controversial questions about the Holocaust and Nazi Germany, with photographs, documents, bibliographies, and several virtual exhibits, **Multimedia Learning Center,** at http://motlc.wiesenthal.com

CHAPTER 28

Europe Divided, 1945–1968

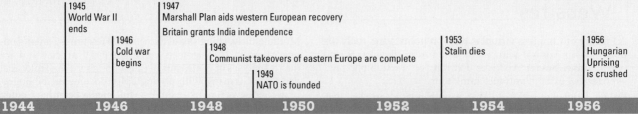

1500 B.C.E.	1000 B.C.E.	500 B.C.E.	1 B.C.E./1 C.E.

1945
World War II
ends

1946
Cold war
begins

1947
Marshall Plan aids western European recovery
Britain grants India independence

1948
Communist takeovers of eastern Europe are complete

1949
NATO is founded

1953
Stalin dies

1956
Hungarian
Uprising
is crushed

1944	1946	1948	1950	1952	1954	1956

Europe Following World War II

Between 1945 and 1989 Europe became divided into two camps struggling for legitimacy in an ideologically polarized world. The borders of European states changed only a little, compared to the settlement following World War I, but the two camps, East and West, were fiercely opposed to each other. What changes on this map reflect this bitter division?

FINLAND

From Finland, 1940–1956

Helsinki

Leningrad

NORWAY

Oslo

Stockholm

SOVIET UNION 1917

SWEDEN

Baltic Sea

ESTONIA to U.S.S.R., 1940

North Sea

DENMARK

Copenhagen

LATVIA to U.S.S.R. 1940

IRELAND

GREAT BRITAIN

London

NETHERLANDS

Amsterdam

U.S. Zone

Bremen

Soviet Zone

British Zone

Berlin

EAST GERMANY 1949

Gdansk (Danzig)

LITHUANIA to U.S.S.R. 1940

Incorporated into U.S.S.R., 1945

Incorporated into Poland, 1945

Warsaw

Brest

BELGIUM

Brussels

Bonn

WEST GERMANY

U.S. Zone

POLAND 1947

From Poland, 1940–1947

Paris

LUX.

French Zone

Prague

UKRAINE

CZECHOSLOVAKIA 1948

From Czechoslovakia, 1945–1947

FRANCE

Munich

Soviet Zone

AUSTRIA

Vienna

Bern

French Zone

U.S. Zone

British Zone

HUNGARY 1949

Budapest

BESSARABIA

From Romania, 1940–1947

SWITZERLAND

Milan

From Italy, 1945

ROMANIA 1947

Yalta

Belgrade

Bucharest

Black Sea

SPAIN

YUGOSLAVIA 1945

From Romania, 1940

Corsica (Fr.)

ITALY

Rome

BULGARIA 1946

Sofia

Balearic Islands (Sp.)

Sardinia (It.)

Istanbul

TURKEY

Tiranë

Mediterranean Sea

Sicily (It.)

ALBANIA 1944

GREECE

Athens

Crete (Gr.)

ALGERIA (Fr.)

TUNISIA (Fr.)

Legend

— Postwar national boundaries, to 1989
Allied occupation of Germany and Austria 1945–1955
Territory lost by Germany
Territory gained by Soviet Union
1945 Year communist control of government gained
— "Iron Curtain" to 1989
→ Baltic
→ Czech
→ Finns
→ Germans
→ Poles
→ Russians
→ Peoples settled by International Refugee Organization

Berlin inset

EAST GERMANY

French Sector

British Sector

West Berlin

U.S. Sector

East Berlin

Soviet Sector

EAST GERMANY

Potsdam

— Berlin Wall (1961–1989)

Scale

0 250 500 Km.
0 250 500 Mi.

Timeline

500 C.E.   1000 C.E.   1500 C.E.   2000 C.E.

1961
Berlin Wall goes up

1968
Martin Luther King Jr. is assassinated

Students and workers strike in France

Prague Spring is crushed

1958
European Economic Community is founded

1962
French grant Algeria independence

1958   1960   1962   1964   1966   1968   1970

Choice

Ana Pauker Submits to the Communist Party

Ana Pauker

Named by *Time* magazine in 1948 as "the most powerful woman alive," Ana Pauker was in charge of the Communist Party in Romania between 1948 and 1953. Yet she never served as the general secretary of the party, for as woman and a Jew, she realized these identities would hamper her authority as the official leader. (Time Life Pictures/Getty Images)

In August 1944, Ana Pauker rode into Bucharest atop a Soviet tank, returning to the city of her troubled youth as a liberator (or conqueror). She had traveled a long and difficult path from her birth to an impoverished Jewish family in northern Romania, at a time and place where antisemitism was popular and where women were regarded as second-class citizens. Intelligent and fearless, she worked hard against this double discrimination and the roles traditionally assigned to women like her. She first chose to study Judaism and then went on to join the Communist Party during World War I, having opposed Romania's entry into the war. Though she spent some years abroad after the war, she returned to Romania to lead underground activities against Romania's unstable governments. During the 1920s and 1930s, she served several prison sentences, the last one at the same time that her husband, Marcel Pauker, was imprisoned by the Soviets during the Great Purges.

Pauker denounced her husband at his 1938 trial in Moscow. At that moment, she understood clearly that she had to pick one of her conflicting loyalties—family or the communist revolution. If she questioned the Moscow party line, she would be betraying her ideological convictions. She chose ideology. By betraying her husband, she aligned herself with Moscow and made herself ready to win control in Romania after the war.

After she returned to Romania in 1944, she retained this all-consuming loyalty. She willingly gave up leadership of the Communist Party in recognition that, as a woman and Jew, she was a liability to the party. Only by downplaying these identities could she be a decision maker in the government. As shadow leader of the party in the Politburo, she oversaw the purging of the precommunist political leadership and the transformation of the state into one modeled after Stalin's vision. In 1948, *Time* magazine named her "the most powerful woman alive."

Yet by 1951, Pauker had come into conflict with other Romanian communist leaders, as well as Stalin, especially over collectivization. Having given so much of her personal life to the party, Pauker assumed she could independently make the most important decisions in this aspect of economic reform. She wanted to collectivize slowly, to ensure that peasants would not come to resent the party. Though she did not come from a peasant family, she cared about the fate of peasants, and though she felt deep personal loyalty to Stalin, she also cared about Romania. Still, many in Romania perceived her as a "foreigner" because of her Jewish origins. In an atmosphere of growing antisemitism, Pauker's competitors in the party used this conflict to accuse her of betraying communism. Only her personal friendship with Stalin saved her life. But in 1953

Pauker was forced to denounce herself as a traitor and renounce her membership in the Communist Party. Once more she sacrificed herself for the sake of the party.

Few people mourned Pauker's departure from the party leadership, as her ruthless style was much feared. But, unlike other communists, Pauker seems to have wanted power not so much for herself but rather in order to carry out her convictions. She passed away two decades later, in anonymity and still much hated by many Romanians.

Introduction

Military hostilities ended in August 1945, but peace did not immediately follow. Instead, many Europeans experienced occupation by "liberating" armies and retribution for war crimes. Yet war memories were quickly silenced by new challenges. By 1949, the United States and the Soviet Union were struggling for global power and parceling up the world into zones of influence. Europe became the first and initially most important site for superpower confrontation, as it was divided between East and West, communism and capitalism, totalitarianism and democracy. Europeans had to realign their identities. For some, like Ana Pauker, the new era meant transforming their societies in the likeness of the Soviet Union. For others, the end of one war was the beginning of a new one to protect democratic values against communism. This war—a cold war—was fought at the highest level of military and diplomatic planning, usually in great secrecy; yet it touched the lives of every person living in Europe and throughout the world.

By the late 1950s, western Europeans had settled into a comfortable view of themselves as the "real" Europe and their enemies as distant contenders. In France and Germany, in particular, economic reconstruction brought about great hopes that Europe could regain its leading role in the world. In the meantime, eastern Europeans were thrown into the challenges of building communism according to Stalin's vision of it. The communist regimes employed harsh policies but achieved some measure of success in modernizing their economies. By the late 1950s, the separation between East and West was entrenched. It took another generation to challenge this division. In the wake of anticolonial movements and a new antiestablishment youth, Europeans were forced to look across the East-West divide more carefully and reexamine their values as events during 1968 shook the political establishment.

The Iron Curtain, 1945–1958

↓ What conflicts over Europe's future paved the way for its division?

↓ How did international relations change in the first two postwar decades?

The end of World War II brought to Europe a tense and precarious stalemate among the winning Allies. There was no comprehensive peace treaty. The United States and Great Britain were at odds with the Soviet Union over the future of the liberated territories and their own role in the process. Initially, each victor had its own methods for dealing with Nazi war crimes. The issue of what to do with the people displaced by the war also posed significant problems. But everything came under the shadow of a growing rift between the United States and the Soviet Union. By 1948 the Soviet Union had given up the pretenses of cooperating with the West and forcefully put an end to democratic politics in eastern Europe. The rift became a division, with the United States assuming the role of protector of western European democracy and capitalism and the Soviet Union as the protector of oppressed peoples everywhere and the counterforce, through the spread of communism, against western imperialism. The United Nations added another dimension to the polarized international system.

Occupation and De-Nazification

At the end of World War II, millions of Europeans were homeless and impoverished. Entire cities and economies lay in ruin. The political leadership of many countries had either perished or been thoroughly compromised by collaboration with the Nazis. To ensure a stable transition to postwar peace, the United States, Britain, France, and the Soviet Union occupied and divided the territories formerly controlled by the Third Reich and its allies. Germany, Austria, and the city of

Chronology

1945 Potsdam Conference discusses how to administer postwar Germany	**1951** European Coal and Steel Community (ECSC) is established
1946 National Health Service Act ensures healthcare for all in Britain	**1953** Stalin dies
1947 India gains independence; Truman Doctrine commits the United States to fight communism worldwide; U.S. Marshall Plan offers reconstruction aid to western Europe	**1954** Vietnam gains independence
	1954–1962 Algerians win independence from the colonial French government
	1955 Warsaw Pact is formed
1947–1948 Communists take over Romania, Czechoslovakia, Hungary, Poland, East Germany, and Bulgaria	**1956** Khrushchev delivers Secret Speech criticizing Stalin; Hungarian Uprising is crushed by Soviets; Egypt nationalizes the Suez Canal
1948 Stalin expels Tito from Cominform; Stalin begins purges of eastern European communist leadership	**1958** European Economic Community is formed
	1958 French Fourth Republic falls; De Gaulle succeeds in French presidential coup
1949 Indonesia gains independence; North Atlantic Treaty Organization (NATO) is founded; Committee for Mutual Economic Assistance (CMEA) is founded; Mao Zedong leads communist takeover in China	**1961** Soviets construct Berlin Wall
	1962 Cuban Missile Crisis
	1968 Prague Spring is crushed by Soviets; Students and workers create national strike in France
1950–1953 Korean War ends in stalemate	

Berlin were divided into four occupation zones, while other areas of Europe fell under the control of the liberating ally.

In 1945, Soviet troops had liberated all the countries east of Berlin and were fully in control of them. A 1944 **percentages agreement** between Winston Churchill and Joseph Stalin assigned Romania and Bulgaria to the Soviet sphere of influence, Czechoslovakia and Greece to the West (Britain, France, and the United States), with Yugoslavia and Hungary in a fifty-fifty arrangement. Subsequently at Yalta (1945), Poland was placed in the hands of the Soviets, while Czechoslovakia's fate remained open.

To be viewed as liberators, the Americans, aided by the British and French, swiftly rounded up Nazi Party members and collaborators. The **Nuremberg Trials** were the most famous of the **de-Nazification** war crime trials that took place everywhere in Europe between 1945 and 1948. These international tribunals brought charges of "crimes against humanity," a new legal concept rooted in Enlightenment notions of hu-

man rights, to sit in judgment on Nazi racism and the Final Solution. But many high-ranking Nazi officials involved in the death camps and most rank-and-file party members escaped trial. Many of them now cast themselves as victims or innocent bystanders. During his trial at Nuremberg, **Hermann Göring,** head of the Luftwaffe, rejected the notion of collective guilt. "It is the leaders of the country who determine the policy,"

percentages agreement Secret agreement reached by Churchill and Stalin in 1944 regarding the division of eastern Europe.

Nuremberg Trials Postwar trials of Nazi leaders and collaborators, held in Nuremberg, Germany, in 1945–1946.

de-Nazification Destruction of Nazism and its influence.

Hermann Göring (1893–1946) Nazi leader, founder of the Gestapo and head of the Luftwaffe, who was convicted at the Nuremberg Trials.

he said cynically, "and it is always a simple matter to drag the people along, whether it is a democracy or a fascist dictatorship."

Using the Nuremberg model, in eastern Europe, as the Soviet sphere was increasingly called, the Soviets orchestrated trials against many military and political leaders who had worked with the Nazis or, more recently, opposed the Soviets. Invariably, those tried were found guilty and executed or sent to prison. In eastern Europe, the de-Nazification trials became both a form of intimidation and an attempt to legitimize the communists—the Communist Party being the only political party that appeared untainted by wartime collaboration with the Nazis. With so many politicians removed, the trials paved the way for the future communist takeovers and created a myth that responsibility for war crimes rested exclusively on the shoulders of the Germans and other foreign fascists.

The de-Nazification trials failed to find all Nazi collaborators and punish them. The prosecutors had neither the ability nor the political will for such a vast task, and many collaborators went into hiding or committed suicide. But the trials did enable survivors to achieve a degree of closure on the Nazi past and get on with their lives. In addition, in light of the growing competition with the Soviet Union, the western allies found it politically expedient to complete de-Nazification quickly in order to shift focus toward economic reconstruction.

Displaced Persons

To get on with their lives, however, many Europeans first had to try to find a home. Entire cities were in rubble, and many Germans and others had fled West as the Soviet armies advanced. At the end of the war, between 11 and 20 million individuals were displaced persons.

Moreover, entire populations were resettled. At the **Potsdam Conference** in July 1945, the western allies agreed that eastern European governments in Poland and Czechoslovakia could forcibly remove all Germans from their countries. In Poland, hundreds of thousands of ethnic Germans were expelled. A similar policy sent hundreds of thousands of Poles from western Ukraine and Belorussia to Poland. Czechoslovakia also expelled its Germans. There was much debate over who exactly was a German, as there were many ethnically mixed marriages and individuals whose families had long lived in the contested areas. A Czech woman married to a Sudeten German would likely become a candidate for expulsion, even though she and her husband had been born subjects of Czechoslovakia and his family had lived there for genera-

MAP 28.1   **UN Mandate for Israel and Palestine, 1947** The UN Mandate, which created the legal framework for international recognition of Israel, left the status of the Arab inhabitants of Palestine unresolved. The conflict that rages today between Israel and the Arab states in the Middle East originated with the formation of the state of Israel in 1948.

tions and had become subjects of the Nazi state only after 1938. Often resettlement was abused by envious neighbors who wanted a piece of property or simply revenge for some past wrong. The process reinforced the power of the state to decide the identity and fate of its inhabitants. Ultimately, more than 13 million ethnic Germans, mostly in eastern Europe, were forcibly removed. In expelling Germans, Czechoslovakia and Poland enforced the racist definitions of nationality developed by the Nazis. Ironically, the western defenders of democracy were enabling the elimination of populations promoted by the Nazis.

Potsdam Conference   Meeting in July 1945 at which the United States, Britain, and the Soviet Union decided how to administer postwar Germany.

Those forced out left almost everything behind. They walked or rode bicycles or donkeys; the lucky had horse-driven carts. In the process, children were sometimes separated from parents and wives from husbands. More than 100,000 families ended up living across the East-West divide, unable to keep in touch with each other for a generation. The process of moving millions of people away from their homes and into potentially hostile communities generated psychic wounds that began to heal only later, primarily through forgetting. An important political result was the reshaping of most of eastern Europe into more ethnically homogeneous countries. Poland, for instance, became almost entirely Polish and Catholic, with Jews, Germans, and Ukrainians gone.

Among the displaced persons were more than 250,000 Jews, located primarily in the American zone, where they were placed in camps. Jewish leaders from Palestine, such as **David Ben-Gurion**, worked with the western allies to decide the fate of these people. More than 130,000 of them settled in British-controlled Palestine, which became Israel in 1948. Those who stayed in Europe were subjected to anti-semitic discrimination and even postwar pogroms, which generated additional emigrations to Israel.

Beginnings of the Cold War

The wartime alliance between the United States and the Soviet Union against a common enemy dissolved into an adversarial relation, as the victors could not agree on postwar goals for Germany and the rest of Europe. Both nations emerged from the war as superpowers, with great international prestige, and each embarked on a struggle for political, economic, and moral-cultural world supremacy. No other state could match their strength, and most European states owed their survival to one or both of them. In this contest, the engagement of the United States in European affairs was a greater departure from past behavior than for the Soviet Union. While after World War I the Soviets had aided communist movements in Europe, the United States had pursued isolationism. After World War II, however, the development of Europe cannot be understood without the essential involvement of the United States.

Europe became the playing field in a struggle between the opposing options of the Americans and the Soviets: liberal democracy versus communism, private property versus state ownership, capitalism and free-market economies versus state-controlled ones, freedom and material comforts versus equality and social justice. Both sides wanted to erase whatever gray areas existed in each European country between these poles. New identities and allegiances were created in connection with the two superpowers, and new enmities developed among old neighbors. The Hungarians, who had been the Austrians' partners in ruling the Habsburg Empire a century earlier, were now to be their enemies by virtue of the barbed wire that separated the two countries. East Germans, under Soviet occupation, were to begin thinking of their West German relatives and friends as imperialist traitors. This division of Europe into East and West came about as a result of the superpower confrontation.

In the contest over world domination, the two superpowers gave different explanations and used different methods. The Soviet Union had lost more people (over 30 million by some accounts) and resources than any other war combatant and wanted to recoup the economic resources spent fighting the war. In fact, since Germany had experienced 80 percent of its casualties at the hands of the Soviets, Stalin was not exaggerating when he claimed that Europe owed the Nazi defeat to his country. To rebuild the Soviet economy, he wanted Soviet troops in the occupied zone to oversee the production and subsequent transfer of goods to the Soviet Union. The Soviets also acted out of fear. Having been attacked by Germany twice in the twentieth century, they wanted a buffer zone in eastern Europe, where friendly political regimes and military resources would protect Soviet security.

The United States, on the other hand, had an overwhelming interest in bringing back democracy and capitalist markets to the regions it had liberated. One lesson from World War I was that a punishing peace could lead to resentment and revenge. This time, the victors focused on rebuilding a Germany committed to their ideals. In addition, the Great Depression's costly economic and political consequences also pointed toward rebuilding markets as a better strategy than exacting high war payments. Strong capitalist economies would bolster political stability, American strategists concluded. These goals were not entirely altruistic. The American economy had grown during the war, and businesses were looking for new markets. European countries had already become deeply dependent on American goods and dollars, and they were a good investment.

The means by which the Soviets pursued their goals in eastern Europe were in keeping with Stalin's personality. He fundamentally distrusted those not

David Ben-Gurion   (1886–1973) Zionist leader central to the establishment of the state of Israel and its first prime minister.

under his control. He sent some of the toughest military leaders and most unquestioning loyalists from the communist parties in eastern Europe, such as Ana Pauker (see Choice), to oversee postwar regimes. The Soviets manipulated the western observers and used any legal means available, as well as illegal and violent ones, to eliminate all political enemies and place Soviet pawns in power. Political legitimacy and the well-being of the populations involved were low on Stalin's agenda.

Stalin had a formidable opponent in U.S. president Harry Truman, who, as vice president, had never trusted the Soviet Union. Following President Franklin D. Roosevelt's death in April 1945, the simple man from Missouri brought his common sense to the presidency and his own strong views about the postwar peace. He followed a careful line of encouraging a stable international environment through the **United Nations (UN)** and an increasingly hard line against the Soviets.

In Europe, Truman was committed to prosperity and democracy through positive, though anti-Soviet, incentives. Instead of sending troops to defend American interests, in March 1947 he issued the **Truman Doctrine**, which offered to help countries fighting communist expansion, specifically Turkey and Greece, where communist partisans in a civil war were receiving help from Yugoslavia and the Soviets. Greece was considered key to the political stability in the Mediterranean and American overseas markets. With substantial American support, the military establishment defeated the communists and imposed its own authoritarian rule.

In addition, the 1947 **Marshall Plan** allocated more than $13 billion in grants and loans to rebuild Europe's economies. This money helped rebuild roads, industries, and housing. The plan found unprecedented support among Americans and generated a host of programs that paved the way for the European Union. American aid came with a price, however. The United States encouraged France, Britain, and Germany to hunt down communist sympathizers who might have infiltrated leftist parties and be plotting communist takeovers. The Marshall Plan also served to further separate western from eastern Europe, where countries occupied by Soviet troops were never in a position to accept U.S. aid.

In Germany, the Soviets dismantled industrial plants in their occupation zone and took no interest in preventing the starvation of German civilians, which drew the criticism of the West. In response, in February 1948 the Soviets set up a blockade to isolate the western zones of Berlin from access by Western powers. To avert military conflict, the United States

sent in supplies by means of the **Berlin airlift**, flying in up to 13,000 tons per day. By May 1949, the Soviets had backed down, and Germany became divided into the Federal Republic of Germany, known as West Germany, and the German Democratic Republic, known as East Germany. Berlin itself was divided into East and West Berlin. Though stabilized, Germany remained at the epicenter of the contest between the United States and the Soviet Union for the next forty years—the **cold war.**

Other developments helped shape the cold war. After the contentious creation of Israel in 1948, the Middle East became an important ground for competition between the Soviets, generally backing Arab states and insurgents, and the Americans, generally supporting Israel, especially from the late 1960s onward. In addition, in 1949, **Mao Zedong** led a successful communist revolution in China, a development that made the Americans more fearful of the spread of communism. Communist China complicated American strategies, as it operated independently of the Soviet Union, unlike other communist states. Finally, after the Soviets exploded an atomic bomb in 1949, the prospect of nuclear war intensified. Fear of total annihilation kept the Soviets and the Americans at some distance, while their ambitions kept them in uncomfortable proximity and often in indirect military confrontation in the regional struggles they wanted to manipulate.

The Soviets' development of nuclear weapons after 1949 ushered in an arms race. Starting in the 1950s, both the United States and the Soviet Union expended huge sums on military technology and espionage, as

United Nations (UN) International organization founded in 1945 to facilitate collaboration among nations; replaced the League of Nations.

Truman Doctrine Policy statement issued by U.S. president Harry S. Truman in 1947 announcing U.S. commitment to fight the spread of communism everywhere in the world.

Marshall Plan Economic recovery plan established by the United States in 1947 that offered grants and low-interest loans to noncommunist European states.

Berlin airlift (1948–1949) U.S. shipment of supplies to Western-controlled sectors of Berlin following a Soviet blockade.

cold war Name by which the 1945–1991 standoff between the superpowers, the United States and the Soviet Union, came to be known.

Mao Zedong (1893–1976) Leader of the communist revolution and, from 1949, the communist regime in China.

each tried to keep up with the other. In 1953, the United States spent $50 billion, or almost 40 percent of the federal budget, on the military. Spending by the Soviet Union for the same purposes reached 25 percent of its revenues during the same period. This obsession with being militarily prepared for global conflict created a predicament, as neither country had enough intelligence about the other's capacity to make reasoned judgments, and the political leadership was easily persuaded about the need for military spending. Unprecedented levels of military spending only increased the fear of conflict and fed the perceived need to spend more.

International Security

The piecemeal peace agreements of the first postwar years secured a somewhat stable relationship between the superpowers in Europe. But the most important step for creating a different international order was the establishment of the United Nations (UN) in 1945. Unlike with the League of Nations, which it never joined, the United States was a founding member of the UN. This organization was similar to the league in its aim to facilitate collaboration among all states by giving all members the same rights regardless of size, military power, or wealth. But the UN was different from its predecessor in how it achieved these goals. It included a governing body, the **Security Council**, on which China, France, Great Britain, the Soviet Union, and the United States sat as permanent members, along with ten rotating members. The UN also acquired financial resources and a military force to take action when necessary. Its large budget enabled it to manage international programs for public health, child protection, and cultural exchange, giving states large and small, poor and rich, access to new opportunities for peaceful cooperation, such as the successful anti-malaria campaigns in Africa and assistance in underdeveloped areas to increase productivity and eradicate poverty.

The UN's **Universal Declaration of Human Rights** (1948) specified unprecedented rights and freedoms, such as the freedom to move from one location to another, the right to education, and the right to be protected from unemployment. Though not legally binding, the declaration became a powerful means whereby citizens could hold their governments accountable for human rights abuses in an international arena. The autonomous International Criminal Court at The Hague became an important forum for punishing human rights abuses and war crimes. Thus, the UN revolutionized international relations and brought

pressure and resources to bear on broad issues from human rights to poverty and health.

However, other international organizations reduced hopes for peaceful solutions to international problems. In 1949, the **North Atlantic Treaty Organization (NATO)**, a military defense alliance aimed primarily against the Soviets' alleged plans for armed global conflict, was created, with collective security as its cardinal principle—an attack on one member was an attack on all, and the security of each individual member depended on the security of all. NATO forced uniform policies on its members and required that each be in a permanent state of military preparedness. The establishment of NATO signaled a formal division of the postwar world between the western democracies, with the twelve NATO members—the United States, Britain, France, Canada, Italy, the Netherlands, Belgium, Luxembourg, Portugal, Denmark, Norway, and Iceland, later joined by West Germany, Greece, and Turkey—at the forefront, and the Soviet-dominated communist camp on the opposite side.

The Soviet Union retaliated by calling for the creation of a communist alliance. First, the **Committee for Mutual Economic Assistance (CMEA)** was formed in 1949 as a counterpart to the Marshall Plan, serving to increase Soviet control over eastern European economies. Subsequently, the **Warsaw Pact** was created in 1955 as a direct response against the rearming of West Germany and counterpart to NATO. But the Warsaw Pact increasingly policed its own communist member states.

In this new international order, European states were pawns rather than major players. Military buildups provide an example. Although NATO presumed that all members would participate actively in military defense, the United States and Britain led in ar-

Security Council Leading body of the United Nations in matters of international security.

Universal Declaration of Human Rights Declaration adopted by the United Nations General Assembly in 1948 outlining universal basic human rights.

North Atlantic Treaty Organization (NATO) Defensive alliance established by Britain, France, and the United States in 1949 with Canada and other western European allies.

Committee for Mutual Economic Assistance (CMEA) Soviet organization created in 1949 to coordinate economic production and trade in communist bloc countries.

Warsaw Pact Organization of communist states created in 1955 as a counterpart to NATO.

mament production, and when Charles de Gaulle attempted to upgrade France's nuclear program, he was hastily rebutted by the Americans and the British. The power imbalance was even more evident in the Warsaw Pact, with the Soviets supervising the production and sale of armaments, even when the factories were in Czechoslovakia.

The Revival of Western Europe

   ↓ Why was western Europe so successful in rebuilding its economic power?
   ↓ What were the political consequences of the commitment to economic recovery?

Given the magnitude of the material destruction and political disarray at the end of the war, western Europe's record recovery has been rightly called a miracle. By 1950, the region was producing at a level 30 percent higher than before the war. This great achievement owes much to the immense financial resources poured into the economies of western Europe, to international stability (if not without tension), and to the expansion of the welfare state, which secured internal social and political stability.

The Economic Miracle

Thanks to the Marshall Plan, France and Italy had surpassed their prewar levels of production by 1950, but West Germany had the most impressive success. Between 1945 and 1950, production shot up 25 percent, 15 percent higher than in 1938. Many West German cities destroyed during the war were completely rebuilt to accommodate former inhabitants and to make room for the more than 12 million refugees from the communist East. By the 1960s, West Germany was the undisputed economic leader in western Europe in industrial production, research and development, and its ability to put its swelling population to work. Even with a tremendous growth in population, the country had virtually no unemployment until the 1960s, when a majority of West Germans were living in unprecedented comfort, able to fill their apartments and homes with refrigerators, television sets, and automatic washing machines.

It is no wonder, then, that **Konrad Adenauer,** the leader who oversaw this economic miracle, continued to dominate the political scene until the 1960s. The founder of the Christian Democratic Union, he was the first postwar chancellor. Like other successful western political leaders after the war, he had a

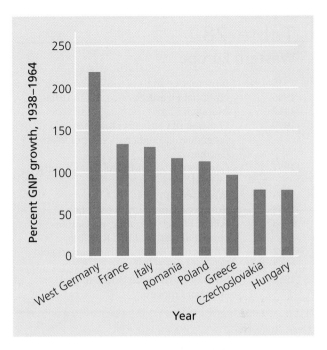

FIGURE 28.1   Economic Growth in Europe, 1938–1964 Between 1945 and 1964 western Europe experienced a virtual economic miracle. In part due to the Marshall Plan, and in part due to successful internal political and economic policies, Germany, France, and Britain regained their economic prominence.   *Source: Wilkinson, James D.; Huges, H. Stuart,* Contemporary Europe: A History, *9th Edition, © 1998, pp. 425. Reprinted by permission of Pearson Education, Inc., Upper Saddle River, NJ.*

record of resistance to the Nazis, a commitment to rebuilding capitalist democracy, and a center-right political orientation. An active opponent of Hitler, he had spent part of the war in a concentration camp, but he was *not* a sympathizer of the left. He used his reputation to push economic recovery and political distance from East Germany. Under his leadership, the great German industries and private business were rebuilt and workers were guaranteed decent wages and healthcare. The Old Man, as he came to be known, masterfully developed a new image of Germany that highlighted the nation's industrious and democratic spirit. His politics gave hope to West Germans and attracted their loyalty, discrediting claims by communist East Germany that it also represented the German people. Adenauer's Christian Democrats, committed to economic recovery and social stability, dominated

Konrad Adenauer   (1876–1967) Christian Democratic conservative opponent of Hitler who was elected the first chancellor of West Germany in 1949.

Table 28.1

Western Europe

1945–1946	Nuremberg Trials
1946	National Health Service Act in Britain
1947	Marshall Plan
1949	Division of Germany; Konrad Adenauer elected chancellor of West Germany
1951	European Coal and Steel Community formed
1955	West Germany Joins NATO
1958	European Community established
1958	Fall of French Republic; de Gaulle coup and birth of Fifth Republic
1961	1 million Volkswagen Transporters sold
1962–1965	Second Vatican Council
1968	Student movements and national strike in France

German politics until 1963. Table 28.1 summarizes key events in western Europe during the postwar period.

Recovery in France

In France, economic recovery was also remarkable, but it was not accompanied immediately by political stability. France had largely escaped physical destruction during the war, and its population had suffered smaller losses than had most other countries. However, France had experienced great shame and humiliation. Reconstruction thus had much to do with resurrecting faith in a vigorous France.

Charles de Gaulle overshadowed all other politicians during this period, even though he did not hold office between 1946 and 1958. Raised in a well-educated Catholic family, de Gaulle embodied some of the oldest and proudest French traditions. He grew up among history and philosophy books and in adolescence opted for a military career in which he could live out his patriotic sentiments. He served in the infantry, almost died at Verdun in 1916, and subsequently volunteered to fight against the Bolshevik Russians in 1919–1920. His family's political leanings were monarchist, but de Gaulle became a republican. Still, party divisions were never to his taste, as he preferred either the strict hierarchy of the army or the direct voice of the people at the ballot box. Above all, de Gaulle saw two fundamental traits in his countrymen: "The desire of privilege and the taste of equality are the dominant and contradictory passions of the French of all times."

France had had a vibrant socialist movement since the nineteenth century, and it was prominent in anti-Nazi resistance. The resistance had also been fertile ground for the communists, yet de Gaulle, who represented the conservative nationalist wing of European politics, led the liberating French forces in 1945. Until 1958, France was bitterly divided between left and right. The left claimed legitimacy based on its wartime efforts, but the communists became compromised by connections with the Soviet Union. The right, dominated by de Gaulle's party and other nationalist movements, had U.S. support. More than nineteen governments rotated in and out of power during this period.

In 1958 a political crisis brought de Gaulle into office and launched the **Fifth Republic,** under a new constitution that gave broad powers to the presidency and limited those of the parliament. He was a more difficult ally for the Americans than Adenauer but no friend of the Soviet Union or the communists. As premier, de Gaulle helped restore people's faith in France as a great nation. His victory in French politics had come primarily at the expense of the left, which became increasingly marginalized in the decade after the war, accused of being a tool of Soviet expansionism. The decline of the left in France was like that in other western European countries with strong socialist and communist movements, such as Germany and Italy.

The European Community

The hardening of the East-West division between 1947 and 1958 served to broaden ties among western European states. These countries began to create stronger internal markets and to cooperate in trade, economic production, and employment policies. Given the nationalist jealousy that had dominated relations between France and Germany since the nineteenth century, this cooperation was remarkable. But European politicians and economists had learned the hard lessons of the Great Depression and were ready to take new directions. In addition, the Marshall Plan stipulated that the recipients were to cooperate in areas of investment, production, and trade.

The main architect of these bold policies was **Robert Schuman,** an economist and the first premier of post-

Fifth Republic Current French political regime established by Charles de Gaulle in 1958 through a presidential coup.

Robert Schuman (1886–1963) First premier of postwar France, instrumental in forming the European Union and the European Coal and Steel Community.

A visionary French economist and politician, Robert Schuman successfully convinced the French public and his West German counterparts to put their nationalist disputes behind them and cooperate for the benefits of prosperity and democracy in their respective countries and in Europe more broadly. *(Bettmann/Corbis)*

war France. Together with other French and German economists and politicians, he put forth a plan to end enmity between Germany and France, promising greater stability and prosperity for both countries. "The solidarity in production thus established," he explained, "will make it plain that any war between France and Germany becomes not merely unthinkable, but materially impossible."

Discussions led in 1951 to the creation of the **European Coal and Steel Community (ECSC)**, with six members—Belgium, France, Germany, Italy, Luxembourg, and the Netherlands. Trade tariffs were lifted for some products, workers from member countries could cross borders to find employment, and investment in coal and steel production across borders was encouraged. The union offered opportunities to entrepreneurs, paving the way for multinational corporations, as well as workers, and extending protections to them in all member states.

The ECSC was a great success, increasing steel and iron production by 75 percent in its first three years, with industrial production rising by 58 percent. It made possible the creation of the European Atomic Energy Community (1957), which oversaw the development of atomic energy for civilian purposes, and finally the European Economic Community (EEC). The 1958 EEC Rome Treaty provided the institutional foundations for four areas of cooperation among members: administrative (Council of the European Union), legislative (European Parliament, largely on paper), economic (European Commission), and judicial (European Court of Justice). The EEC also became known as the **European Community** or the Common Market. This transformation did not mean the end of political independence for the members but ensured cooperation and joint planning to enhance economic growth.

The success of the European Community was also linked to the optimism and self-sacrifice present everywhere in Europe after the war. Most people focused their energies on stability and economic well-being rather than politics. Thus, political leaders could take swift steps toward recovery in the major industries at the expense of consumer goods. The spirit of cooperation also developed among political parties, which began to make connections with across borders with others of similar leanings—from left-wing socialists to center-right Christian Democrats. NATO also induced military cooperation among members.

Yet nationalism continued to pose problems for the European Community. De Gaulle, for example, used France's veto to block Great Britain's membership in this organization in 1963 and 1967. His opposition was based on his negative view of Britain's postwar subservience to the United States and also on his skepticism about Britain's willingness to accept all EEC responsibilities. De Gaulle's concerns were not groundless: given its success in postwar recovery, Britain was slow to show interest in the European Community.

Great Britain and the Welfare State

After the war, Britain's political and economic problems forced its leadership to focus inward. Though a

European Coal and Steel Community (ECSC)
 Organization established in 1951 that created a common customs, production, and labor market for coal and steel.

European Community Precursor of the European Union, founded in 1958 with the creation of the European Economic Community, the European Coal and Steel Community, and the European Atomic Energy Commission.

wartime hero, Churchill was defeated by Labour Party contender **Clement Attlee** in July 1945. The election outcome reflected a widespread desire among the public to shift away from deep involvement in European and world security. For more than five years the British public had been told to sacrifice for others, and they did so at great human and material cost. Now they wanted the government to look out for them.

The Labour Party interpreted its victory as a mandate for welfare programs. The state established firm control over important areas of the economy and public services, from transportation to utilities. The Bank of England was nationalized, as were the coal and steel industries. The National Health Service Act of 1946 placed health insurance under state control while still allowing for private practice. This pioneering law made healthcare accessible to virtually all British citizens. A similarly radical reform established government-funded pensions for all working citizens—a social security fund. Britain thus became a leader in welfare policies and a model for other European countries, which were encouraged to adopt similar policies. The sweeping welfare measures worked both because of the conciliatory mood of the Conservatives, who continued the policies of the Labour Party after they came to power in the 1950s, and because of the generous financial help—more than $3 billion—of the Marshall Plan.

The state also expanded educational opportunities. The 1944 Education Act made education mandatory until age fifteen and increased government funding to create the necessary schools, as well as scholarships for university students. More poor pupils than ever before were able to finish secondary schools and attend college, a development that took place just as rapid modernization escalated the need for educated professionals and skilled workers in the industrial and service sectors. Simultaneously, important shifts in agricultural production pushed new waves of people into urban areas. The population of the countryside fell by 50 percent as urban growth exploded.

Women, however, lagged behind as beneficiaries of these new social welfare programs. Quotas imposed for access into secondary education, even when state mandated and funded, ensured that the number of girls who attended the best schools was always smaller than the number of boys, despite girls' overall superior academic performance. And though more women than ever before were employed, their wages lagged 30 to 50 percent behind men's. They also received insufficient support for child care and often had to leave the labor force for this reason.

Overall, however, the growth of work opportunities, education, and inexpensive or free public services from the state made it possible for record numbers of workers to partake in the consumer culture and enjoy leisure activities. British workers attended concerts, participated in sports, took paid vacations, and traveled abroad. Tourism took off, with more than 100 million people taking trips every year. The working class was looking like and identifying more with the middle class, and old stereotypes about national characteristics weakened as people traveled in other countries and worked together in Common Market projects.

The Restructuring of Eastern Europe

↓ What were the important steps in the communist takeovers in eastern Europe?
↓ What was the effect in the region of Stalin's death?

By 1948, the communists were in power everywhere in eastern Europe, revolutionizing politics, and in the next two decades internal and external forces solidified these regimes. In some cases, communist leaders preferred to follow Moscow to ensure their own political survival. In other cases, local communists attempted to gain legitimacy by portraying themselves as leaders of their nation. But the Soviets reacted swiftly against all who deviated from the interests of communism as defined in Moscow and put down any important attempts at reform. By 1968, all the communist leaders who had dreamed of reform and autonomy from Moscow were gone, generating broad disillusionment with all communist ideals.

The Communist Takeovers

In 1945, the communists were a tiny political group in eastern Europe, except for Czechoslovakia and Yugoslavia. Most members of these parties had perished at the hands of the Nazis or their own governments during the war. Some had escaped to Moscow, as Stalin worked hard to recruit European communists who, like Ana Pauker, were fully devoted to Soviet goals for eastern Europe. By 1945, these communists had been returned to their countries to begin organizing mass movements and building political power.

The only other potential contenders for political power were the representatives of the governments in

Clement Attlee   (1883–1967) British prime minister from 1945 to 1951 and Labour Party leader who oversaw the establishment of the welfare state and the end of British colonialism.

MAP 28.2   East European Stalinism Between 1945 and 1953, the Soviet Union consolidated its grip over the political institutions and economies of its eastern European satellites. Yugoslavia alone remained a thorn in Stalin's side.   Source: Magocsi, Paul R., *Historical Atlas of East Central Europe*, cartographic design by Geoffrey J. Matthews, Seattle: University of Washington Press, 1993. Reprinted by permission.

exile, especially the Poles and Czechoslovaks, as well as the leaders of parties that had not cooperated with the Nazis. The Soviets were able to eliminate many of these during the de-Nazification trials. And with the Soviet troops on the ground at the end of the war, noncommunist politicians stood virtually no chance of resuming office in the new regimes unless they cooperated with the Soviets.

The noncommunist Czechoslovak leader **Edvard Beneš**, for example, had kept channels of communication with Moscow open throughout the war, and after the war his country was not occupied. Instead, the Soviets used Beneš's political and moral authority to smooth the transition to the postwar regime. Beneš won the 1946 presidential election as head of a coalition government led by communists and socialists, who had been fairly strong in Czechoslovakia in the 1920s and 1930s. In contrast to other eastern European countries under Soviet domination, these elections were not outright rigged. By 1947, however, the Soviets had made it clear that Czechoslovakia was not to accept Marshall Plan aid. The electoral popularity of the Czech Communist Party quickly dropped to 20 percent. In February 1948, the Soviets helped the communists force a political coup. Beneš refused to sign the new constitution, which banned all parties save for the Communist Party, and died soon afterward.

In Romania, where the Communist Party had only about a thousand members, the Soviets played a more direct role in the communist takeover. Under the strict oversight of Soviet generals and their troops, Pauker and a handful of other Moscow protégés imprisoned, exiled, or executed all noncommunist politicians. This loyal leadership also followed Moscow's orders in taking over all newspapers and radio stations, the police, the military, and labor unions. By 1947 the communists controlled the elections and orchestrated the victory of their party. The communist takeovers in Hungary, Poland, East Germany, and Bulgaria were similar.

By 1948, the Communist Parties had outmaneuvered their political opponents everywhere in eastern Europe, often due to the presence of Soviet troops. But the victory of communist regimes was also due to the lack of viable political options and to the collapse of democracy long before the Soviet occupation. In Poland, many saw the Soviet Union as the only power interested in securing the Polish borders against future aggression from the West, and Polish communists cast themselves as patriots protecting their nation from another German invasion.

Edvard Beneš (1884–1948) President of Czechoslovakia after World War II who resented the communist takeover in 1948 and resigned.

Jakub Berman Defends the Communist Takeover in Poland

In an interview conducted by Teresa Toranska, a young Polish journalist, in the early 1980s, Jakub Berman, one of the main leaders of the Polish communist regime in the early Stalinist years, staunchly defended the legitimacy of that regime. Like Ana Pauker, Berman had spent the war in Moscow. He returned to his native Poland as part of the Soviet "liberation" of the country but was very much perceived, again like Pauker, as a foreign occupier, in part because he was Jewish. This interview reveals the huge gap between Berman and Toranska's generations in their understanding of communism.

➡ How does Berman describe the communist takeover? Do you agree with this assessment?

Berman: ➡ After all the disasters that had befallen this country, we brought in its ultimate liberation, because we finally got rid of those Germans. We wanted to get this country moving, to breathe life into it; all our hopes were tied up with the new model of Poland, which was the only chance it had had throughout its thousand years of history. We were bound to succeed, because we were right;

not in some irrational, dreamed-up way we'd plucked out of the air, but historically—history was on our side. . . .

Toranska: You're considered the cause of all the evil that has befallen this nation. . . .

Berman: That's the result of mental backwardness. . . . Two great powers arose. → We found ourselves in the Soviet sphere of influence, which was lucky for us. They had to meet with resistance on the part of a population raised on and accustomed to an entirely different set of ideas. . . . Was it plausible at any moment to imagine that Poland would be again the country it had been between the wars? . . . You have to be deaf and blind not to see that we, the Polish communists, rescued Poland from the worst. . . . → Our efforts were stifled by the extraordinary pressure of the cold war atmosphere and by a genuine threat from America. . . . She wanted to invest in Europe (hence the Marshall Plan) in order to make it dependent on her. . . . For us to break away from the Soviet Union would have meant losing the recovered territories. Poland would have become the duchy of Warsaw. . . . The world *has* changed, can't you see that? There aren't any sovereign states any more, only semisovereign ones. . . . Poland can't be uprooted from the Soviet bloc. Poland lies on the road between the Soviet Union and western Europe, and its position is clear: either/or. There are no half shades, because Poland can't float in the air."

To oversee relations with Communist Parties abroad and the new governments of the communist bloc, as communist eastern Europe came to be called, the Soviets established the **Cominform.** Under direct Soviet control, it was a ruthless instrument for purging various Communist Parties. As relations with the West worsened, Stalin became convinced that he was surrounded by enemies, that he could not trust even allies, and that his efforts to win the war had gone unappreciated. The Cominform's close control over the affairs of European Communist Parties reflected his increasingly paranoid view.

Yugoslavia's Independent Course

Yugoslavia was the only country in eastern Europe where the communist victory was due overwhelmingly to internal forces. Communist partisans had effectively struggled against the Nazi occupation and liberated Yugoslavia's territory. To be sure, the Yugoslav communists also abused their power, especially at the expense of populations who had collaborated with the Germans, such as the Croatians. But by 1947, the Yugoslav Communist League was popular and widely viewed as the legitimate political leader.

Josip Broz Tito, the leader of the communist partisans, became the undisputed leader of Yugoslavia, and he stood up against Stalin's designs for eastern Europe. Born to a Slovenian mother and Croat father, Tito embodied a Yugoslav identity devoid of ethnic nationalism. Moreover, he was a veteran communist, initially favored by Moscow. He had fought for the Reds in the Russian Civil War, was trained in Moscow afterward, and ruthlessly followed Stalin's line during World War II. Thus, he considered himself untouchable and after 1945 embarked on an independent plan to industrialize and modernize the economy. He also sought to speed up communist revolution in the Balkans by giving military aid to communists in Greece and

Cominform   Postwar international organization, directed from Moscow, that coordinated Communist Parties abroad, including those in western Europe.

Albania. At a time when all regional relations were subject to Soviet oversight, he sought closer relations with Bulgaria independently of Moscow.

Stalin perceived these moves as a direct challenge to his authority, and Tito's insistence on remaining autonomous soon incurred the wrath of the Soviet leader. Increasingly paranoid about the growing strength of his ideological and personal enemies, Stalin was fixated on punishing anyone who disobeyed. After repeated warnings, Stalin summoned Tito to Moscow in 1948. When the Yugoslav leader failed to appear, Stalin denounced him as a capitalist spy and expelled him from the Cominform. Tito stood his ground and survived, due to internal support and significant help from the West. The United States, perceiving him as an important tool in the cold war, lavished financial aid on Yugoslavia, over $600 million in 1950–1953 alone. In some ways Yugoslavia became another pawn in the superpower game for world domination.

Yet Tito also remained independent of both superpowers, challenging the notion that the world had to be divided into two camps. He became a role model for many **Third World** countries emerging from colonial rule and, after 1948, founded the **Non-Aligned Movement**. Tito saw a great opportunity among newly liberated colonial territories such as India and Indonesia to create a bloc of states independent of the Soviet and American alliances. This movement focused on increasing trade relations among members to reduce their economic dependency on the two superpowers and lobbying the UN to represent their interests, especially in situations of international crisis. For instance, as a supporter of Arab nationalism in the Middle East, Tito used nonalignment to represent the interests of the **Palestine Liberation Organization (PLO)** against Israel.

Anti-Tito Purges

While Tito purged his internal political enemies and skillfully used his position to advance his interests in the international arena, other Soviet bloc countries bore the brunt of the Tito-Stalin split. Stalin took his anger out on the eastern European regimes, as the Soviet Union helped orchestrate vast purges of the communist leadership between 1948 and 1953. Many leaders who had been in Moscow during the war and ruthlessly followed Stalin's orders in the early postwar years were now put on trial for fabricated charges of collaboration with western "imperialist" forces against their own people. In reality, these were sham trials, staged to satisfy Stalin's growing fear of imagined enemies and to reinforce the threat that the communist police state could eliminate anyone at any time, even

its highest leaders. Ostensibly aimed at all communist leaders who had been friendly to Tito before 1948, the anti-Tito campaign actually proved an opportunity for revenge among Communist Party factions, as exemplified in Romania by the purge of Ana Pauker at the hands of her rival, **Gheorghe Gheorghiu-Dej.**

The years 1948–1953 were dominated by fear and violence, similar the Great Purges in the Soviet Union but with the important difference that these purges came about through both internal rivalries and Soviet interference. For many loyalists, this interference tainted the ideals of communism. Any legitimacy the Communist Parties claimed on the basis of having fought the fascist threat and struggled for social justice now eroded. As leaders fell and were replaced by others, who in turn could fall at any time, people learned to keep their heads down in fear and to distrust party ideology. Those who rose to the top of the party hierarchy were not idealists but opportunists.

The most bitter disillusionment came in Czechoslovakia in 1951 with the **Slánský trial.** Like Pauker, Rudolf Slánský had been a ruthless communist, but now he was accused of having spied for the West and plotting against the Soviet Union. Slánský's Jewish background was used against him, and others who were purged with him were Jewish survivors of concentration camps and idealistic communists. Antisemitism had become a feature of Soviet policies in Russia and beyond. In Czechoslovakia, the communist-controlled press identified the Jewish communist leaders alternatively as Zionists and as fascist radicals, once picturing Slánský in an SS uniform. Most troubling, people generally accepted the absurd antisemitic accusations not only out of fear but also because they often shared antisemitic attitudes. By 1953,

Third World   Term coined in 1952 to identify the nations that aligned with neither the West (the First World) nor the Soviet bloc (the Second World) during the cold war.

Non-Aligned Movement   Grouping of states initiated by Josip Broz Tito in 1948 that did not wish to be caught in the East-West cold war and tried not to choose sides.

Palestine Liberation Organization (PLO)   Organization founded in 1964 by Palestinians fighting for an independent Palestinian state in territories claimed by Israel after 1948.

Gheorghe Gheorghiu-Dej (1901–1965)   Leader of communist Romania from 1948 to 1965 who carried out a ruthless campaign of collectivization in the 1950s.

Slánský trial   Anti-Titoist purge trial in 1951 against Rudolf Slánský, leader of the Czechoslovak Communist Party.

most of the top echelon of the communist leadership and government officials in the communist bloc had been removed from power, stripped of their party membership, like Pauker, or executed, like Slánský.

State-Controlled Economies

While implementing these purges, the communist regimes in eastern Europe also began economic reconstruction with the direct Soviet support. Initially, the Soviets focused on rebuilding Russia, and they did so by directly extracting resources from the communist bloc, from wheat and cattle to entire factories. The Soviets justified these seizures as war reparations. Thus, there was little economic growth in eastern Europe during the first few years of communist domination.

Moscow sent observers, usually with military personnel, to oversee economic planning in each country. Instead of imposing a Soviet-style command economy, planners required each country to specialize in certain areas so that the region would collectively achieve economic growth. This clever plan ensured that no one state could gain economic autonomy. Thus, East Germany, Poland, and Czechoslovakia, which were already more industrialized, were to focus on industrial goods, while Romania, Bulgaria, and, to some extent, Hungary were to provide raw materials and agricultural goods to support the industries and consumer needs of the other countries. The Soviets provided energy sources for industrial production in exchange for finished industrial products, at prices set by the Soviets. The Committee for Mutual Economic Assistance coordinated economic exchanges among these countries, with support from the Soviets, but in reality the Soviets controlled all the economic exchanges. For instance, the sale of Czech-produced cars in Poland was subject to Soviet approval.

This formula for economic growth had some payoffs: by 1950, some industrial products, like steel, had surpassed prewar production. But these successes came at great cost for both agricultural and consumer goods. In addition, just as in the Soviet Union, the performance of the economy was judged by production rather than its value on the open market. For this reason, the quality of goods remained inferior to goods produced in western Europe.

Although the goals of economic restructuring were everywhere the same, the processes varied, depending on the relationship of the local communist leadership with Moscow. For instance, the collectivization of agriculture was pursued aggressively in Romania but not in Poland. Polish communists viewed collectivization as potentially destabilizing, while the Romanians were more willing to apply violent means to accomplish it. As a result, by 1958 the Romanian state fully controlled agriculture, and the regime was able to persuade the Soviets to withdraw all troops. The Poles relied on Soviet troops, however, to secure their western borders, which were not recognized by West Germany until the 1960s. Without the incentive of Soviet troop withdrawal, Polish communists allowed most peasants to keep their land but controlled the sale of agricultural products instead.

Economic restructuring produced a social restructuring like that in the Soviet Union in the 1920s and 1930s. Using the Soviet model, each Communist Party attempted to create a larger urban proletariat and eliminate all class enemies, including the old middle classes and rich peasants. In addition, many religious leaders were imprisoned, and writers and artists with a "bourgeois" background were censored or imprisoned to make way for a new atheist communist spirit. Ultimately, the communist regimes in eastern Europe wanted to replicate the total social control achieved by the Soviets in their own country.

The stamp of Soviet domination was made visible also through the renaming of places after Stalin. The old Romanian city BraSov became Stalin; the highest peak in the Tatra Mountains in Poland was renamed Stalin; and one of the largest squares in Budapest took on Stalin's name as well. But no Poles, Bulgarians, and Romanians rushed to name newborns after the Soviet leader, as many in the Soviet Union had done in the first decade of communist control. Many feared Stalin's close embrace; few admired him in the way Russians had looked up to V. I. Lenin in the 1920s.

De-Stalinization

In 1953 Stalin suddenly died. Soviet leaders and the population at large were petrified: Stalin's presence had been so overwhelming that virtually nobody knew how to behave in his absence. The funeral became a performance for anticipating Stalin's successor, as he had not given the issue much thought. Thousands crowded to see the corpse, laid beside Lenin's in the mausoleum in downtown Moscow. Party members paid their respects out of loyalty and fear of the unknown future; average people were mostly curious to see the great man dead. The pallbearers and funeral speakers were viewed as the potential successors, especially **Georgy Malenkov**. He was prime minister and assumed the position of party general secretary.

Georgy Malenkov (1902–1988) Soviet communist leader who lost to Nikita Khrushchev in becoming Stalin's successor.

The Hungarian Uprising of 1956 gained mass support when it shifted from a communist conflict between elites to a national uprising of the Hungarian people against Soviet imperialism. In this photograph, a Hungarian rebel, armed with a Soviet gun, oversees the burning of books by V. I. Lenin, in a symbolic act of defiance. *(Erich Lessing/Magnum Photos)*

Within a year, Khrushchev's newspaper succeeded in tarnishing Malenkov's attempts to paint himself a reformer interested in improving living standards. Like Stalin, Khrushchev worked behind the scenes, and he orchestrated Malenkov's resignation. Between 1955 and 1956, he outmaneuvered other contenders for first place in the collective leadership of the party and in February 1956 made a dramatic move that catapulted him to the top. At the Twentieth Party Congress, Khrushchev delivered a **Secret Speech** that denounced the abuses of Stalin's era and called for a reassessment of that legacy, together with punishment for Stalin's henchmen. Declaring himself the true heir of Lenin, he placed himself in opposition to those who had supported Stalin.

The speech became a watershed in Soviet and communist history. It called for reassessment and encouraged internal criticism of the party, overturning the doctrine of infallibility established by Stalin. Khrushchev made good on this promise by freeing some political prisoners of the Stalin regime, in both the Soviet Union and eastern Europe. Some labor camps were closed down, and the **KGB**'s powers were reduced. At the same time, purges against Stalin's supporters began all over the eastern bloc.

When Khrushchev opened the pages of *Pravda* to criticisms of the party and suggestions for reform, even Poles and Hungarians began reading it, interested in the changes it outlined. But many were aware of Khrushchev's past and realized that his call for reform had limits. That he avoided explanations, but claimed the mantle of Leninist leadership, was a signal to proceed cautiously. The most important test case for **de-Stalinization** came in Hungary in 1956, where two communist factions vied for leadership. One faction, led by **Imre Nagy**, adopted Khrushchev's liberal-

In the following months, a fierce battle took place in the Politburo. Initially, the decision was to revive the principle of collective leadership. At the same time, however, two opponents began to vie for first place: Malenkov and **Nikita Khrushchev**. Khrushchev had been faithful to the party and loyal to Stalin and also cultivated an image as a simple man of the people. Born to an impoverished peasant family, he was the first among them to learn to read and write. He had fought in the Civil War and had worked hard and ruthlessly to become the leader of the Moscow party organization in 1935. At the height of the Great Purges, Khrushchev was one of Stalin's henchmen in Moscow and Ukraine, where he eliminated opponents of collectivization. By 1953, he had a forceful presence in the Politburo and controlled the main party newspaper, *Pravda*.

Nikita Khrushchev (1894–1971) Stalin's successor as leader of the Soviet Union and Soviet Communist Party who criticized Stalin's excesses and opened up a period of mild liberalization.

Secret Speech Speech by Khrushchev in 1956 to a closed party meeting that criticized Stalin and marked the beginning of his campaign to purge Stalin's supporters.

KGB Soviet Union's premier security, secret police, and intelligence agency, from 1954 to 1991.

de-Stalinization Elimination of Stalin's followers from the leadership of Soviet bloc Communist Parties after Stalin's death.

Imre Nagy (1896–1958) Hungarian communist leader who broke with Moscow in 1956 and attempted to establish an independent socialist path for Hungary.

izing attitude and gained the support of the younger generation and lower-ranking party members, while the other wanted to preserve the Stalinist controls over political and economic life. Initially Khrushchev supported the reformers, who became emboldened. In October 1956, the party conflict gave way to a popular uprising that called for the expulsion of all Soviet forces. Nagy announced Hungary's withdrawal from the Warsaw Pact. The insurgents looked with hope to the West, but the United States was unwilling to risk its stable relations with the Soviets to support the **Hungarian Uprising.** And in western Europe, while the conservative parties took the same approach as the United States, their left-wing counterparts followed the Soviet line. A brief and bloody struggle ensued, with the Soviets prevailing through violence. As Soviet tanks rolled over the border and into Budapest, guns and homemade bombs were not enough to stop them. More than half a million Hungarians were imprisoned as a result, several thousand were killed in the initial clashes and the subsequent purges, and thousands managed to flee the country. Eastern European leaders learned the hard way that de-Stalinization would have to proceed at the speed and in the direction approved by Moscow.

Yet de-Stalinization did bring improvements. As people learned to live by the new rules, the violent purges ended. The state began spending more money on housing, public health, and basic consumer goods. Workers now had paid vacation time and opportunities to travel in other countries of the communist bloc. By the beginning of the 1960s, Stalin's legacy seemed a distant memory. His name was removed from Soviet encyclopedias and his photograph taken down in public buildings; places named Stalin were renamed once again. Table 28.2 summarizes key events in Eastern Europe during the postwar period.

Superpower Conflicts and Colonial Independence Movements, 1945–1968

↓ What role did the American-Soviet conflict play in the colonial struggles for independence?
↓ What were the consequences of the liberation movements?

Europe's transformation into the two opposing camps of the cold war coincided with a revolution in the European colonies, most of which gained independence in the two decades after World War II. Yet the degree of actual political and economic autonomy of these postcolonial states varied greatly. Many continued to

Table 28.2

Eastern Europe

1947	Communist takeover in Czechoslovakia
1948	Tito expelled from Cominform; beginning of purges
1948–1949	Berlin blockade
1949	Formation of CMEA
1951	Slánský trial
1953	Stalin dies; Khrushchev comes to power
1955	Warsaw Pact formed
1956	Khrushchev's Secret Speech; Hungarian uprising
1958	Soviet troops withdrawn from Romania
1961	Berlin Wall constructed
1964	Brezhnev comes to power
1968	Prague Spring and Soviet suppression

depend heavily on Europe, now with support from the Americans as well, while others opted to embrace the Soviet side of the cold war. Yet some states chose a third way, nonalignment. Overall, the East-West divide became replicated all over the postcolonial world, with the United States and the Soviet Union coming into conflict in Southeast Asia, the Middle East, and Africa.

Superpower Confrontations

In the 1950s, the United States and Soviet Union became embroiled in Korea in their first direct military confrontation of the cold war. A postwar settlement had divided the former Japanese territory into a communist Democratic People's Republic in the north and the Republic of Korea in the south. What started as a war between the two in 1950 quickly became internationalized in the bipolar world of the cold war. After the Soviets sent military support to the North, the Americans went before the UN Security Council to request a military intervention on behalf of the South. The Security Council agreed, primarily because the Soviets, boycotting the UN at the time, were not present to veto the decision. The United States thus sent in troops under the guise of South Korean requests

Hungarian Uprising   Nationwide uprising against the Soviet occupation and communist regime in 1956 that was violently crushed by the Soviets.

The Korean War, the first cold war military confrontation, resulted in a stalemate that continues today. It was also the first combat action in which U.S. troops were officially integrated. *(Corbis)*

for help and UN endorsement. In reality, the **Korean War** was a heated conflict unfolding between the Soviets' pursuit of a zone of influence in Korea and the Americans' implementation of the Truman Doctrine to aid those fighting the spread of communism. The new Chinese communist regime also became involved, sending military aid to the North Koreans. A truce in 1953 left Korea divided, with families split across the border and unable to communicate. The Soviets and Chinese celebrated a communist victory, while the United States boasted success in stopping the spread of communism.

Yet the Korean War was an abysmal failure. It brought the two superpowers into a military conflict that left nothing resolved; troops remain poised at the border today. The outcome of this conflict for the world scene was twofold: it established that the two superpowers were willing to use military power in their contest for world domination, and it showed the great military and human costs of such actions. If Korea could be a setting for war among the superpowers, then all political leaders of liberation movements in colonial territories had to think carefully about the choices they made.

In the following decade, the contest between the Soviets and the Americans circled the globe and escalated to outer space. Under President Dwight Eisen-

hower, the United States expanded its military alliances and placed nuclear missiles around the world, from France to Pakistan and the Philippines. The Soviets also built a missile arsenal. In 1957 they launched *Sputnik 1,* the first space satellite and a scientific achievement that placed them ahead of the Americans in the space race.

The Soviets attempted to parlay this success by threatening to hand over control of access to West Berlin to the East Germans, hoping to force the Americans out of the city and ending the flow of Germans from East to West. After a three-year standoff, in 1961 East Germany put up the **Berlin Wall,** dividing the city. There was little the Americans could do about it. The wall became a powerful symbol of what the cold war meant for average people.

Korean War (1950–1953) Military conflict between communist-backed North Korea and United States–supported South Korea.

Sputnik 1 Soviet satellite that in 1957 was the first to be launched into earth orbit and began the Soviet-American space race.

Berlin Wall Wall built through Berlin by East Germany in 1961 to prevent its citizens from escaping into West Germany.

In June 1963, U.S. President John F. Kennedy stood on a platform above the Berlin Wall, addressing 12,000 West Berliners and a few East Berliners silently watching on the other side of the wall. Speaking on the themes of freedom and citizenship, he asserted, "Ich bin ein Berliner" (I am a Berliner). By identifying with both West and East Berliners, Kennedy signaled U.S. commitment to the reunification of the country under the West German democracy. *(Corbis)*

The most dangerous confrontation of the Soviets and Americans came in 1962, during the **Cuban Missile Crisis.** After **Fidel Castro** came to power in Cuba in 1959, he was courted by both the Americans and the Soviets. For the United States, Cuba had great economic and strategic interest because of its proximity. For the Soviets, Cuba could be an outpost for nuclear missiles, to counter the American bases in Turkey and Pakistan. After a failed American attempt to depose Castro in 1961, the Soviets offered to bolster the Cuban defenses by bringing in nuclear weapons. For a few days in October 1962, President John F. Kennedy and Khrushchev came close to nuclear war. Each leader called on the other to back down, while both were in fact mobilizing out of fear that the other would strike. Then, when the Americans promised not to invade Cuba and to withdraw their missiles from Turkey, the Soviets removed the missiles from Cuba. The crisis made both powers aware of the need for constant communication.

Colonial Independence Movements

While American and Soviet economic and military power expanded, most European countries with colonies realized that their reduced political, military, and economic resources made it impossible for them to maintain control over vast territories outside of Europe. In Britain, the Labour Party favored liberating the colonies as a matter of ideology and pragmatic consideration. The British led **decolonization** by offering colonies independence and a new, autonomous relationship with Great Britain through the **Commonwealth of Nations,** which focused on economic relations. India was a relatively successful model. Given the large population and great variety of traditions and cultures that existed on the subcontinent, the Indian nationalist movements were remarkably united in their negotiations with the British. The leadership of Mohandas Gandhi gave these movements cohesion and a strategy of peaceful resistance to colonial rule. His protégé **Jawaharlal Nehru** became the first prime minister of independent India. Both resisted

Cuban Missile Crisis Standoff between the United States and the Soviet Union in 1962 over Soviet equipping of Cuba with nuclear missiles.

Fidel Castro (1926–) Leader of Cuban communist revolution in 1956 and president of Cuba since 1959.

decolonization Process by which European imperialist powers moved to withdraw from colonial holdings and ready colonies for independence.

Commonwealth of Nations Association of independent states, originally former British colonies, that was created in 1947 to enhance economic and cultural cooperation.

Jawaharlal Nehru (1889–1964) Leading figure of the Indian independence movement who became the first prime minister of India in 1947.

MAP 28.3   Decolonization Movements, 1945–1968 Between 1945 and 1968 most European colonies gained independence. For some, like Ghana, the process was peaceful. Others, like Vietnam, fought bloody wars. The United States and the Soviet Union became involved in these struggles as the new world power brokers.

the strategy of outright military conflict over India's borders, a serious threat as India was culturally and ethnically divided, most importantly between Hindus and Muslims. In 1947, British India devolved into Muslim-dominated Pakistan and Hindu-dominated India. Border conflicts between the two countries continue today.

The British pursued a similar disengagement policy in their African colonies but proceeded more gradually, as these colonies had not yet developed an indigenous intellectual and economic elite like that in South Asia. In addition, as the white settlers in these African territories were far more numerous than those in Asia and unwilling to give up their homes, the process of decolonization was more contentious and violent. In West Africa, Ghana, and Nigeria were the first to gain independence peacefully. By contrast, a great deal more conflict occurred in Kenya, where white settlers wished to retain their economic privileges after independence, by force if necessary, while indigenous radical groups such as the **Mau Mau** fought for a radical break from the British. After five years of violence, the British won the war but lost the colony. Having become financially overextended, the British pulled out their troops. Kenya became independent in 1963.

The French wanted to preserve greater control over colonies in Africa and Asia and chose to repress independence movements. In Asia, de Gaulle attempted to persuade Vietnam to remain part of the French Union. This arrangement allowed colonial territories to gain more autonomy and become more democratic through enfranchisement of the local population. But administration, education, and commerce would remain heavily dominated by French-educated and -speaking elites.

But the postwar Vietnamese political factions proved impossible to control. The communists were a growing pro-independence group that secured help from the new regime in China. In 1954, the communist leader Ho Chi Minh defeated the French, despite massive financial help from the United States. Vietnam was divided between the communist-controlled north and the western-supported south. The loss of Vietnam produced a political crisis in France that eventually brought colonial rule to an end.

Yet Vietnam remained an important battleground in the cold war. In the early 1960s, the United States sent military advisers and then troops into South Vietnam to forestall what President Lyndon Johnson saw as the threat of communist revolution everywhere in Asia. The **Vietnam War** became increasingly brutal but did not bring any resolution. In 1973, under pressure from the American public, who watched the atrocities committed by both sides every day on tele-

vision, President Richard Nixon reached a truce with North Vietnam and pulled out.

The French had troubles with their overseas territories in Africa as well, with the costliest conflict in Algeria. More than 1 million European settlers had lived there for generations, and the territory had been formally integrated into France as an administrative region. Therefore, when a revolt broke out in 1954, shortly after the humiliating defeat in Vietnam, the French felt a threat to the homeland, and repression of the rebels became a core political issue. Yet the Muslim rebels were committed to fighting for independence from French rule. The **Algerian War** divided France both at home and in North Africa, bringing down the Fourth Republic in 1958. In this civil war, some white settlers and European French citizens sided with the pro-independence insurgents, while some of the North African indigenous populations sided with the French colonial administration. By and large, however, the division was racial—whites against nonwhites—and the abuses committed during the war only reinforced racism in French society. De Gaulle was able to save the state from the brink of collapse in 1958 through a new constitution that strengthened the power of the president and military establishment against the parliament. Yet he eventually gave up Algeria in 1962.

The rest of French Africa, where the French were less invested politically and culturally and the number of European settlers smaller, gained independence with less strife. After Algeria, the French administration was eager to grant independence to the rest of its colonies. Yet, as the level of indigenous economic development remained low, these countries continued in their economic dependence on France.

While disengagement and decolonization dominated the political fate of former colonies in Asia and Africa, the Middle East became a new battleground for the two superpowers, primarily because of its tremendous oil resources. The United States gradually

Mau Mau   (in Kikuyu, "burning spear") Pro-independence Kenyan rebels who advocated violent methods against white settlers in order to reclaim land and political power for indigenous Africans.

Vietnam War   (1959–1975) Successful effort by the communist North Vietnamese to take over South Vietnam, which was supported by the Americans and the French.

Algerian War   (1954–1962) Civil war in which Algerian nationalists eventually defeated the French colonial administration and established an independent state.

These three leaders of the nonaligned movement—Egypt's Gamal Abdel Nasser, Yugoslavia's Josip Broz Tito, and India's Jawaharlal Nehru—saw themselves as the advocates of independence for their nations and critics of imperialist oppression. Inside their states, however, they often appeared more like the autocratic rulers with a taste for luxury rather than the democratic leaders of their people. *(Hulton Archives/ Getty Images)*

replaced the British in the area, trying to broker between the newly established state of Israel and its hostile Arab neighbors while competing with the Soviet Union for alliances with oil-rich Arab leaders.

The development of Arab nationalism was accelerated by the creation of Israel and the failure of the United Nations to create a Palestinian Arab state. On the one hand, Israel came to define itself and be viewed increasingly as a promoter of progressive ideas and of western civilization. After 1967, it was sturdily on the side of American interests in the area. On the other hand, some Arab populations in Palestine and the rest of the Middle East began to look toward the Soviet Union as a better broker for their interests. After 1964, when the PLO established itself as the foremost leader in the Palestinian struggle for statehood, the organization was quickly recognized by and sought the material support of the Soviet Union and other communist states, such as Yugoslavia.

Yet neither communism nor capitalism was the choice of the political leaders of the Middle East. Instead, the region produced a blend of Arab nationalism with strong Muslim influences. Many territories remained kingdoms, while postcolonial states established authoritarian governments with only a thin veneer of parliamentary life. Political institutions in these countries often resembled premodern theocracies, and their oil resources brought great wealth to ruling elites.

States like Saudi Arabia could display the trappings of material civilization in step with Europe while its justice system and suppression of women remained violent. Until the 1970s, neither superpower intervened directly in the internal ideological preferences of these states so long as they could benefit from access to the region's oil resources.

The Nonaligned Movement

By the late 1960s, European colonial rule had come to an end almost everywhere. This process was uneven and very costly in some instances, and it brought about radical change in international relations. The UN General Assembly became dominated numerically by relatively poor postcolonial states. By 1980, the nonaligned movement grew from 25 to 117, becoming the largest bloc in the UN and acting forcefully as a faction when important matters came to a vote. Thus, the nonaligned bloc was able to direct financial assistance to underdeveloped areas, such as South Asia and Africa. This bloc regarded Europe sometimes positively, as an important patron in cultural and economic relations, and at other times with bitterness, as the seat of imperialist oppression. Almost half of the presidents of the assembly have come from postcolonial states of the nonaligned bloc.

Postcolonial regions became a new arena for superpower struggle. The Soviets invested heavily in economic and educational exchanges with the newly independent African states, accompanied by a heavy dose of communist ideology. African rulers often found the Soviet propaganda about western imperialism appealing. By contrast, the United States backed regimes that supported its economic interests. American oil investments in the Persian Gulf, for example, prompted U.S. support for an authoritarian monarchy in Iran that replaced the nationalist republican independence movement.

States such as Indonesia, Egypt, and India maintained more distance from the two superpowers. One important moment in this process was the **Suez Canal Crisis.** In 1956, during the Hungarian Uprising, Egyptian leader **Gamal Abdel Nasser** nationalized the canal. With encouragement from the Soviets, the Egyptians hoped to secure control over this strategic body of water that had been under French, British, and more recently American control. But Khrushchev did not send direct military aid. Thus, in winning the conflict, Nasser established an independence position, able to broker between the superpowers without a direct commitment to either side. Like Tito before him, Nasser also secured hefty financial support for Egypt from both superpowers.

Cultural Developments and Social Protest

↓ Why was there a moral and spiritual crisis in the 1950s?
↓ What were the generational divides behind the revolt of the 1960s?

In the 1950s and 1960s, European culture took many new turns, especially as the very meaning of being European was questioned and redefined. Although a consensus seemed to develop in the 1950s about European identity and culture, a new generation of intellectuals and rebels in the 1960s helped shake it up. Now Europe became divided between old and young, between conformist and antiestablishment factions.

Consumption and Conformity

After the war, western Europeans sought to forget the past, work hard, and acquire material goods. Instead of participating in mass political movements, they sought recognition for individual achievements. Initially success measured by material goods meant simply having a job, a place to live, and food on the table. But as the economic miracle began to make consumer goods more affordable, the culture of consumption

took off. At first, people wanted refrigerators, radios, and comfortable furniture. By the 1960s, they wanted a television, a car, and the leisure activities that a car made possible.

The availability of inexpensive consumer goods was closely connected to technological advances made during and after the war. Plastics made everything cheaper—and also created an unprecedented level of dependency on oil. As consumer goods proliferated, their very availability induced people to want to have more of what other people had. The desire to conform increased as the possibility for purchasing the same goods grew. This kind of social pressure was not new, but it had never before been expressed on a massive scale that defied social class divisions. Ironically, while struggling to be individually successful, people now proclaimed their status by fitting in; conformity and anonymity gave a sense of security. This reaction seemed natural after the wartime years, when many had lived the experience of being singled out in painful ways.

Nothing parallel to consumer culture developed in eastern Europe, but the new communist regimes did place great emphasis on conformity. This conformity was, however, imposed without mercy from above and enforced by manipulating fear. Behavior regarded as deviant was harshly punished, with imprisonment or exile to labor camps. Priests and religious believers were often singled out. Some theological institutes were closed. All denominations were persecuted, but not to the same extent. For instance, members of the Greek Catholic Church, made illegal in Romania in 1948, were harshly punished for any public religious displays, while members of the Roman Catholic Church in the same country were allowed to continue their religious practices in limited ways.

Under the pressure for conformity to the strict party line, people quickly learned to live double lives. A member of an illegal faith might openly abandon his or her religious allegiance but continue religious practice in hiding. Because the communist regimes could not police a person's every action, most eastern Europeans became skilled at shifting between public and hidden identities.

By the beginning of the 1960s, the communist regimes were also using the mass media to enhance

Suez Canal Crisis Military attack on Egypt by Britain, France, and Israel in 1956 after Egypt seized the Suez Canal from British administration.

Gamal Abdel Nasser (1918–1970) President of Egypt from 1956 to 1970 who nationalized the Suez Canal.

conformity and social stability. Radio and television programs, films, and magazines—some glossy and appealingly designed—became effective communist propaganda machines. Starved for information and entertainment, people in eastern Europe often embraced these propaganda products as a form of relaxation and escape.

Moral and Spiritual Crisis

As western European culture became more conformist and consumer oriented, it also became increasingly secular and even unconcerned with questions of morality and spirituality. For many, the war and the Holocaust had unraveled the very concept of civilization. In the first decade after the war, a few intellectuals and spiritual leaders attempted to offer answers to the deep moral questions opened up by the wartime violence, corruption, and utter degradation of the human condition. Yet these answers proved unsatisfactory to the following generation, who challenged the solutions offered by their predecessors.

Intellectuals such as **Albert Camus** and **Jean-Paul Sartre** tried to claim social relevance for literature through personal engagement against injustice. In the Algerian War, these writers took opposite sides— Sartre for postcolonial independence, Camus for retention of links with France. Sartre's position derived from his ideological commitment to communism, while Camus arrived at his stance through direct experience in his native Algeria. Their quarrel became famous in intellectual circles, but, powerful as they were, their writings offered no moral guidance or satisfactory answers to their readers. In fact, it was Camus' gradual distancing from the ideological commitment of Sartre that resonated most strongly. The condition of the postwar generation was one of moral alienation.

This context provided some important opportunities for the Catholic and Protestant churches in western Europe to regain spiritual relevance. But it was not the churches that grew. Instead, it was the Christian Democratic political parties that grew, especially in France, Germany, and Italy and especially when they demonstrated a concern for social justice and progressive measures relating to workers' rights and social welfare. But these parties also represented a social and cultural conservatism that had little appeal to the generation born after the war, which seemed detached from the challenges of the postwar years and unable to find moral and spiritual guidance either in religious parties or in religion itself.

In response to this moral crisis, Pope **John XXIII** attempted to provide a new direction for Catholicism.

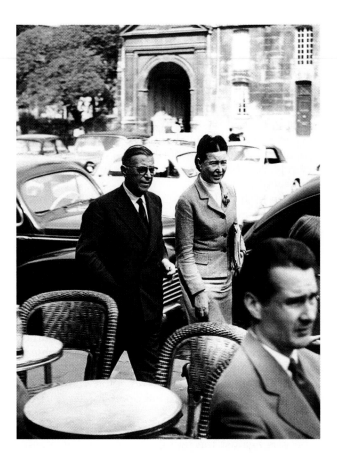

Jean Paul Sartre and Simone de Beauvoir were the most celebrated couple in postwar France—intellectuals committed to political and social causes. Yet de Beauvoir remained for a long time in the shadow of Sartre, her feminism viewed as secondary to his existential philosophy. *(RDA/Hulton Archive/ Getty Images)*

At the **Second Vatican Council**, he presented a broad agenda for changes in all areas of the church's organization and social engagement while attempting to preserve its fundamental mission. Decisions at this

Albert Camus   (1913–1960) Algerian-born French writer and philosopher who opposed Algerian independence and was awarded the Nobel Prize in Literature in 1957.

Jean Paul Sartre   (1905–1980) Most famous French philosopher of the twentieth century, an open communist sympathizer.

John XXIII   (r. 1958–1962) Reformist pope who spearheaded changes in language use and liturgical rituals and initiated the Second Vatican Council.

Second Vatican Council   Meeting of cardinals and bishops of the Roman Catholic Church between 1962 and 1965 to promote church reform.

The English rock band the Who turned youthful rebellion into performance art. In addition to playing well-crafted compositions with great style, Pete Townshend (guitar) and Keith Moon (drums) also took to smashing their instruments on stage at the end of performances. (*Carter Tomassi*)

series of meetings, from 1962 to 1965, allowed churches to use local languages, gave reformist bishops more autonomy, and permitted greater involvement in social activism—for instance, on behalf of the poor in Latin America.

If the primary struggle of churches in western Europe was against the moral and spiritual alienation of the population at large, in the communist bloc, churches and religious believers fought for their very survival in the face of political persecution. The communist regimes tolerated and gradually used some churches both to appease religious believers and to inform on them with the help of corrupt priests. In other instances, however, religious institutions became the seat of spiritual survival against communism. In Poland, the Catholic Church preserved a degree of integrity and moral authority unparalleled anywhere else in eastern Europe. In fact, religiosity among Poles grew, and many gravitated to the church as the one institution uncorrupted by communism. Protestant denominations also offered a secure and morally uplifting refuge. But most eastern Europeans became estranged from religious experience through the aggressive antireligious campaigns of the communist regimes.

Youth and the Counterculture

By the mid-1960s, a new postwar generation was questioning the direction of prosperity and security in western Europe and rejecting the values and lifestyles of their elders. The clash of generations arose from several factors. First, while the direct experience of deprivation and death made the prewar generation overly preoccupied with material comforts, abundance made the postwar generation indifferent to the value of material goods. Those born after 1945 were marked by the culture of conformity and consumption in two ways: on the one hand, they fully enjoyed the fruits of the economic miracle, the availability of cheap material goods, books, records, and other forms of entertainment and information; on the other hand, they wanted more meaning in their lives than the satisfactions their parents found in material goods. They deplored the conformity and cultural boredom of their elders and wanted to engage in meaningful choices and spread their comforts among others less fortunate. Finally, the postwar generation had much greater access to college education.

A new pop culture best expressed the mood of this new generation. Rock and roll developed first in America, but by the mid-1960s, European bands like the Beatles and the Who had taken the new musical form and made it theirs: "Things they do look awful cold / Hope I die before I get old / Talkin' bout my generation."[1] Rock music was rebellious and appealing precisely because it was loud and rough. Young people loved it as much as their parents hated it. Some performers brought a broader political and social content to their lyrics. Bob Dylan, the most powerful voice of the postwar generation, wrote verses

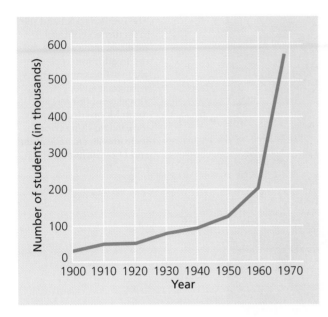

FIGURE 28.2 **Enrollment Figures for French Universities from 1900–1968** After World War II western Europe was fundamentally changed by the great growth in college attendance. The beneficiaries of this growth were especially the poor and women. Source: Wilkinson, James D.; Huges, H. Stuart, *Contemporary Europe: A History,* 9th Edition, © 1998, pp. 425. Reprinted by permission of Pearson Education, Inc., Upper Saddle River, NJ.

that resonated with young people all over western Europe: "I learned to hate the Russians /all through my whole life / If another war comes / it's them we must fight /... with God on my side." [2]

In film, New Wave cinema merged a social and political critique with a harsh style that echoed the loudness of rock music. The films of French director **Jean-Luc Goddard** confronted materialism, sexuality, and political violence. He and other film makers broke free of the conventions and conservative aesthetics of their predecessors. Film, they contended, should not be an escape. It should depict life, and life was neither heroic nor even coherent, but full of violence, breakdown, and loss.

One central unifying element of this new generation was its unprecedented access to education. In France, for instance, university enrollment went up by almost 200 percent in the 1960s, especially among women and working-class people. This dramatic change forced important questions about the quality of education and the political agenda of its content. In the ensuing battles over democratizing university education, both students and teachers became increasingly radical-

ized and involved in political protest, giving rise to a new wave of left-wing activists and politicians.

1968

These generational tensions came to a head in the extraordinary year 1968. In an explosive set of coincidences, the world seemed headed toward a revolution. In the United States, the charismatic civil rights leader **Martin Luther King Jr.** was assassinated. His murder signaled the end of the peaceful civil rights movement and the beginning of more belligerent African American protests. At the same time, protests against the Vietnam War were taking a more radical form. On campuses across America, originally peaceful marches often ended as violent clashes with the police. Television news reports showing long-haired hippies being clobbered by steel-helmeted police made this generational clash real for everyone. To some, the young appeared unruly, self-indulgent, and irresponsible. To others, they were heroic for shaking up the political establishment and addressing large issues such as racism, sexism, postcolonial imperialism, and naked military aggression.

A similar style of protest emerged in Europe, as student antiwar and anticolonial protests erupted from London to Berlin. But the most powerful student movement was centered in Paris, where, in May 1968, under the inspired leadership of **Daniel Cohn-Bendit**, it made common cause with the French workers. Born in the year the war ended Cohn-Bendit embodied many of the characteristics of his generation. He came from a German Jewish family that, having fled the Nazis during the war, had returned to West Germany afterward. His background made him painfully aware of the cost of postwar western European reconstruction—the abandonment of moral imperatives for the sake of material well-being. In the impassioned works of Marxist revolutionaries, Cohn-Bendit found inspiration for challenging all that was accepted around him and struggling for social justice in ways that the tradi-

Jean-Luc Goddard (1930–) Prominent French New Wave filmmaker.

Martin Luther King Jr. (1929–1968) African American Baptist minister and nonviolent leader of the American civil rights movement in the 1960s.

Daniel Cohn-Bendit (1945–) German-born charismatic left-wing leader of the student protests in France in May 1968.

Lyrics from Bob Dylan, "With God on Our Side," from *Times They Are A-Changin'*, Columbia Records, New York, 1964. Reprinted by permission of Bob Dylan Music Company, Special Rider Music Company.

While Czech students protested Soviet oppression in Prague and American students protested the Vietnam War on college campuses, in May 1968 French students took to the streets to support a general strike that brought the country to a standstill and forced politicians of the older generation to pay attention to the students' calls for change. *(Bruno Barbey/Magnum Photos)*

tional left seemed to have abandoned. The national strike Cohn-Bendit led put France on hold for almost a month and helped bring down de Gaulle. Similar student protests across Europe evidenced the reengagement of youth in politics, in support of the anticolonial struggle, social justice, the guerrilla fighters in Algeria and Vietnam, and communist leaders such as Mao in China.

Yet the most important political challenge of 1968 came from inside the communist bloc, in Prague. Until the late 1960s, the Czechoslovaks had avoided de-Stalinization because of their success in industrial production. As long as their industrial production worked to the benefit of the Soviet Union, Khrushchev left the Czechoslovaks alone. By the early 1960s, however, the productivity of the Czechoslovak economy was decreasing, and growing numbers of party members called for economic, social, and cultural reforms. **Alexander Dubček**, a reformer who had spent the wartime years fighting in the anti-Nazi resistance, convinced the Soviets, responding to pressure from dissidents, to allow him to experiment with liberalizing reforms. For a few brief months during the **Prague Spring**, Dubček attempted to create "socialism with a human face"—abolishing censorship of the press, allowing criticism of the communist leadership, and reviving workers' councils. He tried to combine

social policies that would benefit all citizens with policies that would accelerate economic growth. He even pardoned political prisoners, including religious believers, who had been harshly persecuted in the 1950s.

The reforms in Czechoslovakia proved too radical for the Soviets, who recalled the 1956 Hungarian Uprising, even though the Czechoslovak movement proposed not to end communist rule but to reform it. In August 1968, **Leonid Brezhnev** sent tanks into Czechoslovakia to wipe out all opposition. All Warsaw Pact members save Romania also sent in troops. The military intervention was out of proportion, given the fact that Czechoslovak reformers did not put up armed resistance, and the West came to associate the communist leadership of eastern Europe with this crude

Alexander Dubček   (1921–1992) Leader of the Czechoslovak Communist Party during the Prague Spring who initiated liberalizing reforms but was forcibly removed from power.

Prague Spring   Short-lived period of liberalization in Czechoslovakia in 1968 that was violently crushed by the Soviets.

Leonid Brezhnev   (1906–1982) Soviet leader between 1964 and 1983 who oversaw the reversal of the liberalization efforts of the Khrushchev regime.

military response. The crushing of the Prague Spring brought to a tragic end the era of de-Stalinization and reform. Over the next two decades, while the western European youthful protesters became influential in politics, culture, technology, and commerce, their counterparts in eastern Europe spent years in jail or learned not to challenge the system. A lucky few escaped into the West.

Summary

Review Questions

↑ How did the cold war affect international security?

↑ What were the costs of postwar reconstruction in western versus eastern Europe?

↑ How did the new polarization of the world into two superpower-dominated camps and anticolonial independence movements affect Europeans' identity?

World War II transformed Europe from the most powerful seat of democratic tradition, economic development, and cultural progress into a pawn in the struggle between the two superpowers of the cold war—the United States and the Soviet Union. In the process, Europe became divided into two camps: the capitalist West, which became a place for rebuilding democracy, and the communist East, where dictatorial regimes came to power under Soviet control. Western European states embarked on creating social stability through extensive and unprecedented welfare measures.

In the two decades after the war, both sides of this divide tried to legitimate themselves as the "true" Europeans—the West by rebuilding democratic regimes, the East by fighting against capitalist imperialism. Even as the new regimes made important attempts to link themselves to prewar traditions, new multinational organizations like the UN, NATO, and the Warsaw Pact marked an entirely new international order in which European states were often relegated to the sidelines in the contest between the Soviet Union and the United States.

The relationship between Europe and its colonies also changed dramatically, as European states shed their nineteenth-century concerns with empire building. But Europe remained tied culturally, economically, and politically to the postcolonial world. By 1968, however, liberation movements in places like Algeria and Vietnam were also becoming a powerful influence in the opposition movements in Europe.

The experience of the war had a profound impact on Europeans' views of their culture and European identity. The continent that had fostered Christianity and the Enlightenment had also produced hateful mass movements, atrocities, and genocide. Yet few political leaders were prepared to deal with these moral dilemmas in the first postwar decades, and the wartime generation focused instead on hard work. It was the next generation of better-educated, more diverse, and less traumatized Europeans who forced a new period of social and political engagement, moral responsibility, and self-sacrifice. The 1968 student protests brought this generational conflict to a head and prompted Europeans East and West to look back at their past as well as toward their goals for European development in the future.

← Thinking Back, Thinking Ahead →

How were questions of international security confronted and resolved by Europeans in 1918, 1945, and 1968?

ECHO

The Volkswagen Transporter

Today's SUV (sport-utility vehicle), the mark of middle-class America, has as its ancestor a little box on wheels thought up in 1947 by a Dutch car importer, Ben Pon. At that time, the British controlled the Volkswagen (VW) factory in Wolfsburg, which had been developed under Adolf Hitler to produce affordable vehicles for all Germans. Pon met with British authorities to suggest building a vehicle that would, like the original Volkswagen ("people's car") Beetle, be small and affordable, yet more useful for hauling both people and goods. German manufacturers liked the idea and created the first prototype by 1949. The minibus or Transporter, as this hybrid vehicle came to be known, became an instant success, and, though modest by today's standards, it revolutionized transportation. By 1961, more than 1 million had been sold. Minibuses became a fixture all over Europe, even behind the Iron Curtain, because of their great versatility, low price, and great gas mileage. For a small-business owner, the bus could be both workplace and vacation vehicle. It could be easily outfitted with sleeping and eating quarters, becoming the first affordable, compact camper to hit the European market. In fact, the minibus became more than a vehicle: it represented a lifestyle, providing a new generation with a mobility, freedom, and interconnectedness that contrasted with what they saw as the dull conservatism of their parents.

By the late 1960s, traveling bands of young people could be seen driving minibuses on highways in Europe and the United States and parked at music festivals, antiwar protests, and vacation spots. The minibus became the symbol of the "flower power" generation and continues to be so today. Transporters still travel the roads of Europe, especially in postcommunist countries, and in the United States they show up at rainbow gatherings and other Dead Head events. But the sons and daughters of the "flower children" rebelled against their parents by embracing materialism again and turning to bigger, more powerful descendants of the minibus—the minivan, the SUV, and more recently the Hummer—for hauling kids and their gear to and from programmed activities.

Suggested Readings

Caute, David. *The Year of the Barricades: A Journey Through 1968.* New York: HarperCollins, 1990. A survey of international political developments in 1968, including the antiwar and civil rights movements.

Hogan, Michael J. *The Marshall Plan: America, Britain, and the Reconstruction of Western Europe, 1947–1952.* New York: Cambridge University Press, 2005. An analysis of how the Marshall Plan was more than an effort by American officials to refashion western Europe into a smaller version of the U.S. capitalist economy.

Mahoney, Daniel J. *De Gaulle: Statesmanship, Grandeur, and Modern Democracy.* New Brunswick, N.J.: Transaction Publishers, 2000. A comprehensive study of the thought and actions of Charles de Gaulle.

Naimark, Norman. *Fires of Hatred: Ethnic Cleansing in Twentieth-Century Europe.* Cambridge, Mass.: Harvard University Press, 2002. An insightful history of ethnic cleansing and its relationship to genocide and population transfer in the violent twentieth century.

Painter, David. *The Cold War: An International History.* New York: Routledge, 1999. A compact international study that provides a fresh perspective on the cold war.

Rothschild, Joseph, and Nancy M. Wingfield. *Return to Diversity: A Political History of East Central Europe Since World War II.* New York: Oxford University Press, 1999. A comprehensive political history of eastern Europe.

Springhall, John. *Decolonization Since 1945: The Collapse of European Overseas Empires.* New York: Palgrave Macmillan, 2003. A study that focuses on each major European overseas colony.

Websites

Documents and scholarly analyses on the development of the cold war in the military field, **The Parallel History Project on Cooperative Security,** at www.isn.ethz.ch/php

A growing archive of documents pertaining to the cold war, **Cold War International History Project,** at wwics.si.edu/index.cfm?topic_id=1409&fuseaction=topics.home

An archive of documents related to the history of European integration from 1930 until today, **EU History,** at www.eu-history.leidenuniv.nl/index.php3?m=1&c=3&garb=0.3437423344549452&session

CHAPTER 29

Lifting the Iron Curtain, 1969–1991

1500 B.C.E.	1000 B.C.E.	500 B.C.E.	1 B.C.E./1 C.E.

1972
West Germany recognizes East German border
Antiballistic Missile Treaty is signed

1968
Prague Spring
is crushed

1973
Arab oil embargo
begins

1966	1968	1970	1972	1974	1976	1978

From European Community to European Union

In the 1970s and 1980s, the European Community became a source for European integration in economic matters and a springboard for cultural change toward a shared European identity that stood for democratic values, greater tolerance, and decreased nationalist tensions. How does the change in the map of the Common Market suggest changes in the actions and sense of identity of the European Community?

Expansion of European Community

- Original members, 1967
- New members, 1973
- New member, 1981
- New member, 1986
- Members of CMEA

FINLAND

NORWAY

SWEDEN

Oslo Helsinki

Stockholm

SCOTLAND

Leningrad

RUSSIA

ESTONIA

Moscow

NORTHERN IRELAND

North Sea

DENMARK

Copenhagen

Riga LATVIA

LITHUANIA

IRELAND

Dublin

GREAT BRITAIN

WALES

London

NETHERLANDS

The Hague

Amsterdam

Hamburg

Gdansk

Minsk

BELARUSSIA

Lake Ladoga

Volga

S O V I E T   U N I O N

KAZAKHSTAN

ATLANTIC OCEAN

Brussels

BELGIUM

Berlin

GERMANY

POLAND

Warsaw

Bonn

Paris

LUX.

Luxembourg

Prague

Kiev

Kharkov

UKRAINE

Volga

FRANCE

Loire

Seine

Rhine

CZECHOSLOVAKIA

MOLDOVA

Dnieper

Munich

LIECH.

Vienna

Budapest

Bern

SWITZ.

Geneva

AUSTRIA

HUNGARY

ROMANIA

Crimea

Yalta

GEORGIA

Milan

Po

ANDORRA

Marseilles

MONACO

SAN MARINO

Belgrade

Bucharest

Black Sea

AZERBAIJAN

ARMENIA

Lisbon

Madrid

Tagus

Barcelona

Corsica (Fr.)

ITALY

YUGOSLAVIA

BULGARIA

Sofia

SPAIN

Balearic Islands (Sp.)

Sardinia (It.)

Rome

VATICAN CITY

Naples

ALBANIA

Tiranë

Istanbul

Ankara

TURKEY

Gibraltar (U.K.)

Mediterranean Sea

MALTA

GREECE

Athens

Crete (Gr.)

Nicosia

CYPRUS

SYRIA

IRAQ

ALGERIA

LEBANON

TUNISIA

0   250   500 Km.

0   250   500 Mi.

ISRAEL

JORDAN

LYBIA

EGYPT

500 C.E.   1000 C.E.   1500 C.E.   2000 C.E.

1979
Thatcher becomes British prime minister

1980
Polish Solidarity movement begins

1983
First Green Party member is elected to West German parliament

1985
Gorbachev becomes leader of Soviet Union

1989
Berlin Wall falls

1991
Soviet Union collapses

1980   1982   1984   1986   1988   1990   1992

Choic Choice Choice

Václav Havel

In the 1980s, Václav Havel became the face of peaceful anticommunist dissent in eastern Europe. His plays, critical of communism, had already been staged abroad, but he became renowned for his role in the Charter 77 human rights petition, written in Czechoslovakia in 1977, protesting abuses by the communist regime against members of a rock band. In 1989, Havel was elected the first president of postcommunist Czechoslovakia. (AP/Wide World Photos)

Václav Havel Chooses Dissent

To live in truth: this is the deceptively simple choice Václav Havel, the first president of postcommunist Czechoslovakia, made most of his life. In a brave letter to the communist leadership, he wrote: "Even a purely moral act that has no hope of any immediate and visible political effect can gradually and indirectly, over time, gain in political significance." This strong faith in the power of each individual to make a difference in the world by living a moral life guided the famous playwright in his own life and imposed on him costly personal choices—from social isolation to imprisonment—but it also made him an inspiration to people throughout the communist bloc.

During the short-lived Prague Spring, from January to August 1968, Havel was at the forefront of the reform movement that sought full freedom of the press, religion, and assembly in addition to important social and economic changes advocated by the reformist party leadership. Thirty-two at that time, and thus older than most of the students who stood beside him, Havel publicly criticized the injustices of the communist regime even though, as a prominent playwright, he had much to lose. But he believed in truth telling, and in an open letter to the communist leadership, he laid out the major abuses of the regime.

These actions made him a target of the repression that came in 1969, after the Soviets rolled their tanks through Prague. Havel was blacklisted, his plays removed from all theaters: he was forced to choose between being a playwright without a stage or abandoning his political principles. Havel chose neither. He remained an unconcealed opponent of the regime, but as he was not allowed to publish or stage his plays, he created an underground publishing house and arranged to have his plays staged in unlikely places, from barns to restaurants. As he could not make a living as a playwright, he took on a day job stocking barrels in a brewery. In this way, he continued to provide an inspiring example of how one could not only survive but also live in truth under a regime of lies, exposing it for what it really was. His underground press published many texts that opposed the regime, contributing to the development and recognition of an important body of works. Many of these publications were also smuggled abroad, making Havel, his cohort of writers, and, more broadly, Czechoslovakia a place to which western Europeans and Americans looked for signs of a crack in the Soviet bloc.

Havel's best-known act of opposition was his central role in co-writing and publicizing a petition against the Czechoslovak government in 1977. Charter 77, as it became known, pointed out real but undisclosed facts about the abuses of the communist regime, which in 1975 had signed the famous Helsinki Final Act that guaranteed citizens' basic human rights. Charter 77 became the foundation for a new movement for rehumanizing social relations, restoring human dignity, and reenergizing moral conviction. In its most public challenge, the petition asked the government to release the members of a rock band who had been imprisoned for their lyrics and for loud aesthetics—supposedly "unbecoming" of a musical group in a communist state. Charter 77, and Havel in particular, challenged the regime to show how it could claim to support freedom of speech and personal movement while treating people as subjects of a tyranny. For his role in Charter 77, Havel was imprisoned in 1979 and suffered great abuses. In 1983 he almost died from an untreated case of pneumonia, and only under great international pressure was he finally released to recover in a regular hospital. By now he had become a larger-than-life hero of the underground intellectual and civil rights reform movement in the communist world. In 1989, he emerged as leader of the anticommunist opposition and was soon elected as president of a democratic Czechoslovakia. After Slovakia declared its independence in 1991, he remained the president of the Czech Republic until his retirement in February 2003.

Introduction

Václav Havel was one of the many youthful supporters of the 1968 revolt against the pressures for conformity and the lies of governments and politics. The hopes of these young people for a radical change in leadership style and for more direct political participation by the people were dashed by the harsh response of the authorities, from Prague to Paris. But the revolts shook the establishment and put traditional political parties on the defensive, forcing them to redefine themselves if they were to speak to this younger generation. These challenges also pushed governments East and West to learn to live with the idea of permanent threat brought about by the cold war while achieving internal political stability.

Inside western Europe, the political challenges of the 1970s and 1980s came not from traditional political organizations but rather from radical new political formations, like the Greens, feminists, and antinuclear activists. These groups did not propose choosing between capitalism and communism but rather moving beyond the cold war divide and recognizing the greater problems that threatened the well-being of all people, from nuclear obliteration to gender inequality.

An economic crisis that started with the oil embargo of 1973 and continued into the 1980s complicated the political choices of western Europeans, who had to contend with economic depression, unemployment, inflation, and a severe slowdown of the postwar "economic miracle." The European Community also became involved in unprecedented global economic connections.

The economic crisis of the 1970s also brought about radical change in eastern Europe and the Soviet Union. Governments looked for new markets and took advantage of a relaxation of tensions to increase trade. People in the communist bloc started to get a taste of consumer goods through popular culture, travel, and even access to coveted western status symbols, like blue jeans. The same economic crisis finally forced Soviet leader Mikhail Gorbachev to acknowledge that the Soviet Union was financially unable to maintain its hold in eastern Europe and to concede that each state in the bloc should follow its own path. Within three years, all eastern European communist regimes had fallen like a house of cards, and the Soviet Union itself had disappeared, ending the communist experiment initiated by revolution in 1917.

Politics in Western Europe

↓ What role did the relaxation of international tensions play in western Europe?
↓ How did political parties change in the 1970s and 1980s?

In the 1970s, tensions between western and eastern Europe relaxed, and governments began to consider issues on which they could cooperate, such as human rights initiatives. At the same time, the West faced important internal challenges, such as an energy crisis after 1973 and the emergence of radical terrorist groups from Northern Ireland to Italy. Leftist parties were less able to deal with these problems than their center-right counterparts, who gained political control in many places by 1980. Yet, especially in southern Europe and in France, left-wing parties held the power throughout the 1980s. The Common Market expanded but was also burdened by the weaker new members that joined in this decade.

Chronology

1972	West Germany recognizes the East German border; United States and Soviet Union sign the Antiballistic Missile Treaty
1973	Great Britain, Ireland, and Denmark join the Common Market; Egypt and Israel engage in the Yom Kippur War; Arab oil embargo begins
1974	Abortion is decriminalized in France
1975	European states sign Helsinki Final Act
1976–1977	Massive strikes erupt in Poland and Romania
1977	Charter 77 movement in Czechoslovakia begins
1978	Polish cardinal Karol Wojtyła a becomes Pope John Paul II
1979	Soviets invade Afghanistan; Margaret Thatcher becomes British prime minister
1980	Solidarity movement begins in Poland
1981	Greece joins the Common Market; Spain legalizes divorce; Millions march in antinuclear protests in western Europe
1982	Britain defeats Argentina in Falklands War
1983	François Mitterrand becomes president of France; Petra Kelly, first Green Party representative, is elected to the West German parliament; AIDS crisis begins
1985	Mikhail Gorbachev becomes leader of the Soviet Union
1986	Explosion at the Chernobyl nuclear power plant spreads contamination
1989	Berlin Wall is taken down; Communism falls in eastern Europe
1991	Soviet Union collapses

Relaxed Tensions and Renewed Cooperation

The 1968 protests challenged western European parties to define a new kind of politics in which people could participate more directly and be counted. At the same time, the dominant presence of the two superpowers raised questions of European autonomy in international relations, especially in Europe. These two concerns combined to produce two new directions in European politics: a focus on internal stability and a stabilization of international relations.

In the United States, the violent protests of 1968 helped secure the victory of a Republican law-and-order presidential candidate, Richard Nixon. Once defeated by the charismatic John F. Kennedy, Nixon returned to politics by casting himself as a representative of stability and reason. With his secretary of state, Henry Kissinger, Nixon engineered a major shift in international politics, the policy of **détente**. From reconsidering the Vietnam War to opening relations with communist China, Nixon led the way toward relaxing the tough stance that had defined relations between the democratic and communist blocs in the previous decades. He also sought to reengage the United States in Europe by building bridges of communication across the East-West divide.

By the end of the 1960s, not only Nixon but also his Soviet counterpart Leonid Brezhnev and many politicians in western Europe realized that the cold war had achieved a balance of power and military escalation was unlikely. An important departure in the 1970s was the decision by Nixon and Brezhnev to limit their military buildups, evident in the **Antiballistic Missile Treaty** (1972). In agreeing to limit their antiballistic missile systems and put a cap on military spending, the Americans and Soviets conceded that military parity was sufficient for both to feel secure and that to continue spending would in fact increase the possi-

détente (in French, "release from tension") Easing of political relations between the Soviet Union and the United States in the 1970s.

Antiballistic Missile Treaty Treaty signed in 1972 by the Soviet Union and the United States reducing their nuclear arsenals.

bility of conflict, especially nuclear war. This kind of self-limiting thinking was a complete reversal from the military planning of the late 1940s and represented a major step toward a more peaceful international environment.

No longer content to be pawns in the superpower game, European political leaders played an active, even pioneering, role in this process. In West Germany, Chancellor **Willy Brandt** initiated a policy of normalizing relations with East Germany and, years before Nixon and Brezhnev, worked on a policy of reconciliation between the West and the East. His accession to power in 1969 signaled a momentous change in West Germany: it was the first time since the 1920s that the Social Democrats were in power. Brandt had an unimpeachable past. He had been a Social Democrat since the age of seventeen, and in 1933, when the Gestapo tried to arrest him, he fled to Scandinavia, where he became an outspoken journalist and antifascist activist until the end of the Third Reich. He saw these years not as a cowardly flight but rather as "a chance to serve the 'Other Germany,' which did not resign itself submissively to enslavement."

In the Bundestag, which had replaced the Reichstag as West Germany's parliament, Brandt made his mark as a defender of democracy and socialism against communist dictatorship. He was the mayor of West Berlin when the first bricks in the Berlin Wall went up in August 1961. Finding that the contest between the superpowers made him powerless to attend to the well-being of ordinary Germans, he took on a pragmatic view of cold war politics. By 1969, when he was elected chancellor, he had become the foremost spokesman of **Ostpolitik**, the policy of taking small, steady steps toward normalizing relations with East Germany and, by extension, serving as a model for better relations between the East and West in Europe. He was a pioneer in the détente shift in international relations.

Brandt successfully cultivated an international image acceptable to both the United States and the Soviet Union and, at the same time, independent of their whims. Though his politics were far to the left of those of the Christian Democrat Konrad Adenauer, Brandt appeared to Nixon as a peaceful and loyal ally and to Brezhnev as a reasonable representative of socialism.

Brandt proceeded to make good on his promise to open up relations with the East by traveling to Moscow and signing an important nonaggression pact with the Soviets, which paved the way to recognizing the border between East and West Germany in 1972. This action of legitimating the post-1945 rearrangement of European states was, in fact, the final peace treaty of World War II. And this time Europeans themselves acted on their own behalf rather than at

In a symbolic gesture, in December 1970 West German Chancellor Willy Brandt knelt before the Warsaw Ghetto Uprising memorial, asking forgiveness from the Polish people for the violence of the Nazi regime. The gesture greatly improved West German–Polish relations and helped decrease East-West tensions generally in the 1970s. *(Bettmann/Corbis)*

the beckoning of the superpowers, as had been the case in 1945. Brandt also normalized relations with other eastern European countries, most prominently Poland. Possibly the most famous of his gestures of reconciliation was his visit to Warsaw in 1970, where he knelt before the memorial to the Warsaw Ghetto heroes and begged the forgiveness of the Polish nation for the horrors committed by the Third Reich. Brandt's public career was crowned by the Nobel Peace Prize, which he received in 1971 for his leadership role in East-West relations.

Willy Brandt (1913–1992) West German chancellor from 1969 to 1974, Social Democrat and architect of détente.

Ostpolitik (in German, "eastern politics") West German policy of reconciliation with the communist East.

If Ostpolitik and détente meant relaxation, tolerance, and the willingness to sit down at the negotiating table, they also encouraged greater scrutiny and manipulation of the flow of information between East and West. It was a gamble on both sides, and it proved very costly for Brandt. A few dramatic cases of Soviet agents in West Germany caught with important German secrets encouraged the perception that western leaders who promoted détente were not watchful and tough enough on communist threats from over the wall. Brandt became the victim of one such a scandal. Although he had not been personally responsible for the actions of a Soviet spy who had infiltrated his administration, Brandt lost legitimacy at home and finally resigned in 1974. But the policy of détente continued in the hands of other European leaders and with the support of U.S. presidents Gerald Ford and Jimmy Carter.

Brandt's policy of opening up trade with the East in order to improve the quality of life under communism provided an important starting point for a broader international process of European cooperation, and this gave birth to the **Conference on Security and Cooperation in Europe.** The conference represented the first attempt to broadly rethink European international relations not only in terms of the cold war superpower contest, but also in terms of the interests and needs of the European states. All European states participated, as well as the United States and Canada. The process itself, together with the **Helsinki Final Act** (1975) it generated, created a new forum for collaboration between East and West, especially in the area of human rights. All signatories recognized existing European borders and committed themselves to protecting their citizens' human rights, including freedom of religion, free speech, freedom to move or travel, and the right to due process. The Final Act became a guiding principle for the Carter administration's foreign policy. For Europeans, it represented a new basis for international relations that went beyond the political interests and ideologies of the United States and the Soviet Union.

The conference also gave rise to institutions for implementing these agreements. **Helsinki Watch** became one of the important **nongovernmental organizations (NGOs)** reporting on human rights violations, both in the West and in the East. As Helsinki Watch and other NGOs worked with western governments to guide the implementation of the Final Act, they became new players in international relations. Often lobbying on behalf of the powerless, they also worked with western governments to expose abuses by regimes that did not acknowledge their violations of basic human rights and to bring international pressure to bear on them. The United States, for instance, offered reduced tariffs to eastern European countries that abided by the provisions of Helsinki and threatened to cut off economic benefits to regimes with human rights abuses.

Security and Economic Challenges from the Middle East

As tensions across the East-West divide relaxed, Europeans countries faced new security and economic challenges from the Middle East. In October 1973, in alliance with Syria, Egyptian president **Anwar el-Sadat** attacked Israel, to regain territories lost by both states in the **Six-Day War** (1967). The **Yom Kippur War** grew in complexity as Arab states lent support and troops to Egypt, while Israel enlisted the support of the United States and western Europe. Arab states, viewing western support of Israel as a conspiracy against Egypt's legitimate reconquest of territories Israel had seized, retaliated through an **oil embargo** that lasted until March 1974. The embargo sent the world economy into a decade-long crisis. The immediate effect was soaring oil prices, which generated a rise in the price of virtually all products. In addition, most European states were unable to provide sufficient energy resources for their economies. Some went so far as to ration the use of oil and other energy resources. In the United States, the government introduced unprecedented supply and price regulations.

Conference on Security and Cooperation in Europe Meeting of all European states, the United States, and Canada in 1972–1975 to rethink East-West relations.

Helsinki Final Act Accord signed in 1975 by all European states that introduced human rights as a principle in international relations.

Helsinki Watch Nongovernmental organization created to oversee the implementation of the Helsinki Final Act's human rights provisions.

nongovernmental organization (NGO) Voluntary nonprofit organization often focused on humanitarian issues.

Anwar el-Sadat (1918–1981) President of Egypt who contributed to the rise of Arab nationalism in the 1970s.

Six-Day War War fought in 1967 between Israel and its Arab neighbors Egypt, Jordan, and Syria; won by Israel.

Yom Kippur War 1973 war between Egypt and Israel over the Sinai Peninsula and Golan Heights, which had been conquered by Israel in 1967; won by Israel.

oil embargo (1973–1974) Refusal by Arab petroleum-exporting countries to ship petroleum to countries that had supported Israel in the Yom Kippur War.

The energy crisis signaled two important long-term trends in Europe and elsewhere. Economic processes were becoming increasingly **globalized,** so it was no longer possible for the West to be economically self-sufficient. And western Europeans, with only meager internal oil resources, resolved to deal with the crisis by looking into alternative energy resources, from hydroelectric to wind and nuclear. Overall, the energy crisis induced greater cooperation among members of the Common Market in finding alternative fuels and markets that would buffer them from fluctuations in the global economy. During the oil crisis, the Common Market provided important benefits to its members, such as access to nuclear power and coal, but its success was also measured by its general prosperity and growth, as Brandt had been able to reconcile the French to the idea of allowing Great Britain to join in the very year of the oil embargo.

Member countries continued to negotiate and move forward toward a **European Monetary Union.** But in 1979, a second oil crisis brought about by the 1977 **Iranian Revolution,** together with a spike in the value of the dollar, made European currencies more vulnerable on the international markets. As European economies slowed down, further discussions of the monetary union ended. The strongest western European economies—the German and the British—turned inward to solve their problems with rising unemployment and low economic performance instead of pursuing further collaboration with the Common Market.

Overall, by 1979, the era of détente was ending. There were some important changes—the stabilization of European borders and recognition of human rights as an important component of international politics. Yet trust did not catch hold, and ideologues on both sides of the cold war skillfully exploited the fears of average voters about loss of stability. In addition, the Soviets changed their international stance significantly. On Christmas Eve 1979, they invaded Afghanistan. The reason for this intervention seems to have been the fear of the spread of Islamic fundamentalism from Afghanistan into Soviet-controlled Central Asian territories. But the United States read the **Afghanistan invasion** as a challenge to the balance of power in the Persian Gulf, a region to which it had become vulnerable since the 1973 oil embargo. The Americans reacted swiftly and sent military help to the Islamic Afghan rebels who opposed the Soviets.

Thus, a significant change in U.S. relations with the Soviet Union and western Europe took place in the 1980s. American voters viewed Carter's stance on human rights and his response to the Iranian Revolution as weak, and they put Ronald Reagan, an unabashed hawk in international relations, in the White House. The United States shifted toward a renewed military buildup against the Soviet Union, which responded with similar moves. Until 1985, relations between the two superpowers remained extremely tense. NATO became an important institution for rallying western Europe support behind Reagan's vision of military buildup as the guarantee for peace, with Britain as the most outspoken ally. Other Europeans saw themselves cast again as second-tier participants in the superpower contest.

Yet, despite such challenges, western European states moved along toward European integration. The major successes of the 1980s were Greece, Portugal, and Spain, which quietly abandoned authoritarian rule between 1970 and 1975 and in the 1980s were welcomed into the Common Market. By this time, vestiges of the old dictatorships were largely gone in the politics of these countries, while their economies began to flourish and a culture of **pluralism** also developed. Their Common Market membership enhanced their political stability in the face of continued challenges from extremist movements.

The Transformation of the Left

In the 1970s and 1980s, domestic politics in western Europe saw an ebb and flow among traditional parties, but two trends were about to transform them. First, traditional politics seemed to draw less voter support. As 1968 had shown, average citizens were less interested in what politicians had to offer through the regular channels of political platforms and elections. Second, new types of movements—grass-roots politics and radical, secret terrorist organizations—attracted more followers.

In Britain, where the Labour Party had come to

globalization Increasing global connections among national and international economic and cultural forces, starting in the 1970s.

European Monetary Union Unification in 1990–1999 of the fiscal policies of European Community members, with the goal of creating a single currency.

Iranian Revolution Nationalist uprising in 1977 that ousted the Iranian monarchy and destabilized the global oil supply.

Afghanistan invasion Military invasion by Soviet Union in 1979 to prevent the spread of Muslim fundamentalism to the Soviet Republics in Central Asia.

pluralism State of society in which diverse groups can participate while maintaining their interests and traditions.

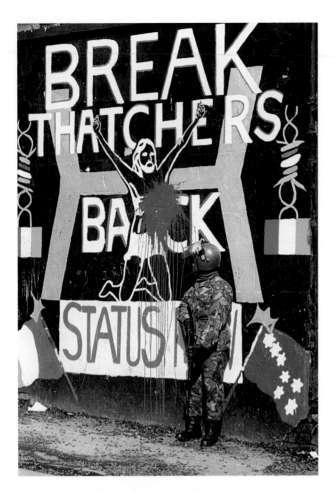

From the late 1960s to the present, the walls of many urban neighborhoods in Northern Ireland became a venue for the Irish Republican Army's quest for legitimacy. This mural, painted during the 1980s, is critical of Margaret Thatcher's government. *(Alain Le Garsmeur/Alamy)*

British politics, with both British and Irish nationalists unwilling to compromise. Instead, violence and terrorism became a way of life for the next generation—both Protestants and Catholics.

In an era of rapid secularization elsewhere in Europe, the people of Ireland went in a different direction, taking religious identity as a rallying point. Religious spaces, religious rituals, and overall religious practice became nationalist and overtly political. The voice of religious authorities on these divisions mattered less than the use of religious language by politicians and terrorists. Friendships across this harsh divide became dangerous, shunned by both communities, even though children grew up speaking the same language and playing the same games.

In Italy the communists made important gains in the early 1970s. The recovery of the Communist Party after the 1956 and 1968 uprisings in Hungary and Czechoslovakia was due to the ability of the Italian communists to project their party as humane. Under **Palmiro Togliatti**, Italian communism succeeded in becoming both a nationalist movement, highlighting the "Italian way," and also a party consistently committed to social justice. Thus, for most of the 1970s, the Communists and the Christian Democrats shared power and succeeded in preserving stability and prosperity.

Yet a parallel development, prompted by a grassroots dissatisfaction with these political compromises, gave rise to terrorist movements on both the left and right. By 1978 the **Red Brigades**, a radical left-wing communist terrorist organization, were regularly staging kidnappings and other terrorist attacks, such as bombings. Their most prominent action was the 1978 murder of **Aldo Moro**, who had been instrumental in

power in 1973, the oil crisis of that same year undermined economic prosperity. Unemployment stayed high, the economy did not bounce back, and the pound remained weak. When the party proved incapable of effective solutions, it lost power in 1979.

The Labour Party also lost support because of its inability to deal with the rise of protests in Northern Ireland. In the late 1960s, the **Northern Ireland Civil Rights Association** sponsored peaceful street protests and began documenting the abuses of the **Unionist** government against Catholics. The government's violent crackdown led to actions by the Irish Republican Army (IRA) that brought the level of violence to unprecedented heights. Car bombings in Protestant communities and assassinations of government loyalists became staple activities of this group. The situation in Ireland soon became a permanent crisis in

Northern Ireland Civil Rights Association
Organization started in the late 1960s by Northern Ireland Catholics to record abuses by the Unionist government.

Unionists Representatives of the British government in Northern Ireland who favored preserving the union with Great Britain.

Palmiro Togliatti (1893–1964) Italian Communist Party leader who devised a compromise with the Christian Democrats that brought stability to the government.

Red Brigades Radical communist group in Italy that led campaign of terrorist actions from street and car bombings to kidnappings.

Aldo Moro (1916–1978) Italian Christian Democratic politician who was instrumental in the compromise with the Italian Communist Party.

the left-center-right compromise. Eager to blame each other for the violence, the left and right broke off their alliance.

The nationalist terrorist movement in Northern Ireland and the communist terrorist movement in Italy were but two examples of a more general trend in Europe. The year 1968 had opened a new era of grass-roots politics, of taking ideas to the streets and using new technologies, especially television, to force action and change outside parliamentary debate, legislation, and election. These terrorist movements were not widespread; most were small, secret organizations that could not operate on a large scale. But, in the beginning at least, they did resonate with a broader population. The IRA specifically used dissatisfaction among the Irish in general to strike against established political institutions.

In France, however, traditional left-wing governments dominated the 1980s. In 1983, **François Mitterrand** gained power and remained president of France for two terms, the first socialist head of government since Léon Blum in 1936. But Mitterrand was moderate and continued many policies of his center-right predecessor, **Valéry Giscard d'Estaing**. After attempting to nationalize important financial institutions and initiate an increase in wages and social benefits, Mitterrand found such policies ineffective in addressing larger problems such as trade deficits and the devaluation of the franc. Within a year, his government returned to many of the previous center-right policies. Yet Mitterrand improved some social services and welfare measures, such as shorter working hours and increased pension benefits.

Spain and Greece also saw the emergence of socialist governments. The Spanish Socialist Workers' Party secured both stability and steady economic growth, despite repeated challenges from the right. King **Juan Carlos** played an important role in restraining the military establishment against the democratic left. The financial commitment of the European Community was also important in this process.

The Antinuclear and Environmental Movements

The 1968 protests expressed opposition to the colonial wars, and as the Vietnam War continued into the 1970s, the peace movement also grew. Many involved in these movements saw themselves as outside the division between capitalism and communism; they viewed themselves as advocates of a world free of the threat of war and of the arms race that dominated U.S.-Soviet relations. They hailed the Antiballistic Mis-

sile Treaty of 1972 as a victory and committed themselves to continuing reductions of the nuclear arsenal. Yet even as the energy crisis of the early 1970s made nuclear power attractive to some, fears of a nuclear disaster gained new dimensions. Table 29.1 summarizes antinuclear protests during this period.

Table 29.1

Antinuclear Protests

1971	Demonstrations against nuclear power plants in France and Germany
1972	Antiballistic Missile Treaty
1978	UN first special session on disarmament
1981	Millions of western Europeans participate in antinuclear street protests
1981–1991	Women's protest at Greenham Common military base in England
1983	Antinuclear Green Party wins twenty-seven seats in West German parliament
March 1983	U.S. Strategic Defense Initiative announced; relations with Soviet Union reach all-time low
October 1983	Protests of millions in western Europe against U.S. intermediate-range nuclear force (INF) deployments
1983–1984	Over forty thousand women resume protests at Greenham
1987	Reagan and Gorbachev sign intermediate-range nuclear force treaty
May 1991	Last U.S. cruise missile leaves Greenham Common military base, site of decade of antinuclear protests organized by women

François Mitterrand (1916–1996) French president from 1982 to 1994, first socialist French president of the postwar era.

Valéry Giscard d'Estaing (1926–) French president from 1974 until 1982 who pursued centrist policies supporting business interests and social welfare services.

Juan Carlos I (r. 1975–) King of Spain who helped smooth the transition from the authoritarian Franco regime to a democratic pluralist government.

For ten years, thousands of women kept a continuous presence at the Greenham Common military base west of London. They camped, held vigils, and engaged in various other forms of protest to signal their commitment to creating a nuclear-free Britain. *(The Press Association [PA Photos])*

The antiwar and antinuclear/environmental movements were closely connected and drew support from a wide range of scientists, student activists, housewives, and people of any or no political persuasion. In Britain, the **Campaign for Nuclear Disarmament,** founded in the 1950s, became the leading organization of the antinuclear movement. It served as a political lobbying force and also a link for people beyond national boundaries, ideologies, and religious beliefs. Other environmental NGOs built communities on an ethic of caring that crossed national borders and promoted a new global identity. Free from the adversities of the ballot box, these NGOs often acted swiftly and also across borders, especially in moments of crisis.

The same concern for environmental issues gave birth to a new left-wing party in Germany, the **Green Party.** The party grew from small local groups that lobbied on behalf of ecological concerns starting in the early 1970s and attracted voters dissatisfied with

the social and environmental policies of the traditional left. This trend was not exclusive to West Germany, but it developed faster and had broader appeal there, in part because of the committed sense of citizenship that was particular to post-1945 German political culture. In the 1980s, the Greens remained a marginal presence in the Bundestag but made steady gains in local politics. Throughout this period they continued to work closely with local environmental NGOs in a new blend of community activism and parliamentary politics.

Campaign for Nuclear Disarmament Antinuclear British organization founded in the 1950s that became a leader in the peace movement of the 1970s and 1980s.

Green Party West German party founded by antinuclear and environmental activists in 1979.

After 1981, as the Reagan administration resumed military buildup in Europe, the antinuclear movement offered increased resistance. Though the British government welcomed the American missiles, the popular support of the generation who had welcomed the Americans as liberators during World War II was almost gone, as the numbers of this generation dwindled through death. Their sons and daughters, taking security and prosperity as a given, opposed nuclear threat of any sort—from West or East. Thus, when the Reagan administration announced the deployment of new Pershing II intermediate-range missiles on U.S. bases in western Europe, almost 1 million people marched in Bonn, London, and Rome in opposition; a month later, half a million protesters gathered in Amsterdam. These protests continued throughout the 1980s, most famously at the **Greenham Common** military base, where an all-woman camp established in 1981 continued until 1991, when the last nuclear missiles were removed from the site.

In April 1986, an explosion at a nuclear power station in **Chernobyl**, in Soviet Ukraine, forced all Europeans to face the reality of environmental nuclear disaster. Though the details were at first suppressed by the Soviet leader, **Mikhail Gorbachev**, the effects were so severe and widespread that Chernobyl became an instant symbol of the dangers of nuclear power. More than thirty thousand square miles of land were contaminated and, according to a 1994 study, almost 5 million people in the region were affected. In western Europe, environmental pressure groups forced the closing of nuclear power plants: France, which had been a leading producer of nuclear energy, had to retool its energy sources. By the end of the 1980s, concerns over with the possibility of nuclear disaster had breached political divisions between East and West to become a common cause across Europe.

The New Conservatism

In the 1980s, with the traditional left losing support and new grass-roots movements still politically underdeveloped, West German and British parliaments were dominated by conservative regimes. In West Germany the Christian Democrats, led by **Helmut Kohl**, assumed control in 1982. As chancellor, Kohl continued the policies of Ostpolitik and the effort to change political culture in Germany. German laws, culture, and educational policies openly acknowledged and discussed the atrocities of the Third Reich and worked to prevent any recurrence. More than any other European state, Germany was quick to condemn extremism and avoid aggression. Kohl also oversaw a tremendous economic recovery of the country that made Germany

the backbone of the Common Market, producing one-third of its exports in the 1980s.

In Britain, the electorate brought back the Conservatives in 1979 under the leadership of **Margaret Thatcher**, the first woman prime minister of Britain. She dominated politics throughout the 1980s, orchestrating a decisive shift in foreign and domestic politics. Thatcher came to be known as the Iron Lady for her resolute support for the Reagan administration's rearmament policies and for her stiff refusal to consider the social welfare costs of her government's support for business and industry. Whether people admired or despised her, Thatcher articulated a new path for conservative politics. Her years in power and policies have reshaped the relationship between the traditional left and right, making Thatcherism an important force in contemporary politics until today. The focus on individual freedoms rather than social programs and on encouraging business rather than favoring labor unions became the trademarks of this movement.

As a woman, Thatcher was an improbable leader of the Conservatives, a party in which women were underrepresented and that generally lined up with areas of political and economic life that were dominated by men—from the armaments industry to the landed aristocracy. Most western European women who entered politics after World War II gravitated to left-wing parties, which tended to have woman-friendly positions on issues such as child care, healthcare, education, and birth control. But Thatcher was not one to fit any particular cliché of a female politician, and she followed her own path. Born in 1925, she became interested in politics as a chemistry student at Oxford. In 1953, as a brand-new mother of twins, she also passed the bar and soon returned to work as a tax specialist. After she won a seat in Parliament at age thirty-four, she fully dedicated her public

Greenham Common   Military air base in England that became the site of a long-standing antinuclear protest from 1981 to 1991.

Chernobyl   City in Soviet Ukraine where the greatest nuclear disaster to date occurred in April 1986, resulting in widespread nuclear contamination.

Mikhail Gorbachev   (1931–) Soviet leader between 1985 and 1991 whose reforms paved the way to the fall of communism in 1991.

Helmut Kohl   (1930–) Christian Democratic chancellor of West Germany from 1982 to 1998 who continued Ostpolitik.

Margaret Thatcher   (1925–) First female British prime minister who led the Conservative government between 1980 and 1992.

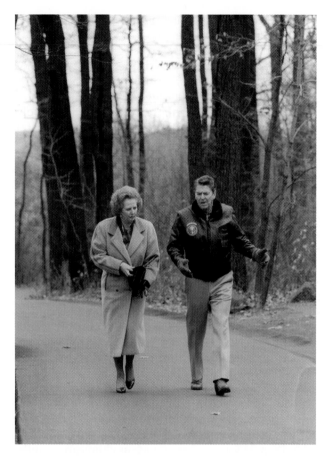

British Prime Minister Margaret Thatcher and U.S. President Ronald Reagan, here at the presidential retreat Camp David in 1986, are generally considered the two staunchest defenders of a tough policy of nonnegotiation with the Soviet Union during the 1980s. Their personal friendship helped resolidify a close British-American alliance that has lasted into the twenty-first century. *(Reagan Presidential Library)*

Britain's international position as a partner with the United States in the cold war.

Thatcher was unapologetically imperialistic, opposing nationalist movements in Wales and Scotland, and offered symbolic victories that drew even the working classes to support her government. Britain's easy victory in the 1982 **Falklands War** helped solidify her reputation. The British Navy came out in full force to confront Argentina's takeover of the tiny Falkland/Malvinas Islands. The conflict lasted only a few weeks, but it inflicted serious casualties on the Argentineans while yielding a victory for Britain that stirred those nostalgic for empire. For many in Britain, disaffected by dull leaders and ineffective government, Thatcher seemed to commanded respect, regardless of party.

In domestic politics, Thatcher deregulated many industries in communications and energy and refused to bow to the pressures from trade unions. The new climate helped generate economic growth, but it also brought higher unemployment rates and diminished spending on social programs. Thatcher favored limiting state interference in social services provided by private businesses. Thus, while she retained national healthcare, she allowed private providers greater freedom. The aim was no longer to serve all populations, especially the poorest, but to harmonize the well-being of private businesses with access to these services.

Although Thatcher did continue funding for public education, her careful pulling back from the universal commitments to social welfare of postwar governments represented an important and permanent departure. She had her share of opponents among the British politicians and public, but her policies of favoring the free market and diminishing state services were never fully reversed after she lost power to the Labour Party in 1990. Thatcherism became a political hallmark of the late twentieth century.

Social Change in the West

↓ How did western European societies change during this period?

↓ How did western European identities alter?

Despite growing prosperity and opportunities for social advancement in western Europe, the years after 1968 saw challenges from various groups. Women de-

life to working for the Conservatives. She served in several cabinets in the 1960s and in the 1970s drew attention as a leader of the Conservative opposition by condemning détente and supporting rearmament: "The men in the Soviet Politburo put guns before butter," she quipped, "while we put just about everything before guns."

These policy stands won her the "Iron Lady" nickname, and she proceeded to make good on it in the 1980s. In foreign policy, she reinvented the "special friendship" with the United States that still defines the relationship between the two countries. She vocally supported Reagan's nuclear rearmament policies and gladly offered British military bases for stationing U.S. nuclear missiles. No other European state took such a friendly view of Reagan's policies regarding the Soviet Union, but her aim was to restore

Falklands War (1982) Conflict won by Great Britain against Argentina over a small archipelago off Argentina, the Falkland/Malvinas Islands.

manded greater social, political, and economic power. Demographic change spurred social change, as birthrates decreased and working populations aged. Newly arrived immigrants and guest workers tested the ability of western governments to deliver the same social services to all those who lived and worked in their countries.

The Feminist Revolution

By 1970, women had made dramatic gains in many areas. More women were employed outside the home and received college degrees than ever before. Yet their economic opportunities were more limited than those of men, their wages were significantly lower (by about one-third), and they were still expected to be primarily wives and mothers. A woman with a college degree in business would more likely become a secretary than a manager. Left-wing parties, which advocated economic and social equality, remained unsympathetic to glaring gender inequalities in politics and the workplace. They were willing to offer social assistance to workers but not to consider housework as labor that was entitled to respect and protection.

Even in left-wing movements, women were relegated to secondary roles—making signs, typing, and making coffee—behind the masculine façade of the protests. Disillusioned, many women left these movements and formed their own, vowing to promote gender equality in structures that rejected the male patriarchal model. "The personal is political" was the motto of this feminist movement, which focused primarily on the social and economic empowerment of women rather than their relationship to men. Celebrating women's identities as women and defining them as worthy of public concern was at the heart of this new movement. Thus, giving birth was viewed not as a personal and private event but as a unique female experience with deep social, emotional, and political implications for the whole community. Feminists also addressed the problem of "compulsory heterosexuality." Lesbian activism developed during this period as a form of celebrating women's identities unencumbered by relations with men. This was the age of universal sisterhood.

The most prominent intellectual figure of the women's movement in Europe, **Simone de Beauvoir**, defined the struggle for women's liberation as an individual quest to gain respect for differences. Her study of women's cultural and psychological conditioning, *The Second Sex* (1949), became an important manifesto for European feminists, who focused on especially family issues. They sought the right to divorce, access to birth control (including abortion), and child care for working mothers. This emphasis was in contrast to American feminists, who also embraced these issues but who generally focused less on difference and complementarity than on equality in economic power and in politics. American feminists, for example, demanded "equal pay for equal work" and full representation in government, business, sports, and education.

De Beauvoir herself had not been interested in taking a public stance on women's issues until 1971, when she signed the **Manifesto of the 343**, acknowledging that she had had an abortion. Since abortion was a criminal act in France, signing this document was an act of civil disobedience, and it became a springboard for securing women's access to birth control. Abortion was legalized three years later, one year after it was also decriminalized in the United States. Other Catholic countries followed suit—Italy in 1978 and Spain in 1985—with women's groups applying the pressure. In 1990, Belgium became the last western European country to decriminalize abortion.

Catholic countries also eventually legalized divorce. Left-wing governments in Italy (1974) and Spain (1981) gave in to grass-roots pressure in which women played a major role. Women were only loosely organized in informal networks that focused mostly on coping with women's burdens. But as more women became educated and understood their burdens as discriminatory treatment that could be changed, they started to act differently in their daily lives. They applied pressure to the Italian government by marching in the streets, a traditional form of protest; but they also withheld household "services" such as cooking and cleaning. These methods made the point, as 60 percent of Italians came to support legalization of divorce in this most Catholic of western European states.

Women's actions on behalf of abortion and divorce had broad effects throughout society. The birthrate dropped significantly, and marriage patterns changed. Couples married later and became more committed to long-term monogamous relationships than in the past. Overall, women were now able to lead freer lives, with more economic and social choices than ever before.

But in traditional politics, women remained marginal. The percentage of women in elected national

Simone de Beauvoir (1908–1986) French philosopher and author of *The Second Sex* (1949), a central text of the second-wave feminist movement.

Manifesto of the 343 Manifesto in support of legalizing abortion in France, signed in 1971 by 343 French women who acknowledged they had had illegal abortions.

Petra Kelly, the first Green Party candidate elected to the West German Bundestag, combined street activism and legislative work on behalf of her deeply held ecologist, pacifist, and feminist beliefs. *(AP/Wide World Photos)*

offices remained disproportionately low, at 5 to 10 percent, with a slightly higher level in local government. Women tended to be appointed to "feminized" government positions—in social services, education, public health, or the arts. At the same time, however, Thatcher's position in Britain, though she represented a conservative party and did not encourage female participation in politics, proved an important milestone toward redefining women's politics.

In leftists parties, women did assume leadership positions. **Petra Kelly,** for example, of West Germany's Green Party, was elected to a seat in the Bundestag in 1983, and she set new directions. At age thirty-six, she was younger than most other members. She focused on environmental safety and antinuclear activism as unifying concerns, "beyond left and right." She was a feminist without making feminism the center of her political struggle. Her strong belief in the need for women's equality was shaped by her experience growing up in the United States in the 1960s, and she was always quick to point out gender biases in the Green movement itself. Kelly was part of a generation that took gender equality as given and simply acted accordingly.

New Populations

Between 1960 and 1990, the natural population growth in European Community states declined by three-quarters. The birthrate decreased dramatically everywhere in western Europe but most remarkably in Catholic countries that legalized abortion during this period. In Spain, for example, the birthrate dropped from 21.5 per thousand in 1960 to 10.3 per thousand in 1990. The downturn in the birthrate raised concerns about a shrinking workforce. At the same time, the number of elderly people who were entitled to retirement benefits was growing. The average age expectancy for western European men in 1980 was 71, and for women 77, while retirement ages averaged 60 for men and 55 for women. Thus, western European states needed to provide retirement and healthcare benefits for an average of twelve years for each retired person.

Petra Kelly (1947–1992) West German feminist who helped found the Green Party and became the first Green Party member to serve in the West German Bundestag.

Overall, it seemed that the number of people contributing to the workforce was going down while the number of those entitled to social services was rising.

To fill needs in the labor force, western European governments opened up their borders to **guest workers** and immigrants. People with skills for critical economic needs were permitted to live temporarily in European Community states as guest workers. The needs most often cited were for low-paying, menial jobs, such as domestic service and janitorial work, and for hard labor in dangerous settings. The migrants had the right to work. They had to pay taxes, but they did not have the right to apply for permanent residency, nor did they have the same social rights as citizens. Healthcare, education, pensions, and vacations were not guaranteed to guest workers. Nor was there any attempt to acculturate them to the language and customs of the host country. Guest workers remained on the margins of their host societies.

Yet foreign nationals reshaped the demographic profile of western Europe. Policies encouraged immigration from the old colonies in Asia, Africa, and the West Indies, and large numbers of Muslims came to work in Germany, the Netherlands, Denmark, Spain, France, and Britain. At first guest workers seemed largely invisible, but as their populations grew cultural differences were exposed. Western European governments were largely unprepared for the presence of large groups of unassimilated migrants. Moreover, just as Italians, Danes, and Germans were starting to identify themselves as Europeans, there were new populations to define themselves against—new people of color and adherents of different religions. Thus new tensions arose over what it meant to be European.

Tensions also arose as guest workers lived in poverty while they worked in prosperous settings. A Turkish worker cleaning toilets in the Frankfurt International Airport, for example, saw the lifestyle available to Germans and knew it would never be possible for him. The loneliness and resentment of guest workers was compounded as they observed ethnic Germans repatriated from eastern Europe gaining citizenship and access to full social services. The significance of race in eligibility for citizenship was clear. The race line was a particular problem for children born to guest workers in the host country: Were they to be "tolerated," or could they become citizens with full rights? As temporary workers lived in host countries for decades, a new generation of children were exposed to the possibility of losing their rights if their parents were deported. And, because they attended European schools and spoke European languages, they began to identify themselves as Europeans. Thousands of families struggled with divided identities.

Growing Crisis in the Communist East

↓ What impact did détente have for the people of the communist bloc?
↓ How did the Soviet Union change from the 1970s to the late 1980s?

For most eastern Europeans, 1968 represented the end of hope. Yet, by the late 1970s, Ostpolitik and détente had increased the availability of consumer goods, allowed people to travel more freely inside the bloc and beyond, and made room for dissidents to express their criticisms. The 1973 economic crisis did not hit eastern Europe as hard as it did the West. But by the beginning of the 1980s, severe inflation and underproduction were forcing the Soviet Union to rethink its economic and foreign policy. At the same time, popular protests in Czechoslovakia and Poland forced communist regimes there to use increasingly brutal repressive measures. Communism was weakening.

Détente and False Prosperity

When Brezhnev pulled Soviet bloc troops from Czechoslovakia in 1969, the hope of reform—so strong during the Prague Spring on 1968—seemed dead. The leaders of the dissident movement had been imprisoned or purged. By directly participating in the invasion, eastern European communist regimes had also signed on to the **Brezhnev Doctrine**, a commitment to crush dissent.

But the communist leaders understood that military force and fear alone were not sufficient to suppress opposition. The era of détente made possible a shift in economic planning from heavy industries toward consumer goods. For the first time, radios and television sets became available. New countries in addition to Czechoslovakia, such as Romania, began to produce their own cars. Only a generation earlier, most transportation had been either by horse and cart or on foot; in contrast, this new emphasis in economic policy was breathtaking. Items formerly considered luxuries were now mass-produced, and western consumer goods began to be imported.

guest workers Citizens of foreign countries temporarily allowed to live and work in western European countries.
Brezhnev Doctrine Policy of Soviet military intervention to secure the interest of communism in Soviet bloc countries, established by Leonid Brezhnev in 1968.

For many eastern Europeans, the early 1970s was an age of prosperity. For the first time, a factory worker could get in his car and take his family on a trip to another country. A Bulgarian teenager could wear jeans and makeup. Polish students spent their summer vacations camping in Romania, sipping Cuban rum and Pepsi at dance clubs that played the latest tunes from the Swedish pop band ABBA. Workers from nonaligned Yugoslavia went to West Germany to work and returned home with western cars, whiskey, or plain cash. Though salaries were relatively low, many people now dreamed less of life in the free West than of vacations and new furniture.

The communist regimes shifted economic priorities partly because oil from the Soviet Union was available at a time when the rest of the world was suffering from the oil crisis and partly because cheap loans were a stimulus. West Germany had been the first to extend cheap loans to East Germany, but soon Poland, Yugoslavia, Romania, and others benefited. After the Helsinki Act, the United States and western European countries extended special loans and lower tariff rates to eastern European countries that agreed to protect human rights and allow the freedom of religion.

This deal afforded the communist regimes new means of "buying off" the loyalty of their citizens. But it also compelled these regimes to conceal their human rights abuses, if not to curb them. And the availability of western goods, especially movies, VCRs, and books, also made many increasingly aware of the prosperous lifestyle of the noncommunist West. People did not regard the new goods as proof of the success of the communist regimes but rather as proof of West's ability to offer superior products.

By the end of the 1970s, the veneer of economic well-being was wearing off. Because they were not producing goods that could be sold abroad, most eastern European states could repay foreign loans only by raising prices for basic goods, such as bread and milk, which had long been subsidized. But wages were not raised, and in 1976–1977 strikes erupted from the Jiu Valley in Romania, to Gdańsk, Poland. At the Lenin shipyards in Gdańsk, violent clashes between workers and police were followed by a crackdown. The government canceled the price hikes but avoided dealing with the underlying economic issues. People went back home, bruised and fearful, but it was clear that the consumerist policies of the early 1970s had backfired.

By the mid-1970s, even the Soviet Union was experiencing economic troubles. There was a sense of stagnation—that things were not getting any better during a period when people expected more. Voices from inside the Soviet Union rose to criticize Brezhnev. **Andrei Sakharov**, a brilliant physicist who had

helped develop the Soviet hydrogen bomb, gave up his privileges when he openly discussed Soviet treatment of dissenters and put his life in danger by speaking out on behalf of human rights. For these efforts, he received the Nobel Peace Prize in 1975, but he was unable to collect it. Placed under house arrest, he continued his activities from his tiny apartment in Gorky and remained one of the important leaders of the movement for peace and human rights until his death in 1989.

Charter 77 and Solidarity

By 1977, it was becoming clear that the governments of eastern Europe had failed in their attempt to win loyalty through consumerism. Centralized economic planning could not sustain the growing demand for consumer goods at the low prices people had come to expect. And with increased expectations about consumer goods, those inside communist countries were more likely to become dissatisfied when such goods disappeared or became too expensive. The strikes were only the most visible sign that the workers' states were facing the revolt of the workers. In Gdańsk, the strikes gave birth to an underground organization, the **Workers' Defense Committee**, which offered assistance to those who lost their jobs in the strikes. This network provided the foundation for an alliance of workers, lawyers, and intellectuals that was a first in eastern Europe.

The Czechoslovaks followed the Polish example with **Charter 77**, which called on the government to abide by the Helsinki Final Act. It listed actions taken by the government, such as imprisoning citizens without due process, which contravened the agreement signed by the Czechoslovak government in 1975. This petition was signed by more than a thousand people, including prominent writers such as **Václav Havel** (see Choice) but also by engineers, workers, and other average people. The petition refused to define itself as a

Andrei Sakharov (1921–1989) Soviet physicist who was the most prominent human rights and antinuclear activist during the Brezhnev era.

Workers' Defense Committee Polish underground organization founded after the 1976 Gdańsk labor strikes to provide assistance to the participants.

Charter 77 Document signed by Czechoslovak citizens in 1977 protesting the communist government's noncompliance with the Helsinki Final Act.

Václav Havel (1936–) Czech playwright and dissident who became the first president of postcommunist Czechoslovakia.

political movement; it simply stood as a grass-roots act. Thus, it became the foundation for a new type of **civil society** that tried to change political culture and government policies from outside traditional political channels. Like citizens in the West, but for different reasons, eastern Europeans were tired of traditional politics and turned toward grass-roots activism to express their criticism. For those living under a dictatorship, the price of such actions was high. Predictably, the leaders of Charter 77 were imprisoned and stripped of their rights. But the crackdown did not match the purges of the early 1950s.

> **civil society**   Nongovernmental institutions and social networks that help negotiate civil rights, social justice, and a public space outside of direct state control.

Voice

Václav Havel Calls on the Power of the Powerless

This essay, written a year after the founding of Charter 77, is Václav Havel's most famous piece. It was first published abroad in an English translation and came out in its original Czech only after 1989; before that, mimeographed copies circulated in the underground. The parable of the greengrocer has become a legendary statement of the corrupting power of totalitarian regimes and the apparently simple, potentially costly, yet fundamentally liberating means of escape from the vicious circle of living within a lie. Note that in calling people to live in truth by rejecting the communist regime as fundamentally untruthful, Havel does not embrace capitalism. He sees the consumerism of Western capitalist societies as a coercive conformity, pressuring individuals into other forms of living within a lie.

> ➡ This is one of the most famous mottos of *The Communist Manifesto*, which adorned the front page of many communist newspapers in the Soviet bloc. Why does he do it?

The manager of a fruit and vegetable shop places in his window, among the onions and carrots, the slogan: ➡ "Workers of the world, unite!" . . . I think it can safely be assumed that the overwhelming majority of shopkeepers never think about the slogans they put in their windows, nor do they use them to express their real opinions. ➡ That poster was delivered to our greengrocer from the enterprise headquarters along with the onions and carrots. He put them all into the window simply because that is the way it has to be. If

> ➡ Why does Havel pick a greengrocer for this parable?

he were to refuse, there could be trouble. He could be reproached for not having the proper "decoration" in his window; someone might even accuse him of disloyalty. He does it because these things must be done if one is to get along in life. It is one of the thousands of details that guarantee him a relatively tranquil life "in harmony with society," as they say. . . .

We have seen that the real meaning of the greengrocer's slogan has nothing to do with what the text of the slogan actually says. Even so, this real meaning is quite clear and generally comprehensible because the code is so familiar: the greengrocer declares his loyalty (and he can do no other if his declaration is to be accepted) in the only way the regime is capable of hearing; that is, by accepting the prescribed *ritual,* by accepting appearances as reality, by accepting the given rules of the game. In doing so, however, he has himself become a player in the

➡️ How does the ritual of displaying the slogan help dictatorship become anonymous? What does it mean for power to become anonymous?

➡️ If the greengrocer helps create the conditions to which he had to adapt, then is he a victim of the regime? Is he powerless?

➡️ What would be the consequences of living within the truth? Is that an easy choice to make and maintain?

game, thus making it possible for the game to go on, for it to exist in the first place. . . . ➡️ Because of this, dictatorship of the ritual, however, power becomes clearly *anonymous*. . . .

[A] woman who ignored the greengrocer's slogan may well have hung a similar slogan just an hour before in the corridor of the office where she works. She did it more or less without thinking, just as our greengrocer did, and she could do so precisely because she was doing it against the background of the general panorama and with some awareness of it, that is, against the background of the panorama of which the greengrocer's shop window forms a part. . . . ➡️ The greengrocer and the office worker have both adapted to the conditions in which they live, but in doing so, they help to create those conditions. . . .

➡️ Let us now imagine that one day something in our greengrocer snaps and he stops putting up the slogans merely to ingratiate himself. He stops voting in elections he knows are a farce. He begins to say what he really thinks at political meetings. And he even finds the strength in himself to express solidarity with those whom his conscience commands him to support. In this revolt the greengrocer steps out of living within the lie. He rejects the ritual and breaks the rules of the game. He discovers once more his suppressed identity and dignity. He gives his freedom a concrete significance. ➡️ His revolt is an attempt to *live within the truth*. . . .

➡️ Are these two forms of noncompliance acts of opposition against the regime? What is their meaning and for whom?

The most devastating challenge to a communist regime came in 1980, when another wave of strikes swept through Poland following a government announcement that it would raise the price of basic foods. The deep economic problems that lay behind the previous round of strikes had not been solved. Poland was defaulting on its international loans, and its economy collapsed. People were forced to wait in line for everything from bread to shoes, as the state became unable to deliver even basic goods.

The strikes in the Gdańsk shipyards were led by **Lech Wałęsa**, a young worker with boundless energy, great charisma, and an unshaken belief in the Catholic Church. Wałęsa was not well educated, nor was he a party member. He was truly of the people, and many came to seem him not only as a workers' representative but also as a Polish patriot. Throughout Poland, most factory workers, teachers, rural workers, and even some party members struck in sympathy with the Gdańsk workers. Poland's economy came to a standstill.

With other dedicated workers, Wałęsa established **Solidarity** to negotiate better working conditions and wages. The organization was independent of communist control and at its height had more than 10 million members. This organization gave hope to most Poles that they could organize themselves and func-

tion independently of the communist regime. Entire communities gave everything they had to make this effort work, from Catholic priests, who described the actions of Solidarity in their sermons, to housewives, who turned their apartments into miniature publishing houses, hostels, and cafeterias. By December 1981, the communist regime regarded Solidarity as enough of a threat to send tanks into the streets of Warsaw. For a year Poland was under martial law. Solidarity leaders were imprisoned, and the state imposed harsh control over all media. But the organization was too strong to be eliminated.

In the following years, Solidarity supporters formed an underground network known as the **flying university**. The government tried to shut it down but had neither the will nor the resources to succeed, as many

Lech Wałęsa (1943–) Shipyard worker who led 1980 labor strikes in Gdańsk, Poland, and leader of the Solidarity union and movement.

Solidarity First noncommunist workers' union of any communist regime in eastern Europe, founded in August 1980 in Poland.

flying university Underground Polish educational network that was a training ground for dissidents in the 1980s.

Poles were no longer afraid. Writers expelled from official publications immediately found employment as teachers and editors in the underground classes set up in churches and farmhouses. Those who still had official jobs used their economic resources to help people in the underground. Virtually everyone in Poland, including party members, either knew someone who was an underground activist or helped in such activities.

The Polish dissident movement was unique in eastern Europe for its long-term worker activism and the organizational structure of the Workers' Defense Committee and also because of the role of the Catholic Church, which opened its doors to the flying university and Solidarity activists after 1981. In addition, in 1978, the Catholic Poles gained one of their most important spokesmen in the international community through the election of Karol Cardinal Wojtyła as Pope **John Paul II.** The first Polish pope, John Paul was an inspiration for all Catholics in Poland and gave them renewed faith. The pope himself became an outspoken, if diplomatic, critic of the communist bloc. Even though there were large groups of Catholics in Slovakia, Hungary, Romania, and Croatia, nowhere else did the Catholic Church provide such a catalyst for mass dissent in the last decade of communism.

Reform in the Soviet Union

In 1985, Mikhail Gorbachev became the new Soviet leader, turning out to be the right man at the right time, as Soviet leaders and the general population had come to see the necessity for change. As the old generation of party activists from World War II passed away, younger people, who had not lived under unconstrained Stalinist terror, came to expect reform to be possible. Gorbachev exemplified this new generation of leaders. He had been just eight years old when Germany invaded the Soviet Union, and when Stalin died he was pursuing a law degree in Moscow. In some ways Gorbachev was typical: an ambitious, hardworking, and talented party activist, rising through the ranks very quickly to become, at age forty-nine, the youngest member of the Politburo. His relative youth made him attractive to those desiring reform.

Once in power, Gorbachev moved swiftly to eliminate most of the upper and midlevel old party leadership, replacing them with younger men he personally trusted. Such a change might have appeared autocratic, but he followed this power consolidation with a much more radical change. Starting in 1986 he introduced the policy of **glasnost,** or openness, which was an invitation to both party members and the media at large to discuss domestic problems honestly.

Initially, the policy was not intended as full freedom of speech. Gorbachev hoped to control reform by positioning trusted party members as critics of the status quo and the advocates of change. He anticipated criticisms of Joseph Stalin and Leonid Brezhnev but also a positive reevaluation of some Leninist legacies, especially the NEP years, as well of Nikita Khrushchev, all intended to reinforce commitment to the central ideals of communism.

The gamble was fundamentally wrongheaded: Gorbachev believed openness would strengthen communist rule and restore the faith of satellite regimes. But reform was too little, too late. Both inside the Soviet Union and elsewhere, many took glasnost to mean openness *not* to choose communism and tested Gorbachev's willingness to deliver on his promise. Within three years the Soviet Union was falling apart.

Still, glasnost had important accomplishments, especially in encouraging the growth of independent organizations that became the kernel of a new civil society, much like Solidarity in Poland. Gorbachev himself oversaw the restoration of civil rights to many political prisoners, including Sakharov, and a new respect for human rights. The new openness also had an intolerant underside. For instance, the organization **Pamiat',** dedicated to the victims of communism, had openly antisemitic overtones and encouraged new forms of **xenophobia.**

Gorbachev saw glasnost as part of a broader agenda, which also included **perestroika,** or restructuring. In 1988, he introduced open elections and set new time limitations to political office. In effect, he was institutionalizing a more democratic process that prized change, rather than stability, as the key to healthy politics.

In the economy perestroika proved more challenging, as some reformers called for decentralizing planning and production, which would have meant a systemwide overhaul. Previous economic reform had focused on fighting corruption, reviving worker control

John Paul II   (r. 1978–2005) Pope who inspired Polish Catholics and encouraged their opposition to the communist regime.

glasnost   (in Russian, "openness) Policy of encouraging constructive criticism of the Communist Party that was introduced by Mikhail Gorbachev in 1985.

Pamiat'   Nongovernmental Soviet organization that fostered antisemitic, radical-right nationalism.

xenophobia   Intense fear of foreigners.

perestroika   (in Russian, "restructuring") Failed economic reforms aimed at decentralizing state control of the economy, initiated under Mikhail Gorbachev.

on the factory floor, and replacing political leaders with able technocrats. Gorbachev himself gained popularity by firing corrupt factory managers and giving speeches about making peasants the new masters of the land. But the Soviet economy was too large and sluggish to be changed just by introducing new laws and possibilities for freer market relations. All signs pointed toward the need to let the market, rather than the party, set prices and production priorities. But neither the party leadership nor the population at large was ready for such a radical change.

The very culture of work needed to be transformed so as to encourage personal incentive and creativity. But neither the manager of a textile factory nor the workingwoman on the floor could make such a switch in thinking. The communist regime had so successfully reshaped the identity of the New Soviet Man and Woman that workers identified more closely with the fixed paycheck they took home every month than with productivity or creativity at work. The security of access to free public health, education, and a meager pension rendered workers supporters of this status quo. Similarly, the communist regime had successfully directed factory managers to respond to party directives: they were not used to having to make decisions about what the factory would produce, for whom, and at what cost. These decisions were made in Moscow, and the manager's job was to simply implement them.

So when Gorbachev's reforms allowed the opening of small individual enterprises and gave more power to factory managers, the response was mixed. Most managers were unwilling to really change: their choice was most often to maintain things as they had been. Workers were no less conservative. And allowing prices to reflect the true market value of products brought inflation, which devalued the savings most people had gathered for years under their mattresses. By the end of the 1980s, the Soviet gross domestic production figures had declined by 17 percent and retail prices had increased by 140 percent. The communist system was collapsing, though the speed with which it unraveled caught the whole world by surprise.

Cultural Leaps over the Wall

⬇ How did cultural concerns shared by people on both sides of the Iron Curtain transform European identities?
⬇ What role did these cultural trends play in challenging the division between West and East?

In the 1970s and 1980s, cultural divisions between East and West became muted. People on both sides of the Iron Curtain had similar cultural concerns. They embraced sexuality as a part of their identity. Intellectuals challenged faith in progress, while many people turned to new religious practices. In eastern Europe these shifts did not directly challenge communism, but they did show the extent to which people no longer believed in government propaganda and tried to create alternative identities.

Whose Sexual Revolution?

The four decades after World War II saw a virtual revolution in sexual identities. Men and women became more open about sex as integral to their identity. New technologies for birth control made it easier to separate reproduction from sexual intercourse. And with methods that allowed both partners to control the process, men and women both became generally more sexually active—earlier and with more partners.

But this new openness did not necessarily bring greater sexual equality between men and women. In the West, feminists lobbied for greater access to birth control, especially the contraceptive pill, as a means for women to eliminate unplanned pregnancies. Yet the pill, first available in Europe in the late 1960s, and other contraceptives increased pressure for women to become sexually active. By the early 1980s, the average age when a girl became sexually active in Sweden was fifteen years and two months and for a boy, two months later. For almost half of these young women, their first sexual encounter was not consensual.

In communist Europe, with abortion having become legal after World War II and with methods of birth control available, especially interuterine devices, there was also a revolution in sexuality. But the revolution here was directed from the top down, as the communist regimes wanted to separate production from reproduction to facilitate the entry of a maximum number of women into the workforce. Indeed, in some eastern European countries, almost 40 percent of women worked, but usually in low-level, poorly paid jobs. More women entered technical professions than in the West (engineering was especially popular), but, as elsewhere, women were less likely to rise to the top of their professional ranks than men.

Yet, by the late 1960s, concerns for women as active workers were replaced by fears of depopulation. Everywhere in Europe, the birthrate was decreasing dramatically, and the total population of many countries was going down. In western Europe, the solution was to bring in guest workers. But communist bloc governments looked to other methods. The most dramatic solution was found in Romania, where, in 1967, on the advice of sociologists and doctors, the

As James Bond, British secret agent 007, Sean Connery became a symbol of a hetero-masculinity that was tough but alluring. His portrayal conveyed so much sexual charisma as to justify casual and frequent erotic encounters as a role model for all men. *(Photofest)*

government of **Nicolae Ceauşescu** recriminalized abortion and eliminated all forms of birth control. Women went overnight from being free to choose any form of birth control to being forced to undergo monthly gynecological examinations to monitor any pregnancy. Women's identity shifted from being partners in the labor force and public life to becoming birthing vessels. Yet mothers were given little assistance by the state, and the quality of healthcare and child care indicated that the regime was interested primarily in the number of children born.

Another important aspect of the sexual revolution was the emerging acceptability of homosexuality as an identity. Underground gay communities and culture had existed for a long time, but in the late 1960s and early 1970s politicians began to consider decriminalizing homosexual acts. Sweden had led the way in 1944. In the 1970s and 1980s, gay rights activists in the West largely achieved decriminalization and a degree of cultural tolerance. Sexual equality was added to the list of human rights that most western European governments protected by law. By contrast, in the communist East homosexuality remained criminalized, and many gay persons were placed in abusive psychiatric wards.

Then, in 1983, the AIDS (acquired immune deficiency syndrome) crisis reignited worldwide fears of sexual promiscuity, especially regarding male homo-sexuals. Despite medical research indicating that heterosexuals were often as likely as homosexuals to become infected with the AIDS virus and that the source of infection could be blood transfusions rather than sexual contact, the myth that AIDS was a homosexual illness or punishment for sexual deviants persists in many places.

These important changes in how sexuality was defined had much to do with social practices, medical advances, and public policy. But equally important was the role of popular culture. The emergence of rock and roll and of youth culture as a product that could be easily marketed, together with the growth of television, helped popularize sexual freedom. Rock stars openly flaunted their sexuality, and their fans imitated these trends. Movies, television programs, billboards, and newspaper advertisements promoted sexually explicit images, reinforcing the notion that people's sexual desires and actions were not shameful taboos but integral components of their identity.

Yet popular culture generally did little to challenge traditional gender and sexual identities. James Bond movies celebrated masculine sexual promiscuity and

Nicolae Ceauşescu (1918–1989) Dictatorial leader of communist Romania from 1965 to 1989.

the ideal of the sexually submissive woman. Later in the 1970s, the lifestyles of rock stars like David Bowie and Elton John challenged the staunchly heterosexual aggressive masculine ideal, but most people in western Europe were not ready to accept their sexual choices as anything more than eccentric. In eastern Europe attitudes changed even more slowly, though by the 1980s an infatuation with western popular culture had introduced important aspects of the sexual revolution in the communist bloc. As men traveled abroad, they brought back copies of pornographic magazines and sexually explicit movies. Yet, untouched by feminism, many women in eastern Europe came to equate freedom from communist oppression with the freedom to be erotically provocative in ways that western feminists might decry as turning themselves into sexual objects for the enjoyment of men.

Religious Revival

In both West and East, the generation coming of age in the 1970s and 1980s turned away from established religious traditions. In the West, those who rejected the increasingly consumerist and materialist society sought a new spirituality. In the East, many who were alienated from the ideas of communism and from the religious institutions that had not opposed communism also became interested in nontraditional religions. Buddhist and Hindu practices, particularly yoga, offered spiritual fulfillment for some. Following the trend set by famous stars like the Beatles, some westerners traveled to Asia to immerse themselves in local traditions. People retreated into either private or highly informal ways of expressing their religious beliefs rather than supporting established religious institutions. Church attendance declined even as interest in spirituality grew.

Ireland and Poland were exceptions, however, as in both the Catholic Church became a focus of national resistance to oppression—imperial in Ireland and communist in Poland. In Northern Ireland, the Catholic population, whether they supported the IRA or not, found in the Catholic Church a space in which to cultivate Irish national identity as separate from Protestant English nationalism. In Poland, there was an upsurge of religious attendance as young people found the church a refuge from their bleak political and economic life.

Other developments revived affiliation with traditional religions. In the case of Judaism, antisemitic policies in eastern Europe and the Soviet Union prompted Jews to reassert their religious identity and request permission to emigrate to Israel. In Poland the turning point was 1968, when Jewish students and in-

tellectuals were targeted in the crackdown against the protest movements. In the Soviet Union, the Jewish population began to demand the implementation of the Helsinki Final Act, but only after Gorbachev came to power were a considerable number of emigration requests granted. With a significant influx of eastern European Jewry in the 1980s, the population of Israel changed dramatically. Many immigrants arrived in Israel barely familiar with the religious and cultural traditions of their new home and had to make a radical transition to assume their role as citizens.

As Jews were leaving Europe, another religious group was growing—Muslims, who arrived as guest workers. Because of their poverty and cultural marginalization by the larger community, most guest workers remained conservative in their religious practices. Their children were often raised in the spirit of strict Muslim traditions in the midst of larger secular communities often intolerant of Islam. These economic and cultural factors combined to reinforce the marginalization of Muslims in their host countries, even in France, where this group had become the second-largest religious denomination by the beginning of the twenty-first century.

Postmodernism

While some Europeans experienced new or renewed religious affiliations, others questioned the essence of faith in progress and western civilization itself. In the formulations of French philosopher **Michel Foucault**, the most important thinker of the postmodern movement, these two critiques were closely intertwined. Born in 1926, Foucault was active in the 1968 political protests. Yet, as a homosexual, he was a closet minority even within that progressive vanguard. In the 1970s he published a series of studies that questioned the concepts of "knowledge" and "truth," arguing that both were products of specific ways of thinking and thus fundamentally subjective. In the postmodernist universe, action was part of a complex web of relations, and individual ideas and deeds did not have meaning outside that web. Postmodernists suggested it was foolish to believe that any political or social system could be reformed from within. The fundamental injustices were in the imbalances of power between those who had economic and other resources and those who started from marginal positions. Thus, it was impossible to pinpoint the causes and conse-

Michel Foucault   (1926–1984) French philosopher and prominent postmodernist author.

quences of any action. The theory generated a fundamental dilemma: if there was no way of establishing a clear relationship between any two actions of even one individual, then knowledge was nothing more than an illusion. To "know" was to insert one's own beliefs into the interpretation of facts. This critique did not point to any way out. The only response was irony and skepticism.

For many intellectuals in both the West and East, postmodernism expressed the contradictions of their age—the promises of plenty and the persistence of poverty, access to education and growing ignorance, the ideals of freedom and the shackles of consumerism. In particular, the ironic stance proposed by postmodernists was a survival tool for many writers behind the Iron Curtain. They were themselves caught in a web of powerlessness vis-à-vis the political leadership, for political repression made it impossible to be true to one's calling as a writer and at the same time the calling compelled them to try to express their ideas. It is no wonder, then, that some of the most original and sophisticated thinkers of the postmodern movement came from eastern Europe. For example, the Slovenian philosopher **Slavoj Žižek**'s preoccupation with the ways in which language is shaped by power, and power by language, was an extension of his experience growing up with a regime in which lies were the norm.

The Americanization of European Popular Culture

While some intellectuals worried about the meaning of postmodernism, most Europeans became addicted to American television. Comedy shows like *Married with Children* and *Roseanne* became very popular in Britain and Germany. At seven o'clock in the evening, families across the entire continent could watch the evening news in their native language or broadcasts of American sitcoms. Late-night shows that tried to replicate David Letterman's format sprang up everywhere. There were local alternatives, but the popularity of the American programs was undeniable.

American musicians from Willie Nelson to Madonna regularly sold out all their European performances. American fast-food franchises such as McDonalds opened everywhere in Europe, including Budapest and Moscow. Some worried that eating Big Macs and watching reruns of *Roseanne* would make European culture bland. In fact, Europeans still read more and watch less television than Americans, and they are less likely to eat fast food. It is not clear whether economic reasons or cultural preferences are behind these differences. But it seems that Europeans have self-

consciously attempted to preserve some distance between their consumption of American popular culture and material goods, on the one hand, and their identification with their local and regional European culture, on the other.

The Collapse of the Soviet System, 1989–1991

↓ What were the immediate causes of the collapse of communism in eastern Europe?

↓ How was the fall of communism different among the communist bloc countries?

By 1989, Gorbachev's attempts at reform in the Soviet Union were failing. Talk of perestroika was not followed by spectacular results at a time when most people were expecting a dramatic rise in their quality of life. Yet, the final blow to Gorbachev's reforms resulted from his unwillingness to hold back the new nationalist wave sweeping through both the Soviet Union and its eastern European clients. Even as he was struggling to revive the Soviet Union's viability, his actions prompted dissident movements in eastern Europe to overthrow the communist regimes. With no hope of support from Moscow, most of these regimes gave up without a struggle. Romania, however, experienced a bloody revolution that brought the end of communism at a much higher price. By the end of 1991, the communist bloc had ceased to exist.

The Velvet Revolution

Under glasnost, many informal groups with an openly non-Russian national character developed in various Soviet Republics. They were most outspoken and well-organized in the Baltic Republics, where massive rallies in 1988 showed popular support for economic independence from Moscow. Perestroika was interpreted there in a nationalist-separatist direction. In addition, by 1988 Gorbachev was speaking clearly about the need to let European nations follow their own paths. This policy reversed the interventionist Brezhnev Doctrine and signaled the beginning of Soviet disengagement from its imperialism in eastern Europe. Though Thatcher and Reagan took credit for pressuring the Soviet leader into making such statements, Gorbachev's position was, in fact, an extension

Slavoj Žižek (1949–) Postmodernist Slovenian philosopher and literary critic.

MAP 29.1 **The Fall of Communism, 1989–1991** Between 1989 and 1991 most of the communist states in Europe collapsed, bringing the cold war to an end.

of the glasnost and perestroika policies he had promoted since his arrival in the Kremlin in 1985. The fall of communism is summarized in Table 29.2.

In eastern Europe, the reversal of the Brezhnev Doctrine was perceived by most of the older party leaders as a personal threat to their authority. Reformers moved quickly to secure a peaceful transition to a younger and more dynamic party leadership. In Poland, Solidarity was the first noncommunist organization to become the engine of change. In early 1989, it held roundtable talks with communist officials who hoped to secure a peaceful transition to a regime that would allow the party to retain some political power. But free elections resulted in a complete victory for Solidarity and in the peaceful ousting of the communists.

A wave of activism followed. In the summer of 1989, Estonians, Latvians, and Lithuanians formed a peaceful human chain more than four hundred miles long in opposition to Soviet rule. The rest of eastern Europe awaited Moscow's reaction to these political challenges. Yet nothing happened—no troops crossed

into Poland, no tanks entered the streets of Riga. This lack of response prompted the Hungarian government to open up its border with Austria. In a few days the East Germans started to leave in droves for West Germany through Czechoslovakia, Hungary, and Austria. The road was tortuous, the lines at the border were long, but nobody could stop the exodus. Driving beat-up Trabants, riding old motorcycles, or walking, people camped out on the side of the road, sharing food, music, and their strong hope that they were finally getting out.

By October 1989, the East German leadership had acknowledged defeat and opened up the border with West Germany. In a frenzy of youthful hope and pent-up hate for the regime, people took axes, hammers, and household knives to the Berlin Wall and tore it down. News of what was happening in Berlin was flashed instantly by Radio Free Europe and Voice of America throughout the communist bloc. From Warsaw to Tirana, people celebrated in the streets or rejoiced quietly at home.

Just as the Berlin Wall became the symbol of the cold war after 1961, this image of West and East Germans dancing together on the wall signaled to all in Europe, West and East, that the cold war was over. Today, in the new Berlin, a small portion of the Wall is preserved as a reminder of these historical events. *(AP/Wide World Photos)*

Table 29.2

The Fall of Communism

1976–1977	Massive strikes in Poland and Romania
1977	Charter 77 movement in Czechoslovakia
1978	Polish cardinal becomes Pope John Paul II
1980–1981	Solidarity movement in Poland
1985	Mikhail Gorbachev becomes leader of Soviet Union
1988	Anti-Soviet demonstrations in Lithuania
April 1989	Roundtable talks between Solidarity and Polish communist regime
June 1989	Anticommunist protests in Tiananmen Square, Beijing
September 1989	Hungary opens border with Austria
September 11, 1989	125,000 East Germans cross into Austria via Hungary
November 9, 1989	Berlin Wall comes down
November 10, 1989	Bulgarian communist leader Todor Zhivkov deposed
November 17–December 29, 1989	Peaceful street demonstrations and deposition of communist regime in Czechoslovakia
December 16–21, 1989	Massive street protests in Romania; thousands killed
December 22, 1989	Romanian communist dictator Nicolae Ceaușescu flees
March 1991	Baltic Republics gain independence from Soviet rule
August 19–21, 1991	Failed coup by authoritarian communist group in Moscow
December 1, 1991	Ukraine declares independence from Soviet Union
December 8, 1991	Commonwealth of Independent States established
December 25, 1991	Soviet flag lowered for last time from Kremlin

In November–December, the **Velvet Revolution** brought down the Czechoslovak government. Although massive student demonstrations in Prague on November 17 were brutally suppressed by the police, peaceful street marches continued. Almost half a million Czechoslovaks joined the protests after the first signs of repression. Unlike in 1968, the government had neither the force nor the political will to continue.

Velvet Revolution The peaceful fall of communism in most of eastern Europe in 1989.

Instead, the communists retreated. On December 29, Václav Havel was elected as president by the "power of the powerless."

Violent Struggle in Romania

In two countries, however, the fall of communism proved much more violent. In Yugoslavia, a bloody civil war set the country on a path of self-destruction that would last a decade. In Romania, a much shorter violent popular uprising became the means by which communist dictatorship was forced out. Nicolae Ceauşescu was alone in disregarding Moscow's encouragements for reform, but that was not a new stance.

Since the 1960s he had acted independently, securing good relations with China when the Soviets were in conflict with that country and, in the 1970s, emulating North Korea by breaking all links with the outside world to show that Romania needed no economic assistance from the West or the East. In reality, the Romanian economy suffered from the same problems of soaring prices and lack of energy resources as the rest of the continent.

By 1989, basic goods such as bread, milk, and toilet paper were unavailable, and Romanians were simply struggling to survive. On December 16, people took to the streets of Timişoara to protest the imprisonment of a prominent local Hungarian clergyman. Despite the climate of terror that had increased in the 1980s, thousands joined the crowd. Then the police attacked, killing some civilians. The street uprising seemed to calm down by evening.

A few days later, on December 21, Ceauşescu decided to demonstrate his power by holding a public gathering in Bucharest. The plan backfired. Within minutes there was loud booing, and the dictator fled the scene. A few hours later he and his wife were seized by a group of secret police, military, and political leaders. By the end of the year, the **National Salvation Front** was in charge. Ceauşescu and his wife had been executed after a sham trial, and some top communist leaders were in prison. But many midlevel communists were part of this new government, led by an old party activist who had known Gorbachev since his youth, **Ion Iliescu.** The Romanians had rid themselves of the most horrible aspects of communism, but they had not achieved a democratic regime. Still, the year 1990 began with great optimism in eastern Europe. The Iron Curtain had been lifted.

The End of the Soviet Union

In the Soviet Union, 1990 began with the recognition that the communist experiment had failed to achieve a viable workers' state. The Soviet political and military establishment realized that Gorbachev's reformist talk had permitted the lawful and peaceful exit of the eastern European communist bloc states and that even Soviet Republics no longer wished to be part of the Union. The Baltic states had already made that clear, and after Gorbachev pulled troops out of Afghanistan in 1989, a growing wave of independence movements swept the republics of Central Asia. Nationalism, whether secular or strongly Muslim in orientation, was challenging the authority of communism and the Russian party elites everywhere.

By August 1991, the party had become sharply divided into two factions: one led by **Boris Yeltsin,** the president of the Russian Republic and a young former supporter of Gorbachev, now disappointed with perestroika's lack of success; the other, a conservative faction, now led by Gorbachev, which tried to undo many of the reforms of the 1980s. The unforeseen consequences of his reforms had pushed Gorbachev to retreat. He was fundamentally still a supporter of the communist project and could not embrace the disintegration of the Soviet Union even though he had provided the means for it. Thus, for a brief period of time, Gorbachev attempted to rein in the nationalist independence movements, with strong support from the military establishment and older party leaders.

Yet Gorbachev was also troubled by his abandonment of the principles of glasnost and perestroika. So, by early 1991, he returned to his reformist stance and, under strong international pressure, allowed the independence of Latvia, Lithuania, and Estonia. By August, together with Yeltsin, he had prepared a new treaty for a looser union with the remaining Soviet Republics. This treaty set the stage for the creation of a **Commonwealth of Independent States (CIS)**, which offered its members autonomy in the management of internal affairs while the CIS would coordinate foreign affairs, security, and some economic policies, such as trade.

National Salvation Front Emergency government that came to power in Romania in 1989 after dictator Nicolae Ceauşescu fled.

Ion Iliescu (1930–) Communist leader of the National Salvation Front in postcommunist Romania who became the first president of the country after elections in 1990

Boris Yeltsin (1931–2007) First president of postcommunist Russia, 1991–1999, who oversaw the dismemberment of the Soviet Union and privatization of the economy.

Commonwealth of Independent States (CIS) Alliance of former Soviet republics that oversees some trade, economic reform, and defense issues.

In August 1991 Boris Yeltsin became an instant symbol of revolt against the old Soviet system as he stood with civilians and soldiers on the top of this tank, demanding the resignation of the Soviet leadership. Shortly after these events he outlawed the Communist Party in the Russian Soviet Socialist Republic. *(Reuters/Corbis)*

In a last-ditch effort to save the status quo, a group of eight conservative party leaders tried to seize power and establish a hard-line authoritarian regime. Working with the KGB, they detained Gorbachev at his summer home on August 19. But Yeltsin remained in Moscow, where he appeared in public, made statements broadcast in the state-controlled media, and rallied around him the support of the people and even many military troops. The most defiant moment of Yeltsin's opposition to the **August coup** came when he stood atop a tank that was supposed to separate the Duma from the population and spoke on live television surrounded by large crowds of supporters. Russians everywhere instantly realized that the army was divided, the coup was a sham, and Yeltsin was the man of the hour. Within three days the conservative coup collapsed and Gorbachev returned to Moscow.

But the real winner was Yeltsin, who had stood up to the hard-liners and confronted the army through an act of passive resistance. Instead of operating behind closed doors to outmaneuver his opponents, as the conservatives had done, Yeltsin had instead stood with the people to protest the abuses of the government. Earlier, when Soviet troops had threatened to intervene in the Baltic Republics, he had flown to Riga to stand by protesters. Now, when the party threatened to take over the government, he called on the people and the lower army ranks to stand by him as a Russian patriot.

Yeltsin thus became the face of democratic Russia. As president of the Russian Republic, he shortly outlawed the Communist Party there, closed down communist newspapers, and transferred most state authority from the Soviet Union's federal level of government to his own Russian Republic. On December 1, Ukraine, the second most populous republic of the Soviet Union, proclaimed its independence. By Christmas Day, 1991, the Soviet Union had ceased to exist. The hammer and sickle flag in Red Square was lowered, and the Russian flag raised. The seventy-year communist experiment had ended, and Russian nationalism was restored.

The collapse of the Soviet Union was surprisingly more peaceful than its beginnings, and it signaled the

August coup   Attempt in August 1991 by communist hard-liners to bring an end to the reforms of Yeltsin and Gorbachev that was crushed by a popular uprising.

end of the cold war. Arguments remain over the most important causes for this collapse: the strong military stance of Reagan and Thatcher, Gorbachev's reforms, or dissent movements in eastern Europe. While the West had won the cold war, the meaning of this victory for Europeans at large was still to be determined, as the communist bloc states remained weak economically and politically.

Summary

Review Questions

↑ What brought down the Iron Curtain?

↑ What were the important challenges to democracy in western Europe?

↑ How did European identities become more varied during this period?

Between 1968 and 1991, Europe went from being divided into two ideologically opposed camps to a continent open to the flow of people, ideas, and goods from all regions. During détente, the actions of Western and Eastern political leaders helped increase the exchange of ideas and goods across the cold war divide. Dissidents took advantage of increased visibility to challenge their governments to honor human rights. Others simply left for the West. And although tensions between the United States and the Soviet Union increased after the Soviet invasion of Afghanistan, Gorbachev reversed the Soviet position in eastern Europe. His policy forced the communist regimes to seek reform or face mass uprisings. By the end of 1991, the communists had lost power everywhere in eastern Europe except Yugoslavia. It seemed obvious that the West had won this struggle and that democracy and capitalism had been victorious.

But western Europe was not without its weaknesses, and some important changes in the 1970s and 1980s signaled the shift in the meaning of democratic rights, politics, and freedoms. Traditional parties were confronted with new types of activism, from the Greens to radical nationalist and terrorist movements. Another important challenge came from the decade-long economic crisis that began in 1973. Western European governments achieved renewed prosperity and stability in the 1980s, but only through the scaling back of welfare programs and the privatization of some economic sectors. Overall, Europe became more vulnerable to shifts in the global economy.

A subtler change took place in the social and cultural outlook of Europeans. Eastern Europeans began to see themselves more as part of a cultural continuum that defied the East-West divide. While people in the East looked to the West, some western Europeans questioned the faith in progress in their societies. Feminists pointed to persisting gender inequalities, antinuclear and environmental activists to growing environmental problems and a growing gap between governments and their citizens, and nationalists to a disregard of governments for minorities. Demographic shifts brought important changes to Europe. Its population was aging and growing more diverse ethnically, religiously, and sexually.

← **Thinking Back, Thinking Ahead** →

Did Europe's division during the cold war enhance or diminish the power of the West in the twentieth century and beyond?

ECHO ECHO ECHO ECHO ECHO

Peace Protests

The peace and other street protests of the twenty-first century have a direct link to the antiwar activism that started in western Europe after World War II and grew to mass proportions in the 1980s. The peace symbol, now recognized throughout the world, originated as the logo of the Campaign for Nuclear Disarmament, a British organization, in the early 1960s. This group and many others are the inspiration for contemporary peace activists.

The first antiwar and antinuclear activists were scientists, students, politicians, and housewives who were drawn to these movements for personal or civic reasons. Most learned about them through word of mouth. Neighbors and friends might post leaflets or chat about peace marches. People acted locally and had few resources to coordinate more than small-scale actions. In the 1960s, antiwar protests grew to massive proportions, partly because they made use of television publicity and so garnered faraway supporters who staged similar protests of their own. In the 1980s, when the United States was rebuilding its nuclear arsenal in Europe, massive peace demonstrations were staged in Britain, Germany, Italy, and other western European countries.

At the dawn of the twenty-first century, when peace protests rose against the military actions in Iraq, they were organized quite differently from early protests. What were formerly loose coalitions became activated by new technologies, such as cellular phones and the Internet. Online groups such as Move On had a catalyzing effect, encouraging not only Internet activism but also local street activism, connecting concerned citizens in specific cities. Activists also became able to respond much more quickly to government actions, and they could instantly make their positions and activities known around the world. The international context also became different, as the world is no longer divided by cold war antagonists. During the 1960s, 1970s, and 1980s, peace activists were protesting the actions of both superpowers as well as U.S. and Soviet nuclear power and the militarization of their societies. After the end of the cold war, the protests focused more squarely on U.S. attempts to maintain its international role as the sole superpower.

Suggested Readings

Garton Ash, Timothy. *The Magic Lantern. The Revolution of '89 Witnessed in Warsaw, Budapest, Berlin, and Prague.* New York: Vintage, 1993. An evocative portrait of the revolutions that swept communism from eastern Europe in 1989.

Hayward, Jack, and Anand Menon, eds. *Governing Europe.* Oxford and New York: Oxford University Press, 2003. A comprehensive survey covering all aspects of politics in western Europe.

Hosking, Geoffrey. *The Awakening of the Soviet Union.* Cambridge, Mass.: Harvard University Press, 1991. Illuminates the social, cultural, and historical developments that created the need—and openness—for the political and economic changes that occurred in the late 1980s.

Kaplan, Gisela. *Contemporary Western European Feminism.* New York: New York University Press, 1992. A sophisticated comparative analysis of the feminist movements in western Europe in the second half of the twentieth century.

Loth, Wilfried. *Overcoming the Cold War: A History of Detente, 1950–1991.* New York: Palgrave, 2003. A major new interpretation of the cold war that offers new information taken from Eastern and Western archives.

McCormick, John, *Understanding the European Union: A Concise Introduction.* New York: Palgrave Macmillan, 2005. A uniquely broad-ranging but concise introduction to the European Union, covering in one volume all major aspects of European integration.

Tismăneanu, Vladimir. *Reinventing Politics: Eastern Europe from Stalin to Havel.* New York: Free Press, 2000. An exciting comparative analysis of the breakup of the Soviet Union's outer empire that follows communist governance in each of the communist bloc countries from postwar Stalinist intervention to the present.

Websites

Library of Congress online exhibit, archive, and bibliography on Soviet-U.S. relations, useful for understanding the international context of the cold war, **Cold War,** at www.ibiblio.org/expo/soviet.exhibit/coldwar.html

Full text of the Helsinki Final Act, **Conference on Security and Co-operation in Europe: Final Act,** at www.osce.org/documents/mcs/1975/08/4044_en.pdf

Documents about the fall of communism in eastern Europe, **The Revolutions of 1989,** at //www.gwu.edu/~nsarchiv/news/19991105

CHAPTER 30

Europe in a Globalizing World, 1991 to the Present

1500 B.C.E.	1000 B.C.E.	500 B.C.E.	1 B.C.E./1 C.E.

	1991 Yugoslav civil wars begin Soviet Union collapses	1993 European Union is inaugurated	1995 World Trade Organization is established		1999 Kosovo War brings NATO intervention

1990	1992	1994	1996	1998	2000

The European Union in 2007

Since 1993, the European Union has been a powerful force in refashioning European identities. Originally an international economic organization, it has gained political and cultural dimensions. Its most remarkable transformation in the twenty-first century has been its enlargement to include most of the former communist bloc countries. How has Europeanness been redefined through the change in EU membership?

Expansion of European Union

- Members, 1989
- German reunification, 1990
- New members, 1995
- New members, 2004
- New members, 2007
- Candidates, 2007

500 C.E.   1000 C.E.   1500 C.E.   2000 C.E.

2001
Terrorists attack
the United States

2002
Euro
goes into
circulation

2003
Iraq War
begins

2004
European Union
gains ten new
members

2005
European Union
Constitution is
defeated

2002   2004   2006   2008   2010

Choice Choice Choice

José Bové

José Bové went from being an antinuclear activist in the 1970s to becoming a leader in the environmental antiglobalization movement that seeks to end the use of genetically modified crops. His activism has often been illegal and at times damaging of private property, leading critics to characterize him as a terrorist. But Bové has always carefully staged his protests against property only, never against people, and has always willingly accepted the legal consequences of his actions. (Serra Antoine/Corbis Sygma)

José Bové Plows Down a McDonald's

One fine summer morning in 1999, José Bové woke up early, as farmers do. Then he stepped behind the wheel of a bulldozer and rolled into the little town of Millau, France, and straight into a McDonald's. This particular fast-food restaurant, one of 31,000 worldwide, was due to open in days. But Bové and other Millau citizens dismantled the building and placed the rubble in front of the town hall as a warning to local politicians that the voice of the people must be heard. With this bold action, Bové became an instant celebrity and a symbol, both loved and despised, of environmental and anticorporate activism.

What drove Bové to destroy property and what his choice means is the story of grass-roots activism in the era of globalization. The action wasn't just about McDonald's; it was part of a larger trade war in which the European Union refused to allow genetically modified beef to be sold on its markets and the United States responded with a ban on the import of Roquefort cheese. It was also part of an even larger contest over the power of multinational corporations and the rights of consumers and small producers, as well as part of an international debate over food supplies, poverty and hunger, ecological balance, and what is really good for the earth and the humans who live on it.

Grass-roots activism was not new for Bové. Born in 1953 to a family of scientists, he grew up in France, Luxembourg, and Berkeley, California. Like many of his generation, he took the affluence of his parents for granted but questioned their values. In high school, he protested the religious content of French state education and was expelled for being "faithless." At seventeen, he refused to serve in the military, instead joining other conscientious objectors who occupied lands slated for military camps and farmed them. With hundreds of local farmers and conscientious objectors, he built a traditional stone sheep barn. The project took almost two years. This creative pacifist action offered farming as a countermodel to militarization—a peaceful and useful, if difficult, lifestyle. Bové began to raise sheep and learned to make Roquefort cheese, which became his livelihood as a farmer and later the springboard for his more aggressive antiglobalization protests.

In the 1980s and 1990s Bové participated in Greenpeace actions, protesting France's testing of nuclear weapons in 1995. About the same time, as multinational corporations spread throughout the world and companies like McDonald's began to bring their products and tastes to Europe, Bové turned his attention to the effects of this new global economy at the local level. In 1997, he destroyed the seed production facility of a company known for its genetically modified grain.

But it was the plowing down of the McDonald's at Millau that turned Bové into an icon of antiglobalization. He was soon a favorite of many around the world who resented the dominant presence of American companies. He was also condemned for this new kind of violence; some labeled him a terrorist. In 1999, antiglobalization protesters at a World Trade Organization meeting in Seattle used his protest model when they destroyed corporate property in full daylight. Looters followed. Bové himself did not participate in any of these actions. He just sat and ate a Roquefort cheese sandwich in front of a downtown McDonald's. Unmoved by the abuses of the looters or the accusations of terrorism leveled against him, Bové acknowledged that violence is not a constructive solution: "Yes, this action was illegal. It's not in this way that social and economic problems are resolved. Through the action which we undertook and for which we are being judged, we kicked off a vast citizens' movement which refuses the use of genetically modified organisms in foodstuffs for animals and for humans. These actions will stop when this mad logic comes to a halt." In the following years, he destroyed fields of genetically modified corn in Brazil and France. By calling these acts civil disobedience, he challenged the core values of western civilization. In what way, he asked, is private property more important than the safety of food?

More recently, Bové traveled to the West Bank and Gaza to protest the Israeli presence and treatment of Palestinians. In 2002 he met with Yasser Arafat, head of the Palestine Liberation Organization. For Bové, economic, environmental, and political concerns are one and the same in a world that is globalized.

Introduction

José Bové's protests embody many of the challenges and changes that have transformed the world since 1991. He represents a new generation of activists who see the globalization of economies, the degradation of the environment, and the continuing violence of weapons and war as the world's most serious problems. The first of these challenges was to undo the economic and political legacies of the cold war. Liberal democracies won the war, and the postcommunist European states now took on new significance for western Europe as trade partners, a source of labor, and simply as neighbors. The creation of the European Union (EU) and then its enlargement eastward have been important steps toward European integration.

Overall, democracy has been secured in Europe, even in Russia and Yugoslavia, and Europeans now live in greater stability and prosperity, and with greater tolerance toward each other's differences, than before. Where such tolerance remains challenged is in accepting the increasing Muslim influences in European societies. While Muslim workers and their families are allowed to live in Europe, they have been generally treated as outsiders.

Europeans have once again become strong players on the international scene as a leading force in the global economy. Though far from united, Europeans have also been active in international conflicts, from the Yugoslav Wars of the 1990s to the War on Terrorism since 2001. Internally, the greatest challenges have been preserving democratic principles in the European Union while stretching its boundaries to include countries of the postcommunist bloc. Externally, the

most important challenge has been how to negotiate with the United States their position as collective winners in the cold war in economic and international security matters. Who has paid the cost of this victory and who is reaping the benefits have remained subjects of contention in American-European relations. People like Bové have tried to preserve the particular character of European culture in this era of increasing homogenization and the dominance of global economic and political concerns.

Eastern Europe After Communism

⬇ What impact did the postcommunist transition have on eastern European states and societies?
⬇ To what extent have these countries become more democratic?

The West won the cold war. By the end of 1991, the Soviet Union was defunct, and all but one eastern European country had renounced communism. Within a few years, Russia became a friend and ally of liberal western Europe, the most remarkable achievement in politics of the last two decades. In eastern Europe, however, Yugoslavia remained a vestige of the old communist order, now transformed into an ethno-nationalist dictatorship. As the postcommunist countries claimed a place in the larger European "home," new challenges arose for countries embarking on democratization. The only politicians with experience were the communists, and the most popular ideas uniting the citizenry were nationalist and often nondemocratic. Eastern European

Chronology

1991	Gulf War begins; Soviet Union is dissolved
1991–1995	Serbs, Croats, and Bosnians fight ethnic-based civil wars in Yugoslavia
1992	Internet society is chartered
1993	Israel and the Palestine Liberation Organization sign Oslo Agreements; EU comes into being after ratification of the Maastricht treaty
1995	World Trade Organization is created; Dayton Agreement ends Bosnian War, establishes an independent Bosnia and Serbian Republic of Bosnia
1996	Poland, Czech Republic, and Hungary join NATO
1997	Tony Blair is elected prime minister of Great Britain
1998	Russian stock market collapses
1999	NATO begins Kosovo War against Serbia; José Bové demolishes the Millau McDonald's
2000	Vladimir Putin is elected president of Russia
2001	Al-Qaeda hijacks passenger planes to attack the World Trade Center in New York and the Pentagon in Washington, D.C.
2002	Euro becomes European currency; Fall of Milošević government; MTV opens local broadcast channel in Romania
2003	Iraq War begins
2004	Al-Qaeda terrorists bomb commuter trains in Madrid; Ten new members, mostly postcommunist countries, join the EU; Russians reinvade Chechnya; George W. Bush is reelected president of the United States
2005	EU Constitution is defeated

politicians had to deal with internal political and social problems while also responding to outside pressures from the West for transparency, increased economic freedoms, and reduced corruption. For Russia, Romania, and Bulgaria, these challenges were difficult to meet, while Poland, Hungary, and the Czech Republic managed this difficult decade effectively. The postcommunist transitions have led countries of the Soviet bloc in different directions, and political democratization has not always brought economic betterment, nor has international investment been a guarantee for democratization. The relationship between the free market and democratic politics still remains problematic in this part of Europe.

Russia from Foe to Partner

Russians woke up on Christmas Day 1991 to a brand-new state: a noncommunist Russia and its Commonwealth of Independent States (CIS). At the helm was Boris Yeltsin, the jovial and forceful politician who had stood up to the fearful Gorbachev and staunch communist old-timers to demand reform and democratization. Yeltsin was hugely popular in the days of the August 1991 coup, when he stood atop a tank and

asked the Russian people to protect him and the reformist politicians from the abuses of the communist leadership. He sounded and looked like a man of the people, and his wild stunt worked in rousing the population.

Yet, Yeltsin was not an outsider to Communist Party politics. He had been handpicked by Mikhail Gorbachev to pursue perestroika in the mid-1980s as party chief in the Moscow region. But dutifully following the rules was not Yeltsin's way. He was certainly ambitious and wanted to rise high in the party. But he had been a thrill seeker since childhood, when he pursued many sports competitively, from volleyball to boxing. As a teenager, he learned the skills of the construction trade and then in college became an engineer and joined the party. He soon rose to top leadership in Sverdlovsk. In 1985 he catapulted into the Politburo, becoming the youngest member and Moscow party chief, where he became broadly popular for his tough stand against corruption.

Unceremoniously fired in 1987 for his daring reforms that pushed perestroika and glasnost too far, Yeltsin returned to a humble job in the construction industry. But in 1989, Gorbachev's reforms in electoral law enabled the people of Moscow to bring

Yeltsin back to the Duma. With broad popular support, Yeltsin quickly rose to become the most outspoken and trusted reformist of the Communist Party elite, in 1990 creating a Democratic Platform group that demanded radical change in the party's leading role, as well as decentralization of the state structure.

By August 1991, when conservatives attempted a coup, Yeltsin was the popularly elected president of Russia. This victory emboldened him to contest the power of the Soviet federal authorities. In fact, he swiftly dissolved the Communist Party in Russia and proceeded to fire officials appointed on the basis of party loyalty. In all these radical changes, Yeltsin risked a great deal of personal and professional safety, but it was in his nature to gamble and think big.

By early 1992, Yeltsin commanded the admiration of the entire world: the amazingly sudden and peaceful transformation of the Soviet Union from the "evil empire" of U.S. president Ronald Reagan's rhetoric into multiparty Russia was one of the most important developments of the post–cold war period. Politicians in the West celebrated the victory of the United States over the Soviet Union. The Soviet people themselves celebrated the end of communist rule as though waking from a bad dream. But these celebrations were short lived. Within months, the reality of the aftermath of political, social, and economic collapse set in.

Yeltsin continued to rule Russia throughout the decade, but his popularity and success were never as high as in 1992. Politically the country became democratic in that the communist monopoly was replaced by a multitude of political parties, but many of them were undemocratic. Measures to transform the state-controlled economy into a market-driven one benefited a narrow stratum of people while most became impoverished. And in matters of national unity and international security, Yeltsin satisfied neither die-hard nationalists nor progressive reformers.

In 1992 the only Russian politicians with experience were communists, and most people who were not already involved in the party had no desire to participate in politics. Therefore, even though Yeltsin's regime introduced full political freedoms, most political parties represented small groups interested in political gains rather than voters' interests. Most prominent among these groups were newly enriched businessmen, who were able to gain control over important economic resources illegally and wanted to protect their businesses. The oil industry became a particularly powerful force in several parties.

Other groups were motivated by the nationalist desire to make sure the new Russia served Russians above other nationalities. These groups grew in the early 1990s, as they spoke to the electorate in terms the people understood. They blamed poverty and personal insecurity on outsiders—the West or enemies within the CIS, such as Ukraine, Georgia, and Moldova, former Soviet Republics now seeking independence from the Russians. Though these parties acknowledged social and economic problems, their solutions, such as increasing military spending to alleviate poverty, were ineffective. Yeltsin tried to balance these new factions and the communists but could not manage to create a popular, reform-minded party of his own.

Given the lack of parties that offered solid solutions to the economic and social problems of the broad electorate, most people did not fare better in these early years of Russian democratization. The economy was swiftly **privatized,** with the state selling or simply giving up its previous control over most economic enterprises, from factories to beauty salons. By 1995, over half of all economic activity was in private hands. It was in these private enterprises that almost 90 percent of the industrial workforce was employed. New service sectors developed, while large public enterprises and services, such as healthcare, social services, and education, remained largely in the hands of the state. State employees such as coal miners and teachers sometimes did not get paid for months, while inflation reduced the buying power of the ruble. Thus, even when the checks arrived, many public employees could not support their families. In 1993 over 30 percent of the population was living in poverty.

During the same period, there was a marked increase in the activities of criminal gangs, who took advantage of irregularities and simply took over many services and state enterprises. The state did not have enough reliable law enforcement agents to deal with corruption. Thus, while some of the signs of privatization looked encouraging, the overall welfare of the people declined. For a majority of Russians, the benefits of democracy were not apparent, and many began celebrating the old national holiday of the Soviet Union (November 7) with parades and even mourning Joseph Stalin's death.

In August 1998 the Russian stock market completely collapsed. Under pressure from international financial organizations such as the **World Bank** and

privatization Replacement of state ownership of property with private ownership in the postcommunist states.

World Bank International financial organization controlled by developed countries in the West that offers discounted loans for economic reform to developing countries.

the **International Monetary Fund**, which had loaned Russia billions of dollars for its economic reform, the government was forced to devalue the ruble. This move was completely unexpected, as Yeltsin had promised time and again never to devalue the ruble. Many lost their life savings and trust in the banking system overnight. The ruble slowly recovered some of its value, but faith in the stock market and in Yeltsin's brand of reform was never fully restored.

Yeltsin's decade in power was also plagued by crises in former Soviet territories. **Chechnya,** where the native Islamic majority had never accepted the Russian takeover of 1859, made a bid for independence in the early days of postcommunism. In 1994 Yeltsin sought to regain control through military invasion. Three years of military conflict ensued, and Yeltsin's popularity plummeted when he signed a shaky truce with the Chechen rebels in 1997. By 1999, Chechnya had become a haven for traffic in illegal weapons and drugs, as well as a training ground for Islamic radicals.

After a decade of political, economic, and international challenges, Yeltsin finally decided to step down. Suffering from severe health problems and battling alcoholism, he had taken steps to secure his successor in the summer of 1999, when he appointed **Vladimir Putin** as premier. On December 31 Yeltsin called Putin into his office and handed over the presidency to him. This choice of a successor may be Yeltsin's most troubled legacy.

The Dismemberment of Yugoslavia

In the 1990s Yugoslavia plunged into a bloody civil war that destroyed the country, brought appalling human losses, and prompted the first major military intervention by NATO. The political and economic troubles that destroyed Yugoslavia had begun as early as 1968, when a new wave of nationalism became apparent in various regions of the country. Yugoslavia had been created after World War I, primarily as an extension of Serbia's ambitions for unifying all the South Slavs; Croats, Bosnians, and Slovenes were brought into this union as unequal partners. World War II had further antagonized the various ethnic groups, as Serbs massacred Croats and Croats massacred Serbs under the watchful eye of the Nazi occupiers. After 1945, Josip Broz Tito had attempted to create "brotherhood and unity" among these embattled ethnic groups.

But when Tito died in 1980, hope for brotherhood and unity vanished. Politicians began to depict inflation and other economic problems in ethnocentric terms. In 1986, a brash Serbian lawyer, **Slobodan Milošević,** attracted attention by laying blame for the

---

Table 30.1

The Dissolution of Yugoslavia

1989	Slobodan Milošević becomes president of Serbia; Kosovo loses autonomous status
1991	Slovenia declares independence; Yugoslavia fails in military attempt to prevent it
1991	Croatia declares independence; civil war begins
1992	Bosnia civil war begins
1993	UN peacekeeping troops on the ground
1995	NATO air strikes
1995	Dayton Agreement
1996	Active military resistance in Kosovo against Serbian government begins
1999	NATO/U.S. air strikes against Serbia
2002	Milošević ousted
2003	Yugoslavia ceases to exist, becoming "Serbia and Montenegro"
2004	Slovenia joins the EU
2006	Montenegro declares independence from Serbia

Serbians' economic problems on the Croats, Bosnians, and Kosovar Albanians. As president of Serbia, Milošević was still a high official in the Communist Party, but he had already begun his transformation into a Serbian ultranationalist. By 1991, he had emerged as the most outspoken proponent of Yugoslavia as the country of Serbs first and other nationalities second. With the state fully in control of politics, the media, and the army, Milošević embarked on a campaign to discredit non-Serbians and liberal economic and political reformers. Table 30.1 summarizes the dissolution of Yugoslavia.

Slovenes and Croats reacted by declaring independence in June 1991. While the Slovenes were able to walk away from the Yugoslav union without any contest, Croatia and then Bosnia, which declared independence in 1992, became engulfed in civil war.

International Monetary Fund International financial organization started in 1946 responsible for managing the global financial system.

Chechnya Region in Central Asia controlled by Russia since 1859, which has a strong independence movement led by radical Islamists.

Vladimir Putin (1952–) President of Russia since 2000, popular because of his nationalist credentials and anticorruption platform.

Slobodan Milošević (1941–2006) Socialist dictatorial president of Serbia and Yugoslavia who was deposed by popular protests and died while on trial for genocidal war crimes.

MAP 30.1 **The Breakup of Yugoslavia** Between 1991 and 2006 the federal, multi-ethnic Yugoslavia fragmented into small and relatively poor independent states. While Slovenia became a success, Montenegro is still struggling to become an economically viable state.

Between 1991 and 1995, Serbs, Croats, and Muslim Bosnians engaged in **ethnic cleansing,** killing each other relentlessly on the basis of ethnic identity. Most of the fighting took place outside Serbia proper, but Milošević's actions as supreme commander of the Yugoslav army and in helping Serbian paramilitary groups in Croatia and Bosnia played a central role in the atrocities committed by the Serbian forces. The exiling, killing, raping, and seizure and destruction of property had the sole purpose of eliminating the presence of these other ethnicities. More than twenty thousand women, most of them Muslim, were systematically raped in Bosnia as part of the Serbian and Croatian ethnic-cleansing campaigns.

By 1994 world opinion prompted belated action against these outrageous crimes. The internationally sanctioned **Geneva Conventions** forbade the mistreatment of civilians and prisoners of war, and the UN attempted to impose **sanctions** and sent in observers, but these measures had little effect. After the publication of evidence about several massacres, the UN finally approved air strikes by NATO, its first military intervention ever. By December 1995, the war

was over, and all parties signed the **Dayton Agreement,** which recognized both an independent Muslim-Croat federation and a Serbian Republic in Bosnia, with a UN peacekeeping force to oversee the postwar transition. While this agreement offered a peaceful resolution, it also created some important problems. In particular, it implicitly endorsed the right of the Milošević government to fight any future pro-independence movements.

ethnic cleansing Eliminating an "enemy" ethnic group by exiling, killing, and raping its members and destroying or taking away their property.

Geneva Conventions Four international treaties that forbid the mistreatment of civilians and prisoners of war during wartime.

sanctions Punitive measures adopted by a country or group of countries against another state for political reasons.

Dayton Agreement Peace agreement signed in 1995 that ended the Bosnian civil war and established the grounds for an independent Bosnia and a Serbian Republic.

Between 1991 and 1995 Yugoslavia endured the bloodiest civil war in Europe since 1918. Serbs, Croats, and Bosnians fought with each other, and many civilians were murdered, giving rise to the term "ethnic cleansing." In this photograph we see Muslims at a funeral of forty-seven civilians killed by Serbs at the beginning of the war and later unearthed an in the village of Ahatovici near Sarajevo on Sunday, July 7, 1996. *(Rikard Larma/AP Images)*

Most post-Yugoslav countries pursued economic and political reconstruction with the aim of "rejoining" Europe. Slovenia quickly developed a free market while maintaining important components of the communist welfare system. By 2004, this country had a per capita GDP of $18,300. It was a complete success story. By contrast, Croatia had more problems, especially given the staunchly nationalist and sometimes illiberal bent of its government in the early 1990s. With much of the economy trying to reinvent itself outside the Yugoslav markets, and with many of its resources having been diverted to civil war, Croatia was slower to move toward a democratic system and free-market economy. Yet, by the end of the 1990s, nationalist excesses were diminishing, trade with western Europe was picking up, and the economy was growing so fast that Croatia began to negotiate joining the EU.

Milošević tried to pull together Yugoslavia's remaining resources. His corrupt regime controlled the media, the military, and political parties with support from abroad, especially Russia. To revive his popularity among nationalist followers, he turned to Kosovo, where tensions between the overwhelmingly Albanian majority (80 percent) and the powerful Serbian minority had festered for a long time. Tensions increased as Kosovars suffered increasingly from economic problems and political oppression. In the summer of 1998, as many as three hundred thousand Kosovo

Albanians were forced to flee their homes, going elsewhere inside Yugoslavia or across the border to Albania, Macedonia, and Greece. This mass exodus raised international concern.

In February 1999, with one civilian massacre by the Serb forces confirmed, American, British, and Russian negotiators attempted a settlement between the Kosovo Albanians and Serbs. Serbians and their Russian supporters walked out of the talks, and on March 24 NATO began air strikes against Serbia. The **Kosovo War** lasted just a few months. Its most spectacular features—the American bombing of the Chinese Embassy and Serbian hospitals—received much media attention, while the number of casualties was disputed because few independent observers were allowed on the ground. The number of Kosovo Albanian refugees skyrocketed to more than 1 million. When the NATO bombing ended on June 10, it was not clear who had won. Inside Serbia, Milošević declared victory. Though his version defied facts by depicting Serbs as victims of a worldwide conspiracy and U.S. president Bill Clinton as another Hitler, Milošević gained popularity in Serbia after the war. In-

Kosovo War (March–June 1999) Military conflict between NATO forces and Serbia over abuses against Kosovo Albanians.

In October 2002 Slobodan Milošević was brought down by a popular street uprising in which young people and Internet communication played an important role. Serbia has struggled since then to fashion an international image of a viable democracy. *(Kamenko Pajic)*

stead of weakening him, the NATO campaign had the adverse result of mobilizing more Serbs, who cast themselves as patriots defending their country against a foreign invasion.

The massive abuses in Kosovo ended, though instances of ethnic hatred have erupted periodically since 1999. The area's stability depends entirely on the continued presence of UN troops. The region is officially still part of Serbia, yet Belgrade has virtually no say in internal affairs. Most refugees (eight hundred thousand) returned, and autonomous government institutions were set up to represent the Albanian population.

The Kosovo War did not bring down Milošević, but in October 2002 a popular revolt, with street protests all over Belgrade, removed him from power. His replacement was Vojislav Koštunica, a constitutional lawyer with strong Serbian nationalist credentials and a more internationally acceptable reputation. The Milošević regime was brought down by its own massive corruption, the impoverishment of the population, general fatigue after a decade of fighting, and the growing sense that their country had become an outcast in Europe.

Postcommunist Transitions in Eastern Europe

The transformation of the other eastern European countries from members of the communist bloc to members of the European international community has been more successful. They have developed constitutional, pluralist governments, with free elections, multiple parties, freedom of the press, and a free-market economy. But each has had specific problems to deal with, and their choices for solutions have differed widely.

Like Yugoslavia, Czechoslovakia was created after World War I. And like Yugoslavia, Czechoslovakia was dismembered in the early postcommunist years under the weight of nationalist pressures. But rather than civil war, the Czechs and Slovaks went their separate ways on the basis of national referendums. At the end of 1992, the population simply voted to split up the country into two republics. Václav Havel, the playwright president, oversaw this peaceful democratic process and accepted its outcome. The important difference between Yugoslavia and Czechoslovakia was that the political leadership, even when nationalist enmities existed, refused to pursue a violent path. Instead, leaders trusted the newly developed democratic institutions, even when these institutions turned them out of power.

Hungary also embraced democratic politics, but with a stronger nationalist element. Some popular politicians of the 1990s openly espoused antisemitism and pushed for special protection for ethnic Hungarians living in other countries, especially Romania. Yet such ethnocentric issues did not play any role in the economic policies pursued by either center-right and left-wing governments. Overall, Hungary was successful in maintaining a talented labor force, attracting foreign investments, and improving the quality of life of its citizens.

Poland saw the return and then departure of Solidarity leader Lech Wałęsa. While in 1980 Wałęsa had been a charismatic unifier of opponents to communism, after 1989 he was ill prepared to assume the responsibilities of governing a democratic regime. He had neither the vision nor the skills to offer good solutions to the challenges of privatization and to the increasing activism of the Catholic Church. Still, though Solidarity lost its initial appeal, it did give rise to numerous other parties and provided the groundwork for a generation of democratic politicians. Poland was also fortunate in that it proceeded quickly with privatization and implemented tough reforms that brought healthy economic growth by the end of the decade.

In social and cultural policies, however, Poland seemed to cling strongly to the past. Having been a main force of opposition under communism, the Catholic Church, with the direct support of Pope John Paul II, proceeded to create its own political following. The church cultivated socially conservative politicians who wanted to make abortion illegal and advocated Catholic "family values," pursuing anti-gay propaganda campaigns. The public presence of the church grew, from television programs to educational institutions. Still, though many in Poland see the Catholic Church as a privileged institution, it coexists alongside secular social and cultural organizations that pursue their own agendas and values.

The Czech Republic, Slovakia, Hungary, and Poland thus implemented democratic reforms and successfully managed antidemocratic forces. They were also the first to engage successfully in regional cooperation. Coming together as the **Visegrád Four** in 1991, they agreed to coordinate internal reforms from education to the environment, with the goal of joining the EU. By building regional trade, the four countries turned their communist economies into competitive capitalist ones. Key to their success were three factors: agreement among the political leadership, public support, and economic and administrative infrastructures that were compatible with reform. In addition, long-standing personal links forged in the communist era among the underground oppositions in Poland, Czechosolvakia, and to some extent Hungary fostered institutional cooperation. Morevoer, both the EU and the United States regarded the economies of these four countries as the most advanced of the former communist states and invested in them both political hopes and financial resources.

Latvia, Lithuania, and Estonia traveled a different road from direct Soviet control to successful democratization. In these Baltic countries, the legacies of communist politics and state economies were more difficult to undo. In Estonia, where a large ethnic Russian population had been brought in, the ethnic antagonism between the two groups ran deep, especially since positions of power had been occupied overwhelmingly by Russians. While Latvians found it relatively easy to tolerate the presence of the Russians without any fears of further russification, the Estonians (and to some extent the Lithuanians) saw ethnic Russians as agents of imperialism even after the dissolution of the Soviet Union. Indeed, Russia remained vocally concerned about the large Russian minority in Estonia but had little power to act on its behalf. Under the influence of growing nationalism, the Estonians have implemented some policies to diminish the public presence of the Russian minority, such as mandating a majority of classroom hours in Estonian, even in towns where only ethnic Russians live. Overall, however, with unemployment relatively low and new economic opportunities opening up, the people of the Baltic states have remained relatively content. All three countries have stable democracies.

Romania and Bulgaria, however, failed to become fully functioning democracies. They did hold free elections in which a multitude of parties competed. But these parties were closer to the kinds of factions that developed in Russia under Yeltsin, led by old Communist Party activists and interested in protecting narrow interests. Political corruption continued to dominate the electoral process, with few checks and balances. Corrupt judges protected corrupt legislators, while local law enforcement agencies worked with administrators to protect each other's interests.

In Romania, Ion Iliescu, a disgruntled protégé of Nicolae Ceauşescu, won the first presidential election and then proceeded to win again after a four-year interregnum by a more reform-minded coalition. Most successful Romanian politicians of this decade espoused some form of nationalism, from mild to radical. There was a short revival of a neofascist party, and one openly antisemitic and anti-Hungarian party won 20 percent of the vote in the 2000 presidential elections.

Romania's most debilitating problem was that no government in the 1990s pursued a thorough policy of privatizing large state enterprises and encouraging investments in competitive new businesses. Instead,

Visegrád Four   Group formed in the early 1990s by Hungary, Poland, the Czech Republic, and Slovakia to coordinate internal reforms toward joining the EU.

political clients won investment bids through bribery and squandered many of the state and private resources for personal gain. Foreign investment was also discouraged by Romania's inability to protect private property. By 2000, the Romanian economy lagged behind that of every country in Europe, save Albania.

Bulgaria fared marginally better. Though plagued by political corruption, its service and tourism industries outperformed those in Romania. Nor did nationalism play a strong rallying role, although small Muslim enclaves remained relatively impoverished and received inadequate support from the government. The country was also relatively freer of organized crime than Romania and Russia, whose economies were sapped of important revenue resources by these criminal organizations.

Overall, economic growth in Romania and Bulgaria has been impeded by the harsh political and economic legacies of the communist period as well as a lack of investment incentives or interest from Western countries. By the time these regimes achieved internal political stability, curbed corruption, and created legislation friendly to foreign investment, the initial enthusiasm of the West to invest in the postcommunist countries had vanished.

European Integration

> ↓ How has the EU transformed European politics and economies?
> ↓ What impact has the EU had on European security matters?

Due to these remarkable changes among the postcommunist states, eastern Europe both transformed and was transformed by the European Union. With the Soviet threat removed, western Europe perceived the future differently. The former communist countries became collaborators in a larger framework of European integration. This process of challenging established divisions and offering new ways of connecting European states and people created unprecedented opportunities to redefine Europe as a political, economic, and cultural community. In the 1990s the Common Market underwent important institutional changes, from a loose economic union to a fiscal unit, a political institution, and a cluster of cultural and social institutions that are today truly multinational and reach into every corner of the continent. Europeans tackled international security challenges on the basis of cooperation. Yet, internal political contests and nationalism continued to test the boundaries of international collaboration. Table 30.2 summarizes the development of the European Union.

Table 30.2
Development of the European Union

1951	European Coal and Steel Community is established (ECSC)
1957	Treaty of Rome establishes the European Economic Community (EEC), made up of Belgium, France, Italy, Luxembourg, the Netherlands, and West Germany
1973	Britain, Denmark, and Ireland join the EEC
1981	Greece joins the EEC
1985	Portugal and Spain join the EEC
1992	Maastricht treaty creates the European Union (EU); European Economic Community is renamed the European Community (EC) as part of the EU
1995	Austria, Finland, and Sweden join the EU; Schengen Agreement goes into effect
2002	The euro becomes EU currency
2003	First EU constitution is drafted
2004	Cyprus, the Czech Republic, Estonia, Hungary, Latvia, Lithuania, Malta, Poland, Slovenia, and Slovakia join the EU
2007	Bulgaria and Romania join the EU

From Community to Union

After 1985, when **Jacques Delors** became the president of the **European Commission**, the highest executive authority of the Common Market, the European Community embarked more forcefully on a plan to create a single-market entity. Delors and other euro-enthusiasts pointed to the outstanding track record of the participating countries since the inception of the Common Market in terms of economic growth, employment, and per capita income, suggesting that greater institutional cooperation among member countries would increasingly benefit them. The growing complexity of economic activities since the 1970s also suggested that greater political cooperation would be needed to sustain the well-being of member countries. To enable the workforce to move across borders in order to effectively match skills and needs, states would have to work out better policies regarding migration, labor rights, and social welfare policies. Closer

Jacques Delors (1925–) French Socialist politician and president of the European Commission from 1985 to 1994 who promoted the creation of the EU.

European Commission Executive branch of the EU, responsible for drafting legislation and enforcing regulations.

coordination of taxation, interest rates, and other fiscal measures would also help businesses operate across borders. For example, for an enterprise such as Airbus, with capital and profits in France, to expand its operations outside of France meant depending on the willingness of Spain and Britain, for example, to protect its business interests and accept its practices. Since the inception of the Common Market, such arrangements had developed through bilateral agreements. By the 1980s, many believed that an international political institution would improve cooperation and serve the interests of both employers and employees.

The unification of institutions and standardization of regulations of economic practice, from taxation to the labeling of agricultural products, was to take place between 1985 and 1992. The process of ratification was cumbersome, for the national governments of Common Market members had to individually ratify all changes. This arrangement respected the sovereignty of each member state but rendered the process vulnerable to political change in any member country.

At the beginning there was a great deal of enthusiasm for the idea of a single market, increased opportunities for investment, and the unrestricted movement of workers and goods across borders. But by 1990 the enthusiasm was largely gone, as politicians, corporations, and consumers began to see that regulations meant to free up access to markets and goods also had a restrictive impact. For instance, agricultural producers were to test, package, and label their goods in accordance with new Common Market regulations. Smaller organic farmers, like **José Bové** (see Choice), suffered in the process, as their costs of production and shipping increased significantly. If they passed these costs on to consumers through higher prices, they would make themselves less competitive than multinational corporations, such as McDonald's, which could produce certified genetically modified products more cheaply.

At a series of intergovernmental meetings in 1991, member countries addressed such issues. Achieving a European Monetary Union demanded a complex plan of coordinating fiscal policies among members. And since such a massive fiscal restructuring had never before been attempted, policymakers and ordinary people alike worried about potential negative consequences. A policy of moving to one single currency, the **euro (€)**, was outlined, with the ultimate goal of having one European Bank and the euro in circulation by 1999. That change actually occurred in 2002.

In addition, the question of political integration raised nationalist fears about the expanded powers of the European Commission and European Parliament at the expense of national governments. The formula

of a loose federation was worked out by the end of 1991. No one country could dominate either of these bodies. Additionally, any legislative measures by the European Parliament would have to be approved by a broad international margin, and the most important measures, such as a European constitution, would have to be ratified by each member. Furthermore, the European Parliament would have the power to check the executive powers of the European Commission.

Another thorny issue was the growth of the German share of the Common Market, especially with the unification of the two Germanies in 1990. Suddenly, this country counted for a quarter of the total population and 27 percent of the European Community's production. Concerns that a strong and ambitious Germany might again threaten the stability of Europe were allayed only when well-respected politicians, in particular French president François Mitterrand and German chancellor Helmut Kohl, pursued a campaign for European integration: "We consider it necessary to accelerate the political construction of the Europe of the Twelve. We believe that it is time to transform relations as a whole among the member states into a European Union . . . and invest this union with the necessary means of action."

The idea of free movement of people across borders became vastly more complicated with the opening of borders in eastern Europe after the fall of communism and the incoming flood of eastern Europeans. A unified EU policy on immigration actually reconstructed the East-West divide. In 1995, most EU members (save Ireland, Britain, and Denmark) began implementing the **Schengen Agreement**, which eliminated the need for citizens of signatory states to obtain visas to travel and work inside the Schengen space. Citizens of most other countries still had to apply for entry, but once they obtained a visa from one of the signatory states, they could travel without additional visas elsewhere in the Schengen space. In practice, it became more difficult for most people outside the Schengen territory to obtain work or permanent residence visas in any of the signatory countries, but it was easier to obtain travel visas. For people

José Bové (1953–) French environmental activist known for his violent protests against genetically modified foods.

euro (€)   Currency introduced in most EU member countries starting in 2002.

Schengen Agreement   Treaty signed by seven members of the Common Market in 1985 allowing the free passage of people and goods across their borders, which went into effect in 1995.

from postcommunist eastern Europe, still having to apply for a visa was a humiliating reminder of their outsider status in Europe.

In February 1992, the Common Market foreign ministers signed the **Maastricht treaty,** which created the European Union, the most important milestone toward European integration since the creation of the European Coal and Steel Community in 1951. Although it was expected that member countries would ratify the treaty without much resistance, there was opposition in Denmark and Britain, where politicians and the populace at large preferred national policies in certain crucial areas. In Britain, the Conservatives retained the policy of deregulating industries and upholding the strength of the pound. In Denmark, the vote went narrowly against the treaty in order to retain environmental and other public policy standards higher than those of the EU; the Danes also feared German domination. In both cases, however, opposition stemmed less from nationalist pride and anxieties than from concern about specific economic and social policies. After a year of negotiations with both countries, the Maastricht treaty went into effect in November 1993 and the European Union came into being.

The European Union in Operation

The EU consists of a set of existing institutions, now with expanded powers, as well as some new bodies. The highest executive body is the **European Council,** composed of heads of state or government and the president of the European Commission. Since 1993 the European Council has met several times a year to discuss issues of interest at the national and international level and on occasion to iron out tensions among member states. This body does not deal with the specific implementation of day-to-day measures passed by the European Parliament but only with broad issues, such as the balance between national political autonomy and international cooperation.

The **Council of Ministers** is charged with implementing EU goals on a practical level. A cross between an executive and legislative body, the Council of Ministers attempts to find a balance in unifying everything from energy to taxation policies so as not to run counter to national prerogatives and to maintain cooperation. For instance, the use of nuclear power for the energy needs of a particular state has to be reconciled with the environmental regulations of the EU as a whole.

The European Commission, whose president also sits on the European Council, also mediates between national and EU interests but works solely as an elected body of the EU. Before 1993, the European Commission was the primary initiator of legislation

and also served as the executive power in dealing with the Council of Ministers and the European Council. After 1993, the European Commission lost some of its legislative authority to the European Parliament, especially in matters of the EU budget. The EU Parliament has also helped restrain the executive powers of the European Commission, especially those of its president.

The development of the **European Parliament** from a symbolic body to a legislative assembly with European-wide powers from taxation to education is one of the most important political developments in Europe since Maastricht, and it has started to reshape European political parties at large. As the number of seats assigned to each country varies but is not strictly proportional, smaller countries have disproportionate influence. Thus, these smaller countries can form coalitions to block the passage of laws they view as harmful to their interests. Yet, representatives in the European Parliament tend to act not only according to their national flags but also according to their ideological platforms, and the body divides more consistently along ideological than national lines. Thus, French delegates are as likely to be at odds with each other over environmental concerns, such as the use of genetically modified organisms in agriculture, as they are to be at odds with their German colleagues. Delegates who are members of Green parties, for example, tend to vote as an international bloc on environmental matters, regardless of what other representatives from their home countries think.

In the 1990s the EU began to consider the question of enlargement to include countries from the former communist bloc. This issue was first broached in 1990, after German reunification, in which the political and economic legacies of communism were assumed directly by West Germany, which was already the strongest economy in the Common Market. When the Visegrád Four began to lobby for admission, the EU had to consider the impact of such a change on its economic strength and also the very criteria for admission. Greece, Portugal, and Spain had all been

Maastricht treaty Treaty signed in 1992 and ratified by all members of the Common Market in 1993 that brought the EU into being.

European Council EU advisory body composed of the heads of state or government of member countries and the president of the European Commission.

Council of Ministers Main legislative body of the EU, composed of ministers from each country, that carries out EU goals in legal measures and policymaking.

European Parliament The directly elected parliamentary body of the European Union.

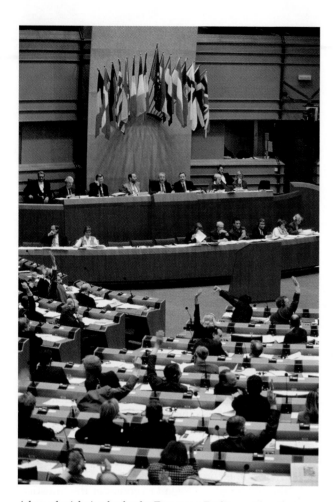

A huge legislative body, the European Parliament has the power to vote (as we see it exercised in this image) on important policies that affect the people, economies, and political institutions of all member countries. *(TM-Photo/Zefa/Corbis)*

By February 2003, eight of the postcommunist countries (the Czech Republic, Estonia, Hungary, Latvia, Lithuania, Poland, Slovakia, and Slovenia) had finally been accepted into the union, along with two other applicants (Cyprus and Malta), bringing the number of member states to twenty-five. In May 2004, these ten countries began to function as members of the EU. The success or failure of this larger union, now with two additional members (Bulgaria and Romania), remains to be seen, especially as the new members prepare for full monetary union. But several issues will continue to be of concern. The larger union means a larger bureaucracy. If all the existing rules regarding governance, balance of power between the Commission and the Parliament, and representation of all languages in the running of the EU are to be maintained, the daily activities of EU institutions are likely to become more expensive and more cumbersome.

The rejection of the EU constitution by France and the Netherlands in 2005 indicates that the institutional growth of the EU is likely to come to a halt. The EU constitution would have given increased powers to the European Parliament and greater protections for human rights in some member countries. Though the French and Dutch broadly support the union's current policies, they do not wish to see the powers of their national governments further eroded. Opposition to the EU constitution came from both right-wing anti-immigration groups concerned about the growing presence of Muslim immigrants, as well as left-wing groups wanting to maintain specific social policies.

Another important test for the criteria and goals of EU enlargement has been Turkey's bid for admission. Turkey was a member of NATO and a functioning democracy long before any eastern European country applied for membership. The thorny question here pertains to the very definition of "European civilization." While many in Istanbul consider themselves European by virtue of their geography, political structure, culture, artistic sensibilities, and lifestyle, many Europeans regard Turkey as a Muslim non-European state. The growth of militant Islam in Turkey and the recent pro-religious policies of the government have reinforced the sense of some EU members that Turkey is turning away from Europe and forging closer ties with the Middle East. Moreover, if Turkey were to be admitted, the proportion of Muslims in the EU would jump from 2.6 percent to around 10 percent. Such statistics pose policy challenges regarding the rights and obligations of citizens and governments as well as broader cultural challenges regarding the character of European cultures and societies. Many are not yet prepared to offer Islam a seat at the European table.

accepted as members in the 1980s on the premise that they had potential for democratic politics, rather than a proven record. Yet, to many EU leaders, the admission of Greece, because of its weak economy in the 1980s, set an unfortunate precedent. Still, some members, such as France, Germany, and Italy, supported the notion of rewarding the stable postcommunist democracies with EU membership. Supporters of enlargement eastward also pointed to the potential larger markets and increased stability in Europe as advantages for the EU. Ultimately, market expansion and European stability became the criteria for enlargement in the next phase. Yet, the way these criteria were applied in some cases raised questions. For instance, many argued that having Estonia, Latvia, and Lithuania, with their sizable Russian minorities, in the EU would, in fact, create new tensions between the EU and Russia, reducing European stability.

Nation-States in a New Context

The EU has not meant European unity, even among the older member countries. In Britain, Germany, and, more recently, Spain, right-wing governments were replaced by left-wing ones, though not necessarily for the same reasons. In Britain in 1997, the Labour Party returned to power with **Tony Blair** as prime minister when the public reacted against the Conservative government's aggressive policies of privatizing national industries and reducing social programs. Blair pursued business-friendly internal policies and a commitment to the EU. To Conservative skepticism about the impact of the EU on the British pound and industries, Blair responded with an enthusiasm for the EU's social and political components. Still, he was careful to continue his support for the pound, even as the rest of the EU was adopting the euro.

The shift toward the left in Germany was both a product of EU integration and the condition for it. While Helmut Kohl was one of the most important players in promoting Maastricht and further EU enlargement, he faced problems at home connected to reunification, including fluctuating unemployment, the democratization and privatization of the former East Germany, and important disparities in the standard of living. The socially conservative chancellor lost some of his popularity during this period, as voters in both parts of reunified Germany began to identify the Christian Democrats with the economic and social problems of reunification.

As a result, the Social Democrats came to power in 1998, with the younger **Gerhard Schroeder** as the first German chancellor to have grown up after the war and also the first to rule in a coalition with the Greens. Schroeder was a disappointment to the more left-leaning Social Democrats and the Greens, as he increased German military involvement in NATO and was unable to reduce unemployment. Still, he secured a second term in 2002. Among his important achievements were the lowering of taxes, preservation of government funding for education, and recognition of homosexual civil unions. More recently, Germany returned the Christian Democrats to power under the leadership of the first East German and first woman chancellor, **Angela Merkel.**

In Spain, a centrist government dominated politics after 1996, overseeing the country's full integration into the EU and a healthy economic growth since 2000. But it lost popularity by 2004 because of Spain's active role in the **Iraq War.** After **al-Qaeda** engineered a series of bombings in Madrid in March of that year, killing and injuring hundreds of people, the Socialist Workers' Party won a close victory. From a staunchly

Catholic conservative country under Francisco Franco, Spain has become a leader in political reforms that surpass the most ambitious EU civil rights policies. In 2005 the Socialist Workers' Party government passed a law that recognizes same-sex marriages and engineered a reconciliation with terrorist Basque separatist groups. It is not clear, however, that it has been equally effective in dealing with the social tensions raised by Spain's growing Muslim and other immigrant populations.

By contrast, in France, Italy, and Austria, left-wing governments have given way to center-right ones. In France, **Jacques Chirac,** the leader of the center-right party, Rally for the Republic, won the presidential election in 1995 in a close contest with the socialists. Chirac had built a strong career as a successor of the Gaullist tradition since the 1970s, and after several unsuccessful bids, he emerged as president in the middle of a decade of slow economic growth and high unemployment. Despite his promise of opposing further EU integration, he became an advocate of the euro. Though he was implicated in several high-level corruption scandals, he managed to distance himself from former close allies who were prosecuted. Chirac also maintained his popularity in France because of his staunchly anti-American position on the Iraq War. In 2007, the center-right Nicholas Sarkozy, who proved tough on Muslim rioters two years back as Minister of the Interior, won a resounding victory as Chirac's successor. Sarkozy has made a mark for himself through critical views of EU expansion, especially regarding Turkey, and through his pro-American stance, which sets him apart from his predecessor.

Tony Blair   (1953–) Labour Party prime minister of Britain from 1997 to 2007, credited with creating a more centrist position for the British left.

Gerhard Schroeder   (1944–) Social Democratic chancellor of Germany from 1998 to 2005 who led a coalition government with the Greens.

Angela Merkel   (1954–) Christian Democratic chancellor of Germany since 2005, the first woman and first East German politician to be elected to this position.

Iraq War   War begun in March 2003 when a U.S.-lead coalition overthrew Iraqi president Saddam Hussein in an attempt to establish a new, democratic regime.

al-Qaeda   Islamic terrorist organization established by Saudi Arabs in 1988 to fight against the Soviet Union in Afghanistan.

Jacques Chirac   (1932–) French president from 1995 to 2007, leader of the center-right party Rally for the Republic and outspoken critic of American policy in Iraq.

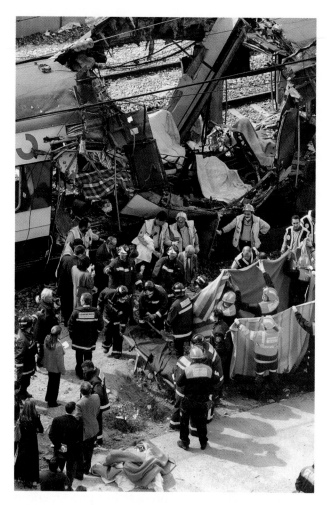

In March 2004, a series of related bombings on commuter trains in Madrid killed 191 and wounded more than 2,050 people. The heavily used commuter system of the Spanish capital came to a standstill. Though horrified by these events, Spanish politicians and the Spanish public only grew increasingly critical of U.S. President George W. Bush's so-called War on Terror. *(Paul White/AP Images)*

ment rates and an economic slowdown. Haider's platform was squarely anti-EU and anti-immigration, with clear elements of antisemitism. He shocked the world with statements praising the orderliness of the Nazis, earning Austria a series of economic and political boycotts in the EU and beyond. The center-right coalition won reelection in 2002. At the same time, though, the Green Party has grown to a sizable 10 percent in the parliament.

In the postcommunist countries of eastern Europe, governments have likewise shifted regularly between center-right and center-left coalitions, as no single party has been able to rule without an alliance. Initially, many observers saw this situation as a weakness, retarding necessary economic reforms. But, in fact, these alliances prompted more moderate ideological platforms and encouraged a political culture more prone to negotiation than posturing. For instance, radical antisemitic and nationalist parties in Romania and Hungary have toned down their rhetoric in order to join ruling coalitions. Those that maintain their nationalist radical ideology are marginal.

By contrast, a nationalist authoritarian mood has been growing in Russia since 2000, when Vladimir Putin assumed the presidency. Chosen by Yeltsin as acting president in 1999, Putin easily won election in 2000. Many outside were puzzled by the broad popularity of an ex-agent of the KGB. But Putin seemed to embody qualities lacking in Yeltsin and much in demand as Russia's economic and political stability floundered. His healthier lifestyle and personal self-restraint were a powerful contrast to Yeltsin's hedonistic outbursts. Putin is a disciplined practitioner of judo who, unlike his predecessor, does not drink alcohol or join in drinking and dancing at official functions. Even more important, his devotion to Orthodox Christianity has bolstered his popularity in Russia, where church attendance has been growing. Many communist politicians had trouble making the transition from a staunchly atheistic and anticlerical ideology to embracing the Orthodox Church as an official religion, but Putin skillfully put his KGB past behind him, inviting high clergy to and incorporating religious elements into official state functions.

Even those who are not particularly religious have embraced Putin's style as embodying Russian national

Between 2001 and 2006, Italian politics were likewise dominated by a center-right government led by **Silvio Berlusconi**, a media mogul turned politician. Having made millions of dollars in the entertainment industry, especially television, in the 1990s Berlusconi developed a party devoted to defeating the communists with a nationalist, business-friendly platform. Like Chirac, he was involved in several high-profile corruption scandals but survived them until 2006, when he lost elections to the center-left coalition of Romano Prodi, who had been premier in the 1990s.

In Austria, a right-wing coalition dominated by the charismatic leader of the Freedom Party, **Jörg Haider**, won elections in 1999, on the heels of high unemploy-

Silvio Berlusconi (1936–) Television mogul, leader of a center-right coalition, and prime minister of Italy from 2001 to 2006.

Jörg Haider (1950–) Leader of the antisemitic Freedom Party and prime minister of Austria from 1999 to 2002.

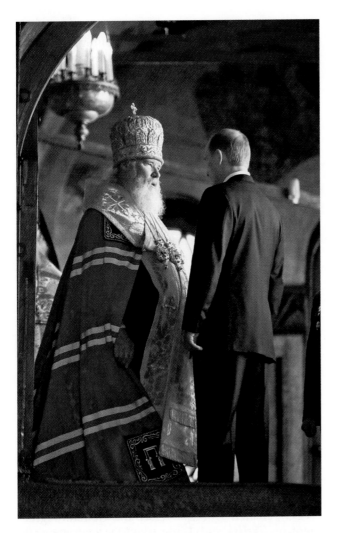

Though a faithful employee of the Soviet secret police, the KGB, and of a state that believed religion was an opiate of the masses, Vladimir Putin has become an open supporter of the Orthodox Church, an institution fundamentally linked to Russian culture and identity, as seen in this photograph from Putin's inauguration as president in Moscow, 2001. *(Alexander Zemilianichenko/Pool/Reuters/Corbis)*

aspirations. Whether dealing with foreign crises, the military, terrorism, or corruption in politics and the economy, Putin has placed his actions in the context of Russia's need to maintain its international standing as a powerful state. He has reasserted the legitimacy of Russian interference in the affairs of independent ex-Soviet states, such as Georgia and Ukraine, where Russia openly supported the pro-Russian presidential candidate in 2004. Such measures have led ethnic Russians to consider Putin their defender and a strong leader, even when his policies do not serve the immediate economic and social needs of the majority of

Russian citizens. But nationalist sentiments continue to be a strong force in Russia, where a stable democratic political culture has yet to be established.

Putin's image as a stalwart crusader against corruption and defender of Russian interests was welcomed by foreign leaders, who had tired of Yeltsin's inconsistency on international matters. Until 2002, the United States preferred not to criticize the foreign policy choices and internal problems of the Russians, treating Putin as an equal partner in matters of international security. Western Europeans were more openly critical of his autocratic tendencies.

By 2004, the rightward shifts in some national elections combined with some negative reactions to the effects of EU integration had produced a general shift to the right in the European Parliament elections, in which various right-wing parties and coalitions garnered over 60 percent of the vote. Almost one-quarter of these representatives are outright opponents of the EU. Thus, debates over the EU's future are guaranteed to remain wide-ranging, from questions about enlargement to specific economic, social, and cultural policies.

European Security and International Organizations

While the EU has successfully met the political challenges of the post–cold war period, it has been less effective in international security matters, where the changing roles of the UN and NATO have also intruded on European states' potential for representing their interests as a bloc. While the UN had been influential in the postcolonial world in security matters and had tried to mediate between the two superpowers and other states, it had not played an important security role in Europe. The ethnic-cleansing atrocities and utter internal chaos of the Yugoslav civil wars, however, convinced the UN to send a peacekeeping force. EU members generally supported this idea, and British, French, and Italian troops figured prominently among peacekeepers. The UN intervention was framed not in terms of countering threats to European security but rather as a globally significant means of halting human rights abuses. Thus, the EU remained marginal in decision making.

The ineffectiveness of UN troops, however, forced the international community to consider more drastic measures, and NATO stepped in to oversee a military intervention against the rebel Serbs in Bosnia. Traditionally, NATO had focused on securing western Europe against threats from the communist East. In the 1990s, however, it transformed itself, partly through this intervention, into a broader alliance to secure democratic Europe, east and west, against external or internal threats. Russia, no longer the main enemy, played a sometimes friendly, if passive, role. Though aligned with Milošević, it never challenged NATO militarily.

As part of its expanded mandate of preserving security and democracy in Europe, NATO also embarked upon a process of eastward enlargement, building **Partnerships for Peace** with postcommunist countries as a bridge toward their full membership in the alliance. Partnerships with thirty countries allowed for increased cooperation in matters of military training, ground operations, and logistical links for future strategy planning. NATO requirements forced reforms, including civilian leadership at the top of the armed services administration and increased expenditures on armaments, equipment, and personnel. In 1996, the Czech Republic, Poland, and Hungary were admitted to NATO, paving the way toward the admission of most other postcommunist eastern European states in the next decade. Thus, NATO became the broadest military alliance representing the security interests of Europe.

The U.S. role in NATO remained central, however, as its largest and most important funding and armament source. Some European states, such as France, urged a more European-centered framework for solving international conflicts on the continent, but most others, especially the postcommunist countries of eastern Europe, were happy to have American troops and military support in their countries, as they were still concerned about Russia's interests in the area. The Kosovo War became the first test of the new members' and partners' commitment to upholding their military obligations, and Poles, Czechs, and Romanians all gave significant help. Since 2000, however, the operations of NATO in Europe have remained minimal, limited to peacekeeping in Serbia, while the bulk of operations have shifted to the Middle East and Central Asia.

Europe and Globalization

↓ How has globalization transformed the economic power of Europe in the world?
↓ What have been the great international challenges since 1991?

Since the early 1990s, a combination of technological, political, and market forces have transformed the world economy into a dynamic, close-knit web of processes. The growth of the EU played a central part in this change, securing Europe a privileged role in globalization. As the speed of global communication has in-

creased, Europeans have become increasingly involved in world affairs and culture while non-Europeans have remained interested in Europe. But the international security problems that emerged after the cold war have been challenging, and Europeans have often been divided over crises in the Middle East and international terrorism.

Economic Globalization

In the 1990s economic production and trade became more closely interwoven on an unprecedented global scale, owing to several developments. New technologies, such as accurate and instant communication of information, computerized assembly lines, and new types of large trucks and refrigerated crates, made it easier to produce and transport more goods anywhere from the United States to Taiwan. Support for free trade among the most powerful countries in the world facilitated the exchange of goods across borders. An already high standard of living in the developed countries meant that people expected access to cheap consumer goods. To feed this process, many American and European businesses, such as Unilever, started to look for production sites with low costs, loose labor and environmental protections, and high product quality. Postcommunist eastern Europe fit this profile, as did China, Vietnam, and other places in the Third World. Evian and Nissan production facilities sprouted from Hungary to Taiwan.

The most important institutional supporter of globalization has been the **World Trade Organization (WTO)**, created 1995 to oversee the **General Agreement on Tariffs and Trade (GATT)**. First signed in 1947, this agreement encouraged free trade in order to generate economic prosperity in the early postwar years. There was no institution to oversee the agreement, which remained loosely enforced by individual countries. For instance, the countries of the Common Market abided by GATT, but countries in eastern Europe and Latin America were less inclined to allow cheaper western goods to be introduced on their

Partnership for Peace NATO project to increase cooperation in military matters between its members and postcommunist states.

World Trade Organization (WTO) International organization created by GATT in 1995 to implement GATT's free-trade principles.

General Agreement on Tariffs and Trade (GATT) International agreement promoting free trade, first signed in 1947, and most recently signed by 123 countries in 1993.

markets. Instead, most developing countries pursued policies that protected internal production so as to reduce their dependency on imports. Equally important were the ideological considerations of countries like China, which feared that the impact of western goods might destabilize communism.

But with the end of the cold war, many of these considerations became obsolete. Starting in 1995, the WTO has allowed countries to become members on the basis of stable trade policies and stable governments. The 149 member countries benefit from reduced tariffs, preferential trade agreements, and access to international loans through connections with the International Monetary Fund (IMF) and World Bank. Entry into this group and policymaking are both accomplished through consensus, not majority vote, an arrangement that has tended to give the wealthiest economies greater power than members with weaker economies. It has also facilitated the operation of large multinational corporations in foreign markets, to the detriment of small producers everywhere, especially in less developed countries. And since most multinational corporations are still overwhelmingly controlled by investors in the United States, western Europe, and Japan, the WTO has enhanced the economic power of these areas at the expense of the rest of the world.

Individually, European countries and corporations might have been at a disadvantage against the greater economic power of the United States or, more recently, China and Russia. But the EU framework has enhanced their competitiveness in the scramble for new markets and cheap labor in the developing world. In the early 1990s the markets in eastern Europe were flooded with chickens from the Netherlands, milk from Italy, and shoes from Spain. These products were often partially manufactured in eastern Europe, but still under western brand names. The flow of goods was overwhelmingly west to east for the first decade after 1989. But western producers have now set up shop in many eastern European locations and are beginning to ship their goods, for example, from Budapest to Paris. For the postcommunist countries now in the EU, this process has reached near-parity, with the new members having achieved greater buying and production power. The EU has also built on the colonial links of its member countries, forging strong relations with developing economies from Indonesia to Nigeria. British Petroleum, for example, is working in South Korea to develop technologies that will be used in Cameroon and Nigeria to extract oil and natural gas.

Producers have successfully used the WTO and other international organizations like the IMF to secure business interests, but human rights, environmental, and consumer activists have not been effective in curbing the deleterious effects of globalization. Questions about product safety, abusive labor practices such as child labor and sweatshops, and environmental damage have not received much attention in private corporations' trade practices, nor have they been the subject of serious international state-sponsored agreements. Even when states have tried to increase legal regulations against such abuses, multinational corporations such as Shell or Nike, with higher annual revenues than some European countries, have used the WTO effectively to lobby on behalf of deregulation in the name of free trade. More recently, however, Amnesty International and other human rights groups have forced the question of human rights abuses by member countries or members-to-be. A precondition for China's admission to the WTO, for example, was the reduction of abuses in labor practices.

International organizations have also been ineffective in dealing with other global problems, such as **global warming**, world poverty, and the AIDS epidemic. Scientists have linked the **greenhouse effect** to rapid industrialization and have urged governments to come to a global agreement over basic environmental regulations that would prevent further erosion of the earth's atmosphere. In 1997 representatives from 160 countries met in Kyoto and signed an agreement to cut greenhouse gas emissions by 10 percent, but the United States, the world's larger industrial producer of greenhouse gases, has declined to ratify it. Without U.S. support, the **Kyoto Agreement** remains ineffectual.

Nor has globalization alleviated world poverty. The UN has worked to bring economic help to the world's poorest areas, such as Africa and South Asia, but even as farmers produce more than enough to feed the world's population, neither the UN's direct aid policies nor the WTO's advocacy for free trade has eliminated starvation as a cause of premature death.

Since the 1990s, another significant global concern has been the persistence of malaria and the spread of the AIDS virus, especially in Africa. Over 25 percent of the population in parts of Africa have the AIDS virus, and while western pharmaceutical companies have developed preventive anti-HIV vaccines and treatments for those already infected, most of the people who need

global warming   Increase in the average temperature of the air and oceans in recent decades and its projected continuation.

greenhouse effect   Effect of gases emitted by human activities, especially polution.

Kyoto Agreement   Agreement signed in 1997 by 160 nations to reduce greenhouse gas emissions; not ratified by the United States.

these medicines are too poor to afford them. Likewise, malaria, for which preventive vaccines have existed for more than a generation, still kills millions of people each year in the poorest areas of the world. The most effective programs in containing these two epidemics have been international philanthropic nongovernmental organizations rather than the World Bank, the UN, or the WTO.

International Security and Terrorism

Since the 1990s, a sweeping transformation has occurred in international relations. Though the Americans and western Europeans were partners in winning the cold war, the United States has largely determined the international agenda since 1991. Security concerns in the West changed from the contained fears about relatively stable communist states to a vague terrorist threat, largely located in the Middle East and in Muslim communities, but often without a state sponsor that could be held accountable through the conventional means of international relations. Overall, this change has reduced the effectiveness of the UN as a means for peacefully alleviating security threats. Its function has shifted instead to poverty, AIDS, and other human rights issues. Though peacekeeping remains one of its functions, the UN has not used its troops to great effect anywhere in the world since the 1990s, from Bosnia to Rwanda. Instead, the United States has come to rely primarily on NATO and other bilateral and broader agreements to further its security interests. Europeans have participated in this process either as members of NATO or more recently as individual allies of the United States in the **War on Terrorism.**

The most intense site of conflict has remained the Middle East. In 1991 Iraq, under the leadership of **Saddam Hussein,** invaded Kuwait, a country rich in oil resources and with close economic ties to the United States. The noncompliance of the Iraqi leader with the UN resolution demanding his withdrawal prompted an international military response. In the **Gulf War,** the United States led a coalition of more than thirty states that included significant forces from Great Britain, France, and Egypt. Even the postcommunist countries sent in specialists to lend logistical support.

This conflict signaled an intensification of tensions that had been building up in the Middle East since World War II. Since the inception of Israel in 1948, the United States, Britain, and other western countries have been committed to its security as an outpost of democratic rule and western civilization. These are

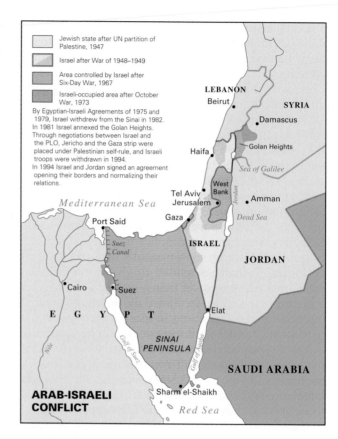

MAP 30.2 **Israel-Palestine Since 1948** The State of Israel and the stateless Palestinians have been at the heart of struggles in the Middle East for economic resources, political legitimacy, and international support.

precisely the reasons that Arab countries in the Middle East came to view the west with mistrust and Israel as a symbol of western imperialism in the area. While Jordan remained relatively friendly to the west, since the mid-1950s, Egypt, Syria, and later Iran and Iraq became open supporters of Arab nationalist claims at the expense of Israel, on occasion testing the strength of this state through military campaigns at its borders.

War on Terrorism Term used by the George W. Bush administration to refer to military, political, and legal actions taken to curb the spread of terrorism since 2001.

Saddam Hussein (1937–2006) Iraqi president from 1979 to 2003 who fought against the United States in the 1991 Gulf War and was deposed during the Iraq War.

Gulf War (1991) War between an international coalition led by the United States against Iraq in response to Iraq's invasion of Kuwait.

The fate of the Muslim and Christian Palestinians in Israeli territories have remained a point of contention between Arab nationalists and Israel. By the 1970s, as peaceful negotiations had not yielded much success for the Palestinian cause, a new method of struggle emerged—**terrorism.** At the 1976 Olympics in Munich, Israeli athletes were taken hostage and killed by Arab nationalist terrorists. After that globally publicized incident, the Palestine Liberation Organization and other such groups continued to pursue terrorist actions against Jewish citizens of Israel and other states. Antisemitism was an important component of these terrorist groups' agenda.

In Iraq, Saddam Hussein managed to fashion himself as a regional protector of Arab nationalism against the west. Hussein had come to power in 1979 as a secularizing popular nationalist, and the United States had assisted his regime because he seemed to offer a counterbalance to the radical Islamic regime in power in Iran since 1977. From the beginning, Hussein cleverly played American concerns and Soviet regional interests to his advantage, securing financial help from both superpowers during the cold war. Content to have him in power and as a supplier of oil for western needs, the United States overlooked the human rights abuses of the regime against religious and ethnic minorities. But when Hussein refashioned himself as a paragon of Arab nationalism against Israel and the west, and attacked Kuwait in 1991, the west reacted with military intervention. During the Gulf War, Hussein launched missile attacks against Israel. This anti-Israeli and more broadly antisemitic agenda continued during the 1990s, when Iraq offered cash to the families of **suicide bombers** who attacked Israelies.

Although the American-led coalition scored a sweeping victory, the Gulf War left complicated legacies that came to haunt the UN, the EU, and the international community in general. Inside Iraq, Hussein became solidly entrenched. The country's Shiite and Kurdish peoples suffered harsh reprisals, including the use of chemical and biological weapons, and the traumatic environmental and psychological effects of the war on both civilians and soldiers are still unfolding. During the 1990s, the European allies in the war remained convinced that UN sanctions and inspection teams could curb Hussein's abuses, while the American leadership began to loose faith in such methods.

One of the most important consequences of the Gulf War was the destabilization of the Middle East, with Israel enlisting the support of the United States and some European governments while many Arab Muslim states began to see themselves as more in conflict with the west than as allies of the Americans in putting down Hussein's bullying actions in the region.

Yet, European countries that had supported the United States in the 1991 war resisted drawing the same clear lines as the Americans between supporting Israel and vilifying its Arab foes, including the Palestine Liberation Organization. In 1993, when President Bill Clinton hosted Israeli and Palestinian leaders and orchestrated the **Oslo Agreements** as a step toward a peaceful resolution of their conflict, Europe remained in the background. Many in Europe viewed the United States as unfairly favoring Israel, though Britain steadily supported the American role.

Terrorist attacks continued in the 1990s in Africa, Southeast Asia, and Europe, but the most important challenge to the post–cold war international order came on **September 11, 2001,** when an al-Qaeda attack brought down the World Trade Center in New York and destroyed part of the Pentagon in Washington, D.C. The 9/11 attacks killed more than three thousand people from more than sixty countries and were the most severe attack on American soil since Pearl Harbor. Although al-Qaeda and similar organizations had undertaken terrorist actions over the previous decade, the attacks on September 11 were perceived as unprecedented in the United States and prompted a major foreign policy shift by the George W. Bush administration.

Within days, President Bush declared a War on Terrorism and embarked on an aggressive policy of employing all American intelligence, diplomatic, and military resources to respond to this grave terrorist threat. Although a significant number of European nationals were killed during the 9/11 attacks, European countries responded to the American call to action in different ways. The initial military campaign in Afghanistan, one of whose goals was to find and capture **Osama bin Laden,** the al-Qaeda leader and

terrorism   Violence or other harmful acts against civilians, often by disempowered groups trying to force political change.

suicide bombers   Individuals who carry out terrorist attacks by setting off explosive devices that also kill themselves.

Oslo Agreements   Agreements signed by Israel and the PLO in 1993 to establish an independent Palestinian state and subsequently repudiated by both sides.

September 11, 2001   Day on which al-Qaeda terrorists crashed hijacked passenger planes into the World Trade Center in New York and the Pentagon in Washington, D.C.

Osama bin Laden   (1957–) Militant Saudi Arabian Islamist who founded al-Qaeda in 1988 and organized the 9/11 attacks on the United States.

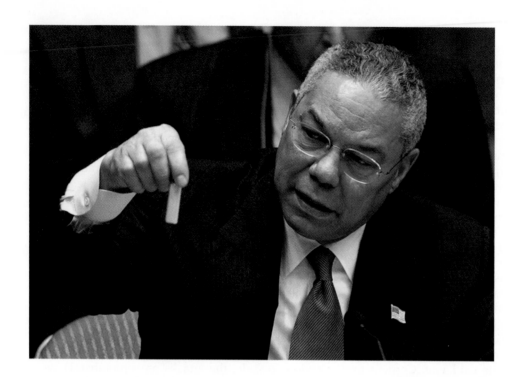

In February 2003 U.S. Secretary of State Colin Powell went before the UN General Assembly to convince the international community that Saddam Hussein was concealing chemical and biological weapons, and to request the approval of the Security Council to commence military action against Iraq. Here he holds up a vial of anthrax, a life-threatening infectious disease reputed to be in the terrorist arsenal. *(Elise Amandola/AP Images)*

mastermind behind the 9/11 attacks, was broadly supported by governments in Europe. NATO members sent military, logistical, and humanitarian support. The European public was less eager to support these actions, however, and massive antiwar protests took place all over western Europe, reminiscent of the peaceful street protests of the 1980s. Unlike in the 1980s, however, when activists had a broad antinuclear agenda but did not single out the Americans, these protests generally identified the United States as the sole country engaged in military and economic imperialism.

When President Bush shifted his focus in the War on Terrorism from Afghanistan to Iraq, European political leaders responded in an increasingly negative manner. The UN was at that time involved in overseeing economic sanctions and inspections to make sure Iraq was destroying its military capabilities, as Saddam Hussein had agreed to do following his defeat in the Gulf War. Starting in 2002, reports about Iraq's nuclear and chemical capabilities in defiance of the 1991 agreements and UN resolutions led the Bush administration to contemplate military action against Iraq. In late 2002 the European countries on the UN Security Council (Great Britain, France, Russia, and Spain) made it clear that they would not support military action by the United States until all peaceful options, especially the international inspections, had been exhausted. In 2003, the inspectors openly stated that there were no weapons of mass destruction left in Iraq.

In a last attempt to convince the UN that collective military action was necessary, in February 2003 U.S. secretary of state **Colin Powell** presented an impassioned report on Iraq's severe violations of the UN resolutions. Some, like Britain and Spain, were convinced, but most other countries were not. The United States went to war against Iraq a month later, its preemptive strike justified as intended to destroy nuclear and biochemical weapons capabilities, but these capabilities proved to be an illusion, as Powell later acknowledged.

The Iraq War split the European political leadership and population, but not along the old cold war lines. The French, Russians, and Germans vehemently opposed the war, while the British, Dutch, Italians, and Spaniards supported it. These different responses were based on different fears regarding terrorist actions; different views on the U.S. disregard for the UN as well as U.S. policies on the Middle East, especially the Israeli-Palestinian conflict; and pragmatic assessments of economic benefits and costs in the aftermath of the war. For instance, the Spanish were concerned about terrorism at home and supported the Americans as a deterrent to their own internal enemies, while the Russians opposed the intervention

Colin Powell   (1937–) U.S. secretary of state under George W. Bush 2000 to 2004.

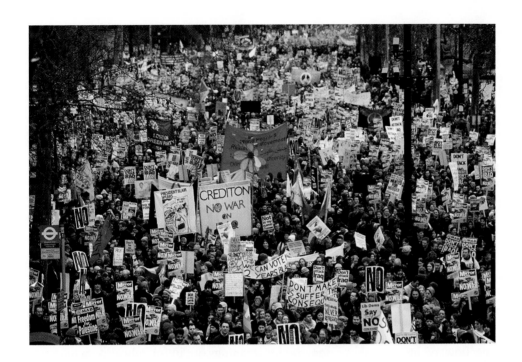

Since 2003 hundreds of thousands of people have marched through the streets of European and North American cities to protest against the American-led War in Iraq. In this photograph, British citizens are seen at a massive anti-war protest. *(Gideon Mendel/Corbis)*

because they did not want to invite terrorist activities in volatile places like Chechnya. The French and Germans resented the American disregard of the UN. The postcommunist countries generally identified Hussein with the kind of tyrannical government that had dominated their region for fifty years and so were eager for a direct military alliance with the United States that would stand against Russia. Romania and Bulgaria welcomed American bases that would deploy troops to Iraq. Yet the level of anti-Americanism in Europe has never been so high, among both politicians and the general public. At the same time, the threat of nuclear proliferation intensified by tests in North Korea has also brought European states, including Russia, in closer cooperation with the United States.

Instant Communication and the Internet

Even as they remain divided over international politics, Europeans and Americans have become more closely connected than ever through new means of communication, information exchange, and entertainment. The end of the twentieth century brought communications revolutions that have made distances insignificant and provided instant access to almost anywhere on earth. The new technologies have brought people greater freedom to relate to each other and to become "virtually" anyone; they have also brought greater power to those who create and implement these technologies.

Cable television, first introduced in the United States in the 1970s, became wildly popular across Europe in the 1990s. Many people in the postcommunist countries went from having access to one or two government-controlled channels to having twenty or more public and private channels through inexpensive cable packages. Overnight, a person sitting in his living room in Sofia, Bulgaria, went from watching the daily dose of communist speeches to being able to choose everything from Scooby-Doo cartoons to live coverage of the O. J. Simpson trial. The impact of the diversity of mostly American programs and channels was tremendous all over the globe.

Another component of the communications revolution was the **Internet,** which, since its inception in 1992, has become the most important means for information gathering and exchange in today's world. Ubiquitous in Europe, it has proved to be an equalizer, as differences in access arise largely from differences in education and technical know-how rather than from economic status. Internet cafés that charge low access fees can be found in even the most provincial

> **Internet** Global computer network created in 1992 that makes it possible to instantly connect to people and information around the world.

settings, and most people under age thirty have an Internet account. Young people have a sense that they can always be connected to others anywhere in the world, and they share ideas and music with people they have never met. But the spread of the Internet has not necessarily encouraged communication across cultures or languages. It has become more of a resource for creating parallel communities of people with similar tastes and interests. Fans of Christina Aguilera, for example, create websites to communicate about her; they rarely explore other types of music. White supremacist groups, too, have found niches where their biases are reinforced by all participants rather than challenged by those who oppose their racist ideologies.

Above all, the Internet has facilitated the possibility of imagining multiple identities, of turning the concept of the self in a community into a more fluid and less concretely bound thing. Fact and fiction blend together in the virtual space, making it easy to converse across national borders and to imagine being anyone or anywhere. The free flow of ideas challenges national allegiances, and authoritarian regimes, such as China, have censored the Internet. But users have ways of getting around such controls.

The Future of the West

⬇ What important challenges are likely to reshape the West in the near future?

⬇ What is the meaning of western civilization in the global future?

The face of the West is likely to become less specifically "western" in the twenty-first century. Even as Europeans are holding on to old institutions, from politics to social relations and culture, they are debating the meaning of these institutions both inside Europe and beyond. Demographically, with migration on the rise and large birthrate differentials among various social categories of Europeans, the face of the west is also likely to change significantly in the next generation. In the short run, the most important challenges and frictions remain between Christian and Muslim populations. In the long run, it is not clear whether the primacy of western civilization, as asserted in the past few thousands years, is likely to endure.

Old Institutions, New Directions

In the twenty-first century, the west seems to have retained important institutions, but their future is some-what uncertain. Nation-states remain the basic political units of government. Nationalism remains an important rallying force for politicians and average citizens, from Washington to Moscow to Beirut. But the multinational EU has created a new model for international political organization and peaceful cooperation among states. Whether the EU can retain this healthy balance remains to be seen after its next round of enlargement, especially if Turkey becomes a member.

In the global economy, most traditional economic institutions have taken on new elements. Small businesses continue to exist, but they are rarely able to operate without some direct or indirect assistance from multinational companies. With oil controlled by the **Organization of Petroleum Exporting Countries (OPEC)** and in the hands of a tiny group of multinational corporations, no one government can dictate the use of these resources, and small businesses are very much at the mercy of rising oil prices. A weaver in Bloomington, Indiana, may succeed or fail in selling her product not only on the basis of its quality or the demand for weavings but ultimately also on the basis of competitive pricing. Yet, the costs for producing those weavings—from paying for yarn transported from elsewhere to paying for the electricity and other utilities in the workshop—are controlled by global market forces, especially the rising cost of energy. Despite such growing concerns, the United States is likely to remain the most powerful economic unit in the global economy, with the EU as a smaller partner or competitor. China is the only economy that might challenge the undisputed first place of the United States.

Even basic social and cultural institutions and traditions are likely to be greatly transformed. The traditional definition of marriage as a social institution, initially sanctioned by religious authorities in the Middle Ages and in the twentieth century identified as a secular institution, has recently been challenged. Gay couples all over the world have demanded changes in the law to recognize same-sex unions as legal marriages. This challenge is testing the boundaries of secularization in the west. For instance, evangelical Christian organizations in the United States have successfully prevented the legalization of same-sex marriage. Yet in South Africa and Europe, even in staunchly Catholic Spain, gay marriages have been legalized without considerable opposition. In the

Organization of Petroleum Exporting Countries (OPEC) International organization that oversees price and supply fluctuations in the production and sales of oil.

realm of civil rights, the EU remains more committed to the traditions of social inclusiveness and tolerance than the United States, where liberty from government interference is still valued more than government protection for the disadvantaged and socially marginal.

Religious institutions are also being challenged from within the ranks of the clergy. With the decrease in young men's willingness to join the Catholic priesthood, some religious reformers have suggested the need to reconsider clerical celibacy. Others have suggested that women should also be allowed into the priesthood. While other Christian denominations, such as the Episcopalians and Methodists, have undertaken some reforms toward greater gender and even sexual inclusion, the Catholic Church has refused to consider any such reforms. Following the death of Pope John Paul II, the election of another conservative cardinal, Pope **Benedict XVI**, has made the church's direction clear and reinforced the primacy of the West and Europe in defining the future of the Catholic Church. Even as the largest areas of growth of the Catholic Church are in Asia, Africa, and Latin America, it was a German pope who was selected to lead the church in 2005. But the Catholic Church no longer holds a central religious, social, or cultural role in defining what it is, or means, to be European.

> **Benedict XVI**   (r. 2005–) German-born pope who has continued the conservative policies of Pope John Paul II.

Voice Voice Voice Voice

Pope Benedict XVI Speaks of the Future of Christianity

In August 2006, in preparation for his first trip to his native Bavaria since assuming the pontificate, Benedict XVI spoke to a Vatican spokesman about his goals for the trip and more generally about his vision for the role of the Roman Catholic Church. The pope's background as a German growing up in the Third Reich has made him the object of criticism by both liberal secular intellectuals and non-German (and especially non-European) Catholics. Pope Benedict XVI has been an outspoken advocate for living in strict accordance with Catholic dogma and has condemned some reformist interpretations of the Second Vatican Council. Regarding relations with other religions, he has spoken about love and reconciliation but also condemned certain Islamic practices in ways that have brought a strong reaction from Muslim leaders.

> ➡ What does Pope Benedict see as the most important spiritual challenge in the West today? How is it tied to globalization?

ZDF: How do you see the present situation of the Catholic Church in Germany?

Benedict XVI: ➡ I would say, first of all, that Germany is part of the West, with its own characteristic colouring obviously, and that in the Western world today we are experiencing a wave of new and drastic enlightenment or secularization, whatever you like to call it. It has become more difficult to believe because the world in which we find ourselves is completely made up of ourselves, and God, so to speak, does not appear directly anymore. We do not drink from the source anymore, but from the vessel which is offered to us already full, and so on. Humanity has rebuilt the world by itself, and finding God inside this world has become more difficult. This is not specific to Germany: it is something that is valid throughout the world, especially in the West. Then again, today the West is being strongly influenced by other cultures in which the original religious element is very powerful. These cultures are horrified when they experience the

West's coldness towards God. This "presence of the sacred" in other cultures, even if often veiled, touches the Western world again, it touches us at the crossroads of so many cultures. The quest for "something bigger" wells up again from the depths of Western people and in Germany. We see how in young people there is the search for something "more," we see how the religious phenomenon is returning, as they say, even if it is a search that is rather indefinite. But with all this the Church is present once more and faith is offered as the answer. . . .

BR: Holy Father, Christianity has spread around the world starting from Europe. Now many people think that the future of the Church is to be found in other continents. Is that true? Or, in other words, what is the future of Christianity in Europe, where it looks like it is being reduced to the private affair of a minority?

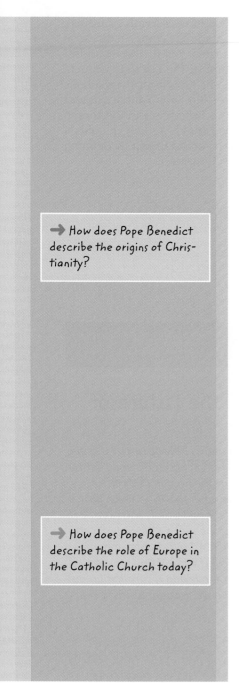

How does Pope Benedict describe the origins of Christianity?

How does Pope Benedict describe the role of Europe in the Catholic Church today?

Benedict XVI: I would like to introduce a few subtleties. → It is true, as we know, that Christianity began in the Near East. And for a long time its main development continued there. Then it spread in Asia, much more than what we think today after the changes brought about by Islam. Precisely for this reason its axis moved noticeably toward the West and Europe. Europe—we are proud and pleased to say so—further developed Christianity in its broader intellectual and cultural dimensions. But I think it is important to remind ourselves about the Eastern Christians because there is the present danger of them emigrating, these Christians who have always been an important minority living in a fruitful relationship with the surrounding reality. There is a great danger that these places where Christianity had its origins will be left without Christians. I think we need to help them a lot so that they can stay. But getting back to your question: Europe definitely became the centre of Christianity and its missionary movement. Today, other continents and other cultures play with equal importance in the concert of world history. In this way the number of voices in the Church grows, and this is a good thing. It is good that different temperaments can express themselves, the special gifts of Africa, Asia and America, Latin America in particular. Of course, they are all touched not only by the word of Christianity, but by the secular message of this world that carries to other continents the disruptive forces we have already experienced. → All the Bishops from different parts of the world say: we still need Europe, even if Europe is only a part of a greater whole. We still carry the responsibility that comes from our experience, from the science and technology that was developed here, from our liturgical experience to our traditions, the ecumenical experiences we have accumulated: all this is very important for the other continents too. So it is important that today we do not give up, feeling sorry for ourselves and saying: "Look at us, we are just a minority, let us at least try and preserve our small number!" We have to keep our dynamism alive, open relationships of exchange, so that new strength for us comes from there.

Source: Benedict XVI's Speech on the Future of Christianity (5 August 2006). © Libreria Editrice Vaticana, 2007. Reprinted by permission of Libreria Editrice Vaticana.

Who Is a European?

The reassertion of European leadership in the Catholic Church is part of continued efforts to define who may be a European and who may not. Thus, just as Catholic institutions remain essentially tied to Europe, Muslim institutions remain defined as largely non-western. The growth of Muslim populations in many European states, such as Holland, Denmark, Spain, Britain, France, and Germany, are forcing non-Muslims to ask themselves about their relationship with these often deeply religious communities that uphold seemingly non-European traditions and cultural values. For instance, a video that depicts the culture of Holland for its immigrant populations includes images of topless women and gay couples kissing as examples of the tolerance and liberal tradition that the Dutch government is proud of. But the video does not also include images of Muslim women in traditional veils, suggesting the limits of what liberal democratic Europe is willing to embrace.

Overall, the decreasing birthrate among secular and Christian Europeans, and the parallel rising birthrate among Muslim Europeans, is posing a serious question about what being a European might mean a generation from now. Israel faces a particularly perplexing dilemma, as the sharp differences in birthrates between Jews and Arabs in that state indicate that in the next generation Muslims will constitute more than a quarter of the Israeli population.

Politically, democratic forms of government have become an important marker of Europeanness. The enlargement of the EU has been tied to how well applicants can demonstrate potential (Greece, Portugal, and Spain) or success (the postcommunist applicants) in creating a democracy. Yet radical antidemocratic movements are still present everywhere in Europe, both as political parties and as militant terrorist cells. One thing is certain: the clear-cut east-west divide between those who belong to the European core and those who are at the margins is vanishing. Not everyone wants to welcome every country, from Iceland to Russia, into the new European home, but it is becoming increasingly difficult to justify any divisions along these lines.

Europeanness has also become identified more closely with highly urbanized and well-educated societies that are secular yet tolerant of religious difference. The vast majority of Europeans live in cities, yet some are choosing to reject the overcrowded, traffic-jammed, polluted urban setting for the simpler country life. This choice has been a response to the excesses of globalization and an embrace of the local resources it endangers. Yet this "simple life" is facilitated by new communication technologies, such as cell phones, luxuries many cannot afford.

Most Europeans have graduated from high school and have attended institutions of higher education. Education has been an important tool in providing greater equality to all people, regardless of gender, class, ethnicity, and religion—one of the great successes of the post-1945 welfare state. Yet the cost of these state services has become so burdensome as to endanger the quality of public education. As a result, private institutions are proliferating, creating new levels of competition and possibly inequality in terms of access to high-quality education.

And even though secularism and religious toler-

Over the past few years the Muslim population in Europe has become more assertive about their civil rights and have demanded that their cultural differences be respected in public institutions and policies. In this image from January 18, 2004, Muslim French women are protesting in Paris against the banning of headscarves in public schools. Their banners read: "Sarko [A reference to Nicolas Sarkozy, then the Minister of Interior, starting in June 2007, the French President], French Islam Doesn't Need Foreign Interference!"; "Why, in the country of the rights of man, women don't have the right to wear what they want?"; and "Beloved France, where is my freedom?" *(Owen Franken/Corbis)*

ance have remained important components of Europeanness, since the 1990s debates over the acceptance of religious differences, especially with regard to Judaism and Islam, have grown. Antisemitism and anti-Muslim attitudes are on the rise, especially since 9/11. The recent ban in French schools against the headscarves that all observant Muslim girls must wear calls into question the level of religious tolerance in the cradle of modern European democracy. Turkey's bid for membership in the EU remains an important test for the question of European definitions of western civilization. If Turkey continues to be rejected, it means that Europeans are fundamentally unable to consider Islamic traditions and culture, even in their most secularized forms, as an integral part of the west. Yet if Turkey does become an EU member, its presence will initiate a fundamental redefinitions of who is a European and what core values western civilization can embrace.

Even though European people like to represent their identity and culture as very different from the American identity and culture, the lifestyle of the average person in Europe is increasingly similar to that of the average person in the United States. The European past, long a mark of European distinctiveness, is becoming more difficult to discern in the face of a shared popular culture. A Polish college student in Warsaw is much closer in her fashion preferences, job options, and hobbies to an American college student in Chicago than she is to her Polish parents who grew up under communism. It is increasingly the past, rather than the future, that is likely to define the West as somehow unique in the world.

Summary

Review Questions

↑ What has the end of the cold war meant for Europe?

↑ How has the European Union enhanced the position of Europe on the globalizing international scene?

↑ How have these recent changes reshaped European identity?

The end of the cold war brought huge opportunities and challenges for all countries in Europe. Overall, the continent has seen increasing democratization. States have had difficulty maintaining their commitment to welfare programs, but overall public services from healthcare to education have remained high on political agendas. Even in Russia, where there has been a clear backlash against democratic politics, the government is still more open to change than was the case in the last days of communism.

The EU helped bolster this commitment to democracy as well as the economic power of Europe in the global economy. Since the mid-1990s, European companies have become serious competitors of U.S. companies in the world market. In terms of economic growth, the EU has been a success. Even in countries that have not joined the union, possibilities for economic growth have increased significantly in the last decade.

Though stronger economically, Europe has not been able to act as a unit in international affairs, especially after the terrorist attacks of 9/11. There has been a growth in popular anti-American attitudes, but governments have reacted differently to international crises, unable to use either the UN or any new European body to present a common international agenda. In particular, while Great Britain, Italy, and most post-communist countries have supported American actions in the War on Terrorism, France, Germany, and Russia have been stalwart opponents.

So, has the idea of Europe triumphed? On the one hand, there is increasing homogeneity across Europe in terms of markers for social advancement, consumer tastes, and the tendency of people to identify themselves as European along with their other national and regional identities. On the other hand, the particular cultural markets that broad cross sections of the population identify with are increasingly similar to those of people living in other places in the world. Europeanness has become tied to a past culture, something significantly unique to their continent, rather than to the current and future aspirations of people living in Europe. It remains to be seen whether the desire to remain different and revel in local particularities, evident in activists like José Bové, will prevail over the desire for a comfortable life.

← **Thinking Back, Thinking Ahead** →

How is nationalism being transformed in the era of globalization?

ECHO ECHO ECHO ECHO ECHO

I Want My MTV

Since 1981, when American MTV hit the airwaves, the genre of video music shows hosted by and addressed primarily to young audiences has become a worldwide industry. Starting in the 1990s, the channel broadcast its New York programs in western Europe, and increasingly in eastern Europe, through cable television packages owned and marketed by American companies. Parents were shocked by the violence and sexuality portrayed in the music videos and came to demonize American culture as superficial and harmful. But young people loved it and began to buy the products advertised directly and indirectly on that channel. To some, MTV seemed to be a subversive weapon of international corporations, meant to indoctrinate the younger generation into consumerist culture. But to most viewers, MTV was a form of generational rebellion against the old-fashioned local culture.

Over time, several MTV stations developed in Europe, so that, if one were to watch the channel, say, in northern Europe, the hosts and studio audience would be Swedish. In eastern Europe, many people got the channel via its Israeli studios. More recently, globalization has become more sophisticated. In Romania, for instance, a local MTV studio began broadcasting in 2002, and the programming includes at least 25 percent Romanian music videos by local artists such as Sarmalele Reci (in Romanian, "Cold Stuffed Cabbage"). The hosts are also young men and women from Romania. And all the publicity is in Romanian.

Does this mean that globalization has met its match—stopped in its tracks by local cultures and products? The morphing of MTV into national music channels has certainly meant that American culture is no longer distributed and accepted wholesale. Both the producers in these local studios and the local musicians have tried to put their personal and sometimes national imprint on the music, fashions, and other products presented on MTV. But all these subtle changes carry with them reminders of the overwhelming presence of the American music industry in all genres of this cultural enterprise. As much as young people everywhere in Europe sometimes try to distance themselves from American influence, they more often than not employ the vocabulary and cultural symbols of American commercial culture.

Suggested Readings

Bremmer, Ian, and Raymond Taras, eds. *New States, New Politics: Building the Post-Soviet Nations.* Cambridge, England: Cambridge University Press, 1996. Comprehensive analysis of nation building in the states that emerged from the Soviet collapse.

Cornish, Paul. *Partnership in Crisis: The US, Europe and the Fall and Rise of NATO.* London: Cassell, 1997. Excellent background reading for understanding the expansion of NATO after 1991.

Friedman, Thomas. *The World Is Flat: A Brief History of the Twenty-First Century.* New York: Farrar, Straus, and Giroux, 2006. A provocative analysis of globalization and its impact on the twenty-first century.

Glenny, Misha. *The Fall of Yugoslavia.* New York: Penguin, 1996. Journalistic, detailed description of the Yugoslav Wars of the 1990s.

Helleiner, Eric. *States and the Re-Emergence of Global Finance: From Bretton Woods to the 1990s.* Ithaca, N.Y.: Cornell University Press, 1996. Accessible account of the transformation of financial institutions and practices during globalization.

Pagden, Anthony, ed. *The Idea of Europe: From Antiquity to the European Union.* Washington, D.C.: Woodrow Wilson Center and Cambridge University Press, 2002. Consideration of what it means, and has meant, to be "European," from antiquity to the end of the twentieth century.

Pinder, John. *The European Union.* New York: Oxford University Press, 2001. Brief account of how the European Union has developed from 1950 to the present.

Websites

Gateway to the European Union's official website containing up-to-date information, including an online historical archive, **Europa,** at http://europa.eu.int

Website containing documents (video and audio), a portal to other websites related to the September 11 attacks, **The September 11 Digital Archive,** at www.911digitalarchive.org

Glossary of terms, documents, and debates regarding globalization, with useful links to websites that focus on international relations, **The Globalization Website,** at www.emory.edu/SOC/globalization/index.html

Shanghai, 704; decolonization and, 825; disengagement policy of, in Africa, 827; dominion over India, 695–699; East India Company and, 521; education in, 638, 816; Factory Acts in, 593; Falklands War and, 846; geography of, 533; Glorious Revolution in, 533; Gordon Riots in, 528, 529; Great Depression in, 771; growth of Royal Navy in, 524; health care in, 816; home front in, 730; income tax in, 644; India and, 524; industrialization in, 654, 718, 719; Industrial Revolution in, 532–534, 598; Ireland and, 640, 844; Labour Party in, 748, 778, 816, 843–844, 848; left-wing governments in, 881; Liberal Party in, 748; Muslim population in, 892; Napoleon's economic warfare against, 556, 558; national identity in, 719; National Unity Government in, 778; negotiation of Sykes-Picot Agreement by, 728; Parliament and, 512; plutocratic society of, 530; politics in, 498; poor in, 517; putting-out system in, 528; railroads in, 601–602; reform in, 588–592; reparations and, 746–747; resistance to Maastricht treaty in, 877; Seven Years' War and, 531; steel output in, 659; under Margaret Thatcher, 847–848; war with France, 555–556; welfare state and, 815–816; women in, 816; workers' rights in, 615; in World War I, 721; in World War II, 791–795. See also England

Great Depression (1929–1941), 775–777; authoritarian solutions, 778–779; democracies' responses, 777–778; effects of, 777; rise of Nazism and, 780–781

Great Expectations (Dickens), 672
Great Fear, 544, 553
Great Fire (1666), 516
Great Northern War (1700–1721), 458
Great Purges, 783, 806
Great Reforms (1861–1876), 649
Great Schism (1378–1417), 384
Great Terror in Paris, 555
Great Trek (1836–1846), 687
Great War, 713. *See also* World War I (1914–1918)
Great Western (steamship), 598
Greece: dictatorship in, 779; independence of, 720; as member of European Union (EU), 878; nationalism in, 586; occupation of, 808; Socialist

Workers' Party in, 845; Truman Doctrine and, 811; in World War I, 721; post World War I, 742, 744, 749, 750; in World War II, 792, 793. *See also* Athens; Sparta
Greek Catholic Church, 829
Greek New Testament, 334
Greek War of Independence, 582
Greenham Common Women's Camp, 847
Greenhouse effect, 885
Green movement, gender biases in, 850
Green Party: in Germany, 846, 850; in Italy, 882
Greenwich Mean Time (GMT), 617
Grey, Edward, 721
Grimm, Jacob, 568–569, 585, 627, 630; writing foreword to *German Dictionary*, 581–582
Grimm, Wilhelm, 568–569, 580, 582, 627, 630
Grossdeutsch solution, 629
Grosz, George, 740
Guadeloupe, 558; French in, 523
Guatemala, in World War I, 727
Guest workers, 851, 856
Guilds, 355, 417
Guillotine, 552
Guinea, 367
Guise family, 426, 431
Guizot, François (1787–1874), 605
Gulags, 784
Gunpowder, introduction of, from China, 359
Gustavus II Adolphus, King of Sweden (r. 1594–1632), 428
Gutenberg, Johannes, 336
Gymnasien, 642

Habsburgs, 358, 361, 418, 430, 449, 451–453, 454
Habsburg War against Islam, 427
Hague conferences and tribunals, 647
Haider, Jörg, 882
Haiti, 558
Halske, Johann, 661
Hambach Festival, 585
Hamburg, population of, 663
Handel, George Fredrick, 518
Hanseatic cities, 344–345
Hanseatic League, 344
Hardenberg, Friedrich von, 573
Hargreaves, James, 531
Harrison, Benjamin, 378
Harvey, William, 484
Hasek, Jaroslav, 740
Havel, Václav, 838–839, 852–853, 862, 875

Haydn, Joseph, 652
Health, public, 666–667
Heart of Darkness (Conrad), 692
Hegel, G. W. F., 618, 674
Helsinki Final Act (1975), 838, 842, 852, 858
Helsinki Watch, 842
Henriade (Voltaire), 488
Henry II, King of France (r. 1547–1559), 361, 362, 426
Henry III, King of Navarre (r. 1572–1610), 426
Henry IV, King of Navarre (r. 1589–1610), 426, 488
Henry the Navigator, Prince (1394–1460), 367
Henry V, King of England (r. 1413–1422), 343
Henry VI, King of England (r. 1421–1461, 1470–1471), 343
Henry VII, King of England (r. 1485–1509), 344, 361
Henry VIII, King of England (r. 1509–1547), 362, 431–434; Catholic Church and, 396–397
Herder, Johann Gottfried von, 582
Herero Revolt (1905–1907), 692
Hertz, Heinrich, 677
Herzl, Theodor (1860–1904), 624–625, 645, 647, 702
Hispaniola: Columbus in, 368; French claims on, 415
History: defined, 10; nature of, 488
Hitler, Adolf, 722, 739, 745, 771, 775, 780–783, 790, 791; consolidation of power by, 784–787; suicide of, 795
Hobbes, Thomas, 486, 487, 501, 573
Hobson, John A., 710–711
Ho Chi Minh, 703
Hoechst, innovations in, 659
Hohenzollern, Frederick William von, 455. *See also* Frederick William, the Great Elector
Holbein, Hans, the Younger, 334
Holland: growth of Muslim population in, 892; in World War I, 721. *See also* Netherlands
Holocaust Memorial Commission, 803
Holy Alliance, 572
Holy Roman Empire: under Charles V, 358–360; eastern Europe and, 344–345; religious war in, 425
Holy Synod, Russia (1721), 459
Homage to Catalonia (Orwell), 774
Home Insurance Building (Chicago), 655
Homer, 431, 439
Homes, medieval, 330

White House, 474
White man's burden, 688–690
White slaves, 535
Whitney, Eli, 532, 596
Who, 831
Widows, medieval, 355
Wilberforce, Samuel, 678
William, Stadtholder of the Dutch Republic (1672–1702), 449, 462, 464
William I, Dutch King, 581
William I, King of Prussia (r. 1861–1888), 579, 627, 632–635, 636
William II, King of Prussia and German Kaiser (r. 1890–1918), 717, 718, 719, 722
William III, King of England, 449, 462, 487
William IV, King of England and Ireland (r. 1830–1837), 585–586
William of Orange (William the Silent) (1533–1584), 420, 421
William Pitt the Elder (1708–1778), 498
William the Silent. See William of Orange (William the Silent) (1533–1584)
Wilno in World War I, 736
Wilson, Woodrow, 737, 738, 746, 747, 749
Wine islands, 524
Winter Palace, 472
Wireless, advances in, 661–662
Witches: hunt for, 417–418
Witches' Sabbaths, 418
Wojtyła, Karol Cardinal (Pope John Paul II), 853
Wollstonecraft, Mary, 502, 551, 574, 593
Woman and Socialism (Bebel), 744
Women: accusation of, as witches, 418; education for, 665, 667; employment of, 609; equal rights movement and, 669; feminist movement and, 847–848; in guilds, 355; humanism and, 326; middle-class, 606; participation in Scientific Revolution and Enlightenment, 477; post World War I, 761; rights of, according to Gouges, Olympe de, 544–545; role of, in food riots, 528; in workforce, 669; work of, 512, 513; in World War I, 728, 730–731; in World War II, 797
Women's Army Auxiliary Corps (WAACs), 730–731
Women's magazines, sex advice columns in, 766

Women's Royal Naval Service (WRENS), 730–731
Women's Section of Communist Party (the Zhenotdel), 744, 760
Woolf, Virginia, 788
Wordsworth, William, 550, 573
Work: patterns of, 513–514; of women, 512, 513
Workday, length of, 659
Worker resistance, forms of, 614–615
Workers' Defense Committee, in Poland, 853
Workforce, women in, 669
Workhouses, 527
Working classes, 611–615; consciousness and trade unionism, 614–615; diversity within, 611–612; in England, 596–597; families in, 613
Works, 388
World Bank, 871–872
World Trade Center (WTC), September 11th terrorism attacks on, 887
World Trade Organization (WTO), 884–885
World War I (1914–1918), 439; Africa in, 727; airplanes in, 720, 726–727; Allies in, 721, 722, 726, 727, 729, 730, 735, 736, 737, 738; assassination of Francis Ferdinand in, 721; casualties in, 723, 726; Central Powers in, 721, 722, 726, 728, 736, 737, 738; end of European era in, 739–740; entry of United States in, 737–738; Estonia in, 738; exhaustion in, 736–737; Finland in, 738; German defeat, 738–739; German victory over Russia, 738; home front in, 727, 730, 737; intellectual responses to, 764–765; nationalism as cause of, 716–717; navy in, 726; postwar political experiments, 751–757; propaganda in, 721, 725, 726, 729–730, 738, 739, 741; rationing in, 729; search for stability after, 745–751; submarines in, 726, 739; as total war, 727, 728–730, 739; trench warfare in, 723–726, 739; turning of tide in, 736–740; War Industries Board in, 737; women in, 728, 730–731
World War II (1939–1945), 439, 791–801; allied victory, 793–796; blitzkrieg in,

791; final solution, 798–801; France in, 791, 793–798; Germany's early triumphs, 791–793; Great Britain in, 792–793; Japan in, 793; major events of, 791; mobilization of civilians, 796–798; in North Africa, 792, 795; resistance movements and, 797; women in, 797; Yugoslavia in, 793, 798
Wren, Christopher, 512
Wright brothers, 662

Xavier, Francis. See Francis Xavier
Xenophobia, 855
X-rays, 677

Yalta, occupation of, 803
Yalta Conference (1945), 796
Yellow fever, 508–509
Yeltsin, Boris, 862, 870–871, 872, 882, 883
Yiddish, 435
Yom Kippur War (1973), 842
Young Germany, 585
Young Italy, 584
Youth, and counterculture, 831–832
Yugoslav Communist League, 819
Yugoslavia: anti-Tito purges, 820–821; civil war in, 862, 872; creation of, 875; dictatorship in, 779; dismemberment of, 872–875; fascist movements in, 779; occupation of, 808; post World War I, 746, 748, 749; resistance movements in, 798; under Tito, 819–820; in World War II, 792, 793

Zacatecas, 373
Zambia, 683, 727
Zenta, Battle of (1697), 453
Zeppelins, 662, 723
Zhenotdel, 740, 760
Zimbabwe, 683
Zimmermann, Arthur, 737
Zionism, 647, 702, 724, 747, 818; creation of modern, 647; Muslims and, 702; Ottoman Empire and, 702
Zola, Émile, 642, 666, 673
Zweig, Stefan, 620
Zwingli, Huldrych, 391
Zyklon B, 800

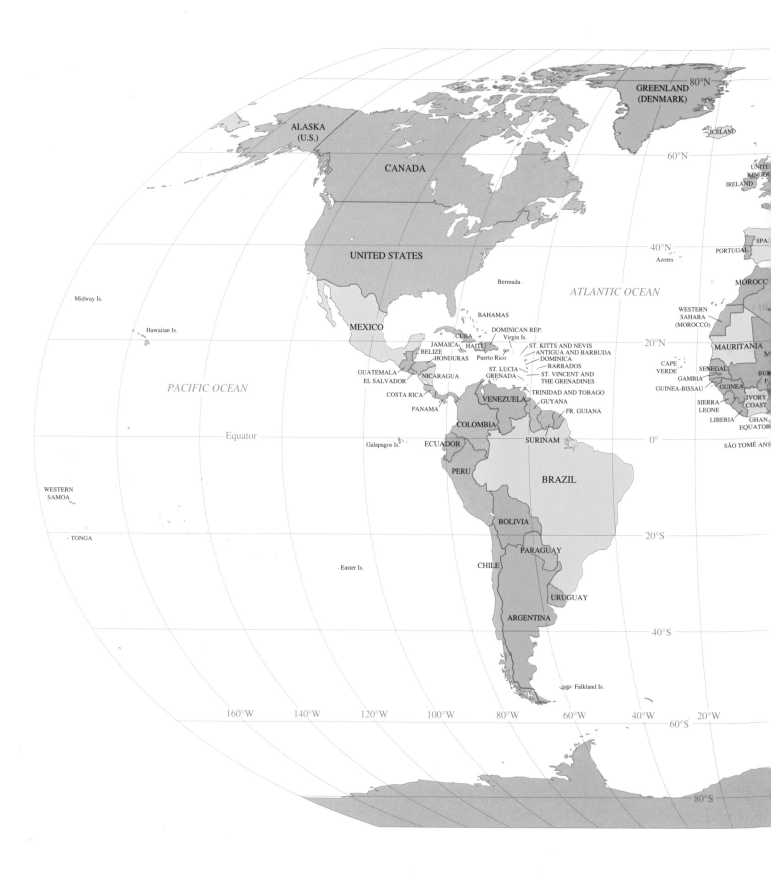

ALASKA
(U.S.)

GREENLAND
(DENMARK)
80°N

ICELAND

CANADA

60°N

UNITE
KINGD

IRELAND

UNITED STATES

40°N

Azores

ATLANTIC OCEAN

SPA

PORTUGAL

MOROCC

Midway Is.

WESTERN
SAHARA
(MOROCCO)

Hawaiian Is.

MEXICO

Bermuda

BAHAMAS

CUBA

DOMINICAN REP.

20°N

MAURITANIA

M

JAMAICA
BELIZE
HONDURAS

HAITI

Virgin Is.

ST. KITTS AND NEVIS
ANTIGUA AND BARBUDA
DOMINICA
BARBADOS
ST. VINCENT AND
THE GRENADINES

Puerto Rico

CAPE
VERDE

SENEGAL

BU

GUATEMALA
EL SALVADOR

NICARAGUA

ST. LUCIA
GRENADA

GAMBIA

F

PACIFIC OCEAN

GUINEA-BISSAU

GUINEA

COSTA RICA

VENEZUELA

TRINIDAD AND TOBAGO

GUYANA

SIERRA
LEONE

IVORY
COAST

PANAMA

LIBERIA

GHAN
EQUATOR

COLOMBIA

FR. GUIANA

Galapagos Is.

ECUADOR

SURINAM

Equator

0°

SÃO TOMÉ AN

PERU

BRAZIL

WESTERN
SAMOA

BOLIVIA

TONGA

20°S

PARAGUAY

Easter Is.

CHILE

URUGUAY

ARGENTINA

40°S

Falkland Is.

160°W   140°W   120°W   100°W   80°W   60°W   40°W   20°W

60°S

80°S